Literature and the Writing Process

THIRD EDITION

ELIZABETH McMAHAN
Illinois State University

SUSAN DAY
Illinois State University

ROBERT FUNK
Eastern Illinois University

MACMILLAN PUBLISHING COMPANY
New York

MAXWELL MACMILLAN CANADA
Toronto

Editor: D. Anthony English
Production Supervisor: France Burke
Production Manager: Paul Smolenski
Text Designer: Jane Edelstein
Cover Designer: Russ Maselli
Cover illustration: James Farrington Gookins. "Hummingbird Hunters," 1884.
Oil on canvas. Sheldon Swope Art Museum, Terre Haute, IN.
Illustrations: Digitype, Inc.

This book was set in 11/12 Janson by Digitype, Inc., and was printed and bound
by Rand McNally. The cover was printed by New England Book Components.

Macmillan Publishing Company
866 Third Avenue, New York, New York 10022

Macmillan Publishing Company is part of
the Maxwell Communication Group of Companies.

Maxwell Macmillan Canada, Inc.
1200 Eglinton Avenue East, Suite 200
Don Mills, Ontario M3C 3N1

Library of Congress Cataloging-in-Publication Data

McMahan, Elizabeth.
   Literature and the writing process / Elizabeth McMahan, Susan Day,
Robert Funk. — 3rd ed.
      p.   cm.
   Includes index.
   ISBN 0-02-379705-3 (paper)
   1. College readers.   2. English language — Rhetoric.
3. Literature — Collections.   I. Day, Susan.   II. Funk, Robert.
III. Title.
PE1417.M45   1992   92–4610
808'.0427 — dc20   CIP

Printing: 1   2   3   4   5   6   7   Year: 3   4   5   6   7   8   9

Acknowledgments

CHINUA ACHEBE: "Dead Men's Path" from *Girls at War and Other Stories* by Chinua Achebe. Copyright ©
   1972, 1973 by Chinua Achebe. Used by permission of Doubleday, a division of Bantam Doubleday Dell
   Publishing Group, Inc., and Harold Ober Associates Incorporated.
EDWARD ALBEE: *The American Dream.* Reprinted by permission of The William Morris Agency, Inc., and
   The Putnam Publishing Group from *The American Dream* by Edward Albee. Copyright © 1960, 1961 by
   Edward Albee. *The American Dream* is the sole property of the author and is fully protected by copyright.
   It may not be acted either by professionals or amateurs without written consent. Public readings, radio
   and television broadcasts likewise are forbidden. All inquiries concerning these rights should be ad-
   dressed to The William Morris Agency, 1350 Avenue of the Americas, New York, NY 10019.
SHERWOOD ANDERSON: "The Untold Lie" from *Winesburg, Ohio* by Sherwood Anderson, Introduction,

Malcolm Cowley. Copyright 1919 by B. W. Huebsch. Copyright 1947 by Eleanor Copenhaver Anderson. Used by permission of Viking Penguin, a division of Penguin Books USA Inc.

FERNANDO ARRABAL: "Picnic on the Battlefield" translated by Barbara Wright from *Guernica and Other Plays* by Fernando Arrabal. Copyright © 1967 by Calder & Boyars Ltd. Used by permission of Grove Press, Inc.

W. H. AUDEN: "Musée des Beaux Arts," "Lullaby," and "The Unknown Citizen" from *W. H. Auden: Collected Poems* by W. H. Auden, edited by Edward Mendelson. Copyright 1940 and renewed 1968 by W. H. Auden. Reprinted by permission of Random House, Inc.

JIMMY SANTIAGO BACA: "There Are Black" from *Immigrants in Our Own Land* by Jimmy Santiago Baca. Copyright © 1982 by Jimmy Santiago Baca. Reprinted by permission of New Directions Publishing Corporation.

IMAMU AMIRI BARAKA (LEROI JONES): "Preface to a Twenty Volume Suicide Note." Reprinted by permission of Sterling Lord Literistic, Inc. Copyright 1961 by Amiri Baraka.

JOHN BERRYMAN: "#14 Life, Friends" from *The Dream Songs* by John Berryman. Copyright © 1969 by John Berryman. Reprinted by permission of Farrar, Straus & Giroux, Inc.

ARNA BONTEMPS: "A Summer Tragedy." Reprinted by permission of Harold Ober Associates Incorporated. Copyright 1933 by Arna Bontemps, renewed.

GWENDOLYN BROOKS: "A Song in the Front Yard," "We Real Cool — The Pool Players. Seven at the Golden Shovel," and "The Bean Eaters" from *Blacks*, © copyright 1987, The David Co., Chicago and © copyright 1991, Third World Press, Chicago. Reprinted by permission of the author.

RAYMOND CARVER: "What We Talk About When We Talk About Love" from *What We Talk About When We Talk About Love* by Raymond Carver. Copyright © 1981 by Raymond Carver. Reprinted by permission of Alfred A. Knopf, Inc.

ANTON CHEKHOV: *The Marriage Proposal.* © Ronald Hingley 1968. Reprinted from *The Oxford Chekhov:* vol. 1, *Short Plays,* translated and edited by Ronald Hingley (1968), by permission of Oxford University Press.

COUNTEE CULLEN: "Incident." Reprinted by permission of GRM Associates, Inc., Agents for the Estate of Ida M. Cullen. From the book *On These I Stand* by Countee Cullen. Copyright © 1925 by Harper & Brothers; copyright renewed 1953 by Ida M. Cullen.

E. E. CUMMINGS: "next to of course god america i," "since feeling is first," "pity this busy monster,manunkind," and "anyone lived in a pretty how town." Reprinted from *Complete Poems, 1913–1962* by e. e. cummings, by permission of Liveright Publishing Corporation. Copyright © 1923, 1925 1931, 1935, 1938, 1939, 1940, 1944, 1945, 1946, 1947, 1948, 1949, 1950, 1951, 1952, 1953, 1954, 1955, 1956, 1957, 1958, 1959, 1960, 1961, 1962 by the Trustees for the e. e. cummings Trust. Copyright © 1961, 1963, 1968 by Marion Morehouse Cummings.

JAMES DICKEY: "The Leap." Reprinted from *Poems 1957–1967,* © 1967 by James Dickey, by permission of Wesleyan University Press.

EMILY DICKINSON: "There's a certain Slant of light," "He put the Belt around my life," "Much Madness is divinest Sense," "Because I could not stop for Death," and "I heard a Fly buzz — when I died." Reprinted by permission of the publishers and the Trustees of Amherst College from *The Poems of Emily Dickinson,* Thomas H. Johnson, ed., Cambridge, Mass.: The Belknap Press of Harvard University Press. Copyright 1951, © 1955, 1979, 1983 by the President and Fellows of Harvard College.

H. D. (HILDA DOOLITTLE): "Heat," from *Selected Poems.* Copyright © 1957 by Norman Holmes Pearson. Reprinted by permission of New Directions Publishing Corporation.

ANDRE DUBUS: "The Fat Girl" from *Adultery and Other Choices* by Andre Dubus. Copyright © 1975 by Andre Dubus. Reprinted by permission of David R. Godine, Publisher.

T. S. ELIOT: "The Love Song of J. Alfred Prufrock" from *Collected Poems 1909–1962* by T. S. Eliot, copyright 1936 by Harcourt Brace Jovanovich, Inc., copyright 1964, 1963 by T. S. Eliot, reprinted by permission of the publisher.

LOUISE ERDRICH: "The Red Convertible" from *Love Medicine* by Louise Erdrich. Copyright © 1984 by Louise Erdrich. Reprinted by permission of Henry Holt and Company, Inc.

WILLIAM FAULKNER: "Dry September" and "A Rose for Emily" from *Collected Stories of William Faulkner* by William Faulkner. Copyright 1930 and renewed 1958 by William Faulkner. Reprinted by permission of Random House, Inc.

ROBERT FROST: "The Silken Tent," "Fire and Ice," "Desert Places," and "Design." From *The Poetry of Robert Frost* edited by Edward Connery Lathem. Copyright 1923, © 1929 by Holt, Rinehart and Winston. Copyright 1936, 1942, 1951 by Robert Frost. Copyright © 1964, 1970 by Lesley Frost Ballantine. Reprinted by permission of Henry Holt and Company, Inc.

ALLEN GINSBERG: "A Supermarket in California" from *Collected Poems 1947–1980* by Allen Ginsberg. Copyright © 1955 by Allen Ginsberg. Reprinted by permission of HarperCollins Publishers.

NIKKI GIOVANNI: "Dreams" from *Black Feelings, Black Talk, Black Judgment* by Nikki Giovanni. Copyright © 1968, 1970 by Nikki Giovanni. Reprinted by permission of William Morrow & Company, Inc. "Kidnap Poem" from *The Women and the Men* by Nikki Giovanni. Copyright © 1970, 1974, 1975 by Nikki Giovanni. Reprinted by permission of William Morrow & Company, Inc.

SUSAN GLASPELL: "A Jury of Her Peers" published in 1917. Reprinted by permission of Daphne C. Cook, and the Estate of Susan Glaspell. *Trifles* from *Plays* by Susan Glaspell. Copyright 1920 by Dodd, Mead, and Co., Inc., renewed 1948 by Susan Glaspell. Reprinted by permission of Daphne C. Cook, and the Estate of Susan Glaspell.

SUSAN GRIFFIN: "I Like to Think of Harriet Tubman" from *Like the Iris of an Eye,* copyright 1976. Reprinted by permission of the author.

THOM GUNN: "On the Move" from *Selected Poems 1950–1975* by Thom Gunn. Copyright © 1979 by Thom Gunn. Reprinted by permission of Farrar, Straus & Giroux, Inc., and Faber and Faber Ltd., publishers.

DONALD HALL: "My Son My Executioner" from *Old and New Poems* by Donald Hall. Copyright © 1990 by Donald Hall. Reprinted by permission of Ticknor & Fields, a Houghton Mifflin Company imprint. All rights reserved.

LORRAINE HANSBERRY: *A Raisin in the Sun* by Lorraine Hansberry. Copyright © 1958 by Robert Nemiroff, as an unpublished work. Copyright © 1959, 1966, 1984 by Robert Nemiroff. Reprinted by permission of Random House, Inc.

THOMAS HARDY: "The Ruined Maid" and "The Darkling Thrush" from *The Complete Poems of Thomas Hardy*, edited by James Gibson (New York: Macmillan, 1978). Courtesy of Macmillan Publishing Company.

ROBERT HAYDEN: "Those Winter Sundays" is reprinted from *Angle of Ascent, New and Selected Poems*, by Robert Hayden, by permission of Liveright Publishing Corporation. Copyright © 1975, 1972, 1970, 1966 by Robert Hayden.

SEAMUS HEANEY: "Digging" from *Selected Poems 1966–1987* by Seamus Heaney. Copyright © 1990 by Seamus Heaney. Reprinted by permission of Farrar, Straus & Giroux, Inc., and Faber & Faber Ltd., publishers.

ERNEST HEMINGWAY: "Hills Like White Elephants." Reprinted with permission of Charles Scribner's Sons, an imprint of Macmillan Publishing Company, from *Men Without Women* by Ernest Hemingway. Copyright 1927 by Charles Scribner's Sons; renewal copyright 1955 by Ernest Hemingway.

HAROLD G. HENDERSON: "Heat Lightning" and "The Sudden Chillness" from *An Introduction to Haiku* by Harold G. Henderson. Copyright © 1958 by Harold G. Henderson. Used by permission of Doubleday, a division of Bantam Doubleday Dell Publishing Group, Inc.

A. E. HOUSMAN: "Eight O'Clock," "Loveliest of trees, the cherry now," and "To an Athlete Dying Young" from *The Collected Poems of A. E. Housman*. Copyright 1939, 1940, © 1965 by Holt, Rinehart and Winston. Copyright 1950 by Barclays Bank Ltd. Copyright © 1967, 1968 by Robert E. Symons. Reprinted by permission of Henry Holt and Company, Inc.

LANGSTON HUGHES: "Daybreak in Alabama" from *Selected Poems of Langston Hughes*. Reprinted by permission of Random House, Inc. "Same in Blues." Copyright 1951 by Langston Hughes. Reprinted from *The Panther and the Lash: Poems of Our Times*, by Langston Hughes, by permission of Alfred A. Knopf. "Theme for English B" from *Mortgage for a Dream Deferred*. Reprinted by permission of Harold Ober Associates Incorporated. Copyright 1951 by Langston Hughes. Copyright renewed 1979 by George Houston Bass. "The Negro Speaks of Rivers" from *Selected Poems* by Langston Hughes. Copyright © 1959 by Langston Hughes. Reprinted by permission of the publisher. "Harlem" from *The Panther and the Lash: Poems of Our Times*, by Langston Hughes. Copyright 1951 by Langston Hughes. Reprinted by permission of Alfred A. Knopf, Inc.

TED HUGHES: "Secretary" from *The Hawk in the Rain* by Ted Hughes. Copyright © 1957 by Ted Hughes. Reprinted by permission of HarperCollins Publishers.

ZORA NEALE HURSTON: "Sweat." Reprinted by permission of Clifford J. Hurston.

HENRIK IBSEN: *A Doll's House* © James McFarlane 1961. Reprinted from *The Oxford Ibsen* translated and edited by James Walter McFarlane, vol. 5 (1961) by permission of Oxford University Press.

SHIRLEY JACKSON: "The Lottery" from *The Lottery* by Shirley Jackson. Copyright © 1948, 1949 by Shirley Jackson. Renewal copyright © 1976, 1977 by Laurence Hyman, Barry Hyman, Mrs. Sarah Webster, Mrs. Joanne Schnurer. Reprinted by permission of Farrar, Straus & Giroux, Inc.

RANDALL JARRELL: "The Death of the Ball Turret Gunner" from *The Complete Poems* by Randall Jarrell. Copyright © 1945 by Mrs. Randall Jarrell. Reprinted by permission of Farrar, Straus & Giroux, Inc. "The Woman at the Washington Zoo," copyright © 1960 by Randall Jarrell from *The Woman at the Washington Zoo* reprinted in *The Complete Poems of Randall Jarrell*, Farrar, Straus & Giroux, 1989. Permission granted by Rhoda Weyr Agency, New York.

JAMES JOYCE: "Araby" and "Eveline" from *Dubliners* by James Joyce. Copyright 1916 by B. W. Huebsch. Definitive text copyright © 1967 by the Estate of James Joyce. Used by permission of Viking Penguin, a division of Penguin Books USA Inc.

DONALD JUSTICE: "Men at Forty" and "The Missing Person." Reprinted from *Night Light*, © 1967 by Donald Justice, by permission of Wesleyan University Press.

FRANZ KAFKA: "A Hunger Artist" from *The Penal Colony* by Franz Kafka, translated by Willa and Edwin Muir. Translation copyright 1948 and renewed 1976 by Schocken Books, Inc. Reprinted by permission of Schocken Books, published by Pantheon Books, a division of Random House, Inc.

CLAIRE KEMP: "Keeping Company" by Claire Kemp. Copyright 1990. This story appeared in the *Chicago Tribune Magazine* on 26 August 1990, pp. 25–27. Reprinted by permission of the PEN Syndicated Fiction Project and "The Sound of Writing," a production of the Project and National Public Radio.

MAXINE KUMIN: "Woodchucks," copyright © 1971 by Maxine Kumin, from *Our Ground Time Here Will Be Brief* by Maxine Kumin. Used by permission of Viking Penguin, a division of Penguin Books USA Inc.

RING LARDNER: "Haircut." Reprinted with permission of Charles Scribner's Sons, an imprint of Macmillan Publishing Company, from *The Love Nest and Other Stories* by Ring Lardner. Copyright 1925 and renewed 1953 by Ellis A. Lardner.

PHILIP LARKIN: "The Poetry of Departures" and "Toads" by Philip Larkin are reprinted from *The Less Deceived* by permission of The Marvell Press, England.

D. H. LAWRENCE: "Piano" and "Snake" from *The Complete Poems of D. H. Lawrence* by D. H. Lawrence.

DUDLEY RANDALL: "Ballad of Birmingham" from *Poem Counterpoem*, copyright 1966, and "To the Mercy Killers," copyright 1966 by *Negro Digest*. Reprinted by permission of the author.

ISHMAEL REED: "beware: do not read this poem." Copyright © 1972 by Ishmael Reed. Reprinted by permission. Ishmael Reed's new novel, *Japanese By Spring*, will be published by Atheneum Publishers in February, 1993.

ADRIENNE RICH: "Diving into the Wreck," "Living in Sin," and "Aunt Jennifer's Tigers." Reprinted from *The Fact of a Doorframe, Poems Selected and New, 1950–1984*, by Adrienne Rich, by permission of W. W. Norton & Company, Inc. Copyright © 1984 by Adrienne Rich. Copyright © 1975, 1978 by W. W. Norton & Company, Inc. Copyright © 1981 by Adrienne Rich.

THEODORE ROETHKE: "My Papa's Waltz," copyright 1942 by Hearst Magazines, Inc. "Root Cellar," copyright 1943 by Modern Poetry Association, Inc. "I Knew a Woman," copyright 1954 by Theodore Roethke. Used by permission of Doubleday, a division of Bantam Doubleday Dell Publishing Group, Inc.

CARL SANDBURG: "Fog" from *Chicago Poems* by Carl Sandburg, copyright 1916 by Holt, Rinehart and Winston, Inc., and renewed 1944 by Carl Sandburg, reprinted by permission of Harcourt Brace Jovanovich, Inc., "Grass" from *Cornhuskers* by Carl Sandburg, copyright 1918 by Holt, Rinehart and Winston, Inc., and renewed 1946 by Carl Sandburg, reprinted by permission of Harcourt Brace Jovanovich, Inc.

DELMORE SCHWARTZ: "The Heavy Bear Who Goes with Me" from *Selected Poems: Summer Knowledge* by Delmore Schwartz. Copyright © 1959 by Delmore Schwartz. Reprinted by permission of the New Directions Publishing Corporation.

ANNE SEXTON: "You All Know the Story of the Other Woman" from *Love Poems* by Anne Sexton. Copyright © 1967, 1968, 1969 by Anne Sexton. Reprinted by permission of Houghton Mifflin Company. All rights reserved. "The Farmer's Wife" from *To Bedlam and Part Way Back* by Anne Sexton. Copyright © 1960 by Anne Sexton. Reprinted by permission of Houghton Mifflin Company. All rights reserved.

WILLIAM SHAKESPEARE: Footnotes to accompany "Othello" from *The Complete Works of Shakespeare* by David Bevington. Copyright © 1980, 1973 by Scott, Foresman and Company. Reprinted by permission of HarperCollins Publishers.

KARL SHAPIRO: "Auto Wreck." Copyright © Karl Shapiro. Reprinted by arrangement with Wieser & Wieser, Inc. 118 East 25th St., New York, NY 10010.

PAUL SIMON: "Richard Cory." Copyright © 1966 Paul Simon. Used by permission of the Publisher.

STEVIE SMITH: "Not Waving but Drowning" from *The Collected Poems of Stevie Smith*. Copyright © 1972 by Stevie Smith. Reprinted by permission of New Directions Publishing Corporation.

W. D. SNODGRASS: "April Inventory." Copyright © 1957 by W. D. Snodgrass. Reprinted from *Heart's Needle* by W. D. Snodgrass, by permission of Alfred A. Knopf, Inc.

SOPHOCLES: *The Antigone of Sophocles*: An English version by Dudley Fitts and Robert Fitzgerald, copyright 1939 by Harcourt Brace Jovanovich, Inc., renewed 1967 by Dudley Fitts and Robert Fitzgerald, reprinted by permission of the publisher. *Caution:* All rights, including professional, amateur, motion picture, recitation, lecturing, performance, public reading, radio broadcasting, and television are strictly reserved. Inquiries on all rights should be addressed to Harcourt Brace Jovanovich, Inc., Orlando, FL 32887.

WOLE SOYINKA: "Telephone Conversation" by Wole Soyinka. Copyright 1960 by Wole Soyinka. Reprinted by permission of Brandt & Brandt Literary Agents, Inc.

JOHN STEINBECK: "The Chrysanthemums" from *The Long Valley* by John Steinbeck. Copyright 1937, renewed © 1965 by John Steinbeck. All rights reserved. Reprinted by permission of Viking Penguin, a division of Penguin Books USA Inc.

WALLACE STEVENS: "Sunday Morning" and "The Emperor of Ice Cream." Copyright 1923 and renewed 1951 by Wallace Stevens. Reprinted from *The Collected Poems of Wallace Stevens*, by permission of Alfred A. Knopf, Inc.

MAY SWENSON: "Pigeon Woman" © 1962 and renewed 1990. First published in *The New Yorker* and used with the permission of the Literary Estate of May Swenson.

DYLAN THOMAS: "Do Not Go Gentle into That Good Night," "The Force That Through the Green Fuse Drives the Flower," and "Fern Hill" from *The Poems of Dylan Thomas*. Copyright 1945 by the Trustees for the Copyrights of Dylan Thomas; 1952 by Dylan Thomas. Reprinted by permission of New Directions Publishing Corporation.

JEAN TOOMER: "Reapers" is reprinted from *Cane* by Jean Toomer, by permission of Liveright Publishing Corporation. Copyright 1923 by Boni & Liveright. Copyright renewed 1951 by Jean Toomer.

JOHN UPDIKE: "A & P" from *Pigeon Feathers and Other Stories* by John Updike. Copyright © 1962 by John Updike. Reprinted by permission of Alfred A. Knopf, Inc. "Ex-Basketball Player" from *The Carpentered Hen and Other Tame Creatures* by John Updike. Copyright © 1957, 1982 by John Updike. Reprinted by permission of Alfred A. Knopf, Inc.

MONA VAN DUYN: "Leda." Reprinted with permission of Atheneum Publishers, an imprint of Macmillan Publishing Company, from *To See, To Take* by Mona Van Duyn. Copyright © 1966, 1970 by Mona Van Duyn.

ALICE WALKER: "Everyday Use" from *In Love & Trouble: Stories of Black Women*, copyright © 1973 by Alice Walker, reprinted by permission of Harcourt Brace Jovanovich, Inc.

EUDORA WELTY: "A Worn Path" from *A Curtain of Green and Other Stories*, copyright 1941 and renewed 1964 by Eudora Welty, reprinted by permission of Harcourt Brace Jovanovich, Inc.

EDITH WHARTON: "Roman Fever." Reprinted with permission of Charles Scribner's Sons, an imprint of Macmillan Publishing Company, from *Roman Fever and Other Stories* by Edith Wharton. Copyright 1934 Liberty Magazine, renewed 1962 by William R. Tyler.

RICHARD WILBUR: "First Snow in Alsace" from *The Beautiful Changes and Other Poems*, copyright 1947 and renewed 1975 by Richard Wilbur, reprinted by permission of Harcourt Brace Jovanovich, Inc. "The Writer" from *The Mind-Reader: New Poems*, copyright © 1971 by Richard Wilbur, reprinted by permission of Harcourt Brace Jovanovich, Inc.

TENNESSEE WILLIAMS: *Cat on a Hot Tin Roof*. Copyright © 1954, 1955, 1971, and 1975 by Tennessee Williams. Reprinted by permission of New Directions Publishing Corporation.

WILLIAM CARLOS WILLIAMS: "Danse Russe" and "The Red Wheelbarrow" from *The Collected Poems of William Carlos Williams, 1909–1939, vol. I.* Copyright 1938 by New Directions Publishing Corporation. Reprinted by permission of New Directions Publishing Corporation.

JAMES WRIGHT: "A Blessing." Reprinted from *The Collected Poems*, © 1971 by James Wright, by permission of Wesleyan University Press.

RICHARD WRIGHT: "The Man Who Was Almost a Man" from the book, *Eight Men* by Richard Wright. Copyright © 1987 by the Estate of Richard Wright. Used by permission of the publisher, Thunder's Mouth Press.

HISAYE YAMAMOTO: "Seventeen Syllables" from *Seventeen Syllables and Other Stories* by Hisaye Yamamoto. Copyright © 1948 by *Partisan Review*, renewed © 1975 by Hisaye Yamamoto. Used by permission of Kitchen Table: Women of Color Press, P.O. Box 908, Latham, NY 12110.

WILLIAM BUTLER YEATS: "The Second Coming." Reprinted with permission of Macmillan Publishing Company from *The Poems of W. B. Yeats: A New Edition*, edited by Richard J. Finneran. Copyright 1924 by Macmillan Publishing Company, renewed 1952 by Bertha Georgie Yeats. "Sailing to Byzantium" and "Leda and the Swan." Reprinted with permission of Macmillan Publishing Company from *The Poems of W. B. Yeats: A New Edition*, edited by Richard J. Finneran. Copyright 1928 by Macmillan Publishing Company, renewed 1956 by Georgie Yeats.

Preface

This text grew out of our long-standing interest in the possibilities of integrating the studies of literature and composition. Many of our students have learned to write preceptively and well by using literature as their subject matter. Great literature is always thought-provoking, always new. Why not mobilize it in the pursuit of critical thinking and improved writing? Toward that end, we have combined an introduction to literature with instruction in writing.

Literature and the Writing Process, third edition, presents literary selections as material for students to read and write about, not as models for them to emulate. The text is designed to guide students step by step through the allied processes of critical reading and critical writing. In order to expand the options for writing, we have added responsive writing topics as well as critical writing topics to each chapter of this edition.

The writing instruction, concurrent with the literary study, follows a well-grounded order, beginning with the larger questions of content and organization and proceeding to particular effects such as word choice, sentence elements, and manuscript form. We have increased the emphasis on the entire process of writing both by adding to the text more suggestions for invention and exploratory writing and by providing in Part I a complete illustration of the preparation of a student's paper, an illustration which includes samples of prewriting, drafting, peer editing, after-writing outlining, revising, and editing. We have included three additional student papers: one illustrates the use of library resources in a short story analysis; one provides a model of close analysis of a brief passage from a novella; and one offers an unusual response to a poem—a response that should spark lively in-class discussion. We have also provided throughout the text further instruction on the difficult matters of devising a sound thesis and discovering theme.

Part I provides an overview of the composition process—prewriting, writing, and rewriting—using James Joyce's short story "Eveline" as subject matter for writing exercises and short papers. Parts II, III, and IV provide chapters offering specific advice for analyzing short fiction, poetry, and drama plus instruction for composing essays about this literature. Each of these sections begins with a set of questions for students to apply to that type of literature and concludes with an anthology of the genre it covers. The drama section has a chapter on using library sources in writing about literature—advice on doing bibliographical work, taking notes, integrating sources, using MLA documentation, and avoiding plagiarism. Realizing that previous writing courses may not have completely eradicated sentence-level problems, we have included at the end of the text a concise handbook for correcting errors. This handbook will serve as a reference tool, as will the glossary of literary and rhetorical terms that follows it.

The composition theory integrated into this textbook has been informed by the valuable work of many researchers, including James Moffett, James Kinneavy, Janet Emig, Nancy Sommers, Frank O'Hare, and Linda Flower. The approach to literature is basically formalist, with some added spice from reader response theory. In revising the literary selections in this text, we have been guided by the advice of our reviewers. Following their suggestions, we now include 39 stories, 156 poems, and 9 plays, which have been chosen for their literary value and for their potential appeal to students.

Our thanks to the reviewers who helped us craft this third edition: Diane Thomas Christian, Angelo State University, San Angelo, Texas; Irene R. Fairley, Northeastern University, Boston, Massachusetts; Carolyn Foster, Clemson University, Clemson, South Carolina; Jack E. Harris, West Liberty State College, West Liberty, Virginia; Jeane Harris, Arkansas State University; Mary Arshagouni Papazian, Oakland University, California; David Smit, Kansas State University, Manhattan, Kansas; Vickey Daley, Deborah E. Bush, Sue Parson, and Patricia Fortney of Stephen F. Austin State University, Texas. Our thanks also to Shannon Perry of Illinois State University for her able research assistance and to Linda Coleman of Eastern Illinois University for her help in improving our poetry chapters. For supporting us in ways from the most practical to the most subtle, our warm gratitude goes to Dan LeSeure, David X Lee, Bill Weber—and to our incomparable editor Tony English.

Elizabeth McMahan
Susan Day
Robert Funk

Brief Contents

Contents

PART II   *Writing About Short Fiction*   53

PART III   *Writing About Poetry*   *457*

CHAPTER 12   *Writing About Poetic Language*   *479*

PART V *The Editing Process* *1011*

A Handbook for Correcting Errors *1013*

PART ONE

Composing: An Overview

This text serves a dual purpose: to enable you to enjoy, understand, and learn from imaginative literature; and to help you to write clearly, intelligently, and correctly about what you have learned. For many people, the most difficult part of the writing process is getting started. We will provide help at this stage and then show you how to follow through to the completion of a finished paper you can be proud of.

1

The Prewriting Process

Your study of writing, as we approach it in this book, will focus on the composing process: prewriting, writing, rewriting, and editing. The first section of the text takes you through each stage, explaining one way of putting together a paper on James Joyce's "Eveline." The following sections, which include more short stories, plus poems and plays, offer further advice for understanding and writing about these various kinds of literature.

We realize, of course, that our chronological, linear (step-by-step) explanations of the writing process are not entirely true to experience; most of us juggle at least two of the steps at a time when we write. We put down half a sentence, go back and revise it, make notes of some details to include later in the essay, and then finish the sentence, perhaps crossing out and correcting a misspelled word—a combination of prewriting, writing, rewriting, and editing. We have adopted the linear, step-by-step presentation because it allows us to explain this complicated process.

Reading for Writing

To prepare for your study of the stages of writing an essay about a literary topic, find a comfortable spot and read the following short story.

James Joyce *1882–1941*

EVELINE

She sat at the window watching the evening invade the avenue. Her head was leaned against the window curtains and in her nostrils was the odour of dusty cretonne. She was tired.

Few people passed. The man out of the last house passed on his way home; she heard his footsteps clacking along the concrete pavement and afterwards crunching on the cinder path before the new red houses. One time there used to be a field there in which they used to play every evening with other people's children. Then a man from Belfast bought the field and built houses in it — not like their little brown houses but bright brick houses with shining roofs. The children of the avenue used to play together in that field — the Devines, the Waters, the Dunns, little Keogh the cripple, she and her brothers and sisters. Ernest, however, never played: he was too grown up. Her father used often to hunt them in out of the field with his blackthorn stick; but usually little Keogh used to keep *nix* and call out when he saw her father coming. Still they seemed to have been rather happy then. Her father was not so bad then; and besides, her mother was alive. That was a long time ago; she and her brothers and sisters were all grown up; her mother was dead. Tizzie Dunn was dead, too, and the Waters had gone back to England. Everything changes. Now she was going to go away like the others, to leave her home.

Home! She looked round the room, reviewing all its familiar objects which she had dusted once a week for so many years, wondering where on earth all the dust came from. Perhaps she would never see again those familiar objects from which she had never dreamed of being divided. And yet during all those years she had never found out the name of the priest whose yellowing photograph hung on the wall above the broken harmonium beside the coloured print of the promises made to Blessed Margaret Mary Alacoque. He had been a school friend of her father. Whenever he showed the photograph to a visitor her father used to pass it with a casual word:

"He is in Melbourne now."

She had consented to go away, to leave her home. Was that wise? She tried to weigh each side of the question. In her home anyway she had shelter and food; she had those whom she had known all her life about her. Of course she had to work hard, both in the house and at business. What would they say of her in the Stores when they found out that she had run away with a fellow? Say she was a fool, perhaps; and her place would be filled up by advertisement. Miss Gavan would be glad. She had always had an edge on her, especially whenever there were people listening.

"Miss Hill, don't you see these ladies are waiting?"

"Look lively, Miss Hill, please."

She would not cry many tears at leaving the Stores.

But in her new home, in a distant unknown country, it would not be like that. Then she would be married — she, Eveline. People would treat her with respect then. She would not be treated as her mother had been. Even now, though she was over nineteen, she sometimes felt herself in danger of her father's violence. She knew it was that that had given her the palpitations. When they were growing up he had never gone for her, like he used to go for Harry and Ernest, because she was a girl; but latterly he had begun to threaten her and say what he would do to her only for her dead mother's sake. And now she had nobody to protect her. Ernest was dead and Harry, who was in the church decorating business, was nearly always down somewhere in the country. Besides, the invariable squabble for money on Saturday nights had begun to weary her unspeakably. She always gave her entire wages — seven shillings — and Harry always sent up what he could but the trouble was to get any money from her father. He said she used to squander the money, that she had no head, that he wasn't going to give her his hard-earned money to throw about the streets, and much more, for he was usually fairly bad on Saturday night. In the end he would give her the money and ask her had she any intention of buying Sunday's dinner. Then she had to rush out as quickly as she could and do her marketing, holding her black leather purse tightly in her hand as she elbowed her way through the crowds and returning home late under her load of provisions. She had hard work to keep the house together and to see that the two young children who had been left to her charge went to school regularly and got their meals regularly. It was hard work — a hard life — but now that she was about to leave it she did not find it a wholly undesirable life.

She was about to explore another life with Frank. Frank was very kind, manly, open-hearted. She was to go away with him by the night-boat to be his wife and to live with him in Buenos Ayres where he had a home waiting for her. How well she remembered the first time she had seen him; he was lodging in a house on the main road where she used to visit. It seemed a few weeks ago. He was standing at the gate, his peaked cap pushed back on his head and his hair tumbled forward over a face of bronze. Then they had come to know each other. He used to meet her outside the Stores every evening and see her home. He took her to see *The Bohemian Girl* and she felt elated as she sat in an unaccustomed part of the theatre with him. He was awfully fond of music and sang a little. People knew that they were courting and, when he sang about the lass that loves a sailor, she always felt pleasantly confused. He used to call her Poppens out of fun. First of all it had been an excitement for her to have a fellow and then she had begun to like him. He had tales of distant countries. He had started as a deck boy at a pound a month on a ship of the Allan Line going out to Canada. He told her the names of the ships he had been on and the names of the different services. He had sailed through the Straits of Magellan and he told her stories of the terrible Patagonians. He had fallen on his feet in Buenos Ayres, he said, and had come over to the old country just for a holiday. Of course, her father had found out the affair and had forbidden her to have anything to say to him.

"I know these sailor chaps," he said.

One day he had quarrelled with Frank and after that she had to meet her lover secretly.

The evening deepened in the avenue. The white of two letters in her lap grew indistinct. One was to Harry; the other was to her father. Ernest had been her favourite but she liked Harry too. Her father was becoming old lately, she noticed; he would miss her. Sometimes he could be very nice. Not long before, when she had been laid up for a day, he had read her out a ghost story and made toast for her at the fire. Another day, when their mother was alive, they had all gone for a picnic to the Hill of Howth. She remembered her father putting on her mother's bonnet to make the children laugh.

like a
refrain

Her time was running out but she continued to sit by the window, leaning her head against the window curtain, inhaling the odour of dusty cretonne. Down far in the avenue she could hear a street organ playing. She knew the air. Strange that it should come that very night to remind her of the promise to her mother, her promise to keep the home together as long as she could. She remembered the last night of her mother's illness; she was again in the close dark room at the other side of the hall and outside she heard a melancholy air of Italy. The organ-player had been ordered to go away and given sixpence. She remembered her father strutting back into the sickroom saying:

"Damned Italians! coming over here!"

As she mused the pitiful vision of her mother's life laid its spell on the very quick of her being — that life of commonplace sacrifices closing in final craziness. She trembled as she heard again her mother's voice saying constantly with foolish insistence:

"Derevaun Seraun! Derevaun Seraun!" [1]

She stood up in a sudden impulse of terror. Escape! She must escape! Frank would save her. He would give her life, perhaps love, too. But she wanted to live. Why should she be unhappy? She had a right to happiness. Frank would take her in his arms, fold her in his arms. He would save her.

She stood among the swaying crowd in the station at the North Wall. He held her hand and she knew that he was speaking to her, saying something about the passage over and over again. The station was full of soldiers with brown baggages. Through the wide doors of the sheds she caught a glimpse of the black mass of the boat, lying in beside the quay wall, with illumined portholes. She answered nothing. She felt her cheek pale and cold and, out of a maze of distress, she prayed to God to direct her, to show her what was her duty. The boat blew a long mournful whistle into the mist. If she went, tomorrow she would be on the sea with Frank, steaming towards Buenos Ayres. This passage had been booked. Could she still draw back after all he had done for her? Her distress awoke a nausea in her body and she kept moving her lips in silent fervent prayer.

A bell clanged upon her heart. She felt him seize her hand:

"Come!"

All the seas of the world tumbled about her heart. He was drawing her into them: he would drown her. She gripped with both hands at the iron railing.

"Come!"

No! No! No! It was impossible. Her hands clutched the iron in frenzy. Amid the seas she sent a cry of anguish.

"Eveline! Evvy!"

He rushed beyond the barrier and called to her to follow. He was shouted at to go on but he still called to her. She set her white face to him, passive, like a helpless animal. Her eyes gave him no sign of love or farewell or recognition.

(1914)

* * * *

Now that your reading of Joyce's story has given you material to mull over, you should consider some questions that good writers think about

---

[1] "The end of pleasure is pain!"

as they prepare to write. Granted, experienced writers might go over some of these prewriting matters almost unconsciously—and perhaps *as* they write instead of before. But in order to explain how to get the process going for you, we will present these considerations one by one.

Who Are My Readers?

Unless you are writing a journal or a diary for your own satisfaction, your writing always has an audience—the person or group of people who will read it. You need to keep this audience in mind as you plan what to say and as you choose the best way to express your ideas.

Analyze the Audience

No doubt you already have considerable audience awareness. You would never write a job application letter using the latest in-group slang, nor would you normally correspond with your dear Aunt Minnie in impersonal formal English. Writing for diverse groups about whom you know little is more difficult than writing for a specific audience whom you know well. In this class, for instance, you will be writing for your fellow students and for your instructor, a mixed group often thrown together by a computer. Although they are diverse, they do share some characteristics. For one thing, when you begin to write a paper about "Eveline," you know that your audience has read the story; thus you need not summarize the plot. Also, the people in your audience are college educated (or becoming so); therefore, you need not avoid difficult words like *epitome*, *eclectic*, or *protean* if they are the appropriate choices. Other shared qualities will become apparent as you get to know your classmates and your instructor.

Prewriting Exercise

Compose a brief letter persuading Eveline that she should (or should not) leave Frank. Your argumentative tactics, your attitude, and even your word choice must be affected by what you know about Eveline from reading the story—her essential timidity, her insecurity, her self-doubt, her capacity for self-deception.

Then, write briefly to her bullying father explaining to him why his dutiful daughter has deserted him.

Finally, write Frank a short letter explaining why Eveline will not be going away with him.

Be prepared to discuss with the class specific ways in which your letters are different when you change your audience.

Why Am I Writing?

Every kind of writing, even a grocery list, has a purpose. You seldom sit down to write without some aim in mind, and this purpose affects your whole approach to writing. The immediate response to the question "Why am I writing?" may be that your teacher or your employer asked you to. But that answer will not help you understand the reasons that make writing worth doing—and worth reading.

Reasons for Writing

Sometimes you may write in order *to express* your own feelings, as in a diary or a love letter. More frequently, though, you will be writing for several other people, and the response you want from these prospective readers will determine your purpose. If, for instance, you want your audience to be amused by your writing (as in an informal essay or friendly letter), your purpose is *to entertain.* If you want your readers to gain some knowledge from your writing (say, how to get to your house from the airport), then you are writing *to inform.* If you want your readers to agree with an opinion or to accept an idea (as in a letter to the editor or an advertisement), then you are writing *to persuade.* Of course, these aims overlap—as do most things in the writing process—but usually one purpose predominates.

Most of your writing in this course, as in real life, will attempt to persuade in one way or another. Your purpose is often to convince your reader to agree with the points you are making. Logical ideas set down in clear, interesting writing should prove convincing and keep your readers reading.

Prewriting Exercise

In writing the three letters to various characters, you have already noticed how audience and purpose can change the way you think and write about "Eveline." After studying the four writing suggestions that follow, reread the story. You may discover that you have more ideas and feelings about it than you first imagined. Thinking about prospective readers and determining your purpose will help you to understand your own views and reactions better.

1. If your purpose is *to express* your personal response:
   Write down your feelings about Eveline in a journal entry or in a brief note to a close friend. Do you sympathize with Eveline? Pity her? Does she irritate you or make you angry? Be as forthright as you can.

2. If your purpose is *to inform* someone else:
   Write a brief summary (less than one hundred words) of "Eveline"

for a fellow student who wants to know if the story is worth reading. Write a slightly longer summary for your instructor (or someone else who has read the story) who wants to know if you have grasped its important points.

Which summary was easier to write? What purposes besides providing information were involved in each summary?

3. If your purpose is *to entertain* yourself or your readers:
How would you rewrite the ending of "Eveline" to make it more positive or romantic — to make it appeal to a wider audience? Would such an ending be consistent with the earlier parts of the story? Would it be true to human experience?

4. If your purpose is *to persuade* your readers:
The author tells us that Eveline held two letters in her lap, but we do not know their contents. Write your version of one of them. Try to construe from evidence in the story what Eveline would have said to convince her father or her brother that she had good reasons for going away with Frank. How would she persuade them to forgive her? Consider also what other purposes Eveline would try to achieve in each of these letters.

What Ideas Should I Use?

Understanding literature involves learning what questions to ask yourself as you examine a literary work. To sharpen your comprehension of the story and develop ideas for writing, you may want to use one of the following methods of discovering ideas, all of which involve questioning. This whole process of deciding what ideas to use in writing is called *invention.*

Self-Questioning

These are the kinds of questions you might ask yourself when studying a work of literature: questions about characters, their circumstances, their motives and conflicts, their fears and expectations, their relations with other characters; questions about the setting in which the story takes place; questions about any repeated details that seem significant; questions about the meaning and value of actions and events. Write out your responses to these questions about "Eveline" and keep them handy as you formulate your essay.

1. What is Eveline's home life like?
2. How does she expect her new life to be different?
3. Do you think this expectation is realistic?
4. Why is the word *dust* mentioned so often?
5. List all the concrete details you can find that describe Eveline's home.

6. How old is Eveline? Is her age important for any reason?

7. What sort of person is her father? What kind of "bad way" is he in on Saturday nights?

8. How does Eveline feel about her father?

9. What sort of person was Eveline's mother? What happened to her? Does Eveline identify with her mother in any way?

10. How does Eveline feel about her dead mother?

11. What do you think her mother meant when she kept repeating "the end of pleasure is pain"? Why would she say this? Was she really crazy — or only worn down?

12. What does Eveline's father mean when he tells her, "I know these sailor chaps"? What possible reasons could he have for trying to break up Eveline's romance?

13. What sort of person is Frank? What does Eveline actually know about him?

14. Has Eveline romanticized Frank in any way? Is her father's objection to him perhaps justified?

15. What is Eveline's duty to her father? What promise did she make to her dying mother?

16. What is her duty to herself? Does she really believe she has a "right to happiness"? Why or why not?

17. How does Eveline feel about leaving her brother?

18. In what ways is Eveline "like a helpless animal"? What is she afraid of?

19. Why do you think her eyes give Frank "no sign of love or farewell or recognition"?

20. Do you think Eveline made the right decision? Why or why not?

During the invention stage, you want to turn up as many ideas as possible. Later, after choosing a focus for your paper, such as characterization or theme, you will then select those story details which you'll be discussing when developing your ideas. Even though you narrow your focus, you still need to consider other elements of the story — imagery, symbolism, setting, point of view — as these elements serve to reveal character or theme.

Directed Freewriting

Many people find that they can best bring ideas to the surface by writing freely, with no restrictions about correctness. When you engage in freewriting in order to "free" ideas from your subconscious mind, you should think of a pertinent question and just start writing.

Consider this question: "Why does Eveline stay with her abusive father?" As you think, start writing. Set down everything that comes to mind. Write in complete sentences, but do not concern yourself with spelling, word choice, or punctuation. You are writing for your own benefit, attempting to discover everything about Eveline's decision that you have in mind after reading and thinking about the story.

After writing for ten minutes (or after you run out of ideas), stop and read over what you have said. Underline any idea that might serve as the focus for a paper. Put stars in the margins beside any ideas that sound useful as support for your interpretation. Figure 1–1 provides an example of freewriting turned out by a student on this same question.

If you find freewriting a good method for generating ideas, you may want to go through the process again. This time write down a statement that you underlined in your first freewriting as a possible approach for your paper. Let's say you decide to focus (as our student did) on the idea that Eveline's sense of insecurity causes her to remain with her father. Put that sentence at the top of a fresh sheet of paper and begin writing. Continue recording your thoughts until you either run out of ideas or run out of time (fifteen minutes is usually enough). Then read over your freewriting, underlining or putting stars by any ideas that you think would be good support to include in your paper.

A word of advice: Do not think of your freewriting as a first draft. The ideas produced here need to be organized into a unified, logical plan — a process discussed in our next chapter.

Problem-Solving

Another method of generating material for a paper involves *problem-solving*. Consider some part of the work that you feel you need to understand better and pose yourself a problem, like this:

> Explain the ending of the story so that it is understandable and believable.

As you seek a solution, ask yourself more questions.

> — Why does Eveline refuse to leave her pinched, narrow life with her father and the younger children?
> — Is there anything about the way she was brought up that makes this action seem reasonable, perhaps inevitable?
> — Would her life have been different if she had been born male instead of female? What happened to her brothers, for instance?
> — Does her religion have any bearing on her decision?

Write down all the reasons you can find to help explain why Eveline does not leave home. Do any of these reasons shed light on the theme — the overall meaning of the story? Do you now perhaps see a meaningful point you could develop that ties in with the theme of the story?

Why does Eveline stay? She feels a sense of duty — to her mother (dying wish / promise). *
Father old, lonely, needs her to run household. She needs to feel _loved_, * to feel she belongs. *
Naturally, she's afraid to leave home for the first time — and go so far away. * She's _insecure_. But she's 19 — must want to test her wings, have a better life than her poor mother's. She's suffocating there in all that dust! Frank represents freedom and romance and _fun_. She thinks she likes him, maybe loves him. She doesn't seem sure. But her father's warned her about Frank. * And how much does she actually know about him? What if he's all promises, promises — and then deserts her halfway around the world? * Maybe her father's right. But try telling a teenager anything! How does she feel about her parents? She knows her mother's life was miserable — she gave herself completely to the family — dies a pitiful death. She fears her * father who must have been responsible for alot of her mother's misery & hardship. But E. has a _strong sense of duty_ — and she does love her father despite his many faults. *

FIGURE 1–1 Directed Freewriting

Clustering

Another useful way of getting ideas out of your head and down on paper involves *clustering*. Begin with a blank sheet of paper. In the center write a crucial question about the story that you want to investigate, and circle the words. Then, draw a line out from that circle, write an idea or a question related to the central idea, and circle that. Spiraling out from that circle, add and circle any further associations that you can make. Continue drawing lines from the center, like spokes radiating from a wheel, and record any other ideas or questions that are related. When you finish, you will have a cluster of related ideas resembling Figure 1–2, which explores the question, "Why does Eveline decide to stay with her father?"

Clustering works just fine with statements, as well as with questions. If you think you might want to write a paper focusing on the characterization of Eveline, you could just write her name in the center of the page and begin recording all that you know about her. Your first ring of circles might include father, mother, siblings, house, church, job, Frank, lifestyle, personality—and spiral out from there.

You can see that this technique works well for exploring any aspect of a work. As you progress through this course, you may decide to write in the middle of the page *point of view, setting, imagery*, or whatever element you think might serve as a meaningful focus for your paper. If you have trouble reeling out enough material, you need to try another element. If you produce too much, you can narrow your focus.

What Point Should I Make?

Besides providing a thorough understanding of the story, these prewriting activities serve to stir up ideas for a thesis—the controlling idea for your paper—and to help you discover evidence to support convincingly the observations you will make in developing that thesis.

Relate a Part to the Whole

One bit of advice that will help you write meaningful literary papers is this:

> Devise a thesis that makes its point by relating some aspect of the work to its theme, i.e., to the meaning of the whole.

Our questions so far have led you to approach Joyce's story by analyzing character and plot. But writing a simple character sketch (in which you discuss what sort of person Eveline is) would not produce a satisfactory literary paper. You need to go beyond that one-dimensional approach and

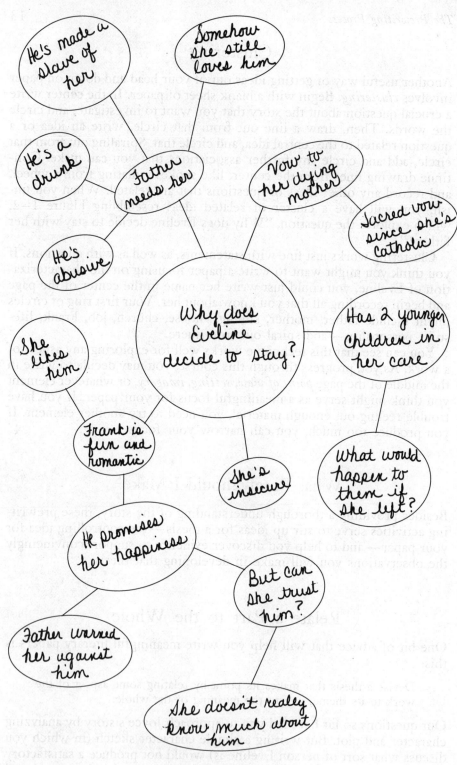

FIGURE 1–2 Clustering

make your essay say something about the story itself. In short, you must relate your analysis of her character to the theme.

How Do I Find the Theme?

You may have learned that the theme of a work is the moral. In a sense that is true, but a moral suggests a neatly stated, preachy comment on some vice or virtue, whereas a literary theme will seldom be so pat and should never sound preachy. In order to discover theme you need to decide what you have learned from reading the story. What did the author reveal about the behavior of human beings, about the conduct of society? Rather than looking for a moral, look for some insight into the human condition.

Sometimes you may have a theme in mind but be unable to express it except in a cliché. You could, for instance, see the theme of "Eveline" as an acceptance of the old adage, "Better the devil you know than the devil you don't." Although this idea is acceptable as a theme, a clearer statement would relate the concept more closely to the story, like this:

> In "Eveline" Joyce focuses on the painful choices a young woman faces concerning her desire for a better life, her duty to her family, and her fear of leaving home.

Certainly her character—the kind of person she is—relates directly to this theme. If, for instance, Eveline had been a willful, disobedient child who grew up into a rebellious, irresponsible young woman, the outcome of the story would surely have been different.

The problem is thus to find a thesis that will allow you to explain how Eveline's upbringing has conditioned her for the inevitable failure of nerve, the return to servitude and security, the relinquishing of hopes and dreams.

Stating the Thesis

A good thesis statement should be a *complete sentence* that clearly conveys the point you plan to make in your paper. Notice the difference between a *topic*, which is not a complete sentence, and a *thesis*, which is.

Topic: A characterization of Eveline

Thesis: Joyce's characterization of Eveline as a dutiful daughter enables us to discover why she makes her strange decision at the end.

Topic: The role of the church in "Eveline"

Thesis: The role of the Catholic church is crucial in shaping Eveline's personality and in helping us understand why she sacrifices herself for her family.

Topic: Dust as a symbol in "Eveline"

Thesis: Joyce's use of dust as a controlling symbol in "Eveline"
           reinforces our understanding of this young woman's dreary,
           suffocating, arid life.

Your thesis sentence should be broad enough to include all the ideas
that are necessary as evidence but narrow enough to make a precise
statement of your main point and focus your thoughts. If your thesis is
too broad—as, for example, "Joyce's characterization of Eveline is extremely well drawn"—you may end up skimming the surface, never
providing a meaningful interpretation of the work. Notice that the previous overly broad thesis is unsatisfactory for another reason: it fails to
make a real point.

A better thesis for a paper on "Eveline" might be stated in any of the
following ways:

Eveline's Catholic upbringing as a dutiful daughter makes impossible
her hopes for a happier life.

If Eveline had been born male instead of female, she might have
escaped her unhappy home life, as her brother did.

Eveline, "trapped like a helpless animal" by her deathbed promise to
her mother, is morally unable to break her vow and flee her miserable
home to seek a new life for herself.

Having been thoroughly beaten down by her brutal, domineering
father, Eveline lacks the self-confidence to flee in search of her own life.

Most of the ideas and details you need to support any of these thesis
statements will appear in the freewriting or clustering that you have
already completed. In the next chapter, we will suggest some ways in
which you might arrange this material in the paper itself.

2

The Writing Process

Now that you have examined your reactions to "Eveline," collected your ideas, and formulated a thesis sentence, you are ready to organize this material into a workable arrangement for writing.

How Should I Organize My Ideas?

A traditional but effective format includes three parts: the beginning (the introduction), the middle (the body), and the end (the conclusion). This simple plan will serve for almost any piece of writing.

The Basic Structure: Beginning, Middle, and End

The *beginning* of the paper has two main functions: to engage your readers' interest and to let them know what point you expect to make. The *middle* portion of your paper develops and supports the main point with details, examples, reasons, and explanations that make the general thesis more specific and more understandable. The *end* of the paper returns your readers to the main point by summarizing or stressing the general idea you want them to perceive from reading your essay. Later in the chapter, we will offer you more specific suggestions about how to begin and end a paper effectively. For now we want to wrestle with the problem of organizing the body—or the middle part—of your paper about "Eveline."

The Basic Approach: Devising a Plan

The thesis statements that we presented in Chapter 1 approached Joyce's story by relating Eveline's character to the meaning of the work. In the prewriting activities, you generated ample insights and observations about Eveline. Now you must find some arrangement for your ideas in order to present them clearly to your audience. Here is a general plan for writing a paper about a character in literature:

1. *Beginning.* Identify the character you are analyzing and state the main point you intend to make about him or her (this point will serve as your thesis sentence).

2. *Middle.* Present the details of the character's personality that led you to your thesis. Pay attention to the following: what the character says, thinks, and does; what other characters say and think about the person; and what the narrator tells about the character.

3. *End.* Conclude your interpretation and reinforce how this character's role functions to reveal theme.

The middle section of your paper can be arranged in several ways. You could organize your writing, for instance, around *central traits,* like "timidity, cowardice, passivity," or around *central events* in the work that make the character's nature clear. Because "Eveline" contains so few events or incidents, you will probably choose to organize this character analysis around central traits. Here is a brief plan for a paper based on one of our sample thesis statements:

1. *Beginning.* Eveline lacks courage to flee from her domineering father and seek her own happiness.

2. *Middle.* Evidence of Eveline's lack of courage can be seen in the following:
   —Her passivity as a female who lacks the resources and imagination to challenge her traditional role;
   —Her physical fear of her father, perhaps generalized to all men;
   —Her reverence for her mother's memory and the promise she made to keep the family together.

3. *End.* Eveline exemplifies how a woman may be trapped by passivity, fear, and obligations.

This plan states the thesis and then indicates the subpoints that will become topic sentences for several paragraphs of development and support.

The following plan organizes the middle of a paper on the same thesis by stating the topic sentences as specific fears that contribute to Eveline's lack of courage:

Eveline's lack of courage is illustrated in these ways:
   —She is afraid to go against her religious beliefs.
   —She is afraid something will happen to her father if she leaves him.
   —She is afraid her mother's memory will continue to haunt her.
   —She is afraid Frank will treat her as her father treated her mother.

By writing out the subpoints, you provide yourself with a plan to follow

in writing the paragraphs that will make up the main part (the body) of
your character analysis.

Ordering the Ideas

As you write the middle section of your essay, you will have to decide
which point to take up first and which ones to use later in the development of your thesis. Ordinarily, you can arrange your topic sentences in
two ways: logical order or chronological order.

Logical order involves arranging ideas in a way that will appeal to your
readers' intelligence and good sense. Many writers begin with a less
crucial idea and work up to their most important one. The logic behind
this arrangement is based on the assumption that since your final point is
the one your readers are most likely to remember, it should also be your
strongest point.

In the second plan for writing just presented to you for a paper on
"Eveline," the topic sentences about fears are arranged according to the
increasing strength of Eveline's feelings: the plan starts with a general
point about religion, moves to more specific fears about leaving her
father and remembering her mother, and concludes with an insight about
what could happen in her life with Frank. The last idea is particularly
appropriate, as it sums up the previous two points by relating Eveline's
anxiety about Frank to her feelings about her parents' relationship.

Chronological order, which is based on time, involves writing about
events in the order in which they occur. Most narratives, such as short
stories and novels, use a chronological approach. Because you will be
writing about literature, your organization for a paper could simply
follow the chronology of the work under consideration. Logical order is
preferable, though, as it provides a more analytical arrangement that will
keep your paper from seeming like a mere plot summary.

Maintaining a Critical Focus

Even though you arrange your ideas logically, the paper could still sound
like a plot summary if you imbed your critical[1] insights in the middle of
paragraphs. In order to achieve a sharp critical focus, the topic sentences
(usually the first one of each paragraph in the body of the paper) should
be critical observations supporting or relating to your thesis. In academic
writing, placing the topic sentences at the beginnings of paragraphs helps
your instructor to follow your thinking. You should in each paragraph
use the plot details to support or prove the critical generalization in the
topic sentence.

[1]As you probably know, the term *critical,* as applied to literature, means an evaluative assessment,
not fault finding.

Distinguishing Critical Comments from Plot Details   Notice the difference between a critical comment and a plot detail:

Plot detail:	Jackson's story opens on a balmy summer day.
Critical comment:	By setting her story on a balmy summer day, Jackson creates a false sense of well being.
Plot detail:	The oiler, who dies, was the strongest of the four men in the boat.
Critical comment:	The oiler's death is ironic because it upsets our expectations of survival of the fittest.

If you want to use both a critical observation and a plot detail in your topic sentence, be sure that the critical comment appears in the independent (main) clause and that the plot detail is placed in a subordinate position:

Plot detail:	Granny detests Cornelia's blue lampshades.
Critical comment:	One of Cornelia's blue lampshades becomes the image of Granny's diminishing spark of life.
Combined:	Although Granny detests Cornelia's blue lampshades, one of them becomes the image of her diminishing spark of life.
Plot detail:	The dog in "To Build a Fire" knows better than to go out in weather fifty below zero.
Critical comment:	The dog serves as a foil for the foolish man in Jack London's "To Build a Fire."
Combined:	In "To Build a Fire" the dog, who knows better than to go out in weather fifty below zero, serves as a foil for the foolish man.

Developing with Details

No matter what organization you choose for the body of your paper, remember to state each critical generalization clearly and to support each one with enough specific references to the story to be convincing. Sort through the observations that you made in your prewriting, and select those that relate to the topic sentences in your plan. The following sample paragraph shows how a writer uses specific detail and brief quotations from the story to develop the idea stated in the topic sentence:

> Eveline lacks courage to seek a life of her own because she fears that her father will not be able to cope if she leaves him. Her anxiety is heightened as she recalls that she and her brothers and sisters are grown up and that her mother is dead. If she leaves, her father will be all alone. She realizes that he is "usually fairly bad on a Saturday night" and recognizes that his drinking problem will not get any better after she leaves. Also she has noticed that "Her father was becoming

old lately" and assumes that "he would miss her." As a dutiful daughter, Eveline seems to feel that going away with Frank means abandoning her aging father, and that may be why she has written a letter to him — to ease the blow of her departure and to soothe her own conscience.

Questions for Consideration

In the sample paragraph, has the writer given adequate support for the topic sentence? What details from the story has the writer cited to develop the main point? What other details could be used? Where does the writer bring in personal opinion (or interpretation)? Do you think the interpretation is reasonable?

How Should I Begin?

Your introduction is crucial to the effectiveness of your essay — and often proves to be the most difficult to write. Try to think of this part as challenging (rather than merely hard to do), and you may find yourself rising to new heights of accomplishment.

Postpone If Nothing Comes

Remember that you do not have to write your introduction first just because it appears first in the finished essay. As long as you have your thesis clearly in mind (or clearly written out on your planning sheet), you can start at once on the body of the paper. Once you begin generating material, you may suddenly perceive an idea that will serve nicely as a beginning. Or, if you postpone your introduction until the next day, your subconscious mind may provide you with the perfect opening. You may find that some of your best ideas come to you in the shower.

Write an Appealing Opening

Work especially hard on your opening sentence. You want to engage the interest of your readers at once. If you begin like this,

"Eveline" is a very interesting short story by James Joyce,

no one other than your loving mother is likely to read any further unless paid to. You should mention the author and title somewhere in your introduction (even though both may appear in your title). But try also to incorporate something specific in that first sentence. You might want to focus your readers' attention on an incident that you consider significant:

> In his short story "Eveline," James Joyce portrays a young woman paralyzed by the need to make a decision that will change the course of her life.

Or you could start this way:

> In James Joyce's "Eveline," we see a tired young woman accustomed to the "odour of dusty cretonne" trying to muster courage to exchange her dreary existence for the unknown excitements of life with a "sailor chap" in exotic Buenos Ayres.

Or you might try this:

> In the closing lines of James Joyce's "Eveline," the young woman of the title stands "passive, like a helpless animal," watching her dreams of romance and excitement fade into the mist.

State the Thesis

Even more important than an arresting opening sentence is the need to let your readers know somewhere in the introductory paragraph what the paper is going to be about. But try to avoid stating your main point too bluntly:

> I am going to show that Eveline stays home with her domineering father because she lacks courage to go with Frank.

The "I am going to show" is not stylistically effective. Try to suggest a bit more subtly the direction of your thought, the case that you will present within your essay. Your thesis should sound more like this:

> Having been thoroughly beaten down by her brutal, domineering father, Eveline lacks the courage to go with Frank in search of her own happiness.

If you combine your thesis with a general statement about the story, you should produce a worthwhile introduction for a short paper:

> In James Joyce's "Eveline," we see a tired young woman accustomed to the "odour of dusty cretonne" trying to muster courage to exchange her dreary existence for the unknown excitements of life with a "sailor chap" in exotic Buenos Ayres. But, having been thoroughly beaten down by her brutal father, Eveline lacks the courage to go with Frank in search of her own happiness.

How Should I End?

Your conclusion is just as important as your introduction—perhaps even more so. You want to leave your readers feeling satisfied that you have written something worth reading, that their time has not been wasted. Do not give them a chance to ask, "Well, so what?" at the end.

Relate the Discussion to Theme

Impress your readers with the value of your discussion by reinforcing in the conclusion how your analysis illuminates the theme, or meaning, of the work. This process may involve echoing your thesis statement in the introduction. But take care to avoid simply repeating what you said at the beginning. Your conclusion should offer a clear expression of how your discussion relates to the theme of the story.

Postpone or Write Ahead

Conclusions, like introductions, do not necessarily have to be written when you come to them. If you should get some additional insight concerning the theme as you work on composing the main part of the paper, take a minute to jot down the idea so that you can later incorporate this insight into your ending. Or, you could stop right then, write the final paragraph, and put it aside until you come to it. Chances are that you may change this conclusion later, but having something to work with is an enormous help—especially if you are getting tired.

If you write your way through the entire paper and still have no inspiration for the conclusion, then force yourself. Write something and keep revising it until you produce a version that pleases you. The following suggestion may help.

Write an Emphatic Final Sentence

No matter how exhausted you are when you compose your final paragraph, do not risk ruining the effect of your entire essay by letting your conclusion trail off at the end with a limp last sentence. Regardless of the brilliance of your middle paragraphs, your readers are going to feel dejected if you end like this:

> All in all, I think "Eveline" was a fine story, and I think anyone would enjoy reading it and maybe even learn something from it.

We have advice for you in the next chapter on how to compose emphatic sentences. Study those suggestions before you rewrite your conclusion. Work *hard* on that last line. Try to come up with a final paragraph that will crystalize your meaning, something like this one:

> Joyce makes clear throughout the story that Eveline's personality has been heavily influenced by her dutiful upbringing; her passivity has been reinforced by her promise to her dying mother. She is herself now doomed to endure that "life of commonplace sacrifices" that led her mother into despair.

Composing the First Draft

At this point you should be ready to compose the first draft of your essay on "Eveline." You have completed the prewriting activities, devised a working thesis statement, arranged your main supporting points, and selected plenty of details to use for development. You may have even written some of your introduction and conclusion. Now is the time to move beyond these preliminary stages and write a complete draft of your paper.

Pausing to Rescan

You may have been told to get your first draft down on paper as quickly as possible and then, once it was completed, to revise it. This is probably not bad advice if you suffer from writer's block, but you should know that recent studies show that most skilled writers go about it in a different way. Experienced writers tend to pause frequently as they compose—to rescan and perhaps reword what they have just written; to think about what to say next; to make additions, substitutions, or deletions; to be sure a sentence says precisely what they want it to say. After the first draft is completed, these accomplished writers revise still further, preferably several hours or even days later so that they can reexamine their writing from a reader's perspective.

If you tend to write headlong without pausing once you begin, perhaps you should try to slow down. Mina Shaughnessy, a noted composition expert, speaks of "the messy process that leads to clarity" in writing. This messy process involves pausing and thinking and reviewing and rewording if you expect to write well.

Citing Your Sources

The Modern Language Association has set a standard way to credit a source when you quote material in an essay. If you are using only a single *primary* source—the work of literature under discussion—you cite in parentheses after the quotation the page (or pages) on which you found that material:

> Eveline admits that hers is "a hard life," yet decides, ". . . now that she was about to leave it she did not find it a wholly undesirable life" (5).

If you are using more than one primary source, you need to include the author's last name in the parentheses—with only a single blank space separating it from the page number—unless you mention the author's name in the text of your paper.

> At the end of the story Eveline is "like a helpless animal" (Joyce 6), and Hulga at the end is similarly helpless, "left sitting on the straw in the dusty sunlight" (O'Connor 391).

Note: If you are using library sources, the situation becomes more complicated. Consult Chapter 17 for complete instructions in writing researched papers.

The Work Cited Sheet   Even if you are citing only your primary source, you need to let your readers know what it is. On a separate page at the end of your essay, center the title (Work Cited or Works Cited) at the top. Using double spacing, provide complete publication information for your source or sources. The Work Cited entry for a paper on "Eveline" using this text would look like this:

Joyce, James. "Eveline." Literature and the

Writing Process. Eds. Elizabeth McMahan,

Susan Day, and Robert Funk. 3rd ed. New

York: Macmillan, 1993. 4-6.

Notice the *hanging* indention: indent all lines after the first one five spaces. Space twice after periods, only once after colons and commas. Use an abbreviated form of the publisher's firm — just Macmillan, not Macmillan Publishing Company, Inc. If you are using more than one source, alphabetize the entries by their authors' last names.

Enlisting Help from Peers

After you have completed a legible first draft, you need to find someone to read your draft carefully for you and let you know where it needs improvement. Tell your reader not to worry at this point about surface errors (that is, errors in grammar, punctuation, or usage). It's not that such mistakes are unimportant; it's just too soon in the writing process to be concerned about them.

An ideal person to help you evaluate your first draft is another member of your own writing class. This person will be familiar with the assignment and will understand why you are writing the paper and for whom. Many composition teachers include *peer evaluation* sessions as part of the regular classroom activities. Students exchange papers in groups of two or three and respond on a separate sheet of paper to any questions submitted by the writer of the draft. In the next section we provide a list of questions that are designed to get at typical concerns in literary papers. If you use this checklist, feel free to add to it any additional questions directed to points in your first draft.

An important part of the peer evaluation process involves group discussion. After returning to the writers the first drafts and the written responses to the questions, every member of the group should quickly study the responses and then discuss them with the person who made the suggestions. If you fail to see why someone suggested a particular revision, politely ask why. Most differences can be quickly resolved in friendly conversation.

Sample Student Paper — First Draft

Here is the first draft of a paper on "Eveline" written by Wendy Dennison, a student at Illinois State University whose directed freewriting for this same paper appears in Figure 1–1. In order to save space, we have combined and summarized the responses made by Wendy's two peer evaluators and by her instructor. Representative comments, suggestions, and questions from all three readers appear in the margin.

Are there too many rhetorical questions??

Wendy Dennison

English 102

January 23, 1991

Mention title of story here
⋁

For Fear of Failing Alone

Eveline, the title character of   [1]
Joyce's short story is given that once-in-a-
lifetime chance--to leave her old life to
begin a new one. But she rejects the offer
Fate--or God--makes, preferring instead to
Isn't it Frank? settle back down into the dusty, abusive life
she has lead. Why does she not go away with
Frank? The obvious responses--duty to her
mother's dying wish, the love of her father,
the love of her home--do not quite ring true,
for Eveline owes little or nothing to her
parents or her home. In fact, leaving seems a
much more logical choice. So why does Eveline
really stay behind? She is afraid of failure.

Do you want to give away your conclusion? What does Eveline really owe her   [2]
mother? Her "promise . . . that she keep the
home together as long as she could" (6) was

unfairly given. It was unfair of her mother to
ask such a thing of her, as it prevents her
from having a life of her own. It is very
likely that Eveline will never marry and leave
her father as long as he is alive, for she
will always recall that promise. Why stay for
this?

Does this ¶ need more details?

Why should we be surprised that [3]
Eveline might wish to leave her father? An
abusive drunk, he has taken advantage of her
promise to her mother. She is forced to keep
house for him, yet must beg from him money
with which to do so. He practically accuses
her of stealing, claiming ". . . she used to
squander the money, that she had no head, that
he wasn't going to give her his hard-earned
money to throw about the streets . . ." (5).
A bully, he has scared her with threats of
beatings, giving her "palpitations" (4).
Eveline reallizes that with her brothers
gone, ther is "nobody to protect her" (5)
from her father's rage. Why would she ever
want to stay with a man of whom she is terribly
afraid? She did remember happy moments with
him when the family went on picnics and he was
jolly and played with the children.

Good intro. of quotation

Does this detail fit?

Eveline's home life is so unhealthy [4]
that she would be wise to leave it all behind.
For all that she does, she still does not feel
quite a part of everything. For example, she
knows nothing about the picture of the priest,
not even his name. The dustiness of the house,
of which Joyce reminds us periodically, is
suggestive of the pervading dirtiness and
squalor of her daily life. It is significant

Why is this important?

best word?

Does this fit? | also that she often thinks about her
unpleasant, unhappy job. Her home is clearly
not conducive to happiness. So why does she   */ Combine sentences?*
stay there?

                  The only real reason why Eveline   [5]
would stay in Irelnad is the fact that she is
desperately afraid of failing on her own. If

Check whole paper
for typos!   she leaves the familiar, no matter how
unpleasant, she risks failure. "She was
about to explore another life with Frank"

Good!   (5). The word "explore" is significant here,
as it brings to mind uncertainty and risk, two
factors that Eveline is not prepared to deal
with. She admits that hers "was a hard life,"

Tense shift?   yet thinks, "now that she was about to leave
it she did not find it an wholly undesirable

Is this sentence life" (5). When she sits in the growing
O.K.?   darkness--the threat of her father returning
from work--with the letters in her lap,
Eveline calls up a couple of good memories to
calm her fears, effectively helping to
convince herself to stay home.

                  Afraid of failing on her own,   [6]
Eveline retreats into the familiar,
convincing herself that life with father
cannot be as frightening as a risky life with

Is this a good
detail to use here? Frank. "Why should she be unhappy? She had a
right to happiness" (6). Indeed, Eveline
decides that a predictable--if abusive and
unhealthy--life is better than one without
direction or pattern.

Well done, Wendy! But please outline this draft to be sure the material is tightly unified.

Work Cited

Not accurate!
Check the MLA
style!

Joyce, James. "Eveline," in <u>Literature and</u>
<u>the Writing Process</u>. Edited by Elizabeth
McMahan, Susan Day, and Robert Funk. NY:
McMillan, 1993. Pages 4-6.

Advice for Writing

If you want to write a paper focusing on character, you will need to choose a suitable work from the short story anthology beginning on page 248. Kate Chopin's "Désirée's Baby" would be a good choice for a brief paper. Read the story once for pleasure. Then turn to Chart 4–1 at the end of Chapter 4. See how many of the questions you can answer after a single reading, but do not be discouraged if you can respond to only a few. You need to read the story again — slowly and carefully, paying attention to details. After a second reading, you should be able to answer most of the questions on the list and begin arriving at an understanding of the story.

In order to come up with ideas, find a sheet of paper and perform one of the prewriting activities discussed in Chapter 1 — self-questioning, directed freewriting, clustering, or whatever works for you. Look at the following "Ideas for Critical Writing" and "Ideas for Responsive Writing" if you need more help. Read the story again — and again — if you are still puzzled about its meaning. We think that the story has two distinct themes, perhaps more. When you have devised a thesis and come up with enough material to support it, write your first draft.

Next, you need to find someone to help you get started revising, someone who will respond in writing to the peer evaluation checklist in Chart 2–1. Perhaps your instructor will provide class time for this activity. If not, find someone who has read or is willing to read the story and can thus give you thoughtful suggestions for improving your paper. In the next chapter, "The Rewriting Process," we explain in detail how you can go about making your changes.

Ideas for Writing

Ideas for Responsive Writing

1. Have you ever known anyone like Désirée? Perhaps your grandmother or mother is this kind of selfless woman whose whole identity revolves around a man. Write a character sketch of this person, using plenty of specific details to make your essay believable and interesting.

CHART 2–1. Peer Evaluation
Checklist for Revision

The following questions and guidelines will help you evaluate your own or another student's first draft. If you are doing peer evaluation in class, exchange papers; read your partner's thoroughly; then write out, in full sentences, responses to the questions and suggestions that follow. Your conscientious evaluation will be valuable to your partner in the revision stage. You will also learn about composition by doing close analysis of an essay, and, of course, another student will give you helpful remarks and advice on your own work in progress.

If you are not doing peer evaluation in the classroom, try to talk a friend into reading your paper and thoughtfully answering these questions:

1. Does the paper have a clear purpose? What is the main point? Does the whole paper relate to the main point? Is the main point interesting or too predictable?

2. Are the ideas consistently clear? Make a note of any sentences or paragraphs that you had to reread. Make a note of any words you found confusing.

3. Does the paper seem well organized? Is it logical? Is there perhaps a better order for the body paragraphs? Are there any paragraphs or supporting ideas that do not seem to belong?

4. Is there enough material in the essay? Does it need further details or examples? Make a note of places where you would like to see more details or examples. Write questions to help your partner add details. For example, if the essay says, "Eveline did not much like her father," you could ask, "Exactly how did she feel about him?"

5. Are all the quotations from the story accurate? Do they appear within quotation marks?

6. Does the opening or the closing need revision? Make suggestions for improvement if you can.

2. Have you ever known anyone like Armand? Perhaps you have a friend who is reckless, self-centered, and lacks the ability to truly love another person. Write a character sketch of this person, using plenty of specific details to make your essay plausible and appealing.

Ideas for Critical Writing

1. In discussing Kate Chopin's story, "Désirée's Baby," focus on Désirée's character to show how being the kind of person she is helps bring about the sad conclusion of the story. Why, after Armand rejects her, does she not take the baby and return home as her mother requests? What is the significance of the white imagery associated with her?

2. Focus on Armand's character to show how being the kind of person he is causes the sad ending. In deciding where the cause of the tragedy really lies, consider Armand's treatment of the slaves, his domination of his wife, and his concern for his proud family name.

The Rewriting Process

You are probably relieved and pleased that you have completed the first draft of your essay. A large portion of your work is finished. But do not be in a rush to type the finished version yet. You need first to do a careful revision of your paper.

What Is Revision?

Revision involves more than just tidying your prose. The process of correcting your spelling, punctuation, and mechanics is called *editing,* but your paper is not ready for that yet. First you need *re-vision,* seeing again to discover ways to make your writing better. Schedule your time so that you are able to lay the rough draft aside at least overnight before attempting to revise. While a draft is still warm from the writing, you cannot look at it objectively. And looking at it objectively is the basis of revision. Your fondness for a well-turned paragraph should not prevent you from cutting it when, in the cold light of morning, you realize that it does not quite relate to your thesis. Your relief at having the words down on paper should not interfere with your crossing them out and rewriting when necessary.

As you examine your cooled-down essay, you may even see that while you were writing, your main point shifted somewhat. Sometimes writers discover what they actually want to say while trying to write something slightly different. You may need to go back and change the thesis, rewrite paragraphs, cut others, and find new support from the literary work before you can consider the paper finished. For example, one student made the point in the first draft of a paper on Flannery O'Connor's "Good Country People" (see pages 378–391) that the main characters are all self-deceived. As she reread her draft, she noticed that she had focused almost entirely on Hulga Joy and her mother but had said almost nothing about the young Bible salesman. After some reflection—and another reading of the story—she decided to change her thesis to emphasize the point that the Bible salesman, who makes his living through willful deception, is the only character who is not self-deceived. By shifting her focus to a consideration of this insight, she discovered a number of related ideas that she had previously overlooked and thus was able to strengthen the content of her analysis.

That student was able to get some distance from her own writing, to look at it as another reader might. In revising, *look at your paper from the reader's point of view.* What questions might a reader want to ask you? These must be answered in the paper, because you will not be around to supply information. Would a reader find your essay consistent? Interesting? Convincing? Are there enough details, illustrations, facts, and evidence from the work you are writing about? Because these considerations may lead you to lengthy rewriting, remember to plan at least as much time for revision as for writing the first draft.

What Should I Add or Take Out?

Revising is hard work, and you may wonder just where and how to start. If you have not been following a plan carefully worked out before you began writing, you should begin the revising process by outlining your first draft.

Outlining After the First Draft

To be sure that your discussion is unified and complete—i.e., to discover whether anything needs to be taken out or added—you should briefly outline your rough draft. It may seem odd to make an outline *after* you have written the paper, but listing your main ideas and supporting details will enable you to review your essay quickly and easily. You can examine its skeleton and decide whether everything fits together properly. This step in the revising process is *essential* if you have written the first draft without an outline or a detailed plan.

Making the Outline

An outline, whether done before or after the first draft, allows you to check for sufficient and logical development of ideas as well as for unity throughout the essay. Your introductory paragraph should contain your thesis, perhaps stated in a general way but stated clearly enough to let your readers know what your focus is. Here is one way to construct an after-writing outline:

1. Take a separate sheet of paper and write your thesis statement at the top.

2. Add the topic sentences stating the main ideas of your paragraphs, along with the supporting points in each one.

Your final paragraph should draw a conclusion concerning the thesis — a conclusion that relates the material in the body of the paper to the theme or purpose of the literary work.

Checking the Outline

Check your outline this way:

1. Make sure that the idea in every topic sentence is a significant critical observation relating directly to your thesis.
2. If not, revise the topic sentence until it clearly supports your thesis — or else delete the whole paragraph.

Just as the topic sentence of each paragraph should relate to the thesis of the paper, every piece of supporting evidence in the paragraph should relate to its topic sentence. So, next check the organization within each paragraph this way:

3. In each body paragraph, examine your supporting details to be sure that each relates directly to the topic sentence.
4. Make sure that none of your points repeats an idea included elsewhere (unless you are repeating for emphasis). Eliminate any careless repetition.
5. Decide whether your support is adequate. Think about whether you have included the most convincing details and whether you have enough of them.
6. If you decide you do not have sufficient support for a topic sentence, you need to rethink the point in order to expand it, or consider omitting the paragraph if the ideas are not essential. Sometimes you can combine the material from two paragraphs into a single new one having a broader topic sentence.

Sample After-Writing Outline

Since one peer reader of Wendy Dennison's paper on "Eveline" noticed that a couple of examples might be out of place, Wendy outlined her first draft. Here is her after-writing outline. (Her draft appeared in Chapter 2.)

> 1. Intro.
>   — Eveline refuses to leave with Frank because she fears failure. (thesis)

2. Her deathbed promise to her mother was unfair.
   — unfair to ask Eveline to give up her own life
3. She has good reasons to want to leave her father.
   — he's a drunk, takes advantage of the promise
   — he's stingy
   — abuses her verbally
   — he's a bully, might actually beat her
   — he was sometimes fun in past, played at picnics
4. Her homelife is so unhealthy she should leave.
   — doesn't feel a part of everything (picture of priest)
   — dust in house = dirtiness, squalor of her life
   — thinks of leaving and remembers her dreary job
5. Her only reason for staying is that she's afraid.
   — leaving the familiar could mean failure
   — quote: "about to explore" suggests uncertainty
   — life is hard so she thinks of good memories to convince herself to stay
6. She retreats into the familiar to avoid risk.
   — feels she has a right to happiness
   — decides a predictable life is better than one without direction and pattern (conclusion)

Examining the Sample Outline

If you examine Wendy's outline carefully, you can see a few problems.

Paragraph 2:   Needs more material about why the promise to her dying mother was unfair.

Paragraph 3:   The last point about "fun at picnics" does not relate to the topic sentence for the paragraph, which focuses on "good reasons to leave."

Paragraph 4:   The last point about Eveline's job does not relate to the topic sentence for the paragraph, which focuses on Eveline's "unhealthy homelife."

Paragraph 5:   The last point about Eveline's "good memories" provides a good place to move the example about "fun at picnics" from paragraph 3.

Paragraph 6:   The first point about Eveline's "right to happiness" does not relate to the topic sentence, which focuses on "Eveline's retreat into the familiar," but could well be moved to paragraph 2 to support the topic sentence idea that "her death-bed promise was unfair."

In the final draft of Wendy's paper, which appears at the end of this chapter, you will see how she took care of the problems revealed by her outline.

Outlining Exercise

For practice in checking the relevance and organization of ideas, outline the following paragraph in the way we just described, putting the topic sentence at the top of the page, and then listing each supporting idea:

> Eveline lacks courage to seek a life of her own because she fears that her father will not be able to cope if she leaves him. Her anxiety is heightened as she recalls that she and her brothers and sisters are grown up and that her mother is dead. If she leaves, her father will soon be all alone. She realizes that he is "usually fairly bad on a Saturday night" (5) and recognizes that his drinking problem will not get any better after she leaves. Also she has noticed that "Her father was becoming old lately" and assumes that ". . . he will miss her" (5). As a dutiful daughter, Eveline seems to feel that going away with Frank means abandoning her aging father, and that may be why she has written a letter to him — to ease the blow of her departure and to soothe her own conscience.

Next, examine your outline. Do you see any irrelevant points? Can you think of any important ideas or details that have been omitted from the paragraph? Are the points arranged in an effective order? Would another arrangement be better?

Now look at the following outline and see whether it matches yours:

> Topic sentence — Eveline fears her father will not be able to manage if she leaves him.
>
> 1. Eveline thinks about his loneliness — children grown, wife dead.
> 2. She fears his drinking problem worsening.
> 3. She worries that he is becoming old lately.
> 4. She assumes "he would miss her."
> 5. She writes letter to ease the blow.

Your outline may not come out exactly like this one, but the main idea is to be sure you have included all of the supporting details.

Here are some observations to consider for a revision of the sample paragraph, based on the outline of its major points:

1. Point 1 could be expanded to include details about the neighbors who have died (Tizzie Dunn) and moved away (the Waters).
2. An earlier draft of the paragraph included the point about Eveline's promise to her mother, but it was dropped as being irrelevant to the topic sentence. Do you agree?
3. The paragraph's supporting points appear in the same order as they do in the story. Is this chronological organization effective? Would some logical order be better?

What Should I Rearrange?

A crucial part of revision involves giving some thought to the order of your paragraphs and the order of the supporting details within them. The order in which they came to your mind is not necessarily the best. Luckily, rearranging is fairly easy once you have an after-writing outline.

Remember that neatness does not count at this stage. If you need to add only a sentence or two, you can perhaps squeeze the new material in between the lines or draw an arrow to the top or bottom margin and write there. If you discover the need to make major additions or to move whole paragraphs, you may want to use scissors on your rough draft. Cut your paper apart, quite literally, and tape in an added section. Or include an extra sheet of paper (numbered, for example, "p. 3 – A"), with a bold notation in the margin at the place on page 3 where you want to include the insert from page 3 – A. Revising the order of ideas is extremely easy to do if you are lucky enough to be using a word processor, which will do your cutting and pasting electronically.

The two principles you need to use in considering how well your points are arranged are *logic* and *emphasis*. Both principles allow you to arrange ideas in a certain sequence. The following questions will help you devise an appropriate arrangement:

1. Should I arrange the paragraphs and details in my essay in the same order in which they appear in the work I am analyzing?

   If you are writing a paragraph supporting the topic that Eveline is timid, you might collect details from throughout the story. You could then put those details in the same order as they appear in the story.

2. Should I organize the descriptions in terms of space?

   In a paper examining the significance of the objects in Eveline's home, you might take up these objects as though presented in a tour around the room. Other descriptions may be arranged from near to far, from outside to inside, from small to large.

3. Should I arrange my main points along a scale of value, of power, of weight, or of forcefulness? Could I use an arrangement of

   negative to positive?
   universal to individual?
   most influential to least influential?
   general to specific?
   least impressive to most impressive?

You can arrange your ideas in either direction along any of these scales — negative to positive or positive to negative, for instance. It is usually effective to place the most emphatic point last in any essay. If you are writing about several of Eveline's reasons for not going with

Frank, and you believe that the most influential reason was her promise to her dying mother, you would include that idea in the last
paragraph of the body of your paper, opening with a transition like
this:

> Though her timidity in general and her fear of her father in
> particular affected Eveline's final decision, her promise to her mother
> was the most powerful influence.

The strongest-point rule is just a guideline, of course. Try to arrange
your ideas in a way your readers will find effective.

Which Sentences Should I Combine?

Once you are satisfied that your ideas proceed smoothly, you need to
consider the possibility of combining sentences to avoid needless repetition of words and to eliminate choppiness. You may also decide to
combine sentences to achieve emphasis and variety. Probably you can
discover many ways to improve your sentences.

Rearranging for Conciseness

If you find that sometimes you are repeating the same word without
meaning to, you may eliminate the problem by combining sentences. For
instance, you might have written something like this:

> Twain savagely attacks conformity in the scene where the villagers
> stone the woman. The woman is suspected of being a witch.

As the repetition of *the woman* serves no useful purpose, the two statements can be more effectively phrased in a single sentence:

> In a scene showing the villagers stoning a woman suspected of being a
> witch, Twain savagely attacks conformity.

When you combine sentences in this way, you take the main idea from
one sentence and tuck it, usually as a modifier of some sort, within
another sentence. We can illustrate the process in reverse to help you see
more clearly what the technique involves. Notice that this sentence
contains two simple statements:

> Theodore, who did not wish to throw a stone, was horrified by the cruelty.

The two main ideas in that sentence are these:

> Theodore was horrified by the cruelty.
> Theodore did not wish to throw a stone.

You can recombine those sentences in various ways, depending upon
which idea you choose to emphasize:

Horrified by the cruelty, Theodore did not wish to throw a stone.

Not wishing to throw a stone, Theodore was horrified by the cruelty.

Sentence combining not only eliminates wordiness but also adds variety and focus. The various combinations provide numerous stylistic choices.

Sentence Combining Exercise

The following sentences, all written by students, include needless repetition and wordiness that can be eliminated by sentence combining. Decide which idea in each pair of sentences should be emphasized, and put that idea in the main (independent) clause. You will, of course, need to change, add, or omit words as you work to improve these sentences, but try not to leave out any significant ideas.

1. The second common stereotype is the dark lady. Usually the dark lady stereotype symbolizes sexual temptation.
2. Kate Chopin wrote a short story called "The Storm." As the title of the story suggests, it is about a rain storm and shows how people respond to the storm.
3. Emily Dickinson's poetry is sometimes elliptical. It is thus sometimes difficult for readers to get even the literal meaning of her poems.
4. There are three major things to consider in understanding Goodman Brown's character. These things include what the author tells us about Brown, what Brown himself says and does, and how other people respond to him.
5. Most of the incidents that inspire Walter Mitty's fantasies have humorous connotations associated with them. These can be broken down into basically two groups, with the first one being his desire to be in charge of a situation.

Rearranging for Emphasis and Variety

When you rewrite to gain emphasis and variety, you probably will restructure sentences as well as combine them. In fact, you may find yourself occasionally dividing a sentence for easier reading or to produce a short emphatic sentence. The following are some techniques to help you in polishing your sentence structure.

Varying the Pattern

The usual way of forming sentences in English is to begin with the subject, follow with the verb, and add a complement (something that completes the verb), like this:

Walter Mitty is not a brave person.

Any time you depart from this expected pattern, you gain variety and some degree of emphasis. Notice the difference:

> A brave person Walter Mitty is not.

Here are other variations that you may want to try:

A Dash at the End

> Twain found constant fault with humanity—with what he called "the damned human race."

An Interrupter Set Off by Dashes or Commas

> Twain considered humanity in general—"the damned human race"—inferior to the so-called lower animals.

A Modifier at the Beginning

> Although he loved individual human beings, Twain professed to loathe what he called "the damned human race."

A Short-Short Sentence   Because most of the sentences you will write are moderately long, you gain considerable emphasis when you follow a sentence of normal length with an extremely short one:

> Plagiarizing, which means borrowing the words or ideas of another writer without giving proper credit, is a serious infraction. Do not do it.

Deliberate Repetition   Just a few pages ago, we cautioned you to combine sentences rather than to repeat words needlessly. That caution still holds. But repeating words for emphasis is a different matter. Purposeful repetition can produce effective and emphatic sentences:

> Twain believed that organized religion was folly, a folly to be ridiculed discreetly.

> One cannot talk well, study well, or write well if one cannot think well.

That last sentence (modeled after one written by Virginia Woolf) repeats the same grammatical structure as well as the same words to achieve a powerful effect.

Exercise on Style

Rewrite the following ordinary sentences to achieve greater emphasis, variety, and conciseness.

1. Edith Wharton was born into a rich, upper-class family, but she was not even allowed to have paper on which to write when she was a child.
2. Her governesses never taught her how to organize ideas in writing, so when she decided to write a book on the decoration of houses, she had to ask her friend Walter Berry to help her write it.

3. She married Teddy Wharton when she was twenty-three years old, and he always carried a one-thousand dollar bill in case she wanted anything.

4. Her good friend, Henry James, gave her advice to help her improve her novels, yet her novels invariably sold far more copies than James's did.

5. She was awarded the Legion of Honor, which is the highest award given by the French government, following World War I for her refugee relief activities.

Which Words Should I Change?

You may have a good thesis and convincing, detailed support for it — but your writing style can make the difference between a dull, boring presentation and a rich, engaging one.

Check Your Verbs

After examining the construction of your sentences, you should look at the specific language you have used. Read through the rough draft and underline the verbs. Look for forms of these useful but well-worn words:

is (are, was, were, etc.)	go	has
get	come	move
do	make	use

Consider substituting a different verb — one that presents an image, visual or otherwise — to your readers. For example, this sentence is grammatically correct but dull:

Eveline does her work with reluctance.

Searching for a more precise verb than *does,* you might write:

Eveline reluctantly plods through her work.

Plods suggests a picture of poor Eveline with slumped shoulders and slow steps, dragging through the day.

Occasionally you can pick up a lively word from somewhere else in a limp sentence and convert it into the main verb:

Eveline is unable to leave her home because she is trapped by a promise to her dead mother.

Trapped is an arresting word in that sentence, and you could shift it to an earlier position to good effect:

A promise to her dead mother traps Eveline in her miserable home.

This revision also cuts unnecessary words out of the first version.

Exercise on Word Choice

Rewrite the following sentences using livelier verbs and fewer words.

1. The narrator's most unusual characteristic is an overactive sense of humor.
2. Jim's constant practical joking finally makes the readers disgusted.
3. Readers of the story get the message that some people are entertained by the misfortunes of others.
4. The readers come to the conclusion that Jim gets what he deserves.
5. Since the narrator's talk makes up the whole story, we have only his point of view.

Use Active Voice Most of the Time

Although the passive voice sometimes offers the best way to construct a sentence, the habitual use of the passive sprinkles your prose with color-less helping verbs, like *is* and *was*. If a sentence is in passive voice, the subject does *not* perform the action implied by the verb:

The paper was written by Janet, Jo's roommate.

The assignment was given poorly.

Her roommate's efforts were hindered by a lack of understanding.

The paper, the assignment, and the roommate's efforts did *not* carry out the writing, the giving, or the hindering. In active voice the subjects of the sentences are the doers or the causes of the action:

Jo's roommate Janet wrote the paper.

The teacher gave the assignment poorly.

Lack of understanding hindered her roommate's efforts.

Use Passive if Appropriate

Sometimes, of course, you may have a good reason for writing in the passive voice. For example, you may want to give a certain word the important position of subject even though it is not the agent of the action. In the sentence,

Sensory details are emphasized in this paragraph.

the *details* are the key point. The writer of the paragraph (the agent of the action) is not important enough even to include. In active voice, the key term would be pushed to the middle of the sentence, a much weaker position:

The writer emphasizes sensory details in this paragraph.

Clearly, you need not shun the passive, but if any of your sentences sound stilted or awkward, check to see if the passive voice may be the culprit.

Exercise on Passive Voice

Change passive voice to active in the following sentences. Feel free to add, delete, or change words.

1. Antigone is treated brutally by Creon because of her struggle to achieve justice.
2. Creon was not convinced by her tirade against his unbending authority.
3. Conflict between male and female was portrayed in the play by the author.
4. If even a small point is won against a tyrant by society, considerable benefit may be experienced.
5. The tragedy was caused by the iron-bound authority exercised by Creon.

Feel the Words

Words have emotional meanings (*connotations*) as well as direct dictionary meanings (*denotations*). You may be invited to a get-together, a soiree, a social gathering, a blowout, a blast, a reception, a bash, or a do, and although all are words for parties, the connotations tell you whether to wear jeans or feathers, whether to bring a case of cheap beer or a bottle of expensive wine.

In writing, take into account the emotional content of the words you use. One of our favorite essays, "The Discus Thrower," opens with this sentence:

I spy on my patients.

The word *spy* immediately captures the imagination with its connotations of intrigue and mystery and its slight flavor of deception. "I watch my patients when they don't know it" is still an interesting sentence because of its denotative content, but essayist Richard Selzer's version commands emotional as well as intellectual engagement.

We are not encouraging you to puff up your prose with strings of adverbs and adjectives; indeed, a single emotionally charged word in a simple sentence can be quite powerful.

Attend to Tone

Tone—the reflection of a writer's attitude—is usually described in terms of emotion: serious, solemn, satirical, humorous, sly, mournful, expectant, and so on. Although most writing about literature calls for a plain, direct tone, other attitudes can be conveyed. Negative book reviews, for instance, sometimes have a sarcastic tone. A writer unsympathetic to Eveline might describe her as "a spineless drudge who enjoys her oppression," whereas a sympathetic reader might state that Eveline is "a pitiful victim of a brutal home life." Someone who wants to remain neutral could describe Eveline as "a young woman trapped by duty and her own fears." These variations in tone, conveyed by word choice, reflect the writers' differing attitudes toward what is being discussed.

Once you establish a tone, you should stick with it. A humorous or sarcastic section set unexpectedly in a straightforward, direct essay will distract or disconcert your readers. Be sure to set your tone in the first paragraph; then your readers will unconsciously adjust their expectations about the rest of the paper.

Use Formal Language

The nature of your audience will also determine the level of usage for your writing. Essays for college classes usually require *formal language,* a style that takes a serious or neutral tone and avoids such informal usage as contractions, slang, and sentence fragments, even intentional ones. (See the "Handbook for Correcting Errors," at the end of this text, for information about fragments.)

Formal writing often involves a third-person approach:

> One can sympathize with Eveline, at the same time regretting her weakness.
>
> The reader sympathizes with Eveline, . . .

Most people today consider the use of first-person plural (*we, us, our, ours*) quite acceptable in formal papers:

> We sympathize with Eveline, . . .
>
> Eveline gains our sympathy, . . .

A growing number of people think the use of the first-person singular (*I, me, my, mine*) also is acceptable in formal writing:

> I sympathize with Eveline, . . .
>
> Eveline gains my sympathy, . . .

But avoid the informal second person, *you.* Do *not* write, "You can see that Eveline is caught in a terrible bind."

Does It Flow?

The best way to examine the flow (the *coherence*) of your prose is to read it aloud. Recording your essays on tape and playing them back enables you to hear with some objectivity how your writing sounds. You might also entice a friend to read your paper aloud to you. Whatever method you use, listen for choppiness or abruptness. Your ideas should be arranged in a clear sequence that is easy to follow. Will your readers experience any confusion when a new idea comes up? If so, you need stronger connections between sentences or between paragraphs — *transitions* that indicate how one idea is related to the next.

For example, when you see the words *for example,* you know what to expect. When you see *furthermore* opening a paragraph, your mind gets ready for some addition to the previous point. By contrast, when you see phrases like *on the other hand* or *by contrast,* you are prepared for something different from the previous point.

These clearly transitional phrases can be supplemented by more subtle echo transitions (in this paragraph, the words *transitional phrases* echo the main idea of the preceding paragraph), and by pronoun reference (in this paragraph, the word *these* refers to the examples in the preceding paragraph). Another technique that increases coherence in writing is the repetition of key terms and structures. In the paragraph you are reading, the key terms are forms of the words *transition, echo, refer,* and *repeat.* In the paragraph preceding this one, notice the repetition of the phrase, *when you see* and, in this paragraph, the repetition of *in this paragraph, the word(s).* Parallel ideas are presented in parallel ways.

In short, here are the techniques for achieving coherence:

1. A clearly sequenced flow of ideas
2. Transitional terms (see Chart 3 – 1 for a handy list)
3. Echo transitions (see "A Handbook for Correcting Errors" for further explanation)
4. Repetition of key terms
5. Repetition of parallel sentence structures.

A "Revising Checklist" to help you review all the important aspects of the revising process apears in Chart 3 – 2.

What Is Editing?

When you get to the editing stage, you can cease being creative. Try to think not about the ideas you have written but about the way you have written them. In order to become a competent editor, you must train yourself to see your own mistakes.

Proofreading: Try Doing It Backwards

To avoid getting so interested in what you have written that you fail to see your errors, try reading your sentences from the last one on the page to the first, that is, from the bottom to the top. Because your ideas will lack continuity in reverse order, you stand a better chance of keeping your attention focused on each sentence *as* a sentence. Be sure that every

CHART 3–1. Transitional Terms
for All Occasions

TO CONTINUE TO A NEW POINT
next, second, third, besides, further, finally

TO MAKE AN ADDITION TO A POINT
too, moreover, in addition, for example, such as, that is, as an
illustration, for instance, furthermore

TO SHOW CAUSE AND EFFECT
therefore, consequently, as a result, accordingly, then, thus, so,
hence

TO SHOW CONTRAST
but, still, on the other hand, nevertheless, however, conversely,
notwithstanding, yet

TO SHOW SIMILARITY
too, similarly, in the same way, likewise, also

TO EMPHASIZE OR RESTATE
again, namely, in other words, finally, especially, without doubt,
indeed, in short, in brief, primarily, chiefly, as a matter of fact, no
doubt

TO CONCLUDE A POINT
finally, in conclusion, to summarize, to sum up, in sum

word is correctly spelled, that each sentence is complete and correctly
punctuated. If you are using a word processor, be sure to run your
spelling checker.

Look for Your Typical Errors

If you know that you often have problems with certain elements of
punctuation or diction, be on guard for these particular errors as you
examine each sentence.

1. Make sure that each sentence really is a sentence, not a fragment—
   especially those beginning with *because, since, which, that, although, as,
   when,* or *what,* and those beginning with words ending in *ing.*
2. Make sure that independent clauses joined by *indeed, moreover, how-*

CHART 3–2. Revising Checklist

1. Is the thesis idea intelligent and clearly stated?
2. Is the main idea of every paragraph directly related to the thesis?
3. Is every paragraph fully developed, with plenty of specific examples or illustrations relating to the topic sentence?
4. Do all of my ideas flow coherently? Is every transition easy to follow? Are there perhaps too many transitions?
5. Is every word, every sentence, completely clear?
6. Is every sentence well structured and accurately worded?
7. Is my introduction pleasing? Does it make clear what the paper will be about without giving all the content away?
8. Is the concluding sentence emphatic or at least convincing?
9. Have I accomplished my purpose? Does the paper make the point I set out to prove?
10. Have I used formal English throughout?
11. Is the manuscript form acceptable?
    —Have I skipped three lines between the title and the first line of the essay?
    —Have I double-spaced throughout?
    —Did I leave at least one-inch margins on all sides, including top and bottom?
    —Have I prepared a title sheet (if requested to do so)?
    —Have I clipped the pages together?

---

ever, nevertheless, thus, and *hence* have a semicolon before those words, not just a comma.
3. Make sure that every modifying phrase or clause is close to the word it modifies.
4. If you know you have a problem with spelling, check every word and look up all questionable ones. Run your spelling checker if you are writing on a word processor.
5. Be especially alert for words that you know you consistently get wrong. If you are aware that you sometimes confuse words that sound alike (*it's/its, your/you're, there/their/they're, effect/affect*), check the accuracy of your usage. Remember that your spelling checker will not help you here.

If you are in doubt about how to correct any of the errors just mentioned, you will find advice in the "Handbook for Correcting Errors" at the end

CHART 3 – 3. Proofreading Checklist

1. Have I mixed up any of these easily confused words?

its/it's	their/they're/there	lie/lay
effect/affect	suppose/supposed	our/are
your/you're	woman/women	use/used
to/too/two	prejudice/prejudiced	then/than
who's/whose	accept/except	cite/site

2. Have I put an apostrophe appropriately in each of my possessive nouns?
3. Have I carelessly repeated any word?
4. Have I carelessly left any words out?
5. Have I omitted the first or final letter from any words?
6. Have I used the proper punctuation at the end of every sentence?
7. Have I spelled every word correctly?

of this text. You will also find a handy "Proofreading Checklist" in Chart 3 – 3.

See Each Word Separately

If you find that you still miss spelling and typographical errors even when reading carefully sentence by sentence from the bottom of the page, you need to go through the paper a second time using an index card with a slit cut in it that allows you to see only a word or two at a time. Fold the card in half and, using a pair of scissors, snip out a viewing slot about a quarter of an inch wide and an inch and a half long. (Cut a somewhat larger opening if your finished drafts are handwritten.) Then, beginning at the bottom of the page, move the card slowly across from *right to left*, checking the spelling of each word as you go. If you are unsure about the spelling of any word, look it up in a dictionary. The easier a word is to spell, the more important it becomes to spell it correctly.

Read the Paper Aloud

In an earlier section, we recommended reading your paper aloud as a means of checking coherence. It's a good idea to read it aloud again at the editing stage to catch words left out or carelessly repeated.

Find a Friend to Help

If you are writing an important paper and have a literate friend who will help you proofread, you are in luck. Ask this kind person to point out errors and also to let you know whether your thesis is made plain at the beginning, whether every sentence is clear throughout, and whether the paper as a whole makes good sense. You risk, of course, having to do further revising should any of your friend's responses prove negative, but try to be grateful for the help. You want to turn in a paper that you can be proud of.

Relying entirely on someone else to do your proofreading, though, is probably unwise. You are sure to encounter writing situations in college that preclude your bringing a friend to help — essay examinations, for instance, and in-class essays. You need to learn to find and correct your own errors as best you can, so that you will not risk failure when forced to go it alone.

Sample Student Paper — Final Draft

Here is the final draft of Wendy Dennison's paper on "Eveline." This finished version reflects the changes she made in organization to correct the problems revealed by her after-writing outline. The paper also includes editing changes she made to achieve precision in word choice and to increase the effectiveness of each individual sentence. The corrections and minor changes made in ink were added during her final proofreading.

Wendy Dennison

English 102

January 23, 1991

Fear of Failure in Joyce's "Eveline"

In his short story "Eveline,"   [1]
James Joyce gives the protagonist an exciting
chance to leave her old life and begin a new
one. But she rejects this offer that Frank--
or Fate--makes, preferring instead to settle
back into the dreary life she has known all
along. Why does she not go away with Frank

when the opportunity seems so attractive? We
need to examine Eveline's timid personality
in order to discover the answer.

    Since Eveline has been raised a   [2]
Catholic, we know she would not take her
deathbed promise to her mother lightly. But
surely her promise to "keep the home together
as long as she could" (6) was given under
extreme circumstances. It was unjust of her
mother to ask such a sacrifice of her, and
Eveline is aware of the unfairness: "Why
should she be unhappy? She had a right to
happiness" (6). We know that Eveline will
always be haunted by that promise, but we do
not expect her to give up her own chance for a
life of her own in order to be a dutiful
daughter. Surely that promise cannot be the
only reason she stays.

    We certainly should not be   [3]
surprised that Eveline might wish to leave
her abusive father. A hot-tempered heavy
drinker, he has taken advantage of his
daughter's promise to her mother. She is
forced to keep house for him, yet must beg for
money to feed the family. He practically
accuses her of stealing, claiming ". . . she
used to squander the money, that she had no
head, that he wasn't going to give her his
hard-earned money to throw about the
streets. . ." (5). He has so frightened her
with threats of beatings that she has
"palpitations" (4). Eveline realizes that
with her brothers gone, there is "nobody to
protect her" (5) from her father's rage. Her
father has treated Eveline badly and may

abuse her even worse *in* the ~~the~~ future. To
leave him would obviously be in her best
interest, yet something keeps her there.

    Eveline's home life is so unhealthy [4]
that we feel she would be wise to leave.
Despite all the chores she performs, she
still does not feel entirely at home in her
father's house. For example, she knows
nothing about the picture of the priest (4),
not even his name, yet the portrait seems
quite important to her father. The dustiness
of the house, of which Joyce reminds us
periodically, suggests the pervasive
dreariness of her daily life, as she looks
around ''wondering where all that dust came
from'' (4). Since her home is clearly not
conducive to happiness, why does she stay
there?

    The ~~only real~~ *main* reason why Eveline [5]
would remain in Ireland is the fact that she
is desperately afraid of the unknown. If she
leaves the familiar, no matter how
unpleasant, she risks failure. ''She was
about to explore another life with Frank''
(5), we are told, in far away Buenos
Ayres. The word ''explore'' is significant,
as it brings to mind uncertainty and risk, two
factors that Eveline is not prepared to deal
with. She admits that hers is ''a hard life,''
yet thinks, ''. . . now that she was about to
leave it she did not find it a wholly
undesirable life'' (5). When she sits in the
growing darkness with the letters in her lap,
Eveline calls up a couple of good memories--
of her father being jolly once on a picnic, of

his kindness ~~to her~~ once when she was
sick. We see her trying to calm her fears,
trying to convince herself that her home life
is more bearable than it is.

Afraid of failing on her own,   [6]
Eveline retreats into the familiar, telling
herself that life with father cannot be as
frightening as a risky, unknown life with
Frank. So strong is her fear of failure that
it overrides her fear of her father. She
seems to decide that a predictable--if dreary
and abusive--life is better than a life
without security or pattern.

Work Cited

Joyce, James. "Eveline." Literature and
     the Writing Process. Ed. Elizabeth
     McMahan, Susan Day, and Robert Funk. 3rd
     ed. New York: Macmillan, 1992. 4-6.

PART TWO

Writing About Short Fiction

This section, focusing on the short story, covers the literary and rhetorical elements that you need to understand in order to write effectively about short fiction.

4

How Do I Read Short Fiction?

As noted author Joyce Carol Oates has observed, short fiction can be difficult to understand "because it demands compression; each sentence must contribute to the effect of the whole. Its strategy is not to include an excess of detail but to exclude, to select, to focus as sharply as possible."[1] In order to grasp the full meaning of a story, you need to read it at least twice. Preferably, let some time elapse between readings so that you can mull the story over in your mind. Your initial reading can be purely for pleasure, but the second reading should involve careful and deliberate study of all the elements that combine to produce a unified whole. You should gain both pleasure and knowledge from reading short fiction. The knowledge frequently stems from understanding the *theme* that usually provides some insight into the human condition, although sometimes contemporary short stories simply raise moral or ethical questions and make no pretense of providing answers.

Notice the Structure

During the second reading, you should notice the way the story is structured. The action (i.e., what happens) is called the *plot* and usually is spurred by some conflict involving the main character (the *protagonist*). Except in some modern works, most short stories have a clear beginning, middle, and end in which the conflict producing the action becomes increasingly intense, building to a climax that sometimes resolves the conflict and sometimes simply concludes it — often in catastrophe. Do not expect many happy endings in serious fiction. A somber conclusion is more likely.

[1] Joyce Carol Oates, Preface, *Story.* Part Two (New York: Heath, 1985), 830.

Usually stories proceed in regular chronological order following a time sequence similar to that in real life. But occasionally an author employs *flashbacks* — stopping the forward action to recount an episode that happened in the past — in order to supply necessary background material or to maintain suspense. By sorting out the numerous flashbacks in Katherine Anne Porter's "The Jilting of Granny Weatherall," readers discover that Granny has been jilted not once but twice. And if William Faulkner had written "A Rose for Emily" chronologically, without the distorted time sequence, the stunning impact of the conclusion would have been lost.

Subplots

Longer works, such as novels, plays, and films, frequently include one or more *subplots*, which produce minor complications in the main action. Often, some quality of a major character is illuminated through interaction with minor characters in a subplot. In a closely unified work, the action of a subplot reinforces the theme. In Joseph Heller's World War II novel, *Catch-22*, the subplot involving Milo Minderbinder and his flourishing business empire satirizes the activities of war profiteers, who gained millions of dollars at the expense of millions of lives. Thus, the subplot strengthens Heller's powerful antiwar theme. Occasionally, though, subplots are introduced simply to provide interest, excitement, or comic relief. As you study a work involving subplots, consider their function. Do they provide action that contributes to the meaning of the work? If so, try to decide how. You may find you can write an interesting paper by focusing on the way a subplot serves to develop character or emphasize theme.

Consider Point of View and Setting

Sometimes the *point of view* — the position from which an author chooses to relate a story — can be crucial to the effectiveness, even to the understanding, of short fiction. In Alice Walker's "Everyday Use," we have the mother's views and feelings about her two quite different daughters. In "The Yellow Wall-Paper," Charlotte Perkins Gilman allows her main character to relate the story through entries in her private journal, a perfect point of view for conveying the distorted perceptions of a mind descending into madness. In other stories the point of view provides access to the thoughts and feelings of more than one character. In Arna Bontemps's "A Summer Tragedy," for example, we know the thoughts of both husband and wife. Ernest Hemingway, in "Hills Like White Elephants," chooses to let his characters tell the story themselves through conversation. This objective *(dramatic)* point of view is revealed by a glance at the pages, which consist primarily of dialogue. Some authors select one character to tell the story firsthand, but these first-person narrators can play quite different roles. In "I Stand Here Ironing," Tillie Olsen creates a strong sense of believability by presenting the reflections running through a mother's mind as she recalls her difficulties in raising a daughter with too little money and no husband to help. In Edgar Allan Poe's "The Fall of the House of Usher," the first-person narrator is essentially an observer, a peripheral character who is present during all of the action reported but who is not himself the focus of it. In James Joyce's "Araby," the narrator recounts an experience from his boyhood but from the vantage point of adulthood, employing adult perceptions.

The *setting* of a story, like the point of view, can sometimes be important, sometimes not. In many of the stories included in this anthology, setting plays a role of some consequence. For instance, John Steinbeck opens "The Chrysanthemums" with this description:

> The high gray-flannel fog of winter closed off the Salinas Valley from the sky and from all the rest of the world. On every side it sat like a lid on the mountains and made of the great valley a closed pot.

The isolation of the valley by the fog suggests the isolation of Elisa Allen, whose energies and experiences are restricted by her living on the ranch. The sea in Kate Chopin's "The Awakening" serves symbolically to heighten Edna Pontellier's dual awakening to selfhood and sexuality as she learns to swim in the sensuous, moonlit waters of the Gulf of Mexico. As you study a short story, give some thought to the setting. Could the events just as well take place somewhere else? Or does the setting seem to play an integral part? How does its time period affect the story? Does the setting in some way add to the meaning of the work?

Study the Characters

As you reread *dialogue*, pay special attention to those passages in quotation marks that characters speak to each other. You can begin to determine characterization from these exchanges, just as you come to know real people partly by what they say. As you form an understanding of a character, you also should notice what other people in the story say about that person, how they respond to that person, as well as what the author reveals of that person's thoughts and past behavior. Because fiction often allows us access to what the characters are thinking (as well as doing), we can sometimes know fictional persons better than we do our closest friends and family members. Sometimes we can be certain of a character's motivation for behaving in a certain way; at other times motivation becomes one of the elements to be determined before we can fully appreciate the work.

In Hawthorne's "Young Goodman Brown," in order to understand why the main character becomes an embittered and distrustful old man, we must examine his motives and his behavior. At the beginning of the story, we see Brown as an apparently well-meaning and trusting young man who enters the forest on an errand of questionable intent, perhaps to test his faith. But we can see finally that he is too easily persuaded to believe the worst of his fellow townspeople. The abundant ambiguities in the story keep us wondering what is actually happening in the forest and what is simply a figment of Brown's imagination. But he is so single-minded that he does not even try to sort out illusion from reality. Instead, he decides that everyone in the village except himself is a sinner. His loss of faith — we might even say his rejection of Faith — extends to all humanity and completely ruins his life.

Foils

A *foil* is a minor character whose role sharpens our understanding of a major character by providing a contrast. Although far more common in drama than in the short story, foils can also prove useful in analyzing works of fiction.

Kate Chopin's "The Awakening" provides abundant examples of the skillful use of foils. Edna, the protagonist, has two foils (Mme. Ratignolle and Mlle. Reisz) who help us chart her progression from a conventional wife and mother to the self-assertive woman she has become at the end. Her husband, Léonce, has a foil in Edna's father, and her lover, Robert, in his brother Victor. In "A Worn Path," Eudora Welty uses minor characters to emphasize several qualities of her main character, Phoenix Jackson. The young hunter who callously points his gun at Phoenix and suggests that her trip is too long for an old woman emphasizes for us just how strong willed and determined she is. The cold professionals who dutifully dole out the state's charity at the clinic underscore the sincerity of Phoenix's self-sacrifice.

After you have read a fictional work, ask yourself why the author included the minor characters. What role do they serve in the work as a whole? Often the role of a minor character will provide an appropriate focus for writing an analysis of a short story, a novel, or a play.

Look for Specialized Literary Techniques

As you study a story on second reading, you may notice irony and foreshadowing that you missed the first time through. Since *irony* involves an upsetting of expectations — having the opposite happen from what would be usual — you sometimes need to know the outcome of an action in order to detect the full extent of the irony. *Foreshadowing* works the same way: you may not be aware of these hints of future happenings until the happenings finally occur. But when you go through a story again, both irony and foreshadowing become easily apparent and contribute to its meaning and effectiveness.

Be alert also for *images* — for words and phrases that put a picture in your mind. These images increase the enjoyment of reading fiction and, if deliberately repeated, can become *motifs* that emphasize some important element in the story and thus convey meaning. The constant images of fungus and decay in Poe's "The Fall of the House of Usher" reinforce our impression of the deterioration of Roderick Usher's mind. If a repeated image gathers significant meaning, it then becomes a *symbol* — to be clearly related to something else in the story. The moldering of the Usher mansion probably symbolizes the decay of Usher's psyche, just as the repeated images of dust and decay in Faulkner's "A Rose for Emily" symbolize the deterioration of Miss Emily's mind and of the fortunes of her once revered family.

Examine the Title

The title may in some way point toward or be related to the meaning. Richard Wright's title, "The Man Who Was Almost a Man," evokes his theme: the difficulty that black males encounter in achieving manhood in America. Sometimes the title identifies the controlling symbol, as in Steinbeck's "The Chrysanthemums" and Gilman's "The Yellow Wall-Paper." Edith Wharton's title, "Roman Fever," carries a double meaning, suggesting both the fever of malaria that Mrs. Ainsley caught in the Colosseum and the fever of passion that propelled her there one fateful night. Conrad's title, "Heart of Darkness," directs us straight to his subject: the evil that lurks at the core of human nature.

Continue Questioning to Discover Theme

Your entire study of these various elements of fiction should lead to an understanding of the meaning, the *theme*, of the story. You need to ponder everything about a short story in order to discover its theme. Keep asking yourself questions until you come up with some meaningful observation about human behavior or the conduct of society. The questions in Chart 4–1 (see page 60) will guide you in exploring any story and perhaps spark that essential insight that leads to understanding.

CHART 4–1. Critical Questions for Reading the Short Story

Before planning an analysis of any of the selections in the anthology of short stories, write out the answers to the following questions to be sure you understand the piece and to help you generate material for your paper.

1. Who is the main character? Does this person's character change during the course of the story? Do you feel sympathetic toward the main character? What sort of person is she or he? Does this character have a foil?

2. What pattern or structure is there to the development of the plot? Can you describe the way the events are organized? Is the structure significant to the meaning?

3. Does surprise play an important role in the plot? Is there foreshadowing? Does the author use flashbacks?

4. Is anything about the story ironic?

5. Is there any symbolism in the story? How does the author make you aware of symbolic actions, people, or objects?

6. What is the setting — the time and location? How important are these elements in the story? Could it be set in another time or place just as well? Is the setting significant to the meaning?

7. Describe the atmosphere of the story, if it is important. How does the author create this atmosphere?

8. Who narrates the story? Is the narrator reliable? What effect does the point of view have on your understanding of the story? What would be gained or lost if the story were told from a different point of view (for example, by another character)?

9. How does the title relate to the other elements in the story and to the overall meaning?

10. What is the theme of the story? Can you state it in a single sentence? How is this theme carried out?

11. Does the author's style of writing affect your interpretation of the story? If so, how would you describe the style? For example, is it conversational or formal? Familiar or unfamiliar? Simple or ornate? Ironic or satiric?

CHAPTER

5

Writing About Structure

When you focus on structure in discussing a literary work, you are examining the way the parts fit together to form a whole. Examining the structure often proves an excellent means of understanding a short story, novel, poem, or play and is also a good way to approach a written literary analysis.

What Is Structure?

Most works of literature have an *underlying, reasoned pattern* that serves as a framework or *structure*. Consider the key terms in our definition.

Underlying:	We mean that the structure is probably not immediately or visually evident. As an analogy, consider the skeleton that gives structure to the body.
Reasoned:	We use this term because structure is usually logically appropriate for the plot and theme of the work.
Pattern:	We use this term to suggest that the structure serves as a plan or design, like an outline for an essay.

Looking at Structure

With our definition of structure in mind, read Alice Walker's "Everyday Use" and try to determine what holds the story together.

Alice Walker *1944–*

EVERYDAY USE

For Your Grandmama

I will wait for her in the yard that Maggie and I made so clean and wavy yesterday afternoon. A yard like this is more comfortable than most people know. It is not just a yard. It is like an extended living room. When the hard clay is swept clean as a floor and the fine sand around the edges lined with tiny, irregular grooves, anyone can come and sit and look up into the elm tree and wait for the breezes that never come inside the house.

Maggie will be nervous until after her sister goes: she will stand hopelessly in corners, homely and ashamed of the burn scars down her arms and legs, eying her sister with a mixture of envy and awe. She thinks her sister has held life always in the palm of one hand, that "no" is a word the world never learned to say to her.

You've no doubt seen those TV shows where the child who has "made it" is confronted, as a surprise, by her own mother and father, tottering in weakly from backstage. (A pleasant surprise, of course: What would they do if parent and child came on the show only to curse out and insult each other?) On TV mother and child embrace and smile into each other's faces. Sometimes the mother and father weep, the child wraps them in her arms and leans across the table to tell how she would not have made it without their help. I have seen these programs.

Sometimes I dream a dream in which Dee and I are suddenly brought together on a TV program of this sort. Out of a dark and soft-seated limousine I am ushered into a bright room filled with many people. There I meet a smiling, gray, sporty man like Johnny Carson who shakes my hand and tells me what a fine girl I have. Then we are on the stage and Dee is embracing me with tears in her eyes. She pins on my dress a large orchid, even though she has told me once that she thinks orchids are tacky flowers.

In real life I am a large, big-boned woman with rough, man-working hands. In the winter I wear flannel nightgowns to bed and overalls during the day. I can kill and clean a hog as mercilessly as a man. My fat keeps me hot in zero weather. I can work outside all day, breaking ice to get water for washing; I can eat pork liver cooked over the open fire minutes after it comes steaming from the hog. One winter I knocked a bull calf straight in the brain between the eyes with a sledge hammer and had the meat hung up to chill before nightfall. But of course all this does not show on television. I am the way my daughter would want me to be: a hundred pounds lighter, my skin like an uncooked barley pancake. My hair glistens in the hot bright lights. Johnny Carson has much to do to keep up with my quick and witty tongue.

But that is a mistake. I know even before I wake up. Who ever knew a Johnson with a quick tongue? Who can even imagine me looking a strange white man in the eye? It seems to me I have talked to them always with one foot raised in flight, with my head turned in whichever way is farthest from them. Dee,

62

though. She would always look anyone in the eye. Hesitation was no part of her nature.

"How do I look, Mama?" Maggie says, showing just enough of her thin body enveloped in pink skirt and red blouse for me to know she's there, almost hidden by the door.

"Come out into the yard," I say.

Have you ever seen a lame animal, perhaps a dog run over by some careless person rich enough to own a car, sidle up to someone who is ignorant enough to be kind to him? That is the way my Maggie walks. She has been like this, chin on chest, eyes on ground, feet in shuffle, ever since the fire that burned the other house to the ground.

Dee is lighter than Maggie, with nicer hair and a fuller figure. She's a woman now, though sometimes I forget. How long ago was it that the other house burned? Ten, twelve years? Sometimes I can still hear the flames and feel Maggie's arms sticking to me, her hair smoking and her dress falling off her in little black papery flakes. Her eyes seemed stretched open, blazed open by the flames reflected in them. And Dee. I see her standing off under the sweet gum tree she used to dig gum out of; a look of concentration on her face as she watched the last dingy gray board of the house fall in toward the red-hot brick chimney. Why don't you do a dance around the ashes? I'd wanted to ask her. She had hated the house that much.

I used to think she hated Maggie, too. But that was before we raised the money, the church and me, to send her to Augusta to school. She used to read to us without pity; forcing words, lies, other folks' habits, whole lives upon us two, sitting trapped and ignorant underneath her voice. She washed us in a river of make-believe, burned us with a lot of knowledge we didn't necessarily need to know. Pressed us to her with the serious way she read, to shove us away at just the moment, like dimwits, we seemed about to understand.

Dee wanted nice things. A yellow organdy dress to wear to her graduation from high school; black pumps to match a green suit she'd made from an old suit somebody gave me. She was determined to stare down any disaster in her efforts. Her eyelids would not flicker for minutes at a time. Often I fought off the temptation to shake her. At sixteen she had a style of her own: and knew what style was.

I never had an education myself. After second grade the school was closed down. Don't ask me why: in 1927 colored asked fewer questions than they do now. Sometimes Maggie reads to me. She stumbles along good-naturedly but can't see well. She knows she is not bright. Like good looks and money, quickness passed her by. She will marry John Thomas (who has mossy teeth in an earnest face) and then I'll be free to sit here and I guess just sing church songs to myself. Although I never was a good singer. Never could carry a tune. I was always better at a man's job. I used to love to milk till I was hooked in the side in '49. Cows are soothing and slow and don't bother you, unless you try to milk them the wrong way.

I have deliberately turned my back on the house. It is three rooms, just like the one that burned, except the roof is tin; they don't make shingle roofs any more. There are no real windows, just some holes cut in the sides, like the portholes in a ship, but not round and not square, with rawhide holding the shutters up on the outside. This house is in a pasture, too, like the other one. No doubt when Dee sees it she will want to tear it down. She wrote me once that no matter where we "choose" to live, she will manage to come see us. But she will never bring her friends. Maggie and I thought about this and Maggie asked me, "Mama, when did Dee ever *have* any friends?"

She had a few. Furtive boys in pink shirts hanging about on washday after school. Nervous girls who never laughed. Impressed with her they worshipped the well-turned phrase, the cute shape, the scalding humor that erupted like bubbles in lye. She read to them.

When she was courting Jimmy T she didn't have much time to pay to us, but turned all her faultfinding power on him. He *flew* to marry a cheap city girl from a family of ignorant flashy people. She hardly had time to recompose herself.

When she comes I will meet — but there they are!

Maggie attempts to make a dash for the house, in her shuffling way, but I stay her with my hand. "Come back here," I say. And she stops and tries to dig a well in the sand with her toe.

It is hard to see them clearly through the strong sun. But even the first glimpse of leg out of the car tells me it is Dee. Her feet were always neat-looking, as if God himself had shaped them with a certain style. From the other side of the car comes a short, stocky man. Hair is all over his head a foot long and hanging from his chin like a kinky mule tail. I hear Maggie suck in her breath. "Uhnnnh," is what it sounds like. Like when you see the wriggling end of a snake just in front of your foot on the road. "Uhnnnh."

Dee next. A dress down to the ground, in this hot weather. A dress so loud it hurts my eyes. There are yellows and oranges enough to throw back the light of the sun. I feel my whole face warming from the heat waves it throws out. Earrings gold, too, and hanging down to her shoulders. Bracelets dangling and making noises when she moves her arm up to shake the folds of the dress out of her armpits. The dress is loose and flows, and as she walks closer, I like it. I hear Maggie go "Uhnnnh" again. It is her sister's hair. It stands straight up like the wool on a sheep. It is black as night and around the edges are two long pigtails that rope about like small lizards disappearing behind her ears.

"Wa-su-zo-Tean-o!" she says, coming on in that gliding way the dress makes her move. The short stocky fellow with the hair to his navel is all grinning and he follows up with "Asalamalakim, my mother and sister!" He moves to hug Maggie but she falls back, right up against the back of my chair. I feel her trembling there and when I look up I see the perspiration falling off her chin.

"Don't get up," says Dee. Since I am stout it takes something of a push. You can see me trying to move a second or two before I make it. She turns, showing white heels through her sandals, and goes back to the car. Out she peeks next with a Polaroid. She stoops down quickly and lines up picture after picture of me sitting there in front of the house with Maggie cowering behind me. She never takes a shot without making sure the house is included. When a cow comes nibbling around the edge of the yard she snaps it and me and Maggie *and* the house. Then she puts the Polaroid in the back seat of the car, and comes up and kisses me on the forehead.

Meanwhile Asalamalakim is going through motions with Maggie's hand. Maggie's hand is as limp as a fish, and probably as cold, despite the sweat, and she keeps trying to pull it back. It looks like Asalamalakim wants to shake hands but wants to do it fancy. Or maybe he don't know how people shake hands. Anyhow, he soon gives up on Maggie.

"Well," I say. "Dee."

"No, Mama," she says. "Not 'Dee,' Wangero Leewanika Kemanjo!"

"What happened to 'Dee'?" I wanted to know.

"She's dead," Wangero said. "I couldn't bear it any longer, being named after the people who oppress me."

"You know as well as me you was named after your aunt Dicie," I said. Dicie is my sister. She named Dee. We called her "Big Dee" after Dee was born.

"But who was *she* named after?" asked Wangero.

"I guess after Grandma Dee," I said.

"And who was she named after?" asked Wangero.

"Her mother," I said, and saw Wangero was getting tired. "That's about as far back as I can trace it," I said. Though, in fact, I probably could have carried it back beyond the Civil War through the branches.

"Well," said Asalamalakim, "there you are."

"Uhnnnh," I heard Maggie say.

"There I was not," I said, "before 'Dicie' cropped up in our family, so why should I try to trace it that far back?"

He just stood there grinning, looking down on me like somebody inspecting a Model A car. Every once in a while he and Wangero sent eye signals over my head.

"How do you pronounce this name?" I asked.

"You don't have to call me by it if you don't want to," said Wangero.

"Why shouldn't I?" I asked. "If that's what you want us to call you, we'll call you."

"I know it might sound awkward at first," said Wangero.

"I'll get used to it," I said. "Ream it out again."

Well, soon we got the name out of the way. Asalamalakim had a name twice as long and three times as hard. After I tripped over it two or three times he told me to just call him Hakim-a-barber. I wanted to ask him was he a barber, but I didn't really think he was, so I didn't ask.

"You must belong to those beef-cattle peoples down the road," I said. They said "Asalamalakim" when they met you, too, but they didn't shake hands. Always too busy: feeding the cattle, fixing the fences, putting up salt-lick shelters, throwing down hay. When the white folks poisoned some of the herd the men stayed up all night with rifles in their hands. I walked a mile and a half just to see the sight.

Hakim-a-barber said, "I accept some of their doctrines, but farming and raising cattle is not my style." (They didn't tell me, and I didn't ask, whether Wangero (Dee) had really gone and married him.)

We sat down to eat and right away he said he didn't eat collards and pork was unclean. Wangero, though, went on through the chitlins and corn bread, the greens and everything else. She talked a blue streak over the sweet potatoes. Everything delighted her. Even the fact that we still used the benches her daddy made for the table when we couldn't afford to buy chairs.

"Oh, Mama!" she cried. Then turned to Hakim-a-barber. "I never knew how lovely these benches are. You can feel the rump prints," she said, running her hands underneath her and along the bench. Then she gave a sigh and her hand closed over Grandma Dee's butter dish. "That's it!" she said. "I knew there was something I wanted to ask you if I could have." She jumped up from the table and went over in the corner where the churn stood, the milk in it clabber by now. She looked at the churn and looked at it.

"This churn top is what I need," she said. "Didn't Uncle Buddy whittle it out of a tree you all used to have?"

"Yes," I said.

"Uh huh," she said happily. "And I want the dasher, too."

"Uncle Buddy whittle that, too?" asked the barber.

Dee (Wangero) looked up at me.

"Aunt Dee's first husband whittled the dash," said Maggie so low you almost couldn't hear her. "His name was Henry, but they called him Stash."

"Maggie's brain is like an elephant's," Wangero said, laughing. "I can use the churn top as a centerpiece for the alcove table," she said, sliding a plate over the churn, "and I'll think of something artistic to do with the dasher."

When she finished wrapping the dasher the handle stuck out. I took it for a moment in my hands. You didn't even have to look close to see where hands pushing the dasher up and down to make butter had left a kind of sink in the wood. In fact, there were a lot of small sinks; you could see where thumbs and fingers had sunk into the wood. It was beautiful light yellow wood, from a tree that grew in the yard where Big Dee and Stash had lived.

After dinner Dee (Wangero) went to the trunk at the foot of my bed and started rifling through it. Maggie hung back in the kitchen over the dishpan. Out came Wangero with two quilts. They had been pieced by Grandma Dee and then Big Dee and me had hung them on the quilt frames on the front porch and quilted them. One was in the Lone Star pattern. The other was Walk Around the Mountain. In both of them were scraps of dresses Grandma Dee had worn fifty and more years ago. Bits and pieces of Grandpa Jarrell's Paisley shirts. And one teeny faded blue piece, about the size of a penny matchbox, that was from Great Grandpa Ezra's uniform that he wore in the Civil War.

"Mama," Wangero said sweet as a bird. "Can I have these old quilts?"

I heard something fall in the kitchen, and a minute later the kitchen door slammed.

"Why don't you take one or two of the others?" I asked. "These old things was just done by me and Big Dee from some tops your grandma pieced before she died."

"No," said Wangero. "I don't want those. They are stitched around the borders by machine."

"That'll make them last better," I said.

"That's not the point," said Wangero. "These are all pieces of dresses Grandma used to wear. She did all this stitching by hand. Imagine!" She held the quilts securely in her arms, stroking them.

"Some of the pieces, like those lavender ones, come from old clothes her mother handed down to her," I said, moving up to touch the quilts. Dee (Wangero) moved back just enough so that I couldn't reach the quilts. They already belonged to her.

"Imagine!" she breathed again, clutching them closely to her bosom.

"The truth is," I said, "I promised to give them quilts to Maggie, for when she marries John Thomas."

She gasped like a bee had stung her.

"Maggie can't appreciate these quilts!" she said. "She'd probably be backward enough to put them to everyday use."

"I reckon she would," I said. "God knows I been saving 'em for long enough with nobody using 'em. I hope she will!" I didn't want to bring up how I had offered Dee (Wangero) a quilt when she went away to college. Then she had told me they were old-fashioned, out of style.

"But they're *priceless*!" she was saying now, furiously; for she has a temper. "Maggie would put them on the bed and in five years they'd be in rags. Less than that!"

"She can always make some more," I said. "Maggie knows how to quilt."

Dee (Wangero) looked at me with hatred. "You just will not understand. The point is these quilts, *these* quilts!"

"Well," I said, stumped. "What would *you* do with them?"

"Hang them," she said. As if that was the only thing you *could* do with quilts.

Maggie by now was standing in the door. I could almost hear the sound her feet made as they scraped over each other.

"She can have them, Mama," she said, like somebody used to never winning anything, or having anything reserved for her. "I can 'member Grandma Dee without the quilts."

I looked at her hard. She had filled her bottom lip with checkerberry snuff and it gave her face a kind of dopey, hangdog look. It was Grandma Dee and Big Dee who taught her how to quilt herself. She stood there with her scarred hands hidden in the folds of her skirt. She looked at her sister with something like fear but she wasn't mad at her. This was Maggie's portion. This was the way she knew God to work.

When I looked at her like that something hit me in the top of my head and ran down to the soles of my feet. Just like when I'm in church and the spirit of God touches me and I get happy and shout. I did something I never had done before: hugged Maggie to me, then dragged her on into the room, snatched the quilts out of Miss Wangero's hands and dumped them into Maggie's lap. Maggie just sat there on my bed with her mouth open.

"Take one or two of the others," I said to Dee.

But she turned without a word and went out to Hakim-a-barber.

"You just don't understand," she said, as Maggie and I came out to the car.

"What don't I understand?" I wanted to know.

"Your heritage," she said. And then she turned to Maggie, kissed her, and said, "You ought to try to make something of yourself, too, Maggie. It's really a new day for us. But from the way you and Mama still live you'd never know it."

She put on some sunglasses that hid everything above the tip of her nose and her chin.

Maggie smiled; maybe at the sunglasses. But a real smile, not scared. After we watched the car dust settle I asked Maggie to bring me a dip of snuff. And then the two of us sat there just enjoying, until it was time to go in the house and go to bed.

(1973)

Prewriting

Before you can begin to write about structure, you must first determine the underlying patterns that serve as a framework for the story.

Finding Patterns

Read the following questions; then carefully reread the story. Write down your answers to the questions.

1. How many parts of the story relate to the title, "Everyday Use"?
2. What is the major source of conflict in the story? That is, what causes tension?
3. How many different time periods are described in the story? Make a list of them in the order they appear in the story. Then organize the list in chronological (historical) order.
4. Look at the story as a series of scenes, like scenes in a play or film. Visualize the scenes. How many separate scenes are there? How can you tell when a scene begins and ends? If you were directing a film of the story, what would you emphasize in each scene?
5. Although we learn much about the lives of the family members, we don't learn everything. List some scenes that are left out of the story. Are there any you would put in if you were making a film?
6. Wangero says that her mother doesn't understand her heritage. What does she mean? Is it true? Which of the scenes in the story help answer these questions about Wangero's statement?

Writing

Once you understand the structure of the story, you need to discover a framework within which you can effectively present your observations — that is, a structure for your own paper.

Grouping Details

Write a sentence that explains something about the author's selection of scenes to include in the story. Next, discuss which details in the story support your explanations. For example, if you mentioned that the selected scenes relate to the idea of heritage, supporting details would include

- the dirt yard
- the first names
- the kitchen benches
- the churn
- the quilts

Relating Details to Theme

An accurate description of the pattern of the story and a convincing list of supporting details will be crucial to any essay about structure. But you also need to work out a thesis—a controlling idea for your paper that relates the structure to the overall impact or meaning of the work. For example, an essay about the structure of "Everyday Use" might have this thesis:

> The order of the episodes that occur or are remembered in "Everyday Use" serves to escalate our distaste for Dee/Wangero and reinforce our identification with her mother, preparing us to take the mother's side in the final confrontation.

Ideas for Writing

Ideas for Responsive Writing

1. Do you perceive any cultural gaps in your own family? For example, does your mother or grandmother find anything about your life-style objectionable or outrageous? Write first about a cultural gap from your own point of view. Then write about the same gap from the other side—that is, take on the opposing point of view.

2. In "Everyday Use," objects take on more importance than their simple functions—the churn and the quilts, for example. Are there any items like this in your life? Which of your belongings do you think your grandchildren will value? Why? Write about how objects acquire special significance.

3. Have you ever changed your name? Have you asked people to call you by a new name—for example, changing from Susie to Susan? Do you know anyone who has? Why do people change their names? Write an essay about what our names mean to us.

Ideas for Critical Writing

The following writing ideas relate structure to meaning. Adopt one of them, revise one, or create your own for a paper on "Everyday Use."

1. The opening and the closing scenes of "Everyday Use," which take place only hours apart, mirror each other and signify the changes Maggie and Mama have undergone in those hours.

2. Alice Walker uses explanatory flashbacks to Dee/Wangero's early life but excludes any depiction of her current life (even such details as whether she is married or where she lives); this character appears from nowhere, ironically suggesting her own lack of heritage or cultural tradition, a lack she is quick to perceive in others.

3. Each memory recorded in "Everyday Use" serves to strengthen the contrast between Dee/Wangero and her mother, a contrast that flares into a clash between two notions of heritage.

4. Certain key objects, such as the burned house and the old quilts, focus the reader's attention on the basic conflict of the story.

Rewriting

Our advice in this section will focus on problems characteristic of writing about a literary work.

Integrating Quotations Gracefully

In any literary essay you will need quotations from the text of the work you are examining. In fact, when you revise your essay, always consider adding more specific evidence straight from the text. This evidence will help your readers understand the general points you make and will show what inspired your thoughts. Quoting directly also serves as a self-check: by finding specific support in the work, you confirm that your ideas are, indeed, grounded in the text and not in your fancy.

Be sure that you enclose these borrowings in quotation marks as you gracefully introduce them into your own sentences. For example:

> Early in the story, Mama remembers that Dee held her family "trapped and ignorant" as she read to them.

> When Wangero arrives, she takes "picture after picture" with her Polaroid, foreshadowing her preoccupation with images.

> Mama describes herself as "a large, big-boned woman with rough, man-working hands"; impassively, she describes Dee as having "nicer hair and a fuller figure [than Maggie's]."

That last example shows how you may add your own words to explain a possibly confusing word in a quotation: use brackets. Most of the time, though, you can devise a way to avoid this awkwardness by rewriting the sentence, perhaps adding more from the source:

> Mama describes herself as "a large, big-boned woman with rough, man-working hands"; impassively, she describes Dee as "lighter than Maggie, with nicer hair and a fuller figure."

6

Writing About Imagery and Symbolism

Imagery and symbolism, two of the most important elements of serious imaginative literature, provide rich sources of insight. The interpretive skill necessary to detect and understand them can be developed with practice. Because the meaning or theme of a literary work is often reinforced through imagery and symbolism, you can effectively devote an entire paper to an examination of a key symbol or a pattern of imagery.

What Are Images?

Images are words, sometimes phrases, that appeal to the senses and often put a picture in your mind. Literary critics classify images roughly into several categories:

visual:	images of sight ("future days strung together like pearls in a rosary" — Mary E. Wilkins Freeman)
auditory:	images of sound ("the loud, iron clanking of the lift machinery" — John Cheever)
gustatory:	images of taste ("the acrid, metallic taste of gunfire" — Alberto Moravia)
kinetic:	images of motion (a thought "bumping like a helium balloon at the ceiling of the brain" — Sandra Cisneros)
thermal:	images of temperature ("the blueblack cold" of early morning — Robert Hayden)
tactile:	images of feeling ("the ache of marriage throbs in the teeth" — Denise Levertov)

Such images enrich our pleasure in reading, and if deliberately repeated, can become *motifs*, or patterns of imagery, that emphasize some element of the story. The repeated bird images in Chopin's "The Awakening" form a significant motif: birds (which soar) are associated with the human soul (which seeks to soar). Since the soul trying to soar to freedom is clearly Edna's, we see the bird images throughout the story associated with Edna. Eudora Welty in "A Worn Path" also uses bird images associated with her main character, Phoenix, whose name is a highly meaningful bird reference.

What Are Symbols?

If a repeated image gathers significant meaning, it then becomes a *symbol*. The bird images discussed above symbolize Edna's soul — or to use a more modern term, selfhood. The dust in Faulkner's "Dry September" settles in our consciousness as symbolizing the absence of spiritual strength in that community. Because spring rains bring renewed life to the earth, water is used in the baptismal service to signify rebirth. Thus, in literature we associate water with a vigorous, living spirit and its opposite — dryness, dust, aridity — with death of the human spirit or the decay of moral values.

Archetypal Symbols

Some symbols, like birds and dust, are considered *archetypal* or universal — supposedly conveying the same meaning in all cultures from the time of earliest civilization. The circle, for instance, is an ancient symbol of wholeness or perfection; the sea has for centuries symbolized the voyage through life. But because white has long been associated with innocence and black with evil, we begin to suspect that these symbols may be "universal" only in Western culture. Be that as it may, in much of the literature you will be reading, these archetypal meanings will be conveyed.

Phallic and Yonic Symbols   Two important and commonly employed symbols are associated with human sexuality. A *phallic* symbol suggests the potency of the male (as does the gun in "The Man Who Was Almost a Man") or the force of male dominance in a patriarchal society (as does the stone pillar in "Désirée's Baby"). Common phallic symbols are towers, spurs, snakes, sleek cars, jet planes, motorcycles — objects resembling in shape the male sex organ. A *yonic* symbol suggests the fecundity of the female or the allure of female sexuality. Common yonic symbols are caves, pots, rooms, full-blown roses — round or concave objects resembling the shape of the primary sex organs of the female. If you think fruit, then bananas are phallic and apples are yonic. Remember, though, that these objects will not always be charged with sexual significance. You must be sure that in context the image can be reasonably associated with sexuality.

How Will I Recognize Symbols?

"How am I supposed to know the significance of all of these things?" you may well ask. Many symbols you already understand through knowledge gathered from experience and observation. You just have to make the association. Spring signifying rebirth, for example, is a connection anyone can make who has seen the earth come alive at winter's end. Pay attention to the way objects and colors gather associations: white for brides, black for funerals, blue for sadness, red for passion or anger. Just keep making associations until you come up with a meaning that seems to fit the symbol in its context.

Reference Works on Symbols

If you draw an absolute blank, you can consult several handy volumes that allow you to look up words to discover their symbolic implications. Your library should have copies of the following works in the humanities reference section:

- Cirlot, J. E. *A Dictionary of Symbols*
- Cooper, J. C. *An Encyclopedia of Traditional Symbols*
- Frazer, Sir James. *The Golden Bough*
- Olderr, Stephen. *Symbolism: A Comprehensive Dictionary*
- Walker, Barbara. *The Woman's Encyclopedia of Myths and Secrets.*

Looking at Images and Symbols

Recognizing images and symbols and responding to them sensitively are requirements for an informed reading of serious fiction. Read the following story by Shirley Jackson and see if you are aware, on first reading, of her use of symbolic imagery.

Shirley Jackson *1919–1965*

THE LOTTERY

The morning of June 27th was clear and sunny, with the fresh warmth of a full-summer day; the flowers were blossoming profusely and the grass was richly green. The people of the village began to gather in the square, between the post office and the bank, around ten o'clock; in some towns there were so many people that the lottery took two days and had to be started on June 26th, but in this village, where there were only about three hundred people, the whole lottery took less than two hours, so it could begin at ten o'clock in the morning and still be through in time to allow the villagers to get home for noon dinner.

The children assembled first, of course. School was recently over for the summer, and the feeling of liberty sat uneasily on most of them; they tended to gather together quietly for a while before they broke into boisterous play, and their talk was still of the classroom and the teacher, of books and reprimands. Bobby Martin had already stuffed his pockets full of stones, and the other boys soon followed his example, selecting the smoothest and roundest stones; Bobby and Harry Jones and Dickie Delacroix—the villagers pronounced his name "Dellacroy"—eventually made a great pile of stones in one corner of the square and guarded it against the raids of the other boys. The girls stood aside, talking among themselves, looking over their shoulders at the boys, and the very small children rolled in the dust or clung to the hands of their older brothers or sisters.

Soon the men began to gather, surveying their own children, speaking of planting and rain, tractors and taxes. They stood together, away from the pile of stones in the corner, and their jokes were quiet and they smiled rather than laughed. The women, wearing faded house dresses and sweaters, came shortly after their menfolk. They greeted one another and exchanged bits of gossip as they went to join their husbands. Soon the women, standing by their husbands, began to call to their children, and the children came reluctantly, having to be called four or five times. Bobby Martin ducked under his mother's grasping hand and ran, laughing, back to the pile of stones. His father spoke up sharply, and Bobby came quickly and took his place between his father and his oldest brother.

The lottery was conducted—as were the square dances, the teen-age club, the Halloween program—by Mr. Summers, who had time and energy to devote to civic activities. He was a round-faced, jovial man and he ran the coal business, and people were sorry for him, because he had no children and his wife was a scold. When he arrived in the square, carrying the black wooden box, there was a murmur of conversation among the villagers, and he waved and called, "Little late today, folks." The postmaster, Mr. Graves, followed him, carrying a three-legged stool, and the stool was put in the center of the square and Mr. Summers set the black box down on it. The villagers kept their distance, leaving a space between themselves and the stool, and when Mr. Summers said, "Some of you fellows want to give me a hand?" there was a hesitation before two men, Mr. Martin and his oldest son, Baxter, came forward to hold the box steady on the stool while Mr. Summers stirred up the paper inside it.

The original paraphernalia for the lottery had been lost long ago, and the black box now resting on the stool had been put into use even before Old Man Warner, the oldest man in town, was born. Mr. Summers spoke frequently to the villagers about making a new box, but no one liked to upset even as much tradition as was represented by the black box. There was a story that the present box had been made with some pieces of the box that had preceded it, the one that had been constructed when the first people settled down to make a village here. Every year, after the lottery, Mr. Summers began talking again about a new box, but every year the subject was allowed to fade off without anything's being done. The black box grew shabbier each year; by now it was no longer completely black but splintered badly along one side to show the original wood color, and in some places faded or stained.

Mr. Martin and his oldest son, Baxter, held the black box securely on the stool until Mr. Summers had stirred the papers thoroughly with his hand. Because so much of the ritual had been forgotten or discarded, Mr. Summers had been successful in having slips of paper substituted for the chips of wood that had been used for generations. Chips of wood, Mr. Summers had argued, had been all very well when the village was tiny, but now that the population was more than three hundred and likely to keep on growing, it was necessary to use something that would fit more easily into the black box. The night before the lottery, Mr. Summers and Mr. Graves made up the slips of paper and put them in the box, and it was then taken to the safe of Mr. Summers' coal company and locked up until Mr. Summers was ready to take it to the square next morning. The rest of the year, the box was put away, sometimes one place, sometimes another; it had spent one year in Mr. Graves's barn and another year underfoot in the post office, and sometimes it was set on a shelf in the Martin grocery and left there.

There was a great deal of fussing to be done before Mr. Summers declared the lottery open. There were the lists to make up—of heads of families, heads of households in each family, members of each household in each family. There was the proper swearing-in of Mr. Summers by the postmaster, as the official of the lottery; at one time, some people remembered, there had been a recital of some sort, performed by the official of the lottery, a perfunctory, tuneless chant that had been rattled off duly each year; some people believed that the official of the lottery used to stand just so when he said or sang it, others believed that he was supposed to walk among the people, but years and years ago this part of the ritual had been allowed to lapse. There had been, also, a ritual salute, which the official of the lottery had had to use in addressing each person who came up to draw from the box, but this also had changed with time, until now it was felt necessary only for the official to speak to each person approaching. Mr. Summers was very good at all this; in his clean white shirt and blue jeans, with one hand resting carelessly on the black box, he seemed very proper and important as he talked interminably to Mr. Graves and the Martins.

Just as Mr. Summers finally left off talking and turned to the assembled villagers, Mrs. Hutchinson came hurriedly along the path to the square, her sweater thrown over her shoulders, and slid into place in the back of the crowd. "Clean forgot what day it was," she said to Mrs. Delacroix, who stood next to her, and they both laughed softly. "Thought my old man was out back stacking wood," Mrs. Hutchinson went on, "and then I looked out the window and the kids were gone, and then I remembered it was the twenty-seventh and came a-running." She dried her hands on her apron, and Mrs. Delacroix said, "You're in time, though. They're still talking away up there."

Mrs. Hutchinson craned her neck to see through the crowd and found her husband and children standing near the front. She tapped Mrs. Delacroix on the arm as a farewell and began to make her way through the crowd. The people separated good-humoredly to let her through; two or three people said, in voices just loud enough to be heard across the crowd, "Here comes your Missus, Hutchinson," and "Bill, she made it after all." Mrs. Hutchinson reached her husband, and Mr. Summers, who had been waiting, said cheerfully, "Thought we were going to have to get on without you, Tessie." Mrs. Hutchinson said, grinning, "Wouldn't have me leave m'dishes in the sink, now, would you, Joe?," and soft laughter ran through the crowd as the people stirred back into position after Mrs. Hutchinson's arrival.

"Well, now," Mr. Summers said soberly, "guess we better get started, get this over with, so's we can go back to work. Anybody ain't here?"

"Dunbar," several people said. "Dunbar, Dunbar."

Mr. Summers consulted his list. "Clyde Dunbar," he said. "That's right. He's broke his leg, hasn't he? Who's drawing for him?"

"Me, I guess," a woman said, and Mr. Summers turned to look at her. "Wife draws for her husband," Mr. Summers said. "Don't you have a grown boy to do it for you, Janey?" Although Mr. Summers and everyone else in the village knew the answer perfectly well, it was the business of the official of the lottery to ask such questions formally. Mr. Summers waited with an expression of polite interest while Mrs. Dunbar answered.

"Horace's not but sixteen yet," Mrs. Dunbar said regretfully. "Guess I gotta fill in for the old man this year."

"Right," Mr. Summers said. He made a note on the list he was holding. Then he asked, "Watson boy drawing this year?"

A tall boy in the crowd raised his hand. "Here," he said. "I'm drawing for m'mother and me." He blinked his eyes nervously and ducked his head as several voices in the crowd said things like "Good fellow, Jack," and "Glad to see your mother's got a man to do it."

"Well," Mr. Summers said, "guess that's everyone. Old Man Warner make it?"

"Here," a voice said, and Mr. Summers nodded.

A sudden hush fell on the crowd as Mr. Summers cleared his throat and looked at the list. "All ready?" he called. "Now, I'll read the names — heads of families first — and the men come up and take a paper out of the box. Keep the paper folded in your hand without looking at it until everyone has had a turn. Everything clear?"

The people had done it so many times that they only half listened to the directions; most of them were quiet, wetting their lips, not looking around. Then Mr. Summers raised one hand high and said, "Adams." A man disengaged himself from the crowd and came forward. "Hi, Steve," Mr. Summers said, and Mr. Adams said, "Hi, Joe." They grinned at one another humorlessly and nervously. Then Mr. Adams reached into the black box and took out a folded paper. He held it firmly by one corner as he turned and went hastily back to his place in the crowd, where he stood a little apart from his family, not looking down at his hand.

"Allen." Mr. Summers said. "Anderson. . . . Bentham."

"Seems like there's no time at all between lotteries any more," Mrs. Delacroix said to Mrs. Graves in the back row. "Seems like we got through with the last one only last week."

"Time sure goes fast," Mrs. Graves said.

"Clark. . . . Delacroix."

"There goes my old man," Mrs. Delacroix said. She held her breath while her husband went forward.

"Dunbar," Mr. Summers said, and Mrs. Dunbar went steadily to the box while one of the women said, "Go on, Janey," and another said, "There she goes."

"We're next," Mrs. Graves said. She watched while Mr. Graves came around from the side of the box, greeted Mr. Summers gravely, and selected a slip of paper from the box. By now, all through the crowd there were men holding the small folded papers in their large hands, turning them over and over nervously. Mrs. Dunbar and her two sons stood together, Mrs. Dunbar holding the slip of paper.

"Harburt. . . . Hutchinson."

"Get up there, Bill," Mrs. Hutchinson said, and the people near her laughed.

"Jones."

"They do say," Mr. Adams said to Old Man Warner, who stood next to him, "that over in the north village they're talking of giving up the lottery."

Old Man Warner snorted. "Pack of crazy fools," he said. "Listening to the young folks, nothing's good enough for *them*. Next thing you know, they'll be wanting to go back to living in caves, nobody work any more, live *that* way for a while. Used to be a saying about 'Lottery in June, corn be heavy soon.' First thing you know, we'd all be eating stewed chickweed and acorns. There's *always* been a lottery," he added petulantly. "Bad enough to see young Joe Summers up there joking with everybody."

"Some places have already quit lotteries," Mrs. Adams said.

"Nothing but trouble in *that*," Old Man Warner said stoutly. "Pack of young fools."

"Martin." And Bobby Martin watched his father go forward. "Overdyke. . . . Percy."

"I wish they'd hurry," Mrs. Dunbar said to her oldest son. "I wish they'd hurry."

"They're almost through," her son said.

"You get ready to run tell Dad," Mrs. Dunbar said.

Mr. Summers called his own name and then stepped forward precisely and selected a slip from the box. Then he called, "Warner."

"Seventy-seventh year I been in the lottery," Old Man Warner said as he went through the crowd. "Seventy-seventh time."

"Watson." The tall boy came awkwardly through the crowd. Someone said, "Don't be nervous, Jack," and Mr. Summers said, "Take your time, son."

"Zanini."

After that, there was a long pause, a breathless pause, until Mr. Summers, holding his slip of paper in the air, said, "All right, fellows." For a minute, no one moved, and then all the slips of paper were opened. Suddenly, all the women began to speak at once, saying, "Who is it?," "Who's got it?," "Is it the Dunbars?," "Is it the Watsons?" Then the voices began to say, "It's Hutchinson. It's Bill," "Bill Hutchinson's got it."

"Go tell your father," Mrs. Dunbar said to her older son.

People began to look around to see the Hutchinsons. Bill Hutchinson was standing quiet, staring down at the paper in his hand. Suddenly, Tessie Hutchinson shouted to Mr. Summers, "You didn't give him time enough to take any paper he wanted. I saw you. It wasn't fair!"

"Be a good sport, Tessie," Mrs. Delacroix called, and Mrs. Graves said, "All of us took the same chance."

"Shut up, Tessie," Bill Hutchinson said.

"Well, everyone," Mr. Summers said, "that was done pretty fast, and now we've got to be hurrying a little more to get it done in time." He consulted his next list. "Bill," he said, "you draw for the Hutchinson family. You got any other households in the Hutchinsons?"

"There's Don and Eva," Mrs. Hutchinson yelled. "Make *them* take their chance!"

"Daughters draw with their husbands' families, Tessie," Mr. Summers said gently. "You know that as well as anyone else."

"It wasn't *fair*," Tessie said.

"I guess not, Joe," Bill Hutchinson said regretfully. "My daughter draws with her husband's family, that's only fair. And I've got no other family except the kids."

"Then, as far as drawing for families is concerned, it's you," Mr. Summers said in explanation, "and as far as drawing for households is concerned, that's you, too. Right?"

"Right," Bill Hutchinson said.

"How many kids, Bill?" Mr. Summers asked formally.

"Three," Bill Hutchinson said. "There's Bill, Jr., and Nancy, and little Dave. And Tessie and me."

"All right, then," Mr. Summers said. "Harry, you got their tickets back?"

Mr. Graves nodded and held up the slips of paper. "Put them in the box, then," Mr. Summers directed. "Take Bill's and put it in."

"I think we ought to start over," Mrs. Hutchinson said, as quietly as she could. "I tell you it wasn't *fair*. You didn't give him time enough to choose. *Every*body saw that."

Mr. Graves had selected the five slips and put them in the box, and he dropped all the papers but those onto the ground, where the breeze caught them and lifted them off.

"Listen, everybody," Mrs. Hutchinson was saying to the people around her.

"Ready, Bill?" Mr. Summers asked, and Bill Hutchinson, with one quick glance around at his wife and children, nodded.

"Remember," Mr. Summers said, "take the slips and keep them folded until each person has taken one. Harry, you help little Dave." Mr. Graves took the hand of the little boy, who came willingly with him up to the box. "Take a paper out of the box, Davy," Mr. Summers said. Davy put his hand into the box and laughed. "Take just *one* paper," Mr. Summers said. "Harry, you hold it for him." Mr. Graves took the child's hand and removed the folded paper from the tight fist and held it while little Dave stood next to him and looked up at him wonderingly.

"Nancy, next," Mr. Summers said. Nancy was twelve, and her school friends breathed heavily as she went forward, switching her skirt, and took a slip daintily from the box. "Bill, Jr.," Mr. Summers said, and Billy, his face red and his feet over-large, nearly knocked the box over as he got a paper out. "Tessie," Mr. Summers said. She hesitated for a minute, looking around defiantly, and then set her lips and went up to the box. She snatched a paper out and held it behind her.

"Bill," Mr. Summers said, and Bill Hutchinson reached into the box and felt around, bringing his hand out at last with the slip of paper in it.

The crowd was quiet. A girl whispered, "I hope it's not Nancy," and the sound of the whisper reached the edges of the crowd.

"It's not the way it used to be," Old Man Warner said clearly. "People ain't the way they used to be."

"All right," Mr. Summers said. "Open the papers. Harry, you open little Dave's."

Mr. Graves opened the slip of paper and there was a general sigh through the crowd as he held it up and everyone could see that it was blank. Nancy and Bill, Jr., opened theirs at the same time, and both beamed and laughed, turning around to the crowd and holding their slips of paper above their heads.

"Tessie," Mr. Summers said. There was a pause, and then Mr. Summers looked at Bill Hutchinson, and Bill unfolded his paper and showed it. It was blank.

"It's Tessie," Mr. Summers said, and his voice was hushed. "Show us her paper, Bill."

Bill Hutchinson went over to his wife and forced the slip of paper out of her hand. It had a black spot on it, the black spot Mr. Summers had made the night before with the heavy pencil in the coal-company office. Bill Hutchinson held it up, and there was a stir in the crowd.

"All right, folks," Mr. Summers said. "Let's finish quickly."

Although the villagers had forgotten the ritual and lost the original black box, they still remembered to use stones. The pile of stones the boys had made earlier was ready; there were stones on the ground with the blowing scraps of paper that had come out of the box. Mrs. Delacroix selected a stone so large she had to pick it up with both hands and turned to Mrs. Dunbar. "Come on," she said. "Hurry up."

Mrs. Dunbar had small stones in both hands, and she said, gasping for breath, "I can't run at all. You'll have to go ahead and I'll catch up with you."

The children had stones already, and someone gave little Davy Hutchinson a few pebbles.

Tessie Hutchinson was in the center of a cleared space by now, and she held her hands out desperately as the villagers moved in on her. "It isn't fair," she said. A stone hit her on the side of the head.

Old Man Warner was saying, "Come on, come on, everyone." Steve Adams was in the front of the crowd of villagers, with Mrs. Graves beside him.

"It isn't fair, it isn't right," Mrs. Hutchinson screamed, and then they were upon her.

(1948)

Prewriting

Since much of the imagery in "The Lottery" carries symbolic significance, we will focus on symbolism as the topic for writing here. Symbols in fiction are not difficult to recognize. Usually an author will give a symbol particular emphasis — by mentioning it repeatedly (like the dust in "Eveline") or even by naming the work after it (as in "The Yellow

Wall-Paper"). A crucial symbol will sometimes be placed in the story's opening or ending.

Interpreting Symbols

Shirley Jackson directs our attention to the lottery by making it the title of her story. She also gives us abundant detail about this traditional ritual: we know the exact date and time, how the lottery is conducted, who draws and in what order, what the box and the slips of paper look like, and so forth. Clearly the lottery is the story's central symbol as well as its title. The meaning of the lottery is the meaning of "The Lottery."

Here are some points and questions to consider as you read the story a second time and try to work out your interpretation of its symbolism.

1. We are told a lot about the lottery, but not its exact purpose. Do the townspeople know? Is this omission significant? Intentional?

2. Why is much of the history of the lottery and the black box uncertain and vague? Why does Mr. Summers have to ask a question that he and everybody else already know the answer to?

3. The box used in the lottery is mentioned almost thirty times in the story—more than ten times in the phrase *the black box*. Why does the author emphasize this object and its color so strongly?

4. The stones are mentioned five times near the beginning of the story and then five or six times more at the end. Why is their presence so important? What are the historical/biblical associations of a "stoning"? Do they apply in this situation?

5. Which characters seem to stand for particular ideas or views? What about Old Man Warner? Look at his speeches and comments throughout the story. Tessie Hutchinson also gets a lot of attention, of course. What is ironic about her being the chosen victim? Does her last name have any significance for you? If not, look up *Hutchinson* in a good encyclopedia.

Writing

The key to a successful essay is a good *thesis*, or controlling idea. Before you get too far in your writing, you should try to state your main point in a single sentence.

Producing a Workable Thesis

A useful thesis should narrow the topic to an idea you can cover within your word limit. It should indicate the direction of your thinking—what you intend to *say* about that idea. Be sure to state your thesis in a complete sentence to indicate the point you plan to make.

Exercise on Thesis Statements

The following thesis statements are too broad to be workable. Figure out how each one can be narrowed and given direction; then write an improved version. Here is an example of the kind of revisions we hope you will produce.

Too broad: Shirley Jackson's "The Lottery" contains a number of significant symbols.

Improved: In "The Lottery" Shirley Jackson uses simple objects — a box, some stones, some slips of paper — to symbolize the narrow-mindedness and brutality that result from superstitious thinking.

1. Shirley Jackson's "The Lottery" is a compelling story about scapegoats.
2. The ritual of the lottery itself serves as a symbol in Shirley Jackson's story.
3. The setting of Shirley Jackson's "The Lottery" is an important element in contributing to the effectiveness of the story.
4. The characters function symbolically in Shirley Jackson's "The Lottery."
5. Shirley Jackson's "The Lottery" reveals a great deal about society and human nature.

Ideas for Writing

Ideas for Responsive Writing

1. What is Shirley Jackson saying about traditional rituals in "The Lottery"? Think of some ritual in our present society that you think ought to be dropped — or at least reconsidered and modified — and write an essay setting forth your views. Consider, for example, proms, weddings, Christmas gift exchanges, dating conventions, beauty pageants, boxing matches, funeral services, graduation ceremonies, fraternity/sorority pledging, and honoring the most prolific mother in the nation on Mother's Day.
2. Can you think of any famous scapegoats — or any who are not famous, for that matter? Write an essay discussing the role that scapegoats play in society, using examples chosen from history, novels, films, or your own experience.

Ideas for Critical Writing

1. Look up the word *scapegoat* in a good dictionary. Then look it up in the *Micropaedia* of the *Encyclopaedia Britannica*, which will give you some historical examples of the use of scapegoats. Formulate a thesis that relates the symbolism of "The Lottery" to the notion of

a scapegoat. Be sure in the conclusion to relate your remarks to the theme of the story.

2. Write an essay focusing on the symbolism of the characters in "The Lottery," especially Tessie Hutchinson, Old Man Warner, Bill Hutchinson, Mr. Graves, and Mr. Summers. Conclude your essay by relating your observations to the story's theme.

3. In the "Anthology of Short Fiction" (a later section of this text), read Nathaniel Hawthorne's "Young Goodman Brown" and write a paper focusing on the symbolism of the forest versus the community, keeping in mind Hawthorne's theme as you devise your thesis. In your conclusion, show how these major symbols function to reveal the meaning of the story.

4. Read Eudora Welty's "A Worn Path" and show how the bird imagery contributes to the effectiveness of the story.

5. Read Ursula LeGuin's "The Ones Who Walk Away from Omelas" and explore the symbolism to show how it serves to reinforce the theme.

Rewriting

As you revise your first draft, try, of course, to improve it in every way possible. Our advice at this point involves ideas for improving your introduction.

Sharpening the Introduction

Look at your introductory paragraph. Does it give your readers a clear idea of the topic and purpose? Will it arouse curiosity and interest, as well as lead into your subject?

One strategy for catching the attention of your readers involves using a pertinent quotation:

> "The less there is to justify a traditional custom," wrote Mark Twain, "the harder it is to get rid of it." This comment accurately describes the situation that Shirley Jackson presents in "The Lottery." Her story illustrates how ignorance and superstition become instilled in human society and lead to unnecessary violence.

Another relevant quotation for this introduction might be Gathorne Cranbrook's observation that "The tradition of preserving traditions became a tradition." Useful quotations like these are available in your library in reference books such as *Bartlett's Familiar Quotations*.

You can also take an arresting or tantalizing quotation from the story itself. Tessie Hutchinson's final scream, "It isn't fair, it isn't right," or Old Man Warner's "There's *always* been a lottery," might serve as an effective opening for an essay on this story.

Another strategy is to pose a startling question, like this:

> Why would the people in a quiet, peaceful village publicly murder one of their neighbors every summer? This is the shocking question that Shirley Jackson forces us to consider in her symbolic story "The Lottery."

Or you can combine some suspense with a *brief* overview of the story:

> The weather is sunny and clear. The residents of a peaceful village have gathered for an important annual event. They smile and chat with one another, while the children scurry about in play. Then someone brings out a black box, and the ordinary people of this ordinary town begin the process of choosing which one of their neighbors they are going to stone to death this summer. This shocking turn of events is the premise for Shirley Jackson's story about the fear and violence that lie beneath the placid surface of human societies. The story is called "The Lottery."

Another way to introduce a critical essay is to use interesting details about the author or the story's background that relate to the focus of your essay:

> In June of 1948 *The New Yorker* magazine published "The Lottery," a story by Shirley Jackson. Within days the magazine began to receive a flood of telephone calls and letters, more than for any other piece of fiction they had ever published. Almost all of those who wrote were outraged or bewildered—sometimes both. Why did this story prompt such reactions? Why does it still shock readers? The answer may lie in the story's strong symbolic representation of the pointless violence and casual inhumanity that exist in all our lives.

Whatever approach you choose, keep the reader in mind. Think about reading an essay yourself: What do you expect from the introduction? Remember that the reader forms an important first impression from your opening paragraph.

Sample Student Paper

On the following left-hand pages appears the uncorrected second draft of an essay written by Todd Hageman, a student at Eastern Illinois University. On the right-hand pages you will see Todd's finished version. The questions in the margins of the final version ask you to consider the changes Todd made when he revised the paper. You will find another sample student paper on "The Lottery," using library sources and illustrating the MLA style, in Chapter 17, which explains the research paper.

Sample Student Paper--Second Draft

Symbollism in The Lottery

Shirley Jackson's "The Lottery" uses
subtle symbollism along with inconngruities
to exemplify the loss of significance of some
rituals & traditions, and supersitions and
flaws of human nature. The first incongruity
used is the day the story takes place, June
27th. Jackson paints a picture of a nice,
sunny summer day in a small "Anytown, USA."
While Jackson paints this picture, though,
the reader feels an uneasy mood and senses
something is going to happen. Jackson does
this by using the words "hesitant" and
"reluctant" to describe the crowd while they
"smile at jokes instead of laugh" (74).
The next, and one of the biggest symbols
used in the story, is the box--the black box
to be more exact. The box is mentioned
repeatedly to bring significance to it,
although the reader isn't sure why until
toward the end of the story. As the lottery
symbolizes

Sample Student Paper--Finished Version

Why did Todd eliminate the second part of his thesis statement (about "incongruities" as well as symbolism)?

Why did Todd make the changes that he did in this opening sentence?

Symbolism in "The Lottery"

In "The Lottery" Shirley Jackson uses subtle symbolism to exemplify the emptiness of some rituals and traditions, as well as to illustrate several flaws of human nature. She begins with an incongruity in the setting on the day the story takes place, June 27th. Jackson paints a picture of a sunny summer day in a small "Anytown, USA." While Jackson introduces this pleasant setting, though, the reader feels uneasy and senses that something bad is going to happen. Jackson creates this tension by using the words "hesitant" and "reluctant" to describe the crowd and by mentioning that they "smiled rather than laughed" at jokes ← 74).

Why did he change "Jackson does this . . ." to "Jackson creates this tension . . ."?

Why did Todd change the quotation?

How did he improve the opening sentence of this paragraph?

The controlling symbol in the story is the box--the black box suggestive of death. The box is mentioned repeatedly to increase its significance, although the reader is not sure why she stresses its importance until toward the end of the story. As the lottery symbolizes empty

<u>Second Draft</u>

tradition, the box symbolizes the lottery.
Mr. Summers, the lottery official, tells
about getting a new box every year, but the
talk seems to "fade off." The box was
described as "faded," "splintered," and
"grew shabbyier each year" (75). The
condition of the box symbolize the tradition
of the lottery, and the need for a new box
symbolizes the need for a new tradition.

There was a need for a new tradition
because the lottery itself had lost its
significance. Parts of the original lottery
ritual had been allowed to lapse, and other
parts, such as the salute of the official had
"changed with the times" (75).The lottery
had lapsed and changed so much from the
original lottery that the people really
didn't know why they were going through it any
more. Probably the only reason they were
going through it was the intellectual
argument used by Old Man Warner, who said,
"There's always been a lottery" (77). When
Mr. Warner is informed that some places have
stopped the lottery, he comes back with such
wit as "Nothing but trouble in that," and
"pack of young fools." (77). The latter idea
expressed brings out the idea that all change
is bad and the young are the ones who make
changes. It is generally aknowledged that the
preceeding

Finished Version

Why did Todd change this quotation from "grew shabbier each year"?

tradition, the box symbolizes the lottery itself. Mr. Summers, the lottery official, speaks about getting a new box every year but his talk seems to "fade off." The box is described as "faded," "splintered," and growing "shabbier each year" (75). The worn out condition of the box symbolizes the tradition of the lottery, while the need for a new box symbolizes the need for a new tradition, but the townspeople fail to see the need for change.

← *Why did Todd add this information?*

There is a need for a new tradition because the lottery itself has lost its significance. Parts of the original lottery ritual have been allowed to lapse, and other parts, such as the salute of the official, have "changed with time" (75). The lottery has lapsed and changed so much from the original that the people really do not know why they are going through it any more.

Why did he eliminate the sarcasm directed at Old Man Warner?

Probably the only reason they continue is solemnly stated by Old Man Warner: "There's always been a lottery" (77). When Mr. Warner is informed that some places have stopped the lottery, he comes back with such meaningless arguments as "Nothing but trouble in that," and "pack of young fools" (77). He simply believes that all change is bad and the young are the ones who make changes. Most people

<u>Second Draft</u>

statement is false, leaving Mr. Warner on thin
ice from which to argue. I think the author
shows the uselessness of the lottery through
Mr. Warner's ignorance.

Human nature is shown very clearliy
through Tessie in the story. Tessie shows up
late at the lottery very lackadaisical and in
a joking mood before she was picked. She even
gave her husband an extra nudge as he went to
draw. When Tessie found out one of her family
would be chosen, her mood changed rather
quickly, screaming "unfair!" She even
wanted her two daughters to take their
chances; which she knew was wrong. Her
"friends" around her showed their flaws by
saying, "Be a good sport," and "We all took
the same chance," and not showing a bit of
pity (78). Tessie's kids also showed no pity,
as they opened their blank pieces of paper,
they were described as "beaming and
laughing" (79) with the crowd, even though
they knew it was going to be Mom or Dad picked.
The final part of human nature exemplified
was when Tessie drew the black dot. Every time
she said, "It isn't fair," the following
sentence was always her getting hit with a
stone, almost as punishment for saying it. The
stones seem to be saying, "You thought it was
fair until you were picked; now take your
medicine."

Finished Version

Can you think of another way to revise the stilted, wordy language of Todd's original statement, "It is generally acknowledged that the preceeding statement is false . . ."? would disagree, for Mr. Warner has little evidence to support his ideas. I think the author emphasizes the uselessness of the lottery through Mr. Warner's ignorant defense of it.

The selfishness in human nature is shown clearly in the story through Tessie. She shows up late at the lottery, lackadaisically joking with her neighbors before she is picked. She even gives her husband an encouraging nudge as he goes to draw. When Tessie finds out one of her family will be chosen, her mood changes quickly, and she screams, "It wasn't fair!" (78). She even wants her two daughters to take their chances along with her, which hardly suggests mother-love. Her "friends" around her show their lack of pity by saying, "Be a good sport," and "All of us took the same chance!"

Would you have put the period in the same place in revising Todd's comma splice? Or would you have used a semicolon? Why or why not? (78). Tessie's children also show no sympathy. As they open their blank pieces of paper, they are described as beaming and laughing with the crowd, even though they know one of their parents is going to be picked. Human cruelty is also exemplified after Tessie draws the black dot. Both times she cries, "It isn't fair!" (79), she gets hit with a stone, almost as punishment for objecting.

How does the addition of one word — "selfishness" — in the opening sentence improve this whole paragraph?

Second Draft

   The story has one key sentence which
puts the whole theme in a nutshell: "Although
the villagers had forgotten the ritual and
lost the original box, they still remembered
to use stones"(79). Through the symbollism
being used, the sentence can be translated
into a theme for the story. The ritual had
changed with the times and lost the original
purpose, but people still remember to look
out for themselves. Every time a villager
threw a stone, he was probably thinking,
"Better you than me."
   A final thought could be about the slips
of paper and what they symbolized. Jackson
mentioned that the unused papers were
"dropped to the ground where the breeze
caught them and lifted them off" (78). The
papers could be meant to symbolize the people
who had been sacrificed through the lottery.
The village people had used both the papers
and the sacrificed people and had discarded
them as trash.

Shirley Jackson, "The Lottery," in   *Is this form*
                                       ✓ *correct?*
   Literature and the Writing Process, New
      York: McMillan, 1993:74-79.
                        ƒ
   Spelled correctly?

Finished Version

Why did Todd move his final paragraph to this position?

The slips of paper also serve a symbolic purpose. Jackson mentions that the unused papers dropped to the ground "where the breeze caught them and lifted them off" (78). The papers could symbolize the people who have been sacrificed through the lottery. The village people make use of both the papers and the sacrificed people, then discard them as trash.

Why did he replace the phrase "in a nutshell"?

The story has one key sentence which captures the whole theme: "Although the villagers had forgotten the ritual and lost the original black box, they still remembered to use stones" (79). Considering the symbolism in the story, the sentence can be translated into a theme. Although the ritual had changed with the times and lost the original purpose, people still remember to look out for themselves. Every time the villagers threw a stone, they were probably

How do these last two sentences that he added improve the paper?

thinking, "Better you than me." Jackson dramatizes for us the harm done by ignorance which causes people to cling to outworn rituals. She also shows the selfishness and cruelty which lie just beneath the civilized surface of human behavior.

Jackson, Shirley. "The Lottery."
    Literature and the Writing Process. Ed.
    Elizabeth McMahan, Susan Day, and Robert
    Funk. 3rd ed. New York: Macmillan,
    1993. 74-79.

7

Writing About Point of View

Learning about point of view in fiction will help you to understand how the author has shaped what you know and how you feel about the events in a story. When the point of view is unusual, you may want to focus your written analysis on the narrator or on the significance of the writer's choice of narrative focus.

What Is Point of View?

In identifying point of view, you decide who tells the story — that is, whose thoughts and feelings the reader has access to. The storyteller, called the *narrator,* is a creation of the author and should not be confused with the author. In the following passage from "Everyday Use," Alice Walker takes the reader into the private world of her narrator's fantasy:

> Sometimes I dream a dream in which Dee and I are suddenly brought together on a TV program of this sort. Out of a dark and soft-seated limousine I am ushered into a bright room filled with many people.

In John Updike's story "A & P," the narrator's distinctive voice is established in the opening lines:

> In walks these three girls in nothing but bathing suits. I'm in the third checkout slot, with my back to the door, so I don't see them until they're over by the bread.

But in the opening of "The Lottery," we are not conscious of a narrator at all:

> The morning of June 27th was clear and sunny, with a fresh warmth of a full-summer day; the flowers were blossoming profusely and the grass was richly green.

Describing Point of View

There are several systems for labeling the point of view in a work of literature. They classify the stance and the identity of the person who records and reports the action — that is, the person whose eyes and mind become ours as we read the story.

In actuality, a great many points of view are possible, and you may find some overlapping among the categories we provide here, but the following should allow you to describe all of the works included in this text.

1. *Omniscient*: an all-knowing narrator freely relates many or all of the characters' thoughts, feelings, and actions. The omniscient narrator is not a character in the story and is not involved in the action. Stephen Crane's "The Open Boat" is told from an omniscient point of view, as is Kate Chopin's "Désirée's Baby."

2. *Limited*: the narration is limited to the thoughts and observations of a single character. In detective fiction, for example, we often see the plot unfold strictly from the main character's (the detective's) point of view. Sometimes our perceptions are limited to those of a minor character; in the Sherlock Holmes stories, for example, the events are reported from the point of view of Dr. Watson, the great detective's sidekick, whose admiration and awe for Holmes's skills become ours.

3. *First person*: the narrator recounts events in which he or she has been involved as a major or minor participant. This narrator, identified as "I" in the story, addresses the reader directly. First-person narrators usually present only their side of the story. For example, Sammy, the first-person narrator in John Updike's "A & P," gives an obviously subjective account of why he quit his job; and in "Everyday Use" we get only Mama's version of her daughter Dee's visit.

4. *Objective*: the narrator disappears and the story seems to tell itself through action and dialogue. An objective narrative does not get into the minds of the characters; it gives the reader only what could be recorded by a camera and a microphone. In reading this kind of story, we have to make judgments and draw conclusions on our own. The objective narrator may edit the tape and direct the camera, but we have to figure out why the characters behave as they do. When you read "The Lottery," you encountered an objective point of view — the narrator presented the events, but you had to determine why they occurred and what they meant.

5. *Shifting*: If a writer tells the same story twice, once through one character and again through a different character, the point of view is still limited, but *shifting*. John Fowles's novel *The Collector* narrates a kidnapping first from the kidnapper's point of view and then from the victim's point of view. The point of view can shift in other ways. Eudora Welty's "A Worn Path," for example, begins in a general, objective way:

It was December — a bright frozen day in the early morning. Far out in the country there was an old Negro woman with her head tied in a red rag, coming along a path through the pinewoods.

But the narration gradually becomes more limited, focusing almost exclusively on the thoughts, words, and actions of Phoenix Jackson, the story's main character.

6. *Unreliable narrator:* If the storyteller misrepresents or misinterprets the facts, purposely or naively, the narrator is considered *unreliable*. A child, an insane person, or a villain, for example, would sometimes be unable or unwilling to give a fully truthful presentation. Writers also sometimes use unreliable narrators to emphasize the subjectivity of experience, as you will see in the following story by Ring Lardner.

Looking at Point of View

As you read Ring Lardner's "Haircut," notice how much the narrator inadvertently reveals about himself and his social circle.

Ring Lardner *1885–1933*

HAIRCUT

I got another barber that comes over from Carterville and helps me out Saturdays, but the rest of the time I can get along all right alone. You can see for yourself that this ain't no New York City and besides that, the most of the boys works all day and don't have no leisure to drop in here and get themselves prettied up.

You're a newcomer, ain't you? I thought I hadn't seen you round before. I hope you like it good enough to stay. As I say, we ain't no New York City or Chicago, but we have pretty good times. Not as good, though, since Jim Kendall got killed. When he was alive, him and Hod Meyers used to keep this town in an uproar. I bet they was more laughin' done here than any town its size in America.

Jim was comical, and Hod was pretty near a match for him. Since Jim's gone, Hod tries to hold his end up just the same as ever, but it's rough goin' when you ain't got nobody to kind of work with.

They used to be plenty fun in here Saturdays. This place is jam-packed Saturdays, from four on. Jim and Hod would show up right after their supper, round six o'clock. Jim would set himself down in that big chair, nearest the blue spittoon. Whoever had been settin' in that chair, why they'd get up when Jim come in and give it to him.

You'd of thought it was a reserved seat like they have sometimes in a theayter. Hod would generally always stand or walk up and down, or some Saturdays, of course, he'd be settin' in this chair part of the time, gettin' a haircut.

Well, Jim would set there a w'ile without openin' his mouth only to spit, and then finally he'd say to me, "Whitey," — my right name, that is, my right first name, is Dick, but everybody round here calls me Whitey — Jim would say,

"Whitey, your nose looks like a rosebud tonight. You must of been drinkin' some of your aw de cologne."

So I'd say, "No, Jim, but you look like you'd been drinking somethin' of that kind or somethin' worse."

Jim would have to laugh at that, but then he'd speak up and say, "No, I ain't had nothin' to drink, but that ain't sayin' I wouldn't like somethin'. I wouldn't even mind if it was wood alcohol."

Then Hod Meyers would say, "Neither would your wife." That would set everybody to laughin' because Jim and his wife wasn't on very good terms. She'd of divorced him only they wasn't no chance to get alimony and she didn't have no way to take care of herself and the kids. She couldn't never understand Jim. He *was* kind of rough, but a good fella at heart.

Him and Hod had all kinds of sport with Milt Sheppard. I don't suppose you've seen Milt. Well, he's got an Adam's apple that looks more like a mushmelon. So I'd be shavin' Milt and when I'd start to shave down here on his neck, Hod would holler, "Hey, Whitey, wait a minute! Before you cut into it, let's make up a pool and see who can guess closest to the number of seeds."

And Jim would say, "If Milt hadn't of been so hoggish, he'd of ordered a half a canteloupe instead of a whole one and it might not of stuck in his throat."

All the boys would roar at this and Milt himself would force a smile, though the joke was on him. Jim certainly was a card!

There's his shavin' mug, settin' on the shelf, right next to Charley Vail's. "Charles M. Vail." That's the druggist. He comes in regular for his shave, three times a week. And Jim's is the cup next to Charley's. "James H. Kendall." Jim won't need no shavin' mug no more, but I'll leave it there just the same for old time's sake. Jim certainly was a character!

Years ago, Jim used to travel for a canned goods concern over in Carterville. They sold canned goods. Jim had the whole northern half of the State and was on the road five days out of every week. He'd drop in here Saturdays and tell his experiences for that week. It was rich.

I guess he paid more attention to playin' jokes than makin' sales. Finally the concern let him out and he come right home here and told everybody he'd been fired instead of sayin' he'd resigned like most fellas would of.

It was a Saturday and the shop was full and Jim got up out of that chair and says, "Gentlemen, I got an important announcement to make. I been fired from my job."

Well, they asked him if he was in earnest and he said he was and nobody could think of nothin' to say till Jim finally broke the ice himself. He says, "I been sellin' canned goods and now I'm canned goods myself."

You see, the concern he'd been workin' for was a factory that made canned goods. Over in Carterville. And now Jim said he was canned himself. He was certainly a card!

For instance, they'd be a sign, "Henry Smith, Dry Goods." Well, Jim would write down the name and the name of the town and when he got to wherever he was goin' he'd mail back a postal card to Henry Smith at Benton and not sign no name to it, but he'd write on the card, well, somethin' like "Ask your wife about that book agent that spent the afternoon last week," or "Ask your Missus who kept her from gettin' lonesome the last time you was in Carterville." And he'd sign the card, "A Friend."

Of course, he never knew what really come of none of these jokes, but he could picture what *probably* happened and that was enough.

Jim didn't work very steady after he lost his position with the Carterville people. What he did earn, doin' odd jobs round town, why he spent pretty near all of it on gin and his family might of starved if the stores hadn't of carried them along. Jim's wife tried her hand at dressmakin', but they ain't nobody goin' to get rich makin' dresses in this town.

As I say, she'd of divorced Jim, only she seen that she couldn't support herself and the kids and she was always hopin' that some day Jim would cut his habits and give her more than two or three dollars a week.

There was a time when she would go to whoever he was workin' for and ask them to give her his wages, but after she done this once or twice, he beat her to it by borrowin' most of his pay in advance. He told it all round town, how he had outfoxed his Missus. He certainly was a caution!

But he wasn't satisfied with just outwittin' her. He was sore the way she had acted, tryin' to grab off his pay. And he made up his mind he'd get even. Well, he waited till Evan's Circus was advertised to come to town. Then he told his wife and kiddies that he was goin' to take them to the circus. The day of the circus, he told them he would get the tickets and meet them outside the entrance to the tent.

Well, he didn't have no intentions of bein' there or buyin' tickets or nothin'. He got full of gin and laid round Wright's poolroom all day. His wife and the kids waited and waited and of course he didn't show up. His wife didn't have a dime with her, or nowhere else, I guess. So she finally had to tell the kids it was all off and they cried like they wasn't never goin' to stop.

Well, it seems, w'ile they was cryin', Doc Stair came along and he asked what was the matter, but Mrs. Kendall was stubborn and wouldn't tell him, but the kids told him and he insisted on takin' them and their mother in the show. Jim found this out afterwards and it was one reason why he had it in for Doc Stair.

Doc Stair come here about a year and a half ago. He's a mighty handsome young fella and his clothes always look like he has them made to order. He goes to Detroit two or three times a year and w'ile he's there he must have a tailor take his measure and then make him a suit to order. They cost pretty near twice as much, but they fit a whole lot better than if you just bought them in a store.

For a w'ile everybody was wonderin' why a young doctor like Doc Stair should come to a town like this where we already got old Doc Gamble and Doc Foote that's both been here for years and all the practice in town was always divided between the two of them.

Then they was a story got round that Doc Stair's gal had thrown him over, a gal up in the Northern Peninsula somewheres, and the reason he come here was to hide himself away and forget it. He said himself that he thought they wasn't nothin' like general practice in a place like ours to fit a man to be a good all round doctor. And that's why he'd came.

Anyways, it wasn't long before he was makin' enough to live on, though they tell me that he never dunned nobody for what they owed him, and the folks here certainly has got the owin' habit, even in my business. If I had all that was comin' to me for just shaves alone, I could go to Carterville and put up at the Mercer for a week and see a different picture every night. For instance, they's old George Purdy—but I guess I shouldn't ought to be gossipin'.

Well, last year, our coroner died, died of the flu. Ken Beatty, that was his name. He was the coroner. So they had to choose another man to be coroner in his place and they picked Doc Stair. He laughed at first and said he didn't want it, but they made him take it. It ain't no job nobody would fight for and what a man makes out of it in a year would just about buy seeds for their garden. Doc's the kind, though, that can't say no to nothin', if you keep at him long enough.

But I was goin' to tell you about a poor boy we got here in town—Paul Dickson. He fell out of a tree when he was about ten years old. Lit on his head and it done somethin' to him and he ain't never been right. No harm in him, but just silly. Jim Kendall used to call him cuckoo; that's a name Jim had for anybody that was off their head, only he called people's head their bean. That was another of his gags, callin' head bean and callin' crazy people cuckoo. Only poor Paul ain't crazy, but just silly.

You can imagine that Jim used to have all kinds of fun with Paul. He'd send him to the White Front Garage for a left-handed monkey wrench. Of course they ain't no such a thing as a left-handed monkey wrench.

And once we had a kind of fair here and they was a baseball game between the fats and the leans and before the game started Jim called Paul over and sent him down to Schrader's hardware store to get a key for the pitcher's box.

They wasn't nothin' in the way of gags that Jim couldn't think up, when he put his mind to it.

Poor Paul was always kind of suspicious of people, maybe on account of how Jim had kept foolin' him. Paul wouldn't have much to do with anybody only his own mother and Doc Stair and a girl here in town named Julie Gregg. That is, she ain't a girl no more, but pretty near thirty or over.

When Doc first come to town, Paul seemed to feel like here was a real friend and he hung around Doc's office most of the w'ile; the only time he wasn't there was when he'd go home to eat or sleep or when he seen Julie Gregg doin' her shoppin'.

When he looked out Doc's window and seen her, he'd run downstairs and join her and tag along with her to the different stores. The poor boy was crazy about Julie and she always treated him mighty nice and made him feel like he was welcome, though of course it wasn't nothin' but pity on her side.

Doc done all he could to improve Paul's mind and he told me once that he really thought the boy was gettin' better, that they was times when he was as bright and sensible as anybody else.

But I was goin' to tell you about Julie Gregg. Old Man Gregg was in the lumber business, but got to drinkin' and lost most of his money and when he died, he didn't leave nothin' but the house and just enough insurance for the girl to skimp along on.

Her mother was a kind of invalid and didn't hardly ever leave the house. Julie wanted to sell the place and move somewheres else after the old man died, but the mother said she was born here and would die here. It was tough on Julie, as for the young people round this town—well, she's too good for them.

She's been away to school and Chicago and New York and different places and they ain't no subject she can't talk on, where you take the rest of the young folks here and you mention anything to them outside of Gloria Swanson or Tommy Meighan and they think you're delirious. Did you see Gloria in *Wages of Virtue?* You missed somethin'!

Well, Doc Stair hadn't been here more than a week when he come in one day to get shaved and I recognized who he was as he had been pointed out to me, so I told him about my old lady. She's been ailin' for a couple years and either Doc Gamble or Doc Foote, neither one, seemed to be helpin' her. So he said he would come out and see her, but if she was able to get out herself, it would be better to bring her to his office where he could make a completer examination.

So I took her to his office and w'ile I was waiting for her in the reception room, in come Julie Gregg. When somebody comes in Doc Stair's office, they's a bell that rings in his inside office so he can tell they's somebody to see him.

So he left my old lady inside and come out to the front office and that's the first time him and Julie met and I guess it was what they call love at first sight. But it wasn't fifty-fifty. This young fella was the slickest lookin' fella she'd ever seen in this town and she went wild over him. To him she was just a young lady that wanted to see the doctor.

She'd came on about the same business I had. Her mother had been doctorin' for years with Doc Gamble and Doc Foote and without no results. So she'd heard they was a new doc in town and decided to give him a try. He promised to call and see her mother that same day.

I said a minute ago that it was love at first sight on her part. I'm not only judgin' by how she acted afterwards but how she looked at him that first day in his office. I ain't no mind reader, but it was wrote all over her face that she was gone.

Now Jim Kendall, besides bein' a jokesmith and a pretty good drinker, well, Jim was quite a lady-killer. I guess he run pretty wild durin' the time he was on the road for them Carterville people, and besides that, he'd had a couple little affairs of the heart right here in town. As I say, his wife could of divorced him, only she couldn't.

But Jim was like the majority of men, and women, too, I guess. He wanted what he couldn't get. He wanted Julie Gregg and worked his head off tryin' to land her. Only he'd of said bean instead of head.

Well, Jim's habits and his jokes didn't appeal to Julie and of course he was a married man, so he didn't have no more chance than, well, than a rabbit. That's an expression of Jim's himself. When somebody didn't have no chance to get elected or somethin', Jim would always say they didn't have no more chance than a rabbit.

He didn't make no bones about how he felt. Right in here, more than once, in front of the whole crowd, he said he was stuck on Julie and anybody that could get her for him was welcome to his house and his wife and kids included. But she wouldn't have nothin' to do with him; wouldn't even speak to him on the street. He finally seen he wasn't gettin' nowheres with his usual line so he decided to try the rough stuff. He went right up to her house one evenin' and when she opened the door he forced his way in and grabbed her. But she broke loose and before he could stop her, she run in the next room and locked the door and phoned to Joe Barnes. Joe's the marshal. Jim could hear who she was phonin' to and he beat it before Joe got there.

Joe was an old friend of Julie's pa. Joe went to Jim the next day and told him what would happen if he ever done it again.

I don't know how the news of this little affair leaked out. Chances is that Joe Barnes told his wife and she told somebody else's wife and they told their husband. Anyways, it did leak out and Hod Meyers had the nerve to kid Jim about it, right here in this shop. Jim didn't deny nothin' and kind of laughed it off and said for us all to wait; that lots of people had tried to make a monkey out of him, but he always got even.

Meanw'ile everybody in town was wise to Julie's bein' wild mad over the Doc.

I don't suppose she had any idear how her face changed when him and her was together; of course she couldn't of, or she'd of kept away from him. And she didn't know that we was all noticin' how many times she made excuses to go up to his office or pass it on the other side of the street and look up in his window to see if he was there. I felt sorry for her and so did most other people.

Hod Meyers kept rubbin' it into Jim about how the Doc had cut him out. Jim didn't pay no attention to the kiddin' and you could see he was plannin' one of his jokes.

One trick Jim had was the knack of changin' his voice. He could make you think he was a girl talkin' and he could mimic any man's voice. To show you how good he was along this line, I'll tell you the joke he played on me once.

You know, in most towns of any size, when a man is dead and needs a shave, why the barber that shaves him soaks him five dollars for the job; that is, he don't soak *him*, but whoever ordered the shave. I just charge three dollars because personally I don't mind much shavin' a dead person. They lay a whole lot stiller than live customers. The only thing is that you don't feel like talkin' to them and you get kind of lonesome.

Well, about the coldest day we ever had here, two years ago last winter, the phone rung at the house w'ile I was home to dinner and I answered the phone and it was a woman's voice and she said she was Mrs. John Scott and her husband was dead and would I come out and shave him.

Old John had always been a good customer of mine. But they live seven miles out in the country, on the Streeter road. Still I didn't see how I could say no.

So I said I would be there, but would have to come in a jitney and it might cost three or four dollars besides the price of the shave. So she, or the voice, said that was all right, so I got Frank Abbott to drive me out to the place and when I got there, who should open the door but old John himself! He wasn't no more dead than, well, than a rabbit.

It didn't take no private detective to figure out who had played me this little joke. Nobody could of thought it up but Jim Kendall. He certainly was a card!

I tell you this incident just to show you how he could disguise his voice and make you believe it was somebody else talkin'. I'd of swore it was Mrs. Scott had called me. Anyways, some woman.

Well, Jim waited till he had Doc Stair's voice down pat; then he went after revenge.

He called Julie up on a night when he knew Doc was over in Carterville. She never questioned but what it was Doc's voice. Jim said he must see her that night; he couldn't wait no longer to tell her somethin'. She was all excited and told him to come to the house. But he said he was expectin' an important long distance call and wouldn't she please forget her manners for once and come to his office. He said they couldn't nothin' hurt her and nobody would see her and he just *must* talk to her a little w'ile. Well, poor Julie fell for it.

Doc always keeps a night light in his office, so it looked to Julie like they was somebody there.

Meanw'ile Jim Kendall had went to Wright's poolroom, where they was a whole gang amusin' themselves. The most of them had drunk plenty of gin, and they was a rough bunch even when sober. They was always strong for Jim's jokes and when he told them to come with him and see some fun they give up their card games and pool games and followed along.

Doc's office is on the second floor. Right outside his door they's a flight of stairs leadin' to the floor above. Jim and his gang hid in the dark behind these stairs.

Well, Julie come up to Doc's door and rung the bell and they was nothin' doin'. She rung it again and she rung it seven or eight times. Then she tried the door and found it locked. Then Jim made some kind of a noise and she heard it and waited a minute, and then she says, "Is that you, Ralph?" Ralph is Doc's first name.

They was no answer and it must of came to her all of a sudden that she'd been bunked. She pretty near fell downstairs and the whole gang after her. They chased her all the way home, hollerin', "Is that you, Ralph?" and "Oh, Ralphie, dear, is that you?" Jim says he couldn't holler it himself, as he was laughin' too hard.

Poor Julie! She didn't show up here on Main Street for a long, long time afterward.

And of course Jim and his gang told everybody in town, everybody but Doc Stair. They was scared to tell him, and he might of never knowed only for Paul Dickson. The poor cuckoo, as Jim called him, he was here in the shop one night when Jim was still gloatin' yet over what he'd done to Julie. And Paul took in as much of it as he could understand and he run to Doc with the story.

It's a cinch Doc went up in the air and swore he'd make Jim suffer. But it was a kind of delicate thing, because if it got out that he had beat Jim up, Julie was bound to hear of it and then she'd know that Doc knew and of course knowin' that he knew would make it worse for her than ever. He was goin' to do somethin', but it took a lot of figurin'.

Well, it was a couple of days later when Jim was here in the shop again, and so was the cuckoo. Jim was goin' duck-shootin' the next day and had come in lookin' for Hod Meyers to go with him. I happened to know that Hod went over to Carterville and wouldn't be home till the end of the week. So Jim said he hated to go alone and he guessed he would call it off. Then poor Paul spoke up and said if Jim would take him he would go along. Jim thought a w'ile and then he said, well, he guessed a halfwit was better than nothin'.

I suppose he was plottin' to get Paul out in the boat and play some joke on him, like pushin' him in the water. Anyways, he said Paul could go. He asked him had he ever shot a duck and Paul said no, he'd never even had a gun in his hands. So Jim said he could set in the boat and watch him and if he behaved himself, he might lend him his gun for a couple of shots. They made a date to meet in the mornin' and that's the last I seen of Jim alive.

Next mornin', I hadn't been open more than ten minutes when Doc Stair come in. He looked kind of nervous. He asked me had I seen Paul Dickson. I said no, but I knew where he was, out duck-shootin' with Jim Kendall. So Doc says that's what he had heard, and he couldn't understand it because Paul had told him he wouldn't never have no more to do with Jim as long as he lived.

He said Paul had told him about the joke Jim played on Julie. He said Paul had asked him what he thought of the joke and the Doc had told him anybody that would do a thing like that ought not to be let live.

I said it had been a kind of raw thing, but Jim just couldn't resist no kind of a joke, no matter how raw. I said I thought he was all right at heart, but just bubblin' over with mischief. Doc turned and walked out.

At noon he got a phone call from old John Scott. The lake where Jim and Paul had went shootin' is on John's place. Paul had come runnin' up to the house a few minutes before and said they'd been an accident. Jim had shot a few ducks and then give the gun to Paul and told him to try his luck. Paul hadn't never handled a gun and he was nervous. He was shakin' so hard that he couldn't control the gun. He let fire and Jim sunk back in the boat, dead.

Doc Stair, bein' the coroner, jumped in Frank Abbott's flivver and rushed out to Scott's farm. Paul and old John was down on the shore of the lake. Paul had rowed the boat to shore, but they'd left the body in it, waitin' for Doc to come.

Doc examined the body and said they might as well fetch it back to town. They was no use leavin' it there or callin' a jury, as it was a plain case of accidental shootin'.

Personally I wouldn't never leave a person shoot a gun in the same boat I was in unless I was sure they knew somethin' about guns. Jim was a sucker to leave a new beginner have his gun, let alone a half-wit. It probably served Jim right, what he got. But still we miss him round here. He certainly was a card!

Comb it wet or dry?

(1925)

Prewriting

To help you examine the point of view of "Haircut" and to see how it affects other elements of the story, write out answers to the following questions.

Identifying Point of View

1. Reread the first two paragraphs of "Haircut." Who is speaking? Identify words and phrases in the first two paragraphs that give you an impression of the speaker. How would you summarize that impression?

2. Reread the rest of the story. Who is really the main character?

3. Why did the author choose the town's barber as narrator of this story? What stereotypes is Lardner drawing on in his choice of narrator?

4. How do your feelings about the other characters in the story (Hod, Doc Stair, Julie, Paul) affect your responses to Whitey and Jim?

5. How does Whitey react when Jim plays a trick on him? What does his reaction tell you about Whitey?

6. Where does Whitey get his information about people and incidents in the town? How much is first-hand? Does Whitey ever question or doubt what he hears?

7. What do other characters in the story think about Jim? Cite examples. Does Whitey seem to pay any attention to these views?

8. What do you think of Whitey's explanation of Jim's death? Why is he unable to draw the obvious conclusion about the shooting?

9. Do Whitey's views match Ring Lardner's? How do you know?

Writing

Before you decide to focus your paper on point of view, you need to determine its importance in the story. An analysis of point of view may not always merit a full-length paper: a first-person, reliable main character's narration of a personal story is such a natural and appropriate choice that there is little to say about it. But often, as in "Haircut," analysis of the point of view is the key to the story.

Relating Point of View to Theme

Once we become aware that Whitey has been unconsciously exposing Jim Kendall's viciousness, we need to relate that perception to the main point or impact of the story. Why is this particular point of view effective for this particular story?

Ideas for Writing
Ideas for Responsive Writing

1. Write a description of Jim from the point of view of another character in the story: Hud, Julie, or Doc Stair.
2. Imagine that you are conducting an inquiry into the death of Jim. Write a report of your findings. Be sure to include your evaluation of Whitey's testimony.
3. Do you know someone whose word is not reliable? Write a comparison between Whitey and the person you know.
4. Did you have the same reaction to Whitey as you had to Mama, the narrator of "Everyday Use"? Discuss the similarities and differences in your response to these two first-person narrators.

Ideas for Critical Writing

Here are some possible thesis statements that focus on point of view. Choose one of these statements, revise one, or make up your own thesis.

1. The narrator's attitude toward Jim Kendall and his pranks slowly reveals the backbiting nature of small-town life and of the narrator himself.
2. Ring Lardner uses an unreliable narrator, developing his unreliability throughout the story so that readers are allowed to draw their own conclusions about Jim's death.
3. Whitey's mostly innocent lack of sympathy and self-awareness enhances, by comparison, our discovery of the malice of Jim Kendall, "the card," the main character.

4. Whitey, seemingly a normal resident of the little town, is the perfect choice of narrator for "Haircut," a story fundamentally about small-town life.

Rewriting

When you revise, do not neglect your conclusion just because it comes last. It has a psychologically important place in your paper. Ask yourself, "Does my closing restate the main idea in a too obvious, repetitive way? Will the readers feel let down, dropped off, cut short?" If so, consider some of these ways to make your ending more lively.

Sharpening the Conclusion

1. *Description.* After a discussion of the viciousness that underlies the placid, small-town life in "Haircut," you might write the following:

   Finally, the reader may envision Whitey's customer leaving the barbershop, settling his hat on his new haircut as he surveys the sleepy, serene streets of town, getting into his car, and leaving as fast as possible, forever.

2. *Humor or irony.* (If appropriate to the tone of your essay.) You can probably never match Lardner's gem, "Comb it wet or dry?" which stands in telling ironic contrast to the previous description of murder.

3. *A quotation from the story.* Remember that it must be integrated into your own sentence, perhaps like this:

   The design of the story surely leads us to question the breadth of the "we" in Whitey's statement about Jim, "But still we miss him around here."

4. *An echo from your introduction.* If you wrote of "Jim Kendall's ten 'jokes'" in your opening, for example, you could conclude with "Jim Kendall played ten big jokes; the eleventh one was on him."

5. *A thought-provoking question, suggestion, or statement.*

   Does Lardner imply that such human cruelty is inevitable?

   Is a neighborhood in a big city that different from the world of "Haircut"?

8

Writing About Setting and Atmosphere

Setting and atmosphere contribute to the effectiveness of short stories in various ways. Sometimes these elements assume enough importance to become the focus of a literary analysis.

What Are Setting and Atmosphere?

Of course you know the meaning of *setting* in reference to a work of literature: the setting includes the location and time of the action in a story, novel, play, or poem. Sometimes the setting conveys an *atmosphere* — the emotional effect of the setting and events — that contributes to the impact or to the meaning of the work. Atmosphere (or mood) is that feeling of chill foreboding that Poe creates by setting his tale of "The Fall of the House of Usher" in a remote, moldering mansion on the edge of a black, stagnant pool and then having eerie things happen. Atmosphere can also be used to increase irony, as Shirley Jackson does in "The Lottery" by conveying the deceptive feeling of carefree summer festivity just before turning her tale abruptly toward ritual murder. Usually, though, setting and atmosphere reflect the dominant tone and theme of a work.

In deciding whether to focus on setting or atmosphere in writing a literary paper, you need to ask yourself not only how much the effect of the work would be changed if these elements were different but also how much you have to say about them — especially concerning their contribution to the effectiveness of the piece. For instance, the barbershop in which Ring Lardner's "Haircut" takes place seems the perfect setting for that story. We can scarcely imagine its being set as effectively anywhere else. How much more can you think of to say about the setting and atmosphere?

Looking at Setting and Atmosphere

As you read the following story, first published in 1892, consider how crucial setting and atmosphere are in contributing to its effect.

Charlotte Perkins Gilman *1860–1935*

THE YELLOW WALL-PAPER

It is very seldom that mere ordinary people like John and myself secure ancestral halls for the summer.

A colonial mansion, a hereditary estate, I would say a haunted house, and reach the height of romantic felicity—but that would be asking too much of fate!

Still I will proudly declare that there is something queer about it.

Else, why should it be let so cheaply? And why have stood so long untenanted?

John laughs at me, of course, but one expects that in marriage.

John is practical in the extreme. He has no patience with faith, an intense horror of superstition, and he scoffs openly at any talk of things not to be felt or seen and put down in figures.

John is a physician, and *perhaps*—(I would not say it to a living soul, of course, but this is dead paper and a great relief to my mind)—*perhaps* that is one reason I do not get well faster.

You see he does not believe I am sick! And what can one do?

If a physician of high standing, and one's own husband, assures friends and relatives that there is really nothing the matter with one but temporary nervous depression—a slight hysterical tendency—what is one to do?

My brother is also a physician, and also of high standing, and he says the same thing.

So I take phosphates or phosphites—whichever it is—and tonics, and journeys, and air, and exercise, and am absolutely forbidden to "work" until I am well again.

Personally, I disagree with their ideas.

Personally, I believe that congenial work, with excitement and change, would do me good.

But what is one to do?

I did write for a while in spite of them; but it *does* exhaust me a good deal—having to be so sly about it, or else meet with heavy opposition.

I sometimes fancy that in my condition if I had less opposition and more society and stimulus—but John says the very worst thing I can do is to think about my condition, and I confess it always makes me feel bad.

So I will let it alone and talk about the house.

The most beautiful place! It is quite alone, standing well back from the road, quite three miles from the village. It makes me think of English places that you read about, for there are hedges and walls and gates that lock, and lots of separate little houses for the gardeners and people.

There is a *delicious* garden! I never saw such a garden—large and shady, full of box-bordered paths, and lined with long grape-covered arbors with seats under them.

There were greenhouses, too, but they are all broken now.

There was some legal trouble, I believe, something about the heirs and co-heirs; anyhow, the place has been empty for years.

That spoils my ghostliness, I am afraid, but I don't care—there is something strange about the house—I can feel it.

I even said so to John one moonlight evening, but he said what I felt was a draft, and shut the window.

I get unreasonably angry with John sometimes. I'm sure I never used to be so sensitive. I think it is due to this nervous condition.

But John says if I feel so I shall neglect proper self-control; so I take pains to control myself—before him, at least, and that makes me very tired.

I don't like our room a bit. I wanted one downstairs that opened on the piazza and had roses all over the window, and such pretty old-fashioned chintz hangings! But John would not hear of it.

He said there was only one window and not room for two beds, and no near room for him if he took another.

He is very careful and loving, and hardly lets me stir without special direction.

I have a schedule prescription for each hour in the day; he takes all care from me, and so I feel basely ungrateful not to value it more.

He said we came here solely on my account, that I was to have perfect rest and all the air I could get. "Your exercise depends on your strength, my dear," said he, "and your food somewhat on your appetite; but air you can absorb all the time." So we took the nursery at the top of the house.

It is a big, airy room, the whole floor nearly, with windows that look all ways, and air and sunshine galore. It was nursery first and then playroom and gymnasium, I should judge; for the windows are barred for little children, and there are rings and things in the walls.

The paint and paper look as if a boys' school had used it. It is stripped off—the paper—in great patches all around the head of my bed, about as far as I can reach, and in a great place on the other side of the room low down. I never saw a worse paper in my life.

One of those sprawling flamboyant patterns committing every artistic sin.

It is dull enough to confuse the eye in following, pronounced enough constantly to irritate and provoke study, and when you follow the lame uncertain curves for a little distance they suddenly commit suicide—plunge off at outrageous angles, destroy themselves in unheard of contradictions.

The color is repellent, almost revolting; a smoldering unclean yellow, strangely faded by the slow-turning sunlight.

It is a dull yet lurid orange in some places, a sickly sulphur tint in others.

No wonder the children hated it! I should hate it myself if I had to live in this room long.

There comes John, and I must put this away—he hates to have me write a word.

We have been here two weeks, and I haven't felt like writing before, since that first day.

I am sitting by the window now, up in this atrocious nursery, and there is nothing to hinder my writing as much as I please, save lack of strength.

John is away all day, and even some nights when his cases are serious.

I am glad my case is not serious!

But these nervous troubles are dreadfully depressing.

John does not know how much I really suffer. He knows there is no *reason* to suffer, and that satisfies him.

Of course it is only nervousness. It does weigh on me so not to do my duty in any way!

I meant to be such a help to John, such a real rest and comfort, and here I am a comparative burden already!

Nobody would believe what an effort it is to do what little I am able — to dress and entertain, and order things.

It is fortunate Mary is so good with the baby. Such a dear baby!

And yet I *cannot* be with him, it makes me so nervous.

I suppose John never was nervous in his life. He laughs at me so about this wall-paper!

At first he meant to repaper the room, but afterwards he said that I was letting it get the better of me, and that nothing was worse for a nervous patient than to give way to such fancies.

He said that after the wall-paper was changed it would be the heavy bedstead, and then the barred windows, and then that gate at the head of the stairs, and so on.

"You know the place is doing you good," he said, "and really, dear, I don't care to renovate the house just for a three months' rental."

"Then do let us go downstairs," I said, "there are such pretty rooms there."

Then he took me in his arms and called me a blessed little goose, and said he would go down cellar, if I wished, and have it whitewashed into the bargain.

But he is right enough about the beds and windows and things.

It is an airy and comfortable room as any one need wish, and, of course, I would not be so silly as to make him uncomfortable just for a whim.

I'm really getting quite fond of the big room, all but that horrid paper.

Out of one window I can see the garden, those mysterious deep-shaded arbors, the riotous old-fashioned flowers, and bushes and gnarly trees.

Out of another I get a lovely view of the bay and a little private wharf belonging to the estate. There is a beautiful shaded lane that runs down there from the house. I always fancy I see people walking in these numerous paths and arbors, but John has cautioned me not to give way to fancy in the least. He says that with my imaginative power and habit of story-making, a nervous weakness like mine is sure to lead to all manner of excited fancies, and that I ought to use my will and good sense to check the tendency. So I try.

I think sometimes that if I were only well enough to write a little it would relieve the press of ideas and rest me.

But I find I get pretty tired when I try.

It is so discouraging not to have any advice and companionship about my work. When I get really well, John says we will ask Cousin Henry and Julia down for a long visit; but he says he would as soon put fireworks in my pillowcase as to let me have those stimulating people about now.

I wish I could get well faster.

But I must not think about that. This paper looks to me as if it *knew* what a vicious influence it had!

There is a recurrent spot where the pattern lolls like a broken neck and two bulbous eyes stare at you upside down.

I get positively angry with the impertinence of it and the everlastingness. Up and down and sideways they crawl, and those absurd, unblinking eyes are everywhere. There is one place where two breadths didn't match, and the eyes go all up and down the line, one a little higher than the other.

I never saw so much expression in an inanimate thing before, and we all know how much expression they have! I used to lie awake as a child and get more entertainment and terror out of blank walls and plain furniture than most children could find in a toy-store.

I remember what a kindly wink the knobs of our big, old bureau used to have, and there was one chair that always seemed like a strong friend.

I used to feel that if any of the other things looked too fierce I could always hop into that chair and be safe.

The furniture in this room is no worse than inharmonious, however, for we had to bring it all from downstairs. I suppose when this was used as a playroom they had to take the nursery things out, and no wonder! I never saw such ravages as the children have made here.

The wall-paper, as I said before, is torn off in spots, and it sticketh closer than a brother—they must have had perseverance as well as hatred. *[margin: Bible]*

Then the floor is scratched and gouged and splintered, the plaster itself is dug out here and there, and this great heavy bed which is all we found in the room, looks as if it had been through the wars.

But I don't mind it a bit—only the paper.

There comes John's sister. Such a dear girl as she is, and so careful of me! I must not let her find me writing.

She is a perfect and enthusiastic housekeeper, and hopes for no better profession. I verily believe she thinks it is the writing which made me sick!

But I can write when she is out, and see her a long way off from these windows.

There is one that commands the road, a lovely shaded winding road, and one that just looks off over the country. A lovely country, too, full of great elms and velvet meadows.

This wall-paper has a kind of sub-pattern in a different shade, a particularly irritating one, for you can only see it in certain lights, and not clearly then. *[margin: Woman]*

But in the places where it isn't faded and where the sun is just so—I can see a strange, provoking, formless sort of figure, that seems to skulk about behind that silly and conspicuous front design. *[margin: behind the Paper.]*

There's sister on the stairs!

Well, the Fourth of July is over! The people are all gone and I am tired out. John thought it might do me good to see a little company, so we just had mother and Nellie and the children down for a week.

Of course I didn't do a thing. Jennie sees to everything now.

But it tired me all the same.

John says if I don't pick up faster he shall send me to Weir Mitchell[1] in the fall.

But I don't want to go there at all. I had a friend who was in his hands once, and she says he is just like John and my brother, only more so!

Besides, it is such an undertaking to go so far.

I don't feel as if it was worth while to turn my hand over for anything, and I'm getting dreadfully fretful and querulous.

[margin: Cries] I cry at nothing, and cry most of the time.

Of course I don't when John is here, or anybody else, but when I am alone.

[1]S. Weir Mitchell (1829–1914), a noted physician who specialized in treating neurasthenic women, attended both Charlotte Perkins Gilman and Edith Wharton when they suffered from "nerves."

And I am alone a good deal just now. John is kept in town very often by serious cases, and Jennie is good and lets me alone when I want her to.

So I walk a little in the garden or down that lovely lane, sit on the porch under the roses, and lie down up here a good deal.

I'm getting really fond of the room in spite of the wall-paper. Perhaps *because* of the wall-paper.

It dwells in my mind so!

I lie here on this great immovable bed—it is nailed down, I believe—and follow that pattern about by the hour. It is as good as gymnastics, I assure you. I start, we'll say, at the bottom, down in the corner over there where it has not been touched, and I determine for the thousandth time that I *will* follow that pointless pattern to some sort of a conclusion.

I know a little of the principle of design, and I know this thing was not arranged on any laws of radiation, or alternation, or repetition, or symmetry, or anything else that I ever heard of.

It is repeated, of course, by the breadths, but not otherwise.

Looked at in one way each breadth stands alone, the bloated curves and flourishes—a kind of "debased Romanesque" with delirium tremens—go waddling up and down in isolated columns of fatuity.

But, on the other hand, they connect diagonally, and the sprawling outlines run off in great slanting waves of optic horror, like a lot of wallowing seaweeds in full chase.

The whole thing goes horizontally, too, at least it seems so, and I exhaust myself trying to distinguish the order of its going in that direction.

They have used a horizontal breadth for a frieze, and that adds wonderfully to the confusion.

There is one end of the room where it is almost intact, and there, when the crosslights fade and the low sun shines directly upon it, I can almost fancy radiation after all,—the interminable grotesques seem to form around a common center and rush off in headlong plunges of equal distraction.

It makes me tired to follow it. I will take a nap I guess.

I don't know why I should write this.

I don't want to.

I don't feel able.

And I know John would think it absurd. But I *must* say what I feel and think in some way—it is such a relief!

But the effort is getting to be greater than the relief.

Half the time now I am awfully lazy, and lie down ever so much.

John says I mustn't lose my strength, and has me take cod liver oil and lots of tonics and things, to say nothing of ale and wine and rare meat.

Dear John! He loves me very dearly, and hates to have me sick. I tried to have a real earnest reasonable talk with him the other day, and tell him how I wish he would let me go and make a visit to Cousin Henry and Julia.

But he said I wasn't able to go, nor able to stand it after I got there; and I did not make out a very good case for myself, for I was crying before I had finished.

It is getting to be a great effort for me to think straight. Just this nervous weakness I suppose.

And dear John gathered me up in his arms, and just carried me upstairs and laid me on the bed, and sat by me and read to me till it tired my head.

He said I was his darling and his comfort and all he had, and that I must take care of myself for his sake, and keep well.

He says no one but myself can help me out of it, that I must use my will and self-control and not let any silly fancies run away with me.

There's one comfort, the baby is well and happy, and does not have to occupy this nursery with the horrid wall-paper.

If we had not used it, that blessed child would have! What a fortunate escape! Why, I wouldn't have a child of mine, an impressionable little thing, live in such a room for worlds.

I never thought of it before, but it is lucky that John kept me here after all, I can stand it so much easier than a baby, you see.

Of course I never mention it to them any more — I am too wise — but I keep watch for it all the same.

There are things in that paper that nobody knows but me, or ever will. *woman*

Behind that outside pattern the dim shapes get clearer every day. *behind*

It is always the same shape, only very numerous. *The*

And it is like a woman stooping down and creeping about behind that pattern. *paper*
I don't like it a bit. I wonder — I begin to think — I wish John would take me away from here!

It is so hard to talk with John about my case, because he is so wise, and because he loves me so.

But I tried it last night.

It was moonlight. The moon shines in all around just as the sun does.

I hate to see it sometimes, it creeps so slowly, and always comes in by one window or another.

John was asleep and I hated to waken him, so I kept still and watched the moonlight on that undulating wall-paper till I felt creepy.

The faint figure behind seemed to shake the pattern, just as if she wanted to get out.

I got up softly and went to feel and see if the paper *did* move, and when I came back John was awake.

"What is it, little girl?" he said. "Don't go walking about like that — you'll get cold."

I thought it was a good time to talk so I told him that I really was not gaining here, and that I wished he would take me away.

"Why darling!" said he, "our lease will be up in three weeks, and I can't see how to leave before.

"The repairs are not done at home, and I cannot possibly leave town just now. Of course if you were in any danger, I could and would, but you really are better, dear, whether you can see it or not. I am a doctor, dear, and I know. You are gaining flesh and color, your appetite is better. I feel really much easier about you."

"I don't weigh a bit more," said I, "nor as much; and my appetite may be better in the evening when you are here, but it is worse in the morning when you are away!"

"Bless her little heart!" said he with a big hug, "she shall be as sick as she pleases! But now let's improve the shining hours by going to sleep, and talk about it in the morning!"

"And you won't go away?" I asked gloomily.

"Why, how can I, dear? It is only three weeks more and then we will take a nice little trip of a few days while Jennie is getting the house ready. Really, dear, you are better!"

"Better in body perhaps—" I began, and stopped short, for he sat up straight and looked at me with such a stern, reproachful look that I could not say another word.

"My darling," said he, "I beg of you, for my sake and for our child's sake, as well as for your own, that you will never for one instant let that idea enter your mind! There is nothing so dangerous, so fascinating, to a temperament like yours. It is a false and foolish fancy. Can you not trust me as a physician when I tell you so?"

So of course I said no more on that score, and we went to sleep before long. He thought I was asleep first, but I wasn't, and lay there for hours trying to decide whether that front pattern and the back pattern really did move together or separately.

On a pattern like this, by daylight, there is a lack of sequence, a defiance of law, that is a constant irritant to a normal mind.

The color is hideous enough, and unreliable enough, and infuriating enough, but the pattern is torturing.

You think you have mastered it, but just as you get well underway in following, it turns a back-somersault and there you are. It slaps you in the face, knocks you down, and tramples upon you. It is like a bad dream.

The outside pattern is a florid arabesque, reminding one of a fungus. If you can imagine a toadstool in joints, an interminable string of toadstools, budding and sprouting in endless convolutions—why, that is something like it.

That is, sometimes!

There is one marked peculiarity about this paper, a thing nobody seems to notice but myself, and that is that it changes as the light changes.

When the sun shoots in through the east window—I always watch for that first, long, straight ray—it changes so quickly that I never can quite believe it. That is why I watch it always.

By moonlight—the moon shines in all night when there is a moon—I wouldn't know it was the same paper.

At night in any kind of light, in twilight, candlelight, lamplight, and worst of all by moonlight, it becomes bars! The outside pattern I mean, and the woman behind it is as plain as can be.

I didn't realize for a long time what the thing was that showed behind, that dim sub-pattern, but now I am quite sure it is a woman.

By daylight she is subdued, quiet. I fancy it is the pattern that keeps her so still. It is so puzzling. It keeps me quiet by the hour.

I lie down ever so much now. John says it is good for me, and to sleep all I can.

Indeed he started the habit by making me lie down for an hour after each meal.

It is a very bad habit I am convinced, for you see I don't sleep.

And that cultivates deceit, for I don't tell them I'm awake—O, no!

The fact is I am getting a little afraid of John.

He seems very queer sometimes, and even Jennie has an inexplicable look.

It strikes me occasionally, just as a scientific hypothesis, that perhaps it is the paper!

I have watched John when he did not know I was looking, and come into the room suddenly on the most innocent excuses, and I've caught him several times *looking at the paper!* And Jennie too. I caught Jennie with her hand on it once.

She didn't know I was in the room, and when I asked her in a quiet, a very quiet voice, with the most restrained manner possible, what she was doing with the paper — she turned around as if she had been caught stealing, and looked quite angry — asked me why I should frighten her so!

Then she said that the paper stained everything it touched, that she had found yellow smooches on all my clothes and John's, and she wished we would be more careful!

Did not that sound innocent? But I know she was studying that pattern, and I am determined that nobody shall find it out but myself!

Life is very much more exciting now than it used to be. You see I have something more to expect, to look forward to, to watch. I really do eat better, and am more quiet than I was.

John is so pleased to see me improve! He laughed a little the other day, and said I seemed to be flourishing in spite of my wall-paper.

I turned it off with a laugh. I had no intention of telling him it was *because* of the wall-paper — he would make fun of me. He might even want to take me away.

I don't want to leave now until I have found it out. There is a week more, and I think that will be enough.

I'm feeling ever so much better! I don't sleep much at night, for it is so interesting to watch developments; but I sleep a good deal in the daytime.

In the daytime it is tiresome and perplexing.

There are always new shoots on the fungus, and new shades of yellow all over it. I cannot keep count of them, though I have tried conscientiously.

It is the strangest yellow, that wall-paper! It makes me think of all the yellow things I ever saw — not beautiful ones like buttercups, but old foul, bad yellow things.

But there is something else about that paper — the smell! I noticed it the moment we came into the room, but with so much air and sun it was not bad. Now we have had a week of fog and rain, and whether the windows are open or not, the smell is here.

It creeps all over the house.

I find it hovering in the dining-room, skulking in the parlor, hiding in the hall, lying in wait for me on the stairs.

It gets into my hair.

Even when I go to ride, if I turn my head suddenly and surprise it — there is that smell!

Such a peculiar odor, too! I have spent hours in trying to analyze it, to find what it smelled like.

It is not bad — at first, and very gentle, but quite the subtlest, most enduring odor I ever met.

In this damp weather it is awful, I wake up in the night and find it hanging over me.

It used to disturb me at first. I thought seriously of burning the house — to reach the smell.

But now I am used to it. The only thing I can think of that it is like is the *color* of the paper! A yellow smell.

There is a very funny mark on this wall, low down, near the mopboard. A streak that runs round the room. It goes behind every piece of furniture, except the bed, a long, straight, even *smooch*, as if it had been rubbed over and over.

I wonder how it was done and who did it, and what they did it for. Round and round and round—round and round and round—it makes me dizzy!

I really have discovered something at last.

Through watching so much at night, when it changes so, I have finally found out.

The front pattern *does* move—and no wonder! The woman behind shakes it!

Sometimes I think there are a great many women behind, and sometimes only one, and she crawls around fast, and her crawling shakes it all over.

Then in the very bright spots she keeps still, and in the very shady spots she just takes hold of the bars and shakes them hard.

And she is all the time trying to climb through. But nobody could climb through that pattern—it strangles so; I think that is why it has so many heads.

They get through, and then the pattern strangles them off and turns them upside down, and makes their eyes white!

If those heads were covered or taken off it would not be half so bad.

I think that woman gets out in the daytime!

And I'll tell you why—privately—I've seen her!

I can see her out of every one of my windows!

It is the same woman, I know, for she is always creeping, and most women do not creep by daylight.

I see her in that long shaded lane, creeping up and down. I see her in those dark grape arbors, creeping all around the garden.

I see her on that long road under the trees, creeping along, and when a carriage comes she hides under the blackberry vines.

I don't blame her a bit. It must be very humiliating to be caught creeping by daylight!

I always lock the door when I creep by daylight. I can't do it at night, for I know John would suspect something at once.

And John is so queer now, that I don't want to irritate him. I wish he would take another room! Besides, I don't want anybody to get that woman out at night but myself.

I often wonder if I could see her out of all the windows at once.

But, turn as fast as I can, I can only see out of one at one time.

And though I always see her, she *may* be able to creep faster than I can turn!

I have watched her sometimes away off in the open country, creeping as fast as a cloud shadow in a high wind.

If only that top pattern could be gotten off from the under one! I mean to try it, little by little.

I have found out another funny thing, but I shan't tell it this time! It does not do to trust people too much.

There are only two more days to get this paper off, and I believe John is beginning to notice. I don't like the look in his eyes.

And I heard him ask Jennie a lot of professional questions about me. She had a very good report to give.

She said I slept a good deal in the daytime.

John knows I don't sleep very well at night, for all I'm so quiet!

He asked me all sorts of questions, too, and pretended to be very loving and kind.

As if I couldn't see through him!

Still, I don't wonder he acts so, sleeping under this paper for three months.

It only interests me, but I feel sure John and Jennie are secretly affected by it.

Hurrah! This is the last day, but it is enough. John to stay in town over night, and won't be out until this evening.

Jennie wanted to sleep with me — the sly thing! but I told her I should undoubtedly rest better for a night all alone.

That was clever, for really I wasn't alone a bit! As soon as it was moonlight and that poor thing began to crawl and shake the pattern, I got up and ran to help her.

I pulled and she shook, I shook and she pulled, and before morning we had peeled off yards of that paper.

A strip about as high as my head and half around the room.

And then when the sun came and that awful pattern began to laugh at me, I declared I would finish it to-day!

We go away to-morrow, and they are moving all my furniture down again to leave things as they were before.

Jennie looked at the wall in amazement, but I told her merrily that I did it out of pure spite at the vicious thing.

She laughed and said she wouldn't mind doing it herself, but I must not get tired.

How she betrayed herself that time!

But I am here, and no person touches this paper but Me — not *alive!*

She tried to get me out of the room — it was too patent! But I said it was so quiet and empty and clean now that I believed I would lie down again and sleep all I could; and not to wake me even for dinner — I would call when I woke.

So now she is gone, and the servants are gone, and the things are gone, and there is nothing left but the great bedstead nailed down, with the canvas mattress we found on it.

We shall sleep downstairs to-night, and take the boat home to-morrow.

I quite enjoy the room, now it is bare again.

How those children did tear about here!

This bedstead is fairly gnawed!

But I must get to work.

I have locked the door and thrown the key down into the front path.

I don't want to go out, and I don't want to have anybody come in, till John comes.

I want to astonish him.

I've got a rope up here that even Jennie did not find. If that woman does get out, and tries to get away, I can tie her!

But I forgot I could not reach far without anything to stand on!

This bed will *not* move!

I tried to lift and push it until I was lame, and then I got so angry I bit off a little piece at one corner — but it hurt my teeth.

Then I peeled off all the paper I could reach standing on the floor. It sticks

horribly and the pattern just enjoys it! All those strangled heads and bulbous eyes
and waddling fungus growths just shriek with derision!

I am getting angry enough to do something desperate. To jump out of the
window would be admirable exercise, but the bars are too strong even to try.

Besides I wouldn't do it. Of course not. I know well enough that a step like
that is improper and might be misconstrued.

I don't like to *look* out the windows even—there are so many of those
creeping women, and they creep so fast.

I wonder if they all come out of that wall-paper as I did?

But I am securely fastened now by my well-hidden rope—you don't get *me*
out in the road there!

I suppose I shall have to get back behind the pattern when it comes night, and
that is hard!

It is so pleasant to be out in this great room and creep around as I please!

I don't want to go outside. I won't, even if Jennie asks me to.

For outside you have to creep on the ground, and everything is green instead
of yellow.

But here I can creep smoothly on the floor, and my shoulder just fits in that
long smooch around the wall, so I cannot lose my way.

Why there's John at the door!

It is no use, young man, you can't open it!

How he does call and pound!

Now he's crying for an axe.

It would be a shame to break down that beautiful door!

"John dear!" said I in the gentlest voice, "the key is down by the front steps,
under a plantain leaf!"

That silenced him for a few moments.

Then he said, very quietly indeed, "Open the door, my darling!"

"I can't," said I. "The key is down by the front door under a plantain leaf!"

And then I said it again, several times, very gently and slowly, and said it so
often that he had to go and see, and he got it of course, and came in. He stopped
short by the door.

"What is the matter?" he cried. "For God's sake, what are you doing!"

I kept on creeping just the same, but I looked at him over my shoulder.

"I've got out at last," said I, "in spite of you and Jane. And I've pulled off most
of the paper, so you can't put me back!"

Now why should that man have fainted? But he did, and right across my path
by the wall, so that I had to creep over him every time!

(1892)

Prewriting

As you read the story carefully a second time, pay particular attention to
the descriptive passages that appeal to the senses—especially, in this
story, to sight and smell. Underline any specific words or phrases that
you think contribute to the atmosphere. List, as you go along, the unusual
words that Gilman uses in her descriptions, like *skulk, waddling, smooches.*

Prewriting Exercise

1. List at least five words that describe the atmosphere created in this story. Use your thesaurus if you get stuck. Your instructor might want to have you discuss these word choices with the class. Try to decide which are the most appropriate — and why.

2. In a paragraph of about one hundred words, describe the house — and especially the room — in which the narrator is confined. Decide which details are crucial to the story. As you read the story again, be sure you have not overlooked any significant descriptive details.

3. Before planning your paper, write your responses to the following questions.
   a. Why is it fitting that the narrator's husband chooses the nursery as her room? (Is it indeed a nursery?)
   b. What would the narrator *like* to be doing? Why can't she? Does her illness alone prevent her from doing as she wishes?
   c. What do the sunshine and the moonlight contribute to the story?
   d. What would be gained or lost if the wallpaper were the kind found in a typical bathroom or kitchen or child's room today (e.g., with little animals)?
   e. What are the similarities between the narrator and the woman she sees behind the wallpaper?
   f. What significance can you attach to the narrator's discovery that the woman escapes and creeps around outside? Why do you think the narrator asserts that "most women do not creep by daylight"? Is it significant that by the end of the story the narrator sees *many* women creeping about the countryside?
   g. Who does the narrator think she is at the end of the story?

Writing

Now that you have become familiar with the story, you need to ask yourself still more questions: How can I make a statement about the function of setting in relation to theme? What, indeed, does the setting contribute to the overall effectiveness of the story? What does the atmosphere contribute? How do both relate to the meaning of the story? Do they simply *heighten* the theme, or do they actually help the reader to understand what the story is about? As you think about answers to these questions, review your prewriting material and continue consulting the story for clues.

Discovering an Organization

As you are trying to solve the problems posed by the questions in the preceding paragraph, write down all the likely ideas that strike you. Do not trust your memory, or some of your best inspirations may slip away.

Then try to think of some point you can make about the story that will allow you to use this information. Once you have discovered an interesting point to pursue, write out this idea in a single, clear sentence. This idea will be your thesis. Then sort through the details related to setting in the story and ask yourself: What generalizations can I make about these details in support of my thesis? You might, for instance, group your material spatially — arranging details describing the landscape outside the house, details of the inside, details within the narrator's room, and finally details of the yellow wallpaper itself. Conclude with a statement summarizing the effectiveness of these details in documenting the narrator's descent into madness.

Ideas for Writing
Ideas for Responsive Writing

1. "The Yellow Wall-Paper" reflects accurately the standard treatment of well-to-do women with nervous disorders in the nineteenth century. What do you think of it? Why might the authorities of the time consider this treatment effective? What would really be the best treatment, in your opinion?

2. We all have limitations on our freedom; the narrator of "The Yellow Wall-Paper" has more than most of us. Write about the limitations on your freedom and how they affect you. You might organize your writing by dividing the limitations into those that are voluntary and those that are involuntary.

Ideas for Critical Writing

1. Discuss the importance of the setting in understanding the relationship between the dominant husband and submissive wife — a relationship that ultimately drives the narrator insane.

2. Show how the atmosphere of strangeness that Gilman creates throughout the story intensifies her portrayal of the narrator's growing mental imbalance.

Rewriting: Organization and Style

Once you have written out your ideas, you will try to improve every element of that draft — from the overall organization to the individual sentences.

Checking Your Organization

Each paragraph should have a topic, a main point that you can summarize in a sentence. On a separate sheet of paper, list the topics of your paragraphs. When you see the bare bones of your essay this way, you can ask yourself questions about your organization:

1. Do any of the topics repeat each other? If so, think about combining them or placing them close together. If there is a fine distinction between them, go back to the essay and express the distinction clearly.

2. Is each topic fully supported? Compare the topic as stated on your outline with the paragraph in your essay. Make sure that you can see how each sentence in the paragraph relates to the topic. Weed out sentences that only repeat the topic. Add specific details from the literary work instead.

3. Does the order of topics make sense? You might have originally written your paragraphs in the order the topics occurred to you, but that may not be the most reasonable organization for the final essay. Group similar topics together — for example, all the topics that relate setting to character should be close to each other, and so should all the topics that relate setting to theme. At the beginning of each paragraph, write a word, phrase, clause, or sentence that shows that paragraph's relationship to the paragraph before it. These transitions will help your readers know what to expect and prepare them for what comes next.

Improving the Style: Balanced Sentences

Sound organization is vital to the success of your essay; graceful style is an added gift to your reader. One stylistic plus is the balanced or parallel sentence, which puts similar ideas into similar grammatical structures, like this:

> Chopin is admired for the *grace, precision,* and *economy* of her style.
>
> Good writers acknowledge the necessity of *thinking, planning, writing, revising, resting,* and then *thinking* and *revising* still further.

In the following sentence, though, the third item in the italicized series does not match. Compare it to the corrected version:

> *Unbalanced:* The main character would not willingly give up the *carefree, extravagant,* and *drinking and staying out late* as he did when a bachelor.
>
> *Balanced:* The main character would not willingly give up the *carefree, extravagant, carousing* ways of his bachelorhood.

Probably you can already handle such balancing in ordinary sentences. But pay attention during revising to make sure that all items in series are indeed balanced.

If you need an emphatic sentence for your introduction or conclusion, a good way to learn to write impressive balanced sentences is through *sentence modeling*. Many expert writers — Robert Louis Stevenson, Abraham Lincoln, Winston Churchill, Somerset Maugham — attest that they perfected their writing by studiously copying and imitating the sentences of stylists whom they admired.

Sentence Modeling Exercise

Examine the model sentence below to discover its structure. How is it formed? Does it use balanced phrases, clauses, or single words? Does it include any deliberate repetition of words as well as structures? Does it build to a climax at the end? If so, how? By adding ideas of increasing importance? By establishing a pattern that gathers momentum?

Once you have discovered the structure of the model sentence, write one as nearly like it as possible *using your own words and subject matter*. Then, repeat this process of imitation four more times, changing your ideas with each new sentence, like this:

> *Model:*   "Until the young are informed as much about the courage of pacifists as about the obedience of soldiers, they aren't educated."
>
> *—Coleman McCarthy*
>
> *Imitation:* Until Americans become as interested in the speeches of candidates as about the performance of athletes, they aren't ideal citizens.
>
> *Imitation:* Until men are interested as much by the minds of women as by the bodies of women, they will be seen as sexist.

First, copy each of the numbered sentences carefully — including the exact punctuation. Then imitate each one at least five times.

1. "He sees no seams or joints or points of intersection — only irrevocable wholes."

   —Mina Shaughnessy

2. "We made meals and changed diapers and took out the garbage and paid bills — while other people died."

   —Ellen Goodman

3. "The refrigerator was full of sulfurous scraps, dark crusts, furry oddments."

   —Alice Munro

4. "It is sober without being dull; massive without being oppressive."
   —*Sir Kenneth Clark*

5. "Joint by joint, line by line, pill by pill, the use of illegal drugs has become a crisis for American business."
   —*Newsweek* (1983)

CHAPTER

9

Writing About Theme

A story's theme or meaning grows out of all the elements of imaginative fiction — character, structure, symbolism, point of view, and setting. The theme is usually not an obvious moral or message, and it may be difficult to sum up succinctly. But thinking about the theme of a story and trying to state it in your own words will help to focus your scattered reactions and to make your understanding of the author's purpose more certain.

What Is Theme?

Theme has been defined in many ways: the central idea or thesis; the central thought; the underlying meaning, either implied or directly stated; the general idea or insight revealed by the entire story; the central truth; the dominating idea; the abstract concept that is made concrete through representation in person, action, and image.

Because the theme involves ideas and insights, we usually state it in general terms. "Eveline," for instance, concerns the conflicts of a specific character, but the story's central truth — its theme — relates to abstract qualities like *duty* and *fear*. If someone asks what "Eveline" is *about*, we might respond with details about the title character's encounter with Frank and her failure to go away with him. But if someone asks for the story's *theme*, we would answer with a general statement of ideas or values: "Eveline" shows how people can be trapped by fear and obligation.

It is easy to confuse *subject* with *theme*. The subject is the topic or material the story examines — love, death, war, human relations, growing up, and so forth. But the theme is the direct or implied statement that the story makes *about* the subject. For example, the *subject* of "Everyday Use" is mother-daughter relationships, but the *theme* emerges from what the story says about Mama, Maggie, and Dee and why these characters interact as they do. The theme, then, is the insight that we gain from thinking about what we have read.

Looking at Theme

As you read "The Open Boat" by Stephen Crane, think about how this tale of shipwreck and survival relates to other areas of human experience.

Stephen Crane *1871–1900*

THE OPEN BOAT

A TALE INTENDED TO BE AFTER THE FACT:
BEING THE EXPERIENCE OF FOUR MEN
FROM THE SUNK STEAMER *COMMODORE*

I

None of them knew the color of the sky. Their eyes glanced level, and were fastened upon the waves that swept toward them. These waves were of the hue of slate, save for the tops, which were of foaming white, and all of the men knew the colors of the sea. The horizon narrowed and widened, and dipped and rose, and at all times its edge was jagged with waves that seemed thrust up in points like rocks.

Many a man ought to have a bathtub larger than the boat which here rode upon the sea. These waves were most wrongfully and barbarously abrupt and tall, and each froth-top was a problem in small-boat navigation.

The cook squatted in the bottom, and looked with both eyes at the six inches of gunwale which separated him from the ocean. His sleeves were rolled over his fat forearms, and the two flaps of his unbuttoned vest dangled as he bent to bail out the boat. Often he said, "Gawd! that was a narrow clip." As he remarked it he invariably gazed eastward over the broken sea.

The oiler, steering with one of the two oars in the boat, sometimes raised himself suddenly to keep clear of water that swirled in over the stern. It was a thin little oar, and it seemed often ready to snap.

The correspondent,[1] pulling at the other oar, watched the waves and wondered why he was there.

The injured captain, lying in the bow, was at this time buried in that profound dejection and indifference which comes, temporarily at least, to even the bravest and most enduring when, willy-nilly, the firm fails, the army loses, the ship goes down. The mind of the master of a vessel is rooted deep in the timbers of her, though he command for a day or a decade; and this captain had on him the stern impression of a scene in the grays of dawn of seven turned faces, and later a stump of a topmast with a white ball on it, that slashed to and fro at the waves, went low and lower, and down. Thereafter there was something strange in his voice. Although steady, it was deep with mourning, and of a quality beyond oration or tears.

"Keep'er a little more south, Billie," said he.

"A little more south, sir," said the oiler at the stern.

A seat in this boat was not unlike a seat upon a bucking broncho, and by the same token a broncho is not much smaller. The craft pranced and reared and plunged like an animal. As each wave came, and she rose for it, she seemed like a horse making at a fence outrageously high. The manner of her scramble over these walls of water is a mystic thing, and, moreover, at the top of them were

---

[1] A foreign correspondent, newspaper reporter.

ordinarily these problems in white water, the foam racing down from the summit of each wave requiring a new leap, and a leap from the air. Then, after scornfully bumping a crest, she would slide and race and splash down a long incline, and arrive bobbing and nodding in front of the next menace.

A singular disadvantage of the sea lies in the fact that after successfully surmounting one wave you discover that there is another behind it just as important and just as nervously anxious to do something effective in the way of swamping boats. In a ten-foot dinghy one can get an idea of the resources of the sea in the line of waves that is not probable to the average experience, which is never at sea in a dinghy. As each slaty wall of water approached, it shut all else from the view of the men in the boat, and it was not difficult to imagine that this particular wave was the final outburst of the ocean, the last effort of the grim water. There was a terrible grace in the move of the waves, and they came in silence, save for the snarling of the crests.

In the wan light the faces of the men must have been gray. Their eyes must have glinted in strange ways as they gazed steadily astern. Viewed from a balcony, the whole thing would doubtless have been weirdly picturesque. But the men in the boat had no time to see it, and if they had had leisure, there were other things to occupy their minds. The sun swung steadily up the sky, and they knew it was broad day because the color of the sea changed from slate to emerald-green streaked with amber lights, and the foam was like tumbling snow. The process of the breaking day was unknown to them. They were aware only of this effect upon the color of the waves that rolled toward them.

In disjointed sentences the cook and the correspondent argued as to the difference between a life-saving station and a house of refuge. The cook had said: "There's a house of refuge just north of the Mosquito Inlet Light, and as soon as they see us they'll come off in their boat and pick us up."

"As soon as who sees us?" said the correspondent.

"The crew," said the cook.

"Houses of refuge don't have crews," said the correspondent. "As I understand them, they are only places where clothes and grub are stored for the benefit of shipwrecked people. They don't carry crews."

"Oh, yes, they do," said the cook.

"No, they don't," said the correspondent.

"Well, we're not there yet, anyhow," said the oiler, in the stern.

"Well," said the cook, "perhaps it's not a house of refuge that I'm thinking of as being near Mosquito Inlet Light; perhaps it's a life-saving station."

"We're not there yet," said the oiler in the stern.

II

As the boat bounced from the top of each wave the wind tore through the hair of the hatless men, and as the craft plopped her stern down again the spray splashed past them. The crest of each of these waves was a hill, from the top of which the men surveyed for a moment a broad tumultuous expanse, shining and wind-riven. It was probably splendid, it was probably glorious, this play of the free sea, wild with lights of emerald and white and amber.

"Bully good thing it's an onshore wind," said the cook. "If not, where would we be? Wouldn't have a show."

"That's right," said the correspondent.

The busy oiler nodded his assent.

Then the captain, in the bow, chuckled in a way that expressed humor, contempt, tragedy, all in one. "Do you think we've got much of a show now, boys?" said he.

Whereupon the three were silent, save for a trifle of hemming and hawing. To express any particular optimism at this time they felt to be childish and stupid, but they all doubtless possessed this sense of the situation in their minds. A young man thinks doggedly at such times. On the other hand, the ethics of their condition was decidedly against any open suggestion of hopelessness. So they were silent.

"Oh, well," said the captain, soothing his children, "we'll get ashore all right."

But there was that in his tone which made them think; so the oiler quoth, "Yes! if this wind holds."

The cook was bailing. "Yes! if we don't catch hell in the surf."

Canton-flannel[2] gulls flew near and far. Sometimes they sat down on the sea, near patches of brown seaweed that rolled over the waves with a movement like carpets on a line in a gale. The birds sat comfortably in groups, and they were envied by some in the dinghy, for the wrath of the sea was no more to them than it was to a covey of prairie chickens a thousand miles inland. Often they came very close and stared at the men with black bead-like eyes. At these times they were uncanny and sinister in their unblinking scrutiny, and the men hooted angrily at them, telling them to be gone. One came, and evidently decided to alight on the top of the captain's head. The bird flew parallel to the boat and did not circle, but made short sidelong jumps in the air in chicken fashion. His black eyes were wistfully fixed upon the captain's head. "Ugly brute," said the oiler to the bird. "You look as if you were made with a jackknife." The cook and the correspondent swore darkly at the creature. The captain naturally wished to knock it away with the end of the heavy painter, but he did not dare do it, because anything resembling an emphatic gesture would have capsized this freighted boat; and so, with his open hand, the captain gently and carefully waved the gull away. After it had been discouraged from the pursuit the captain breathed easier on account of his hair, and others breathed easier because the bird struck their minds at this time as being somehow gruesome and ominous.

In the meantime the oiler and the correspondent rowed. And also they rowed. They sat together in the same seat, and each rowed an oar. Then the oiler took both oars; then the correspondent took both oars; then the oiler; then the correspondent. They rowed and they rowed. The very ticklish part of the business was when the time came for the reclining one in the stern to take his turn at the oars. By the very last star of truth, it is easier to steal eggs from under a hen than it was to change seats in the dinghy. First the man in the stern slid his hand along the thwart and moved with care, as if he were of Sèvres.[3] Then the man in the rowing-seat slid his hand along the other thwart. It was all done with the most extraordinary care. As the two sidled past each other, the whole party kept watchful eyes on the coming wave, and the captain cried: "Look out, now! Steady, there!"

---

[2]A comparison to sturdy cotton flannel.

[3]Delicate, expensive chinaware made in this French town.

The brown mats of seaweed that appeared from time to time were like islands, bits of earth. They were traveling, apparently, neither one way nor the other. They were, to all intents, stationary. They informed the men in the boat that it was making progress slowly toward the land.

The captain, rearing cautiously in the bow after the dinghy soared on a great swell, said that he had seen the lighthouse at Mosquito Inlet. Presently the cook remarked that he had seen it. The correspondent was at the oars then, and for some reason he too wished to look at the lighthouse; but his back was toward the far shore, and the waves were important, and for some time he could not seize an opportunity to turn his head. But at last there came a wave more gentle than the others, and when at the crest of it he swiftly scoured the western horizon.

"See it?" said the captain.

"No," said the correspondent, slowly; "I didn't see anything."

"Look again," said the captain. He pointed. "It's exactly in that direction."

At the top of another wave the correspondent did as he was bid, and this time his eyes chanced on a small, still thing on the edge of the swaying horizon. It was precisely like the point of a pin. It took an anxious eye to find a lighthouse so tiny.

"Think we'll make it, Captain?"

"If this wind holds and the boat don't swamp, we can't do much else," said the captain.

The little boat, lifted by each towering sea and splashed viciously by the crests, made progress that in the absence of seaweed was not apparent to those in her. She seemed just a wee thing wallowing, miraculously top up, at the mercy of five oceans. Occasionally a great spread of water, like white flames, swarmed into her.

"Bail her, cook," said the captain, serenely.

"All right, Captain," said the cheerful cook.

III

It would be difficult to describe the subtle brotherhood of men that was here established on the seas. No one said that it was so. No one mentioned it. But it dwelt in the boat, and each man felt it warm him. They were a captain, an oiler, a cook, and a correspondent, and they were friends — friends in a more curiously ironbound degree than may be common. The hurt captain, lying against the water jar in the bow, spoke always in a low voice and calmly; but he could never command a more ready and swiftly obedient crew than the motley three of the dinghy. It was more than a mere recognition of what was best for the common safety. There was surely in it a quality that was personal and heartfelt. And after this devotion to the commander of the boat, there was this comradeship, that the correspondent, for instance, who had been taught to be cynical of men, knew even at the time was the best experience of his life. But no one said that it was so. No one mentioned it.

"I wish we had a sail," remarked the captain. "We might try my overcoat on the end of an oar, and give you two boys a chance to rest." So the cook and the correspondent held the mast and spread wide the overcoat; the oiler steered; and the little boat made good way with her new rig. Sometimes the oiler had to scull sharply to keep a sea from breaking into the boat, but otherwise sailing was a success.

Meanwhile the lighthouse had been growing slowly larger. It had now almost assumed color, and appeared like a little gray shadow on the sky. The man at the oars could not be prevented from turning his head rather often to try for a glimpse of this little gray shadow.

At last, from the top of each wave, the men in the tossing boat could see land. Even as the lighthouse was an upright shadow on the sky, this land seemed but a long black shadow on the sea. It certainly was thinner than paper. "We must be about opposite New Smyrna,"[4] said the cook, who had coasted this shore often in schooners. "Captain, by the way, I believe they abandoned that life-saving station there about a year ago."

"Did they?" said the captain.

The wind slowly died away. The cook and the correspondent were not now obliged to slave in order to hold high the oar. But the waves continued their old impetuous swooping at the dinghy, and the little craft, no longer under way, struggled woundily over them. The oiler or the correspondent took the oars again.

Shipwrecks are *apropos* of nothing. If men could only train for them and have them occur when the men had reached pink condition, there would be less drowning at sea. Of the four in the dinghy none had slept any time worth mentioning for two days and two nights previous to embarking in the dinghy, and in the excitement of clambering about the deck of a foundering ship they had also forgotten to eat heartily.

For these reasons, and for others, neither the oiler nor the correspondent was fond of rowing at this time. The correspondent wondered ingenuously how in the name of all that was sane could there be people who thought it amusing to row a boat. It was not an amusement; it was a diabolical punishment, and even a genius of mental aberrations could never conclude that it was anything but a horror to the muscles and a crime against the back. He mentioned to the boat in general how the amusement of rowing struck him, and the weary-faced oiler smiled in full sympathy. Previously to the foundering, by the way, the oiler had worked a double watch in the engine room of the ship.

"Take her easy now, boys," said the captain. "Don't spend yourselves. If we have to run a surf you'll need all your strength, because we'll sure have to swim for it. Take your time."

Slowly the land arose from the sea. From a black line it became a line of black and a line of white — trees and sand. Finally the captain said that he could make out a house on the shore. "That's the house of refuge, sure," said the cook. "They'll see us before long, and come out after us."

The distant lighthouse reared high. "The keeper ought to be able to make us out now, if he's looking through a glass," said the captain. "He'll notify the life-saving people."

"None of those other boats could have got ashore to give word of this wreck," said the oiler, in a low voice, "else the lifeboat would be out hunting us."

Slowly and beautifully the land loomed out of the sea. The wind came again. It had veered from the northeast to the southeast. Finally a new sound struck the ears of the men in the boat. It was the low thunder of the surf on the shore. "We'll never be able to make the lighthouse now," said the captain. "Swing her head a little more north, Billie."

---

[4]Coastal town just south of Daytona Beach, Florida.

"A little more north, sir," said the oiler.

Whereupon the little boat turned her nose once more down the wind, and all but the oarsman watched the shore grow. Under the influence of this expansion doubt and direful apprehension were leaving the minds of the men. The management of the boat was still most absorbing, but it could not prevent a quiet cheerfulness. In an hour, perhaps, they would be ashore.

Their backbones had become thoroughly used to balancing in the boat, and they now rode this wild colt of a dinghy like circus men. The correspondent thought that he had been drenched to the skin, but happening to feel in the top pocket of his coat, he found therein eight cigars. Four of them were soaked with seawater; four were perfectly scatheless. After a search, somebody produced three dry matches; and thereupon the four waifs rode impudently in their little boat and, with an assurance of an impending rescue shining in their eyes, puffed at the big cigars, and judged well and ill of all men. Everybody took a drink of water.

IV

"Cook," remarked the captain, "there don't seem to be any signs of life about your house of refuge."

"No," replied the cook. "Funny they don't see us!"

A broad stretch of lowly coast lay before the eyes of the men. It was of low dunes topped with dark vegetation. The roar of the surf was plain, and sometimes they could see the white lip of a wave as it spun up the beach. A tiny house was blocked out black upon the sky. Southward, the slim lighthouse lifted its little gray length.

Tide, wind, and waves were swinging the dinghy northward. "Funny they don't see us," said the men.

The surf's roar was here dulled, but its tone was nevertheless thunderous and mighty. As the boat swam over the great rollers the men sat listening to this roar. "We'll swamp sure," said everybody.

It is fair to say here that there was not a life-saving station within twenty miles in either direction; but the men did not know this fact, and in consequence they made dark and opprobrious remarks concerning the eyesight of the nation's lifesavers. Four scowling men sat in the dinghy and surpassed records in the invention of epithets.

"Funny they don't see us."

The light-heartedness of a former time had completely faded. To their sharpened minds it was easy to conjure pictures of all kinds of incompetency and blindness and, indeed, cowardice. There was the shore of the populous land, and it was bitter and bitter to them that from it came no sign.

"Well," said the captain, ultimately, "I suppose we'll have to make a try for ourselves. If we stay out here too long, we'll none of us have strength left to swim after the boat swamps."

And so the oiler, who was at the oars, turned the boat straight for the shore. There was a sudden tightening of muscles. There was some thinking.

"If we don't all get ashore," said the captain—"if we don't all get ashore, I suppose you fellows know where to send news of my finish?"

They then briefly exchanged some addresses and admonitions. As for the reflections of the men, there was a great deal of rage in them. Perchance they might be formulated thus: "If I am going to be drowned—if I am going to be drowned—if I am going to be drowned, why, in the name of the seven mad gods who rule the sea, was I allowed to come thus far and contemplate sand and trees? Was I brought here merely to have my nose dragged away as I was about to nibble the sacred cheese of life? It is preposterous. If this old ninny-woman, Fate, cannot do better than this, she should be deprived of the management of men's fortunes. She is an old hen who knows not her intention. If she has decided to drown me, why did she not do it in the beginning and save me all this trouble? The whole affair is absurd. . . . But no; she cannot mean to drown me. She dare not drown me. She cannot drown me. Not after all this work." Afterward the man might have had an impulse to shake his fist at the clouds. "Just you drown me, now, and then hear what I call you!"

The billows that came at this time were formidable. They seemed always just about to break and roll over the little boat in a turmoil of foam. There was a preparatory and long growl in the speech of them. No mind unused to the sea would have concluded that the dinghy could ascend these sheer heights in time. The shore was still afar. The oiler was a wily surfman. "Boys," he said swiftly, "she won't live three minutes more, and we're too far out to swim. Shall I take her to sea again, Captain?"

"Yes; go ahead!" said the captain.

This oiler, by a series of quick miracles and fast and steady oarsmanship, turned the boat in the middle of the surf and took her safely to sea again.

There was a considerable silence as the boat bumped over the furrowed sea to deeper water. Then somebody in gloom spoke: "Well, anyhow, they must have seen us from the shore by now."

The gulls went in slanting flight up the wind toward the gray, desolate east. A squall, marked by dingy clouds and clouds brick-red, like smoke from a burning building, appeared from the southeast.

"What do you think of those life-saving people? Ain't they peaches?"

"Funny they haven't seen us."

"Maybe they think we're out here for sport! Maybe they think we're fishin'. Maybe they think we're damned fools."

It was a long afternoon. A changed tide tried to force them southward, but wind and wave said northward. Far ahead, where coastline, sea, and sky formed their mighty angle, there were little dots which seemed to indicate a city on the shore.

"St. Augustine?"

The captain shook his head. "Too near Mosquito Inlet."

And the oiler rowed, and then the correspondent rowed; then the oiler rowed. It was a weary business. The human back can become the seat of more aches and pains than are registered in books for the composite anatomy of a regiment. It is a limited area, but it can become the theater of innumerable muscular conflicts, tangles, wrenches, knots, and other comforts.

"Did you ever like to row, Billie?" asked the correspondent.

"No," said the oiler; "hang it!"

When one exchanged the rowing-seat for a place in the bottom of the boat, he suffered a bodily depression that caused him to be careless of everything save an obligation to wiggle one finger. There was cold seawater swashing to and fro in the boat, and he lay in it. His head, pillowed on a thwart, was within an inch of the swirl of a wave-crest, and sometimes a particularly obstreperous sea came inboard and drenched him once more. But these matters did not annoy him. It is almost certain that if the boat had capsized he would have tumbled comfortably out upon the ocean as if he felt sure that it was a great soft mattress.

"Look! There's a man on the shore!"

"Where?"

"There! See 'im? See 'im?"

"Yes, sure! He's walking along."

"Now he's stopped. Look! He's facing us!"

"He's waving at us!"

"So he is! By thunder!"

"Ah, now we're all right! Now we're all right! There'll be a boat out here for us in half an hour."

"He's going on. He's running. He's going up to that house there."

The remote beach seemed lower than the sea, and it required a searching glance to discern the little black figure. The captain saw a floating stick, and they rowed to it. A bath towel was by some weird chance in the boat, and, tying this on the stick, the captain waved it. The oarsman did not dare turn his head, so he was obliged to ask questions.

"What's he doing now?"

"He's standing still again. He's looking, I think. . . . There he goes again — toward the house. . . . Now he's stopped again."

"Is he waving at us?"

"No, not now; he was, though."

"Look! There comes another man!"

"He's running."

"Look at him go, would you!"

"Why, he's on a bicycle. Now he's met the other man. They're both waving at us. Look!"

"There comes something up the beach."

"What the devil is that thing?"

"Why, it looks like a boat."

"Why, certainly, it's a boat."

"No; it's on wheels."

"Yes, so it is. Well, that must be the lifeboat. They drag them along shore on a wagon."

"That's the lifeboat, sure."

"No, by God, it's — it's an omnibus."

"I tell you it's a lifeboat."

"It is not! It's an omnibus. I can see it plain. See? One of these big hotel omnibuses."

"By thunder, you're right. It's an omnibus, sure as fate. What do you suppose they are doing with an omnibus? Maybe they are going around collecting the life-crew, hey?"

"That's it, likely. Look! There's a fellow waving a little black flag. He's standing on the steps of the omnibus. There come those other two fellows. Now they're all talking together. Look at the fellow with the flag. Maybe he ain't waving it!"

"That ain't a flag, is it? That's his coat. Why, certainly, that's his coat."

"So it is; it's his coat. He's taken it off and is waving it around his head. But would you look at him swing it!"

"Oh, say, there isn't any life-saving station there. That's just a winter-resort hotel omnibus that has brought over some of the boarders to see us drown."

"What's that idiot with the coat mean? What's he signaling, anyhow?"

"It looks as if he were trying to tell us to go north. There must be a life-saving station up there."

"No; he thinks we're fishing. Just giving us a merry hand. See? Ah, there, Willie!"

"Well, I wish I could make something out of those signals. What do you suppose he means?"

"He don't mean anything; he's just playing."

"Well, if he'd just signal us to try the surf again, or to go to sea and wait, or go north, or go south, or go to hell, there would be some reason in it. But look at him! He just stands there and keeps his coat revolving like a wheel. The ass!"

"There come more people."

"Now there's quite a mob. Look! Isn't that a boat?"

"Where? Oh, I see where you mean. No, that's no boat."

"That fellow is still waving his coat."

"He must think we like to see him do that. Why don't he quit it? It don't mean anything."

"I don't know. I think he is trying to make us go north. It must be that there's a life-saving station there somewhere."

"Say, he ain't tired yet. Look at 'im wave!"

"Wonder how long he can keep that up. He's been revolving his coat ever since he caught sight of us. He's an idiot. Why aren't they getting men to bring a boat out? A fishing boat — one of those big yawls — could come out here all right. Why don't he do something?"

"Oh, it's all right now."

"They'll have a boat out here for us in less than no time, now that they've seen us."

A faint yellow tone came into the sky over the low land. The shadows on the sea slowly deepened. The wind bore coldness with it, and the men began to shiver.

"Holy smoke!" said one, allowing his voice to express his impious mood, "if we keep on monkeying out here! If we've got to flounder out here all night!"

"Oh, we'll never have to stay here all night! Don't you worry. They've seen us now, and it won't be long before they'll come chasing out after us."

The shore grew dusky. The man waving a coat blended gradually into this gloom, and it swallowed in the same manner the omnibus and the group of people. The spray, when it dashed uproariously over the side, made the voyagers shrink and swear like men who were being branded.

"I'd like to catch the chump who waved the coat. I feel like socking him one, just for luck."

"Why? What did he do?"

"Oh, nothing, but then he seemed so damned cheerful."

In the meantime the oiler rowed, and then the correspondent rowed, and then the oiler rowed. Gray-faced and bowed forward, they mechanically, turn by turn, plied the leaden oars. The form of the lighthouse had vanished from the southern horizon, but finally a pale star appeared, just lifting from the sea. The streaked saffron in the west passed before the all-merging darkness, and the sea to the east was black. The land had vanished, and was expressed only by the low and drear thunder of the surf.

"If I am going to be drowned — if I am going to be drowned — if I am going to be drowned, why, in the name of the seven mad gods who rule the sea, was I allowed to come thus far and contemplate sand and trees? Was I brought here merely to have my nose dragged away as I was about to nibble the sacred cheese of life?"

The patient captain, drooped over the water jar, was sometimes obliged to speak to the oarsman.

"Keep her head up! Keep her head up!"

"Keep her head up, sir." The voices were weary and low.

This was surely a quiet evening. All save the oarsman lay heavily and listlessly in the boat's bottom. As for him, his eyes were just capable of noting the tall black waves that swept forward in a most sinister silence, save for an occasional subdued growl of a crest.

The cook's head was on a thwart, and he looked without interest at the water under his nose. He was deep in other scenes. Finally he spoke. "Billie," he murmured, dreamfully, "what kind of pie do you like best?"

V

"Pie!" said the oiler and the correspondent, agitatedly. "Don't talk about those things, blast you!"

"Well," said the cook, "I was just thinking about ham sandwiches, and—"

A night on the sea in an open boat is a long night. As darkness settled finally, the shine of the light, lifting from the sea in the south, changed to full gold. On the northern horizon a new light appeared, a small bluish gleam on the edge of the waters. These two lights were the furniture of the world. Otherwise there was nothing but waves.

Two men huddled in the stern, and distances were so magnificent in the dinghy that the rower was enabled to keep his feet partly warm by thrusting them under his companions. Their legs indeed extended far under the rowing-seat until they touched the feet of the captain forward. Sometimes, despite the efforts of the tired oarsman, a wave came piling into the boat, an icy wave of the night, and the chilling water soaked them anew. They would twist their bodies for a moment and groan, and sleep the dead sleep once more, while the water in the boat gurgled about them as the craft rocked.

The plan of the oiler and the correspondent was for one to row until he lost the ability, and then arouse the other from his seawater couch in the bottom of the boat.

The oiler plied the oars until his head drooped forward and the overpowering sleep blinded him; and he rowed yet afterward. Then he touched a man in the bottom of the boat, and called his name. "Will you spell me for a little while?" he said meekly.

"Sure, Billie," said the correspondent, awaking and dragging himself to a sitting position. They exchanged places carefully, and the oiler, cuddling down in the seawater at the cook's side, seemed to go to sleep instantly.

The particular violence of the sea had ceased. The waves came without snarling. The obligation of the man at the oars was to keep the boat headed so that the tilt of the rollers would not capsize her, and to preserve her from filling when the crests rushed past. The black waves were silent and hard to be seen in the darkness. Often one was almost upon the boat before the oarsman was aware.

In a low voice the correspondent addressed the captain. He was not sure that the captain was awake, although this iron man seemed to be always awake. "Captain, shall I keep her making for that light north, sir?"

The same steady voice answered him. "Yes. Keep it about two points off the port bow."

The cook had tied a lifebelt around himself in order to get even the warmth which this clumsy cork contrivance could donate, and he seemed almost stove-like when a rower, whose teeth invariably chattered wildly as soon as he ceased his labor, dropped down to sleep.

The correspondent, as he rowed, looked down at the two men sleeping underfoot. The cook's arm was around the oiler's shoulders, and, with their fragmentary clothing and haggard faces, they were the babes of the sea — a grotesque rendering of the old babes in the wood.

Later he must have grown stupid at his work, for suddenly there was a growling of water, and a crest came with a roar and a swash into the boat, and it was a wonder that it did not set the cook afloat in his lifebelt. The cook continued to sleep, but the oiler sat up, blinking his eyes and shaking with the new cold.

"Oh, I'm awful sorry, Billie," said the correspondent, contritely.

"That's all right, old boy," said the oiler, and lay down again and was asleep.

Presently it seemed that even the captain dozed, and the correspondent thought that he was the one man afloat on all the oceans. The wind had a voice as it came over the waves, and it was sadder than the end.

There was a long, loud swishing astern of the boat, and a gleaming trail of phosphorescence, like a blue flame, was furrowed on the black waters. It might have been made by a monstrous knife.

Then there came a stillness, while the correspondent breathed with open mouth and looked at the sea.

Suddenly there was another swish and another long flash of bluish light, and this time it was alongside the boat, and might almost have been reached with an oar. The correspondent saw an enormous fin speed like a shadow through the water, hurling the crystalline spray and leaving the long glowing trail.

The correspondent looked over his shoulder at the captain. His face was hidden, and he seemed to be asleep. He looked at the babes of the sea. They certainly were asleep. So, being bereft of sympathy, he leaned a little way to one side and swore softly into the sea.

But the thing did not then leave the vicinity of the boat. Ahead or astern, on one side or the other, at intervals long or short, fled the long sparkling streak, and there was to be heard the *whirroo* of the dark fin. The speed and power of the thing was greatly to be admired. It cut the water like a gigantic and keen projectile.

The presence of this biding thing did not affect the man with the same horror that it would if he had been a picnicker. He simply looked at the sea dully and swore in an undertone.

Nevertheless, it is true that he did not wish to be alone with the thing. He wished one of his companions to awake by chance and keep him company with it. But the captain hung motionless over the water jug, and the oiler and the cook in the bottom of the boat were plunged in slumber.

VI

"If I am going to be drowned — if I am going to be drowned — if I am going to be drowned, why, in the name of the seven mad gods who rule the sea, was I allowed to come thus far and contemplate sand and trees?"

During this dismal night, it may be remarked that a man would conclude that it was really the intention of the seven mad gods to drown him, despite the abominable injustice of it. For it was certainly an abominable injustice to drown a man who had worked so hard, so hard. The man felt it would be a crime most unnatural. Other people had drowned at sea since galleys swarmed with painted sails, but still —

When it occurs to a man that nature does not regard him as important, and that she feels she would not maim the universe by disposing of him, he at first wishes to throw bricks at the temple, and he hates deeply the fact that there are no bricks and no temples. Any visible expression of nature would surely be pelleted with his jeers.

Then, if there be no tangible thing to hoot, he feels, perhaps, the desire to confront a personification and indulge in pleas, bowed to one knee, and with hands supplicant, saying, "Yes, but I love myself."

A high cold star on a winter's night is the word he feels that she says to him. Thereafter he knows the pathos of his situation.

The men in the dinghy had not discussed these matters, but each had, no doubt, reflected upon them in silence and according to his mind. There was seldom any expression upon their faces save the general one of complete weariness. Speech was devoted to the business of the boat.

To chime the notes of his emotion, a verse mysteriously entered the correspondent's head. He had even forgotten that he had forgotten this verse, but it suddenly was in his mind.

A soldier of the Legion lay dying in Algiers;
There was a lack of woman's nursing, there was dearth of woman's tears;
But a comrade stood beside him, and he took that comrade's hand,
And he said, "I never more shall see my own, my native land."[5]

In his childhood the correspondent had been made acquainted with the fact that a soldier of the Legion lay dying in Algiers, but he had never regarded the fact as important. Myriads of his school-fellows had informed him of the soldier's plight, but the dinning had naturally ended by making him perfectly indifferent. He had never considered it his affair that a soldier of the Legion lay dying in Algiers, nor had it appeared to him as a matter for sorrow. It was less to him than the breaking of a pencil's point.

Now, however, it quaintly came to him as a human, living thing. It was no longer merely a picture of a few throes in the breast of a poet, meanwhile

[5]From "Bingen on the Rhine," a popular poem by Caroline Norton (1808–1877), frequently recited by students in class.

drinking tea and warming his feet at the grate; it was an actuality—stern, mournful, and fine.

The correspondent plainly saw the soldier. He lay on the sand with his feet out straight and still. While his pale left hand was upon his chest in an attempt to thwart the going of his life, the blood came between his fingers. In the far Algerian distance, a city of low square forms was set against a sky that was faint with the last sunset hues. The correspondent, plying the oars and dreaming of the slow and slower movements of the lips of the soldier, was moved by a profound and perfectly impersonal comprehension. He was sorry for the soldier of the Legion who lay dying in Algiers.

The thing which had followed the boat and waited had evidently grown bored at the delay. There was no longer to be heard the slash of the cut-water, and there was no longer the flame of the long trail. The light in the north still glimmered, but it was apparently no nearer to the boat. Sometimes the boom of the surf rang in the correspondent's ears, and he turned the craft seaward then and rowed harder. Southward, some one had evidently built a watch fire on the beach. It was too low and too far to be seen, but it made a shimmering, roseate reflection upon the bluff in back of it, and this could be discerned from the boat. The wind came stronger, and sometimes a wave suddenly raged out like a mountain cat, and there was to be seen the sheen and sparkle of a broken crest.

The captain, in the bow, moved on his water jar and sat erect. "Pretty long night," he observed to the correspondent. He looked at the shore. "Those life-saving people take their time."

"Did you see that shark playing around?"

"Yes, I saw him. He was a big fellow, all right."

"Wish I had known you were awake."

Later the correspondent spoke into the bottom of the boat. "Billie!" There was a slow and gradual disentanglement. "Billie, will you spell me?"

"Sure," said the oiler.

As soon as the correspondent touched the cold, comfortable seawater in the bottom of the boat and had huddled close to the cook's lifebelt he was deep in sleep, despite the fact that his teeth played all the popular airs. This sleep was so good to him that it was but a moment before he heard a voice call his name in a tone that demonstrated the last stages of exhaustion. "Will you spell me?"

"Sure, Billie."

The light in the north had mysteriously vanished, but the correspondent took his course from the wide-awake captain.

Later in the night they took the boat farther out to sea, and the captain directed the cook to take one oar at the stern and keep the boat facing the seas. He was to call out if he should hear the thunder of the surf. This plan enabled the oiler and the correspondent to get respite together. "We'll give those boys a chance to get into shape again," said the captain. They curled down and, after a few preliminary chatterings and trembles, slept once more the dead sleep. Neither knew they had bequeathed to the cook the company of another shark, or perhaps the same shark.

As the boat caroused on the waves, spray occasionally bumped over the side and gave them a fresh soaking, but this had no power to break their repose. The ominous slash of the wind and the water affected them as it would have affected mummies.

"Boys," said the cook, with the notes of every reluctance in his voice, "she's drifted in pretty close. I guess one of you had better take her to sea again." The correspondent, aroused, heard the crash of the toppled crests.

As he was rowing, the captain gave him some whiskey-and-water, and this steadied the chills out of him. "If I ever get ashore and anybody shows me even a photograph of an oar —"

At last there was a short conversation.

"Billie! . . . Billie, will you spell me?"

"Sure," said the oiler.

VII

When the correspondent again opened his eyes, the sea and the sky were each of the gray hue of the dawning. Later, carmine and gold was painted upon the waters. The morning appeared finally, in its splendor, with a sky of pure blue, and the sunlight flamed on the tips of the waves.

On the distant dunes were set many little black cottages, and a tall white windmill reared above them. No man, nor dog, nor bicycle appeared on the beach. The cottages might have formed a deserted village.

The voyagers scanned the shore. A conference was held in the boat. "Well," said the captain, "if no help is coming, we might better try a run through the surf right away. If we stay out here much longer we will be too weak to do anything for ourselves at all." The others silently acquiesced in this reasoning. The boat was headed for the beach. The correspondent wondered if none ever ascended the tall wind-tower, and if then they never looked seaward. This tower was a giant, standing with its back to the plight of the ants. It represented in a degree, to the correspondent, the serenity of nature amid the struggles of the individual — nature in the wind, and nature in the vision of men. She did not seem cruel to him then, nor beneficent, nor treacherous, nor wise. But she was indifferent, flatly indifferent. It is, perhaps, plausible that a man in this situation, impressed with the unconcern of the universe, should see the innumerable flaws of his life, and have them taste wickedly in his mind, and wish for another chance. A distinction between right and wrong seems absurdly clear to him, then, in this new ignorance of the grave-edge, and he understands that if he were given another opportunity he would mend his conduct and his words, and be better and brighter during an introduction or at a tea.

"Now, boys," said the captain, "she is going to swamp sure. All we can do is to work her in as far as possible, and then when she swamps, pile out and scramble for the beach. Keep cool now, and don't jump until she swamps sure."

The oiler took the oars. Over his shoulders he scanned the surf. "Captain," he said, "I think I'd better bring her about and keep her head-on to the seas and back her in."

"All right, Billie," said the captain. "Back her in." The oiler swung the boat then, and, seated in the stern, the cook and the correspondent were obliged to look over their shoulders to contemplate the lonely and indifferent shore.

The monstrous inshore rollers heaved the boat high until the men were again enabled to see the white sheets of water scudding up the slanted beach. "We won't get in very close," said the captain. Each time a man could wrest his attention from the rollers, he turned his glance toward the shore, and in the expression of the eyes during this contemplation there was a singular quality.

The correspondent, observing the others, knew that they were not afraid, but the full meaning of their glances was shrouded.

As for himself, he was too tired to grapple fundamentally with the fact. He tried to coerce his mind into thinking of it, but the mind was dominated at this time by the muscles, and the muscles said they did not care. It merely occurred to him that if he should drown it would be a shame.

There were no hurried words, no pallor, no plain agitation. The men simply looked at the shore. "Now, remember to get well clear of the boat when you jump," said the captain.

Seaward the crest of a roller suddenly fell with a thunderous crash, and the long white comber came roaring down upon the boat.

"Steady now," said the captain. The men were silent. They turned their eyes from the shore to the comber and waited. The boat slid up the incline, leaped at the furious top, bounced over it, and swung down the long back of the wave. Some water had been shipped, and the cook bailed it out.

But the next crest crashed also. The tumbling, boiling flood of white water caught the boat and whirled it almost perpendicular. Water swarmed in from all sides. The correspondent had his hands on the gunwhale at this time, and when the water entered at that place he swiftly withdrew his fingers, as if he objected to wetting them.

The little boat, drunken with this weight of water, reeled and snuggled deeper into the sea.

"Bail her out, cook! Bail her out!" said the captain.

"All right, Captain," said the cook.

"Now boys, the next one will do us for sure," said the oiler. "Mind to jump clear of the boat."

The third wave moved forward, huge, furious, implacable. It fairly swallowed the dinghy, and almost simultaneously the men tumbled into the sea. A piece of lifebelt had lain in the bottom of the boat, and as the correspondent went overboard he held this to his chest with his left hand.

The January water was icy, and he reflected immediately that it was colder than he had expected to find it off the coast of Florida. This appeared to his dazed mind as a fact important enough to be noted at the time. The coldness of the water was sad; it was tragic. This fact was somehow mixed and confused with his opinion of his own situation, so that it seemed almost a proper reason for tears. The water was cold.

When he came to surface he was conscious of little but the noisy water. Afterward he saw his companions in the sea. The oiler was ahead in the race. He was swimming strongly and rapidly. Off to the correspondent's left, the cook's great white and corked back bulged out of the water; and in the rear the captain was hanging with his one good hand to the keel of the overturned dinghy.

There is a certain immovable quality to a shore, and the correspondent wondered at it amid the confusion of the sea.

It seemed also very attractive; but the correspondent knew that it was a long journey, and he paddled leisurely. The piece of life preserver lay under him, and sometimes he whirled down the incline of a wave as if he were on a hand-sled.

But finally he arrived at a place in the sea where travel was beset with difficulty. He did not pause swimming to inquire what manner of current had caught him, but there his progress ceased. The shore was set before him like a bit of scenery on a stage, and he looked at it and understood with his eyes each detail of it.

As the cook passed, much farther to the left, the captain was calling to him, "Turn over on your back, cook! Turn over on your back and use the oar."

"All right, sir." The cook turned on his back, and, paddling with an oar, went ahead as if he were a canoe.

Presently the boat also passed to the left of the correspondent, with the captain clinging with one hand to the keel. He would have appeared like a man raising himself to look over a board fence if it were not for the extraordinary gymnastics of the boat. The correspondent marveled that the captain could still hold to it.

They passed on nearer to shore—the oiler, the cook, the captain—and following them went the water jar, bouncing gaily over the seas.

The correspondent remained in the grip of this strange new enemy—a current. The shore, with its white slope of sand and its green bluff topped with little silent cottages, was spread like a picture before him. It was very near to him then, but he was impressed as one who, in a gallery, looks at a scene from Brittany or Algiers.

He thought: "I am going to drown? Can it be possible? Can it be possible? Can it be possible?" Perhaps an individual must consider his own death to be the final phenomenon of nature.

But later a wave perhaps whirled him out of this small deadly current, for he found suddenly that he could again make progress toward the shore. Later still he was aware that the captain, clinging with one hand to the keel of the dinghy, had his face turned away from the shore and toward him, and was calling his name. "Come to the boat! Come to the boat!"

In his struggle to reach the captain and the boat, he reflected that when one gets properly wearied drowning must really be a comfortable arrangement—a cessation of hostilities accompanied by a large degree of relief; and he was glad of it, for the main thing in his mind for some moments had been horror of the temporary agony. He did not wish to be hurt.

Presently he saw a man running along the shore. He was undressing with most remarkable speed. Coat, trousers, shirt, everything flew magically off him.

"Come to the boat!" called the captain.

"All right, Captain." As the correspondent paddled, he saw the captain let himself down to bottom and leave the boat. Then the correspondent performed his one little marvel of the voyage. A large wave caught him and flung him with ease and supreme speed completely over the boat and far beyond it. It struck him even then as an event in gymnastics and a true miracle of the sea. An overturned boat in the surf is not a plaything to a swimming man.

The correspondent arrived in water that reached only to his waist, but his condition did not enable him to stand for more than a moment. Each wave knocked him into a heap, and the undertow pulled at him.

Then he saw the man who had been running and undressing, and undressing and running, come bounding into the water. He dragged ashore the cook, and then waded toward the captain; but the captain waved him away and sent him to the correspondent. He was naked—naked as a tree in winter; but a halo was about his head, and he shone like a saint. He gave a strong pull, and a long drag, and a bully heave at the correspondent's hand. The correspondent, schooled in the minor formulae, said, "Thanks, old man." But suddenly the man cried, "What's that?" He pointed a swift finger. The correspondent said, "Go."

In the shallows, face downward, lay the oiler. His forehead touched sand that was periodically, between each wave, clear of the sea.

The correspondent did not know all that transpired afterward. When he achieved safe ground he fell, striking the sand with each particular part of his body. It was as if he had dropped from a roof, but the thud was grateful to him.

It seems that instantly the beach was populated with men with blankets, clothes, and flasks, and women with coffeepots and all the remedies sacred to their minds. The welcome of the land to the men from the sea was warm and generous; but a still and dripping shape was carried slowly up the beach, and the land's welcome for it could only be the different and sinister hospitality of the grave.

When it came night, the white waves paced to and fro in the moonlight, and the wind brought the sound of the great sea's voice to the men on the shore, and they felt that they could then be interpreters.

(1898)

Prewriting

Understanding the theme of a piece of literature involves figuring out what the whole work means. Your prewriting task here is to ask yourself questions that lead to the meaning of the story you just read. You should then try to express that idea in a complete sentence. You may need to rewrite the sentence several times until you can express the theme satisfactorily.

Figuring Out the Theme

Reread "The Open Boat" and formulate specific leading questions about the following elements of the story:

1. The title
2. The setting, especially the repeated descriptions of the sky, the waves, and the wind
3. The men in the boat
4. Any significant object or images, such as the people on the shore, the gulls, the shark
5. Any changes that you notice in the four men and their feeling for one another
6. Any observations about life or human nature that the all-knowing narrator makes
7. The ending.

Stating the Theme

After writing out the answers to the questions you have set for yourself, sum up the theme of this story in a single statement. Then express the theme in another way, using other words. Are both statements valid? Are there any secondary themes that enrich the story and add to the primary theme? Write those down, too.

Take one of the statements of theme that you have formulated, and write it at the top of a blank sheet of paper. Fill the page with freewriting about this idea, expressing as quickly as you can your thoughts and feelings about Crane's vision of life and the struggle for survival.

Writing

We have emphasized that your essays should be rich in supporting details from your source. Without specific references to the literary work you are analyzing, your judgments and conclusions may be vague and unconvincing.

Choosing Supporting Details

During a close second reading of a story, pay special attention to the descriptive details. In "The Open Boat," you will notice that images of light and the color of the sky appear frequently. After identifying these images, go back through the story one more time and put a check mark next to each one. During this third examination, you may come up with an insight about the meaning of these images — perhaps something like

> The changing color of the light in the sky parallels the shifting fortunes of the men in the open boat.

You now have a good topic sentence for a paragraph or a section of your paper.

A list of specific examples from the story could support your topic sentence, but a mere list would not reveal much insight. So, if possible, *classify* the details. In this case, sometimes the light is natural and sometimes it appears to come from human sources on the shore. Quote one or two examples of each kind, and then — most important — explain the significance of these details. In this story, the natural light is an accurate indicator of the men's fortunes, while the lights on the shore are illusory and create false hope.

Approach writing about one of the following ideas by rereading the story with the topic in mind. As you read, jot down any details that seem relevant. Review your notes and see what general observations you can make concerning the topic; then sort out these supporting details and comment on their significance.

Ideas for Writing
Ideas for Responsive Writing

1. Do you think nature is hostile, benign, or neutral? Drawing on your own experiences, explain your view of nature and relate it to the view that Crane presents in "The Open Boat."

2. "The Open Boat" is based on an actual event: in 1897 Crane was shipwrecked off the coast of Florida and escaped in a ten-foot lifeboat with the ship's captain and two members of the crew. Have you had a life-threatening experience? How did it affect you? How does it compare to Crane's? Describe your experience, and comment on its effect (or lack of effect) on your values and beliefs.

3. Do you find it ironic that the oiler is the one person to die? How do you feel about his death?

Ideas for Critical Writing

1. How do you define *heroism*? Who is the hero of "The Open Boat"?

2. Some critics think that "The Open Boat" is an allegory for our travels on the sea of life and the boat a microcosm of society. Write an essay in which you agree or disagree with this interpretation.

3. Explain the story's last sentence. Of what can the survivors now "be interpreters"?

Rewriting

When you revise, you should make sure that your paper *flows* — that your readers can follow your ideas easily.

Achieving Coherence

The best way to make your writing *coherent* — to make it hold together and be easy to follow — is to have a clear thesis and to make sure that all your subpoints pertain to that thesis. If you organize the development of your ideas carefully, your paragraphs should unfold in a logical, connected way. Continuity also comes when you think out your ideas completely and develop them adequately. Leaps in thought and shifts in meaning often result from too much generalization and too little development.

Checking for Coherence   Type up or print out a clean copy of the latest draft of your essay. In the margins, write a word or phrase that states the point or describes the purpose of every group of related sentences. These words and phrases are called "glosses." (You can even use short sentences if you want.) To help write glosses for your sentences and paragraphs, ask yourself these questions: What have I said here? How many ideas are in this passage? What does this sentence/paragraph contribute to the development of my main idea—my thesis?

When you have finished putting glosses in the margins of your essay, go back and review the glosses. Can you see a clear sequence of points? Are there any sentences or passages that you could not write a gloss for? Is there any place where you digress or introduce an unrelated idea? Using the glosses as a guide, make revisions that will improve the coherence of your essay: fill in gaps, combine repetitive sentences, cut out irrelevant material, add transitions (see Chart 3–1: Transitional Terms for All Occasions and "Writing Smooth Transitions" in "A Handbook for Correcting Errors."

Editing: Improving Connections

Here are some other ways to help you strengthen the flow and coherence of your sentences:

Repeat Words and Synonyms

Repeat key words for coherence as well as for emphasis:

> I do not want *to read another gothic romance*. I especially do not want *to read another* long *gothic romance*.

If repetition is tiresome or you want more variety, use a synonym:

> It was a rare *caper*, planned to the last second. Such elaborate *heists* seem to come right from a detective novel.

Take care when you repeat words. These words should be important or emphatic. Do not repeat a common, limp term because you are too lazy to find a synonym.[1] The following introduction to a student paper suffers because the writer needlessly repeats the same uninteresting verb:

> Shirley Jackson's "The Lottery" is a complex story that deals with a fundamental part of human psychology, the *using* of scapegoats. Scapegoats have been *used* throughout history to justify actions. Many times scapegoats are *used* to conceal human errors or misbeliefs. Scapegoats are, in fact, still *used* today. [italics added]

Notice that the repetition of the key word *scapegoats* is emphatic. The ineffective repetition can be revised this way:

> Shirley Jackson's "The Lottery" is a complex story that deals with a fundamental element of human psychology—*using* scapegoats. Scapegoats have been *created* throughout history to justify actions. Many times they are *employed* to conceal human errors or misbeliefs. In fact, scapegoats still *exist* today.

[1]But you must be aware that synonyms are not always interchangeable. Be sure to check the meaning of any word you are not sure of.

Try Parallel Structure

Repeat a grammatical pattern to tie points and details together:

> In the morning Madam Bovary ate breakfast with her husband; in the afternoon she picnicked with her paramour.

> The play was about to end: the lovers kissed, the curtain fell, and the audience applauded wildly.

Be sure that your grammatical pattern actually *is* parallel. If your phrases or clauses are not precisely balanced (i.e., all grammatically similar), you will lose the good effect:

Not parallel: In "The Lottery" these characteristics include *unwillingness to change, being stuck in tradition, fear of peer pressure,* and *fear itself.*

Parallel: In "The Lottery" these characteristics include *unwillingness to change, enslavement to tradition, fear of peer pressure,* and *fear of the unknown.*

Not parallel: Many times scapegoats are used to conceal *human errors* or *misbeliefs people have.*

Parallel: Many times scapegoats are used to conceal human *errors* or *misbeliefs.*

Sample Student Paper

In the following critical paper, Sandra Bettis, a student at Illinois State University, closely analyzes the details in a brief scene from Kate Chopin's novella *The Awakening.* Sandy's analysis focuses on the function of this scene in revealing the novel's theme.

Sandra Bettis

English 102

February 10, 1991

Edna's Emerging Selfhood

The "hammock scene" (Chapter XI, pages 183-84) in Kate Chopin's The Awakening illuminates the marital relationship of the Pontelliers and marks a significant stage in the

development of Edna's emerging identity. As her husband Léonce
attempts to get Edna to come inside the house (because he wishes
to go to bed), Edna chafes at his insistence and becomes
determined to remain outside in the hammock. Ordinarily, she
would have "unthinkingly" obeyed her husband, but this time
she is acutely aware of her own desires--and she does not wish
to go to bed right now. Léonce epitomizes a controlling
husband, and Edna's resistance to his coercion aptly
illustrates her emerging sense of self and her desire to do as
she wishes and not what her nineteenth-century role as
submissive wife dictates.

Submissive behavior is a part of Edna's wifely role. In
fact, it has become such a "habit" that Edna responds
"unthinkingly" to her husband's requests, as she goes
"through the daily treadmill of the life which has been
portioned out to us." But on this particular summer night,
her senses are heightened, sleep does not come quickly, and
Léonce's suggestions that she come inside are met with strong
resistance.

Edna recognizes Léonce's assumed attitude of concern for
his wife's welfare--" 'You will take cold out there' " and
" 'The mosquitoes will devour you' "--as nothing more than a
ploy by her husband to entice her to do his bidding. As she
replies, " 'It isn't cold; I have my shawl' " and " 'There are no
mosquitoes,' " Léonce communicates his disapproval by "moving
about the room; every sound indicating impatience and
irritation." Léonce then makes one more appeal for Edna to
come inside, which she rebuffs, before he issues a command that
she " 'must come in the house instantly.' " Her husband's
totally dominating attitude causes Edna's resistance to flare
up even stronger; and as she burrows deeper into the hammock,
she wonders "if her husband had ever spoken to her like that
before, and if she had submitted to his command." She knows
that she has, but with her newly-awakened consciousness that

that night, she "could not realize why or how she should have yielded. . . ." And yield is not what she is about to do tonight.

Realizing that Edna is not going to heed his demands, Léonce has to save face and at the same time assert his masculine prerogative of control over the situation. So instead of going to bed and leaving Edna to the privacy of her own space and thoughts, he prepares to outwait her. After fortifying himself with wine, he goes outside where he assumes a dominating posture by placing his feet above her "on the rail" and smokes cigars while Edna remains in the hammock until "the physical need for sleep" begins to overtake her. Then she goes inside. Léonce has won the power struggle, and he even lingers outside to finish his cigar--and savor his triumph. He may have won the battle, but he has lost the war.

As Chopin shows us throughout this novel, Edna's unwillingness to yield to Léonce's overtures this night is but a harbinger of her newly-found strength and determination to break out of the mold into which she has been cast--a mold which stifles her desire to control her own life. The night's experiences represent a great deal of inner turmoil as Edna struggles with Léonce's dominating attitude and her own growing awareness of her sense of selfhood and her awakening desires; but as she says in her own words at the conclusion of the novella, "perhaps it is better to wake up after all, even to suffer, rather than to remain a dupe to illusions all one's life" (243).

Work Cited

Chopin, Kate. <u>The Awakening</u>. <u>Literature</u> <u>and</u> <u>the</u> <u>Writing</u> <u>Pro-</u>
<u>cess</u>. Ed. Elizabeth McMahan, Susan Day, and Robert
Funk. 3rd ed. New York: Macmillan, 1993. 162-247.

Anthology of Short Fiction

Nathaniel Hawthorne *1804–1864*

YOUNG GOODMAN BROWN

Young Goodman Brown came forth at sunset, into the street of Salem village, but put his head back, after crossing the threshold, to exchange a parting kiss with his young wife. And Faith, as the wife was aptly named, thrust her own pretty head into the street, letting the wind play with the pink ribbons of her cap, while she called to Goodman Brown.

"Dearest heart," whispered she, softly and rather sadly, when her lips were close to his ear, "prithee, put off your journey until sunrise, and sleep in your own bed to-night. A lone woman is troubled with such dreams and such thoughts, that she's afeard of herself, sometimes. Pray, tarry with me this night, dear husband, of all nights in the year!"

"My love and my Faith," replied young Goodman Brown, "of all nights in the year, this one night must I tarry away from thee. My journey, as thou callest it, forth and back again, must needs be done 'twixt now and sunrise. Why, my sweet, pretty wife, dost thou doubt me already, and we but three months married?"

"Then God bless you!" said Faith with the pink ribbons, "and may you find all well, when you come back."

"Amen!" cried Goodman Brown. "Say thy prayers, dear Faith, and go to bed at dusk, and no harm will come to thee."

So they parted; and the young man pursued his way, until, being about to turn the corner by the meeting-house, he looked back and saw the head of Faith still peeping after him, with a melancholy air, in spite of her pink ribbons.

"Poor little Faith!" thought he, for his heart smote him. "What a wretch am I, to leave her on such an errand! She talks of dreams, too. Methought, as she spoke, there was trouble in her face, as if a dream had warned her what work is to be done to-night. But no, no! 't would kill her to think it. Well she's a blessed angel on earth; and after this one night I'll cling to her skirts and follow her to Heaven."

With this excellent resolve for the future, Goodman Brown felt himself justified in making more haste on his present evil purpose. He had taken a dreary road, darkened by all the gloomiest trees of the forest, which barely stood aside

149

to let the narrow path creep through, and closed immediately behind. It was as lonely as could be; and there is this peculiarity in such a solitude, that the traveller knows not who may be concealed by the innumerable trunks and the thick boughs overhead; so that, with lonely footsteps, he may yet be passing through an unseen multitude.

"There may be a devilish Indian behind every tree," said Goodman Brown to himself; and he glanced fearfully behind him, as he added, "What if the devil himself should be at my very elbow!"

His head being turned back, he passed a crook of the road, and looking forward again, beheld the figure of a man, in grave and decent attire, seated at the foot of an old tree. He arose at Goodman Brown's approach, and walked onward, side by side with him.

"You are late, Goodman Brown," said he. "The clock of the Old South was striking, as I came through Boston; and that is full fifteen minutes agone."

"Faith kept me back awhile," replied the young man, with a tremor in his voice, caused by the sudden appearance of his companion, though not wholly unexpected.

It was now deep dusk in the forest, and deepest in that part of it where these two were journeying. As nearly as could be discerned, the second traveller was about fifty years old, apparently in the same rank of life as Goodman Brown, and bearing a considerable resemblance to him, though perhaps more in expression than features. Still, they might have been taken for father and son. And yet, though the elder person was as simply clad as the younger, and as simple in manner too, he had an indescribable air of one who knew the world, and would not have felt abashed at the governor's dinner-table, or in King William's court, were it possible that his affairs should call him thither. But the only thing about him that could be fixed upon as remarkable, was his staff, which bore the likeness of a great black snake, so curiously wrought, that it might almost be seen to twist and wriggle itself like a living serpent. This, of course, must have been an ocular deception, assisted by the uncertain light.

"Come, Goodman Brown!" cried his fellow-traveller, "this is a dull pace for the beginning of a journey. Take my staff, if you are so soon weary."

"Friend," said the other, exchanging his slow pace for a full stop, "having kept covenant by meeting thee here, it is my purpose now to return whence I came. I have scruples, touching the matter thou wot'st of."

"Sayest thou so?" replied he of the serpent, smiling apart. "Let us walk on, nevertheless, reasoning as we go, and if I convince thee not, thou shalt turn back. We are but a little way in the forest, yet."

"Too far, too far!" exclaimed the goodman, unconsciously resuming his walk. "My father never went into the woods on such an errand, nor his father before him. We have been a race of honest men and good Christians, since the days of the martyrs. And shall I be the first of the name of Brown that ever took this path and kept—"

"Such company, thou wouldst say," observed the elder person, interrupting his pause. "Well said, Goodman Brown! I have been as well acquainted with your family as with ever a one among the Puritans; and that's no trifle to say. I helped your grandfather, the constable, when he lashed the Quaker woman so smartly through the streets of Salem. And it was I that brought your father a pitch-pine knot, kindled at my own hearth, to set fire to an Indian village, in King Philip's war. They were my good friends, both; and many a pleasant walk have we had along this path, and returned merrily after midnight. I would fain be friends with you, for their sake."

"If it be as thou sayest," replied Goodman Brown, "I marvel they never spoke of these matters. Or, verily, I marvel not, seeing that the least rumor of the sort would have driven them from New England. We are a people of prayer, and good works to boot, and abide no such wickedness."

"Wickedness or not," said the traveller with the twisted staff, "I have a very general acquaintance here in New England. The deacons of many a church have drunk the communion wine with me; the selectmen, of divers towns, make me their chairman; and a majority of the Great and General Court are firm supporters of my interest. The governor and I, too—but these are state secrets."

"Can this be so!" cried Goodman Brown, with a stare of amazement at his undisturbed companion. "Howbeit, I have nothing to do with the governor and council; they have their own ways, and are no rule for a simple husbandman like me. But, were I to go on with thee, how should I meet the eye of that good old man, our minister, at Salem village? Oh, his voice would make me tremble, both Sabbath-day and lecture-day!"

Thus far, the elder traveller had listened with due gravity, but now burst into a fit of irrepressible mirth, shaking himself so violently, that his snakelike staff actually seemed to wriggle in sympathy.

"Ha, ha, ha!" shouted he, again and again; then composing himself, "Well, go on, Goodman Brown, go on; but, prithee, don't kill me with laughing!"

"Well, then, to end the matter at once," said Goodman Brown, considerably nettled, "there is my wife, Faith. It would break her dear little heart; and I'd rather break my own!"

"Nay, if that be the case," answered the other, "e'en go thy ways, Goodman Brown. I would not, for twenty old women like the one hobbling before us, that Faith should come to any harm."

As he spoke, he pointed his staff at a female figure on the path, in whom Goodman Brown recognized a very pious and exemplary dame, who had taught him his catechism in youth, and was still his moral and spiritual adviser, jointly with the minister and Deacon Gookin.

"A marvel, truly, that Goody Cloyse should be so far in the wilderness, at nightfall!" said he. "But, with your leave, friend, I shall take a cut through the woods, until we have left this Christian woman behind. Being a stranger to you, she might ask whom I was consorting with, and whither I was going."

"Be it so," said his fellow-traveller. "Betake you to the woods, and let me keep the path."

Accordingly, the young man turned aside, but took care to watch his companion, who advanced softly along the road, until he had come within a staff's length of the old dame. She, meanwhile, was making the best of her way, with singular speed for so aged a woman, and mumbling some indistinct words, a prayer, doubtless, as she went. The traveller put forth his staff, and touched her withered neck with what seemed the serpent's tail.

"The devil!" screamed the pious old lady.

"Then Goody Cloyse knows her old friend?" observed the traveller, confronting her, and leaning on his writhing stick.

"Ah, forsooth, and is it your worship, indeed?" cried the good dame. "Yea, truly is it, and in the very image of my old gossip, Goodman Brown, the grandfather of the silly fellow that now is. But, would your worship believe it?

my broomstick hath strangely disappeared, stolen, as I suspect, by that unhanged witch, Goody Cory, and that, too, when I was all anointed with the juice of smallage and cinque-foil and wolf's-bane —"

"Mingled with fine wheat and the fat of a new-born babe," said the shape of old Goodman Brown.

"Ah, your worship knows the recipe," cried the old lady, cackling aloud. "So, as I was saying, being all ready for the meeting, and no horse to ride on, I made up my mind to foot it; for they tell me there is a nice young man to be taken into communion to-night. But now your good worship will lend me your arm, and we shall be there in a twinkling."

"That can hardly be," answered her friend. "I may not spare you my arm, Goody Cloyse, but here is my staff, if you will."

So saying, he threw it down at her feet where, perhaps, it assumed life, being one of the rods which its owner had formerly lent to the Egyptian Magi. Of this fact, however, Goodman Brown could not take cognizance. He had cast up his eyes in astonishment, and looking down again, beheld neither Goody Cloyse nor the serpentine staff, but his fellow-traveller alone, who waited for him as calmly as if nothing had happened.

"That old woman taught me my catechism!" said the young man; and there was a world of meaning in this simple comment.

They continued to walk onward, while the elder traveller exhorted his companion to make good speed and persevere in the path, discoursing so aptly, that his arguments seemed rather to spring up in the bosom of his auditor, than to be suggested by himself. As they went he plucked a branch of maple, to serve for a walking-stick, and began to strip it of the twigs and little boughs, which were wet with evening dew. The moment his fingers touched them, they became strangely withered and dried up, as with a week's sunshine. Thus the pair proceeded, at a good free pace, until suddenly, in a gloomy hollow of the road, Goodman Brown sat himself down on the stump of a tree, and refused to go any farther.

"Friend," said he, stubbornly, "my mind is made up. Not another step will I budge on this errand. What if a wretched old woman do choose to go to the devil, when I thought she was going to Heaven! Is that any reason why I should quit my dear Faith, and go after her?"

"You will think better of this by and by," said his acquaintance, composedly. "Sit here and rest yourself awhile; and when you feel like moving again, there is my staff to help you along."

Without more words, he threw his companion the maple stick, and was as speedily out of sight as if he had vanished into the deepening gloom. The young man sat a few moments by the roadside, applauding himself greatly, and thinking with how clear a conscience he should meet the minister, in his morning walk, nor shrink from the eye of good old Deacon Gookin. And what calm sleep would be his, that very night, which was to have been spent so wickedly, but purely and sweetly now, in the arms of Faith! Amidst these pleasant and praise-worthy meditations, Goodman Brown heard the tramp of horses along the road, and deemed it advisable to conceal himself within the verge of the forest, conscious of the guilty purpose that had brought him thither, though now so happily turned from it.

On came the hoof-tramps and the voices of the riders, two grave old voices, conversing soberly as they drew near. These mingled sounds appeared to pass along the road, within a few yards of the young man's hiding-place; but owing, doubtless, to the depth of the gloom, at that particular spot, neither the travellers nor their steeds were visible. Though their figures brushed the small boughs by the wayside, it could not be seen that they intercepted, even for a moment, the faint gleam from the strip of bright sky, athwart which they must have passed. Goodman Brown alternately crouched and stood on tiptoe, pulling aside the branches, and thrusting forth his head as far as he durst, without discerning so much as a shadow. It vexed him the more, because he could have sworn, were such a thing possible, that he recognized the voices of the minister and Deacon Gookin, jogging along quietly, as they were wont to do, when bound to some ordination or ecclesiastical council. While yet within hearing, one of the riders stopped to pluck a switch.

"Of the two, reverend Sir," said the voice like the deacon's, "I had rather miss an ordination dinner than to-night's meeting. They tell me that some of our community are to be here from Falmouth and beyond, and others from Connecticut and Rhode Island; besides several of the Indian powwows, who, after their fashion, know almost as much deviltry as the best of us. Moreover, there is a goodly young woman to be taken into communion."

"Mighty well, Deacon Gookin!" replied the solemn old tones of the minister. "Spur up, or we shall be late. Nothing can be done, you know, until I get on the ground."

The hoofs clattered again, and the voices, talking so strangely in the empty air, passed on through the forest, where no church had ever been gathered, nor solitary Christian prayed. Whither, then, could these holy men be journeying, so deep into the heathen wilderness? Young Goodman Brown caught hold of a tree, for support, being ready to sink down on the ground, faint and over-burthened with the heavy sickness of his heart. He looked up to the sky, doubting whether there really was a Heaven above him. Yet, there was the blue arch, and the stars brightening in it.

"With Heaven above, and Faith below, I will yet stand firm against the devil!" cried Goodman Brown.

While he still gazed upward, into the deep arch of the firmament, and had lifted his hands to pray, a cloud, though no wind was stirring, hurried across the zenith, and hid the brightening stars. The blue sky was still visible, except directly overhead, where this black mass of cloud was sweeping swiftly northward. Aloft in the air, as if from the depths of the cloud, came a confused and doubtful sound of voices. Once, the listener fancied that he could distinguish the accents of townspeople of his own, men and women, both pious and ungodly, many of whom he had met at the communion-table, and had seen others rioting at the tavern. The next moment, so indistinct were the sounds, he doubted whether he had heard aught but the murmur of the old forest, whispering without a wind. Then came a stronger swell of those familiar tones, heard daily in the sunshine, at Salem village, but never, until now, from a cloud at night. There was one voice, of a young woman, uttering lamentations, yet with an uncertain sorrow, and entreating for some favor, which, perhaps, it would grieve her to obtain. And all the unseen multitude, both saints and sinners, seemed to encourage her onward.

"Faith!" shouted Goodman Brown, in a voice of agony and desperation; and the echoes of the forest mocked him, crying — "Faith! Faith!" as if bewildered wretches were seeking her, all through the wilderness.

The cry of grief, rage, and terror was yet piercing the night, when the unhappy husband held his breath for a response. There was a scream, drowned immediately in a louder murmur of voices fading into far-off laughter, as the dark cloud swept away, leaving the clear and silent sky above Goodman Brown. But something fluttered lightly down through the air, and caught on the branch of a tree. The young man seized it and beheld a pink ribbon.

"My Faith is gone!" cried he, after one stupefied moment. "There is no good on earth, and sin is but a name. Come, devil! for to thee is this world given."

And maddened with despair, so that he laughed loud and long, did Goodman Brown grasp his staff and set forth again, at such a rate, that he seemed to fly along the forest path, rather than to walk or run. The road grew wilder and drearier, and more faintly traced, and vanished at length, leaving him in the heart of the dark wilderness, still rushing onward, with the instinct that guides mortal man to evil. The whole forest was peopled with frightful sounds: the creaking of the trees, the howling of wild beasts, and the yell of Indians; while, sometimes, the wind tolled like a distant church bell, and sometimes gave a broad roar around the traveller, as if all Nature was laughing him to scorn. But he was himself the chief horror of the scene, and shrank not from its other horrors.

"Ha! ha! ha!" roared Goodman Brown, when the wind laughed at him. "Let us hear which will laugh loudest! Think not to frighten me with your deviltry! Come witch, come wizard, come Indian powwow, come devil himself! and here comes Goodman Brown. You may as well fear him as he fear you!"

In truth, all through the haunted forest, there could be nothing more frightful than the figure of Goodman Brown. On he flew, among the black pines, brandishing his staff with frenzied gestures, now giving vent to an inspiration of horrid blasphemy, and now shouting forth such laughter, as set all the echoes of the forest laughing like demons around him. The fiend in his own shape is less hideous, than when he rages in the breast of man. Thus sped the demoniac on his course, until, quivering among the trees, he saw a red light before him, as when the felled trunks and branches of a clearing have been set on fire, and throw up their lurid blaze against the sky, at the hour of midnight. He paused, in a lull of the tempest that had driven him onward, and heard the swell of what seemed a hymn, rolling solemnly from a distance, with the weight of many voices. He knew the tune. It was a familiar one in the choir of the village meeting-house. The verse died heavily away, and was lengthened by a chorus, not of human voices, but of all the sounds of the benighted wilderness, pealing in awful harmony together. Goodman Brown cried out; and his cry was lost to his own ear, by its unison with the cry of the desert.

In the interval of silence, he stole forward, until the light glared full upon his eyes. At one extremity of an open space, hemmed in by the dark wall of the forest, arose a rock, bearing some rude, natural resemblance either to an altar or a pulpit, and surrounded by four blazing pines, their tops aflame, their stems untouched, like candles at an evening meeting. The mass of foliage, that had overgrown the summit of the rock, was all on fire, blazing high into the night, and fitfully illuminating the whole field. Each pendent twig and leafy festoon was in a blaze. As the red light arose and fell, a numerous congregation alternately shone forth, then disappeared in shadow, and again grew, as it were, out of the darkness, peopling the heart of the solitary woods at once.

"A grave and dark-clad company!" quoth Goodman Brown.

In truth, they were such. Among them, quivering to-and-fro, between gloom and splendor, appeared faces that would be seen, next day, at the council-board of the province, and others which, Sabbath after Sabbath, looked devoutly heavenward, and benignantly over the crowded pews, from the holiest pulpits in the land. Some affirm, that the lady of the governor was there. At least, there were high dames well known to her, and wives of honored husbands, and widows a great multitude, and ancient maidens, all of excellent repute, and fair young girls, who trembled lest their mothers should espy them. Either the sudden gleams of light, flashing over the obscure field, bedazzled Goodman Brown, or he recognized a score of the church members of Salem village, famous for their especial sanctity. Good old Deacon Gookin had arrived, and waited at the skirts of that venerable saint, his reverend pastor. But, irreverently consorting with these grave, reputable, and pious people, these elders of the church, these chaste dames and dewy virgins, there were men of dissolute lives and women of spotted fame, wretches given over to all mean and filthy vice, and suspected even of horrid crimes. It was strange to see, that the good shrank not from the wicked, nor were the sinners abashed by the saints. Scattered, also, among their pale-faced enemies, were the Indian priests, or powwows, who had often scared their native forest with more hideous incantations than any known to English witchcraft.

"But, where is Faith?" thought Goodman Brown; and, as hope came into his heart, he trembled.

Another verse of the hymn arose, a slow and mournful strain, such as the pious love, but joined to words which expressed all that our nature can conceive of sin, and darkly hinted at far more. Unfathomable to mere mortals is the lore of fiends. Verse after verse was sung, and still the chorus of the desert swelled between, like the deepest tone of a mighty organ. And, with the final peal of that dreadful anthem, there came a sound, as if the roaring wind, the rushing streams, the howling beasts, and every other voice of the unconverted wilderness were mingling and according with the voice of guilty man, in homage to the prince of all. The four blazing pines threw up a loftier flame, and obscurely discovered shapes and visages of horror on the smoke-wreaths, above the impious assembly. At the same moment, the fire on the rock shot redly forth, and formed a glowing arch above its base, where now appeared a figure. With reverence be it spoken, the apparition bore no slight similitude, both in garb and manner, to some grave divine of the New England churches.

"Bring forth the converts!" cried a voice, that echoed through the field and rolled into the forest.

At the word, Goodman Brown stepped forth from the shadow of the trees, and approached the congregation, with whom he felt a loathful brotherhood, by the sympathy of all that was wicked in his heart. He could have well-nigh sworn, that the shape of his own dead father beckoned him to advance, looking downward from a smoke-wreath, while a woman, with dim features of despair, threw out her hand to warn him back. Was it his mother? But he had no power to retreat one step, nor to resist, even in thought, when the minister and good old Deacon Gookin seized his arms, and led him to the blazing rock. Thither came also the slender form of a veiled female, led between Goody Cloyse, that pious teacher of the catechism, and Martha Carrier, who had received the devil's promise to be queen of hell. A rampant hag was she! And there stood the proselytes, beneath the canopy of fire.

"Welcome, my children," said the dark figure, "to the communion of your race! Ye have found, thus young, your nature and your destiny. My children, look behind you!"

They turned; and flashing forth, as it were, in a sheet of flame, the fiend-worshippers were seen; the smile of welcome gleamed darkly on every visage.

"There," resumed the sable form, "are all whom ye have reverenced from youth. Ye deemed them holier than yourselves, and shrank from your own sin, contrasting it with their lives of righteousness and prayerful aspirations heavenward. Yet, here are they all, in my worshipping assembly! This night it shall be granted you to know their secret deeds; how hoary-bearded elders of the church have whispered wanton words to the young maids of their households; how many a woman, eager for widow's weeds, has given her husband a drink at bedtime, and let him sleep his last sleep in her bosom; how beardless youths have made haste to inherit their father's wealth; and how fair damsels—blush not, sweet ones!—have dug little graves in the garden, and bidden me, the sole guest, to an infant's funeral. By the sympathy of your human hearts for sin, ye shall scent out all the places—whether in church, bed-chamber, street, field, or forest—where crime has been committed, and shall exult to behold the whole earth one stain of guilt, one mighty blood-spot. Far more than this! It shall be yours to penetrate, in every bosom, the deep mystery of sin, the fountain of all wicked arts, and which inexhaustibly supplies more evil impulses than human power—than my power, at its utmost!—can make manifest in deeds. And now, my children, look upon each other."

They did so; and, by the blaze of the hell-kindled torches, the wretched man beheld his Faith, and the wife her husband, trembling before that unhallowed altar.

"Lo! there ye stand, my children," said the figure, in a deep and solemn tone, almost sad, with its despairing awfulness, as if his once angelic nature could yet mourn for our miserable race. "Depending upon one another's hearts, ye had still hoped that virtue were not all a dream! Now are ye undeceived!—Evil is the nature of mankind. Evil must be your only happiness. Welcome, again, my children, to the communion of your race!"

"Welcome!" repeated the fiend-worshippers, in one cry of despair and triumph.

And there they stood, the only pair, as it seemed, who were yet hesitating on the verge of wickedness, in this dark world. A basin was hollowed, naturally, in the rock. Did it contain water, reddened by the lurid light? or was it blood? or, perchance, a liquid flame? Herein did the Shape of Evil dip his hand, and prepare to lay the mark of baptism upon their foreheads, that they might be partakers of the mystery of sin, more conscious of the secret guilt of others, both in deed and thought, than they could now be of their own. The husband cast one look at his pale wife, and Faith at him. What polluted wretches would the next glance show them to each other, shuddering alike at what they disclosed and what they saw!

"Faith! Faith!" cried the husband. "Look up to Heaven, and resist the Wicked One!"

Whether Faith obeyed, he knew not. Hardly had he spoken, when he found himself amid calm night and solitude, listening to a roar of the wind, which died heavily away through the forest. He staggered against the rock, and felt it chill and damp, while a hanging twig, that had been all on fire, besprinkled his cheek with the coldest dew.

The next morning, young Goodman Brown came slowly into the street of

Salem village staring around him like a bewildered man. The good old minister was taking a walk along the grave-yard, to get an appetite for breakfast and meditate his sermon, and bestowed a blessing, as he passed, on Goodman Brown. He shrank from the venerable saint, as if to avoid an anathema. Old Deacon Gookin was at domestic worship, and the holy words of his prayer were heard through the open window. "What God doth the wizard pray to?" quoth Goodman Brown. Goody Cloyse, that excellent old Christian, stood in the early sunshine, at her own lattice, catechising a little girl, who had brought her a pint of morning's milk. Goodman Brown snatched away the child, as from the grasp of the fiend himself. Turning the corner by the meeting-house, he spied the head of Faith, with the pink ribbons, gazing anxiously forth, and bursting into such joy at sight of him that she skipt along the street, and almost kissed her husband before the whole village. But Goodman Brown looked sternly and sadly into her face, and passed on without a greeting.

Had Goodman Brown fallen asleep in the forest, and only dreamed a wild dream of a witch-meeting?

Be it so, if you will. But, alas! it was a dream of evil omen for young Goodman Brown. A stern, a sad, a darkly meditative, a distrustful, if not a desperate man did he become, from the night of that fearful dream. On the Sabbath day, when the congregation were singing a holy psalm, he could not listen, because an anthem of sin rushed loudly upon his ear, and drowned all the blessed strain. When the minister spoke from the pulpit, with power and fervid eloquence, and with his hand on the open Bible, of the sacred truths of our religion, and of saint-like lives and triumphant deaths, and of future bliss or misery unutterable, then did Goodman Brown turn pale, dreading lest the roof should thunder down upon the gray blasphemer and his hearers. Often, awaking suddenly at midnight, he shrank from the bosom of Faith, and at morning or eventide, when the family knelt down at prayer, he scowled, and muttered to himself, and gazed sternly at his wife, and turned away. And when he had lived long, and was borne to his grave, a hoary corpse, followed by Faith, an aged woman, and children and grand-children, a goodly procession, besides neighbors not a few, they carved no hopeful verse upon his tombstone; for his dying hour was gloom.

(1835)

Edgar Allan Poe *1809–1849*

THE CASK OF AMONTILLADO

The thousand injuries of Fortunato I had borne as I best could, but when he ventured upon insult I vowed revenge. You, who so well know the nature of my soul, will not suppose, however, that I gave utterance to a threat. *At length* I would be avenged; this was a point definitely settled — but the very definitiveness with which it was resolved precluded the idea of risk. I must not only punish but punish with impunity. A wrong is unredressed when retribution overtakes its redresser. It is equally unredressed when the avenger fails to make himself felt as such to him who has done the wrong.

It must be understood that neither by word nor by deed had I given Fortunato cause to doubt my good will. I continued, as was my wont, to smile in his face, and he did not perceive that my smile *now* was at the thought of his immolation.

He had a weak point — this Fortunato — although in other regards he was a man to be respected and even feared. He prided himself on his connoisseurship in wine. Few Italians have the true virtuoso spirit. For the most part their enthusiasm is adopted to suit the time and opportunity, to practise imposture upon the British and Austrian *millionaires*. In painting and gemmary, Fortunato, like his countrymen, was a quack, but in the matter of old wines he was sincere. In this respect I did not differ from him materially; — I was skillful in the Italian vintages myself, and bought largely whenever I could.

It was about dusk, one evening during the supreme madness of the carnival season, that I encountered my friend. He accosted me with excessive warmth, for he had been drinking much. The man wore motley. He had on a tight-fitting parti-striped dress, and his head was surmounted by the conical cap and bells. I was so pleased to see him that I thought I should never have done wringing his hand.

I said to him — "My dear Fortunato, you are luckily met. How remarkably well you are looking to-day. But I have received a pipe of what passes for Amontillado, and I have my doubts."

"How?" said he. "Amontillado? A pipe? Impossible! And in the middle of the carnival!"

"I have my doubts," I replied; "and I was silly enough to pay the full Amontillado price without consulting you in the matter. You were not to be found, and I was fearful of losing a bargain."

"Amontillado!"

"I have my doubts."

"Amontillado!"

"And I must satisfy them."

"Amontillado!"

"As you are engaged, I am on my way to Luchresi. If any one has a critical turn it is he. He will tell me———"

"Luchresi cannot tell Amontillado from Sherry."

"And yet some fools will have it that his taste is a match for your own."

"Come, let us go."

"Whither?"

"To your vaults."

"My friend, no; I will not impose upon your good nature. I perceive you have an engagement. Luchresi————"

"I have no engagement;—come."

"My friend, no. It is not the engagement, but the severe cold with which I perceive you are afflicted. The vaults are insufferably damp. They are encrusted with nitre."

"Let us go, nevertheless. The cold is merely nothing. Amontillado! You have been imposed upon. And as for Luchresi, he cannot distinguish Sherry from Amontillado."

Thus speaking, Fortunato possessed himself of my arm; and putting on a mask of black silk and drawing a *roquelaire* closely about my person, I suffered him to hurry me to my palazzo.

There were no attendants at home; they had absconded to make merry in honor of the time. I had told them that I should not return until the morning, and had given them explicit orders not to stir from the house. These orders were sufficient, I well knew, to insure their immediate disappearance, one and all, as soon as my back was turned.

I took from their sconces two flambeaux, and giving one to Fortunato, bowed him through several suites of rooms to the archway that led into the vaults. I passed down a long and winding staircase, requesting him to be cautious as he followed. We came at length to the foot of the descent, and stood together upon the damp ground of the catacombs of the Montresors.

The gait of my friend was unsteady, and the bells upon his cap jingled as he strode.

"The pipe," he said.

"It is farther on," said I; "but observe the white web-work which gleams from these cavern walls."

He turned towards me, and looked into my eyes with two filmy orbs that distilled the rheum of intoxication.

"Nitre?" he asked at length.

"Nitre," I replied. "How long have you had that cough?"

"Ugh! ugh! ugh!—ugh! ugh! ugh!—ugh! ugh! ugh!—ugh! ugh! ugh! —ugh! ugh! ugh!"

My poor friend found it impossible to reply for many minutes.

"It is nothing," he said at last.

Come," I said, with decision, "we will go back; your health is precious. You are rich, respected, admired, beloved; you are happy, as once I was. You are a man to be missed. For me it is no matter. We will go back; you will be ill, and I cannot be responsible. Besides, there is Luchresi————"

"Enough," he said; "the cough is a mere nothing; it will not kill me. I shall not die of a cough."

"True—true," I replied; "and, indeed, I had no intentions of alarming you unnecessarily—but you should use all proper caution. A draught of this Medoc will defend us from the damps."

Here I knocked off the neck of a bottle which I drew from a long row of its fellows that lay upon the mould.

"Drink," I said, presenting him the wine.

He raised it to his lips with a leer. He paused and nodded to me familiarly, while his bells jingled.

"I drink," he said, "to the buried that repose around us."

"And I to your long life."

He again took my arm, and we proceeded.

"These vaults," he said, "are extensive."

"The Montresors," I replied, "were a great and numerous family."

"I forget your arms."

"A huge human foot d'or, in a field azure; the foot crushes a serpent rampant whose fangs are imbedded in the heel."

"And the motto?"

"Nemo me impune lacessit."[1]

"Good!" he said.

The wine sparkled in his eyes and the bells jingled. My own fancy grew warm with the Medoc. We had passed through long walls of piled skeletons, with casks and puncheons intermingling, into the inmost recesses of the catacombs. I paused again, and this time I made bold to seize Fortunato by an arm above the elbow.

"The nitre!" I said; "see, it increases. It hangs like moss upon the vaults. We are below the river's bed. The drops of moisture trickle among the bones. Come, we will go back ere it is too late. Your cough————"

"It is nothing," he said; "let us go on. But first, another draught of the Medoc."

I broke and reached him a flagon of De Grâve. He emptied it at a breath. His eyes flashed with a fierce light. He laughed and threw the bottle upwards with a gesticulation I did not understand.

I looked at him in surprise. He repeated the movement—a grotesque one.

"You do not comprehend?" he said.

"Not I," I replied.

"Then you are not of the brotherhood."

"How?"

"You are not of the masons."

"Yes, yes," I said; "yes, yes."

"You? Impossible! A mason?"

"A mason," I replied.

"A sign," he said, "a sign."

"It is this," I answered, producing from beneath the folds of my *roquelaire* a trowel.

"You jest," he exclaimed, recoiling a few paces. "But let us proceed to the Amontillado."

"Be it so," I said, replacing the tool beneath the cloak and again offering him my arm. He leaned upon it heavily. We continued our route in search of the Amontillado. We passed through a range of low arches, descended, passed on, and descending again, arrived at a deep crypt, in which the foulness of the air caused our flambeaux rather to glow than flame.

At the most remote end of the crypt there appeared another less spacious. Its walls had been lined with human remains, piled to the vault overhead, in the fashion of the great catacombs of Paris. Three sides of this interior crypt were still ornamented in this manner. From the fourth side the bones had been thrown down, and lay promiscuously upon the earth, forming at one point a mound of

---

[1]"No one attacks me without paying dearly."

some size. Within the wall thus exposed by the displacing of the bones, we perceived a still interior crypt or recess, in depth about four feet, in width three, in height six or seven. It seemed to have been constructed for no especial use within itself, but formed merely the interval between two of the colossal supports of the roof of the catacombs, and was backed by one of their circumscribing walls of solid granite.

It was in vain that Fortunato, uplifting his dull torch, endeavored to pry into the depth of the recess. Its termination the feeble light did not enable us to see.

"Proceed," I said; "herein is the Amontillado. As for Luchresi————"

"He is an ignoramus," interrupted my friend, as he stepped unsteadily forward, while I followed immediately at his heels. In an instant he had reached the extremity of the niche, and finding his progress arrested by the rock, stood stupidly bewildered. A moment more and I had fettered him to the granite. In its surface were two iron staples, distant from each other about two feet, horizontally. From one of these depended a short chain, from the other a padlock. Throwing the links about his waist, it was but the work of a few seconds to secure it. He was too much astounded to resist. Withdrawing the key I stepped back from the recess.

"Pass your hand," I said, "over the wall; you cannot help feeling the nitre. Indeed, it is *very* damp. Once more let me *implore* you to return. No? Then I must positively leave you. But I must first render you all the little attentions in my power."

"The Amontillado!" ejaculated my friend, not yet recovered from his astonishment.

"True," I replied; "the Amontillado."

As I said these words I busied myself among the pile of bones of which I have before spoken. Throwing them aside, I soon uncovered a quantity of building stone and mortar. With these materials and with the aid of my trowel, I began vigorously to wall up the entrance of the niche.

I had scarcely laid the first tier of the masonry when I discovered that the intoxication of Fortunato had in a great measure worn off. The earliest indication I had of this was a low moaning cry from the depth of the recess. It was *not* the cry of a drunken man. There was a long and obstinate silence. I laid the second tier, and the third, and the fourth; and then I heard the furious vibrations of the chain. The noise lasted for several minutes, during which, that I might hearken to it with the more satisfaction, I ceased my labors and sat down upon the bones. When at last the clanking subsided, I resumed the trowel, and finished without interruption the fifth, the sixth, and the seventh tier. The wall was now nearly upon a level with my breast. I again paused, and holding the flambeaux over the mason-work, threw a few feeble rays upon the figure within.

A succession of loud and shrill screams, bursting suddenly from the throat of the chained form, seemed to thrust me violently back. For a brief moment I hesitated, I trembled. Unsheathing my rapier, I began to grope with it about the recess; but the thought of an instant reassured me. I placed my hand upon the solid fabric of the catacombs, and felt satisfied. I reapproached the wall; I replied to the yells of him who clamoured. I re-echoed, I aided, I surpassed them in volume and in strength. I did this, and the clamourer grew still.

It was now midnight, and my task was drawing to a close. I had completed the eighth, the ninth, and the tenth tier. I had finished a portion of the last and the eleventh; there remained but a single stone to be fitted and plastered in. I struggled with its weight; I placed it partially in its destined position. But now there came from out the niche a low laugh that erected the hairs upon my head. It was succeeded by a sad voice, which I had difficulty in recognizing as that of the noble Fortunato. The voice said—

"Ha! ha! ha!—he! he ! he!—a very good joke, indeed—an excellent jest. We will have many a rich laugh about it at the palazzo—he! he! he!—over our wine—he! he! he!"

"The Amontillado!" I said.

"He! he! he!—he! he! he!—yes, the Amontillado. But is it not getting late? Will not they be awaiting us at the palazzo, the Lady Fortunato and the rest? Let us be gone."

"Yes," I said, "let us be gone."

"*For the love of God, Montresor!*"

"Yes," I said, "for the love of God."

But to these words I hearkened in vain for a reply. I grew impatient. I called aloud—

"Fortunato!"

No answer. I called again—

"Fortunato!"

No answer still. I thrust a torch through the remaining aperture and let it fall within. There came forth in return only a jingling of the bells. My heart grew sick; it was the dampness of the catacombs that made it so. I hastened to make an end of my labour. I forced the last stone into its position; I plastered it up. Against the new masonry I re-erected the old rampart of bones. For the half of a century no mortal has disturbed them. *In pace requiescat!*[2]

(1846)

---

[2] Let him rest in peace!

Kate Chopin *1851–1904*

THE AWAKENING

I

A green and yellow parrot, which hung in a cage outside the door, kept repeating over and over:

"*Allez vous-en! Allez vous-en! Sapristi!* That's all right!"

He could speak a little Spanish, and also a language which nobody understood, unless it was the mocking-bird that hung on the other side of the door, whistling his fluty notes out upon the breeze with maddening persistence.

Mr. Pontellier, unable to read his newspaper with any degree of comfort, arose with an expression and an exclamation of disgust. He walked down the gallery and across the narrow "bridges" which connected the Lebrun cottages one with the other. He had been seated before the door of the main house. The parrot and the mocking-bird were the property of Madame Lebrun, and they had the right to make all the noise they wished. Mr. Pontellier had the privilege of quitting their society when they ceased to be entertaining.

He stopped before the door of his own cottage, which was the fourth one from the main building and next to the last. Seating himself in a wicker rocker which was there, he once more applied himself to the task of reading the newspaper. The day was Sunday; the paper was a day old. The Sunday papers had not yet reached Grand Isle. He was already acquainted with the market reports, and he glanced restlessly over the editorials and bits of news which he had not had time to read before quitting New Orleans the day before.

Mr. Pontellier wore eye-glasses. He was a man of forty, of medium height and rather slender build; he stooped a little. His hair was brown and straight, parted on one side. His beard was neatly and closely trimmed.

Once in a while he withdrew his glance from the newspaper and looked about him. There was more noise than ever over at the house. The main building was called "the house," to distinguish it from the cottages. The chattering and whistling birds were still at it. Two young girls, the Farival twins, were playing a duet from "Zampa" upon the piano. Madame Lebrun was bustling in and out, giving orders in a high key to a yard-boy whenever she got inside the house, and directions in an equally high voice to a dining-room servant whenever she got outside. She was a fresh, pretty woman, clad always in white with elbow sleeves. Her starched skirts crinkled as she came and went. Farther down, before one of the cottages, a lady in black was walking demurely up and down, telling her beads. A good many persons of the *pension* had gone over to the *Chênière Caminada* in Beaudelet's lugger to hear mass. Some young people were out under the water-oaks playing croquet. Mr. Pontellier's two children were there — sturdy little fellows of four and five. A quadroon nurse followed them about with a far-away, meditative air.

Mr. Pontellier finally lit a cigar and began to smoke, letting the paper drag idly from his hand. He fixed his gaze upon a white sunshade that was advancing at snail's pace from the beach. He could see it plainly between the gaunt trunks of the water-oaks and across the stretch of yellow camomile. The gulf looked far away, melting hazily into the blue of the horizon. The sunshade continued to approach slowly. Beneath its pink-lined shelter were his wife, Mrs. Pontellier, and young Robert Lebrun. When they reached the cottage, the two seated themselves with some appearance of fatigue upon the upper step of the porch, facing each other, each leaning against a supporting post.

"What folly! to bathe at such an hour in such heat!" exclaimed Mr. Pontellier. He himself had taken a plunge at daylight. That was why the morning seemed long to him.

"You are burnt beyond recognition," he added, looking at his wife as one looks at a valuable piece of personal property which has suffered some damage. She held up her hands, strong, shapely hands, and surveyed them critically, drawing up her lawn sleeves above the wrists. Looking at them reminded her of her rings, which she had given to her husband before leaving for the beach. She silently reached out to him, and he, understanding, took the rings from his vest pocket and dropped them into her open palm. She slipped them upon her fingers; then clasping her knees, she looked across at Robert and began to laugh. The rings sparkled upon her fingers. He sent back an answering smile.

"What is it?" asked Pontellier, looking lazily and amused from one to the other. It was some utter nonsense; some adventure out there in the water, and they both tried to relate it at once. It did not seem half so amusing when told. They realized this, and so did Mr. Pontellier. He yawned and stretched himself. Then he got up, saying he had half a mind to go over to Klein's hotel and play a game of billiards.

"Come go along, Lebrun," he proposed to Robert. But Robert admitted quite frankly that he preferred to stay where he was and talk to Mrs. Pontellier.

"Well, send him about his business when he bores you, Edna," instructed her husband as he prepared to leave.

"Here, take the umbrella," she exclaimed, holding it out to him. He accepted the sunshade, and lifting it over his head descended the steps and walked away.

"Coming back to dinner?" his wife called after him. He halted a moment and shrugged his shoulders. He felt in his vest pocket; there was a ten-dollar bill there. He did not know; perhaps he would return for the early dinner and perhaps he would not. It all depended upon the company which he found over at Klein's and the size of "the game." He did not say this, but she understood it, and laughed, nodding good-by to him.

Both children wanted to follow their father when they saw him starting out. He kissed them and promised to bring them back bonbons and peanuts.

II

Mrs. Pontellier's eyes were quick and bright; they were a yellowish brown, about the color of her hair. She had a way of turning them swiftly upon an object and holding them there as if lost in some inward maze of contemplation or thought.

Her eyebrows were a shade darker than her hair. They were thick and almost horizontal, emphasizing the depth of her eyes. She was rather handsome than beautiful. Her face was captivating by reason of a certain frankness of expression and a contradictory subtle play of features. Her manner was engaging.

Robert rolled a cigarette. He smoked cigarettes because he could not afford cigars, he said. He had a cigar in his pocket which Mr. Pontellier had presented him with, and he was saving it for his after-dinner smoke.

This seemed quite proper and natural on his part. In coloring he was not unlike his companion. A clean-shaved face made the resemblance more pronounced than it would otherwise have been. There rested no shadow of care upon his open countenance. His eyes gathered in and reflected the light and languor of the summer day.

Mrs. Pontellier reached over for a palm-leaf fan that lay on the porch and began to fan herself, while Robert sent between his lips light puffs from his cigarette. They chatted incessantly: about the things around them; their amusing adventure out in the water — it had again assumed its entertaining aspect; about the wind, the trees, the people who had gone to the *Chênière;* about the children playing croquet under the oaks, and the Farival twins, who were now performing the overture to "The Poet and the Peasant."

Robert talked a good deal about himself. He was very young, and did not know any better. Mrs. Pontellier talked a little about herself for the same reason. Each was interested in what the other said. Robert spoke of his intention to go to Mexico in the autumn, where fortune awaited him. He was always intending to go to Mexico, but some way never got there. Meanwhile he held on to his modest position in a mercantile house in New Orleans, where an equal familiarity with English, French and Spanish gave him no small value as a clerk and correspondent.

He was spending his summer vacation, as he always did, with his mother at Grand Isle. In former times, before Robert could remember, "the house" had been a summer luxury of the Lebruns. Now, flanked by its dozen or more cottages, which were always filled with exclusive visitors from the *"Quartier Français,"* it enabled Madame Lebrun to maintain the easy and comfortable existence which appeared to be her birthright.

Mrs. Pontellier talked about her father's Mississippi plantation and her girlhood home in the old Kentucky blue-grass country. She was an American woman, with a small infusion of French which seemed to have been lost in dilution. She read a letter from her sister, who was away in the East, and who had engaged herself to be married. Robert was interested, and wanted to know what manner of girls the sisters were, what the father was like, and how long the mother had been dead.

When Mrs. Pontellier folded the letter it was time for her to dress for the early dinner.

"I see Léonce isn't coming back," she said, with a glance in the direction whence her husband had disappeared. Robert supposed he was not, as there were a good many New Orleans club men over at Klein's.

When Mrs. Pontellier left him to enter her room, the young man descended the steps and strolled over toward the croquet players, where, during the half-hour before dinner, he amused himself with the little Pontellier children, who were very fond of him.

III

It was eleven o'clock that night when Mr. Pontellier returned from Klein's hotel. He was in an excellent humor, in high spirits, and very talkative. His entrance awoke his wife, who was in bed and fast asleep when he came in. He talked to her while he undressed, telling her anecdotes and bits of news and gossip that he had gathered during the day. From his trousers pockets he took a fistful of crumpled bank notes and a good deal of silver coin, which he piled on the bureau indiscriminately with keys, knife, handkerchief, and whatever else happened to be in his pockets. She was overcome with sleep, and answered him with little half utterances.

He thought it very discouraging that his wife, who was the sole object of his existence, evinced so little interest in things which concerned him, and valued so little his conversation.

Mr. Pontellier had forgotten the bonbons and peanuts for the boys. Notwithstanding he loved them very much, and went into the adjoining room where they slept to take a look at them and make sure that they were resting comfortably. The result of his investigation was far from satisfactory. He turned and shifted the youngsters about in bed. One of them began to kick and talk about a basket full of crabs.

Mr. Pontellier returned to his wife with the information that Raoul had a high fever and needed looking after. Then he lit a cigar and went and sat near the open door to smoke it.

Mrs. Pontellier was quite sure Raoul had no fever. He had gone to bed perfectly well, she said, and nothing had ailed him all day. Mr. Pontellier was too well acquainted with fever symptoms to be mistaken. He assured her the child was consuming at that moment in the next room.

He reproached his wife with her inattention, her habitual neglect of the children. If it was not a mother's place to look after children, whose on earth was it? He himself had his hands full with his brokerage business. He could not be in two places at once; making a living for his family on the street, and staying at home to see that no harm befell them. He talked in a monotonous, insistent way.

Mrs. Pontellier sprang out of bed and went into the next room. She soon came back and sat on the edge of the bed, leaning her head down on the pillow. She said nothing, and refused to answer her husband when he questioned her. When his cigar was smoked out he went to bed, and in half a minute he was fast asleep.

Mrs. Pontellier was by that time thoroughly awake. She began to cry a little, and wiped her eyes on the sleeve of her *peignoir*. Blowing out the candle, which her husband had left burning, she slipped her bare feet into a pair of satin *mules* at the foot of the bed and went out on the porch, where she sat down in the wicker chair and began to rock gently to and fro.

It was then past midnight. The cottages were all dark. A single faint light gleamed out from the hallway of the house. There was no sound abroad except the hooting of an old owl in the top of a water-oak, and the everlasting voice of the sea, that was not uplifted at that soft hour. It broke like a mournful lullaby upon the night.

The tears came so fast to Mrs. Pontellier's eyes that the damp sleeve of her *peignoir* no longer served to dry them. She was holding the back of her chair with one hand; her loose sleeve had slipped almost to the shoulder of her uplifted arm. Turning, she thrust her face, steaming and wet, into the bend of her arm, and she went on crying there, not caring any longer to dry her face, her eyes, her arms. She could not have told why she was crying. Such experiences as the foregoing were not uncommon in her married life. They seemed never before to have weighed much against the abundance of her husband's kindness and a uniform devotion which had come to be tacit and self-understood.

An indescribable oppression, which seemed to generate in some unfamiliar part of her consciousness, filled her whole being with a vague anguish. It was like a shadow, like a mist passing across her soul's summer day. It was strange and unfamiliar; it was a mood. She did not sit there inwardly upbraiding her husband, lamenting at Fate, which had directed her footsteps to the path which they had taken. She was just having a good cry all to herself. The mosquitoes made merry over her, biting her firm, round arms and nipping at her bare insteps.

The little stinging, buzzing imps succeeded in dispelling a mood which might have held her there in the darkness half a night longer.

The following morning Mr. Pontellier was up in good time to take the rockaway which was to convey him to the steamer at the wharf. He was returning to the city to his business, and they would not see him again at the Island till the coming Saturday. He had regained his composure, which seemed to have been somewhat impaired the night before. He was eager to be gone, as he looked forward to a lively week in Carondelet Street.

Mr. Pontellier gave his wife half of the money which he had brought away from Klein's hotel the evening before. She liked money as well as most women, and accepted it with no little satisfaction.

"It will buy a handsome wedding present for Sister Janet!" she exclaimed, smoothing out the bills as she counted them one by one.

"Oh! we'll treat Sister Janet better than that, my dear," he laughed, as he prepared to kiss her good-by.

The boys were tumbling about, clinging to his legs, imploring that numerous things be brought back to them. Mr. Pontellier was a great favorite, and ladies, men, children, even nurses, were always on hand to say good-by to him. His wife stood smiling and waving, the boys shouting, as he disappeared in the old rockaway down the sandy road.

A few days later a box arrived for Mrs. Pontellier from New Orleans. It was from her husband. It was filled with *friandises*, with luscious and toothsome bits—the finest of fruits, *patés*, a rare bottle or two, delicious syrups, and bonbons in abundance.

Mrs. Pontellier was always very generous with the contents of such a box; she was quite used to receiving them when away from home. The *patés* and fruit were brought to the dining-room; the bonbons were passed around. And the ladies, selecting with dainty and discriminating fingers and a little greedily, all declared that Mr. Pontellier was the best husband in the world. Mrs. Pontellier was forced to admit that she knew of none better.

IV

It would have been a difficult matter for Mr. Pontellier to define to his own satisfaction or any one else's wherein his wife failed in her duty toward their children. It was something which he felt rather than perceived, and he never voiced the feeling without subsequent regret and ample atonement.

If one of the little Pontellier boys took a tumble whilst at play, he was not apt to rush crying to his mother's arms for comfort; he would more likely pick himself up, wipe the water out of his eyes and the sand out of his mouth, and go on playing. Tots as they were, they pulled together and stood their ground in childish battles with doubled fists and uplifted voices, which usually prevailed against the other brother-tots. The quadroon nurse was looked upon as a huge encumbrance, only good to button up waists and panties and to brush and part hair; since it seemed to be a law of society that hair must be parted and brushed.

In short, Mrs. Pontellier was not a mother-woman. The mother-women seemed to prevail that summer at Grand Isle. It was easy to know them, fluttering about with extended, protecting wings when any harm, real or imaginary, threatened their precious brood. They were women who idolized their children, worshiped their husbands, and esteemed it a holy privilege to efface themselves as individuals and grow wings as ministering angels.

Many of them were delicious in the rôle; one of them was the embodiment of every womanly grace and charm. If her husband did not adore her, he was a brute, deserving of death by slow torture. Her name was Adèle Ratignolle. There are no words to describe her save the old ones that have served so often to picture the bygone heroine of romance and the fair lady of our dreams. There was nothing subtle or hidden about her charms; her beauty was all there, flaming and apparent: the spungold hair that comb nor confining pin could restrain; the blue eyes that were like nothing but sapphires; two lips that pouted, that were so red one could only think of cherries or some other delicious crimson fruit in looking at them. She was growing a little stout, but it did not seem to detract an iota from the grace of every step, pose, gesture. One would not have wanted her white neck a mite less full or her beautiful arms more slender. Never were hands more exquisite than hers, and it was a joy to look at them when she threaded her needle or adjusted her gold thimble to her taper middle finger as she sewed away on the little night-drawers or fashioned a bodice or a bib.

Madame Ratignolle was very fond of Mrs. Pontellier, and often she took her sewing and went over to sit with her in the afternoons. She was sitting there the afternoon of the day the box arrived from New Orleans. She had possession of the rocker, and she was busily engaged in sewing upon a diminutive pair of night-drawers.

She had brought the pattern of the drawers for Mrs. Pontellier to cut out — a marvel of construction, fashioned to enclose a baby's body so effectually that only two small eyes might look out from the garment, like an Eskimo's. They were designed for winter wear, when treacherous drafts came down chimneys and insidious currents of deadly cold found their way through key-holes.

Mrs. Pontellier's mind was quite at rest concerning the present material needs of her children, and she could not see the use of anticipating and making winter night garments the subject of her summer meditations. But she did not want to appear unamiable and uninterested, so she had brought forth newspapers, which she spread upon the floor of the gallery, and under Madame Ratignolle's directions she had cut a pattern of the impervious garment.

Robert was there, seated as he had been the Sunday before, and Mrs. Pontellier also occupied her former position on the upper step, leaning listlessly against the post. Beside her was a box of bonbons, which she held out at intervals to Madame Ratignolle.

That lady seemed at a loss to make a selection, but finally settled upon a stick of nougat, wondering if it were not too rich; whether it could possibly hurt her. Madame Ratignolle had been married seven years. About every two years she had a baby. At that time she had three babies, and was beginning to think of a fourth one. She was always talking about her "condition." Her "condition" was in no way apparent, and no one would have known a thing about it but for her persistence in making it the subject of conversation.

Robert started to reassure her, asserting that he had known a lady who had subsisted upon nougat during the entire — but seeing the color mount into Mrs. Pontellier's face he checked himself and changed the subject.

Mrs. Pontellier, though she had married a Creole, was not thoroughly at home in the society of Creoles; never before had she been thrown so intimately among them. There were only Creoles that summer at Lebrun's. They all knew each other, and felt like one large family, among whom existed the most amicable relations. A characteristic which distinguished them and which impressed Mrs. Pontellier most forcibly was their entire absence of prudery. Their freedom of expression was at first incomprehensible to her, though she had no difficulty in reconciling it with a lofty chastity which in the Creole woman seems to be inborn and unmistakable.

Never would Edna Pontellier forget the shock with which she heard Madame Ratignolle relating to old Monsieur Farival the harrowing story of one of her *accouchements*, withholding no intimate detail. She was growing accustomed to like shocks, but she could not keep the mounting color back from her cheeks. Oftener than once her coming had interrupted the droll story with which Robert was entertaining some amused group of married women.

A book had gone the rounds of the *pension*. When it came her turn to read it, she did so with profound astonishment. She felt moved to read the book in secret and solitude, though none of the others had done so — to hide it from view at the sound of approaching footsteps. It was openly criticized and freely discussed at table. Mrs. Pontellier gave over being astonished, and concluded that wonders would never cease.

V

They formed a congenial group sitting there that summer afternoon — Madame Ratignolle sewing away, often stopping to relate a story or incident with much expressive gesture of her perfect hands; Robert and Mrs. Pontellier sitting idle, exchanging occasional words, glances or smiles which indicated a certain advanced stage of intimacy and *camaraderie*.

He had lived in her shadow during the past month. No one thought anything of it. Many had predicted that Robert would devote himself to Mrs. Pontellier when he arrived. Since the age of fifteen, which was eleven years before, Robert each summer at Grand Isle had constituted himself the devoted attendant of some fair dame or damsel. Sometimes it was a young girl, again a widow; but as often as not it was some interesting married woman.

For two consecutive seasons he lived in the sunlight of Mademoiselle Duvigné's presence. But she died between summers; then Robert posed as an inconsolable, prostrating himself at the feet of Madame Ratignolle for whatever crumbs of sympathy and comfort she might be pleased to vouchsafe.

Mrs. Pontellier liked to sit and gaze at her fair companion as she might look upon a faultless Madonna.

"Could any one fathom the cruelty beneath that fair exterior?" murmured Robert. "She knew that I adored her once, and she let me adore her. It was 'Robert, come; go; stand up; sit down; do this; do that; see if the baby sleeps; my thimble, please, that I left God knows where. Come and read Daudet to me while I sew.'"

"*Par example!* I never had to ask. You were always there under my feet, like a troublesome cat."

"You mean like an adoring dog. And just as soon as Ratignolle appeared on the scene, then it *was* like a dog. '*Passez! Adieu! Allez vous-en!*'"

"Perhaps I feared to make Alphonse jealous," she interjoined, with excessive naïveté. That made them all laugh. The right hand jealous of the left! The heart jealous of the soul! But for that matter, the Creole husband is never jealous; with him the gangrene passion is one which has become dwarfed by disuse.

Meanwhile Robert, addressing Mrs. Pontellier, continued to tell of his one time hopeless passion for Madame Ratignolle; of sleepless nights, of consuming flames till the very sea sizzled when he took his daily plunge. While the lady at the needle kept up a little running, contemptuous comment:

"*Blagueur—farceur—gros bête, va!*"

He never assumed this serio-comic tone when alone with Mrs. Pontellier. She never knew precisely what to make of it; at that moment it was impossible for her to guess how much of it was jest and what proportion was earnest. It was understood that he had often spoken words of love to Madame Ratignolle, without any thought of being taken seriously. Mrs. Pontellier was glad he had not assumed a similar rôle toward herself. It would have been unacceptable and annoying.

Mrs. Pontellier had brought her sketching materials, which she sometimes dabbled with in an unprofessional way. She liked the dabbling. She felt in it satisfaction of a kind which no other employment afforded her.

She had long wished to try herself on Madame Ratignolle. Never had that lady seemed a more tempting subject than at that moment, seated there like some sensuous Madonna, with the gleam of the fading day enriching her splendid color.

Robert crossed over and seated himself upon the step below Mrs. Pontellier, that he might watch her work. She handled her brushes with a certain ease and freedom which came, not from long and close acquaintance with them, but from a natural aptitude. Robert followed her work with close attention, giving forth little ejaculatory expressions of appreciation in French, which he addressed to Madame Ratignolle.

"*Mais ce n'est pas mal! Elle s'y connait, elle a de la force, oui.*"

During his oblivious attention he once quietly rested his head against Mrs. Pontellier's arm. As gently she repulsed him. Once again he repeated the offense. She could not but believe it to be thoughtlessness on his part; yet that was no reason she should submit to it. She did not remonstrate, except again to repulse him quietly but firmly. He offered no apology.

The picture completed bore no resemblance to Madame Ratignolle. She was greatly disappointed to find that it did not look like her. But it was a fair enough piece of work, and in many respects satisfying.

Mrs. Pontellier evidently did not think so. After surveying the sketch critically she drew a broad smudge of paint across its surface, and crumpled the paper between her hands.

The youngsters came tumbling up the steps, the quadroon following at the respectful distance which they required her to observe. Mrs. Pontellier made them carry her paints and things into the house. She sought to detain them for a little talk and some pleasantry. But they were greatly in earnest. They had only come to investigate the contents of the bonbon box. They accepted without murmuring what she chose to give them, each holding out two chubby hands scoop-like, in the vain hope that they might be filled; and then away they went.

The sun was low in the west, and the breeze soft and languorous that came up from the south, charged with the seductive odor of the sea. Children, freshly befurbelowed, were gathering for their games under the oaks. Their voices were high and penetrating.

Madame Ratignolle folded her sewing, placing thimble, scissors and thread all neatly together in the roll, which she pinned securely. She complained of faintness. Mrs. Pontellier flew for the cologne water and a fan. She bathed Madame Ratignolle's face with cologne, while Robert plied the fan with unnecessary vigor.

The spell was soon over, and Mrs. Pontellier could not help wondering if there were not a little imagination responsible for its origin, for the rose tint had never faded from her friend's face.

She stood watching the fair woman walk down the long line of galleries with the grace and majesty which queens are sometimes supposed to possess. Her little ones ran to meet her. Two of them clung about her white skirts, the third she took from its nurse and with a thousand endearments bore it along in her own fond, encircling arms. Though, as everybody well knew, the doctor had forbidden her to lift so much as a pin!

"Are you going bathing?" asked Robert of Mrs. Pontellier. It was not so much a question as a reminder.

"Oh, no," she answered, with a tone of indecision. "I'm tired; I think not." Her glance wandered from his face away toward the Gulf, whose sonorous murmur reached her like a loving but imperative entreaty.

"Oh, come!" he insisted. "You mustn't miss your bath. Come on. The water must be delicious; it will not hurt you. Come."

He reached up for her big, rough straw hat that hung on a peg outside the door, and put it on her head. They descended the steps, and walked away together toward the beach. The sun was low in the west and the breeze was soft and warm.

VI

Edna Pontellier could not have told why, wishing to go to the beach with Robert, she should in the first place have declined, and in the second place have followed in obedience to one of the two contradictory impulses which impelled her.

A certain light was beginning to dawn dimly within her, — the light which, showing the way, forbids it.

At that early period it served but to bewilder her. It moved her to dreams, to thoughtfulness, to the shadowy anguish which had overcome her the midnight when she had abandoned herself to tears.

In short, Mrs. Pontellier was beginning to realize her position in the universe as a human being, and to recognize her relations as an individual to the world within and about her. This may seem like a ponderous weight of wisdom to descend upon the soul of a young woman of twenty-eight—perhaps more wisdom than the Holy Ghost is usually pleased to vouchsafe to any woman.

But the beginning of things, of a world especially, is necessarily vague, tangled, chaotic, and exceedingly disturbing. How few of us ever emerge from such beginning! How many souls perish in its tumult!

The voice of the sea is seductive; never ceasing, whispering, clamoring, murmuring, inviting the soul to wander for a spell in abysses of solitude; to lose itself in mazes of inward contemplation.

The voice of the sea speaks to the soul. The touch of the sea is sensuous, enfolding the body in its soft, close embrace.

VII

Mrs. Pontellier was not a woman given to confidences, a characteristic hitherto contrary to her nature. Even as a child she had lived her own small life all within herself. At a very early period she had apprehended instinctively the dual life—that outward existence which conforms, the inward life which questions.

That summer at Grand Isle she began to loosen a little the mantle of reserve that had always enveloped her. There may have been—there must have been—influences, both subtle and apparent, working in their several ways to induce her to do this; but the most obvious was the influence of Adèle Ratignolle. The excessive physical charm of the Creole had first attracted her, for Edna had a sensuous susceptibility to beauty. Then the candor of the woman's whole existence, which every one might read, and which formed so striking a contrast to her own habitual reserve—this might have furnished a link. Who can tell what metals the gods use in forging the subtle bond which we call sympathy, which we might as well call love.

The two women went away one morning to the beach together, arm in arm, under the huge white sunshade. Edna had prevailed upon Madame Ratignolle to leave the children behind, though she could not induce her to relinquish a diminutive roll of needlework, which Adèle begged to be allowed to slip into the depths of her pocket. In some unaccountable way they had escaped from Robert.

The walk to the beach was no inconsiderable one, consisting as it did of a long, sandy path, upon which a sporadic and tangled growth that bordered it on either side made frequent and unexpected inroads. There were acres of yellow camomile reaching out on either hand. Further away still, vegetable gardens abounded, with frequent small plantations of orange or lemon trees intervening. The dark green clusters glistened from afar in the sun.

The women were both of goodly height, Madame Ratignolle possessing the more feminine and matronly figure. The charm of Edna Pontellier's physique stole insensibly upon you. The lines of her body were long, clean and symmetrical; it was a body which occasionally fell into splendid poses; there was no suggestion of the trim, stereotyped fashion-plate about it. A casual and indiscriminating observer, in passing, might not cast a second glance upon the figure. But with more feeling and discernment he would have recognized the noble beauty of its modeling, and the graceful severity of poise and movement, which made Edna Pontellier different from the crowd.

She wore a cool muslin that morning—white, with a waving vertical line of brown running through it; also a white linen collar and the big straw hat which she had taken from the peg outside the door. The hat rested any way on her yellow-brown hair, that waved a little, was heavy, and clung close to her head.

Madame Ratignolle, more careful of her complexion, had twined a gauze veil about her head. She wore doeskin gloves, with gauntlets that protected her wrists. She was dressed in pure white, with a fluffiness of ruffles that became her. The draperies and fluttering things which she wore suited her rich, luxuriant beauty as a greater severity of line could not have done.

There were a number of bath-houses along the beach, of rough but solid construction, built with small, protecting galleries facing the water. Each house consisted of two compartments, and each family at Lebrun's possessed a compartment for itself, fitted out with all the essential paraphernalia of the bath and whatever other conveniences the owners might desire. The two women had no intention of bathing; they had just strolled down to the beach for a walk and to be alone and near the water. The Pontellier and Ratignolle compartments adjoined one another under the same roof.

Mrs. Pontellier had brought down her key through force of habit. Unlocking the door of her bath-room she went inside, and soon emerged, bringing a rug, which she spread upon the floor of the gallery, and two huge hair pillows covered with crash, which she placed against the front of the building.

The two seated themselves there in the shade of the porch, side by side, with their backs against the pillows and their feet extended. Madame Ratignolle removed her veil, wiped her face with a rather delicate handkerchief, and fanned herself with the fan which she always carried suspended somewhere about her person by a long, narrow ribbon. Edna removed her collar and opened her dress at the throat. She took the fan from Madame Ratignolle and began to fan both herself and her companion. It was very warm, and for a while they did nothing but exchange remarks about the heat, the sun, the glare. But there was a breeze blowing, a choppy, stiff wind that whipped the water into froth. It fluttered the skirts of the two women and kept them for a while engaged in adjusting, readjusting, tucking in, securing hair-pins and hat-pins. A few persons were sporting some distance away in the water. The beach was very still of human sound at that hour. The lady in black was reading her morning devotions on the porch of a neighboring bath-house. Two young lovers were exchanging their hearts' yearnings beneath the children's tent, which they had found unoccupied.

Edna Pontellier, casting her eyes about, had finally kept them at rest upon the sea. The day was clear and carried the gaze out as far as the blue sky went; there were a few white clouds suspended idly over the horizon. A lateen sail was visible in the direction of Cat Island, and others to the south seemed almost motionless in the far distance.

"Of whom—of what are you thinking?" asked Adèle of her companion, whose countenance she had been watching with a little amused attention, arrested by the absorbed expression which seemed to have seized and fixed every feature into a statuesque repose.

"Nothing," returned Mrs. Pontellier, with a start, adding at once: "How stupid! But it seems to me it is the reply we make instinctively to such a question. Let me see," she went on, throwing back her head and narrowing her fine eyes till they shone like two vivid points of light. "Let me see. I was really not conscious of thinking of anything; but perhaps I can retrace my thoughts."

"Oh! never mind!" laughed Madame Ratignolle. "I am not quite so exacting. I will let you off this time. It is really too hot to think, especially to think about thinking."

"But for the fun of it," persisted Edna. "First of all, the sight of the water stretching so far away, those motionless sails against the blue sky, made a delicious picture that I just wanted to sit and look at. The hot wind beating in my face made me think — without any connection that I can trace — of a summer day in Kentucky, of a meadow that seemed as big as the ocean to the very little girl walking through the grass, which was higher than her waist. She threw out her arms as if swimming when she walked, beating the tall grass as one strikes out in the water. Oh, I see the connection now!"

"Where were you going that day in Kentucky, walking through the grass?"

"I don't remember now. I was just walking diagonally across a big field. My sun-bonnet obstructed the view. I could see only the stretch of green before me, and I felt as if I must walk on forever, without coming to the end of it. I don't remember whether I was frightened or pleased. I must have been entertained.

"Likely as not it was Sunday," she laughed; "and I was running away from prayers, from the Presbyterian service, read in a spirit of gloom by my father that chills me yet to think of."

"And have you been running away from prayer ever since, *ma chère?*" asked Madame Ratignolle, amused.

"No! oh, no!" Edna hastened to say. "I was a little unthinking child in those days, just following a misleading impulse without question. On the contrary, during one period of my life religion took a firm hold upon me; after I was twelve and until — until — why, I suppose until now, though I never thought much about it — just driven along by habit. But do you know," she broke off, turning her quick eyes upon Madame Ratignolle and leaning forward a little so as to bring her face quite close to that of her companion, "sometimes I feel this summer as if I were walking through the green meadow again; idly, aimlessly, unthinking and unguided."

Madame Ratignolle laid her hand over that of Mrs. Pontellier, which was near her. Seeing that the hand was not withdrawn, she clasped it firmly and warmly. She even stroked it a little fondly, with the other hand, murmuring in an undertone, *"Pauvre chérie."*

The action was at first a little confusing to Edna, but she soon lent herself readily to the Creole's gentle caress. She was not accustomed to an outward and spoken expression of affection, either in herself or in others. She and her younger sister, Janet, had quarreled a good deal through force of unfortunate habit. Her older sister, Margaret, was matronly and dignified, probably from having assumed matronly and housewifely responsibilities too early in life, their mother having died when they were quite young. Margaret was not effusive: she was practical. Edna had had an occasional girl friend, but whether accidentally or not, they seemed to have been all of one type — the self-contained. She never realized that the reserve of her own character had much, perhaps everything, to do with this. Her most intimate friend at school had been one of rather exceptional intellectual gifts, who wrote fine-sounding essays, which Edna admired and strove to imitate; and with her she talked and glowed over the English classics, and sometimes held religious and political controversies.

Edna often wondered at one propensity which sometimes had inwardly disturbed her without causing any outward show or manifestation on her part. At a very early age — perhaps it was when she traversed the ocean of waving grass —

she remembered that she had been passionately enamored of a dignified and sad-eyed cavalry officer who visited her father in Kentucky. She could not leave his presence when he was there, nor remove her eyes from his face, which was something like Napoleon's, with a lock of black hair falling across the forehead. But the cavalry officer melted imperceptibly out of her existence.

At another time her affections were deeply engaged by a young gentleman who visited a lady on a neighboring plantation. It was after they went to Mississippi to live. The young man was engaged to be married to the young lady, and they sometimes called upon Margaret, driving over of afternoons in a buggy. Edna was a little miss, just merging into her teens; and the realization that she herself was nothing, nothing, nothing to the engaged young man was a bitter affliction to her. But he, too, went the way of dreams.

She was a grown young woman when she was overtaken by what she supposed to be the climax of her fate. It was when the face and figure of a great tragedian began to haunt her imagination and stir her senses. The persistence of the infatuation lent it an aspect of genuineness. The hopelessness of it colored it with the lofty tones of a great passion.

The picture of the tragedian stood enframed upon her desk. Any one may possess the portrait of a tragedian without exciting suspicion or comment. (This was a sinister reflection which she cherished.) In the presence of others she expressed admiration for his exalted gifts, as she handed the photograph around and dwelt upon the fidelity of the likeness. When alone she sometimes picked it up and kissed the cold glass passionately.

Her marriage to Léonce Pontellier was purely an accident, in this respect resembling many other marriages which masquerade as the decrees of Fate. It was in the midst of her secret great passion that she met him. He fell in love, as men are in the habit of doing, and pressed his suit with an earnestness and an ardor which left nothing to be desired. He pleased her; his absolute devotion flattered her. She fancied there was a sympathy of thought and taste between them, in which fancy she was mistaken. Add to this the violent opposition of her father and her sister Margaret to her marriage with a Catholic, and we need seek no further for the motives which led her to accept Monsieur Pontellier for her husband.

The acme of bliss, which would have been a marriage with the tragedian, was not for her in this world. As the devoted wife of a man who worshiped her, she felt she would take her place with a certain dignity in the world of reality, closing the portals forever behind her upon the realm of romance and dreams.

But it was not long before the tragedian had gone to join the cavalry officer and the engaged young man and a few others; and Edna found herself face to face with the realities. She grew fond of her husband, realizing with some unaccountable satisfaction that no trace of passion or excessive and fictitious warmth colored her affection, thereby threatening its dissolution.

She was fond of her children in an uneven, impulsive way. She would sometimes gather them passionately to her heart; she would sometimes forget them. The year before they had spent part of the summer with their grandmother Pontellier in Iberville. Feeling secure regarding their happiness and welfare, she did not miss them except with an occasional intense longing. Their absence was a sort of relief, though she did not admit this, even to herself. It seemed to free her of a responsibility which she had blindly assumed and for which Fate had not fitted her.

Edna did not reveal so much as all this to Madame Ratignolle that summer day when they sat with faces turned to the sea. But a good part of it escaped her. She had put her head down on Madame Ratignolle's shoulder. She was flushed and felt intoxicated with the sound of her own voice and the unaccustomed taste of candor. It muddled her like wine, or like a first breath of freedom.

There was the sound of approaching voices. It was Robert, surrounded by a troop of children, searching for them. The two little Pontelliers were with him, and he carried Madame Ratignolle's little girl in his arms. There were other children beside, and two nurse-maids followed, looking disagreeable and resigned.

The women at once rose and began to shake out their draperies and relax their muscles. Mrs. Pontellier threw the cushions and rug into the bath-house. The children all scampered off to the awning, and they stood there in a line, gazing upon the intruding lovers, still exchanging their vows and sighs. The lovers got up, with only a silent protest, and walked slowly away somewhere else.

The children possessed themselves of the tent, and Mrs. Pontellier went over to join them.

Madame Ratignolle begged Robert to accompany her to the house; she complained of cramp in her limbs and stiffness of the joints. She leaned draggingly upon his arm as they walked.

VIII

"Do me a favor, Robert," spoke the pretty woman at his side, almost as soon as she and Robert had started on their slow, homeward way. She looked up in his face, leaning on his arm beneath the encircling shadow of the umbrella which he had lifted.

"Granted; as many as you like," he returned, glancing down into her eyes that were full of thoughtfulness and some speculation.

"I only ask for one; let Mrs. Pontellier alone."

"*Tiens!*" he exclaimed, with a sudden, boyish laugh. "*Voilá que Madame Ratignolle est jalouse!*"

"Nonsense! I'm in earnest; I mean what I say. Let Mrs. Pontellier alone."

"Why?" he asked; himself growing serious at his companion's solicitation.

"She is not one of us; she is not like us. She might make the unfortunate blunder of taking you seriously."

His face flushed with annoyance, and taking off his soft hat he began to beat it impatiently against his leg as he walked. "Why shouldn't she take me seriously?" he demanded sharply. "Am I a comedian, a clown, a jack-in-the-box? Why shouldn't she? You Creoles! I have no patience with you! Am I always to be regarded as a feature of an amusing programme? I hope Mrs. Pontellier does take me seriously. I hope she has discernment enough to find in me something besides the *blagueur*. If I thought there was any doubt—"

"Oh, enough, Robert!" she broke into his heated outburst. "You are not thinking of what you are saying. You speak with about as little reflection as we might expect from one of those children down there playing in the sand. If your attentions to any married women here were ever offered with any intention of being convincing, you would not be the gentleman we all know you to be, and you would be unfit to associate with the wives and daughters of the people who trust you."

Madame Ratignolle had spoken what she believed to be the law and the gospel. The young man shrugged his shoulders impatiently.

"Oh! well! That isn't it," slamming his hat down vehemently upon his head. "You ought to feel that such things are not flattering to say to a fellow."

"Should our whole intercourse consist of an exchange of compliments? *Ma foi!*"

"It isn't pleasant to have a woman tell you—" he went on, unheedingly, but breaking off suddenly: "Now if I were like Arobin—you remember Alcée Arobin and that story of the consul's wife at Biloxi?" And he related the story of Alcée Arobin and the consul's wife; and another about the tenor of the French Opera, who received letters which should never have been written; and still other stories, grave and gay, till Mrs. Pontellier and her possible propensity for taking young men seriously was apparently forgotten.

Madame Ratignolle, when they had regained her cottage, went in to take the hour's rest which she considered helpful. Before leaving her, Robert begged her pardon for the impatience—he called it rudeness—with which he had received her well-meant caution.

"You made one mistake, Adèle," he said, with a light smile; "there is no earthly possibility of Mrs. Pontellier ever taking me seriously. You should have warned me against taking myself seriously. Your advice might then have carried some weight and given me subject for some reflection. *Au revoir*. But you look tired," he added, solicitously. "Would you like a cup of bouillon? Shall I stir you a toddy? Let me mix you a toddy with a drop of Angostura."

She acceded to the suggestion of bouillon, which was grateful and acceptable. He went himself to the kitchen, which was a building apart from the cottages and lying to the rear of the house. And he himself brought her the golden-brown bouillon, in a dainty Sèvres cup, with a flaky cracker or two on the saucer.

She thrust a bare, white arm from the curtain which shielded her open door, and received the cup from his hands. She told him he was a *bon garçon* and she meant it. Robert thanked her and turned away toward "the house."

The lovers were just entering the grounds of the *pension*. They were leaning toward each other as the water-oaks bent from the sea. There was not a particle of earth beneath their feet. Their heads might have been turned upside-down, so absolutely did they tread upon blue ether. The lady in black, creeping behind them, looked a trifle paler and more jaded than usual. There was no sign of Mrs. Pontellier and the children. Robert scanned the distance for any such apparition. They would doubtless remain away till the dinner hour. The young man ascended to his mother's room. It was situated at the top of the house, made up of odd angles and a queer, sloping ceiling. Two broad dormer windows looked out toward the Gulf, and as far across it as a man's eye might reach. The furnishings of the room were light, cool, and practical.

Madame Lebrun was busily engaged at the sewing-machine. A little black girl sat on the floor, and with her hands worked the treadle of the machine. The Creole woman does not take any chances which may be avoided of imperiling her health.

Robert went over and seated himself on the broad sill of one of the dormer windows. He took a book from his pocket and began energetically to read it, judging by the precision and frequency with which he turned the leaves. The sewing-machine made a resounding clatter in the room; it was of a ponderous, by-gone make. In the lulls, Robert and his mother exchanged bits of desultory conversation.

"Where is Mrs. Pontellier?"

"Down at the beach with the children."

"I promised to lend her the Goncourt. Don't forget to take it down when you go; it's there on the bookshelf over the small table." Clatter, clatter, clatter, bang! for the next five or eight minutes.

"Where is Victor going with the rockaway?"

"The rockaway? Victor?"

"Yes; down there in front. He seems to be getting ready to drive away somewhere."

"Call him." Clatter, clatter!

Robert uttered a shrill, piercing whistle which might have been heard back at the wharf.

"He won't look up."

Madame Lebrun flew to the window. She called "Victor!" She waved a handkerchief and called again. The young fellow below got into the vehicle and started the horse off at a gallop.

Madame Lebrun went back to the machine, crimson with annoyance. Victor was the younger son and brother—a *tête montée*, with a temper which invited violence and a will which no ax could break.

"Whenever you say the word I'm ready to thrash any amount of reason into him that he's able to hold."

"If your father had only lived!" Clatter, clatter, clatter, clatter, bang! It was a fixed belief with Madame Lebrun that the conduct of the universe and all things pertaining thereto would have been manifestly of a more intelligent and higher order had not Monsieur Lebrun been removed to other spheres during the early years of their married life.

"What do you hear from Montel?" Montel was a middle-aged gentleman whose vain ambition and desire for the past twenty years had been to fill the void which Monsieur Lebrun's taking off had left in the Lebrun household. Clatter, clatter, bang, clatter!

"I have a letter somewhere," looking in the machine drawer and finding the letter in the bottom of the work-basket. "He says to tell you he will be in Vera Cruz the beginning of next month"—clatter, clatter!—"and if you still have the intention of joining him"—bang! clatter, clatter, bang!

"Why didn't you tell me so before, mother? You know I wanted—" Clatter, clatter, clatter!

"Do you see Mrs. Pontellier starting back with the children? She will be in late to luncheon again. She never starts to get ready for luncheon till the last minute." Clatter, clatter! "Where are you going?"

"Where did you say the Goncourt was?"

IX

Every light in the hall was ablaze; every lamp turned as high as it could be without smoking the chimney or threatening explosion. The lamps were fixed at intervals against the wall, encircling the whole room. Some one had gathered orange and lemon branches, and with these fashioned graceful festoons between. The dark green of the branches stood out and glistened against the white muslin curtains which draped the windows, and which puffed, floated, and flapped at the capricious will of a stiff breeze that swept up from the Gulf.

It was Saturday night a few weeks after the intimate conversation held between Robert and Madame Ratignolle on their way from the beach. An unusual number of husbands, fathers, and friends had come down to stay over Sunday; and they were being suitably entertained by their families, with the material help of Madame Lebrun. The dining tables had all been removed to one end of the hall, and the chairs ranged about in rows and in clusters. Each little family group had had its say and exchanged its domestic gossip earlier in the evening. There was now an apparent disposition to relax; to widen the circle of confidences and give a more general tone to the conversation.

Many of the children had been permitted to sit up beyond their usual bedtime. A small band of them were lying on their stomachs on the floor looking at the colored sheets of the comic papers which Mr. Pontellier had brought down. The little Pontellier boys were permitting them to do so, and making their authority felt.

Music, dancing, and a recitation or two were the entertainments furnished, or rather, offered. But there was nothing systematic about the programme, no appearance of prearrangement nor even premeditation.

At an early hour in the evening the Farival twins were prevailed upon to play the piano. They were girls of fourteen, always clad in the Virgin's colors, blue and white, having been dedicated to the Blessed Virgin at their baptism. They played a duet from "Zampa," and at the earnest solicitation of every one present followed it with the overture to "The Poet and the Peasant."

"*Allez vous-en! Sapristi!*" shrieked the parrot outside the door. He was the only being present who possessed sufficient candor to admit that he was not listening to these gracious performances for the first time that summer. Old Monsieur Farival, grandfather of the twins, grew indignant over the interruption, and insisted upon having the bird removed and consigned to regions of darkness. Victor Lebrun objected; and his decrees were as immutable as those of Fate. The parrot fortunately offered no further interruption to the entertainment, the whole venom of his nature apparently having been cherished up and hurled against the twins in that one impetuous outburst.

Later a young brother and sister gave recitations, which every one present had heard many times at winter evening entertainments in the city.

A little girl performed a skirt dance in the center of the floor. The mother played her accompaniments and at the same time watched her daughter with greedy admiration and nervous apprehension. She need have had no apprehension. The child was mistress of the situation. She had been properly dressed for the occasion in black tulle and black silk tights. Her little neck and arms were bare, and her hair, artificially crimped, stood out like fluffy black plumes over her head. Her poses were full of grace, and her little black-shod toes twinkled as they shot out and upward with a rapidity and suddenness which were bewildering.

But there was no reason why every one should not dance. Madame Ratignolle could not, so it was she who gaily consented to play for the others. She played very well, keeping excellent waltz time and infusing an expression into the strains which was indeed inspiring. She was keeping up her music on account of the children, she said; because she and her husband both considered it a means of brightening the home and making it attractive.

Almost every one danced but the twins, who could not be induced to separate during the brief period when one or the other should be whirling around the room in the arms of a man. They might have danced together, but they did not think of it.

The children were sent to bed. Some went submissively; others with shrieks and protests as they were dragged away. They had been permitted to sit up till after the ice-cream, which naturally marked the limit of human indulgence.

The ice-cream was passed around with cake — gold and silver cake arranged on platters in alternate slices; it had been made and frozen during the afternoon back of the kitchen by two black women, under the supervision of Victor. It was pronounced a great success — excellent if it had only contained a little less vanilla or a little more sugar, if it had been frozen a degree harder, and if the salt might have been kept out of portions of it. Victor was proud of his achievement, and went about recommending it and urging every one to partake of it to excess.

After Mrs. Pontellier had danced twice with her husband, once with Robert, and once with Monsieur Ratignolle, who was thin and tall and swayed like a reed in the wind when he danced, she went out on the gallery and seated herself on the low window-sill, where she commanded a view of all that went on in the hall and could look out toward the Gulf. There was a soft effulgence in the east. The moon was coming up, and its mystic shimmer was casting a million lights across the distant, restless water.

"Would you like to hear Mademoiselle Reisz play?" asked Robert, coming out on the porch where she was. Of course Edna would like to hear Mademoiselle Reisz play; but she feared it would be useless to entreat her.

"I'll ask her," he said. "I'll tell her that you want to hear her. She likes you. She will come." He turned and hurried away to one of the far cottages, where Mademoiselle Reisz was shuffling away. She was dragging a chair in and out of her room, and at intervals objecting to the crying of a baby, which a nurse in the adjoining cottage was endeavoring to put to sleep. She was a disagreeable little woman, no longer young, who had quarreled with almost every one, owing to a temper which was self-assertive and a disposition to trample upon the rights of others. Robert prevailed upon her without any too great difficulty.

She entered the hall with him during a lull in the dance. She made an awkward, imperious little bow as she went in. She was a homely woman, with a small weazened face and body and eyes that glowed. She had absolutely no taste in dress, and wore a batch of rusty black lace with a bunch of artificial violets pinned to the side of her hair.

"Ask Mrs. Pontellier what she would like to hear me play," she requested of Robert. She sat perfectly still before the piano, not touching the keys, while Robert carried her message to Edna at the window. A general air of surprise and genuine satisfaction fell upon every one as they saw the pianist enter. There was a settling down, and a prevailing air of expectancy everywhere. Edna was a trifle embarrassed at being thus signaled out for the imperious little woman's favor. She would not dare to choose, and begged that Mademoiselle Reisz would please herself in her selections.

Edna was what she herself called very fond of music. Musical strains, well rendered, had a way of evoking pictures in her mind. She sometimes liked to sit in the room of mornings when Madame Ratignolle played or practiced. One piece which that lady played Edna had entitled "Solitude." It was a short, plaintive, minor strain. The name of the piece was something else, but she called it "Solitude." When she heard it there came before her imagination the figure of a man standing beside a desolate rock on the seashore. He was naked. His attitude was one of hopeless resignation as he looked toward a distant bird winging its flight away from him.

Another piece called to her mind a dainty young woman clad in an Empire gown, taking mincing dancing steps as she came down a long avenue between tall hedges. Again, another reminded her of children at play, and still another of nothing on earth but a demure lady stroking a cat.

The very first chords which Mademoiselle Reisz struck upon the piano sent a keen tremor down Mrs. Pontellier's spinal column. It was not the first time she had heard an artist at the piano. Perhaps it was the first time she was ready, perhaps the first time her being was tempered to take an impress of the abiding truth.

She waited for the material pictures which she thought would gather and blaze before her imagination. She waited in vain. She saw no pictures of solitude, of hope, of longing, or of despair. But the very passions themselves were aroused within her soul, swaying it, lashing it, as the waves daily beat upon her splendid body. She trembled, she was choking, and the tears blinded her.

Mademoiselle had finished. She arose, and bowing her stiff, lofty bow, she went away, stopping for neither thanks nor applause. As she passed along the gallery she patted Edna upon the shoulder.

"Well, how did you like my music?" she asked. The young woman was unable to answer; she pressed the hand of the pianist convulsively. Mademoiselle Reisz perceived her agitation and even her tears. She patted her again upon the shoulder as she said:

"You are the only one worth playing for. Those others? Bah!" and she went shuffling and sidling on down the gallery toward her room.

But she was mistaken about "those others." Her playing had aroused a fever of enthusiasm. "What passion!" "What an artist!" "I have always said no one could play Chopin like Mademoiselle Reisz!" "That last prelude! Bon Dieu! It shakes a man!"

It was growing late, and there was a general disposition to disband. But some one, perhaps it was Robert, thought of a bath at that mystic hour and under that mystic moon.

X

At all events Robert proposed it, and there was not a dissenting voice. There was not one but was ready to follow when he led the way. He did not lead the way, however, he directed the way; and he himself loitered behind with the lovers, who had betrayed a disposition to linger and hold themselves apart. He walked between them, whether with malicious or mischievous intent was not wholly clear, even to himself.

The Pontelliers and Ratignolles walked ahead; the women leaning upon the arms of their husbands. Edna could hear Robert's voice behind them, and could sometimes hear what he said. She wondered why he did not join them. It was unlike him not to. Of late he had sometimes held away from her for an entire day, redoubling his devotion upon the next and the next, as though to make up for hours that had been lost. She missed him the days when some pretext served to take him away from her, just as one misses the sun on a cloudy day without having thought much about the sun when it was shining.

The people walked in little groups toward the beach. They talked and laughed; some of them sang. There was a band playing down at Klein's hotel, and the strains reached them faintly, tempered by the distance. There were strange, rare odors abroad — a tangle of the sea smell and of weeds and damp, new-plowed earth, mingled with the heavy perfume of a field of white blossoms somewhere near. But the night sat lightly upon the sea and the land. There was no weight of darkness; there were no shadows. The white light of the moon had fallen upon the world like the mystery and the softness of sleep.

Most of them walked into the water as though into a native element. The sea was quiet now, and swelled lazily in broad billows that melted into one another and did not break except upon the beach in little foamy crests that coiled back like slow, white serpents.

Edna had attempted all summer to learn to swim. She had received instructions from both the men and women; in some instances from the children. Robert had pursued a system of lessons almost daily; and he was nearly at the point of discouragement in realizing the futility of his efforts. A certain ungovernable dread hung about her when in the water, unless there was a hand near by that might reach out and reassure her.

But that night she was like the little tottering, stumbling, clutching child, who of a sudden realizes its powers, and walks for the first time alone, boldly and with over-confidence. She could have shouted for joy. She did shout for joy, as with a sweeping stroke or two she lifted her body to the surface of the water.

A feeling of exultation overtook her, as if some power of significant import had been given her to control the working of her body and her soul. She grew daring and reckless, overestimating her strength. She wanted to swim far out, where no woman had swum before.

Her unlooked-for achievement was the subject of wonder, applause, and admiration. Each one congratulated himself that his special teachings had accomplished this desired end.

"How easy it is!" she thought. "It is nothing," she said aloud; "why did I not discover before that it was nothing? Think of the time I have lost splashing about like a baby!" She would not join the groups in their sports and bouts, but intoxicated with her newly conquered power, she swam out alone.

She turned her face seaward to gather in an impression of space and solitude, which the vast expanse of water, meeting and melting with the moonlit sky, conveyed to her excited fancy. As she swam she seemed to be reaching out for the unlimited in which to lose herself.

Once she turned and looked toward the shore, toward the people she had left there. She had not gone any great distance — that is, what would have been a great distance for an experienced swimmer. But to her unaccustomed vision the stretch of water behind her assumed the aspect of a barrier which her unaided strength would never be able to overcome.

A quick vision of death smote her soul, and for a second of time appalled and enfeebled her senses. But by an effort she rallied her staggering faculties and managed to regain the land.

She made no mention of her encounter with death and her flash of terror, except to say to her husband, "I thought I should have perished out there alone."

"You were not so very far, my dear; I was watching you," he told her.

Edna went at once to the bath-house, and she had put on her dry clothes and was ready to return home before the others had left the water. She started to walk away alone. They all called to her and shouted to her. She waved a dissenting hand, and went on, paying no further heed to their renewed cries which sought to detain her.

"Sometimes I am tempted to think that Mrs. Pontellier is capricious," said Madame Lebrun, who was amusing herself immensely and feared that Edna's abrupt departure might put an end to the pleasure.

"I know she is," assented Mr. Pontellier; "sometimes, not often."

Edna had not traversed a quarter of the distance on her way home before she was overtaken by Robert.

"Did you think I was afraid?" she asked him, without a shade of annoyance.

"No; I knew you weren't afraid."

"Then why did you come? Why didn't you stay out there with the others?"

"I never thought of it."

"Thought of what?"

"Of anything. What difference does it make?"

"I'm very tired," she uttered, complainingly.

"I know you are."

"You don't know anything about it. Why should you know? I never was so exhausted in my life. But it isn't unpleasant. A thousand emotions have swept through me to-night. I don't comprehend half of them. Don't mind what I'm saying; I am just thinking aloud. I wonder if I shall ever be stirred again as Mademoiselle Reisz's playing moved me to-night. I wonder if any night on earth will ever again be like this one. It is like a night in a dream. The people about me are like some uncanny, half-human beings. There must be spirits abroad to-night."

"There are," whispered Robert. "Didn't you know this was the twenty-eighth of August?"

"The twenty-eighth of August?"

"Yes. On the twenty-eighth of August, at the hour of midnight, and if the moon is shining — the moon must be shining — a spirit that has haunted these shores for ages rises up from the Gulf. With its own penetrating vision the spirit seeks some one mortal worthy to hold him company, worthy of being exalted for a few hours into realms of the semi-celestials. His search has always hitherto been fruitless, and he has sunk back, disheartened, into the sea. But to-night he found Mrs. Pontellier. Perhaps he will never wholly release her from the spell. Perhaps she will never again suffer a poor, unworthy earthling to walk in the shadow of her divine presence."

"Don't banter me," she said, wounded at what appeared to be his flippancy. He did not mind the entreaty, but the tone with its delicate note of pathos was like a reproach. He could not explain; he could not tell her that he had penetrated her mood and understood. He said nothing except to offer her his arm, for, by her own admission, she was exhausted. She had been walking alone with her arms hanging limp, letting her white skirts trail along the dewy path. She took his arm, but she did not lean upon it. She let her hand lie listlessly, as though her thoughts were elsewhere — somewhere in advance of her body, and she was striving to overtake them.

Robert assisted her into the hammock which swung from the post before her door out to the trunk of a tree.

"Will you stay out here and wait for Mr. Pontellier?" he asked.

"I'll stay out here. Good-night."

"Shall I get you a pillow?"

"There's one here," she said, feeling about, for they were in the shadow.

"It must be soiled; the children have been tumbling it about."

"No matter." And having discovered the pillow, she adjusted it beneath her head. She extended herself in the hammock with a deep breath of relief. She was not a supercilious or an over-dainty woman. She was not much given to reclining in the hammock, and when she did so it was with no cat-like suggestion of voluptuous ease, but with a beneficent repose which seemed to invade her whole body.

"Shall I stay with you till Mr. Pontellier comes?" asked Robert, seating himself on the outer edge of one of the steps and taking hold of the hammock rope which was fastened to the post.

"If you wish. Don't swing the hammock. Will you get my white shawl which I left on the window-sill over at the house?"

"Are you chilly?"

"No; but I shall be presently."

"Presently?" he laughed. "Do you know what time it is? How long are you going to stay out here?"

"I don't know. Will you get the shawl?"

"Of course I will," he said, rising. He went over to the house, walking along the grass. She watched his figure pass in and out of the strips of moonlight. It was past midnight. It was very quiet.

When he returned with the shawl she took it and kept it in her hand. She did not put it around her.

"Did you say I should stay till Mr. Pontellier came back?"

"I said you might if you wished to."

He seated himself again and rolled a cigarette, which he smoked in silence. Neither did Mrs. Pontellier speak. No multitude of words could have been more significant than those moments of silence, or more pregnant with the first-felt throbbings of desire.

When the voices of the bathers were heard approaching, Robert said good-night. She did not answer him. He thought she was asleep. Again she watched his figure pass in and out of the strips of moonlight as he walked away.

XI

"What are you doing out here, Edna? I thought I should find you in bed," said her husband, when he discovered her lying there. He had walked up with Madame Lebrun and left her at the house. His wife did not reply.

"Are you asleep?" he asked, bending down close to look at her.

"No." Her eyes gleamed bright and intense, with no sleepy shadows, as they looked into his.

"Do you know it is past one o'clock? Come on," and he mounted the steps and went into their room.

"Edna!" called Mr. Pontellier from within, after a few moments had gone by. "Don't wait for me," she answered. He thrust his head through the door. "You will take cold out there," he said, irritably. "What folly is this? Why don't you come in?"

"It isn't cold; I have my shawl."

"The mosquitoes will devour you."

"There are no mosquitoes."

She heard him moving about the room; every sound indicating impatience and irritation. Another time she would have gone in at his request. She would, through habit, have yielded to his desire; not with any sense of submission or obedience to his compelling wishes, but unthinkingly, as we walk, move, sit, stand, go through the daily treadmill of the life which has been portioned out to us.

"Edna, dear, are you not coming in soon?" he asked again, this time fondly, with a note of entreaty.

"No; I am going to stay out here."

"This is more than folly," he blurted out. "I can't permit you to stay out there all night. You must come in the house instantly."

With a writhing motion she settled herself more securely in the hammock. She perceived that her will had blazed up, stubborn and resistant. She could not at that moment have done other than denied and resisted. She wondered if her husband had ever spoken to her like that before, and if she had submitted to his command. Of course she had; she remembered that she had. But she could not realize why or how she should have yielded, feeling as she then did.

"Léonce, go to bed," she said. "I mean to stay out here. I don't wish to go in, and I don't intend to. Don't speak to me like that again; I shall not answer you."

Mr. Pontellier had prepared for bed, but he slipped on an extra garment. He opened a bottle of wine, of which he kept a small and select supply in a buffet of his own. He drank a glass of the wine and went out on the gallery and offered a glass to his wife. She did not wish any. He drew up the rocker, hoisted his slippered feet on the rail, and proceeded to smoke a cigar. He smoked two cigars; then he went inside and drank another glass of wine. Mrs. Pontellier again declined to accept a glass when it was offered to her. Mr. Pontellier once more seated himself with elevated feet, and after a reasonable interval of time smoked some more cigars.

Edna began to feel like one who awakens gradually out of a dream, a delicious, grotesque, impossible dream, to feel again the realities pressing into her soul. The physical need for sleep began to overtake her; the exuberance which had sustained and exalted her spirit left her helpless and yielding to the conditions which crowded her in.

The stillest hour of the night had come, the hour before dawn, when the world seems to hold its breath. The moon hung low, and had turned from silver to copper in the sleeping sky. The old owl no longer hooted, and the water-oaks had ceased to moan as they bent their heads.

Edna arose, cramped from lying so long and still in the hammock. She tottered up the steps, clutching feebly at the post before passing into the house.

"Are you coming in, Léonce?" she asked, turning her face toward her husband.

"Yes, dear," he answered, with a glance following a misty puff of smoke. "Just as soon as I have finished my cigar."

XII

She slept but a few hours. They were troubled and feverish hours, disturbed with dreams that were intangible, that eluded her, leaving only an impression upon her half-awakened senses of something unattainable. She was up and dressed in the cool of the early morning. The air was invigorating and steadied somewhat her faculties. However, she was not seeking refreshment or help from any source, either external or from within. She was blindly following whatever impulse moved her, as if she had placed herself in alien hands for direction, and freed her soul of responsibility.

Most of the people at that early hour were still in bed and asleep. A few, who intended to go over to the *Chênière* for mass, were moving about. The lovers, who had laid their plans the night before, were already strolling toward the wharf. The lady in black, with her Sunday prayer-book, velvet and gold-clasped, and her Sunday silver beads, was following them at no great distance. Old Monsieur Farival was up, and was more than half inclined to do anything that suggested itself. He put on his big straw hat, and taking his umbrella from the stand in the hall, followed the lady in black, never overtaking her.

The little negro girl who worked Madame Lebrun's sewing-machine was sweeping the galleries with long, absent-minded strokes of the broom. Edna sent her up into the house to awaken Robert.

"Tell him I am going to the *Chênière*. The boat is ready; tell him to hurry."

He had soon joined her. She had never sent for him before. She had never asked for him. She had never seemed to want him before. She did not appear conscious that she had done anything unusual in commanding his presence. He was apparently equally unconscious of anything extraordinary in the situation. But his face was suffused with a quiet glow when he met her.

They went together back to the kitchen to drink coffee. There was no time to wait for any nicety of service. They stood outside the window and the cook passed them their coffee and a roll, which they drank and ate from the window-sill. Edna said it tasted good. She had not thought of coffee nor of anything. He told her he had often noticed that she lacked forethought.

"Wasn't it enough to think of going to the *Chênière* and waking you up?" she laughed. "Do I have to think of everything? — as Léonce says when he's in a bad humor. I don't blame him; he'd never be in a bad humor if it weren't for me."

They took a short cut across the sands. At a distance they could see the curious procession moving toward the wharf — the lovers, shoulder to shoulder, creeping; the lady in black, gaining steadily upon them; old Monsieur Farival, losing ground inch by inch, and a young barefooted Spanish girl, with a red kerchief on her head and a basket on her arm, bringing up the rear.

Robert knew the girl, and he talked to her a little in the boat. No one present understood what they said. Her name was Mariequita. She had a round, sly, piquant face and pretty black eyes. Her hands were small, and she kept them folded over the handle of her basket. Her feet were broad and coarse. She did not strive to hide them. Edna looked at her feet, and noticed the sand and slime between her brown toes.

Beaudelet grumbled because Mariequita was there, taking up so much room. In reality he was annoyed at having old Monsieur Farival, who considered himself the better sailor of the two. But he would not quarrel with so old a man as Monsieur Farival, so he quarreled with Mariequita. The girl was deprecatory at one moment, appealing to Robert. She was saucy the next, moving her head up and down, making "eyes" at Robert and making "mouths" at Beaudelet.

The lovers were all alone. They saw nothing, they heard nothing. The lady in black was counting her beads for the third time. Old Monsieur Farival talked incessantly of what he knew about handling a boat, and of what Beaudelet did not know on the same subject.

Edna liked it all. She looked Mariequita up and down, from her ugly brown toes to her pretty black eyes, and back again.

"Why does she look at me like that?" inquired the girl of Robert.

"Maybe she thinks you are pretty. Shall I ask her?"

"No. Is she your sweetheart?"

"She's a married lady, and has two children."

"Oh! well! Francisco ran away with Sylvano's wife, who had four children. They took all his money and one of the children and stole his boat."

"Shut up!"

"Does she understand?"

"Oh, hush!"

"Are those two married over there — leaning on each other?"

"Of course not," laughed Robert.

"Of course not," echoed Mariequita, with a serious, confirmatory bob of the head.

The sun was high up and beginning to bite. The swift breeze seemed to Edna to bury the sting of it into the pores of her face and hands. Robert held his umbrella over her.

As they went cutting sidewise through the water, the sails bellied taut, with the wind filling and overflowing them. Old Monsieur Farival laughed sardonically at something as he looked at the sails, and Beaudelet swore at the old man under his breath.

Sailing across the bay to the *Chênière Caminada*, Edna felt as if she were being borne away from some anchorage which had held her fast, whose chains had been loosening — had snapped the night before when the mystic spirit was abroad, leaving her free to drift whithersoever she chose to set her sails. Robert spoke to her incessantly; he no longer noticed Mariequita. The girl had shrimps in her bamboo basket. They were covered with Spanish moss. She beat the moss down impatiently, and muttered to herself sullenly.

"Let us go to Grande Terre to-morrow," said Robert in a low voice.

"What shall we do there?"

"Climb up the hill to the old fort and look at the little wriggling gold snakes, and watch the lizards sun themselves."

She gazed away toward Grande Terre and thought she would like to be alone there with Robert, in the sun, listening to the ocean's roar and watching the slimy lizards writhe in and out among the ruins of the old fort.

"And the next day or the next we can sail to the Bayou Brulow," he went on.

"What shall we do there?"

"Anything — cast bait for fish."

"No; we'll go back to Grande Terre. Let the fish alone."

"We'll go wherever you like," he said. "I'll have Tonie come over and help me patch and trim my boat. We shall not need Beaudelet nor any one. Are you afraid of the pirogue?"

"Oh, no."

"Then I'll take you some night in the pirogue when the moon shines. Maybe your Gulf spirit will whisper to you in which of these islands the treasures are hidden — direct you to the very spot, perhaps."

"And in a day we should be rich!" she laughed. "I'd give it all to you, the pirate gold and every bit of treasure we could dig up. I think you would know how to spend it. Pirate gold isn't a thing to be hoarded or utilized. It is something to squander and throw to the four winds, for the fun of seeing the golden specks fly."

"We'd share it, and scatter it together," he said. His face flushed.

They all went together up to the quaint little Gothic church of Our Lady of Lourdes, gleaming all brown and yellow with paint in the sun's glare.

Only Beaudelet remained behind, tinkering at his boat, and Mariequita walked away with her basket of shrimps, casting a look of childish ill-humor and reproach at Robert from the corner of her eye.

XIII

A feeling of oppression and drowsiness overcame Edna during the service. Her head began to ache, and the lights on the altar swayed before her eyes. Another time she might have made an effort to regain her composure; but her one thought was to quit the stifling atmosphere of the church and reach the open air. She arose, climbing over Robert's feet with a muttered apology. Old Monsieur Farival, flurried, curious, stood up, but upon seeing that Robert had followed Mrs. Pontellier, he sank back into his seat. He whispered an anxious inquiry of the lady in black, who did not notice him or reply, but kept her eyes fastened upon the pages of her velvet prayer-book.

"I felt giddy and almost overcome," Edna said, lifting her hands instinctively to her head and pushing her straw hat up from her forehead. "I couldn't have stayed through the service." They were outside in the shadow of the church. Robert was full of solicitude.

"It was folly to have thought of going in the first place, let alone staying. Come over to Madame Antoine's; you can rest there." He took her arm and led her away, looking anxiously and continuously down into her face.

How still it was, with only the voice of the sea whispering through the reeds that grew in the salt-water pools! The long line of little gray, weather-beaten houses nestled peacefully among the orange trees. It must always have been God's day on that low, drowsy island, Edna thought. They stopped, leaning over a jagged fence made of sea-drift, to ask for water. A youth, a mild-faced Acadian, was drawing water from the cistern, which was nothing more than a rusty buoy, with an opening on one side, sunk in the ground. The water which the youth handed to them in a tin pail was not cold to taste, but it was cool to her heated face, and it greatly revived and refreshed her.

Madame Antoine's cot was at the far end of the village. She welcomed them with all the native hospitality, as she would have opened her door to let the sunlight in. She was fat, and walked heavily and clumsily across the floor. She could speak no English, but when Robert made her understand that the lady who accompanied him was ill and desired to rest, she was all eagerness to make Edna feel at home and to dispose of her comfortably.

The whole place was immaculately clean, and the big, four-posted bed, snow-white, invited one to repose. It stood in a small side room which looked out across a narrow grass plot toward the shed, where there was a disabled boat lying keel upward.

Madame Antoine had not gone to mass. Her son Tonie had, but she supposed he would soon be back, and she invited Robert to be seated and wait for him. But he went and sat outside the door and smoked. Madame Antoine busied herself in the large front room preparing dinner. She was boiling mullets over a few red coals in the huge fireplace.

Edna, left alone in the little side room, loosened her clothes, removing the greater part of them. She bathed her face, her neck and arms in the basin that stood between the windows. She took off her shoes and stockings and stretched herself in the very center of the high, white bed. How luxurious it felt to rest thus in a strange, quaint bed, with its sweet country odor of laurel lingering about the sheets and mattress! She stretched her strong limbs that ached a little. She ran her fingers through her loosened hair for a while. She looked at her round arms as she held them straight up and rubbed them one after the other, observing closely, as if it were something she saw for the first time, the fine, firm quality and texture of her flesh. She clasped her hands easily above her head, and it was thus she fell asleep.

She slept lightly at first, half awake and drowsily attentive to the things about her. She could hear Madame Antoine's heavy, scraping tread as she walked back and forth on the sanded floor. Some chickens were clucking outside the windows, scratching for bits of gravel in the grass. Later she half heard the voices of Robert and Tonie talking under the shed. She did not stir. Even her eyelids rested numb and heavily over her sleepy eyes. The voices went on—Tonie's slow, Acadian drawl, Robert's quick, soft, smooth French. She understood French imperfectly unless directly addressed, and the voices were only part of the other drowsy, muffled sounds lulling her senses.

When Edna awoke it was with the conviction that she had slept long and soundly. The voices were hushed under the shed. Madame Antoine's step was no longer to be heard in the adjoining room. Even the chickens had gone elsewhere to scratch and cluck. The mosquito bar was drawn over her; the old woman had come in while she slept and let down the bar. Edna arose quietly from the bed, and looking between the curtains of the window, she saw by the slanting rays of the sun that the afternoon was far advanced. Robert was out there under the shed, reclining in the shade against the sloping keel of the overturned boat. He was reading from a book. Tonie was no longer with him. She wondered what had become of the rest of the party. She peeped out at him two or three times as she stood washing herself in the little basin between the windows.

Madame Antoine had laid some coarse, clean towels upon a chair, and had placed a box of *poudre de riz* within easy reach. Edna dabbed the powder upon her nose and cheeks as she looked at herself closely in the little distorted mirror which hung on the wall above the basin. Her eyes were bright and wide awake and her face glowed.

When she had completed her toilet she walked into the adjoining room. She was very hungry. No one was there. But there was a cloth spread upon the table that stood against the wall, and a cover was laid for one, with a crusty brown loaf and a bottle of wine beside the plate. Edna bit a piece from the brown loaf, tearing it with her strong, white teeth. She poured some of the wine into the glass and drank it down. Then she went softly out of doors, and plucking an orange from the low-hanging bough of a tree, threw it at Robert, who did not know she was awake and up.

An illumination broke over his whole face when he saw her and joined her under the orange tree.

"How many years have I slept?" she inquired. "The whole island seems changed. A new race of beings must have sprung up, leaving only you and me as past relics. How many ages ago did Madame Antoine and Tonie die? and when did our people from Grand Isle disappear from the earth?"

He familiarly adjusted a ruffle upon her shoulder.

"You have slept precisely one hundred years. I was left here to guard your slumbers; and for one hundred years I have been out under the shed reading a book. The only evil I couldn't prevent was to keep a broiled fowl from drying up."

"If it has turned to stone, still will I eat it," said Edna, moving with him into the house. "But really, what has become of Monsieur Farival and the others?"

"Gone hours ago. When they found that you were sleeping they thought it best not to awake you. Any way, I wouldn't have let them. What was I here for?"

"I wonder if Léonce will be uneasy!" she speculated, as she seated herself at table.

"Of course not; he knows you are with me," Robert replied, as he busied himself among sundry pans and covered dishes which had been left standing on the hearth.

"Where are Madame Antoine and her son?" asked Edna.

"Gone to Vespers, and to visit some friends, I believe. I am to take you back in Tonie's boat whenever you are ready to go."

He stirred the smoldering ashes till the broiled fowl began to sizzle afresh. He served her with no mean repast, dripping the coffee anew and sharing it with her. Madame Antoine had cooked little else than the mullets, but while Edna slept Robert had foraged the island. He was childishly gratified to discover her appetite, and to see the relish with which she ate the food which he had procured for her.

"Shall we go right away?" she asked, after draining her glass and brushing together the crumbs of the crusty loaf.

"The sun isn't as low as it will be in two hours," he answered.

"The sun will be gone in two hours."

"Well, let it go; who cares!"

They waited a good while under the orange trees, till Madame Antoine came back, panting, waddling, with a thousand apologies to explain her absence. Tonie did not dare to return. He was shy, and would not willingly face any woman except his mother.

It was very pleasant to stay there under the orange trees, while the sun dipped lower and lower, turning the western sky to flaming copper and gold. The shadows lengthened and crept out like stealthy, grotesque monsters across the grass.

Edna and Robert both sat upon the ground — that is, he lay upon the ground beside her, occasionally picking at the hem of her muslin gown.

Madame Antoine seated her fat body, broad and squat, upon a bench beside the door. She had been talking all the afternoon, and had wound herself up to the story-telling pitch.

And what stories she told them! But twice in her life she had left the *Chênière*

Caminada, and then for the briefest span. All her years she had squatted and waddled there upon the island, gathering legends of the Baratarians and the sea. The night came on, with the moon to lighten it. Edna could hear the whispering voices of dead men and the click of muffled gold.

When she and Robert stepped into Tonie's boat, with the red lateen sail, misty spirit forms were prowling in the shadows and among the reeds, and upon the water were phantom ships, speeding to cover.

XIV

The youngest boy, Etienne, had been very naughty, Madame Ratignolle said, as she delivered him into the hands of his mother. He had been unwilling to go to bed and had made a scene; whereupon she had taken charge of him and pacified him as well as she could. Raoul had been in bed and asleep for two hours.

The youngster was in his long white nightgown, that kept tripping him up as Madame Ratignolle led him along by the hand. With the other chubby fist he rubbed his eyes, which were heavy with sleep and ill humor. Edna took him in her arms, and seating herself in the rocker, began to coddle and caress him, calling him all manner of tender names, soothing him to sleep.

It was not more than nine o'clock. No one had yet gone to bed but the children.

Léonce had been very uneasy at first, Madame Ratignolle said, and had wanted to start at once for the *Chênière.* But Monsieur Farival had assured him that his wife was only overcome with sleep and fatigue, that Tonie would bring her safely back later in the day; and he had thus been dissuaded from crossing the bay. He had gone over to Klein's, looking up some cotton broker whom he wished to see in regard to securities, exchanges, stocks, bonds, or something of the sort, Madame Ratignolle did not remember what. He said he would not remain away late. She herself was suffering from heat and oppression, she said. She carried a bottle of salts and a large fan. She would not consent to remain with Edna, for Monsieur Ratignolle was alone, and he detested above all things to be left alone.

When Etienne had fallen asleep Edna bore him into the back room, and Robert went and lifted the mosquito bar that she might lay the child comfortably in his bed. The quadroon had vanished. When they emerged from the cottage Robert bade Edna good-night.

"Do you know we have been together the whole livelong day, Robert—since early this morning?" she said at parting.

"All but the hundred years when you were sleeping. Good-night."

He pressed her hand and went away in the direction of the beach. He did not join any of the others, but walked alone toward the Gulf.

Edna stayed outside, awaiting her husband's return. She had no desire to sleep or to retire; nor did she feel like going over to sit with the Ratignolles, or to join Madame Lebrun and a group whose animated voices reached her as they sat in conversation before the house. She let her mind wander back over her stay at Grand Isle; and she tried to discover wherein this summer had been different from any and every other summer of her life. She could only realize that she herself—her present self—was in some way different from the other self. That she was seeing with different eyes and making the acquaintance of new condi-

tions in herself that colored and changed her environment, she did not yet
suspect.

She wondered why Robert had gone away and left her. It did not occur to her
to think he might have grown tired of being with her the livelong day. She was
not tired, and she felt that he was not. She regretted that he had gone. It was so
much more natural to have him stay when he was not absolutely required to leave
her.

As Edna waited for her husband she sang low a little song that Robert had sung
as they crossed the bay. It began with "Ah! *Si tu savais*,"[1] and every verse ended
with "*si tu savais.*"

Robert's voice was not pretentious. It was musical and true. The voice, the
notes, the whole refrain haunted her memory.

XV

When Edna entered the dining-room one evening a little late, as was her habit,
an unusually animated conversation seemed to be going on. Several persons were
talking at once, and Victor's voice was predominating, even over that of his
mother. Edna had returned late from her bath, had dressed in some haste, and her
face was flushed. Her head, set off by her dainty white gown, suggested a rich,
rare blossom. She took her seat at table between old Monsieur Farival and
Madame Ratignolle.

As she seated herself and was about to begin to eat her soup, which had been
served when she entered the room, several persons informed her simultaneously
that Robert was going to Mexico. She laid her spoon down and looked about her
bewildered. He had been with her, reading to her all the morning, and had never
even mentioned such a place as Mexico. She had not seen him during the
afternoon; she had heard some one say he was at the house, upstairs with his
mother. This she had thought nothing of, though she was surprised when he did
not join her later in the afternoon, when she went down to the beach.

She looked across at him, where he sat beside Madame Lebrun, who presided.
Edna's face was a blank picture of bewilderment, which she never thought of
disguising. He lifted his eyebrows with the pretext of a smile as he returned her
glance. He looked embarrassed and uneasy.

"When is he going?" she asked of everybody in general, as if Robert were not
there to answer for himself.

"To-night!" "This very evening!" "Did you ever!" "What possesses him!"
were some of the replies she gathered, uttered simultaneously in French and
English.

"Impossible!" she exclaimed. "How can a person start off from Grand Isle to
Mexico at a moment's notice, as if he were going over to Klein's or to the wharf
or down to the beach?"

"I said all along I was going to Mexico; I've been saying so for years!" cried
Robert, in an excited and irritable tone, with the air of a man defending himself
against a swarm of stinging insects.

Madame Lebrun knocked on the table with her knife handle.

[1]"If only you knew."

"Please let Robert explain why he is going, and why he is going to-night," she called out. "Really, this table is getting to be more and more like Bedlam every day, with everybody talking at once. Sometimes — I hope God will forgive me — but positively, sometimes I wish Victor would lose the power of speech."

Victor laughed sardonically as he thanked his mother for her holy wish, of which he failed to see the benefit to anybody, except that it might afford her a more ample opportunity and license to talk herself.

Monsieur Farival thought that Victor should have been taken out in midocean in his earliest youth and drowned. Victor thought there would be more logic in thus disposing of old people with an established claim for making themselves universally obnoxious. Madame Lebrun grew a trifle hysterical; Robert called his brother some sharp, hard names.

"There's nothing much to explain, mother," he said; though he explained, nevertheless — looking chiefly at Edna — that he could only meet the gentleman whom he intended to join at Vera Cruz by taking such and such a steamer, which left New Orleans on such a day; that Beaudelet was going out with his lugger-load of vegetables that night, which gave him an opportunity of reaching the city and making his vessel in time.

"But when did you make up your mind to all this?" demanded Monsieur Farival.

"This afternoon," returned Robert, with a shade of annoyance.

"At what time this afternoon?" persisted the old gentleman, with nagging determination, as if he were cross-questioning a criminal in a court of justice.

"At four o'clock this afternoon, Monsieur Farival," Robert replied, in a high voice and with a lofty air, which reminded Edna of some gentleman on the stage.

She had forced herself to eat most of her soup, and now she was picking the flaky bits of a *court bouillon* with her fork.

The lovers were profiting by the general conversation on Mexico to speak in whispers of matters which they rightly considered were interesting to no one but themselves. The lady in black had once received a pair of prayer-beads of curious workmanship from Mexico, with very special indulgence attached to them, but she had never been able to ascertain whether the indulgence extended outside the Mexican border. Father Fochel of the Cathedral had attempted to explain it; but he had not done so to her satisfaction. And she begged that Robert would interest himself, and discover, if possible, whether she was entitled to the indulgence accompanying the remarkably curious Mexican prayer-beads.

Madame Ratignolle hoped that Robert would exercise extreme caution in dealing with the Mexicans, who, she considered, were a treacherous people, unscrupulous and revengeful. She trusted she did them no injustice in thus condemning them as a race. She had known personally but one Mexican, who made and sold excellent tamales, and whom she would have trusted implicitly, so soft-spoken was he. One day he was arrested for stabbing his wife. She never knew whether he had been hanged or not.

Victor had grown hilarious, and was attempting to tell an anecdote about a Mexican girl who served chocolate one winter in a restaurant in Dauphine Street. No one would listen to him but old Monsieur Farival, who went into convulsions over the droll story.

Edna wondered if they had all gone mad, to be talking and clamoring at that rate. She herself could think of nothing to say about Mexico or the Mexicans.

"At what time do you leave?" she asked Robert.

"At ten," he told her. "Beaudelet wants to wait for the moon."

"Are you all ready to go?"

"Quite ready. I shall only take a hand-bag, and shall pack my trunk in the city."

He turned to answer some question put to him by his mother, and Edna, having finished her black coffee, left the table.

She went directly to her room. The little cottage was close and stuffy after leaving the outer air. But she did not mind; there appeared to be a hundred different things demanding her attention indoors. She began to set the toilet-stand to rights, grumbling at the negligence of the quadroon, who was in the adjoining room putting the children to bed. She gathered together stray garments that were hanging on the backs of chairs, and put each where it belonged in closet or bureau drawer. She changed her gown for a more comfortable and commodious wrapper. She rearranged her hair, combing and brushing it with unusual energy. Then she went in and assisted the quadroon in getting the boys to bed.

They were very playful and inclined to talk — to do anything but lie quiet and go to sleep. Edna sent the quadroon away to her supper and told her she need not return. Then she sat and told the children a story. Instead of soothing it excited them, and added to their wakefulness. She left them in heated argument, specu-lating about the conclusion of the tale which their mother promised to finish the following night.

The little black girl came in to say that Madame Lebrun would like to have Mrs. Pontellier go and sit with them over at the house till Mr. Robert went away. Edna returned answer that she had already undressed, that she did not feel quite well, but perhaps she would go over to the house later. She started to dress again, and got as far advanced as to remove her *peignoir*. But changing her mind once more she resumed the *peignoir*, and went outside and sat down before her door. She was over-heated and irritable, and fanned herself energetically for a while. Madame Ratignolle came down to discover what was the matter.

"All that noise and confusion at the table must have upset me," replied Edna, "and moreover, I hate shocks and surprises. The idea of Robert starting off in such a ridiculously sudden and dramatic way! As if it were a matter of life and death! Never saying a word about it all morning when he was with me."

"Yes," agreed Madame Ratignolle. "I think it was showing us all — you especially — very little consideration. It wouldn't have surprised me in any of the others; those Lebruns are all given to heroics. But I must say I should never have expected such a thing from Robert. Are you not coming down? Come on, dear; it doesn't look friendly."

"No," said Edna, a little sullenly. "I can't go to the trouble of dressing again; I don't feel like it."

"You needn't dress; you look all right; fasten a belt around your waist. Just look at me!"

"No," persisted Edna; "but you go on. Madame Lebrun might be offended if we both stayed away."

Madame Ratignolle kissed Edna good-night, and went away, being in truth rather desirous of joining in the general and animated conversation which was still in progress concerning Mexico and the Mexicans.

Somewhat later Robert came up, carrying his hand-bag.

"Aren't you feeling well?" he asked.

"Oh, well enough. Are you going right away?"

He lit a match and looked at his watch. "In twenty minutes," he said. The sudden and brief flare of the match emphasized the darkness for a while. He sat down upon a stool which the children had left out on the porch.

"Get a chair," said Edna.

"This will do," he replied. He put on his soft hat and nervously took it off again, and wiping his face with his handkerchief, complained of the heat.

"Take the fan," said Edna, offering it to him.

"Oh, no! Thank you. It does no good; you have to stop fanning some time, and feel all the more uncomfortable afterward."

"That's one of the ridiculous things which men always say. I have never known one to speak otherwise of fanning. How long will you be gone?"

"Forever, perhaps. I don't know. It depends upon a good many things."

"Well, in case it shouldn't be forever, how long will it be?"

"I don't know."

"This seems to me perfectly preposterous and uncalled for. I don't like it. I don't understand your motive for silence and mystery, never saying a word to me about it this morning." He remained silent, not offering to defend himself. He only said, after a moment:

"Don't part from me in an ill-humor. I never knew you to be out of patience with me before."

"I don't want to part in any ill-humor," she said. "But can't you understand? I've grown used to seeing you, to having you with me all the time, and your action seems unfriendly, even unkind. You don't even offer an excuse for it. Why, I was planning to be together, thinking of how pleasant it would be to see you in the city next winter."

"So was I," he blurted. "Perhaps that's the—" He stood up suddenly and held out his hand. "Good-by, my dear Mrs. Pontellier; good-by. You won't—I hope you won't completely forget me." She clung to his hand, striving to detain him.

"Write to me when you get there, won't you, Robert?" she entreated.

"I will, thank you. Good-by."

How unlike Robert! The merest acquaintance would have said something more emphatic than "I will, thank you; good-by," to such a request.

He had evidently already taken leave of the people over at the house, for he descended the steps and went to join Beaudelet, who was out there with an oar across his shoulder waiting for Robert. They walked away in the darkness. She could only hear Beaudelet's voice; Robert had apparently not even spoken a word of greeting to his companion.

Edna bit her handkerchief convulsively, striving to hold back and to hide, even from herself as she would have hidden from another, the emotion which was troubling—tearing—her. Her eyes were brimming with tears.

For the first time she recognized anew the symptoms of infatuation which she had felt incipiently as a child, as a girl in her earliest teens, and later as a young woman. The recognition did not lessen the reality, the poignancy of the revelation by any suggestion or promise of instability. The past was nothing to her; offered no lesson which she was willing to heed. The future was a mystery which she never attempted to penetrate. The present alone was significant; was hers, to torture her as it was doing then with the biting conviction that she had lost that which she had held, that she had been denied that which her impassioned, newly awakened being demanded.

XVI

"Do you miss your friend greatly?" asked Mademoiselle Reisz one morning as she came creeping up behind Edna, who had just left her cottage on her way to the beach. She spent much of her time in the water since she had acquired finally the art of swimming. As their stay at Grand Isle drew near its close, she felt that she could not give too much time to a diversion which afforded her the only real pleasurable moments that she knew. When Mademoiselle Reisz came and touched her upon the shoulder and spoke to her, the woman seemed to echo the thought which was ever in Edna's mind; or better, the feeling which constantly possessed her.

Robert's going had some way taken the brightness, the color, the meaning out of everything. The conditions of her life were in no way changed, but her whole existence was dulled, like a faded garment which seems to be no longer worth wearing. She sought him everywhere—in others whom she induced to talk about him. She went up in the mornings to Madame Lebrun's room, braving the clatter of the old sewing-machine. She sat there and chatted at intervals as Robert had done. She gazed around the room at the pictures and photographs hanging upon the wall, and discovered in some corner an old family album, which she examined with the keenest interest, appealing to Madame Lebrun for enlightenment concerning the many figures and faces which she discovered between its pages.

There was a picture of Madame Lebrun with Robert as a baby, seated in her lap, a round-faced infant with a fist in his mouth. The eyes alone in the baby suggested the man. And that he was also in kilts, at the age of five, wearing long curls and holding a whip in his hand. It made Edna laugh, and she laughed, too, at the portrait in his first long trousers; while another interested her, taken when he left for college, looking thin, long-faced, with eyes full of fire, ambition and great intentions. But there was no recent picture, none which suggested the Robert who had gone away five days ago, leaving a void and wilderness behind him.

"Oh, Robert stopped having his pictures taken when he had to pay for them himself! He found wiser use for his money, he says," explained Madame Lebrun. She had a letter from him, written before he left New Orleans. Edna wished to see the letter, and Madame Lebrun told her to look for it either on the table or the dresser, or perhaps it was on the mantelpiece.

The letter was on the bookshelf. It possessed the greatest interest and attraction for Edna; the envelope, its size and shape, the post-mark, the handwriting. She examined every detail of the outside before opening it. There were only a few lines, setting forth that he would leave the city that afternoon, that he had packed his trunk in good shape, that he was well, and sent her his love and begged to be affectionately remembered to all. There was no special message to Edna except a postscript saying that if Mrs. Pontellier desired to finish the book which he had been reading to her, his mother would find it in his room, among other books there on the table. Edna experienced a pang of jealousy because he had written to his mother rather than to her.

Every one seemed to take for granted that she missed him. Even her husband, when he came down the Saturday following Robert's departure, expressed regret that he had gone.

"How do you get on without him, Edna?" he asked.

"It's very dull without him," she admitted. Mr. Pontellier had seen Robert in the city, and Edna asked him a dozen questions or more. Where had they met? On Carondelet Street, in the morning. They had gone "in" and had a drink and a cigar together. What had they talked about? Chiefly about his prospects in Mexico, which Mr. Pontellier thought were promising. How did he look? How did he seem — grave, or gay, or how? Quite cheerful, and wholly taken up with the idea of his trip, which Mr. Pontellier found altogether natural in a young fellow about to seek fortune and adventure in a strange, queer country.

Edna tapped her foot impatiently, and wondered why the children persisted in playing in the sun when they might be under the trees. She went down and led them out of the sun, scolding the quadroon for not being more attentive.

It did not strike her as in the least grotesque that she should be making of Robert the object of conversation and leading her husband to speak of him. The sentiment which she entertained for Robert in no way resembled that which she felt for her husband, or had ever felt, or ever expected to feel. She had all her life long been accustomed to harbor thoughts and emotions which never voiced themselves. They had never taken the form of struggles. They belonged to her and were her own, and she entertained the conviction that she had a right to them and that they concerned no one but herself. Edna had once told Madame Ratignolle that she would never sacrifice herself for her children, or for any one. Then had followed a rather heated argument; the two women did not appear to understand each other or to be talking the same language. Edna tried to appease her friend, to explain.

"I would give up the unessential; I would give my money, I would give my life for my children; but I wouldn't give myself. I can't make it more clear; it's only something which I am beginning to comprehend, which is revealing itself to me."

"I don't know what you would call the essential, or what you mean by the unessential," said Madame Ratignolle, cheerfully; "but a woman who would give her life for her children could do no more than that — your Bible tells you so. I'm sure I couldn't do more than that."

"Oh, yes you could!" laughed Edna.

She was not surprised at Mademoiselle Reisz's question the morning that lady, following her to the beach, tapped her on the shoulder and asked if she did not greatly miss her young friend.

"Oh, good morning, Mademoiselle; is it you? Why, of course I miss Robert. Are you going down to bathe?"

"Why should I go down to bathe at the very end of the season when I haven't been in the surf all summer?" replied the woman, disagreeably.

"I beg your pardon," offered Edna, in some embarrassment, for she should have remembered that Mademoiselle Reisz's avoidance of the water had furnished a theme for much pleasantry. Some among them thought it was on account of her false hair, or the dread of getting the violets wet, while others attributed it to the natural aversion for water sometimes believed to accompany the artistic temperament. Mademoiselle offered Edna some chocolates in a paper bag, which she took from her pocket, by way of showing that she bore no ill feeling. She habitually ate chocolates for their sustaining quality; they contained much nutrient in small compass, she said. They saved her from starvation, as Madame Lebrun's table was utterly impossible; and no one save so impertinent a woman as Madame Lebrun could think of offering such food to people and requiring them to pay for it.

"She must feel very lonely without her son," said Edna, desiring to change the subject. "Her favorite son, too. It must have been quite hard to let him go."

Mademoiselle laughed maliciously.

"Her favorite son! Oh, dear! Who could have been imposing such a tale upon you? Aline Lebrun lives for Victor, and for Victor alone. She has spoiled him into the worthless creature he is. She worships him and the ground he walks on. Robert is very well in a way, to give up all the money he can earn to the family, and keep the barest pittance for himself. Favorite son, indeed! I miss the poor fellow myself, my dear. I liked to see him and to hear him about the place — the only Lebrun who is worth a pinch of salt. He comes to see me often in the city. I like to play to him. That Victor! hanging would be too good for him. It's a wonder Robert hasn't beaten him to death long ago."

"I thought he had great patience with his brother," offered Edna, glad to be talking about Robert, no matter what was said.

"Oh! he thrashed him well enough a year or two ago," said Mademoiselle. "It was about a Spanish girl, whom Victor considered that he had some sort of claim upon. He met Robert one day talking to the girl, or walking with her, or bathing with her, or carrying her basket — I don't remember what; — and he became so insulting and abusive that Robert gave him a thrashing on the spot that has kept him comparatively in order for a good while. It's about time he was getting another."

"Was her name Mariequita?" asked Edna.

"Mariequita — yes, that was it; Mariequita. I had forgotten. Oh, she's a sly one, and a bad one, that Mariequita!"

Edna looked down at Mademoiselle Reisz and wondered how she could have listened to her venom so long. For some reason she felt depressed, almost unhappy. She had not intended to go into the water; but she donned her bathing suit, and left Mademoiselle alone, seated under the shade of the children's tent. The water was growing cooler as the season advanced. Edna plunged and swam about with an abandon that thrilled and invigorated her. She remained a long time in the water, half hoping that Mademoiselle Reisz would not wait for her.

But Mademoiselle waited. She was very amiable during the walk back, and raved much over Edna's appearance in her bathing suit. She talked about music. She hoped that Edna would go to see her in the city, and wrote her address with the stub of a pencil on a piece of card which she found in her pocket.

"When do you leave?" asked Edna.

"Next Monday; and you?"

"The following week," answered Edna, adding, "It has been a pleasant summer, hasn't it, Mademoiselle?"

"Well," agreed Mademoiselle Reisz, with a shrug, "rather pleasant, if it hadn't been for the mosquitoes and the Farival twins."

XVII

The Pontelliers possessed a very charming home on Esplanade Street in New Orleans. It was a large, double cottage, with a broad front veranda, whose round, fluted columns supported the sloping roof. The house was painted a dazzling white; the outside shutters, or jalousies, were green. In the yard, which was kept scrupulously neat, were flowers and plants of every description which flourish in South Louisiana. Within doors the appointments were perfect after the conventional type. The softest carpets and rugs covered the floors; rich and tasteful draperies hung at doors and windows. There were paintings, selected with judgment and discrimination, upon the walls. The cut glass, the silver, the heavy damask which daily appeared upon the table were the envy of many women whose husbands were less generous than Mr. Pontellier.

Mr. Pontellier was very fond of walking about his house examining its various appointments and details, to see that nothing was amiss. He greatly valued his possessions, chiefly because they were his, and derived genuine pleasure from contemplating a painting, a statuette, a rare lace curtain — no matter what — after he had bought it and placed it among his household goods.

On Tuesday afternoons — Tuesday being Mrs. Pontellier's reception day — there was a constant stream of callers — women who came in carriages or in the street cars, or walked when the air was soft and distance permitted. A light-colored mulatto boy, in dress coat and bearing a diminutive silver tray for the reception of cards, admitted them. A maid, in white fluted cap, offered the callers liqueur, coffee, or chocolate, as they might desire. Mrs. Pontellier, attired in a handsome reception gown, remained in the drawing-room the entire afternoon receiving her visitors. Men sometimes called in the evening with their wives.

This had been the programme which Mrs. Pontellier had religiously followed since her marriage, six years before. Certain evenings during the week she and her husband attended the opera or sometimes the play.

Mr. Pontellier left his home in the mornings between nine and ten o'clock, and rarely returned before half-past six or seven in the evening — dinner being served at half-past seven.

He and his wife seated themselves at table one Tuesday evening, a few weeks after their return from Grand Isle. They were alone together. The boys were being put to bed; the patter of their bare, escaping feet could be heard occasionally, as well as the pursuing voice of the quadroon, lifted in mild protest and entreaty. Mrs. Pontellier did not wear her usual Tuesday reception gown; she was in ordinary house dress. Mr. Pontellier, who was observant about such things, noticed it, as he served the soup and handed it to the boy in waiting.

"Tired out, Edna? Whom did you have? Many callers?" he asked. He tasted his soup and began to season it with pepper, salt, vinegar, mustard — everything within reach.

"There were a good many," replied Edna, who was eating her soup with evident satisfaction. "I found their cards when I got home; I was out."

"Out!" exclaimed her husband, with something like genuine consternation in his voice as he laid down the vinegar cruet and looked at her through his glasses. "Why, what could have taken you out on Tuesday? What did you have to do?"

"Nothing. I simply felt like going out, and I went out."

"Well, I hope you left some suitable excuse," said her husband, somewhat appeased, as he added a dash of cayenne pepper to the soup.

"No, I left no excuse. I told Joe to say I was out, that was all."

"Why, my dear, I should think you'd understand by this time that people don't do such things; we've got to observe *les convenances* if we ever expect to get on and keep up with the procession. If you felt that you had to leave home this afternoon, you should have left some suitable explanation for your absence.

"This soup is really impossible; it's strange that woman hasn't learned yet to make a decent soup. Any free-lunch stand in town serves a better one. Was Mrs. Belthrop here?"

"Bring the tray with the cards, Joe. I don't remember who was here."

The boy retired and returned after a moment, bringing the tiny silver tray, which was covered with ladies' visiting cards. He handed it to Mrs. Pontellier.

"Give it to Mr. Pontellier," she said.

Joe offered the tray to Mr. Pontellier, and removed the soup.

Mr. Pontellier scanned the names of his wife's callers, reading some of them aloud, with comments as he read.

"'The Misses Delasidas.' I worked a big deal in futures for their father this morning; nice girls; it's time they were getting married. 'Mrs. Belthrop.' I tell you what it is, Edna; you can't afford to snub Mrs. Belthrop. Why, Belthrop could buy and sell us ten times over. His business is worth a good, round sum to me. You'd better write her a note. 'Mrs. James Highcamp.' Hugh! the less you have to do with Mrs. Highcamp, the better. 'Madame Laforcé.' Came all the way from Carrolton, too, poor old soul. 'Miss Wiggs,' 'Mrs. Eleanor Boltons.'" He pushed the cards aside.

"Mercy!" exclaimed Edna, who had been fuming. "Why are you taking the thing so seriously and making such a fuss over it?"

"I'm not making any fuss over it. But it's just such seeming trifles that we've got to take seriously; such things count."

The fish was scorched. Mr. Pontellier would not touch it. Edna said she did not mind a little scorched taste. The roast was in some way not to his fancy, and he did not like the manner in which the vegetables were served.

"It seems to me," he said, "we spend money enough in this house to procure at least one meal a day which a man could eat and retain his self-respect."

"You used to think the cook was a treasure," returned Edna, indifferently.

"Perhaps she was when she first came; but cooks are only human. They need looking after, like any other class of persons that you employ. Suppose I didn't look after the clerks in my office, just let them run things their own way; they'd soon make a nice mess of me and my business."

"Where are you going?" asked Edna, seeing that her husband arose from table without having eaten a morsel except a taste of the highly-seasoned soup.

"I'm going to get my dinner at the club. Good night." He went into the hall, took his hat and stick from the stand, and left the house.

She was somewhat familiar with such scenes. They had often made her very unhappy. On a few previous occasions she had been completely deprived of any desire to finish her dinner. Sometimes she had gone into the kitchen to administer a tardy rebuke to the cook. Once she went to her room and studied the cookbook during an entire evening, finally writing out a menu for the week, which left her harassed with a feeling that, after all, she had accomplished no good that was worth the name.

But that evening Edna finished her dinner alone, with forced deliberation. Her face was flushed and her eyes flamed with some inward fire that lighted them. After finishing her dinner she went to her room, having instructed the boy to tell any other callers that she was indisposed.

It was a large, beautiful room, rich and picturesque in the soft, dim light which the maid had turned low. She went and stood at an open window and looked out upon the deep tangle of the garden below. All the mystery and witchery of the night seemed to have gathered there amid the perfumes and the dusky and tortuous outlines of flowers and foliage. She was seeking herself and finding herself in just such sweet, half-darkness which met her moods. But the voices were not soothing that came to her from the darkness and the sky above and the stars. They jeered and sounded mournful notes without promise, devoid even of hope. She turned back into the room and began to walk to and fro down its whole length, without stopping, without resting. She carried in her hands a thin handkerchief, which she tore into ribbons, rolled into a ball, and flung from her. Once she stopped, and taking off her wedding ring, flung it upon the carpet. When she saw it lying there, she stamped her heel upon it, striving to crush it. But her small boot heel did not make an indenture, not a mark upon the little glittering circlet.

In a sweeping passion she seized a glass vase from the table and flung it upon the tiles of the hearth. She wanted to destroy something. The crash and clatter were what she wanted to hear.

A maid, alarmed at the din of breaking glass, entered the room to discover what was the matter.

"A vase fell upon the hearth," said Edna. "Never mind; leave it till morning."

"Oh! you might get some of the glass in your feet, ma'am," insisted the young woman, picking up bits of the broken vase that were scattered upon the carpet. "And here's your ring, ma'am, under the chair."

Edna held out her hand, and taking the ring, slipped it upon her finger.

XVIII

The following morning Mr. Pontellier, upon leaving for his office, asked Edna if she would not meet him in town in order to look at some new fixtures for the library.

"I hardly think we need new fixtures, Léonce. Don't let us get anything new; you are too extravagant. I don't believe you ever think of saving or putting by."

"The way to become rich is to make money, my dear Edna, not to save it," he said. He regretted that she did not feel inclined to go with him and select new fixtures. He kissed her good-by, and told her she was not looking well and must take care of herself. She was unusually pale and very quiet.

She stood on the front veranda as he quitted the house, and absently picked a few sprays of jessamine that grew upon a trellis near by. She inhaled the odor of the blossoms and thrust them into the bosom of her white morning gown. The boys were dragging along the banquette a small "express wagon," which they had filled with blocks and sticks. The quadroon was following them with little quick steps, having assumed a fictitious animation and alacrity for the occasion. A fruit vender was crying his wares in the street.

Edna looked straight before her with a self-absorbed expression upon her face. She felt no interest in anything about her. The street, the children, the fruit vender, the flowers growing there under her eyes, were all part and parcel of an alien world which had suddenly become antagonistic.

She went back into the house. She had thought of speaking to the cook concerning her blunders of the previous night; but Mr. Pontellier had saved her that disagreeable mission, for which she was so poorly fitted. Mr. Pontellier's arguments were usually convincing with those whom he employed. He left home feeling quite sure that he and Edna would sit down that evening, and possibly a few subsequent evenings, to a dinner deserving of the name.

Edna spent an hour or two in looking over some of her old sketches. She could see their shortcomings and defects, which were glaring in her eyes. She tried to work a little, but found she was not in the humor. Finally she gathered together a few of the sketches — those which she considered the least discreditable; and she carried them with her when, a little later, she dressed and left the house. She looked handsome and distinguished in her street gown. The tan of the seashore had left her face, and her forehead was smooth, white, and polished beneath her heavy, yellow-brown hair. There were a few freckles on her face, and a small, dark mole near the under lip and one on the temple, half-hidden in her hair.

As Edna walked along the street she was thinking of Robert. She was still under the spell of her infatuation. She had tried to forget him, realizing the inutility of remembering. But the thought of him was like an obsession, ever pressing itself upon her. It was not that she dwelt upon details of their acquaintance, or recalled in any special or peculiar way his personality; it was his being, his existence, which dominated her thought, fading sometimes as if it would melt into the mist of the forgotten, reviving again with an intensity which filled her with an incomprehensible longing.

Edna was on her way to Madame Ratignolle's. Their intimacy, begun at Grand Isle, had not declined, and they had seen each other with some frequency since their return to the city. The Ratignolles lived at no great distance from Edna's home, on the corner of a side street, where Monsieur Ratignolle owned and conducted a drug store which enjoyed a steady and prosperous trade. His father had been in the business before him, and Monsieur Ratignolle stood well in the community and bore an enviable reputation for integrity and clear-headedness. His family lived in commodious apartments over the store, having an entrance on the side within the *porte cochère.* There was something which Edna thought very French, very foreign, about their whole manner of living. In the large and pleasant salon which extended across the width of the house, the Ratignolles entertained their friends once a fortnight with a *soirée musicale,* sometimes diversified by card-playing. There was a friend who played upon the 'cello. One brought his flute and another his violin, while there were some who sang and a number who performed upon the piano with various degrees of taste and agility. The Ratignolles' *soirées musicales* were widely known, and it was considered a privilege to be invited to them.

Edna found her friend engaged in assorting the clothes which had returned that morning from the laundry. She at once abandoned her occupation upon seeing Edna, who had been ushered without ceremony into her presence.

" 'Cité can do it as well as I; it is really her business," she explained to Edna, who apologized for interrupting her. And she summoned a young black woman, whom she instructed, in French, to be very careful in checking off the list which she handed her. She told her to notice particularly if a fine linen handkerchief of Monsieur Ratignolle's, which was missing last week, had been returned; and to be sure to set to one side such pieces as required mending and darning.

Then placing an arm around Edna's waist, she led her to the front of the house, to the salon, where it was cool and sweet with the odor of great roses that stood upon the hearth in jars.

Madame Ratignolle looked more beautiful than ever there at home, in a négligée which left her arms almost wholly bare and exposed the rich, melting curves of her white throat.

"Perhaps I shall be able to paint your picture some day," said Edna with a smile when they were seated. She produced the roll of sketches and started to unfold them. "I believe I ought to work again. I feel as if I wanted to be doing something. What do you think of them? Do you think it worth while to take it up again and study some more? I might study for a while with Laidpore."

She knew that Madame Ratignolle's opinion in such a matter would be next to valueless, that she herself had not alone decided, but determined; but she sought the words of praise and encouragement that would help her to put heart into her venture.

"Your talent is immense, dear!"

"Nonsense!" protested Edna, well pleased.

"Immense, I tell you," persisted Madame Ratignolle, surveying the sketches one by one, at close range, then holding them at arm's length, narrowing her eyes, and dropping her head on one side. "Surely, this Bavarian peasant is worthy of framing; and this basket of apples! Never have I seen anything more lifelike. One might almost be tempted to reach out a hand and take one."

Edna could not control a feeling which bordered upon complacency at her friend's praise, even realizing, as she did, its true worth. She retained a few of the sketches, and gave all the rest to Madame Ratignolle, who appreciated the gift far beyond its value and proudly exhibited the pictures to her husband when he came up from the store a little later for his midday dinner.

Mr. Ratignolle was one of those men who are called the salt of the earth. His cheerfulness was unbounded, and it was matched by his goodness of heart, his broad charity, and common sense. He and his wife spoke English with an accent which was only discernible through its un-English emphasis and a certain carefulness and deliberation. Edna's husband spoke English with no accent whatever. The Ratignolles understood each other perfectly. If ever the fusion of two human beings into one has been accomplished on this sphere it was surely in their union.

As Edna seated herself at table with them she thought, "Better a dinner of herbs," though it did not take her long to discover that [it] was no dinner of herbs, but a delicious repast, simple, choice, and in every way satisfying.

Monsieur Ratignolle was delighted to see her, though he found her looking not so well as at Grand Isle, and he advised a tonic. He talked a good deal on various topics, a little politics, some city news and neighborhood gossip. He spoke with an animation and earnestness that gave an exaggerated importance to every syllable he uttered. His wife was keenly interested in everything he said, laying down her fork the better to listen, chiming in, taking the words out of his mouth.

Edna felt depressed rather than soothed after leaving them. The little glimpse of domestic harmony which had been offered her, gave her no regret, no longing. It was not a condition of life which fitted her, and she could see in it but an appalling and hopeless ennui. She was moved by a kind of commiseration for Madame Ratignolle,—a pity for that colorless existence which never uplifted its possessor beyond the region of blind contentment, in which no moment of anguish ever visited her soul, in which she would never have the taste of life's delirium. Edna vaguely wondered what she meant by "life's delirium." It had crossed her thought like some unsought extraneous impression.

XIX

Edna could not help but think that it was very foolish, very childish, to have stamped upon her wedding ring and smashed the crystal vase upon the tiles. She was visited by no more outbursts, moving her to such futile expedients. She began to do as she liked and to feel as she liked. She completely abandoned her Tuesdays at home, and did not return the visits of those who had called upon her. She made no ineffectual efforts to conduct her household *en bonne ménagère*, going and coming as it suited her fancy, and, so far as she was able, lending herself to any passing caprice.

Mr. Pontellier had been a rather courteous husband so long as he met a certain tacit submissiveness in his wife. But her new and unexpected line of conduct completely bewildered him. It shocked him. Then her absolute disregard for her duties as a wife angered him. When Mr. Pontellier became rude, Edna grew insolent. She had resolved never to take another step backward.

"It seems to me the utmost folly for a woman at the head of a household, and the mother of children, to spend in an atelier days which would be better employed contriving for the comfort of her family."

"I feel like painting," answered Edna. "Perhaps I shan't always feel like it."

"Then in God's name paint! but don't let the family go to the devil. There's Madame Ratignolle; because she keeps up her music, she doesn't let everything else go to chaos. And she's more of a musician than you are a painter."

"She isn't a musician, and I'm not a painter. It isn't on account of painting that I let things go."

"On account of what, then?"

"Oh! I don't know. Let me alone; you bother me."

It sometimes entered Mr. Pontellier's mind to wonder if his wife were not growing a little unbalanced mentally. He could see plainly that she was not herself. That is, he could not see that she was becoming herself and daily casting aside that fictitious self which we assume like a garment with which to appear before the world.

Her husband let her alone as she requested, and went away to his office. Edna went up to her atelier — a bright room in the top of the house. She was working with great energy and interest, without accomplishing anything, however, which satisfied her even in the smallest degree. For a time she had the whole household enrolled in the service of art. The boys posed for her. They thought it amusing at first, but the occupation soon lost its attractiveness when they discovered that it was not a game arranged especially for their entertainment. The quadroon sat for hours before Edna's palette, patient as a savage, while the house-maid took charge of the children, and the drawing-room went undusted. But the house-maid, too, served her term as model when Edna perceived that the young woman's back and shoulders were molded on classic lines, and that her hair, loosened from its confining cap, became an inspiration. While Edna worked she sometimes sang low the little air, *"Ah! si tu savais!"*

It moved her with recollections. She could hear again the ripple of the water, the flapping sail. She could see the glint of the moon upon the bay, and could feel the soft, gusty beating of the hot south wind. A subtle current of desire passed through her body, weakening her hold upon the brushes and making her eyes burn.

There were days when she was very happy without knowing why. She was happy to be alive and breathing, when her whole being seemed to be one with the sunlight, the color, the odors, the luxuriant warmth of some perfect Southern day. She liked then to wander alone into strange and unfamiliar places. She discovered many a sunny, sleepy corner, fashioned to dream in. And she found it good to dream and to be alone and unmolested.

There were days when she was unhappy, she did not know why, — when it did not seem worth while to be glad or sorry, to be alive or dead; when life appeared to her like a grotesque pandemonium and humanity like worms struggling blindly toward inevitable annihilation. She would not work on such a day, nor weave fancies to stir her pulses and warm her blood.

XX

It was during such a mood that Edna hunted up Mademoiselle Reisz. She had not forgotten the rather disagreeable impression left upon her by their last interview; but she nevertheless felt a desire to see her — above all, to listen while she played upon the piano. Quite early in the afternoon she started upon her quest for the pianist. Unfortunately she had mislaid or lost Mademoiselle Reisz's card, and looking up her address in the city directory, she found that the woman lived on Bienville Street, some distance away. The directory which fell into her hands was a year or more old, however, and upon reaching the number indicated, Edna discovered that the house was occupied by a respectable family of mulattoes who had *chambres garnies* to let. They had been living there for six months, and knew absolutely nothing of a Mademoiselle Reisz. In fact, they knew nothing of any of their neighbors; their lodgers were all people of the highest distinction, they assured Edna. She did not linger to discuss class distinctions with Madame Pouponne, but hastened to a neighboring grocery store, feeling sure that Mademoiselle would have left her address with the proprietor.

He knew Mademoiselle Reisz a good deal better than he wanted to know her, he informed his questioner. In truth, he did not want to know her at all, or anything concerning her — the most disagreeable and unpopular woman who ever lived in Bienville Street. He thanked heaven she had left the neighborhood, and was equally thankful that he did not know where she had gone.

Edna's desire to see Mademoiselle Reisz had increased tenfold since these unlooked-for obstacles had arisen to thwart it. She was wondering who could give her the information she sought, when it suddenly occurred to her that Madame Lebrun would be the one most likely to do so. She knew it was useless to ask Madame Ratignolle, who was on the most distant terms with the musician, and preferred to know nothing concerning her. She had once been almost as emphatic in expressing herself upon the subject as the corner grocer.

Edna knew that Madame Lebrun had returned to the city, for it was the middle of November. And she also knew where the Lebruns lived, on Chartres Street. Their home from the outside looked like a prison, with iron bars before the door and lower windows. The iron bars were a relic of the old *régime,* and no one had ever thought of dislodging them. At the side was a high fence enclosing the garden. A gate or door opening upon the street was locked. Edna rang the bell at this side garden gate, and stood upon the banquette, waiting to be admitted.

It was Victor who opened the gate for her. A black woman, wiping her hands upon her apron, was close at his heels. Before she saw them Edna could hear them in altercation, the woman — plainly an anomaly — claiming the right to be allowed to perform her duties, one of which was to answer the bell.

Victor was surprised and delighted to see Mrs. Pontellier, and he made no attempt to conceal either his astonishment or his delight. He was a dark-browed, good-looking youngster of nineteen, greatly resembling his mother, but with ten times her impetuosity. He instructed the black woman to go at once and inform Madame Lebrun that Mrs. Pontellier desired to see her. The woman grumbled a refusal to do part of her duty when she had not been permitted to do it all, and started back to her interrupted task of weeding the garden. Whereupon Victor administered a rebuke in the form of a volley of abuse, which, owing to its rapidity and incoherence, was all but incomprehensible to Edna. Whatever it was, the rebuke was convincing, for the woman dropped her hoe and went mumbling into the house.

Edna did not wish to enter. It was very pleasant there on the side porch, where there were chairs, a wicker lounge, and a small table. She seated herself, for she was tired from her long tramp; and she began to rock gently and smooth out the folds of her silk parasol. Victor drew up his chair beside her. He at once explained that the black woman's offensive conduct was all due to imperfect training, as he was not there to take her in hand. He had only come up from the island the morning before, and expected to return next day. He stayed all winter at the island; he lived there, and kept the place in order and got things ready for the summer visitors.

But a man needed occasional relaxation, he informed Mrs. Pontellier, and every now and again he drummed up a pretext to bring him to the city. My! but he had had a time of it the evening before! He wouldn't want his mother to know, and he began to talk in a whisper. He was scintillant with recollections. Of course, he couldn't think of telling Mrs. Pontellier all about it, she being a woman and not comprehending such things. But it all began with a girl peeping and smiling at him through the shutters as he passed by. Oh! but she was a beauty! Certainly he smiled back, and went up and talked to her. Mrs. Pontellier did not know him if she supposed he was one to let an opportunity like that escape him. Despite herself, the youngster amused her. She must have betrayed in her look some degree of interest or entertainment. The boy grew more daring, and Mrs. Pontellier might have found herself, in a little while, listening to a highly colored story but for the timely appearance of Madame Lebrun.

That lady was still clad in white, according to her custom of the summer. Her eyes beamed an effusive welcome. Would not Mrs. Pontellier go inside? Would she partake of some refreshment? Why had she not been there before? How was that dear Mr. Pontellier and how were those sweet children? Had Mrs. Pontellier ever known such a warm November?

Victor went and reclined on the wicker lounge behind his mother's chair, where he commanded a view of Edna's face. He had taken her parasol from her hands while he spoke to her, and he now lifted it and twirled it above him as he lay on his back. When Madame Lebrun complained that it was *so* dull coming back to the city; that she saw *so* few people now; that even Victor, when he came up from the island for a day or two, had *so* much to occupy him and engage his time; then it was that the youth went into contortions on the lounge and winked mischievously at Edna. She somehow felt like a confederate in crime, and tried to look severe and disapproving.

There had been but two letters from Robert, with little in them, they told her. Victor said it was really not worth while to go inside for the letters, when his mother entreated him to go in search of them. He remembered the contents, which in truth he rattled off very glibly when put to the test.

One letter was written from Vera Cruz and the other from the City of Mexico. He had met Montel, who was doing everything toward his advancement. So far, the financial situation was no improvement over the one he had left in New Orleans, but of course the prospects were vastly better. He wrote of the City of Mexico, the buildings, the people and their habits, the conditions of life which he found there. He sent his love to the family. He inclosed a check to his mother, and hoped she would affectionately remember him to all his friends. That was about the substance of the two letters. Edna felt that if there had been a message for her, she would have received it. The despondent frame of mind in which she had left home began again to overtake her, and she remembered that she wished to find Mademoiselle Reisz.

Madame Lebrun knew where Mademoiselle Reisz lived. She gave Edna the address, regretting that she would not consent to stay and spend the remainder of the afternoon, and pay a visit to Mademoiselle Reisz some other day. The afternoon was already well advanced.

Victor escorted her out upon the banquette, lifted her parasol, and held it over her while he walked to the car with her. He entreated her to bear in mind that the disclosures of the afternoon were strictly confidential. She laughed and bantered him a little, remembering too late that she should have been dignified and reserved.

"How handsome Mrs. Pontellier looked!" said Madame Lebrun to her son.

"Ravishing!" he admitted. "The city atmosphere has improved her. Some way she doesn't seem like the same woman."

XXI

Some people contended that the reason Mademoiselle Reisz always chose apartments up under the roof was to discourage the approach of beggars, peddlars and callers. There were plenty of windows in her little front room. They were for the most part dingy, but as they were nearly always open it did not make so much difference. They often admitted into the room a good deal of smoke and soot; but at the same time all the light and air that there was came through them. From her windows could be seen the crescent of the river, the masts of ships and the big chimneys of the Mississippi steamers. A magnificent piano crowded the apartment. In the next room she slept, and in the third and last she harbored a gasoline stove on which she cooked her meals when disinclined to descend to the neighboring restaurant. It was there also that she ate, keeping her belongings in a rare old buffet, dingy and battered from a hundred years of use.

When Edna knocked at Mademoiselle Reisz's front room door and entered, she discovered that person standing beside the window, engaged in mending or patching an old prunella gaiter. The little musician laughed all over when she saw Edna. Her laugh consisted of a contortion of the face and all the muscles of the body. She seemed strikingly homely, standing there in the afternoon light. She still wore the shabby lace and the artificial bunch of violets on the side of her head.

"So you remembered me at last," said Mademoiselle. "I had said to myself, 'Ah, bah! she will never come.'"

"Did you want me to come?" asked Edna with a smile.

"I had not thought much about it," answered Mademoiselle. The two had seated themselves on a little bumpy sofa which stood against the wall. "I am glad, however, that you came. I have the water boiling back there, and was just about to make some coffee. You will drink a cup with me. And how is *la belle dame?* Always handsome! always healthy! always contented!" She took Edna's hand between her strong wiry fingers, holding it loosely without warmth, and executing a sort of double theme upon the back and palm.

"Yes," she went on; "I sometimes thought: 'She will never come. She promised as those women in society always do, without meaning it. She will not come.' For I really don't believe you like me, Mrs. Pontellier."

"I don't know whether I like you or not," replied Edna, gazing down at the little woman with a quizzical look.

The candor of Mrs. Pontellier's admission greatly pleased Mademoiselle Reisz. She expressed her gratification by repairing forthwith to the region of the gasoline stove and rewarding her guest with the promised cup of coffee. The coffee and the biscuit accompanying it proved very acceptable to Edna, who had declined refreshment at Madame Lebrun's and was now beginning to feel hungry. Mademoiselle set the tray which she brought in upon a small table near at hand, and seated herself once again on the lumpy sofa.

"I have had a letter from your friend," she remarked, as she poured a little cream into Edna's cup and handed it to her.

"My friend?"

"Yes, your friend Robert. He wrote to me from the City of Mexico."

"Wrote to *you?*" repeated Edna in amazement, stirring her coffee absently.

"Yes, to me. Why not? Don't stir all the warmth out of your coffee; drink it. Though the letter might as well have been sent to you; it was nothing but Mrs. Pontellier from beginning to end."

"Let me see it," requested the young woman, entreatingly.

"No; a letter concerns no one but the person who writes it and the one to whom it is written."

"Haven't you just said it concerned me from beginning to end?"

"It was written about you, not to you. 'Have you seen Mrs. Pontellier? How is she looking?' he asks. 'As Mrs. Pontellier says,' or 'as Mrs. Pontellier once said.' 'If Mrs. Pontellier should call upon you, play for her that Impromptu of Chopin's, my favorite. I heard it here a day or two ago, but not as you play it. I should like to know how it affects her,' and so on, as if he supposed we were constantly in each other's society."

"Let me see the letter."

"Oh, no."

"Have you answered it?"

"No."

"Let me see the letter."

"No, and again, no."

"Then play the Impromptu for me."

"It is growing late; what time do you have to be home?"

"Time doesn't concern me. Your question seems a little rude. Play the Impromptu."

"But you have told me nothing of yourself. What are you doing?"

"Painting!" laughed Edna. "I am becoming an artist. Think of it!"

"Ah! an artist! You have pretensions, Madame."

"Why pretensions? Do you think I could not become an artist?"

"I do not know you well enough to say. I do not know your talent or your temperament. To be an artist includes much; one must possess many gifts — absolute gifts — which have not been acquired by one's own effort. And, moreover, to succeed, the artist must possess the courageous soul."

"What do you mean by the courageous soul?"

"Courageous, *ma foi!* The brave soul. The soul that dares and defies."

"Show me the letter and play for me the Impromptu. You see that I have persistence. Does that quality count for anything in art?"

"It counts with a foolish old woman whom you have captivated," replied Mademoiselle, with her wriggling laugh.

The letter was right there at hand in the drawer of the little table upon which Edna had just placed her coffee cup. Mademoiselle opened the drawer and drew forth the letter, the topmost one. She placed it in Edna's hands, and without further comment arose and went to the piano.

Mademoiselle played a soft interlude. It was an improvisation. She sat low at the instrument, and the lines of her body settled into ungraceful curves and angles that gave it an appearance of deformity. Gradually and imperceptibly the interlude melted into the soft opening minor chords of the Chopin Impromptu.

Edna did not know when the Impromptu began or ended. She sat in the sofa corner reading Robert's letter by the fading light. Mademoiselle had glided from the Chopin into the quivering love-notes of Isolde's song, and back again to the Impromptu with its soulful and poignant longing.

The shadows deepened in the little room. The music grew strange and fantastic — turbulent, insistent, plaintive and soft with entreaty. The shadows grew deeper. The music filled the room. It floated out upon the night, over the housetops, the crescent of the river, losing itself in the silence of the upper air.

Edna was sobbing, just as she had wept one midnight at Grand Isle when strange, new voices awoke in her. She arose in some agitation to take her departure. "May I come again, Mademoiselle?" she asked at the threshold.

"Come whenever you feel like it. Be careful; the stairs and landings are dark; don't stumble."

Mademoiselle reëntered and lit a candle. Robert's letter was on the floor. She stooped and picked it up. It was crumpled and damp with tears. Mademoiselle smoothed the letter out, restored it to the envelope, and replaced it in the table drawer.

XXII

One morning on his way into town Mr. Pontellier stopped at the house of his old friend and family physician, Doctor Mandelet. The Doctor was a semi-retired physician, resting, as the saying is, upon his laurels. He bore a reputation for wisdom rather than skill — leaving the active practice of medicine to his assistants and younger contemporaries — and was much sought for in matters of consultation. A few families, united to him by bonds of friendship, he still attended when they required the services of a physician. The Pontelliers were among these.

Mr. Pontellier found the Doctor reading at the open window of his study. His house stood rather far back from the street, in the center of a delightful garden, so that it was quiet and peaceful at the old gentleman's study window. He was a great reader. He stared up disapprovingly over his eye-glasses as Mr. Pontellier entered, wondering who had the temerity to disturb him at that hour of the morning.

"Ah, Pontellier! Not sick, I hope. Come and have a seat. What news do you bring this morning?" He was quite portly, with a profusion of gray hair, and small blue eyes which age had robbed of much of their brightness but none of their penetration.

"Oh! I'm never sick, Doctor. You know that I come of tough fiber — of that old Creole race of Pontelliers that dry up and finally blow away. I came to consult — no, not precisely to consult — to talk to you about Edna. I don't know what ails her."

"Madame Pontellier not well?" marveled the Doctor. "Why, I saw her — I think it was a week ago — walking along Canal Street, the picture of health, it seemed to me."

"Yes, yes; she seems quite well," said Mr. Pontellier, leaning forward and whirling his stick between his two hands; "but she doesn't act well. She's odd, she's not like herself. I can't make her out, and I thought perhaps you'd help me."

"How does she act?" inquired the doctor.

"Well, it isn't easy to explain," said Mr. Pontellier, throwing himself back in his chair. "She lets the housekeeping go to the dickens."

"Well, well; women are not all alike, my dear Pontellier. We've got to consider — "

"I know that; I told you I couldn't explain. Her whole attitude — toward me and everybody and everything — has changed. You know I have a quick temper, but I don't want to quarrel or be rude to a woman, especially my wife; yet I'm driven to it, and feel like ten thousand devils after I've made a fool of myself. She's making it devilishly uncomfortable for me," he went on nervously. "She's got some sort of notion in her head concerning the eternal rights of women; and — you understand — we meet in the morning at the breakfast table."

The old gentleman lifted his shaggy eyebrows, protruded his thick nether lip, and tapped the arms of his chair with his cushioned fingertips.

"What have you been doing to her, Pontellier?"

"Doing! *Parbleu!*"

"Has she," asked the Doctor, with a smile, "has she been associating of late with a circle of pseudo-intellectual women — super-spiritual superior beings? My wife has been telling me about them."

"That's the trouble," broke in Mr. Pontellier, "she hasn't been associating with any one. She has abandoned her Tuesdays at home, has thrown over all her acquaintances, and goes tramping about by herself, moping in the street-cars, getting in after dark. I tell you she's peculiar. I don't like it; I feel a little worried over it."

This was a new aspect for the Doctor. "Nothing hereditary?" he asked, seriously. "Nothing peculiar about her family antecedents, is there?"

"Oh, no, indeed! She comes of sound old Presbyterian Kentucky stock. The old gentleman, her father, I have heard, used to atone for his weekday sins with his Sunday devotions. I know for a fact, that his race horses literally ran away with the prettiest bit of Kentucky farming land I ever laid eyes upon. Margaret —you know Margaret—she has all the Presbyterianism undiluted. And the youngest is something of a vixen. By the way, she gets married in a couple of weeks from now."

"Send your wife up to the wedding," exclaimed the Doctor, foreseeing a happy solution. "Let her stay among her own people for a while; it will do her good."

"That's what I want her to do. She won't go to the marriage. She says a wedding is one of the most lamentable spectacles on earth. Nice thing for a woman to say to her husband!" exclaimed Mr. Pontellier, fuming anew at the recollection.

"Pontellier," said the Doctor, after a moment's reflection, "let your wife alone for a while. Don't bother her, and don't let her bother you. Woman, my dear friend, is a very peculiar and delicate organism—a sensitive and highly organized woman, such as I know Mrs. Pontellier to be, is especially peculiar. It would require an inspired psychologist to deal successfully with them. And when ordinary fellows like you and me attempt to cope with their idiosyncrasies the result is bungling. Most women are moody and whimsical. This is some passing whim of your wife, due to some cause or causes which you and I needn't try to fathom. But it will pass happily over, especially if you let her alone. Send her around to see me."

"Oh! I couldn't do that; there'd be no reason for it," objected Mr. Pontellier.

"Then I'll go around and see her," said the Doctor. "I'll drop in to dinner some evening *en bon ami.*"

"Do! by all means," urged Mr. Pontellier. "What evening will you come? Say Thursday. Will you come Thursday?" he asked, rising to take his leave.

"Very well; Thursday. My wife may possibly have some engagement for me Thursday. In case she has, I shall let you know. Otherwise, you may expect me."

Mr. Pontellier turned before leaving to say:

"I am going to New York on business very soon. I have a big scheme on hand, and want to be on the field proper to pull the ropes and handle the ribbons. We'll let you in on the inside if you say so, Doctor," he laughed.

"No, I thank you, my dear sir," returned the Doctor. "I leave such ventures to you younger men with the fever of life still in your blood."

"What I wanted to say," continued Mr. Pontellier, with his hand on the knob; "I may have to be absent a good while. Would you advise me to take Edna along?"

"By all means, if she wishes to go. If not, leave her here. Don't contradict her. The mood will pass, I assure you. It may take a month, two, three months— possibly longer, but it will pass; have patience."

"Well, good-by, *à jeudi,*" said Mr. Pontellier, as he let himself out.

The doctor would have liked during the course of conversation to ask, "Is there any man in the case?" but he knew his Creole too well to make such a blunder as that.

He did not resume his book immediately, but sat for a while meditatively looking out into the garden.

XXIII

Edna's father was in the city, and had been with them several days. She was not very warmly or deeply attached to him, but they had certain tastes in common, and when together they were companionable. His coming was in the nature of a welcome disturbance; it seemed to furnish a new direction for her emotions.

He had come to purchase a wedding gift for his daughter, Janet, and an outfit for himself in which he might make a creditable appearance at her marriage. Mr. Pontellier had selected the bridal gift, as every one immediately connected with him always deferred to his taste in such matters. And his suggestions on the question of dress — which too often assumes the nature of a problem — were of inestimable value to his father-in-law. But for the past few days the old gentleman had been upon Edna's hands, and in his society she was becoming acquainted with a new set of sensations. He had been a colonel in the Confederate army, and still maintained, with the title, the military bearing which had always accompanied it. His hair and mustache were white and silky, emphasizing the rugged bronze of his face. He was tall and thin, and wore his coats padded, which gave a fictitious breadth and depth to his shoulders and chest. Edna and her father looked very distinguished together, and excited a good deal of notice during their perambulations. Upon his arrival she began by introducing him to her atelier and making a sketch of him. He took the whole matter very seriously. If her talent had been ten-fold greater than it was, it would not have surprised him, convinced as he was that he had bequeathed to all of his daughters the germs of a masterful capability, which only depended upon their own efforts to be directed toward successful achievement.

Before her pencil he sat rigid and unflinching, as he had faced the cannon's mouth in days gone by. He resented the intrusion of the children, who gaped with wondering eyes at him, sitting so stiff up there in their mother's bright atelier. When they drew near he motioned them away with an expressive action of the foot, loath to disturb the fixed lines of his countenance, his arms, or his rigid shoulders.

Edna, anxious to entertain him, invited Mademoiselle Reisz to meet him, having promised him a treat in her piano playing; but Mademoiselle declined the invitation. So together they attended a *soirée musicale* at the Ratignolle's. Monsieur and Madame Ratignolle made much of the Colonel, installing him as the guest of honor and engaging him at once to dine with them the following Sunday, or any day which he might select. Madame coquetted with him in the most captivating and naïve manner, with eyes, gestures, and a profusion of compliments, till the Colonel's old head felt thirty years younger on his padded shoulders. Edna marveled, not comprehending. She herself was almost devoid of coquetry.

There were one or two men whom she observed at the *soirée musicale*; but she would never have felt moved to any kittenish display to attract their notice — to any feline or feminine wiles to express herself toward them. Their personality attracted her in an agreeable way. Her fancy selected them, and she was glad when a lull in the music gave them an opportunity to meet her and talk with her. Often on the street the glance of strange eyes had lingered in her memory, and sometimes had disturbed her.

Mr. Pontellier did not attend these *soirées musicales*. He considered them *bourgeois*, and found more diversion at the club. To Madame Ratignolle he said the music dispensed at her *soirées* was too "heavy," too far beyond his untrained comprehension. His excuse flattered her. But she disapproved of Mr. Pontellier's club, and she was frank enough to tell Edna so.

"It's a pity Mr. Pontellier doesn't stay home more in the evenings. I think you would be more — well, if you don't mind my saying it — more united, if he did."

"Oh! dear no!" said Edna, with a blank look in her eyes. "What should I do if he stayed home? We wouldn't have anything to say to each other."

She had not much of anything to say to her father, for that matter; but he did not antagonize her. She discovered that he interested her, though she realized that he might not interest her long; and for the first time in her life she felt as if she were thoroughly acquainted with him. He kept her busy serving him and ministering to his wants. It amused her to do so. She would not permit a servant or one of the children to do anything for him which she might do herself. Her husband noticed, and thought it was the expression of a deep filial attachment which he had never suspected.

The Colonel drank numerous "toddies" during the course of the day, which left him, however, imperturbed. He was an expert at concocting strong drinks. He had even invented some, to which he had given fantastic names, and for whose manufacture he required diverse ingredients that it devolved upon Edna to procure for him.

When Doctor Mandelet dined with the Pontelliers on Thursday he could discern in Mrs. Pontellier no trace of that morbid condition which her husband had reported to him. She was excited and in a manner radiant. She and her father had been to the race course, and their thoughts when they seated themselves at table were still occupied with the events of the afternoon, and their talk was still of the track. The Doctor had not kept pace with turf affairs. He had certain recollections of racing in what he called "the good old times" when the Lecompte stables flourished, and he drew upon this fund of memories so that he might not be left out and seem wholly devoid of the modern spirit. But he failed to impose upon the Colonel, and was even far from impressing him with this trumped-up knowledge of bygone days. Edna had staked her father on his last venture, with the most gratifying results to both of them. Besides, they had met some very charming people, according to the Colonel's impressions. Mrs. Mortimer Merriman and Mrs. James Highcamp, who were there with Alcée Arobin, had joined them and had enlivened the hours in a fashion that warmed him to think of.

Mr. Pontellier himself had no particular leaning toward horse-racing, and was even rather inclined to discourage it as a pastime, especially when he considered the fate of that blue-grass farm in Kentucky. He endeavored in a general way, to express a particular disapproval, and only succeeded in arousing the ire and opposition of his father-in-law. A pretty dispute followed, in which Edna warmly espoused her father's cause and the Doctor remained neutral.

He observed his hostess attentively from under his shaggy brows, and noted a subtle change which had transformed her from the listless woman he had known into a being who, for the moment, seemed palpitant with the forces of life. Her speech was warm and energetic. There was no repression in her glance or gesture. She reminded him of some beautiful, sleek animal waking up in the sun.

The dinner was excellent. The claret was warm and the champagne was cold, and under their beneficent influence the threatened unpleasantness melted and vanished with the fumes of the wine.

Mr. Pontellier warmed up and grew reminiscent. He told some amusing plantation experiences, recollections of old Iberville and his youth, when he hunted 'possum in company with some friendly darky; thrashed the pecan trees, shot the grosbec, and roamed the woods and fields in mischievous idleness.

The Colonel, with little sense of humor and of the fitness of things, related a somber episode of those dark and bitter days, in which he had acted a conspicuous part and always formed a central figure. Nor was the Doctor happier in his selection, when he told the old, ever new and curious story of the waning of a woman's love, seeking strange, new channels, only to return to its legitimate source after days of fierce unrest. It was one of the many little human documents which had been unfolded to him during his long career as a physician. The story did not seem especially to impress Edna. She had one of her own to tell, of a woman who paddled away with her lover one night in a pirogue and never came back. They were lost amid the Baratarian Islands, and no one ever heard of them or found trace of them from that day to this. It was a pure invention. She said that Madame Antoine had related it to her. That, also, was an invention. Perhaps it was a dream she had had. But every glowing word seemed real to those who listened. They could feel the hot breath of the Southern night; they could hear the long sweep of the pirogue through the glistening moonlit water, the beating of birds' wings, rising startled from among the reeds in the salt-water pools; they could see the faces of the lovers, pale, close together, rapt in oblivious forgetfulness, drifting into the unknown.

The champagne was cold, and its subtle fumes played fantastic tricks with Edna's memory that night.

Outside, away from the glow of the fire and the soft lamplight, the night was chill and murky. The Doctor doubled his old-fashioned cloak across his breast as he strode home through the darkness. He knew his fellow-creatures better than most men; knew that inner life which so seldom unfolds itself to unanointed eyes. He was sorry he had accepted Pontellier's invitation. He was growing old, and beginning to need rest and an imperturbed spirit. He did not want the secrets of other lives thrust upon him.

"I hope it isn't Arobin," he muttered to himself as he walked. "I hope to heaven it isn't Alcée Arobin."

XXIV

Edna and her father had a warm, and almost violent dispute upon the subject of her refusal to attend her sister's wedding. Mr. Pontellier declined to interfere, to interpose either his influence or his authority. He was following Doctor Mandelet's advice, and letting her do as she liked. The Colonel reproached his daughter for her lack of filial kindness and respect, her want of sisterly affection and womanly consideration. His arguments were labored and unconvincing. He doubted if Janet would accept any excuse — forgetting that Edna had offered none. He doubted if Janet would ever speak to her again, and he was sure Margaret would not.

Edna was glad to be rid of her father when he finally took himself off with his wedding garments and his bridal gifts, with his padded shoulders, his Bible reading, his "toddies" and ponderous oaths.

Mr. Pontellier followed him closely. He meant to stop at the wedding on his way to New York and endeavor by every means which money and love could devise to atone somewhat for Edna's incomprehensible action.

"You are too lenient, too lenient by far, Léonce," asserted the Colonel. "Authority, coercion are what is needed. Put your foot down good and hard; the only way to manage a wife. Take my word for it."

The Colonel was perhaps unaware that he had coerced his own wife into her grave. Mr. Pontellier had a vague suspicion of it which he thought it needless to mention at that late day.

Edna was not so consciously gratified at her husband's leaving home as she had been over the departure of her father. As the day approached when he was to leave her for a comparatively long stay, she grew melting and affectionate, remembering his many acts of consideration and his repeated expressions of an ardent attachment. She was solicitous about his health and his welfare. She bustled around, looking after his clothing, thinking about heavy underwear, quite as Madame Ratignolle would have done under similar circumstances. She cried when he went away, calling him her dear, good friend, and she was quite certain she would grow lonely before very long and go to join him in New York.

But after all, a radiant peace settled upon her when she at last found herself alone. Even the children were gone. Old Madame Pontellier had come herself and carried them off to Iberville with their quadroon. The old Madame did not venture to say she was afraid they would be neglected during Léonce's absence; she hardly ventured to think so. She was hungry for them — even a little fierce in her attachment. She did not want them to be wholly "children of the pavement," she always said when begging to have them for a space. She wished them to know the country, with its streams, its fields, its woods, its freedom, so delicious to the young. She wished them to taste something of the life their father had lived and known and loved when he, too, was a little child.

When Edna was at last alone, she breathed a big, genuine sigh of relief. A feeling that was unfamiliar but very delicious came over her. She walked all through the house, from one room to another, as if inspecting it for the first time. She tried the various chairs and lounges, as if she had never sat and reclined upon them before. And she perambulated around the outside of the house, investigating, looking to see if windows and shutters were secure and in order. The flowers were like new acquaintances; she approached them in a familiar spirit, and made herself at home among them. The garden walks were damp, and Edna called to the maid to bring out her rubber sandals. And there she stayed, and stooped, digging around the plants, trimming, picking dead, dry leaves. The children's little dog came out, interfering, getting in her way. She scolded him, laughed at him, played with him. The garden smelled so good and looked so pretty in the afternoon sunlight. Edna plucked all the bright flowers she could find, and went into the house with them, she and the little dog.

Even the kitchen assumed a sudden interesting character which she had never before perceived. She went in to give directions to the cook, to say that the butcher would have to bring much less meat, that they would require only half their usual quantity of bread, of milk and groceries. She told the cook that she herself would be greatly occupied during Mr. Pontellier's absence, and she begged her to take all thought and responsibility of the larder upon her own shoulders.

That night Edna dined alone. The candelabra, with a few candles in the center of the table, gave all the light she needed. Outside the circle of light in which she sat, the large dining-room looked solemn and shadowy. The cook, placed upon her mettle, served a delicious repast — a luscious tenderloin broiled *à point*. The wine tasted good; the *marron glacé* seemed to be just what she wanted. It was so pleasant, too, to dine in a comfortable *peignoir*.

She thought a little sentimentally about Léonce and the children, and wondered what they were doing. As she gave a dainty scrap or two to the doggie, she talked intimately to him about Etienne and Raoul. He was beside himself with astonishment and delight over these companionable advances, and showed his appreciation by his little quick, snappy barks and a lively agitation.

Then Edna sat in the library after dinner and read Emerson until she grew sleepy. She realized that she had neglected her reading, and determined to start anew upon a course of improving studies, now that her time was completely her own to do with as she liked.

After a refreshing bath, Edna went to bed. And as she snuggled comfortably beneath the eiderdown a sense of restfulness invaded her, such as she had not known before.

XXV

When the weather was dark and cloudy Edna could not work. She needed the sun to mellow and temper her mood to the sticking point. She had reached a stage when she seemed to be no longer feeling her way, working, when in the humor, with sureness and ease. And being devoid of ambition, and striving not toward accomplishment, she drew satisfaction from the work in itself.

On rainy or melancholy days Edna went out and sought the society of the friends she had made at Grand Isle. Or else she stayed indoors and nursed a mood with which she was becoming too familiar for her own comfort and peace of mind. It was not despair; but it seemed to her as if life were passing by, leaving its promise broken and unfulfilled. Yet there were other days when she listened, was led on and deceived by fresh promises which her youth held out to her.

She went again to the races, and again. Alcée Arobin and Mrs. Highcamp called for her one bright afternoon in Arobin's drag. Mrs. Highcamp was a worldly but unaffected, intelligent, slim, tall blonde woman in the forties, with an indifferent manner and blue eyes that stared. She had a daughter who served her as a pretext for cultivating the society of young men of fashion. Alcée Arobin was one of them. He was a familiar figure at the race course, the opera, the fashionable clubs. There was a perpetual smile in his eyes, which seldom failed to awaken a corresponding cheerfulness in any one who looked into them and listened to his good-humored voice. His manner was quiet, and at times a little insolent. He possessed a good figure, a pleasing face, not overburdened with depth of thought or feeling; and his dress was that of the conventional man of fashion.

He admired Edna extravagantly, after meeting her at the races with her father. He had met her before on other occasions, but she had seemed to him unapproachable until that day. It was at his instigation that Mrs. Highcamp called to ask her to go with them to the Jockey Club to witness the turf event of the season.

There were possibly a few track men out there who knew the race horse as well as Edna, but there was certainly none who knew it better. She sat between her two companions as one having authority to speak. She laughed at Arobin's pretensions, and deplored Mrs. Highcamp's ignorance. The race horse was a friend and intimate associate of her childhood. The atmosphere of the stable and the breath of the blue grass paddock revived in her memory and lingered in her nostrils. She did not perceive that she was talking like her father as the sleek geldings ambled in review before them. She played for very high stakes, and fortune favored her. The fever of the game flamed in her cheeks and eyes, and it got into her blood and into her brain like an intoxicant. People turned their heads to look at her, and more than one lent an attentive ear to her utterances, hoping thereby to secure the elusive but everdesired "tip." Arobin caught the contagion of excitement which drew him to Edna like a magnet. Mrs. Highcamp remained, as usual, unmoved, with her indifferent stare and uplifted eyebrows.

Edna stayed and dined with Mrs. Highcamp upon being urged to do so. Arobin also remained and sent away his drag.

The dinner was quiet and uninteresting, save for the cheerful efforts of Arobin to enliven things. Mrs. Highcamp deplored the absence of her daughter from the races, and tried to convey to her what she had missed by going to the "Dante reading" instead of joining them. The girl held a geranium leaf up to her nose and said nothing, but looked knowing and noncommittal. Mr. Highcamp was a plain, bald-headed man, who only talked under compulsion. He was unresponsive. Mrs. Highcamp was full of delicate courtesy and consideration toward her husband. She addressed most of her conversation to him at table. They sat in the library after dinner and read the evening papers together under the droplight; while the younger people went into the drawing-room near by and talked. Miss Highcamp played some selections from Grieg upon the piano. She seemed to have apprehended all of the composer's coldness and none of his poetry. While Edna listened she could not help wondering if she had lost her taste for music.

When the time came for her to go home, Mr. Highcamp grunted a lame offer to escort her, looking down at his slippered feet with tactless concern. It was Arobin who took her home. The car ride was long, and it was late when they reached Esplanade Street. Arobin asked permission to enter for a second to light his cigarette — his match safe was empty. He filled his match safe, but did not light his cigarette until he left her, after she had expressed her willingness to go to the races with him again.

Edna was neither tired nor sleepy. She was hungry again, for the Highcamp dinner, though of excellent quality, had lacked abundance. She rummaged in the larder and brought forth a slice of Gruyère and some crackers. She opened a bottle of beer which she found in the icebox. Edna felt extremely restless and excited. She vacantly hummed a fantastic tune as she poked at the wood embers on the hearth and munched a cracker.

She wanted something to happen — something, anything; she did not know what. She regretted that she had not made Arobin stay a half hour to talk over the horses with her. She counted the money she had won. But there was nothing else to do, so she went to bed, and tossed there for hours in a sort of monotonous agitation.

In the middle of the night she remembered that she had forgotten to write her regular letter to her husband; and she decided to do so next day and tell him about her afternoon at the Jockey Club. She lay wide awake composing a letter which was nothing like the one which she wrote next day. When the maid awoke her in the morning Edna was dreaming of Mr. Highcamp playing the piano at the entrance of a music store on Canal Street, while his wife was saying to Alcée Arobin, as they boarded an Esplanade Street car:

"What a pity that so much talent has been neglected! but I must go."

When, a few days later, Alcée Arobin again called for Edna in his drag, Mrs. Highcamp was not with him. He said they would pick her up. But as that lady had not been apprised of his intention of picking her up, she was not at home. The daughter was just leaving the house to attend the meeting of a branch Folk Lore Society, and regretted that she could not accompany them. Arobin appeared nonplused, and asked Edna if there were any one else she cared to ask.

She did not deem it worth while to go in search of any of the fashionable acquaintances from whom she had withdrawn herself. She thought of Madame Ratignolle, but knew that her fair friend did not leave the house, except to take a languid walk around the block with her husband after nightfall. Mademoiselle Reisz would have laughed at such a request from Edna. Madame Lebrun might have enjoyed the outing, but for some reason Edna did not want her. So they went alone, she and Arobin.

The afternoon was intensely interesting to her. The excitement came back upon her like a remittent fever. Her talk grew familiar and confidential. It was no labor to become intimate with Arobin. His manner invited easy confidence. The preliminary stage of becoming acquainted was one which he always endeavored to ignore when a pretty and engaging woman was concerned.

He stayed and dined with Edna. He stayed and sat beside the wood fire. They laughed and talked; and before it was time to go he was telling her how different life might have been if he had known her years before. With ingenuous frankness he spoke of what a wicked, ill-disciplined boy he had been, and impulsively drew up his cuff to exhibit upon his wrist the scar from a saber cut which he had received in a duel outside of Paris when he was nineteen. She touched his hand as she scanned the red cicatrice on the inside of his white wrist. A quick impulse that was somewhat spasmodic impelled her fingers to close in a sort of clutch upon his hand. He felt the pressure of her pointed nails in the flesh of his palm.

She arose hastily and walked toward the mantel.

"The sight of a wound or scar always agitates and sickens me," she said. "I shouldn't have looked at it."

"I beg your pardon," he entreated, following her; "it never occurred to me that it might be repulsive."

He stood close to her, and the effrontery in his eyes repelled the old, vanishing self in her, yet drew all her awakening sensuousness. He saw enough in her face to impel him to take her hand and hold it while he said his lingering good night.

"Will you go to the races again?" he asked.

"No," she said. "I've had enough of the races. I don't want to lose all the money I've won, and I've got to work when the weather is bright, instead of—"

"Yes; work; to be sure. You promised to show me your work. What morning may I come up to your atelier? To-morrow?"

"No!"

"Day after?"

"No, no."

"Oh, please don't refuse me! I know something of such things. I might help you with a stray suggestion or two."

"No. Good night. Why don't you go after you have said good night? I don't like you," she went on in a high, excited pitch, attempting to draw away her hand. She felt that her words lacked dignity and sincerity, and she knew that he felt it.

"I'm sorry you don't like me. I'm sorry I offended you. How have I offended you? What have I done? Can't you forgive me?" And he bent and pressed his lips upon her hand as if he wished never more to withdraw them.

"Mr. Arobin," she complained, "I'm greatly upset by the excitement of the afternoon; I'm not myself. My manner must have misled you in some way. I wish you to go, please." She spoke in a monotonous, dull tone. He took his hat from the table, and stood with eyes turned from her, looking into the dying fire. For a moment or two he kept an impressive silence.

"Your manner has not misled me, Mrs. Pontellier," he said finally. "My own emotions have done that. I couldn't help it. When I'm near you, how could I help it? Don't think anything of it, don't bother, please. You see, I go when you command me. If you wish me to stay away, I shall do so. If you let me come back, I—oh! you will let me come back?"

He cast one appealing glance at her, to which she made no response. Alcée Arobin's manner was so genuine that it often deceived even himself.

Edna did not care or think whether it were genuine or not. When she was alone she looked mechanically at the back of her hand which he had kissed so warmly. Then she leaned her head down on the mantelpiece. She felt somewhat like a woman who in a moment of passion is betrayed into an act of infidelity, and realizes the significance of the act without being wholly awakened from its glamour. The thought was passing vaguely through her mind, "What would he think?"

She did not mean her husband; she was thinking of Robert Lebrun. Her husband seemed to her now like a person whom she had married without love as an excuse.

She lit a candle and went up to her room. Alcée Arobin was absolutely nothing to her. Yet his presence, his manners, the warmth of his glances, and above all the touch of his lips upon her hand had acted like a narcotic upon her.

She slept a languorous sleep, interwoven with vanishing dreams.

XXVI

Alcée Arobin wrote Edna an elaborate note of apology, palpitant with sincerity. It embarrassed her; for in a cooler, quieter moment it appeared to her absurd that she should have taken his action so seriously, so dramatically. She felt sure that the significance of the whole occurrence had lain in her own self-consciousness. If she ignored his note it would give undue importance to a trivial affair. If she replied to it in a serious spirit it would still leave in his mind the impression that she had in a susceptible moment yielded to his influence. After all, it was no great matter to have one's hand kissed. She was provoked at his having written the apology. She answered in as light and bantering a spirit as she fancied it deserved, and said she would be glad to have him look in upon her at work whenever he felt the inclination and his business gave him the opportunity.

He responded at once by presenting himself at her home with all his disarming naïveté. And then there was scarcely a day which followed that she did not see him or was not reminded of him. He was prolific in pretexts. His attitude became one of good-humored subservience and tacit adoration. He was ready at all times to submit to her moods, which were as often kind as they were cold. She grew accustomed to him. They became intimate and friendly by impercepti- ble degrees, and then by leaps. He sometimes talked in a way that astonished her at first and brought the crimson into her face; in a way that pleased her at last, appealing to the animalism that stirred impatiently within her.

There was nothing which so quieted the turmoil of Edna's senses as a visit to Mademoiselle Reisz. It was then, in the presence of that personality which was offensive to her, that the woman, by her divine art, seemed to reach Edna's spirit and set it free.

It was misty, with heavy, lowering atmosphere, one afternoon, when Edna climbed the stairs to the pianist's apartments under the roof. Her clothes were dripping with moisture. She felt chilled and pinched as she entered the room. Mademoiselle was poking at a rusty stove that smoked a little and warmed the room indifferently. She was endeavoring to heat a pot of chocolate on the stove. The room looked cheerless and dingy to Edna as she entered. A bust of Beethoven, covered with a hood of dust, scowled at her from the mantelpiece.

"Ah! here comes the sunlight!" exclaimed Mademoiselle, rising from her knees before the stove. "Now it will be warm and bright enough; I can let the fire alone."

She closed the stove door with a bang, and approaching, assisted in removing Edna's dripping mackintosh.

"You are cold; you look miserable. The chocolate will soon be hot. But would you rather have a taste of brandy? I have scarcely touched the bottle which you brought me for my cold." A piece of red flannel was wrapped around Mademoiselle's throat; a stiff neck compelled her to hold her head on one side.

"I will take some brandy," said Edna, shivering as she removed her gloves and overshoes. She drank the liquor from the glass as a man would have done. Then flinging herself upon the uncomfortable sofa she said, "Mademoiselle, I am going to move away from my house on Esplanade Street."

"Ah!" ejaculated the musician, neither surprised nor especially interested. Nothing ever seemed to astonish her very much. She was endeavoring to adjust the bunch of violets which had become loose from its fastening in her hair. Edna drew her down upon the sofa, and taking a pin from her own hair, secured the shabby artificial flowers in their accustomed place.

"Aren't you astonished?"

"Passably. Where are you going? to New York? to Iberville? to your father in Mississippi? where?"

"Just two steps away," laughed Edna, "in a little four-room house around the corner. It looks so cozy, so inviting and restful, whenever I pass by; and it's for rent. I'm tired looking after that big house. It never seemed like mine, anyway —like home. It's too much trouble. I have to keep too many servants. I am tired bothering with them."

"That is not your true reason, *ma belle*. There is no use in telling me lies. I don't know your reason, but you have not told me the truth." Edna did not protest or endeavor to justify herself.

"The house, the money that provides for it, are not mine. Isn't that enough reason?"

"They are your husband's," returned Mademoiselle, with a shrug and a malicious elevation of the eyebrows.

"Oh! I see there is no deceiving you. Then let me tell you: It is a caprice. I have a little money of my own from my mother's estate, which my father sends me by driblets. I won a large sum this winter on the races, and I am beginning to sell my sketches. Laidpore is more and more pleased with my work; he says it grows in force and individuality. I cannot judge of that myself, but I feel that I have gained in ease and confidence. However, as I said, I have sold a good many through Laidpore. I can live in the tiny house for little or nothing, with one servant. Old Celestine, who works occasionally for me, says she will come stay with me and do my work. I know I shall like it, like the feeling of freedom and independence."

"What does your husband say?"

"I have not told him yet. I only thought of it this morning. He will think I am demented, no doubt. Perhaps you think so."

Mademoiselle shook her head slowly. "Your reason is not yet clear to me," she said.

Neither was it quite clear to Edna herself; but it unfolded itself as she sat for a while in silence. Instinct had prompted her to put away her husband's bounty in casting off her allegiance. She did not know how it would be when he returned. There would have to be an understanding, an explanation. Conditions would some way adjust themselves, she felt; but whatever came, she had resolved never again to belong to another than herself.

"I shall give a grand dinner before I leave the old house!" Edna exclaimed. "You will have to come to it, Mademoiselle. I will give you everything that you like to eat and to drink. We shall sing and laugh and be merry for once." And she uttered a sigh that came from the very depths of her being.

If Mademoiselle happened to have received a letter from Robert during the interval of Edna's visits, she would give her the letter unsolicited. And she would seat herself at the piano and play as her humor prompted her while the young woman read the letter.

The little stove was roaring; it was red-hot, and the chocolate in the tin sizzled and sputtered. Edna went forward and opened the stove door, and Mademoiselle rising, took a letter from under the bust of Beethoven and handed it to Edna.

"Another! so soon!" she exclaimed, her eyes filled with delight. "Tell me, Mademoiselle, does he know that I see his letters?"

"Never in the world! He would be angry and would never write to me again if he thought so. Does he write to you? Never a line. Does he send you a message? Never a word. It is because he loves you, poor fool, and is trying to forget you, since you are not free to listen to him or to belong to him."

"Why do you show me his letters, then?"

"Haven't you begged for them? Can I refuse you anything? Oh! you cannot deceive me," and Mademoiselle approached her beloved instrument and began to play. Edna did not at once read the letter. She sat holding it in her hand, while the music penetrated her whole being like an effulgence, warming and brightening the dark places of her soul. It prepared her for joy and exultation.

"Oh!" she exclaimed, letting the letter fall to the floor. "Why did you not tell me?" She went and grasped Mademoiselle's hands up from the keys. "Oh! unkind! malicious! Why did you not tell me?"

"That he was coming back? No great news, *ma foi*. I wonder he did not come long ago."

"But when, when?" cried Edna, impatiently. "He does not say when."

"He says 'very soon.' You know as much about it as I do; it is all in the letter."

"But why? Why is he coming? Oh, if I thought — " and she snatched the letter from the floor and turned the pages this way and that way, looking for the reason, which was left untold.

"If I were young and in love with a man," said Mademoiselle, turning on the stool and pressing her wiry hands between her knees as she looked down at Edna, who sat on the floor holding the letter, "it seems to me he would have to be some *grand esprit;* a man with lofty aims and ability to reach them; one who stood high enough to attract the notice of his fellow-men. It seems to me if I were young and in love I should never deem a man of ordinary caliber worthy of my devotion."

"Now it is you who are telling lies and seeking to deceive me, Mademoiselle; or else you have never been in love, and know nothing about it. Why," went on Edna, clasping her knees and looking up into Mademoiselle's twisted face, "do you suppose a woman knows why she loves? Does she select? Does she say to herself: 'Go to! Here is a distinguished statesman with presidential possibilities; I shall proceed to fall in love with him.' Or, 'I shall set my heart upon this musician, whose fame is on every tongue?' Or, 'This financier, who controls the world's money markets?'"

"You are purposely misunderstanding me, *ma reine.* Are you in love with Robert?"

"Yes," said Edna. It was the first time she had admitted it, and a glow overspread her face, blotching it with red spots.

"Why?" asked her companion. "Why do you love him when you ought not to?"

Edna, with a motion or two, dragged herself on her knees before Mademoiselle Reisz, who took the glowing face between her two hands.

"Why? Because his hair is brown and grows away from his temples; because he opens and shuts his eyes, and his nose is a little out of drawing; because he has two lips and a square chin, and a little finger which he can't straighten from having played baseball too energetically in his youth. Because—"

"Because you do, in short," laughed Mademoiselle. "What will you do when he comes back?" she asked.

"Do? Nothing, except feel glad and happy to be alive."

She was already glad and happy to be alive at the mere thought of his return. The murky, lowering sky, which had depressed her a few hours before, seemed bracing and invigorating as she splashed through the streets on her way home.

She stopped at a confectioner's and ordered a huge box of bonbons for the children in Iberville. She slipped a card in the box, on which she scribbled a tender message and sent an abundance of kisses.

Before dinner in the evening Edna wrote a charming letter to her husband, telling him of her intention to move for a while into the little house around the block, and to give a farewell dinner before leaving, regretting that he was not there to share it, to help her out with the menu and assist her in entertaining the guests. Her letter was brilliant and brimming with cheerfulness.

XXVII

"What is the matter with you?" asked Arobin that evening. "I never found you in such a happy mood." Edna was tired by that time, and was reclining on the lounge before the fire.

"Don't you know the weather prophet has told us we shall see the sun pretty soon?"

"Well, that ought to be reason enough," he acquiesced. "You wouldn't give me another if I sat here all night imploring you." He sat close to her on a low tabouret, and as he spoke his fingers lightly touched the hair that fell a little over her forehead. She liked the touch of his fingers through her hair, and closed her eyes sensitively.

"One of these days," she said, "I'm going to pull myself together for a while and think—try to determine what character of a woman I am; for, candidly, I don't know. By all the codes which I am acquainted with, I am a devilishly wicked specimen of the sex. But some way I can't convince myself that I am. I must think about it."

"Don't. What's the use? Why should you bother thinking about it when I can tell you what manner of woman you are." His fingers strayed occasionally down to her warm, smooth cheeks and firm chin, which was growing a little full and double.

"Oh, yes! You will tell me that I am adorable; everything that is captivating. Spare yourself the effort."

"No; I shan't tell you anything of the sort, though I shouldn't be lying if I did."

"Do you know Mademoiselle Reisz?" she asked irrelevantly.

"The pianist? I know her by sight. I've heard her play."

"She says queer things sometimes in a bantering way that you don't notice at the time and you find yourself thinking about afterward."

"For instance?"

"Well, for instance, when I left her to-day, she put her arms around me and felt my shoulder blades, to see if my wings were strong, she said. 'The bird that would soar above the level plain of tradition and prejudice must have strong wings. It is a sad spectacle to see the weaklings bruised, exhausted, fluttering back to earth.'"

"Whither would you soar?"

"I'm not thinking of any extraordinary flights. I only half comprehend her."

"I've heard she's partially demented," said Arobin.

"She seems to me wonderfully sane," Edna replied.

"I'm told she's extremely disagreeable and unpleasant. Why have you introduced her at a moment when I desired to talk of you?"

"Oh! talk of me if you like," cried Edna, clasping her hands beneath her head; "but let me think of something else while you do."

"I'm jealous of your thoughts to-night. They're making you a little kinder than usual; but some way I feel as if they were wandering, as if they were not here with me." She only looked at him and smiled. His eyes were very near. He leaned upon the lounge with an arm extended across her, while the other hand still rested upon her hair. They continued silently to look into each other's eyes. When he leaned forward and kissed her, she clasped his head, holding his lips to hers.

It was the first kiss of her life to which her nature had really responded. It was a flaming torch that kindled desire.

XXVIII

Edna cried a little that night after Arobin left her. It was only one phase of the multitudinous emotions which had assailed her. There was with her an overwhelming feeling of irresponsibility. There was the shock of the unexpected and the unaccustomed. There was her husband's reproach looking at her from the external things around her which he had provided for her external existence. There was Robert's reproach making itself felt by a quicker, fiercer, more overpowering love, which had awakened within her toward him. Above all, there was understanding. She felt as if a mist had been lifted from her eyes, enabling her to look upon and comprehend the significance of life, that monster made up of beauty and brutality. But among the conflicting sensations which assailed her, there was neither shame nor remorse. There was a dull pang of regret because it was not the kiss of love which had inflamed her, because it was not love which had held this cup of life to her lips.

XXIX

Without even waiting for an answer from her husband regarding his opinion or wishes in the matter, Edna hastened her preparations for quitting her home on Esplanade Street and moving into the little house around the block. A feverish anxiety attended her every action in that direction. There was no moment of deliberation, no interval of repose between the thought and its fulfillment. Early upon the morning following those hours passed in Arobin's society, Edna set about securing her new abode and hurrying her arrangements for occupying it. Within the precincts of her home she felt like one who has entered and lingered within the portals of some forbidden temple in which a thousand muffled voices bade her begone.

Whatever was her own in the house, everything which she had acquired aside from her husband's bounty, she caused to be transported to the other house, supplying simple and meager deficiencies from her own resources.

Arobin found her with rolled sleeves, working in company with the house-maid when he looked in during the afternoon. She was splendid and robust, and had never appeared handsomer than in the old blue gown, with a red silk handkerchief knotted at random around her head to protect her hair from the dust. She was mounted upon a high step-ladder, unhooking a picture from the wall when he entered. He had found the front door open, and had followed his ring by walking in unceremoniously.

"Come down!" he said. "Do you want to kill yourself?" She greeted him with affected carelessness, and appeared absorbed in her occupation.

If he had expected to find her languishing, reproachful, or indulging in sentimental tears, he must have been greatly surprised.

He was no doubt prepared for any emergency, ready for any one of the foregoing attitudes, just as he bent himself easily and naturally to the situation which confronted him.

"Please come down," he insisted, holding the ladder and looking up at her.

"No," she answered; "Ellen is afraid to mount the ladder. Joe is working over at the 'pigeon house'—that's the name Ellen gives it, because it's so small and looks like a pigeon house—and some one has to do this."

Arobin pulled off his coat, and expressed himself ready and willing to tempt fate in her place. Ellen brought him one of her dust-caps, and went into contortions of mirth, which she found it impossible to control, when she saw him put it on before the mirror as grotesquely as he could. Edna herself could not refrain from smiling when she fastened it at his request. So it was he who in turn mounted the ladder, unhooking pictures and curtains, and dislodging ornaments as Edna directed. When he had finished he took off his dust-cap and went out to wash his hands.

Edna was sitting on the tabouret, idly brushing the tips of a feather duster along the carpet when he came in again.

"Is there anything more you will let me do?" he asked.

"That is all," she answered. "Ellen can manage the rest." She kept the young woman occupied in the drawing-room, unwilling to be left alone with Arobin.

"What about the dinner?" he asked; "the grand event, the *coup d'état?*"

"It will be day after to-morrow. Why do you call it the *'coup d'état'?* Oh! it will be very fine; all my best of everything — crystal, silver and gold, Sèvres, flowers, music, and champagne to swim in. I'll let Léonce pay the bills. I wonder what he'll say when he sees the bills."

"And you ask me why I call it a *coup d'état?*" Arobin had put on his coat, and he stood before her and asked if his cravat was plumb. She told him it was, looking no higher than the tip of his collar.

"When do you go to the 'pigeon house?' — with all due acknowledgement to Ellen."

"Day after to-morrow, after the dinner. I shall sleep there."

"Ellen, will you very kindly get me a glass of water?" asked Arobin. "The dust in the curtains, if you will pardon me for hinting such a thing, has parched my throat to a crisp."

"While Ellen gets the water," said Edna, rising, "I will say good-by and let you go. I must get rid of this grime, and I have a million things to do and think of."

"When shall I see you?" asked Arobin, seeking to detain her, the maid having left the room.

"At the dinner, of course. You are invited."

"Not before? — not to-night or to-morrow morning or to-morrow noon or night? or the day after morning or noon? Can't you see yourself, without my telling you, what an eternity it is?"

He had followed her into the hall and to the foot of the stairway, looking up at her as she mounted with her face half turned to him.

"Not an instant sooner," she said. But she laughed and looked at him with eyes that at once gave him courage to wait and made it torture to wait.

XXX

Though Edna had spoken of the dinner as a very grand affair, it was in truth a very small affair and very select, in so much as the guests invited were few and were selected with discrimination. She had counted upon an even dozen seating themselves at her round mahogany board, forgetting for the moment that Madame Ratignolle was to the last degree *souffrante* and unpresentable, and not foreseeing that Madame Lebrun would send a thousand regrets at the last moment. So there were only ten, after all, which made a cozy, comfortable number.

There were Mr. and Mrs. Merriman, a pretty, vivacious little woman in the thirties; her husband, a jovial fellow, something of a shallow-pate, who laughed a good deal at other people's witticisms, and had thereby made himself extremely popular. Mrs. Highcamp had accompanied them. Of course, there was Alcée Arobin; and Mademoiselle Reisz had consented to come. Edna had sent her a fresh bunch of violets with black lace trimmings for her hair. Monsieur Ratignolle brought himself and his wife's excuses. Victor Lebrun, who happened to be in the city, bent upon relaxation, had accepted with alacrity. There was a Miss Mayblunt, no longer in her teens, who looked at the world through lorgnettes and with the keenest interest. It was thought and said that she was intellectual; it was suspected of her that she wrote under a *nom de guerre*. She had come with a gentleman by the name of Gouvernail, connected with one of the daily papers, of whom nothing special could be said, except that he was observant and seemed quiet and inoffensive. Edna herself made the tenth, and at half-past eight they seated themselves at table, Arobin and Monsieur Ratignolle on either side of their hostess.

Mrs. Highcamp sat between Arobin and Victor Lebrun. Then came Mrs. Merriman, Mr. Gouvernail, Miss Mayblunt, Mr. Merriman, and Mademoiselle Reisz next to Monsieur Ratignolle.

There was something extremely gorgeous about the appearance of the table, an effect of splendor conveyed by a cover of pale yellow satin under strips of lace-work. There were wax candles in massive brass candelabra, burning softly under yellow silk shades; full, fragrant roses, yellow and red, abounded. There were silver and gold, as she had said there would be, and crystal which glittered like the gems which the women wore.

The ordinary stiff dining chairs had been discarded for the occasion and replaced by the most commodious and luxurious which could be collected throughout the house. Mademoiselle Reisz, being exceedingly diminutive, was elevated upon cushions, as small children are sometimes hoisted at table upon bulky volumes.

"Something new, Edna?" exclaimed Miss Mayblunt, with lorgnette directed toward a magnificent cluster of diamonds that sparkled, that almost sputtered, in Edna's hair, just over the center of her forehead.

"Quite new; 'brand' new, in fact; a present from my husband. It arrived this morning from New York. I may as well admit that this is my birthday, and that I am twenty-nine. In good time I expect you to drink my health. Meanwhile, I shall ask you to begin with this cocktail, composed—would you say 'composed?'" with an appeal to Miss Mayblunt—"composed by my father in honor of Sister Janet's wedding."

Before each guest stood a tiny glass that looked and sparkled like a garnet gem.

"Then, all things considered," spoke Arobin, "it might not be amiss to start out by drinking the Colonel's health in the cocktail which he composed, on the birthday of the most charming of women—the daughter whom he invented."

Mr. Merriman's laugh at this sally was such a genuine outburst and so contagious that it started the dinner with an agreeable swing that never slackened.

Miss Mayblunt begged to be allowed to keep her cocktail untouched before her, just to look at. The color was marvelous! She could compare it to nothing she had ever seen, and the garnet lights which it emitted were unspeakably rare. She pronounced the Colonel an artist, and stuck to it.

Monsieur Ratignolle was prepared to take things seriously: the *mets*, the *entre-mets*, the service, the decorations, even the people. He looked up from his pompano and inquired of Arobin if he were related to the gentleman of that name who formed one of the firm of Laitner and Arobin, lawyers. The young man admitted that Laitner was a warm personal friend, who permitted Arobin's name to decorate the firm's letterheads and to appear upon a shingle that graced Perdido Street.

"There are so many inquisitive people and institutions abounding," said Arobin, "that one is really forced as a matter of convenience these days to assume the virtue of an occupation if he has it not."

Monsieur Ratignolle stared a little, and turned to ask Mademoiselle Reisz if she considered the symphony concerts up to the standard which had been set the previous winter. Mademoiselle Reisz answered Monsieur Ratignolle in French, which Edna thought a little rude, under the circumstances, but characteristic. Mademoiselle had only disagreeable things to say of the symphony concerts, and insulting remarks to make of all the musicians of New Orleans, singly and collectively. All her interest seemed to be centered upon the delicacies placed before her.

Mr. Merriman said that Mr. Arobin's remark about inquisitive people reminded him of a man from Waco the other day at the St. Charles Hotel — but as Mr. Merriman's stories were always lame and lacking point, his wife seldom permitted him to complete them. She interrupted him to ask if he remembered the name of the author whose book she had bought the week before to send to a friend in Geneva. She was talking "books" with Mr. Gouvernail and trying to draw from him his opinion upon current literary topics. Her husband told the story of the Waco man privately to Miss Mayblunt, who pretended to be greatly amused and to think it extremely clever.

Mrs. Highcamp hung with languid but unaffected interest upon the warm and impetuous volubility of her left-hand neighbor, Victor Lebrun. Her attention was never for a moment withdrawn from him after seating herself at table; and when he turned to Mrs. Merriman, who was prettier and more vivacious than Mrs. Highcamp, she waited with easy indifference for an opportunity to reclaim his attention. There was the occasional sound of music, of mandolins, sufficiently removed to be an agreeable accompaniment rather than an interruption to the conversation. Outside the soft, monotonous splash of a fountain could be heard; the sound penetrated into the room with the heavy odor of jessamine that came through the open windows.

The golden shimmer of Edna's satin gown spread in rich folds on either side of her. There was a soft fall of lace encircling her shoulders. It was the color of her skin, without the glow, the myriad living tints that one may sometimes discover in vibrant flesh. There was something in her attitude, in her whole appearance when she leaned her head against the high-backed chair and spread her arms, which suggested the regal woman, the one who rules, who looks on, who stands alone.

But as she sat there amid her guests, she felt the old ennui overtaking her; the hopelessness which so often assailed her, which came upon her like an obsession, like something extraneous, independent of volition. It was something which announced itself; a chill breath that seemed to issue from some vast cavern wherein discords wailed. There came over her the acute longing which always summoned into her spiritual vision the presence of the beloved one, overpowering her at once with a sense of the unattainable.

The moments glided on, while a feeling of good fellowship passed around the circle like a mystic cord, holding and binding these people together with jest and laughter. Monsieur Ratignolle was the first to break the pleasant charm. At ten o'clock he excused himself. Madame Ratignolle was waiting for him at home. She was *bien souffrante,* and she was filled with vague dread, which only her husband's presence could allay.

Mademoiselle Reisz arose with Monsieur Ratignolle, who offered to escort her to the car. She had eaten well; she had tasted the good, rich wines, and they must have turned her head, for she bowed pleasantly to all as she withdrew from table. She kissed Edna upon the shoulder, and whispered: *"Bonne nuit, ma reine; soyez sage."* She had been a little bewildered upon rising, or rather, descending from her cushions, and Monsieur Ratignolle gallantly took her arm and led her away.

Mrs. Highcamp was weaving a garland of roses, yellow and red. When she had finished the garland, she laid it lightly upon Victor's black curls. He was reclining far back in the luxurious chair, holding a glass of champagne to the light.

As if a magician's wand had touched him, the garland of roses transformed him into a vision of Oriental beauty. His cheeks were the color of crushed grapes, and his dusky eyes glowed with a languishing fire.

"Sapristi!" exclaimed Arobin.

But Mrs. Highcamp had one more touch to add to the picture. She took from the back of her chair a white silken scarf, with which she had covered her shoulders in the early part of the evening. She draped it across the boy in graceful folds, and in a way to conceal his black, conventional evening dress. He did not seem to mind what she did to him, only smiled showing a faint gleam of white teeth, while he continued to gaze with narrowing eyes at the light through his glass of champagne.

"Oh! to be able to paint in color rather than in words!" exclaimed Miss Mayblunt, losing herself in a rhapsodic dream as she looked at him.

> "'There was a graven image of Desire
> Painted with red blood on a ground of gold.'"

murmured Gouvernail, under his breath.

The effect of the wine upon Victor was to change his accustomed volubility into silence. He seemed to have abandoned himself to a reverie, and to be seeing pleasing visions in the amber bead.

"Sing," entreated Mrs. Highcamp. "Won't you sing to us?"

"Let him alone," said Arobin.

"He's posing," offered Mr. Merriman; "let him have it out."

"I believe he's paralyzed," laughed Mrs. Merriman. And leaning over the youth's chair, she took the glass from his hand and held it to his lips. He sipped the wine slowly, and when he had drained the glass she laid it upon the table and wiped his lips with her little filmy handkerchief.

"Yes, I'll sing for you," he said, turning in his chair toward Mrs. Highcamp. He clasped his hands behind his head, and looking up at the ceiling began to hum a little, trying his voice like a musician tuning an instrument. Then, looking at Edna, he began to sing:

> "Ah! si tu savais!"

"Stop!" she cried, "don't sing that. I don't want you to sing it," and she laid her glass so impetuously and blindly upon the table as to shatter it against a carafe. The wine spilled over Arobin's legs and some of it trickled down upon Mrs. Highcamp's black gauze gown. Victor had lost all idea of courtesy, or else he thought his hostess was not in earnest, for he laughed and went on:

> "Ah! si tu savais
> Ce que tes yeux me disent" —

"Oh! you mustn't! you mustn't," exclaimed Edna, and pushing back her chair she got up, and going behind him placed her hand over his mouth. He kissed the soft palm that pressed upon his lips.

"No, no, I won't, Mrs. Pontellier. I didn't know you meant it," looking up at her with caressing eyes. The touch of his lips was like a pleasing sting to her hand. She lifted the garland of roses from his head and flung it across the room.

"Come, Victor; you've posed long enough. Give Mrs. Highcamp her scarf."

Mrs. Highcamp undraped the scarf from about him with her own hands. Miss Mayblunt and Mr. Gouvernail suddenly conceived the notion that it was time to say good night. And Mr. and Mrs. Merriman wondered how it could be so late.

Before parting from Victor, Mrs. Highcamp invited him to call upon her daughter, who she knew would be charmed to meet him and talk French and sing French songs with him. Victor expressed his desire and intention to call upon Miss Highcamp at the first opportunity which presented itself. He asked if Arobin were going his way. Arobin was not.

The mandolin players had long since stolen away. A profound stillness had fallen upon the broad, beautiful street. The voices of Edna's disbanding guests jarred like a discordant note upon the quiet harmony of the night.

XXXI

"Well?" questioned Arobin, who had remained with Edna after the others had departed.

"Well," she reiterated, and stood up, stretching her arms, and feeling the need to relax her muscles after having been so long seated.

"What next?" he asked.

"The servants are all gone. They left when the musicians did. I have dismissed them. The house has to be closed and locked, and I shall trot around to the pigeon house, and shall send Celestine over in the morning to straighten things up."

He looked around, and began to turn out some of the lights.

"What about upstairs?" he inquired.

"I think it is all right; but there may be a window or two unlatched. We had better look; you might take a candle and see. And bring me my wrap and hat on the foot of the bed in the middle room."

He went up with the light, and Edna began closing doors and windows. She hated to shut in the smoke and the fumes of the wine. Arobin found her cape and hat, which he brought down and helped her to put on.

When everything was secured and the lights put out, they left through the front door, Arobin locking it and taking the key, which he carried for Edna. He helped her down the steps.

"Will you have a spray of jessamine?" he asked, breaking off a few blossoms as he passed.

"No; I don't want anything."

She seemed disheartened, and had nothing to say. She took his arm, which he offered her, holding up the weight of her satin train with the other hand. She looked down, noticing the black line of his leg moving in and out so close to her against the yellow shimmer of her gown. There was the whistle of a railway train somewhere in the distance, and the midnight bells were ringing. They met no one in their short walk.

The "pigeon-house" stood behind a locked gate, and a shallow *parterre* that had been somewhat neglected. There was a small front porch, upon which a long window and the front door opened. The door opened directly into the parlor; there was no side entry. Back in the yard was a room for servants, in which old Celestine had been ensconced.

Edna had left a lamp burning low upon the table. She had succeeded in making the room look habitable and homelike. There were some books on the table and a lounge near at hand. On the floor was a fresh matting, covered with a rug or two; and on the walls hung a few tasteful pictures. But the room was filled with flowers. These were a surprise to her. Arobin had sent them, and had had Celestine distribute them during Edna's absence. Her bedroom was adjoining, and across a small passage were the dining-room and kitchen.

Edna seated herself with every appearance of discomfort.

"Are you tired?" he asked.

"Yes, and chilled, and miserable. I feel as if I had been wound up to a certain pitch — too tight — and something inside of me had snapped."

She rested her head against the table upon her bare arm.

"You want to rest," he said, "and to be quiet. I'll go; I'll leave you and let you rest."

"Yes," she replied.

He stood up beside her and smoothed her hair with his soft, magnetic hand. His touch conveyed to her a certain physical comfort. She could have fallen quietly asleep there if he had continued to pass his hand over her hair. He brushed the hair upward from the nape of her neck.

"I hope you will feel better and happier in the morning," he said. "You have tried to do too much in the past few days. The dinner was the last straw; you might have dispensed with it."

"Yes," she admitted; "it was stupid."

"No, it was delightful; but it has worn you out." His hand strayed to her beautiful shoulders, and he could feel the response of her flesh to his touch. He seated himself beside her and kissed her lightly upon the shoulder.

"I thought you were going away," she said, in an uneven voice.

"I am, after I have said good night."

"Good night," she murmured.

He did not answer, except to continue to caress her. He did not say good night until she had become supple to his gentle, seductive entreaties.

XXXII

When Mr. Pontellier learned of his wife's intention to abandon her home and take up her residence elsewhere he immediately wrote her a letter of unqualified disapproval and remonstrance. She had given reasons which he was unwilling to acknowledge as adequate. He hoped she had not acted upon her rash impulse;

and he begged her to consider first, foremost, and above all else, what people would say. He was not dreaming of scandal when he uttered this warning; that was a thing which would never have entered into his mind to consider in connection with his wife's name or his own. He was simply thinking of his financial integrity. It might get noised about that the Pontelliers had met with reverses, and were forced to conduct their *ménage* on a humbler scale than heretofore. It might do incalculable mischief to his business prospects.

But remembering Edna's whimsical turn of mind of late, and foreseeing that she had immediately acted upon her impetuous determination, he grasped the situation with his usual promptness and handled it with his well-known business tact and cleverness.

The same mail which brought to Edna his letter of disapproval carried instructions—the most minute instructions—to a well-known architect concerning the remodeling of his home, changes which he had long contemplated, and which he desired carried forward during his temporary absence.

Expert and reliable packers and movers were engaged to convey the furniture, carpets, pictures—everything movable, in short—to places of security. And in an incredibly short time the Pontellier house was turned over to the artisans. There was to be an addition—a small snuggery; there was to be frescoing, and hardwood flooring was to be put into such rooms as had not yet been subjected to this improvement.

Furthermore, in one of the daily papers appeared a brief notice to the effect that Mr. and Mrs. Pontellier were contemplating a summer sojourn abroad, and that their handsome residence on Esplanade Street was undergoing sumptuous alterations, and would not be ready for occupancy until their return. Mr. Pontellier had saved appearances!

Edna admired the skill of his maneuver, and avoided any occasion to balk his intentions. When the situation as set forth by Mr. Pontellier was accepted and taken for granted, she was apparently satisfied that it should be so.

The pigeon-house pleased her. It at once assumed the intimate character of a home, while she herself invested it with a charm which it reflected like a warm glow. There was with her a feeling of having descended in the social scale, with a corresponding sense of having risen in the spiritual. Every step which she took toward relieving herself from obligations added to her strength and expansion as an individual. She began to look with her own eyes; to see and to apprehend the deeper undercurrents of life. No longer was she content to "feed upon opinion" when her own soul had invited her.

After a little while, a few days, in fact, Edna went up and spent a week with her children in Iberville. They were delicious February days, with all the summer's promise hovering in the air.

How glad she was to see the children! She wept for very pleasure when she felt their little arms clasping her; their hard, ruddy cheeks pressed against her own glowing cheeks. She looked into their faces with hungry eyes that could not be satisfied with looking. And what stories they had to tell their mother! About the pigs, the cows, the mules! About riding to the mill behind Gluglu; fishing back in the lake with their Uncle Jasper; picking pecans with Lidie's little black brood, and hauling chips in their express wagon. It was a thousand times more fun to haul real chips for old lame Susie's real fire than to drag painted blocks along the banquette on Esplanade Street!

She went with them herself to see the pigs and the cows, to look at the darkies laying the cane, to thrash the pecan trees, and catch fish in the back lake. She lived with them a whole week long, giving them all of herself, and gathering and filling herself with their young existence. They listened, breathless, when she told them the house in Esplanade Street was crowded with workmen, hammering, nailing, sawing, and filling the place with clatter. They wanted to know where their bed was; what had been done with their rocking-horse; and where did Joe sleep, and where had Ellen gone, and the cook? But, above all, they were fired with a desire to see the little house around the block. Was there any place to play? Were there any boys next door? Raoul, with pessimistic foreboding, was convinced that there were only girls next door. Where would they sleep, and where would papa sleep? She told them the fairies would fix it all right.

The old Madame was charmed with Edna's visit, and showered all manner of delicate attentions upon her. She was delighted to know that the Esplanade Street house was in a dismantled condition. It gave her the promise and pretext to keep the children indefinitely.

It was with a wrench and a pang that Edna left her children. She carried away with her the sound of their voices and the touch of their cheeks. All along the journey homeward their presence lingered with her like the memory of a delicious song. But by the time she had regained the city the song no longer echoed in her soul. She was again alone.

XXXIII

It happened sometimes when Edna went to see Mademoiselle Reisz that the little musician was absent, giving a lesson or making some small necessary household purchase. The key was always left in a secret hiding-place in the entry, which Edna knew. If Mademoiselle happened to be away, Edna would usually enter and wait for her return.

When she knocked at Mademoiselle Reisz's door one afternoon there was no response; so unlocking the door, as usual, she entered and found the apartment deserted, as she had expected. Her day had been quite filled up, and it was for a rest, for a refuge, and to talk about Robert, that she sought out her friend.

She had worked at her canvas—a young Italian character study—all the morning, completing the work without the model; but there had been many interruptions, some incident to her modest housekeeping, and others of a social nature.

Madame Ratignolle had dragged herself over, avoiding the too public thoroughfares, she said. She complained that Edna had neglected her much of late. Besides, she was consumed with curiosity to see the little house and the manner in which it was conducted. She wanted to hear all about the dinner party; Monsieur Ratignolle had left *so* early. What had happened after he left? The champagne and grapes which Edna sent over were *too* delicious. She had so little appetite; they had refreshed and toned her stomach. Where on earth was she going to put Mr. Pontellier in that little house, and the boys? And then she made Edna promise to go to her when her hour of trial overtook her.

"At any time—any time of the day or night, dear," Edna assured her.

Before leaving Madame Ratignolle said:

"In some way you seem to me like a child, Edna. You seem to act without a certain amount of reflection which is necessary in this life. That is the reason I want to say you mustn't mind if I advise you to be a little careful while you are living here alone. Why don't you have some one come and stay with you? Wouldn't Mademoiselle Reisz come?"

"No; she wouldn't wish to come, and I shouldn't want her always with me."

"Well, the reason — you know how evil-minded the world is — some one was talking of Alcée Arobin visiting you. Of course, it wouldn't matter if Mr. Arobin had not such a dreadful reputation. Monsieur Ratignolle was telling me that his attentions alone are considered enough to ruin a woman's name."

"Does he boast of his successes?" asked Edna, indifferently, squinting at her picture.

"No, I think not. I believe he is a decent fellow as far as that goes. But his character is so well known among the men. I shan't be able to come back and see you; it was very, very imprudent to-day."

"Mind the step!" cried Edna.

"Don't neglect me," entreated Madame Ratignolle; "and don't mind what I said about Arobin, or having some one to stay with you."

"Of course not," Edna laughed. "You may say anything you like to me." They kissed each other good-by. Madame Ratignolle had not far to go, and Edna stood on the porch a while watching her walk down the street.

Then in the afternoon Mrs. Merriman and Mrs. Highcamp had made their "party call." Edna felt that they might have dispensed with the formality. They had also come to invite her to play *vingt-et-un* one evening at Mrs. Merriman's. She was asked to go early, to dinner, and Mr. Merriman or Mr. Arobin would take her home. Edna accepted in a half-hearted way. She sometimes felt very tired of Mrs. Highcamp and Mrs. Merriman.

Late in the afternoon she sought refuge with Mademoiselle Reisz, and stayed there alone, waiting for her, feeling a kind of repose invade her with the very atmosphere of the shabby, unpretentious little room.

Edna sat at the window, which looked out over the house-tops and across the river. The window frame was filled with pots of flowers, and she sat and picked the dry leaves from a rose geranium. The day was warm, and the breeze which blew from the river was very pleasant. She removed her hat and laid it on the piano. She went on picking the leaves and digging around the plants with her hat pin. Once she thought she heard Mademoiselle Reisz approaching. But it was a young black girl, who came in, bringing a small bundle of laundry, which she deposited in the adjoining room, and went away.

Edna seated herself at the piano, and softly picked out with one hand the bars of a piece of music which lay open before her. A half-hour went by. There was the occasional sound of people going and coming in the lower hall. She was growing interested in her occupation of picking out the aria, when there was a second rap at the door. She vaguely wondered what these people did when they found Mademoiselle's door locked.

"Come in," she called, turning her face toward the door. And this time it was Robert Lebrun who presented himself. She attempted to rise; she could not have done so without betraying the agitation which mastered her at sight of him, so she fell back upon the stool, only exclaiming, "Why, Robert!"

He came and clasped her hand, seemingly without knowing what he was saying or doing.

"Mrs. Pontellier! How do you happen — oh! how well you look! Is Mademoiselle Reisz not here? I never expected to see you."

"When did you come back?" asked Edna in an unsteady voice, wiping her face with her handkerchief. She seemed ill at ease on the piano stool, and he begged her to take the chair by the window. She did so, mechanically, while he seated himself on the stool.

"I returned day before yesterday," he answered, while he leaned his arm on the keys, bringing forth a crash of discordant sound.

"Day before yesterday!" she repeated, aloud; and went on thinking to herself, "day before yesterday," in a sort of an uncomprehending way. She had pictured him seeking her at the very first hour, and he had lived under the same sky since day before yesterday; while only by accident had he stumbled upon her. Mademoiselle must have lied when she said, "Poor fool, he loves you."

"Day before yesterday," she repeated, breaking off a spray of Mademoiselle's geranium; "then if you had not met me here to-day you wouldn't — when — that is, didn't you mean to come and see me?"

"Of course, I should have gone to see you. There have been so many things —" he turned the leaves of Mademoiselle's music nervously. "I started in at once yesterday with the old firm. After all there is as much chance for me here as there was there — that is, I might find it profitable some day. The Mexicans were not very congenial."

So he had come back because the Mexicans were not congenial; because business was as profitable here as there; because of reason, and not because he cared to be near her. She remembered the day she sat on the floor, turning the pages of his letter, seeking the reason which was left untold.

She had not noticed how he looked — only feeling his presence; but she turned deliberately and observed him. After all, he had been absent but a few months, and was not changed. His hair — the color of hers — waved back from his temples in the same way as before. His skin was not more burned than it had been at Grand Isle. She found in his eyes, when he looked at her for one silent moment, the same tender caress, with an added warmth and entreaty which had not been there before — the same glance which had penetrated to the sleeping places of her soul and awakened them.

A hundred times Edna had pictured Robert's return, and imagined their first meeting. It was usually at her home, whither he had sought her out at once. She always fancied him expressing or betraying in some way his love for her. And here, the reality was that they sat ten feet apart, she at the window, crushing geranium leaves in her hand and smelling them, he twirling around on the piano stool, saying:

"I was very much surprised to hear of Mr. Pontellier's absence; it's a wonder Mademoiselle Reisz did not tell me; and your moving — mother told me yesterday. I should think you would have gone to New York with him, or to Iberville with the children, rather than be bothered here with housekeeping. And you are going abroad, too, I hear. We shan't have you at Grand Isle next summer; it won't seem — do you see much of Mademoiselle Reisz? She often spoke of you in the few letters she wrote."

"Do you remember that you promised to write to me when you went away?" A flush overspread his whole face.

"I couldn't believe that my letters would be of any interest to you."

"That is an excuse; it isn't the truth." Edna reached for her hat on the piano. She adjusted it, sticking the hat pin through the heavy coil of hair with some deliberation.

"Are you not going to wait for Mademoiselle Reisz?" asked Robert.

"No; I have found when she is absent this long, she is liable not to come back till late." She drew on her gloves, and Robert picked up his hat.

"Won't you wait for her?" asked Edna.

"Not if you think she will not be back till late," adding, as if suddenly aware of some discourtesy in his speech, "and I should miss the pleasure of walking home with you." Edna locked the door and put the key back in its hiding-place.

They went together, picking their way across muddy streets and side-walks encumbered with the cheap display of small tradesmen. Part of the distance they rode in the car, and after disembarking, passed the Pontellier mansion, which looked broken and half torn asunder. Robert had never known the house, and looked at it with interest.

"I never knew you in your home," he remarked.

"I am glad you did not."

"Why?" She did not answer. They went on around the corner, and it seemed as if her dreams were coming true after all, when he followed her into the little house.

"You must stay and dine with me, Robert. You see I am all alone, and it is so long since I have seen you. There is so much I want to ask you."

She took off her hat and gloves. He stood irresolute, making some excuse about his mother who expected him; he even muttered something about an engagement. She struck a match and lit the lamp on the table; it was growing dusk. When he saw her face in the lamp-light, looking pained, with all the soft lines gone out of it, he threw his hat aside and seated himself.

"Oh! you know I want to stay if you will let me!" he exclaimed. All the softness came back. She laughed, and went and put her hand on his shoulder.

"This is the first moment you have seemed like the old Robert. I'll go tell Celestine." She hurried away to tell Celestine to set an extra place. She even sent her off in search of some added delicacy which she had not thought of for herself. And she recommended great care in dripping the coffee and having the omelet done to a proper turn.

When she reëntered, Robert was turning over magazines, sketches and things that lay upon the table in great disorder. He picked up a photograph, and exclaimed:

"Alcée Arobin! What on earth is his picture doing here?"

"I tried to make a sketch of his head one day," answered Edna, "and he thought the photograph might help me. It was at the other house. I thought it had been left there. I must have packed it up with my drawing materials."

"I should think you would give it back to him if you have finished with it."

"Oh! I have a great many such photographs. I never think of returning them. They don't amount to anything." Robert kept on looking at the picture.

"It seems to me — do you think his head worth drawing? Is he a friend of Mr. Pontellier's? You never said you knew him."

"He isn't a friend of Mr. Pontellier's; he's a friend of mine. I always knew him — that is, it is only of late that I know him pretty well. But I'd rather talk about you, and know what you have been seeing and doing and feeling out there in Mexico." Robert threw aside the picture.

"I've been seeing the waves and the white beach of Grand Isle; the quiet, grassy street of the *Chênière*; the old fort at Grande Terre. I've been working like a machine, and feeling like a lost soul. There was nothing interesting."

She leaned her head upon her hand to shade her eyes from the light.

"And what have you been seeing and doing and feeling all these days?" he asked.

"I've been seeing the waves and the white beach of Grand Isle; the quiet, grassy street of the *Chênière Caminada;* the old sunny fort at Grande Terre. I've been working with a little more comprehension than a machine, and still feeling like a lost soul. There was nothing interesting."

"Mrs. Pontellier, you are cruel," he said, with feeling, closing his eyes and resting his head back in his chair. They remained in silence till old Celestine announced dinner.

XXXIV

The dining-room was very small. Edna's round mahogany would have almost filled it. As it was there was but a step or two from the little table to the kitchen, to the mantel, the small buffet, and the side door that opened out on the narrow brick-paved yard.

A certain degree of ceremony settled upon them with the announcement of dinner. There was no return to personalities. Robert related incidents of his sojourn in Mexico, and Edna talked of events likely to interest him, which had occurred during his absence. The dinner was of ordinary quality, except for the few delicacies which she had sent out to purchase. Old Celestine, with a bandana *tignon* twisted about her head, hobbled in and out, taking a personal interest in everything; and she lingered occasionally to talk patois with Robert, whom she had known as a boy.

He went out to a neighboring cigar stand to purchase cigarette papers, and when he came back he found that Celestine had served the black coffee in the parlor.

"Perhaps I shouldn't have come back," he said. "When you are tired of me, tell me to go."

"You never tire me. You must have forgotten the hours and hours at Grand Isle in which we grew accustomed to each other and used to being together."

"I have forgotten nothing at Grand Isle," he said, not looking at her, but rolling a cigarette. His tobacco pouch, which he laid upon the table, was a fantastic embroidered silk affair, evidently the handiwork of a woman.

"You used to carry your tobacco in a rubber pouch," said Edna, picking up the pouch and examining the needle work.

"Yes; it was lost."

"Where did you buy this one? In Mexico?"

"It was given to me by a Vera Cruz girl; they are very generous," he replied, striking a match and lighting his cigarette.

"They are very handsome, I suppose, those Mexican women; very picturesque, with their black eyes and their lace scarfs."

"Some are; others are hideous. Just as you find women everywhere."

"What was she like — the one who gave you the pouch? You must have known her very well."

"She was very ordinary. She wasn't of the slightest importance. I knew her well enough."

"Did you visit at her house? Was it interesting? I should like to know and hear about the people you met, and the impressions they made on you."

"There are some people who leave impressions not so lasting as the imprint of an oar upon the water."

"Was she such a one?"

"It would be ungenerous for me to admit that she was of that order and kind." He thrust the pouch back in his pocket, as if to put away the subject with the trifle which had brought it up.

Arobin dropped in with a message from Mrs. Merriman, to say that the card party was postponed on account of the illness of one of her children.

"How do you do, Arobin?" said Robert, rising from the obscurity.

"Oh! Lebrun. To be sure! I heard yesterday you were back. How did they treat you down in Mexique?"

"Fairly well."

"But not well enough to keep you there. Stunning girls, though, in Mexico. I thought I should never get away from Vera Cruz when I was down there a couple of years ago."

"Did they embroider slippers and tobacco pouches and hat-bands and things for you?" asked Edna.

"Oh! my! no! I didn't get so deep in their regard. I fear they made more impression on me than I made on them."

"You were less fortunate than Robert, then."

"I am always less fortunate than Robert. Has he been imparting tender confidences?"

"I've been imposing myself long enough," said Robert, rising, and shaking hands with Edna. "Please convey my regards to Mr. Pontellier when you write."

He shook hands with Arobin and went away.

"Fine fellow, that Lebrun," said Arobin when Robert had gone. "I never heard you speak of him."

"I knew him last summer at Grand Isle," she replied. "Here is that photograph of yours. Don't you want it?"

"What do I want with it? Throw it away." She threw it back on the table.

"I'm not going to Mrs. Merriman's," she said. "If you see her, tell her so. But perhaps I had better write. I think I shall write now, and say that I am sorry her child is sick, and tell her not to count on me."

"It would be a good scheme," acquiesced Arobin. "I don't blame you; stupid lot!"

Edna opened the blotter, and having procured paper and pen, began to write the note. Arobin lit a cigar and read the evening paper, which he had in his pocket.

"What is the date?" she asked. He told her.

"Will you mail this for me when you go out?"

"Certainly." He read to her little bits out of the newspaper, while she straightened things on the table.

"What do you want to do?" he asked, throwing aside the paper. "Do you want to go out for a walk or a drive or anything? It would be a fine night to drive."

"No; I don't want to do anything but just be quiet. You go away and amuse yourself. Don't stay."

"I'll go away if I must; but I shan't amuse myself. You know that I only live when I am near you."

He stood up to bid her good night.

"Is that one of the things you always say to women?"

"I have said it before, but I don't think I ever came so near meaning it," he answered with a smile. There were no warm lights in her eyes; only a dreamy, absent look.

"Good night. I adore you. Sleep well," he said, and he kissed her hand and went away.

She stayed alone in a kind of reverie—a sort of stupor. Step by step she lived over every instant of the time she had been with Robert after he had entered Mademoiselle Reisz's door. She recalled his words, his looks. How few and meager they had been for her hungry heart! A vision—a transcendently seductive vision of a Mexican girl arose before her. She writhed with a jealous pang. She wondered when he would come back. He had not said he would come back. She had been with him, had heard his voice and touched his hand. But some way he had seemed nearer to her off there in Mexico.

XXXV

The morning was full of sunlight and hope. Edna could see before her no denial—only the promise of excessive joy. She lay in bed awake, with bright eyes full of speculation. "He loves you, poor fool." If she could but get that conviction firmly fixed in her mind, what mattered about the rest? She felt she had been childish and unwise the night before in giving herself over to despondency. She recapitulated the motives which no doubt explained Robert's reserve. They were not insurmountable; they would not hold if he really loved her; they could not hold against her own passion, which he must come to realize in time. She pictured him going to his business that morning. She even saw how he was dressed; how he walked down one street, and turned the corner of another; saw him bending over his desk, talking to people who entered the office, going to his lunch, and perhaps watching for her on the street. He would come to her in the afternoon or evening, sit and roll his cigarette, talk a little, and go away as he had done the night before. But how delicious it would be to have him there with her! She would have no regrets, nor seek to penetrate his reserve if he still chose to wear it.

Edna ate her breakfast only half dressed. The maid brought her a delicious printed scrawl from Raoul, expressing his love, asking her to send him some bonbons, and telling her they had found that morning ten tiny white pigs all lying in a row beside Lidie's big white pig.

A letter also came from her husband, saying he hoped to be back early in March, and then they would get ready for that journey abroad which he had promised her so long, which he felt now fully able to afford; he felt able to travel as people should, without any thought of small economies—thanks to his recent speculations in Wall Street.

Much to her surprise she received a note from Arobin, written at midnight from the club. It was to say good morning to her, to hope she had slept well, to assure her of his devotion, which he trusted she in some faintest manner returned.

All these letters were pleasing to her. She answered the children in a cheerful frame of mind, promising them bonbons, and congratulating them upon their happy find of the little pigs.

She answered her husband with friendly evasiveness,—not with any fixed design to mislead him, only because all sense of reality had gone out of her life; she had abandoned herself to Fate, and awaited the consequences with indifference.

To Arobin's note she made no reply. She put it under Celestine's stove-lid. Edna worked several hours with much spirit. She saw no one but a picture dealer, who asked her if it were true that she was going abroad to study in Paris.

She said possibly she might, and he negotiated with her for some Parisian studies to reach him in time for the holiday trade in December.

Robert did not come that day. She was keenly disappointed. He did not come the following day, nor the next. Each morning she awoke with hope, and each night she was a prey to despondency. She was tempted to seek him out. But far from yielding to the impulse, she avoided any occasion which might throw her in his way. She did not go to Mademoiselle Reisz's nor pass by Madame Lebrun's, as she might have done if he had still been in Mexico.

When Arobin, one night, urged her to drive with him, she went—out to the lake, on the Shell Road. His horses were full of mettle, and even a little unmanageable. She liked the rapid gait at which they spun along, and the quick, sharp sound of the horses' hoofs on the hard road. They did not stop anywhere to eat or to drink. Arobin was not needlessly imprudent. But they ate and they drank when they regained Edna's little dining-room—which was comparatively early in the evening.

It was late when he left her. It was getting to be more than a passing whim with Arobin to see her and be with her. He had detected the latent sensuality, which unfolded under his delicate sense of her nature's requirements like a torpid, torrid, sensitive blossom.

There was no despondency when she fell asleep that night; nor was there hope when she awoke in the morning.

XXXVI

There was a garden out in the suburbs; a small, leafy corner, with a few green tables under the orange trees. An old cat slept all day on the stone step in the sun, and an old *mulatresse* slept her idle hours away in her chair at the open window, till some one happened to knock on one of the green tables. She had milk and cream cheese to sell, and bread and butter. There was no one who could make such excellent coffee or fry a chicken so golden brown as she.

The place was too modest to attract the attention of people of fashion, and so quiet as to have escaped the notice of those in search of pleasure and dissipation. Edna had discovered it accidentally one day when the high-board gate stood ajar. She caught sight of a little green table, blotched with the checkered sunlight that filtered through the quivering leaves overhead. Within she had found the slumbering *mulatresse*, the drowsy cat, and a glass of milk which reminded her of the milk she had tasted in Iberville.

She often stopped there during her perambulations; sometimes taking a book with her, and sitting an hour or two under the trees when she found the place deserted. Once or twice she took a quiet dinner there alone, having instructed Celestine beforehand to prepare no dinner at home. It was the last place in the city where she would have expected to meet any one she knew.

Still she was not astonished when, as she was partaking of a modest dinner late in the afternoon, looking into an open book, stroking the cat, which had made friends with her—she was not greatly astonished to see Robert come in at the tall garden gate.

"I am destined to see you only by accident," she said, shoving the cat off the chair beside her. He was surprised, ill at ease, almost embarrassed at meeting her thus so unexpectedly.

"Do you come here often?" he asked.

"I almost live here," she said.

"I used to drop in very often for a cup of Catiche's good coffee. This is the first time since I came back."

"She'll bring you a plate, and you will share my dinner. There's always enough for two — even three." Edna had intended to be indifferent and as reserved as he when she met him; she had reached the determination by a laborious train of reasoning, incident to one of her despondent moods. But her resolve melted when she saw him before her, seated there beside her in the little garden, as if a designing Providence had led him into her path.

"Why have you kept away from me, Robert?" she asked, closing the book that lay open upon the table.

"Why are you so personal, Mrs. Pontellier? Why do you force me to idiotic subterfuges?" he exclaimed with sudden warmth. "I suppose there's no use telling you I've been very busy, or that I've been sick, or that I've been to see you and not found you at home. Please let me off with any one of these excuses."

"You are the embodiment of selfishness," she said. "You save yourself something — I don't know what — but there is some selfish motive, and in sparing yourself you never consider for a moment what I think, or how I feel your neglect and indifference. I suppose this is what you would call unwomanly; but I have got into a habit of expressing myself. It doesn't matter to me, and you may think me unwomanly if you like."

"No; I only think you cruel, as I said the other day. Maybe not intentionally cruel; but you seem to be forcing me into disclosures which can result in nothing; as if you would have me bare a wound for the pleasure of looking at it, without the intention or power of healing it."

"I'm spoiling your dinner, Robert; never mind what I say. You haven't eaten a morsel."

"I only came in for a cup of coffee." His sensitive face was all disfigured with excitement.

"Isn't this a delightful place?" she remarked. "I am so glad it has never actually been discovered. It is so quiet, so sweet, here. Do you notice there is scarcely a sound to be heard? It's so out of the way; and a good walk from the car. However, I don't mind walking. I always feel so sorry for women who don't like to walk; they miss so much — so many rare little glimpses of life; and we women learn so little of life on the whole.

"Catiche's coffee is always hot. I don't know how she manages it, here in open air. Celestine's coffee gets cold bringing it from the kitchen to the dining-room. Three lumps! How can you drink it so sweet? Take some of the cress with your chop; it's so biting and crisp. Then there's the advantage of being able to smoke with your coffee out here. Now, in the city — aren't you going to smoke?"

"After a while," he said, laying a cigar on the table.

"Who gave it to you?" she laughed.

"I bought it. I suppose I'm getting reckless; I bought a whole box." She was determined not to be personal again and make him uncomfortable.

The cat made friends with him, and climbed into his lap when he smoked his cigar. He stroked her silky fur, and talked a little about her. He looked at Edna's book, which he had read; and he told her the end, to save her the trouble of wading through it, he said.

Again he accompanied her back to her home; and it was after dusk when they reached the little "pigeon-house." She did not ask him to remain, which he was grateful for, as it permitted him to stay without the discomfort of blundering through an excuse which he had no intention of considering. He helped her to light the lamp; then she went into her room to take off her hat and to bathe her face and hands.

When she came back Robert was not examining the pictures and magazines as before; he sat off in the shadow, leaning his head back on the chair as if in a reverie. Edna lingered a moment beside the table, arranging the books there. Then she went across the room to where he sat. She bent over the arm of his chair and called his name.

"Robert," she said, "are you asleep?"

"No," he answered, looking up at her.

She leaned over and kissed him — a soft, cool, delicate kiss, whose voluptuous sting penetrated his whole being — then she moved away from him. He followed, and took her in his arms, just holding her close to him. She put her hand up to his face and pressed his cheek against her own. The action was full of love and tenderness. He sought her lips again. Then he drew her down upon the sofa beside him and held her hand in both of his.

"Now you know," he said, "now you know what I have been fighting against since last summer at Grand Isle; what drove me away and drove me back again."

"Why have you been fighting against it?" she asked. Her face glowed with soft lights.

"Why? Because you were not free; you were Léonce Pontellier's wife. I couldn't help loving you if you were ten times his wife; but so long as I went away from you and kept away I could help telling you so." She put her free hand up to his shoulder, and then against his cheek, rubbing it softly. He kissed her again. His face was warm and flushed.

"There in Mexico I was thinking of you all the time, and longing for you."

"But not writing to me," she interrupted.

"Something put into my head that you cared for me; and I lost my senses. I forgot everything but a wild dream of your some way becoming my wife."

"Your wife!"

"Religion, loyalty, everything would give way if only you cared."

"Then you must have forgotten that I was Léonce Pontellier's wife."

"Oh! I was demented, dreaming of wild, impossible things, recalling men who had set their wives free, we have heard of such things."

"Yes, we have heard of such things."

"I came back full of vague, mad intentions. And when I got here — "

"When you got here you never came near me!" She was still caressing his cheek.

"I realized what a cur I was to dream of such a thing, even if you had been willing."

She took his face between her hands and looked into it as if she would never withdraw her eyes more. She kissed him on the forehead, the eyes, the cheeks, and the lips.

"You have been a very, very foolish boy, wasting your time dreaming of impossible things when you speak of Mr. Pontellier setting me free! I am no longer one of Mr. Pontellier's possessions to dispose of or not. I give myself where I choose. If he were to say, 'Here, Robert, take her and be happy; she is yours,' I should laugh at you both."

His face grew a little white. "What do you mean?" he asked.

There was a knock at the door. Old Celestine came in to say that Madame Ratignolle's servant had come around the back way with a message that Madame had been taken sick and begged Mrs. Pontellier to go to her immediately.

"Yes, yes," said Edna, rising; "I promised. Tell her yes — to wait for me. I'll go back with her."

"Let me walk over with you," offered Robert.

"No," she said; "I will go with the servant." She went into her room to put on her hat, and when she came in again she sat once more upon the sofa beside him. He had not stirred. She put her arms about his neck.

"Good-by, my sweet Robert. Tell me good-by." He kissed her with a degree of passion which had not before entered into his caress, and strained her to him.

"I love you," she whispered, "only you; no one but you. It was you who woke me last summer out of life-long, stupid dream. Oh! you have made me so unhappy with your indifference. Oh! I have suffered, suffered! Now you are here we shall love each other, my Robert. We shall be everything to each other. Nothing else in the world is of any consequence. I must go to my friend; but you will wait for me? No matter how late; you will wait for me, Robert?"

"Don't go; don't go! Oh! Edna, stay with me," he pleaded. "Why should you go? Stay with me, stay with me."

"I shall come back as soon as I can; I shall find you here." She buried her face in his neck, and said good-by again. Her seductive voice, together with his great love for her, had enthralled his senses, had deprived him of every impulse but the longing to hold her and keep her.

XXXVII

Edna looked in at the drug store. Monsieur Ratignolle was putting up a mixture himself, very carefully, dropping a red liquid into a tiny glass. He was grateful to Edna for having come; her presence would be a comfort to his wife. Madame Ratignolle's sister, who had always been with her at such trying times, had not been able to come up from the plantation, and Adèle had been inconsolable until Mrs. Pontellier so kindly promised to come to her. The nurse had been with them at night for the past week, as she lived a great distance away. And Dr. Mandelet had been coming and going all the afternoon. They were then looking for him any moment.

Edna hastened upstairs by a private stairway that led from the rear of the store to the apartment above. The children were all sleeping in a back room. Madame Ratignolle was in the salon, whither she had strayed in her suffering impatience. She sat on the sofa, clad in an ample white *peignoir*, holding a handkerchief tight in her hand with a nervous clutch. Her face was drawn and pinched, her sweet blue eyes haggard and unnatural. All her beautiful hair had been drawn back and plaited. It lay in a long braid on the sofa pillow, coiled like a golden serpent. The nurse, a comfortable looking *Griffe* woman in white apron and cap, was urging her to return to her bedroom.

"There is no use, there is no use," she said at once to Edna. "We must get rid of Mandelet; he is getting too old and careless. He said he would be here at half-past seven; now it must be eight. See what time it is, Joséphine."

The woman was possessed of a cheerful nature, and refused to take any situation too seriously, especially a situation with which she was so familiar. She urged Madame to have courage and patience. But Madame only set her teeth hard into her under lip, and Edna saw the sweat gather in beads on her white forehead. After a moment or two she uttered a profound sigh and wiped her face with the handkerchief rolled in a ball. She appeared exhausted. The nurse gave her a fresh handkerchief, sprinkled with cologne water.

"This is too much!" she cried. "Mandelet ought to be killed! Where is Alphonse? Is it possible I am to be abandoned like this — neglected by every one?"

"Neglected, indeed!" exclaimed the nurse. Wasn't she there? And here was Mrs. Pontellier leaving, no doubt, a pleasant evening at home to devote to her? And wasn't Monsieur Ratignolle coming that very instant through the hall? And Joséphine was quite sure she had heard Doctor Mandelet's coupé. Yes, there it was, down at the door.

Adèle consented to go back to her room. She sat on the edge of a little low couch next to her bed.

Doctor Mandelet paid no attention to Madame Ratignolle's upbraidings. He was accustomed to them at such times, and was too well convinced of her loyalty to doubt it.

He was glad to see Edna, and wanted her to go with him into the salon and entertain him. But Madame Ratignolle would not consent that Edna should leave her for an instant. Between agonizing moments, she chatted a little, and said it took her mind off her sufferings.

Edna began to feel uneasy. She was seized with a vague dread. Her own like experiences seemed far away, unreal, and only half remembered. She recalled faintly an ecstasy of pain, the heavy odor of chloroform, a stupor which had deadened sensation, and an awakening to find a little new life to which she had given being, added to the great unnumbered multitude of souls that come and go.

She began to wish she had not come; her presence was not necessary. She might have invented a pretext for staying away; she might even invent a pretext now for going. But Edna did not go. With an inward agony, with a flaming, outspoken revolt against the ways of Nature, she witnessed the scene [of] torture.

She was still stunned and speechless with emotion when later she leaned over her friend to kiss her and softly say good-by. Adèle, pressing her cheek, whispered in an exhausted voice: "Think of the children, Edna. Oh, think of the children! Remember them!"

XXXVIII

Edna still felt dazed when she got outside in the open air. The Doctor's coupé had returned for him and stood before the *porte cochère*. She did not wish to enter the coupé, and told Doctor Mandelet she would walk; she was not afraid, and would go alone. He directed his carriage to meet him at Mrs. Pontellier's, and he started to walk home with her.

Up — away up, over the narrow street between the tall houses, the stars were blazing. The air was mild and caressing, but cool with the breath of spring and the night. They walked slowly, the Doctor with a heavy, measured tread and his hands behind him; Edna, in an absent-minded way, as she had walked one night at Grand Isle, as if her thoughts had gone ahead of her and she was striving to overtake them.

"You shouldn't have been there, Mrs. Pontellier," he said. "That was no place for you. Adèle is full of whims at such times. There were a dozen women she might have had with her, unimpressionable women. I felt that it was cruel, cruel. You shouldn't have gone."

"Oh, well!" she answered, indifferently. "I don't know that it matters after all. One has to think of the children some time or other; the sooner the better."

"When is Léonce coming back?"

"Quite soon. Some time in March."

"And you are going abroad?"

"Perhaps—no, I am not going. I'm not going to be forced into doing things. I don't want to go abroad. I want to be let alone. Nobody has any right—except children, perhaps—and even then, it seems to me—or it did seem—" She felt that her speech was voicing the incoherency of her thoughts, and stopped abruptly.

"The trouble is," sighed the Doctor, grasping her meaning intuitively, "that youth is given up to illusions. It seems to be a provision of Nature; a decoy to secure mothers for the race. And Nature takes no account of moral consequences, or arbitrary conditions which we create, and which we feel obliged to maintain at any cost."

"Yes," she said. "The years that are gone seem like dreams—if one might go on sleeping and dreaming—but to wake up and find—oh! well! perhaps it is better to wake up after all, even to suffer, rather than to remain a dupe to illusions all one's life."

"It seems to me, my dear child," said the Doctor at parting, holding her hand, "you seem to me to be in trouble. I am not going to ask for your confidence. I will only say that if ever you feel moved to give it to me, perhaps I might help you. I know I would understand, and I tell you there are not many who would—not many, my dear."

"Some way I don't feel moved to speak of things that trouble me. Don't think I am ungrateful or that I don't appreciate your sympathy. There are periods of despondency and suffering which take possession of me. But I don't want anything but my own way. That is wanting a good deal, of course, when you have to trample upon the lives, the hearts, the prejudices of others—but no matter—still, I shouldn't want to trample upon the little lives. Oh! I don't know what I'm saying, Doctor. Good night. Don't blame me for anything."

"Yes, I will blame you if you don't come and see me soon. We will talk of things you never have dreamt of talking about before. It will do us both good. I don't want you to blame yourself, whatever comes. Good night, my child."

She let herself in at the gate, but instead of entering she sat upon the step of the porch. The night was quiet and soothing. All the tearing emotion of the last few hours seemed to fall away from her like a somber, uncomfortable garment, which she had but to loosen to be rid of. She went back to that hour before Adèle had sent for her; and her senses kindled afresh in thinking of Robert's words, the pressure of his arms, and the feeling of his lips upon her own. She could picture at the moment no greater bliss on earth than possession of the beloved one. His expression of love had already given him to her in part. When she thought that he was there at hand, waiting for her, she grew numb with the intoxication of expectancy. It was so late; he would be asleep perhaps. She would awaken him with a kiss. She hoped he would be asleep that she might arouse him with her caresses.

Still, she remembered Adèle's voice whispering, "Think of the children; think of them." She meant to think of them; that determination had driven into her soul like a death wound—but not to-night. To-morrow would be time to think of everything.

Robert was not waiting for her in the little parlor. He was nowhere at hand. The house was empty. But he had scrawled on a piece of paper that lay in the lamplight:

"I love you. Good-by—because I love you."

Edna grew faint when she read the words. She went and sat on the sofa. Then she stretched herself out there, never uttering a sound. She did not sleep. She did not go to bed. The lamp sputtered and went out. She was still awake in the morning, when Celestine unlocked the kitchen door and came in to light the fire.

XXXIX

Victor, with hammer and nails and scraps of scantling, was patching a corner of one of the galleries. Mariequita sat near by, dangling her legs, watching him work, and handing him nails from the tool-box. The sun was beating down upon them. The girl covered her head with her apron folded into a square pad. They had been talking for an hour or more. She was never tired of hearing Victor describe the dinner at Mrs. Pontellier's. He exaggerated every detail, making it appear a veritable Lucullean feast. The flowers were in tubs, he said. The champagne was quaffed from huge golden goblets. Venus rising from the foam could have presented no more entrancing a spectacle than Mrs. Pontellier, blazing with beauty and diamonds at the head of the board, while the other women were all of them youthful houris, possessed of incomparable charms.

She got it into her head that Victor was in love with Mrs. Pontellier, and he gave her evasive answers, framed so as to confirm her belief. She grew sullen and cried a little, threatening to go off and leave him to his fine ladies. There were a dozen men crazy about her at the *Chênière*; and since it was the fashion to be in love with married people, why, she could run away any time she liked to New Orleans with Célina's husband.

Célina's husband was a fool, a coward, and a pig, and to prove it to her, Victor intended to hammer his head into a jelly the next time he encountered him. This assurance was very consoling to Mariequita. She dried her eyes, and grew cheerful at the prospect.

They were still talking of the dinner and the allurements of city life when Mrs. Pontellier herself slipped around the corner of the house. The two youngsters stayed dumb with amazement before what they considered to be an apparition. But it was really she in flesh and blood, looking tired and a little travel-stained.

"I walked up from the wharf," she said, "and heard the hammering. I supposed it was you, mending the porch. It's a good thing. I was always tripping over those loose planks last summer. How dreary and deserted everything looks!"

It took Victor some time to comprehend that she had come in Beaudelet's lugger, that she had come alone, and for no purpose but to rest.

"There's nothing fixed up yet, you see. I'll give you my room; it's the only place."

"Any corner will do," she assured him.

"And if you can stand Philomel's cooking," he went on, "though I might try to get her mother while you are here. Do you think she would come?" turning to Mariequita.

Mariequita thought that perhaps Philomel's mother might come for a few days, and money enough.

Beholding Mrs. Pontellier make her appearance, the girl had at once suspected a lovers' rendezvous. But Victor's astonishment was so genuine, and Mrs. Pontellier's indifference so apparent, that the disturbing notion did not lodge long in her brain. She contemplated with the greatest interest this woman who gave the most sumptuous dinners in America, and who had all the men in New Orleans at her feet.

"What time will you have dinner?" asked Edna. "I'm very hungry; but don't get anything extra."

"I'll have it ready in little or no time," he said, bustling and packing away his tools. "You may go to my room to brush up and rest yourself. Mariequita will show you."

"Thank you," said Edna. "But, do you know, I have a notion to go down to the beach and take a good wash and even a little swim, before dinner?"

"The water is too cold!" they both exclaimed. "Don't think of it."

"Well, I might go down and try—dip my toes in. Why, it seems to me the sun is hot enough to have warmed the very depths of the ocean. Could you get me a couple of towels? I'd better go right away, so as to be back in time. It would be a little too chilly if I waited till this afternoon."

Mariequita ran over to Victor's room, and returned with some towels, which she gave to Edna.

"I hope you have fish for dinner," said Edna, as she started to walk away; "but don't do anything extra if you haven't."

"Run and find Philomel's mother," Victor instructed the girl. "I'll go to the kitchen and see what I can do. By Gimminy! Women have no consideration! She might have sent me word."

Edna walked on down to the beach rather mechanically, not noticing anything special except that the sun was hot. She was not dwelling upon any particular train of thought. She had done all the thinking which was necessary after Robert went away, when she lay awake upon the sofa till morning.

She had said over and over to herself: "To-day it is Arobin; to-morrow it will be some one else. It makes no difference to me, it doesn't matter about Léonce Pontellier—but Raoul and Etienne!" She understood now clearly what she had meant long ago when she said to Adèle Ratignolle that she would give up the unessential, but she would never sacrifice herself for her children.

Despondency had come upon her there in the wakeful night, and had never lifted. There was no one thing in the world that she desired. There was no human being whom she wanted near her except Robert; and she even realized that the day would come when he, too, and the thought of him would melt out of her existence, leaving her alone. The children appeared before her like antagonists who had overcome her; who had overpowered and sought to drag her into the soul's slavery for the rest of her days. But she knew a way to elude them. She was not thinking of these things when she walked down to the beach.

The water of the Gulf stretched out before her, gleaming with the million lights of the sun. The voice of the sea is seductive, never ceasing, whispering, clamoring, murmuring, inviting the soul to wander in abysses of solitude. All along the white beach, up and down, there was no living thing in sight. A bird with a broken wing was beating the air above, reeling, fluttering, circling disabled down, down to the water.

Edna had found her old bathing suit still hanging, faded, upon its accustomed peg.

She put it on, leaving her clothing in the bath-house. But when she was there beside the sea, absolutely alone, she cast the unpleasant, pricking garments from her, and for the first time in her life she stood naked in the open air, at the mercy of the sun, the breeze that beat upon her, and the waves that invited her.

How strange and awful it seemed to stand naked under the sky! how delicious! She felt like some new-born creature, opening its eyes in a familiar world that it had never known.

The foamy wavelets curled up to her white feet, and coiled like serpents above her ankles. She walked out. The water was chill, but she walked on. The water was deep, but she lifted her white body and reached out with a long, sweeping stroke. The touch of the sea is sensuous, enfolding the body in its soft, close embrace.

She went on and on. She remembered the night she swam far out, and recalled the terror that seized her at the fear of being unable to regain the shore. She did not look back now, but went on and on, thinking of the blue-grass meadow that she had traversed when a little child, believing that it had no beginning and no end.

Her arms and legs were growing tired.

She thought of Léonce and the children. They were a part of her life. But they need not have thought that they could possess her, body and soul. How Mademoiselle Reisz would have laughed, perhaps sneered, if she knew! "And you call yourself an artist! What pretensions, Madame! The artist must possess the courageous soul that dares and defies."

Exhaustion was pressing upon and overpowering her.

"Good-by—because I love you." He did not know; he did not understand. He would never understand. Perhaps Doctor Mandelet would have understood if she had seen him—but it was too late; the shore was far behind her, and her strength was gone.

She looked into the distance, and the old terror flamed up for an instant, then sank again. Edna heard her father's voice and her sister Margaret's. She heard the barking of an old dog that was chained to the sycamore tree. The spurs of the cavalry officer clanged as he walked across the porch. There was the hum of bees, and the musky odor of pinks filled the air.

(1899)

Kate Chopin *1851–1904*

DÉSIRÉE'S BABY

As the day was pleasant, Madame Valmondé drove over to L'Abri to see Désirée and the baby.

It made her laugh to think of Désirée with a baby. Why, it seemed but yesterday that Désirée was little more than a baby herself; when Monsieur in riding through the gateway of Valmondé had found her lying asleep in the shadow of the big stone pillar.

The little one awoke in his arms and began to cry for "Dada." That was as much as she could do or say. Some people thought she might have strayed there of her own accord, for she was of the toddling age. The prevailing belief was that she had been purposely left by a party of Texans, whose canvas-covered wagon, late in the day, had crossed the ferry that Coton Maïs kept, just below the plantation. In time Madame Valmondé abandoned every speculation but the one that Désirée had been sent to her by a beneficent Providence to be the child of her affection, seeing that she was without child of the flesh. For the girl grew to be beautiful and gentle, affectionate and sincere, — the idol of Valmondé.

It was no wonder, when she stood one day against the stone pillar in whose shadow she had lain asleep, eighteen years before, that Armand Aubigny riding by and seeing her there, had fallen in love with her. That was the way all the Aubignys fell in love, as if struck by a pistol shot. The wonder was that he had not loved her before; for he had known her since his father brought him home from Paris, a boy of eight, after his mother died there. The passion that awoke in him that day, when he saw her at the gate, swept along like an avalanche, or like a prairie fire, or like anything that drives headlong over all obstacles.

Monsieur Valmondé grew practical and wanted things well considered: that is, the girl's obscure origin. Armand looked into her eyes and did not care. He was reminded that she was nameless. What did it matter about a name when he could give her one of the oldest and proudest in Louisiana? He ordered the *corbeille* from Paris, and contained himself with what patience he could until it arrived; then they were married.

Madame Valmondé had not seen Désirée and the baby for four weeks. When she reached L'Abri she shuddered at the first sight of it, as she always did. It was a sad looking place, which for many years had not known the gentle presence of a mistress, old Monsieur Aubigny having married and buried his wife in France, and she having loved her own land too well ever to leave it. The roof came down steep and black like a cowl, reaching out beyond the wide galleries that encircled the yellow stuccoed house. Big, solemn oaks grew close to it, and their thick-leaved, far-reaching branches shadowed it like a pall. Young Aubigny's rule was a strict one, too, and under it his negroes had forgotten how to be gay, as they had been during the old master's easy-going and indulgent lifetime.

The young mother was recovering slowly, and lay full length, in her soft white muslins and laces, upon a couch. The baby was beside her, upon her arm, where he had fallen asleep, at her breast. The yellow nurse woman sat beside a window fanning herself.

Madame Valmondé bent her portly figure over Désirée and kissed her, holding her an instant tenderly in her arms. Then she turned to the child.

"This is not the baby!" she exclaimed, in startled tones. French was the language spoken at Valmondé in those days.

"I knew you would be astonished," laughed Désirée, "at the way he has grown. The little *cochon de lait*! Look at his legs, mamma, and his hands and finger-nails, — real finger-nails. Zandrine had to cut them this morning. Isn't it true, Zandrine?"

The woman bowed her turbaned head majestically, "Mais si, Madame."

"And the way he cries," went on Désirée, "is deafening. Armand heard him the other day as far away as La Blanche's cabin."

Madame Valmondé had never removed her eyes from the child. She lifted it and walked with it over to the window that was lightest. She scanned the baby narrowly, then looked as searchingly at Zandrine, whose face was turned to gaze across the fields.

"Yes, the child has grown, has changed," said Madame Valmondé, slowly, as she replaced it beside its mother. "What does Armand say?"

Désirée's face became suffused with a glow that was happiness itself.

"Oh, Armand is the proudest father in the parish, I believe, chiefly because it is a boy, to bear his name; though he says not, — that he would have loved a girl as well. But I know it isn't true. I know he says that to please me. And mamma," she added, drawing Madame Valmondé's head down to her, and speaking in a whisper, "he hasn't punished one of them — not one of them — since baby is born. Even Négrillon, who pretended to have burnt his leg that he might rest from work — he only laughed, and said Négrillon was a great scamp. Oh, mamma, I'm so happy; it frightens me."

What Désirée said was true. Marriage, and later the birth of his son, had softened Armand Aubigny's imperious and exacting nature greatly. This was what made the gentle Désirée so happy, for she loved him desperately. When he frowned she trembled, but loved him. When he smiled, she asked no greater blessing of God. But Armand's dark, handsome face had not often been disfigured by frowns since the day he fell in love with her.

When the baby was about three months old, Désirée awoke one day to the conviction that there was something in the air menacing her peace. It was at first too subtle to grasp. It had only been a disquieting suggestion; an air of mystery among the blacks; unexpected visits from far-off neighbors who could hardly account for their coming. Then a strange, an awful change in her husband's manner, which she dared not ask him to explain. When he spoke to her, it was with averted eyes, from which the old love-light seemed to have gone out. He absented himself from home; and when there, avoided her presence and that of her child, without excuse. And the very spirit of Satan seemed suddenly to take hold of him in his dealings with the slaves. Désirée was miserable enough to die.

She sat in her room, one hot afternoon, in her *peignoir*, listlessly drawing through her fingers the strands of her long, silky brown hair that hung about her shoulders. The baby, half naked, lay asleep upon her own great mahogany bed, that was like a sumptuous throne, with its satin-lined half-canopy. One of La Blanche's little quadroon boys — half naked too — stood fanning the child slowly with a fan of peacock feathers. Désirée's eyes had been fixed absently and sadly upon the baby, while she was striving to penetrate the threatening mist that she felt closing about her. She looked from her child to the boy who stood beside him, and back again; over and over. "Ah!" It was a cry that she could not help; which she was not conscious of having uttered. The blood turned like ice in her veins, and a clammy moisture gathered upon her face.

She tried to speak to the little quadroon boy; but no sound would come, at first. When he heard his name uttered, he looked up, and his mistress was pointing to the door. He laid aside the great, soft fan, and obediently stole away, over the polished floor, on his bare tiptoes.

She stayed motionless, with gaze riveted upon her child, and her face the picture of fright.

Presently her husband entered the room, and without noticing her, went to a table and began to search among some papers which covered it.

"Armand," she called to him, in a voice which must have stabbed him, if he was human. But he did not notice. "Armand," she said again. Then she rose and tottered towards him. "Armand," she panted once more, clutching his arm, "look at our child. What does it mean? tell me."

He coldly but gently loosened her fingers from about his arm and thrust the hand away from him. "Tell me what it means!" she cried despairingly.

"It means," he answered lightly, "that the child is not white; it means that you are not white."

A quick conception of all that this accusation meant for her nerved her with unwonted courage to deny it. "It is a lie; it is not true, I am white! Look at my hair, it is brown; and my eyes are gray, Armand, you know they are gray. And my skin is fair," seizing his wrist. "Look at my hand; whiter than yours, Armand," she laughed hysterically.

"As white as La Blanche's," he returned cruelly; and went away leaving her alone with their child.

When she could hold a pen in her hand, she sent a despairing letter to Madame Valmondé.

"My mother, they tell me I am not white. Armand has told me I am not white. For God's sake tell them it is not true. You must know it is not true. I shall die. I must die. I cannot be so unhappy, and live."

The answer that came was as brief:

"My own Désirée: Come home to Valmondé; back to your mother who loves you. Come with your child."

When the letter reached Désirée she went with it to her husband's study, and laid it open upon the desk before which he sat. She was like a stone image: silent, white, motionless after she placed it there.

In silence he ran his cold eyes over the written words. He said nothing. "Shall I go, Armand?" she asked in tones sharp with agonized suspense.

"Yes, go."

"Do you want me to go?"

"Yes, I want you to go."

He thought Almighty God had dealt cruelly and unjustly with him; and felt, somehow, that he was paying Him back in kind when he stabbed thus into his wife's soul. Moreover he no longer loved her, because of the unconscious injury she had brought upon his home and his name.

She turned away like one stunned by a blow, and walked slowly towards the door, hoping he could call her back.

"Good-by, Armand," she moaned.

He did not answer her. That was his last blow at fate.

Désirée went in search of her child. Zandrine was pacing the sombre gallery with it. She took the little one from the nurse's arms with no word of explanation, and descending the steps, walked away, under the live-oak branches.

It was an October afternoon; the sun was just sinking. Out in the still fields the negroes were picking cotton.

Désirée had not changed the thin white garment nor the slippers she wore. Her hair was uncovered and the sun's rays brought a golden gleam from its brown meshes. She did not take the broad, beaten road which led to the far-off plantation of Valmondé. She walked across a deserted field, where the stubble bruised her tender feet, so delicately shod, and tore her thin gown to shreds.

She disappeared among the reeds and willows that grew thick along the banks of the deep, sluggish bayou; and she did not come back again.

Some weeks later there was a curious scene enacted at L'Abri. In the centre of the smoothly swept back yard was a great bonfire. Armand Aubigny sat in the wide hallway that commanded a view of the spectacle; and it was he who dealt out to a half dozen negroes the material which kept this fire ablaze.

A graceful cradle of willow, with all its dainty furbishings, was laid upon the pyre, which had already been fed with the richness of a priceless *layette*. Then there were silk gowns, and velvet and satin ones added to these; laces, too, and embroideries; bonnets and gloves; for the *corbeille* had been of rare quality.

The last thing to go was a tiny bundle of letters; innocent little scribblings that Désirée had sent to him during the days of their espousal. There was the remnant of one back in the drawer from which he took them. But it was not Désirée's; it was part of an old letter from his mother to his father. He read it. She was thanking God for the blessing of her husband's love: —

"But, above all," she wrote, "night and day, I thank God for having so arranged our lives that our dear Armand will never know that his mother, who adores him, belongs to the race that is cursed with the brand of slavery."

(1893)

Kate Chopin *1851–1905*

THE STORY OF AN HOUR

Knowing that Mrs. Mallard was afflicted with a heart trouble, great care was taken to break to her as gently as possible the news of her husband's death.

It was her sister Josephine who told her, in broken sentences; veiled hints that revealed in half concealing. Her husband's friend Richards was there, too, near her. It was he who had been in the newspaper office when intelligence of the railroad disaster was received, with Brently Mallard's name leading the list of "killed." He had only taken the time to assure himself of its truth by a second telegram, and had hastened to forestall any less careful, less tender friend in bearing the sad message.

She did not hear the story as many women have heard the same, with a paralyzed inability to accept its significance. She wept at once, with sudden, wild abandonment, in her sister's arms. When the storm of grief had spent itself she went away to her room alone. She would have no one follow her.

There stood, facing the open window, a comfortable, roomy armchair. Into this she sank, pressed down by a physical exhaustion that haunted her body and seemed to reach into her soul.

She could see in the open square before her house the tops of trees that were all aquiver with the new spring life. The delicious breath of rain was in the air. In the street below a peddler was crying his wares. The notes of a distant song which some one was singing reached her faintly, and countless sparrows were twittering in the eaves.

There were patches of blue sky showing here and there through the clouds that had met and piled one above the other in the west facing her window.

She sat with her head thrown back upon the cushion of the chair, quite motionless, except when a sob came up into her throat and shook her, as a child who has cried herself to sleep continues to sob in its dreams.

She was young, with a fair, calm face, whose lines bespoke repression and even a certain strength. But now there was a dull stare in her eyes, whose gaze was fixed away off yonder on one of those patches of blue sky. It was not a glance of reflection, but rather indicated a suspension of intelligent thought.

There was something coming to her and she was waiting for it, fearfully. What was it? She did not know; it was too subtle and elusive to name. But she felt it, creeping out of the sky, reaching toward her through the sounds, the scents, the color that filled the air.

Now her bosom rose and fell tumultuously. She was beginning to recognize this thing that was approaching to possess her, and she was striving to beat it back with her will—as powerless as her two white slender hands would have been.

When she abandoned herself a little whispered word escaped her slightly parted lips. She said it over and over under her breath: "free, free, free!" The vacant stare and the look of terror that had followed it went from her eyes. They stayed keen and bright. Her pulses beat fast, and the coursing blood warmed and relaxed every inch of her body.

She did not stop to ask if it were or were not a monstrous joy that held her. A clear and exalted perception enabled her to dismiss the suggestion as trivial.

She knew that she would weep again when she saw the kind, tender hands folded in death; the face that had never looked save with love upon her, fixed and gray and dead. But she saw beyond that bitter moment a long procession of years to come that would belong to her absolutely. And she opened and spread her arms out to them in welcome.

There would be no one to live for her during those coming years; she would live for herself. There would be no powerful will bending hers in that blind persistence with which men and women believe they have a right to impose a private will upon a fellow-creature. A kind intention or a cruel intention made the act seem no less a crime as she looked upon it in that brief moment of illumination.

And yet she had loved him—sometimes. Often she had not. What did it matter! What could love, the unsolved mystery, count for in face of this possession of self-assertion which she suddenly recognized as the strongest impulse of her being!

"Free! Body and soul free!" she kept whispering.

Josephine was kneeling before the closed door with her lips to the keyhole, imploring for admission. "Louise, open the door! I beg; open the door—you will make yourself ill. What are you doing, Louise? For heaven's sake open the door."

"Go away. I am not making myself ill." No; she was drinking in a very elixir of life through that open window.

Her fancy was running riot along those days ahead of her. Spring days, and summer days, and all sorts of days that would be her own. She breathed a quick prayer that life might be long. It was only yesterday she had thought with a shudder that life might be long.

She arose at length and opened the door to her sister's importunities. There was a feverish triumph in her eyes, and she carried herself unwittingly like a goddess of Victory. She clasped her sister's waist, and together they descended the stairs. Richards stood waiting for them at the bottom.

Some one was opening the front door with a latchkey. It was Brently Mallard who entered, a little travel-stained, composedly carrying his grip-sack and umbrella. He had been far from the scene of accident, and did not even know there had been one. He stood amazed at Josephine's piercing cry; at Richards' quick motion to screen him from the view of his wife.

But Richards was too late.

When the doctors came they said she had died of heart disease—of joy that kills.

                                                                      (1894)

Anton Chekhov *1860–1904*

THE LAMENT

It is twilight. A thick wet snow is slowly twirling around the newly lighted street lamps, and lying in soft thin layers on roofs, on horses' backs, on people's shoulders and hats. The cab-driver Iona Potapov is quite white, and looks like a phantom; he is bent double as far as a human body can bend double; he is seated on his box; he never makes a move. If a whole snowdrift fell on him, it seems as if he would not find it necessary to shake it off. His little horse is also quite white, and remains motionless; its immobility, its angularity, and its straight wooden-looking legs, even close by, give it the appearance of a gingerbread horse worth a *kopek*. It is, no doubt, plunged in deep thought. If you were snatched from the plow, from your usual gray surroundings, and were thrown into this slough full of monstrous lights, unceasing noise, and hurrying people, you too would find it difficult not to think.

Iona and his little horse have not moved from their place for a long while. They left their yard before dinner, and up to now, not a fare. The evening mist is descending over the town, the white lights of the lamps replacing brighter rays, and the hubbub of the street getting louder. "Cabby for Viborg way!" suddenly hears Iona. "Cabby!"

Iona jumps, and through his snow-covered eyelashes sees an officer in a greatcoat, with his hood over his head.

"Viborg way!" the officer repeats. "Are you asleep, eh? Viborg way!"

With a nod of assent Iona picks up the reins, in consequence of which layers of snow slip off the horse's back and neck. The officer seats himself in the sleigh, the cabdriver smacks his lips to encourage his horse, stretches out his neck like a swan, sits up, and, more from habit than necessity, brandishes his whip. The little horse also stretches its neck, bends its wooden-looking legs, and makes a move undecidedly.

"What are you doing, werewolf!" is the exclamation Iona hears from the dark mass moving to and fro, as soon as they have started.

"Where the devil are you going? To the r-r-right!"

"You do not know how to drive. Keep to the right!" calls the officer angrily.

A coachman from a private carriage swears at him; a passerby, who has run across the road and rubbed his shoulder against the horse's nose, looks at him furiously as he sweeps the snow from his sleeve. Iona shifts about on his seat as if he were on needles, moves his elbows as if he were trying to keep his equilibrium, and gapes about like someone suffocating, who does not understand why and wherefore he is there.

"What scoundrels they all are!" jokes the officer; "one would think they had all entered into an agreement to jostle you or fall under your horse."

Iona looks round at the officer, and moves his lips. He evidently wants to say something, but the only sound that issues is a snuffle.

"What?" asks the officer.

Iona twists his mouth into a smile, and with an effort says hoarsely:

"My son, *barin*, died this week."

"Hm! What did he die of?"

Iona turns with his body toward his fare, and says:

"And who knows! They say high fever. He was three days in the hospital, and then died. . . . God's will be done."

"Turn round! The devil!" sounds from the darkness. "Have you popped off, old doggie, eh? Use your eyes!"

"Go on, go on," says the officer, "otherwise we shall not get there by tomorrow. Hurry up a bit!"

The cabdriver again stretches his neck, sits up, and, with a bad grace, brandishes his whip. Several times again he turns to look at his fare, but the latter has closed his eyes, and apparently is not disposed to listen. Having deposited the officer in the Viborg, he stops by the tavern, doubles himself up on his seat, and again remains motionless, while the snow once more begins to cover him and his horse. An hour, and another. . . . Then, along the footpath, with a squeak of galoshes, and quarreling, come three young men, two of them tall and lanky, the third one short and humpbacked.

"Cabby, to the Police Bridge!" in a cracked voice calls the humpback. "The three of us for two *griveniks!*"

Iona picks up his reins, and smacks his lips. Two *griveniks* is not a fair price, but he does not mind whether it is a *rouble* or five *kopeks*—to him it is all the same now, so long as they are fares. The young men, jostling each other and using bad language, approach the sleigh, and all three at once try to get onto the seat; then begins a discussion as to which two shall sit and who shall be the one to stand. After wrangling, abusing each other, and much petulance, it is at last decided that the humpback shall stand, as he is the smallest.

"Now then, hurry up!" says the humpback in a twanging voice, as he takes his place and breathes in Iona's neck. "Old furry! Here, mate, what a cap you have! There is not a worse one to be found in all Petersburg! . . ."

"He-he!—he-he!" giggles Iona. "Such a . . ."

"Now you, 'such a,' hurry up, are you going the whole way at this pace? Are you? . . . Do you want it in the neck?"

"My head feels like bursting," says one of the lanky ones. "Last night at the Donkmasovs, Vaska and I drank the whole of four bottles of cognac."

"I don't understand what you lie for," says the other lanky one angrily; "you lie like a brute."

"God strike me, it's the truth!"

"It's as much the truth as that a louse coughs!"

"He, he," grins Iona, "what gay young gentlemen!"

"Pshaw, go to the devil!" says the humpback indignantly.

"Are you going to get on or not, you old pest? Is that the way to drive? Use the whip a bit! Go on, devil, go on, give it to him well!"

Iona feels at his back the little man wriggling, and the tremble in his voice. He listens to the insults hurled at him, sees the people, and little by little the feeling of loneliness leaves him. The humpback goes on swearing until he gets mixed up in some elaborate six-foot oath, or chokes with coughing. The lankies begin to talk about a certain Nadejda Petrovna. Iona looks round at them several times; he waits for a temporary silence, then, turning round again, he murmurs:

"My son . . . died this week."

"We must all die," sighs the humpback, wiping his lips after an attack of coughing. "Now, hurry up, hurry up! Gentlemen, I really cannot go any farther like this! When will he get us there?"

"Well, just you stimulate him a little in the neck!"

"You old pest, do you hear, I'll bone your neck for you! If one treated the like of you with ceremony one would have to go on foot! Do you hear, old serpent Gorinytch![1] Or do you not care a spit?"

Iona hears rather than feels the blows they deal him.

"He, he," he laughs. "They are gay young gentlemen, God bless 'em!"

"Cabby, are you married?" asks a lanky one.

"I? He, he, gay young gentlemen! Now I have only a wife and the moist ground. . . . He, ho, ho . . . that is to say, the grave. My son has died, and I am alive. . . . A wonderful thing, death mistook the door . . . instead of coming to me, it went to my son. . . ."

Iona turns round to tell them how his son died, but at this moment, the humpback, giving a little sigh, announces, "Thank God, we have at last reached our destination," and Iona watches them disappear through the dark entrance. Once more he is alone, and again surrounded by silence. . . . His grief, which has abated for a short while, returns and rends his heart with greater force. With an anxious and hurried look, he searches among the crowds passing on either side of the street to find whether there may be just one person who will listen to him. But the crowds hurry by without noticing him or his trouble. Yet it is such an immense, illimitable grief. Should his heart break and the grief pour out, it would flow over the whole earth, so it seems, and yet no one sees it. It has managed to conceal itself in such an insignificant shell that no one can see it even by day and with a light.

Iona sees a hall porter with some sacking, and decides to talk to him.

"Friend, what sort of time is it?" he asks.

"Past nine. What are you standing here for? Move on."

Iona moves on a few steps, doubles himself up, and abandons himself to his grief. He sees it is useless to turn to people for help. In less than five minutes he straightens himself, holds up his head as if he felt some sharp pain, and gives a tug at the reins; he can bear it no longer. "The stables," he thinks, and the little horse, as if it understood, starts off at a trot.

About an hour and a half later Iona is seated by a large dirty stove. Around the stove, on the floor, on the benches, people are snoring; the air is thick and suffocatingly hot. Iona looks at the sleepers, scratches himself, and regrets having returned so early.

"I have not even earned my fodder," he thinks. "That's what's my trouble. A man who knows his job, who has had enough to eat, and his horse too, can always sleep peacefully."

A young cabdriver in one of the corners half gets up, grunts sleepily, and stretches towards a bucket of water.

"Do you want a drink?" Iona asks him.

"Don't I want a drink!"

"That's so? Your good health! But listen, mate—you know, my son is dead. . . . Did you hear? This week, in the hospital. . . . It's a long story."

Iona looks to see what effect his words have, but sees none—the young man has hidden his face and is fast asleep again. The old man sighs, and scratches his head. Just as much as the young one wants to drink, the old man wants to talk. It will soon be a week since his son died, and he has not been able to speak about it properly to anyone. One must tell it slowly and carefully; how his son fell ill,

---

[1] a character in Russian folklore

how he suffered, what he said before he died, how he died. One must describe every detail of the funeral, and the journey to the hospital to fetch the dead son's clothes. His daughter Anissia has remained in the village—one must talk about her too. Is it nothing he has to tell? Surely the listener would gasp and sigh, and sympathize with him? It is better, too, to talk to women; although they are stupid, two words are enough to make them sob.

"I'll go and look after my horse," thinks Iona; "there's always time to sleep. No fear of that!"

He puts on his coat, and goes to the stables to his horse; he thinks of the corn, the hay, the weather. When he is alone, he dares not think of his son; he can speak about him to anyone, but to think of him, and picture him to himself, is unbearably painful.

"Are you tucking in?" Iona asks his horse, looking at its bright eyes; "go on, tuck in, though we've not earned our corn, we can eat hay. Yes! I am too old to drive—my son could have, not I. He was a first-rate cabdriver. If only he had lived!"

Iona is silent for a moment, then continues:

"That's how it is, my old horse. There's no more Kuzma Ionitch. He has left us to live, and he went off pop. Now let's say, you had a foal, you were the foal's mother, and suddenly, let's say, that foal went and left you to live after him. It would be sad, wouldn't it?"

The little horse munches, listens, and breathes over its master's hand. . . .

Iona's feelings are too much for him, and he tells the little horse the whole story.

(1885)

Edith Wharton *1862–1937*

ROMAN FEVER

I

From the table at which they had been lunching two American ladies of ripe but well-cared-for middle age moved across the lofty terrace of the Roman restaurant and, leaning on its parapet, looked first at each other, and then down on the outspread glories of the Palatine and the Forum, with the same expression of vague but benevolent approval.

As they leaned there a girlish voice echoed up gaily from the stairs leading to the court below. "Well, come along, then," it cried, not to them but to an invisible companion, "and let's leave the young things to their knitting"; and a voice as fresh laughed back: "Oh, look here, Babs, not actually *knitting*—" "Well, I mean figuratively," rejoined the first. "After all, we haven't left our poor parents much else to do . . . " and at that point the turn of the stairs engulfed the dialogue.

The two ladies looked at each other again, this time with a tinge of smiling embarrassment, and the smaller and paler one shook her head and coloured slightly.

"Barbara!" she murmured, sending an unheard rebuke after the mocking voice in the stairway.

The other lady, who was fuller, and higher in colour, with a small determined nose supported by vigorous black eyebrows, gave a good-humoured laugh. "That's what our daughters think of us!"

Her companion replied by a deprecating gesture. "Not of us individually. We must remember that. It's just the collective modern idea of Mothers. And you see—" Half guiltily she drew from her handsomely mounted black hand-bag a twist of crimson silk run through by two fine knitting needles. "One never knows," she murmured. "The new system has certainly given us a good deal of time to kill; and sometimes I get tired just looking—even at this." Her gesture was now addressed to the stupendous scene at their feet.

The dark lady laughed again, and they both relapsed upon the view, contemplating it in silence, with a sort of diffused serenity which might have been borrowed from the spring effulgence of the Roman skies. The luncheon-hour was long past, and the two had their end of the vast terrace to themselves. At its opposite extremity a few groups, detained by a lingering look at the outspread city, were gathering up guide-books and fumbling for tips. The last of them scattered, and the two ladies were alone on the air-washed height.

"Well, I don't see why we shouldn't just stay here," said Mrs. Slade, the lady of the high colour and energetic brows. Two derelict basket-chairs stood near, and she pushed them into the angle of the parapet, and settled herself in one, her gaze upon the Palatine. "After all, it's still the most beautiful view in the world."

"It always will be, to me," assented her friend Mrs. Ansley, with so slight a stress on the "me" that Mrs. Slade, though she noticed it, wondered if it were not merely accidental, like the random underlinings of old-fashioned letter-writers.

"Grace Ansley was always old-fashioned," she thought; and added aloud, with a retrospective smile: "It's a view we've both been familiar with for a good many years. When we first met here we were younger than our girls are now. You remember?"

"Oh, yes, I remember," murmured Mrs. Ansley, with the same undefinable stress. — "There's that head-waiter wondering," she interpolated. She was evidently far less sure than her companion of herself and of her rights in the world.

"I'll cure him of wondering," said Mrs. Slade, stretching her hand toward a bag as discreetly opulent-looking as Mrs. Ansley's. Signing to the head-waiter, she explained that she and her friend were old lovers of Rome, and would like to spend the end of the afternoon looking down on the view — that is, if it did not disturb the service? The head-waiter, bowing over her gratuity, assured her that the ladies were most welcome, and would be still more so if they would condescend to remain for dinner. A full moon night, they would remember. . . .

Mrs. Slade's black brows drew together, as though references to the moon were out-of-place and even unwelcome. But she smiled away her frown as the head-waiter retreated. "Well, why not? We might do worse. There's no knowing, I suppose, when the girls will be back. Do you even know back from *where?* I don't!"

Mrs. Ansley again coloured slightly. "I think those young Italian aviators we met at the Embassy invited them to fly to Tarquinia for tea. I suppose they'll want to wait and fly back by moonlight."

"Moonlight — moonlight! What a part it still plays. Do you suppose they're as sentimental as we were?"

"I've come to the conclusion that I don't in the least know what they are," said Mrs. Ansley. "And perhaps we didn't know much more about each other."

"No; perhaps we didn't."

Her friend gave her a shy glance. "I never should have supposed you were sentimental, Alida."

"Well, perhaps I wasn't." Mrs. Slade drew her lids together in retrospect; and for a few moments the two ladies, who had been intimate since childhood, reflected how little they knew each other. Each one, of course, had a label ready to attach to the other's name; Mrs. Delphin Slade, for instance, would have told herself, or any one who asked her, that Mrs. Horace Ansley, twenty-five years ago, had been exquisitely lovely — no, you wouldn't believe it, would you? . . . though, of course, still charming, distinguished. . . . Well, as a girl she had been exquisite; far more beautiful than her daughter Barbara, though certainly Babs, according to the new standards at any rate, was more effective — had more *edge*, as they say. Funny where she got it, with those two nullities as parents. Yes; Horace Ansley was — well, just the duplicate of his wife. Museum specimens of old New York. Good-looking, irreproachable, exemplary. Mrs. Slade and Mrs. Ansley had lived opposite each other — actually as well as figuratively — for years. When the drawing-room curtains in No. 20 East 73rd Street were renewed, No. 23, across the way, was always aware of it. And of all the movings, buyings, travels, anniversaries, illnesses — the tame chronicle of an estimable pair. Little of it escaped Mrs. Slade. But she had grown bored with it by the time her husband made his big *coup* in Wall Street, and when they bought in upper Park Avenue had already begun to think: "I'd rather live opposite a speak-easy for a change; at least one might see it raided." The idea of seeing Grace raided was so amusing that (before the move) she launched it at a woman's lunch. It made a hit, and went the rounds — she sometimes wondered if it had crossed the street, and reached Mrs. Ansley. She hoped not, but didn't much mind. Those were the days when respectability was at a discount, and it did the irreproachable no harm to laugh at them a little.

A few years later, and not many months apart, both ladies lost their husbands. There was an appropriate exchange of wreaths and condolences, and a brief renewal of intimacy in the half-shadow of their mourning; and now, after another interval, they had run across each other in Rome, at the same hotel, each of them the modest appendage of a salient daughter. The similarity of their lot had again drawn them together, lending itself to mild jokes, and the mutual confession that, if in old days it must have been tiring to "keep up" with daughters, it was now, at times, a little dull not to.

No doubt, Mrs. Slade reflected, she felt her unemployment more than poor Grace ever would. It was a big drop from being the wife of Delphin Slade to being his widow. She had always regarded herself (with a certain conjugal pride) as his equal in social gifts, as contributing her full share to the making of the exceptional couple they were: but the difference after his death was irremediable. As the wife of the famous corporation lawyer, always with an international case or two on hand, every day brought its exciting and unexpected obligation: the impromptu entertaining of eminent colleagues from abroad, the hurried dashes on legal business to London, Paris or Rome, where the entertaining was so handsomely reciprocated; the amusement of hearing in her wake: "What, that handsome woman with the good clothes and the eyes is Mrs. Slade — *the* Slade's wife? Really? Generally the wives of celebrities are such frumps."

Yes; being *the* Slade's widow was a dullish business after that. In living up to such a husband all her faculties had been engaged; now she had only her daughter to live up to, for the son who seemed to have inherited his father's gifts had died suddenly in boyhood. She had fought through that agony because her husband was there, to be helped and to help; now, after the father's death, the thought of the boy had become unbearable. There was nothing left but to mother her daughter; and dear Jenny was such a perfect daughter that she needed no excessive mothering. "Now with Babs Ansley I don't know that I *should* be so quiet," Mrs. Slade sometimes half-enviously reflected; but Jenny, who was younger than her brilliant friend, was that rare accident, an extremely pretty girl who somehow made youth and prettiness seem as safe as their absence. It was all perplexing — and to Mrs. Slade a little boring. She wished that Jenny would fall in love — with the wrong man, even; that she might have to be watched, out-manoeuvred, rescued. And instead, it was Jenny who watched her mother, kept her out of draughts, made sure that she had taken her tonic. . . .

Mrs. Ansley was much less articulate than her friend, and her mental portrait of Mrs. Slade was slighter, and drawn with fainter touches. "Alida Slade's awfully brilliant; but not as brilliant as she thinks," would have summed it up; though she would have added, for the enlightenment of strangers, that Mrs. Slade had been an extremely dashing girl; much more so than her daughter, who was pretty, of course, and clever in a way, but had none of her mother's — well, "vividness," some one had once called it. Mrs. Ansley would take up current words like this, and cite them in quotation marks, as unheard-of audacities. No; Jenny was not like her mother. Sometimes Mrs. Ansley thought Alida Slade was disappointed; on the whole she had had a sad life. Full of failures and mistakes; Mrs. Ansley had always been rather sorry for her. . . .

So these two ladies visualized each other, each through the wrong end of her little telescope.

II

For a long time they continued to sit side by side without speaking. It seemed as though, to both, there was a relief in laying down their somewhat futile activities in the presence of the vast Memento Mori which faced them. Mrs. Slade sat quite still, her eyes fixed on the golden slope of the Palace of the Cæsars, and after a while Mrs. Ansley ceased to fidget with her bag, and she too sank into meditation. Like many intimate friends, the two ladies had never before had occasion to be silent together, and Mrs. Ansley was slightly embarrassed by what seemed, after so many years, a new stage in their intimacy, and one with which she did not yet know how to deal.

Suddenly the air was full of that deep clangour of bells which periodically covers Rome with a roof of silver. Mrs. Slade glanced at her wrist-watch. "Five o'clock already," she said, as though surprised.

Mrs. Ansley suggested interrogatively: "There's bridge at the Embassy at five." For a long time Mrs. Slade did not answer. She appeared to be lost in contemplation, and Mrs. Ansley thought the remark had escaped her. But after a while she said, as if speaking out of a dream: "Bridge, did you say? Not unless you want to. . . . But I don't think I will, you know."

"Oh, no," Mrs. Ansley hastened to assure her. "I don't care to at all. It's so lovely here; and so full of old memories, as you say." She settled herself in her chair, and almost furtively drew forth her knitting. Mrs. Slade took sideway note of this activity, but her own beautifully cared-for hands remained motionless on her knee.

"I was just thinking," she said slowly, "what different things Rome stands for to each generation of travellers. To our grandmothers, Roman fever; to our mothers, sentimental dangers—how we used to be guarded!—to our daughters, no more dangers than the middle of Main Street. They don't know it—but how much they're missing!"

The long golden light was beginning to pale, and Mrs. Ansley lifted her knitting a little closer to her eyes. "Yes; how we were guarded!"

"I always used to think," Mrs. Slade continued, "that our mothers had a much more difficult job than our grandmothers. When Roman fever stalked the streets it must have been comparatively easy to gather in the girls at the danger hour; but when you and I were young, with such beauty calling us, and the spice of disobedience thrown in, and no worse risk than catching cold during the cool hour after sunset, the mothers used to be put to it to keep us in—didn't they?"

She turned again toward Mrs. Ansley, but the latter had reached a delicate point in her knitting. "One, two, three—slip two; yes, they must have been," she assented, without looking up.

Mrs. Slade's eyes rested on her with a deepened attention. "She can knit—in the face of *this*! How like her. . . . "

Mrs. Slade leaned back, brooding, her eyes ranging from the ruins which faced her to the long green hollow of the Forum, the fading glow of the church fronts beyond it, and the outlying immensity of the Colosseum. Suddenly she thought: "It's all very well to say that our girls have done away with sentiment and moonlight. But if Babs Ansley isn't out to catch that young aviator—the one who's a Marchese—then I don't know anything. And Jenny has no chance beside her. I know that too. I wonder if that's why Grace Ansley likes the two girls to go everywhere together? My poor Jenny as a foil—!" Mrs. Slade gave a hardly audible laugh, and at the sound Mrs. Ansley dropped her knitting.

"Yes—?"

"I—oh, nothing. I was only thinking how your Babs carries everything before her. That Campolieri boy is one of the best matches in Rome. Don't look so innocent, my dear—you know he is. And I was wondering, ever so respectfully, you understand . . . wondering how two such exemplary characters as you and Horace had managed to produce anything quite so dynamic." Mrs. Slade laughed again, with a touch of asperity.

Mrs. Ansley's hands lay inert across her needles. She looked straight out at the great accumulated wreckage of passion and splendour at her feet. But her small profile was almost expressionless. At length she said: "I think you overrate Babs, my dear."

Mrs. Slade's tone grew easier. "No; I don't. I appreciate her. And perhaps envy you. Oh, my girl's perfect; if I were a chronic invalid I'd—well, I think I'd rather be in Jenny's hands. There must be times . . . but there! I always wanted a brilliant daughter . . . and never quite understood why I got an angel instead."

Mrs. Ansley echoed her laugh in a faint murmur. "Babs is an angel too."

"Of course—of course! But she's got rainbow wings. Well, they're wandering by the sea with their young men; and here we sit . . . and it all brings back the past a little too acutely."

Mrs. Ansley had resumed her knitting. One might almost have imagined (if one had known her less well, Mrs. Slade reflected) that, for her also, too many memories rose from the lengthening shadows of those august ruins. But no; she was simply absorbed in her work. What was there for her to worry about? She knew that Babs would almost certainly come back engaged to the extremely eligible Campolieri. "And she'll sell the New York house, and settle down near them in Rome, and never be in their way . . . she's much too tactful. But she'll have an excellent cook, and just the right people in for bridge and cock- tails . . . and a perfectly peaceful old age among her grandchildren."

Mrs. Slade broke off this prophetic flight with a recoil of self-disgust. There was no one of whom she had less right to think unkindly than of Grace Ansley. Would she never cure herself of envying her? Perhaps she had begun too long ago.

She stood up and leaned against the parapet, filling her troubled eyes with the tranquillizing magic of the hour. But instead of tranquillizing her the sight seemed to increase her exasperation. Her gaze turned toward the Colosseum. Already its golden flank was drowned in purple shadow, and above it the sky curved crystal clear, without light or colour. It was the moment when afternoon and evening hang balanced in mid-heaven.

Mrs. Slade turned back and laid her hand on her friend's arm. The gesture was so abrupt that Mrs. Ansley looked up, startled.

"The sun's set. You're not afraid, my dear?"

"Afraid—?"

"Of Roman fever or pneumonia? I remember how ill you were that winter. As a girl you had a very delicate throat, hadn't you?"

"Oh, we're all right up here. Down below, in the Forum, it does get deathly cold, all of a sudden . . . but not here."

"Ah, of course you know because you had to be so careful." Mrs. Slade turned back to the parapet. She thought: "I must make one more effort not to hate her." Aloud she said: "Whenever I look at the Forum from up here, I remember that story about a great-aunt of yours, wasn't she? A dreadfully wicked great-aunt?"

"Oh, yes; Great-aunt Harriet. The one who was supposed to have sent her young sister out to the Forum after sunset to gather a nightblooming flower for her album. All our great-aunts and grandmothers used to have albums of dried flowers."

Mrs. Slade nodded. "But she really sent her because they were in love with the same man—"

"Well, that was the family tradition. They said Aunt Harriet confessed it years afterward. At any rate, the poor little sister caught the fever and died. Mother used to frighten us with the story when we were children."

"And you frightened *me* with it, that winter when you and I were here as girls. The winter I was engaged to Delphin."

Mrs. Ansley gave a faint laugh. "Oh, did I? Really frightened you? I don't believe you're easily frightened."

"Not often; but I was then. I was easily frightened because I was too happy. I wonder if you know what that means?"

"I—yes . . . " Mrs. Ansley faltered.

"Well, I suppose that was why the story of your wicked aunt made such an impression on me. And I thought: 'There's no more Roman fever, but the Forum is deathly cold after sunset—especially after a hot day. And the Colosseum's even colder and damper.'"

"The Colosseum—?"

"Yes. It wasn't easy to get in, after the gates were locked for the night. Far from easy. Still, in those days it could be managed; it *was* managed, often. Lovers met there who couldn't meet elsewhere. You knew that?"

"I—I daresay. I don't remember."

"You don't remember? You don't remember going to visit some ruins or other one evening, just after dark, and catching a bad chill? You were supposed to have gone to see the moon rise. People always said that expedition was what caused your illness."

There was a moment's silence; then Mrs. Ansley rejoined: "Did they? It was all so long ago."

"Yes. And you got well again—so it didn't matter. But I suppose it struck your friends—the reason given for your illness, I mean—because everybody knew you were so prudent on account of your throat, and your mother took such care of you. . . . You *had* been out late sight-seeing, hadn't you, that night?"

"Perhaps I had. The most prudent girls aren't always prudent. What made you think of it now?"

Mrs. Slade seemed to have no answer ready. But after a moment she broke out: "Because I simply can't bear it any longer—!"

Mrs. Ansley lifted her head quickly. Her eyes were wide and very pale. "Can't bear what?"

"Why—your not knowing that I've always known why you went."

"Why I went—?"

"Yes. You think I'm bluffing, don't you? Well, you went to meet the man I was engaged to—and I can repeat every word of the letter that took you there."

While Mrs. Slade spoke Mrs. Ansley had risen unsteadily to her feet. Her bag, her knitting and gloves, slid in a panic-stricken heap to the ground. She looked at Mrs. Slade as though she were looking at a ghost.

"No, no—don't," she faltered out.

"Why not? Listen, if you don't believe me. 'My one darling, things can't go on like this. I must see you alone. Come to the Colosseum immediately after dark tomorrow. There will be somebody to let you in. No one whom you need fear will suspect'—but perhaps you've forgotten what the letter said?"

Mrs. Ansley met the challenge with an unexpected composure. Steadying herself against the chair she looked at her friend, and replied: "No; I know it by heart too."

"And the signature? 'Only *your* D.S.' Was that it? I'm right, am I? That was the letter that took you out that evening after dark?"

Mrs. Ansley was still looking at her. It seemed to Mrs. Slade that a slow struggle was going on behind the voluntarily controlled mask of her small quiet face. "I shouldn't have thought she had herself so well in hand," Mrs. Slade reflected, almost resentfully. But at this moment Mrs. Ansley spoke. "I don't know how you knew. I burnt that letter at once."

"Yes; you would, naturally—you're so prudent!" The sneer was open now. "And if you burnt the letter you're wondering how on earth I know what was in it. That's it, isn't it?"

Mrs. Slade waited, but Mrs. Ansley did not speak.

"Well, my dear, I know what was in that letter because I wrote it!"

"You wrote it?"

"Yes."

The two women stood for a minute staring at each other in the last golden light. Then Mrs. Ansley dropped back into her chair. "Oh," she murmured, and covered her face with her hands.

Mrs. Slade waited nervously for another word or movement. None came, and at length she broke out: "I horrify you."

Mrs. Ansley's hands dropped to her knee. The face they uncovered was streaked with tears. "I wasn't thinking of you. I was thinking—it was the only letter I ever had from him!"

"And I wrote it. Yes; I wrote it! But I was the girl he was engaged to. Did you happen to remember that?"

Mrs. Ansley's head drooped again. "I'm not trying to excuse myself. . . . I remembered. . . . "

"And you still went?"

"Still I went."

Mrs. Slade stood looking down on the small bowed figure at her side. The flame of her wrath had already sunk, and she wondered why she had ever thought there would be any satisfaction in inflicting so purposeless a wound on her friend. But she had to justify herself.

"You do understand? I'd found out—and I hated you, hated you. I knew you were in love with Delphin—and I was afraid; afraid of you, of your quiet ways, your sweetness . . . your . . . well, I wanted you out of the way, that's all.

Just for a few weeks; just till I was sure of him. So in a blind fury I wrote that letter. . . . I don't know why I'm telling you now."

"I suppose," said Mrs. Ansley slowly, "it's because you've always gone on hating me."

"Perhaps. Or because I wanted to get the whole thing off my mind." She paused. "I'm glad you destroyed the letter. Of course I never thought you'd die."

Mrs. Ansley relapsed into silence, and Mrs. Slade, leaning above her, was conscious of a strange sense of isolation, of being cut off from the warm current of human communion. "You think me a monster!"

"I don't know. . . . It was the only letter I had, and you say he didn't write it?"

"Ah, how you care for him, still!"

"I cared for that memory," said Mrs. Ansley.

Mrs. Slade continued to look down on her. She seemed physically reduced by the blow — as if, when she got up, the wind might scatter her like a puff of dust. Mrs. Slade's jealousy suddenly leapt up again at the sight. All these years the woman had been living on that letter. How she must have loved him, to treasure the mere memory of its ashes! The letter of the man her friend was engaged to. Wasn't it she who was the monster?

"You tried your best to get him away from me, didn't you? But you failed; and I kept him. That's all."

"Yes. That's all."

"I wish now I hadn't told you. I'd no idea you'd feel about it as you do; I thought you'd be amused. It all happened so long ago, as you say; and you must do me the justice to remember that I had no reason to think you'd ever taken it seriously. How could I, when you were married to Horace Ansley two months afterward? As soon as you could get out of bed your mother rushed you off to Florence and married you. People were rather surprised — they wondered at its being done so quickly; but I thought I knew. I had an idea you did it out of *pique* — to be able to say you'd got ahead of Delphin and me. Girls have such silly reasons for doing the most serious things. And your marrying so soon convinced me that you'd never really cared."

"Yes. I suppose it would," Mrs. Ansley assented.

The clear heaven overhead was emptied of all its gold. Dusk spread over it, abruptly darkening the Seven Hills. Here and there lights began to twinkle through the foliage at their feet. Steps were coming and going on the deserted terrace — waiters looking out of the doorway at the head of the stairs, then reappearing with trays and napkins and flasks of wine. Tables were moved, chairs straightened. A feeble string of electric lights flickered out. Some vases of faded flowers were carried away, and brought back replenished. A stout lady in a dust-coat suddenly appeared, asking in broken Italian if any one had seen the elastic band which held together her tattered Baedeker. She poked with her stick under the table at which she had lunched, the waiters assisting.

The corner where Mrs. Slade and Mrs. Ansley sat was still shadowy and deserted. For a long time neither of them spoke. At length Mrs. Slade began again: "I suppose I did it as a sort of joke —"

"A joke?"

"Well, girls are ferocious sometimes, you know. Girls in love especially. And I remember laughing to myself all that evening at the idea that you were waiting around there in the dark, dodging out of sight, listening for every sound, trying to get in —. Of course I was upset when I heard you were so ill afterward."

Mrs. Ansley had not moved for a long time. But now she turned slowly toward her companion. "But I didn't wait. He'd arranged everything. He was there. We were let in at once," she said.

Mrs. Slade sprang up from her leaning position. "Delphin there? They let you in? — Ah, now you're lying!" she burst out with violence.

Mrs. Ansley's voice grew clearer, and full of surprise. "But of course he was there. Naturally he came — "

"Came? How did he know he'd find you there? You must be raving!"

Mrs. Ansley hesitated, as though reflecting. "But I answered the letter. I told him I'd be there. So he came."

Mrs. Slade flung her hands up to her face. "Oh, God — you answered! I never thought of your answering. . . . "

"It's odd you never thought of it, if you wrote the letter."

"Yes. I was blind with rage."

Mrs. Ansley rose, and drew her fur scarf about her. "It is cold here. We'd better go. . . . I'm sorry for you," she said, as she clasped the fur about her throat.

The unexpected words sent a pang through Mrs. Slade. "Yes; we'd better go." She gathered up her bag and cloak. "I don't know why you should be sorry for me," she muttered.

Mrs. Ansley stood looking away from her toward the dusky secret mass of the Colosseum. "Well — because I didn't have to wait that night."

Mrs. Slade gave an unquiet laugh. "Yes; I was beaten there. But I oughtn't to begrudge it to you, I suppose. At the end of all these years. After all, I had everything; I had him for twenty-five years. And you had nothing but that one letter that he didn't write."

Mrs. Ansley was again silent. At length she turned toward the door of the terrace. She took a step, and turned back, facing her companion.

"I had Barbara," she said, and began to move ahead of Mrs. Slade toward the stairway.

(1934)

Sherwood Anderson *1876–1941*

rural

THE UNTOLD LIE

Ray Pearson and Hal Winters were farm hands employed on a farm three miles north of Winesburg. On Saturday afternoons they came into town and wandered about through the streets with other fellows from the country.

Ray was a quiet, rather nervous man of perhaps fifty with a brown beard and shoulders rounded by too much and too hard labor. In his nature he was as unlike Hal Winters as two men can be unlike.

Ray was an altogether serious man and had a little sharp-featured wife who had also a sharp voice. The two, with half a dozen thin-legged children, lived in a tumbledown frame house beside a creek at the back end of the Wills farm where Ray was employed.

Hal Winters, his fellow employee, was a young fellow. He was not of the Ned Winters family, who were very respectable people in Winesburg, but was one of the three sons of the old man called Windpeter Winters who had a sawmill near Unionville, six miles away, and who was looked upon by everyone in Winesburg as a confirmed old reprobate.

People from the part of Northern Ohio in which Winesburg lies will remember old Windpeter by his unusual and tragic death. He got drunk one evening in town and started to drive home to Unionville along the railroad tracks. Henry Brattenburg, the butcher, who lived out that way, stopped him at the edge of town and told him he was sure to meet the down train but Windpeter slashed at him with his whip and drove on. When the train struck and killed him and his two horses a farmer and his wife who were driving home along a nearby road saw the accident. They said that old Windpeter stood up on the seat of the wagon, raving and swearing at the onrushing locomotive, and that he fairly screamed with delight when the team, maddened by his incessant slashing at them, rushed straight ahead to certain death. Boys like George Willard and Seth Richmond will remember the incident quite vividly because, although everyone in our town said that the old man would go straight to hell and that the community was better off without him, they had a secret conviction that he knew what he was doing and admired his foolish courage. Most boys have seasons of wishing they could die gloriously instead of just being grocery clerks and going on with their humdrum lives.

But this is not the story of Windpeter Winters nor yet of his son Hal who worked on the Wills farm with Ray Pearson. It is Ray's story. It will, however, be necessary to talk a little of young Hal so that you will get into the spirit of it.

Hal was a bad one. Everyone said that. There were three of the Winters boys in the family, John, Hal, and Edward, all broad-shouldered big fellows like old Windpeter himself and all fighters and woman-chasers and generally all-around bad ones.

Hal was the worst of the lot and always up to some devilment. He once stole a load of boards from his father's mill and sold them in Winesburg. With the money he bought himself a suit of cheap, flashy clothes. Then he got drunk and when his father came raving into town to find him, they met and fought with their fists on Main Street and were arrested and put into jail together.

Hal went to work on the Wills farm because there was a country school

267

teacher out that way who had taken his fancy. He was only twenty-one then but had already been in two or three of what were spoken of in Winesburg as "women scrapes." Everyone who heard of his infatuation for the school teacher was sure it would turn out badly. "He'll only get her into trouble, you'll see," was the word that went around.

And so these two men, Ray and Hal, were at work in a field on a day in the late October. They were husking corn and occasionally something was said and they laughed. Then came silence. Ray, who was the more sensitive and always minded things more, had chapped hands and they hurt. He put them into his coat pockets and looked away across the fields. He was in a sad, distracted mood and was affected by the beauty of the country. If you knew the Winesburg country in the fall and how the low hills are all splashed with yellows and reds you would understand his feeling. He began to think of the time, long ago when he was a young fellow living with his father, then a baker in Winesburg, and how on such days he had wandered away to the woods to gather nuts, hunt rabbits, or just to loaf about and smoke his pipe. His marriage had come about through one of his days of wandering. He had induced a girl who waited on trade in his father's shop to go with him and something had happened. He was thinking of that afternoon and how it had affected his whole life when a spirit of protest awoke in him. He had forgotten about Hal and muttered words. "Tricked by Gad, that's what I was, tricked by life and made a fool of," he said in a low voice.

As though understanding his thoughts, Hal Winters spoke up. "Well, has it been worth while? What about it, eh? What about marriage and all that?" he asked and then laughed. Hal tried to keep on laughing but he too was in an earnest mood. He began to talk earnestly. "Has a fellow got to do it?" he asked. "Has he got to be harnessed up and driven through life like a horse?"

Hal didn't wait for an answer but sprang to his feet and began to walk back and forth between the corn shocks. He was getting more and more excited. Bending down suddenly he picked up an ear of yellow corn and threw it at the fence. "I've got Nell Gunther in trouble," he said. "I'm telling you, but you keep your mouth shut."

Ray Pearson arose and stood staring. He was almost a foot shorter than Hal, and when the younger man came and put his two hands on the older man's shoulders they made a picture. There they stood in the big empty field with the quiet corn shocks standing in rows behind them and the red and yellow hills in the distance, and from being just two indifferent workmen they had become all alive to each other. Hal sensed it and because that was his way he laughed. "Well, old daddy," he said awkwardly, "come on, advise me. I've got Nell in trouble. Perhaps you've been in the same fix yourself. I know what everyone would say is the right thing to do, but what do you say? Shall I marry and settle down? Shall I put myself into the harness to be worn out like an old horse? You know me, Ray. There can't anyone break me but I can break myself. Shall I do it or shall I tell Nell to go to the devil? Come on, you tell me. Whatever you say, Ray, I'll do."

Ray couldn't answer. He shook Hal's hands loose and turning walked straight away toward the barn. He was a sensitive man and there were tears in his eyes. He knew there was only one thing to say to Hal Winters, son of old Windpeter Winters, only one thing that all his own training and all the beliefs of the people he knew would approve, but for his life he couldn't say what he knew he should say.

At half-past four that afternoon Ray was puttering about the barnyard when his wife came up the land along the creek and called him. After the talk with Hal he hadn't returned to the cornfield but worked about the barn. He had already done the evening chores and had seen Hal, dressed and ready for a roistering night in town, come out of the farmhouse and go into the road. Along the path to his own house he trudged behind his wife, looking at the ground and thinking. He couldn't make out what was wrong. Every time he raised his eyes and saw the beauty of the country in the failing light he wanted to do something he had never done before, shout or scream or hit his wife with his fists or something equally unexpected and terrifying. Along the path he went scratching his head and trying to make it out. He looked hard at his wife's back but she seemed all right.

She only wanted him to go into town for groceries and as soon as she had told him what she wanted began to scold. "You're always puttering," she said. "Now I want you to hustle. There isn't anything in the house for supper and you've got to get to town and back in a hurry."

Ray went into his own house and took an overcoat from a hook back of the door. It was torn about the pockets and the collar was shiny. His wife went into the bedroom and presently came out with a soiled cloth in one hand and three silver dollars in the other. Somewhere in the house a child wept bitterly and a dog that had been sleeping by the stove arose and yawned. Again the wife scolded. "The children will cry and cry. Why are you always puttering?" she asked.

Ray went out of the house and climbed the fence into a field. It was just growing dark and the scene that lay before him was lovely. All the low hills were washed with color and even the little clusters of bushes in the corners by the fences were alive with beauty. The whole world seemed to Ray Pearson to have become alive with something just as he and Hal had suddenly become alive when they stood in the corn field staring into each other's eyes.

The beauty of the country about Winesburg was too much for Ray on that fall evening. That is all there was to it. He could not stand it. Of a sudden he forgot all about being a quiet old farm hand and throwing off the torn overcoat began to run across the field. As he ran he shouted a protest against his life, against all life, against everything that makes life ugly. "There was no promise made," he cried into the empty spaces that lay about him. "I didn't promise my Minnie anything and Hal hasn't made any promise to Nell. I know he hasn't. She went into the woods with him because she wanted to go. What he wanted she wanted. Why should I pay? Why should Hal pay? Why should anyone pay? I don't want Hal to become old and worn out. I'll tell him. I won't let it go on. I'll catch Hal before he gets to town and I'll tell him."

Ray ran clumsily and once he stumbled and fell down. "I must catch Hal and tell him," he kept thinking, and although his breath came in gasps he kept running harder and harder. As he ran he thought of things that hadn't come into his mind for years — how at the time he married he had planned to go west to his uncle in Portland, Oregon — how he hadn't wanted to be a farm hand, but had thought when he got out West he would go to sea and be a sailor or get a job on a ranch and ride a horse into Western towns, shooting and laughing and waking the people in the houses with his wild cries. Then as he ran he remembered his children and in fancy felt their hands clutching at him. All of his thoughts of himself were involved with the thoughts of Hal and he thought the children were clutching at the younger man also. "They are the accidents of life, Hal," he cried. "They are not mine or yours. I had nothing to do with them."

Darkness began to spread over the fields as Ray Pearson ran on and on. His breath came in little sobs. When he came to the fence at the edge of the road and confronted Hal Winters, all dressed up and smoking a pipe as he walked jauntily along, he could not have told what he thought or what he wanted.

Ray Pearson lost his nerve and this is really the end of the story of what happened to him. It was almost dark when he got to the fence and he put his hands on the top bar and stood staring. Hal Winters jumped a ditch and coming up close to Ray put his hands into his pockets and laughed. He seemed to have lost his own sense of what had happened in the corn field and when he put up a strong hand and took hold of the lapel of Ray's coat he shook the old man as he might have shaken a dog that had misbehaved.

"You came to tell me, eh?" he said. "Well, never mind telling me anything. I'm not a coward and I've already made up my mind." He laughed again and jumped back across the ditch. "Nell ain't no fool," he said. "She didn't ask me to marry her. I want to marry her. I want to settle down and have kids."

Ray Pearson also laughed. He felt like laughing at himself and all the world.

As the form of Hal Winters disappeared in the dusk that lay over the road that led to Winesburg, he turned and walked slowly back across the fields to where he had left his torn overcoat. As he went some memory of pleasant evenings spent with the thin-legged children in the tumble-down house by the creek must have come into his mind, for he muttered words. "It's just as well. Whatever I told him would have been a lie," he said softly, and then his form also disappeared into the darkness of the fields.

(1919)

Susan Glaspell *1882–1948*

A JURY OF HER PEERS

When Martha Hale opened the storm-door and got a cut of the north wind, she ran back for her big woolen scarf. As she hurriedly wound that round her head her eye made a scandalized sweep of her kitchen. It was no ordinary thing that called her away—it was probably farther from ordinary than anything that had ever happened in Dickson County. But what her eye took in was that her kitchen was in no shape for leaving: her bread all ready for mixing, half the flour sifted and half unsifted.

She hated to see things half done; but she had been at that when the team from town stopped to get Mr. Hale, and then the sheriff came running in to say his wife wished Mrs. Hale would come too—adding, with a grin, that he guessed she was getting scarey and wanted another woman along. So she had dropped everything right where it was.

"Martha!" now came her husband's impatient voice. "Don't keep folks waiting out here in the cold."

She again opened the storm-door, and this time joined the three men and the one woman waiting for her in the big two-seated buggy.

After she had the robes tucked around her she took another look at the woman who sat beside her on the back seat. She had met Mrs. Peters the year before at the county fair, and the thing she remembered about her was that she didn't seem like a sheriff's wife. She was small and thin and didn't have a strong voice. Mrs. Gorman, sheriff's wife before Gorman went out and Peters came in, had a voice that somehow seemed to be backing up the law with every word. But if Mrs. Peters didn't look like a sheriff's wife, Peters made it up in looking like a sheriff. He was to a dot the kind of man who could get himself elected sheriff—a heavy man with a big voice, who was particularly genial with the law-abiding, as if to make it plain that he knew the difference between criminals and non-criminals. And right there it came into Mrs. Hale's mind, with a stab, that this man who was so pleasant and lively with all of them was going to the Wrights' now as a sheriff.

"The country's not very pleasant this time of year," Mrs. Peters at last ventured, as if she felt they ought to be talking as well as the men.

Mrs. Hale scarcely finished her reply, for they had gone up a little hill and could see the Wright place now, and seeing it did not make her feel like talking. It looked very lonesome this cold March morning. It had always been a lonesome-looking place. It was down in a hollow, and the poplar trees around it were lonesome-looking trees. The men were looking at it and talking about what had happened. The county attorney was bending to one side of the buggy, and kept looking steadily at the place as they drew up to it.

"I'm glad you came with me," Mrs. Peters said nervously, as the two women were about to follow the men in through the kitchen door.

Even after she had her foot on the door-step, her hand on the knob, Martha Hale had a moment of feeling she could not cross that threshold. And the reason it seemed she couldn't cross it now was simply because she hadn't crossed it before. Time and time again it had been in her mind, "I ought to go over and see Minnie Foster"—she still thought of her as Minnie Foster, though for twenty years she had been Mrs. Wright. And then there was always something to do and Minnie Foster would go from her mind. But *now* she could come.

The men went over to the stove. The women stood close together by the door. Young Henderson, the county attorney, turned around and said, "Come up to the fire, ladies."

Mrs. Peters took a step forward, then stopped. "I'm not—cold," she said.

And so the two women stood by the door, at first not even so much as looking around the kitchen.

The men talked for a minute about what a good thing it was the sheriff had sent his deputy out that morning to make a fire for them, and then Sheriff Peters stepped back from the stove, unbuttoned his outer coat, and leaned his hands on the kitchen table in a way that seemed to mark the beginning of official business. "Now, Mr. Hale," he said in a sort of semi-official voice, "before we move things about, you tell Mr. Henderson just what it was you saw when you came here yesterday morning."

The county attorney was looking around the kitchen.

"By the way," he said, "has anything been moved?" He turned to the sheriff. "Are things just as you left them yesterday?"

Peters looked from cupboard to sink; from that to a small worn rocker a little to one side of the kitchen table.

"It's just the same."

"Somebody should have been left here yesterday," said the county attorney.

"Oh—yesterday," returned the sheriff, with a little gesture as of yesterday having been more than he could bear to think of. "When I had to send Frank to Morris Center for that man who went crazy—let me tell you, I had my hands full *yesterday*. I knew you could get back from Omaha by to-day, George, and as long as I went over everything here myself—"

"Well, Mr. Hale," said the county attorney, in a way of letting what was past and gone go, "tell just what happened when you came here yesterday morning."

Mrs. Hale, still leaning against the door, had that sinking feeling of the mother whose child is about to speak a piece. Lewis often wandered along and got things mixed up in a story. She hoped he would tell this straight and plain, and not say unnecessary things that would just make things harder for Minnie Foster. He didn't begin at once, and she noticed that he looked queer—as if standing in that kitchen and having to tell what he had seen there yesterday morning made him almost sick.

"Yes, Mr. Hale?" the county attorney reminded.

"Harry and I had started to town with a load of potatoes," Mrs. Hale's husband began.

Harry was Mrs. Hale's oldest boy. He wasn't with them now, for the very good reason that those potatoes never got to town yesterday and he was taking them this morning, so he hadn't been home when the sheriff stopped to say he wanted Mr. Hale to come over to the Wright place and tell the county attorney his story there, where he could point it all out. With all Mrs. Hale's other emotions came the fear that maybe Harry wasn't dressed warm enough—they hadn't any of them realized how that north wind did bite.

"We come along this road," Hale was going on, with a motion of his hand to the road over which they had just come, "and as we got in sight of the house I says to Harry, 'I'm goin' to see if I can't get John Wright to take a telephone.' You see," he explained to Henderson, "unless I can get somebody to go in with me they won't come out this branch road except for a price *I* can't pay. I'd spoke to Wright about it once before; but he put me off, saying folks talked too much anyway, and all he asked was peace and quiet — guess you know about how much he talked himself. But I thought maybe if I went to the house and talked about it before his wife, and said all the women-folks liked the telephones, and that in this lonesome stretch of road it would be a good thing — well, I said to Harry that that was what I was going to say — though I said at the same time that I didn't know as what his wife wanted made much difference to John — "

Now, there he was! — saying things he didn't need to say. Mrs. Hale tried to catch her husband's eye, but fortunately the county attorney interrupted with:

"Let's talk about that a little later, Mr. Hale. I do want to talk about that, but I'm anxious now to get along to just what happened when you got here."

When he began this time, it was very deliberately and carefully:

"I didn't see or hear anything. I knocked at the door. And still it was all quiet inside. I knew they must be up — it was past eight o'clock. So I knocked again, louder, and I thought I heard somebody say 'Come in.' I wasn't sure — I'm not sure yet. But I opened the door — this door," jerking a hand toward the door by which the two women stood, "and there, in that rocker" — pointing to it — "sat Mrs. Wright."

Every one in the kitchen looked at the rocker. It came into Mrs. Hale's mind that that rocker didn't look in the least like Minnie Foster — the Minnie Foster of twenty years before. It was a dingy red, with wooden rungs up the back, and the middle rung was gone, and the chair sagged to one side.

"How did she — look?" the county attorney was inquiring.

"Well," said Hale, "she looked — queer."

"How do you mean — queer?"

As he asked it he took out a note-book and pencil. Mrs. Hale did not like the sight of that pencil. She kept her eye fixed on her husband, as if to keep him from saying unnecessary things that would go into that note-book and make trouble.

Hale did speak guardedly, as if the pencil had affected him too.

"Well, as if she didn't know what she was going to do next. And kind of — done up."

"How did she seem to feel about your coming?"

"Why, I don't think she minded — one way or other. She didn't pay much attention. I said, 'Ho' do, Mrs. Wright? It's cold, ain't it?' And she said, 'Is it?' — and went on pleatin' at her apron.

"Well, I was surprised. She didn't ask me to come up to the stove, or to sit down, but just set there, not even lookin' at me. And so I said: 'I want to see John.'

"And then she — laughed. I guess you would call it a laugh.

"I thought of Harry and the team outside, so I said, a little sharp, 'Can I see John?' 'No,' says she — kind of dull like. 'Ain't he home?' says I. Then she looked at me. 'Yes,' says she, 'he's home.' 'Then why can't I see him?' I asked her, out of patience with her now. ''Cause he's dead,' says she, just as quiet and dull — and fell to pleatin' her apron. 'Dead?' says I, like you do when you can't take in what you've heard.

"She just nodded her head, not getting a bit excited, but rockin' back and forth.

"'Why — where is he?' says I, not knowing *what* to say.

"She just pointed upstairs — like this" — pointing to the room above.

"I got up, with the idea of going up there myself. By this time I — didn't know what to do. I walked from there to here; then I says: 'Why, what did he die of?'

"'He died of a rope around his neck,' says she; and just went on pleatin' at her apron."

Hale stopped speaking, and stood staring at the rocker, as if he were still seeing the woman who had sat there the morning before. Nobody spoke; it was as if every one were seeing the woman who had sat there the morning before.

"And what did you do then?" the county attorney at last broke the silence.

"I went out and called Harry. I thought I might — need help. I got Harry in, and we went upstairs." His voice fell almost to a whisper. "There he was — lying over the — "

"I think I'd rather have you go into that upstairs," the county attorney interrupted, "where you can point it all out. Just go on now with the rest of the story."

"Well, my first thought was to get that rope off. It looked — "

He stopped, his face twitching.

"But Harry, he went up to him, and he said, 'No, he's dead all right, and we'd better not touch anything.' So we went downstairs.

"She was still sitting that same way. 'Has anybody been notified?' I asked. 'No,' says she, unconcerned.

"'Who did this, Mrs. Wright?' said Harry. He said it business-like, and she stopped pleatin' at her apron. 'I don't know,' she says. 'You don't *know*?' says Harry. 'Weren't you sleepin' in the bed with him?' 'Yes,' says she, 'but I was on the inside.' 'Somebody slipped a rope round his neck and strangled him, and you didn't wake up?' says Harry. 'I didn't wake up,' she said after him.

"We may have looked as if we didn't see how that could be, for after a minute she said, 'I sleep sound.'

"Harry was going to ask her more questions, but I said maybe that weren't our business; maybe we ought to let her tell her story first to the coroner or the sheriff. So Harry went fast as he could over to High Road — the Rivers' place, where there's a telephone."

"And what did she do when she knew you had gone for the coroner?" The attorney got his pencil in his hand all ready for writing.

"She moved from that chair to this one over here" — Hale pointed to a small chair in the corner — "and just sat there with her hands held together and looking down. I got a feeling that I ought to make some conversation, so I said I had come in to see if John wanted to put in a telephone; and at that she started to laugh, and then she stopped and looked at me — scared."

At the sound of a moving pencil the man who was telling the story looked up.

"I dunno — maybe it wasn't scared," he hastened; "I wouldn't like to say it was. Soon Harry got back, and then Dr. Lloyd came, and you, Mr. Peters, and so I guess that's all I know that you don't."

He said that last with relief, and moved a little, as if relaxing. Every one moved a little. The county attorney walked toward the stair door.

"I guess we'll go upstairs first — then out to the barn and around there."

He paused and looked around the kitchen.

"You're convinced there was nothing important here?" he asked the sheriff. "Nothing that would — point to any motive?"

The sheriff too looked all around, as if to re-convince himself.

"Nothing here but kitchen things," he said, with a little laugh for the insignificance of kitchen things.

The county attorney was looking at the cupboard—a peculiar, ungainly structure, half closet and half cupboard, the upper part of it being built in the wall, and the lower part just the old-fashioned kitchen cupboard. As if its queerness attracted him, he got a chair and opened the upper part and looked in. After a moment he drew his hand away sticky.

"Here's a nice mess," he said resentfully.

The two women had drawn nearer, and now the sheriff's wife spoke.

"Oh—her fruit," she said, looking to Mrs. Hale for sympathetic understanding. She turned back to the county attorney and explained: "She worried about that when it turned so cold last night. She said the fire would go out and her jars might burst."

Mrs. Peters' husband broke into a laugh.

"Well, can you beat the woman! Held for murder, and worrying about her preserves!"

The young attorney set his lips.

"I guess before we're through with her she may have something more serious than preserves to worry about."

"Oh, well," said Mrs. Hale's husband, with good-natured superiority, "women are used to worrying over trifles."

The two women moved a little closer together. Neither of them spoke. The county attorney seemed suddenly to remember his manners—and think of his future.

"And yet," said he, with the gallantry of a young politician, "for all their worries, what would we do without the ladies?"

The women did not speak, did not unbend. He went to the sink and began washing his hands. He turned to wipe them on the roller towel—whirled it for a cleaner place.

"Dirty towels! Not much of a housekeeper, would you say, ladies?"

He kicked his foot against some dirty pans under the sink.

"There's a great deal of work to be done on a farm," said Mrs. Hale stiffly.

"To be sure. And yet"—with a little bow to her—"I know there are some Dickinson County farm-houses that do not have such roller towels." He gave it a pull to expose its full length again.

"Those towels get dirty awful quick. Men's hands aren't always as clean as they might be."

"Ah, loyal to your sex, I see," he laughed. He stopped and gave her a keen look. "But you and Mrs. Wright were neighbors. I suppose you were friends, too."

Martha Hale shook her head.

"I've seen little enough of her of late years. I've not been in this house—it's more than a year."

"And why was that? You didn't like her?"

"I liked her well enough," she replied with spirit. "Farmers' wives have their hands full, Mr. Henderson. And then"—She looked around the kitchen.

"Yes?" he encouraged.

"It never seemed a very cheerful place," said she, more to herself than to him.

"No," he agreed; "I don't think any one would call it cheerful. I shouldn't say she had the home-making instinct."

"Well, I don't know as Wright had, either," she muttered.

"You mean they didn't get on very well?" he was quick to ask.

"No; I don't mean anything," she answered, with decision. As she turned a little away from him, she added: "But I don't think a place would be any the cheerfuler for John Wright's bein' in it."

"I'd like to talk to you about that a little later, Mrs. Hale," he said. "I'm anxious to get the lay of things upstairs now."

He moved toward the stair door, followed by the two men.

"I suppose anything Mrs. Peters does'll be all right?" the sheriff inquired. "She was to take in some clothes for her, you know — and a few little things. We left in such a hurry yesterday."

The county attorney looked at the two women whom they were leaving alone there among the kitchen things.

"Yes — Mrs. Peters," he said, his glance resting on the woman who was not Mrs. Peters, the big farmer woman who stood behind the sheriff's wife. "Of course Mrs. Peters is one of us," he said, in a manner of entrusting responsibility. "And keep your eye out, Mrs. Peters, for anything that might be of use. No telling; you women might come upon a clue to the motive — and that's the thing we need."

Mr. Hale rubbed his face after the fashion of a show man getting ready for a pleasantry.

"But would the women know a clue if they did come upon it?" he said; and, having delivered himself of this, he followed the others through the stair door.

The women stood motionless and silent, listening to the footsteps, first upon the stairs, then in the room above them.

Then, as if releasing herself from something strange, Mrs. Hale began to arrange the dirty pans under the sink, which the county attorney's disdainful push of the foot had deranged.

"I'd hate to have men comin' into my kitchen," she said testily — "snoopin' round and criticizin'."

"Of course it's no more than their duty," said the sheriff's wife, in her manner of timid acquiescence.

"Duty's all right," replied Mrs. Hale bluffly; "but I guess that deputy sheriff that come out to make the fire might have got a little of this on." She gave the roller towel a pull. "Wish I'd thought of that sooner! Seems mean to talk about her for not having things slicked up, when she had to come away in such a hurry."

She looked around the kitchen. Certainly it was not "slicked up." Her eye was held by a bucket of sugar on a low shelf. The cover was off the wooden bucket, and beside it was a paper bag — half full.

Mrs. Hale moved toward it.

"She was putting this in there," she said to herself — slowly.

She thought of the flour in her kitchen at home — half sifted, half not sifted. She had been interrupted, and had left things half done. What had interrupted Minnie Foster? Why had that work been left half done? She made a move as if to finish it, — unfinished things always bothered her, — and then she glanced around and saw that Mrs. Peters was watching her — and she didn't want Mrs. Peters to get that feeling she had got of work begun and then — for some reason — not finished.

"It's a shame about her fruit," she said, and walked toward the cupboard that the county attorney had opened, and got on the chair, murmuring: "I wonder if it's all gone."

It was a sorry enough looking sight, but "Here's one that's all right," she said at last. She held it toward the light. "This is cherries, too." She looked again. "I declare I believe that's the only one."

With a sigh, she got down from the chair, went to the sink, and wiped off the bottle.

"She'll feel awful bad, after all her hard work in the hot weather. I remember the afternoon I put up my cherries last summer."

She set the bottle on the table, and, with another sigh, started to sit down in the rocker. But she did not sit down. Something kept her from sitting down in that chair. She straightened — stepped back, and, half turned away, stood looking at it, seeing the woman who sat there "pleatin' at her apron."

The thin voice of the sheriff's wife broke in upon her: "I must be getting those things from the front room closet." She opened the door into the other room, started in, stepped back. "You coming with me, Mrs. Hale?" she asked nervously. "You — you could help me get them."

They were soon back — the stark coldness of that shut-up room was not a thing to linger in.

"My!" said Mrs. Peters, dropping the things on the table and hurrying to the stove.

Mrs. Hale stood examining the clothes the woman who was being detained in town had said she wanted.

"Wright was close!" she exclaimed, holding up a shabby black skirt that bore the marks of much making over. "I think maybe that's why she kept so much to herself. I s'pose she felt she couldn't do her part; and then, you don't enjoy things when you feel shabby. She used to wear pretty clothes and be lively — when she was Minnie Foster, one of the town girls, singing in the choir. But that — oh, that was twenty years ago."

With a carefulness in which there was something tender, she folded the shabby clothes and piled them at one corner of the table. She looked at Mrs. Peters, and there was something in the other woman's look that irritated her.

"She don't care," she said to herself. "Much difference it makes to her whether Minnie Foster had pretty clothes when she was a girl."

Then she looked again, and she wasn't so sure; in fact, she hadn't at any time been perfectly sure about Mrs. Peters. She had that shrinking manner, and yet her eyes looked as if they could see a long way into things.

"This all you was to take in?" asked Mrs. Hale.

"No," said the sheriff's wife; "she said she wanted an apron. Funny thing to want," she ventured in her nervous little way, "for there's not much to get you dirty in jail, goodness knows. But I suppose just to make her feel more natural. If you're used to wearing an apron —. She said they were in the bottom drawer of this cupboard. Yes — here they are. And then her little shawl that always hung on the stair door."

She took the small gray shawl from behind the door leading upstairs, and stood a minute looking at it.

Suddenly Mrs. Hale took a quick step toward the other woman.

"Mrs. Peters!"

"Yes, Mrs. Hale?"

"Do you think she — did it?"

A frightened look blurred the other things in Mrs. Peters' eyes.

"Oh, I don't know," she said, in a voice that seemed to shrink away from the subject.

"Well, I don't think she did," affirmed Mrs. Hale stoutly. "Asking for an apron, and her little shawl. Worryin' about her fruit."

"Mr. Peters says—." Footsteps were heard in the room above; she stopped, looked up, then went on in a lowered voice: "Mr. Peters says—it looks bad for her. Mr. Henderson is awful sarcastic in a speech, and he's going to make fun of her saying she didn't—wake up."

For a moment Mrs. Hale had no answer. Then, "Well, I guess John Wright didn't wake up—when they was slippin' that rope under his neck," she muttered.

"No, it's *strange*," breathed Mrs. Peters. "They think it was such a—funny way to kill a man."

She began to laugh; at sound of the laugh, abruptly stopped.

"That's just what Mr. Hale said," said Mrs. Hale, in a resolutely natural voice. "There was a gun in the house. He says that's what he can't understand."

"Mr. Henderson said, coming out, that what was needed for the case was a motive. Something to show anger—or sudden feeling."

"Well, I don't see any signs of anger around here," said Mrs. Hale. "I don't—"

She stopped. It was as if her mind tripped on something. He eye was caught by a dish-towel in the middle of the kitchen table. Slowly she moved toward the table. One half of it was wiped clean, the other half messy. Her eyes made a slow, almost unwilling turn to the bucket of sugar and the half empty bag beside it. Things begun—and not finished.

After a moment she stepped back, and said, in that manner of releasing herself: "Wonder how they're finding things upstairs? I hope she had it a little more red up up there. You know,"—she paused, and feeling gathered,—"it seems kind of *sneaking*; locking her up in town and coming out here to get her own house to turn against her!"

"But, Mrs. Hale," said the sheriff's wife, "the law is the law."

"I s'pose 'tis," answered Mrs. Hale shortly.

She turned to the stove, saying something about that fire not being much to brag of. She worked with it a minute, and when she straightened up she said aggressively:

"The law is the law—and a bad stove is a bad stove. How'd you like to cook on this?"—pointing with the poker to the broken lining. She opened the oven door and started to express her opinion of the oven; but she was swept into her own thoughts, thinking of what it would mean, year after year, to have that stove to wrestle with. The thought of Minnie Foster trying to bake in that oven—and the thought of her never going over to see Minnie Foster—.

She was startled by hearing Mrs. Peters say: "A person gets discouraged—and loses heart."

The sheriff's wife had looked from the stove to the sink—to the pail of water which had been carried in from outside. The two women stood there silent, above them the footsteps of the men who were looking for evidence against the woman who had worked in that kitchen. That look of seeing into things, of seeing through a thing to something else, was in the eyes of the sheriff's wife now. When Mrs. Hale next spoke to her, it was gently:

"Better loosen up your things, Mrs. Peters. We'll not feel them when we go out."

Mrs. Peters went to the back of the room to hang up the fur tippet she was wearing. A moment later she exclaimed, "Why, she was piecing a quilt," and held up a large sewing basket piled high with quilt pieces.

Mrs. Hale spread some of the blocks on the table.

"It's log-cabin pattern," she said, putting several of them together. "Pretty, isn't it?"

They were so engaged with the quilt that they did not hear the footsteps on the stairs. Just as the stair door opened Mrs. Hale was saying:

"Do you suppose she was going to quilt it or just knot it?"

The sheriff threw up his hands.

"They wonder whether she was going to quilt it or just knot it!"

There was a laugh for the ways of women, a warming of hands over the stove, and then the county attorney said briskly:

"Well, let's go right out to the barn and get that cleared up."

"I don't see as there's anything so strange," Mrs. Hale said resentfully, after the outside door had closed on the three men—"our taking up our time with little things while we're waiting for them to get the evidence. I don't see as it's anything to laugh about."

"Of course they've got awful important things on their minds," said the sheriff's wife apologetically.

They returned to an inspection of the blocks for the quilt. Mrs. Hale was looking at the fine, even sewing, and preoccupied with thoughts of the woman who had done that sewing, when she heard the sheriff's wife say, in a queer tone:

"Why, look at this one."

She turned to take the block held out to her.

"The sewing," said Mrs. Peters, in a troubled way. "All the rest of them have been so nice and even—but—this one. Why, it looks as if she didn't know what she was about!"

Their eyes met—something flashed to life, passed between them; then, as if with an effort, they seemed to pull away from each other. A moment Mrs. Hale sat there, her hands folded over that sewing which was so unlike all the rest of the sewing. Then she had pulled a knot and drawn the threads.

"Oh, what are you doing, Mrs. Hale?" asked the sheriff's wife, startled.

"Just pulling out a stitch or two that's not sewed very good," said Mrs. Hale mildly.

"I don't think we ought to touch things," Mrs. Peters said, a little helplessly.

"I'll just finish up this end," answered Mrs. Hale, still in that mild, matter-of-fact fashion.

She threaded a needle and started to replace bad sewing with good. For a little while she sewed in silence. Then, in that thin, timid voice, she heard:

"Mrs. Hale!"

"Yes, Mrs. Peters?"

"What do you suppose she was so—nervous about?"

"Oh, *I* don't know," said Mrs. Hale, as if dismissing a thing not important enough to spend much time on. "I don't know as she was—nervous. I sew awful queer sometimes when I'm just tired."

She cut a thread, and out of the corner of her eye looked up at Mrs. Peters. The small, lean face of the sheriff's wife seemed to have tightened up. Her eyes had that look of peering into something. But the next moment she moved, and said in her thin, indecisive way:

"Well, I must get those clothes wrapped. They may be through sooner than we think. I wonder where I could find a piece of paper—and string."

"In that cupboard, maybe," suggested Mrs. Hale, after a glance around.

One piece of the crazy sewing remained unripped. Mrs. Peters' back turned, Martha Hale now scrutinized that piece, compared it with the dainty, accurate sewing of the other blocks. The difference was startling. Holding this block made her feel queer, as if the distracted thoughts of the woman who had perhaps turned to it to try and quiet herself were communicating themselves to her.

Mrs. Peters' voice roused her.

"Here's a bird-cage," she said. "Did she have a bird, Mrs. Hale?"

"Why, I don't know whether she did or not." She turned to look at the cage Mrs. Peters was holding up. "I've not been here in so long." She sighed. "There was a man round last year selling canaries cheap—but I don't know as she took one. Maybe she did. She used to sing real pretty herself."

Mrs. Peters looked around the kitchen.

"Seems kind of funny to think of a bird here." She half-laughed—an attempt to put up a barrier. "But she must have had one—or why would she have a cage? I wonder what happened to it."

"I suppose maybe the cat got it," suggested Mrs. Hale, resuming her sewing.

"No; she didn't have a cat. She's got that feeling some people have about cats—being afraid of them. When they brought her to our house yesterday, my cat got in the room, and she was real upset and asked me to take it out."

"My sister Bessie was like that," laughed Mrs. Hale.

The sheriff's wife did not reply. The silence made Mrs. Hale turn around. Mrs. Peters was examining the bird-cage.

"Look at this door," she said slowly. "It's broke. One hinge has been pulled apart."

Mrs. Hale came nearer.

"Looks as if some one must have been—rough with it."

Again their eyes met—startled, questioning, apprehensive. For a moment neither spoke nor stirred. Then Mrs. Hale, turning away, said brusquely:

"If they're going to find any evidence, I wish they'd be about it. I don't like this place."

"But I'm awful glad you came with me, Mrs. Hale." Mrs. Peters put the bird-cage on the table and sat down. "It would be lonesome for me—sitting here alone."

"Yes, it would, wouldn't it?" agreed Mrs. Hale, a certain determined natural-ness in her voice. She picked up the sewing, but now it dropped in her lap, and she murmured in a different voice: "But I tell you what I *do* wish, Mrs. Peters. I wish I had come over sometimes when she was here. I wish—I had."

"But of course you were awful busy, Mrs. Hale. Your house—and your children."

"I could've come," retorted Mrs. Hale shortly. "I stayed away because it weren't cheerful—and that's why I ought to have come. I"—she looked around—"I've never liked this place. Maybe because it's down in a hollow and you don't see the road. I don't know what it is, but it's a lonesome place, and always was. I wish I had come over to see Minnie Foster sometimes. I can see now—" She did not put it into words.

"Well, you mustn't reproach yourself," counseled Mrs. Peters. "Somehow, we just don't see how it is with other folks till—something comes up."

"Not having children makes less work," mused Mrs. Hale, after a silence, "but it makes a quiet house — and Wright out to work all day — and no company when he did come in. Did you know John Wright, Mrs. Peters?"

"Not to know him. I've seen him in town. They say he was a good man."

"Yes — good," conceded John Wright's neighbor grimly. "He didn't drink, and kept his word as well as most, I guess, and paid his debts. But he was a hard man, Mrs. Peters. Just to pass the time of day with him —." She stopped, shivered a little. "Like a raw wind that gets to the bone." Her eye fell upon the cage on the table before her, and she added, almost bitterly: "I should think she would've wanted a bird!"

Suddenly she leaned forward, looking intently at the cage. "But what do you s'pose went wrong with it?"

"I don't know," returned Mrs. Peters; "unless it got sick and died."

But after she said it she reached over and swung the broken door. Both women watched it as if somehow held by it.

"You didn't know — her?" Mrs. Hale asked, a gentler note in her voice.

"Not till they brought her yesterday," said the sheriff's wife.

"She — come to think of it, she was kind of like a bird herself. Real sweet and pretty, but kind of timid and — fluttery. How — she — did — change."

That held her for a long time. Finally, as if struck with a happy thought and relieved to get back to everyday things, she exclaimed:

"Tell you what, Mrs. Peters, why don't you take the quilt in with you? It might take up her mind."

"Why, I think that's a real nice idea, Mrs. Hale," agreed the sheriff's wife, as if she too were glad to come into the atmosphere of a simple kindness. "There couldn't possibly be any objection to that, could there? Now, just what will I take? I wonder if her patches are in here — and her things."

They turned to the sewing basket.

"Here's some red," said Mrs. Hale, bringing out a roll of cloth. Underneath that was a box. "Here, maybe her scissors are in here — and her things." She held it up. "What a pretty box! I'll warrant that was something she had a long time ago — when she was a girl."

She held it in her hand a moment; then, with a little sigh, opened it.

Instantly her hand went to her nose.

"Why —!"

Mrs. Peters drew nearer — then turned away.

"There's something wrapped up in this piece of silk," faltered Mrs. Hale.

"This isn't her scissors," said Mrs. Peters in a shrinking voice.

Her hand not steady, Mrs. Hale raised the piece of silk. "Oh, Mrs. Peters!" she cried. "It's —"

Mrs. Peters bent closer.

"It's the bird," she whispered.

"But, Mrs. Peters!" cried Mrs. Hale. "*Look* at it! Its neck — look at its neck! It's all — other side *to*."

She held the box away from her.

The sheriff's wife again bent closer.

"Somebody wrung its neck," said she, in a voice that was slow and deep.

And then again the eyes of the two women met — this time clung together in a look of dawning comprehension, of growing horror. Mrs. Peters looked from the dead bird to the broken door of the cage. Again their eyes met. And just then there was a sound at the outside door.

Mrs. Hale slipped the box under the quilt pieces in the basket, and sank into the chair before it. Mrs. Peters stood holding to the table. The county attorney and the sheriff came in from outside.

"Well, ladies," said the county attorney, as one turning from serious things to little pleasantries, "have you decided whether she was going to quilt it or knot it?"

"We think," began the sheriff's wife in a flurried voice, "that she was going to — knot it."

He was too preoccupied to notice the change that came in her voice on that last.

"Well, that's very interesting, I'm sure," he said tolerantly. He caught sight of the bird-cage. "Has the bird flown?"

"We think the cat got it," said Mrs. Hale in a voice curiously even.

He was walking up and down, as if thinking something out.

"Is there a cat?" he asked absently.

Mrs. Hale shot a look up at the sheriff's wife.

"Well, not *now*," said Mrs. Peters. "They're superstitious, you know; they leave."

She sank into her chair.

The county attorney did not heed her. "No sign at all of any one having come in from the outside," he said to Peters, in the manner of continuing an interrupted conversation. "Their own rope. Now let's go upstairs again and go over it, piece by piece. It would have to have been some one who knew just the — "

The stair door closed behind them and their voices were lost.

The two women sat motionless, not looking at each other, but as if peering into something and at the same time holding back. When they spoke now it was as if they were afraid of what they were saying, but as if they could not help saying it.

"She liked the bird," said Martha Hale, low and slowly. "She was going to bury it in that pretty box."

"When I was a girl," said Mrs. Peters, under her breath, "my kitten — there was a boy took a hatchet, and before my eyes — before I could get there — " She covered her face an instant. "If they hadn't held me back I would have — " she caught herself, looked upstairs where footsteps were heard, and finished weakly — "hurt him."

Then they sat without speaking or moving.

"I wonder how it would seem," Mrs. Hale at last began, as if feeling her way over strange ground — "never to have had any children around?" Her eyes made a slow sweep of the kitchen, as if seeing what that kitchen had meant through all the years. "No, Wright wouldn't like the bird," she said after that — "a thing that sang. She used to sing. He killed that too." Her voice tightened.

Mrs. Peters moved uneasily.

"Of course we don't know who killed the bird."

"I knew John Wright," was Mrs. Hale's answer.

"It was an awful thing was done in this house that night, Mrs. Hale," said the sheriff's wife. "Killing a man while he slept — slipping a thing round his neck that choked the life out of him."

Mrs. Hale's hand went out to the bird-cage.

"His neck. Choked the life out of him."

"We don't *know* who killed him," whispered Mrs. Peters wildly. "We don't *know*."

Mrs. Hale had not moved. "If there had been years and years of—nothing, then a bird to sing to you, it would be awful—still—after the bird was still."

It was as if something within her not herself had spoken, and it found in Mrs. Peters something she did not know as herself.

"I know what stillness is," she said, in a queer, monotonous voice. "When we homesteaded in Dakota, and my first baby died—after he was two years old—and me with no other then—"

Mrs. Hale stirred.

"How soon do you suppose they'll be through looking for evidence?"

"I know what stillness is," repeated Mrs. Peters, in just that same way. Then she too pulled back. "The law has got to punish crime, Mrs. Hale," she said in her tight little way.

"I wish you'd seen Minnie Foster," was the answer, "when she wore a white dress with blue ribbons, and stood up there in the choir and sang."

The picture of that girl, the fact that she had lived neighbor to that girl for twenty years, and had let her die for lack of life, was suddenly more than she could bear.

"Oh, I *wish* I'd come over here once in a while!" she cried. "That was a crime! That was a crime! Who's going to punish that?"

"We mustn't take on," said Mrs. Peters, with a frightened look toward the stairs.

"I might 'a' *known* she needed help! I tell you, it's *queer*, Mrs. Peters. We live close together, and we live far apart. We all go through the same things—it's all just a different kind of the same thing! If it weren't—why do you and I *understand*? Why do we *know*—what we know this minute?"

She dashed her hand across her eyes. Then, seeing the jar of fruit on the table, she reached for it and choked out:

"If I was you I wouldn't *tell* her her fruit was gone! Tell her it *ain't*. Tell her it's all right—all of it. Here—take this in to prove it to her! She—she may never know whether it was broke or not."

She turned away.

Mrs. Peters reached out for the bottle of fruit as if she were glad to take it—as if touching a familiar thing, having something to do, could keep her from something else. She got up, looked about for something to wrap the fruit in, took a petticoat from the pile of clothes she had brought from the front room, and nervously started winding that round the bottle.

"My!" she began, in a high, false voice, "it's a good thing the men couldn't hear us! Getting all stirred up over a little thing like a—dead canary." She hurried over that. "As if that could have anything to do with—with—My, wouldn't they *laugh*?"

Footsteps were heard on the stairs.

"Maybe they would," muttered Mrs. Hale—"maybe they wouldn't."

"No, Peters," said the county attorney incisively; "it's all perfectly clear, except the reason for doing it. But you know juries when it comes to women. If there was some definite thing—something to show. Something to make a story about. A thing that would connect up with this clumsy way of doing it."

In a covert way Mrs. Hale looked at Mrs. Peters. Mrs. Peters was looking at her. Quickly they looked away from each other. The outer door opened and Mr. Hale came in.

"I've got the team round now," he said. "Pretty cold out there."

"I'm going to stay here awhile by myself," the county attorney suddenly announced. "You can send Frank out for me, can't you?" he asked the sheriff. "I want to go over everything. I'm not satisfied we can't do better."

Again, for one brief moment, the two women's eyes found one another.

The sheriff came up to the table.

"Did you want to see what Mrs. Peters was going to take in?"

The county attorney picked up the apron. He laughed.

"Oh, I guess they're not very dangerous things the ladies have picked out."

Mrs. Hale's hand was on the sewing basket in which the box was concealed. She felt that she ought to take her hand off the basket. She did not seem able to. He picked up one of the quilt blocks which she had piled on to cover the box. Her eyes felt like fire. She had a feeling that if he took up the basket she would snatch it from him.

But he did not take it up. With another little laugh, he turned away, saying:

"No; Mrs. Peters doesn't need supervising. For that matter, a sheriff's wife is married to the law. Ever think of it that way, Mrs. Peters?"

Mrs. Peters was standing beside the table. Mrs. Hale shot a look up at her; but she could not see her face. Mrs. Peters had turned away. When she spoke, her voice was muffled.

"Not—just that way," she said.

"Married to the law!" chuckled Mrs. Peters' husband. He moved toward the door into the front room, and said to the county attorney:

"I just want you to come in here a minute, George. We ought to take a look at these windows."

"Oh—windows," said the county attorney scoffingly.

"We'll be right out, Mr. Hale," said the sheriff to the farmer, who was still waiting by the door.

Hale went to look after the horses. The sheriff followed the county attorney into the other room. Again—for one moment—the two women were alone in that kitchen.

Martha Hale sprang up, her hands tight together, looking at that other woman, with whom it rested. At first she could not see her eyes, for the sheriff's wife had not turned back since she turned away at that suggestion of being married to the law. But now Mrs. Hale made her turn back. Her eyes made her turn back. Slowly, unwillingly, Mrs. Peters turned her head until her eyes met the eyes of the other woman. There was a moment when they held each other in a steady, burning look in which there was no evasion nor flinching. Then Martha Hale's eyes pointed the way to the basket in which was hidden the thing that would make certain the conviction of the other woman—that woman who was not there and yet who had been there with them all through the hour.

For a moment Mrs. Peters did not move. And then she did it. With a rush forward, she threw back the quilt pieces, got the box, tried to put it in her handbag. It was too big. Desperately she opened it, started to take the bird out. But there she broke—she could not touch the bird. She stood helpless, foolish.

There was the sound of a knob turning in the inner door. Martha Hale snatched the box from the sheriff's wife, and got it in the pocket of her big coat just as the sheriff and the county attorney came back into the kitchen.

"Well, Henry," said the county attorney facetiously, "at least we found out that she was not going to quilt it. She was going to—what is it you call it, ladies?"

Mrs. Hale's hand was against the pocket of her coat.

"We call it—knot it, Mr. Henderson."

(1917)

James Joyce *1882–1941*

ARABY

North Richmond Street, being blind, was a quiet street except at the hour when the Christian Brothers' School set the boys free. An uninhabited house of two storeys stood at the blind end, detached from its neighbours in a square ground. The other houses of the street, conscious of decent lives within them, gazed at one another with brown imperturbable faces.

The former tenant of our house, a priest, had died in the back drawing-room. Air, musty from having been long enclosed, hung in all the rooms, and the waste room behind the kitchen was littered with old useless papers. Among these I found a few paper-covered books, the pages of which were curled and damp: *The Abbot*, by Walter Scott, *The Devout Communicant* and *The Memoirs of Vidocq*. I liked the last best because its leaves were yellow. The wild garden behind the house contained a central apple-tree and a few straggling bushes under one of which I found the late tenant's rusty bicycle-pump. He had been a very charitable priest; in his will he had left all his money to institutions and the furniture of his house to his sister.

When the short days of winter came dusk fell before we had well eaten our dinners. When we met in the street the houses had grown sombre. The space of sky above us was the colour of ever-changing violet and towards it the lamps of the street lifted their feeble lanterns. The cold air stung us and we played till our bodies glowed. Our shouts echoed in the silent street. The career of our play brought us through the dark muddy lanes behind the houses where we ran the gauntlet of the rough tribes from the cottages, to the back doors of the dark dripping gardens where odours arose from the ashpits, to the dark odorous stables where a coachman smoothed and combed the horse or shook music from the buckled harness. When we returned to the street light from the kitchen windows had filled the areas. If my uncle was seen turning the corner we hid in the shadow until we had seen him safely housed. Or if Mangan's sister came out on the doorstep to call her brother in to his tea we watched her from our shadow peer up and down the street. We waited to see whether she would remain or go in and, if she remained, we left our shadow and walked up to Mangan's steps resignedly. She was waiting for us, her figure defined by the light from the half-opened door. Her brother always teased her before he obeyed and I stood by the railings looking at her. Her dress swung as she moved her body and the soft rope of her hair tossed from side to side.

Every morning I lay on the floor in the front parlour watching her door. The blind was pulled down to within an inch of the sash so that I could not be seen. When she came out on the doorstep my heart leaped. I ran to the hall, seized my books and followed her. I kept her brown figure always in my eye and, when we came near the point at which our ways diverged, I quickened my pace and passed her. This happened morning after morning. I had never spoken to her, except for a few casual words, and yet her name was like a summons to all my foolish blood.

Her image accompanied me even in places the most hostile to romance. On Saturday evenings when my aunt went marketing I had to go to carry some of the parcels. We walked through the flaring streets, jostled by drunken men and bargaining women, amid the curse of labourers, the shrill litanies of shop-boys who stood on guard by the barrels of pigs' cheeks, the nasal chanting of street-singers, who sang a *come-all-you* about O'Donovan Rossa, or a ballad about the troubles in our native land. These noises converged in a single sensation of life for me: I imagined that I bore my chalice safely through a throng of foes. Her name sprang to my lips at moments in strange prayers and praises which I myself did not understand. My eyes were often full of tears (I could not tell why) and at times a flood from my heart seemed to pour itself out into my bosom. I thought little of the future. I did not know whether I would ever speak to her or not or, if I spoke to her, how I could tell her of my confused adoration. But my body was like a harp and her words and gestures were like fingers running upon the wires.

One evening I went into the back drawing-room in which the priest had died. It was a dark rainy evening and there was no sound in the house. Through one of the broken panes I heard the rain impinge upon the earth, the fine incessant needles of water playing in the sodden beds. Some distant lamp or lighted window gleamed below me. I was thankful that I could see so little. All my senses seemed to desire to veil themselves and, feeling that I was about to slip from them, I pressed the palms of my hands together until they trembled, murmuring: "*O love! O love!*" many times.

At last she spoke to me. When she addressed the first words to me I was so confused that I did not know what to answer. She asked me was I going to *Araby*. I forgot whether I answered yes or no. It would be a splendid bazaar, she said; she would love to go.

"And why can't you?" I asked.

While she spoke she turned a silver bracelet round and round her wrist. She could not go, she said, because there would be a retreat that week in her convent. Her brother and two other boys were fighting for their caps and I was alone at the railings. She held one of the spikes, bowing her head towards me. The light from the lamp opposite our door caught the white curve of her neck, lit up her hair that rested there and, falling, lit up the hand upon the railing. It fell over one side of her dress and caught the white border of a petticoat just visible as she stood at ease.

"It's well for you," she said.

"If I go," I said, "I will bring you something."

What innumerable follies laid waste my waking and sleeping thoughts after that evening! I wished to annihilate the tedious intervening days. I chafed against the work of school. At night in my bedroom and by day in the classroom her image came between me and the page I strove to read. The syllables of the word *Araby* were called to me through the silence in which my soul luxuriated and cast an Eastern enchantment over me. I asked for leave to go to the bazaar on Saturday night. My aunt was surprised and hoped it was not some Freemason affair. I answered few questions in class. I watched my master's face pass from amiability to sternness; he hoped I was not beginning to idle. I could not call my wandering thoughts together. I had hardly any patience with the serious work of life which, now that it stood between me and my desire, seemed to me child's play, ugly monotonous child's play.

On Saturday morning I reminded my uncle that I wished to go to the bazaar in the evening. He was fussing at the hall-stand, looking for the hat-brush, and answered me curtly:

"Yes, boy, I know."

As he was in the hall I could not go into the front parlour and lie at the window. I left the house in bad humour and walked slowly towards the school. The air was pitilessly raw and already my heart misgave me.

When I came home to dinner my uncle had not yet been home. Still it was early. I sat staring at the clock for some time and, when its ticking began to irritate me, I left the room. I mounted the staircase and gained the upper part of the house. The high cold empty gloomy rooms liberated me and I went from room to room singing. From the front window I saw my companions playing below in the street. Their cries reached me weakened and indistinct and, leaning my forehead against the cool glass, I looked over at the dark house where she lived. I may have stood there for an hour, seeing nothing but the brown-clad figure cast by my imagination, touched discreetly by the lamplight at the curved neck, at the hand upon the railings and at the border below the dress.

When I came downstairs again I found Mrs. Mercer sitting at the fire. She was an old garrulous woman, a pawnbroker's widow, who collected used stamps for some pious purpose. I had to endure the gossip of the tea-table. The meal was prolonged beyond an hour and still my uncle did not come. Mrs. Mercer stood up to go: she was very sorry she couldn't wait any longer, but it was after eight o'clock and she did not like to be out late, as the night air was bad for her. When she had gone I began to walk up and down the room, clenching my fists. My aunt said:

"I'm afraid you may put off your bazaar for this night of Our Lord."

At nine o'clock I heard my uncle's latchkey in the halldoor. I heard him talking to himself and heard the hallstand rocking when it had received the weight of his overcoat. I could interpret these signs. When he was midway through his dinner I asked him to give me the money to go to the bazaar. He had forgotten.

"The people are in bed and after their first sleep now," he said.

I did not smile. My aunt said to him energetically:

"Can't you give him the money and let him go? You've kept him late enough as it is."

My uncle said he was very sorry he had forgotten. He said he believed in the old saying: "All work and no play makes Jack a dull boy." He asked me where I was going and, when I had told him a second time he asked me did I know *The Arab's Farewell to his Steed*. When I left the kitchen he was about to recite the opening lines of the piece to my aunt.

I held a florin tightly in my hand as I strode down Buckingham Street towards the station. The sight of the streets thronged with buyers and glaring with gas recalled to me the purpose of my journey. I took my seat in a third-class carriage of a deserted train. After an intolerable delay the train moved out of the station slowly. It crept onward among ruinous houses and over the twinkling river. At Westland Row Station a crowd of people pressed to the carriage doors; but the porters moved them back, saying that it was a special train for the bazaar. I remained alone in the bare carriage. In a few minutes the train drew up beside an improvised wooden platform. I passed out on to the road and saw by the lighted dial of a clock that it was ten minutes to ten. In front of me was a large building which displayed the magical name.

I could not find any sixpenny entrance and, fearing that the bazaar would be closed, I passed quickly through a turnstile, handing a shilling to a weary-looking man. I found myself in a big hall girdled at half its height by a gallery. Nearly all the stalls were closed and the greater part of the hall was in darkness. I recognized a silence like that which pervades a church after a service. I walked into the centre of the bazaar timidly. A few people were gathered about the stalls which were still open. Before a curtain, over which the words *Café Chantant* were written in coloured lamps, two men were counting money on a salver. I listened to the fall of the coins.

Remembering with difficulty why I had come I went over to one of the stalls and examined porcelain vases and flowered tea-sets. At the door of the stall a young lady was talking and laughing with two young gentlemen. I remarked their English accents and listened vaguely to their conversation.

"O, I never said such a thing!"

"O, but you did!"

"O, but I didn't!"

"Didn't she say that?"

"Yes. I heard her."

"O, there's a . . . fib!"

Observing me the young lady came over and asked me did I wish to buy anything. The tone of her voice was not encouraging; she seemed to have spoken to me out of a sense of duty. I looked humbly at the great jars that stood like eastern guards at either side of the dark entrance to the stall and murmured:

"No, thank you."

The young lady changed the position of one of the vases and went back to the two young men. They began to talk of the same subject. Once or twice the young lady glanced at me over her shoulder.

I lingered before her stall, though I knew my stay was useless, to make my interest in her wares seem the more real. Then I turned away slowly and walked down the middle of the bazaar. I allowed the two pennies to fall against the sixpence in my pocket. I heard a voice call from one end of the gallery that the light was out. The upper part of the hall was now completely dark.

Gazing up into the darkness I saw myself as a creature driven and derided by vanity; and my eyes burned with anguish and anger.

                                                                                    (1914)

Franz Kafka *1883–1924*

A HUNGER ARTIST

During these last decades the interest in professional fasting has markedly diminished. It used to pay very well to stage such great performances under one's own management, but today that is quite impossible. We live in a different world now. At one time the whole town took a lively interest in the hunger artist; from day to day of his fast the excitement mounted; everybody wanted to see him at least once a day; there were people who bought season tickets for the last few days and sat from morning till night in front of his small barred cage; even in the nighttime there were visiting hours, when the whole effect was heightened by torch flares; on fine days the cage was set out in the open air, and then it was the children's special treat to see the hunger artist; for their elders he was often just a joke that happened to be in fashion, but the children stood open-mouthed, holding each other's hands for greater security, marvelling at him as he sat there pallid in black tights, with his ribs sticking out so prominently, not even on a seat but down among straw on the ground, sometimes giving a courteous nod, answering questions with a constrained smile, or perhaps stretching an arm through the bars so that one might feel how thin it was, and then again withdrawing deep into himself, paying no attention to anyone or anything, not even to the all-important striking of the clock that was the only piece of furniture in his cage, but merely staring into vacancy with half-shut eyes, now and then taking a sip from a tiny glass of water to moisten his lips.

Besides casual onlookers there were also relays of permanent watchers se-lected by the public, usually butchers, strangely enough, and it was their task to watch the hunger artist day and night, three of them at a time, in case he should have some secret recourse to nourishment. This was nothing but a formality, instituted to reassure the masses, for the initiates knew well enough that during his fast the artist would never in any circumstances, not even under forcible compulsion, swallow the smallest morsel of food; the honor of his profession forbade it. Not every watcher, of course, was capable of understanding this, there were often groups of night watchers who were very lax in carrying out their duties and deliberately huddled together in a retired corner to play cards with great absorption, obviously intending to give the hunger artist the chance of a little refreshment, which they supposed he could draw from some private hoard. Nothing annoyed the artist more than such watchers; they made him miserable; they made his fast seem unendurable; sometimes he mastered his feebleness sufficiently to sing during their watch for as long as he could keep going, to show them how unjust their suspicions were. But that was of little use; they only wondered at his cleverness in being able to fill his mouth even while singing. Much more to his taste were the watchers who sat close up to the bars, who were not content with the dim night lighting of the hall but focused him in the full glare of the electric pocket torch given them by the impresario. The harsh light did not trouble him at all. In any case he could never sleep properly, and he could always drowse a little, whatever the light, at any hour, even when the hall was thronged with noisy onlookers. He was quite happy at the prospect of spending a sleepless night with such watchers; he was ready to exchange jokes with them, to tell them stories out of his nomadic life, anything at all to keep them awake and demonstrate to them again that he had no eatables in his cage and that he was fasting as not one of them could fast. But his happiest moment was when the morning came and an enormous breakfast was brought them, at his expense, on which they flung themselves with the keen appetite of healthy men after a weary night of wakefulness. Of course there were people who argued that this breakfast was an unfair attempt to bribe the watchers, but that was going rather too far, and when they were invited to take on a night's vigil without a breakfast, merely for the sake of the cause, they made themselves scarce, although they stuck stubbornly to their suspicions.

Such suspicions, anyhow, were a necessary accompaniment to the profession of fasting. No one could possibly watch the hunger artist continuously, day and night, and so no one could produce first-hand evidence that the fast had really been rigorous and continuous; only the artist himself could know that; he was therefore bound to be the sole completely satisfied spectator of his own fast. Yet for other reasons he was never satisfied; it was not perhaps mere fasting that had brought him to such skeleton thinness that many people had regretfully to keep away from his exhibitions, because the sight of him was too much for them, perhaps it was dissatisfaction with himself that had worn him down. For he alone knew, what no other initiate knew, how easy it was to fast. It was the easiest thing in the world. He made no secret of this, yet people did not believe him; at the best they set him down as modest; most of them, however, thought he was out for publicity or else was some kind of cheat who found it easy to fast because he had discovered a way of making it easy, and then had the impudence to admit the fact, more or less. He had to put up with all that, and in the course of time had got used to it, but his inner dissatisfaction always rankled, and never yet, after any term of fasting—this must be granted to his credit—had he left the cage of his own free will. The longest period of fasting was fixed by his impresario at forty days, beyond that term he was not allowed to go, not even in great cities, and there was good reason for it, too. Experience had proved that for about forty days the interest of the public could be stimulated by a steadily increasing pressure of advertisement, but after that the town began to lose interest, sympathetic support began notably to fall off; there were of course local variations as between one town and another or one country and another, but as a general rule forty days marked the limit. So on the fortieth day the flower-be-decked cage was opened, enthusiastic spectators filled the hall, a military band played, two doctors entered the cage to measure the results of the fast, which were announced through a megaphone, and finally two young ladies appeared, blissful at having been selected for the honor, to help the hunger artist down the few steps leading to a small table on which was spread a carefully chosen invalid repast. And at this very moment the artist always turned stubborn. True, he would entrust his bony arms to the outstretched helping hands of the ladies bending over him, but stand up he would not. Why stop fasting at this particular moment, after forty days of it? He had held out for a long time, an illimitably long time; why stop now, when he was in his best fasting form, or rather, not yet quite in his best fasting form? Why should he be cheated of the fame he would get for fasting longer, for being not only the record hunger artist of all time, which presumably he was already, but for beating his own record by a performance beyond human imagination, since he felt that there were no limits to his capacity for fasting? His public pretended to admire him so much, why should it have so little patience with him; if he could endure fasting longer, why shouldn't the public endure it? Besides, he was tired, he was comfortable sitting in the straw, and now he was supposed to lift himself to his full height and go down to a meal the very thought of which gave him a nausea that only the presence of the ladies kept him from betraying, and even that with an effort. And he looked up into the eyes of the ladies who were apparently so friendly and in reality so cruel, and shook his head, which felt too heavy on its strengthless neck. But then there happened yet again what always happened. The impresario came forward, without a word—for the band made speech impossible—lifted his arms in the air above the artist, as if inviting Heaven to look down upon its creature here in the straw, this suffering martyr, which indeed he was, although in quite another sense; grasped him round the emaciated waist, with exaggerated caution, so that the frail condition he was in might be appreciated; and committed him to the care of the blenching ladies, not without secretly giving him a shaking so that his legs and body tottered and swayed. The artist now submitted completely; his head lolled on his breast as if it had landed there by chance; his body was hollowed out; his legs in a spasm of self-preservation clung close to each other at the knees, yet scraped on the ground as if it were not really solid ground, as if they were only trying to find solid ground; and the whole weight of his body, a featherweight after all, relapsed onto one of the ladies, who, looking round for help and panting a little—this post of honor was not at all what she had expected it to be—first stretched her neck as far as she could to keep her face at least free from contact with the artist, then finding this impossible, and her more fortunate companion not coming to her aid but merely holding extended on her own trembling hand the little bunch of knucklebones that was the artist's, to the great delight of the spectators burst into tears and had to be replaced by an attendant who had long been stationed in readiness. Then came the food, a little of which the impresario managed to get between the artist's lips, while he sat in a kind of half-fainting trance, to the accompaniment of cheerful patter designed to distract the public's attention from the artist's condition; after that, a toast was drunk to the public, supposedly prompted by a whisper from the artist in the impresario's ear; the band confirmed it with a mighty flourish, the spectators melted away, and no one had any cause to be dissatisfied with the proceedings, no one except the hunger artist himself, he only, as always.

So he lived for many years, with small regular intervals of recuperation, in visible glory, honored by the world, yet in spite of that troubled in spirit, and all the more troubled because no one would take his trouble seriously. What comfort could he possibly need? What more could he possibly wish for? And if some good-natured person, feeling sorry for him, tried to console him by pointing out that his melancholy was probably caused by fasting, it could happen, especially when he had been fasting for some time, that he reacted with an outburst of fury and to the general alarm began to shake the bars of his cage like a wild animal. Yet the impresario had a way of punishing these outbreaks which he rather enjoyed putting into operation. He would apologize publicly for the artist's behavior, which was only to be excused, he admitted, because of the irritability caused by fasting; a condition hardly to be understood by well-fed people; then by natural transition he went on to mention the artist's equally incomprehensible boast that he could fast for much longer than he was doing; he praised the high ambition, the good will, the great self-denial undoubtedly implicit in such a statement; and then quite simply countered it by bringing out photographs, which were also on sale to the public, showing the artist on the fortieth day of a fast lying in bed almost dead from exhaustion. This perversion of the truth, familiar to the artist though it was, always unnerved him afresh and proved too much for him. What was a consequence of the premature ending of his fast was here presented as the cause of it! To fight against this lack of understanding, against a whole world of nonunderstanding, was impossible. Time and again in good faith he stood by the bars listening to the impresario, but as soon as the photographs appeared he always let go and sank with a groan back onto his straw, and the reassured public could once more come close and gaze at him.

A few years later when the witnesses of such scenes called them to mind, they often failed to understand themselves at all. For meanwhile the aforementioned change in public interest had set in; it seemed to happen almost overnight; there may have been profound causes for it, but who was going to bother about that; at any rate the pampered hunger artist suddenly found himself deserted one fine day by the amusement seekers, who went streaming past him to other more favored attractions. For the last time the impresario hurried him over half Europe to discover whether the old interest might still survive here and there; all in vain; everywhere, as if by secret agreement, a positive revulsion from professional fasting was in evidence. Of course it could not really have sprung up so suddenly as all that, and many premonitory symptoms which had not been sufficiently remarked or suppressed during the rush and glitter of success now came retrospectively to mind, but it was now too late to take any countermeasures. Fasting would surely come into fashion again at some future date, yet that was no comfort for those living in the present. What, then, was the hunger artist to do? He had been applauded by thousands in his time and could hardly come down to showing himself in a street booth at village fairs, and as for adopting another profession, he was not only too old for that but too fanatically devoted to fasting. So he took leave of the impresario, his partner in an unparalleled career, and hired himself to a large circus; in order to spare his own feelings he avoided reading the conditions of his contract.

A large circus with its enormous traffic in replacing and recruiting men, animals and apparatus can always find a use for people at any time, even for a hunger artist, provided of course that he does not ask too much, and in this particular case anyhow it was not only the artist who was taken on but his famous and long-known name as well; indeed considering the peculiar nature of his performance, which was not impaired by advancing age, it could not be objected that here was an artist past his prime, no longer at the height of his professional skill, seeking a refuge in some quiet corner of a circus; on the contrary, the hunger artist averred that he could fast as well as ever, which was entirely credible; he even alleged that if he were allowed to fast as he liked, and this was at once promised him without more ado, he could astound the world by establishing a record never yet achieved, a statement which certainly provoked a smile among the other professionals, since it left out of account the change in public opinion, which the hunger artist in his zeal conveniently forgot.

He had not, however, actually lost his sense of the real situation and took it as a matter of course that he and his cage should be stationed, not in the middle of the ring as a main attraction, but outside, near the animal cages, on a site that was after all easily accessible. Large and gaily painted placards made a frame for the cage and announced what was to be seen inside it. When the public came thronging out in the intervals to see the animals, they could hardly avoid passing the hunger artist's cage and stopping there for a moment perhaps they might even have stayed longer had not those pressing behind them in the narrow gangway, who did not understand why they should be held up on their way towards the excitements of the menagerie, made it impossible for anyone to stand gazing quietly for any length of time. And that was the reason why the hunger artist, who had of course been looking forward to these visiting hours as the main achievement of his life, began instead to shrink from them. At first he could hardly wait for the intervals; it was exhilarating to watch the crowds come streaming his way, until only too soon — not even the most obstinate self-deception, clung to almost consciously, could hold out against the fact — the conviction was borne in upon him that these people, most of them, to judge from their actions, again and again, without exception, were all on their way to the menagerie. And the first sight of them from the distance remained the best. For when they reached his cage he was at once deafened by the storm of shouting and abuse that arose from the two contending factions, which renewed themselves continuously, of those who wanted to stop and stare at him — he soon began to dislike them more than the others — not out of real interest but only out of obstinate self-assertiveness, and those who wanted to go straight on to the animals. When the first great rush was past, the stragglers came along, and these, whom nothing could have prevented from stopping to look at him as long as they had breath, raced past with long strides, hardly even glancing at him, in their haste to get to the menagerie in time. And all too rarely did it happen that he had a stroke of luck, when some father of a family fetched up before him with his children, pointed a finger at the hunger artist and explained at length what the phenomenon meant, telling stories of earlier years when he himself had watched similar but much more thrilling performances, and the children, still rather uncomprehending, since neither inside nor outside school had they been sufficiently prepared for this lesson — what did they care about fasting? — yet showed by the brightness of their intent eyes that new and better times might be coming. Perhaps, said the hunger artist to himself many a time, things would be a little better if his cage were set not quite so near the menagerie. That made it too easy for people to make their choice, to say nothing of what he suffered from the stench of the menagerie, the animals' restlessness by night, the carrying past of raw lumps of flesh for the beasts of prey, the roaring at feeding times, which depressed him continually. But he did not dare to lodge a complaint with the management; after all, he had the animals to thank for the troops of people who passed his cage, among whom there might always be one here and there to take an interest in him, and who could tell where they might seclude him if he called attention to his existence and thereby to the fact that, strictly speaking, he was only an impediment on the way to the menagerie.

A small impediment, to be sure, one that grew steadily less. People grew familiar with the strange idea that they could be expected, in times like these, to take an interest in a hunger artist, and with this familiarity the verdict went out against him. He might fast as much as he could, and he did so; but nothing could save him now, people passed him by. Just try to explain to anyone the art of fasting! Anyone who has no feeling for it cannot be made to understand it. The fine placards grew dirty and illegible, they were torn down; the little notice board telling the number of fast days achieved, which at first was changed carefully every day, had long stayed at the same figure, for after the first few weeks even this small task seemed pointless to the staff; and so the artist simply fasted on and on, as he had always foretold, but no one counted the days, no one, not even the artist himself, knew what records he was already breaking, and his heart grew heavy. And when once in a time some leisurely passer-by stopped, made merry over the old figure on the board and spoke of swindling, that was in its way the stupidest lie ever invented by indifference and inborn malice, since it was not the hunger artist who was cheating; he was working honestly, but the world was cheating him of his reward.

Many more days went by, however, and that too came to an end. An overseer's eye fell on the cage one day and he asked the attendants why this perfectly good cage should be left standing there unused with dirty straw inside it; nobody knew, until one man, helped out by the notice board, remembered about the hunger artist. They poked into the straw with sticks and found him in it. "Are you still fasting?" asked the overseer. "When on earth do you mean to stop?" "Forgive me, everybody," whispered the hunger artist; only the overseer, who had his ear to the bars, understood him. "Of course," said the overseer, and tapped his forehead with a finger to let the attendants know what state the man was in, "we forgive you." "I always wanted you to admire my fasting," said the hunger artist. "We do admire it," said the overseer, affably. "But you shouldn't admire it," said the hunger artist. "Well, then we don't admire it," said the overseer, "but why shouldn't we admire it?" "Because I have to fast, I can't help it," said the hunger artist. "What a fellow you are," said the overseer, "and why can't you help it?" "Because," said the hunger artist, lifting his head a little and speaking, with his lips pursed, as if for a kiss, right into the overseer's ear, so that no syllable might be lost, "because I couldn't find the food I liked. If I had found it, believe me, I should have made no fuss and stuffed myself like you or anyone else." These were his last words, but in his dimming eyes remained the firm though no longer proud persuasion that he was still continuing to fast.

"Well, clear this out now!" said the overseer, and they buried the hunger artist, straw and all. Into the cage they put a young panther. Even the most insensitive felt it refreshing to see this wild creature leaping around the cage that had so long been dreary. The panther was all right. The food he liked was brought him without hesitation by the attendants; he seemed not even to miss his freedom; his noble body, furnished almost to the bursting point with all that it needed, seemed to carry freedom around with it too; somewhere in his jaws it seemed to lurk; and the joy of life streamed with such ardent passion from his throat that for the onlookers it was not easy to stand the shock of it. But they braced themselves, crowded round the cage, and did not want ever to move away.

(1922)

Translated by Willa and Edwin Muir

Katherine Anne Porter *1890–1980*

THE JILTING OF GRANNY WEATHERALL

She flicked her wrist neatly out of Doctor Harry's pudgy careful fingers and pulled the sheet up to her chin. The brat ought to be in knee breeches. Doctoring around the country with spectacles on his nose! "Get along now, take your schoolbooks and go. There's nothing wrong with me."

Doctor Harry spread a warm paw like a cushion on her forehead where the forked green vein danced and made her eyelids twitch. "Now, now, be a good girl, and we'll have you up in no time."

"That's no way to speak to a woman nearly eighty years old just because she's down. I'd have you respect your elders, young man."

"Well, Missy, excuse me." Doctor Harry patted her cheek. "But I've got to warn you, haven't I? You're a marvel, but you must be careful or you're going to be good and sorry."

"Don't tell me what I'm going to be. I'm on my feet now, morally speaking. It's Cornelia. I had to go to bed to get rid of her."

Her bones felt loose, and floated around in her skin, and Doctor Harry floated like a balloon around the foot of the bed. He floated and pulled down his waistcoat and swung his glasses on a cord. "Well, stay where you are, it certainly can't hurt you."

"Get along and doctor your sick," said Granny Weatherall. "Leave a well woman alone. I'll call for you when I want you. . . . Where were you forty years ago when I pulled through milk-leg and double pneumonia? You weren't even born. Don't let Cornelia lead you on," she shouted, because Doctor Harry appeared to float up to the ceiling and out. "I pay my own bills, and I don't throw my money away on nonsense!"

She meant to wave good-by, but it was too much trouble. Her eyes closed of themselves, it was like a dark curtain drawn around the bed. The pillow rose and floated under her, pleasant as a hammock in a light wind. She listened to the leaves rustling outside the window. No, somebody was swishing newspapers: no, Cornelia and Doctor Harry were whispering together. She leaped broad awake, thinking they whispered in her ear.

"She was never like this, *never* like this!" "Well, what can we expect?" "Yes, eighty years old. . . . "

Well, and what if she was? She still had ears. It was like Cornelia to whisper around doors. She always kept things secret in such a public way. She was always being tactful and kind. Cornelia was dutiful; that was the trouble with her. Dutiful and good: "So good and dutiful," said Granny, "that I'd like to spank her." She saw herself spanking Cornelia and making a fine job of it.

"What'd you say, Mother?"

Granny felt her face tying up in hard knots.

"Can't a body think, I'd like to know?"

"I thought you might want something."

"I do. I want a lot of things. First off, go away and don't whisper."

She lay and drowsed, hoping in her sleep that the children would keep out and let her rest a minute. It had been a long day. Not that she was tired. It was always pleasant to snatch a minute now and then. There was always so much to be done, let me see: tomorrow.

Tomorrow was far away and there was nothing to trouble about. Things were finished somehow when the time came; thank God there was always a little margin over for peace: then a person could spread out the plan of life and tuck in the edges orderly. It was good to have everything clean and folded away, with the hair brushes and tonic bottles sitting straight on the white embroidered linen: the day started without fuss and the pantry shelves laid out with rows of jelly glasses and brown jugs and white stone-china jars with blue whirligigs and words painted on them: coffee, tea, sugar, ginger, cinnamon, allspice: and the bronze clock with the lion on top nicely dusted off. The dust that lion could collect in twenty-four hours! The box in the attic with all those letters tied up, well she'd have to go through that tomorrow. All those letters—George's letters and John's letters and her letters to them both—lying around for the children to find afterwards made her uneasy. Yes, that would be tomorrow's business. No use to let them know how silly she had been once.

While she was rummaging around she found death in her mind and it felt clammy and unfamiliar. She had spent so much time preparing for death there was no need for bringing it up again. Let it take care of itself now. When she was sixty she had felt very old, finished, and went around making farewell trips to see her children and grandchildren, with a secret in her mind: This is the very last of your mother, children! Then she made her will and came down with a long fever. That was all just a notion like a lot of other things, but it was lucky too, for she had once for all got over the idea of dying for a long time. Now she couldn't be worried. She hoped she had better sense now. Her father had lived to be one hundred and two years old and had drunk a noggin of strong hot toddy on his last birthday. He told the reporters it was his daily habit, and he owed his long life to that. He had made quite a scandal and was very pleased about it. She believed she'd just plague Cornelia a little.

"Cornelia! Cornelia!" No footsteps, but a sudden hand on her cheek. "Bless you, where have you been?"

"Here, mother."

"Well, Cornelia, I want a noggin of hot toddy."

"Are you cold, darling?"

"I'm chilly, Cornelia. Lying in bed stops the circulation. I must have told you that a thousand times."

Well, she could just hear Cornelia telling her husband that Mother was getting childish and they'd have to humor her. The thing that most annoyed her was that Cornelia thought she was deaf, dumb, and blind. Little hasty glances and tiny gestures tossed around her and over her head saying, "Don't cross her, let her have her way, she's eighty years old," and she sitting there as if she lived in a thin glass cage. Sometimes Granny almost made up her mind to pack up and move back to her own house where nobody could remind her every minute that she was old. Wait, wait, Cornelia, till your own children whisper behind your back!

In her day she had kept a better house and had got more work done. She wasn't too old yet for Lydia to be driving eighty miles for advice when one of the children jumped the track, and Jimmy still dropped in and talked things over: "Now, Mammy, you've a good business head, I want to know what you think of this? . . . " Old Cornelia couldn't change the furniture around without asking.

Little things, little things! They had been so sweet when they were little. Granny wished the old days were back again with the children young and everything to be done over. It had been a hard pull, but not too much for her. When she thought of all the food she had cooked, and all the clothes she had cut and sewed, and all the gardens she had made—well, the children showed it. There they were, made out of her, and they couldn't get away from that. Sometimes she wanted to see John again and point to them and say, Well, I didn't do so badly, did I? But that would have to wait. That was for tomorrow. She used to think of him as a man, but now all the children were older than their father, and he would be a child beside her if she saw him now. It seemed strange and there was something wrong in the idea. Why, he couldn't possibly recognize her. She had fenced in a hundred acres once, digging the post holes herself and clamping the wires with just a negro boy to help. That changed a woman. John would be looking for a young woman with the peaked Spanish comb in her hair and the painted fan. Digging post holes changed a woman. Riding country roads in the winter when women had their babies was another thing: sitting up nights with sick horses and sick negroes and sick children and hardly ever losing one. John, I hardly ever lost one of them! John would see that in a minute, that would be something he could understand, she wouldn't have to explain anything!

It made her feel like rolling up her sleeves and putting the whole place to rights again. No matter if Cornelia was determined to be everywhere at once, there were a great many things left undone on this place. She would start tomorrow and do them. It was good to be strong enough for everything, even if all you made melted and changed and slipped under your hands, so that by the time you finished you almost forgot what you were working for. What was it I set out to do? she asked herself intently, but she could not remember. A fog rose over the valley, she saw it marching across the creek swallowing the trees and moving up the hill like an army of ghosts. Soon it would be at the near edge of the orchard, and then it was time to go in and light the lamps. Come in, children, don't stay out in the night air.

Lighting the lamps had been beautiful. The children huddled up to her and breathed like little calves waiting at the bars in the twilight. Their eyes followed the match and watched the flame rise and settle in a blue curve, then they moved away from her. The lamp was lit, they didn't have to be scared and hang on to mother any more. Never, never, never more. God, for all my life I thank Thee. Without Thee, my God, I could never have done it. Hail, Mary, full of grace.

I want you to pick all the fruit this year and see that nothing is wasted. There's always someone who can use it. Don't let good things rot for want of using. You waste life when you waste good food. Don't let things get lost. It's bitter to lose things. Now, don't let me get to thinking, not when I am tired and taking a little nap before supper. . . .

The pillow rose about her shoulders and pressed against her heart and the memory was being squeezed out of it: oh, push down the pillow, somebody: it would smother her if she tried to hold it. Such a fresh breeze blowing and such a green day with no threats in it. But he had not come, just the same. What does a woman do when she has put on the white veil and set out the white cake for a man and he doesn't come? She tried to remember. No, I swear he never harmed me but in that. He never harmed me but in that . . . and what if he did? There was the day, the day, but a whirl of dark smoke rose and covered it, crept up and over into the bright field where everything was planted so carefully in orderly rows. That was hell, she knew hell when she saw it. For sixty years she had prayed against remembering him and against losing her soul in the deep pit of hell, and now the two things were mingled in one and the thought of him was a smoky cloud from hell that moved and crept in her head when she had just got rid of Doctor Harry and was trying to rest a minute: Wounded vanity, Ellen, said a sharp voice in the top of her mind. Don't let your wounded vanity get the upper hand of you. Plenty of girls get jilted. You were jilted, weren't you? Then stand up to it. Her eyelids wavered and let in streamers of blue-gray light like tissue paper over her eyes. She must get up and pull the shades down or she'd never sleep. She was in bed again and the shades were not down. How could that happen? Better turn over, hide from the light, sleeping in the light gave you nightmares. "Mother, how do you feel now?" and a stinging wetness on her forehead. But I don't like having my face washed in cold water!

Hapsy? George? Lydia? Jimmy? No, Cornelia, and her features were swollen and full of little puddles. "They're coming, darling, they'll all be here soon." Go wash your face, child, you look funny.

Instead of obeying, Cornelia knelt down and put her head on the pillow. She seemed to be talking but there was no sound. "Well, are you tongue-tied? Whose birthday is it? Are you going to give a party?"

Cornelia's mouth moved urgently in strange shapes. "Don't do that, you bother me, daughter."

"Oh, no, Mother, Oh, no. . . . "

Nonsense. It was strange about children. They disputed your every word. "No what, Cornelia?"

"Here's Doctor Harry."

"I won't see that boy again. He just left five minutes ago."

"That was this morning, Mother. It's night now. Here's the nurse."

"This is Doctor Harry, Mrs. Weatherall. I never saw you look so young and happy!"

"Ah, I'll never be young again—but I'd be happy if they'd let me be in peace and get rested."

She thought she spoke up loudly, but no one answered. A warm weight on her forehead, a warm bracelet on her wrist, and a breeze went on whispering, trying to tell her something. A shuffle of leaves in the everlasting hand of God. He blew on them and they danced and rattled. "Mother, don't mind, we're going to give you a little hypodermic." "Look here, daughter, how do ants get in this bed? I saw sugar ants yesterday." Did you send for Hapsy too?

It was Hapsy she really wanted. She had to go a long way back through a great many rooms to find Hapsy standing with a baby on her arm. She seemed to herself to be Hapsy also, and the baby on Hapsy's arm was Hapsy and himself and herself, all at once, and there was no surprise in the meeting. Then Hapsy melted from within and turned flimsy as gray gauze and the baby was a gauzy shadow, and Hapsy came up close and said, "I thought you'd never come," and looked at her very searchingly and said, "You haven't changed a bit!" They leaned forward to kiss, when Cornelia began whispering from a long way off, "Oh, is there anything you want to tell me? Is there anything I can do for you?"

Yes, she had changed her mind after sixty years and she would like to see George. I want you to find George. Find him and be sure to tell him I forgot him. I want him to know I had my husband just the same and my children and my house like any other woman. A good house too and a good husband that I loved and fine children out of him. Better than I hoped for even. Tell him I was given back everything he took away and more. Oh, no, oh, God, no, there was something else besides the house and the man and the children. Oh, surely they were not all? What was it? Something not given back. . . . Her breath crowded down under her ribs and grew into a monstrous frightening shape with cutting edges; it bored up into her head, and the agony was unbelievable: Yes, John, get the doctor now, no more talk, my time has come.

When this one was born it should be the last. The last. It should have been born first, for it was the one she had truly wanted. Everything came in good time. Nothing left out, left over. She was strong, in three days she would be as well as ever. Better. A woman needed milk in her to have her full health.

"Mother, do you hear me?"

"I've been telling you—"

"Mother, Father Connolly's here."

"I went to Holy Communion only last week. Tell him I'm not so sinful as all that."

"Father just wants to speak to you."

He could speak as much as he pleased. It was like him to drop in and inquire about her soul as if it were a teething baby, and then stay on for a cup of tea and a round of cards and gossip. He always had a funny story of some sort, usually about an Irishman who made his little mistakes and confessed them, and the point lay in some absurd thing he would blurt out in the confessional showing his struggles between native piety and original sin. Granny felt easy about her soul. Cornelia, where are your manners? Give Father Connolly a chair. She had her secret, comfortable understanding with a few favorite saints who cleared a straight road to God for her. All as surely signed and sealed as the papers for the new Forty Acres. Forever . . . heirs and assigns forever. Since the day the wedding cake was not cut, but thrown out and wasted. The whole bottom dropped out of the world, and there she was blind and sweating with nothing under her feet and the walls falling away. His hand had caught her under the breast, she had not fallen, there was the freshly polished floor with the green rug on it, just as before. He had cursed like a sailor's parrot and said, "I'll kill him for you." Don't lay a hand on him, for my sake leave something to God. "Now, Ellen, you must believe what I tell you. . . . "

So there was nothing, nothing to worry about any more, except sometimes in the night one of the children screamed in a nightmare, and they both hustled out shaking and hunting for the matches and calling, "There, wait a minute, here we are!" John, get the doctor now. Hapsy's time has come. But there was Hapsy standing by the bed in a white cap. "Cornelia, tell Hapsy to take off her cap. I can't see her plain."

Her eyes opened very wide and the room stood out like a picture she had seen somewhere. Dark colors with the shadows rising towards the ceiling in long angles. The tall black dresser gleamed with nothing on it but John's picture, enlarged from a little one, with John's eyes very black when they should have been blue. You never saw him, so how do you know how he looked? But the man insisted the copy was perfect, it was very rich and handsome. For a picture, yes, but it's not my husband. The table by the bed had a linen cover and a candle and a crucifix. The light was blue from Cornelia's silk lampshades. No sort of light at all, just frippery. You had to live forty years with kerosene lamps to appreciate honest electricity. She felt very strong and she saw Doctor Harry with a rosy nimbus around him.

"You look like a saint, Doctor Harry, and I vow that's as near as you'll ever come to it."

"She's saying something."

"I heard you, Cornelia. What's all this carrying-on?"

"Father Connolly's saying—"

Cornelia's voice staggered and bumped like a cart in a bad road. It rounded corners and turned back again and arrived nowhere. Granny stepped up in the cart very lightly and reached for the reins, but a man sat beside her and she knew him by his hands, driving the cart. She did not look in his face, for she knew without seeing, but looked instead down the road where the trees leaned over and bowed to each other and a thousand birds were singing a Mass. She felt like singing too, but she put her hand in the bosom of her dress and pulled out a rosary, and Father Connolly murmured Latin in a very solemn voice and tickled her feet. My God, will you stop that nonsense? I'm a married woman. What if he did run away and leave me to face the priest by myself? I found another a whole world better. I wouldn't have exchanged my husband for anybody except St. Michael himself, and you may tell him that for me with a thank you in the bargain.

Light flashed on her closed eyelids, and a deep roaring shook her. Cornelia, is that lightning? I hear thunder. There's going to be a storm. Close all the windows. Call the children in. . . . "Mother, here we are, all of us." "Is that you, Hapsy?" "Oh, no, I'm Lydia. We drove as fast as we could." Their faces drifted above her, drifted away. The rosary fell out of her hands and Lydia put it back. Jimmy tried to help, their hands fumbled together, and Granny closed two fingers around Jimmy's thumb. Beads wouldn't do it, it must be something alive. She was so amazed her thoughts ran round and round. So, my dear Lord, this is my death and I wasn't even thinking about it. My children have come to see me die. But I can't, it's not time. Oh, I always hated surprises. I wanted to give Cornelia the amethyst set—Cornelia, you're to have the amethyst set, but Hapsy's to wear it when she wants, and, Doctor Harry, do shut up. Nobody sent for you. Oh, my dear Lord, do wait a minute. I meant to do something about the Forty Acres, Jimmy doesn't need it and Lydia will later on, with that worthless husband of hers. I meant to finish the altar cloth and send six bottles of wine to Sister Borgia for her dyspepsia. I want to send six bottles of wine to Sister Borgia, Father Connolly, now don't let me forget.

Cornelia's voice made short turns and tilted over and crashed. "Oh, Mother, oh, Mother, oh, Mother. . . ."

"I'm not going Cornelia. I'm taken by surprise. I can't go."

You'll see Hapsy again. What about her? "I thought you'd never come." Granny made a long journey outward, looking for Hapsy. What if I don't find her? What then? Her heart sank down and down, there was no bottom to death, she couldn't come to the end of it. The blue light from Cornelia's lampshade drew into a tiny point in the center of her brain, it flickered and winked like an eye, quietly it fluttered and dwindled. Granny lay curled down within herself, amazed and watchful, staring at the point of light that was herself; her body was now only a deeper mass of shadow in an endless darkness and this darkness would curl around the light and swallow it up. God, give a sign!

For the second time there was no sign. Again no bridegroom and the priest in the house. She could not remember any other sorrow because this grief wiped them all away. Oh, no, there's nothing more cruel than this — I'll never forgive it. She stretched herself with a deep breath and blew out the light.

(1930)

William Faulkner *1897–1962*

DRY SEPTEMBER

Through the bloody September twilight, aftermath of sixty-two rainless days, it had gone like a fire in dry grass—the rumor, the story, whatever it was. Something about Miss Minnie Cooper and a Negro. Attacked, insulted, frightened: none of them, gathered in the barber shop on that Saturday evening where the ceiling fan stirred, without freshening it, the vitiated air, sending back upon them, in recurrent surges of stale pomade and lotion, their own stale breath and odors, knew exactly what had happened.

"Except it wasn't Will Mayes," a barber said. He was a man of middle age; a thin, sand-colored man with a mild face, who was shaving a client. "I know Will Mayes. He's a good nigger. And I know Miss Minnie Cooper, too."

"What do you know about her?" a second barber said.

"Who is she?" the client said. "A young girl?"

"No," the barber said. "She's about forty, I reckon. She aint married. That's why I dont believe—"

"Believe, hell!" a hulking youth in a sweat-stained silk shirt said. "Wont you take a white woman's word before a nigger's?"

"I dont believe Will Mayes did it," the barber said. "I know Will Mayes."

"Maybe you know who did it, then. Maybe you already got him out of town, you damn niggerlover."

"I dont believe anybody did anything. I dont believe anything happened. I leave it to you fellows if them ladies that get old without getting married dont have notions that a man cant—"

"Then you are a hell of a white man," the client said. He moved under the cloth. The youth had sprung to his feet.

"You dont?" he said. "Do you accuse a white woman of lying?"

The barber held the razor poised above the half-risen client. He did not look around.

"It's this durn weather," another said. "It's enough to make a man do anything. Even to her."

Nobody laughed. The barber said in his mild, stubborn tone: "I aint accusing nobody of nothing. I just know and you fellows know how a woman that never—"

"You damn niggerlover!" the youth said.

"Shut up, Butch," another said. "We'll get the facts in plenty of time to act."

"Who is? Who's getting them?" the youth said. "Facts, hell! I—"

"You're a fine white man," the client said. "Aint you?" In his frothy beard he looked like a desert rat in the moving pictures. "You tell them, Jack," he said to the youth. "If there aint any white men in this town, you can count on me, even if I aint only a drummer and a stranger."

"That's right, boys," the barber said. "Find out the truth first. I know Will Mayes."

"Well, by God!" the youth shouted. "To think that a white man in this town—"

"Shut up, Butch," the second speaker said. "We got plenty of time."

302

The client sat up. He looked at the speaker. "Do you claim that anything excuses a nigger attacking a white woman? Do you mean to tell me you are a white man and you'll stand for it? You better go back North where you came from. The South dont want your kind here."

"North what?" the second said. "I was born and raised in this town."

"Well, by God!" the youth said. He looked about with a strained, baffled gaze, as if he was trying to remember what it was he wanted to say or to do. He drew his sleeve across his sweating face. "Damn if I'm going to let a white woman —"

"You tell them, Jack," the drummer said. "By God, if they —"

The screen door crashed open. A man stood in the floor, his feet apart and his heavy-set body poised easily. His white shirt was open at the throat; he wore a felt hat. His hot, bold glance swept the group. His name was McLendon. He had commanded troops at the front in France and had been decorated for valor.

"Well," he said, "are you going to sit there and let a black son rape a white woman on the streets of Jefferson?"

Butch sprang up again. The silk of his shirt clung flat to his heavy shoulders. At each armpit was a dark halfmoon. "That's what I been telling them! That's what I —"

"Did it really happen?" a third said. "This aint the first man scare she ever had, like Hawkshaw says. Wasn't there something about a man on the kitchen roof, watching her undress, about a year ago?"

"What?" the client said. "What's that?" The barber had been slowly forcing him back into the chair; he arrested himself reclining, his head lifted, the barber still pressing him down.

McLendon whirled on the third speaker. "Happen? What the hell difference does it make? Are you going to let the black sons get away with it until one really does it?"

"That's what I'm telling them!" Butch shouted. He cursed, long and steady, pointless.

"Here, here," a fourth said. "Not so loud. Dont talk so loud."

"Sure," McLendon said; "no talking necessary at all. I've done my talking. Who's with me?" He poised on the balls of his feet, roving his gaze.

The barber held the drummer's face down, the razor poised. "Find the facts first, boys. I know Willy Mayes. It wasn't him. Let's get the sheriff and do this thing right."

McLendon whirled upon him his furious, rigid face. The barber did not look away. They looked like men of different races. The other barbers had ceased also above their prone clients. "You mean to tell me," McLendon said, "that you'd take a nigger's word before a white woman's? Why, you damn niggerloving —"

The third speaker rose and grasped McLendon's arm; he too had been a soldier. "Now, now. Let's figure this thing out. Who knows anything about what really happened?"

"Figure out hell!" McLendon jerked his arm free. "All that're with me get up from there. The ones that aint —" He roved his gaze, dragging his sleeve across his face.

Three men rose. The drummer in the chair sat up. "Here," he said, jerking at the cloth about his neck; "get this rag off me. I'm with him. I dont live here, but by God, if our mothers and wives and sisters —" He smeared the cloth over his face and flung it to the floor. McLendon stood in the floor and cursed the others.

Another rose and moved toward him. The remainder sat uncomfortable, not looking at one another, then one by one they rose and joined him.

The barber picked the cloth from the floor. He began to fold it neatly. "Boys, dont do that. Will Mayes never done it. I know."

"Come on," McLendon said. He whirled. From his hip pocket protruded the butt of a heavy automatic pistol. They went out. The screen door crashed behind them reverberant in the dead air.

The barber wiped the razor carefully and swiftly, and put it away, and ran to the rear, and took his hat from the wall. "I'll be back as soon as I can," he said to the other barbers. "I cant let—" He went out, running. The two other barbers followed him to the door and caught it on the rebound, leaning out and looking up the street after him. The air was flat and dead. It had a metallic taste at the base of the tongue.

"What can he do?" the first said. The second one was saying "Jees Christ, Jees Christ" under his breath. "I'd just as lief be Will Mayes as Hawk, if he gets McLendon riled."

"Jees Christ, Jees Christ," the second whispered.

"You reckon he really done it to her?" the first said.

II

She was thirty-eight or thirty-nine. She lived in a small frame house with her invalid mother and a thin, sallow, unflagging aunt, where each morning between ten and eleven she would appear on the porch in a lace-trimmed boudoir cap, to sit swinging in the porch swing until noon. After dinner she lay down for a while, until the afternoon began to cool. Then, in one of the three or four new voile dresses which she had each summer, she would go downtown to spend the afternoon in the stores with the other ladies, where they would handle the goods and haggle over the prices in cold, immediate voices, without any intention of buying.

She was of comfortable people—not the best in Jefferson, but good people enough—and she was still on the slender side of ordinary looking, with a bright, faintly haggard manner and dress. When she was young she had had a slender, nervous body and a sort of hard vivacity which had enabled her for a time to ride upon the crest of the town's social life as exemplified by the high school party and church social period of her contemporaries while still children enough to be unclassconscious.

She was the last to realize that she was losing ground; that those among whom she had been a little brighter and louder flame than any other were beginning to learn the pleasure of snobbery—male—and retaliation—female. That was when her face began to wear that bright, haggard look. She still carried it to parties on shadowy porticoes and summer lawns, like a mask or a flag, with that bafflement of furious repudiation of truth in her eyes. One evening at a party she heard a boy and two girls, all schoolmates, talking. She never accepted another invitation.

She watched the girls with whom she had grown up as they married and got homes and children, but no man ever called on her steadily until the children of the other girls had been calling her "aunty" for several years, the while their mothers told them in bright voices about how popular Aunt Minnie had been as a girl. Then the town began to see her driving on Sunday afternoons with the cashier in the bank. He was a widower of about forty—a high-colored man, smelling always faintly of the barber shop or of whisky. He owned the first automobile in town, a red runabout; Minnie had the first motoring bonnet and veil the town ever saw. Then the town began to say: "Poor Minnie." "But she is old enough to take care of herself," others said. That was when she began to ask her old schoolmates that their children call her "cousin" instead of "aunty."

It was twelve years now since she had been relegated into adultery by public opinion, and eight years since the cashier had gone to a Memphis bank, returning for one day each Christmas, which he spent at an annual bachelors' party at the hunting club on the river. From behind their curtains the neighbors would see the party pass, and during the over-the-way Christmas day visiting they would tell her about him, about how well he looked, and how they heard that he was prospering in the city, watching with bright, secret eyes her haggard, bright face. Usually by that hour there would be the scent of whisky on her breath. It was supplied her by a youth, a clerk at the soda fountain: "Sure; I buy it for the old gal. I reckon she's entitled to a little fun."

Her mother kept to her room altogether now; the gaunt aunt ran the house. Against that background Minnie's bright dresses, her idle and empty days, had a quality of furious unreality. She went out in the evenings only with women now, neighbors, to the moving pictures. Each afternoon she dressed in one of the new dresses and went downtown alone, where her young "cousins" were already strolling in the late afternoons with their delicate, silken heads and thin, awkward arms and conscious hips, clinging to one another or shrieking and giggling with paired boys in the soda fountain when she passed and went on along the serried store fronts, in the doors of which the sitting and lounging men did not even follow her with their eyes any more.

III

The barber went swiftly up the street where the sparse lights, insect-swirled, glared in rigid and violent suspension in the lifeless air. The day had died in a pall of dust; above the darkened square, shrouded by the spent dust, the sky was as clear as the inside of a brass bell. Below the east was a rumor of the twice-waxed moon.

When he overtook them McLendon and three others were getting into a car parked in an alley. McLendon stooped his thick head, peering out beneath the top. "Changed your mind, did you?" he said. "Damn good thing; by God, tomorrow when this town hears about how you talked tonight—"

"Now, now," the other ex-soldier said. "Hawkshaw's all right. Come on, Hawk; jump in."

"Will Mayes never done it, boys," the barber said. "If anybody done it. Why, you all know well as I do there aint any town where they got better niggers than us. And you know how a lady will kind of think things about men when there aint any reason to, and Miss Minnie anyway—"

"Sure, sure," the soldier said. "We're just going to talk to him a little; that's all."

"Talk hell!" Butch said. "When we're through with the—"

"Shut up, for God's sake!" the soldier said. "Do you want everybody in town—"

"Tell them, by God!" McLendon said. "Tell every one of the sons that'll let a white woman—"

"Let's go; let's go: here's the other car." The second car slid squealing out of a cloud of dust at the alley mouth. McLendon started his car and took the lead. Dust lay like fog in the street. The street lights hung nimbused as in water. They drove on out of town.

A rutted lane turned at right angles. Dust hung above it too, and above all the land. The dark bulk of the ice plant, where the Negro Mayes was night watchman, rose against the sky. "Better stop here, hadn't we?" the soldier said. McLendon did not reply. He hurled the car up and slammed to a stop, the headlights glaring on the blank wall.

"Listen here, boys," the barber said; "if he's here, dont that prove he never done it? Dont it? If it was him, he would run. Dont you see he would?" The second car came up and stopped. McLendon got down; Butch sprang down beside him. "Listen, boys," the barber said.

"Cut the lights off!" McLendon said. The breathless dark rushed down. There was no sound in it save their lungs as they sought air in the parched dust in which for two months they had lived; then the diminishing crunch of McLendon's and Butch's feet, and a moment later McLendon's voice:

"Will! . . . Will!"

Below the east the wan hemorrhage of the moon increased. It heaved above the ridge, silvering the air, the dust, so that they seemed to breathe, live, in a bowl of molten lead. There was no sound of nightbird nor insect, no sound save their breathing and a faint ticking of contracting metal about the cars. Where their bodies touched one another they seemed to sweat dryly, for no more moisture came. "Christ!" a voice said; "let's get out of here."

But they didn't move until vague noises began to grow out of the darkness ahead; then they got out and waited tensely in the breathless dark. There was another sound: a blow, a hissing expulsion of breath and McLendon cursing in undertone. They stood a moment longer, then they ran forward. They ran in a stumbling clump, as though they were fleeing something. "Kill him, kill the son," a voice whispered. McLendon flung them back.

"Not here," he said. "Get him into the car." "Kill him, kill the black son!" the voice murmured. They dragged the Negro to the car. The barber had waited beside the car. He could feel himself sweating and he knew he was going to be sick at the stomach.

"What is it, captains?" the Negro said. "I aint done nothing. 'Fore God, Mr John." Someone produced handcuffs. They worked busily about the Negro as though he were a post, quiet, intent, getting in one another's way. He submitted to the handcuffs, looking swiftly and constantly from dim face to dim face. "Who's here, captains?" he said, leaning to peer into the faces until they could feel his breath and smell his sweaty reek. He spoke a name or two. "What you all say I done, Mr John?"

McLendon jerked the car door open. "Get in!" he said.

The Negro did not move. "What you all going to do with me, Mr John? I aint done nothing. White folks, captains, I aint done nothing: I swear 'fore God." He called another name.

"Get in!" McLendon said. He struck the Negro. The others expelled their breath in a dry hissing and struck him with random blows and he whirled and cursed them, and swept his manacled hands across their faces and slashed the barber upon the mouth, and the barber struck him also. "Get him in there," McLendon said. They pushed at him. He ceased struggling and got in and sat quietly as the others took their places. He sat between the barber and the soldier, drawing his limbs in so as not to touch them, his eyes going swiftly and constantly from face to face. Butch clung to the running board. The car moved on. The barber nursed his mouth with his handkerchief.

"What's the matter, Hawk?" the soldier said.

"Nothing," the barber said. They regained the high road and turned away from town. The second car dropped back out of the dust. They went on, gaining speed; the final fringe of houses dropped behind.

"Goddamn, he stinks!" the soldier said.

"We'll fix that," the drummer in the front beside McLendon said. On the running board Butch cursed into the hot rush of air. The barber leaned suddenly forward and touched McLendon's arm.

"Let me out, John," he said.

"Jump out, niggerlover," McLendon said without turning his head. He drove swiftly. Behind them the sourceless lights of the second car glared in the dust. Presently McLendon turned into a narrow road. It was rutted with disuse. It led back to an abandoned brick kiln—a series of reddish mounds and weed- and vine-choked vats without bottom. It had been used for pasture once, until one day the owner missed one of his mules. Although he prodded carefully in the vats with a long pole, he could not even find the bottom of them.

"John," the barber said.

"Jump out, then," McLendon said, hurling the car along the ruts. Beside the barber the Negro spoke:

"Mr Henry."

The barber sat forward. The narrow tunnel of the road rushed up and past. Their motion was like an extinct furnace blast; cooler, but utterly dead. The car bounded from rut to rut.

"Mr Henry," the Negro said.

The barber began to tug furiously at the door. "Look out, there!" the soldier said, but the barber had already kicked the door open and swung onto the running board. The soldier leaned across the Negro and grasped at him, but he had already jumped. The car went on without checking speed.

The impetus hurled him crashing through dust-sheathed weeds, into the ditch. Dust puffed about him, and in a thin, vicious crackling of sapless stems he lay choking and retching until the second car passed and died away. Then he rose and limped on until he reached the high road and turned toward town, brushing at his clothes with his hands. The moon was higher, riding high and clear of the dust at last, and after a while the town began to glare beneath the dust. He went on, limping. Presently he heard cars and the glow of them grew in the dust behind him and he left the road and crouched again in the weeds until they passed. McLendon's car came last now. There were four people in it and Butch was not on the running board.

They went on; the dust swallowed them; the glare and the sound died away. The dust of them hung for a while, but soon the eternal dust absorbed it again. The barber climbed back onto the road and limped on toward town.

IV

As she dressed for supper on that Saturday evening, her own flesh felt like fever. Her hands trembled among the hooks and eyes and her eyes had a feverish look, and her hair swirled crisp and crackling under the comb. While she was still dressing the friends called for her and sat while she donned her sheerest underthings and stockings and a new voile dress. "Do you feel strong enough to go out?" they said, their eyes bright too, with a dark glitter. "When you have had time to get over the shock, you must tell us what happened. What he said and did; everything."

In the leafed darkness, as they walked toward the square, she began to breathe deeply, something like a swimmer preparing to dive, until she ceased trembling, the four of them walking slowly because of the terrible heat and out of solicitude for her. But as they neared the square she began to tremble again, walking with her head up, her hands clenched at her sides, their voices about her murmurous, also with that feverish, glittering quality of their eyes. They entered the square, she in the center of the group, fragile in her fresh dress. She was trembling worse. She walked slower and slower, as children eat ice cream, her head up and her eyes bright in the haggard banner of her face, passing the hotel and the coatless drummers in chairs along the curb looking around at her: "That's the one: see? The one in pink in the middle." "Is that her? What did they do with the nigger? Did they—?" "Sure. He's all right." "All right, is he?" "Sure. He went on a little trip." Then the drug store, where even the young men lounging in the doorway tipped their hats and followed with their eyes the motion of her hips and legs when she passed.

They went on, passing the lifted hats of the gentlemen, the suddenly ceased voices, deferent, protective. "Do you see?" the friends said. Their voices sounded like long, hovering sighs of hissing exultation. "There's not a Negro on the square. Not one."

They reached the picture show. It was like a miniature fairyland with its lighted lobby and colored lithographs of life caught in its terrible and beautiful mutations. Her lips began to tingle. In the dark, when the picture began, it would be all right; she could hold back the laughing so it would not waste away so fast and so soon. So she hurried on before the turning faces, the undertones of low astonishment, and they took their accustomed places where she could see the aisle against the silver glare and the young men and girls coming in two and two against it.

The lights flicked away; the screen glowed silver, and soon life began to unfold, beautiful and passionate and sad, while still the young men and girls entered, scented and sibilant in the half dark, their paired backs in silhouette delicate and sleek, their slim, quick bodies awkward, divinely young, while beyond them the silver dream accumulated, inevitably on and on. She began to laugh. In trying to suppress it, it made more noise than ever; heads began to turn. Still laughing, her friends raised her and led her out, and she stood at the curb, laughing on a high, sustained note, until the taxi came up and they helped her in.

They removed the pink voile and the sheer underthings and the stockings, and put her to bed, and cracked ice for her temples, and sent for the doctor. He was hard to locate, so they ministered to her with hushed ejaculations, renewing the ice and fanning her. While the ice was fresh and cold she stopped laughing and lay still for a time, moaning only a little. But soon the laughing welled again and her voice rose screaming.

"Shhhhhhhhhhh! Shhhhhhhhhhhhhhh!" they said, freshening the icepack, smoothing her hair, examining it for gray; "poor girl!" Then to one another: "Do you suppose anything really happened?" their eyes darkly aglitter, secret and passionate. "Shhhhhhhhhh! Poor girl! Poor Minnie!"

V

It was midnight when McLendon drove up to his neat new house. It was trim and fresh as a birdcage and almost as small, with its clean, green-and-white paint. He locked the car and mounted the porch and entered. His wife rose from a chair beside the reading lamp. McLendon stopped in the floor and stared at her until she looked down.

"Look at that clock," he said, lifting his arm, pointing. She stood before him, her face lowered, a magazine in her hands. Her face was pale, strained, and weary-looking. "Haven't I told you about sitting up like this, waiting to see when I come in?"

"John," she said. She laid the magazine down. Poised on the balls of his feet, he glared at her with his hot eyes, his sweating face.

"Didn't I tell you?" He went toward her. She looked up then. He caught her shoulder. She stood passive, looking at him.

"Don't, John. I couldn't sleep. . . . The heat; something. Please, John. You're hurting me."

"Didn't I tell you?" He released her and half struck, half flung her across the chair, and she lay there and watched him quietly as he left the room.

He went on through the house, ripping off his shirt, and on the dark, screened porch at the rear he stood and mopped his head and shoulders with the shirt and flung it away. He took the pistol from his hip and laid it on the table beside the bed, and sat on the bed and removed his shoes, and rose and slipped his trousers off. He was sweating again already, and he stooped and hunted furiously for the shirt. At last he found it and wiped his body again, and, with his body pressed against the dusty screen, he stood panting. There was no movement, no sound, not even an insect. The dark world seemed to lie stricken beneath the cold moon and the lidless stars.

(1931)

William Faulkner *1897–1962*

A ROSE FOR EMILY

I

When Miss Emily Grierson died, our whole town went to her funeral: the men through a sort of respectful affection for a fallen monument, the women mostly out of curiosity to see the inside of her house, which no one save an old manservant—a combined gardener and cook—had seen in at least ten years.

It was a big, squarish frame house that had once been white, decorated with cupolas and spires and scrolled balconies in the heavily lightsome style of the seventies, set on what had once been our most select street. But garages and cotton gins had encroached and obliterated even the august names of that neighborhood; only Miss Emily's house was left, lifting its stubborn and coquettish decay above the cotton wagons and the gasoline pumps—an eyesore among eyesores. And now Miss Emily had gone to join the representatives of those august names where they lay in the cedar-bemused cemetery among the ranked and anonymous graves of Union and Confederate soldiers who fell at the battle of Jefferson.

Alive, Miss Emily had been a tradition, a duty, and a care; a sort of hereditary obligation upon the town, dating from that day in 1894 when Colonel Sartoris, the mayor—he who fathered the edict that no Negro woman should appear on the streets without an apron—remitted her taxes, the dispensation dating from the death of her father on into perpetuity. Not that Miss Emily would have accepted charity. Colonel Sartoris invented an involved tale to the effect that Miss Emily's father had loaned money to the town, which the town, as a matter of business, preferred this way of repaying. Only a man of Colonel Sartoris' generation and thought could have invented it, and only a woman could have believed it.

When the next generation, with its more modern ideas, became mayors and aldermen, this arrangement created some little dissatisfaction. On the first of the year they mailed her a tax notice. February came, and there was no reply. They wrote her a formal letter, asking her to call at the sheriff's office at her convenience. A week later the mayor wrote her himself, offering to call or to send his car for her, and received in reply a note on paper of an archaic shape, in a thin, flowing calligraphy in faded ink, to the effect that she no longer went out at all. The tax notice was also enclosed, without comment.

They called a special meeting of the Board of Aldermen. A deputation waited upon her, knocked at the door through which no visitor has passed since she ceased giving china-painting lessons eight or ten years earlier. They were admitted by the old Negro into a dim hall from which a stairway mounted into still more shadow. It smelled of dust and disuse—a close, dank smell. The Negro led them into the parlor. It was furnished in heavy, leather-covered furniture. When the Negro opened the blinds of one window, they could see that the leather was cracked; and when they sat down, a faint dust rose sluggishly about their thighs, spinning with slow motes in the single sun-ray. On a tarnished gilt easel before the fireplace stood a crayon portrait of Miss Emily's father.

They rose when she entered — a small, fat woman in black, with a thin gold chain descending to her waist and vanishing into her belt, leaning on an ebony cane with a tarnished gold head. Her skeleton was small and spare; perhaps that was why what would have been merely plumpness in another was obesity in her. She looked bloated, like a body long submerged in motionless water, and of that pallid hue. Her eyes, lost in the fatty ridges of her face, looked like two small pieces of coal pressed into a lump of dough as they moved from one face to another while the visitors stated their errand.

She did not ask them to sit. She just stood in the door and listened quietly until the spokesman came to a stumbling halt. Then they could hear the invisible watch ticking at the end of the gold chain.

Her voice was dry and cold. "I have no taxes in Jefferson. Colonel Sartoris explained it to me. Perhaps one of you can gain access to the city records and satisfy yourselves."

"But we have. We are the city authorities, Miss Emily. Didn't you get a notice from the sheriff, signed by him?"

"I received a paper, yes," Miss Emily said. "Perhaps he considers himself the sheriff. . . . I have no taxes in Jefferson."

"But there is nothing on the books to show that, you see. We must go by the — "

"See Colonel Sartoris. I have no taxes in Jefferson."

"But, Miss Emily — "

"See Colonel Sartoris." (Colonel Sartoris had been dead almost ten years.) "I have no taxes in Jefferson. Tobe!" The Negro appeared. "Show these gentlemen out."

II

So she vanquished them, horse and foot, just as she had vanquished their fathers thirty years before about the smell. That was two years after her father's death and a short time after her sweetheart — the one we believed would marry her — had deserted her. After her father's death she went out very little; after her sweetheart went away, people hardly saw her at all. A few of the ladies had the temerity to call, but were not received, and the only sign of life about the place was the Negro man — a young man then — going in and out with a market basket.

"Just as if a man — any man — could keep a kitchen properly," the ladies said; so they were not surprised when the smell developed. It was another link between the gross, teeming world and the high and mighty Griersons.

A neighbor, a woman, complained to the mayor, Judge Stevens, eighty years old.

"But what will you have me do about it, madam?" he said.

"Why, send her word to stop it," the woman said. "Isn't there a law?"

"I'm sure that won't be necessary," Judge Stevens said. "It's probably just a snake or a rat that nigger of hers killed in the yard. I'll speak to him about it."

The next day he received two more complaints, one from a man who came in diffident deprecation. "We really must do something about it, Judge. I'd be the last one in the world to bother Miss Emily, but we've got to do something." That night the Board of Aldermen met — three graybeards and one younger man, a member of the rising generation.

"It's simple enough," he said. "Send her word to have her place cleaned up. Give her a certain time to do it in, and if she don't. . . . "

"Dammit, sir," Judge Stevens said, "will you accuse a lady to her face of smelling bad?"

So the next night, after midnight, four men crossed Miss Emily's lawn and slunk about the house like burglars, sniffing along the base of the brickwork and at the cellar openings while one of them performed a regular sowing motion with his hand out of a sack slung from his shoulder. They broke open the cellar door and sprinkled lime there, and in all the outbuildings. As they recrossed the lawn, a window that had been dark was lighted and Miss Emily sat in it, the light behind her, and her upright torso motionless as that of an idol. They crept quietly across the lawn and into the shadow of the locusts that lined the street. After a week or two the smell went away.

That was when people had begun to feel really sorry for her. People in our town, remembering how old lady Wyatt, her great-aunt, had gone completely crazy at last, believed that the Griersons held themselves a little too high for what they really were. None of the young men were quite good enough for Miss Emily and such. We had long thought of them as a tableau, Miss Emily a slender figure in white in the background, her father a spraddled silhouette in the foreground, his back to her and clutching a horsewhip, the two of them framed by the backflung front door. So when she got to be thirty and was still single, we were not pleased exactly, but vindicated; even with insanity in the family she wouldn't have turned down all of her chances if they had really materialized.

When her father died, it got about that the house was all that was left to her; and in a way, people were glad. At last they could pity Miss Emily. Being left alone, and a pauper, she had become humanized. Now she too would know the old thrill and the old despair of a penny more or less.

The day after his death all the ladies prepared to call at the house and offer condolence and aid, as is our custom. Miss Emily met them at the door, dressed as usual and with no trace of grief on her face. She told them that her father was not dead. She did that for three days, with the ministers calling on her, and the doctors, trying to persuade her to let them dispose of the body. Just as they were about to resort to law and force, she broke down, and they buried her father quickly.

We did not say she was crazy then. We believed she had to do that. We remembered all the young men her father had driven away, and we knew that with nothing left, she would have to cling to that which had robbed her, as people will.

III

She was sick for a long time. When we saw her again, her hair was cut short, making her look like a girl, with a vague resemblance to those angels in colored church windows — sort of tragic and serene.

The town had just let the contracts for paving the sidewalks, and in the summer after her father's death they began the work. The construction company came with niggers and mules and machinery, and a foreman named Homer Barron, a Yankee — a big, dark, ready man, with a big voice and eyes lighter than his face. The little boys would follow in groups to hear him cuss the niggers, and the niggers singing in time to the rise and fall of picks. Pretty soon he knew everybody in town. Whenever you heard a lot of laughing anywhere about the square, Homer Barron would be in the center of the group. Presently, we began to see him and Miss Emily on Sunday afternoons driving in the yellow-wheeled buggy and the matched team of bays from the livery stable.

At first we were glad that Miss Emily would have an interest, because the ladies all said, "Of course a Grierson would not think seriously of a Northerner, a day laborer." But there were still others, older people, who said that even grief could not cause a real lady to forget *noblesse oblige*—without calling it *noblesse oblige*. They just said, "Poor Emily. Her kinsfolk should come to her." She had some kin in Alabama; but years ago her father had fallen out with them over the estate of old lady Wyatt, the crazy woman, and there was no communication between the two families. They had not even been represented at the funeral.

And as soon as the old people said, "Poor Emily," the whispering began. "Do you suppose it's really so?" they said to one another. "Of course it is. What else could. . . ." This behind their hands; rustling of craned silk and satin behind jalousies closed upon the sun of Sunday afternoon as the thin, swift clop-clop-clop of the matched team passed: "Poor Emily."

She carried her head high enough—even when we believed that she was fallen. It was as if she demanded more than ever the recognition of her dignity as the last Grierson; as if it had wanted that touch of earthiness to reaffirm her imperviousness. Like when she bought the rat poison, the arsenic. That was over a year after they had begun to say "Poor Emily," and while the two female cousins were visiting her.

"I want some poison," she said to the druggist. She was over thirty then, still a slight woman, though thinner than usual, with cold, haughty black eyes in a face the flesh of which was strained across the temples and about the eyesockets as you imagine a lighthouse-keeper's face ought to look. "I want some poison," she said.

"Yes, Miss Emily. What kind? For rats and such? I'd recom——"

"I want the best you have. I don't care what kind."

The druggist named several. "They'll kill anything up to an elephant. But what you want is——"

"Arsenic," Miss Emily said. "Is that a good one?"

"Is . . . arsenic? Yes, ma'am. But what you want——"

"I want arsenic."

The druggist looked down at her. She looked back at him, erect, her face like a strained flag. "Why, of course," the druggist said. "If that's what you want. But the law requires you to tell what you are going to use it for."

Miss Emily just stared at him, her head tilted back in order to look him eye for eye, until he looked away and went and got the arsenic and wrapped it up. The Negro delivery boy brought her the package; the druggist didn't come back. When she opened the package at home there was written on the box, under the skull and bones: "For rats."

IV

So the next day we all said, "She will kill herself"; and we said it would be the best thing. When she had first begun to be seen with Homer Barron, we had said, "She will marry him." Then we said, "She will persuade him yet," because Homer himself had remarked — he liked men, and it was known that he drank with the younger men in the Elks' Club — that he was not a marrying man. Later we said, "Poor Emily" behind the jalousies as they passed on Sunday afternoon in the glittering buggy, Miss Emily with her head high and Homer Barron with his hat cocked and a cigar in his teeth, reins and whip in a yellow glove.

Then some of the ladies began to say that it was a disgrace to the town and a bad example to the young people. The men did not want to interfere, but at last the ladies forced the Baptist minister — Miss Emily's people were Episcopal — to call upon her. He would never divulge what happened during that interview, but he refused to go back again. The next Sunday they again drove about the streets, and the following day the minister's wife wrote to Miss Emily's relations in Alabama.

So she had blood-kin under her roof again and we sat back to watch developments. At first nothing happened. Then we were sure that they were to be married. We learned that Miss Emily had been to the jeweler's and ordered a man's toilet set in silver, with the letters H.B. on each piece. Two days later we learned that she had bought a complete outfit of men's clothing, including a nightshirt, and we said, "They are married." We were really glad. We were glad because the two female cousins were even more Grierson than Miss Emily had ever been.

So we were not surprised when Homer Barron — the streets had been finished some time since — was gone. We were a little disappointed that there was not a public blowing-off, but we believed that he had gone on to prepare for Miss Emily's coming, or to give her a chance to get rid of the cousins. (By that time it was a cabal, and we were all Miss Emily's allies to help circumvent the cousins.) Sure enough, after another week they departed. And, as we had expected all along, within three days Homer Barron was back in town. A neighbor saw the Negro man admit him at the kitchen door at dusk one evening.

And that was the last we saw of Homer Barron. And of Miss Emily for some time. The Negro man went in and out with the market basket, but the front door remained closed. Now and then we would see her at the window for a moment, as the men did that night when they sprinkled the lime, but for almost six months she did not appear on the streets. Then we knew that this was to be expected too; as if that quality of her father which had thwarted her woman's life so many times had been too virulent and too furious to die.

When we next saw Miss Emily, she had grown fat and her hair was turning gray. During the next few years it grew grayer and grayer until it attained an even pepper-and-salt iron-gray, when it ceased turning. Up to the day of her death at seventy-four it was still that vigorous iron-gray, like the hair of an active man.

From that time on her front door remained closed, save during a period of six or seven years, when she was about forty, during which she gave lessons in china-painting. She fitted up a studio in one of the downstairs rooms, where the daughters and granddaughters of Colonel Sartoris' contemporaries were sent to her with the same regularity and in the same spirit that they were sent to church on Sundays with a twenty-five-cent piece for the collection plate. Meanwhile her taxes had been remitted.

Then the newer generation became the backbone and the spirit of the town, and the painting pupils grew up and fell away and did not send their children to her with boxes of color and tedious brushes and pictures cut from the ladies' magazines. The front door closed upon the last one and remained closed for good. When the town got free postal delivery, Miss Emily alone refused to let them fasten the metal numbers above her door and attach a mailbox to it. She would not listen to them.

Daily, monthly, yearly we watched the Negro grow grayer and more stooped, going in and out with the market basket. Each December we sent her a tax notice, which would be returned by the post office a week later, unclaimed. Now and then we would see her in one of the downstairs windows — she had evidently shut up the top floor of the house — like the carven torso of an idol in a niche, looking or not looking at us, we could never tell which. Thus she passed from generation to generation — dear, inescapable, impervious, tranquil, and perverse.

And so she died. Fell ill in the house filled with dust and shadows, with only a doddering Negro man to wait on her. We did not even know she was sick; we had long since given up trying to get any information from the Negro. He talked to no one, probably not even to her, for his voice had grown harsh and rusty, as if from disuse.

She died in one of the downstairs rooms, in a heavy walnut bed with a curtain, her gray head propped on a pillow yellow and moldy with age and lack of sunlight.

V

The Negro met the first of the ladies at the front door and let them in, with their hushed, sibilant voices and their quick, curious glances, and then he disappeared. He walked right through the house and out the back and was not seen again.

The two female cousins came at once. They held the funeral on the second day, with the town coming to look at Miss Emily beneath a mass of bought flowers, with the crayon face of her father musing profoundly above the bier and the ladies sibilant and macabre; and the very old men — some in their brushed Confederate uniforms — on the porch and the lawn, talking of Miss Emily as if she had been a contemporary of theirs, believing that they had danced with her and courted her perhaps, confusing time with its mathematical progression, as the old do, to whom all the past is not a diminishing road but, instead, a huge meadow which no winter ever quite touches, divided from them now by the narrow bottleneck of the most recent decade of years.

Already we knew that there was one room in that region above stairs which no one had seen in forty years, and which would have to be forced. They waited until Miss Emily was decently in the ground before they opened it.

The violence of breaking down the door seemed to fill this room with pervading dust. A thin, acrid pall as of the tomb seemed to lie everywhere upon this room decked and furnished as for a bridal: upon the valance curtains of faded rose color, upon the rose-shaded lights, upon the dressing table, upon the delicate array of crystal and the man's toilet things backed with tarnished silver, silver so tarnished that the monogram was obscured. Among them lay a collar and tie, as if they had just been removed, which, lifted, left upon the surface a pale crescent in the dust. Upon a chair hung the suit, carefully folded; beneath it the two mute shoes and the discarded socks.

The man himself lay in the bed.

For a long while we just stood there, looking down at the profound and fleshless grin. The body had apparently once lain in the attitude of an embrace, but now the long sleep that outlasts love, that conquers even the grimace of love, had cuckolded him. What was left of him, rotted beneath what was left of the nightshirt, had become inextricable from the bed in which he lay; and upon him and upon the pillow beside him lay that even coating of the patient and biding dust.

Then we noticed that in the second pillow was the indentation of a head. One of us lifted something from it, and leaning forward, that faint and invisible dust dry and acrid in the nostrils, we saw a long strand of iron-gray hair.

(1931)

Ernest Hemingway *1899–1961*

HILLS LIKE WHITE ELEPHANTS

The hills across the valley of the Ebro were long and white. On this side there was no shade and no trees and the station was between two lines of rails in the sun. Close against the side of the station there was the warm shadow of the building and a curtain, made of strings of bamboo beads, hung across the open door into the bar, to keep out flies. The American and the girl with him sat at a table in the shade, outside the building. It was very hot and the express from Barcelona would come in forty minutes. It stopped at this junction for two minutes and went on to Madrid.

"What should we drink?" the girl asked. She had taken off her hat and put it on the table.

"It's pretty hot," the man said.

"Let's drink beer."

"Dos cervezas," the man said into the curtain.

"Big ones?" a woman asked from the doorway.

"Yes. Two big ones."

The woman brought two glasses of beer and two felt pads. She put the felt pads and the beer glasses on the table and looked at the man and the girl. The girl was looking off at the line of hills. They were white in the sun and the country was brown and dry.

"They look like white elephants," she said.

"I've never seen one," the man drank his beer.

"No, you wouldn't have."

"I might have," the man said. "Just because you say I wouldn't have doesn't prove anything."

The girl looked at the bead curtain. "They've painted something on it," she said. "What does it say?"

"Anis del Toro. It's a drink."

"Could we try it?"

The man called "Listen" through the curtain. The woman came out from the bar.

"Four reales."

"We want two Anis del Toro."

"With water?"

"Do you want it with water?"

"I don't know," the girl said. "Is it good with water?"

"It's all right."

"You want them with water?" asked the woman.

"Yes, with water."

"It tastes like licorice," the girl said and put the glass down.

"That's the way with everything."

"Yes," said the girl. "Everything tastes of licorice. Especially all the things you've waited so long for, like absinthe."

"Oh, cut it out."

"You started it," the girl said. "I was being amused. I was having a fine time."

"Well, let's try and have a fine time."

"All right. I was trying. I said the mountains looked like white elephants. Wasn't that bright?"

"That was bright."

"I wanted to try this new drink. That's all we do, isn't it — look at things and try new drinks?"

"I guess so."

The girl looked across at the hills.

"They're lovely hills," she said. "They don't really look like white elephants. I just meant the coloring of their skin through the trees."

"Should we have another drink?"

"All right."

The warm wind blew the bead curtain against the table.

"The beer's nice and cool," the man said.

"It's lovely," the girl said.

"It's really an awfully simple operation, Jig," the man said. "It's not really an operation at all."

The girl looked at the ground the table legs rested on.

"I know you wouldn't mind it, Jig. It's really not anything. It's just to let the air in."

The girl did not say anything.

"I'll go with you and I'll stay with you all the time. They just let the air in and then it's all perfectly natural."

"Then what will we do afterward?"

"We'll be fine afterward. Just like we were before."

"What makes you think so?"

"That's the only thing that bothers us. It's the only thing that's made us unhappy."

The girl looked at the bead curtain, put her hand out and took hold of two of the strings of beads.

"And you think then we'll be all right and be happy."

"I know we will. You don't have to be afraid. I've known lots of people that have done it."

"So have I," said the girl. "And afterward they were all so happy."

"Well," the man said, "if you don't want to you don't have to. I wouldn't have you do it if you didn't want to. But I know it's perfectly simple."

"And you really want to?"

"I think it's the best thing to do. But I don't want you to do it if you don't really want to."

"And if I do it you'll be happy and things will be like they were and you'll love me?"

"I love you now. You know I love you."

"I know. But if I do it, then it will be nice again if I say things are like white elephants, and you'll like it?"

"I'll love it. I love it now but I just can't think about it. You know how I get when I worry."

"If I do it you won't ever worry?"

"I won't worry about that because it's perfectly simple."

"Then I'll do it. Because I don't care about me."

"What do you mean?"

"I don't care about me."

"Well, I care about you."

"Oh, yes. But I don't care about me. And I'll do it and then everything will be fine."

"I don't want you to do it if you feel that way."

The girl stood up and walked to the end of the station. Across, on the other side, were fields of grain and trees along the banks of the Ebro. Far away, beyond the river, were mountains. The shadow of a cloud moved across the field of grain and she saw the river through the trees.

"And we could have all this," she said. "And we could have everything and every day we make it more impossible."

"What did you say?"

"I said we could have everything."

"We can have everything."

"No, we can't."

"We can have the whole world."

"No, we can't."

"We can go everywhere."

"No, we can't. It isn't ours any more."

"It's ours."

"No, it isn't. And once they take it away, you never get it back."

"But they haven't taken it away."

"We'll wait and see."

"Come on back in the shade," he said. "You mustn't feel that way."

"I don't feel any way," the girl said. "I just know things."

"I don't want you to do anything that you don't want to do—"

"Nor that isn't good for me," she said. "I know. Could we have another beer?"

"All right. But you've got to realize—"

"I realize," the girl said. "Can't we maybe stop talking?"

They sat down at the table and the girl looked across at the hills on the dry side of the valley and the man looked at her and at the table.

"You've got to realize," he said, "that I don't want you to do it if you don't want to. I'm perfectly willing to go through with it if it means anything to you."

"Doesn't it mean anything to you? We could get along."

"Of course it does. But I don't want anybody but you. I don't want anyone else. And I know it's perfectly simple."

"Yes, you know it's perfectly simple."

"It's all right for you to say that, but I do know it."

"Would you do something for me now?"

"I'd do anything for you."

"Would you please please please please please please please stop talking?"

He did not say anything but looked at the bags against the wall of the station. There were labels on them from all the hotels where they had spent nights.

"But I don't want you to," he said. "I don't care anything about it."

"I'll scream," the girl said.

The woman came out through the curtains with two glasses of beer and put them down on the damp felt pads. "The train comes in five minutes," she said.

"What did she say?" asked the girl.

"That the train is coming in five minutes."

The girl smiled brightly at the woman, to thank her.

"I'd better take the bags over to the other side of the station," the man said. She smiled at him.

"All right. Then come back and we'll finish the beer."

He picked up the two heavy bags and carried them around the station to the other tracks. He looked up the tracks but could not see the train. Coming back, he walked through the barroom, where people waiting for the train were drinking. He drank an Anis at the bar and looked at the people. They were all waiting reasonably for the train. He went out through the bead curtain. She was sitting at the table and smiled at him.

"Do you feel better?" he asked.

"I feel fine," she said. "There's nothing wrong with me. I feel fine."

(1927)

Zora Neale Hurston *c. 1901–1960*

SWEAT

It was eleven o'clock of a Spring night in Florida. It was Sunday. Any other night, Delia Jones would have been in bed for two hours by this time. But she was a washwoman, and Monday morning meant a great deal to her. So she collected the soiled clothes on Saturday when she returned the clean things. Sunday night after church, she sorted them and put the white things to soak. It saved her almost a half day's start. A great hamper in the bedroom held the clothes that she brought home. It was so much neater than a number of bundles lying around.

She squatted in the kitchen floor beside the great pile of clothes, sorting them into small heaps according to color, and humming a song in a mournful key, but wondering through it all where Sykes, her husband, had gone with her horse and buckboard.

Just then something long, round, limp and black fell upon her shoulders and slithered to the floor beside her. A great terror took hold of her. It softened her knees and dried her mouth so that it was a full minute before she could cry out or move. Then she saw that it was the big bull whip her husband liked to carry when he drove.

She lifted her eyes to the door and saw him standing there bent over with laughter at her fright. She screamed at him.

"Sykes, what you throw dat whip on me like dat? You know it would skeer me—looks like a snake, an' you knows how skeered Ah is of snakes."

"Course Ah knowed it! That's how come Ah done it." He slapped his leg with his hand and almost rolled on the ground in his mirth. "If you such a big fool dat you got to have a fit over a earth worm or a string, Ah don't keer how bad Ah skeer you."

"You aint got no business doing it. Gawd knows it's a sin. Some day Ah'm gointuh drop dead from some of yo' foolishness. 'Nother thing, where you been wid mah rig? Ah feeds dat pony. He aint fuh you to be drivin' wid no bull whip."

"You sho is one aggravatin' nigger woman!" he declared and stepped into the room. She resumed her work and did not answer him at once. "Ah done tole you time and again to keep them white folks' clothes outa dis house."

He picked up the whip and glared down at her. Delia went on with her work. She went out into the yard and returned with a galvanized tub and set it on the washbench. She saw that Sykes had kicked all of the clothes together again, and now stood in her way truculently, his whole manner hoping, *praying*, for an argument. But she walked calmly around him and commenced to re-sort the things.

"Next time, Ah'm gointer kick 'em outdoors," he threatened as he struck a match along the leg of his corduroy breeches.

Delia never looked up from her work, and her thin, stooped shoulders sagged further.

"Ah aint for no fuss t'night, Sykes. Ah just come from taking sacrament at the church house."

He snorted scornfully. "Yeah, you just come from de church house on a Sunday night, but heah you is gone to work on them clothes. You aint nothing but a hypocrite. One of them amen-corner Christians — sing, whoop, and shout, then come home and wash white folks' clothes on the Sabbath."

He stepped roughly upon the whitest pile of things, kicking them helter-skelter as he crossed the room. His wife gave a little scream of dismay, and quickly gathered them together again.

"Sykes, you quit grindin' dirt into these clothes! How can Ah git through by Sat'day if Ah don't start on Sunday?"

"Ah don't keer if you never git through. Anyhow, Ah done promised Gawd and a couple of other men, Ah aint gointer have it in mah house. Don't gimme no lip neither, else Ah'll throw 'em out and put mah fist up side yo' head to boot."

Delia's habitual meekness seemed to slip from her shoulders like a blown scarf. She was on her feet; her poor little body, her bare knuckly hands bravely defying the strapping hulk before her.

"Looka heah, Sykes, you done gone too fur. Ah been married to you fur fifteen years, and Ah been takin' in washin' fur fifteen years. Sweat, sweat, sweat! Work and sweat, cry and sweat, pray and sweat!"

"What's that got to do with me?" he asked brutally.

"What's it got to do with you, Sykes? Mah tub of suds is filled yo' belly with vittles more times than yo' hands is filled it. Mah sweat is done paid for this house and Ah reckon Ah kin keep on sweatin' in it."

She seized the iron skillet from the stove and struck a defensive pose, which act surprised him greatly, coming from her. It cowed him and he did not strike her as he usually did.

"Naw you won't," she panted, "that ole snaggle-toothed black woman you runnin' with aint comin' heah to pile up on *mah* sweat and blood. You aint paid for nothin' on this place, and Ah'm gointer stay right heah till Ah'm toted out foot foremost."

"Well, you better quit gittin' me riled up, else they'll be totin' you out sooner than you expect. Ah'm so tired of you Ah don't know whut to do. Gawd! how Ah hates skinny wimmen!"

A little awed by his new Delia, he sidled out of the door and slammed the back gate after him. He did not say where he had gone, but she knew too well. She knew very well that he would not return until nearly daybreak also. Her work over, she went on to bed but not to sleep at once. Things had come to a pretty pass!

She lay awake, gazing upon the debris that cluttered their matrimonial trail. Not an image left standing along the way. Anything like flowers had long ago been drowned in the salty stream that had been pressed from her heart. Her tears, her sweat, her blood. She had brought love to the union and he had brought a longing after the flesh. Two months after the wedding, he had given her the first brutal beating. She had the memory of his numerous trips to Orlando with all of his wages when he had returned to her penniless, even before the first year had passed. She was young and soft then, but now she thought of her knotty, muscled limbs, her harsh knuckly hands, and drew herself up into an unhappy little ball in the middle of the big feather bed. Too late now to hope for love, even if it were not Bertha it would be someone else. This case differed from the others only in that she was bolder than the others. Too late for everything except her little home. She had built it for her old days, and planted one by one the trees and flowers there. It was lovely to her, lovely.

Somehow, before sleep came, she found herself saying aloud: "Oh well, whatever goes over the Devil's back, is got to come under his belly. Sometime or ruther, Sykes, like everybody else, is gointer reap his sowing." After that she was able to build a spiritual earthworks against her husband. His shells could no longer reach her. *Amen.* She went to sleep and slept until he announced his presence by kicking her feet and rudely snatching the covers away.

"Gimme some kivah heah, an' git yo' damn foots over on yo' own side! Ah oughter mash you in yo' mouf fuh drawing dat skillet on me."

Delia went clear to the rail without answering him. A triumphant indifference to all that he was or did.

The week was full of work for Delia as all other weeks, and Saturday found her behind her little pony, collecting and delivering clothes.

It was a hot, hot day near the end of July. The village men on Joe Clarke's porch even chewed cane listlessly. They did not hurl the caneknots as usual. They let them dribble over the edge of the porch. Even conversation had collapsed under the heat.

"Heah come Delia Jones," Jim Merchant said, as the shaggy pony came 'round the bend of the road toward them. The rusty buckboard was heaped with baskets of crisp, clean laundry.

"Yep," Joe Lindsay agreed. "Hot or col', rain or shine, jes ez reg'lar ez de weeks roll roun' Delia carries 'em an' fetches 'em on Sat'day."

"She better if she wanter eat," said Moss. "Syke Jones aint wuth de shot an' powder hit would tek tuh kill 'em. Not to *huh* he aint."

"He sho' aint," Walter Thomas chimed in. "It's too bad, too, cause she wuz a right pritty lil trick when he got huh. Ah'd uh mah'ied huh mahseff if he hadnter beat me to it."

Delia nodded briefly at the men as she drove past.

"Too much knockin' will ruin *any* 'oman. He done beat huh 'nough tuh kill three women, let 'lone change they looks," said Elijah Moseley. "How Syke kin stommuck dat big black greasy Mogul he's layin' roun' wid, gits me. Ah swear dat eight-rock couldn't kiss a sardine can Ah done thowed out de back do' 'way las' yeah."

"Aw, she's fat, thass how come. He's allus been crazy 'bout fat women," put in Merchant. "He'd a' been tied up wid one long time ago if he could a' found one tuh have him. Did Ah tell yuh 'bout him come sidlin' in' roun' *mah* wife — bringin' her a basket uh peecans outa his yard fuh a present? Yessir, mah wife! She tol' him tuh take em right straight back home, cause Delia works so hard ovah dat wash tub she reckon everything on de place taste lak sweat an' soapsuds. Ah jus' wisht Ah'd a caught 'im 'roun' dere! Ah'd a' made his hips ketch on fiah down dat shell road."

"Ah know he done it, too. Ah sees 'im grinnin' at every 'oman dat passes," Walter Thomas said. "But even so, he useter eat some mighty big hunks uh humble pie tuh git dat lil' 'oman he got. She wuz ez pritty ez a speckled pup! Dat wuz fifteen yeahs ago. He useter be so skeered uh losin' huh, she could make him do some parts of a husband's duty. Dey never wuz de same in de mind."

"There oughter be a law about him," said Lindsay. "He aint fit tuh carry guts tuh a bear."

Clarke spoke for the first time. "Taint no law on earth dat kin make a man be decent if it aint in 'im. There's plenty men dat takes a wife lak dey do a joint uh sugar-cane. It's round, juicy an' sweet when dey gits it. But dey squeeze an' grind, squeeze an' grind an' wring tell dey wring every drop uh pleasure dat's in 'em out. When dey's satisfied dat dey is wrung dry, dey treats 'em jes lak dey do a cane-chew. Dey throws 'em away. Dey knows whut dey is doin' while dey is at it, an' hates theirselves fuh it but they keeps on hangin' after huh tell she's empty. Den dey hates huh fuh bein' a cane-chew an' in de way."

"We oughter take Syke an' dat stray 'oman uh his'n down in Lake Howell swamp an' lay on de rawhide till dey cain't say 'Lawd a' mussy.' He allus wuz uh ovahbearin' niggah, but since dat white 'oman from up north done teached 'im how to run a automobile, he done got too biggety to live—an' we oughter kill 'im," old man Anderson advised.

A grunt of approval went around the porch. But the heat was melting their civic virtue and Elijah Moseley began to bait Joe Clarke.

"Come on, Joe, git a melon outa dere an' slice it up for yo' customers. We'se all sufferin' wid de heat. De bear's done got *me!*"

"Thass right, Joe, a watermelon is jes' whut Ah needs tuh cure de eppizu-dicks," Walter Thomas joined forces with Moseley. "Come on dere, Joe. We all is steady customers an' you aint set us up in a long time. Ah chooses dat long, bowlegged Floridy favorite."

"A god, an' be dough. You all gimme twenty cents and slice way," Clarke retorted. "Ah needs a col' slice m'self. Heah, everybody chip in. Ah'll lend y'll mah meat knife."

The money was quickly subscribed and the huge melon brought forth. At that moment, Sykes and Bertha arrived. A determined silence fell on the porch and the melon was put away again.

Merchant snapped down the blade of his jackknife and moved toward the store door.

"Come on in, Joe, an' gimme a slab uh sow belly an' uh pound uh coffee— almost fuhgot 'twas Sat'day. Got to git on home." Most of the men left also.

Just then Delia drove past on her way home, as Sykes was ordering magnifi-cently for Bertha. It pleased him for Delia to see.

"Git whutsoever yo' heart desires, Honey. Wait a minute, Joe. Give huh two bottles uh strawberry soda-water, uh quart uh parched ground-peas, an' a block uh chewin' gum."

With all this they left the store, with Sykes reminding Bertha that this was his town and she could have it if she wanted it.

The men returned soon after they left, and held their watermelon feast.

"Where did Syke Jones git da 'oman from nohow?" Lindsay asked.

"Ovah Apopka. Guess dey musta been cleanin' out de town when she lef'. She don't look lak a thing but a hunk uh liver wid hair on it."

"Well, she sho' kin squall," Dave Carter contributed. "When she gits ready tuh laff, she jes' opens huh mouf an' latches it back tuh de las' notch. No ole grandpa alligator down in Lake Bell aint got nothin' on huh."

Bertha had been in town three months now. Sykes was still paying her room rent at Della Lewis'—the only house in town that would have taken her in. Sykes took her frequently to Winter Park to "stomps." He still assured her that he was the swellest man in the state.

"Sho' you kin have dat lil' ole house soon's Ah kin git dat 'oman outa dere. Everything b'longs tuh me an' you sho' kin have it. Ah sho' 'bominates uh skinny 'oman. Lawdy, you sho' is got one portly shape on you! You kin git *anything* you wants. Dis is *mah* town an' you sho' kin have it."

Delia's work-worn knees crawled over the earth in Gethesemane and up the rocks of Calvary many, many times during these months. She avoided the villagers and meeting places in her efforts to be blind and deaf. But Bertha nullified this to a degree, by coming to Delia's house to call Sykes out to her at the gate.

Delia and Sykes fought all the time now with no peaceful interludes. They slept and ate in silence. Two or three times Delia had attempted a timid friendliness, but she was repulsed each time. It was plain that the breaches must remain agape.

The sun had burned July to August. The heat streamed down like a million hot arrows, smiting all things living upon the earth. Grass withered, leaves browned, snakes went blind in shedding and men and dogs went mad. Dog days!

Delia came home one day and found Sykes there before her. She wondered, but started to go on into the house without speaking, even though he was standing in the kitchen door and she must either stoop under his arm or ask him to move. He made no room for her. She noticed a soap box beside the steps, but paid no particular attention to it, knowing that he must have brought it there. As she was stooping to pass under his outstretched arm, he suddenly pushed her backward, laughingly.

"Look in de box dere Delia, Ah done brung yuh somethin'!"

She nearly fell upon the box in her stumbling, and when she saw what it held, she all but fainted outright.

"Syke! Syke, mah Gawd! You take dat rattlesnake 'way from heah! You *gottuh.* Oh, Jesus, have mussy!"

"Ah aint gut tuh do nuthin' uh de kin'—fact is Ah aint got tuh do nothin' but die. Taint no use uh you puttin' on airs makin' out lak you skeered uh dat snake—he's gointer stay right heah tell he die. He wouldn't bite me cause Ah knows how tuh handle 'im. Nohow he wouldn't risk breakin' out his fangs 'gin yo' skinny laigs."

"Naw, now Syke, don't keep dat thing 'roun' heah tuh skeer me tuh death. You knows Ah'm even feared uh earth worms. Thass de biggest snake Ah evah did see. Kill 'im Syke, please."

"Doan ast me tuh do nothin' fuh yuh. Goin' 'roun' tryin' tuh be so damn asterperious. Naw, Ah aint gonna kill it. Ah think uh damn sight mo' uh him dan you! Dat's a nice snake an' anybody doan lak 'im kin jes' hit de grit."

The village soon heard that Sykes had the snake, and came to see and ask questions.

"How de hen-fire did you ketch dat six-foot rattler, Syke?" Thomas asked.

"He's full uh frogs so he caint hardly move, thass how Ah eased up on 'm. But Ah'm a snake charmer an' knows how tuh handle 'em. Shux, dat aint nothin'. Ah could ketch one eve'y day if Ah so wanted tuh."

"Whut he needs is a heavy hick'ry club leaned real heavy on his head. Dat's de bes' way tuh charm a rattlesnake."

"Naw, Walt, y'll jes' don't understand dese diamon' backs lak Ah do," said Sykes in a superior tone of voice.

The village agreed with Walter, but the snake stayed on. His box remained by the kitchen door with its screen wire covering. Two or three days later it had

digested its meal of frogs and literally came to life. It rattled at every movement
in the kitchen or the yard. One day as Delia came down the kitchen steps she saw
his chalky-white fangs curved like scimitars hung in the wire meshes. This time
she did not run away with averted eyes as usual. She stood for a long time in the
doorway in a red fury that grew bloodier for every second that she regarded the
creature that was her torment.

That night she broached the subject as soon as Sykes sat down to the table.
"Syke, Ah wants you tuh take dat snake 'way fum heah. You done starved me
an' Ah put up widcher, you done beat me an Ah took dat, but you done kilt all
mah insides bringin' dat varmint heah."

Sykes poured out a saucer full of coffee and drank it deliberately before he
answered her.

"A whole lot Ah keer 'bout how you feels inside uh out. Dat snake aint goin'
no damn wheah till Ah gits ready fuh 'im tuh go. So fur as beatin' is concerned,
yuh aint took near all dat you gointer take ef yuh stay 'roun' *me.*"

Delia pushed back her plate and got up from the table. "Ah hates you, Sykes,"
she said calmly. "Ah hates you tuh de same degree dat Ah useter love yuh. Ah
done took an' took till mah belly is full up tuh mah neck. Dat's de reason Ah got
mah letter fum de church an' moved mah membership tuh Woodbridge — so Ah
don't haftuh take no sacrament wid yuh. Ah don't wantuh see yuh 'roun' me atall.
Lay 'roun' wid dat 'oman all yuh wants tuh, but gwan 'way fum me an' mah
house. Ah hates yuh lak uh suck-egg dog."

Sykes almost let the huge wad of corn bread and collard greens he was
chewing fall out of his mouth in amazement. He had a hard time whipping
himself up to the proper fury to try to answer Delia.

"Well, Ah'm glad you does hate me. Ah'm sho' tiahed uh you hangin' ontuh
me. Ah don't want yuh. Look at yuh stringey ole neck! Yo' rawbony laigs an'
arms is enough tuh cut uh man tuh death. You looks jes' lak de devvul's doll-baby
tuh *me.* You cain't hate me no worse dan Ah hates you. Ah been hatin' *you* fuh
years."

"Yo' ole black hide don't look lak nothin' tuh me, but uh passle uh wrinkled
up rubber, wid yo' big ole yeahs flappin' on each side lak uh paih uh buzzard
wings. Don't think Ah'm gointuh be run 'way fum mah house neither. Ah'm
goin' tuh de white folks bout *you,* mah young man, de very nex' time you lay yo'
han's on me. Mah cup is done run ovah."

Delia said this with no signs of fear and Sykes departed from the house,
threatening her, but made not the slightest move to carry out any of them.

That night he did not return at all, and the next day being Sunday, Delia was
glad she did not have to quarrel before she hitched up her pony and drove the
four miles to Woodbridge.

She stayed to the night service — "love feast" — which was very warm and full
of spirit. In the emotional winds her domestic trials were borne far and wide so
that she sang as she drove homeward,

> "Jurden water, black an' col'
> Chills de body, not de soul
> An' Ah wantah cross Jurden in uh calm time."

She came from the barn to the kitchen door and stopped.

"Whut's de mattah, ol' satan, you aint kickin' up yo' racket?" She addressed
the snake's box. Complete silence. She went on into the house with a new hope

in its birth struggles. Perhaps her threat to go to the white folks had frightened Sykes! Perhaps he was sorry! Fifteen years of misery and suppression had brought Delia to the place where she would hope *anything* that looked towards a way over or through her wall of inhibitions.

She felt in the match safe behind the stove at once for a match. There was only one there.

"Dat niggah wouldn't fetch nothin' heah tuh save his rotten neck, but he kin run thew whut Ah brings quick enough. Now he done toted off nigh on tuh haff uh box uh matches. He done had dat 'oman heah in mah house too."

Nobody but a woman could tell how she knew this even before she struck the match. But she did and it put her into a new fury.

Presently she brought in the tubs to put the white things to soak. This time she decided she need not bring the hamper out of the bedroom: she would go in there and do the sorting. She picked up the pot-bellied lamp and went in. The room was small and the hamper stood hard by the foot of the white iron bed. She could sit and reach through the bedposts—resting as she worked.

"Ah wantah cross Jurden in uh calm time." She was singing again. The mood of the "love feast" had returned. She threw back the lid of the basket almost gaily. Then, moved by both horror and terror, she sprang back toward the door. *There lay the snake in the basket!* He moved sluggishly at first, but even as she turned round and round, jumped up and down in an insanity of fear, he began to stir vigorously. She saw him pouring his awful beauty from the basket upon the bed, then she seized the lamp and ran as fast as she could to the kitchen. The wind from the open door blew out the light and the darkness added to her terror. She sped to the darkness of the yard, slamming the door after her before she thought to set down the lamp. She did not feel safe even on the ground, so she climbed up in the hay barn.

There for an hour or more she lay sprawled upon the hay a gibbering wreck.

Finally she grew quiet, and after that, coherent thought. With this, stalked through her a cold, bloody rage. Hours of this. A period of introspection, a space of retrospection, then a mixture of both. Out of this an awful calm.

"Well, Ah done de bes' Ah could. If things aint right, Gawd knows taint mah fault."

She went to sleep—a twitchy sleep—and woke up to a faint gray sky. There was a loud hollow sound below. She peered out. Sykes was at the wood-pile, demolishing a wire-covered box.

He hurried to the kitchen door, but hung outside there some minutes before he entered, and stood some minutes more inside before he closed it after him.

The gray in the sky was spreading. Delia descended without fear now, and crouched beneath the low bedroom window. The drawn shade shut out the dawn, shut in the night. But the thin walls held back no sound.

"Dat ol' scratch is woke up now!" She mused at the tremendous whirr inside, which every woodsman knows, is one of the sound illusions. The rattler is a ventriloquist. His whirr sounds to the right, to the left, straight ahead, behind, close under foot—everywhere but where it is. Woe to him who guesses wrong unless he is prepared to hold up his end of the argument! Sometimes he strikes without rattling at all.

Inside, Sykes heard nothing until he knocked a pot lid off the stove while trying to reach the match safe in the dark. He had emptied his pockets at Bertha's.

The snake seemed to wake up under the stove and Sykes made a quick leap into the bedroom. In spite of the gin he had had, his head was clearing now.

"Mah Gawd!" he chattered, "ef Ah could on'y strack uh light!"

The rattling ceased for a moment as he stood paralyzed. He waited. It seemed that the snake waited also.

"Oh, fuh de light! Ah thought he'd be too sick"—Sykes was muttering to himself when the whirr began again, closer, right underfoot this time. Long before this, Sykes' ability to think had been flattened down to primitive instinct and he leaped—onto the bed.

Outside Delia heard a cry that might have come from a maddened chimpanzee, a stricken gorilla. All the terror, all the horror, all the rage that man possibly could express, without a recognizable human sound.

A tremendous stir inside there, another series of animal screams, the intermittent whirr of the reptile. The shade torn violently down from the window, letting in the red dawn, a huge brown hand seizing the window stick, great dull blows upon the wooden floor punctuating the gibberish of sound long after the rattle of the snake had abruptly subsided. All this Delia could see and hear from her place beneath the window, and it made her ill. She crept over to the four-o'clocks and stretched herself on the cool earth to recover.

She lay there. "Delia, Delia!" She could hear Sykes calling in a most despairing tone as one who expected no answer. The sun crept on up, and he called. Delia could not move—her legs were gone flabby. She never moved, he called, and the sun kept rising.

"Mah Gawd!" She heard him moan, "Mah Gawd fum Heben!" She heard him stumbling about and got up from her flower-bed. The sun was growing warm. As she approached the door she heard him call out hopefully, "Delia, is dat you Ah heah?

She saw him on his hands and knees as soon as she reached the door. He crept an inch or two toward her—all that he was able, and she saw his horribly swollen neck and his one open eye shining with hope. A surge of pity too strong to support bore her away from that eye that must, could not, fail to see the tubs. He would see the lamp. Orlando with its doctors was too far. She could scarcely reach the Chinaberry tree, where she waited in the growing heat while inside she knew the cold river was creeping up and up to extinguish that eye which must know by now that she knew.

(1926)

Arna Bontemps *1902–1973*

A SUMMER TRAGEDY

Old Jeff Patton, the black share farmer, fumbled with his bow tie. His fingers trembled and the high, stiff collar pinched his throat. A fellow loses his hand for such vanities after thirty or forty years of simple life. Once a year, or maybe twice if there's a wedding among his kinfolks, he may spruce up, but generally fancy clothes do nothing but adorn the wall of the big room and feed the moths. That had been Jeff Patton's experience. He had not worn his stiff-bosomed shirt more than a dozen times in all his married life. His swallow-tailed coat lay on the bed beside him, freshly brushed and pressed, but it was as full of holes as the overalls in which he worked on weekdays. The moths had used it badly. Jeff twisted his mouth into a hideous toothless grimace as he contended with the obstinate bow. He stamped his good foot and decided to give up the struggle.

"Jennie," he called.

"What's that, Jeff?" His wife's shrunken voice came out of the adjoining room like an echo. It was hardly bigger than a whisper.

"I reckon you'll have to he'p me wid this heah bow tie, baby," he said meekly. "Dog if I can hitch it up."

Her answer was not strong enough to reach him, but presently the old woman came to the door, feeling her way with a stick. She had a wasted, dead-leaf appearance. Her body, as scrawny and gnarled as a string bean, seemed less than nothing in the ocean of frayed and faded petticoats that surrounded her. These hung an inch or two above the tops of her heavy unlaced shoes and showed little grotesque piles where the stockings had fallen down from her negligible legs.

"You oughta could do a heap mo' wid a thing like that'n me — beingst as you got yo' good sight."

"Looks like I oughta could," he admitted. "But my fingers is gone democrat on me. I get all mixed up in the looking glass an' can't tell wicha way to twist the devilish thing."

Jennie sat on the side of the bed, and old Jeff Patton got down on one knee while she tied the bow knot. It was a slow and painful ordeal for each of them in this position. Jeff's bones cracked, his knee ached, and it was only after a half dozen attempts that Jennie worked a semblance of a bow into the tie.

"I got to dress maself now," the old woman whispered. "These is ma old shoes an' stockings, and I ain't so much as unwrapped ma dress."

"Well, don't worry 'bout me no mo', baby," Jeff said. "That 'bout finishes me. All I gotta do now is slip on that old coat 'n ves' an' I'll be fixed to leave."

Jennie disappeared again through the dim passage into the shed room. Being blind was no handicap to her in that black hole. Jeff heard the cane placed against the wall beside the door and knew that his wife was on easy ground. He put on his coat, took a battered top hat from the bed post, and hobbled to the front door. He was ready to travel. As soon as Jennie could get on her Sunday shoes and her old black silk dress, they would start.

Outside the tiny log house, the day was warm and mellow with sunshine. A host of wasps were humming with busy excitement in the trunk of a dead sycamore. Gray squirrels were searching through the grass for hickory nuts, and blue jays were in the trees, hopping from branch to branch. Pine woods stretched away to the left like a black sea. Among them were scattered scores of log houses like Jeff's, houses of black share farmers. Cows and pigs wandered freely among the trees. There was no danger of loss. Each farmer knew his own stock and knew his neighbor's as well as he knew his neighbor's children.

Down the slope to the right were the cultivated acres on which the colored folks worked. They extended to the river, more than two miles away, and they were today green with the unmade cotton crop. A tiny thread of a road, which passed directly in front of Jeff's place, ran through these green fields like a pencil mark.

Jeff, standing outside the door, with his absurd hat in his left hand, surveyed the wide scene tenderly. He had been forty-five years on these acres. He loved them with the unexplained affection that others have for the countries to which they belong.

The sun was hot on his head, his collar still pinched his throat, and the Sunday clothes were intolerably hot. Jeff transferred the hat to his right hand and began fanning with it. Suddenly the whisper that was Jennie's voice came out of the shed room.

"You can bring the car round front whilst you's waitin'," it said feebly. There was a tired pause; then it added, "I'll soon be fixed to go."

"A'right, baby," Jeff answered. "I'll get it in a minute."

But he didn't move. A thought struck him that made his mouth fall open. The mention of the car brought to his mind with new intensity, the trip he and Jennie were about to take. Fear came into his eyes; excitement took his breath. Lord, Jesus!

"Jeff. . . . O Jeff," the old woman's whisper called.

He awakened with a jolt. "Hunh, baby?"

"What you doin'?"

"Nuthin. Jes studyin'. I jes been turnin' things round 'n round in ma mind."

"You could be gettin' the car," she said.

"Oh yes, right away, baby."

He started round to the shed, limping heavily on his bad leg. There were three frizzly chickens in the yard. All his other chickens had been killed or stolen recently. But the frizzly chickens had been saved somehow. That was fortunate indeed, for these curious creatures had a way of devouring "poison" from the yard and in that way protecting against conjure and black luck and spells. But even the frizzly chickens seemed now to be in a stupor. Jeff thought they had some ailment; he expected all three of them to die shortly.

The shed in which the old T-model Ford stood was only a grass roof held up by four corner poles. It had been built by tremulous hands at a time when the little rattletrap car had been regarded as a peculiar treasure. And, miraculously, despite wind and downpour, it still stood.

Jeff adjusted the crank and put his weight upon it. The engine came to life with a sputter and bang that rattled the old car from radiator to tail light. Jeff hopped into the seat and put his foot on the accelerator. The sputtering and banging increased. The rattling became more violent. That was good. It was good banging, good sputtering and rattling, and it meant that the aged car was still in running condition. She could be depended on for this trip.

Again Jeff's thought halted as if paralyzed. The suggestion of the trip fell into the machinery of his mind like a wrench. He felt dazed and weak. He swung the car out into the yard, made a half turn, and drove around to the front door. When he took his hands off the wheel, he noticed that he was trembling violently. He cut off the motor and climbed to the ground to wait for Jennie.

A few minutes later she was at the window, her voice rattling against the pane like a broken shutter.

"I'm ready, Jeff."

He did not answer, but limped into the house and took her by the arm. He led her slowly through the big room, down the step, and across the yard.

"You reckon I'd oughta lock the do'?" he asked softly.

They stopped and Jennie weighed the question. Finally she shook her head. "Ne' mind the do'," she said. "I don't see no cause to lock up things."

"You right," Jeff agreed. "No cause to lock up."

Jeff opened the door and helped his wife into the car. A quick shudder passed over him. Jesus! Again he trembled.

"How come you shaking so?" Jennie whispered.

"I don't know," he said.

"You mus' be scairt, Jeff."

"No, baby, I ain't scairt."

He slammed the door after her and went around to crank up again. The motor started easily. Jeff wished that it had not been so responsive. He would have liked a few more minutes in which to turn things around in his head. As it was, with Jennie chiding him about being afraid, he had to keep going. He swung the car into the little pencil-mark road and started off toward the river, driving very slowly, very cautiously.

Chugging across the green countryside, the small battered Ford seemed tiny indeed. Jeff felt a familiar excitement, a thrill, as they came down the first slope to the immense levels on which the cotton was growing. He could not help reflecting that the crops were good. He knew what that meant, too; he had made forty-five of them with his own hands. It was true that he had worn out nearly a dozen mules, but that was the fault of old man Stevenson, the owner of the land. Major Stevenson had the old notion that one mule was all a share farmer needed to work a thirty-acre plot. It was an expensive notion, the way it killed mules from overwork but the old man held to it. Jeff thought it killed a good many share farmers as well as mules, but he had no sympathy for them. He had always been strong, and he had been taught to have no patience with weakness in men. Women or children might be tolerated if they were puny, but a weak man was a curse. Of course, his own children —

Jeff's thought halted there. He and Jennie never mentioned their dead children any more. And naturally, he did not wish to dwell upon them in his mind. Before he knew it, some remark would slip out of his mouth and that would make Jennie feel blue. Perhaps she would cry. A woman like Jennie could not easily throw off the grief that comes from losing five grown children within two years. Even Jeff was still staggered by the blow. His memory had not been much good recently. He frequently talked to himself. And, although he had kept it a secret, he knew that his courage had left him. He was terrified by the least unfamiliar sound at night. He was reluctant to venture far from home in the daytime. And that habit of trembling when he felt fearful was now far beyond his control. Sometimes he became afraid and trembled without knowing what had frightened him. The feeling would just come over him like a chill.

The car rattled slowly over the dusty road. Jennie sat erect and silent with a little absurd hat pinned to her hair. Her useless eyes seemed very large, very white in their deep sockets. Suddenly Jeff heard her voice, and he inclined his head to catch the words.

"Is we passed Delia Moore's house yet?" she asked.

"Not yet," he said.

"You must be drivin' mighty slow, Jeff."

"We just as well take our time, baby."

There was a pause. A little puff of steam was coming out of the radiator of the car. Heat wavered above the hood. Delia Moore's house was nearly half a mile away. After a moment Jennie spoke again.

"You ain't really scairt, is you, Jeff?"

"Nah, baby, I ain't scairt."

"You know how we agreed — we gotta keep on goin'."

Jewels of perspiration appeared on Jeff's forehead. His eyes rounded, blinked, became fixed on the road.

"I don't know," he said with a shiver, "I reckon it's the only thing to do."

"Hm."

A flock of guinea fowls, pecking in the road, were scattered by the passing car. Some of them took to their wings; others hid under bushes. A blue jay, swaying on a leafy twig, was annoying a roadside squirrel. Jeff held an even speed till he came near Delia's place. Then he slowed down noticeably.

Delia's house was really no house at all, but an abandoned store building converted into a dwelling. It sat near a crossroads, beneath a single black cedar tree. There Delia, a cattish old creature of Jennie's age, lived alone. She had been there more years than anybody could remember, and long ago had won the disfavor of such women as Jennie. For in her young days Delia had been gayer, yellower, and saucier than seemed proper in those parts. Her ways with men-folks had been dark and suspicious. And the fact that she had had as many husbands as children did not help her reputation.

"Yonder's old Delia," Jeff said as they passed.

"What she doin'?"

"Jes sittin' in the do'," he said.

"She see us?"

"Hm," Jeff said. "Musta did."

That relieved Jennie. It strengthened her to know that her old enemy had seen her pass in her best clothes. That would give the old she-devil something to chew her gums and fret about, Jennie thought. Wouldn't she have a fit if she didn't find out? Old evil Delia! This would be just the thing for her. It would pay her back for being so evil. It would also pay her, Jennie thought, for the way she used to grin at Jeff — long ago, when her teeth were good.

The road became smooth and red, and Jeff could tell by the smell of the air that they were nearing the river. He could see the rise where the road turned and ran along parallel to the stream. The car chugged on monotonously. After a long silent spell, Jennie leaned against Jeff and spoke.

"How many bale o' cotton you think we got standin'?" she said.

Jeff wrinkled his forehead as he calculated.

"'Bout twenty-five, I reckon."

"How many you make las' year?"

"Twenty-eight," he said. "How come you ask that?"

"I's jes thinkin'," Jennie said quietly.

"It don't make a speck o' difference though," Jeff reflected. "If we get much or if we get little, we still gonna be in debt to old man Stevenson when he gets through counting up agin us. It's took us a long time to learn that."

Jennie was not listening to these words. She had fallen into a trancelike meditation. Her lips twitched. She chewed her gums and rubbed her gnarled hands nervously. Suddenly, she leaned forward, buried her face in the nervous hands, and burst into tears. She cried aloud in a dry, cracked voice that suggested the rattle of fodder on dead stalks. She cried aloud like a child, for she had never learned to suppress a genuine sob. Her slight old frame shook heavily and seemed hardly able to sustain such violent grief.

"What's the matter, baby?" Jeff asked awkwardly. "Why you cryin' like all that?"

"I's jes thinkin'," she said.

"So you the one what's scairt now, hunh?"

"I ain't scairt, Jeff. I's jes thinkin' 'bout leavin' eve'thing like this—eve'thing we been used to. It's right sad-like."

Jeff did not answer, and presently Jennie buried her face again and cried.

The sun was almost overhead. It beat down furiously on the dusty wagon-path road, on the parched roadside grass and the tiny battered car. Jeff's hands, gripping the wheel, became wet with perspiration; his forehead sparkled. Jeff's lips parted. His mouth shaped a hideous grimace. His face suggested the face of a man being burned. But the torture passed and his expression softened again.

"You mustn't cry, baby," he said to his wife. "We gotta be strong. We can't break down."

Jennie waited a few seconds, then said, "You reckon we oughta do it, Jeff? You reckon we oughta go 'head an' do it, really?"

Jeff's voice choked; his eyes blurred. He was terrified to hear Jennie say the thing that had been in his mind all morning. She had egged him on when he had wanted more than anything in the world to wait, to reconsider, to think things over a little longer. Now she was getting cold feet. Actually, there was no need of thinking the question through again. It would only end in making the same painful decision once more. Jeff knew that. There was no need of fooling around longer.

"We jes as well to do like we planned," he said. "They ain't nothin' else for us now—it's the bes' thing."

Jeff thought of the handicaps, the near impossibility, of making another crop with his leg bothering him more and more each week. Then there was always the chance that he would have another stroke, like the one that had made him lame. Another one might kill him. The least it could do would be to leave him helpless. Jeff gasped—Lord Jesus! He could not bear to think of being helpless, like a baby, on Jennie's hands. Frail, blind Jennie.

The little pounding motor of the car worked harder and harder. The puff of steam from the cracked radiator became larger. Jeff realized that they were climbing a little rise. A moment later the road turned abruptly, and he looked down upon the face of the river.

"Jeff."

"Hunh?"

"Is that the water I hear?"

"Hm. Tha's it."

"Well, which way you goin' now?"

"Down this-a way," he said. "The road runs 'long 'side o' the water a lil piece."

She waited a while calmly. Then she said, "Drive faster."

"A'right, baby," Jeff said.

The water roared in the bed of the river. It was fifty or sixty feet below the level of the road. Between the road and the water there was a long smooth slope, sharply inclined. The slope was dry, the clay hardened by prolonged summer heat. The water below, roaring in a narrow channel, was noisy and wild.

"Jeff."

"Hunh?"

"How far you goin'?"

"Jes a lil piece down the road."

"You ain't scairt, is you, Jeff?"

"Nah, baby," he said trembling. "I ain't scairt."

"Remember how we planned it, Jeff. We gotta do it like we said. Bravelike."

"Hm."

Jeff's brain darkened. Things suddenly seemed unreal, like figures in a dream. Thoughts swam in his mind foolishly, hysterically, like little blind fish in a pool within a dense cave. They rushed again. Jeff soon became dizzy. He shuddered violently and turned to his wife.

"Jennie, I can't do it. I can't." His voice broke pitifully.

She did not appear to be listening. All the grief had gone from her face. She sat erect, her unseeing eyes wide open, strained and frightful. Her glossy black skin had become dull. She seemed as thin, as sharp and bony, as a starved bird. Now, having suffered and endured the sadness of tearing herself away from beloved things, she showed no anguish. She was absorbed with her own thoughts, and she didn't even hear Jeff's voice shouting in her ear.

Jeff said nothing more. For an instant there was light in his cavernous brain. The great chamber was, for less than a second, peopled by characters he knew and loved. They were simple, healthy creatures, and they behaved in a manner that he could understand. They had quality. But since he had already taken leave of them long ago, the remembrance did not break his heart again. Young Jeff Patton was among them, the Jeff Patton of fifty years ago who went down to New Orleans with a crowd of country boys to the Mardi Gras doings. The gay young crowd, boys with candystriped shirts and rouged brown girls in noisy silks, was like a picture in his head. Yet it did not make him sad. On that very trip Slim Burns had killed Joe Beasley — the crowd had been broken up. Since then Jeff Patton's world had been the Greenbriar Plantation. If there had been other Mardi Gras carnivals, he had not heard of them. Since then there had been no time; the years had fallen on him like waves. Now he was old, worn out. Another paralytic stroke (like the one he had already suffered) would put him on his back for keeps. In that condition, with a frail blind woman to look after him, he would be worse off than if he were dead.

Suddenly Jeff's hands became steady. He actually felt brave. He slowed down the motor of the car and carefully pulled off the road. Below, the water of the stream boomed, a soft thunder in the deep channel. Jeff ran the car onto the clay slope, pointed it directly toward the stream, and put his foot heavily on the accelerator. The little car leaped furiously down the steep incline toward the water. The movement was nearly as swift and direct as a fall. The two old black folks, sitting quietly side by side, showed no excitement. In another instant the car hit the water and dropped immediately out of sight.

A little later it lodged in the mud of a shallow place. One wheel of the crushed and upturned little Ford became visible above the rushing water.

(1933)

John Steinbeck 1902-1968

THE CHRYSANTHEMUMS

The high gray-flannel fog of winter closed off the Salinas Valley from the sky and from all the rest of the world. On every side it sat like a lid on the mountains and made of the great valley a closed pot. On the broad, level land floor the gang plows bit deep and left the black earth shining like metal where the shares had cut. On the foothill ranches across the Salinas River, the yellow stubble fields seemed to be bathed in pale cold sunshine, but there was no sunshine in the valley now in December. The thick willow scrub along the river flamed with sharp and positive yellow leaves.

It was a time of quiet and of waiting. The air was cold and tender. A light wind blew up from the southwest so that the farmers were mildly hopeful of a good rain before long; but fog and rain do not go together.

Across the river, on Henry Allen's foothill ranch there was little work to be done, for the hay was cut and stored and the orchards were plowed up to receive the rain deeply when it should come. The cattle on the higher slopes were becoming shaggy and rough-coated.

Elisa Allen, working in her flower garden, looked down across the yard and saw Henry, her husband, talking to two men in business suits. The three of them stood by the tractor shed, each man with one foot on the side of the little Fordson. They smoked cigarettes and studied the machine as they talked.

Elisa watched them for a moment and then went back to her work. She was thirty-five. Her face was lean and strong and her eyes were as clear as water. Her figure looked blocked and heavy in her gardening costume, a man's black hat pulled down over her eyes, clodhopper shoes, a figured print dress almost completely covered by a big corduroy apron with four big pockets to hold the snips, the trowel and scratcher, the seeds and the knife she worked with. She wore heavy leather gloves to protect her hands while she worked.

She was cutting down the old year's chrysanthemum stalks with a pair of short and powerful scissors. She looked down toward the men by the tractor shed now and then. Her face was eager and mature and handsome; even her work with the scissors was over-eager, over-powerful. The chrysanthemum stems seemed too small and easy for her energy.

She brushed a cloud of hair out of her eyes with the back of her glove, and left a smudge of earth on her cheek in doing it. Behind her stood the neat white farm house with red geraniums close-banked around it as high as the windows. It was a hard-swept looking little house, with hard-polished windows, and a clean mud-mat on the front steps.

Elisa cast another glance toward the tractor shed. The strangers were getting into their Ford coupe. She took off a glove and put her strong fingers down into the forest of new green chrysanthemum sprouts that were growing around the old roots. She spread the leaves and looked down among the close-growing stems. No aphids were there, no sowbugs or snails or cutworms. Her terrier fingers destroyed such pests before they could get started.

Elisa started at the sound of her husband's voice. He had come near quietly, and he leaned over the wire fence that protected her flower garden from cattle and dogs and chickens.

"At it again," he said. "You've got a strong new crop coming."

Elisa straightened her back and pulled on the gardening glove again. "Yes. They'll be strong this coming year." In her tone and on her face there was a little smugness.

"You've got a gift with things," Henry observed. "Some of those yellow chrysanthemums you had this year were ten inches across. I wish you'd work out in the orchard and raise some apples that big."

Her eyes sharpened. "Maybe I could do it, too. I've a gift with things, all right. My mother had it. She could stick anything in the ground and make it grow. She said it was having planters' hands that knew how to do it."

"Well, it sure works with flowers," he said.

"Henry, who were those men you were talking to?"

"Why, sure, that's what I came to tell you. They were from the Western Meat Company. I sold them those thirty head of three-year-old steers. Got nearly my own price, too."

"Good," she said. "Good for you."

"And I thought," he continued, "I thought how it's Saturday afternoon, and we might go into Salinas for dinner at a restaurant, and then to a picture show — to celebrate, you see."

"Good," she repeated. "Oh, yes. That will be good."

Henry put on his joking tone. "There's fights tonight. How'd you like to go to the fights?"

"Oh, no," she said breathlessly. "No, I wouldn't like fights."

"Just fooling, Elisa. We'll go to a movie. Let's see. It's two now. I'm going to take Scotty and bring down those steers from the hill. It'll take us maybe two hours. We'll go in town about five and have dinner at the Cominos Hotel. Like that?"

"Of course I'll like it. It's good to eat away from home."

"All right, then. I'll go get up a couple of horses."

She said, "I'll have plenty of time to transplant some of these sets, I guess."

She heard her husband calling Scotty down by the barn. And a little later she saw the two men ride up the pale yellow hillside in search of the steers.

There was a little square sandy bed kept for rooting the chrysanthemums. With her trowel she turned the soil over and over, and smoothed it and patted it firm. Then she dug ten parallel trenches to receive the sets. Back at the chrysanthemum bed she pulled out the little crisp shoots, trimmed off the leaves of each one with her scissors and laid it on a small orderly pile.

A squeak of wheels and plod of hoofs came from the road. Elisa looked up. The country road ran along the dense bank of willows and cottonwoods that bordered the river, and up this road came a curious vehicle, curiously drawn. It was an old spring-wagon, with a round canvas top on it like the cover of a prairie schooner. It was drawn by an old bay horse and a little gray-and-white burro. A big stubble-bearded man sat between the cover flaps and drove the crawling team. Underneath the wagon, between the hind wheels, a lean and rangy mongrel dog walked sedately. Words were painted on the canvas, in clumsy, crooked letters. "Pots, pans, knives, sisors, lawn mores, Fixed." Two rows of articles, and the triumphantly definitive "Fixed" below. The black paint had run down in little sharp points beneath each letter.

Elisa, squatting on the ground, watched to see the crazy, loose-jointed wagon pass by. But it didn't pass. It turned into the farm road in front of her house, crooked old wheels skirling and squeaking. The rangy dog darted from between the wheels and ran ahead. Instantly the two ranch shepherds flew out at him. Then all three stopped and with stiff and quivering tails, with taut straight legs, with ambassadorial dignity, they slowly circled, sniffing daintily. The caravan pulled up to Elisa's wire fence and stopped. Now the newcomer dog, feeling out-numbered, lowered his tail and retired under the wagon with raised hackles and bared teeth.

The man on the wagon seat called out, "That's a bad dog in a fight when he gets started."

Elisa laughed. "I see he is. How soon does he generally get started?"

The man caught up her laughter and echoed it heartily. "Sometimes not for weeks and weeks," he said. He climbed stiffly down, over the wheel. The horse and the donkey drooped like unwatered flowers.

Elisa saw that he was a very big man. Although his hair and beard were graying, he did not look old. His worn black suit was wrinkled and spotted with grease. The laugher had disappeared from his face and eyes the moment his laughing voice ceased. His eyes were dark, and they were full of the brooding that gets in the eyes of teamsters and of sailors. The calloused hands he rested on the wire fence were cracked, and every crack was a black line. He took off his battered hat.

"I'm off my general road, ma'am," he said. "Does this dirt road cut over across the river to the Los Angeles highway?"

Elisa stood up and shoved the thick scissors in her apron pocket. "Well, yes, it does, but it winds around and then fords the river. I don't think your team could pull through the sand."

He replied with some asperity, "It might surprise you what them beasts can pull through."

"When they get started?" she asked.

He smiled for a second. "Yes. When they get started."

"Well," said Elisa, "I think you'll save time if you go back to the Salinas road and pick up the highway there."

He drew a big finger down the chicken wire and made it sing. "I ain't in any hurry, ma'am. I go from Seattle to San Diego and back every year. Takes all my time. About six months each way. I aim to follow nice weather."

Elisa took off her gloves and stuffed them in the apron pocket with the scissors. She touched the under edge of her man's hat, searching for fugitive hairs. "That sounds like a nice kind of way to live," she said.

He leaned confidentially over the fence. "Maybe you noticed the writing on my wagon. I mend pots and sharpen knives and scissors. You got any of them things to do?"

"Oh, no," she said quickly. "Nothing like that." Her eyes hardened with resistance.

"Scissors is the worst thing," he explained. "Most people just ruin scissors trying to sharpen 'em, but I know how. I got a special tool. It's a little bobbit kind of thing, and patented. But it sure does the trick."

"No. My scissors are all sharp."

"All right, then. Take a pot," he continued earnestly, "a bent pot, or a pot with a hole. I can make it like new so you don't have to buy no new ones. That's a saving for you."

"No," she said shortly. "I tell you I have nothing like that for you to do."

His face fell to an exaggerated sadness. His voice took on a whining under-tone. "I ain't had a thing to do today. Maybe I won't have no supper tonight. You see I'm off my regular road. I know folks on the highway clear from Seattle to San Diego. They save their things for me to sharpen up because they know I do it so good and save them money."

"I'm sorry," Elisa said irritably. "I haven't anything for you to do."

His eyes left her face and fell to searching the ground. They roamed about until they came to the chrysanthemum bed where she had been working. "What's them plants, ma'am?"

The irritation and resistance melted from Elisa's face. "Oh, those are chrysan-themums, giant whites and yellows. I raise them every year, bigger than anybody around here."

"Kind of a long-stemmed flower? Looks like a quick puff of colored smoke?" he asked.

"That's it. What a nice way to describe them."

"They smell kind of nasty till you get used to them," he said.

"It's a good bitter smell," she retorted, "not nasty at all."

He changed his tone quickly. "I like the smell myself."

"I had ten-inch blooms this year," she said.

The man leaned farther over the fence. "Look. I know a lady down the road a piece, has got the nicest garden you ever seen. Got nearly every kind of flower but no chrysanthemums. Last time I was mending a copper-bottom washtub for her (that's a hard job but I do it good), she said to me, 'If you ever run acrost some nice chrysanthemums I wish you'd try to get me a few seeds.' That's what she told me."

Elisa's eyes grew alert and eager. "She couldn't have known much about chrysanthemums. You *can* raise them from seed, but it's much easier to root the little sprouts you see there."

"Oh," he said. "I s'pose I can't take none to her, then."

"Why yes you can," Elisa cried. "I can put some in damp sand, and you can carry them right along with you. They'll take root in the pot if you keep them damp. And then she can transplant them."

"She'd sure like to have some, ma'am. You say they're nice ones?"

"Beautiful," she said. "Oh, beautiful." Her eyes shone. She tore off the battered hat and shook out her dark pretty hair. "I'll put them in a flower pot, and you can take them right with you. Come into the yard."

While the man came through the picket gate Elisa ran excitedly along the geranium-bordered path to the back of the house. And she returned carrying a big red flower pot. The gloves were forgotten now. She kneeled on the ground by the starting bed and dug up the sandy soil with her fingers and scooped it into the bright new flower pot. Then she picked up the little pile of shoots she had prepared. With her strong fingers she pressed them into the sand and tamped around them with her knuckles. The man stood over her. "I'll tell you what to do," she said. "You remember so you can tell the lady."

"Yes, I'll try to remember."

"Well, look. These will take root in about a month. Then she must set them out, about a foot apart in good rich earth like this, see?" She lifted a handful of dark soil for him to look at. "They'll grow fast and tall. Now remember this: In July tell her to cut them down, about eight inches from the ground."

"Before they bloom?" he asked.

"Yes, before they bloom." Her face was tight with eagerness. "They'll grow right up again. About the last of September the buds will start."

She stopped and seemed perplexed. "It's the budding that takes the most care," she said hesitantly. "I don't know how to tell you." She looked deep into his eyes, searchingly. Her mouth opened a little, and she seemed to be listening. "I'll try to tell you," she said. "Did you ever hear of planting hands?"

"Can't say I have, ma'am."

"Well, I can only tell you what it feels like. It's when you're picking off the buds you don't want. Everything goes right down into your fingertips. You watch your fingers work. They do it themselves. You can feel how it is. They pick and pick the buds. They never make a mistake. They're with the plant. Do you see? Your fingers and the plant. You can feel that, right up your arm. They know. They never make a mistake. You can feel it. When you're like that you can't do anything wrong. Do you see that? Can you understand that?"

She was kneeling on the ground looking up at him. Her breast swelled passionately.

The man's eyes narrowed. He looked away self-consciously. "Maybe I know," he said. "Sometimes in the night in the wagon there —"

Elisa's voice grew husky. She broke in on him, "I've never lived as you do, but I know what you mean. When the night is dark — why, the stars are sharp-pointed, and there's quiet. Why, you rise up and up! Every pointed star gets driven into your body. It's like that. Hot and sharp and — lovely."

Kneeling there, her hand went out toward his legs in the greasy black trousers. Her hesitant fingers almost touched the cloth. Then her hand dropped to the ground. She crouched low like a fawning dog.

He said, "It's nice, just like you say. Only when you don't have no dinner, it ain't."

She stood up then, very straight, and her face was ashamed. She held the flower pot out to him and placed it gently in his arms. "Here. Put it in your wagon, on the seat, where you can watch it. Maybe I can find something for you to do."

At the back of the house she dug in the can pile and found two old and battered aluminum saucepans. She carried them back and gave them to him. "Here, maybe you can fix these."

His manner changed. He became professional. "Good as new I can fix them." At the back of his wagon he set a little anvil, and out of an oily tool box dug a small machine hammer. Elisa came through the gate to watch him while he pounded out the dents in the kettles. His mouth grew sure and knowing. At a difficult part of the work he sucked his underlip.

"You sleep right in the wagon?" Elisa asked.

"Right in the wagon, ma'am. Rain or shine I'm dry as a cow in there."

"It must be nice," she said. "It must be very nice. I wish women could do such things."

"It ain't the right kind of life for a woman."

Her upper lip raised a little, showing her teeth. "How do you know? How can you tell?" she said.

"I don't know, ma'am," he protested. "Of course I don't know. Now here's your kettles, done. You don't have to buy no new ones."

"How much?"

"Oh, fifty cents'll do. I keep my prices down and my work good. That's why I have all them satisfied customers up and down the highway."

Elisa brought him a fifty-cent piece from the house and dropped it in his hand. "You might be surprised to have a rival some time. I can sharpen scissors, too. And I can beat the dents out of little pots. I could show you what a woman might do."

He put his hammer back in the oily box and shoved the little anvil out of sight. "It would be a lonely life for a woman, ma'am, and a scarey life, too, with animals creeping under the wagon all night." He climbed over the singletree, steadying himself with a hand on the burro's white rump. He settled himself in the seat, picked up the lines. "Thank you kindly, ma'am," he said. "I'll do like you told me; I'll go back and catch the Salinas road."

"Mind," she called, "if you're long in getting there, keep the sand damp."

"Sand, ma'am? . . . Sand? Oh, sure. You mean around the chrysanthemums. Sure I will." He clucked his tongue. The beasts leaned luxuriously into their collars. The mongrel dog took his place between the back wheels. The wagon turned and crawled out the entrance road and back the way it had come, along the river.

Elisa stood in front of her wire fence watching the slow progress of the caravan. Her shoulders were straight, her head thrown back, her eyes half-closed, so that the scene came vaguely into them. Her lips moved silently, forming the words "Good-bye—good-bye." Then she whispered, "That's a bright direction. There's a glowing there." The sound of her whisper startled her. She shook herself free and looked about to see whether anyone had been listening. Only the dogs had heard. They lifted their heads toward her from their sleeping in the dust, and then stretched out their chins and settled asleep again. Elisa turned and ran hurriedly into the house.

In the kitchen she reached behind the stove and felt the water tank. It was full of hot water from the noonday cooking. In the bathroom she tore off her soiled clothes and flung them into the corner. And then she scrubbed herself with a little block of pumice, legs and thighs, loins and chest and arms, until her skin was scratched and red. When she had dried herself she stood in front of a mirror in her bedroom and looked at her body. She tightened her stomach and threw out her chest. She turned and looked over her shoulder at her back.

After a while she began to dress slowly. She put on her newest underclothing and her nicest stockings and the dress which was the symbol of her prettiness. She worked carefully on her hair, penciled her eyebrows and rouged her lips.

Before she was finished she heard the little thunder of hoofs and the shouts of Henry and his helper as they drove the red steers into the corral. She heard the gate bang shut and set herself for Henry's arrival.

His steps sounded on the porch. He entered the house calling, "Elisa, where are you?"

"In my room dressing. I'm not ready. There's hot water for your bath. Hurry up. It's getting late."

When she heard him splashing in the tub, Elisa laid his dark suit on the bed, and shirt and socks and tie beside it. She stood his polished shoes on the floor beside the bed. Then she went to the porch and sat primly and stiffly down. She looked toward the river road where the willow-line was still yellow with frosted leaves so that under the high gray fog they seemed a thin band of sunshine. This was the only color in the gray afternoon. She sat unmoved for a long time. Her eyes blinked rarely.

Henry came banging out of the door, shoving his tie inside his vest as he came. Elisa stiffened and her face grew tight. Henry stopped short and looked at her. "Why — why, Elisa. You look so nice!"

"Nice? You think I look nice? What do you mean by 'nice'?"

Henry blundered on. "I don't know. I mean you look different, strong and happy."

"I am strong? Yes, strong. What do you mean 'strong'?"

He looked bewildered. "You're playing some kind of a game," he said helplessly. "It's a kind of a play. You look strong enough to break a calf over your knee, happy enough to eat it like a watermelon."

For a second she lost her rigidity. "Henry! Don't talk like that. You didn't know what you said." She grew complete again. "I'm strong," she boasted. "I never knew before how strong."

Henry looked down toward the tractor shed, and when he brought his eyes back to her, they were his own again. "I'll get out the car. You can put on your coat while I'm starting."

Elisa went into the house. She heard him drive to the gate and idle down his motor, and then she took a long time to put on her hat. She pulled it here and pressed it there. When Henry turned the motor off she slipped into her coat and went out.

The little roadster bounced along on the dirt road by the river, raising the birds and driving the rabbits into the brush. Two cranes flapped heavily over the willow-line and dropped into the riverbed.

Far ahead on the road Elisa saw a dark speck. She knew.

She tried not to look as they passed it, but her eyes would not obey. She whispered to herself sadly, "He might have thrown them off the road. That wouldn't have been much trouble, not very much. But he kept the pot," she explained. "He had to keep the pot. That's why he couldn't get them off the road."

The roadster turned a bend and she saw the caravan ahead. She swung full around toward her husband so she could not see the little covered wagon and the mismatched team as the car passed them.

In a moment it was over. The thing was done. She did not look back.

She said loudly, to be heard above the motor, "It will be good, tonight, a good dinner."

"Now you're changed again," Henry complained. He took one hand from the wheel and patted her knee. "I ought to take you in to dinner oftener. It would be good for both of us. We get so heavy out on the ranch."

"Henry," she asked, "could we have wine at dinner?"

"Sure we could. Say! That will be fine."

She was silent for a while; then she said, "Henry, at those prize fights, do the men hurt each other very much?"

"Sometimes a little, not often. Why?"

"Well, I've read how they break noses, and blood runs down their chests. I've read how the fighting gloves get heavy and soggy with blood."

He looked around at her. "What's the matter, Elisa? I didn't know you read things like that." He brought the car to a stop, then turned to the right over the Salinas River bridge.

"Do any women ever go to the fights?" she asked.

"Oh, sure, some. What's the matter, Elisa? Do you want to go? I don't think you'd like it, but I'll take you if you really want to go."

She relaxed limply in the seat. "Oh, no. No. I don't want to go. I'm sure I don't." Her face was turned away from him. "It will be enough if we can have wine. It will be plenty." She turned up her coat collar so he could not see that she was crying weakly—like an old woman.

(1937)

Alberto Moravia 1907–1990

THE CHASE

I have never been a sportsman — or, rather, I have been a sportsman only once, and that was the first and last time. I was a child, and one day, for some reason or other, I found myself together with my father, who was holding a gun in his hand, behind a bush, watching a bird that had perched on a branch not very far away. It was a large, gray bird — or perhaps it was brown — with a long — or perhaps a short — beak; I don't remember. I only remember what I felt at that moment as I looked at it. It was like watching an animal whose vitality was rendered more intense by the very fact of my watching it and of the animal's not knowing that I was watching it.

At that moment, I say, the notion of wildness entered my mind, never again to leave it: everything is wild which is autonomous and unpredictable and does not depend upon us. Then all of a sudden there was an explosion; I could no longer see the bird and I thought it had flown away. But my father was leading the way, walking in front of me through the undergrowth. Finally he stooped down, picked up something and put it in my hand. I was aware of something warm and soft and I lowered my eyes: there was the bird in the palm of my hand, its dangling, shattered head crowned with a plume of already-thickening blood. I burst into tears and dropped the corpse on the ground, and that was the end of my shooting experience.

I thought again of this remote episode in my life this very day after watching my wife, for the first and also the last time, as she was walking through the streets of the city. But let us take things in order.

What had my wife been like; what was she like now? She once had been, to put it briefly, "wild" — that is, entirely autonomous and unpredictable; latterly she had become "tame" — that is, predictable and dependent. For a long time she had been like the bird that, on that far-off morning in my childhood, I had seen perching on the bough; latterly, I am sorry to say, she had become like a hen about which one knows everything in advance — how it moves, how it eats, how it lays eggs, how it sleeps, and so on.

Nevertheless I would not wish anyone to think that my wife's wildness consisted of an uncouth, rough, rebellious character. Apart from being extremely beautiful, she is the gentlest, politest, most discreet person in the world. Rather her wildness consisted of the air of charming unpredictability, of independence in her way of living, with which during the first years of our marriage she acted in my presence, both at home and abroad. Wildness signified intimacy, privacy, secrecy. Yes, my wife as she sat in front of her dressing table, her eyes fixed on the looking glass, passing the hairbrush with a repeated motion over her long, loose hair, was just as wild as the solitary quail hopping forward along a sun-filled furrow or the furtive fox coming out into a clearing and stopping to look around before running on. She was wild because I, as I looked at her, could never manage to foresee when she would give a last stroke with the hairbrush and rise and come toward me; wild to such a degree that sometimes when I went into our bedroom the smell of her, floating in the air, would have something of the acrid quality of a wild beast's lair.

Gradually she became less wild, tamer. I had had a fox, a quail, in the house, as I have said; then one day I realized that I had a hen. What effect does a hen have on someone who watches it? It has the effect of being, so to speak, an automaton in the form of a bird; automatic are the brief, rapid steps with which it moves about; automatic its hard, terse pecking; automatic the glance of the round eyes in its head that nods and turns; automatic its ready crouching down under the cock; automatic the dropping of the egg wherever it may be and the cry with which it announces that the egg has been laid. Good-by to the fox; good-by to the quail. And her smell — this no longer brought to my mind, in any way, the innocent odor of a wild animal; rather I detected in it the chemical suavity of some ordinary French perfume.

Our flat is on the first floor of a big building in a modern quarter of the town; our windows look out on a square in which there is a small public garden, the haunt of nurses and children and dogs. One day I was standing at the window, looking in a melancholy way at the garden. My wife, shortly before, had dressed to go out; and once again, watching her, I had noticed the irrevocable and, so to speak, invisible character of her gestures and personality: something which gave one the feeling of a thing already seen and already done and which therefore evaded even the most determined observation. And now, as I stood looking at the garden and at the same time wondering why the adorable wildness of former times had so completely disappeared, suddenly my wife came into my range of vision as she walked quickly across the garden in the direction of the bus stop. I watched her and then I almost jumped for joy; in a movement she was making to pull down a fold of her narrow skirt and smooth it over her thigh with the tips of her long, sharp nails, in this movement I recognized the wildness that in the past had made me love her. It was only an instant, but in that instant I said to myself: She's become wild again because she's convinced that I am not there and am not watching her. Then I left the window and rushed out.

But I did not join her at the bus stop; I felt that I must not allow myself to be seen. Instead I hurried to my car, which was standing nearby, got in and waited. A bus came and she got in together with some other people; the bus started off again and I began following it. Then there came back to me the memory of that one shooting expedition in which I had taken part as a child, and I saw that the bus was the undergrowth with its bushes and trees, my wife the bird perching on the bough while I, unseen, watched it living before my eyes. And the whole town, during this pursuit, became, as though by magic, a fact of nature like the countryside: the houses were hills, the streets valleys, the vehicles hedges and woods, and even the passers-by on the pavements had something unpredictable and autonomous — that is, wild — about them. And in my mouth, behind my clenched teeth, there was the acrid, metallic taste of gunfire; and my eyes, usually listless and wandering, had become sharp, watchful, attentive.

These eyes were fixed intently upon the exit door when the bus came to the end of its run. A number of people got out, and then I saw my wife getting out. Once again I recognized, in the manner in which she broke free of the crowd and started off toward a neighboring street, the wildness that pleased me so much. I jumped out of the car and started following her.

She was walking in front of me, ignorant of my presence, a tall woman with an elegant figure, long-legged, narrow-hipped, broad-backed, her brown hair falling on her shoulders.

Men turned around as she went past; perhaps they were aware of what I myself was now sensing with an intensity that quickened the beating of my heart and took my breath away: the unrestricted, steadily increasing, irresistible character of her mysterious wildness.

She walked hurriedly, having evidently some purpose in view, and even the fact that she had a purpose of which I was ignorant added to her wildness; I did not know where she was going, just as on that far-off morning I had not known what the bird perching on the bough was about to do. Moreover I thought the gradual, steady increase in this quality of wildness came partly from the fact that as she drew nearer to the object of this mysterious walk there was an increase in her—how shall I express it?—of biological tension, of existential excitement, of vital effervescence. Then, unexpectedly, with the suddenness of a film, her purpose was revealed.

A fair-haired young man in a leather jacket and a pair of corduroy trousers was leaning against the wall of a house in that ancient, narrow street. He was idly smoking as he looked in front of him. But as my wife passed close to him, he threw away his cigarette with a decisive gesture, took a step forward and seized her arm. I was expecting her to rebuff him, to move away from him, but nothing happened: evidently obeying the rules of some kind of erotic ritual, she went on walking beside the young man. Then after a few steps, with a movement that confirmed her own complicity, she put her arm around her companion's waist and he put his around her.

I understood then that this unknown man who took such liberties with my wife was also attracted by wildness. And so, instead of making a conventional appointment with her, instead of meeting in a café with a handshake, a falsely friendly and respectful welcome, he had preferred, by agreement with her, to take her by surprise—or, rather, to pretend to do so—while she was apparently taking a walk on her own account. All this I perceived by intuition, noticing that at the very moment when he stepped forward and took her arm her wildness had, so to speak, given an upward bound. It was years since I had seen my wife so alive, but alas, the source of this life could not be traced to me.

They walked on thus entwined and then, without any preliminaries, just like two wild animals, they did an unexpected thing: they went into one of the dark doorways in order to kiss. I stopped and watched them from a distance, peering into the darkness of the entrance. My wife was turned away from me and was bending back with the pressure of his body, her hair hanging free. I looked at that long, thick mane of brown hair, which as she leaned back fell free of her shoulders, and I felt at that moment her vitality reached its diapason, just as happens with wild animals when they couple and their customary wildness is redoubled by the violence of love. I watched for a long time and then, since this kiss went on and on and in fact seemed to be prolonged beyond the limits of my power of endurance, I saw that I would have to intervene.

I would have to go forward, seize my wife by the arm—or actually by that hair, which hung down and conveyed so well the feeling of feminine passivity —then hurl myself with clenched fists upon the blond young man. After this encounter I would carry off my wife, weeping, mortified, ashamed, while I was raging and broken-hearted, upbraiding her and pouring scorn upon her.

But what else would this intervention amount to but the shot my father fired at that free, unknowing bird as it perched on the bough? The disorder and confusion, the mortification, the shame, that would follow would irreparably destroy the rare and precious moment of wildness that I was witnessing inside the dark doorway. It was true that this wildness was directed against me; but I had to remember that wildness, always and everywhere, is directed against everything and everybody. After the scene of my intervention it might be possible for me to regain control of my wife, but I should find her shattered and lifeless in my arms like the bird that my father placed in my hand so that I might throw it into the shooting bag.

The kiss went on and on: well, it was a kiss of passion — that could not be denied. I waited until they finished, until they came out of the doorway, until they walked on again still linked together. Then I turned back.

(1969)

Translated by Angus Davidson

Richard Wright *1908–1960*

THE MAN WHO WAS ALMOST A MAN

Dave struck out across the fields, looking homeward through paling light. Whut's the use of talkin wid em niggers in the field? Anyhow, his mother was putting supper on the table. Them niggers can't understan nothing. One of these days he was going to get a gun and practice shooting, then they couldn't talk to him as though he were a little boy. He slowed, looking at the ground. Shucks, Ah ain scareda them even ef they are biggern me! Aw, Ah know whut Ahma do. Ahm going by ol Joe's sto n git that Sears Roebuck catlog n look at them guns. Mebbe Ma will lemme buy one when she gits mah pay from ol man Hawkins. Ahma beg her t gimme some money. Ahm ol ernough to hava gun. Ahm seventeen. Almost a man. He strode, feeling his long loose-jointed limbs. Shucks, a man oughta hava little gun aftah he done worked hard all day.

He came in sight of Joe's store. A yellow lantern glowed on the front porch. He mounted steps and went through the screen door, hearing it bang behind him. There was a strong smell of coal oil and mackerel fish. He felt very confident until he saw fat Joe walk in through the rear door, then his courage began to ooze.

"Howdy, Dave! Whutcha want?"

"How yuh, Mistah Joe? Aw, Ah don wanna buy nothing. Ah jus wanted t see ef yuhd lemme look at tha catlog erwhile."

"Sure! You wanna see it here?"

"Nawsuh. Ah wans t take it home wid me. Ah'll bring it back termorrow when Ah come in from the fiels."

"You plannin on buying something?"

"Yessuh."

"Your ma lettin you have your own money now?"

"Shucks. Mistah Joe, Ahm gittin t be a man like anybody else!"

Joe laughed and wiped his greasy white face with a red bandanna.

"Whut you plannin on buyin?"

Dave looked at the floor, scratched his head, scratched his thigh, and smiled. Then he looked up shyly.

"Ah'll tell yuh, Mistah Joe, ef yuh promise yuh won't tell."

"I promise."

"Waal, Ahma buy a gun."

"A gun? Whut you want with a gun?"

"Ah wanna keep it."

"You ain't nothing but a boy. You don't need a gun."

"Aw, lemme have the catlog, Mistah Joe. Ah'll bring it back."

Joe walked through the rear door. Dave was elated. He looked around at barrels of sugar and flour. He heard Joe coming back. He craned his neck to see if he were bringing the book. Yeah, he's got it. Gawddog, he's got it!

"Here, but be sure you bring it back. It's the only one I got."

"Sho, Mistah Joe."

"Say, if you wanna buy a gun, why don't you buy one from me? I gotta gun to sell."

"Will it shoot?"

"Sure it'll shoot."

"Whut kind is it?"

"Oh, it's kinda old . . . a left-hand Wheeler. A pistol. A big one."

"Is it got bullets in it?"

"It's loaded."

"Kin Ah see it?"

"Where's your money?"

"Whut yuh wan fer it?"

"I'll let you have it for two dollars."

"Just two dollahs? Shucks, Ah could buy tha when Ah git mah pay."

"I'll have it here when you want it."

"Awright, suh. Ah be in fer it."

He went through the door, hearing a slam again behind him. Ahma git some money from Ma n buy me a gun! Only two dollahs! He tucked the thick catalogue under his arm and hurried.

"Where yuh been, boy?" His mother held a steaming dish of black-eyed peas.

"Aw, Ma, Ah jus stopped down the road t talk wid the boys."

"Yuh know bettah t keep suppah waitin."

He sat down, resting the catalogue on the edge of the table.

"Yuh git up from there and git to the well n wash yoself! Ah ain feedin no hogs in mah house!"

She grabbed his shoulder and pushed him. He stumbled out of the room, then came back to get the catalogue.

"Whut this?"

"Aw, Ma, it's jusa catlog."

"Who yuh git it from?"

"From Joe, down at the sto."

"Waal, thas good. We kin use it in the outhouse."

"Naw, Ma." He grabbed for it. "Gimme ma catlog, Ma."

She held onto it and glared at him.

"Quit hollerin at me! Whut's wrong wid yuh? Yuh crazy?"

"But Ma, please. It ain mine! It's Joe's! He tol me t bring it back t im termorrow."

She gave up the book. He stumbled down the back steps, hugging the thick book under his arm. When he had splashed water on his face and hands, he groped back to the kitchen and fumbled in a corner for the towel. He bumped into a chair; it clattered to the floor. The catalogue sprawled at his feet. When he had dried his eyes he snatched up the book and held it again under his arm. His mother stood watching him.

"Now, ef yuh gonna act a fool over that ol book, Ah'll take it n burn it up."

"Naw, Ma, please."

"Waal, set down n be still!"

He sat down and drew the oil lamp close. He thumbed page after page, unaware of the food his mother set on the table. His father came in. Then his small brother.

"Whutcha got there, Dave?" his father asked.

"Jusa catlog," he answered, not looking up.

"Yeah, here they is!" His eyes glowed at blue-and-black revolvers. He glanced up, feeling sudden guilt. His father was watching him. He eased the book under the table and rested it on his knees. After the blessing was asked, he ate. He scooped up peas and swallowed fat meat without chewing. Buttermilk helped to wash it down. He did not want to mention money before his father. He would do much better by cornering his mother when she was alone. He looked at his father uneasily out of the edge of his eye.

"Boy, how come yuh don quit foolin wid tha book n eat yo suppah?"

"Yessuh."

"How you n ol man Hawkins gitten erlong?"

"Suh?"

"Can't yuh hear? Why don yuh lissen? Ah ast yu how wuz yuh n ol man Hawkins gittin erlong?"

"Oh, swell, Pa. Ah plows mo lan than anybody over there."

"Waal, yuh oughta keep yo mind on whut yuh doin."

"Yessuh."

He poured his plate full of molasses and sopped it up slowly with a chunk of cornbread. When his father and brother had left the kitchen, he still sat and looked again at the guns in the catalogue, longing to muster courage enough to present his case to his mother. Lawd, ef Ah only had tha pretty one! He could almost feel the slickness of the weapon with his fingers. If he had a gun like that he would polish it and keep it shining so it would never rust. N Ah'd keep it loaded, by Gawd!

"Ma?" His voice was hesitant.

"Hunh?"

"Ol man Hawkins give yuh mah money yit?"

"Yeah, but ain no usa yuh thinking bout throwin nona it erway. Ahm keepin tha money sos yuh kin have cloes t go to school this winter."

He rose and went to her side with the open catalogue in his palms. She was washing dishes, her head bent low over a pan. Shyly he raised the book. When he spoke, his voice was husky, faint.

"Ma, Gawd knows Ah wans one of these."

"One of whut?" she asked, not raising her eyes.

"One of these," he said again, not daring even to point. She glanced up at the page, then at him with wide eyes.

"Nigger, is yuh gone plumb crazy?"

"Aw, Ma—"

"Git outta here! Don yuh talk t me bout no gun! Yuh a fool!"

"Ma, Ah kin buy one fer two dollahs."

"Not ef Ah knows it, yuh ain!"

"But yuh promised me one—"

"Ah don care whut Ah promised! Yuh ain nothing but a boy yit!"

"Ma, ef yuh lemme buy one Ah'll *never* ast yuh fer nothing no mo."

"Ah tol yuh t git outta here! Yuh ain gonna toucha penny of tha money fer no gun! Thas how come Ah has Mistah Hawkins t pay yo wages t me, cause Ah knows yuh ain got no sense."

"But, Ma, we needa gun. Pa ain got no gun. We needa gun in the house. Yuh kin never tell whut might happen."

"Now don yuh try to maka fool outta me, boy! Ef we did hava gun, yuh wouldn't have it!"

He laid the catalogue down and slipped his arm around her waist.

"Aw, Ma, Ah done worked hard alla summer n ain ast yuh fer nothin, is Ah, now?"

"Thas whut yuh spose t do!"

"But Ma, Ah wans a gun. Yuh kin lemme have two dollahs outta mah money. Please, Ma. I kin give it to Pa. . . . Please, Ma! Ah loves yuh, Ma."

When she spoke her voice came soft and low.

"Whut yu wan wida gun, Dave? Yuh don need no gun. Yuh'll git in trouble. N ef yo pa jus thought Ah let yuh have money t buy a gun he'd hava fit."

"Ah'll hide it, Ma. It ain but two dollahs."

"Lawd, chil, whut's wrong wid yuh?"

"Ain nothin wrong, Ma. Ahm almos a man now. Ah wans a gun."

"Who gonna sell yuh a gun?"

"Ol Joe at the sto."

"N it don cos but two dollahs?"

"Thas all, Ma. Jus two dollahs. Please, Ma."

She was stacking the plates away; her hands moved slowly, reflectively. Dave kept an anxious silence. Finally, she turned to him.

"Ah'll let yuh git tha gun ef yuh promise me one thing."

"Whut's tha, Ma?"

"Yuh bring it straight back t me, yuh hear? It be fer Pa."

"Yessum! Lemme go now, Ma."

She stopped, turned slightly to one side, raised the hem of her dress, rolled down the top of her stocking, and came up with a slender wad of bills.

"Here," she said. "Lawd knows yuh don need no gun. But yer pa does. Yuh bring it right back t me, yuh hear? Ahma put it up. Now ef yuh don, Ahma have yuh pa lick yuh so hard yuh won fergit it."

"Yessum."

He took the money, ran down the steps, and across the yard.

"Dave! Yuuuuuh Daaaaave!"

He heard, but he was not going to stop now. "Naw, Lawd!"

The first movement he made the following morning was to reach under his pillow for the gun. In the gray light of dawn he held it loosely, feeling a sense of power. Could kill a man with a gun like this. Kill anybody, black or white. And if he were holding his gun in his hand, nobody could run over him; they would have to respect him. It was a big gun, with a long barrel and a heavy handle. He raised and lowered it in his hand, marveling at its weight.

He had not come straight home with it as his mother had asked; instead he had stayed out in the fields, holding the weapon in his hand, aiming it now and then at some imaginary foe. But he had not fired it; he had been afraid that his father might hear. Also he was not sure he knew how to fire it.

To avoid surrendering the pistol he had not come into the house until he knew that they were all asleep. When his mother had tiptoed to his bedside late that night and demanded the gun, he had first played possum; then he had told her that the gun was hidden outdoors, that he would bring it to her in the morning. Now he lay turning it slowly in his hands. He broke it, took out the cartridges, felt them, and then put them back.

He slid out of bed, got a long strip of old flannel from a trunk, wrapped the gun in it, and tied it to his naked thigh while it was still loaded. He did not go in

to breakfast. Even though it was not yet daylight, he started for Jim Hawkins'
plantation. Just as the sun was rising he reached the barns where the mules and
plows were kept.

"Hey! That you, Dave?"

He turned. Jim Hawkins stood eying him suspiciously.

"What're yuh doing here so early?"

"Ah didn't know Ah wuz gittin up so early, Mistah Hawkins. Ah wuz fixin t
hitch up ol Jenny n take her t the fiels."

"Good. Since you're so early, how about plowing that stretch down by the
woods?"

"Suits me, Mistah Hawkins."

"O.K. Go to it!"

He hitched Jenny to a plow and started across the fields. Hot dog! This was
just what he wanted. If he could get down by the woods, he could shoot his gun
and nobody would hear. He walked behind the plow, hearing the traces creaking,
feeling the gun tied tight to his thigh.

When he reached the woods, he plowed two whole rows before he decided to
take out the gun. Finally, he stopped, looked in all directions, then untied the gun
and held it in his hand. He turned to the mule and smiled.

"Know whut this is, Jenny? Naw, yuh wouldn know! Yuhs jusa ol mule!
Anyhow, this is a gun, n it kin shoot, by Gawd!"

He held the gun at arm's length. Whut t hell, Ahma shoot this thing! He
looked at Jenny again.

"Lissen here, Jenny! When Ah pull this ol trigger, Ah don wan yuh t run n
acka fool now!"

Jenny stood with head down, her short ears pricked straight. Dave walked off
about twenty feet, held the gun far out from him at arm's length, and turned his
head. Hell, he told himself, Ah ain afraid. The gun felt loose in his fingers; he
waved it wildly for a moment. Then he shut his eyes and tightened his forefinger. Bloom! A report half deafened him and he thought his right hand was torn
from his arm. He heard Jenny whinnying and galloping over the field, and he
found himself on his knees, squeezing his fingers hard between his legs. His
hand was numb; he jammed it into his mouth, trying to warm it, trying to stop
the pain. The gun lay at his feet. He did not quite know what had happened. He
stood up and stared at the gun as though it were a living thing. He gritted his
teeth and kicked the gun. Yuh almos broke mah arm! He turned to look for
Jenny; she was far over the fields, tossing her head and kicking wildly.

"Hol on there, ol mule!"

When he caught up with her she stood trembling, walling her big white eyes
at him. The plow was far away; the traces had broken. Then Dave stopped short,
looking, not believing. Jenny was bleeding. Her left side was red and wet with
blood. He went closer. Lawd, have mercy! Wondah did Ah shoot this mule? He
grabbed for Jenny's mane. She flinched, snorted, whirled, tossing her head.

"Hol on now! Hol on."

Then he saw the hole in Jenny's side, right between the ribs. It was round,
wet, red. A crimson stream streaked down the front leg, flowing fast. Good
Gawd! Ah wuzn't shootin at tha mule. He felt panic. He knew he had to stop that
blood, or Jenny would bleed to death. He had never seen so much blood in all his
life. He chased the mule for half a mile, trying to catch her. Finally she stopped,
breathing hard, stumpy tail half arched. He caught her mane and led her back to

where the plow and gun lay. Then he stooped and grabbed handfuls of damp black earth and tried to plug the bullet hole. Jenny shuddered, whinnied, and broke from him.

"Hol on! Hol on now!"

He tried to plug it again, but blood came anyhow. His fingers were hot and sticky. He rubbed dirt into his palms, trying to dry them. Then again he attempted to plug the bullet hole, but Jenny shied away, kicking her heels high. He stood helpless. He had to do something. He ran at Jenny; she dodged him. He watched a red stream of blood flow down Jenny's leg and form a bright pool at her feet.

"Jenny . . . Jenny," he called weakly.

His lips trembled. She's bleeding t death! He looked in the direction of home, wanting to go back, wanting to get help. But he saw the pistol lying in the damp black clay. He had a queer feeling that if he only did something, this would not be; Jenny would not be there bleeding to death.

When he went to her this time, she did not move. She stood with sleepy, dreamy eyes; and when he touched her she gave a low-pitched whinny and knelt to the ground, her front knees slopping in blood.

"Jenny . . . Jenny . . . " he whispered.

For a long time she held her neck erect; then her head sank, slowly. Her ribs swelled with a mighty heave and she went over.

Dave's stomach felt empty, very empty. He picked up the gun and held it gingerly between his thumb and forefinger. He buried it at the foot of a tree. He took a stick and tried to cover the pool of blood with dirt — but what was the use? There was Jenny lying with her mouth open and her eyes walled and glassy. He could not tell Jim Hawkins he had shot his mule. But he had to tell something. Yeah, Ah'll tell em Jenny started gittin wil n fell on the joint of the plow. . . . But that would hardly happen to a mule. He walked across the field slowly, head down.

It was sunset. Two of Jim Hawkins' men were over near the edge of the woods digging a hole in which to bury Jenny. Dave was surrounded by a knot of people, all of whom were looking down at the dead mule.

"I don't see how in the world it happened," said Jim Hawkins for the tenth time.

The crowd parted and Dave's mother, father, and small brother pushed into the center.

"Where Dave?" his mother called.

"There he is," said Jim Hawkins.

His mother grabbed him.

"Whut happened, Dave? Whut yuh done?"

"Nothin."

"C'mon, boy, talk," his father said.

Dave took a deep breath and told the story he knew nobody believed.

"Waal," he drawled. "Ah brung ol Jenny down here sos Ah could do mah plowin. Ah plowed bout two rows, just like yuh see." He stopped and pointed at the long rows of upturned earth. "Then somethin musta been wrong wid ol Jenny. She wouldn ack right a-tall. She started snortin n kickin her heels. Ah tried t hol her, but she pulled erway, rearin n goin in. Then when the point of the plow was stickin up in the air, she swung erroun n twisted herself back on it. . . . She stuck herself n started t bleed. N fo Ah could do anything, she wuz dead."

"Did you ever hear of anything like that in all your life?" asked Jim Hawkins.

There were white and black standing in the crowd. They murmured. Dave's mother came close to him and looked hard into his face. "Tell the truth, Dave," she said.

"Looks like a bullet hole to me," said one man.

"Dave, whut yuh do wid the gun?" his mother asked.

The crowd surged in, looking at him. He jammed his hands into his pockets, shook his head slowly from left to right, and backed away. His eyes were wide and painful.

"Did he hava gun?" asked Jim Hawkins.

"By Gawd, Ah tol yuh tha wuz a gun wound," said a man, slapping his thigh.

His father caught his shoulders and shook him till his teeth rattled.

"Tell whut happened, yuh rascal! Tell whut . . . "

Dave looked at Jenny's stiff legs and began to cry.

"Whut yuh do wid tha gun?" his mother asked.

"Whut wuz he doin wida gun?" his father asked.

"Come on and tell the truth," said Hawkins. "Ain't nobody going to hurt you. . . . "

His mother crowded close to him.

"Did yuh shoot tha mule, Dave?"

Dave cried, seeing blurred white and black faces.

"Ahh ddinn gggo tt sshooot hher. . . . Ah ssswear ffo Gawd Ahh ddin. . . . Ah wuz a-tryin t sssee ef the old gggun would sshoot—"

"Where yuh git the gun from?" his father asked.

"Ah got it from Joe, at the sto."

"Where yuh git the money?"

"Ma give it t me."

"He kept worryin me, Bob. Ah had t. Ah tol im t bring the gun right back t me. . . . It was fer yuh, the gun."

"But how yuh happen to shoot that mule?" asked Jim Hawkins.

"Ah wuzn shootin at the mule, Mistah Hawkins. The gun jumped when Ah pulled the trigger. . . . N fo Ah knowed anythin Jenny was there a-bleedin."

Somebody in the crowd laughed. Jim Hawkins walked close to Dave and looked into his face.

"Well, looks like you have bought you a mule, Dave."

"Ah swear fo Gawd, Ah didn go t kill the mule, Mistah Hawkins!"

"But you killed her!"

All the crowd was laughing now. They stood on tiptoe and poked heads over one another's shoulders.

"Well, boy, looks like yuh done bought a dead mule! Hahaha!"

"Ain tha ershame."

"Hohohohoho."

Dave stood, head down, twisting his feet in the dirt.

"Well, you needn't worry about it, Bob," said Jim Hawkins to Dave's father. "Just let the boy keep on working and pay me two dollars a month."

"Whut yuh wan fer yo mule, Mistah Hawkins?"

Jim Hawkins screwed up his eyes.

"Fifty dollars."

"Whut yuh do wid tha gun?" Dave's father demanded.

Dave said nothing.

"Yuh wan me t take a tree n beat yuh till yuh talk!"

"Nawsuh!"

"Whut yuh do wid it?"

"Ah throwed it erway."

"Where?"

"Ah . . . Ah throwed it in the creek."

"Waal, c'mon home. N firs thing in the mawnin git to tha creek n fin tha gun."

"Yessuh."

"Whut yuh pay fer it?"

"Two dollahs."

"Take tha gun n git yo money back n carry it t Mistah Hawkins, yuh hear? N don fergit Ahma lam you black bottom good fer this! Now march yosef on home, suh!"

Dave turned and walked slowly. He heard people laughing. Dave glared, his eyes welling with tears. Hot anger bubbled in him. Then he swallowed and stumbled on.

That night Dave did not sleep. He was glad that he had gotten out of killing the mule so easily, but he was hurt. Something hot seemed to turn over inside him each time he remembered how they had laughed. He tossed on his bed, feeling his hard pillow. N Pa says he's gonna beat me. . . . He remembered other beatings, and his back quivered. Naw, naw, Ah sho don wan im t beat me tha way no mo. Dam em all! Nobody ever gave him anything. All he did was work. They treat me like a mule, n then they beat me. He gritted his teeth. N Ma had t tell on me.

Well, if he had to, he would take old man Hawkins that two dollars. But that meant selling the gun. And he wanted to keep that gun. Fifty dollars for a dead mule.

He turned over, thinking how he had fired the gun. He had an itch to fire it again. Ef other men kin shoota gun, by Gawd, Ah kin! He was still, listening. Mebbe they all sleepin now. The house was still. He heard the soft breathing of his brother. Yes, now! He would go down and get that gun and see if he could fire it! He eased out of bed and slipped into overalls.

The moon was bright. He ran almost all the way to the edge of the woods. He stumbled over the ground, looking for the spot where he had buried the gun. Yeah, here it is. Like a hungry dog scratching for a bone, he pawed it up. He puffed his black cheeks and blew dirt from the trigger and barrel. He broke it and found four cartridges unshot. He looked around; the fields were filled with silence and moonlight. He clutched the gun stiff and hard in his fingers. But, as soon as he wanted to pull the trigger, he shut his eyes and turned his head. Naw, Ah can't shoot wid mah eyes closed n mah head turned. With effort he held his eyes open; then he squeezed. *Blooooom!* He was stiff, not breathing. The gun was still in his hands. Dammit, he'd done it! He fired again. *Blooooom!* He smiled. *Blooooom! Blooooom! Click, click.* There! It was empty. If anybody could shoot a gun, he could. He put the gun into his hip pocket and started across the fields.

When he reached the top of a ridge he stood straight and proud in the moonlight, looking at Jim Hawkins' big white house, feeling the gun sagging in his pocket. Lawd, ef Ah had just one mo bullet Ah'd taka shot at tha house. Ah'd

like t scare ol man Hawkins jusa little. . . . Jusa enough t let im know Dave
Saunders is a man.

To his left the road curved, running to the tracks of the Illinois Central. He
jerked his head, listening. From far off came a faint *hoooof-hoooof; hoooof-hoooof;
hoooof-hoooof.* . . . He stood rigid. Two dollahs a mont. Les see now. . . . Tha
means it'll take bout two years. Shucks! Ah'll be dam!

He started down the road, toward the tracks. Yeah, here she comes! He stood
beside the track and held himself stiffly. Here she comes, erroun the ben. . . . C
mon, yuh slow poke! C mon! He had his hand on his gun; something quivered in
his stomach. Then the train thundered past, the gray and brown box cars
rumbling and clinking. He gripped the gun tightly; then he jerked his hand out of
his pocket. Ah betcha Bill wouldn't do it! Ah betcha. . . . The cars slid past,
steel grinding upon steel. Ahm ridin yuh ternight, so hep me Gawd! He was hot
all over. He hesitated just a moment; then he grabbed, pulled atop of a car, and
lay flat. He felt his pocket; the gun was still there. Ahead the long rails were
glinting in the moonlight, stretching away, away to somewhere, somewhere
where he could be a man. . . .

                                                                        (1940)

Eudora Welty *1909–*

A WORN PATH

It was December—a bright frozen day in the early morning. Far out in the country there was an old Negro woman with her head tied in a red rag, coming along a path through the pinewoods. Her name was Phoenix Jackson. She was very old and small and she walked slowly in the dark pine shadows, moving a little from side to side in her steps, with the balanced heaviness and lightness of a pendulum in a grandfather clock. She carried a thin, small cane made from an umbrella, and with this she kept tapping the frozen earth in front of her. This made a grave and persistent noise in the still air, that seemed meditative like the chirping of a solitary little bird.

She wore a dark striped dress reaching down to her shoe tops, and an equally long apron of bleached sugar sacks, with a full pocket: all neat and tidy, but every time she took a step she might have fallen over her shoelaces, which dragged from her unlaced shoes. She looked straight ahead. Her eyes were blue with age. Her skin had a pattern all its own of numberless branching wrinkles and as though a whole little tree stood in the middle of her forehead, but a golden color ran underneath, and the two knobs of her cheeks were illumined by a yellow burning under the dark. Under the red rag her hair came down on her neck in the frailest of ringlets, still black, and with an odor like copper.

Now and then there was a quivering in the thicket. Old Phoenix said, "Out of my way, all you foxes, owls, beetles, jack rabbits, coons and wild animals! . . . Keep out from under these feet, little bob-whites. . . . Keep the big wild hogs out of my path. Don't let none of those come running my direction. I got a long way." Under her small black-freckled hand her cane, limber as a buggy whip, would switch at the brush as if to rouse up any hiding things.

On she went. The woods were deep and still. The sun made the pine needles almost too bright to look at, up where the wind rocked. The cones dropped as light as feathers. Down in the hollow was the mourning dove—it was not too late for him.

The path ran up a hill. "Seem like there is chains about my feet, time I get this far," she said, in the voice of argument old people keep to use with themselves. "Something always take a hold of me on this hill—pleads I should stay."

After she got to the top she turned and gave a full, severe look behind her where she had come. "Up through pines," she said at length. "Now down through oaks."

Her eyes opened their widest, and she started down gently. But before she got to the bottom of the hill a bush caught her dress.

Her fingers were busy and intent, but her skirts were full and long, so that before she could pull them free in one place they were caught in another. It was not possible to allow the dress to tear. "I in the thorny bush," she said. "Thorns, you doing your appointed work. Never want to let folks pass, no sir. Old eyes thought you was a pretty little *green* bush."

Finally, trembling all over, she stood free, and after a moment dared to stoop for her cane.

"Sun so high!" she cried, leaning back and looking, while the thick tears went over her eyes. "The time getting all gone here."

At the foot of this hill was a place where a log was laid across the creek. "Now comes the trial," said Phoenix.

Putting her right foot out, she mounted the log and shut her eyes. Lifting her skirt, leveling her cane fiercely before her, like a festival figure in some parade, she began to march across. Then she opened her eyes and she was safe on the other side.

"I wasn't as old as I thought," she said.

But she sat down to rest. She spread her skirts on the bank around her and folded her hands over her knees. Up above her was a tree in a pearly cloud of mistletoe. She did not dare to close her eyes, and when a little boy brought her a plate with a slice of marble-cake on it she spoke to him. "That would be acceptable," she said. But when she went to take it there was just her own hand in the air.

So she left that tree, and had to go through a barbed-wire fence. There she had to creep and crawl, spreading her knees and stretching her fingers like a baby trying to climb the steps. But she talked loudly to herself: she could not let her dress be torn now, so late in the day, and she could not pay for having her arm or her leg sawed off if she got caught fast where she was.

At last she was safe through the fence and risen up out in the clearing. Big dead trees, like black men with one arm, were standing in the purple stalks of the withered cotton field. There sat a buzzard.

"Who you watching?"

In the furrow she made her way along.

"Glad this not the season for bulls," she said, looking sideways, "and the good Lord made his snakes to curl up and sleep in the winter. A pleasure I don't see no two-headed snake coming around that tree, where it come once. It took a while to get by him, back in the summer."

She passed through the old cotton and went into a field of dead corn. It whispered and shook and was taller than her head. "Through the maze now," she said, for there was no path.

Then there was something tall, black, and skinny there, moving before her.

At first she took it for a man. It could have been a man dancing in the field. But she stood still and listened, and it did not make a sound. It was as silent as a ghost.

"Ghost," she said sharply, "who be you the ghost of? For I have heard of nary death close by."

But there was no answer—only the ragged dancing in the wind.

She shut her eyes, reached out her hand, and touched a sleeve. She found a coat and inside that an emptiness, cold as ice.

"You scarecrow," she said. Her face lighted. "I ought to be shut up for good," she said with laughter. "My senses is gone. I too old. I the oldest people I ever know. Dance, old scarecrow," she said, "while I dancing with you."

She kicked her foot over the furrow and, with mouth drawn down, shook her head once or twice in a little strutting way. Some husks blew down and whirled in streamers about her skirts.

Then she went on, parting her way from side to side with the cane, through the whispering field. At last she came to the end, to a wagon track where the silver grass blew between the red ruts. The quail were walking around like pullets, seeming all dainty and unseen.

"Walk pretty," she said. "This the easy place. This the easy going."

She followed the track, swaying through the quiet bare fields, through the little strings of trees silver in their dead leaves, past cabins silver from weather, with the doors and windows boarded shut, all like old women under a spell sitting there. "I walking in their sleep," she said, nodding her head vigorously.

In a ravine she went where a spring was silently flowing through a hollow log. Old Phoenix bent and drank. "Sweet-gum makes the water sweet," she said, and drank more. "Nobody know who made this well, for it was here when I was born."

The track crossed a swampy part where the moss hung as white as lace from every limb. "Sleep on, alligators, and blow your bubbles." Then the track went into the road.

Deep, deep the road went down between the high green-colored banks. Overhead the live-oaks met, and it was as dark as a cave.

A black dog with a lolling tongue came up out of the weeds by the ditch. She was meditating, and not ready, and when he came at her she only hit him a little with her cane. Over she went in the ditch, like a little puff of milkweed.

Down there, her senses drifted away. A dream visited her, and she reached her hand up, but nothing reached down and gave her a pull. So she lay there and presently went to talking. "Old woman," she said to herself, "that black dog come up out of the weeds to stall you off, and now there he sitting on his fine tail, smiling at you."

A white man finally came along and found her — a hunter, a young man, with his dog on a chain.

"Well, Granny!" he laughed. "What are you doing there?"

"Lying on my back like a June-bug waiting to be turned over, mister," she said, reaching up her hand.

He lifted her up, gave her a swing in the air, and set her down. "Anything broken, Granny?"

"No sir, them old dead weeds is springy enough," said Phoenix, when she had got her breath. "I thank you for your trouble."

"Where do you live, Granny?" he asked, while the two dogs were growling at each other.

"Away back yonder, sir, behind the ridge. You can't even see it from here."

"On your way home?"

"No sir, I going to town."

"Why, that's too far! That's as far as I walk when I come out myself, and I get something for my trouble." He patted the stuffed bag he carried, and there hung down a little closed claw. It was one of the bob-whites, with its beak hooked bitterly to show it was dead. "Now you go on home, Granny!"

"I bound to go to town, mister," said Phoenix. "The time come around."

He gave another laugh, filling the whole landscape. "I know you old colored people! Wouldn't miss going to town to see Santa Claus!"

But something held old Phoenix very still. The deep lines in her face went into a fierce and different radiation. Without warning, she had seen with her own eyes a flashing nickel fall out of the man's pocket onto the ground.

"How old are you, Granny?" he was saying.

"There is no telling, mister," she said, "no telling."

Then she gave a little cry and clapped her hands and said, "Git on away from here, dog! Look! Look at that dog!" She laughed as if in admiration. "He ain't scared of nobody. He a big black dog." She whispered, "Sic him!"

"Watch me get rid of that cur," said the man. "Sic him, Pete! Sic him!"

Phoenix heard the dogs fighting, and heard the man running and throwing sticks. She even heard a gunshot. But she was slowly bending forward by that time, further and further forward, the lids stretched down over her eyes, as if she were doing this in her sleep. Her chin was lowered almost to her knees. The yellow palm of her hand came out from the fold of her apron. Her fingers slid down and along the ground under the piece of money with the grace and care they would have in lifting an egg from under a setting hen. Then she slowly straightened up, she stood erect, and the nickel was in her apron pocket. A bird flew by. Her lips moved. "God watching me the whole time. I come to stealing."

The man came back, and his own dog panted about them. "Well, I scared him off that time," he said, and then he laughed and lifted his gun and pointed it at Phoenix.

She stood straight and faced him.

"Doesn't the gun scare you?" he said, still pointing it.

"No, sir, I seen plenty go off closer by, in my day, and for less than what I done," she said, holding utterly still.

He smiled, and shouldered the gun. "Well, Granny," he said, "you must be a hundred years old, and scared of nothing. I'd give you a dime if I had any money with me. But you take my advice and stay home, and nothing will happen to you."

"I bound to go on my way, mister," said Phoenix. She inclined her head in the red rag. Then they went in different directions, but she could hear the gun shooting again and again over the hill.

She walked on. The shadows hung from the oak trees to the road like curtains. Then she smelled wood-smoke, and smelled the river, and she saw a steeple and the cabins on their steep steps. Dozens of little black children whirled around her. There ahead was Natchez shining. Bells were ringing. She walked on.

In the paved city it was Christmas time. There were red and green electric lights strung and criss-crossed everywhere, and all turned on in the daytime. Old Phoenix would have been lost if she had not distrusted her eyesight and depended on her feet to know where to take her.

She paused quietly on the sidewalk where people were passing by. A lady came along in the crowd, carrying an armful of red-, green- and silver-wrapped presents: she gave off perfume like the red roses in hot summer, and Phoenix stopped her.

"Please, missy, will you lace up my shoe?" She held up her foot.

"What do you want, Grandma?"

"See my shoe," said Phoenix. "Do all right for out in the country, but wouldn't look right to go in a big building."

"Stand still then, Grandma," said the lady. She put her packages down on the sidewalk beside her and laced and tied both shoes tightly.

"Can't lace 'em with a cane," said Phoenix. "Thank you, missy, I doesn't mind asking a nice lady to tie up my shoe, when I gets out on the street."

Moving slowly and from side to side, she went into the big building, and into a tower of steps, where she walked up and around and around until her feet knew to stop.

She entered a door, and there she saw nailed up on the wall the document that had been stamped with the gold seal and framed in the gold frame, which matched the dream that was hung up in her head.

"Here I be," she said. There was a fixed and ceremonial stiffness over her body.

"A charity case, I suppose," said an attendant who sat at the desk before her.

But Phoenix only looked above her head. There was sweat on her face, the wrinkles in her skin shone like a bright net.

"Speak up, Grandma," the woman said. "What's your name? We must have your history, you know. Have you been here before? What seems to be the trouble with you?"

Old Phoenix only gave a twitch to her face as if a fly were bothering her.

"Are you deaf?" cried the attendant.

But then the nurse came in.

"Oh, that's just old Aunt Phoenix," she said. "She doesn't come for herself —she has a little grandson. She makes these trips just as regular as clockwork. She lives away back off the Old Natchez Trace." She bent down. "Well, Aunt Phoenix, why don't you just take a seat? We won't keep you standing after your long trip." She pointed.

The old woman sat down, bolt upright in the chair.

"Now, how is the boy?" asked the nurse.

Old Phoenix did not speak.

"I said, how is the boy?"

But Phoenix only waited and stared straight ahead, her face very solemn and withdrawn into rigidity.

"Is his throat any better?" asked the nurse. "Aunt Phoenix, don't you hear me? Is your grandson's throat any better since the last time you came for the medicine?"

With her hands on her knees, the old woman waited, silent, erect and motionless, just as if she were in armor.

"You mustn't take up our time this way, Aunt Phoenix," the nurse said. "Tell us quickly about your grandson, and get it over. He isn't dead, is he?"

At last there came a flicker and then a flame of comprehension across her face, and she spoke.

"My grandson. It was my memory had left me. There I sat and forgot why I made my long trip."

"Forgot?" The nurse frowned. "After you came so far?"

Then Phoenix was like an old woman begging a dignified forgiveness for waking up frightened in the night. "I never did go to school, I was too old at the Surrender," she said in a soft voice. "I'm an old woman without an education. It was my memory fail me. My little grandson, he is just the same, and I forgot it in the coming."

"Throat never heals, does it?" said the nurse, speaking in a loud, sure voice to old Phoenix. By now she had a card with something written on it, a little list. "Yes. Swallowed lye. When was it?—January—two—three years ago—"

Phoenix spoke unasked now. "No, missy, he not dead, he just the same. Every little while his throat begin to close up again, and he not able to swallow. He not get his breath. He not able to help himself. So the time come around, and I go on another trip for the soothing medicine."

"All right. The doctor said as long as you came to get it, you could have it," said the nurse. "But it's an obstinate case."

"My little grandson, he sit up there in the house all wrapped up, waiting by himself," Phoenix went on. "We is the only two left in the world. He suffer and it don't seem to put him back at all. He got a sweet look. He going to last. He wear a little patch quilt and peep out holding his mouth open like a little bird. I remembers so plain now. I not going to forget him again, no, the whole enduring time. I could tell him from all the others in creation."

"All right." The nurse was trying to hush her now. She brought her a bottle of medicine. "Charity," she said, making a checkmark in a book.

Old Phoenix held the bottle close to her eyes, and then carefully put it into her pocket.

"I thank you," she said.

"It's Christmas time, Grandma," said the attendant. "Could I give you a few pennies out of my purse?"

"Five pennies is a nickel," said Phoenix stiffly.

"Here's a nickel," said the attendant.

Phoenix rose carefully and held out her hand. She received the nickel and then fished the other nickel out of her pocket and laid it beside the new one. She stared at her palm closely, with her head on one side.

Then she gave a tap with her cane on the floor.

"This is what come to me to do," she said. "I going to the store and buy my child a little windmill they sells, made out of paper. He going to find it hard to believe there such a thing in the world. I'll march myself back where he waiting, holding it straight up in this hand."

She lifted her free hand, gave a little nod, turned around, and walked out of the doctor's office. Then her slow step began on the stairs, going down.

(1941)

Tillie Olsen *1913–*

I STAND HERE IRONING

I stand here ironing, and what you asked me moves tormented back and forth with the iron.

"I wish you would manage the time to come in and talk with me about your daughter. I'm sure you can help me understand her. She's a youngster who needs help and whom I'm deeply interested in helping."

"Who needs help?" Even if I came what good would it do? You think because I am her mother I have a key, or that in some way you could use me as a key? She has lived for nineteen years. There is all that life that has happened outside of me, beyond me.

And when is there time to remember, to sift, to weigh, to estimate, to total? I will start and there will be an interruption and I will have to gather it all together again. Or I will become engulfed with all I did or did not do, with what should have been and what cannot be helped.

She was a beautiful baby. The first and only one of our five that was beautiful at birth. You do not guess how new and uneasy her tenancy in her now-loveliness. You did not know her all those years she was thought homely, or see her poring over her baby pictures, making me tell her over and over how beautiful she had been — and would be, I would tell her — and was now, to the seeing eye. But the seeing eyes were few or nonexistent. Including mine.

I nursed her. They feel that's important nowadays. I nursed all the children, but with her, with all the fierce rigidity of first motherhood, I did like the books then said. Though her cries battered me to trembling and my breasts ached with swollenness, I waited till the clock decreed.

Why do I put that first? I do not even know if it matters, or if it explains anything.

She was a beautiful baby. She blew shining bubbles of sound. She loved motion, loved light, loved color and music and textures. She would lie on the floor in her blue overalls patting the surface so hard in ecstasy her hands and feet would blur. She was a miracle to me, but when she was eight months old I had to leave her daytimes with the woman downstairs to whom she was no miracle at all, for I worked or looked for work and for Emily's father, who "could no longer endure" (he wrote in his good-by note) "sharing want with us."

I was nineteen. It was the pre-relief, pre-WPA world of the depression. I would start running as soon as I got off the streetcar, running up the stairs, the place smelling sour, and awake or asleep to startle awake, when she saw me she would break into a clogged weeping that could not be comforted, a weeping I can yet hear.

After a while I found a job hashing at night so I could be with her days, and it was better. But it came to where I had to bring her to his family and leave her.

It took a long time to raise the money for her fare back. Then she got chicken pox and I had to wait longer. When she finally came, I hardly knew her, walking quick and nervous like her father, looking like her father, thin, and dressed in a shoddy red that yellowed her skin and glared at the pockmarks. All the baby loveliness gone.

She was two. Old enough for nursery school they said, and I did not know

363

then what I know now—the fatigue of the long day, and the lacerations of group life in the kinds of nurseries that are only parking places for children.

Except that it would have made no difference if I had known. It was the only place there was. It was the only way we could be together, the only way I could hold a job.

And even without knowing, I knew. I knew the teacher that was evil because all these years it has curdled into my memory, the little boy hunched in the corner, her rasp, "why aren't you outside, because Alvin hits you? that's no reason, go out, scaredy." I knew Emily hated it even if she did not clutch and implore "don't go Mommy" like the other children, mornings.

She always had a reason why we should stay home. Momma, you look sick. Momma, I feel sick. Momma, the teachers aren't there today, they're sick. Momma, we can't go, there was a fire there last night. Momma it's a holiday today, no school, they told me.

But never a direct protest, never rebellion. I think of our others in their three-, four-year-oldness—the explosions, the tempers, the denunciations, the demands—and I feel suddenly ill. I put the iron down. What in me demanded that goodness in her? And what was the cost, the cost to her of such goodness?

The old man living in the back once said in his gentle way: "You should smile at Emily more when you look at her." What *was* in my face when I looked at her? I loved her. There were all the acts of love.

It was only with the others I remembered what he said, so that it was the face of joy, and not of care or tightness or worry I turned to them—too late for Emily. She does not smile easily, let alone almost always as her brothers and sisters do. Her face is closed and somber, but when she wants, how fluid. You must have seen it in her pantomimes, you spoke of her rare gift for comedy on the stage that rouses a laughter out of the audience so dear they applaud and applaud and do not want to let her go.

Where does it come from, that comedy? There was none of it in her when she came back to me that second time, after I had had to send her away again. She had a new daddy now to learn to love, and I think perhaps it was a better time.

Except when we left her alone nights, telling ourselves she was old enough.

"Can't you go some other time, Mommy, like tomorrow?" she would ask. "Will it be just a little while you'll be gone? Do you promise?"

The time we came back, the front door open, the clock on the floor in the hall. She rigid awake. "It wasn't just a little while. I didn't cry. Three times I called you, just three times, and then I ran downstairs to open the door so you could come faster. The clock talked loud, I threw it away, it scared me when it talked."

She said the clock talked loud that night I went to the hospital to have Susan. She was delirious with the fever that comes before red measles, but she was fully conscious all the week I was gone and the week after we were home when she could not come near the new baby or me.

She did not get well. She stayed skeleton thin, not wanting to eat, and night after night she had nightmares. She would call for me, and I would sleepily call back, "you're all right, darling, go to sleep, it's just a dream," and if she still called, in a sterner voice, "now go to sleep, Emily, there's nothing to hurt you." Twice, only twice, when I had to get up for Susan anyway, I went in to sit with her.

Now when it is too late (as if she would let me hold and comfort her like I do the others) I get up and go to her at her moan or restless stirring. "Are you awake? Can I get you something?" And the answer is always the same: "No, I'm all right, go back to sleep Mother."

They persuaded me at the clinic to send her away to a convalescent home in the country where "she can have the kind of food and care you can't manage for her, and you'll be free to concentrate on the new baby." They still send children to that place. I see pictures on the society page of sleek young women planning affairs to raise money for it, or dancing at the affairs, or decorating Easter eggs or filling Christmas stockings for children.

They never have a picture of the children so I do not know if they still wear those gigantic red bows and the ravaged looks on the every other Sunday when parents can come to visit "unless otherwise notified"—as we were notified the first six weeks.

Oh it is a handsome place, green lawns and tall trees and fluted flower beds. High up on the balconies of each cottage the children stand, the girls in their red bows and white dresses, the boys in white suits and giant red ties. The parents stand below shrieking up to be heard and the children shriek down to be heard, and between them the invisible wall "Not To Be Contaminated by Parental Germs or Physical Affection."

There was a tiny girl who always stood hand in hand with Emily. Her parents never came. One visit she was gone. "They moved her to Rose Cottage," Emily shouted in explanation. "They don't like you to love anybody here."

She wrote once a week, the labored writing of a seven-year-old. "I am fine. How is the baby. If I write my leter nicly I will have a star. Love." There was never a star. We wrote every other day, letters she could never hold or keep but only hear read—once. "We simply do not have room for children to keep any personal possessions," they patiently explained when we pieced one Sunday's shrieking together to plead how much it would mean to Emily to keep her letters and cards.

Each visit she looked frailer. "She isn't eating," they told us.

(They had runny eggs for breakfast or mush with lumps, Emily said later, I'd hold it in my mouth and not swallow. Nothing ever tasted good, just when they had chicken.)

It took us eight months to get her released home, and only the fact that she gained back so little of her seven lost pounds convinced the social worker.

I used to try to hold and love her after she came back, but her body would stay stiff, and after a while she'd push away. She ate little. Food sickened her, and I think much of life too. Oh she had physical lightness and brightness, twinkling by on skates, bouncing like a ball up and down up and down over the jump rope, skimming over the hill; but these were momentary.

She fretted about her appearance, thin and dark and foreign-looking at a time when every little girl was supposed to look or thought she should look a chubby blond replica of Shirley Temple. The doorbell sometimes rang for her, but no one seemed to come and play in the house or be a best friend. Maybe because we moved so much.

There was a boy she loved painfully through two school semesters. Months later she told me how she had taken pennies from my purse to buy him candy. "Licorice was his favorite and I bought him some every day, but he still liked Jennifer better'n me. Why, Mommy?" The kind of question for which there is no answer.

School was a worry to her. She was not glib or quick in a world where glibness and quickness were easily confused with ability to learn. To her over-worked and exasperated teachers she was an over-conscientious "slow learner" who kept trying to catch up and was absent entirely too often.

I let her be absent, though sometimes the illness was imaginary. How different from my now-strictness about attendance with the others. I wasn't working. We had a new baby, I was home anyhow. Sometimes, after Susan grew old enough, I would keep her home from school, too, to have them all together.

Mostly Emily had asthma, and her breathing, harsh and labored, would fill the house with a curiously tranquil sound. I would bring the two old dresser mirrors and her boxes of collections to her bed. She would select beads and single earrings, bottle tops and shells, dried flowers and pebbles, old postcards and scraps, all sorts of oddments; then she and Susan would play Kingdom, setting up landscapes and furniture, peopling them with action.

Those were the only times of peaceful companionship between her and Susan. I have edged away from it, that poisonous feeling between them, that terrible balancing of hurts and needs I had to do between the two, and did so badly, those earlier years.

Oh there are conflicts between the others too, each one human, needing, demanding, hurting, taking—but only between Emily and Susan, no, Emily toward Susan that corroding resentment. It seems so obvious on the surface, yet it is not obvious. Susan, the second child, Susan, golden and curly haired and chubby, quick and articulate and assured, everything in appearance and manner Emily was not; Susan, not able to resist Emily's precious things, losing or sometimes clumsily breaking them; Susan telling jokes and riddles to company for applause while Emily sat silent (to say to me later: that was *my* riddle, Mother, I told it to Susan); Susan, who for all the five years' difference in age was just a year behind Emily in developing physically.

I am glad for that slow physical development that widened the difference between her and her contemporaries, though she suffered over it. She was too vulnerable for that terrible world of youthful competition, of preening and parading, of constant measuring of yourself against every other, of envy: "If I had that copper hair," or "If I had that skin. . . ." She tormented herself enough about not looking like the others, there was enough of the unsureness, the having to be conscious of words before you speak, the constant caring—what are they thinking of me? what kind of an impression am I making—without having it all magnified unendurably by the merciless physical drives.

Ronnie is calling. He is wet and I change him. It is rare there is such a cry now. That time of motherhood is almost behind me when the ear is not one's own but must always be racked and listening for the child cry, the child call. We sit for a while and I hold him, looking out over the city spread in charcoal with its soft aisles of light. "*Shoogily*," he breathes and curls closer. I carry him back to bed, asleep. *Shoogily*. A funny word, a family word, inherited from Emily, invented by her to say: *comfort*.

In this and other ways she leaves her seal, I say aloud. And startle at my saying it. What do I mean? What did I start to gather together, to try and make coherent? I was at the terrible, growing years. War years. I do not remember them well. I was working again, there were four smaller ones now, there was no time for her. She had to help be a mother, and housekeeper, and shopper. She had to set her seal. Mornings of crisis and near hysteria trying to get lunches packed, hair combed, coats and shoes found, everyone to school or Child Care on time, the baby ready for transportation. And always the paper scribbled on by a smaller one, the book looked at by Susan then mislaid, the homework not done. Running out to that huge school where she was one, she was lost, she was a drop; suffering over her unpreparedness, stammering and unsure in her classes.

There was so little left at night after the kids were bedded down. She would struggle over her books, always eating (it was in those years she developed her enormous appetite that is legendary in our family) and I would be ironing, or preparing food for the next day, or writing V-mail to Bill, or tending the baby. Sometimes, to make me laugh, or out of her despair, she would imitate happenings or types at school.

I think I said once: "Why don't you do something like this in the school amateur show?" One morning she phoned me at work, hardly understandable through the weeping: "Mother, I did it. I won, I won; they gave me first prize; they clapped and clapped and wouldn't let me go."

Now suddenly she was Somebody, and as imprisoned in her difference as she had been in her anonymity.

She began to be asked to perform at other high schools, even in colleges, then at city and state-wide affairs. The first one we went to, I only recognized her that first moment when thin, shy, she almost drowned herself into the curtains. Then: Was this Emily? The control, the command, the convulsing and deadly clowning, the spell, then the roaring, stamping audience, unwilling to let this rare and precious laughter out of their lives.

Afterwards: You ought to do something about her with a gift like that—but without money or knowing how, what does one do? We have left it all to her, and the gift has as often eddied inside, clogged and clotted, as been used and growing.

She is coming. She runs up the stairs two at a time with her light graceful step, and I know she is happy tonight. Whatever it was that occasioned your call did not happen today.

"Aren't you ever going to finish the ironing, Mother? Whistler painted his mother in a rocker. I'd have to paint mine standing over an ironing board." This is one of the communicative nights and she tells me everything and nothing as she fixes herself a plate of food out of the icebox.

She is so lovely. Why did you want me to come in at all? Why were you concerned? She will find her way.

She starts up the stairs to bed. "Don't get *me* up with the rest in the morning." "But I thought you were having midterms." "Oh, those," she comes back in, kisses me, and says quite lightly, "in a couple of years when we'll all be atom-dead they won't matter a bit."

She has said it before. She *believes* it. But because I have been dredging the past, and all that compounds a human being is so heavy and meaningful in me, I cannot endure it tonight.

I will never total it all. I will never come in to say: She was a child seldom smiled at. Her father left me before she was a year old. I had to work away from her her first six years when there was work, or I sent her home and to his relatives. There were years she had care she hated. She was dark and thin and foreign-looking in a world where the prestige went to blondness and curly hair and dimples, she was slow where glibness was prized. She was a child of anxious, not proud, love. We were poor and could not afford for her the soil of easy growth. I was a young mother, I was a distracted mother. There were the other children pushing up, demanding. Her younger sister seemed all that she was not. There were years she did not want me to touch her. She kept too much in herself, her life was such she had to keep too much in herself. My wisdom came too late. She has much to her and probably little will come of it. She is a child of her age, of depression, of war, of fear.

Let her be. So all that is in her will not bloom — but in how many does it? There is still enough left to live by. Only help her to know — help make it so there is cause for her to know — that she is more than this dress on the ironing board, helpless before the iron.

(1961)

depression

war

fear

has mother felt helpless before the iron?
(circumstances beyond her control?)
what is function of Ronnie incident?

Hisaye Yamamoto *1921–*

SEVENTEEN SYLLABLES

The first Rosie knew that her mother had taken to writing poems was one evening when she finished one and read it aloud for her daughter's approval. It was about cats, and Rosie pretended to understand it thoroughly and appreciate it no end, partly because she hesitated to disillusion her mother about the quantity and quality of Japanese she had learned in all the years now that she had been going to Japanese school every Saturday (and Wednesday, too, in the summer). Even so, her mother must have been skeptical about the depth of Rosie's understanding, because she explained afterwards about the kind of poem she was trying to write.

See, Rosie, she said, it was a *haiku*, a poem in which she must pack all her meaning into seventeen syllables only, which were divided into three lines of five, seven, and five syllables. In the one she had just read, she had tried to capture the charm of a kitten, as well as comment on the superstition that owning a cat of three colors meant good luck.

"Yes, yes, I understand. How utterly lovely," Rosie said, and her mother, either satisfied or seeing through the deception and resigned, went back to composing.

The truth was that Rosie was lazy; English lay ready on the tongue but Japanese had to be searched for and examined, and even then put forth tentatively (probably to meet with laughter). It was so much easier to say yes, yes, even when one meant no, no. Besides, this was what was in her mind to say: I was looking through one of your magazines from Japan last night, Mother, and towards the back I found some *haiku* in English that delighted me. There was one that made me giggle off and on until I fell asleep—

> It is morning, and lo!
> I lie awake, comme il faut,
> sighing for some dough.

Now, how to reach her mother, how to communicate the melancholy song? Rosie knew formal Japanese by fits and starts, her mother had even less English, no French. It was much more possible to say yes, yes.

It developed that her mother was writing the *haiku* for a daily newspaper, the *Mainichi Shimbun*, that was published in San Francisco. Los Angeles, to be sure, was closer to the farming community in which the Hayashi family lived and several Japanese vernaculars were printed there, but Rosie's parents said they preferred the tone of the northern paper. Once a week, the *Mainichi* would have a section devoted to *haiku*, and her mother became an extravagant contributor, taking for herself the blossoming pen name, Ume Hanazono.

So Rosie and her father lived for awhile with two women, her mother and Ume Hanazono. Her mother (Tome Hayashi by name) kept house, cooked, washed, and, along with her husband and the Carrascos, the Mexican family hired for the harvest, did her ample share of picking tomatoes out in the sweltering fields and boxing them in tidy strata in the cool packing shed. Ume Hanazono, who came to life after the dinner dishes were done, was an earnest,

369

muttering stranger who often neglected speaking when spoken to and stayed busy at the parlor table as late as midnight scribbling with pencil on scratch paper or carefully copying characters on good paper with her fat, pale green Parker.

The new interest had some repercussions on the household routine. Before, Rosie had been accustomed to her parents and herself taking their hot baths early and going to bed almost immediately afterwards, unless her parents challenged each other to a game of flower cards or unless company dropped in. Now if her father wanted to play cards, he had to resort to solitaire (at which he always cheated fearlessly), and if a group of friends came over, it was bound to contain someone who was also writing *haiku*, and the small assemblage would be split in two, her father entertaining the non-literary members and her mother comparing ecstatic notes with the visiting poet.

If they went out, it was more of the same thing. But Ume Hanazono's life span, even for a poet's, was very brief—perhaps three months at most.

One night they went over to see the Hayano family in the neighboring town to the west, an adventure both painful and attractive to Rosie. It was attractive because there were four Hayano girls, all lovely and each one named after a season of the year (Haru, Natsu, Aki, Fuyu), painful because something had been wrong with Mrs. Hayano ever since the birth of her first child. Rosie would sometimes watch Mrs. Hayano, reputed to have been the belle of her native village, making her way about a room, stooped, slowly shuffling, violently trembling (*always* trembling), and she would be reminded that this woman, in this same condition, had carried and given issue to three babies. She would look wonderingly at Mr. Hayano, handsome, tall, and strong, and she would look at her four pretty friends. But it was not a matter she could come to any decision about.

On this visit, however, Mrs. Hayano sat all evening in the rocker, as motionless and unobtrusive as it was possible for her to be, and Rosie found the greater part of the evening practically anaesthetic. Too, Rosie spent most of it in the girls' room, because Haru, the garrulous one, said almost as soon as the bows and other greetings were over, "Oh, you must see my new coat!"

It was a pale plaid of grey, sand, and blue, with an enormous collar, and Rosie, seeing nothing special in it, said, "Gee, how nice."

"Nice?" said Haru, indignantly. "Is that all you can say about it? It's gorgeous! And so cheap, too. Only seventeen-ninety-eight, because it was a sale. The saleslady said it was twenty-five dollars regular."

"Gee," said Rosie. Natsu, who never said much and when she said anything said it shyly, fingered the coat covetously and Haru pulled it away.

"Mine," she said, putting it on. She minced in the aisle between the two large beds and smiled happily. "Let's see how your mother likes it."

She broke into the front room and the adult conversation and went to stand in front of Rosie's mother, while the rest watched from the door. Rosie's mother was properly envious. "May I inherit it when you're through with it?"

Haru, pleased, giggled and said yes, she could, but Natsu reminded gravely from the door, "You promised me, Haru."

Everyone laughed but Natsu, who shamefacedly retreated into the bedroom. Haru came in laughing, taking off the coat. "We were only kidding, Natsu," she said. "Here, you try it on now."

After Natsu buttoned herself into the coat, inspected herself solemnly in the bureau mirror, and reluctantly shed it, Rosie, Aki, and Fuyu got their turns, and Fuyu, who was eight, drowned in it while her sisters and Rosie doubled up in amusement. They all went into the front room later, because Haru's mother quaveringly called to her to fix the tea and rice cakes and open a can of sliced peaches for everybody. Rosie noticed that her mother and Mr. Hayano were talking together at the little table—they were discussing a *haiku* that Mr. Hayano was planning to send to the *Mainichi*, while her father was sitting at one end of the sofa looking through a copy of *Life*, the new picture magazine. *alone* Occasionally, her father would comment on a photograph, holding it toward Mrs. Hayano and speaking to her as he always did—loudly, as though he thought someone such as she must surely be at least a trifle deaf also.

The five girls had their refreshments at the kitchen table, and it was while Rosie was showing the sisters her trick of swallowing peach slices without chewing (she chased each slippery crescent down with a swig of tea) that her father brought his empty teacup and untouched saucer to the sink and said, "Come on, Rosie, we're going home now."

"Already?" asked Rosie.

"Work tomorrow," he said. *leave early*

Father He sounded irritated, and Rosie, puzzled, gulped one last yellow slice and stood up to go, while the sisters began protesting, as was their wont.

"We have to get up at five-thirty," he told them, going into the front room quickly, so that they did not have their usual chance to hang onto his hands and plead for an extension of time.

Rosie, following, saw that her mother and Mr. Hayano were sipping tea and still talking together, while Mrs. Hayano concentrated, quivering, on raising the handleless Japanese cup to her lips with both her hands and lowering it back to her lap. Her father, saying nothing, went out the door, onto the bright porch, and down the steps. Her mother looked up and asked, "Where is he going?"

"Where is he going?" Rosie said. "He said we were going home now."

"Going home?" Her mother looked with embarrassment at Mr. Hayano and his absorbed wife and then forced a smile. "He must be tired," she said.

Haru was not giving up yet. "May Rosie stay overnight?" she asked, and Natsu, Aki, and Fuyu came to reinforce their sister's plea by helping her make a circle around Rosie's mother. Rosie, for once having no desire to stay, was relieved when her mother, apologizing to the perturbed Mr. and Mrs. Hayano for her father's abruptness at the same time, managed to shake her head no at the quartet, kindly but adamant, so that they broke their circle and let her go.

Rosie's father looked ahead into the windshield as the two joined him. "I'm sorry," her mother said. "You must be tired." Her father, stepping on the starter, said nothing. "You know how I get when it's *haiku*," she continued, "I forget what time it is." He only grunted.

As they rode homeward silently, Rosie, sitting between, felt a rush of hate for ╱ both—for her mother for begging, for her father for denying her mother. I wish this old Ford would crash, right now, she thought, then immediately, no, no, I wish my father would laugh, but it was too late: already the vision had passed through her mind of the green pick-up crumpled in the dark against one of the mighty eucalyptus trees they were just riding past, of the three contorted, bleeding bodies, one of them hers.

change of scene

Rosie ran between two patches of tomatoes, her heart working more ram-
bunctiously than she had ever known it to. How lucky it was that Aunt Taka and
Uncle Gimpachi had come tonight, though, how very lucky. Otherwise she
might not have really kept her half-promise to meet Jesus Carrasco. Jesus was
going to be a senior in September at the same school she went to, and his parents
were the ones helping with the tomatoes this year. She and Jesus, who hardly
remembered seeing each other at Cleveland High where there were so many
other people and two whole grades between them, had become great friends this
summer—he always had a joke for her when he periodically drove the loaded
pick-up up from the fields to the shed where she was usually sorting while her
mother and father did the packing, and they laughed a great deal together over
infinitesimal repartee during the afternoon break for chilled watermelon or ice
cream in the shade of the shed.

What she enjoyed most was racing him to see which could finish picking a
double row first. He, who could work faster, would tease her by slowing down
until she thought she would surely pass him this time, then speeding up furiously
to leave her several sprawling vines behind. Once he had made her screech
hideously by crossing over, while her back was turned, to place atop the tomatoes in her green-stained bucket a truly monstrous, pale green worm (it had
looked more like an infant snake). And it was when they had finished a contest
this morning, after she had pantingly pointed a green finger at the immature
tomatoes evident in the lugs at the end of his row and he had returned the
accusation (with justice), that he had startlingly brought up the matter of their
possibly meeting outside the range of both their parents' dubious eyes.

"What for?" she had asked.

"I've got a secret I want to tell you," he said.

"Tell me now," she demanded.

"It won't be ready till tonight," he said.

She laughed. "Tell me tomorrow then."

"It'll be gone tomorrow," he threatened.

"Well, for seven hakes, what is it?" she had asked, more than twice, and when
he had suggested that the packing shed would be an appropriate place to find out,
she had cautiously answered maybe. She had not been certain she was going to
keep the appointment until the arrival of mother's sister and her husband. Their
coming seemed a sort of signal of permission, of grace, and she had definitely
made up her mind to lie and leave as she was bowing them welcome.

So as soon as everyone appeared settled back for the evening, she announced
loudly that she was going to the privy outside. "I'm going to the *benjo*!" and
slipped out the door. And now that she was actually on her way, her heart
pumped in such an undisciplined way that she could hear it with her ears. It's
because I'm running, she told herself, slowing to a walk. The shed was up ahead,
one more patch away, in the middle of the fields. Its bulk, looming in the
dimness, took on a sinisterness that was funny when Rosie reminded herself that
it was only a wooden frame with a canvas roof and three canvas walls that made a
slapping noise on breezy days.

Jesus was sitting on the narrow plank that was the sorting platform and she
went around to the other side and jumped backwards to seat herself on the rim of

a packing stand. "Well, tell me," she said without greeting, thinking her voice sounded reassuringly familiar.

"I saw you coming out the door," Jesus said. "I heard you running part of the way, too."

"Uh-huh," Rosie said. "Now tell me the secret."

"I was afraid you wouldn't come," he said.

Rosie delved around on the chicken-wire bottom of the stall for number two tomatoes, ripe, which she was sitting beside, and came up with a left-over that felt edible. She bit into it and began sucking out the pulp and seeds. "I'm here," she pointed out.

"Rosie, are you sorry you came?"

"Sorry? What for?" she said. "You said you were going to tell me something."

"I will, I will," Jesus said, but his voice contained disappointment, and Rosie fleetingly felt the older of the two, realizing a brand-new power which vanished without category under her recognition.

"I have to go back in a minute," she said. "My aunt and uncle are here from Wintersburg. I told them I was going to the privy."

Jesus laughed. "You funny thing," he said. "You slay me!"

"Just because you have a bathroom *inside*," Rosie said. "Come on, tell me."

Chuckling, Jesus came around to lean on the stand facing her. They still could not see each other very clearly, but Rosie noticed that Jesus became very sober again as he took the hollow tomato from her hand and dropped it back into the stall. When he took hold of her empty hand, she could find no words to protest; her vocabulary had become distressingly constricted and she thought desperately that all that remained intact now was yes and no and oh, and even these few sounds would not easily out. Thus, kissed by Jesus, Rosie fell for the first time entirely victim to a helplessness delectable beyond speech. But the terrible, beautiful sensation lasted no more than a second, and the reality of Jesus' lips and tongue and teeth and hands made her pull away with such strength that she nearly tumbled.

Rosie stopped running as she approached the lights from the windows of home. How long since she had left? She could not guess, but gasping yet, she went to the privy in back and locked herself in. Her own breathing deafened her in the dark, close space, and she sat and waited until she could hear at last the nightly calling of the frogs and crickets. Even then, all she could think to say was oh, my, and the pressure of Jesus' face against her face would not leave.

No one had missed her in the parlor, however, and Rosie walked in and through quickly, announcing that she was next going to take a bath. "Your father's in the bathhouse," her mother said, and Rosie, in her room, recalled that she had not seen him when she entered. There had been only Aunt Taka and Uncle Gimpachi with her mother at the table, drinking tea. She got her robe and straw sandals and crossed the parlor again to go outside. Her mother was telling them about the *haiku* competition in the *Mainichi* and the poem she had entered.

Rosie met her father coming out of the bathhouse. "Are you through, Father?" she asked. "I was going to ask you to scrub my back."

"Scrub your own back," he said shortly, going toward the main house.

"What have I done now?" she yelled after him. She suddenly felt like doing a lot of yelling. But he did not answer, and she went into the bathhouse. Turning on the dangling light, she removed her denims and T-shirt and threw them in the big carton for dirty clothes standing next to the washing machine. Her other things she took with her into the bath compartment to wash after her bath. After she had scooped a basin of hot water from the square wooden tub, she sat on the grey cement of the floor and soaped herself at exaggerated leisure, singing "Red Sails in the Sunset" at the top of her voice and using da-da-da where she suspected her words. Then, standing up, still singing, for she was possessed by the notion that any attempt now to analyze would result in spoilage and she believed that the larger her volume the less she would be able to hear herself think, she obtained more hot water and poured it on until she was free of lather. Only then did she allow herself to step into the steaming vat, one leg first, then the remainder of her body inch by inch until the water no longer stung and she could move around at will.

She took a long time soaking, afterwards remembering to go around outside to stoke the embers of the tin-lined fireplace beneath the tub and to throw on a few more sticks so that the water might keep its heat for her mother, and when she finally returned to the parlor, she found her mother still talking *haiku* with her aunt and uncle, the three of them on another round of tea. Her father was nowhere in sight.

At Japanese school the next day (Wednesday, it was), Rosie was grave and giddy by turns. Preoccupied at her desk in the row for students on Book Eight, she made up for it at recess by performing wild mimicry for the benefit of her friend Chizuko. She held her nose and whined a witticism or two in what she considered was the manner of Fred Allen; she assumed intoxication and a British accent to go over the climax of the Rudy Vallee recording of the pub conversation about William Ewart Gladstone; she was the child Shirley Temple piping, "On the Good Ship Lollipop"; she was the gentleman soprano of the Four Inkspots trilling, "If I Didn't Care." And she felt reasonably satisfied when Chizuko wept and gasped, "Oh, Rosie, you ought to be in the movies!"

Her father came after her at noon, bringing her sandwiches of minced ham and two nectarines to eat while she rode, so that she could pitch right into the sorting when they got home. The lugs were piling up, he said, and the ripe tomatoes in them would probably have to be taken to the cannery tomorrow if they were not ready for the produce haulers tonight. "This heat's not doing them any good. And we've got no time for a break today."

It *was* hot, probably the hottest day of the year, and Rosie's blouse stuck damply to her back even under the protection of the canvas. But she worked as efficiently as a flawless machine and kept the stalls heaped, with one part of her mind listening in to the parental murmuring about the heat and the tomatoes and with another part planning the exact words she would say to Jesus when he drove up with the first load of the afternoon. But when at last she saw that the pick-up was coming, her hands went berserk and the tomatoes started falling in the wrong stalls, and her father said, "Hey, hey! Rosie, watch what you're doing!"

"Well, I have to go to the *benjo*," she said, hiding panic.

"Go in the weeds over there," he said, only half-joking.

"Oh, Father!" she protested.

"Oh, go on home," her mother said. "We'll make out for awhile."

In the privy Rosie peered through a knothole toward the fields, watching as much as she could of Jesus. Happily she thought she saw him look in the direction of the house from time to time before he finished unloading and went back toward the patch where his mother and father worked. As she was heading for the shed, a very presentable black car purred up the dirt driveway to the house and its driver motioned to her. Was this the Hayashi home, he wanted to know. She nodded. Was she a Hayashi? Yes, she said, thinking that he was a good-looking man. He got out of the car with a huge, flat package and she saw that he warmly wore a business suit. "I have something here for your mother then," he said, in a more elegant Japanese than she was used to.

She told him where her mother was and he came along with her, patting his face with an immaculate white handkerchief and saying something about the coolness of San Francisco. To her surprised mother and father, he bowed and introduced himself as, among other things, the *haiku* editor of the *Mainichi Shimbun*, saying that since he had been coming as far as Los Angeles anyway, he had decided to bring her the first prize she had won in the recent contest.

"First prize?" her mother echoed, believing and not believing, pleased and overwhelmed. Handed the package with a bow, she bobbed her head up and down numerous times to express her utter gratitude.

"It is nothing much," he added, "but I hope it will serve as a token of our great appreciation for your contributions and our great admiration of your considerable talent."

"I am not worthy," she said, falling easily into his style. "It is I who should make some sign of my humble thanks for being permitted to contribute."

"No, no, to the contrary," he said, bowing again.

But Rosie's mother insisted, and then saying that she knew she was being unorthodox, she asked if she might open the package because her curiosity was so great. Certainly she might. In fact, he would like her reaction to it, for personally, it was one of his favorite *Hiroshiges*.

Rosie thought it was a pleasant picture, which looked to have been sketched with delicate quickness. There were pink clouds, containing some graceful calligraphy, and a sea that was a pale blue except at the edges, containing four sampans with indications of people in them. Pines edged the water and on the far-off beach there was a cluster of thatched huts towered over by pine-dotted mountains of grey and blue. The frame was scalloped and gilt.

After Rosie's mother pronounced it without peer and somewhat prodded her father into nodding agreement, she said Mr. Kuroda must at least have a cup of tea after coming all this way, and although Mr. Kuroda did not want to impose, he soon agreed that a cup of tea would be refreshing and went along with her to the house, carrying the picture for her.

"Ha, your mother's crazy!" Rosie's father said, and Rosie laughed uneasily as she resumed judgment on the tomatoes. She had emptied six lugs when he broke into an imaginary conversation with Jesus to tell her to go and remind her mother of the tomatoes, and she went slowly.

Mr. Kuroda was in his shirtsleeves expounding some *haiku* theory as he munched a rice cake, and her mother was rapt. Abashed in the great man's presence, Rosie stood next to her mother's chair until her mother looked up inquiringly, and then she started to whisper the message, but her mother pushed her gently away and reproached, "You are not being very polite to our guest."

"Father says the tomatoes . . . " Rosie said aloud, smiling foolishly.

"Tell him I shall only be a minute," her mother said, speaking the language of Mr. Kuroda.

When Rosie carried the reply to her father, he did not seem to hear and she said again, "Mother says she'll be back in a minute."

"All right, all right," he nodded, and they worked again in silence. But suddenly, her father uttered an incredible noise, exactly like the cork of a bottle popping, and the next Rosie knew, he was stalking angrily toward the house, almost running in fact, and she chased after him crying, "Father! Father! What are you going to do?"

He stopped long enough to order her back to the shed. "Never mind!" he shouted. "Get on with the sorting!"

And from the place in the fields where she stood, frightened and vacillating, Rosie saw her father enter the house. Soon Mr. Kuroda came out alone, putting on his coat. Mr. Kuroda got into his car and backed out down the driveway onto the highway. Next her father emerged, also alone, something in his arms (it was the picture, she realized), and, going over to the bathhouse woodpile, he threw the picture on the ground and picked up the axe. Smashing the picture, glass and all (she heard the explosion faintly), he reached over for the kerosene that was used to encourage the bath fire and poured it over the wreckage. I am dreaming, Rosie said to herself, I am dreaming, but her father, having made sure that his act of cremation was irrevocable, was even then returning to the fields.

Rosie ran past him and toward the house. What had become of her mother? She burst into the parlor and found her mother at the back window watching the dying fire. They watched together until there remained only a feeble smoke under the blazing sun. Her mother was very calm.

"Do you know why I married your father?" she said without turning.

"No," said Rosie. It was the most frightening question she had ever been called upon to answer. Don't tell me now, she wanted to say, tell me tomorrow, tell me next week, don't tell me today. But she knew she would be told now, that the telling would combine with the other violence of the hot afternoon to level her life, her world to the very ground.

It was like a story out of the magazines illustrated in sepia, which she had consumed so greedily for a period until the information had somehow reached her that those wretchedly unhappy autobiographies, offered to her as the testimonials of living men and women, were largely inventions: Her mother, at nineteen, had come to America and married her father as an alternative to suicide.

At eighteen she had been in love with the first son of one of the well-to-do families in her village. The two had met whenever and wherever they could, secretly, because it would not have done for his family to see him favor her — her father had no money; he was a drunkard and a gambler besides. She had learned she was with child; an excellent match had already been arranged for her lover. Despised by her family, she had given premature birth to a stillborn son, who would be seventeen now. Her family did not turn her out, but she could no longer project herself in any direction without refreshing in them the memory of her indiscretion. She wrote to Aunt Taka, her favorite sister in America, threatening to kill herself if Aunt Taka would not send for her. Aunt Taka hastily arranged a marriage with a young man of whom she knew, but lately arrived from Japan, a young man of simple mind, it was said, but of kindly heart. The young man was never told why his unseen betrothed was so eager to hasten the day of meeting.

The story was told perfectly, with neither groping for words nor untoward passion. It was as though her mother had memorized it by heart, reciting it to herself so many times over that its nagging vileness had long since gone.

"I had a brother then?" Rosie asked, for this was what seemed to matter now; she would think about the other later, she assured herself, pushing back the illumination which threatened all that darkness that had hitherto been merely mysterious or even glamorous. "A half-brother?"

"Yes."

"I would have liked a brother," she said.

Suddenly, her mother knelt on the floor and took her by the wrists. "Rosie," she said urgently, "Promise me you will never marry!" Shocked more by the request than the revelation, Rosie stared at her mother's face. Jesus, Jesus, she called silently, not certain whether she was invoking the help of the son of the Carrascos or of God, until there returned sweetly the memory of Jesus' hand, how it had touched her and where. Still her mother waited for an answer, holding her wrists so tightly that her hands were going numb. She tried to pull free. Promise, her mother whispered fiercely, promise. Yes, yes, I promise, Rosie said. But for an instant she turned away, and her mother, hearing the familiar glib agreement, released her. Oh, you, you, you, her eyes and twisted mouth said, you fool. Rosie, covering her face, began at last to cry, and the embrace and consoling hand came much later than she expected.

(1949)

Flannery O'Connor *1925–1964*

GOOD COUNTRY PEOPLE

Besides the neutral expression that she wore when she was alone, Mrs. Freeman had two others, forward and reverse, that she used for all her human dealings. Her forward expression was steady and driving like the advance of a heavy truck. Her eyes never swerved to left or right but turned as the story turned as if they followed a yellow line down the center of it. She seldom used the other expression because it was not often necessary for her to retract a statement, but when she did, her face came to a complete stop, there was an almost imperceptible movement of her black eyes, during which they seemed to be receding, and then the observer would see that Mrs. Freeman, though she might stand there as real as several grain sacks thrown on top of each other, was no longer there in spirit. As for getting anything across to her when this was the case, Mrs. Hopewell had given it up. She might talk her head off. Mrs. Freeman could never be brought to admit herself wrong on any point. She would stand there and if she could be brought to say anything, it was something like, "Well, I wouldn't of said it was and I wouldn't of said it wasn't" or letting her gaze range over the top kitchen shelf where there was an assortment of dusty bottles, she might remark, "I see you ain't ate many of them figs you put up last summer."

They carried on their most important business in the kitchen at breakfast. Every morning Mrs. Hopewell got up at seven o'clock and lit her gas heater and Joy's. Joy was her daughter, a large blonde girl who had an artificial leg. Mrs. Hopewell thought of her as a child though she was thirty-two years old and highly educated. Joy would get up while her mother was eating and lumber into the bathroom and slam the door, and before long, Mrs. Freeman would arrive at the back door. Joy would hear her mother call, "Come on in," and then they would talk for a while in low voices that were indistinguishable in the bathroom. By the time Joy came in, they had usually finished the weather report and were on one or the other of Mrs. Freeman's daughters, Glynese or Carramae. Joy called them Glycerin and Caramel. Glynese, a redhead, was eighteen and had many admirers; Carramae, a blonde, was only fifteen but already married and pregnant. She could not keep anything on her stomach. Every morning Mrs. Freeman told Mrs. Hopewell how many times she had vomited since the last report.

Mrs. Hopewell liked to tell people that Glynese and Carramae were two of the finest girls she knew and that Mrs. Freeman was a *lady* and that she was never ashamed to take her anywhere or introduce her to anybody they might meet. Then she would tell how she had happened to hire the Freemans in the first place and how they were a godsend to her and how she had had them four years. The reason for her keeping them so long was that they were not trash. They were good country people. She had telephoned the man whose name they had given as reference and he had told her that Mr. Freeman was a good farmer but that his wife was the nosiest woman ever to walk the earth. "She's got to be into everything," the man said. "If she don't get there before the dust settles, you can bet she's dead, that's all. She'll want to know all your business. I can stand him real good," he had said, "but me nor my wife neither could have stood that woman one more minute on this place." That had put Mrs. Hopewell off for a few days.

She had hired them in the end because there were no other applicants but she had made up her mind beforehand exactly how she would handle the woman. Since she was the type who had to be into everything, then, Mrs. Hopewell had decided, she would not only let her be into everything, she would *see to it* that she was into everything—she would give her the responsibility of everything, she would put her in charge. Mrs. Hopewell had no bad qualities of her own but she was able to use other people's in such a constructive way that she had kept them four years.

Nothing is perfect. This was one of Mrs. Hopewell's favorite sayings. Another was: that is life! And still another, the most important, was: well, other people have their opinions too. She would make these statements, usually at the table, in a tone of gentle insistence as if no one held them but her, and the large hulking Joy, whose constant outrage had obliterated every expression from her face, would stare just a little to the side of her, her eyes icy blue, with the look of someone who has achieved blindness by an act of will and means to keep it.

When Mrs. Hopewell said to Mrs. Freeman that life was like that, Mrs. Freeman would say, "I always said so myself." Nothing had been arrived at by anyone that had not first been arrived at by her. She was quicker than Mr. Freeman. When Mrs. Hopewell said to her after they had been on the place a while, "You know, you're the wheel behind the wheel," and winked, Mrs. Freeman had said, "I know it. I've always been quick. It's some that are quicker than others."

"Everybody is different," Mrs. Hopewell said.

"Yes, most people is," Mrs. Freeman said.

"It takes all kinds to make the world."

"I always said it did myself."

The girl was used to this kind of dialogue for breakfast and more of it for dinner; sometimes they had it for supper too. When they had no guest they ate in the kitchen because that was easier. Mrs. Freeman always managed to arrive at some point during the meal and to watch them finish it. She would stand in the doorway if it were summer but in the winter she would stand with one elbow on top of the refrigerator and look down on them, or she would stand by the gas heater, lifting the back of her skirt slightly. Occasionally she would stand against the wall and roll her head from side to side. At no time was she in any hurry to leave. All this was very trying on Mrs. Hopewell but she was a woman of great patience. She realized that nothing is perfect and that in the Freemans she had good country people and that if, in this day and age, you get good country people, you had better hang onto them.

She had had plenty of experience with trash. Before the Freemans she had averaged one tenant family a year. The wives of these farmers were not the kind you would want to be around you for very long. Mrs. Hopewell, who had divorced her husband long ago, needed someone to walk over the fields with her; and when Joy had to be impressed for these services, her remarks were usually so ugly and her face so glum that Mrs. Hopewell would say, "If you can't come pleasantly, I don't want you at all," to which the girl, standing square and rigid-shouldered with her neck thrust slightly forward, would reply, "If you want me, here I am—LIKE I AM."

Mrs. Hopewell excused this attitude because of the leg (which had been shot off in a hunting accident when Joy was ten). It was hard for Mrs. Hopewell to realize that her child was thirty-two now and that for more than twenty years she had had only one leg. She thought of her still as a child because it tore her heart to think instead of the poor stout girl in her thirties who had never danced a step or had any *normal* good times. Her name was really Joy but as soon as she was twenty-one and away from home, she had had it legally changed. Mrs. Hopewell was certain that she had thought and thought until she had hit upon the ugliest name in any language. Then she had gone and had the beautiful name, Joy, changed without telling her mother until after she had done it. Her legal name was Hulga.

When Mrs. Hopewell thought the name, Hulga, she thought of the broad blank hull of a battleship. She would not use it. She continued to call her Joy to which the girl responded but in a purely mechanical way.

Hulga had learned to tolerate Mrs. Freeman who saved her from taking walks with her mother. Even Glynese and Carramae were useful when they occupied attention that might otherwise have been directed at her. At first she had thought she could not stand Mrs. Freeman for she had found that it was not possible to be rude to her. Mrs. Freeman would take on strange resentments and for days together she would be sullen but the source of her displeasure was always obscure; a direct attack, a positive leer, blatant ugliness to her face — these never touched her. And without warning one day, she began calling her Hulga.

She did not call her that in front of Mrs. Hopewell who would have been incensed but when she and the girl happened to be out of the house together, she would say something and add the name Hulga to the end of it, and the big spectacled Joy-Hulga would scowl and redden as if her privacy had been intruded upon. She considered the name her personal affair. She had arrived at it first purely on the basis of its ugly sound and then the full genius of its fitness had struck her. She had a vision of the name working like the ugly sweating Vulcan who stayed in the furnace and to whom, presumably, the goddess had to come when called. She saw it as the name of her highest creative act. One of her major triumphs was that her mother had not been able to turn her dust into Joy, but the greater one was that she had been able to turn it herself into Hulga. However, Mrs. Freeman's relish for using the name only irritated her. It was as if Mrs. Freeman's beady steel-pointed eyes had penetrated far enough behind her face to reach some secret fact. Something about her seemed to fascinate Mrs. Freeman and then one day Hulga realized that it was the artificial leg. Mrs. Freeman had a special fondness for the details of secret infections, hidden deformities, assaults upon children. Of diseases, she preferred the lingering or incurable. Hulga had heard Mrs. Hopewell give her the details of the hunting accident, how the leg had been literally blasted off, how she had never lost consciousness. Mrs. Freeman could listen to it any time as if it had happened an hour ago.

When Hulga stumped into the kitchen in the morning (she could walk without making the awful noise but she made it — Mrs. Hopewell was certain — because it was ugly-sounding), she glanced at them and did not speak. Mrs. Hopewell would be in her red kimono with her hair tied around her head in rags. She would be sitting at the table, finishing her breakfast and Mrs. Freeman would be hanging by her elbow outward from the refrigerator, looking down at the table. Hulga always put her eggs on the stove to boil and then stood over them with her arms folded, and Mrs. Hopewell would look at her — a kind of indirect gaze divided between her and Mrs. Freeman — and would think that if she would only keep herself up a little, she wouldn't be so bad looking. There was nothing wrong with her face that a pleasant expression wouldn't help. Mrs. Hopewell said that people who looked on the bright side of things would be beautiful even if they were not.

Whenever she looked at Joy this way, she could not help but feel that it would have been better if the child had not taken the Ph.D. It had certainly not brought her out any and now that she had it, there was no more excuse for her to go to school again. Mrs. Hopewell thought it was nice for girls to go to school to have a good time but Joy had "gone through." Anyhow, she would not have been strong enough to go again. The doctors had told Mrs. Hopewell that with the best of care, Joy might see forty-five. She had a weak heart. Joy had made it plain that if it had not been for this condition, she would be far from these red hills and good country people. She would be in a university lecturing to people who knew what she was talking about. And Mrs. Hopewell could very well picture her there, looking like a scarecrow and lecturing to more of the same. Here she went about all day in a six-year-old skirt and a yellow sweat shirt with a faded cowboy on a horse embossed on it. She thought this was funny; Mrs. Hopewell thought it was idiotic and showed simply that she was still a child. She was brilliant but she didn't have a grain of sense. It seemed to Mrs. Hopewell that every year she grew less like other people and more like herself — bloated, rude, and squint-eyed. And she said such strange things! To her own mother she had said — without warning, without excuse, standing up in the middle of a meal with her face purple and her mouth half full — "Woman! do you ever look inside? Do you ever look inside and see what you are *not?* God!" she had cried sinking down again and staring at her plate, "Malebranche[1] was right: we are not our own light. We are not our own light!" Mrs. Hopewell had no idea to this day what brought that on. She had only made the remark, hoping Joy would take it in, that a smile never hurt anyone.

The girl had taken the Ph.D. in philosophy and this left Mrs. Hopewell at a complete loss. You could say, "My daughter is a nurse," or "My daughter is a school teacher," or even, "My daughter is a chemical engineer." You could not say, "My daughter is a philosopher." That was something that had ended with the Greeks and Romans. All day Joy sat on her neck in a deep chair, reading. Sometimes she went for walks but she didn't like dogs or cats or birds or flowers or nature or nice young men. She looked at nice young men as if she could smell their stupidity.

One day Mrs. Hopewell had picked up one of the books the girl had just put down and opening it at random, she read, "Science, on the other hand, has to assert its soberness and seriousness afresh and declare that it is concerned solely with what-is. Nothing — how can it be for science anything but a horror and a phantasm? If science is right, then one thing stands firm: science wishes to know nothing of nothing. Such is after all the strictly scientific approach to Nothing. We know it by wishing to know nothing of Nothing." These words had been underlined with a blue pencil and they worked on Mrs. Hopewell like some evil incantation in gibberish. She shut the book quickly and went out of the room as if she were having a chill.

This morning when the girl came in, Mrs. Freeman was on Carramae. "She

---

[1] Nicolas Malebranche, 1638–1715, French philosopher

thrown up four times after supper," she said, "and was up twict in the night after three o'clock. Yesterday she didn't do nothing but ramble in the bureau drawer. All she did. Stand up there and see what she could run up on."

"She's got to eat," Mrs. Hopewell muttered, sipping her coffee, while she watched Joy's back at the stove. She was wondering what the child had said to the Bible salesman. She could not imagine what kind of a conversation she could possibly have had with him.

He was a tall gaunt hatless youth who had called yesterday to sell them a Bible. He had appeared at the door, carrying a large black suitcase that weighted him so heavily on one side that he had to brace himself against the door facing. He seemed on the point of collapse but he said in a cheerful voice, "Good morning, Mrs. Cedars!" and set the suitcase down on the mat. He was not a bad-looking young man though he had on a bright blue suit and yellow socks that were not pulled up far enough. He had prominent face bones and a streak of sticky-looking brown hair falling across his forehead.

"I'm Mrs. Hopewell," she said.

"Oh!" he said, pretending to look puzzled but with his eyes sparkling, "I saw it said 'The Cedars,' on the mailbox so I thought you was Mrs. Cedars!" and he burst out in a pleasant laugh. He picked up the satchel and under cover of a pant, he fell forward into her hall. It was rather as if the suitcase had moved first, jerking him after it. "Mrs. Hopewell!" he said and grabbed her hand. "I hope you are well!" and he laughed again and then all at once his face sobered completely. He paused and gave her a straight earnest look and said, "Lady, I've come to speak of serious things."

"Well, come in," she muttered, none too pleased because her dinner was almost ready. He came into the parlor and sat down on the edge of a straight chair and put the suitcase between his feet and glanced around the room as if he were sizing her up by it. Her silver gleamed on the two sideboards; she decided he had never been in a room as elegant as this.

"Mrs. Hopewell," he began, using her name in a way that sounded almost intimate, "I know you believe in Chrustian service."

"Well yes," she murmured.

"I know," he said and paused, looking very wise with his head cocked on one side, "that you're a good woman. Friends have told me."

Mrs. Hopewell never liked to be taken for a fool. "What are you selling?" she asked.

"Bibles," the young man said and his eye raced around the room before he added, "I see you have no family Bible in your parlor, I see that is the one lack you got!"

Mrs. Hopewell could not say, "My daughter is an atheist and won't let me keep the Bible in the parlor." She said, stiffening slightly, "I keep my Bible by my bedside." This was not the truth. It was in the attic somewhere.

"Lady," he said, "the word of God ought to be in the parlor."

"Well, I think that's a matter of taste," she began. "I think. . . . "

"Lady," he said, "for a Chrustian, the word of God ought to be in every room in the house besides in his heart. I know you're a Chrustian because I can see it in every line of your face."

She stood up and said, "Well, young man, I don't want to buy a Bible and I smell my dinner burning."

He didn't get up. He began to twist his hands and looking down at them, he said softly, "Well lady, I'll tell you the truth — not many people want to buy one nowadays and besides, I know I'm real simple. I don't know how to say a thing but to say it. I'm just a country boy." He glanced up into her unfriendly face. "People like you don't like to fool with country people like me!"

"Why!" she cried, "good country people are the salt of the earth! Besides, we all have different ways of doing, it takes all kinds to make the world go 'round. That's life!"

"You said a mouthful," he said.

"Why, I think there aren't enough good country people in the world!" she said, stirred. "I think that's what's wrong with it!"

His face had brightened. "I didn't inraduce myself," he said. "I'm Manley Pointer from out in the country around Willohobie, not even from a place, just from near a place."

"You wait a minute," she said. "I have to see about my dinner." She went out to the kitchen and found Joy standing near the door where she had been listening.

"Get rid of the salt of the earth," she said, "and let's eat."

Mrs. Hopewell gave her a pained look and turned the heat down under the vegetables. "*I* can't be rude to anybody," she murmured and went back into the parlor.

He had opened the suitcase and was sitting with a Bible on each knee.

"You might as well put those up," she told him. "I don't want one."

"I appreciate your honesty," he said. "You don't see any more real honest people unless you go way out in the country."

"I know," she said, "real genuine folks!" Through the crack in the door she heard a groan.

"I guess a lot of boys come telling you they're working their way through college," he said, "but I'm not going to tell you that. Somehow," he said, "I don't want to go to college. I want to devote my life to Chrustian service. See," he said, lowering his voice, "I got this heart condition. I may not live long. When you know it's something wrong with you and you may not live long, well then, lady. . . . " He paused, with his mouth open, and stared at her.

He and Joy had the same condition! She knew that her eyes were filling with tears but she collected herself quickly and murmured, "Won't you stay for dinner? We'd love to have you!" and was sorry the instant she heard herself say it.

"Yes mam," he said in an abashed voice, "I would sher love to do that!"

Joy had given him one look on being introduced to him and then throughout the meal had not glanced at him again. He had addressed several remarks to her, which she had pretended not to hear. Mrs. Hopewell could not understand deliberate rudeness, although she lived with it, and she felt she had always to overflow with hospitality to make up for Joy's lack of courtesy. She urged him to talk about himself and he did. He said he was the seventh child of twelve and that his father had been crushed under a tree when he himself was eight years old. He had been crushed very badly, in fact, almost cut in two and was practically not recognizable. His mother had got along the best she could by hard working and she had always seen that her children went to Sunday School and that they read the Bible every evening. He was now nineteen years old and he had been selling Bibles for four months. In that time he had sold seventy-seven Bibles and had the promise of two more sales. He wanted to become a missionary because he

thought that was the way you could do most for people. "He who losest his life
shall find it," he said simply and he was so sincere, so genuine and earnest that
Mrs. Hopewell would not for the world have smiled. He prevented his peas from
sliding onto the table by blocking them with a piece of bread which he later
cleaned his plate with. She could see Joy observing sidewise how he handled his
knife and fork and she saw too that every few minutes, the boy would dart a keen
appraising glance at the girl as if he were trying to attract her attention.

After dinner Joy cleared the dishes off the table and disappeared and Mrs.
Hopewell was left to talk with him. He told her again about his childhood and
his father's accident and about various things that had happened to him. Every
five minutes or so she would stifle a yawn. He sat for two hours until finally she
told him she must go because she had an appointment in town. He packed his
Bibles and thanked her and prepared to leave, but in the doorway he stopped and
wrung her hand and said that not on any of his trips had he met a lady as nice as
her and he asked if he could come again. She had said she would always be happy
to see him.

Joy had been standing in the road, apparently looking at something in the
distance, when he came down the steps toward her, bent to the side with his
heavy valise. He stopped where she was standing and confronted her directly.
Mrs. Hopewell could not hear what he said but she trembled to think what Joy
would say to him. She could see that after a minute Joy said something and that
then the boy began to speak again, making an excited gesture with his free hand.
After a minute Joy said something else at which the boy began to speak once
more. Then to her amazement, Mrs. Hopewell saw the two of them walk off
together, toward the gate. Joy had walked all the way to the gate with him and
Mrs. Hopewell could not imagine what they had said to each other, and she had
not yet dared to ask.

Mrs. Freeman was insisting upon her attention. She had moved from the
refrigerator to the heater so that Mrs. Hopewell had to turn and face her in order
to seem to be listening. "Glynese gone out with Harvey Hill again last night,"
she said. "She had this sty."

"Hill," Mrs. Hopewell said absently, "is that the one who works in the
garage?"

"Nome, he's the one that goes to chiropracter school," Mrs. Freeman said.
"She had this sty. Been had it two days. So she says when he brought her in the
other night he says, 'Lemme get rid of that sty for you,' and she says, 'How?' and
he says, 'You just lay yourself down acrost the seat of that car and I'll show you.'
So she done it and he popped her neck. Kept on a-popping it several times until
she made him quit. This morning," Mrs. Freeman said, "she ain't got no sty. She
ain't got no traces of a sty."

"I never heard of that before," Mrs. Hopewell said.

"He ast her to marry him before the Ordinary,"[2] Mrs. Freeman went on, "and
she told him she wasn't going to be married in no *office*."

"Well, Glynese is a fine girl," Mrs. Hopewell said. "Glynese and Carramae
are both fine girls."

"Carramae said when her and Lyman was married Lyman said it sure felt
sacred to him. She said he said he wouldn't take five hundred dollars for being
married by a preacher."

[2]Judge of probate.

"How much would he take?" the girl asked from the stove.

"He said he wouldn't take five hundred dollars," Mrs. Freeman repeated.

"Well we all have work to do," Mrs. Hopewell said.

"Lyman said it just felt more sacred to him," Mrs. Freeman said. "The doctor wants Carramae to eat prunes. Says instead of medicine. Says them cramps is coming from pressure. You know where I think it is?"

"She'll be better in a few weeks," Mrs. Hopewell said.

"In the tube," Mrs. Freeman said. "Else she wouldn't be as sick as she is."

Hulga had cracked her two eggs into a saucer and was bringing them to the table along with a cup of coffee that she had filled too full. She sat down carefully and began to eat, meaning to keep Mrs. Freeman there by questions if for any reason she showed an inclination to leave. She could perceive her mother's eye on her. The first round-about question would be about the Bible salesman and she did not wish to bring it on. "How did he pop her neck?" she asked.

Mrs. Freeman went into a description of how he had popped her neck. She said he owned a '55 Mercury but that Glynese said she would rather marry a man with only a '36 Plymouth who would be married by a preacher. The girl asked what if he had a '32 Plymouth and Mrs. Freeman said what Glynese had said was a '36 Plymouth.

Mrs. Hopewell said there were not many girls with Glynese's common sense. She said what she admired in those girls was their common sense. She said that reminded her that they had had a nice visitor yesterday, a young man selling Bibles. "Lord," she said, "he bored me to death but he was so sincere and genuine I couldn't be rude to him. He was just good country people, you know," she said, "—just the salt of the earth."

"I seen him walk up," Mrs. Freeman said, "and then later—I seen him walk off," and Hulga could feel the slight shift in her voice, the slight insinuation, that he had not walked off alone, had he? Her face remained expressionless but the color rose into her neck and she seemed to swallow it down with the next spoonful of egg. Mrs. Freeman was looking at her as if they had a secret together.

"Well, it takes all kinds of people to make the world go 'round," Mrs. Hopewell said. "It's very good we aren't all alike."

"Some people are more alike than others," Mrs. Freeman said.

Hulga got up and stumped, with about twice the noise that was necessary, into her room and locked the door. She was to meet the Bible salesman at ten o'clock at the gate. She had thought about it half the night. She had started thinking of it as a great joke and then she had begun to see profound implications in it. She had lain in bed imagining dialogues for them that were insane on the surface but that reached below to depths that no Bible salesman would be aware of. Their conversation yesterday had been of this kind.

He had stopped in front of her and had simply stood there. His face was bony and sweaty and bright, with a little pointed nose in the center of it, and his look was different from what it had been at the dinner table. He was gazing at her with open curiosity, with fascination, like a child watching a new fantastic animal at the zoo, and he was breathing as if he had run a great distance to reach her. His gaze seemed somehow familiar but she could not think where she had been regarded with it before. For almost a minute he didn't say anything. Then on what seemed an insuck of breath, he whispered, "You ever ate a chicken that was two days old?"

The girl looked at him stonily. He might have just put this question up for consideration at the meeting of a philosophical association. "Yes," she presently replied as if she had considered it from all angles.

"It must have been mighty small!" he said triumphantly and shook all over with little nervous giggles, getting very red in the face, and subsiding finally into his gaze of complete admiration, while the girl's expression remained exactly the same.

"How old are you?" he asked softly.

She waited some time before she answered. Then in a flat voice she said, "Seventeen."

His smiles came in succession like waves breaking on the surface of a little lake. "I see you got a wooden leg," he said. "I think you're real brave. I think you're real sweet."

The girl stood blank and solid and silent.

"Walk to the gate with me," he said. "You're a brave sweet little thing and I liked you the minute I seen you walk in the door."

Hulga began to move forward.

"What's your name?" he asked, smiling down on the top of her head.

"Hulga," she said.

"Hulga," he murmured, "Hulga. Hulga. I never heard of anybody name Hulga before. You're shy, aren't you, Hulga?" he asked.

She nodded, watching his large red hand on the handle of the giant valise.

"I like girls that wear glasses," he said. "I think a lot. I'm not like these people that a serious thought don't ever enter their heads. It's because I may die."

"I may die too," she said suddenly and looked up at him. His eyes were very small and brown, glittering feverishly.

"Listen," he said, "don't you think some people was meant to meet on account of what all they got in common and all? Like they both think serious thoughts and all?" He shifted the valise to his other hand so that the hand nearest her was free. He caught hold of her elbow and shook it a little. "I don't work on Saturday," he said. "I like to walk in the woods and see what Mother Nature is wearing. O'er the hills and far away. Picnics and things. Couldn't we go on a picnic tomorrow? Say yes, Hulga," he said and gave her a dying look as if he felt his insides about to drop out of him. He had even seemed to sway slightly toward her.

During the night she had imagined that she seduced him. She imagined that the two of them walked on the place until they came to the storage barn beyond the two back fields and there, she imagined, that things came to such a pass that she very easily seduced him and that then, of course, she had to reckon with his remorse. True genius can get an idea across even to an inferior mind. She imagined that she took his remorse in hand and changed it into a deeper understanding of life. She took all his shame away and turned it into something useful.

She set off for the gate at exactly ten o'clock, escaping without drawing Mrs. Hopewell's attention. She didn't take anything to eat, forgetting that food is usually taken on a picnic. She wore a pair of slacks and a dirty white shirt, and as an afterthought, she had put some Vapex on the collar of it since she did not own any perfume. When she reached the gate no one was there.

She looked up and down the empty highway and had the furious feeling that she had been tricked, that he had only meant to make her walk to the gate after the idea of him. Then suddenly he stood up, very tall, from behind a bush on the opposite embankment. Smiling, he lifted his hat which was new and wide-brimmed. He had not worn it yesterday and she wondered if he had bought it for the occasion. It was toast-colored with a red and white band around it and was slightly too large for him. He stepped from behind the bush still carrying the black valise. He had on the same suit and the same yellow socks sucked down in his shoes from walking. He crossed the highway and said, "I knew you'd come!"

The girl wondered acidly how he had known this. She pointed to the valise and asked, "Why did you bring your Bibles?"

He took her elbow, smiling down on her as if he could not stop. "You can never tell when you'll need the word of God, Hulga," he said. She had a moment in which she doubted that this was actually happening and then they began to climb the embankment. They went down into the pasture toward the woods. The boy walked lightly by her side, bouncing on his toes. The valise did not seem to be heavy today; he even swung it. They crossed half the pasture without saying anything and then, putting his hand easily on the small of her back, he asked softly, "Where does your wooden leg join on?"

She turned an ugly red and glared at him and for an instant the boy looked abashed. "I didn't mean you no harm," he said. "I only meant you're so brave and all. I guess God takes care of you."

"No," she said, looking forward and walking fast, "I don't even believe in God."

At this he stopped and whistled. "No!" he exclaimed as if he were too astonished to say anything else.

She walked on and in a second he was bouncing at her side, fanning with his hat. "That's very unusual for a girl," he remarked, watching her out of the corner of his eye. When they reached the edge of the wood, he put his hand on her back again and drew her against him without a word and kissed her heavily.

The kiss, which had more pressure than feeling behind it, produced that extra surge of adrenalin in the girl that enables one to carry a packed trunk out of a burning house, but in her, the power went at once to the brain. Even before he released her, her mind, clear and detached and ironic anyway, was regarding him from a great distance, with amusement but with pity. She had never been kissed before and she was pleased to discover that it was an unexceptional experience and all a matter of the mind's control. Some people might enjoy drain water if they were told it was vodka. When the boy, looking expectant but uncertain, pushed her gently away, she turned and walked on, saying nothing as if such business, for her, were common enough.

He came along panting at her side, trying to help her when he saw a root that she might trip over. He caught and held back the long swaying blades of thorn vine until she had passed beyond them. She led the way and he came breathing heavily behind her. Then they came out on a sunlit hillside, sloping softly into another one a little smaller. Beyond, they could see the rusted top of the old barn where the extra hay was stored.

The hill was sprinkled with small pink weeds. "Then you ain't saved?" he asked suddenly, stopping.

The girl smiled. It was the first time she had smiled at him at all. "In my economy," she said, "I'm saved and you are damned but I told you I didn't believe in God."

Nothing seemed to destroy the boy's look of admiration. He gazed at her now as if the fantastic animal at the zoo had put its paw through the bars and given him a loving poke. She thought he looked as if he wanted to kiss her again and she walked on before he had the chance.

"Ain't there somewheres we can sit down sometime?" he murmured, his voice softening toward the end of the sentence.

"In that barn," she said.

They made for it rapidly as if it might slide away like a train. It was a large two-story barn, cool and dark inside. The boy pointed up the ladder that led into the loft and said, "It's too bad we can't go up there."

"Why can't we?" she asked.

"Yer leg," he said reverently.

The girl gave him a contemptuous look and putting both hands on the ladder, she climbed it while he stood below, apparently awestruck. She pulled herself expertly through the opening and then looked down at him and said, "Well, come on if you're coming," and he began to climb the ladder, awkwardly bringing the suitcase with him.

"We won't need the Bible," she observed.

"You never can tell," he said, panting. After he had got into the loft, he was a few seconds catching his breath. She had sat down in a pile of straw. A wide sheath of sunlight, filled with dust particles, slanted over her. She lay back against a bale, her face turned away, looking out the front opening of the barn where hay was thrown from a wagon into the loft. The two pink-speckled hillsides lay back against a dark ridge of woods. The sky was cloudless and cold blue. The boy dropped down by her side and put one arm under her and the other over her and began methodically kissing her face, making little noises like a fish. He did not remove his hat but it was pushed far enough back not to interfere. When her glasses got in his way, he took them off of her and slipped them into his pocket.

The girl at first did not return any of the kisses but presently she began to and after she had put several on his cheek, she reached his lips and remained there, kissing him again and again as if she were trying to draw all the breath out of him. His breath was clear and sweet like a child's and the kisses were sticky like a child's. He mumbled about loving her and about knowing when he first seen her that he loved her, but the mumbling was like the sleepy fretting of a child being put to sleep by his mother. Her mind, throughout this, never stopped or lost itself for a second to her feelings. "You ain't said you loved me none," he whispered finally, pulling back from her. "You got to say that."

She looked away from him off into the hollow sky and then down at a black ridge and then down farther into what appeared to be two green swelling lakes. She didn't realize he had taken her glasses but this landscape could not seem exceptional to her for she seldom paid any close attention to her surroundings.

"You got to say it," he repeated. "You got to say you love me."

She was always careful how she committed herself. "In a sense," she began, "if you use the word loosely, you might say that. But it's not a word I use. I don't have illusions. I'm one of those people who see *through* to nothing."

The boy was frowning. "You got to say it. I said it and you got to say it," he said.

The girl looked at him almost tenderly. "You poor baby," she murmured. "It's just as well you don't understand," and she pulled him by the neck, face-down, against her. "We are all damned," she said, "but some of us have taken off our blindfolds and see that there's nothing to see. It's a kind of salvation."

The boy's astonished eyes looked blankly through the ends of her hair. "Okay," he almost whined, "but do you love me or don'tcher?"

"Yes," she said and added, "in a sense. But I must tell you something. There mustn't be anything dishonest between us." She lifted his head and looked him in the eye. "I am thirty years old," she said. "I have a number of degrees."

The boy's look was irritated but dogged. "I don't care," he said. "I don't care a thing about what all you done. I just want to know if you love me or don'tcher?" and he caught her to him and wildly planted her face with kisses until she said, "Yes, yes."

"Okay then," he said, letting her go. "Prove it."

She smiled, looking dreamily out on the shifty landscape. She had seduced him without even making up her mind to try. "How?" she asked, feeling that he should be delayed a little.

He leaned over and put his lips to her ear. "Show me where your wooden leg joins on," he whispered.

The girl uttered a sharp little cry and her face instantly drained of color. The obscenity of the suggestion was not what shocked her. As a child she had sometimes been subject to feelings of shame but education had removed the last traces of that as a good surgeon scrapes for cancer; she would no more have felt it over what he was asking than she would have believed in his Bible. But she was as sensitive about the artificial leg as a peacock about his tail. No one ever touched it but her. She took care of it as someone else would his soul, in private and almost with her own eyes turned away. "No," she said.

"I known it," he muttered, sitting up. "You're just playing me for a sucker."

"Oh no no!" she cried. "It joins on at the knee. Only at the knee. Why do you want to see it?"

The boy gave her a long penetrating look. "Because," he said, "it's what makes you different. You ain't like anybody else."

She sat staring at him. There was nothing about her face or her round freezing-blue eyes to indicate that this had moved her; but she felt as if her heart had stopped and left her mind to pump her blood. She decided that for the first time in her life she was face to face with real innocence. This boy, with an instinct that came from beyond wisdom, had touched the truth about her. When after a minute, she said in a hoarse high voice, "All right," it was like surrendering to him completely. It was like losing her own life and finding it again, miraculously, in his.

Very gently he began to roll the slack leg up. The artificial limb, in a white sock and brown flat shoe, was bound in a heavy material like canvas and ended in an ugly jointure where it was attached to the stump. The boy's face and his voice were entirely reverent as he uncovered it and said, "Now show me how to take it off and on."

She took it off for him and put it back on again and then he took it off himself, handling it as tenderly as if it were a real one. "See!" he said with a delighted child's face. "Now I can do it myself!"

"Put it back on," she said. She was thinking that she would run away with him and that every night he would take the leg off and every morning put it back on again. "Put it back on," she said.

"Not yet," he murmured, setting it on its foot out of her reach. "Leave it off for awhile. You got me instead."

She gave a little cry of alarm but he pushed her down and began to kiss her again. Without the leg she felt entirely dependent on him. Her brain seemed to have stopped thinking altogether and to be about some other function that it was not very good at. Different expressions raced back and forth over her face. Every now and then the boy, his eyes like two steel spikes, would glance behind him, where the leg stood. Finally she pushed him off and said, "Put it back on me now."

"Wait," he said. He leaned the other way and pulled the valise toward him and opened it. It had a pale blue spotted lining and there were only two Bibles in it. He took one of these out and opened the cover of it. It was hollow and contained a pocket flask of whiskey, a pack of cards, and a small blue box with printing on it. He laid these out in front of her one at a time in an evenly-spaced row, like one presenting offerings at the shrine of a goddess. He put the blue box in her hand. THIS PRODUCT TO BE USED ONLY FOR THE PREVENTION OF DISEASE, she read, and dropped it. The boy was unscrewing the top of the flask. He stopped and pointed, with a smile, to the deck of cards. It was not an ordinary deck but one with an obscene picture on the back of each card. "Take a swig," he said, offering her the bottle first. He held it in front of her, but like one mesmerized, she did not move.

Her voice when she spoke had an almost pleading sound. "Aren't you," she murmured, "aren't you just good country people?"

The boy cocked his head. He looked as if he were just beginning to understand that she might be trying to insult him. "Yeah," he said, curling his lip slightly, "but it ain't held me back none. I'm as good as you any day in the week."

"Give me my leg," she said.

He pushed it farther away with his foot. "Come on now, let's begin to have us a good time," he said coaxingly. "We ain't got to know one another good yet."

"Give me my leg!" she screamed and tried to lunge for it but he pushed her down easily.

"What's the matter with you all of a sudden?" he asked, frowning as he screwed the top on the flask and put it quickly back inside the Bible. "You just a while ago said you didn't believe in nothing. I thought you was some girl!"

Her face was almost purple. "You're a Christian!" she hissed. "You're a fine Christian! You're just like them all — say one thing and do another. You're a perfect Christian, you're . . . "

The boy's mouth was set angrily. "I hope you don't think," he said in a lofty indignant tone, "that I believe in that crap! I may sell Bibles but I know which end is up and I wasn't born yesterday and I know where I'm going!"

"Give me my leg!" she screeched. He jumped up so quickly that she barely saw him sweep the cards and the blue box back into the Bible and throw the Bible into the valise. She saw him grab the leg and then she saw it for an instant slanted forlornly across the inside of the suitcase with a Bible at either side of its opposite ends. He slammed the lid shut and snatched up the valise and swung it down the hole and then stepped through himself.

When all of him had passed but his head, he turned and regarded her with a look that no longer had any admiration in it. "I've gotten a lot of interesting things," he said. "One time I got a woman's glass eye this way. And you needn't to think you'll catch me because Pointer ain't really my name. I use a different name at every house I call at and don't stay nowhere long. And I'll tell you another thing, Hulga," he said, using the name as if he didn't think much of it, "you ain't so smart. I been believing in nothing ever since I was born!" and then the toast-colored hat disappeared down the hole and the girl was left, sitting on the straw in the dusty sunlight. When she turned her churning face toward the opening, she saw his blue figure struggling successfully over the green speckled lake.

Mrs. Hopewell and Mrs. Freeman, who were in the back pasture, digging up onions, saw him emerge a little later from the woods and head across the meadow toward the highway. "Why, that looks like that nice dull young man that tried to sell me a Bible yesterday," Mrs. Hopewell said, squinting. "He must have been selling them to the Negroes back in there. He was so simple," she said, "but I guess the world would be better off if we were all that simple."

Mrs. Freeman's gaze drove forward and just touched him before he disappeared under the hill. Then she returned her attention to the evil-smelling onion shoot she was lifting from the ground. "Some can't be that simple," she said. "I know I never could."

(1955)

Ursula K. Le Guin *1929–*

THE ONES WHO WALK AWAY FROM OMELAS

With a clamor of bells that set the swallows soaring, the Festival of Summer came to the city Omelas, bright-towered by the sea. The rigging of the boats in harbor sparkled with flags. In the streets between houses with red roofs and painted walls, between old moss-grown gardens and under avenues of trees, past great parks and public buildings, processions moved. Some were decorous: old people in long stiff robes of mauve and gray, grave master workmen, quiet, merry women carrying their babies and chatting as they walked. In other streets the music beat faster, a shimmering of gong and tambourine, and the people went dancing, the procession was a dance. Children dodged in and out, their high calls rising like the swallows' crossing flights over the music and the singing. All the processions wound towards the north side of the city, where on the great water-meadow called the Green Fields boys and girls, naked in the bright air, with mud-stained feet and ankles and long, lithe arms, exercised their restive horses before the race. The horses wore no gear at all but a halter without bit. Their manes were braided with streamers of silver, gold, and green. They flared their nostrils and pranced and boasted to one another; they were vastly excited, the horse being the only animal who had adopted our ceremonies as his own. Far off to the north and west the mountains stood up half encircling Omelas on her bay. The air of morning was so clear that the snow still crowning the Eighteen Peaks burned with white-gold fire across the miles of sunlit air, under the dark blue of the sky. There was just enough wind to make the banners that marked the racecourse snap and flutter now and then. In the silence of the broad green meadows one could hear the music winding through the city streets, farther and nearer and ever approaching, a cheerful faint sweetness of the air that from time to time trembled and gathered together and broke out into the great joyous clanging of the bells.

Joyous! How is one to tell about joy? How describe the citizens of Omelas?

They were not simple folk, you see, though they were happy. But we do not say the words of cheer much any more. All smiles have become archaic. Given a description such as this one tends to make certain assumptions. Given a description such as this one tends to look next for the King, mounted on a splendid stallion and surrounded by his noble knights, or perhaps in a golden litter borne by great-muscled slaves. But there was no king. They did not use swords, or keep slaves. They were not barbarians. I do not know the rules and laws of their society, but I suspect that they were singularly few. As they did without monarchy and slavery, so they also got on without the stock exchange, the advertisement, the secret police, and the bomb. Yet I repeat that these were not simple folk, not dulcet shepherds, noble savages, bland utopians. They were not less complex than us. The trouble is that we have a bad habit, encouraged by pedants and sophisticates, of considering happiness as something rather stupid. Only pain is intellectual, only evil interesting. This is the treason of the artist: a refusal to admit the banality of evil and the terrible boredom of pain. If you can't lick 'em, join 'em. If it hurts, repeat it. But to praise despair is to condemn delight, to embrace violence is to lose hold of everything else. We have almost lost hold; we can no longer describe a happy man, nor make any celebration of joy. How can I tell you about the people of Omelas? They were not naïve and happy children — though their children were, in fact, happy. They were mature, intelligent, passionate adults whose lives were not wretched. O miracle! but I wish I could describe it better. I wish I could convince you. Omelas sounds in my words like a city in a fairy tale, long ago and far away, once upon a time. Perhaps it would be best if you imagined it as your own fancy bids, assuming it will rise to the occasion, for certainly I cannot suit you all. For instance, how about technology? I think that there would be no cars or helicopters in and above the streets; this follows from the fact that the people of Omelas are happy people. Happiness is based on a just discrimination of what is necessary, what is neither necessary nor destructive, and what is destructive. In the middle category, however — that of the unnecessary but undestructive, that of comfort, luxury, exuberance, etc. — they could perfectly well have central heating, subway trains, washing machines, and all kinds of marvelous devices not yet invented here, floating light-sources, fuelless power, a cure for the common cold. Or they could have none of that: it doesn't matter. As you like it. I incline to think that people from towns up and down the coast have been coming in to Omelas during the last days before the Festival on very fast little trains and double-decked trams, and that the train station of Omelas is actually the handsomest building in town, though plainer than the magnificent Farmers' Market. But even granted trains, I fear that Omelas so far strikes some of you as goodygoody. Smiles, bells, parades, horses, bleh. If so, please add an orgy. If an orgy would help, don't hesitate. Let us not, however, have temples from which issue beautiful nude priests and priestesses already half in ecstasy and ready to copulate with any man or woman, lover or stranger, who desires union with the deep godhead of the blood, although that was my first idea. But really it would be better not to have any temples in Omelas — at least, not manned temples. Religion yes, clergy no. Surely the beautiful nudes can just wander about, offering themselves like divine soufflés to the hunger of the needy and the rapture of the flesh. Let them join the processions. Let tambourines be struck above the copulations, and the glory of desire be proclaimed upon the gongs, and (a not unimportant point) let the offspring of these delightful rituals be beloved and looked after by all. One thing I know there is none of in Omelas is guilt. But what else should there be? I thought at first there were no drugs, but that is puritanical. For those who like it, the faint insistent sweetness of *drooz* may perfume the ways of the city, *drooz* which first brings a great lightness and brilliance to the mind and limbs, and then after some hours a dreamy languor, and wonderful visions at last of the very arcana and inmost secrets of the Universe, as well as exciting the pleasure of sex beyond all belief; and it is not habit-forming. For more modest tastes I think there ought to be beer. What else, what else belongs in the joyous city? The sense of victory, surely, the celebration of courage. But as we did without clergy, let us do without soldiers. The joy built upon successful slaughter is not the right kind of joy; it will not do; it is fearful and it is trivial. A boundless and generous contentment, a magnanimous triumph felt not against some outer enemy but in communion with the finest and fairest in the souls of all men everywhere and the splendor of the world's summer: this is what swells the hearts of the people of Omelas, and the victory they celebrate is that of life. I really don't think many of them need to take *drooz*.

Most of the processions have reached the Green Fields by now. A marvelous smell of cooking goes forth from the red and blue tents of the provisioners. The faces of small children are amiably sticky; in the benign gray beard of a man a couple of crumbs of rich pastry are entangled. The youths and girls have mounted their horses and are beginning to group around the starting line of the course. An old woman, small, fat, and laughing, is passing out flowers from a basket, and tall young men wear her flowers in their shining hair. A child of nine or ten sits at the edge of the crowd, alone, playing on a wooden flute. People pause to listen, and they smile, but they do not speak to him; for he never ceases playing and never sees them, his dark eyes wholly rapt in the sweet, thin magic of the tune.

He finishes and slowly lowers his hands holding the wooden flute.

As if that little private silence were the signal, all at once a trumpet sounds from the pavilion near the starting line: imperious, melancholy, piercing. The horses rear on their slender legs, and some of them neigh in answer. Sober-faced, the young riders stroke the horses' necks and soothe them, whispering, "Quiet, quiet, there my beauty, my hope. . . ." They begin to form in rank along the starting line. The crowds along the racecourse are like a field of grass and flowers in the wind. The Festival of Summer has begun.

Do you believe? Do you accept the festival, the city, the joy? No? Then let me describe one more thing.

In a basement under one of the beautiful public buildings of Omelas, or perhaps in the cellar of one of its spacious private homes, there is a room. It has one locked door, and no window. A little light seeps in dustily between cracks in the boards, second-hand from a cobwebbed window somewhere across the cellar. In one corner of the little room a couple of mops, with stiff, clotted, foul-smelling heads, stand near a rusty bucket. The floor is dirt, a little damp to the touch, as cellar dirt usually is. The room is about three paces long and two wide: a mere broom closet or disused tool room. In the room a child is sitting. It could be a boy or a girl. It looks about six, but actually is nearly ten. It is feeble-minded. Perhaps it was born defective, or perhaps it has become imbecile through fear, malnutrition, and neglect. It picks its nose and occasionally fumbles vaguely with its toes or genitals, as it sits hunched in the corner farthest from the bucket and the two mops. It is afraid of the mops. It finds them horrible. It shuts its eyes, but it knows the mops are still standing there; and the door is locked; and nobody will come. The door is always locked; and nobody ever comes, except that sometimes — the child has no understanding of time or interval — sometimes the door rattles terribly and opens, and a person, or several people, are there. One of them may come in and kick the child to make it stand up. The others never come close, but peer in at it with frightened, disgusted eyes. The food bowl and the water jug are hastily filled, the door is locked, the eyes disappear. The people at the door never say anything, but the child, who has not always lived in the tool room, and can remember sunlight and its mother's voice, sometimes speaks. "I will be good," it says. "Please let me out. I will be good!" They never answer. The child used to scream for help at night, and cry a good deal, but now it only makes a kind of whining, "eh-haa, eh-haa," and it speaks less and less often. It is so thin there are no calves to its legs; its belly protrudes; it lives on a half-bowl of corn meal and grease a day. It is naked. Its buttocks and thighs are a mass of festered sores, as it sits in its own excrement continually.

They all know it is there, all the people of Omelas. Some of them have come to see it, others are content merely to know it is there. They all know that it has to be there. Some of them understand why, and some do not, but they all understand that their happiness, the beauty of their city, the tenderness of their friendships, the health of their children, the wisdom of their scholars, the skill of their makers, even the abundance of their harvest and the kindly weathers of their skies, depend wholly on this child's abominable misery.

This is usually explained to children when they are between eight and twelve, whenever they seem capable of understanding; and most of those who come to see the child are young people, though often enough an adult comes, or comes back, to see the child. No matter how well the matter has been explained to them, these young spectators are always shocked and sickened at the sight. They feel disgust, which they had thought themselves superior to. They feel anger, outrage, impotence, despite all the explanations. They would like to do something for the child. But there is nothing they can do. If the child were brought up into the sunlight out of that vile place, if it were cleaned and fed and comforted, that would be a good thing, indeed; but if it were done, in that day and hour all the prosperity and beauty and delight of Omelas would wither and be destroyed. Those are the terms. To exchange all the goodness and grace of every life in Omelas for that single, small improvement: to throw away the happiness of thousands for the chance of the happiness of one: that would be to let guilt within the walls indeed.

The terms are strict and absolute; there may not even be a kind word spoken to the child.

Often the young people go home in tears, or in a tearless rage, when they have seen the child and faced this terrible paradox. They may brood over it for weeks or years. But as time goes on they begin to realize that even if the child could be released, it would not get much good of its freedom: a little vague pleasure of warmth and food, no doubt, but little more. It is too degraded and imbecile to know any real joy. It has been afraid too long ever to be free of fear. Its habits are too uncouth for it to respond to humane treatment. Indeed, after so long it would probably be wretched without walls about it to protect it, and darkness for its eyes, and its own excrement to sit in. Their tears at the bitter injustice dry when they begin to perceive the terrible justice of reality, and to accept it. Yet it is their tears and anger, the trying of their generosity and the acceptance of their helplessness, which are perhaps the true source of the splendor of their lives. Theirs is no vapid, irresponsible happiness. They know that they, like the child, are not free. They know compassion. It is the existence of the child, and their knowledge of its existence, that makes possible the nobility of their architecture, the poignancy of their music, the profundity of their science. It is because of the child that they are so gentle with children. They know that if the wretched one were not there sniveling in the dark, the other one, the flute-player, could make no joyful music as the young riders line up in their beauty for the race in the sunlight of the first morning of summer.

Now do you believe in them? Are they not more credible? But there is one more thing to tell, and this is quite incredible.

At times one of the adolescent girls or boys who go to see the child does not go home to weep or rage, does not, in fact, go home at all. Sometimes also a man or woman much older falls silent for a day or two, and then leaves home. These people go out into the street, and walk down the street alone. They keep walking, and walk straight out of the city of Omelas, through the beautiful gates.

They keep walking across the farmlands of Omelas. Each one goes alone, youth or girl, man or woman. Night falls; the traveler must pass down village streets, between the houses with yellow-lit windows, and on out into the darkness of the fields. Each alone, they go west or north, towards the mountains. They go on. They leave Omelas, they walk ahead into the darkness, and they do not come back. The place they go towards is a place even less imaginable to most of us than the city of happiness. I cannot describe it at all. It is possible that it does not exist. But they seem to know where they are going, the ones who walk away from Omelas.

(1975)

Chinua Achebe 1930–

DEAD MEN'S PATH

Michael Obi's hopes were fulfilled much earlier than he had expected. He was appointed headmaster of Ndume Central School in January 1949. It had always been an unprogressive school, so the Mission authorities decided to send a young and energetic man to run it. Obi accepted this responsibility with enthusiasm. He had many wonderful ideas and this was an opportunity to put them into practice. He had had sound secondary school education which designated him a "pivotal teacher" in the official records and set him apart from the other headmasters in the mission field. He was outspoken in his condemnation of the narrow views of these older and often less-educated ones.

"We shall make a good job of it, shan't we?" he asked his young wife when they first heard the joyful news of his promotion.

"We shall do our best," she replied. "We shall have such beautiful gardens and everything will be just *modern* and delightful. . . ." In their two years of married life she had become completely infected by his passion for "modern methods" and his denigration of "these old and superannuated people in the teaching field who would be better employed as traders in the Onitsha market." She began to see herself already as the admired wife of the young headmaster, the queen of the school.

The wives of the other teachers would envy her position. She would set the fashion in everything. . . . Then, suddenly, it occurred to her that there might not be other wives. Wavering between hope and fear, she asked her husband, looking anxiously at him.

"All our colleagues are young and unmarried," he said with enthusiasm which for once she did not share. "Which is a good thing," he continued.

"Why?"

"Why? They will give all their time and energy to the school."

Nancy was downcast. For a few minutes she became sceptical about the new school; but it was only for a few minutes. Her little personal misfortune could not blind her to her husband's happy prospects. She looked at him as he sat folded up in a chair. He was stoop-shouldered and looked frail. But he sometimes surprised people with sudden bursts of physical energy. In his present posture, however, all his bodily strength seemed to have retired behind his deep-set eyes, giving them an extraordinary power of penetration. He was only twenty-six, but looked thirty or more. On the whole, he was not unhandsome.

"A penny for your thoughts, Mike," said Nancy after a while, imitating the woman's magazine she read.

"I was thinking what a grand opportunity we've got at last to show these people how a school should be run."

Ndume School was backward in every sense of the word. Mr. Obi put his whole life into the work, and his wife hers too. He had two aims. A high standard of teaching was insisted upon, and the school compound was to be turned into a place of beauty. Nancy's dream-gardens came to life with the coming of the rains, and blossomed. Beautiful hibiscus and allamanda hedges in brilliant red and yellow marked out the carefully tended school compound from the rank neighbourhood bushes.

One evening as Obi was admiring his work he was scandalized to see an old woman from the village hobble right across the compound, through a marigold flower-bed and the hedges. On going up there he found faint signs of an almost disused path from the village across the school compound to the bush on the other side.

"It amazes me," said Obi to one of his teachers who had been three years in the school, "that you people allowed the villagers to make use of this footpath. It is simply incredible." He shook his head.

"The path," said the teacher apologetically, "appears to be very important to them. Although it is hardly used, it connects the village shrine with their place of burial."

"And what has that got to do with the school?" asked the headmaster.

"Well, I don't know," replied the other with a shrug of the shoulders. "But I remember there was a big row some time ago when we attempted to close it."

"That was some time ago. But it will not be used now," said Obi as he walked away. "What will the Government Education Officer think of this when he comes to inspect the school next week? The villagers might, for all I know, decide to use the schoolroom for a pagan ritual during the inspection."

Heavy sticks were planted closely across the path at the two places where it entered and left the school premises. These were further strengthened with barbed wire.

Three days later the village priest of *Ani* called on the headmaster. He was an old man and walked with a slight stoop. He carried a stout walking-stick which he usually tapped on the floor, by way of emphasis, each time he made a point in his argument.

"I have heard," he said after the usual exchange of cordialities, "that our ancestral footpath has recently been closed. . . ."

"Yes," replied Mr. Obi. "We cannot allow people to make a highway of our school compound."

"Look here, my son," said the priest bringing down his walking-stick, "this path was here before you were born and before your father was born. The whole life of this village depends on it. Our dead relatives depart by it and our ancestors visit us by it. But most important, it is the path of children coming in to be born. . . ."

Mr. Obi listened with a satisfied smile on his face.

"The whole purpose of our school," he said finally, "is to eradicate just such beliefs as that. Dead men do not require footpaths. The whole idea is just fantastic. Our duty is to teach your children to laugh at such ideas."

"What you say may be true," replied the priest, "but we follow the practices of our fathers. If you reopen the path we shall have nothing to quarrel about. What I always say is: let the hawk perch and let the eagle perch." He rose to go.

"I am sorry," said the young headmaster. "But the school compound cannot be a thoroughfare. It is against our regulations. I would suggest your constructing another path, skirting our premises. We can even get our boys to help in building it. I don't suppose the ancestors will find the little detour too burdensome."

"I have no more words to say," said the old priest, already outside.

Two days later a young woman in the village died in childbed. A diviner was immediately consulted and he prescribed heavy sacrifices to propitiate ancestors insulted by the fence.

Obi woke up next morning among the ruins of his work. The beautiful hedges were torn up not just near the path but right round the school, the flowers trampled to death and one of the school buildings pulled down. . . . That day, the white Supervisor came to inspect the school and wrote a nasty report on the state of the premises but more seriously about the "tribal-war situation developing between the school and the village, arising in part from the misguided zeal of the new headmaster."

(1953)

Alice Munro 1931–

BOYS AND GIRLS

My father was a fox farmer. That is, he raised silver foxes, in pens; and in the fall
and early winter, when their fur was prime, he killed them and skinned them and
sold their pelts to the Hudson's Bay Company or the Montreal Fur Traders.
These companies supplied us with heroic calendars to hang, one on each side of
the kitchen door. Against a background of cold blue sky and black pine forests
and treacherous northern rivers, plumed adventurers planted the flags of England or of France; magnificent savages bent their backs to the portage.

For several weeks before Christmas, my father worked after supper in the
cellar of our house. The cellar was whitewashed, and lit by a hundred-watt bulb
over the worktable. My brother Laird and I sat on the top step and watched. My
father removed the pelt inside-out from the body of the fox, which looked
surprisingly small, mean and rat-like, deprived of its arrogant weight of fur. The
naked, slippery bodies were collected in a sack and buried at the dump. One time
the hired man, Henry Bailey, had taken a swipe at me with his sack, saying,
"Christmas present!" My mother thought that was not funny. In fact she disliked
the whole pelting operation — that was what the killing, skinning, and preparation of the furs was called — and wished it did not have to take place in the
house. There was the smell. After the pelt had been stretched inside-out on a
long board my father scraped away delicately, removing the little clotted webs of
blood vessels, the bubbles of fat; the smell of blood and animal fat, with the
strong primitive odour of the fox itself, penetrated all parts of the house. I found
it reassuringly seasonal, like the smell of oranges and pine needles.

Henry Bailey suffered from bronchial troubles. He would cough and cough
until his narrow face turned scarlet, and his light blue, derisive eyes filled up
with tears; then he took the lid off the stove, and, standing well back, shot out a
great clot of phlegm — hsss — straight into the heart of the flames. We admired
him for this performance and for his ability to make his stomach growl at will,
and for his laughter, which was full of high whistlings and gurglings and
involved the whole faulty machinery of his chest. It was sometimes hard to tell
what he was laughing at, and always possible that it might be us.

After we had been sent to bed we could still smell fox and still hear Henry's
laugh, but these things, reminders of the warm, safe, brightly lit downstairs
world, seemed lost and diminished, floating on the stale cold air upstairs. We
were afraid at night in the winter. We were not afraid of *outside* though this was
the time of year when snowdrifts curled around our house like sleeping whales
and the wind harassed us all night, coming up from the buried fields, the frozen
swamp, with its old bugbear chorus of threats and misery. We were afraid of
inside, the room where we slept. At this time the upstairs of our house was not
finished. A brick chimney went up one wall. In the middle of the floor was a
square hole, with a wooden railing around it; that was where the stairs came up.
On the other side of the stairwell were the things that nobody had any use for
any more — a soldiery roll of linoleum, standing on end, a wicker baby carriage,
a fern basket, china jugs and basins with cracks in them, a picture of the Battle of
Balaclava, very sad to look at. I had told Laird, as soon as he was old enough to
understand such things, that bats and skeletons lived over there; whenever a man

escaped from the county jail, twenty miles away, I imagined that he had some-how let himself in the window and was hiding behind the linoleum. But we had rules to keep us safe. When the light was on, we were safe as long as we did not step off the square of worn carpet which defined our bedroom-space; when the light was off no place was safe but the beds themselves. I had to turn out the light kneeling on the end of my bed, and stretching as far as I could to reach the cord.

In the dark we lay on our beds, our narrow life rafts, and fixed our eyes on the faint light coming up the stairwell, and sang songs. Laird sang "Jingle Bells," which he would sing any time, whether it was Christmas or not, and I sang "Danny Boy." I loved the sound of my own voice, frail and supplicating, rising in the dark. We could make out the tall frosted shapes of the windows now, gloomy and white. When I came to the part, *When I am dead, as dead I well may be*—a fit of shivering caused not by the cold sheets but by pleasurable emotion almost silenced me. *You'll kneel and say, an Ave there above me*—What was an Ave? Every day I forgot to find out.

Laird went straight from singing to sleep. I could hear his long, satisfied, bubbly breaths. Now for the time that remained to me, the most perfectly private and perhaps the best time of the whole day, I arranged myself tightly under the covers and went on with one of the stories I was telling myself from night to night. These stories were about myself, when I had grown a little older; they took place in a world that was recognizably mine, yet one that presented opportunities for courage, boldness and self-sacrifice, as mine never did. I rescued people from a bombed building (it discouraged me that the real war had gone on so far away from Jubilee). I shot two rabid wolves who were menacing the schoolyard (the teachers cowered terrified at my back). I rode a fine horse spiritedly down the main street of Jubilee, acknowledging the townspeople's gratitude for some yet-to-be-worked-out piece of heroism (nobody ever rode a horse there, except King Billy in the Orangemen's Day parade). There was always riding and shooting in these stories, though I had only been on a horse twice—bareback because we did not own a saddle—and the second time I had slid right around and dropped under the horse's feet; it had stepped placidly over me. I really was learning to shoot, but I could not hit anything yet, not even tin cans on fence posts.

Alive, the foxes inhabited a world my father made for them. It was surrounded by a high guard fence, like a medieval town, with a gate that was padlocked at night. Along the streets of this town were ranged large, sturdy pens. Each of them had a real door that a man could go through, a wooden ramp along the wire, for the foxes to run up and down on, and a kennel—something like a clothes chest with airholes—where they slept and stayed in winter and had their young. There were feeding and watering dishes attached to the wire in such a way that they could be emptied and cleaned from the outside. The dishes were made of old tin cans, and the ramps and kennels of odds and ends of old lumber. Everything was tidy and ingenious; my father was tirelessly inventive and his favourite book in the world was Robinson Crusoe. He had fitted a tin drum on a wheelbarrow, for bringing water down to the pens. This was my job in summer, when the foxes had to have water twice a day. Between nine and ten o'clock in the morning, and again after supper, I filled the drum at the pump and trundled it down through the barnyard to the pens, where I parked it, and filled my watering can and went along the streets. Laird came too, with his little cream and green gardening can, filled too full and knocking against his legs and slopping water on his canvas shoes. I had the real watering can, my father's, though I could only carry it three-quarters full.

The foxes all had names, which were printed on a tin plate and hung beside their doors. They were not named when they were born, but when they survived the first year's pelting and were added to the breeding stock. Those my father had named were called names like Prince, Bob, Wally and Betty. Those I had named were called Star or Turk, or Maureen or Diana. Laird named one Maud after a hired girl we had when he was little, one Harold after a boy at school, and one Mexico, he did not say why.

Naming them did not make pets out of them, or anything like it. Nobody but my father ever went into the pens, and he had twice had blood-poisoning from bites. When I was bringing them their water they prowled up and down on the paths they had made inside their pens, barking seldom — they saved that for nighttime, when they might get up a chorus of community frenzy — but always watching me, their eyes burning, clear gold, in their pointed, malevolent faces. They were beautiful for their delicate legs and heavy, aristocratic tails and the bright fur sprinkled on dark down their backs — which gave them their name — but especially for their faces, drawn exquisitely sharp in pure hostility, and their golden eyes.

Besides carrying water I helped my father when he cut the long grass, and the lamb's quarter and flowering money-musk, that grew between the pens. He cut with the scythe and I raked into piles. Then he took a pitchfork and threw fresh-cut grass all over the top of the pens, to keep the foxes cooler and shade their coats, which were browned by too much sun. My father did not talk to me unless it was about the job we were doing. In this he was quite different from my mother, who, if she was feeling cheerful, would tell me all sorts of things — the name of a dog she had had when she was a little girl, the names of boys she had gone out with later on when she was grown up, and what certain dresses of hers had looked like — she could not imagine now what had become of them. Whatever thoughts and stories my father had were private, and I was shy of him and would never ask him questions. Nevertheless I worked willingly under his eyes, and with a feeling of pride. One time a feed salesman came down into the pens to talk to him and my father said, "Like to have you meet my new hired man." I turned away and raked furiously, red in the face with pleasure.

"Could of fooled me," said the salesman. "I thought it was only a girl."

After the grass was cut, it seemed suddenly much later in the year. I walked on stubble in the earlier evening, aware of the reddening skies, the entering silences, of fall. When I wheeled the tank out of the gate and put the padlock on, it was almost dark. One night at this time I saw my mother and father standing talking on the little rise of ground we called the gangway, in front of the barn. My father had just come from the meathouse; he had his stiff bloody apron on, and a pail of cut-up meat in his hand.

It was an odd thing to see my mother down at the barn. She did not often come out of the house unless it was to do something — hang out the wash or dig potatoes in the garden. She looked out of place, with her bare lumpy legs, not touched by the sun, her apron still on and damp across the stomach from the supper dishes. Her hair was tied up in a kerchief, wisps of it falling out. She would tie her hair up like this in the morning, saying she did not have time to do it properly, and it would stay tied up all day. It was true, too; she really did not have time. These days our back porch was piled with baskets of peaches and grapes and pears, bought in town, and onions and tomatoes and cucumbers grown at home, all waiting to be made into jelly and jam and preserves, pickles and chili sauce. In the kitchen there was a fire in the stove all day, jars clinked in boiling water, sometimes a cheesecloth bag was strung on a pole between two chairs, straining blue-black grape pulp for jelly. I was given jobs to do and I would sit at the table peeling peaches that had been soaked in the hot water, or cutting up onions, my eyes smarting and streaming. As soon as I was done I ran out of the house, trying to get out of earshot before my mother thought of what she wanted me to do next. I hated the hot dark kitchen in summer, the green blinds and the flypapers, the same old oilcloth table and wavy mirror and bumpy linoleum. My mother was too tired and preoccupied to talk to me, she had no heart to tell about the Normal School Graduation Dance; sweat trickled over her face and she was always counting under her breath, pointing at jars, dumping cups of sugar. It seemed to me that work in the house was endless, dreary and peculiarly depressing; work done out of doors, and in my father's service, was ritualistically important.

I wheeled the tank up to the barn, where it was kept, and I heard my mother saying, "Wait till Laird gets a little bigger, then you'll have a real help."

What my father said I did not hear. I was pleased by the way he stood listening, politely as he would to a salesman or a stranger, but with an air of wanting to get on with his real work. I felt my mother had no business down here and I wanted him to feel the same way. What did she mean about Laird? He was no help to anybody. Where was he now? Swinging himself sick on the swing, going around in circles, or trying to catch caterpillars. He never once stayed with me till I was finished.

"And then I can use her more in the house," I heard my mother say. She had a dead-quiet, regretful way of talking about me that always made me uneasy. "I just get my back turned and she runs off. It's not like I had a girl in the family at all."

I went and sat on a feed bag in the corner of the barn, not wanting to appear when this conversation was going on. My mother, I felt, was not to be trusted. She was kinder than my father and more easily fooled, but you could not depend on her, and the real reasons for the things she said and did were not to be known. She loved me, and she sat up late at night making a dress of the difficult style I wanted, for me to wear when school started, but she was also my enemy. She was always plotting. She was plotting now to get me to stay in the house more, although she knew I hated it (*because* she knew I hated it) and keep me from working for my father. It seemed to me she would do this simply out of perversity, and to try her power. It did not occur to me that she could be lonely, or jealous. No grown-up could be; they were too fortunate. I sat and kicked my heels monotonously against a feedbag, raising dust, and did not come out till she was gone.

At any rate, I did not expect my father to pay any attention to what she said. Who could imagine Laird doing my work — Laird remembering the padlock and cleaning out the watering-dishes with a leaf on the end of a stick, or even wheeling the tank without it tumbling over? It showed how little my mother knew about the way things really were.

I have forgotten to say what the foxes were fed. My father's bloody apron reminded me. They were fed horsemeat. At this time most farmers still kept horses, and when a horse got too old to work, or broke a leg or got down and would not get up, as they sometimes did, the owner would call my father, and he and Henry went out to the farm in the truck. Usually they shot and butchered the horse there, paying the farmer from five to twelve dollars. If they had already too much meat on hand, they would bring the horse back alive, and keep it for a few days or weeks in our stable, until the meat was needed. After the war the farmers were buying tractors and gradually getting rid of horses altogether, so it sometimes happened that we got a good healthy horse, that there was just no use for any more. If this happened in the winter we might keep the horse in our stable till spring, for we had plenty of hay and if there was a lot of snow — and the plow did not always get our road cleared — it was convenient to be able to go to town with a horse and cutter.

The winter I was eleven years old we had two horses in the stable. We did not know what names they had had before, so we called them Mack and Flora. Mack was an old black workhorse, sooty and indifferent. Flora was a sorrel mare, a driver. We took them both out in the cutter. Mack was slow and easy to handle. Flora was given to fits of violent alarm, veering at cars and even at other horses, but we loved her speed and high-stepping, her general air of gallantry and abandon. On Saturdays we went down to the stable and as soon as we opened the door on its cosy, animal-smelling darkness Flora threw up her head, rolled her eyes, whinnied despairingly and pulled herself through a crisis of nerves on the spot. It was not safe to go into her stall; she would kick.

This winter also I began to hear a great deal more on the theme my mother had sounded when she had been talking in front of the barn. I no longer felt safe. It seemed that in the minds of the people around me there was a steady undercurrent of thought, not to be deflected, on this one subject. The word *girl* had formerly seemed to me innocent and unburdened, like the word *child*; now it appeared that it was no such thing. A girl was not, as I had supposed, simply what I was; it was what I had to become. It was a definition, always touched with emphasis, with reproach and disappointment. Also it was a joke on me. Once Laird and I were fighting, and for the first time ever I had to use all my strength against him; even so, he caught and pinned my arm for a moment, really hurting me. Henry saw this, and laughed, saying, "Oh, that there Laird's gonna show you, one of these days!" Laird was getting a lot bigger. But I was getting bigger too.

My grandmother came to stay with us for a few weeks and I heard other things. "Girls don't slam doors like that." "Girls keep their knees together when they sit down." And worse still, when I asked some questions, "That's none of girls' business." I continued to slam the doors and sit as awkwardly as possible, thinking that by such measures I kept myself free.

When spring came, the horses were let out in the barnyard. Mack stood against the barn wall trying to scratch his neck and haunches, but Flora trotted up and down and reared at the fences, clattering her hooves against the rails. Snow drifts dwindled quickly, revealing the hard grey and brown earth, the familiar rise and fall of the ground, plain and bare after the fantastic landscape of winter. There was a great feeling of opening-out, of release. We just wore rubbers now, over our shoes; our feet felt ridiculously light. One Saturday we went out to the stable and found all the doors open, letting in the unaccustomed sunlight and fresh air. Henry was there, just idling around looking at his collection of calendars which were tacked up behind the stalls in a part of the stable my mother had probably never seen.

"Come to say goodbye to your old friend Mack?" Henry said. "Here, you give him a taste of oats." He poured some oats into Laird's cupped hands and Laird went to feed Mack. Mack's teeth were in bad shape. He ate very slowly, patiently shifting the oats around in his mouth, trying to find a stump of a molar to grind it on. "Poor old Mack," said Henry mournfully. "When a horse's teeth's gone, he's gone. That's about the way."

"Are you going to shoot him today?" I said. Mack and Flora had been in the stable so long I had almost forgotten they were going to be shot.

Henry didn't answer me. Instead he started to sing in a high, trembly, mocking-sorrowful voice, *Oh, there's no more work, for poor Uncle Ned, he's gone where the good darkies go.* Mack's thick, blackish tongue worked diligently at Laird's hand. I went out before the song was ended and sat down on the gangway.

I had never seen them shoot a horse, but I knew where it was done. Last summer Laird and I had come upon a horse's entrails before they were buried. We had thought it was a big black snake, coiled up in the sun. That was around in the field that ran up beside the barn. I thought that if we went inside the barn, and found a wide crack or a knothole to look through, we would be able to see them do it. It was not something I wanted to see; just the same, if a thing really happened, it was better to see it, and know.

My father came down from the house, carrying the gun.

"What are you doing here?" he said.

"Nothing."

"Go on up and play around the house."

He sent Laird out of the stable. I said to Laird, "Do you want to see them shoot Mack?" and without waiting for an answer led him around to the front door of the barn, opened it carefully, and went in. "Be quiet or they'll hear us," I said. We could hear Henry and my father talking in the stable, then the heavy, shuffling steps of Mack being backed out of his stall.

In the loft it was cold and dark. Thin, crisscrossed beams of sunlight fell through the cracks. The hay was low. It was a rolling country, hills and hollows, slipping under our feet. About four feet up was a beam going around the walls. We piled hay up in one corner and I boosted Laird up and hoisted myself. The beam was not very wide; we crept along it with our hands flat on the barn walls. There were plenty of knotholes, and I found one that gave me the view I wanted—a corner of the barnyard, the gate, part of the field. Laird did not have a knothole and began to complain.

I showed him a widened crack between two boards. "Be quiet and wait. If they hear you you'll get us in trouble."

My father came in sight carrying the gun. Henry was leading Mack by the halter. He dropped it and took out his cigarette papers and tobacco; he rolled cigarettes for my father and himself. While this was going on Mack nosed around in the old, dead grass along the fence. Then my father opened the gate and they took Mack through. Henry led Mack away from the path to a patch of ground and they talked together, not loud enough for us to hear. Mack again began searching for a mouthful of fresh grass, which was not to be found. My father walked away in a straight line, and stopped short at a distance which seemed to suit him. Henry was walking away from Mack too, but sideways, still negligently holding on to the halter. My father raised the gun and Mack looked up as if he had noticed something and my father shot him.

Mack did not collapse at once but swayed, lurched sideways and fell, first on his side; then he rolled over on his back and, amazingly, kicked his legs for a few seconds in the air. At this Henry laughed, as if Mack had done a trick for him. Laird, who had drawn a long, groaning breath of surprise when the shot was fired, said out loud, "He's not dead." And it seemed to me it might be true. But his legs stopped, he rolled on his side again, his muscles quivered and sank. The two men walked over and looked at him in a businesslike way; they bent down and examined his forehead where the bullet had gone in, and now I saw his blood on the brown grass.

"Now they just skin him and cut him up," I said. "Let's go." My legs were a little shaky and I jumped gratefully down into the hay. "Now you've seen how they shoot a horse," I said in a congratulatory way, as if I had seen it many times before. "Let's see if any barn cat's had kittens in the hay." Laird jumped. He seemed young and obedient again. Suddenly I remembered how, when he was little, I had brought him into the barn and told him to climb the ladder to the top beam. That was in the spring, too, when the hay was low. I had done it out of a need for excitement, a desire for something to happen so that I could tell about it. He was wearing a little bulky brown and white checked coat, made down from one of mine. He went all the way up, just as I told him, and sat down on the top beam with the hay far below him on one side, and the barn floor and some old machinery on the other. Then I ran screaming to my father, "Laird's up on the top beam!" My father came, my mother came, my father went up the ladder talking very quietly and brought Laird down under his arm, at which my mother leaned against the ladder and began to cry. They said to me, "Why weren't you watching him?" but nobody ever knew the truth. Laird did not know enough to tell. But whenever I saw the brown and white checked coat hanging in the closet, or at the bottom of the rag bag, which was where it ended up, I felt a weight in my stomach, the sadness of unexorcized guilt.

I looked at Laird who did not even remember this, and I did not like the look on this thin, winter-pale face. His expression was not frightened or upset, but remote, concentrating. "Listen," I said, in an unusually bright and friendly voice, "you aren't going to tell, are you?"

"No," he said absently.

"Promise."

"Promise," he said. I grabbed the hand behind his back to make sure he was not crossing his fingers. Even so, he might have a nightmare; it might come out that way. I decided I had better work hard to get all thoughts of what he had seen out of his mind — which, it seemed to me, could not hold very many things at a time. I got some money I had saved and that afternoon we went into Jubilee and saw a show, with Judy Canova, at which we both laughed a great deal. After that I thought it would be all right.

Two weeks later I knew they were going to shoot Flora. I knew from the night before, when I heard my mother ask if the hay was holding out all right, and my father said, "Well, after tomorrow there'll just be the cow, and we should be able to put her out to grass in another week." So I knew it was Flora's turn in the morning.

This time I didn't think of watching it. That was something to see just one time. I had not thought about it very often since, but sometimes when I was busy, working at school, or standing in front of the mirror combing my hair and wondering if I would be pretty when I grew up, the whole scene would flash into my mind: I would see the easy, practised way my father raised the gun, and hear Henry laughing when Mack kicked his legs in the air. I did not have any great feeling of horror and opposition, such as a city child might have had; I was too used to seeing the death of animals as a necessity by which we lived. Yet I felt a little ashamed, and there was a new wariness, a sense of holding-off, in my attitude to my father and his work.

It was a fine day, and we were going around the yard picking up tree branches that had been torn off in winter storms. This was something we had been told to do, and also we wanted to use them to make a teepee. We heard Flora whinny, and then my father's voice and Henry's shouting, and we ran down to the barnyard to see what was going on.

The stable door was open. Henry had just brought Flora out, and she had broken away from him. She was running free in the barnyard, from one end to the other. We climbed up on the fence. It was exciting to see her running, whinnying, going up on her hind legs, prancing and threatening like a horse in a Western movie, an unbroken ranch horse, though she was just an old driver, an old sorrel mare. My father and Henry ran after her and tried to grab the dangling halter. They tried to work her into a corner, and they had almost succeeded when she made a run between them, wild-eyed, and disappeared around the corner of the barn. We heard the rails clatter down as she got over the fence, and Henry yelled, "She's into the field now!"

That meant she was in the long L-shaped field that ran up by the house. If she got around the center, heading towards the lane, the gate was open; the truck had been driven into the field this morning. My father shouted to me, because I was on the other side of the fence, nearest the lane, "Go shut the gate!"

I could run very fast. I ran across the garden, past the tree where our swing was hung, and jumped across a ditch into the lane. There was the open gate. She had not got out, I could not see her up on the road; she must have run to the other end of the field. The gate was heavy. I lifted it out of the gravel and carried it across the roadway. I had it half-way across when she came in sight, galloping straight towards me. There was just time to get the chain on. Laird came scrambling through the ditch to help me.

Instead of shutting the gate, I opened it as wide as I could. I did not make any decision to do this, it was just what I did. Flora never slowed down; she galloped straight past me, and Laird jumped up and down, yelling, "Shut it, shut it!" even after it was too late. My father and Henry appeared in the field a moment too late to see what I had done. They only saw Flora heading for the township road. They would think I had not got there in time.

They did not waste any time asking about it. They went back to the barn and got the gun and the knives they used, and put these in the truck; then they turned the truck around and came bouncing up the field toward us. Laird called to them, "Let me go too, let me go too!" and Henry stopped the truck and they took him in. I shut the gate after they were all gone.

I supposed Laird would tell. I wondered what would happen to me. I had never disobeyed my father before, and I could not understand why I had done it. Flora would not really get away. They would catch up with her in the truck. Or if they did not catch her this morning somebody would see her and telephone us this afternoon or tomorrow. There was no wild country here for her to run to, only farms. What was more, my father had paid for her, we needed the meat to feed the foxes, we needed the foxes to make our living. All I had done was make more work for my father who worked hard enough already. And when my father found out about it he was not going to trust me any more; he would know that I was not entirely on his side. I was on Flora's side, and that made me no use to anybody, not even to her. Just the same, I did not regret it; when she came running at me and I held the gate open, that was the only thing I could do.

I went back to the house, and my mother said, "What's all the commotion?" I told her that Flora had kicked down the fence and got away. "Your poor father," she said, "now he'll have to go chasing over the countryside. Well, there isn't any use planning dinner before one." She put up the ironing board. I wanted to tell her, but thought better of it and went upstairs and sat on my bed.

Lately I had been trying to make my part of the room fancy, spreading the bed with old lace curtains, and fixing myself a dressing-table with some leftovers of cretonne for a skirt. I planned to put up some kind of barricade between my bed and Laird's, to keep my section separate from his. In the sunlight, the lace curtains were just dusty rags. We did not sing at night any more. One night when I was singing Laird said, "You sound silly," and I went right on but the next night I did not start. There was not so much need to anyway, we were no longer afraid. We knew it was just old furniture over there, old jumble and confusion. We did not keep to the rules. I still stayed awake after Laird was asleep and told myself stories, but even in these stories something different was happening, mysterious alterations took place. A story might start off in the old way, with a spectacular danger, a fire or wild animals, and for a while I might rescue people; then things would change around, and instead, somebody would be rescuing me. It might be a boy from our class at school, or even Mr. Campbell, our teacher, who tickled girls under the arms. And at this point the story concerned itself at great length with what I looked like—how long my hair was, and what kind of dress I had on; by the time I had these details worked out the real excitement of the story was lost.

It was later than one o'clock when the truck came back. The tarpaulin was over the back, which meant there was meat in it. My mother had to heat dinner up all over again. Henry and my father had changed from their bloody overalls into ordinary working overalls in the barn, and they washed their arms and necks and faces at the sink, and splashed water on their hair and combed it. Laird lifted his arm to show off a streak of blood. "We shot old Flora," he said, "and cut her up in fifty pieces."

"Well I don't want to hear about it," my mother said. "And don't come to my table like that."

My father made him go and wash the blood off.

We sat down and my father said grace and Henry pasted his chewing-gum on the end of his fork, the way he always did; when he took it off he would have us admire the pattern. We began to pass the bowls of steaming, overcooked vegetables. Laird looked across the table at me and said proudly, distinctly, "Anyway it was her fault Flora got away."

"What?" my father said.

"She could of shut the gate and she didn't. She just open' it up and Flora run out."

"Is that right?" my father said.

Everybody at the table was looking at me. I nodded, swallowing food with great difficulty. To my shame, tears flooded my eyes.

My father made a curt sound of disgust. "What did you do that for?"

I did not answer. I put down my fork and waited to be sent from the table, still not looking up.

But this did not happen. For some time nobody said anything, then Laird said matter-of-factly, "She's crying."

"Never mind," my father said. He spoke with resignation, even good humour, the words which absolved and dismissed me for good. "She's only a girl," he said.

I didn't protest that, even in my heart. Maybe it was true.

(1968)

John Updike *1932–*

A & P

In walks these three girls in nothing but bathing suits. I'm in the third checkout slot, with my back to the door, so I don't see them until they're over by the bread. The one that caught my eye first was the one in the plaid green two-piece. She was a chunky kid, with a good tan and a sweet broad soft-looking can with those two crescents of white just under it, where the sun never seems to hit, at the top of the backs of her legs. I stood there with my hand on a box of HiHo crackers trying to remember if I rang it up or not. I ring it up again and the customer starts giving me hell. She's one of these cash-register-watchers, a witch about fifty with rouge on her cheekbones and no eyebrows, and I know it made her day to trip me up. She'd been watching cash registers for fifty years and probably never seen a mistake before.

By the time I got her feathers smoothed and her goodies into a bag — she gives me a little snort in passing, if she'd been born at the right time they would have burned her over in Salem — by the time I get her on her way the girls had circled around the bread and were coming back, without a pushcart, back my way along the counters, in the aisle between the checkouts and the Special bins. They didn't even have shoes on. There was this chunky one, with the two-piece — it was bright green and the seams on the bra were still sharp and her belly was still pretty pale so I guessed she just got it (the suit) — there was this one, with one of those chubby berry-faces, the lips all bunched together under her nose, this one, and a tall one, with black hair that hadn't quite frizzed right, and one of these sunburns right across under the eyes and a chin that was too long — you know, the kind of girl other girls think is very "striking" and "attractive" but never quite makes it, as they very well know, which is why they like her so much — and then the third one, that wasn't quite so tall. She was the queen. She kind of led them, the other two peeking around and making their shoulders round. She didn't look around, not this queen, she just walked straight on slowly, on these long white prima-donna legs. She came down a little hard on her heels, as if she didn't walk in bare feet that much, putting down her heels and then letting the weight move along to her toes as if she was testing the floor with every step, putting a little deliberate extra action into it. You never know for sure how girls' minds work (do you really think it's a mind in there or just a little buzz like a bee in a glass jar?) but you got the idea she had talked the other two into coming in here with her, and now she was showing them how to do it, walk slow and hold yourself straight.

She had on a kind of dirty-pink — beige maybe, I don't know — bathing suit with a little nubble all over it and, what got me, the straps were down. They were off her shoulders looped loose around the cool tops of her arms, and I guess as a result the suit had slipped a little on her, so all around the top of the cloth there was this shining rim. If it hadn't been there you wouldn't have known there could have been anything whiter than those shoulders. With the straps pushed off, there was nothing between the top of the suit and the top of her head except just *her*, this clean bare plane of the top of her chest down from the shoulder bones like a dented sheet of metal tilted in the light. I mean, it was more than pretty.

She had a sort of oaky hair that the sun and salt had bleached, done up in a bun that was unraveling, and a kind of prim face. Walking into the A & P with your straps down, I suppose it's the only kind of face you *can* have. She held her head so high her neck, coming up out of those white shoulders, looked kind of stretched, but I didn't mind. The longer her neck was, the more of her there was.

She must have felt in the corner of her eye me and over my shoulder Stokesie in the second slot watching, but she didn't tip. Not this queen. She kept her eyes moving across the racks, and stopped, and turned so slow it made my stomach rub the inside of my apron, and buzzed to the other two, who kind of huddled against her for relief, and then they all three of them went up the cat – and – dog – food – breakfast – cereal – macaroni – rice – raisins – seasonings – spreads – spaghetti – soft-drinks – crackers – and – cookies aisle. From the third slot I look straight up this aisle to the meat counter, and I watched them all the way. The fat one with the tan sort of fumbled with the cookies, but on second thought she put the package back. The sheep pushing their carts down the aisle — the girls were walking against the usual traffic (not that we have one-way signs or anything) — were pretty hilarious. You could see them, when Queenie's white shoulders dawned on them, kind of jerk, or hop, or hiccup, but their eyes snapped back to their own baskets and on they pushed. I bet you could set off dynamite in an A & P and the people would by and large keep reaching and checking oatmeal off their lists and muttering "Let me see, there was a third thing, began with A, asparagus, no, ah, yes, applesauce!" or whatever it is they do mutter. But there was no doubt, this jiggled them. A few houseslaves in pin curlers even looked around after pushing their carts past to make sure what they had seen was correct.

You know, it's one thing to have a girl in a bathing suit down on the beach, where what with the glare nobody can look at each other much anyway, and another thing in the cool of the A & P, under the fluorescent lights, against all those stacked packages, with her feet paddling along naked over our checker-board green-and-cream rubber-tile floor.

"Oh Daddy," Stokesie said beside me. "I feel so faint."

"Darling," I said. "Hold me tight." Stokesie's married, with two babies chalked up on his fuselage already, but as far as I can tell that's the only difference. He's twenty-two, and I was nineteen this April.

"Is it done?" he asks, the responsible married man finding his voice. I forgot to say he thinks he's going to be manager some sunny day, maybe in 1990 when it's called the Great Alexandrov and Petrooshki Tea Company or something.

What he meant was, our town is five miles from a beach, with a big summer colony out on the Point, but we're right in the middle of town, and the women generally put on a shirt or shorts or something before they get out of the car into the street. And anyway these are usually women with six children and varicose veins mapping their legs and nobody, including them, could care less. As I say, we're right in the middle of town, and if you stand at our front doors you can see two banks and the Congregational church and the newspaper store and three real-estate offices and about twenty-seven old freeloaders tearing up Central Street because the sewer broke again. It's not as if we're on the Cape; we're north of Boston and there's people in this town haven't seen the ocean for twenty years.

The girls had reached the meat counter and were asking McMahon something. He pointed, they pointed, and they shuffled out of sight behind a pyramid of Diet Delight peaches. All that was left for us to see was old McMahon patting his mouth and looking after them sizing up their joints. Poor kids, I began to feel sorry for them, they couldn't help it.

Now here comes the sad part of the story, at least my family says it's sad, but I don't think it's so sad myself. The store's pretty empty, it being Thursday afternoon, so there was nothing much to do except lean on the register and wait for the girls to show up again. The whole store was like a pinball machine and I didn't know which tunnel they'd come out of. After a while they come around out of the far aisle, around the light bulbs, records at discount of the Caribbean Six or Tony Martin Sings or some such gunk you wonder they waste the wax on, six-packs of candy bars, and plastic toys done up in cellophane that fall apart when a kid looks at them anyway. Around they come, Queenie still leading the way, and holding a little gray jar in her hand. Slots Three through Seven are unmanned and I could see her wondering between Stokes and me, but Stokesie with his usual luck draws an old party in baggy gray pants who stumbles up with four giant cans of pineapple juice (what do these bums *do* with all that pineapple juice? I've often asked myself) so the girls come to me. Queenie puts down the jar and I take it into my fingers icy cold. Kingfish Fancy Herring Snacks in Pure Sour Cream: 49¢. Now her hands are empty, not a ring or a bracelet, bare as God made them, and I wonder where the money's coming from. Still with that prim look she lifts a folded dollar bill out of the hollow at the center of her nubbled pink top. The jar went heavy in my hand. Really, I thought that was so cute.

Then everybody's luck begins to run out. Lengel comes in from haggling with a truck full of cabbages on the lot and is about to scuttle into that door marked MANAGER behind which he hides all day when the girls touch his eye. Lengel's pretty dreary, teaches Sunday school and the rest, but he doesn't miss that much. He comes over and says, "Girls, this isn't the beach."

Queenie blushes, though maybe it's just a brush of sunburn I was noticing for first time, now that she was so close. "My mother asked me to pick up a jar of herring snacks." Her voice kind of startled me, the way voices do when you see the people first, coming out so flat and dumb yet kind of tony, too, the way it ticked over "pick up" and "snacks." All of a sudden I slid right down her voice into her living room. Her father and the other men were standing around in ice-cream coats and bow ties and the women were in sandals picking up herring snacks on toothpicks off a big glass plate and they were all holding drinks the color of water with olives and sprigs of mint in them. When my parents have somebody over they get lemonade and if it's a real racy affair Schlitz in tall glasses with "They'll Do It Every Time" cartoons stencilled on.

"That's all right," Lengel said. "But this isn't the beach." His repeating this struck me as funny, as if it had just occurred to him, and he had been thinking all these years the A & P was a great big dune and he was the head lifeguard. He didn't like my smiling—as I say he doesn't miss much—but he concentrates on giving the girls that sad Sunday-school-superintendent stare.

Queenie's blush is no sunburn now, and the plump one in plaid, that I liked better from the back—a really sweet can—pipes up, "We weren't doing any shopping. We just came in for the one thing."

"That makes no difference," Lengel tells her, and I could see from the way his eyes went that he hadn't noticed she was wearing a two-piece before. "We want you decently dressed when you come in here."

"We *are* decent," Queenie says suddenly, her lower lip pushing, getting sore now that she remembers her place, a place from which the crowd that runs the A & P must look pretty crummy. Fancy Herring Snacks flashed in her very blue eyes.

"Girls, I don't want to argue with you. After this come in here with your shoulders covered. It's our policy." He turns his back. That's policy for you. Policy is what the kingpins want. What the others want is juvenile delinquency.

All this while, the customers had been showing up with their carts but, you know, sheep, seeing a scene, they had all bunched up on Stokesie, who shook open a paper bag as gently as peeling a peach, not wanting to miss a word. I could feel in the silence everybody getting nervous, most of all Lengel, who asks me, "Sammy, have you rung up their purchase?"

I thought and said "No" but it wasn't about that I was thinking. I go through the punches, 4, 9, GROC, TOT—it's more complicated than you think, and after you do it often enough, it begins to make a little song, that you hear words to, in my case "Hello (*bing*) there, you (*gung*) hap-py *pee*-pul (*splat*)!"—the *splat* being the drawer flying out. I uncrease the bill, tenderly as you may imagine, it just having come from between the two smoothest scoops of vanilla I had ever known there were, and pass a half and a penny into her narrow pink palm, and nestle the herrings in a bag and twist its neck and hand it over, all the time thinking.

The girls, and who'd blame them, are in a hurry to get out, so I say "I quit" to Lengel quick enough for them to hear, hoping they'll stop and watch me, their unsuspected hero. They keep right on going, into the electric eye; the door flies open and they flicker across the lot to their car, Queenie and Plaid and Big Tall Goony-Goony (not that as raw material she was so bad), leaving me with Lengel and a kink in his eyebrow.

"Did you say something, Sammy?"

"I said I quit."

"I thought you did."

"You didn't have to embarrass them."

"It was they who were embarrassing us."

I started to say something that came out "Fiddle-de-do." It's a saying of my grandmother's, and I know she would have been pleased.

"I don't think you know what you're saying," Lengel said.

"I know you don't," I said. "But I do."

I pull the bow at the back of my apron and start shrugging it off my shoulders. A couple of customers that had been heading for my slot begin to knock against each other, like scared pigs in a chute.

Lengel sighs and begins to look very patient and old and gray. He's been a friend of my parents for years. "Sammy, you don't want to do this to your Mom and Dad," he tells me. It's true, I don't. But it seems to me that once you begin a gesture it's fatal not to go through with it. I fold the apron, "Sammy" stitched in red on the pocket, and put it on the counter, and drop the bow tie on top of it. The bow tie is theirs, if you've ever wondered. "You'll feel this for the rest of your life," Lengel says, and I know that's true, too, but remembering how he made that pretty girl blush makes me so scrunchy inside I punch the No Sale tab and the machine whirs "pee-pul" and the drawer splats out. One advantage to this scene taking place in summer, I can follow this up with a clean exit, there's no fumbling around getting your coat and galoshes, I just saunter into the electric eye in my white shirt that my mother ironed the night before, and the door heaves itself open, and outside the sunshine is skating around on the asphalt.

I look around for my girls, but they're gone, of course. There wasn't anybody but some young married screaming with her children about some candy they didn't get by the door of a powder-blue Falcon station wagon. Looking back in the big windows, over the bags of peat moss and aluminum lawn furniture stacked on the pavement, I could see Lengel in my place in the slot, checking the sheep through. His face was dark gray and his back stiff, as if he's just had an injection of iron, and my stomach kind of fell as I felt how hard the world was going to be to me hereafter.

                                                                                                (1962)

Andre Dubus *1936–*

THE FAT GIRL

Her name was Louise. Once when she was sixteen a boy kissed her at a barbecue; he was drunk and he jammed his tongue into her mouth and ran his hands up and down her hips. Her father kissed her often. He was thin and kind and she could see in his eyes when he looked at her the lights of love and pity.

It started when Louise was nine. You must start watching what you eat, her mother would say. I can see you have my metabolism. Louise also had her mother's pale blonde hair. Her mother was slim and pretty, carried herself erectly, and ate very little. The two of them would eat bare lunches, while her older brother ate sandwiches and potato chips, and then her mother would sit smoking while Louise eyed the bread box, the pantry, the refrigerator. Wasn't that good, her mother would say. In five years you'll be in high school and if you're fat the boys won't like you; they won't ask you out. Boys were as far away as five years, and she would go to her room and wait for nearly an hour until she knew her mother was no longer thinking of her, then she would creep into the kitchen and, listening to her mother talking on the phone, or her footsteps upstairs, she would open the bread box, the pantry, the jar of peanut butter. She would put the sandwich under her shirt and go outside or to the bathroom to eat it.

Her father was a lawyer and made a lot of money and came home looking pale and happy. Martinis put color back in his face, and at dinner he talked to his wife and two children. Oh give her a potato, he would say to Louise's mother. She's a growing girl. Her mother's voice then became tense: If she has a potato she shouldn't have dessert. She should have both, her father would say, and he would reach over and touch Louise's cheek or hand or arm.

In high school she had two girl friends and at night and on week-ends they rode in a car or went to movies. In movies she was fascinated by fat actresses. She wondered why they were fat. She knew why she was fat: she was fat because she was Louise. Because God had made her that way. Because she wasn't like her friends Joan and Marjorie, who drank milk shakes after school and were all bones and tight skin. But what about those actresses, with their talents, with their broad and profound faces? Did they eat as heedlessly as Bishop Humphries and his wife who sometimes came to dinner and, as Louise's mother said, gorged between amenities? Or did they try to lose weight, did they go about hungry and angry and thinking of food? She thought of them eating lean meats and salads with friends, and then going home and building strange large sandwiches with French bread. But mostly she believed they did not go through these failures; they were fat because they chose to be. And she was certain of something else too: she could see it in their faces: they did not eat secretly. Which she did: her creeping to the kitchen when she was nine became, in high school, a ritual of deceit and pleasure. She was a furtive eater of sweets. Even her two friends did not know her secret.

Joan was thin, gangling, and flat-chested; she was attractive enough and all she needed was someone to take a second look at her face, but the school was large and there were pretty girls in every classroom and walking all the corridors, so no one ever needed to take a second look at Joan. Marjorie was thin too, an intense, heavy-smoking girl with brittle laughter. She was very intelligent, and with boys she was shy because she knew she made them uncomfortable, and because she was smarter than they were and so could not understand or could not believe the levels they lived on. She was to have a nervous breakdown before earning her Ph.D. in philosophy at the University of California, where she met and married a physicist and discovered within herself an untrammelled passion: she made love with her husband on the couch, the carpet, in the bathtub, and on the washing machine. By that time much had happened to her and she never thought of Louise. Joan would finally stop growing and begin moving with grace and confidence. In college she would have two lovers and then several more during the six years she spent in Boston before marrying a middle-aged editor who had two sons in their early teens, who drank too much, who was tenderly, boyishly grateful for her love, and whose wife had been killed while rock-climbing in New Hampshire with her lover. She would not think of Louise either, except in an earlier time, when lovers were still new to her and she was ecstatically surprised each time one of them loved her and, sometimes at night, lying in a man's arms, she would tell how in high school no one dated her, she had been thin and plain (she would still believe that: that she had been plain; it had never been true) and so had been forced into the week-end and night-time company of a neurotic smart girl and a shy fat girl. She would say this with self-pity exaggerated by Scotch and her need to be more deeply loved by the man who held her.

She never eats, Joan and Marjorie said of Louise. They ate lunch with her at school, watched her refusing potatoes, ravioli, fried fish. Sometimes she got through the cafeteria line with only a salad. That is how they would remember her: a girl whose hapless body was destined to be fat. No one saw the sandwiches she made and took to her room when she came home from school. No one saw the store of Milky Ways, Butterfingers, Almond Joys, and Hersheys far back on her closet shelf, behind the stuffed animals of her childhood. She was not a hypocrite. When she was out of the house she truly believed she was dieting; she forgot about the candy, as a man speaking into his office dictaphone may forget the lewd photographs hidden in an old shoe in his closet. At other times, away from home, she thought of the waiting candy with near lust. One night driving home from a movie, Marjorie said: "You're lucky you don't smoke; it's incredible what I go through to hide it from my parents." Louise turned to her a smile which was elusive and mysterious; she yearned to be home in bed, eating chocolate in the dark. She did not need to smoke; she already had a vice that was insular and destructive.

She brought it with her to college. She thought she would leave it behind. A move from one place to another, a new room without the haunted closet shelf, would do for her what she could not do for herself. She packed her large dresses and went. For two weeks she was busy with registration, with shyness, with classes; then she began to feel at home. Her room was no longer like a motel. Its walls had stopped watching her, she felt they were her friends, and she gave them her secret. Away from her mother, she did not have to be as elaborate; she kept the candy in her drawer now.

The school was in Massachusetts, a girls' school. When she chose it, when she and her father and mother talked about it in the evenings, everyone so carefully avoided the word boys that sometimes the conversations seemed to be about nothing but boys. There are no boys there, the neuter words said; you will not have to contend with that. In her father's eyes were pity and encouragement; in her mother's was disappointment, and her voice was crisp. They spoke of courses, of small classes where Louise would get more attention. She imagined herself in those small classes; she saw herself as a teacher would see her, as the other girls would; she would get no attention.

The girls at the school were from wealthy families, but most of them wore the uniform of another class: blue jeans and work shirts, and many wore overalls. Louise bought some overalls, washed them until the dark blue faded, and wore them to classes. In the cafeteria she ate as she had in high school, not to lose weight nor even to sustain her lie, but because eating lightly in public had become as habitual as good manners. Everyone had to take gym, and in the locker room with the other girls, and wearing shorts on the volleyball and badminton courts, she hated her body. She liked her body most when she was unaware of it: in bed at night, as sleep gently took her out of her day, out of herself. And she liked parts of her body. She liked her brown eyes and sometimes looked at them in the mirror: they were not shallow eyes, she thought; they were indeed windows of a tender soul, a good heart. She liked her lips and nose, and her chin, finely shaped between her wide and sagging cheeks. Most of all she liked her long pale blonde hair, she liked washing and drying it and lying naked on her bed, smelling of shampoo, and feeling the soft hair at her neck and shoulders and back.

Her friend at college was Carrie, who was thin and wore thick glasses and often at night she cried in Louise's room. She did not know why she was crying. She was crying, she said, because she was unhappy. She could say no more. Louise said she was unhappy too, and Carrie moved in with her. One night Carrie talked for hours, sadly and bitterly, about her parents and what they did to each other. When she finished she hugged Louise and they went to bed. Then in the dark Carrie spoke across the room: "Louise? I just wanted to tell you. One night last week I woke up and smelled chocolate. You were eating chocolate, in your bed. I wish you'd eat it in front of me, Louise, whenever you feel like it."

Stiffened in her bed, Louise could think of nothing to say. In the silence she was afraid Carrie would think she was asleep and would tell her again in the morning or tomorrow night. Finally she said Okay. Then after a moment she told Carrie if she ever wanted any she could feel free to help herself; the candy was in the top drawer. Then she said thank you.

They were roommates for four years and in the summers they exchanged letters. Each fall they greeted with embraces, laughter, tears, and moved into their old room, which had been stripped and cleansed of them for the summer. Neither girl enjoyed summer. Carrie did not like being at home because her parents did not love each other. Louise lived in a small city in Louisiana. She did not like summer because she had lost touch with Joan and Marjorie; they saw each other, but it was not the same. She liked being with her father but with no one else. The flicker of disappointment in her mother's eyes at the airport was a vanguard of the army of relatives and acquaintances who awaited her: they would see her on the streets, in stores, at the country club, in her home, and in theirs; in the first moments of greeting, their eyes would tell her she was still fat Louise, who had been fat as long as they could remember, who had gone to college and returned as fat as ever. Then their eyes dismissed her, and she longed for school and Carrie, and she wrote letters to her friend. But that saddened her too. It wasn't simply that Carrie was her only friend, and when they finished college they might never see each other again. It was that her existence in the world was so divided; it had begun when she was a child creeping to the kitchen; now that division was much sharper, and her friendship with Carrie seemed disproportionate and perilous. The world she was destined to live in had nothing to do with the intimate nights in their room at school.

In the summer before their senior year, Carrier fell in love. She wrote to Louise about him, but she did not write much, and this hurt Louise more than if Carrie had shown the joy her writing tried to conceal. That fall they returned to their room; they were still close and warm, Carrie still needed Louise's ears and heart at night as she spoke of her parents and her recurring malaise whose source the two friends never discovered. But on most week-ends Carrie left, and caught a bus to Boston where her boy friend studied music. During the week she often spoke hesitantly of sex; she was not sure if she liked it. But Louise, eating candy and listening, did not know whether Carrie was telling the truth or whether, as in her letters of the past summer, Carrie was keeping from her those delights she may never experience.

Then one Sunday night when Carrie had just returned from Boston and was unpacking her overnight bag, she looked at Louise and said: "I was thinking about you. On the bus coming home tonight." Looking at Carrie's concerned, determined face, Louise prepared herself for humiliation. "I was thinking about when we graduate. What you're going to do. What's to become of you. I want you to be loved the way I love you. Louise, if I help you, *really* help you, will you go on a diet?"

Louise entered a period of her life she would remember always, the way some people remember having endured poverty. Her diet did not begin the next day. Carrie told her to eat on Monday as though it were the last day of her life. So for the first time since grammar school Louise went into a school cafeteria and ate everything she wanted. At breakfast and lunch and dinner she glanced around the table to see if the other girls noticed the food on her tray. They did not. She felt there was a lesson in this, but it lay beyond her grasp. That night in their room she ate the four remaining candy bars. During the day Carrie rented a small refrigerator, bought an electric skillet, an electric broiler, and bathroom scales.

On Tuesday morning Louise stood on the scales, and Carrie wrote in her notebook: *October 14: 184 lbs.* Then she made Louise a cup of black coffee and scrambled one egg and sat with her while she ate. When Carrie went to the dining room for breakfast, Louise walked about the campus for thirty minutes. That was part of the plan. The campus was pretty, on its lawns grew at least one of every tree native to New England, and in the warm morning sun Louise felt a new hope. At noon they met in their room, and Carrie broiled her a piece of hamburger and served it with lettuce. Then while Carrie ate in the dining room Louise walked again. She was weak with hunger and she felt queasy. During her afternoon classes she was nervous and tense, and she chewed her pencil and tapped her heels on the floor and tightened her calves. When she returned to her room late that afternoon, she was so glad to see Carrie that she embraced her; she had felt she could not bear another minute of hunger, but now with Carrie she knew she could make it at least through tonight. Then she would sleep and face tomorrow when it came. Carrie broiled her a steak and served it with lettuce. Louise studied while Carrie ate dinner, then they went for a walk.

That was her ritual and her diet for the rest of the year, Carrie alternating fish and chicken breasts with the steaks for dinner, and every day was nearly as bad as the first. In the evenings she was irritable. In all her life she had never been afflicted by ill temper and she looked upon it now as a demon which, along with hunger, was taking possession of her soul. Often she spoke sharply to Carrie. One night during their after-dinner walk Carrie talked sadly of night, of how darkness made her more aware of herself, and at night she did not know why she was in college, why she studied, why she was walking the earth with other people. They were standing on a wooden foot bridge, looking down at a dark pond. Carrie kept talking; perhaps soon she would cry. Suddenly Louise said: "I'm sick of lettuce. I never want to see a piece of lettuce for the rest of my life. I hate it. We shouldn't even buy it, it's immoral."

Carrie was quiet. Louise glanced at her, and the pain and irritation in Carrie's face soothed her. Then she was ashamed. Before she could say she was sorry, Carrie turned to her and said gently: "I know. I know how terrible it is."

Carrie did all the shopping, telling Louise she knew how hard it was to go into a supermarket when you were hungry. And Louise was always hungry. She drank diet soft drinks and started smoking Carrie's cigarettes, learned to enjoy inhaling, thought of cancer and emphysema but they were as far away as those boys her mother had talked about when she was nine. By Thanksgiving she was smoking over a pack a day and her weight in Carrie's notebook was one hundred and sixty-two pounds. Carrie was afraid if Louise went home at Thanksgiving she would lapse from the diet, so Louise spent the vacation with Carrie, in Philadelphia. Carrie wrote her family about the diet, and told Louise that she had. On the phone to Philadelphia, Louise said: "I feel like a bedwetter. When I was a little girl I had a friend who used to come spend the night and Mother would put a rubber sheet on the bed and we all pretended there wasn't a rubber sheet and that she hadn't wet the bed. Even me, and I slept with her." At Thanksgiving dinner she lowered her eyes as Carrie's father put two slices of white meat on her plate and passed it to her over the bowls of steaming food.

When she went home at Christmas she weighed a hundred and fifty-five pounds; at the airport her mother marvelled. Her father laughed and hugged her and said: "But now there's less of you to love." He was troubled by her smoking but only mentioned it once; he told her she was beautiful and, as always, his eyes bathed her with love. During the long vacation her mother cooked for her as Carrie had, and Louise returned to school weighing a hundred and forty-six pounds.

Flying north on the plane she warmly recalled the surprised and congratulatory eyes of her relatives and acquaintances. She had not seen Joan or Marjorie. She thought of returning home in May, weighing the hundred and fifteen pounds which Carrie had in October set as their goal. Looking toward the stoic days ahead, she felt strong. She thought of those hungry days of fall and early winter (and now: she was hungry now: with almost a frown, almost a brusque shake of the head, she refused peanuts from the stewardess): those first weeks of the diet when she was the pawn of an irascibility which still, conditioned to her ritual as she was, could at any moment take command of her. She thought of the nights of trying to sleep while her stomach growled. She thought of her addiction to cigarettes. She thought of the people at school: not one teacher, not one girl, had spoken to her about her loss of weight, not even about her absence from meals. And without warning her spirit collapsed. She did not feel strong, she did not feel she was committed to and within reach of achieving a valuable goal. She felt that somehow she had lost more than pounds of fat; that some time during her dieting she had lost herself too. She tried to remember what it had felt like to be Louise before she had started living on meat and fish, as an unhappy adult may look sadly in the memory of childhood for lost virtues and hopes. She looked down at the earth far below, and it seemed to her that her soul, like her body aboard the plane, was in some rootless flight. She neither knew its destination nor where it had departed from; it was on some passage she could not even define.

During the next few weeks she lost weight more slowly and once for eight days Carrie's daily recording stayed at a hundred and thirty-six. Louise woke in the morning thinking of the one hundred and thirty-six and then she stood on the scales and they echoed her. She became obsessed with that number, and there wasn't a day when she didn't say it aloud, and through the days and nights the number stayed in her mind, and if a teacher had spoken those digits in a classroom she would have opened her mouth to speak. What if that's me, she said to Carrie. I mean what if a hundred and thirty-six is my real weight and I just can't lose anymore. Walking hand-in-hand with her despair was a longing for this to be true, and that longing angered her and wearied her, and every day she was gloomy. On the ninth day she weighed a hundred and thirty-five and a half pounds. She was not relieved; she thought bitterly of the months ahead, the shedding of the last twenty and a half pounds.

On Easter Sunday, which she spent at Carrie's, she weighed one hundred and twenty pounds, and she ate one slice of glazed pineapple with her ham and lettuce. She did not enjoy it: she felt she was being friendly with a recalcitrant enemy who had once tried to destroy her. Carrie's parents were laudative. She liked them and she wished they would touch sometimes, and look at each other when they spoke. She guessed they would divorce when Carrie left home, and she vowed that her own marriage would be one of affection and tenderness. She could think about that now: marriage. At school she had read in a Boston paper that this summer the cicadas would come out of their seventeen year hibernation on Cape Cod, for a month they would mate and then die, leaving their young to burrow into the ground where they would stay for seventeen years. That's me, she had said to Carrie. Only my hibernation lasted twenty-one years.

Often her mother asked in letters and on the phone about the diet, but Louise answered vaguely. When she flew home in late May she weighed a hundred thirteen pounds, and at the airport her mother cried and hugged her and said again and again: You're so *beautiful*. Her father blushed and bought her a martini. For days her relatives and acquaintances congratulated her, and the applause in their eyes lasted the entire summer, and she loved their eyes, and swam in the country club pool, the first time she had done this since she was a child.

She lived at home and ate the way her mother did and every morning she weighed herself on the scales in her bathroom. Her mother liked to take her shopping and buy her dresses and they put her old ones in the Goodwill box at the shopping center; Louise thought of them existing on the body of a poor woman whose cheap meals kept her fat. Louise's mother had a photographer come to the house, and Louise posed on the couch and standing beneath a live oak and sitting in a wicker lawn chair next to an azalea bush. The new clothes and the photographer made her feel she was going to another country or becoming a citizen of a new one. In the fall she took a job of no consequence, to give herself something to do.

Also in the fall a young lawyer joined her father's firm, he came one night to dinner, and they started seeing each other. He was the first man outside her family to kiss her since the barbecue when she was sixteen. Louise celebrated Thanksgiving not with rice dressing and candied sweet potatoes and mince meat and pumpkin pies, but by giving Richard her virginity which she realized, at the very last moment of its existence, she had embarked on giving him over thirteen months ago, on that Tuesday in October when Carrie had made her a cup of black coffee and scrambled one egg. She wrote this to Carrie, who replied happily by return mail. She also, through glance and smile and innuendo, tried to tell her mother too. But finally she controlled that impulse, because Richard felt guilty about making love with the daughter of his partner and friend. In the spring they married. The wedding was a large one, in the Episcopal church, and Carrie flew from Boston to be maid of honor. Her parents had recently separated and she was living with the musician and was still victim of her unpredictable malaise. It overcame her on the night before the wedding, so Louise was up with her until past three and woke next morning from a sleep so heavy that she did not want to leave it.

Richard was a lean, tall, energetic man with the metabolism of a pencil sharpener. Louise fed him everything he wanted. He liked Italian food and she got recipes from her mother and watched him eating spaghetti with the sauce she had only tasted, and ravioli and lasagna, while she ate antipasto with her chianti. He made a lot of money and borrowed more and they bought a house whose lawn sloped down to the shore of a lake; they had a wharf and a boathouse, and Richard bought a boat and they took friends waterskiing. Richard bought her a car and they spent his vacations in Mexico, Canada, the Bahamas, and in the fifth year of their marriage they went to Europe and, according to their plan, she conceived a child in Paris. On the plane back, as she looked out the window and beyond the sparkling sea and saw her country, she felt that it was waiting for her, as her home by the lake was, and her parents, and her good friends who rode in the boat and waterskied; she thought of the accumulated warmth and pelf of her marriage, and how by slimming her body she had bought into the pleasures of the nation. She felt cunning, and she smiled to herself, and took Richard's hand.

But these moments of triumph were sparse. On most days she went about her routine of leisure with a sense of certainty about herself that came merely from not thinking. But there were times, with her friends, or with Richard, or alone in the house, when she was suddenly assaulted by the feeling that she had taken the wrong train and arrived at a place where no one knew her, and where she ought not to be. Often, in bed with Richard, she talked of being fat: "I was the one who started the friendship with Carrie, I chose her, I started the conversations. When I understood that she was my friend I understood something else: I had chosen her for the same reason I'd chosen Joan and Marjorie. They were all thin. I was always thinking about what people saw when they looked at me and I didn't want them to see two fat girls. When I was alone I didn't mind being fat but then I'd have to leave the house again and then I didn't want to look like me. But at home I didn't mind except when I was getting dressed to go out of the house and when Mother looked at me. But I stopped looking at her when she looked at me. And in college I felt good with Carrie; there weren't any boys and I didn't have any other friends and so when I wasn't with Carrie I thought about her and I tried to ignore the other people around me, I tried to make them not exist. A lot of the time I could do that. It was strange, and I felt like a spy."

If Richard was bored by her repetition he pretended not to be. But she knew the story meant very little to him. She could have been telling him of a childhood illness, or wearing braces, or a broken heart at sixteen. He could not see her as she was when she was fat. She felt as though she were trying to tell a foreign lover about her life in the United States, and if only she could command the language he would know and love all of her and she would feel complete. Some of the acquaintances of her childhood were her friends now, and even they did not seem to remember her when she was fat.

Now her body was growing again, and when she put on a maternity dress for the first time she shivered with fear. Richard did not smoke and he asked her, in a voice just short of demand, to stop during her pregnancy. She did. She ate carrots and celery instead of smoking, and at cocktail parties she tried to eat nothing, but after her first drink she ate nuts and cheese and crackers and dips. Always at these parties Richard had talked with his friends and she had rarely spoken to him until they drove home. But now when he noticed her at the hors d'oeuvres table he crossed the room and, smiling, led her back to his group. His smile and his hand on her arm told her he was doing his clumsy, husbandly best to help her through a time of female mystery.

She was gaining weight but she told herself it was only the baby, and would leave with its birth. But at other times she knew quite clearly that she was losing the discipline she had fought so hard to gain during her last year with Carrie. She was hungry now as she had been in college, and she ate between meals and after dinner and tried to eat only carrots and celery, but she grew to hate them, and her desire for sweets was as vicious as it had been long ago. At home she ate bread and jam and when she shopped for groceries she bought a candy bar and ate it driving home and put the wrapper in her purse and then in the garbage can under the sink. Her cheeks had filled out, there was loose flesh under her chin, her arms and legs were plump, and her mother was concerned. So was Richard. One night when she brought pie and milk to the living room where they were watching television, he said: "You already had a piece. At dinner."

She did not look at him.

"You're gaining weight. It's not all water, either. It's fat. It'll be summertime. You'll want to get into your bathing suit."

The pie was cherry. She looked at it as her fork cut through it; she speared the piece and rubbed it in the red juice on the plate before lifting it to her mouth.

"You never used to eat pie," he said. "I just think you ought to watch it a bit. It's going to be tough on you this summer."

In her seventh month, with a delight reminiscent of climbing the stairs to Richard's apartment before they were married, she returned to her world of secret gratification. She began hiding candy in her underwear drawer. She ate it during the day and at night while Richard slept, and at breakfast she was distracted, waiting for him to leave.

She gave birth to a son, brought him home, and nursed both him and her appetites. During this time of celibacy she enjoyed her body through her son's mouth; while he suckled she stroked his small head and back. She was hiding candy but she did not conceal her other indulgences: she was smoking again but still she ate between meals, and at dinner she ate what Richard did, and coldly he watched her, he grew petulant, and when the date marking the end of their celibacy came they let it pass. Often in the afternoons her mother visited and scolded her and Louise sat looking at the baby and said nothing until finally, to end it, she promised to diet. When her mother and father came for dinners, her father kissed her and held the baby and her mother said nothing about Louise's body, and her voice was tense. Returning from work in the evenings Richard looked at a soiled plate and glass on the table beside her chair as if detecting traces of infidelity, and at every dinner they fought.

"Look at you," he said. "Lasagna, for God's sake. When are you going to start? It's not simply that you haven't lost any weight. You're gaining. I can see it. I can feel it when you get in bed. Pretty soon you'll weigh more than I do and I'll be sleeping on a trampoline."

"You never touch me anymore."

"I don't want to touch you. Why should I? Have you *looked* at yourself?"

"You're cruel," she said. "I never knew how cruel you were."

She ate, watching him. He did not look at her. Glaring at his plate, he worked with fork and knife like a hurried man at a lunch counter.

"I bet you didn't either," she said.

That night when he was asleep she took a Milky Way to the bathroom. For a while she stood eating in the dark, then she turned on the light. Chewing, she looked at herself in the mirror; she looked at her eyes and hair. Then she stood on the scales and looking at the numbers between her feet, one hundred and sixty-two, she remembered when she had weighed a hundred and thirty-six pounds for eight days. Her memory of those eight days was fond and amusing, as though she were recalling an Easter egg hunt when she was six. She stepped off the scales and pushed them under the lavatory and did not stand on them again.

It was summer and she bought loose dresses and when Richard took friends out on the boat she did not wear a bathing suit or shorts; her friends gave her mischievous glances, and Richard did not look at her. She stopped riding on the boat. She told them she wanted to stay with the baby, and she sat inside holding him until she heard the boat leave the wharf. Then she took him to the front lawn and walked with him in the shade of the trees and talked to him about the blue jays and mockingbirds and cardinals she saw on their branches. Sometimes she stopped and watched the boat out on the lake and the friend skiing behind it.

Every day Richard quarrelled, and because his rage went no further than her weight and shape, she felt excluded from it, and she remained calm within layers of flesh and spirit, and watched his frustration, his impotence. He truly believed they were arguing about her weight. She knew better: she knew that beneath the argument lay the question of who Richard was. She thought of him smiling at the wheel of his boat, and long ago courting his slender girl, the daughter of his partner and friend. She thought of Carrie telling her of smelling chocolate in the dark and, after that, watching her eat it night after night. She smiled at Richard, teasing his anger.

He is angry now. He stands in the center of the living room, raging at her, and he wakes the baby. Beneath Richard's voice she hears the soft crying, feels it in her heart, and quietly she rises from her chair and goes upstairs to the child's room and takes him from the crib. She brings him to the living room and sits holding him in her lap, pressing him gently against the folds of fat at her waist. Now Richard is pleading with her. Louise thinks tenderly of Carrie broiling meat and fish in their room, and walking with her in the evenings. She wonders if Carrie still has the malaise. Perhaps she will come for a visit. In Louise's arms now the boy sleeps.

"I'll help you," Richard says. "I'll eat the same things you eat."

But his face does not approach the compassion and determination and love she had seen in Carrie's during what she now recognizes as the worst year of her life. She can remember nothing about that year except hunger, and the meals in her room. She is hungry now. When she puts the boy to bed she will get a candy bar from her room. She will eat it here, in front of Richard. This room will be hers soon. She considers the possibilities: all these rooms and the lawn where she can do whatever she wishes. She knows he will leave soon. It has been in his eyes all summer. She stands, using one hand to pull herself out of the chair. She carries the boy to his crib, feels him against her large breasts, feels that his sleeping body touches her soul. With a surge of vindication and relief she holds him. Then she kisses his forehead and places him in the crib. She goes to the bedroom and in the dark takes a bar of candy from her drawer. Slowly she descends the stairs. She knows Richard is waiting but she feels his departure so happily that, when she enters the living room, unwrapping the candy, she is surprised to see him standing there.

(1975)

Claire Kemp *1936–*

KEEPING COMPANY

William wakes me with water. He sprays me through the window screen and I am introduced to morning under tangled sheets, sprinkled damp and rolled like laundry ready for the iron. He's whistling. When he sings, "Lazy Mary, will you get up?", I do and go outside in my nightdress to stand barefoot on the cool wet cement close to William. "Hello, wife," he says.

Two men walking to the beach smile and wave a hand in greeting. I raise my hand to wave to them but William checks me with a look. He aims the hose at the street but the pressure is down and the water falls short. "Missed by a mile," he says. "I'm losing my touch."

"They're not bothering anyone. What do you care?"

"They're bothering me and I care." A small muscle in his cheek keeps an angry beat.

"You'll be late for work," I tell him and run inside to make his eggs, soft boiled on white toast.

"Never happen," he says. The hose, a fat green snake, uncoils and follows obediently wherever he walks.

Mornings I go to the beach. I go alone because William won't. Certain young men come to stroll on this beach. Their walk is a slow dance, graceful and sure. They glide on pewter sand like skaters do on ice. In their brief suits, satin bands of azure blue, magenta, yellow, emerald green, they appear as exotic flowers blooming in the desert. I am taken with their beauty and don't mind sitting in their shade. Not unkindly they dismiss me with their eyes, unencumbered souls walking free at water's edge with perhaps a scarlet towel over one tanned shoulder or a small cloth bag worn around the neck to hold the treasures of the moment. They have smiles for each other but not for me. I'm a cabbage in their garden, a woman large with child, a different species altogether. Next year, I'll have someone to keep me company. I'll teach her how to make castles with turrets from paper cups and wet sand. Swizzle sticks will make a fine bridge to span the moat. Perhaps we'll place cocktail parasols for color in the sand palace courtyard. And I'll take her home before the tide comes in to take it down. She's with me now, tumbling and turning in her water bed and dancing on my ribs with tiny heels and toes. She's coming to term and letting me know. It won't be long.

Afternoons I tend my flowers. Today, I see an open truck parked next door. And a piano on the porch. Two men are discussing how to get it through the door. One goes inside to pull; the other stays out to push. I think of the piano as a stubborn horse, its mahogany rump splendid in the sun. "Perhaps, if you offer it sugar," I suggest. The outside man grins. "Hello," he says and vaults over his porch rail. I brush potting soil from my hands and reach to shake his hand.

"I'm James," he says. His eyes are gray blue and direct. When he smiles his features merge brightly like a photograph in focus. He has a good face. He says, "Dennis is inside. He might come out or he might not. He's shy." Behind him, someone parts the lace curtain at one window and lets it fall.

I tell James my name and he says, "It's nice to meet you, Nora. Your flowers are lovely." But he's not looking at my flowers. Just at me. He nods in affirmation of some private thought and says, "Moving's more work than I bargained for. I'd better get back to it."

"Yes, see you again" I reply and bend to the task of breaking off the blooms gone by. The aroma of geranium is so strong it seems to leave a taste on my tongue. When I go inside to make myself a cup of tea, the piano has made it through the door and there is no one in sight.

After dinner, I tell William we have neighbors and he tells me he's not blind. He uncaps a beer and tilts the bottle to his lips. He wipes foam from his beard with the back of his hand and gives me a long look I'm meant to pay attention to. "Don't bother with them, Nora. They're not our kind." From next door I hear a tentative chord or two. I listen for more but the night air is still, not another note. I listen for sounds from their house over the sounds of our house all evening long. I don't know why I would. After a while the heat leaves the house and it's cool enough for sleep and still I listen.

James brings me a croissant sprinkled with cinnamon and sugar. I put down my watering can and take it from his hand. Dennis is practicing scales and I remember how it felt to play, my eyes on the page, not on the keys.

"What are you hoping for?" James asks shyly.

"It's a girl. We already know. Doctors can tell in advance now. We've named her Sara."

"Imagine," he says but his eyes are worried as if he marvels at giving credibility to someone who can't yet breathe on her own. "She's like a present, as yet unwrapped," he says. Abruptly the music stops. I picture Dennis closing the piano, covering the keys and going to another part of his house.

"Dennis is tired," James explains. He has already turned from me toward the silence and I am left holding the still warm pastry in one hand and nothing in the other.

I hang the wash, William's work shirts, dish cloths and towels, heavy sheets that pull on my arms. Next door, James and Dennis talking, always talking. Their voices rise and fall and blend together. They have so much to say. They never seem to tire of talk. Their screen door opens and shuts throughout the day as they come and go. When they are out of each other's sight, one calls out and the other answers.

Late in the day, I take in the dry clothes, stripping the line and folding as I go along, leaving the clothespins to bob like small wooden birds. Dennis and James head for the beach. Dennis wears a light jacket zipped to the neck as if he is cold. His short sandy hair curls up around his cap, leaving the back of his neck bare, like a young boy's. I can tell James would walk faster if he was alone. Perhaps he would run. As it is, he holds back to keep the pace that Dennis sets but his energy shows itself in the enthusiastic swing of his arms and the quick, attentive way he inclines his head to catch the words that Dennis speaks. When they're out of sight beyond the dunes, I go inside to wait for William.

James is teaching me backgammon. We sit on his patio under the Cinzano umbrella and drink iced tea with lemon slices on the rim of tall oddly shaped amber glasses, no two alike. Dennis will not play but once he points out a move for me and seems quietly pleased when I take that game from James. I do not tell

William where I spend my summer afternoons. I'm where I belong when he gets home. He slides his arms around me and rubs my face with his beard and says proudly, "Nora, I swear, you're as big as a house." "I am," I agree, laughing. "I'm Sara's house." He does not ask me what I do all day and I would not tell him if he did. I know something about myself that I didn't know before. I'm successful at sins of omission, never really lying, never telling truth. I hoard secrets like a dog who buries bones to relish at some future time. I wonder if when that time comes, I will remember why or where I dug the holes.

William comes home early, tires spinning in the sand on the lane between our house and theirs. I'm caught and stand up fast from James' table and hurry home leaving James in the middle of a play.

"I don't want you over there," William tells me. "Is that clear?"

"But why? They're good company."

"They can keep each other company. Not you. I'm your good company. The only company you'll ever need."

William sighs when he looks at me as though I'm a chore he must complete.

Dennis gives a concert in my honor, all my favorite pieces played perfect, without flaw or fault. I sit on my front step as evening falls to dark and listen till he's done.

William is building a wall. To make certain he's within his rights, he engages a surveyor to determine the exact boundaries of our land. After supper and on Saturdays he works on his wall. There are guidelines he must follow as to height. I know if permitted he would make it six feet high, five inches taller than the top of my head, but the law won't allow it. Its purpose is to keep me in my place. When he's done, he calls me out to admire his work and I do. I tell him it's a fine wall which is what he wants to hear. James, on his porch, raises his glass in a silent toast. I send him my best smile, an apology big enough for both William and myself.

William has gone south to deliver a boat and won't be home before midnight at least. James invites me for dinner. I'm invited, so I go. Their kitchen is yellow and blue, quaint, like a woman's sitting room. There are many plants I can't begin to name in clay pots and hanging baskets. I sit on paisley cushions in a wicker chair by the window watching James make stew from scratch. While James chops vegetables, his hand on the knife making quick, precise cuts, Dennis copies the recipe in his spidery script on a card for me to take home. I set the table, lace cloth from Ireland, tall rose colored candles in crystal, linen napkins in shell rings and sterling silver by the plates. James holds my chair and seats me as if I am a lady and not a country girl in faded shorts and one of William's shirts. Dennis searches the yard for hibiscus blooms. He floats them in a shallow blue bowl for a centerpiece. I have gone over the wall.

Unlike Cinderella, I'm home well before midnight in my own kitchen, with a bowl of stew for William over a low flame on my stove. He eats out of the pan. "What are these yellow things?" he asks, poking with his fork.

"Parsnips."

"OK," he says. "Next time peas. Otherwise, not bad at all."

I let him think I made the stew myself which of course I could have done. And maybe will someday. The recipe is out of sight in the bottom of my sewing box.

We are in a tropical depression. Hot steady rain for a week and thick humid air that leaves me worn out and sleepy. I stay inside, an idle woman, changing in spite of myself like a mushroom growing at a furious rate in this damp and fertile season. We lose our power and Dennis brings candles. He hands the bag to William and runs off without a proper thank you. William hands it quick to me as if its contents are not candles but sticks of dynamite that could go off at any minute. He follows me like the tail of a kite as I place lighted candles on waxed saucers in each room of our house. "The wall is holding," he says. "Can you believe it?" I say, "Yes, I believe it."

In September, Sara will be born.

When the storms give in to sun I'm glad, but it reigns in the sky like a lion. Its heat is fierce. I have not seen Dennis or James. The piano does not play. I knock on their door and finally James is there behind the screen. He doesn't lift the latch. I say, "How are you? I miss you two." "Not to worry," he assures me without meeting my eyes. When I ask for Dennis, James shrugs as if Dennis is someone he's lost track of somehow and can't be bothered getting back, which I know for sure is not the truth. He laughs then, a short harsh sound like a bark. "Sorry," he says. "Dennis is in the hospital. I don't know that he'll be coming home." He says this like he's asking a question, like he's asking me for an answer. I put my hand on my side of the screen and James touches it briefly with his. We stand for a moment, like visitors in prison before he closes the inside door and shuts me out. I wish I could take back the days.

I go home where I belong. There is laundry to fold, chores to do, an entire house to put to order. I do a proper job of every task, a proper penance. Before bed, I tell William. I know as I begin to speak that it will not go well but I'm bound to tell it, to lay it out like a soiled cloth on our clean table.

"Dennis is sick," I say and at just that moment I know that this truth is another bone I buried.

William says, "Yes, he is. Very sick. Have you been over there again? I told you to stay away from them. I warned you. But, knowing you. . . ."

"You don't."

"Don't what?"

"Know me." I stand up. There is a knot of sorrow that drops in me like a sinker in a tidal pool. I walk out the door and away from William. At the jetty, I climb the slick black rocks, heedless of the cruel pockets of stone that could snap a limb as easy as not. I find a smooth stone that makes a good seat. I'm surprised to know I'm crying. Our porch light comes on and there is William, his pale hair like a halo under its glow. He calls me. "Nora, come home," but the tide takes his voice and swallows my name. When I'm thoroughly chilled and empty of anger, I leave my perch and travel north on the wet sand, close to the cool fingers of incoming tide. I'm a small but competent ship sailing the coast line. I set my own course. I hear someone running in my wake and it's William, breathless from the chase. He passes me on fast feet, then turns, dancing backward like a boxer until I stop just shy of the circle of his arms. He carries my sweater, which he puts around my shoulders with great care, as if it is a precious fur he wraps me in and I too am precious. He buttons one button under my chin with clumsy fingers. "Let's go back," he says, so we do. We do not talk about anything, simply walk forward in silence, which is the way it is between husbands and wives, with married people.

(1990)

Raymond Carver *1938-1988*

WHAT WE TALK ABOUT WHEN WE TALK ABOUT LOVE

My friend Mel McGinnis was talking. Mel McGinnis is a cardiologist, and sometimes that gives him the right.

The four of us were sitting around his kitchen table drinking gin. Sunlight filled the kitchen from the big window behind the sink. There were Mel and me and his second wife, Teresa—Terri, we called her—and my wife, Laura. We lived in Albuquerque then. But we were all from somewhere else.

There was an ice bucket on the table. The gin and the tonic water kept going around, and we somehow got on the subject of love. Mel thought real love was nothing less than spiritual love. He said he'd spent five years in a seminary before quitting to go to medical school. He said he still looked back on those years in the seminary as the most important years in his life.

Terri said the man she lived with before she lived with Mel loved her so much he tried to kill her. Then Terri said, "He beat me up one night. He dragged me around the living room by my ankles. He kept saying, 'I love you, I love you, you bitch.' He went on dragging me around the living room. My head kept knocking on things." Terri looked around the table. "What do you do with love like that?"

She was a bone-thin woman with a pretty face, dark eyes, and brown hair that hung down her back. She liked necklaces made of turquoise, and long pendant earrings.

"My God, don't be silly. That's not love, and you know it," Mel said. "I don't know what you'd call it, but I sure know you wouldn't call it love."

"Say what you want to, but I know it was," Terri said. "It may sound crazy to you, but it's true just the same. People are different, Mel. Sure, sometimes he may have acted crazy. Okay. But he loved me. In his own way maybe, but he loved me. There was love there, Mel. Don't say there wasn't."

Mel let out his breath. He held his glass and turned to Laura and me. "The man threatened to kill me," Mel said. He finished his drink and reached for the gin bottle. "Terri's a romantic. Terri's of the kick-me-so-I'll-know-you-love-me school. Terri, hon, don't look that way." Mel reached across the table and touched Terri's cheek with his fingers. He grinned at her.

"Now he wants to make up," Terri said.

"Make up what?" Mel said. "What is there to make up? I know what I know. That's all."

"How'd we get started on this subject, anyway?" Terri said. She raised her glass and drank from it. "Mel always has love on his mind," she said. "Don't you, honey?" She smiled, and I thought that was the last of it.

"I just wouldn't call Ed's behavior love. That's all I'm saying, honey," Mel said. "What about you guys?" Mel said to Laura and me. "Does that sound like love to you?"

"I'm the wrong person to ask," I said. "I didn't even know the man. I've only heard his name mentioned in passing. I wouldn't know. You'd have to know the particulars. But I think what you're saying is that love is an absolute."

Mel said, "The kind of love I'm talking about is. The kind of love I'm talking about, you don't try to kill people."

Laura said, "I don't know anything about Ed, or anything about the situation. But who can judge anyone else's situation?"

I touched the back of Laura's hand. She gave me a quick smile. I picked up Laura's hand. It was warm, the nails polished, perfectly manicured. I encircled the broad wrist with my fingers, and I held her.

"When I left, he drank rat poison," Terri said. She clasped her arms with her hands. "They took him to the hospital in Santa Fe. That's where we lived then, about ten miles out. They saved his life. But his gums went crazy from it. I mean they pulled away from his teeth. After that, his teeth stood out like fangs. My God," Terri said. She waited a minute, then let go of her arms and picked up her glass.

"What people won't do!" Laura said.

"He's out of the action now," Mel said. "He's dead."

Mel handed me the saucer of limes. I took a section, squeezed it over my drink, and stirred the ice cubes with my finger.

"It gets worse," Terri said. "He shot himself in the mouth. But he bungled that too. Poor Ed," she said. Terri shook her head.

"Poor Ed nothing," Mel said. "He was dangerous."

Mel was forty-five years old. He was tall and rangy with curly soft hair. His face and arms were brown from the tennis he played. When he was sober, his gestures, all his movements, were precise, very careful.

"He did love me though, Mel. Grant me that," Terri said. "That's all I'm asking. He didn't love me the way you love me. I'm not saying that. But he loved me. You can grant me that, can't you?"

"What do you mean, he bungled it?" I said.

Laura leaned forward with her glass. She put her elbows on the table and held her glass in both hands. She glanced from Mel to Terri and waited with a look of bewilderment on her open face, as if amazed that such things happened to people you were friendly with.

"How'd he bungle it when he killed himself?" I said.

"I'll tell you what happened," Mel said. "He took this twenty-two pistol he'd bought to threaten Terri and me with. Oh, I'm serious, the man was always threatening. You should have seen the way we lived in those days. Like fugitives. I even bought a gun myself. Can you believe it? A guy like me? But I did. I bought one for self-defense and carried it in the glove compartment. Sometimes I'd have to leave the apartment in the middle of the night. To go to the hospital, you know? Terri and I weren't married then, and my first wife had the house and kids, the dog, everything, and Terri and I were living in this apartment here. Sometimes, as I say, I'd get a call in the middle of the night and have to go in to the hospital at two or three in the morning. It'd be dark out there in the parking lot, and I'd break into a sweat before I could even get to my car. I never knew if he was going to come up out of the shrubbery or from behind a car and start shooting. I mean, the man was crazy. He was capable of wiring a bomb, anything. He used to call my service at all hours and say he needed to talk to the doctor, and when I'd return the call, he'd say, 'Son of a bitch, your days are numbered.' Little things like that. It was scary, I'm telling you."

"I still feel sorry for him," Terri said.

"It sounds like a nightmare," Laura said. "But what exactly happened after he shot himself?"

Laura is a legal secretary. We'd met in a professional capacity. Before we knew it, it was a courtship. She's thirty-five, three years younger than I am. In addition to being in love, we like each other and enjoy one another's company. She's easy to be with.

"What happened?" Laura said.

Mel said, "He shot himself in the mouth in his room. Someone heard the shot and told the manager. They came in with a passkey, saw what had happened, and called an ambulance. I happened to be there when they brought him in, alive but past recall. The man lived for three days. His head swelled up to twice the size of a normal head. I'd never seen anything like it, and I hope I never do again. Terri wanted to go in and sit with him when she found out about it. We had a fight over it. I didn't think she should see him like that. I didn't think she should see him, and I still don't."

"Who won the fight?" Laura said.

"I was in the room with him when he died," Terri said. "He never came up out of it. But I sat with him. He didn't have anyone else."

"He was dangerous," Mel said. "If you call that love, you can have it."

"It was love," Terri said. "Sure, it's abnormal in most people's eyes. But he was willing to die for it. He did die for it."

"I sure as hell wouldn't call it love," Mel said. "I mean, no one knows what he did it for. I've seen a lot of suicides, and I couldn't say anyone ever knew what they did it for."

Mel put his hands behind his neck and tilted his chair back. "I'm not interested in that kind of love," he said. "If that's love, you can have it."

Terri said, "We were afraid. Mel even made a will out and wrote to his brother in California who used to be a Green Beret. Mel told him who to look for if something happened to him."

Terri drank from her glass. She said, "But Mel's right — we lived like fugitives. We were afraid. Mel was, weren't you, honey? I even called the police at one point, but they were no help. They said they couldn't do anything until Ed actually did something. Isn't that a laugh?" Terri said.

She poured the last of the gin into her glass and waggled the bottle. Mel got up from the table and went to the cupboard. He took down another bottle.

"Well, Nick and I know what love is," Laura said. "For us, I mean," Laura said. She bumped my knee with her knee. "You're supposed to say something now," Laura said, and turned her smile on me.

For an answer, I took Laura's hand and raised it to my lips. I made a big production out of kissing her hand. Everyone was amused.

"We're lucky," I said.

"You guys," Terri said. "Stop that now. You're making me sick. You're still on the honeymoon, for God's sake. You're still gaga, for crying out loud. Just wait. How long have you been together now? How long has it been? A year? Longer than a year?"

"Going on a year and a half," Laura said, flushed and smiling.

"Oh, now," Terri said. "Wait awhile."

She held her drink and gazed at Laura.

"I'm only kidding," Terri said.

Mel opened the gin and went around the table with the bottle.

"Here, you guys," he said. "Let's have a toast. I want to propose a toast. A toast to love. To true love," Mel said.

We touched glasses.

"To love," we said.

Outside in the backyard, one of the dogs began to bark. The leaves of the aspen that leaned past the window ticked against the glass. The afternoon sun was like a presence in this room, the spacious light of ease and generosity. We could have been anywhere, somewhere enchanted. We raised our glasses again and grinned at each other like children who had agreed on something forbidden.

"I'll tell you what real love is," Mel said. "I mean, I'll give you a good example. And then you can draw your own conclusions." He poured more gin into his glass. He added an ice cube and a sliver of lime. We waited and sipped our drinks. Laura and I touched knees again. I put a hand on her warm thigh and left it there.

"What do any of us really know about love?" Mel said. "It seems to me we're just beginners at love. We say we love each other and we do, I don't doubt it. I love Terri and Terri loves me, and you guys love each other too. You know the kind of love I'm talking about now. Physical love, that impulse that drives you to someone special, as well as love of the other person's being, his or her essence, as it were. Carnal love and, well, call it sentimental love, the day-to-day caring about the other person. But sometimes I have a hard time accounting for the fact that I must have loved my first wife too. But I did, I know I did. So I suppose I am like Terri in that regard. Terri and Ed." He thought about it and then he went on. "There was a time when I thought I loved my first wife more than life itself. But now I hate her guts. I do. How do you explain that? What happened to that love? What happened to it, is what I'd like to know. I wish someone could tell me. Then there's Ed. Okay, we're back to Ed. He loves Terri so much he tries to kill her and he winds up killing himself." Mel stopped talking and swallowed from his glass. "You guys have been together eighteen months and you love each other. It shows all over you. You glow with it. But you both loved other people before you met each other. You've both been married before, just like us. And you probably loved other people before that too, even. Terri and I have been together five years, been married for four. And the terrible thing, the terrible thing is, but the good thing too, the saving grace, you might say, is that if something happened to one of us — excuse me for saying this — but if something happened to one of us tomorrow, I think the other one, the other person, would grieve for a while, you know, but then the surviving party would go out and love again, have someone else soon enough. All this, all of this love we're talking about, it would just be a memory. Maybe not even a memory. Am I wrong? Am I way off base? Because I want you to set me straight if you think I'm wrong. I want to know. I mean, I don't know anything, and I'm the first one to admit it."

"Mel, for God's sake," Terri said. She reached out and took hold of his wrist. "Are you getting drunk? Honey? Are you drunk?"

"Honey, I'm just talking," Mel said. "All right? I don't have to be drunk to say what I think. I mean, we're all just talking, right?" Mel said. He fixed his eyes on her.

"Sweetie, I'm not criticizing," Terri said.

She picked up her glass.

"I'm not on call today," Mel said. "Let me remind you of that. I am not on call," he said.

"Mel, we love you," Laura said.

Mel looked at Laura. He looked at her as if he could not place her, as if she was not the woman she was.

"Love you too, Laura," Mel said. "And you, Nick, love you too. You know something?" Mel said. "You guys are our pals," Mel said.

He picked up his glass.

Mel said, "I was going to tell you about something. I mean, I was going to prove a point. You see, this happened a few months ago, but it's still going on right now, and it ought to make us feel ashamed when we talk like we know what we're talking about when we talk about love."

"Come on now," Terri said. "Don't talk like you're drunk if you're not drunk."

"Just shut up for once in your life," Mel said very quietly. "Will you do me a favor and do that for a minute? So as I was saying, there's this old couple who had this car wreck out on the interstate. A kid hit them and they were all torn to shit and nobody was giving them much chance to pull through."

Terri looked at us and then back at Mel. She seemed anxious, or maybe that's too strong a word.

Mel was handing the bottle around the table.

"I was on call that night," Mel said. "It was May or maybe it was June. Terri and I had just sat down to dinner when the hospital called. There'd been this thing out on the interstate. Drunk kid, teenager, plowed his dad's pickup into this camper with this old couple in it. They were up in their mid-seventies, that couple. The kid—eighteen, nineteen, something—he was DOA. Taken the steering wheel through his sternum. The old couple, they were alive, you understand. I mean, just barely. But they had everything. Multiple fractures, internal injuries, hemorrhaging, contusions, lacerations, the works, and they each of them had themselves concussions. They were in a bad way, believe me. And, of course, their age was two strikes against them. I'd say she was worse off than he was. Ruptured spleen along with everything else. Both kneecaps broken. But they'd been wearing their seatbelts and, God knows, that's what saved them for the time being."

"Folks, this is an advertisement for the National Safety Council," Terri said. "This is your spokesman, Dr. Melvin R. McGinnis, talking." Terri laughed. "Mel," she said, "sometimes you're just too much. But I love you, hon," she said.

"Honey, I love you," Mel said.

He leaned across the table. Terri met him halfway. They kissed.

"Terri's right," Mel said as he settled himself again. "Get those seatbelts on. But seriously, they were in some shape, those oldsters. By the time I got down there, the kid was dead, as I said. He was off in a corner, laid out on a gurney. I took one look at the old couple and told the ER nurse to get me a neurologist and an orthopedic man and a couple of surgeons down there right away."

He drank from his glass. "I'll try to keep this short," he said. "So we took the two of them up to the OR and worked like fuck on them most of the night. They had these incredible reserves, those two. You see that once in a while. So we did everything that could be done, and toward morning we're giving them a fifty-

fifty chance, maybe less than that for her. So here they are, still alive the next morning. So, okay, we move them into the ICU, which is where they both kept plugging away at it for two weeks, hitting it better and better on all the scopes. So we transfer them out to their own room."

Mel stopped talking. "Here," he said, "let's drink this cheapo gin the hell up. Then we're going to dinner, right? Terri and I know a new place. That's where we'll go, to this new place we know about. But we're not going until we finish up this cut-rate, lousy gin."

Terri said, "We haven't actually eaten there yet. But it looks good. From the outside, you know."

"I like food," Mel said. "If I had it to do all over again, I'd be a chef, you know? Right, Terri?" Mel said.

He laughed. He fingered the ice in his glass.

"Terri knows," he said. "Terri can tell you. But let me say this. If I could come back again in a different life, a different time and all, you know what? I'd like to come back as a knight. You were pretty safe wearing all that armor. It was all right being a knight until gunpowder and muskets and pistols came along."

"Mel would like to ride a horse and carry a lance," Terri said.

"Carry a woman's scarf with you everywhere," Laura said.

"Or just a woman," Mel said.

"Shame on you," Laura said.

Terri said, "Suppose you came back as a serf. The serfs didn't have it so good in those days," Terri said.

"The serfs never had it good," Mel said. "But I guess even the knights were vessels to someone. Isn't that the way it worked? But then everyone is always a vessel to someone. Isn't that right? Terri? But what I liked about knights, besides their ladies, was that they had that suit of armor, you know, and they couldn't get hurt very easy. No cars in those days, you know? No drunk teenagers to tear into your ass."

"Vassals," Terri said.

"What?" Mel said.

"Vassals," Terri said. "They were called vassals, not vessels."

"Vassals, vessels," Mel said, "what the fuck's the difference? You knew what I meant anyway. All right," Mel said. "So I'm not educated. I learned my stuff. I'm a heart surgeon, sure, but I'm just a mechanic. I go in and fuck around and I fix things. Shit," Mel said.

"Modesty doesn't become you," Terri said.

"He's just a humble sawbones," I said. "But sometimes they suffocated in all that armor, Mel. They'd even have heart attacks if it got too hot and they were too tired and worn out. I read somewhere that they'd fall off their horses and not be able to get up because they were too tired to stand with all that armor on them. They got trampled by their own horses sometimes."

"That's terrible," Mel said. "That's a terrible thing, Nicky. I guess they'd just lay there and wait until somebody came along and made a shish kebab out of them."

"Some other vessel," Terri said.

"That's right," Mel said. "Some vassal would come along and spear the bastard in the name of love. Or whatever the fuck it was they fought over in those days."

"Same things we fight over these days," Terri said.

Laura said, "Nothing's changed."

The color was still high in Laura's cheeks. Her eyes were bright. She brought her glass to her lips.

Mel poured himself another drink. He looked at the label closely as if studying a long row of numbers. Then he slowly put the bottle down on the table and slowly reached for the tonic water.

"What about the old couple?" Laura said. "You didn't finish that story you started."

Laura was having a hard time lighting her cigarette. Her matches kept going out.

The sunshine inside the room was different now, changing, getting thinner. But the leaves outside the window were still shimmering, and I stared at the pattern they made on the panes and on the Formica counter. They weren't the same patterns, of course.

"What about the old couple?" I said.

"Older but wiser," Terri said.

Mel stared at her.

Terri said, "Go on with your story, hon. I was only kidding. Then what happened?"

"Terri, sometimes," Mel said.

"Please, Mel," Terri said. "Don't always be so serious, sweetie. Can't you take a joke?"

"Where's the joke?" Mel said.

He held his glass and gazed steadily at his wife.

"What happened?" Laura said.

Mel fastened his eyes on Laura. He said, "Laura, if I didn't have Terri and if I didn't love her so much, and if Nick wasn't my best friend, I'd fall in love with you. I'd carry you off, honey," he said.

"Tell your story," Terri said. "Then we'll go to that new place, okay?"

"Okay," Mel said. "Where was I?" he said. He stared at the table and then he began again.

"I dropped in to see each of them every day, sometimes twice a day if I was up doing other calls anyway. Casts and bandages, head to foot, the both of them. You know, you've seen it in the movies. That's just the way they looked, just like in the movies. Little eye-holes and nose-holes and mouth-holes. And she had to have her legs slung up on top of it. Well, the husband was very depressed for the longest while. Even after he found out that his wife was going to pull through, he was still very depressed. Not about the accident, though. I mean, the accident was one thing, but it wasn't everything. I'd get up to his mouth-hole, you know, and he'd say no, it wasn't the accident exactly but it was because he couldn't see her through his eye-holes. He said that was what was making him feel so bad. Can you imagine? I'm telling you, the man's heart was breaking because he couldn't turn his goddamn head and *see* his goddamn wife."

Mel looked around the table and shook his head at what he was going to say.

"I mean, it was killing the old fart just because he couldn't *look* at the fucking woman."

We all looked at Mel.

"Do you see what I'm saying?" he said.

Maybe we were a little drunk by then. I know it was hard keeping things in focus. The light was draining out of the room, going back through the window where it had come from. Yet nobody made a move to get up from the table to turn on the overhead light.

"Listen," Mel said. "Let's finish this fucking gin. There's about enough here for one shooter all around. Then let's go eat. Let's go to the new place."

"He's depressed," Terri said. "Mel, why don't you take a pill?"

Mel shook his head. "I've taken everything there is."

"We all need a pill now and then," I said.

"Some people are born needing them," Terri said.

She was using her finger to rub at something on the table. Then she stopped rubbing.

"I think I want to call my kids," Mel said. "Is that all right with everybody? I'll call my kids," he said.

Terri said, "What if Marjorie answers the phone? You guys, you've heard us on the subject of Marjorie? Honey, you know you don't want to talk to Marjorie. It'll make you feel even worse."

"I don't want to talk to Marjorie," Mel said. "But I want to talk to my kids."

"There isn't a day goes by that Mel doesn't say he wishes she'd get married again. Or else die," Terri said. "For one thing," Terri said, "she's bankrupting us. Mel says it's just to spite him that she won't get married again. She has a boyfriend who lives with her and the kids, so Mel is supporting the boyfriend too."

"She's allergic to bees," Mel said. "If I'm not praying she'll get married again, I'm praying she'll get herself stung to death by a swarm of fucking bees."

"Shame on you," Laura said.

"Bzzzzzzz," Mel said, turning his fingers into bees and buzzing them at Terri's throat. Then he let his hands drop all the way to his sides.

"She's vicious," Mel said. "Sometimes I think I'll go up there dressed like a beekeeper. You know, that hat that's like a helmet with the plate that comes down over your face, the big gloves, and the padded coat? I'll knock on the door and let loose a hive of bees in the house. But first I'd make sure the kids were out, of course."

He crossed one leg over the other. It seemed to take him a lot of time to do it. Then he put both feet on the floor and leaned forward, elbows on the table, his chin cupped in his hands.

"Maybe I won't call the kids, after all. Maybe it isn't such a hot idea. Maybe we'll just go eat. How does that sound?"

"Sounds fine to me," I said. "Eat or not eat. Or keep drinking. I could head right on out into the sunset."

"What does that mean, honey?" Laura said.

"It just means what I said," I said. "It means I could just keep going. That's all it means."

"I could eat something myself," Laura said. "I don't think I've ever been so hungry in my life. Is there something to nibble on?"

"I'll put out some cheese and crackers," Terri said.

But Terri just sat there. She did not get up to get anything.

Mel turned his glass over. He spilled it out on the table.

"Gin's gone," Mel said.

Terri said, "Now what?"

I could hear my heart beating. I could hear everyone's heart. I could hear the human noise we sat there making, not one of us moving, not even when the room went dark.

(1981)

Joyce Carol Oates *1938–*

WHERE ARE YOU GOING, WHERE HAVE YOU BEEN?

FOR BOB DYLAN[1]

Her name was Connie. She was fifteen and she had a quick, nervous giggling habit of craning her neck to glance into mirrors or checking other people's faces to make sure her own was all right. Her mother, who noticed everything and knew everything and who hadn't much reason any longer to look at her own face, always scolded Connie about it. "Stop gawking at yourself. Who are you? You think you're so pretty?" she would say. Connie would raise her eyebrows at these familiar old complaints and look right through her mother, into a shadowy vision of herself as she was right at that moment: she knew she was pretty and that was everything. Her mother had been pretty once too, if you could believe those old snapshots in the album, but now her looks were gone and that was why she was always after Connie.

"Why don't you keep your room clean like your sister? How've you got your hair fixed—what the hell stinks? Hair spray? You don't see your sister using that junk."

Her sister June was twenty-four and still lived at home. She was a secretary in the high school Connie attended, and if that wasn't bad enough—with her in the same building—she was so plain and chunky and steady that Connie had to hear her praised all the time by her mother and her mother's sisters. June did this, June did that, she saved money and helped clean the house and cooked and Connie couldn't do a thing, her mind was all filled with trashy daydreams. Their father was away at work most of the time and when he came home he wanted supper and he read the newspaper at supper and after supper he went to bed. He didn't bother talking much to them, but around his bent head Connie's mother kept picking at her until Connie wished her mother was dead and she herself was dead and it was all over. "She makes me want to throw up sometimes," she complained to her friends. She had a high, breathless, amused voice that made everything she said sound a little forced, whether it was sincere or not.

There was one good thing: June went places with girl friends of hers, girls who were just as plain and steady as she, and so when Connie wanted to do that her mother had no objections. The father of Connie's best girl friend drove the girls the three miles to town and left them at a shopping plaza so they could walk through the stores or go to a movie, and when he came to pick them up again at eleven he never bothered to ask what they had done.

They must have been familiar sights, walking around the shopping plaza in their shorts and flat ballerina slippers that always scuffed the sidewalk, with charm bracelets jingling on their thin wrists; they would lean together to whisper and laugh secretly if someone passed who amused or interested them. Connie had long dark blond hair that drew anyone's eye to it, and she wore part

---

[1]Bob Dylan (1941–) is the composer, author, and singer who devised and popularized folk-rock during the 1960s. Joyce Carol Oates has said that Dylan's song "It's All Over Now, Baby Blue" was on her mind at the time she wrote the story.

of it pulled up on her head and puffed out and the rest of it she let fall down her back. She wore a pull-over jersey blouse that looked one way when she was at home and another way when she was away from home. Everything about her had two sides to it, one for home and one for anywhere that was not home: her walk, which could be childlike and bobbing, or languid enough to make anyone think she was hearing music in her head; her mouth, which was pale and smirking most of the time, but bright and pink on these evenings out; her laugh, which was cynical and drawling at home — "Ha, ha, very funny," — but high-pitched and nervous anywhere else, like the jingling of the charms on her bracelet.

Sometimes they did go shopping or to a movie, but sometimes they went across the highway, ducking fast across the busy road, to a drive-in restaurant where older kids hung out. The restaurant was shaped like a big bottle, though squatter than a real bottle, and on its cap was a revolving figure of a grinning boy holding a hamburger aloft. One night in mid-summer they ran across, breathless with daring, and right away someone leaned out a car window and invited them over, but it was just a boy from high school they didn't like. It made them feel good to be able to ignore him. They went up through the maze of parked and cruising cars to the bright-lit, fly-infested restaurant, their faces pleased and expectant as if they were entering a sacred building that loomed up out of the night to give them what haven and blessing they yearned for. They sat at the counter and crossed their legs at the ankles, their thin shoulders rigid with excitement, and listened to the music that made everything so good: the music was always in the background, like music at a church service; it was something to depend upon.

A boy named Eddie came in to talk with them. He sat backwards on his stool, turning himself jerkily around in semi-circles and then stopping and turning back again, and after a while he asked Connie if she would like something to eat. She said she would and so she tapped her friend's arm on her way out — her friend pulled her face up into a brave, droll look — and Connie said she would meet her at eleven, across the way. "I just hate to leave her like that," Connie said earnestly, but the boy said that she wouldn't be alone for long. So they went out to his car, and on the way Connie couldn't help but let her eyes wander over the windshields and faces all around her, her face gleaming with a joy that had nothing to do with Eddie or even this place; it might have been the music. She drew her shoulders up and sucked in her breath with the pure pleasure of being alive, and just at that moment she happened to glance at a face just a few feet from hers. It was a boy with shaggy black hair, in a convertible jalopy painted gold. He stared at her and then his lips widened into a grin. Connie slit her eyes at him and turned away, but she couldn't help glancing back and there he was, still watching her. He wagged a finger and laughed and said, "Gonna get you, baby," and Connie turned away again without Eddie noticing anything.

She spent three hours with him, at the restaurant where they ate hamburgers and drank Cokes in wax cups that were always sweating, and then down an alley a mile or so away, and when he left her off at five to eleven only the movie house was still open at the plaza. Her girl friend was there, talking with a boy. When Connie came up, the two girls smiled at each other and Connie said, "How was the movie?" and the girl said, "*You* should know." They rode off with the girl's father, sleepy and pleased, and Connie couldn't help but look back at the darkened shopping plaza with its big empty parking lot and its signs that were faded and ghostly now, and over at the drive-in restaurant where cars were still circling tirelessly. She couldn't hear the music at this distance.

Next morning June asked her how the movie was and Connie said, "So-so."

She and that girl and occasionally another girl went out several times a week, and the rest of the time Connie spent around the house—it was summer vacation—getting in her mother's way and thinking, dreaming about the boys she met. But all the boys fell back and dissolved into a single face that was not even a face but an idea, a feeling, mixed up with the urgent insistent pounding of the music and the humid night air of July. Connie's mother kept dragging her back to the daylight by finding things for her to do or saying suddenly, "What's this about the Pettinger girl?"

And Connie would say nervously, "Oh, her. That dope." She always drew thick clear lines between herself and such girls, and her mother was simple and kind enough to believe it. Her mother was so simple, Connie thought, that it was maybe cruel to fool her so much. Her mother went scuffling around the house in old bedroom slippers and complained over the telephone to one sister about the other, then the other called up and the two of them complained about the third one. If June's name was mentioned her mother's tone was approving, and if Connie's name was mentioned it was disapproving. This did not really mean she disliked Connie, and actually Connie thought that her mother preferred her to June just because she was prettier, but the two of them kept up a pretense of exasperation, a sense that they were tugging and struggling over something of little value to either of them. Sometimes, over coffee, they were almost friends, but something would come up—some vexation that was like a fly buzzing suddenly around their heads—and their faces went hard with contempt.

One Sunday Connie got up at eleven—none of them bothered with church—and washed her hair so that it could dry all day long in the sun. Her parents and sister were going to a barbecue at an aunt's house and Connie said no, she wasn't interested, rolling her eyes to let her mother know just what she thought of it. "Stay home alone then," her mother said sharply. Connie sat out back in a lawn chair and watched them drive away, her father quiet and bald, hunched around so that he could back the car out, her mother with a look that was still angry and not at all softened through the windshield, and in the back seat poor old June, all dressed up as if she didn't know what a barbecue was, with all the running yelling kids and the flies. Connie sat with her eyes closed in the sun, dreaming and dazed with the warmth about her as if this were a kind of love, the caresses of love, and her mind slipped over onto thoughts of the boy she had been with the night before and how nice he had been, how sweet it always was, not the way someone like June would suppose but sweet, gentle, the way it was in movies and promised in songs; and when she opened her eyes she hardly knew where she was, the back yard ran off into weeds and a fence-like line of trees and behind it the sky was perfectly blue and still. The asbestos "ranch house" that was now three years old startled her—it looked small. She shook her head as if to get awake.

It was too hot. She went inside the house and turned on the radio to drown out the quiet. She sat on the edge of her bed, barefoot, and listened for an hour and a half to a program called XYZ Sunday Jamboree, record after record of hard, fast, shrieking songs she sang along with, interspersed by exclamations from "Bobby King": "An' look here, you girls at Napoleon's—Son and Charley want you to pay real close attention to this song coming up!"

And Connie paid close attention herself, bathed in a glow of slow-pulsed joy that seemed to rise mysteriously out of the music itself and lay languidly about the airless little room, breathed in and breathed out with each gentle rise and fall of her chest.

After a while she heard a car coming up the drive. She sat up at once, startled, because it couldn't be her father so soon. The gravel kept crunching all the way in from the road—the driveway was long—and Connie ran to the window. It was a car she didn't know. It was an open jalopy, painted a bright gold that caught the sunlight opaquely. Her heart began to pound and her fingers snatched at her hair, checking it, and she whispered, "Christ. Christ," wondering how bad she looked. The car came to a stop at the side door and the horn sounded four short taps, as if this were a signal Connie knew.

She went into the kitchen and approached the door slowly, then hung out the screen door, her bare toes curling down off the step. There were two boys in the car and now she recognized the driver: he had shaggy, shabby black hair that looked crazy as a wig and he was grinning at her.

"I ain't late, am I?" he said.

"Who the hell do you think you are?" Connie said.

"Toldja I'd be out, didn't I?"

"I don't even know who you are."

She spoke sullenly, careful to show no interest or pleasure, and he spoke in a fast, bright monotone. Connie looked past him to the other boy, taking her time. He had fair brown hair, with a lock that fell onto his forehead. His sideburns gave him a fierce, embarrassed look, but so far he hadn't even bothered to glance at her. Both boys wore sunglasses. The driver's glasses were metallic and mirrored everything in miniature.

"You wanna come for a ride?" he said.

Connie smirked and let her hair fall loose over one shoulder.

"Don'tcha like my car? New paint job," he said. "Hey."

"What?"

"You're cute."

She pretended to fidget, chasing flies away from the door.

"Don'tcha believe me, or what?" he said.

"Look, I don't even know who you are," Connie said in disgust.

"Hey, Ellie's got a radio, see. Mine broke down." He lifted his friend's arm and showed her the little transistor radio the boy was holding, and now Connie began to hear the music. It was the same program that was playing inside the house.

"Bobby King?" she said.

"I listen to him all the time. I think he's great."

"He's kind of great," Connie said reluctantly.

"Listen, that guy's *great*. He knows where the action is."

Connie blushed a little, because the glasses made it impossible for her to see just what this boy was looking at. She couldn't decide if she liked him or if he was just a jerk, and so she dawdled in the doorway and wouldn't come down or go back inside. She said, "What's all that stuff painted on your car?"

"Can'tcha read it?" He opened the door very carefully, as if he were afraid it might fall off. He slid out just as carefully, planting his feet firmly on the ground, the tiny metallic world in his glasses slowing down like gelatine hardening, and in the midst of it Connie's bright green blouse. "This here is my name, to begin with," he said. ARNOLD FRIEND was written in tarlike black letters on the side, with a drawing of a round, grinning face that reminded Connie of a pumpkin, except it wore sunglasses. "I wanta introduce myself, I'm Arnold Friend and that's my real name and I'm gonna be your friend, honey, and inside the car's Ellie Oscar, he's kinda shy." Ellie brought his transistor radio up to his shoulder and balanced it there. "Now, these numbers are a secret code, honey," Arnold Friend explained. He read off the numbers 33, 19, 17 and raised his eyebrows at her to see what she thought of that, but she didn't think much of it. The left rear fender had been smashed and around it was written, on the gleaming gold background: DONE BY CRAZY WOMAN DRIVER. Connie had to laugh at that. Arnold Friend was pleased at her laughter and looked up at her. "Around the other side's a lot more — you wanta come and see them?"

"No."

"Why not?"

"Why should I?"

"Don'tcha wanta see what's on the car? Don'tcha wanta go for a ride?"

"I don't know."

"Why not?"

"I got things to do."

"Like what?"

"Things."

He laughed as if she had said something funny. He slapped his thigh. He was standing in a strange way, leaning back against the car as if he were balancing himself. He wasn't tall, only an inch or so taller than she would be if she came down to him. Connie liked the way he was dressed, which was the way all of them dressed: tight faded jeans stuffed into black, scuffed boots, a belt that pulled his waist in and showed how lean he was, and a white pull-over shirt that was a little soiled and showed the hard small muscles of his arms and shoulders. He looked as if he probably did hard work, lifting and carrying things. Even his neck looked muscular. And his face was a familiar face, somehow: the jaw and chin and cheeks slightly darkened because he hadn't shaved for a day or two, and the nose long and hawklike, sniffing as if she were a treat he was going to gobble up and it was all a joke.

"Connie, you ain't telling the truth. This is your day set aside for a ride with me and you know it," he said, still laughing. The way he straightened and recovered from his fit of laughing showed that it had been all fake.

"How do you know what my name is?" she said suspiciously.

"It's Connie."

"Maybe and maybe not."

"I know my Connie," he said, wagging his finger. Now she remembered him even better, back at the restaurant, and her cheeks warmed at the thought of how she had sucked in her breath just at the moment she passed him — how she must have looked to him. And he had remembered her. "Ellie and I come out here especially for you," he said. "Ellie can sit in back. How about it?"

"Where?"

"Where what?"

"Where're we going?"

He looked at her. He took off the sunglasses and she saw how pale the skin around his eyes was, like holes that were not in shadow but instead in light. His eyes were like chips of broken glass that catch the light in an amiable way. He smiled. It was as if the idea of going for a ride somewhere, to someplace, was a new idea to him.

"Just for a ride, Connie sweetheart."

"I never said my name was Connie," she said.

"But I know what it is. I know your name and all about you, lots of things," Arnold Friend said. He had not moved yet but stood still leaning back against the side of his jalopy. "I took a special interest in you, such a pretty girl, and found out all about you—like I know your parents and sister are gone somewheres and I know where and how long they're going to be gone, and I know who you were with last night, and your best girl friend's name is Betty. Right?"

He spoke in a simple lilting voice, exactly as if he were reciting the words to a song. His smile assured her that everything was fine. In the car Ellie turned up the volume of his radio and did not bother to look around at them.

"Ellie can sit in the back seat," Arnold Friend said. He indicated his friend with a casual jerk of his chin, as if Ellie did not count and she should not bother with him.

"How'd you find out all that stuff?" Connie said.

"Listen: Betty Schultz and Tony Fitch and Jimmy Pettinger and Nancy Pettinger," he said in a chant. "Raymond Stanley and Bob Hutter—"

"Do you know all those kids?"

"I know everybody."

"Look, you're kidding. You're not from around here."

"Sure."

"But—how come we never saw you before?"

"Sure you saw me before," he said. He looked down at his boots, as if he were a little offended. "You just don't remember."

"I guess I'd remember you," Connie said.

"Yeah?" He looked up at this, beaming. He was pleased. He began to mark time with the music from Ellie's radio, tapping his fists lightly together. Connie looked away from his smile to the car, which was painted so bright it almost hurt her eyes to look at it. She looked at that name, ARNOLD FRIEND. And up at the front fender was an expression that was familiar—MAN THE FLYING SAUCERS. It was an expression kids had used the year before but didn't use this year. She looked at it for a while as if the words meant something to her that she did not yet know.

"What're you thinking about? Huh?" Arnold Friend demanded. "Not worried about your hair blowing around in the car, are you?"

"No."

"Think I maybe can't drive good?"

"How do I know?"

"You're a hard girl to handle. How come?" he said. "Don't you know I'm your friend? Didn't you see me put my sign in the air when you walked by?"

"What sign?"

"My sign." And he drew an X in the air, leaning out toward her. They were maybe ten feet apart. After his hand fell back to his side the X was still in the air, almost visible. Connie let the screen door close and stood perfectly still inside it, listening to the music from her radio and the boy's blend together. She stared at Arnold Friend. He stood there so stiffly relaxed, pretending to be relaxed, with one hand idly on the door handle as if he were keeping himself up that way and had no intention of ever moving again. She recognized most things about him, the tight jeans that showed his thighs and buttocks and the greasy leather boots and the tight shirt, and even that slippery friendly smile of his, that sleepy dreamy smile that all the boys used to get across ideas they didn't want to put into words. She recognized all this and also the sing-song way he talked, slightly mocking, kidding, but serious and a little melancholy, and she recognized the way he tapped one fist against the other in homage to the perpetual music behind him. But all these things did not come together.

She said suddenly, "Hey, how old are you?"

His smile faded. She could see then that he wasn't a kid, he was much older — thirty, maybe more. At this knowledge her heart began to pound faster. "That's a crazy thing to ask. Can'tcha see I'm your own age?"

"Like hell you are."

"Or maybe a coupla years older. I'm eighteen."

"Eighteen?" she said doubtfully.

He grinned to reassure her and lines appeared at the corners of his mouth. His teeth were big and white. He grinned so broadly his eyes became slits and she saw how thick the lashes were, thick and black as if painted with a black tarlike material. Then, abruptly, he seemed to become embarrassed and looked over his shoulder at Ellie. "*Him*, he's crazy," he said. "Ain't he a riot? He's a nut, a real character." Ellie was still listening to the music. His sunglasses told nothing about what he was thinking. He wore a bright orange shirt unbuttoned halfway to show his chest, which was a pale, bluish chest and not muscular like Arnold Friend's. His shirt collar was turned up all around and the very tips of the collar pointed out past his chin as if they were protecting him. He was pressing the transistor radio up against his ear and sat there in a kind of daze, right in the sun.

"He's kinda strange," Connie said.

"Hey, she says you're kinda strange! Kinda strange!" Arnold Friend cried. He pounded on the car to get Ellie's attention. Ellie turned for the first time and Connie saw with shock that he wasn't a kid either — he had a fair, hairless face, cheeks reddened slightly as if the veins grew too close to the surface of his skin, the face of a forty-year-old baby. Connie felt a wave of dizziness rise in her at this sight and she stared at him as if waiting for something to change the shock of the moment, make it all right again. Ellie's lips kept shaping words, mumbling along with the words blasting in his ear.

"Maybe you two better go away," Connie said faintly.

"What? How come?" Arnold Friend cried. "We come out here to take you for a ride. It's Sunday." He had the voice of the man on the radio now. It was the same voice, Connie thought. "Don'tcha know it's Sunday all day? And honey, no matter who you were with last night, today you're with Arnold Friend and don't you forget it! Maybe you better step out here," he said, and this last was in a different voice. It was a little flatter, as if the heat was finally getting to him.

"No. I got things to do."

"Hey."

"You two better leave."

"We ain't leaving until you come with us."

"Like hell I am —"

"Connie, don't fool around with me. I mean — I mean, don't fool *around*," he said, shaking his head. He laughed incredulously. He placed his sunglasses on top of his head, carefully, as if he were indeed wearing a wig, and brought the stems down behind his ears. Connie stared at him, another wave of dizziness and fear rising in her so that for a moment he wasn't even in focus but was just a blur standing there against his gold car, and she had the idea that he had driven up the driveway all right but had come from nowhere before that and belonged nowhere and that everything about him and even about the music that was so familiar to her was only half real.

"If my father comes and sees you—"

"He ain't coming. He's at a barbecue."

"How do you know that?"

"Aunt Tillie's. Right now they're—uh—they're drinking. Sitting around," he said vaguely, squinting as if he were staring all the way to town and over to Aunt Tillie's back yard. Then the vision seemed to get clear and he nodded energetically. "Yeah. Sitting around. There's your sister in a blue dress, huh? And high heels, the poor sad bitch—nothing like you, sweetheart! And your mother's helping some fat woman with the corn, they're cleaning the corn—husking the corn—"

"What fat woman?" Connie cried.

"How do I know what fat woman, I don't know every goddamn fat woman in the world!" Arnold Friend laughed.

"Oh, that's Mrs. Hornsby. . . . Who invited her?" Connie said. She felt a little lightheaded. Her breath was coming quickly.

"She's too fat. I don't like them fat. I like them the way you are, honey," he said, smiling sleepily at her. They stared at each other for a while through the screen door. He said softly, "Now, what you're going to do is this: you're going to come out that door. You're going to sit up front with me and Ellie's going to sit in the back, the hell with Ellie, right? This isn't Ellie's date. You're my date. I'm your lover, honey."

"What? You're crazy—"

"Yes, I'm your lover. You don't know what that is but you will," he said. "I know that too. I know all about you. But look: it's real nice and you couldn't ask for nobody better than me, or more polite. I always keep my word. I'll tell you how it is, I'm always nice at first, the first time. I'll hold you so tight you won't think you have to try to get away or pretend anything because you'll know you can't. And I'll come inside you where it's all secret and you'll give in to me and you'll love me—"

"Shut up! You're crazy!" Connie said. She backed away from the door. She put her hands up against her ears as if she'd heard something terrible, something not meant for her. "People don't talk like that, you're crazy," she muttered. Her heart was almost too big for her chest and its pumping made sweat break out all over her. She looked out to see Arnold Friend pause and then take a step toward the porch, lurching. He almost fell. But, like a clever drunken man, he managed to catch his balance. He wobbled in his high boots and grabbed hold of one of the porch posts.

"Honey?" he said. "You still listening?"

"Get the hell out of here!"

"Be nice, honey. Listen."

"I'm going to call the police—"

He wobbled again and out of the side of his mouth came a fast spat curse, an aside not meant for her to hear. But even this "Christ!" sounded forced. Then he began to smile again. She watched this smile come, awkward as if he were smiling from inside a mask. His whole face was a mask, she thought wildly, tanned down to this throat but then running out as if he had plastered make-up on his face but had forgotten about his throat.

"Honey—? Listen, here's how it is. I always tell the truth and I promise you this: I ain't coming in that house after you."

"You better not! I'm going to call the police if you—if you don't—"

"Honey," he said, talking right through her voice, "honey, I'm not coming in there but you are coming out here. You know why?"

She was panting. The kitchen looked like a place she had never seen before, some room she had run inside but that wasn't good enough, wasn't going to help her. The kitchen window had never had a curtain, after three years, and there were dishes in the sink for her to do—probably—and if you ran your hand across the table you'd probably feel something sticky there.

"You listening honey? Hey?"

"—going to call the police—"

"Soon as you touch the phone I don't need to keep my promise and can come inside. You won't want that."

She rushed forward and tried to lock the door. Her fingers were shaking. "But why lock it," Arnold Friend said gently, talking right into her face. "It's just a screen door. It's just nothing." One of his boots was at a strange angle, as if his foot wasn't in it. It pointed out to the left, bent at the ankle. "I mean, anybody can break through a screen door and glass and wood and iron or anything else if he needs to, anybody at all, and especially Arnold Friend. If the place got lit up with a fire, honey, you'd come runnin' out into my arms, right into my arms an' safe at home—like you knew I was your lover and'd stopped fooling around. I don't mind a nice shy girl but I don't like no fooling around." Part of those words were spoken with a slight rhythmic lilt, and Connie somehow recognized them—the echo of a song from last year, about a girl rushing into her boy friend's arms and coming home again—

Connie stood barefoot on the linoleum floor, staring at him. "What do you want?" she whispered.

"I want you," he said.

"What?"

"Seen you that night and thought, that's the one, yes sir. I never needed to look anymore."

"But my father's coming back. He's coming to get me. I had to wash my hair first—" She spoke in a dry, rapid voice, hardly raising it for him to hear.

"No, your daddy is not coming and yes, you had to wash your hair and you washed it for me. It's nice and shining and all for me. I thank you sweetheart," he said with a mock bow, but again he almost lost his balance. He had to bend and adjust his boots. Evidently his feet did not go all the way down; the boots must have been stuffed with something so that he would seem taller. Connie stared out at him and behind him at Ellie in the car, who seemed to be looking off toward Connie's right, into nothing. This Ellie said, pulling the words out of the air one after another as if he were just discovering them, "You want me to pull out the phone?"

"Shut your mouth and keep it shut," Arnold Friend said, his face red from bending over or maybe from embarrassment because Connie had seen his boots. "This ain't none of your business."

"What—what are you doing? What do you want?" Connie said. "If I call the police they'll get you, they'll arrest you—"

"Promise was not to come in unless you touch that phone, and I'll keep that promise," he said. He resumed his erect position and tried to force his shoulders back. He sounded like a hero in a movie, declaring something important. But he spoke too loudly and it was as if he were speaking to someone behind Connie. "I ain't made plans for coming in that house where I don't belong but just for you to come out to me, the way you should. Don't you know who I am?"

"You're crazy," she whispered. She backed away from the door but did not want to go into another part of the house, as if this would give him permission to come through the door. "What do you . . . you're crazy, you. . . ."

"Huh? What're you saying, honey?"

Her eyes darted everywhere in the kitchen. She could not remember what it was, this room.

"This is how it is, honey: you come out and we'll drive away, have a nice ride. But if you don't come out we're gonna wait till your people come home and then they're all going to get it."

"You want that telephone pulled out?" Ellie said. He held the radio away from his ear and grimaced, as if without the radio the air was too much for him.

"I toldja shut up, Ellie," Arnold Friend said, "you're deaf, get a hearing aid, right? Fix yourself up. This little girl's no trouble and's gonna be nice to me, so Ellie keep to yourself, this ain't your date—right? Don't hem in on me, don't hog, don't crush, don't bird dog, don't trail me," he said in a rapid, meaningless voice, as if he were running through all the expressions he'd learned but was no longer sure which of them was in style, then rushing on to new ones, making them up with his eyes closed. "Don't crawl under my fence, don't squeeze in my chipmunk hole, don't sniff my glue, suck my popsicle, keep your own greasy fingers on yourself!" He shaded his eyes and peered in at Connie, who was backed against the kitchen table. "Don't mind him, honey, he's just a creep. He's a dope. Right? I'm the boy for you and like I said, you come out here nice like a lady and give me your hand, and nobody else gets hurt, I mean, your nice old bald-headed daddy and your mummy and your sister in her high heels. Because listen: why bring them in this?"

"Leave me alone," Connie whispered.

"Hey, you know that old woman down the road, the one with the chickens and stuff—you know her?"

"She's dead!"

"Dead? What? You know her?" Arnold Friend said.

"She's dead—"

"Don't you like her?"

"She's dead—she's—she isn't here any more—"

"But don't you like her, I mean, you got something against her? Some grudge or something?" Then his voice dipped as if he were conscious of a rudeness. He touched the sunglasses perched up on top of his head as if to make sure they were still there. "Now, you be a good girl."

"What are you going to do?"

"Just two things, or maybe three," Arnold Friend said. "But I promise it won't last long and you'll like me the way you get to like people you're close to. You will. It's all over for you here, so come on out. You don't want your people in any trouble, do you?"

She turned and bumped against a chair or something, hurting her leg, but she ran into the back room and picked up the telephone. Something roared in her ear, a tiny roaring, and she was so sick with fear that she could do nothing but listen to it — the telephone was clammy and very heavy and her fingers groped down to the dial but were too weak to touch it. She began to scream into the phone, into the roaring. She cried out, she cried for her mother, she felt her breath start jerking back and forth in her lungs as if it were something Arnold Friend was stabbing her with again and again with no tenderness. A noisy sorrowful wailing rose all about her and she was locked inside it the way she was locked inside this house.

After a while she could hear again. She was sitting on the floor with her wet back against the wall.

Arnold Friend was saying from the door, "That's a good girl. Put the phone back."

She kicked the phone away from her.

"No, honey. Pick it up. Put it back right."

She picked it up and put it back. The dial tone stopped.

"That's a good girl. Now, you come outside."

She was hollow with what had been fear but what was now just an emptiness. All that screaming had blasted it out of her. She sat, one leg cramped under her, and deep inside her brain was something like a pinpoint of light that kept going and would not let her relax. She thought, I'm not going to see my mother again. She thought, I'm not going to sleep in my bed again. Her bright green blouse was all wet.

Arnold Friend said, in a gentle-loud voice that was like a stage voice, "The place where you came from ain't there any more, and where you had in mind to go is cancelled out. This place you are now — inside your daddy's house — is nothing but a cardboard box I can knock down any time. You know that and always did know it. You hear me?"

She thought, I have got to think. I have got to know what to do.

"We'll go out to a nice field, out in the country here where it smells so nice and it's sunny," Arnold Friend said. "I'll have my arms tight around you so you won't need to try to get away and I'll show you what love is like, what it does. The hell with this house! It looks solid all right," he said. He ran a fingernail down the screen and the noise did not make Connie shiver, as it would have the day before. "Now, put your hand on your heart, honey. Feel that? That feels solid too but we know better. Be nice to me, be sweet like you can because what else is there for a girl like you but to be sweet and pretty and give in? — and get away before her people come back?"

She felt her pounding heart. Her hand seemed to enclose it. She thought for the first time in her life that it was nothing that was hers, that belonged to her, but just a pounding, living thing inside this body that wasn't really hers either.

"You don't want them to get hurt," Arnold Friend went on. "Now, get up, honey. Get up all by yourself."

She stood.

"Now, turn this way. That's right. Come over here to me. — Ellie, put that away, didn't I tell you? You dope. You miserable creepy dope," Arnold Friend said. His words were not angry but only part of an incantation. The incantation was kindly. "Now, come out through the kitchen to me, honey, and let's see a smile, try it, you're a brave, sweet little girl and now they're eating corn and hot dogs cooked to bursting over an outdoor fire, and they don't know one thing about you and never did and honey, you're better than them because not a one of them would have done this for you."

Connie felt the linoleum under her feet; it was cool. She brushed her hair back out of her eyes. Arnold Friend let go of the post tentatively and opened his arms for her, his elbows pointing in toward each other and his wrists limp, to show that this was an embarrassed embrace and a little mocking, he didn't want to make her self-conscious.

She put out her hand against the screen. She watched herself push the door slowly open as if she were back safe somewhere in the other doorway, watching this body and this head of long hair moving out into the sunlight where Arnold Friend waited.

"My sweet little blue-eyed girl," he said in a half-sung sigh that had nothing to do with her brown eyes but was taken up just the same by the vast sunlit reaches of the land behind him and on all sides of him — so much land that Connie had never seen before and did not recognize except to know that she was going to it.

(1966)

Louise Erdrich *1954–*

THE RED CONVERTIBLE

I was the first one to drive a convertible on my reservation. And of course it was red, a red Olds. I owned that car along with my brother Henry Junior. We owned it together until his boots filled with water on a windy night and he bought out my share. Now Henry owns the whole car, and his younger brother Lyman (that's myself), Lyman walks everywhere he goes.

How did I earn enough money to buy my share in the first place? My one talent was I could always make money. I had a touch for it, unusual in a Chippewa. From the first I was different that way, and everyone recognized it. I was the only kid they let in the American Legion Hall to shine shoes, for example, and one Christmas I sold spiritual bouquets for the mission door to door. The nuns let me keep a percentage. Once I started, it seemed the more money I made the easier the money came. Everyone encouraged it. When I was fifteen I got a job washing dishes at the Joliet Café, and that was where my first big break happened.

It wasn't long before I was promoted to bussing tables, and then the short-order cook quit and I was hired to take her place. No sooner than you know it I was managing the Joliet. The rest is history. I went on managing. I soon become part owner, and of course there was no stopping me then. It wasn't long before the whole thing was mine.

After I'd owned the Joliet for one year, it blew over in the worst tornado ever seen around here. The whole operation was smashed to bits. A total loss. The fryalator was up in a tree, the grill torn in half like it was paper. I was only sixteen. I had it all in my mother's name, and I lost it quick, but before I lost it I had every one of my relatives, and their relatives, to dinner, and I also bought that red Olds I mentioned, along with Henry.

The first time we saw it! I'll tell you when we first saw it. We had gotten a ride up to Winnipeg, and both of us had money. Don't ask me why, because we never mentioned a car or anything, we just had all our money. Mine was cash, a big bankroll from the Joliet's insurance. Henry had two checks—a week's extra pay for being laid off, and his regular check from the Jewel Bearing Plant.

We were walking down Portage anyway, seeing the sights, when we saw it. There it was, parked, large as life. Really as *if* it was alive. I thought of the word *repose*, because the car wasn't simply stopped, parked, or whatever. That car reposed, calm and gleaming, a FOR SALE sign in its left front window. Then, before we had thought it over at all, the car belonged to us and our pockets were empty. We had just enough money for gas back home.

We went to places in that car, me and Henry. We took off driving all one whole summer. We started off toward the Little Knife River and Mandaree in Fort Berthold and then we found ourselves down in Wakpala somehow, and then suddenly we were over in Montana on the Rocky Boys, and yet the summer was not even half over. Some people hang on to details when they travel, but we didn't let them bother us and just lived our everyday lives here to there.

I do remember this one place with willows. I remember I laid under those trees and it was comfortable. So comfortable. The branches bent down all around me like a tent or a stable. And quiet, it was quiet, even though there was a powwow close enough so I could see it going on. The air was not too still, not too windy either. When the dust rises up and hangs in the air around the dancers like that, I feel good. Henry was asleep with his arms thrown wide. Later on, he woke up and we started driving again. We were somewhere in Montana, or maybe on the Blood Reserve—it could have been anywhere. Anyway it was where we met the girl.

All her hair was in buns around her ears, that's the first thing I noticed about her. She was posed alongside the road with her arm out, so we stopped. That girl was short, so short her lumber shirt looked comical on her, like a nightgown. She had jeans on and fancy moccasins and she carried a little suitcase.

"Hop on in," says Henry. So she climbs in between us.

"We'll take you home," I says. "Where do you live?"

"Chicken," she says.

"Where the hell's that?" I ask her.

"Alaska."

"Okay," says Henry, and we drive.

We got up there and never wanted to leave. The sun doesn't truly set there in summer, and the night is more a soft dusk. You might doze off, sometimes, but before you know it you're up again, like an animal in nature. You never feel like you have to sleep hard or put away the world. And things would grow up there. One day just dirt or moss, the next day flowers and long grass. The girl's name was Susy. Her family really took to us. They fed us and put us up. We had our own tent to live in by their house, and the kids would be in and out of there all day and night. They couldn't get over me and Henry being brothers, we looked so different. We told them we knew we had the same mother, anyway.

One night Susy came in to visit us. We sat around in the tent talking of this thing and that. The season was changing. It was getting darker by that time, and the cold was even getting just a little mean. I told her it was time for us to go. She stood up on a chair.

"You never seen my hair," Susy said.

That was true. She was standing on a chair, but still, when she unclipped her buns the hair reached all the way to the ground. Our eyes opened. You couldn't tell how much hair she had when it was rolled up so neatly. Then my brother Henry did something funny. He went up to the chair and said, "Jump on my shoulders." So she did that, and her hair reached down past his waist, and he started twirling, this way and that, so her hair was flung out from side to side.

"I always wondered what it was like to have long pretty hair," Henry says. Well we laughed. It was a funny sight, the way he did it. The next morning we got up and took leave of those people.

On to greener pastures, as they say. It was down through Spokane and across Idaho then Montana and very soon we were racing the weather right along under the Canadian border through Columbus, Des Lacs, and then we were in Bottineau County and soon home. We'd made most of the trip, that summer, without putting up the car hood at all. We got home just in time, it turned out, for the army to remember Henry had signed up to join it.

I don't wonder that the army was so glad to get my brother that they turned him into a Marine. He was built like a brick outhouse anyway. We liked to tease him that they really wanted him for his Indian nose. He had a nose big and sharp as a hatchet, like the nose on Red Tomahawk, the Indian who killed Sitting Bull, whose profile is on signs all along the North Dakota highways. Henry went off to training camp, came home once during Christmas, then the next thing you know we got an overseas letter from him. It was 1970, and he said he was stationed up in the northern hill country. Whereabouts I did not know. He wasn't such a hot letter writer, and only got off two before the enemy caught him. I could never keep it straight, which direction those good Vietnam soldiers were from.

I wrote him back several times, even though I didn't know if those letters would get through. I kept him informed all about the car. Most of the time I had it up on blocks in the yard or half taken apart, because that long trip did a hard job on it under the hood.

I always had good luck with numbers, and never worried about the draft myself. I never even had to think about what my number was. But Henry was never lucky in the same way as me. It was at least three years before Henry came home. By then I guess the whole war was solved in the government's mind, but for him it would keep on going. In those years I'd put his car into almost perfect shape. I always thought of it as his car while he was gone, even though when he left he said, "Now it's yours," and threw me his key.

"Thanks for the extra key," I'd said. "I'll put it up in your drawer just in case I need it." He laughed.

When he came home, though, Henry was very different, and I'll say this: the change was no good. You could hardly expect him to change for the better, I know. But he was quiet, so quiet, and never comfortable sitting still anywhere but always up and moving around. I thought back to times we'd sat still for whole afternoons, never moving a muscle, just shifting our weight along the ground, talking to whoever sat with us, watching things. He'd always had a joke, then, too, and now you couldn't get him to laugh, or when he did it was more the sound of a man choking, a sound that stopped up the throats of other people around him. They got to leaving him alone most of the time, and I didn't blame them. It was a fact: Henry was jumpy and mean.

I'd bought a color TV set for my mom and the rest of us while Henry was away. Money still came very easy. I was sorry I'd ever bought it though, because of Henry. I was also sorry I'd bought color, because with black-and-white the pictures seem older and farther away. But what are you going to do? He sat in front of it, watching it, and that was the only time he was completely still. But it was the kind of stillness that you see in a rabbit when it freezes and before it will bolt. He was not easy. He sat in his chair gripping the armrests with all his might, as if the chair itself was moving at a high speed and if he let go at all he would rocket forward and maybe crash right through the set.

Once I was in the room watching TV with Henry and I heard his teeth click at something. I looked over, and he'd bitten through his lip. Blood was going down his chin. I tell you right then I wanted to smash that tube to pieces. I went over to it but Henry must have known what I was up to. He rushed from his chair and shoved me out of the way, against the wall. I told myself he didn't know what he was doing.

My mom came in, turned the set off real quiet, and told us she had made something for supper. So we went and sat down. There was still blood going down Henry's chin, but he didn't notice it and no one said anything, even though every time he took a bite of his bread his blood fell onto it until he was eating his own blood mixed in with the food.

While Henry was not around we talked about what was going to happen to him. There were no Indian doctors on the reservation, and my mom was afraid of trusting Old Man Pillager because he courted her long ago and was jealous of her husbands. He might take revenge through her son. We were afraid that if we brought Henry to a regular hospital they would keep him.

"They don't fix them in those places," Mom said; "they just give them drugs."

"We wouldn't get him there in the first place," I agreed, "so let's just forget about it."

Then I thought about the car.

Henry had not even looked at the car since he'd gotten home, though like I said, it was in tip-top condition and ready to drive. I thought the car might bring the old Henry back somehow. So I bided my time and waited for my chance to interest him in the vehicle.

One night Henry was off somewhere. I took myself a hammer. I went out to that car and I did a number on its underside. Whacked it up. Bent the tail pipe double. Ripped the muffler loose. By the time I was done with the car it looked worse than any typical Indian car that has been driven all its life on reservation roads, which they always say are like government promises — full of holes. It just about hurt me, I'll tell you that! I threw dirt in the carburetor and I ripped all the electric tape off the seats. I made it look just as beat up as I could. Then I sat back and waited for Henry to find it.

Still, it took him over a month. That was all right, because it was just getting warm enough, not melting, but warm enough to work outside.

"Lyman," he says, walking in one day, "that red car looks like shit."

"Well it's old," I says. "You got to expect that."

"No way!" says Henry. "That car's a classic! But you went and ran the piss right out of it, Lyman, and you know it don't deserve that. I kept that car in A-one shape. You don't remember. You're too young. But when I left, that car was running like a watch. Now I don't even know if I can get it to start again, let alone get it anywhere near its old condition."

"Well you try," I said, like I was getting mad, "but I say it's a piece of junk."

Then I walked out before he could realize I knew he'd strung together more than six words at once.

After that I thought he'd freeze himself to death working on that car. He was out there all day, and at night he rigged up a little lamp, ran a cord out the window, and had himself some light to see by while he worked. He was better than he had been before, but that's still not saying much. It was easier for him to do the things the rest of us did. He ate more slowly and didn't jump up and down during the meal to get this or that or look out the window. I put my hand in the back of the TV set, I admit, and fiddled around with it good, so that it was almost impossible now to get a clear picture. He didn't look at it very often anyway. He was always out with that car or going off to get parts for it. By the time it was really melting outside, he had it fixed.

I had been feeling down in the dumps about Henry around this time. We had always been together before. Henry and Lyman. But he was such a loner now that I didn't know how to take it. So I jumped at the chance one day when Henry seemed friendly. It's not that he smiled or anything. He just said, "Let's take that old shitbox for a spin." Just the way he said it made me think he could be coming around.

We went out to the car. It was spring. The sun was shining very bright. My only sister, Bonita, who was just eleven years old, came out and made us stand together for a picture. Henry leaned his elbow on the red car's windshield, and he took his other arm and put it over my shoulder, very carefully, as though it was heavy for him to lift and he didn't want to bring the weight down all at once.

"Smile," Bonita said, and he did.

That picture. I never look at it anymore. A few months ago, I don't know why, I got his picture out and tacked it on the wall. I felt good about Henry at the time, close to him. I felt good having his picture on the wall, until one night when I was looking at television. I was a little drunk and stoned. I looked up at the wall and Henry was staring at me. I don't know what it was, but his smile had changed, or maybe it was gone. All I know is I couldn't stay in the same room with that picture. I was shaking. I got up, closed the door, and went into the kitchen. A little later my friend Ray came over and we both went back into that room. We put the picture in a brown bag, folded the bag over and over tightly, then put it way back in a closet.

I still see that picture now, as if it tugs at me, whenever I pass that closet door. The picture is very clear in my mind. It was so sunny that day Henry had to squint against the glare. Or maybe the camera Bonita held flashed like a mirror, blinding him, before she snapped the picture. My face is right out in the sun, big and round. But he might have drawn back, because the shadows on his face are deep as holes. There are two shadows curved like little hooks around the ends of his smile, as if to frame it and try to keep it there — that one, first smile that looked like it might have hurt his face. He has his field jacket on and the worn-in clothes he'd come back in and kept wearing ever since. After Bonita took the picture, she went into the house and we got into the car. There was a full cooler in the trunk. We started off, east, toward Pembina and the Red River because Henry said he wanted to see the high water.

The trip over there was beautiful. When everything starts changing, drying up, clearing off, you feel like your whole life is starting. Henry felt it, too. The top was down and the car hummed like a top. He'd really put it back in shape, even the tape on the seats was very carefully put down and glued back in layers. It's not that he smiled again or even joked, but his face looked to me as if it was clear, more peaceful. It looked as though he wasn't thinking of anything in particular except the bare fields and windbreaks and houses we were passing.

The river was high and full of winter trash when we got there. The sun was still out, but it was colder by the river. There were still little clumps of dirty snow here and there on the banks. The water hadn't gone over the banks yet, but it would, you could tell. It was just at its limit, hard swollen, glossy like an old gray scar. We made ourselves a fire, and we sat down and watched the current go. As I watched it I felt something squeezing inside me and tightening and trying to let go all at the same time. I knew I was not just feeling it myself; I knew I was feeling what Henry was going through at that moment. Except that I couldn't stand it, the closing and opening. I jumped to my feet. I took Henry by the shoulders, and I started shaking him. "Wake up," I says, "wake up, wake up, wake up!" I didn't know what had come over me. I sat down beside him again.

His face was totally white and hard. Then it broke, like stones break all of a sudden when water boils up inside them.

"I know it," he says. "I know it. I can't help it. It's no use."

We start talking. He said he knew what I'd done with the car. It was obvious it had been whacked out of shape and not just neglected. He said he wanted to give the car to me for good now, it was no use. He said he'd fixed it just to give it back and I should take it.

"No way," I says, "I don't want it."

"That's okay," he says, "you take it."

"I don't want it, though," I says back to him, and then to emphasize, just to emphasize, you understand, I touch his shoulder. He slaps my hand off.

"Take that car," he says.

"No," I say, "make me," I say, and then he grabs my jacket and rips the arm loose. That jacket is a class act, suede with tags and zippers. I push Henry backwards, off the log. He jumps up and bowls me over. We go down in a clinch and come up swinging hard, for all we're worth, with our fists. He socks my jaw so hard I feel like it swings loose. Then I'm at his ribcage and land a good one under his chin so his head snaps back. He's dazzled. He looks at me and I look at him and then his eyes are full of tears and blood and at first I think he's crying. But no, he's laughing. "Ha! Ha!" he says. "Ha! Ha! Take good care of it."

"Okay," I says, "okay, no problem. Ha! Ha!"

I can't help it, and I start laughing, too. My face feels fat and strange, and after a while I get a beer from the cooler in the trunk, and when I hand it to Henry he takes his shirt and wipes my germs off. "Hoof-and-mouth disease," he says. For some reason this cracks me up, and so we're really laughing for a while, and then we drink all the rest of the beers one by one and throw them in the river and see how far, how fast, the current takes them before they fill up and sink.

"You want to go back?" I ask after a while. "Maybe we could snag a couple nice Kashpaw girls."

He says nothing. But I can tell his mood is turning again.

"They're all crazy, the girls up here, every damn one of them."

"You're crazy too," I say, to jolly him up. "Crazy Lamartine boys!"

He looks as though he will take this wrong at first. His face twists, then clears, and he jumps up on his feet. "That's right!" he says. "Crazier 'n hell. Crazy Indians!"

I think it's the old Henry again. He throws off his jacket and starts swinging his legs out from the knees like a fancy dancer. He's down doing something between a grouse dance and a bunny hop, no kind of dance I ever saw before, but neither has anyone else on all this green growing earth. He's wild. He wants to pitch whoopee! He's up and at me and all over. All this time I'm laughing so hard, so hard my belly is getting tied up in a knot.

"Got to cool me off!" he shouts all of a sudden. Then he runs over to the river and jumps in.

There's boards and other things in the current. It's so high. No sound comes from the river after the splash he makes, so I run right over. I look around. It's getting dark. I see he's halfway across the water already, and I know he didn't swim there but the current took him. It's far. I hear his voice, though, very clearly across it.

"My boots are filling," he says.

He says this in a normal voice, like he just noticed and he doesn't know what to think of it. Then he's gone. A branch comes by. Another branch. And I go in.

By the time I get out of the river, off the snag I pulled myself onto, the sun is down. I walk back to the car, turn on the high beams, and drive it up the bank. I put it in first gear and then I take my foot off the clutch. I get out, close the door, and watch it plow softly into the water. The headlights reach in as they go down, searching, still lighted even after the water swirls over the back end. I wait. The wires short out. It is all finally dark. And then there is only the water, the sound of it going and running and going and running and running.

(1984)

PART THREE

Writing About Poetry

The language of poetry is even more compressed than the language of the short story. You need to give yourself willingly to the understanding of poetry. The pleasure of reading it derives from the beauty of the language—the delight of the sounds and the images—as well as the power of the emotion and the depth of the insights conveyed. Poetry may seem difficult, but it can also be intensely rewarding.

10

How Do I Read Poetry?

In order to enjoy discovering the meaning of poetry, you must approach it with a positive attitude—a willingness to understand. Poetry invites your creative participation. More than any other form of literature, poetry allows you as reader to inform its meaning as you bring your own knowledge and experience to bear in interpreting images, motifs, and symbols.

Begin by reading the poem aloud—or at least by sounding the words aloud in your mind. Rhyme and rhythm work in subtle ways to emphasize key words and clarify meaning. As you reread, go slowly, paying careful attention to every word, looking up in a good dictionary any words that are unclear, and examining again and again any difficult lines.

Get the Literal Meaning First: Paraphrase

Before you begin interpreting a poem, you must be sure that you understand the literal meaning. Because one of the delights of poetry stems from the unusual ways in which poets put words together, you may sometimes need to straighten out the syntax. For instance, Thomas Hardy writes,

> And why unblooms the best hope ever sown?

The usual way of expressing that question would be something like this:

> And why does the best hope ever sown not bloom?

Occasionally you may need to fill in words that the poet has deliberately omitted through ellipsis. When Walt Whitman writes,

> But I with mournful tread,
> Walk the deck my captain lies,
> Fallen cold and dead,

we can tell that he means "the deck [on which] my Captain lies, / Fallen cold and dead."

Pay close attention to punctuation; it can provide clues to meaning. But do not be distressed if you discover that poets (like Emily Dickinson and Stevie Smith) sometimes use punctuation in strange ways or (like e e cummings) not at all. Along with the deliberate fracturing of syntax, this unusual use of punctuation comes under the heading of poetic license.

Always you must look up any words that you do not know — as well as any familiar words that fail to make complete sense in the context. When you read this line from Whitman,

> Passing the apple-tree blows of white and pink in the orchards,

the word "'blows" seems a strange choice. If you consult your dictionary, you will discover an unusual definition of blows: "masses of blossoms," a meaning which fits exactly.

Make Associations for Meaning

Once you understand the literal meaning of a poem, you can begin to expand that meaning into an interpretation. As you do so, keep asking yourself questions: Who is the speaker? Who is being addressed? What is the message? What do the images contribute? What do the symbols suggest? How does it all fit together?

When, for instance, Emily Dickinson in the following lines envisions "Rowing in Eden," how do you respond to this image?

> Rowing in Eden —
> Ah, the Sea!
> Might I but moor — Tonight —
> In Thee!

Can she mean *literally* rowing in Eden? Not unless you picture a lake in the Garden, which is, of course, a possibility. What do you associate with Eden? Complete bliss? Surely. Innocence, perhaps — the innocence of Adam and Eve before the Fall? Or their lustful sensuality after the Fall? Given the opening lines of the poem,

> Wild Nights — Wild Nights!
> Were I with thee
> Wild Nights should be
> Our luxury!

one fitting response might be that "Rowing in Eden" suggests paddling through sexual innocence in a far from chaste anticipation of reaching the port of ecstasy: to "Moor — Tonight — / In Thee!"

Sometimes poems, like stories and plays, contain *allusions* (indirect references to famous persons, events, places, or to other works of litera-

CHART 10-1 Critical Questions for Reading Poetry

Before planning an analysis of any selection in the anthology of poetry, write out your answers to the following questions to confirm your understanding of the poem and to generate material for the paper.

1. Can you paraphrase the poem if necessary?
2. Who is the speaker in the poem? How would you describe this persona?
3. What is the speaker's tone? Which words reveal this tone? Is the poem perhaps ironic?
4. What heavily connotative words are used? What words have unusual or special meanings? Are any words or phrases repeated? If so, why? Which words do you need to look up?
5. What images does the poet use? How do the images relate to one another? Do these images form a unified pattern (a motif) throughout the poem? Is there a central, controlling image?
6. What figures of speech are used? How do they contribute to the tone and meaning of the poem?
7. Are there any symbols? What do they mean? Are they universal symbols, or do they arise from the particular context of this poem?
8. Is the occasion for or the setting of the poem important in understanding its meaning? If so, why?
9. What is the theme (the central idea) of this poem? Can you state it in a single sentence?
10. How important is the role of metrics (sound effects), such as rhyme and rhythm? How do they affect tone and meaning?
11. How important is the contribution of form, such as rhyme scheme and line arrangement? How does the form influence the overall effect of the poem?

ture) that add to the meaning. Some allusions are fairly easy to perceive. When Eliot's Prufrock, in his famous love song, observes,

> No! I am not Prince Hamlet, nor was meant to be,

we know that he declines to compare himself with Shakespeare's Hamlet, a character who also had difficulty taking decisive action. Some allusions,

though, are more subtle. You need to know these lines from Ernest
Dowson,

> Last night, ah, yesternight, betwixt her lips and mine,
> There fell thy shadow, Cynara!

in order to catch the allusion to them in Eliot's "The Hollow Men":

> Between the motion
> And the act
> Falls the shadow.

Many allusions you can simply look up. If you are puzzled by Swin-
burne's line

> Thou has conquered, O pale Galilean,

your dictionary will identify the Galilean as Jesus Christ. For less well-
known figures or events, you may need to consult a dictionary of Biblical
characters, a dictionary of classical mythology, or a good encyclopedia.

Other valuable reference tools are Sir James Frazer's *The Golden Bough*,
which discusses preclassical myth, magic, and religion; and Cirlot's *A
Dictionary of Symbols*, which traces through mythology and world literature the significance of various archetypal (i.e., universal) symbols — the
sea, the seasons, colors, numbers, islands, serpents, and a host of others.

Thus, learning to understand poetry — like learning to understand any
imaginative literature — involves asking yourself questions, then specu-
lating and researching until you come up with satisfying answers.

11

Writing About Persona and Tone

Tone, which can be important in analyzing a short story, is crucial to the interpretation of poetry. Persona is closely related to tone. In order to identify persona and determine tone, you need (as usual) to ask yourself questions about the poem.

Who Is Speaking?

A good question to begin with is this: Who is the speaker in the poem? Often the most obvious answer seems to be "the poet," especially if the poem is written in the first person. When Emily Dickinson begins,

> This is my letter to the world
> That never wrote to me —

we can be fairly sure that she is writing in her own voice — that the poem itself is her "letter to the world." But poets often adopt a *persona*; that is, they speak through the voice of a character they have created. Stevie Smith, herself a middle-aged woman, adopts a persona of a different age and of the opposite sex in these lines:

> An old man of seventy-three
> I lay with my young bride in my arms. . . .

Thomas Hardy in "The Ruined Maid" (on pages 465 – 466) composes a dramatic monologue with a dual persona (or two personae), two young women who converse throughout the poem. The speaker in Auden's "The Unknown Citizen" (on pages 466 – 467) is apparently a spokesperson for the bureaucracy—but most certainly is not Auden himself. Thus, in order to be strictly accurate, you should avoid "The poet says . . . " and use instead, "The speaker in the poem says . . . " or "The persona in the poem says. . . . "

What Is Tone?

After deciding who the speaker is, your next question might be, "What is the tone of this poetic voice?" Tone in poetry is essentially the same as in fiction: the attitude of the writer toward the subject matter of the poem. And tone in a piece of writing is always similar to tone of voice in speaking. If a friend finds you on the verge of tears and comments, "You certainly look cheerful today," the tone of voice—as well as the absurdity of the statement—lets you know that your friend is being ironic—that she means the opposite of what she says. When Stephen Crane begins a poem,

> Do not weep, maiden, for war is kind,

any alert person perceives the ironic tone at once from the word *kind,* which war definitely is not. But irony can be much more subtle. Sometimes you need to put together a number of verbal clues in order to be sure of the irony.

One of your chief problems in identifying tone involves finding exactly the right word or words to describe it. Even after you have detected that a work is ironic, you sometimes need to decide whether the irony is gentle or bitter, whether it is light or scathing in tone. You need a number of adjectives at your command. As you analyze tone in the poems that follow, keep these terms in mind to see whether any may prove useful: humorous, joyous, playful, light, hopeful, brisk, lyrical, admiring, celebratory, laudatory, expectant, wistful, sad, mournful, dreary, tragic, elegiac, solemn, somber, poignant, earnest, blasé, disillusioned, straightforward, curt, hostile, sarcastic, cynical, ambivalent, ambiguous.

Looking at Persona and Tone

Read the following five poems for pleasure. Then, as you read through them again slowly and carefully, pay attention to the persona and try to identify the tone of this speaker's voice. Is the speaker angry, frightened, astonished, admiring? Or perhaps sincere, sarcastic, humorous, or deceptive?

Theodore Roethke *1908–1963*

MY PAPA'S WALTZ

The whiskey on your breath
Could make a small boy dizzy;
But I hung on like death:
Such waltzing was not easy.

We romped until the pans
Slid from the kitchen shelf;
My mother's countenance
Could not unfrown itself.

The hand that held my wrist
Was battered on one knuckle;   10
At every step you missed
My right ear scraped a buckle.

You beat time on my head
With a palm caked hard by dirt,
Then waltzed me off to bed
Still clinging to your shirt.

(1948)

Thomas Hardy *1840–1928*

THE RUINED MAID

"O 'Melia, my dear, this does everything crown!
Who could have supposed I should meet you in Town?
And whence such fair garments, such prosperi-ty?"—
"O didn't you know I'd been ruined?" said she.

—"You left us in tatters, without shoes or socks,
Tired of digging potatoes, and spudding up docks;
And now you've gay bracelets and bright feathers three!"—
"Yes: that's how we dress when we're ruined," said she.

—"At home in the barton[1] you said 'thee' and 'thou,'
And 'thik oon,' and 'theas oon,' and 't'other'; but now   10
Your talking quite fits 'ee for high compa-ny!"—
"Some polish is gained with one's ruin," said she.

—"Your hands were like paws then, your face blue and bleak,
But now I'm bewitched by your delicate cheek,
And your little gloves fit as on any la-dy!"—
"We never do work when we're ruined," said she.

[1]farmyard

—"You used to call home-life a hag-ridden dream,
And you'd sigh, and you'd sock;[2] but at present you seem
To know not of megrims[3] or melancho-ly!"—
"True. One's pretty lively when ruined," said she.　　　　　　　20

—"I wish I had feathers, a fine sweeping gown,
And a delicate face, and could strut about Town!"—
"My dear—a raw country girl, such as you be,
Cannot quite expect that. You ain't ruined," said she.

　　　　　　　　　　　　　　　　　　　　　　　　(1866)

W. H. Auden *1907–1973*

THE UNKNOWN CITIZEN

(To JS/07/M/378
This Marble Monument
Is Erected by the State)

He was found by the Bureau of Statistics to be
One against whom there was no official complaint,
And all the reports on his conduct agree
That, in the modern sense of an old-fashioned word, he was a saint,
For in everything he did he served the Greater Community.
Except for the War till the day he retired
He worked in a factory and never got fired,
But satisfied his employers, Fudge Motors Inc.
Yet he wasn't a scab or odd in his views,
For his Union reports that he paid his dues,　　　　　　　10
(Our report on his Union shows it was sound)
And our Social Psychology workers found
That he was popular with his mates and liked a drink.
The Press are convinced that he bought a paper every day
And that his reactions to advertisements were normal in every way.
Policies taken out in his name prove that he was fully insured,
And his Health-card shows he was once in hospital but left it cured.
Both Producers Research and High-Grade Living declare
He was fully sensible to the advantages of the Installment Plan
And had everything necessary to the Modern Man,　　　　　　　20
A phonograph, a radio, a car and a frigidaire.
Our researchers into Public Opinion are content
That he held the proper opinions for the time of year;
When there was peace, he was for peace; when there was war, he went.
He was married and added five children to the population,

[2]Moan.
[3]Sadness.

Which our Eugenist says was the right number for a parent of his
  generation,
And our teachers report that he never interfered with their education.
Was he free? Was he happy? The question is absurd:
Had anything been wrong, we should certainly have heard.

(1940)

Edmund Waller *1607–1687*

GO, LOVELY ROSE

Go, lovely Rose,
Tell her that wastes her time and me,
   that now she knows,
When I resemble her to thee,
How sweet and fair she seems to be.

Tell her that's young,
And shuns to have her graces spied,
   that had'st thou sprung
In deserts where no men abide,
Thou must have uncommended died.   10

Small is the worth
Of beauty from the light retir'd:
   Bid her come forth,
Suffer herself to be desir'd,
And not blush so to be admir'd.

Then die, that she
The common fate of all things rare
   May read in thee,
How small a part of time they share,
That are so wondrous sweet and fair.   20

(1645)

Dorothy Parker *1893–1967*

ONE PERFECT ROSE

A single flow'r he sent me, since we met.
   All tenderly his messenger he chose;
Deep-hearted, pure, with scented dew still wet—
   One perfect rose.

I knew the language of the floweret;
   "My fragile leaves," it said, "his heart enclose."

Love long has taken for his amulet
 One perfect rose.

Why is it no one ever sent me yet
 One perfect limousine, do you suppose?   10
Ah no, it's always just my luck to get
 One perfect rose.

(1926)

Prewriting

As you search for a fuller understanding of a poem and for a possible writing thesis, remember to keep rereading the poem (or at least pertinent parts of it). The questions you pose for yourself will become easier to answer and your responses more enlightened.

Asking Questions About the Speaker in "My Papa's Waltz"

If a poem lends itself to an approach through persona or tone, you will, of course, find something unusual or perhaps puzzling about the speaker or the poetic voice. Consider Theodore Roethke's "My Papa's Waltz," which you just read. Ask youself first, "Who is the speaker?" You know from line 2: "a small boy." But the past tense verbs suggest that the boy may be grown now, remembering a childhood experience. Sometimes this adult perspective requires additional consideration.

Next, ask yourself, "What is the speaker's attitude toward his father?" The boy's feelings about his father become the crucial issue in determining the tone of the poem. You need to look carefully at details and word choice to discover your answer. Consider, for instance, these questions:

1. Is it pleasant or unpleasant to be made dizzy from the smell of whiskey on someone's breath?
2. Does it sound like fun to hang on "like death"?
3. How does it change the usually pleasant experience of waltzing to call it "not easy"?
4. What sort of "romping" would be necessary to cause pans to slide from a shelf?
5. Is it unusual to hold your dancing partner by the wrist? How is this different from being held by the hand?
6. Would it be enjoyable or painful to have your ear scraped repeatedly by a buckle?
7. Would you like or resent having someone "beat time" on your head with a hard, dirty hand?

8. If the father is gripping the boy's wrist with one hand and thumping his head with the other, does this explain why the boy must hang on for dear life?

9. What other line in the poem does the last line echo?

If your answers to these questions lead you to conclude that this waltzing was not fun for the boy, then you could describe the tone as ironic (because of the discrepancy between the pleasant idea of the waltz and the boy's unpleasant experience). You could, possibly, describe the tone as detached, because the boy gives no clear indication of his feelings. We have to deduce them from details in the poem. You could even describe the tone as reminiscent, but this term is too general to indicate the meaning carried by the tone.

We all bring our own experience to bear in interpreting a poem. What you should be careful about is allowing your personal experience to carry too much weight in your response. If, for instance, you had an abusive father, you might so strongly identify with the boy's discomfort that you would call the tone resentful. On the other hand, if you enjoyed a loving relationship with your father, you might well find, as does X. J. Kennedy[1], "the speaker's attitude toward his father warmly affectionate, and take this recollection of childhood to be a happy one." Kennedy cites as evidence "the rollicking rhythms of the poem; the playfulness of a rhyme like *dizzy* and *easy*; the joyful suggestions of the words *waltz, waltzing,* and *romped*." He suggests that a reader who sees the tone as resentful fails "to visualize this scene in all its comedy, with kitchen pans falling and the father happily using his son's head for a drum." Kennedy also feels in the last line the suggestion of "the boy *still clinging* with persistent love."[1]

Devising a Thesis   Since your prewriting questioning has been directed toward discovering the attitude of the speaker in the poem, you could formulate a thesis that allows you to focus on the importance of understanding the persona in order to perceive the tone of the poem. Of course, the way you interpret the poem will determine the way you state your thesis. You could write a convincing paper on any one of the following thesis statements:

> The attitude of the boy toward his father in Roethke's "My Papa's Waltz" conveys to us the poet's ambivalent tone.

> The attitude of the boy toward his father in Roethke's "My Papa's Waltz" allows us to perceive the poet's ironic tone.

> The attitude of the boy toward his father in Roethke's "My Papa's Waltz" reinforces the poet's loving, nostalgic tone.

If you wrote on the first thesis, you would focus on the conflicting evidence suggesting that the boy is delighted by his father's attention but

[1]*An Introduction to Poetry*, 4th ed. (Boston: Little, Brown, 1971), 10.

frightened by the coercion of the dance. If you wrote on the second thesis, you would cite evidence of the boy's discomfort and argue that the "waltz" in the title and the rollicking meter are thus clearly ironic. If you wrote on the last thesis, you would emphasize the sprightly meter and playful rhymes, which present the dance as a frisky romp and show that the boy is having a splendid time.

Describing the Tone in "The Ruined Maid"

You can see by now that speaker and tone are all but impossible to separate. In order to get at the tone of Hardy's poem, write out responses to the following questions and be prepared to discuss the tone in class.

1. Who are the two speakers in this poem?
2. What does the term *maid* mean in the title? Look it up in your dictionary if you are not sure.
3. What different meanings does your dictionary give for *ruined*? Which one applies in the poem?
4. How does the ruined maid probably make her living? What details suggest this?
5. Describe how the tone of the country maid's speeches changes during the course of the poem.
6. What tone does the ruined maid use in addressing her former friend?
7. How does the final line undercut the ruined maiden's boast that she gained "polish" with her ruin?
8. What is Hardy's tone — that is, the tone of the poem itself?

Discovering a Thesis If you are going to write on tone in "The Ruined Maid," you might devise a statement focusing on the way we, as readers, discover the irony in the poem. Your thesis could read something like this:

> In Hardy's poem the discrepancy between the supposedly "ruined" woman's present condition and her previous wretched state reveals the ironic tone.

If you wanted instead to write about the dual personae in the poem, you might think about how they function — to figure out why Hardy chose to present the poem through two speakers instead of the usual one. Perhaps he chose this technique because the two voices enable him to convey his theme convincingly. You might invent a thesis along these lines:

> Hardy employs dual personae in "The Ruined Maid" to convince us that prostitution, long considered a fate "worse than death," is actually much preferable to grinding poverty.

In each paper, although your focus would be different, the evidence you use in presenting the contrast would be essentially the same.

Describing the Tone in "The Unknown Citizen"

1. How is the "he" being referred to in the poem identified in the italicized epigraph?
2. Who is the speaker in the poem? Why does the speaker use *our* and *we* instead of *my* and *I?*
3. Is *Fudge Motors Inc.* a serious name for a corporation? What is the effect of rhyming *Inc.* (line 8) with *drink* (line 13)?
4. Why does Auden capitalize so many words and phrases that normally would not be capitalized (like Greater Community, Installment Plan, Modern Man, Public Opinion, etc.)?
5. What is the attitude of the poetic voice toward the Unknown Citizen? What is Auden's attitude toward the Unknown Citizen? What is Auden's attitude toward the speaker in the poem?
6. What, then, is the tone of the poem?

Discovering a Thesis If you were going to write on tone in Auden's "The Unknown Citizen," you would focus on the features of the poem that reveal that tone — beginning or ending perhaps with the epigraph of the poem (the citizen's epitaph), in which he is referred to as a number, not a name. You might frame a thesis something like this:

> Auden's sharply ironic tone reveals to us that the Unknown Citizen is being honored not for his accomplishments but for being a model of conformity to the policies of the State.

As you develop this thesis, you can focus on the discrepancies you recognize between the solemn praise offered by the speaker and your recognition of these qualities as far from admirable.

Discovering Tone in "Go, Lovely Rose"

1. What has happened between the speaker and the woman before the poem was written?
2. Why does he choose a rose to carry his message?
3. What does *uncommended* mean in line 10?
4. Can you detect a tone slightly different in lines 2 and 7 from the speaker's admiring tone in the poem as a whole?
5. How do you respond to his telling the rose to die so that the woman may be reminded of how quickly her beauty will also die?

6. Does the title "Song," as the poem is sometimes called, convey any hint about the tone?

7. How would you describe the tone of this poem?

Discovering Tone in "One Perfect Rose"

1. What are the similarities between Parker's poem and Waller's?
2. What are the major differences?
3. Why does Parker put an apostrophe in *flow'r*?
4. What is an *amulet*?
5. How does the tone of the poem change in the last stanza? Can you explain why this happens?
6. What is the tone of the entire poem?

Writing

Because you may find poetry more difficult to write about than short stories, first be sure that you understand the poem. If the poem is difficult, write a complete *paraphrase* in which you straighten out the word order and replace any unfamiliar words or phrases with everyday language. Yes, you damage the poem when you paraphrase it, but the poem will survive.

After you are sure you have a firm grasp on the literal level, you can then begin to examine the images, make associations, and flesh out the meanings that will eventually lead you to an interpretation of the poem. By this time, you should have generated sufficient material to write about the work. The writing process is essentially the same as it is for analyzing a short story.

Explicating and Analyzing

In explicating a poem, you proceed carefully through the text, interpreting it, usually, line by line. Because of the attention to detail, explication is best suited to writing about a short poem or a key section of a longer work. As an explicator you may look at any or all elements of the poem — tone, persona, images, symbolism, metrics — as you discuss the way these elements function together to form the poem. Although you may paraphrase an occasional line, your explication will be concerned mainly with revealing hidden meanings in the poem. Probably most of your class discussions involve a kind of informal explication of poems, stories, or plays.

A written explication is easy to organize: you start with the first line and work straight through the poem. But explicating well requires a discerning eye. You have to make numerous decisions about what to comment on and how far to pursue a point, and you also have to pull various strands together in the end to arrive at a conclusion involving a statement of the theme or purpose of the poem. This approach, if poorly handled, can be a mechanical task, but if well done, explication can prove a rewarding way to examine a rich and complex work.

A written analysis involves explication but differs by focusing on some element of the poem and examining how that element (tone, persona, imagery, symbolism, metrics) contributes to an understanding of the meaning or purpose of the whole. You can see that an analysis is more challenging to write because you must exercise more options in selecting and organizing your material. Your instructor will let you know if it matters which type of paper you compose.

Ideas for Writing

Ideas for Responsive Writing

1. Were you ever frightened or hurt as a child, like the boy in Roethke's poem, by being handled too roughly by an adult? Describe the experience, explaining not only how you felt but also what you now think the adult's motives might have been.

2. Using Dorothy Parker's "One Perfect Rose" as a guide, write an ironic or humorous response to Marlowe's "The Passionate Shepherd to His Love" (page 514) or compose the woman's reply to Andrew Marvell's "To His Coy Mistress" (page 520).

3. Do you know anyone well who is a conformist, a person very much like Auden's Unknown Citizen? If so, write an updated ironic tribute to the type of person who always goes along with the crowd. Write your satirical praise as a speech, an essay, or a poem.

Ideas for Critical Writing

1. Choose one of the sample thesis statements included in the "Prewriting" section of this chapter and write an essay exploring that thesis.

2. Both "My Papa's Waltz" (page 465) by Theodore Roethke and "Piano" by D. H. Lawrence (page 560) concern the childhood experience of a young boy. Study both poems until you are sure you understand them; then compare or contrast their tones.

3. Compare Waller's "Go, Lovely Rose" with Parker's parody "One Perfect Rose" by focusing on the differences in tone.

4. Stevie Smith's "Not Waving but Drowning" (see page 576) seems difficult until you realize that two voices are speaking—the "I" of the first and third stanzas and the "they" of the second. Once you understand the implications of this dual perspective, write an explication of the poem.

5. Discuss the satirical effectiveness of Auden's deadpan narrator in "The Unknown Citizen."

Editing

In this section we will explain a few conventions that you should observe in writing about poetry. If you have often written papers analyzing poetry, you probably incorporate these small but useful bits of mechanical usage automatically. If not, take time during the revising or editing stage to get them right.

Punctuating Poetry in Essays

The following are the main conventions to observe when quoting poetry in writing.

Inserting Slash Marks

When quoting only a couple of lines, use a slash mark to indicate the end of each line (except the last):

> Whitman similarly describes the soul's position in the universe in these lines: "And you O my soul where you stand, Surrounded, detached, in measureless oceans of space" (6–7).

Citing Line Numbers

Cite line numbers in parentheses after the quotation marks and before the period when quoting complete lines, as in the previous example. When quoting only a phrase, cite the line number immediately after closing the quotation marks, even if your sentence continues:

> In the italicized portion of the poem, the bird sings a carol in praise of "lovely and soothing death" (135) to help the persona overcome his grief.

Adjusting End Punctuation

Since you are using the lines you quote in a different context from that in the poem, adjust the punctuation of the last line you quote to make it fit your sentence. Here is a line from Whitman's "When lilacs last in the dooryard bloom'd":

> To adorn the burial-house of him I love?

Notice how the end punctuation is dropped in order to suit the writer's sentence:

> The persona brings visions of the varying beauty of the entire country, as he says, "To adorn the burial-house of him I love" (80).

Using Square Brackets

If you need to change a word, a capital letter or some punctuation *within* the/or lines you quote, enclose the changed letter or mark of punctuation in square brackets (not parentheses):

> The persona brings visions of the varying beauty of the entire country "[t]o adorn the burial-house of him [he] love[s]" (80).

Remember that you do not have to quote complete lines. Rather than clutter your sentence with three sets of brackets, you could simply begin your quotation with the second word in that line:

> The persona brings visions of the varying beauty of the entire country to "adorn the burial-house of him [he] love[s]" (80).

Quoting Multiple Lines

If you are quoting more than two or three lines, indent ten spaces and omit the quotation marks (since the indention tells your readers that the material is quoted):

> After describing the carnage of war dead, the persona realizes that his sympathies have been misplaced:
>
> > They themselves were fully at rest, they suffer'd not,
> > The living remain'd and suffer'd, the mother suffer'd,
> > And the wife and the child and the musing comrade suffer'd
> > And the armies that remain'd suffer'd. (181–84)

The indented material should still be double-spaced (unless your instructor asks you to single-space the lines).

Sample Student Paper

The following student paper was written in response to A. E. Housman's poem "To an Athlete Dying Young" and is included here not as a model but to generate class discussion. Read the poem, which appears on page 546, and then decide if you agree with the student's views about the tone and persona of Housman's poem.

Kenric L. Bond
Eng. 1002
October 2, 1991

Death at an Early Age

Wouldn't it be great to die in your prime, not to   [1]
be remembered as old and feeble but as still strong and vibrant?
A. E. Housman's poem "To an Athlete Dying Young" tells of an

athlete who died a hero not too long after winning a record-
setting race.

The first stanza tells of an athlete coming home   [2]
after winning a race: "The time you won your town the race/ We
chaired you through the market-place" (1-2). But the next
stanza begins, "To-day, the road all runners come,/ Shoulder-
high we bring you home" (5-6). The similarity between these
two scenes is startling. We would not ordinarily link the
picture of pallbearers carrying the deceased home in a casket
with a hero being carried on the shoulders of his cheering
fans. These first two stanzas set up the contrast between
triumph and death that continues through the rest of the poem.

The third stanza deals with this issue of dying   [3]
in one's prime by mentioning "the laurel," which grows
"early" but "withers quicker than the rose" (11-12). The
laurel represents fame for winning the race, but it is forgotten
sooner than the brief life of a rose. This point about the
brevity of fame is repeated in the last stanza:

> And round that early-laurelled head
> Will flock to gaze the strengthless dead,
> And find unwithered on its curls
> The garland briefer than a girl's. (25-28)

The victory garland, awarded after the race, is still green
with life on the dead athlete's head; the fame of winning the
race is shorter than a girl's innocence and purity. So, Housman
implies, the time to die is while the recent victory is still
being discussed among the living in the area coffee shops and
beauty salons.

During the poem, A. E. Housman tries to convince   [4]
us that it is best to die young: "Smart lad, to slip betimes
away/ From fields where glory does not stay" (9-10). Housman
calls the athlete smart for dying while the memory of victory is
still fresh in the minds of a society where positive
accomplishments are easily forgotten. The poet also applauds

the athlete's death because then the runner won't have to face
the disheartening sight of a new runner breaking his records
and stealing the glory he once enjoyed: "Eyes the shady night
has shut/ Cannot see the record cut" (13-14).

As a runner myself, I know that I will someday see   [5]
all the records that I set in high school broken. I have already
witnessed a few of my marks reset by other runners. If I had
died right after my high school years, I could have missed these
superficial disappointments. But an athlete shouldn't be so
shallow that he or she can't bear to live and see such trivial
things as records broken. They are just names on a wall or
trophies in a case. I hope that somebody does break my records
because that's why I made them--to be broken.

A. E. Housman seems to think that setting records   [6]
and living in the limelight are all that athletes are looking
for in their lives. The poet suggests that it would be too
difficult for an athlete to live and see the record books
rewritten and that a victorious athlete would be vain enough to
worry about what other people think of his physical state after
he's dead. Well, I think the poet is wrong. I'm one athlete
who has more than records and glory to live for.

Analyzing an Essay

After rereading Housman's poem, write an analysis of the above student response. (Or, if you prefer, write your own analysis of "To an Athlete Dying Young.") The following questions may help you:

1. Does the student have a clear understanding of the poem's main theme? Where does he state the theme? Do you agree with his statement of the theme?

2. Does the student identify the speaker in the poem? Are the speaker and the poet the same person? How do you know?

3. Does the student identify the poem's tone? Could the speaker's attitude toward death be ironic? Does the student see any irony in the poem? Does the student ever use any irony himself?

4. Do you agree with the student's statement of Housman's purpose (first sentence of paragraph 4)? How does this statement of purpose relate to the student's understanding of the poem's tone?

5. How do the student's own experiences influence his responses to the poem? How does the student feel about the poet's attitude toward athletes? Do you agree with the reactions expressed in the last two paragraphs?

CHAPTER

12

Writing About Poetic Language

In no other form of literature are words so important as in poetry. As you study the language of poetry—its freshness, precision, and beauty—you can learn ways in which to use words effectively in your own prose writing.

What Do the Words Suggest?

Your sensitivity to poetic language will be enhanced if you learn the meaning of a few terms in literary criticism. (The important term *allusion* has been defined in Chapter 10, page 460.)

indirect reference to famous person, place, etc

Connotation and Denotation

Many single words carry a rich load of meaning, both denotative and connotative. The *denotation* of a word is the definition you will find in the dictionary. The *connotation* of a word is the emotional overtones you may feel when encountering the term. Consider the word *mother*. Most people would respond positively with feelings of warmth, security, and love associated with bedtime stories, a warm lap, and fresh apple pies. So, when Stephen Crane includes the word in these moving lines,

> Mother whose heart hung humble as a button
> On the bright splendid shroud of your son,
> Do not weep.
> War is kind.

the connotations of the word *mother* probably account for part of our emotional response.

Figures of Speech

The most common figures of speech—metaphor, simile, and personification—appear in our everyday language. You might say, if you keep
forgetting things, "My mind is a sieve," creating a metaphor. Or you
might note, "That dog looks like a dust mop without a handle," making a
simile. Or you might complain, "My typewriter can't spell worth a darn,"
using personification. Of course, poets use figures of speech that are
much fresher and more imaginative than the kind most of us employ—
one of the cardinal reasons for considering them poets.

Metaphor and Simile   A metaphor is an imaginative comparison that
makes use of the connotative values of words. When Shakespeare writes
to a young lover that "Thy eternal summer shall not fade," he is comparing her youth to the joys of summertime. In "Dulce Et Decorum Est," a
compelling anti-war poem, Wilfred Owen uses the metaphors "drunk
with fatigue," "blood-shod," "like old beggars under sacks," "coughing
like hags," "flound'ring like a man in fire or lime," and "his hanging face,
like a devil's sick of sin." The last four of these singularly grim comparisons would usually be called *similes* because they include the connective
like, but you can also find similes that use *as* and other explicitly comparative words. In fact, you may use the broader term *metaphor* to refer to a
figure of speech that is either a metaphor or a simile.

Personification   "Daylight is nobody's friend," writes Anne Sexton in a
metaphor that compares daylight to a friend, but more exactly it is a
personification, because it makes a nonhuman thing sound like a human
being. T. S. Eliot uses personification when he writes " . . . the afternoon, the evening, sleeps so peacefully," as does Andrew Marvell in "fate
with jealous eyes does see."

Imagery

Perhaps personification is so widely used in poetry because it gives us a
clear image of something otherwise vague or abstract, like daylight or
fate. *Imagery* is the term we use to speak of these sensory impressions
literature gives us. Robert Frost, in a famous poem, describes a sleigh
driver " . . . stopping here/ To watch his woods fill up with snow,"
providing a visual image that most readers find easy to picture. In the
same poem, Frost gives us an apt auditory image: "The only other
sound's the sweep/ Of easy wind and downy flake." And anyone who has
spent time in a big airport surely agrees with Yvor Winters' image of
one: " . . . the light gives perfect vision, false and hard;/ The metal
glitters, deep and bright."

Symbol

A *symbol* is an image that becomes so suggestive that it takes on much more meaning than its descriptive value. The connotations of the words, repetition, placement, and the meaning it may gather from the rest of the poem help identify an image as a symbol. Blue skies and fresh spring breezes can certainly be just that, but they can also symbolize freedom. Look at the first stanza of a W. H. Auden poem:

> As I walked out one evening
> Walking down Bristol Street
> The people on the pavement
> Were fields of harvest wheat.

The image in lines 3 and 4 is descriptive: you can envision a crowd of moving people seeming to ripple like wheat. The observation is also symbolic, because harvest wheat is just about to be cut down; the rest of the poem endorses a rather dim view of human hopes and dreams.

Paradox

The same poem says, "You shall love your crooked neighbor/ With your crooked heart." An inexperienced reader might say, "Now, that doesn't make any sense! *Crooked heart* and *love* seem contradictory." Others, though, would be sensitive to the paradox in those lines. A *paradox* is a phrase or statement that on the surface seems contradictory but makes some kind of emotional sense. Looking back at the Yvor Winters' description of the San Francisco airport at night, you will find the phrase "perfect vision, false and hard." How can perfect vision be false instead of true? Only as a paradox. Paradoxical also are the "sounds of silence," which is the title of a Paul Simon song. And popular singer Carly Simon tells her lover paradoxically that "Nobody does it better/ Makes me feel bad so good." The standard Christian paradox is stated in the motto of Mary, Queen of Scots: "In my end is my beginning." In order to make sense of that statement, all we need to know is the customary Christian belief that after death begins a better life in heaven.

Oxymoron Another figure of speech that appears occasionally in both poetry and prose is an *oxymoron*, an extreme paradox in which two words having opposite meanings are juxtaposed, as in "deafening silence" or "elaborately simple."

Looking at Poetic Language

The six poems you are about to study exemplify elements of poetic language. As you read them over several times, identify figures of speech, imagery, symbol, and paradox.

Walt Whitman *1819–1892*

A NOISELESS PATIENT SPIDER

A noiseless patient spider,
I mark'd where on a little promontory it stood isolated,
Mark'd how to explore the vacant vast surrounding,
It launched forth filament, filament, filament, out of itself,
Ever unreeling them, ever tirelessly speeding them.

And you O my soul where you stand,
Surrounded, detached, in measureless oceans of space,
Ceaselessly musing, venturing, throwing, seeking the spheres to
    connect them,
Till the bridge you will need be form'd, till the ductile anchor hold,
Till the gossamer thread you fling catch somewhere, O my soul.   10

(1881)

William Shakespeare *1564–1616*

SHALL I COMPARE THEE TO A SUMMER'S DAY?

Shall I compare thee to a summer's day?
Thou art more lovely and more temperate:
Rough winds do shake the darling buds of May,
And summer's lease hath all too short a date:
Sometimes too hot the eye of heaven shines,
And often is his gold complexion dimmed;
And every fair from fair sometimes declines,
By chance or nature's changing course untrimmed;
But thy eternal summer shall not fade,
Nor lose possession of that fair thou ow'st;   10
Nor shall death brag thou wander'st in his shade,
When in eternal lines to time thou grow'st:
So long as men can breathe, or eyes can see,
So long lives this, and this gives life to thee.

(1609)

H. D. *1886–1961*

HEAT

Oh wind, rend open the heat,
cut apart the heat,
rend it to tatters.

Fruit cannot drop
through this thick air—
fruit cannot fall into heat
that presses up and blunts
the points of pears
and rounds the grapes.

Cut the heat—   10
plough through it,
turning it on either side
of your path.

(1916)

Robert Frost *1874–1963*

THE SILKEN TENT

She is as in a field a silken tent
At midday when a sunny summer breeze
Has dried the dew and all its ropes relent,
So that in guys it gently sways at ease,
And its supporting central cedar pole,
That is its pinnacle to heavenward
And signifies the sureness of the soul,
Seems to owe naught to any single cord,
But strictly held by none, is loosely bound
By countless silken ties of love and thought   10
To everything on earth the compass round,
And only by one's going slightly taut
In the capriciousness of summer air
Is of the slightest bondage made aware.

(1942)

Donald Hall *1928–*

MY SON MY EXECUTIONER

My son, my executioner,
  I take you in my arms,
Quiet and small and just astir,
  And whom my body warms.

Sweet death, small son, our instrument
  Of immortality,
Your cries and hungers document
  Our bodily decay.

We twenty-five and twenty-two,
   Who seemed to live forever,   10
Observe enduring life in you
   And start to die together.

                                                 (1955)

Adrienne Rich ,1929–

AUNT JENNIFER'S TIGERS

Aunt Jennifer's tigers prance across a screen,
Bright topaz denizens of a world of green.
They do not fear the men beneath the tree;
They pace in sleek chivalric certainty.

Aunt Jennifer's fingers fluttering through her wool
Find even the ivory needle hard to pull.
The massive weight of Uncle's wedding band
Sits heavily upon Aunt Jennifer's hand.

When Aunt is dead, her terrified hands will lie
Still ringed with ordeals she was mastered by.   10
The tigers in the panel that she made
Will go on prancing, proud and unafraid.

                                                 (1951)

[handwritten annotations: "tigers are denizens", "No fear", "sleek", "certainty", "embroidery", "Jen much mussel", "Not much", "his wedding band", "heavy", "Contrast"]

Prewriting

The following exercises will help you analyze the use of language in the poems that you just read in preparation for writing a paper focusing on that approach.

Examining Poetic Language

1. Why could one say that "Shall I compare thee to a summer's day?" presents contrast rather than comparison?

2. In a group of classmates, attempt to write a companion poem to "Shall I compare thee to a summer's day?"only with the extended metaphor being, "Shall I compare thee to a winter's day?" Try to use connotative language.

3. What is the main comparison made in "A Noiseless Patient Spider"? What is personified? Using a thesaurus, paraphrase the poem,

substituting near synonyms for some of the original words. Comment on the differences in meaning and tone you create. (Imagine, for example, if the spider "launched forth string, string, string, out of itself.")

4. "Heat" identifies the abstract conditions of heat and wind with concrete things, but does not do so explicitly. What concrete things represent the heat and the wind in the poem's basic image?

5. Make a sketch of the silken tent in Frost's poem. What do the different parts of the tent symbolize? What is Frost's attitude toward "She," and what words let you know it?

6. Explain the paradox that is central to "My Son My Executioner."

7. The basic comparison in "Aunt Jennifer's Tigers" is the one between the woman herself and the tigers she embroiders. Make a paired list of words that describe Aunt Jennifer and words that describe the tigers. Why is "Uncle's wedding band" used instead of "her wedding band"? What, then, does the wedding band symbolize in the poem?

Writing

Poetic language is one of the richest veins of material for writing. You could, for example, analyze the role of nature imagery in "Heat," in "Shall I compare thee to a summer's day" and in "A Noiseless, Patient Spider." Or you could examine the cumulative effect of the extended simile in "The Silken Tent." One way to approach a paper on poetic language is through comparison.

Comparing and Contrasting

Noticing similarities and differences between poems will sharpen your sensitivity to each of them. If you listed all the words in the short poem "My Son My Executioner" and scrambled them, then listed all the words in "Heat" and scrambled them, putting the two lists side by side, you might see for the first time that "Heat" has no words over two syllables, that it has few abstract terms, and that in contrast with "My Son My Executioner" it has few words that convey emotion. Taking the comparison further, you might say that "Heat" focuses on creating a strong, sensual image, while "My Son My Executioner" focuses on expression of ideas and feelings.

Also, as you have seen from your prewriting exercise on "Aunt Jennifer's Tigers," comparisons of images and language within a poem may give you access to its meaning. The following writing assignments suggest some meaningful comparisons to explore.

Ideas for Writing
Ideas for Responsive Writing

1. Whitman's poem comparing the explorations of the spider to the searchings of his soul makes the totally abstract idea of the soul's search for meaning clear and concrete. Think of some abstraction that you might want to explain to a five-year-old child—something like gentleness, aggression, wisdom, slyness, or perseverance. Then think of an appropriate animal or insect to illustrate the quality, and write a poem or a fable to show the child why the quality is good or bad. Remember to keep your vocabulary simple and your lines or sentences short.

2. Would you like to be the "She" in Frost's "A Silken Tent"? Write an essay explaining why or why not.

3. Write a paper explaining how Frost's poem would have to be changed if it began with "He" instead of "She."

4. Have you ever known a woman like Aunt Jennifer in Adrienne Rich's poem? Write a brief character sketch of this person, and then explain why you think she stayed in the marriage.

Ideas for Critical Writing

1. Analyze the poetic language of "The Silken Tent" and "Aunt Jennifer's Tigers" to make a statement about the poems' attitudes toward traditional women's roles.

2. Compare the two kinds of love described in "A Valediction: Forbidding Mourning" (page 519 in the anthology), using the images associated with each kind, to discover what Donne considers the nature of true love.

3. Discuss the symbol of the spider in "Design" (page 553 in the anthology) and "A Noiseless Patient Spider" (page 482).

4. Show how the language of "To the Mercy Killers" (page 584) and "Root Cellar" (page 580) is similarly effective.

5. Compare and contrast the nature imagery in Shakespeare's Sonnet 18 ("Shall I compare thee to a summer's day?") (page 482) and Sonnet 73 ("That time of year thou mayst in me behold" on page 516 in the anthology).

Rewriting: Style

After looking so closely at poetic language, you should have a grasp of how important every word is to the total effect of a piece of writing.

Choosing Vivid, Descriptive Terms

Dudley Randall's "To the Mercy Killers" draws its strength almost exclusively from the vividness of its language: he describes himself as "a clot, an aching clench,/ A stub, a stump, a butt, a scab, a knob,/ A roaring pain, a putrefying stench." While your expository prose should not be quite so packed with arresting terminology, it can probably be improved by some attention to descriptive wording. Look at several of your back papers from this class. See whether you can identify your pet vacant words: Do you always express positive evaluations with *nice* or *beautiful*? Do you usually intensify an adjective with the word *very*? Do you refer to everything from ideas to irises as *things*? And do you describe anything that causes a faint stir in your being as *interesting*, causing you to come up with vapid sentences like, "This beautiful poem is full of very interesting things"? If so, you need to find livelier, more exact terms.

Finding Lively Words

Two quite different sources of help can work together in your quest for a more descriptive style. The first is your imagination: when you see that word *interesting* crop up as you write your rough draft, put a check in the margin; later, as you rewrite, ask yourself what you really meant. Sometimes you mean *significant* or *meaningful*; sometimes you mean *unusual* or *odd*; sometimes you even mean *perplexing* or *disturbing*.

If you are not completely pleased with your efforts, try using a thesaurus to jog your memory. Under *interesting* in our Roget's *Thesaurus*, we find "racy, spicy, breezy, salty; succulent, piquant, appealing, zestful, glamorous, colorful, picturesque; absorbing, enthralling, engrossing, fascinating, entertaining, ageless, dateless," as well as cross references to more lists at *amusement, attention, attraction*, and *right*. Somewhere in this large selection you should be able to find a word that conveys a clearer image than *interesting* does. Never choose an unfamiliar word, though, without first looking it up in a collegiate dictionary to be sure it conveys the exact meaning you want.

Exercise on Diction

Find five to ten sentences in your back papers (from this class or others) that can be improved by the use of livelier, more descriptive words. Write down the original, using every other line on your page. Then revise each sentence, crossing out expressionless words and writing in the new ones on the blank lines.

Sample Student Paper

Here are the second and third drafts of an essay analyzing poetic imagery
written by a student at Eastern Illinois University.

Comparison Exercise

After you have read both drafts, go over them again, making point-by-
point comparisons. Notice that the writer went beyond the instructor's
specific suggestions in her final revision. Write your response to the
following topics, and be prepared to discuss your findings in class.

1. Identify five cases in which the writer made changes in word
   choice (diction). Using a dictionary, explain the rationale for the
   changes.
2. Identify two sentences that have been significantly changed. Explain
   the reasons for the changes.
3. Closely analyze all the alterations in the third paragraph of the essay.

Sample Student Paper-Second Draft

Sonya Weaver

English 1002

April 3, 1991

Images of a Love

The speaker in John Donne's poem "A
Valediction: Forbidding Mourning" is an
unromantic man who is sternly forbidding his
wife to be sorrowful at his parting. This
description is not true of course, but it is
the way the speaker might be perceived if all
comparisons, contrasts, and images were
taken out of the poem. In order to appreciate

the beauty of this poem and interpret it correctly, it is necessary to take a close look at each image or comparison.

The first comparison we come to likens the speaker's parting to the quiet and easy death of virtuous men. The speaker paints a picture of a virtuous or upright man who, because he does not fear it, is passing peacefully into death. His deathbed is surrounded by his friends who are having trouble deciding if he has actually passed away or if he is still quietly breathing. The speaker says that his departure from his wife should be just as calm. He says, "let us melt" (5) which implies slowly and easily parting without any noise or tears. He explains that showing great emotion would *vague reference* expose their love to the common people and he does not want (this) because he believes their love is special, and that exposure would *Best word choice?* lower their love.

The speaker next contrasts their love to the love of common people. He states that common people notice earthquakes, but not trepidations or tremblings that take place among the stars. He is illustrating that common people's love is earthly, but that *misleading reference?* (their) love is heavenly. He goes on to say that "sublunary" (13) or earthly lovers cannot be apart from each other because when *needs rephrasing* they are, they lose their love because it is only physical. He claims that he and his wife *weak reference* not like (this). He feels that their love (his

and his wife's) is spiritual and refined and
that it is so great that it is above their
understanding ("ourselves know not what it
is" [18]). They do not have to worry about
their spouse being unfaithful, as earthly
lovers do, because their love is not just
physical.

      Next the speaker compares the
malleability of gold to the distance that
their souls can stretch (21-24). The speaker
says that temporary separation should not be
viewed as a break. He believes that even
though they may be many miles apart, they are
still one. He claims their souls can expand
over distances equal to the malleability of
gold or 250 square feet. This is a truly
beautiful image.

      The last image is another very beautiful
one. It compares their two souls to twin
compasses (25-36). The speaker believes that
if their souls are two (instead of one), they
are still linked to each other, as are the
parts of a compass. He likens his wife to the
foot in the center. She makes no attempt on
her own to move. She does so only if he
does. She is also like the center foot in
that if he leaves, she leans after him and
then becomes upright when he returns home as
does the center foot of a compass when the
outer foot is at a distance drawing a
circle. He says that there will be times when
he must leave but that he will always return
to her even as a compass returns to its
starting point upon completion of a circle.

      Without its images, this poem would be

rephrase

Maybe expand with other associations of gold

Clarify

nothing more than a husband prohibiting his
wife from being sad at his departure.
However, Donne's images transform this rough
message into a beautiful and romantic love

weak closing
line

poem. Images <u>are</u> important!

This is a good second draft showing sensitivity to the images
I have marked a few places where your style needs more clarity
and grace as well as one paragraph whose content could be expanded.

Donne, John. "A Valediction: Forbidding
Mourning." <u>Literature and the Writing</u>
<u>Process</u>. Ed. Elizabeth McMahan, Susan Day,
and Robert Funk. 3rd ed. New York:
Macmillan, 1993. 519.

Final Draft

Images of a Love

The speaker in John Donne's poem "A Valediction:
Forbidding Mourning" is an unromantic man who is sternly
forbidding his wife to be sorrowful at his parting. This
description is not true, of course, but it is the way the speaker
might be perceived if all comparisons, contrasts, and images
were taken out of the poem. In order to appreciate the beauty
of this poem and interpret it accurately, each image or
comparison must be closely analyzed.

The first comparison we come to likens the speaker's
parting to the quiet and easy death of virtuous men. The
speaker paints a picture of a virtuous or upright man who,
because he does not fear it, is passing peacefully into
death. His deathbed is surrounded by his friends who are having
trouble deciding if he has actually passed away or if he is
still quietly breathing. The speaker suggests that his
departure from his wife should be just as calm. He says, "let
us melt" (5) which implies slow and easy movement, without any
clamor or sobbing. He explains that showing great emotion
would display their love to the common people, and he does not
want this display because he believes it would make their
special love seem common.

The speaker next contrasts their special love to common
love. He states that common people notice earthquakes, but not
trepidations or tremblings that take place among the stars. He
is illustrating that common people's love is earthly, but that
the love between him and his wife is heavenly. He goes on to say
that "sublunary" (13) or earthly lovers mourn physical
separation because their love is limited to the physical
realm. He claims that he and his wife are not thus

limited. Their love is so spiritual and refined that it is even
beyond their own understanding ("ourselves know not what it
is" [18]). They do not have to worry about unfaithfulness, as
earthly lovers do, because their love is not merely defined by
the physical.

Next the speaker compares their love to the rare, precious,
and beautiful metal gold (21-24). Not only does the comparison
suggest that their love shares these three qualities, but it
also shares gold's malleability. An ounce of gold can be spread
thin enough to cover 250 square feet. The speaker compares
this span to the distance that their souls can stretch. The
speaker says that temporary separation should not be viewed as
a break. He believes that even though they may be many miles
apart, they are still one, like a continuous sheet of spread
gold--an unusual and expressive image.

The last image is another very eloquent one. It compares
their two souls to twin compasses (25-36). The speaker believes
that if their souls are two (instead of one), they are still
linked to each other, as are the parts of a compass. He likens
his wife to the foot in the center. She makes no attempt on her
own to move but does so only if he does. She is also like the
center foot in that if he leaves, she leans after him and then
becomes upright when he returns home, behaving like the center
foot of a compass when the outer foot draws a circle and then
folds into the center. He says that there will be times when he
must leave but that he will always return to her even as a
compass returns to its starting point upon completion of a circle.

Without its images, this poem would be nothing more than a
husband's prohibiting his wife from being sad at his departure.
However, Donne's often extraordinary images transform this
austere message into a beautiful and romantic love poem.

Work Cited

Donne, John. "A Valediction: Forbidding Mourning." Literature
   and the Writing Process. Ed. Elizabeth McMahan, Susan Day,
   and Robert Funk. 3rd ed. New York: Macmillan, 1993. 519.

13

Writing About Poetic Form

When we say that poetry has *form*, we mean it has design or structure. All poems have some kind of form. Many elements go into making the forms of poetry, but they all involve arranging the words in patterns. Sometimes sound controls the pattern; sometimes the number of words or the length of the lines determines the form.

What Are the Forms of Poetry?

Poetic forms can be divided into those that use sound effects (rhythm, rhyme), those that involve the length and organization of lines (stanza), and those that artistically manipulate word order (syntax).

Rhythm and Rhyme

Sound effects are produced by organized repetition. Systematically stressing or accenting words and syllables produces *rhythm*; repeating similar sounds in an effective scheme produces *rhyme*. Both effects intensify the meaning of a poem, arouse interest, and give pleasure. Once we notice a pattern of sound, we expect it to continue, and this expectation makes us more attentive to subtleties in the entire poem.

Rhythm can affect us powerfully. We respond almost automatically to the beat of a drum, the thumping of our heart, the pulsing of an engine. Poetic rhythm, usually more subtle, is created by repeating stresses and pauses. Rhythm conveys no verbal meaning itself, but when used skillfully it reinforces the meaning and tone of a poem. Consider how Theo-

dore Roethke captures the raucous spirit of "My Papa's Waltz" in the
recurring three-stress rhythm of these lines:

> We romped until the pans
> Slid from the kitchen shelf; . . .
> Then waltzed me off to bed
> Still clinging to your shirt.

For more details about the rhythms of poetry, see Chart 13 – 1 on meter.

   Rhyme, a recurring pattern of similar sounds, also enhances tone and
meaning. Because rhymed language is special language, it helps to set
poetry apart from ordinary expression and calls attention to the sense,
feeling, and tone of the words. Rhyme also gives a certain pleasure to the
reader by fulfilling the expectation of the sound patterns. Rhyme, which
usually depends on sound, not spelling, occurs when accented syllables
contain the same or similar vowel sound with identical consonants following the vowel: *right* and *bite, knuckle* and *buckle*. Rhymes are commonly used at regular intervals within a poem, often at the ends of lines:

> Yet he wasn't a scab or odd in his views,
> For his Union reports that he paid his dues.

Alliteration, Assonance, and Consonance

Closely allied to rhyme are other verbal devices that depend on the
correspondence of sounds. *Alliteration* is the repetition of consonant
sounds either at the beginning of words or in stressed syllables: "The
Soul selects her own Society—" or "Nature's first green is gold,/Her
hardest hue to hold." *Assonance* is the repetition of similar vowel sounds
that are not followed by identical consonant sounds: *grave* and *gain, shine*
and *bright. Consonance* is a kind of half-rhyme in which the consonants
are parallel but the vowels change: *blade* and *blood, flash* and *flesh*. Alliteration, assonance, and consonance are likely to be used occasionally and
not in regular, recurring patterns; but these devices of sound do focus our
attention and affect the tone, melody, and tempo of poetic expression.

Exercise on Poetic Form

Listen to a favorite popular song and copy down the lyrics (you may have
to listen several times). Now arrange the lines on the page as you think
they would be printed. What patterns of rhythm and sound do you see?
Did you notice them before you wrote the words down and arranged the
lines? Does the lineation (the arrangement into lines of poetry) help make
the meaning any clearer? If possible, compare your written version with a

printed one (on the album cover or album liner or in a magazine that publishes song lyrics).

Stanzaic Form: Closed and Open Forms

In the past, almost all poems were written in *closed form*: poetry with lines of equal length arranged in fixed patterns of stress and rhyme. Although these elements of form are still much in evidence today, modern poets prefer the greater freedom of *open form poetry*, which uses lines of varying length and avoids rigid patterns of rhyme or rhythm.

Closed forms give definition and shape to poetic expression. *Rhyme schemes* and *stanza patterns* demand the careful arrangement of words and lines into units of meaning that guide both writer and reader in understanding poetry.

Couplets and Quatrains Stanzas can be created on the basis of the number of lines, the length of the lines, the pattern of stressed syllables (the meter), and the rhyme scheme (the order in which rhymed words recur). The simplest stanza form is the *couplet*: two rhymed lines, usually of equal length and similar meter. W. H. Auden's "The Unknown Citizen" (pages 466–467) is written in rhyming couplets, although the lines vary in length and sometimes in rhythm. The most common stanza in English poetry is the *quatrain*, a group of four lines with any number of rhyme schemes. "Aunt Jennifer's Tigers" (page 484) is composed of three quatrains in which the lines rhyme as couplets (critics indicate this pattern of rhyme with letters: *a a b b*). The same rhyme scheme and stanza form are used in "The Ruined Maid" (page 465), while the quatrains of "My Papa's Waltz" (page 465) employ an alternating rhyme pattern (*a b a b*). Longer stanza patterns are used, of course, but the quatrain and the couplet remain the basic components of closed form poetry.

Sonnets The fixed form that has been used most frequently by the greatest variety of notable poets in England and America is the *sonnet*. Originated in Italy in the fourteenth century, the sonnet became a staple of English poetry in the sixteenth century and has continued to attract practitioners ever since.

The form of the sonnet is firmly fixed: fourteen lines, with ten syllables per line, arranged in a set rhyme scheme. The *Shakespearean sonnet* uses the rhyme scheme most common for sonnets in English: *a b a b, c d c d, e f e f, g g*. You will notice the rhyme scheme falls into three quatrains and an ending couplet, with a total of seven rhymes. "Shall I compare thee to a summer's day?" (page 482) and "That time of year thou mayst in me behold" (page 516) are splendid examples of Shakespeare's mastery of the sonnet (he wrote 154 of them) and illustrate why this traditional verse form continues to entice and stir both poets and readers.

CHART 13–1 Meter: The Rhythms of Poetry

When the rhythm has a regular pattern—that is, when the stress recurs at regular intervals—the result is **meter**. Not all poems are metered, but many are written in one pervasive pattern.

Number of Feet   Poetic meter is measured in *feet*, units of stressed and unstressed syllables. A line of poetry may be written in *monometer* (having one foot), *dimeter* (two feet), *trimeter* (three feet), *tetrameter* (four feet), *pentameter* (five feet), *hexameter* (six feet), and so on.

Kinds of Feet   The syllables in a line can occur in regular patterns. The most common pattern for poetry written in English is **iambic**, an unstressed syllable (˘) followed by a stressed one (´):

My mĭs | tress' eýes | are nó | thing líke | the sún

This line is written in *iambic pentameter*: it has five iambic feet.

Three other meters are of some importance in English poetry:

trochaic (a stressed syllable followed by an unstressed one):

Téll me | nót in | moúrn ful | núm bers

anapestic (two unstressed syllables followed by a stressed one):

'Twas the níght | be fore Chríst | mas and áll | through the house

dactylic (a stressed syllable followed by two unstressed ones):

Híg gle dy | píg gle dy | Prés i dent | Jéff er son

Robert Frost's "The Silken Tent" (page 483) is an intriguing example of a modern Shakespearean sonnet.

The Italian sonnet, not too common in English poetry, uses fewer rhymes (five) and has only two groupings of lines, the first eight called the *octave*, and the last six the *sestet*. Frost has created a chilling Italian sonnet in "Design" (page 553).

Free Verse   A poem written in *open form* generally has no rhyme scheme and no basic meter for the entire selection. Rhyme and rhythm do occur, of course, but not in the fixed patterns that are required of stanzas and sonnets. Many readers think that open form poetry is easy to write, but that is not the case. Only careless poetry is easy to write, and even closed forms can be sloppily written. Open forms demand their own special arrangements; without the fixed patterns of traditional forms to guide them, modern poets must discover these structures on their own. Walt Whitman's "A Noiseless Patient Spider" (page 483) demonstrates how open form still uses sound and rhythm to create tone, enhance meaning, and guide the responses of the reader.

Poetic Syntax

Rhyme, rhythm, and stanza are not the only resources of form available to poets. Writers can also manipulate the way the words are arranged into sentences. For instance, the short, staccato sentences of "We Real Cool" (pages 499 – 500) impress us in a way entirely different from the effect of the intricate expression of "The Silken Tent" (page 483), which is a single sentence stretching over fourteen lines. Words in English sentences must be arranged in fairly standard patterns. If we reverse the order of "John struck the ball" to "The ball struck John," the words take on a new meaning altogether. As with stanza form and rhyme scheme, poets can either stick with the rigidity of English sentence structure (syntax) or try to achieve unusual effects through inversion. e. e. cummings, for example, forces his readers to pay close attention to the line "anyone lived in a pretty how town" by rearranging the words in an unexpected way. (In the standard pattern of an exclamation, the line would read "How pretty a town anyone lived in!")

Looking at the Forms of Poetry

The following poems illustrate many of the variations of sound and organization that we have just discussed. As you read these poems, be alert for the special effects that the poets create with rhythm, rhyme, stanza form, and syntax. You may have to read some selections several times to appreciate how thoroughly form and meaning work together.

Gwendolyn Brooks *1917–*

WE REAL COOL

The Pool Players
Seven at the Golden Shovel

We real cool. We
Left school. We

Lurk late. We
Strike straight. We

Sing sin. We
Thin gin. We

Jazz June. We
Die soon.

(1960)

A. E. Housman *1859–1936*

EIGHT O'CLOCK

He stood, and heard the steeple
      Sprinkle the quarters on the morning town.
One, two, three, four, to market-place and people
      It tossed them down.

Strapped, noosed, nighing his hour,
      He stood and counted them and cursed his luck;
And then the clock collected in the tower
      Its strength, and struck.

(1922)

e. e. cummings *1894–1962*

anyone lived in a pretty how town

anyone lived in a pretty how town
(with up so floating many bells down)
spring summer autumn winter
he sang his didn't he danced his did.

Women and men(both little and small)
cared for anyone not at all
they sowed their isn't they reaped their same
sun moon stars rain

children guessed (but only a few
and down they forgot as up they grew   10
autumn winter spring summer)
that noone loved him more by more

when by now and tree by leaf
she laughed his joy she cried his grief
bird by snow and stir by still
anyone's any was all to her

someones married their everyones
laughed their cryings and did their dance
(sleep wake hope and then) they
said their nevers they slept their dream   20

stars rain sun moon
(and only the snow can begin to explain
how children are apt to forget to remember
with up so floating many bells down)

one day anyone died i guess
(and noone stooped to kiss his face)
busy folk buried them side by side
little by little and was by was

all by all and deep by deep
and more by more they dream their sleep   30
noone and anyone earth by april
wish by spirit and if by yes.

Women and men (both dong and ding)
summer autumn winter spring
reaped their sowing and went their came
sun moon stars rain

     (1940)

Wole Soyinka *1934–*

TELEPHONE CONVERSATION

The price seemed reasonable, location
Indifferent. The landlady swore she lived
Off premises. Nothing remained
But self-confession. 'Madam,' I warned,
'I hate a wasted journey—I am African.'
Silence. Silenced transmission of
Pressurized good-breeding. Voice, when it came,
Lipstick coated, long gold-rolled
Cigarette-holder pipped. Caught I was, foully.
'HOW DARK?' . . . I had not misheard . . . 'ARE YOU LIGHT   10
OR VERY DARK?' Button B. Button A. Stench
Of rancid breath of public hide-and-speak.
Red booth. Red pillar-box. Red double-tiered
Omnibus squelching tar. It *was* real! Shamed
By ill-mannered silence, surrender
Pushed dumbfoundment to beg simplification.
Considerate she was, varying the emphasis—
'ARE YOU DARK? OR VERY LIGHT?' Revelation came.
'You mean—like plain or milk chocolate?'
Her assent was clinical, crushing in its light
Impersonality. Rapidly, wave-length adjusted,   20
I chose. 'West African sepia'—and as afterthought,
'Down in my passport.' Silence for spectroscopic
Flight of fancy, till truthfulness clanged her accent

Hard on the mouthpiece. 'WHAT'S THAT?' conceding
'DON'T KNOW WHAT THAT IS.' 'Like brunette.'
'THAT'S DARK, ISN'T IT?' 'Not altogether.
Facially, I am brunette, but madam, you should see
The rest of me. Palm of my hand, soles of my feet
Are a peroxide blond. Friction, caused —   30
Foolishly madam — by sitting down, has turned
My bottom raven black — One moment madam!' — sensing
Her receiver rearing on the thunderclap
About my ears — 'Madam,' I pleaded, 'wouldn't you rather
See for yourself?'
                                                                   (1960)

Arthur W. Monks

TWILIGHT'S LAST GLEAMING

Higgledy-piggledy
President Jefferson
Gave up the ghost on the
Fourth of July.

So did John Adams, which
Shows that such patriots
Propagandistically
Knew how to die.

                                                                   (1967)

William Wordsworth *(1770–1850)*

NUNS FRET NOT

Nuns fret not at their convent's narrow room;
And hermits are contented with their cells;
And students with their pensive citadels;
Maids at the wheel, the weaver at his loom,
Sit blithe and happy; bees that soar for bloom,
High as the highest Peak of Furness-fells,[1]
Will murmur by the hour in foxglove bells:[2]
In truth the prison, unto which we doom
Ourselves, no prison is: and hence for me,
In sundry moods, 'twas pastime to be bound   10

[1]mountains near Wordsworth's home.
[2]wild flowers.

Within the sonnet's scanty plot of ground;
Pleased if some souls (for such there needs must be)
Who have felt the weight of too much liberty,
Should find brief solace there, as I have found.

(1807)

Prewriting

Writing about poetic form is challenging. Because it is impossible to separate form from meaning, you must be sure that you understand what a poem says before you try to analyze how its formal characteristics contribute to your understanding and appreciation. In completing the following exercises, you should read the poems aloud, if possible, and reread the difficult passages a number of times before you decide upon your answers.

Experimenting with Poetic Forms

1. Write out the following poem, filling in the blanks with one of the choices given in parentheses to the right of each line. Use sound, rhyme, and context to determine your choices.

The Death of the Ball Turret Gunner

From my mother's _____ I fell into the State, (womb, sleep)
And I _____ in its belly till my wet   (hunched, crouched)
    _____ froze.   (skin, fur)
Six miles from earth, _____ from its   (freed, loosed)
    dream of life,
I woke to black flak and the _____   (loud, nightmare)
    fighters.
When I died they _____ me out of the   (washed, flushed)
    turret with a _____.   (mop, hose)

Now turn to page 584 and compare your choices with the poet's. Can you explain why each word was chosen?

2. Examine "We Real Cool" by Gwendolyn Brooks (page 499). How would you describe the rhythm of this poem? How does the rhythm affect your perception of the speakers (the "We" of the poem)? Why are all the sentences in the last four stanzas only three words long? What is the effect of placing the subject of those sentences ("We") at the ends of the lines?

3. Look at the alliteration in "Eight O'Clock" by A. E. Housman (page 500). What events or feelings are emphasized by alliteration? How do other elements of form — rhyme, stress, stanza pattern — influence the tone and point of the brief drama described in the

poem? Write an objective account of the events in "Eight O'Clock."
What did you have to leave out of your account?

4. Study the rhyme schemes and line variations of the following
   poems, all of which are written in quatrains:

   "Eight O'Clock" (page 500)   "My Son My Executioner"
   "London" (page 524)   (page 483)
   "anyone lived in a pretty   "One Perfect Rose (page 467)
      how town" (page 500)   "Piano" (page 560)
   "A Valediction: Forbidding Mourning" (page 519)

   In which of the poems do the stanza divisions indicate a change of
   time or the beginning of a new point? Do any of the poets
   disregard the stanza patterns? Try to decide why all of these poets
   used quatrains.

5. Complete as many of the following quatrains as you can by
   supplying a last line. Try to write a line that puts a picture in the
   reader's mind.

   > She even thinks that up in heaven
   >   Her class lies late and snores,
   > While poor black cherubs rise at seven
   >   _____.

   > The golf links lie so near the mill
   >   That almost every day
   > The laboring children can look out
   >   _____.

   > As I walked out one evening,
   >   Walking down Bristol Street,
   > The crowds upon the pavement
   >   _____.

   > Whose woods these are I think I know.
   > His house is in the village though;
   > He will not see me stopping here
   >   _____.

   Compare your creations with the originals, which your teacher can
   supply.

6. Rewrite the following lines—from "The Unknown Citizen" and
   "anyone lived in a pretty how town"—putting them in the word
   order you would ordinarily expect them to follow:

   > For in everything he did he served the Greater Community.

   > Except for the War till the day he retired
   > He worked in a factory. . . .

   > anyone lived in a pretty how town
   > (with up so floating many bells down)

> Women and men (both little and small)
> cared for anyone not at all

7. Ogden Nash was the whimsical master of outrageous rhymes and comical couplets. Often playful and nonsensical, Nash's verse could also be pointed and critical. Read the following rhymed couplets by Ogden Nash and then try to imitate them. In writing your own couplets you will probably want to follow Nash's practice of using a title to set up the theme of your two-line commentaries.

> ### Common Sense
> Why did the Lord give us agility
> If not to evade responsibility?

> ### The Cow
> The cow is of the bovine ilk;
> One end is moo, the other, milk.

> ### Reflection on Ingenuity
> Here's a good rule of thumb:
> Too clever is dumb.

> ### The Parent
> Children aren't happy with nothing to ignore,
> And that's what parents were created for.

> ### Grandpa Is Ashamed
> A child need not be very clever
> To learn that "Later, dear" means "Never."

Writing

Since rhythm, rhyme, syntax, and stanza convey no meaning in themselves, you probably will not write an entire essay on form alone. Instead you can use what you have learned about poetic form to help you analyze and interpret a poem (or poems) with greater understanding and confidence.

Relating Form to Theme

You can use observations about form to confirm and develop your ideas about the meaning or theme of a poem. Looking at a poem's formal characteristics will help you to answer such important questions as these: What is the tone? Is the speaker being ironic? What are the key words and images? And how does the main idea advance through the poem?

Specifically, elements of form offer clues like these:

1. Close, obvious rhyme often indicates a comic or ironic tone. Subtle rhymes support more serious tones.

2. Heavy stress can be humorous, but it can also suggest anger, defiance, strength, or fear.

3. Alliteration can be humorous, but it can also be chillingly serious; it serves to provide emphasis by slowing the reading of the line.

4. Assonance can provide a rich, solemn effect, a certain grandeur perhaps, or even a sensuous effect.

5. Rhythm and repetition emphasize key words.

6. Stanzas and rhyme schemes mark out patterns of thought and can serve as guides to development of theme.

7. Important images are often underscored with rhyme and stress.

8. Syntax calls attention to complex ideas.

9. A combination of elements can indicate a change in speaker or a shift in tone or thought.

10. Typographical effects can call attention to significant feelings or ideas.

This list does not exhaust the possibilities, but it should alert you to the various ways that form relates to thought and meaning in poetry.

Ideas for Writing
Ideas for Expressive Writing

1. **Write an original haiku.**
   A *haiku* is a rhymeless Japanese poem. Its form is based on syllables: seventeen syllables usually arranged in three lines, often following a pattern of five, seven, and five. Haiku written in English, however, do not always follow the original Japanese syllable pattern and may even be rhymed. Because of their brevity, haiku compress their expression by focusing on images and letting the closely observed details suggest the feelings and meanings. The following haiku, some translated from Japanese originals and some written in English, provide a variety of models for you to follow:

> The piercing chill I feel:
>   my dead wife's comb, in our bedroom,
>   under my heel . . .
>   —*Taniguchi Buson* (trans. *Harold G. Henderson*)

> Sprayed with strong poison
>   my roses are crisp this year
> in the crystal vase.
>   —*Paul Goodman*

> the old woman holds
> lilac buds
> to her good ear
> > —*Raymond Roseliep*

> Heat-lightning streak—
> through darkness pierces
> the heron's shriek.
> > —*Matsuo Basho*

Notice that the images in these haiku convey strong sensory experiences implying a great deal more than a mere description would suggest.

2. **Write an original limerick.**
The *limerick* is a form of humorous verse popularized in the nineteenth century by Englishman Edward Lear. Its form is fairly simple—a five-line stanza built on two rhymes (*a a b b a*) with the third and fourth lines one beat shorter than the other three. The meter (or rhythm pattern) usually involves two unstressed syllables followed by an accented syllable, giving the lines a kind of playful skipping or jogging sound when they are recited or read aloud.

Lear's limericks depended on a curious or fantastic "plot" for their effects:

> There was a Young Lady whose chin
> Resembled the point of a pin;
> > So she had it made sharp
> > And purchased a harp,
> And played several tunes with her chin.

More contemporary limericks take delight in giving the last line an extra twist with a surprise rhyme or an absurd idea. Some modern limericks make their point by using outrageous spellings or tricks of typography:

> There was a young fellow named Tate
> Who dined with his girl at 8.8,
> > But I'd hate to relate
> > What that person named Tate
> And his tête-à-tête ate at 8.8.
> > —*Carolyn Wells*

> There was a young lady of Warwick,
> Who lived in a castle histarwick,
> > On the damp castle mould
> > She contracted a could,
> And the doctor prescribed paregarwick.
> > —*Anonymous*

These often ingenious and slightly mad little verses continue to entertain readers and writers alike.

Wear and Tear
There was an old man of the Cape,
Who made himself garments of crêpe.
When asked, "Do they tear?"
He replied, "Here and there,
But they're perfectly splendid for shape!"

—*Robert Louis Stevenson*

There was a young virgin named Wilde,
Who kept herself quite undefiled,
By thinking of Jesus,
Contagious diseases,
And the bother of having a child.

—*Anonymous*

Ideas for Critical Writing

1. Show how rhythm, repetition, and rhyme affect the tone and meaning in "We Real Cool" and "Eight O'Clock." Are the effects the same in both poems?

2. Write an interpretation of "anyone lived in a pretty how town" or "Telephone Conversation." Give particular attention to the way that meter, rhyme, alliteration, syntax, and stanza form contribute to your understanding of the poem.

3. Explain the humorous use of language and poetic form in "Twilight's Last Gleaming."

4. Analyze the series of metaphors in "Nuns Fret Not." What is Wordsworth saying about writing sonnets and using traditional closed forms of poetry?

5. Compare one of Shakespeare's sonnets (page 482 or page 516) with a modern sonnet, such as Frost's "Design" (page 553) or Dudley Randall's "To the Mercy Killers" (page 584). Why do the modern poems *not* seem like sonnets? Pay close attention to the syntax and the way the rhyme scheme subdivides each poem.

Rewriting: Style

As a writer, you must choose your words carefully. Many English words are to some extent synonymous, even interchangeable, but often the distinctions between synonyms are as important as their similarities. "The difference between the right word and the almost right word," said Mark Twain, "is the difference between lightning and the lightning bug." When you revise your essay, focus on the accuracy and precision of the words you use.

Finding the Exact Word

You must take care that both the denotations and connotations of the words you use are the ones you intend. You do not want to write *heroics* when you really mean *heroism*. You do not want to "*expose* three main topics" when you really intend to *explore* them. Here are some problem areas to consider as you look at the words you have used in your essay:

1. **Distinguish among synonyms.**
   Exact writing demands that you choose among different shades of meaning. Although *feeling* and *sensation* are synonyms, they are certainly not interchangeable. Neither are *funny* and *laughable* or *famous* and *notorious*. Consult your dictionary for help in choosing the word that says exactly what you mean.

Exercise on Diction

Explain the differences in meaning among the following groups of words and phrases:
   a. a *renowned* politician, a *famous* politician, a *notorious* politician
   b. an *indifferent* parent, a *detached* parent, an *unconcerned* parent
   c. to *condone* an action, to *excuse* an action, to *forgive* an action
   d. *pilfer, steal, rob, burglarize, loot, ransack*
   e. an *apparent* error, a *visible* error, an *egregious* error
   f. a *proud* person, a *pompous* person, an *arrogant* person

2. **Watch out for words with similar sound or spelling.**
   Homonyms (words that have the same pronunciation but different meanings and different spellings) are sometimes a source of confusion. The student who wrote that a song conveyed the composer's "piece of mind" let the sound of the word override her knowledge of spelling and meaning. Words that are similar in sound and spelling can also be confusing. If you are not careful, you can easily confuse *eminent* with *imminent* or write *quiet* when you mean *quite*.

Exercise on Diction

Explain the difference in meaning in the following pairs of words:
   a. apprise, appraise
   b. anecdote, antidote
   c. chord, cord
   d. elicit, illicit
   e. martial, marital
   f. statue, statute
   g. human, humane

   h. lose, loose
   i. idol, idle
   j. accept, except
   k. simple, simplistic
   l. beside, besides
   m. isle, aisle
   n. weather, whether
   o. incidence, incident

3. **Choose the precise adjective form.**
   Many words have two or more adjective forms: a *questioning* remark is not the same as a *questionable* remark. As with homonyms and other words that sound alike, do not let the similarity in spelling and pronunciation mislead you.

Exercise on Diction

Point out the connotative differences in meaning in the following pairs of adjectives:
   a. an intelligible essay, an intelligent essay
   b. a hateful sibling, a hated sibling
   c. a likely roommate, a likable roommate
   d. an informed speaker, an informative speaker
   e. a workable thesis, a working thesis
   f. a liberal man, a liberated man

4. **Watch out for malapropisms.**
   Misused words are often unintentionally funny. These humorous confusions and near-misses are called malapropisms. You may get a laugh from your readers if you write "My car insurance collapsed last week," but you will not be impressing them with your command of the language.

Exercise on Diction

In the following sentences, what do you think the writer probably meant to say?
   a. He has only a *supercilious* knowledge of the subject.
   b. She was the *pineapple* of perfection.
   c. They burned the *refuge.*
   d. He passed his civil service *eliminations.*
   e. They are in for a *shrewd* awakening.

5. **Be sure the words fit the context.**
   Sentences can be unclear if all the words do not have the same emotional associations. For instance, "The thief brandished his gun

and angrily requested the money" is confusing because *brandished* and *angrily* suggest a different emotion from *requested*.

Exercise on Diction

Explain why the italicized words are inappropriate in the following sentences. What words would you use as replacements?

a. Her *stubbornness* in the face of danger saved our lives.
b. The use of violence to obtain a goal is too *poignantly* barbaric for most people to *sympathize* with.
c. The mob shouted in *displeasure*.

Anthology of Poetry

Anonymous *(English lyric)*

WESTERN WIND

Western wind, when wilt thou blow,
The small rain down can rain?
Christ, if my love were in my arms
And I in my bed again!

(ca. 1500)

Thomas Wyatt *1503–1542*

THEY FLEE FROM ME

They flee from me, that sometime did me seek,
With naked foot, stalking in my chamber:
I have seen them gentle, tame, and meek,
That now are wild, and do not remember
That sometime they put themselves in danger
To take bread at my hand; and now they range,
Busily seeking with a continual change.

Thankéd be fortune, it hath been otherwise
Twenty times better; but once, in special,
In thin array, after a pleasant guise,
When her loose gown from her shoulders did fall,
And she me caught in her arms long and small,

10

513

Therewithal sweetly did me kiss,
And softly said, "Dear heart, how like you this?"

It was no dream; I lay broad waking.
But all is turned, thorough my gentleness,
Into a strange fashion of forsaking;
And I have leave to go of her goodness,
And she also to use new-fangleness.
But since that I so kindely am served,   20
I would fain know what she hath deserved.

                                                   (ca. 1535)

Christopher Marlowe *1564–1593*

THE PASSIONATE SHEPHERD TO HIS LOVE

Come live with me and be my love,
And we will all the pleasures prove,
That valleys, groves, hills and fields,
Woods, or steepy mountain yields.

And we will sit upon the rocks,
And see the shepherds feed their flocks,
By shallow rivers to whose falls
Melodious birds sing madrigals.

And I will make thee beds of roses
With a thousand fragrant posies,   10
A cap of flowers, and a kirtle
Embroidered all with leaves of myrtle;

A gown made of the finest wool
Which from our pretty lambs we pull;
Fair lined slippers for the cold,
With buckles of the purest gold;

A belt of straw and ivy buds,
With coral clasps and amber studs:
And if these pleasures may thee move,
Come live with me and be my love.   20

The shepherds' swains shall dance and sing
For thy delight each May morning:
If these delights thy mind may move,
Then live with me and be my love.

                                                     (1600)

Sir Walter Raleigh *1552?–1618*

THE NYMPH'S REPLY TO THE SHEPHERD

If all the world and love were young,
And truth in every shepherd's tongue,
These pretty pleasures might me move,
To live with thee, and be thy love.

Time drives the flocks from field to fold,
When rivers rage, and rocks grow cold,
And Philomel becometh dumb,
The rest complains of cares to come.

The flowers do fade, and wanton fields,
To wayward winter reckoning yields,   10
A honey tongue, a heart of gall,
Is fancy's spring, but sorrow's fall.

Thy gowns, thy shoes, thy beds of roses,
Thy cap, thy kirtle, and thy posies,
Soon break, soon wither, soon forgotten:
In folly ripe, in reason rotten.

Thy belt of straw and ivy buds,
Thy coral clasps and amber studs,
All these in me no means can move,
To come to thee, and be thy love.   20

But could youth last, and love still breed,
Had joys no date, nor age no need,
Then these delights my mind might move,
To live with thee and be thy love.

(1600)

William Shakespeare *1564–1616*

LET ME NOT TO THE MARRIAGE OF TRUE MINDS

Let me not to the marriage of true minds
Admit impediments. Love is not love
Which alters when it alteration finds,
Or bends with the remover to remove:
O, no! it is an ever-fixéd mark
That looks on tempests and is never shaken;
It is the star to every wandering bark,
Whose worth's unknown, although his height be taken.

Love's not Time's fool, though rosy lips and cheeks
Within his bending sickle's compass come;   10
Love alters not with his brief hours and weeks,
But bears it out even to the edge of doom.
If this be error and upon me proved,
I never writ, nor no man ever loved.

(1609)

THAT TIME OF YEAR THOU MAYST IN ME BEHOLD

That time of year thou mayst in me behold
When yellow leaves, or none, or few, do hang
Upon those boughs which shake against the cold,
Bare ruined choirs, where late the sweet birds sang.
In me thou see'st the twilight of such day
As after sunset fadeth in the west,
Which by and by black night doth take away,
Death's second self that seals up all in rest.
In me thou see'st the glowing of such fire,
That on the ashes of his youth doth lie,   10
As the death-bed, whereon it must expire
Consumed with that which it was nourished by.
This thou perceiv'st, which makes thy love more strong
To love that well, which thou must leave ere long.

(1609)

MY MISTRESS' EYES ARE NOTHING LIKE THE SUN

My mistress' eyes are nothing like the sun;
Coral is far more red than her lips' red;
If snow be white, why then her breasts are dun;
If hairs be wires, black wires grow on her head.
I have seen roses damask'd, red and white,
But no such roses see I in her cheeks,
And in some perfumes there is more delight
Than in the breath that from my mistress reeks.
I love to hear her speak, yet well I know
That music hath a far more pleasing sound.   10
I grant I never saw a goddess go;
My mistress, when she walks, treads on the ground:
And yet, by heaven, I think my love as rare
As any she belied with false compare.

(1609)

TWO LOVES I HAVE OF COMFORT
AND DESPAIR

Two loves I have of comfort and despair,
Which like two spirits do suggest me still:
The better angel is a man right fair,
The worser spirit a woman colored ill.
To win me soon to hell, my female evil
Tempteth my better angel from my side,
And would corrupt my saint to be a devil,
Wooing his purity with her foul pride.
And whether that my angel be turn'd fiend,
Suspect I may, yet not directly tell,   10
But being both from me, both to each friend,
I guess one angel in another's hell.
Yet this shall I ne'er know but live in doubt,
Till my bad angel fire my good one out.

(1609)

John Donne *1572–1631*

SONG

Go and catch a falling star,
    Get with child a mandrake root,
Tell me where all past years are,
    Or who cleft the devil's foot,
Teach me to hear mermaids singing,
Or to keep off envy's stinging,
      And find
      What wind
Serves to advance an honest mind.

If thou be'st born to strange sights,   10
    Things invisible to see,
Ride ten thousand days and nights,
    Till age snow white hairs on thee.
Thou, when thou return'st, wilt tell me,
All strange wonders that befell thee,
      And swear,
      No where
Lives a woman true and fair.

If thou find'st one, let me know;
    Such a pilgrimage were sweet.   20
Yet do not, I would not go,
    Though at next door we might meet:

Though she were true when you met her,
And last till you write your letter,
    Yet she
    Will be
False, ere I come, to two or three.

(1633)

THE BAIT

Come live with me, and be my love,
And we will some new pleasures prove,[1]
Of golden sands, and crystal brooks,
With silken lines, and silver hooks.

There will the river whispering run,
Warmed by thy eyes more than the sun.
And there th' enamoured fish will stay,
Begging themselves they may betray.

When thou wilt swim in that live bath,
Each fish, which every channel hath,   10
Will amorously to thee swim,
Gladder to catch thee, than thou him.

If thou, to be so seen, beest loath,
By sun or moon, thou dark'nest both;
And if myself have leave to see,
I need not their light, having thee.

Let others freeze with angling reeds,
And cut their legs with shells and weeds,
Or treacherously poor fish beset
With strangling snare, or windowy net.   20

Let coarse bold hands from slimy nest
The bedded fish in banks out-wrest,
Or curious traitors, sleave-silk flies,
Bewitch poor fishes' wandering eyes.

For thee, thou need'st no such deceit,
For thou thyself art thine own bait;
That fish that is not catched thereby,
Alas, is wiser far than I.

(1633)

[1]Test.

A VALEDICTION: FORBIDDING MOURNING

As virtuous men pass mildly away,
 And whisper to their souls, to go,
Whilst some of their sad friends do say,
 The breath goes now, and some say, no:

So let us melt, and make no noise,
 No tear-floods, nor sigh-tempests move,
T'were profanation of our joys
 To tell the laity our love.

Moving of th' earth brings harms and fears,
 Men reckon what it did and meant,   10
But trepidation of the spheres,
 Though greater far, is innocent.

Dull sublunary lovers' love
 (Whose soul is sense) cannot admit
Absence, because it doth remove
 Those things which elemented it.

But we by a love, so much refined
 That our selves know not what it is,
Inter-assuréd of the mind,
 Care less, eyes, lips, and hands to miss.   20

Our two souls therefore, which are one,
 Though I must go, endure not yet
A breach, but an expansion,
 Like gold to airy thinness beat.

If they be two, they are two so
 As stiff twin compasses are two,
Thy soul, the fixt foot, makes no show
 To move, but doth, if th' other do.

And though it in the center sit,
 Yet when the other far doth roam,   30
It leans, and hearkens after it,
 And grows erect, as that comes home.

Such wilt thou be to me, who must
 Like th' other foot, obliquely run;
Thy firmness makes my circle just,
 And makes me end, where I begun.

                (1633)

DEATH BE NOT PROUD

Death, be not proud, though some have calléd thee
Mighty and dreadful, for thou art not so,

For those whom thou think'st thou dost overthrow
Die not, poor Death, nor yet canst thou kill me.
From rest and sleep, which but thy pictures be,
Much pleasure, then from thee much more must flow;
And soonest our best men with thee do go —
Rest of their bones and souls' delivery!
Thou'rt slave to fate, chance, kings, and desperate men,
And dost with poison, war, and sickness dwell,   10
And poppy or charms can make us sleep as well,
And better than thy stroke; why swell'st thou then?
One short sleep past, we wake eternally,
And death shall be no more: Death, thou shalt die!

(1633)

Richard Lovelace *1618–1657*

TO LUCASTA, ON GOING TO THE WARS

Tell me not, sweet, I am unkind,
    That from the nunnery
Of thy chaste breast and quiet mind
    To war and arms I fly.

True, a new mistress now I chase,
    The first foe in the field;
And with a stronger faith embrace
    A sword, a horse, a shield.

Yet this inconstancy is such
    As thou too shalt adore;   10
I could not love thee, dear, so much,
    Loved I not honor more.

(1649)

Andrew Marvell *1621–1678*

TO HIS COY MISTRESS

Had we but world enough, and time,
This coyness,[1] lady, were no crime.
We would sit down, and think which way

[1]Modesty, reluctance.

To walk, and pass our long love's day.
Thou by the Indian Ganges' side
Shouldst rubies find: I by the tide
Of Humber[2] would complain. I would
Love you ten years before the Flood:
And you should if you please refuse
Till the conversion of the Jews. 10
My vegetable love should grow
Vaster than empires, and more slow.
An hundred years should go to praise
Thine eyes, and on thy forehead gaze.
Two hundred to adore each breast:
But thirty thousand to the rest.
An age at least to every part,
And the last age should show your heart.
For, lady, you deserve this state;
Nor would I love at lower rate. 20
    But at my back I always hear
Time's wingéd chariot hurrying near:
And yonder all before us lie
Deserts of vast eternity.
Thy beauty shall no more be found,
Nor, in thy marble vault, shall sound
My echoing song; then worms shall try
That long preserved virginity:
And your quaint honour turn to dust;
And into ashes all my lust. 30
The grave's a fine and private place,
But none, I think, do there embrace.
    Now therefore, while the youthful hue
Sits on thy skin like morning dew,
And while thy willing soul transpires
At every pore with instant fires,
Now let us sport us while we may;
And now, like am'rous birds of prey,
Rather at once our time devour,
Than languish in his slow-chapped[3] pow'r. 40
Let us roll all our strength, and all
Our sweetness, up into one ball:
And tear our pleasures with rough strife,
Through the iron gates of life.
Thus, though we cannot make our sun
Stand still, yet we will make him run.

(1681)

[2]A river in northern England.
[3]Slow-chewing.

Anne Finch, Countess of Winchilsea *1661–1720*

THE INTRODUCTION[1]

Did I my lines intend for public view,
How many censures would their faults pursue!
Some would, because such words they do affect,
Cry they're insipid, empty, uncorrect.
And many have attained, dull and untaught,
The name of wit, only by finding fault.
True judges might condemn their want of wit;
And all might say, they're by a woman writ.
Alas! a woman that attempts the pen,
Such an intruder on the rights of men,   10
Such a presumptuous creature is esteemed,
The fault can by no virtue be redeemed.
They tell us we mistake our sex and way;
Good breeding, fashion, dancing, dressing, play
Are the accomplishments we should desire;
To write, or read, or think, or to enquire,
Would cloud our beauty, and exhaust our time,
And interrupt the conquests of our prime;
Whilst the dull manage of a servile house
Is held by some our utmost art and use.   20
    Sure 'twas not ever thus, nor are we told
Fables, of women that excelled of old;
To whom, by the diffusive hand of heaven,
Some share of wit and poetry was given.
On that glad day on which the Ark[2] returned,
The holy pledge for which the land had mourned,
The joyful tribes attend it on the way,
The Levites do the sacred charge convey,
Whilst various instruments before it play;
Here holy virgins in the concert join,   30
The louder notes to soften and refine,
And with alternate verse complete the hymn divine.
    Lo! the young poet,[3] after God's own heart,
By Him inspired and taught the Muses' art,
Returned from conquest a bright chorus meets.
That sing his slain ten thousand in the streets.
In such loud numbers they his acts declare,
Proclaim the wonders of his early war,

---

[1]The poem reprinted here is the introduction to a longer work in which the poet continues her argument that the talents of women should not be suppressed. Her biblical examples are designed to counter the common practice in her day of using biblical texts to keep women subservient to men.
[2]The biblical Ark of the Covenant, a sacred relic containing the Ten Commandments.
[3]David, King of Israel and Judah.

That Saul upon the vast applause does frown,
And feels its mighty thunder shake the crown. 40
What can the threatened judgment now prolong?[4]
Half of the kingdom is already gone;
The fairest half, whose judgment guides the rest,
Have David's empire o'er their hearts confessed.
   A woman here leads fainting Israel on,
She fights, she wins, she triumphs with a song.[5]
Devout, majestic, for the subject fit,
And far above her arms, exalts her wit,
Then to the peaceful, shady palm withdraws,
And rules the rescued nation with her laws. 50
   How are we fallen! fallen by mistaken rules,
And education's, more than nature's fools;
Debarred from all improvements of the mind,
And to be dull, expected and designed;[6]
And if some one would soar above the rest,
With warmer fancy and ambition pressed,
So strong the opposing faction still appears,
The hopes to thrive can ne'er outweigh the fears.
Be cautioned, then, my Muse, and still retired;
Nor be despised, aiming to be admired; 60
Conscious of wants, still with contracted wing,
To some few friends and to thy sorrows sing.
For groves of laurel thou wert never meant;
Be dark enough thy shades, and be thou there content.

(1689?)

William Blake *1757–1827*

THE LAMB

From SONGS OF INNOCENCE

Little Lamb, who made thee?
Dost thou know who made thee?
Gave thee life, and bid thee feed
By the stream and o'er the mead;
Gave thee clothing of delight,
Softest clothing, wooly, bright;
Gave thee such a tender voice,
Making all the vales rejoice?
     Little Lamb, who made thee?
     Dost thou know who made thee? 10

---

[4]*Prolong*: hold off.
[5]Deborah, prophet and judge, won a victory for the Lord and sang His praises.
[6]*Designed*: as intended.

Little Lamb, I'll tell thee,
Little Lamb, I'll tell thee:
He is calléd by thy name,
For he calls himself a Lamb.
He is meek, and he is mild;
He became a little child.
I a child, and thou a lamb,
We are calléd by his name.
    Little Lamb, God bless thee!
    Little Lamb, God bless thee!   20
                                      (1789)

THE TYGER

From SONGS OF EXPERIENCE

Tyger, Tyger, burning bright
In the forests of the night,
What immortal hand or eye
Could frame thy fearful symmetry?

In what distant deeps or skies
Burnt the fire of thine eyes?
On what wings dare he aspire?
What the hand dare seize the fire?

And what shoulder and what art
Could twist the sinews of thy heart?   10
And, when thy heart began to beat,
What dread hand? and what dread feet?

What the hammer? What the chain?
In what furnace was thy brain?
What the anvil? What dread grasp
Dare its deadly terrors clasp?

When the stars threw down their spears,
And watered heaven with their tears,
Did He smile his work to see?
Did He who made the lamb make thee?   20

Tyger, Tyger, burning bright
In the forests of the night,
What immortal hand or eye
Dare frame thy fearful symmetry?

                                      (1794)

LONDON

I wander through each chartered street,
Near where the chartered Thames does flow,

And mark in every face I meet
Marks of weakness, marks of woe.

In every cry of every man,
In every infant's cry of fear,
In every voice, in every ban,
The mind-forged manacles I hear.

How the Chimney-sweeper's cry
Every black'ning church appalls;   10
And the hapless soldier's sigh
Runs in blood down palace walls.

But most through midnight streets I hear
How the youthful harlot's curse
Blasts the new-born infant's tear,
And blights with plagues the marriage hearse.

(1794)

THE GARDEN OF LOVE

I went to the Garden of Love,
And saw what I never had seen:
A Chapel was built in the midst,
Where I used to play on the green.

And the gates of this Chapel were shut,
And "Thou shalt not" writ over the door;
So I turned to the Garden of Love
That so many sweet flowers bore;

And I saw it was filled with graves,
And tombstones where flowers should be;   10
And priests in black gowns were walking their rounds,
And binding with briars my joys and desires.

(1794)

William Wordsworth *1770–1850*

THE WORLD IS TOO MUCH WITH US

The world is too much with us; late and soon,
Getting and spending, we lay waste our powers;
Little we see in Nature that is ours;
We have given our hearts away, a sordid boon![1]
This Sea that bares her bosom to the moon,

[1]Blessing.

The winds that will be howling at all hours,
And are up-gathered now like sleeping flowers,
For this, for everything, we are out of tune;
It moves us not. — Great God! I'd rather be
A Pagan suckled in a creed outworn;   10
So might I, standing on this pleasant lea,[2]
Have glimpses that would make me less forlorn;
Have sight of Proteus[3] rising from the sea;
Or hear old Triton[4] blow his wreathéd horn.

(1807)

Samuel Taylor Coleridge *1772–1834*

KUBLA KHAN

In Xanadu did Kubla Khan
  A stately pleasure-dome decree:
Where Alph, the sacred river, ran
Through caverns measureless to man
  Down to a sunless sea.
So twice five miles of fertile ground
With walls and towers were girdled round:
And there were gardens bright with sinuous rills
Where blossomed many an incense-bearing tree;
And here were forests ancient as the hills,   10
Enfolding sunny spots of greenery.

But O, that deep romantic chasm which slanted
Down the green hill athwart a cedarn cover![1]
A savage place! as holy and enchanted
As e'er beneath a waning moon was haunted
By woman wailing for her demon-lover!
And from this chasm, with ceaseless turmoil seething
As if this earth in fast thick pants were breathing,
A mighty fountain momently[2] was forced;
Amid whose swift half-intermitted burst   20
Huge fragments vaulted like rebounding hail,
Or chaffy grain beneath the thresher's flail:
And 'mid these dancing rocks at once and ever
It flung up momently the sacred river.
Five miles meandering with a mazy motion
Through wood and dale the sacred river ran,

---

[2]Meadow.
[3]A sea god who could change shape.
[4]A sea god whose top half was man and bottom half fish.
[1]Across a cedar woods.
[2]Every moment.

Then reached the caverns measureless to man,
And sank in tumult to a lifeless ocean:
And 'mid this tumult Kubla heard from far
Ancestral voices prophesying war!   30
    The shadow of the dome of pleasure
      Floated midway on the waves;
    Where was heard the mingled measure
      From the fountain and the caves.
It was a miracle of rare device,
A sunny pleasure-dome with caves of ice!

    A damsel with a dulcimer[3]
      In a vision once I saw:
    It was an Abyssinian maid,
      And on her dulcimer she played,   40
    Singing of Mount Abora.
    Could I revive within me,
      Her symphony and song,
To such a deep delight 'twould win me,
That with music loud and long,
I would build that dome in air,
That sunny dome! those caves of ice!
And all who heard should see them there,
And all should cry, Beware! Beware!
His flashing eyes, his floating hair!   50
Weave a circle round him thrice,
    And close your eyes with holy dread,
    For he on honey-dew hath fed,
And drunk the milk of Paradise.

                          (1816)

George Gordon, Lord Byron *1788–1824*

SHE WALKS IN BEAUTY

She walks in beauty, like the night
    Of cloudless climes and starry skies;
And all that's best of dark and bright
    Meet in her aspect and her eyes:
Thus mellowed to that tender light
    Which Heaven to gaudy day denies.

One shade the more, one ray the less,
    Had half impaired the nameless grace
Which waves in every raven tress,
    Or softly lightens o'er her face;   10

[3]A musical instrument like a small harp.

Where thoughts serenely sweet express,
   How pure, how dear their dwelling-place.

And on that cheek, and o'er that brow,
   So soft, so calm, yet eloquent,
The smiles that win, the tints that glow,
   But tell of days in goodness spent,
A mind at peace with all below,
   A heart whose love is innocent!

                        (1814)

Percy Bysshe Shelley *1792–1822*

OZYMANDIAS

I met a traveller from an antique land
Who said: Two vast and trunkless legs of stone
Stand in the desert . . . Near them, on the sand,
Half sunk, a shattered visage lies, whose frown,
And wrinkled lip, and sneer of cold command,
Tell that its sculptor well those passions read
Which yet survive, stamped on these lifeless things,
The hand that mocked them, and the heart that fed:
And on the pedestal these words appear:
"My name is Ozymandias, king of kings: 10
Look on my works, ye Mighty, and despair!"
Nothing beside remains. Round the decay
Of that colossal wreck, boundless and bare
The lone and level sands stretch far away.

                        (1817)

John Keats *1795–1821*

ON FIRST LOOKING INTO
CHAPMAN'S HOMER[1]

Much have I travelled in the realms of gold,
And many goodly states and kingdoms seen:
Round many western islands have I been
Which bards in fealty to Apollo[2] hold.
Oft of one wide expanse had I been told

---

[1]George Chapman published translations of both *The Iliad* (1611) and *The Odyssey* (1616).
[2]God of poetic inspiration.

That deep-browed Homer ruled as his demesne;[3]
Yet did I never breathe its pure serene
Till I heard Chapman speak out loud and bold:
Then felt I like some watcher of the skies
When a new planet swims into his ken;   10
Or like stout Cortez[4] when with eagle eyes
He stared at the Pacific — and all his men
Looked at each other with a wild surmise —
Silent, upon a peak in Darien.

(1816)

ODE ON A GRECIAN URN

Thou still unravished bride of quietness,
    Thou foster-child of silence and slow time,
Sylvan historian, who canst thus express
    A flowery tale more sweetly than our rhyme:
What leaf-fringed legend haunts about thy shape
Of deities or mortals, or of both,
    In Tempe[1] or the dales of Arcady?[2]
What men or gods are these? What maidens loth?
    What mad pursuit? What struggle to escape?
    What pipes and timbrels? What wild ecstasy?   10

Heard melodies are sweet, but those unheard
    Are sweeter; therefore, ye soft pipes, play on;
Not to the sensual ear, but, more endeared,
    Pipe to the spirit ditties of no tone:
Fair youth, beneath the trees, thou canst not leave
    Thy song, nor ever can those trees be bare;
    Bold Lover, never, never canst thou kiss,
Though winning near the goal — yet, do not grieve;
    She cannot fade, though thou hast not thy bliss,
    For ever wilt thou love, and she be fair!   20

Ah, happy, happy boughs! that cannot shed
    Your leaves, nor ever bid the spring adieu;
And, happy melodist, unweariéd,
    For ever piping songs for ever new;
More happy love! more happy, happy love!
    For ever warm and still to be enjoyed,
    For ever panting, and for ever young;

[3]Domain.
[4]Actually Vasco de Balboa first sighted the Pacific.
[1]Valley in Thessaly, noted for its natural beauty.
[2]Region in Greece, a traditional setting for pastoral poetry.

All breathing human passion far above,
　　That leaves a heart high-sorrowful and cloyed,
　　　A burning forehead, and a parching tongue.　　　　　30

Who are these coming to the sacrifice?
　　To what green altar, O mysterious priest,
Lead'st thou that heifer lowing at the skies,
　　And all her silken flanks with garlands dressed?
What little town by river or sea shore,
　　Or mountain-built with peaceful citadel,
　　　Is emptied of this folk, this pious morn?
And, little town, thy streets for evermore
　　Will silent be; and not a soul to tell
　　　Why thou art desolate, can e'er return.　　　　　40

O Attic[3] shape! Fair attitude! with brede[4]
Of marble men and maidens overwrought,
With forest branches and the trodden weed;
　　Thou, silent form, dost tease us out of thought
As doth eternity: Cold Pastoral!
　　When old age shall this generation waste,
　　　Thou shalt remain, in midst of other woe
Than ours, a friend to man, to whom thou say'st,
　　"Beauty is truth, truth beauty," — that is all
　　Ye know on earth, and all ye need to know.　　　　　50
　　　　　　　　　　　　　　　　　　　　　　　　(1819)

Alfred, Lord Tennyson *1809–1892*

ULYSSES[1]

It little profits that an idle king,
By this still hearth, among these barren crags,
Matched with an agéd wife,[2] I mete and dole
Unequal laws unto a savage race,
That hoard, and sleep, and feed, and know not me.
I cannot rest from travel; I will drink
Life to the lees. All times I have enjoyed
Greatly, have suffered greatly, both with those
That loved me, and alone; on shore, and when
Through scudding drifts the rainy Hyades[3]　　　　　10
Vext the dim sea. I am become a name;

[3]Of Attica, thus, classic in grace and simplicity.
[4]Design, decoration.
[1]Tennyson's depiction of the hero of *The Odyssey* owes much to *The Inferno* of Dante, who presented a restless man eager to continue searching for knowledge and truth.
[2]Penelope.
[3]Constellation that, when rising with the sun, was thought to be a sign of rain.

For always roaming with a hungry heart
Much have I seen and known, — cities of men
And manners, climates, councils, governments,
Myself not least, but honored of them all, —
And drunk delight of battle with my peers,
Far on the ringing plains of windy Troy.
I am a part of all that I have met;
Yet all experience is an arch wherethrough
Gleams that untravelled world whose margin fades   20
For ever and for ever when I move.
How dull it is to pause, to make an end,
To rust unburnished, not to shine in use!
As though to breathe were life! Life piled on life
Were all too little, and of one to me
Little remains; but every hour is saved
From that eternal silence, something more,
A bringer of new things; and vile it were
For some three suns to store and hoard myself,
And this gray spirit yearning in desire   30
To follow knowledge like a sinking star,
Beyond the utmost bound of human thought.
          This is my son, mine own Telemachus,
To whom I leave the sceptre and the isle,[4]
Well-loved of me, discerning to fulfill
This labor, by slow prudence to make mild
A rugged people, and through soft degrees
Subdue them to the useful and the good.
Most blameless is he, centred in the sphere
Of common duties, decent not to fail   40
In offices of tenderness, and pay
Meet adoration to my household gods,
When I am gone. He works his work, I mine.
          There lies the port; the vessel puffs her sail;
There gloom the dark, broad seas. My mariners,
Souls that have toiled, and wrought, and thought with me, —
That ever with a frolic welcome took
The thunder and the sunshine, and opposed
Free hearts, free foreheads, — you and I are old;
Old age hath yet his honor and his toil.   50
Death closes all; but something ere the end,
Some work of noble note, may yet be done,
Not unbecoming men that strove with Gods.
The lights begin to twinkle from the rocks;
The long day wanes; the slow moon climbs; the deep
Moans round with many voices. Come, my friends.
'Tis not too late to seek a newer world.
Push off, and sitting well in order smite
The sounding furrows; for my purpose holds

[4]Ithaca.

To sail beyond the sunset, and the baths   60
Of all the western stars, until I die.
It may be that the gulfs will wash us down;
It may be we shall touch the Happy Isles,[5]
And see the great Achilles,[6] whom we knew.
Though much is taken, much abides; and though
We are not now that strength which in old days
Moved earth and heaven, that which we are, we are,—
One equal temper of heroic hearts,
Made weak by time and fate, but strong in will
To strive, to seek, to find, and not to yield.   70
                                                                   (1842)

THE EAGLE

He clasps the crag with crooked hands;
Close to the sun in lonely lands,
Ringed with the azure world, he stands.

The wrinkled sea beneath him crawls;
He watches from his mountain walls,
And like a thunderbolt he falls.

                                                                   (1851)

Robert Browning *1812–1889*

MY LAST DUCHESS

FERRARA

That's my last Duchess painted on the wall,
Looking as if she were alive; I call
That piece a wonder, now: Frà Pandolf's[1] hands
Worked busily a day, and there she stands.
Will't please you sit and look at her? I said
"Frà Pandolf" by design, for never read
Strangers like you that pictured countenance,
The depth and passion of its earnest glance,
But to myself they turned (since none puts by
The curtain I have drawn for you, but I)   10

[5]Elysium, a paradise thought to lie in the western extremity of the ocean.
[6]Major hero of the Trojan War, in which he was killed.
[1]A fictitious artist.

And seemed as they would ask me, if they durst,
How such a glance came there; so, not the first
Are you to turn and ask thus. Sir, 'twas not
Her husband's presence only, called that spot
Of joy into the Duchess' cheek: perhaps
Frà Pandolf chanced to say "Her mantle laps
Over my Lady's wrist too much," or "Paint
Must never hope to reproduce the faint
Half-flush that dies along her throat": such stuff
Was courtesy, she thought, and cause enough   20
For calling up that spot of joy. She had
A heart—how shall I say?—too soon made glad,
Too easily impressed; she liked whate'er
She looked on, and her looks went everywhere.
Sir, 'twas all one! My favor at her breast,
The dropping of the daylight in the West,
The bough of cherries some officious fool
Broke in the orchard for her, the white mule
She rode with round the terrace—all and each
Would draw from her alike the approving speech,   30
Or blush, at least. She thanked men,—good; but thanked
Somehow—I know not how—as if she ranked
My gift of a nine-hundred-years-old name
With anybody's gift. Who'd stoop to blame
This sort of trifling? Even had you skill
In speech—(which I have not)—to make your will
Quite clear to such an one, and say, "Just this
Or that in you disgusts me; here you miss,
Or there exceed the mark"—and if she let
Herself be lessoned so, nor plainly set   40
Her wits to yours, forsooth, and made excuse,
—E'en then would be some stooping, and I choose
Never to stoop. Oh, Sir, she smiled, no doubt,
Whene'er I passed her; but who passed without
Much the same smile? This grew; I gave commands;
Then all smiles stopped together. There she stands
As if alive. Will't please you rise? We'll meet
The company below, then. I repeat,
The Count your Master's known munificence
Is ample warrant that no just pretence   50
Of mine for dowry will be disallowed;
Though his fair daughter's self, as I avowed
At starting, is my object. Nay, we'll go
Together down, Sir! Notice Neptune, though,
Taming a sea-horse, thought a rarity,
Which Claus of Innsbruck[2] cast in bronze for me.

(1842)

---

[2]Another fictitious artist.

Walt Whitman *1819–1892*

WHEN LILACS LAST IN THE DOORYARD BLOOM'D

1

When lilacs last in the dooryard bloom'd,
And the great star early droop'd in the western sky in the night,
I mourn'd, and yet shall mourn with ever-returning spring.

Ever-returning spring, trinity sure to me you bring,
Lilac blooming perennial and drooping star in the west,
And thought of him I love.

2

O powerful western fallen star!
O shades of night—O moody, tearful night!
O great star disappear'd—O the black murk that hides the star!
O cruel hands that hold me powerless—O helpless soul of me!   10
O harsh surrounding cloud that will not free my soul.

3

In the dooryard fronting an old farm-house near the white-wash'd palings,
Stands the lilac-bush tall-growing with heart-shaped leaves of rich green,
With many a pointed blossom rising delicate, with the perfume strong
    I love,
With every leaf a miracle—and from this bush in the dooryard,
With delicate-color'd blossoms and heart-shaped leaves of rich green,
A sprig with its flower I break.

4

In the swamp in secluded recesses,
A shy and hidden bird is warbling a song.

Solitary the thrush,   20
The hermit withdrawn to himself, avoiding the settlements,
Sings by himself a song.

Song of the bleeding throat,
Death's outlet song of life, (for well dear brother I know,
If thou was not granted to sing thou would'st surely die.)

5

Over the breast of the spring, the land, amid cities,
Amid lanes and through old woods, where lately the violets peep'd
    from the ground, spotting the gray debris,
Amid the grass in the fields each side of the lanes, passing the endless grass,
Passing the yellow-spear'd wheat, every grain from its shroud in the
    dark-brown fields uprisen,
Passing the apple-tree blows of white and pink in the orchards,   30
Carrying a corpse to where it shall rest in the grave,
Night and day journeys a coffin.

6

Coffin that passes through lanes and streets,
Through day and night with the great cloud darkening the land,
With the pomp of the inloop'd flags with the cities draped in black,
With the show of the States themselves as of crape-veil'd women standing,
With processions long and winding and the flambeaus of the night,
With the countless torches lit, with the silent sea of faces and the
    unbared heads,
With the waiting depot, the arriving coffin, and the sombre faces,
With dirges through the night, with the thousand voices rising strong
    and solemn,   40
With all the mournful voices of the dirges pour'd around the coffin,
The dim-lit churches and the shuddering organs—where amid these
    you journey,
With the tolling tolling bells' perpetual clang,
Here, coffin that slowly passes,
I give you my sprig of lilac.

7

(Nor for you, for one alone,
Blossoms and branches green to coffins all I bring,
For fresh as the morning, thus would I chant a song for you O sane
    and sacred death.
All over bouquets of roses,
O death, I cover you over with roses and early lilies,   50
But mostly and now the lilac that blooms the first,
Copious I break, I break the sprigs from the bushes,
With loaded arms I come, pouring for you,
For you and the coffins all of you O death.)

8

O western orb sailing the heaven,
Now I know what you must have meant as a month since I walk'd,
As I walk'd in silence the transparent shadowy night,
As I saw you had something to tell as you bent to me night after night,
As you droop'd from the sky low down as if to my side, (while the
    other stars all look'd on,)
As we wander'd together the solemn night, (for something I know not
    what kept me from sleep,)   60
As the night advanced, and I saw on the rim of the west how full you
    were of woe,
As I stood on the rising ground in the breeze in the cool transparent night,
As I watch'd where you pass'd and was lost in the netherward black of
    the night,
As my soul in its trouble dissatisfied sank, as where you sad orb,
Concluded, dropt in the night, and was gone.

9

Sing on there in the swamp,
O singer bashful and tender, I hear your notes, I hear your call,
I hear, I come presently, I understand you,

But a moment I linger, for the lustrous star has detain'd me,
The star my departing comrade holds and detains me.   70

10

O how shall I warble myself for the dead one there I loved?
And how shall I deck my song for the large sweet soul that has gone?
And what shall my perfume be for the grave of him I love?

Sea-winds blown from east and west,
Blown from the Eastern sea and blown from the Western sea, till
   there on the prairies meeting,
These and with these and the breath of my chant,
I'll perfume the grave of him I love.

11

O what shall I hang on the chamber walls?
And what shall the pictures be that I hang on the walls,
To adorn the burial-house of him I love?   80

Pictures of growing spring and farms and homes,
With the Fourth-month eve at sundown, and the gray smoke lucid and
   bright,
With floods of the yellow gold of the gorgeous, indolent, sinking sun,
   burning, expanding the air,
With the fresh sweet herbage under foot, and the pale green leaves of
   the trees prolific,
In the distance the flowing glaze, the breast of the river, with a
   wind-dapple here and there,
With ranging hills on the banks, with many a line against the sky, and
   shadows,
And the city at hand with dwellings so dense, and stacks of chimneys,
And all the scenes of life and the workshops, and the workmen
   homeward returning.

12

Lo, body and soul—this land,
My own Manhattan with spires, and the sparkling and hurrying tides,
   and the ships,   90
The varied and ample land, the South and the North in the light,
   Ohio's shores and flashing Missouri,
And ever the far-spreading prairies cover'd with grass and corn.

Lo, the most excellent sun so calm and haughty,
The violet and purple morn with just-felt breezes,
The gentle soft-born measureless light,
The miracle spreading bathing all, the fulfill'd noon,
The coming eve delicious, the welcome night and the stars,
Over my cities shining all, enveloping man and land.

13

Sing on, sing on you gray-brown bird,
Sing from the swamps, the recesses, pour your chant from the bushes,   100
Limitless out of the dusk, out of the cedars and pines.

Sing on dearest brother, warble your reedy song,
Loud human song, with voice of uttermost woe.

O liquid and free and tender!
O wild and loose to my soul—O wondrous singer!
You only I hear—yet the star holds me, (but will soon depart,)
Yet the lilac with mastering odor holds me.

14

Now while I sat in the day and look'd forth,
In the close of the day with its light and the fields of spring, and the
    farmers preparing their crops,
In the large unconscious scenery of my land with its lakes and forests,   110
In the heavenly aerial beauty, (after the perturb'd winds and the storms,)
Under the arching heavens of the afternoon swift passing, and the
    voices of children and women,
The many-moving sea-tides, and I saw the ships how they sail'd,
And the summer approaching with richness, and the fields all busy
    with labor,
And the infinite separate houses, how they all went on, each with its
    meals and minutia of daily usages,
And the streets how their throbbings throbb'd, and the cities pent—lo,
    then and there,
Falling upon them all and among them all, enveloping me with the rest,
Appear'd the cloud, appear'd the long black trail,
And I knew death, its thought, and the sacred knowledge of death.

Then with the knowledge of death as walking one side of me,   120
And the thought of death close-walking the other side of me,
And I in the middle as with companions, and as holding the hands of
    companions,
I fled forth to the hiding receiving night that talks not,
Down to the shores of the water, the path by the swamp in the dimness,
To the solemn shadowy cedars and ghostly pines so still.

And the singer so shy to the rest receiv'd me,
The gray-brown bird I know receiv'd us comrades three,
And he sang the carol of death, and a verse for him I love.

From deep secluded recesses,
From the fragrant cedars and the ghostly pines so still,   130
Came the carol of the bird.

And the charm of the carol rapt me,
As I held as if by their hands my comrades in the night,
And the voice of my spirit tallied the song of the bird.

Come lovely and soothing death,
Undulate round the world, serenely arriving, arriving,
In the day, in the night, to all, to each,
Sooner or later delicate death.

Prais'd be the fathomless universe,
For life and joy, and for objects and knowledge curious,   140
And for love, sweet love—but praise! praise! praise!
For the sure-enwinding arms of cool-enfolding death.

Dark mother always gliding near with soft feet,
Have none chanted for thee a chant of fullest welcome?
Then I chant it for thee, I glorify thee above all,
I bring thee a song that when thou must indeed come, come unfalteringly.

Approach strong deliveress,
When it is so, when thou hast taken them I joyously sing the dead,
Lost in the loving floating ocean of thee,
Laved in the flood of thy bliss O death.   150

From me to thee glad serenades,
Dances for thee I propose saluting thee, adornments and feastings for thee,
And the sights of the open landscape and the high-spread sky are fitting,
And life and the fields, and the huge and thoughtful night.

The night in silence under many a star,
The ocean shore and the husky whispering wave whose voice I know,
And the soul turning to thee O vast and well-veil'd death,
And the body gratefully nestling close to thee.

Over the tree-tops I float thee a song,
Over the rising and sinking waves, over the myriad fields and the
*   prairies wide,*   160
Over the dense-pack'd cities all and the teeming wharves and ways,
I float this carol with joy, with joy to thee O death.

15

To the tally of my soul,
Loud and strong kept up the gray-brown bird,
With pure deliberate notes spreading filling the night.

Loud in the pines and cedars dim,
Clear in the freshness moist and the swamp-perfume,
And I with my comrades there in the night.

While my sight that was bound in my eyes unclosed,
As to long panoramas of visions.   170

And I saw askant the armies,
I saw as in noiseless dreams hundreds of battle-flags,
Borne through the smoke of the battles and pierc'd with missiles I saw
    them,
And carried hither and yon through the smoke, and torn and bloody,
And at last but a few shreds left on the staffs, (and all in silence,)
And the staffs all splinter'd and broken.

I saw battle-corpses, myriads of them,
And the white skeletons of young men, I saw them,
I saw the debris and debris of all the slain soldiers of the war,
But I saw they were not as was thought,   180
They themselves were fully at rest, they suffer'd not,
The living remain'd and suffer'd, the mother suffer'd,
And the wife and the child and the musing comrade suffer'd,
And the armies that remain'd suffer'd.

16

Passing the visions, passing the night,
Passing, unloosing the hold of my comrades' hands,
Passing the song of the hermit bird and the tallying song of my soul,
Victorious song, death's outlet song, yet varying ever-altering song.
As low and wailing, yet clear the notes, rising and falling, flooding the
    night,
Sadly sinking and fainting, as warning and warning, and yet again
    bursting with joy, 190
Covering the earth and filling the spread of the heaven,
As that powerful psalm in the night I heard from recesses,
Passing, I leave thee lilac with heart-shaped leaves,
I leave thee there in the door-yard, blooming, returning with spring.

I cease from any song for thee,
From my gaze on thee in the west, fronting the west, communing with
    thee,
O comrade lustrous with silver face in the night.

Yet each to keep and all, retrievements out of the night,
The song, the wondrous chant of the gray-brown bird,
And the tallying chant, the echo arous'd in my soul, 200
With the lustrous and drooping star with the countenance full of woe,
With the holders holding my hand nearing the call of the bird,
Comrades mine and I in the midst, and their memory even to keep,
    for the dead I loved so well,
For the sweetest, wisest soul of all my days and lands—and this for
    his dear sake,
Lilac and star and bird twined with the chant of my soul,
There in the fragrant pines and the cedars dusk and dim.

(1867)

Matthew Arnold *1822–1888*

DOVER BEACH

The sea is calm to-night,
The tide is full, the moon lies fair
Upon the Straits;—on the French coast, the light
Gleams, and is gone; the cliffs of England stand,
Glimmering and vast, out in the tranquil bay.
Come to the window, sweet is the night air!
Only, from the long line of spray
Where the ebb meets the moon-blanched sand,
Listen! you hear the grating roar
Of pebbles which the waves suck back, and fling, 10
At their return, up the high strand,
Begin, and cease, and then again begin,

With tremulous cadence slow, and bring
The eternal note of sadness in.

    Sophocles[1] long ago
Heard it on the Aegean, and it brought
Into his mind the turbid ebb and flow
Of human misery; we
Find also in the sound a thought,
Hearing it by this distant northern sea.   20

The sea of faith
Was once, too, at the full, and round earth's shore
Lay like the folds of a bright girdle furled;
But now I only hear
Its melancholy, long, withdrawing roar,
Retreating to the breath
Of the night-wind down the vast edges drear
And naked shingles[2] of the world.

Ah, love, let us be true
To one another! for the world, which seems   30
To lie before us like a land of dreams,
So various, so beautiful, so new,
Hath really neither joy, nor love, nor light,
Nor certitude, nor peace, nor help for pain;
And we are here as on a darkling[3] plain
Swept with confused alarms of struggle and flight,
Where ignorant armies clash by night.

                          (1867)

Emily Dickinson *1830–1886*

SAFE IN THEIR ALABASTER CHAMBERS

Safe in their Alabaster Chambers —
Untouched by Morning —
And untouched by Noon —
Lie the meek members of the Resurrection —
Rafter of Satin — and Roof of Stone!

Grand go the Years — in the Crescent — above them —
Worlds scoop their Arcs —
And Firmaments — row[1] —

[1]In *Antigone* the Greek dramatist Sophocles likens the curse of heaven to the ebb and flow of the sea.
[2]Gravel beaches.
[3]Darkened.
[1]The heavens cast light downward.

Diadems — drop — and Doges[2] — surrender —
Soundless as dots — on a Disc of Snow —

(1859)

THERE'S A CERTAIN SLANT OF LIGHT

There's a certain Slant of light,
Winter Afternoons —
That oppresses, like the Heft[1]
Of Cathedral Tunes —

Heavenly Hurt, it gives us —
We can find no scar,
But internal difference,
Where the Meanings, are —

None may teach it — Any —
'Tis the Seal Despair —   10
An imperial affliction
Sent us of the Air —

When it comes, the Landscape listens —
Shadows — hold their breath —
When it goes, 'tis like the Distance
On the look of Death —

(ca. 1861)

HE PUT THE BELT AROUND MY LIFE

He put the Belt around my life —
I heard the Buckle snap —
And turned away, imperial,
My Lifetime folding up —
Deliberate, as a Duke would do
A Kingdom's Title Deed —
Henceforth, a Dedicated sort —
A Member of the Cloud.

Yet not too far to come at call —
And do the little Toils   10
That make the Circuit of the Rest —
And deal occasional smiles
To lives that stoop to notice mine —
And kindly ask it in —

[2]Early rulers in Venice.
[1]Heaviness.

Whose invitation, know you not
For Whom I must decline?

(ca. 1861)

MUCH MADNESS IS DIVINEST SENSE

Much Madness is divinest Sense —
To a discerning Eye —
Much Sense — the starkest Madness —
'Tis the Majority
In this, as All, prevail —
Assent — and you are sane —
Demur — you're straightway dangerous —
And handled with a Chain —

(ca. 1862)

BECAUSE I COULD NOT STOP FOR DEATH

Because I could not stop for Death —
He kindly stopped for me —
The Carriage held but just Ourselves —
And Immortality —

We slowly drove — He knew no haste
And I had put away
My labor and my leisure too,
For His Civility —

We passed the School, where Children strove
At Recess — in the Ring —   10
We passed the Fields of Gazing Grain —
We passed the Setting Sun —

Or rather — He passed Us —
The Dews drew quivering and chill —
For only Gossamer,[1] my Gown —
My Tippet[2] — only Tulle[3] —

We paused before a House that seemed
A Swelling of the Ground —
The Roof was scarcely visible —
The Cornice — in the Ground —   20

Since then — 'tis Centuries — and yet
Feels shorter than the Day

[1]Thin, sheer.
[2]Short cape covering just the shoulders.
[3]Soft net fabric.

I first surmised the Horses' Heads
Were toward Eternity—

(ca. 1863)

I HEARD A FLY BUZZ—WHEN I DIED

I heard a Fly buzz—when I died—
The Stillness in the Room
Was like the Stillness in the Air—
Between the Heaves of Storm—

The Eyes around—had wrung them dry—
And Breaths were gathering firm
For that last Onset—when the King
Be witnessed—in the Room—

I willed my Keepsakes—Signed away
What portion of me be   10
Assignable—and then it was
There interposed a Fly—

With Blue—uncertain stumbling Buzz—
Between the light—and me—
And then the Windows failed—and then
I could not see to see—

(1862?)

Christina Rossetti *1830–1894*

IN AN ARTIST'S STUDIO

One face looks out from all his canvases,
   One selfsame figure sits or walks or leans:
   We found her hidden just behind those screens,
That mirror gave back all her loveliness.
A queen in opal or in ruby dress,
   A nameless girl in freshest summer-greens,
   A saint, an angel—every canvas means
The same one meaning, neither more nor less.
He feeds upon her face by day and night,
   And she with true kind eyes looks back on him,   10
Fair as the moon and joyful as the light:
   Not wan with waiting, not with sorrow dim;
Not as she is, but was when hope shone bright;
   Not as she is, but as she fills his dream.

(1861)

Thomas Hardy *1840–1928*

THE DARKLING THRUSH

DECEMBER 31, 1900

I leant upon a coppice[1] gate
    When Frost was spectre-gray,
And Winter's dregs made desolate
    The weakening eye of day.
The tangled bine-stems[2] scored the sky
    Like strings of broken lyres,
And all mankind that haunted nigh
    Had sought their household fires.

The land's sharp features seemed to be
    The Century's corpse outleant,   10
His crypt the cloudy canopy,
    The wind his death-lament.
The ancient pulse of germ and birth
    Was shrunken hard and dry,
And every spirit upon earth
    Seemed fervorless as I.

At once a voice arose among
    The bleak twigs overhead
In a full-hearted evensong
    Of joy illimited;   20
An agéd thrush, frail, gaunt, and small,
    In blast-beruffled plume,
Had chosen thus to fling his soul
    Upon the growing gloom.

So little cause for carolings
    Of such ecstatic sound
Was written on terrestrial things
    Afar or nigh around,
That I could think there trembled through
    His happy good-night air   30
Some blessed Hope, whereof he knew
    And I was unaware.

                               (1902)

[1] A small thicket.
[2] Twining shoots of a climbing plant.

Gerard Manley Hopkins *1844–1889*

PIED BEAUTY

Glory be to God for dappled things—
    For skies of couple-color as a brinded[1] cow;
        For rose-moles all in stipple[2] upon trout that swim;
Fresh-firecoal chestnut-falls;[3] finches' wings;
    Landscape plotted and pieced—fold, fallow, and plow;
    And áll trádes, their gear and tackle and trim.[4]

All things counter, original, spare, strange;
    Whatever is fickle, freckled (who knows how?)
        With swift, slow; sweet, sour; adazzle, dim;
He fathers-forth whose beauty is past change:
    Praise him.   10

        (1877)

SPRING AND FALL

To a Young Child

Márgarét áre you gríeving
Over Goldengrove unleaving?
Leáves, líke the things of man, you
With your fresh thoughts care for, can you?
Áh! ás the heart grows older
It will come to such sights colder
By and by, nor spare a sigh
Though worlds of wanwood[1] leafmeal[2] lie;
And yet you *will* weep and know why.
Now no matter, child, the name: 10
Sórrow's spríngs áre the same.
Nor mouth had, no nor mind, expressed
What heart heard of, ghost[3] guessed:
It ís the blight man was born for,
It is Margaret you mourn for.

        (1880)

[1]Striped.
[2]Small dots.
[3]Chestnuts fresh from the fire with their hulls off.
[4]Tools.
[1]Pale woods, as though bloodless.
[2]Fallen leaf by leaf.
[3]Spirit, soul.

A. E. Housman *1859–1936*

TO AN ATHLETE DYING YOUNG

The time you won your town the race
We chaired you through the market-place;
Man and boy stood cheering by,
And home we brought you shoulder-high.

To-day, the road all runners come,
Shoulder-high we bring you home,
And set you at your threshold down,
Townsman of a stiller town.

Smart lad, to slip betimes away
From fields where glory does not stay,   10
And early though the laurel grows
It withers quicker than the rose.

Eyes the shady night has shut
Cannot see the record cut,
And silence sounds no worse than cheers
After earth has stopped the ears.

Now you will not swell the rout
Of lads that wore their honors out,
Runners whom renown outran
And the name died before the man.   20

So set, before its echoes fade,
The fleet foot on the sill of shade,
And hold to the low lintel up
The still-defended challenge-cup.

And round that early-laurelled head
Will flock to gaze the strengthless dead,
And find unwithered on its curls
The garland briefer than a girl's.

                                                    (1896)

LOVELIEST OF TREES

Loveliest of trees, the cherry now
Is hung with bloom along the bough,
And stands about the woodland ride,
Wearing white for Eastertide.

Now, of my threescore years and ten,
Twenty will not come again,
And take from seventy springs a score,
It only leaves me fifty more.

And since to look at things in bloom
Fifty springs are little room,   10
About the woodlands I will go
To see the cherry hung with snow.

(1896)

William Butler Yeats *1865–1939*

THE SECOND COMING

Turning and turning in the widening gyre[1]
The falcon cannot hear the falconer;
Things fall apart; the centre cannot hold;
Mere anarchy is loosed upon the world,
The blood-dimmed tide is loosed, and everywhere
The ceremony of innocence is drowned;
The best lack all conviction, while the worst
Are full of passionate intensity.

Surely some revelation is at hand;
Surely the Second Coming is at hand.   10
The Second Coming! Hardly are those words out
When a vast image out of *Spiritus Mundi*[2]
Troubles my sight: somewhere in sands of the desert
A shape with lion body and the head of a man,
A gaze blank and pitiless as the sun,
Is moving its slow thighs, while all about it
Reel shadows of the indignant desert birds.
The darkness drops again; but now I know
That twenty centuries of stony sleep
Were vexed to nightmare by a rocking cradle,   20
And what rough beast, its hour come round at last,
Slouches towards Bethlehem to be born?

(1921)

LEDA AND THE SWAN

A sudden blow: the great wings beating still
Above the staggering girl, her thighs caressed
By the dark webs, her nape caught in his bill,
He holds her helpless breast upon his breast.

---

[1]A spiral motion, used by Yeats to suggest the cycles of history.
[2]The Soul of the World, a collective unconscious from which humans draw memories, symbols,
dreams.

How can those terrified vague fingers push
The feathered glory from her loosening thighs?
And how can body, laid in that white rush,
But feel the strange heart beating where it lies?

A shudder in the loins engenders there
The broken wall, the burning roof and tower
And Agamemnon dead.　　　　　　　　　　　　　　10
　　　　　　　　　Being so caught up,
So mastered by the brute blood of the air,
Did she put on his knowledge with his power
Before the indifferent beak could let her drop?

　　　　　　　　　　　　　　　　　　　(1923)

SAILING TO BYZANTIUM[1]

That is no country for old men. The young
In one another's arms, birds in the trees
— Those dying generations — at their song,
The salmon-falls, the mackerel-crowded seas,
Fish, flesh, or fowl, commend all summer long
Whatever is begotten, born, and dies.
Caught in that sensual music all neglect
Monuments of unaging intellect.

An agéd man is but a paltry thing,
A tattered coat upon a stick, unless　　　　　　10
Soul clap its hands and sing, and louder sing
For every tatter in its mortal dress,
Nor is there singing school but studying
Monuments of its own magnificence;
And therefore I have sailed the seas and come
To the holy city of Byzantium.

O sages standing in God's holy fire
As in the gold mosaic of a wall,
Come from the holy fire, perne in a gyre,[2]
And be the singing-masters of my soul.　　　　　20
Consume my heart away; sick with desire
And fastened to a dying animal
It knows not what it is; and gather me
Into the artifice of eternity.

Once out of nature I shall never take
My bodily form from any natural thing,
But such a form as Grecian goldsmiths make

---

[1]The capital of the Byzantine Empire, the city now called Istanbul; for Yeats, a symbol of life
perfected by art.
　[2]The spiraling motion that Yeats associates with the whirling of fate; see "The Second Coming."

Of hammered gold and gold enamelling
To keep a drowsy Emperor awake;
Or set upon a golden bough to sing   30
To lords and ladies of Byzantium
Of what is past, or passing, or to come.

(1928)

Edwin Arlington Robinson *1869–1935*

RICHARD CORY

Whenever Richard Cory went downtown,
We people on the pavement looked at him;
He was a gentleman from sole to crown,
Clean favored, and imperially slim.

And he was always quietly arrayed,
And he was always human when he talked;
But still he fluttered pulses when he said,
"Good-morning," and he glittered when he walked.

And he was rich — yes, richer than a king —
And admirably schooled in every grace: 10
In fine,[1] we thought that he was everything
To make us wish that we were in his place.

So on we worked, and waited for the light,
And went without the meat, and cursed the bread;
And Richard Cory, one calm summer night,
Went home and put a bullet through his head.

(1896)

Stephen Crane *1871–1900*

A MAN SAID TO THE UNIVERSE

A man said to the universe:
"Sir, I exist!"
"However," replied the universe,
"The fact has not created in me
A sense of obligation."

(1899)

[1] In truth.

WAR IS KIND

Do not weep, maiden, for war is kind.
Because your lover threw wild hands toward the sky
And the affrighted steed ran on alone,
Do not weep.
War is kind.

    Hoarse, booming drums of the regiment,
    Little souls who thirst for fight,
    These men were born to drill and die.
    The unexplained glory flies above them,
    Great is the Battle-God, great, and his Kingdom —   10
    A field where a thousand corpses lie.

Do not weep, babe, for war is kind.
Because your father tumbled in the yellow trenches,
Raged at his breast, gulped and died,
Do not weep.
War is kind.

    Swift blazing flag of the regiment,
    Eagle with crest of red and gold,
    These men were born to drill and die.
    Point for them the virtue of slaughter,   20
    Make plain to them the excellence of killing
    And a field where a thousand corpses lie.

Mother whose heart hung humble as a button
On the bright spendid shroud of your son,
Do not weep.
War is kind.

(1899)

Paul Laurence Dunbar *1872–1906*

WE WEAR THE MASK

We wear the mask that grins and lies,
It hides our cheeks and shades our eyes, —
This debt we pay to human guile;
With torn and bleeding hearts we smile,
And mouth with myriad subtleties.

Why should the world be overwise,
In counting all our tears and sighs?
Nay, let them only see us, while
    We wear the mask.

We smile, but, O great Christ, our cries   10
To thee from tortured souls arise.

We sing, but oh the clay is vile
Beneath our feet, and long the mile;
But let the world dream otherwise,
We wear the mask!

(1895)

Robert Frost *1874–1963*

MENDING WALL

Something there is that doesn't love a wall,
That sends the frozen-ground-swell under it
And spills the upper boulders in the sun,
And makes gaps even two can pass abreast.
The work of hunters is another thing:
I have come after them and made repair
Where they have left not one stone on a stone,
But they would have the rabbit out of hiding,
To please the yelping dogs. The gaps I mean,
No one has seen them made or heard them made,   10
But at spring mending-time we find them there.
I let my neighbor know beyond the hill;
And on a day we meet to walk the line
And set the wall between us once again.
We keep the wall between us as we go.
To each the boulders that have fallen to each.
And some are loaves and some so nearly balls
We have to use a spell to make them balance:
"Stay where you are until our backs are turned!"
We wear our fingers rough with handling them.   20
Oh, just another kind of outdoor game,
One on a side. It comes to little more:
There where it is we do not need the wall:
He is all pine and I am apple orchard.
My apple trees will never get across
And eat the cones under his pines, I tell him.
He only says, "Good fences make good neighbors."
Spring is the mischief in me, and I wonder
If I could put a notion in his head:
"*Why* do they make good neighbors? Isn't it   30
Where there are cows? But here there are no cows.
Before I built a wall I'd ask to know   *alliteration*
What I was walling in or walling out,
And to whom I was like to give offense.
Something there is that doesn't love a wall,
That wants it down." I could say "Elves" to him,
But it's not elves exactly, and I'd rather

He said it for himself. I see him there,
Bringing a stone grasped firmly by the top
In each hand, like an old-stone savage armed.   40
He moves in darkness as it seems to me,
Not of woods only and the shade of trees.
He will not go behind his father's saying,
And he likes having thought of it so well
He says again, "Good fences make good neighbors."

(1914)

FIRE AND ICE

Some say the world will end in fire,
Some say in ice.
From what I've tasted of desire
I hold with those who favor fire.
But if it had to perish twice,
I think I know enough of hate
To say that for destruction ice
Is also great
And would suffice.

(1923)

DESERT PLACES

Snow falling and night falling fast, oh, fast
In a field I looked into going past,
And the ground almost covered smooth in snow,
But a few weeds and stubble showing last.

The woods around it have it—it is theirs.
All animals are smothered in their lairs.
I am too absent-spirited to count;
The loneliness includes me unawares.

And lonely as it is, that loneliness
Will be more lonely ere it will be less—
A blanker whiteness of benighted snow   10
With no expression, nothing to express.

They cannot scare me with their empty spaces
Between stars—on stars where no human race is.
I have it in me so much nearer home
To scare myself with my own desert places.

(1934)

DESIGN

I found a dimpled spider, fat and white,
On a white heal-all, holding up a moth
Like a white piece of rigid satin cloth —
Assorted characters of death and blight
Mixed ready to begin the morning right,
Like the ingredients of a witches' broth —
A snow-drop spider, a flower like a froth,
And dead wings carried like a paper kite.

What had that flower to do with being white,
The wayside blue and innocent heal-all?   10
What brought the kindred spider to that height,
Then steered the white moth thither in the night?
What but design of darkness to appall? —
If design govern in a thing so small.

(1936)

Amy Lowell *1874–1925*

PATTERNS

I walk down the garden-paths,
And all the daffodils
Are blowing, and the bright blue squills.
I walk down the patterned garden-paths
In my stiff, brocaded gown.
With my powdered hair and jeweled fan,
I too am a rare
Pattern. As I wander down
The garden-paths,
My dress is richly figured,
And the train
Makes a pink and silver stain
On the gravel, and the thrift
Of the borders.
Just a plate of current fashion,
Tripping by in high-heeled, ribboned shoes.
Not a softness anywhere about me,
Only whalebone and brocade.
And I sink on a seat in the shade
Of a lime tree. For my passion   20
Wars against the stiff brocade.
The daffodils and squills
Flutter in the breeze
As they please.

And I weep;
For the lime-tree is in blossom
And one small flower has dropped upon my bosom.

And the plashing of waterdrops
In the marble fountain
Comes down the garden-paths.   30
The dripping never stops.
Underneath my stiffened gown
Is the softness of a woman bathing in a marble basin,
A basin in the midst of hedges grown
So thick, she cannot see her lover hiding,
But she guesses he is near,
And the sliding of the water
Seems the stroking of a dear
Hand upon her.
What is Summer in a fine brocaded gown!   40
I should like to see it lying in a heap upon the ground.
All the pink and silver crumpled up on the ground.
I would be the pink and silver as I ran along the paths,
And he would stumble after,
Bewildered by my laughter.
I should see the sun flashing from his sword-hilt and the buckles on his
    shoes.
I would choose
To lead him in a maze along the patterned paths,
A bright and laughing maze for my heavy-booted lover.
Till he caught me in the shade,   50
And the buttons of his waistcoat bruised my body as he clasped me,
Aching, melting, unafraid.
With the shadows of the leaves and the sundrops,
And the plopping of the waterdrops,
All about us in the open afternoon—
I am very like to swoon
With the weight of this brocade,
For the sun sifts through the shade.

Underneath the fallen blossom
In my bosom   60
Is a letter I have hid.
It was brought to me this morning by a rider from the Duke.
"Madam, we regret to inform you that Lord Hartwell
Died in action Thursday se'ennight."
As I read it in the white, morning sunlight,
The letters squirmed like snakes.
"Any answer, Madam," said my footman.
"No," I told him.
"See that the messenger takes some refreshment.
No, no answer."   70
And I walked into the garden,
Up and down the patterned paths,

In my stiff, correct brocade.
The blue and yellow flowers stood up proudly in the sun,
Each one.
I stood upright too,
Held rigid to the pattern
By the stiffness of my gown;
Up and down I walked,
Up and down.   80

In a month he would have been my husband.
In a month, here, underneath this lime,
We would have broke the pattern;
He for me, and I for him,
He as Colonel, I as Lady,
On this shady seat.
He had a whim
That sunlight carried blessing.
And I answered, "It shall be as you have said."
Now he is dead.   90

In Summer and in Winter I shall walk
Up and down
The patterned garden-paths.
In my stiff, brocaded gown.
The squills and daffodils
Will give place to pillared roses, and to asters, and to snow.
I shall go
Up and down
In my gown.
Gorgeously arrayed,
Boned and stayed.   100
And the softness of my body will be guarded from embrace
By each button, hook, and lace.
For the man who should loose me is dead,
Fighting with the Duke in Flanders,
In a pattern called a war.
Christ! What are patterns for?

                                                              (1916)

Carl Sandburg *1878–1967*

FOG

The fog comes
on little cat feet.

It sits looking
over harbor and city
on silent haunches
and then moves on.

                                                              (1916)

GRASS

Pile the bodies high at Austerlitz and Waterloo.[1]
Shovel them under and let me work —
      I am the grass; I cover all.

And pile them high at Gettysburg[2]
And pile them high at Ypres and Verdun.[3]
Shovel them under and let me work.
Two years, ten years, and passengers ask the conductor:
        What place is this?
        Where are we now?

      I am the grass.   10
      Let me work.

                                     (1918)

Wallace Stevens *1879–1955*

SUNDAY MORNING

1

Complacencies of the peignoir, and late
Coffee and oranges in a sunny chair,
And the green freedom of a cockatoo
Upon a rug mingle to dissipate
The holy hush of ancient sacrifice.
She dreams a little, and she feels the dark
Encroachment of that old catastrophe,
As a calm darkens among water-lights.
The pungent oranges and bright, green wings
Seem things in some procession of the dead,   10
Winding across wide water, without sound.
The day is like wide water, without sound,
Stilled for the passing of her dreaming feet
Over the seas, to silent Palestine,
Dominion of the blood and sepulchre.

2

Why should she give her bounty to the dead?
What is divinity if it can come
Only in silent shadows and in dreams?
Shall she not find in comforts of the sun,
In pungent fruit and bright, green wings, or else   20

[1]Battlefields of the Napoleonic Wars.
[2]Civil War battlefield.
[3]Battlefields in World War I.

In any balm or beauty of the earth,
Things to be cherished like the thought of heaven?
Divinity must live within herself:
Passions of rain, or moods in falling snow;
Grievings in loneliness, or unsubdued
Elations when the forest blooms; gusty
Emotions on wet roads on autumn nights;
All pleasures and all pains, remembering
The bough of summer and the winter branch.
These are the measures destined for her soul.   30

3

Jove in the clouds had his inhuman birth.
No mother suckled him, no sweet land gave
Large-mannered motions to his mythy mind
He moved among us, as a muttering king,
Magnificent, would move among his hinds,
Until our blood, commingling, virginal,
With heaven, brought such requital to desire
The very hinds discerned it, in a star.
Shall our blood fail? Or shall it come to be
The blood of paradise? And shall the earth   40
Seem all of paradise that we shall know?
The sky will be much friendlier then than now,
A part of labor and a part of pain,
And next in glory to enduring love,
Not this dividing and indifferent blue.

4

She says, "I am content when wakened birds,
Before they fly, test the reality
Of misty fields, by their sweet questionings;
But when the birds are gone, and their warm fields
Return no more, where, then, is paradise?"   50
There is not any haunt of prophecy,
Nor any old chimera of the grave,
Neither the golden underground, nor isle
Melodious, where spirits gat them home,
Nor visionary south, nor cloudy palm
Remote on heaven's hill, that has endured
As April's green endures; or will endure
Like her remembrance of awakened birds,
Or her desire for June and evening, tipped
By the consummation of the swallow's wings.   60

5

She says, "But in contentment I still feel
The need of some imperishable bliss."
Death is the mother of beauty; hence from her,
Alone, shall come fulfilment to our dreams
And our desires. Although she strews the leaves
Of sure obliteration on our paths,

The path sick sorrow took, the many paths
Where triumph rang its brassy phrase, or love
Whispered a little out of tenderness,
She makes the willow shiver in the sun   70
For maidens who were wont to sit and gaze
Upon the grass, relinquished to their feet.
She causes boys to pile new plums and pears
On disregarded plate. The maidens taste
And stray impassioned in the littering leaves.

6

Is there no change of death in paradise?
Does ripe fruit never fall? Or do the boughs
Hang always heavy in that perfect sky,
Unchanging, yet so like our perishing earth,
With rivers like our own that seek for seas   80
They never find, the same receding shores
That never touch with inarticulate pang?
Why set the pear upon those river-banks
Or spice the shores with odors of the plum?
Alas, that they should wear our colors there,
The silken weavings of our afternoons,
And pick the strings of our insipid lutes!
Death is the mother of beauty, mystical,
Within whose burning bosom we devise
Our earthly mothers waiting, sleeplessly.   90

7

Supple and turbulent, a ring of men
Shall chant in orgy on a summer morn
Their boisterous devotion to the sun,
Not as a god, but as a god might be,
Naked among them, like a savage source.
Their chant shall be a chant of paradise,
Out of their blood, returning to the sky;
And in their chant shall enter, voice by voice,
The windy lake wherein their lord delights,
The trees, like serafin, and echoing hills,   100
That choir among themselves long afterward.
They shall know well the heavenly fellowship
Of men that perish and of summer morn.
And whence they came and whither they shall go
The dew upon their feet shall manifest.

8

She hears, upon that water without sound,
A voice that cries, "The tomb in Palestine
Is not the porch of spirits lingering.
It is the grave of Jesus, where he lay."
We live in an old chaos of the sun,   110
Or old dependency of day and night,

Or island solitude, unsponsored, free,
Of that wide water, inescapable.
Deer walk upon our mountains, and the quail
Whistle about us their spontaneous cries;
Sweet berries ripen in the wilderness;
And, in the isolation of the sky,
At evening, casual flocks of pigeons make
Ambiguous undulations as they sink,
Downward to darkness, on extended wings.　　120

(1915)

THE EMPEROR OF ICE-CREAM

Call the roller of big cigars,
The muscular one, and bid him whip
In kitchen cups concupiscent curds.
Let the wenches dawdle in such dress
As they are used to wear, and let the boys
Bring flowers in last month's newspapers.
Let be be finale of seem.
The only emperor is the emperor of ice-cream.

Take from the dresser of deal,
Lacking the three glass knobs, that sheet　　10
On which she embroidered fantails once
And spread it so as to cover her face.
If her horny feet protrude, they come
To show how cold she is, and dumb.
Let the lamp affix its beam.
The only emperor is the emperor of ice-cream.

(1923)

William Carlos Williams *1883–1963*

DANSE RUSSE

If when my wife is sleeping
and the baby and Kathleen
are sleeping
and the sun is a flame-white disc
in silken mists
above shining trees, —
if I in my north room
dance naked, grotesquely
before my mirror
waving my shirt round my head　　10

and singing softly to myself:
"I am lonely, lonely.
I was born to be lonely,
I am best so!"
If I admire my arms, my face,
my shoulders, flanks, buttocks
against the yellow drawn shades,—

Who shall say I am not
the happy genius of my household?

(1916)

THE RED WHEELBARROW

so much depends
upon

a red wheel
barrow

glazed with rain
water

beside the white
chickens.

(1923)

D. H. Lawrence *1885–1930*

PIANO

Softly, in the dusk, a woman is singing to me;
Taking me back down the vista of years, till I see
A child sitting under the piano, in the boom of the tingling strings
And pressing the small, poised feet of a mother who smiles as she sings.

In spite of myself, the insidious mastery of song
Betrays me back, till the heart of me weeps to belong
To the old Sunday evenings at home, with winter outside
And hymns in the cozy parlour, the tinkling piano our guide.

So now it is vain for the singer to burst into clamour
With the great black piano appassionato. The glamour

10

Of childish days is upon me, my manhood is cast
Down in the flood of remembrance, I weep like a child for the past.

(1918)

SNAKE

A snake came to my water-trough
On a hot, hot day, and I in pyjamas for the heat,
To drink there.

In the deep, strange-scented shade of the great dark carob tree
I came down the steps with my pitcher
And must wait, must stand and wait, for there he was at the trough
    before me.

He reached down from a fissure in the earth-wall in the gloom
And trailed his yellow-brown slackness soft-bellied down, over the edge
    of the stone trough
And rested his throat upon the stone bottom,
And where the water had dripped from the tap, in a small clearness,   10
He sipped with his straight mouth,
Softly drank through his straight gums, into his slack long body,
Silently.

Someone was before me at my water-trough,
And I, like a second comer, waiting.

He lifted his head from his drinking, as cattle do,
And looked at me vaguely, as drinking cattle do,
And flickered his two-forked tongue from his lips, and mused a
    moment,
And stooped and drank a little more,
Being earth-brown, earth-golden from the burning bowels of the earth   20
On the day of Sicilian July, with Etna smoking.

The voice of my education said to me
He must be killed,
For in Sicily the black, black snakes are innocent, the gold are
    venomous.

And voices in me said, If you were a man
You would take a stick and break him now, and finish him off.

But must I confess how I liked him,
How glad I was he had come like a guest in quiet, to drink at my water-
    trough
And depart peaceful, pacified, and thankless
Into the burning bowels of this earth?   30

Was it cowardice, that I dared not kill him?
Was it perversity, that I longed to talk to him?
Was it humility, to feel so honoured?
I felt so honoured.

And yet those voices:
If you were not afraid, you would kill him!

And truly I was afraid, I was most afraid,
But even so, honoured still more
That he should seek my hospitality
From out the dark door of the secret earth.   40

He drank enough
And lifted his head, dreamily, as one who has drunken,
And flickered his tongue like a forked night on the air, so black,
Seeming to lick his lips,
And looked around like a god, unseeing, into the air,
And slowly turned his head,
And slowly, very slowly, as if thrice adream,
Proceeded to draw his slow length curving round
And climb again the broken bank of my wall-face.

And as he put his head into that dreadful hole,   50
And as he slowly drew up, snake-easing his shoulders, and entered
     farther,
A sort of horror, a sort of protest again his withdrawing into that
     horrid black hole,
Deliberately going into the blackness, and slowly drawing himself after,
Overcame me now his back was turned.

I looked around, I put down my pitcher,
I picked up a clumsy log
And threw it at the water-trough with a clatter.

I think I did not hit him,
But suddenly that part of him that was left behind convulsed in
     undignified haste,
Writhed like lightning, and was gone   60
Into the black hole, the earth-lipped fissure in the wall-front,
At which, in the intense still noon, I stared with fascination.

And immediately I regretted it.
I thought how paltry, how vulgar, what a mean act!
I despised myself and the voices of my accursed human education.

And I thought of the albatross,
And I wished he would come back, my snake.

For he seemed to me again like a king,
Like a king in exile, uncrowned in the underworld.
Now due to be crowned again.   70

And so, I missed my chance with one of the lords
Of life.
And I have something to expiate;
A pettiness.

                                                          (1923)

Ezra Pound *1885–1972*

IN A STATION OF THE METRO[1]

The apparition of these faces in the crowd;
Petals on a wet, black bough.

(1913)

THE RIVER-MERCHANT'S WIFE: A LETTER

While my hair was still cut straight across my forehead
I played about the front gate, pulling flowers.
You came by on bamboo stilts, playing horse,
You walked about my seat, playing with blue plums.
And we went on living in the village of Chokan:
Two small people, without dislike or suspicion.

At fourteen I married My Lord you.
I never laughed, being bashful.
Lowering my head, I looked at the wall.
Called to, a thousand times, I never looked back.   10

At fifteen I stopped scowling,
I desired my dust to be mingled with yours
Forever and forever and forever.
Why should I climb the look out?

At sixteen you departed,
You went into far Ku-to-yen, by the river of swirling eddies,
And you have been gone five months.
The monkeys make sorrowful noise overhead.

You dragged your feet when you went out.
By the gate now, the moss is grown, the different mosses,   20
Too deep to clear them away!
The leaves fall early this autumn, in wind.
The paired butterflies are already yellow with August
Over the grass in the West garden;
They hurt me. I grow older.
If you are coming down through the narrows of the river Kiang,
Please let me know beforehand,
And I will come out to meet you
            As far as Cho-fu-Sa.

by Rihaku[1] (1915)

---

[1]Subway in Paris.
[1]Japanese name for the poet Li Po (eighth century).

Marianne Moore *1887–1972*

POETRY

I, too, dislike it: there are things that are important beyond all this
fiddle.
　　Reading it, however, with a perfect contempt for it, one discovers
　　in it after all, a place for the genuine.
　　　　Hands that can grasp, eyes
　　　　that can dilate, hair that can rise
　　　　　　if it must, these things are important not because a

high-sounding interpretation can be put upon them but because they are
useful. When they become so derivative as to become unintelligible,
　　the same thing may be said for all of us, that we
　　　　do not admire what   10
　　　　we cannot understand: the bat
　　　　　　holding on upside down or in quest of something to

eat, elephants pushing, a wild horse taking a roll, a tireless wolf under
a tree, the immovable critic twitching his skin like a horse that
　　feels a flea, the base-
　　　　ball fan, the statistician —
　　　　　　nor is it valid
　　　　　　　　to discriminate against "business documents and

school-books";[1] all these phenomena are important. One must make a
distinction
however: when dragged into prominence by half poets, the result is   20
　　not poetry,
　　nor till the poets among us can be
　　　　"literalists of
　　the imagination"[2] — above
　　　　insolence and triviality and can present

for inspection, "imaginary gardens with real toads in them," shall we
have
　　it. In the meantime, if you demand on the one hand,
　　the raw material of poetry in
　　　　all its rawness and
　　that which is on the other hand
　　　　genuine, you are interested in poetry.

                                                                          (1921)

<hr />

[1]Quotation from Russian author Leo Tolstoy, who wrote: "poetry is everything with the exception of business documents and school books."

[2]Quotation from poet W. B. Yeats, who characterized William Blake as "a too literal realist of imagination."

T. S. Eliot *1888–1965*

THE LOVE SONG OF J. ALFRED PRUFROCK

S'io credesse che mia risposta fosse
A persona che mai tornasse al mondo,
Questa fiamma staria senza piu scosse.
Ma perciocche giammai di questo fondo
Non torno vivo alcun, s'i'odo il vero,
Senze tema d'infamia ti rispondo.[1]

Let us go then, you and I,
When the evening is spread out against the sky
Like a patient etherised upon a table;
Let us go, through certain half-deserted streets,
The muttering retreats
Of restless nights in one-night cheap hotels
And sawdust restaurants with oyster-shells:
Streets that follow like a tedious argument
Of insidious intent
To lead you to an overwhelming question . . .   10
Oh, do not ask, "What is it?"
Let us go and make our visit.

In the room the women come and go
Talking of Michelangelo.

The yellow fog that rubs its back upon the window-panes,
The yellow smoke that rubs its muzzle on the window-panes
Licked its tongue into the corners of the evening,
Lingered upon the pools that stand in drains,
Let fall upon its back the soot that falls from chimneys,
Slipped by the terrace, made a sudden leap,   20
And seeing that it was a soft October night,
Curled once about the house, and fell asleep.

And indeed there will be time
For the yellow smoke that slides along the street
Rubbing its back upon the window-panes;
There will be time, there will be time
To prepare a face to meet the faces that you meet;
There will be time to murder and create,
And time for all the works and days of hands
That lift and drop a question on your plate;   30

---

[1]The epigraph is from Dante's *Inferno*—the speech of one dead and damned, Count Guido da
Montefeltro, who thinks his hearer is also going to remain in Hell; he offers to tell Dante his story:
"If I thought my reply were to someone who could ever return to the world, this flame would waver
no more. But since, I'm told, nobody ever escapes from this pit, I'll tell you without fear of ill fame."

Time for you and time for me,
And time yet for a hundred indecisions,
And for a hundred visions and revisions,
Before the taking of a toast and tea.

In the room the women come and go
Talking of Michelangelo.

And indeed there will be time
To wonder, "Do I dare?" and, "Do I dare?"
Time to turn back and descend the stair,
With a bald spot in the middle of my hair —   40
(They will say: "How his hair is growing thin!")
My morning coat, my collar mounting firmly to the chin,
My necktie rich and modest, but asserted by a simple pin —
(They will say: "But how his arms and legs are thin!")
Do I dare
Disturb the universe?
In a minute there is time
For decisions and revisions which a minute will reverse.

For I have known them all already, known them all —
Have known the evenings, mornings, afternoons,   50
I have measured out my life with coffee spoons;
I know the voices dying with a dying fall
Beneath the music from a farther room.
         So how should I presume?

And I have known the eyes already, known them all —
The eyes that fix you in a formulated phrase,
And when I am formulated, sprawling on a pin,
When I am pinned and wriggling on the wall,
Then how should I begin
To spit out all the butt-ends of my days and ways?   60
         And how should I presume?

And I have known the arms already, known them all —
Arms that are braceleted and white and bare
(But in the lamplight, downed with light brown hair!)
Is it perfume from a dress
That makes me so digress?
Arms that lie along a table, or wrap about a shawl.
         And should I then presume?
         And how should I begin?
                    . . .

Shall I say, I have gone at dusk through narrow streets   70
And watched the smoke that rises from the pipes
Of lonely men in shirt-sleeves, leaning out of windows? . . .

I should have been a pair of ragged claws
Scuttling across the floors of silent seas.
                    . . .
After the afternoon, the evening, sleeps so peacefully!
Smoothed by long fingers,

Asleep . . . tired . . . or it malingers,
Stretched on the floor, here beside you and me.
Should I, after tea and cakes and ices,
Have the strength to force the moment to its crisis? 80
But though I have wept and fasted, wept and prayed,
Though I have seen my head (grown slightly bald) brought in upon a
  platter,[2]
I am no prophet—and here's no great matter;
I have seen the moment of my greatness flicker,
And I have seen the eternal Footman hold my coat, and snicker,
And in short, I was afraid.

And would it have been worth it, after all,
After the cups, the marmalade, the tea,
Among the porcelain, among some talk of you and me,
Would it have been worth while, 90
To have bitten off the matter with a smile,
To have squeezed the universe into a ball
To roll it toward some overwhelming question,
To say: "I am Lazarus,[3] come from the dead,
Come back to tell you all, I shall tell you all"—
If one, settling a pillow by her head,
    Should say: "That is not what I meant at all;
    That is not it, at all."

And would it have been worth it, after all,
Would it have been worth while, 100
After the sunsets and the dooryards and the sprinkled streets,
After the novels, after the teacups, after the skirts that trail along the
  floor—
And this, and so much more?—
It is impossible to say just what I mean!
But as if a magic lantern threw the nerves in patterns on a screen:
Would it have been worth while
If one, settling a pillow or throwing off a shawl,
And turning toward the window, should say:
    "That is not it at all,
    That is not what I meant, at all." 110
            . . .
No! I am not Prince Hamlet, nor was meant to be;
Am an attendant lord, one that will do
To swell a progress, start a scene or two,
Advise the prince; no doubt, an easy tool,
Deferential, glad to be of use,
Politic, cautious, and meticulous;
Full of high sentence, but a bit obtuse;
At times, indeed, almost ridiculous—
Almost, at times, the Fool.

[2]The head of John the Baptist was presented to Salome on a platter. See Matthew 14:1–11.
[3]Jesus raised Lazarus from the dead. See John 11:1–44.

I grow old . . . I grow old . . .   120
I shall wear the bottoms of my trousers rolled.

Shall I part my hair behind? Do I dare to eat a peach?
I shall wear white flannel trousers, and walk upon the beach.
I have heard the mermaids singing, each to each.

I do not think that they will sing to me.

I have seen them riding seaward on the waves
Combing the white hair of the waves blown back
When the wind blows the water white and black.

We have lingered in the chambers of the sea
By sea-girls wreathed with seaweed red and brown   130
Till human voices wake us, and we drown.

                                                         (1917)

Claude McKay *1890–1948*

AMERICA

Although she feeds me bread of bitterness,
And sinks into my throat her tiger's tooth,
Stealing my breath of life, I will confess
I love this cultured hell that tests my youth!
Her vigor flows like tides into my blood,
Giving me strength erect against her hate.
Her bigness sweeps my being like a flood,
Yet as a rebel fronts a king in state,
I stand within her walls with not a shred
Of terror, malice, not a word of jeer.   10
Darkly I gaze into the days ahead,
And see her might and granite wonders there,
Beneath the touch of Time's unerring hand,
Like priceless treasures sinking in the sand.

                                                         (1920)

Edna St. Vincent Millay *1892–1950*

LOVE IS NOT ALL

Love is not all: it is not meat nor drink
Nor slumber nor a roof against the rain;
Nor yet a floating spar to men that sink
And rise and sink and rise and sink again;

Love can not fill the thickened lung with breath,
Nor clean the blood, nor set the fractured bone;
Yet many a man is making friends with death
Even as I speak, for lack of love alone.
It well may be that in a difficult hour,
Pinned down by pain and moaning for release,   10
Or nagged by want past resolution's power,
I might be driven to sell your love for peace,
Or trade the memory of this night for food.
It well may be. I do not think I would.

                                                  (1931)

FIRST FIG

My candle burns at both ends;
    It will not last the night;
But ah, my foes, and oh, my friends —
    It gives a lovely light!

                                                  (1920)

THE SPRING AND THE FALL

In the spring of the year, in the spring of the year,
I walked the road beside my dear.
The trees were black where the bark was wet.
I see them yet, in the spring of the year.
He broke me a bough of the blossoming peach
That was out of the way and hard to reach.

In the fall of the year, in the fall of the year,
I walked the road beside my dear.
The rooks went up with a raucous trill.
I hear them still, in the fall of the year.   10
He laughed at all I dared to praise,
And broke my heart, in little ways.

Year be springing or year be falling,
The bark will drip and the birds be calling.
There's much that's fine to see and hear
In the spring of a year, in the fall of a year.
Tis not love's going hurts my days,
But that it went in little ways.

                                                  (1923)

Archibald MacLeish *1892–1982*

ARS POETICA

A poem should be palpable and mute
As a globed fruit,

Dumb
As old medallions to the thumb,

Silent as the sleeve-worn stone
Of casement ledges where the moss has grown—

A poem should be wordless
As the flight of birds.

   . . .

A poem should be motionless in time
As the moon climbs,   10

Leaving, as the moon releases
Twig by twig the night-entangled trees,

Leaving, as the moon behind the winter leaves,
Memory by memory the mind—

A poem should be motionless in time
As the moon climbs.

   . . .

A poem should be equal to:
Not true.

For all the history of grief
An empty doorway and a maple leaf   20

For love
The leaning grasses and two lights above the sea—

A poem should not mean
But be.

(1926)

Wilfred Owen *1893–1918*

DULCE ET DECORUM EST

Bent double, like old beggars under sacks,
Knock-kneed, coughing like hags, we cursed through sludge,
Till on the haunting flares we turned our backs
And towards our distant rest began to trudge.
Men marched asleep. Many had lost their boots
But limped on, blood-shod. All went lame; all blind;

Drunk with fatigue; deaf even to the hoots
Of tired, outstripped Five-Nines that dropped behind.

Gas! Gas! Quick, boys! — An ecstasy of fumbling,
Fitting the clumsy helmets just in time;   10
But someone still was yelling out and stumbling
And flound'ring like a man in fire or lime . . .
Dim, through the misty panes and thick green light,
As under a green sea, I saw him drowning.
In all my dreams before my helpless sight,
He plunges at me, guttering, choking, drowning.

If in some smothering dreams you too could pace
Behind the wagon that we flung him in,
And watch the white eyes writhing in his face,
His hanging face, like a devil's sick of sin;   20
If you could hear, at every jolt, the blood
Come gargling from the froth-corrupted lungs,
Obscene as cancer, bitter as the cud
Of vile, incurable sores on innocent tongues, —
My friend, you would not tell with such high zest
To children ardent for some desperate glory,
The old Lie: Dulce et decorum est
Pro patria mori.[1]

          (1920)

e. e. cummings *1894–1962*

next to of course god america i

"next to of course god america i
love you land of the pilgrims' and so forth oh
say can you see by the dawn's early my
country 'tis of centuries come and go
and are no more what of it we should worry
in every language even deafanddumb
thy sons acclaim your glorious name by gorry
by jingo by gee by gosh by gum
why talk of beauty what could be more beautiful than these heroic happy dead   10
who rushed like lions to the roaring slaughter
they did not stop to think they died instead
then shall the voice of liberty be mute?"

He spoke.   And drank rapidly a glass of water

          (1926)

---

[1]The quotation is from the Latin poet Horace, meaning "It is sweet and fitting to die for one's country."

since feeling is first

since feeling is first
who pays any attention
to the syntax of things
will never wholly kiss you;

wholly to be a fool
while Spring is in the world

my blood approves,
and kisses are a better fate
than wisdom
lady i swear by all flowers. Don't cry   10
—the best gesture of my brain is less than
your eyelids' flutter which says

we are for each other: then
laugh, leaning back in my arms
for life's not a paragraph

And death i think is no parenthesis

                                                        (1926)

pity this busy monster,manunkind

pity this busy monster,manunkind,

not. Progress is a comfortable disease:
your victim(death and life safely beyond)

plays with the bigness of his littleness
—electrons deify one razorblade
into a mountainrange;lenses extend

unwish through curving wherewhen till unwish
return on its unself

                    A world of made
is not a world of born — pity poor flesh   10

and trees,poor stars and stones,but never this
fine specimen of hypermagical

ultraomnipotence. We doctors know

a hopeless case if—listen:there's a hell
of a good universe next door;let's go

                                                        (1944)

Jean Toomer *1894–1967*

REAPERS

Black reapers with the sound of steel on stones
Are sharpening scythes. I see them place the hones
In their hip-pockets as a thing that's done,
And start their silent swinging, one by one.

Black horses drive a mower through the weeds,
And there, a field rat, startled, squealing bleeds,
His belly close to ground. I see the blade,
Blood-stained, continue cutting weeds and shade.

(1923)

Langston Hughes *1902–1967*

DAYBREAK IN ALABAMA

When I get to be a composer
I'm gonna write me some music about
Daybreak in Alabama
And I'm gonna put the purtiest songs in it
Rising out of the ground like a swamp mist
And falling out of heaven like soft dew.
I'm gonna put some tall tall trees in it
And the scent of pine needles
And the smell of red clay after rain
And long red necks   10
And poppy colored faces
And big brown arms
And the field daisy eyes
Of black and white black white black people
And I'm gonna put white hands
And black hands and brown and yellow hands
And red clay earth hands in it
Touching everybody with kind fingers
And touching each other natural as dew
In that dawn of music when I   20
Get to be a composer
And write about daybreak
In Alabama.

(1948)

SAME IN BLUES

I said to my baby,
Baby, take it slow.
I can't, she said, I can't!
I got to go!

> *There's certain*
> *amount of traveling*
> *in a dream deferred.*

Lulu said to Leonard,
I want a diamond ring.
Leonard said to Lulu,   10
You won't get a goddamn thing!

> *A certain*
> *amount of nothing*
> *in a dream deferred.*

Daddy, daddy, daddy,
All I want is you.
You can have me, baby —
but my lovin' days is through.

> *A certain*
> *amount of impotence*   20
> *in a dream deferred.*

Three parties
On my party line —
But that third party,
Lord, ain't mine!

> *There's liable*
> *to be confusion*
> *in a dream deferred.*

From river to river,
Uptown and down,   30
There's liable to be confusion
when a dream gets kicked around.

(1951)

THEME FOR ENGLISH B

The instructor said,

> *Go home and write*
> *a page tonight.*
> *And let that page come out of you —*
> *Then, it will be true.*

I wonder if it's that simple?
I am twenty-two, colored, born in Winston-Salem.
I went to school there, then Durham, then here
to this college on the hill above Harlem.
I am the only colored student in my class.   10
The steps from the hill lead down into Harlem,
through a park, then I cross St. Nicholas,
Eighth Avenue, Seventh, and I come to the Y,
the Harlem Branch Y, where I take the elevator
up to my room, sit down, and write this page:

It's not easy to know what is true for you or me
at twenty-two, my age. But I guess I'm what
I feel and see and hear, Harlem, I hear you:
hear you, hear me — we two — you, me, talk on this page.
(I hear New York, too.) Me — who?   20
Well, I like to eat, sleep, drink, and be in love.
I like to work, read, learn, and understand life.
I like a pipe for a Christmas present,
or records — Bessie, bop, or Bach.
I guess being colored doesn't make me *not* like
the same things other folks like who are other races.
So will my page be colored that I write?
Being me, it will not be white.
But it will be
a part of you, instructor.   30
You are white —
yet a part of me, as I am a part of you.
That's American.
Sometimes perhaps you don't want to be a part of me.
Nor do I often want to be a part of you.
But we are, that's true!
I guess you learn from me —
although you're older — and white —
and somewhat more free.

This is my page for English B.   40
(1951)

THE NEGRO SPEAKS OF RIVERS

(To W. E. B. Du Bois)

I've known rivers:
I've known rivers ancient as the world and older than the
    flow of human blood in human veins.

My soul has grown deep like the rivers.

I bathed in the Euphrates when dawns were young.
I built my hut near the Congo and it lulled me to sleep.
I looked upon the Nile and raised the pyramids above it.
I heard the singing of the Mississippi when Abe Lincoln
    went down to New Orleans, and I've seen its muddy
    bosom turn all golden in the sunset.   10

I've known rivers:
Ancient, dusky rivers.

My soul has grown deep like the rivers.

                           (1926)

Stevie Smith *1902–1971*

NOT WAVING BUT DROWNING

Nobody heard him, the dead man,
But still he lay moaning:
I was much further out than you thought
And not waving but drowning.

Poor chap, he always loved larking
And now he's dead
It must have been too cold for him his heart gave way,
They said.

Oh, no no no, it was too cold always
(Still the dead one lay moaning)   10
I was much too far out all my life
And not waving but drowning.

                           (1957)

Countee Cullen *1903–1946*

INCIDENT

(For Eric Walrond)

Once riding in old Baltimore,
    Heart-filled, head-filled with glee,
I saw a Baltimorean
    Keep looking straight at me.

Now I was eight and very small,
    And he was no whit bigger,
And so I smiled, but he poked out
    His tongue, and called me, "Nigger."

I saw the whole of Baltimore
    From May until December;   10
Of all the things that happened there
    That's all that I remember.

                                             (1925)

Pablo Neruda *1904–1973*

THE UNITED FRUIT CO.[1]

When the trumpet sounded, it was
all prepared on the earth,
and Jehovah parceled out the earth
to Coca-Cola, Inc., Anaconda,
Ford Motors, and other entities:
The Fruit Company, Inc.
reserved for itself the most succulent,
the central coast of my own land,
the delicate waist of America.
It rechristened its territories   10
as the "Banana Republics"
and over the sleeping dead,
over the restless heroes
who brought about the greatness,
the liberty and the flags,
it established the comic opera:
abolished the independencies,
presented crowns of Caesar,
unsheathed envy, attracted
the dictatorship of the flies,   20
Trujillo flies, Tacho flies,
Carias flies, Martinez flies,
Ubico flies, damp flies
of modest blood and marmalade,
drunken flies who zoom
over the ordinary graves,
circus flies, wise flies
well trained in tyranny.
Among the bloodthirsty flies
the Fruit Company lands its ships,   30
taking off the coffee and the fruit;

[1]"The Betrayed Sand" (a long poem by Neruda) concentrates on the men who allowed South American nations to fall back on colonialism of the United States, and on the men who support United States' interests today. He mentions the pressure from U.S. companies to keep wages low. He describes especially events in the year 1946, while he was senator in Chile. We have chosen one of the poems in the center of the section, on the United Fruit Company. (*Translator's note*)

the treasure of our submerged
territories flows as though
on plates into the ships.

Meanwhile Indians are falling
into the sugared chasms
of the harbors, wrapped
for burial in the mist of the dawn:
a body rolls, a thing
that has no name, a fallen cipher,   40
a cluster of dead fruit
thrown down on the dump.

                                                        (1971)
                                        Translated by Robert Bly

W. H. Auden *1907–1973*

MUSÉE DES BEAUX ARTS[1]

About suffering they were never wrong,
The Old Masters: how well they understood
Its human position; how it takes place
While someone else is eating or opening a window or just
    walking dully along;
How, when the aged are reverently, passionately waiting
For the miraculous birth, there always must be
Children who did not specially want it to happen, skating
On a pond at the edge of the wood:
They never forgot
That even the dreadful martyrdom must run its course   10
Anyhow in a corner, some untidy spot
Where the dogs go on with their doggy life and the torturer's
    horse
Scratches its innocent behind on a tree.

In Brueghel's *Icarus*,[2] for instance: how everything turns away
Quite leisurely from the disaster; the ploughman may
Have heard the splash, the forsaken cry,
But for him it was not an important failure; the sun shone
As it had to on the white legs disappearing into the green
Water; and the expensive delicate ship that must have seen

[1]Museum of Fine Arts.
[2]Painting by Pieter Brueghel (1520–1569) that depicts the fall of Icarus, who in Greek mythology
had flown too close to the sun on wings made of feathers and wax.

Something amazing, a boy falling out of the sky,   20
Had somewhere to get to and sailed calmly on.

(1940)

LULLABY

Lay your sleeping head, my love,
Human on my faithless arm;
Time and fevers burn away
Individual beauty from
Thoughtful children, and the grave
Proves the child ephemeral:
But in my arms till break of day
Let the living creature lie,
Mortal, guilty, but to me
The entirely beautiful.   10

Soul and body have no bounds:
To lovers as they lie upon
Her tolerant enchanted slope
In their ordinary swoon,
Grave the vision Venus sends
Of supernatural sympathy,
Universal love and hope;
While an abstract insight wakes
Among the glaciers and the rocks
The hermit's sensual ecstasy.   20

Certainly, fidelity
On the stroke of midnight pass
Like vibrations of a bell,
And fashionable madmen raise
Their pedantic boring cry:
Every farthing of the cost,
All the dreaded cards foretell,
Shall be paid, but from this night
Not a whisper, not a thought,
Not a kiss nor look be lost.   30

Beauty, midnight, vision dies:
Let the winds of dawn that blow
Softly round your dreaming head
Such a day of sweetness show
Eye and knocking heart may bless,
Find the mortal world enough;
Noons of dryness see you fed
By the involuntary powers,
Nights of insult let you pass
Watched by every human love.   40

(1940)

Theodore Roethke *1908–1963*

ROOT CELLAR

Nothing would sleep in that cellar, dank as a ditch,
Bulbs broke out of boxes hunting for chinks in the dark,
Shoots dangled and drooped,
Lolling obscenely from mildewed crates,
Hung down long yellow evil necks, like tropical snakes.
And what a congress of stinks! —
Roots ripe as old bait,
Pulpy stems, rank, silo-rich,
Leaf-mold, manure, lime, piled against slippery planks.
Nothing would give up life: 10
Even the dirt kept breathing a small breath.

(1948)

I KNEW A WOMAN

I knew a woman, lovely in her bones,
When small birds sighed, she would sigh back at them;
Ah, when she moved, she moved more ways than one:
The shapes a bright container can contain!
Of her choice virtues only gods should speak,
Or English poets who grew up on Greek
(I'd have them sing in chorus, cheek to cheek).

How well her wishes went! She stroked my chin,
She taught me Turn, and Counter-turn, and Stand;
She taught me Touch, that undulant white skin;   10
I nibbled meekly from her proffered hand;
She was the sickle; I, poor I, the rake,
Coming behind her for her pretty sake
(But what prodigious mowing we did make).

Love likes a gander, and adores a goose:
Her full lips pursed, the errant note to seize;
She played it quick, she played it light and loose;
My eyes, they dazzled at her flowing knees;
Her several parts could keep a pure repose,
Or one hip quiver with a mobile nose   20
(She moved in circles, and those circles moved).

Let seed be grass, and grass turn into hay:
I'm martyr to a motion not my own;
What's freedom for? To know eternity.
I swear she cast a shadow white as stone.
But who would count eternity in days?

These old bones live to learn her wanton ways:
(I measure time by how a body sways).

(1958)

Delmore Schwartz *1913–1966*

THE HEAVY BEAR WHO GOES WITH ME

"The withness of the body"
—Whitehead

The heavy bear who goes with me,
A manifold honey to smear his face,
Clumsy and lumbering here and there,
The central ton of every place,
The hungry beating brutish one
In love with candy, anger, and sleep,
Crazy factotum, dishevelling all,
Climbs the building, kicks the football,
Boxes his brother in the hate-ridden city.

Breathing at my side, that heavy animal,   10
That heavy bear who sleeps with me,
Howls in his sleep for a world of sugar,
A sweetness intimate as the water's clasp,
Howls in his sleep because the tight-rope
Trembles and shows the darkness beneath.
—The strutting show-off is terrified,
Dressed in his dress-suit, bulging his pants,
Trembles to think that his quivering meat
Must finally wince to nothing at all.

That inescapable animal walks with me,   20
Has followed me since the black womb held,
Moves where I move, distorting my gesture,
A caricature, a swollen shadow,
A stupid clown of the spirit's motive,
Perplexes and affronts with his own darkness,
The secret life of belly and bone,
Opaque, too near, my private, yet unknown,

Stretches to embrace the very dear
With whom I would walk without him near,
Touches her grossly, although a word   30
Would bare my heart and make me clear,
Stumbles, flounders, and strives to be fed
Dragging me with him in his mouthing care,
Amid the hundred million of his kind,
The scrimmage of appetite everywhere.

(1938)

Robert Hayden *1913–1980*

THOSE WINTER SUNDAYS

Sundays too my father got up early
and put his clothes on in the blueblack cold,
then with cracked hands that ached
from labor in the weekday weather made
banked fires blaze. No one ever thanked him.

I'd wake and hear the cold splintering, breaking.
When the rooms were warm, he'd call,
and slowly I would rise and dress,
fearing the chronic angers of that house,

Speaking indifferently to him,   10
who had driven out the cold
and polished my good shoes as well.
What did I know, what did I know
of love's austere and lonely offices?

                                                        (1966)

Karl Shapiro *1913–*

AUTO WRECK

Its quick soft silver bell beating, beating,
And down the dark one ruby flare
Pulsing out red light like an artery,
The ambulance at top speed floating down
Past beacons and illuminated clocks
Wings in a heavy curve, dips down,
And brakes speed, entering the crowd.
The doors leap open, emptying light;
Stretchers are laid out, the mangled lifted
And stowed into the little hospital.   10
Then the bell, breaking the hush, tolls once,
And the ambulance with its terrible cargo
Rocking, slightly rocking, moves away,
As the doors, an afterthought, are closed.

We are deranged, walking among the cops
Who sweep glass and are large and composed.
One is still making notes under the light.
One with a bucket douches ponds of blood
Into the street and gutter.
One hangs lanterns on the wrecks that cling,   20
Empty husks of locusts, to iron poles.

Our throats were tight as tourniquets,
Our feet were bound with splints, but now,
Like convalescents intimate and gauche,
We speak through sickly smiles and warn
With the stubborn saw of common sense,
The grim joke and the banal resolution.
The traffic moves around with care,
But we remain, touching a wound
That opens to our richest horror.   30

Already old, the question Who shall die?
Becomes unspoken Who is innocent?
For death in war is done by hands;
Suicide has cause and stillbirth, logic;
And cancer, simple as a flower, blooms.
But this invites the occult mind,
Cancels our physics with a sneer,
And spatters all we knew of denouement
Across the expedient and wicked stones.

(1942)

Dudley Randall *1914–*

BALLAD OF BIRMINGHAM

*(on the bombing of a church in
Birmingham, Alabama, 1963)*

"Mother dear, may I go downtown
instead of out to play,
and march the streets of Birmingham
in a freedom march today?"

"No, baby, no, you may not go,
for the dogs are fierce and wild,
and clubs and hoses, guns and jails
aren't good for a little child."

"But, mother, I won't be alone.
Other children will go with me,   10
and march the streets of Birmingham
to make our country free."

"No, baby, no, you may not go,
for I fear those guns will fire.
But you may go to church instead,
and sing in the children's choir."

She has combed and brushed her nightdark hair,
and bathed rose petal sweet,
and drawn white gloves on her small brown hands,
and white shoes on her feet.   20

The mother smiled to know her child
was in the sacred place,
but that smile was the last smile
to come upon her face.

For when she heard the explosion,
her eyes grew wet and wild.
She raced through the streets of Birmingham
calling for her child.

She clawed through bits of glass and brick,
then lifted out a shoe.   30
"O, here's the shoe my baby wore,
but, baby, where are you?"

                                                      (1968)

TO THE MERCY KILLERS

If ever mercy move you murder me,
I pray you, kindly killers, let me live.
Never conspire with death to set me free,
but let me know such life as pain can give.
Even though I be a clot, an aching clench,
a stub, a stump, a butt, a scab, a knob,
a screaming pain, a putrefying stench,
still let me live, so long as life shall throb.
Even though I turn such traitor to myself
as beg to die, do not accomplice me.   10
Even though I seem not human, a mute shelf
of glucose, bottled blood, machinery
to swell the lung and pump the heart — even so,
do not put out my life. Let me still glow.

                                                      (1973)

Randall Jarrell *1914–1965*

THE DEATH OF THE BALL TURRET GUNNER

From my mother's sleep I fell into the State,
And I hunched in its belly till my wet fur froze.
Six miles from earth, loosed from its dream of life,
I woke to black flak and the nightmare fighters.
When I died they washed me out of the turret with a hose.

                                                      (1945)

THE WOMAN AT THE WASHINGTON ZOO

The saris go by me from the embassies.

Cloth from the moon. Cloth from another planet.
They look back at the leopard like the leopard.

And I. . . .
                    this print of mine, that has kept its color
Alive through so many cleanings; this dull null
Navy I wear to work, and wear from work, and so
To my bed, so to my grave, with no
Complaints, no comment: neither from my chief,
The Deputy Chief Assistant, nor his chief—
Only I complain. . . . this serviceable   10
Body that no sunlight dyes, no hand suffuses
But, dome-shadowed, withering among columns,
Wavy beneath fountains—small, far-off, shining
In the eyes of animals, these beings trapped
As I am trapped but not, themselves, the trap,
Aging, but without knowledge of their age,
Kept safe here, knowing not of death, for death—
Oh, bars of my own body, open, open!

The world goes by my cage and never sees me.
And there come not to me, as come to these,   20
The wild beasts, sparrows pecking the llamas' grain,
Pigeons settling on the bears' bread, buzzards
Tearing the meat the flies have clouded. . . .
                                        Vulture,
When you come for the white rat that the foxes left,
Take off the red helmet of your head, the black
Wings that have shadowed me, and step to me as man:
The wild brother at whose feet the white wolves fawn,
To whose hand of power the great lioness

Stalks, purring. . . .
                    You know what I was,
You see what I am: change me, change me!   30
                                                              (1960)

John Berryman *1914–1972*

LIFE, FRIENDS, IS BORING.
WE MUST NOT SAY SO

Life, friends, is boring. We must not say so.
After all, the sky flashes, the great sea yearns,
we ourselves flash and yearn,

and moreover my mother told me as a boy
(repeatingly) 'Ever to confess you're bored
means you have no

Inner Resources.' I conclude now I have no
inner resources, because I am heavy bored.
Peoples bore me.
literature bores me, especially great literature,   10
Henry bores me, with his plights & gripes
as bad as achilles,

who loves people and valiant art, which bores me.
And the tranquil hills, & gin, look like a drag
and somehow a dog
has taken itself & its tail considerably away
into mountains or sea or sky, leaving
behind: me, wag.

                                                                  (1964)

Dylan Thomas *1914–1953*

THE FORCE THAT THROUGH THE GREEN FUSE DRIVES THE FLOWER

The force that through the green fuse drives the flower
Drives my green age; that blasts the roots of trees
Is my destroyer.
And I am dumb to tell the crooked rose
My youth is bent by the same wintry fever.

The force that drives the water through the rocks
Drives my red blood; that dries the mouthing streams
Turns mine to wax.
And I am dumb to mouth unto my veins
How at the mountain spring the same mouth sucks.   10

The hand that whirls the water in the pool
Stirs the quicksand; that ropes the blowing wind
Hauls my shroud sail.
And I am dumb to tell the hanging man
How of my clay is made the hangman's lime.

The lips of time leech to the fountain head;
Love drips and gathers, but the fallen blood
Shall calm her sores.
And I am dumb to tell a weather's wind
How time has ticked a heaven round the stars.   20

And I am dumb to tell the lover's tomb
How at my sheet goes the same crooked worm.

                                                                  (1934)

DO NOT GO GENTLE INTO THAT
GOOD NIGHT

Do not go gentle into that good night,
Old age should burn and rave at close of day;
Rage, rage against the dying of the light.

Though wise men at their end know dark is right,
Because their words had forked no lightning they
Do not go gentle into that good night.

Good men, the last wave by, crying how bright
Their frail deeds might have danced in a green bay,
Rage, rage against the dying of the light.

Wild men who caught and sang the sun in flight,   10
And learn, too late, they grieved it on its way,
Do not go gentle into that good night.

Grave men, near death, who see with blinding sight
Blind eyes could blaze like meteors and be gay,
Rage, rage against the dying of the light.

And you, my father, there on the sad height,
Curse, bless, me now with your fierce tears, I pray.
Do not go gentle into that good night.
Rage, rage against the dying of the light.

(1952)

FERN HILL

Now as I was young and easy under the apple boughs
About the lilting house and happy as the grass was green,
   The night above the dingle starry,
    Time let me hail and climb
   Golden in the heydays of his eyes,
And honored among wagons I was prince of the apple towns
And once below a time I lordly had the trees and leaves
    Trail with daisies and barley
   Down the rivers of the windfall light.

And as I was green and carefree, famous among the barns   10
About the happy yard and singing as the farm was home,
   In the sun that is young once only,
    Time let me play and be
   Golden in the mercy of his means,
And green and golden I was huntsman and herdsman, the calves
Sang to my horn, the foxes on the hills barked clear and cold,
    And the sabbath rang slowly
   In the pebbles of the holy streams.

All the sun long it was running, it was lovely, the hay
Fields high as the house, the tunes from the chimneys, it was air   20
    And playing, lovely and watery
        And fire green as grass.
    And nightly under the simple stars
As I rode to sleep the owls were bearing the farm away,
All the moon long I heard, blessed among stables, the night-jars
    Flying with the ricks, and the horses
        Flashing into the dark.

And then to awake, and the farm, like a wanderer white
With the dew, come back, the cock on his shoulder: it was all
    Shining, it was Adam and maiden,   30
        The sky gathered again
    And the sun grew round that very day.
So it must have been after the birth of the simple light
In the first, spinning place, the spellbound horses walking warm
    Out of the whinnying green stable
        On to the fields of praise.

And honored among foxes and pheasants by the gay house
Under the new made clouds and happy as the heart was long,
    In the sun born over and over,
        I ran my heedless ways,   40
    My wishes raced through the house high hay
And nothing I cared, at my sky blue trades, that time allows
In all his tuneful turning so few and such morning songs
    Before the children green and golden
        Follow him out of grace,

Nothing I cared, in the lamb white days, that time would take me
Up to the swallow thronged loft by the shadow of my hand,
    In the moon that is always rising,
        Nor that riding to sleep
    I should hear him fly with the high fields   50
And wake to the farm forever fled from the childless land.
Oh as I was young and easy in the mercy of his means,
    Time held me green and dying
    Though I sang in my chains like the sea.

                                (1946)

Gwendolyn Brooks *1917–*

A SONG IN THE FRONT YARD

I've stayed in the front yard all my life.
I want a peek at the back
Where it's rough and untended and hungry weed grows.
A girl gets sick of a rose.

I want to go in the back yard now
And maybe down the alley,
To where the charity children play.
I want a good time today.

They do some wonderful things.
They have some wonderful fun: 10
My mother sneers, but I say it's fine
How they don't have to go in at quarter to nine.

My mother, she tells me that Johnnie Mae
Will grow up to be a bad woman.
That George'll be taken to Jail soon or late
(On account of last winter he sold our back gate).

But I say it's fine. Honest, I do.
And I'd like to be a bad woman, too,
And wear the brave stockings of night-black lace
And strut down the streets with paint on my face.   20

                                                         (1945)

THE BEAN EATERS

They eat beans mostly, this old yellow pair.
Dinner is a casual affair.
Plain chipware on a plain and creaking wood,
Tin flatware.

Two who are Mostly Good.
Two who have lived their day,
But keep on putting on their clothes
And putting things away.

And remembering . . .
Remembering, with twinklings and twinges,   10
As they lean over the beans in their rented back room that
    is full of beads and receipts and dolls and cloths,
    tobacco crumbs, vases and fringes.

                                                         (1945)

May Swenson *1919–1989*

PIGEON WOMAN

Slate, or dirty-marble-colored,
or rusty-iron-colored, the pigeons
on the flagstones in front of the
Public Library make a sharp lake

into which the pigeon woman wades
at exactly 1:30. She wears a
plastic pink raincoat with a round
collar (Looking like a little

girl) and flat gym shoes,
her hair square-cut, orange.   10
Wide-apart feet carefully enter
the spinning, crooning waves

(as if she'd just learned how
to walk, each step conscious,
an accomplishment); blue knots in the
calves of her bare legs (uglied marble),

age in angled cords of jaw
and neck, her pimento-colored hair,
hanging in thin tassels, is gray
around a balding crown.   20

The day-old bread drops down
from her veined hand dipping out
of a paper sack. Choppy, shadowy ripples,
the pigeons strike around her legs.

Sack empty, she squats and seems to rinse
her hands in them — the rainy greens and
oily purples of their necks. Almost
they let her wet her thirsty fingertips —

but drain away in an untouchable tide.
A make-believe trade   30
she has come to, in her lostness
or illness or age — to treat the motley

city pigeons at 1:30 every day, in all
weathers. It is for them she colors
her own feathers. Ruddy-footed
on the lime-stained paving,

purling to meet her when she comes,
they are a lake of love. Retreating
from her hands as soon as empty,
they are the flints of love.   40
                                                               (1971)

Richard Wilbur *1921–*

FIRST SNOW IN ALSACE

The snow came down last night like moths
Burned on the moon; it fell till dawn,
Covered the town with simple cloths.

Absolute snow lies rumpled on
What shellbursts scattered and deranged,
Entangled railings, crevassed lawn.

As if it did not know they'd changed,
Snow smoothly clasps the roofs of homes
Fear-gutted, trustless and estranged.

The ration stacks are milky domes;   10
Across the ammunition pile
The snow has climbed in sparkling combs.

You think: beyond the town a mile
Or two, this snowfall fills the eyes
Of soldiers dead a little while.

Persons and persons in disguise,
Walking the new air white and fine,
Trade glances quick with shared surprise.

At children's windows, heaped, benign,
As always, winter shines the most,   20
And frost makes marvelous designs.

The night guard coming from his post,
Ten first-snows back in thought, walks slow
And warms him with a boyish boast:

He was the first to see the snow.

(1947)

THE WRITER

In her room at the prow of the house
Where light breaks, and the windows are tossed with linden,
My daughter is writing a story.

I pause in the stairwell, hearing
From her shut door a commotion of typewriter-keys
Like a chain hauled over a gunwale.

Young as she is, the stuff
Of her life is a great cargo, and some of it heavy:
I wish her a lucky passage.

But now it is she who pauses,   10
As if to reject my thought and its easy figure.
A stillness greatens, in which

The whole house seems to be thinking,
And then she is at it again with a bunched clamor
Of strokes, and again is silent.

I remember the dazed starling
Which was trapped in that very room, two years ago;
How we stole in, lifted a sash

And retreated, not to affright it;
And how for a helpless hour, through the crack of the door,   20
We watched the sleek, wild, dark

And iridescent creature
Batter against the brilliance, drop like a glove
To the hard floor, or the desk-top,

And wait then, humped and bloody,
For the wits to try it again; and how our spirits
Rose when, suddenly sure,

It lifted off from a chair-back,
Beating a smooth course for the right window
And clearing the sill of the world.   30

It is always a matter, my darling,
Of life or death, as I had forgotten. I wish
What I wished you before, but harder.

                                                                    (1971)

Mona Van Duyn *1921–*

LEDA

"Did she put on his knowledge with his power
Before the indifferent beak could let her drop?"

Not even for a moment. He knew, for one thing, what he was.
When he saw the swan in her eyes he could let her drop.
In the first look of love men find their great disguise,
and collecting these rare pictures of himself was his life.

Her body became the consequence of his juice,
while her mind closed on a bird and went to sleep.
Later, with the children in school, she opened her eyes
and saw her own openness, and felt relief.

In men's stories her life ended with his loss.
She stiffened under the storm of his wings to a glassy shape,   10
stricken and mysterious and immortal. But the fact is,
she was not, for such an ending, abstract enough.

She tried for a while to understand what it was
that had happened, and then decided to let it drop.
She married a smaller man with a beaky nose,
and melted away in the storm of everyday life.

                                                                    (1964)

Philip Larkin *1922–1985*

POETRY OF DEPARTURES

Sometimes you hear, fifth-hand,
As epitaph:
He chucked up everything
And just cleared off,
And always the voice will sound
Certain you approve
This audacious, purifying,
Elemental move.
And they are right, I think.
We all hate home   10
And having to be there:
I detest my room,
Its specially-chosen junk,
The good books, the good bed,
And my life, in perfect order:
So to hear it said
He walked out on the whole crowd
Leaves me flushed and stirred,
Like *Then she undid her dress*
Or *Take that you bastard*;   20
Surely I can, if he did?
And that helps me stay
Sober and industrious.
But I'd go today,
Yes, swagger the nut-strewn roads,
Crouch in the fo'c'sle
Stubbly with goodness, if
It weren't so artificial,
Such a deliberate step backwards
To create an object: 30
Books; china; a life
Reprehensibly perfect.

(1955)

TOADS

Why should I let the toad *work*
    Squat on my life?
Can't I use my wit as a pitchfork
    And drive the brute off?

Six days of the week it soils
    With its sickening poison —

Just for paying a few bills!
  That's out of proportion.

Lots of folk live on their wits:
  Lecturers, lispers,
Losels, loblolly-men,[1] louts —   10
  They don't end as paupers;

Lots of folk live up lanes
  With fires in a bucket,
Eat windfalls and tinned sardines —
  They seem to like it.

Their nippers[2] have got bare feet,
  Their unspeakable wives
Are skinny as whippets[3] — and yet
  No one actually *starves*.   20

Ah, were I courageous enough
  To shout *Stuff your pension*!
But I know, all too well, that's the stuff
  That dreams are made on:

For something sufficiently toad-like
  Squats in me, too;
Its hunkers[4] are heavy as hard luck,
  And cold as snow,

And will never allow me to blarney
  My way to getting   30
The fame and the girl and the money
  All at one sitting.

I don't say, one bodies the other
  One's spiritual truth;
But I do say it's hard to lose either,
  When you have both.

(1955)

James Dickey *1923–*

THE LEAP

The only thing I have of Jane MacNaughton
Is one instant of a dancing-class dance.
She was the fastest runner in the seventh grade,

[1]Losers; clods.
[2]Young boys.
[3]Sleek, thin dogs.
[4]Haunches.

My scrapbook says, even when boys were beginning
To be as big as the girls,
But I do not have her running in my mind,
Though Frances Lane is there, Agnes Fraser,
Fat Betty Lou Black in the boys-against-girls
Relays we ran at recess: she must have run

Like the other girls, with her skirts tucked up   10
So they would be like bloomers,
But I cannot tell; that part of her is gone.
What I do have is when she came,
With the hem of her skirt where it should be
For a young lady, into the annual dance
Of the dancing class we all hated, and with a light
Grave leap, jumped up and touched the end
Of one of the paper-ring decorations

To see if she could reach it. She could,
And reached me now as well, hanging in my mind   20
From a brown chain of brittle paper, thin
And muscular, wide-mouthed, eager to prove
Whatever it proves when you leap
In a new dress, a new womanhood, among the boys
Whom you easily left in the dust
Of the passionless playground. If I said I saw
In the paper where Jane MacNaughton Hill,

Mother of four, leapt to her death from a window
Of a downtown hotel, and that her body crushed-in
The top of a parked taxi, and that I held   30
Without trembling a picture of her lying cradled
In that papery steel as though lying in the grass,
One shoe idly off, arms folded across her breast,
I would not believe myself. I would say
The convenient thing, that it was a bad dream
Of maturity, to see that eternal process

Most obsessively wrong with the world
Come out of her light, earth-spurning feet
Grown heavy: would say that in the dusty heels
Of the playground some boy who did not depend   40
On speed of foot, caught and betrayed her.
Jane, stay where you are in my first mind:
It was odd in that school, at that dance.
I and the other slow-footed yokels sat in corners
Cutting rings out of drawing paper

Before you leapt in your new dress
And touched the end of something I began,
Above the couples struggling on the floor,
New men and women clutching at each other
And prancing foolishly as bears: hold on   50
To that ring I made for you, Jane —

My feet are nailed to the ground
By dust I swallowed thirty years ago—
While I examine my hands.

                                                                        (1967)

Denise Levertov *1923–*

THE ACHE OF MARRIAGE

The ache of marriage:

thigh and tongue, beloved,
are heavy with it,
it throbs in the teeth

We look for communion
and are turned away, beloved,
each and each

It is leviathan and we
in its belly
looking for joy, some joy   10
not to be known outside it

two by two in the ark of
the ache of it.

                                                                        (1964)

COME INTO ANIMAL PRESENCE

Come into animal presence.
No man is so guileless as
the serpent. The lonely white
rabbit on the roof is a star
twitching its ears at the rain.
The llama intricately
folding its hind legs to be seated
not disdains but mildly
disregards human approval.
What joy when the insouciant   10
armadillo glances at us and doesn't
quicken his trotting
across the track into the palm brush.

What is this joy? That no animal
falters, but knows what it must do?
That the snake has no blemish,
that the rabbit inspects his strange surroundings

in white star-silence? The llama
rests in dignity, the armadillo
has some intention to pursue in the palm-forest.   20
Those who were sacred have remained so,
holiness does not dissolve, it is a presence
of bronze, only the sight that saw it
faltered and turned from it.
And old joy returns in holy presence.

(1961)

Donald Justice *1925*–

MEN AT FORTY

Men at forty
Learn to close softly
The doors to rooms they will not be
Coming back to.

At rest on a stair landing,
They feel it
Moving beneath them now like the deck of a ship,
Though the swell is gentle.

And deep in mirrors
They rediscover   10
The face of the boy as he practices tying
His father's tie there in secret

And the face of that father,
Still warm with the mystery of lather.
They are more fathers than sons themselves now.
Something is filling them, something

That is like the twilight sound
Of the crickets, immense,
Filling the woods at the foot of the slope
Behind their mortgaged houses.   20

(1965)

THE MISSING PERSON

He has come to report himself
A missing person.

The authorities
Hand him the forms.

He knows how they have waited
With the learned patience of barbers

In small shops, idle,
Stropping their razors.

But now that these spaces in his life
Stare up at him blankly,   10

Waiting to be filled in,
He does not know how to begin.

Afraid that he may not answer
To his description of himself,

He asks for a mirror.
They reassure him

That he can be nowhere
But wherever he finds himself

From moment to moment
Which, for the moment, is here.   20

And he might like to believe them.
But in the mirror

He sees what is missing.
It is himself

He sees there emerging
Slowly, as from the dark

Of a furnished room
Only by darkness,

One who receives no mail
And is known to the landlady only   30

For keeping himself to himself,
And for whom it will be years yet

Before he can trust to the light
This last disguise, himself.

                                                                (1965)

Maxine Kumin *1925–*

WOODCHUCKS

Gassing the woodchucks didn't turn out right.
The knockout bomb from the Feed and Grain Exchange
was featured as merciful, quick at the bone
and the case we had against them was airtight,
both exits shoehorned shut with puddingstone,
but they had a sub-sub-basement out of range.

Next morning they turned up again, no worse
for the cyanide than we for our cigarettes
and state-store Scotch, all of us up to scratch.
They brought down the marigolds as a matter of course 10
and then took over the vegetable patch
nipping the broccoli shoots, beheading the carrots.

The food from our mouths, I said, righteously thrilling
to the feel of the .22, the bullets' neat noses.
I, a lapsed pacifist fallen from grace
puffed with Darwinian pieties for killing,
now drew a bead on the littlest woodchuck's face.
He died down in the everbearing roses.

Ten minutes later I dropped the mother. She
flipflopped in the air and fell, her needle teeth 20
still hooked in a leaf of early Swiss chard.
Another baby next. O one-two-three
the murderer inside me rose up hard,
the hawkeye killer came on stage forthwith.

There's one chuck left. Old wily fellow, he keeps
me cocked and ready day after day after day.
All night I hunt his humped-up form. I dream
I sight along the barrel in my sleep.
If only they'd all consented to die unseen
gassed underground the quiet Nazi way. 30

(1972)

W. D. Snodgrass *1926–*

APRIL INVENTORY

The green catalpa tree has turned
All white; the cherry blooms once more.
In one whole year I haven't learned
A blessed thing they pay you for.
The blossoms snow down in my hair;
The trees and I will soon be bare.

The trees have more than I to spare.
The sleek, expensive girls I teach,
Younger and pinker every year,
Bloom gradually out of reach. 10
The pear tree lets its petals drop
Like dandruff on a tabletop.

The girls have grown so girlish now
I have to nudge myself to stare.
This year they smile and mind me how

My teeth are falling with my hair.
In thirty years I may not get
Younger, shrewder, or out of debt.

The tenth time, just a year ago,
I made myself a little list   20
Of all the things I'd ought to know,
Then told my parents, analyst,
And everyone who's trusted me
I'd be substantial, presently.

I haven't read one book about
A book or memorized one plot.
Or found a mind I did not doubt.
I learned one date. And then forgot.
And one by one the solid scholars
Get the degrees, the jobs, the dollars.   30

And smile above their starchy collars.
I taught my classes Whitehead's[1] notions;
One lovely girl, a song of Mahler's.[2]
Lacking a source book and promotions,
I taught one child the colors of
A luna moth and how to love.

I taught myself to name my name,
To bark back, loosen love and crying;
To ease my woman so she came,
To ease an old man who was dying.   40
I have not learned how often I
Can win, can love, but choose to die.

I have not learned there is a lie
Love shall be blonder, slimmer, younger;
That my equivocating eye
Loves only by my body's hunger;
That I have forces, true to feel,
Or that the lovely world is real.

While scholars speak authority
And wear their ulcers on their sleeves,   50
My eyes in spectacles shall see
These trees procure and spend their leaves.
There is a value underneath
The gold and silver in my teeth.

Though trees turn bare and girls turn wives,
We shall afford our costly seasons;

---

[1]Alfred North Whitehead (1861–1947), British mathematician and philosopher.
[2]Gustav Mahler (1860–1911), Austrian composer.

> There is a gentleness survives
> That will outspeak and has its reasons.
> There is a loveliness exists,
> Preserves us; not for specialists.

60

(1957)

Allen Ginsberg *1926–*

A SUPERMARKET IN CALIFORNIA

What thoughts I have of you tonight, Walt Whitman, for I walked down the sidestreets under the trees with a headache self-conscious looking at the full moon.

In my hungry fatigue, and shopping for images, I went into the neon fruit supermarket, dreaming of your enumerations!

What peaches and what penumbras! Whole families shopping at night! Aisles full of husbands! Wives in the avocados, babies in the tomatoes! — and you, García Lorca, what were you doing down by the watermelons?

I saw you, Walt Whitman, childless, lonely old grubber, poking among the meats in the refrigerator and eyeing the grocery boys.

I heard you asking questions of each: Who killed the pork chops? What price bananas? Are you my Angel?

I wandered in and out of the brilliant stacks of cans following you, and followed in my imagination by the store detective.

We strode down the open corridors together in our solitary fancy tasting artichokes, possessing every frozen delicacy, and never passing the cashier.

Where are we going, Walt Whitman? The doors close in an hour. Which way does your beard point tonight?

(I touch your book and dream of our odyssey in the supermarket and feel absurd.)

Will we walk all night through solitary streets? The trees add shade to shade, lights out in the houses, we'll both be lonely.

10

Will we stroll dreaming of the lost America of love past blue automobiles in driveways, home to our silent cottage?

Ah, dear father, graybeard, lonely old courage-teacher, what America did you have when Charon quit poling his ferry and you got out on a smoking bank and stood watching the boat disappear on the black waters of Lethe?

(1956)

James Wright *1927–1980*

A BLESSING

Just off the highway to Rochester, Minnesota,
Twilight bounds softly forth on the grass.
And the eyes of those two Indian ponies
Darken with kindness.
They have come gladly out of the willows
To welcome my friend and me.
We step over the barbed wire into the pasture
Where they have been grazing all day, alone.
They ripple tensely, they can hardly contain their happiness
That we have come.   10
They bow shyly as wet swans. They love each other.
There is no loneliness like theirs.
At home once more,
They begin munching the young tufts of spring in the darkness.
I would like to hold the slenderer one in my arms,
For she has walked over to me
And nuzzled my left hand.
She is black and white,
Her mane falls wild on her forehead,
And the light breeze moves me to caress her long ear   20
That is delicate as the skin over a girl's wrist.
Suddenly I realize
That if I stepped out of my body I would break
Into blossom.

                                                                              (1961)

Anne Sexton *1928–1974*

YOU ALL KNOW THE STORY OF THE OTHER WOMAN

It's a little Walden.
She is private in her breathbed
as his body takes off and flies,
flies straight as an arrow.
But it's a bad translation.
Daylight is nobody's friend.
God comes in like a landlord
and flashes on his brassy lamp.
Now she is just so-so.   10
He puts his bones back on,

turning the clock back an hour.
She knows flesh, that skin balloon,
the unbound limbs, the boards,
the roof, the removable roof.
She is his selection, part time.
You know the story too! Look,
when it is over he places her,
like a phone, back on the hook.

(1967)

THE FARMER'S WIFE

From the hodge porridge
of their country lust,
their local life in Illinois,
where all their acres look
like a sprouting broom factory,
they name just ten years now
that she has been his habit;
as again tonight he'll say
honey bunch let's go
and she will not say how there   10
must be more to living
than this brief bright bridge
of the raucous bed or even
the slow braille touch of him
like a heavy god grown light,
that old pantomime of love
that she wants although
it leaves her still alone,
built back again at last,
minds apart from him, living   20
her own self in her own words
and hating the sweat of the house
they keep when they finally lie
each in separate dreams
and then how she watches him,
still strong in the blowzy bag
of his usual sleep while
her young years bungle past
their same marriage bed
and she wishes him cripple, or poet,   30
or even lonely, or sometimes,
better, my lover, dead.

(1960)

Thom Gunn *1929–*

ON THE MOVE

'Man, you gotta Go.'

The blue jay scuffling in the bushes follows
Some hidden purpose, and the gust of birds
That spurts across the field, the wheeling swallows,
Have nested in the trees and undergrowth.
Seeking their instinct, or their poise, or both,
One moves with an uncertain violence
Under the dust thrown by a baffled sense
Or the dull thunder of approximate words.

On motorcycles, up the road, they come:
Small, black, as flies hanging in heat, the Boys,   10
Until the distance throws them forth, their hum
Bulges to thunder held by calf and thigh.
In goggles, donned impersonality,
In gleaming jackets trophied with the dust,
They strap in doubt — by hiding it, robust —
And almost hear a meaning in their noise.

Exact conclusion of their hardiness
Has no shape yet, but from known whereabouts
They ride, direction where the tires press.
They scare a flight of birds across the field: 20
Much that is natural, to the will must yield.
Men manufacture both machine and soul,
And use what they imperfectly control
To dare a future from the taken routes.

It is a part solution, after all.
One is not necessarily discord
On earth; or damned because, half animal,
One lacks direct instinct, because one wakes
Afloat on movement that divides and breaks.
One joins the movement in a valueless world,   30
Choosing it, till, both hurler and the hurled,
One moves as well, always toward, toward.

A minute holds them, who have come to go:
The self-defined, astride the created will
They burst away; the towns they travel through
Are home for neither bird nor holiness,
For birds and saints complete their purposes.
At worse, one is in motion; and at best,
Reaching no absolute, in which to rest,
One is always nearer by not keeping still.   40

(1957)

Adrienne Rich *1929–*

DIVING INTO THE WRECK

First having read the book of myths,
and loaded the camera,
and checked the edge of the knife-blade,
I put on
the body-armor of black rubber
the absurd flippers
the grave and awkward mask.
I am having to do this
not like Cousteau with his
assiduous team   10
aboard the sun-flooded schooner
but here alone.

There is a ladder.
The ladder is always there
hanging innocently
close to the side of the schooner.
We know what it is for,
we who have used it.
Otherwise
it's a piece of maritime floss   20
some sundry equipment.

I go down.
Rung after rung and still
the oxygen immerses me
the blue light
the clear atoms
of our human air.
I go down.
My flippers cripple me,
I crawl like an insect down the ladder   30
and there is no one
to tell me when the ocean
will begin.

First the air is blue and then
it is bluer and then green and then
black I am blacking out and yet
my mask is powerful
it pumps my blood with power
the sea is another story
the sea is not a question of power   40
I have to learn alone
to turn my body without force
in the deep element.

And now: it is easy to forget
what I came for
among so many who have always
lived here
swaying their crenellated fans
between the reefs
and besides   50
you breathe differently down here.

I came to explore the wreck.
The words are purposes.
The words are maps.
I came to see the damage that was done
and the treasures that prevail.
I stroke the beam of my lamp
slowly along the flank
of something more permanent
than fish or weed   60

the thing I came for:
the wreck and not the story of the wreck
the thing itself and not the myth
the drowned face always staring
toward the sun
the evidence of damage
worn by salt and sway into this threadbare beauty
the ribs of the disaster
curving their assertion
among the tentative haunters.   70

This is the place.
And I am here, the mermaid whose dark hair
streams black, the merman in his armored body.
We circle silently
about the wreck
we dive into the hold.
I am she: I am he

whose drowned face sleeps with open eyes
whose breasts still bear the stress
whose silver, copper, vermeil cargo lies   80
obscurely inside barrels
half-wedged and left to rot
we are the half-destroyed instruments
that once held to a course
the water-eaten log
the fouled compass

We are, I am, you are
by cowardice or courage
the ones who find our way
back to this scene   90
carrying a knife, a camera

a book of myths
in which
our names do not appear.

(1972)

LIVING IN SIN

She had thought the studio would keep itself;
No dust upon the furniture of love.
Half heresy, to wish the taps less vocal,
The panes relieved of grime. A plate of pears,
A piano with a Persian shawl, a cat
Stalking the picturesque amusing mouse
Had been her vision when he pleaded "Come."
Not that at five each separate stair would writhe
Under the milkman's tramp; that morning light
So coldly would delineate the scraps   10
Of last night's cheese and blank sepulchral bottles;
That on the kitchen shelf among the saucers
A pair of beetle-eyes would fix her own —
Envoy from some black village in the mouldings . . .
Meanwhile her night's companion, with a yawn
Sounded a dozen notes upon the keyboard,
Declared it out of tune, inspected whistling
A twelve hours' beard, went out for cigarettes;
While she, contending with a woman's demons,
Pulled back the sheets and made the bed and found   20
A fallen towel to dust the table-top,
And wondered how it was a man could wake
From night to day and take the day for granted.
By evening she was back in love again,
Though not so wholly but throughout the night
She woke sometimes to feel the daylight coming
Like a relentless milkman up the stairs.

(1955)

Ted Hughes *1930–*

SECRETARY

If I should touch her she would shriek and weeping
Crawl off to nurse the terrible wound: all
Day like a starling under the bellies of bulls
She hurries among men, ducking, peeping,

Off in a whirl at the first move of a horn.
At dusk she scuttles down the gauntlet of lust
Like a clockwork mouse. Safe home at last
She mends socks with holes, shirts that are torn

For father and brother, and a delicate supper cooks:
Goes to bed early, shuts out with the light   10
Her thirty years, and lies with buttocks tight,
Hiding her lovely eyes until day break.

(1956)

Sylvia Plath *1932–1963*

THE APPLICANT

First, are you our sort of a person?
Do you wear
A glass eye, false teeth or a crutch,
A brace or a hook,
Rubber breasts or a rubber crotch,

Stitches to show something's missing? No, no? Then
How can we give you a thing?
Stop crying.
Open your hand.
Empty? Empty. Here is a hand   10

To fill it and willing
To bring teacups and roll away headaches
And do whatever you tell it.
Will you marry it?
It is guaranteed

To thumb shut your eyes at the end
And dissolve of sorrow.
We make new stock from the salt.
I notice you are stark naked.
How about this suit—   20

Black and stiff, but not a bad fit.
Will you marry it?
It is waterproof, shatterproof, proof
Against fire and bombs through the roof.
Believe me, they'll bury you in it.

Now your head, excuse me, is empty.
I have the ticket for that.
Come here, sweetie, out of the closet.
Well, what do you think of *that*?
Naked as paper to start   30

But in twenty-five years she'll be silver,
In fifty, gold.
A living doll, everywhere you look.
It can sew, it can cook,
It can talk, talk, talk.

It works, there is nothing wrong with it.
You have a hole, it's a poultice.
You have an eye, it's an image.
My boy, it's your last resort.
Will you marry it, marry it, marry it?   40

(1962)

METAPHORS

I'm a riddle in nine syllables,
An elephant, a ponderous house,
A melon strolling on two tendrils.
O red fruit, ivory, fine timbers!
This loaf's big with its yeasty rising.
Money's new-minted in this fat purse.
I'm a means, a stage, a cow in calf.
I've eaten a bag of green apples,
Boarded the train there's no getting off.

(1960)

DADDY

You do not do, you do not do
Any more, black shoe
In which I have lived like a foot
For thirty years, poor and white,
Barely daring to breathe or Achoo.

Daddy, I have had to kill you.
You died before I had time —
Marble-heavy, a bag full of God,
Ghastly statue with one grey toe
Big as a Frisco seal   10

And a head in the freakish Atlantic
Where it pours bean green over blue
In the waters off beautiful Nauset.[1]
I used to pray to recover you.
Ach, du.[2]

---

[1]Beach and harbor on Cape Cod.
[2]German for "Ah, you."

In the German tongue, in the Polish town
Scraped flat by the roller
Of wars, wars, wars.
But the name of the town is common.
My Polack friend   20

Says there are a dozen or two.
So I never could tell where you
Put your foot, your root,
I never could talk to you.
The tongue stuck in my jaw.

It stuck in a barb wire snare.
Ich, ich, ich, ich,[3]
I could hardly speak.
I thought every German was you.
And the language obscene   30

An engine, an engine
Chuffing me off like a Jew.
A Jew to Dachau, Auschwitz, Belsen.[4]
I began to talk like a Jew.
I think I may well be a Jew.

The snows of the Tyrol, the clear beer of Vienna
Are not very pure or true.
With my gypsy ancestress and my weird luck
And my Taroc pack[5] and my Taroc pack
I may be a bit of a Jew.   40

I have always been scared of *you*,
With your Luftwaffe,[6] your gobbledygoo.
And your neat moustache
And your Aryan eye, bright blue.
Panzer[7]-man, panzer-man, O You—

Not God but a swastika
So black no sky could squeak through.
Every woman adores a Fascist,
The boot in the face, the brute
Brute heart of a brute like you.   50

You stand at the blackboard, daddy,
In the picture I have of you,
A cleft in your chin instead of your foot
But no less a devil for that, no not
Any less the black man who

---

[3]German for "I, I, I, I."
[4]Nazi concentration camps.
[5]Tarot cards, used in fortune telling.
[6]The German air force in World War II.
[7]Referring to a German tank unit in World War II.

Bit my pretty red heart in two.
I was ten when they buried you.
At twenty I tried to die
And get back, back, back to you.
I thought even the bones would do.   60

But they pulled me out of the sack,
And they stuck me together with glue.
And then I knew what to do.
I made a model of you,
A man in black with a Meinkampf[8] look

And a love of the rack and the screw.
And I said I do, I do.
So daddy, I'm finally through.
The black telephone's off at the root,
The voices just can't worm through.   70

If I've killed one man, I've killed two—
The vampire who said he was you
And drank my blood for a year,
Seven years, if you want to know.
Daddy, you can lie back now.

There's a stake in your fat black heart
And the villagers never liked you.
They are dancing and stamping on you.
They always *knew* it was you.
Daddy, daddy, you bastard, I'm through.   80
                                                  (1963)

John Updike *1932–*

EX-BASKETBALL PLAYER

Pearl Avenue runs past the high-school lot,
Bends with the trolley tracks, and stops, cut off
Before it has a chance to go two blocks,
At Colonel McComsky Plaza. Berth's Garage
Is on the corner facing west, and there,
Most days, you'll find Flick Webb, who helps Berth out.

Flick stands tall among the idiot pumps—
Five on a side, the old bubble-head style,
Their rubber elbows hanging loose and low.
One's nostrils are two S's, and his eyes   10
An E and O. And one is squat, without
A head at all—more of a football type.

---

[8]*My Struggle*, the title of Adolf Hitler's political autobiography.

Once Flick played for the high-school team, the Wizards.
He was good: in fact, the best. In '46
He bucketed three hundred ninety points,
A county record still. The ball loved Flick.
I saw him rack up thirty-eight or forty
In one home game. His hands were like wild birds.

He never learned a trade, he just sells gas,
Checks oil, and changes flats. Once in a while,   20
As a gag, he dribbles an inner tube,
But most of us remember anyway.
His hands are fine and nervous on the lug wrench.
It makes no difference to the lug wrench, though.

Off work, he hangs around Mae's luncheonette.
Grease-gray and kind of coiled, he plays pinball,
Smokes those thin cigars, nurses lemon phosphates.
Flick seldom says a word to Mae, just nods
Beyond her face toward bright applauding tiers
Of Necco Wafers, Nibs, and Juju Beads.   30

                                                                  (1958)

Imamu Amiri Baraka [LeRoi Jones] *1934–*

PREFACE TO A TWENTY VOLUME SUICIDE NOTE

For Kellie Jones, Born 16 May 1959

Lately, I've become accustomed to the way
The ground opens up and envelopes me
Each time I go out to walk the dog.
Or the broad edged silly music the wind
Makes when I run for a bus . . .

Things have come to that.

And now, each night I count the stars,
And each night I get the same number.
And when they will not come to be counted,
I count the holes they leave.   10

Nobody sings anymore.

And then last night I tiptoed up
To my daughter's room and heard her
Talking to someone, and when I opened
The door, there was no one there . . .
Only she on her knees, peeking into

Her own clasped hands.

                                                                  (1961)

Audre Lorde *1934–*

HANGING FIRE

I am fourteen
and my skin has betrayed me
the boy I cannot live without
still sucks his thumb
in secret
how come my knees are
always so ashy
what if I die
before morning
and momma's in the bedroom   10
with the door closed.

I have to learn how to dance
in time for the next party
my room is too small for me
suppose I die before graduation
they will sing sad melodies
but finally
tell the truth about me
There is nothing I want to do
and too much   20
that has to be done
and momma's in the bedroom
with the door closed.

Nobody even stops to think
about my side of it
I should have been on Math Team
my marks were better than his
why do I have to be
the one
wearing braces   30
I have nothing to wear tomorrow
will I live long enough
to grow up
and momma's in the bedroom
with the door closed.

     (1978)

Marge Piercy *1936–*

BARBIE DOLL

This girlchild was born as usual
and presented dolls that did pee-pee

and miniature GE stoves and irons
and wee lipsticks the color of cherry candy.
Then in the magic of puberty, a classmate said:
You have a great big nose and fat legs.

She was healthy, tested intelligent,
possessed strong arms and back,
abundant sexual drive and manual dexterity.
She went to and fro apologizing.   10
Everyone saw a fat nose on thick legs.

She was advised to play coy,
exhorted to come on hearty,
exercise, diet, smile and wheedle.
Her good nature wore out
like a fan belt.
So she cut off her nose and her legs
and offered them up.

In the casket displayed on satin she lay
with the undertaker's cosmetics painted on,   20
a turned-up putty nose,
dressed in a pink and white nightie.
Doesn't she look pretty? everyone said.
Consummation at last.
To every woman a happy ending.

(1973)

Ishmael Reed *1938–*

beware: do not read this poem

tonite , *thriller* was
abt an ol woman , so vain she
surrounded her self w /
          many mirrors

it got so bad that finally she
locked herself indoors & her
whole life became the
          mirrors

one day the villagers broke
into her house , but she was too   10
swift for them . she disappeared
          into a mirror
each tenant who bought the house
after that, lost a loved one to
          the ol woman in the mirror :
          first a little girl

then a young woman
then the young woman /s husband

the hunger of this poem is legendary
it has taken in many victims   20
    back off from this poem
    it has drawn in yr feet
    back off from this poem
    it has drawn in yr legs
    back off from this poem
    it is a greedy mirror
    you are into this poem . from
      the waist down
    nobody can hear you can they ?
    this poem has had you up to here   30
      belch
    this poem aint got no manners
    you cant call out frm this poem
    relax now & go w/this poem
    move & roll on to this poem

    do not resist this poem
    this poem has yr eyes
    this poem has his head
    this poem has his arms
    this poem has his fingers   40
    this poem has his fingertips

    this poem is the reader & the
    reader this poem

statistic: the us bureau of missing persons reports
    that in 1968 over 100,000 people disappeared
    leaving no solid clues
      nor trace   only
a space   in the lives of their friends

                (1972)

Seamus Heaney *1939*–

DIGGING

Between my finger and my thumb
The squat pen rests; snug as a gun.

Under my window, a clean rasping sound
When the spade sinks into gravelly ground:
My father, digging. I look down

Till his straining rump among the flowerbeds
Bends low, comes up twenty years away

Stooping in rhythm through potato drills
Where he was digging.

The coarse boot nestled on the lug, the shaft   10
Against the inside knee was levered firmly.
He rooted out tall tops, buried the bright edge deep
To scatter new potatoes that we picked
Loving their cool hardness in our hands.

By God, the old man could handle a spade.
Just like his old man.

My grandfather cut more turf in a day
Than any other man on Toner's bog.
Once I carried him milk in a bottle
Corked sloppily with paper. He straightened up   20
To drink it, then fell to right away

Nicking and slicing neatly, heaving sods
Over his shoulder, going down and down
For the good turf. Digging.

The cold smell of potato mould, the squelch and slap
Of soggy peat, the curt cuts of an edge
Through living roots awaken in my head.
But I've no spade to follow men like them.

Between my finger and my thumb
The squat pen rests.   30
I'll dig with it.

                                                          (1966)

John Lennon *1940–1980*
Paul McCartney *1942–*

ELEANOR RIGBY

Ah, look at all the lonely people!
Ah, look at all the lonely people!

Eleanor Rigby
Picks up the rice in the church where a wedding has been,
Lives in a dream,
Waits at the window
Wearing the face that she keeps in a jar by the door.
Who is it for?

All the lonely people,
Where do they all come from?   10
All the lonely people,
Where do they all belong?

Father McKenzie,
Writing the words of a sermon that no one will hear,
No one comes near
Look at him working,
Darning his socks in the night when there's nobody there.
What does he care?

All the lonely people,
Where do they all come from?   20
All the lonely people,
Where do they all belong?

Eleanor Rigby
Died in the church and was buried along with her name.
Nobody came.
Father McKenzie,
Wiping the dirt from his hands as he walks from the grave,
No one was saved.

All the lonely people,
Where do they all come from?   30
All the lonely people,
Where do they all belong?

Ah, look at all the lonely people!
Ah, look at all the lonely people!

        (1966)

Sharon Olds *1942–*

LENINGRAD CEMETERY, WINTER OF 1941[1]

That winter, the dead could not be buried.
The ground was frozen, the gravediggers weak from hunger,
the coffin wood used for fuel. So they were covered with
   something
and taken on a child's sled to the cemetery
in the sub-zero air. They lay on the soil,
some of them wrapped in dark cloth
bound with rope like the tree's ball of roots
when it waits to be planted; others wound in sheets,
their pale, gauze, tapered shapes
stiff as cocoons that will split down the center   10
when the new life inside is prepared;
but most lay like corpses, their coverings
coming undone, naked calves
hard as corded wood spilling

[1]The siege of Leningrad in World War II took place during the winter of 1941.

from under a cloak, a hand reaching out
with no sign of peace, wanting to come back
even to the bread made of glue and sawdust,
even to the icy winter, and the siege.

(1979)

SEX WITHOUT LOVE

How do they do it, the ones who make love
without love? Beautiful as dancers,
gliding over each other like ice-skaters
over the ice, fingers hooked
inside each other's bodies, faces
red as steak, wine, wet as the
children at birth whose mothers are going to
give them away. How do they come to the
come to the   come to the   God   come to the
still waters, and not love   10
the one who came there with them, light
rising slowly as steam off their joined
skin? These are the true religious,
the purists, the pros, the ones who will not
accept a false Messiah, love the
priest instead of the God. They do not
mistake the lover for their own pleasure,
they are like great runners: they know they are alone
with the road surface, the cold, the wind,
the fit of their shoes, their over-all cardio-   20
vascular health—just factors, like the partner
in the bed, and not the truth, which is the
single body alone in the universe
against its own best time.

(1984)

Paul Simon *1942–*

RICHARD CORY

They say that Richard Cory owns one half of this whole town
With political connections to spread his wealth around.
Born into society, a banker's only child,
He had everything a man could want: power grace and style

But I work in his factory
And I curse the life I'm livin'
And I curse my poverty

And I wish that I could be
Oh I wish that I could be
Oh I wish that I could be   10
Richard Cory.

The papers print his picture almost everywhere he goes;
Richard Cory at the opera, Richard Cory at a show,
And the rumour of his parties and the orgies on his yacht,
Oh he surely must be happy with everything he's got.

But I work in his factory
And I curse the live I'm livin'
And I curse my poverty
And I wish that I could be
Oh I wish that I could be   20
Oh I wish that I could be
Richard Cory

He freely gave to charity, he had the common touch,
And they were thankful for his patronage and they thanked him very
    much,
So my mind was filled with wonder when the evening headlines read:
"Richard Cory went home last night and put a bullet through his head."

But I work in his factory
And I curse the life I'm livin'
And I curse my poverty
And I wish that I could be   30
Oh I wish that I could be
Oh I wish that I could be
Richard Cory

                                                        (1966)

Nikki Giovanni *1943–*

DREAMS

        in my younger years
        before i learned
        black people aren't
        suppose to dream
        i wanted to be
        a raelet
        and say "dr o wn d in my youn tears"
        or "tal kin bout tal kin bout"
        or marjorie hendricks and grind
        all up against the mic   10
        and scream
        "baaaaaby nightandday
        baaaaaby nightandday"

then as i grew and matured
i became more sensible
and decided i would
settle down
and just become
a sweet inspiration

(1968)

KIDNAP POEM

ever been kidnapped
by a poet
if i were a poet
i'd kidnap you
put you in my phrases and meter
you to jones beach
or maybe coney island
or maybe just to my house
lyric you in lilacs
dash you in the rain   10
blend into the beach
to complement my see
play the lyre for you
ode you with my love song
anything to win you
wrap you in the red Black green
show you off to mama
yeah if i were a poet i'd kid
nap you

(1970)

Susan Griffin *1943*–

I LIKE TO THINK OF HARRIET TUBMAN[1]

I like to think of Harriet Tubman.
Harriet Tubman who carried a revolver,
who had a scar on her head from a rock thrown
by a slave-master (because she
talked back), and who
had a ransom on her head
of thousands of dollars and who

[1]Harriet Tubman was an escaped slave who worked on the underground railroad spiriting other slaves to the North.

was never caught, and who
had no use for the law
when the law was wrong,   10
who defied the law. I like
to think of her.
I like to think of her especially
when I think of the problem of
feeding children.

The legal answer
to the problem of feeding children
is ten free lunches every month,
being equal, in the child's real life,
to eating lunch every other day.   20
Monday but not Tuesday.
I like to think of the President
eating lunch Monday, but not
Tuesday.
And when I think of the President
and the law, and the problem of
feeding children, I like to
think of Harriet Tubman
and her revolver.

And then sometimes   30
I think of the President
and other men,
men who practice the law,
who revere the law,
who make the law,
who enforce the law,
who live behind
and operate through
and feed themselves
at the expense of   40
starving children
because of the law.

Men who sit in paneled offices
and think about vacations
and tell women
whose care it is
to feed children
not be be hysterical
not to be hysterical as in the word
hysterikos, the greek for   50
womb suffering,
not to suffer in their
wombs,
not to care,
not to bother the men
because they want to think

of other things
and do not want
to take the women seriously.
I want them   60
to take women seriously.

I want them to think about Harriet Tubman,
and remember,
remember she was beat by a white man
and she lived
and she lived to redress her grievances,
and she lived in swamps
and wore the clothes of a man
bringing hundreds of fugitives from
slavery, and was never caught,   70
and led an army,
and won a battle,
and defied the laws
because the laws were wrong, I want men
to take us seriously.
I am tired wanting them to think
about right and wrong.
I want them to fear.
I want them to feel fear now
as I have felt suffering in the womb, and   80
I want them
to know
that there is always a time
there is always a time to make right
what is wrong,
there is always a time
for retribution
and that time
is beginning.

(1976)

Jimmy Santiago Baca *1952–*

THERE ARE BLACK

There are black guards slamming cell gates
on black men,
And brown guards saying hello to brown men
with numbers on their backs,
And white guards laughing with white cons,
and red guards, few, say nothing
to red inmates as they walk by to chow and cells.

There you have it, the little antpile . . .
convicts marching in straight lines, guards flying
on badged wings, permits to sting, to glut themselves
at the cost of secluding themselves from their people . . .
     Turning off their minds like watertaps
wrapped in gunnysacks that insulate the pipes
carrying the pale weak water to their hearts.

     It gets bad when you see these same guards
carrying buckets of blood out of cells,
see them puking at the smell, the people,
their own people slashing their wrists,
hanging themselves with belts from light outlets;
it gets bad to see them clean up the mess,
carry the blue cold body out under sheets,
and then retake their places in guard cages,
watching their people maul and mangle themselves,

     And over this blood-rutted land,
the sun shines, the guards talk of horses and guns,
go to the store and buy new boots,
and the longer they work here the more powerful they become,
taking on the presence of some ancient mummy,
down in the dungeons of prison, a mummy
that will not listen, but has a strange power
in this dark world, to be so utterly disgusting in ignorance,
and yet so proudly command so many men. . . .

     And the convicts themselves, at the mummy's
feet, blood-splattered leather, at this one's feet,
they become cobras sucking life out of their brothers,
they fight for rings and money and drugs,
in this pit of pain their teeth bare fangs,
to fight for what morsels they can. . . .

     And the other convicts, guilty
of nothing but their born color, guilty of being innocent,
they slowly turn to dust in the nightly winds here,
flying in the wind back to their farms and cities.
From the gash in their hearts, sand flies up spraying
over houses and through trees,

       look at the sand blow over this deserted place,
you are looking at them.

(1979)

10

20

30

40

PART FOUR

Writing About Drama

This section, focusing on drama and including brief discussions of its beginnings and more recent developments in contemporary theater, completes our literary and rhetorical instruction.

CHAPTER

14

How Do I Read a Play?

A play is written to be performed. Although most drama begins with a written script, the author of a play counts on the collaboration of others —actors, directors, set designers, costumers, make-up artists, lighting and sound engineers—to translate the written words into a performance on stage or film or videotape. Unlike novelists and poets, playwrights do not necessarily expect their words to be read by the audience.

The performance goal of drama does not mean, however, that you cannot read and study a play as you would a story or a poem. Plays share many literary qualities with other types of creative writing: character, plot, structure, atmosphere, theme, symbolism, and point of view. But it is important to recognize the differences between reading a play and seeing one performed.

Listen to the Lines

The major difference between reading and watching a play is that, as reader, you do not have the actors' voices and gestures to interpret the lines and establish the characters for you. Because playwrights rely almost entirely on speeches or conversations (called *dialogue*) to define charac-ter, develop plot, and convey theme, it will be your task as a reader to listen to the lines in your mind. Read the dialogue as you would expect to hear it spoken. For example, when you read Antigone's response to Creon,

> Your edict, King, was strong,
> But all your strength is weakness itself against
> The immortal unrecorded laws of God,

do you hear the assurance and defiance in her voice? Or when you read Maggie's speech to her husband at the end of *Cat on a Hot Tin Roof*, can you detect the mixture of tenderness and regret in her words? "Oh, you weak people, you weak, beautiful people who give up with such grace.

627

What you want is someone to — take hold of you. — Gently, gently with love hand your life back to you."Of course the tone of these lines is not as clear when they are taken out of context, but even these brief quotations illustrate the charged nature of language you should expect when you read a play.

You can actually read the lines out loud to yourself or enlist some fellow students to act out some scenes with you. These oral readings will force you to decide how to interpret the words. But most of the time you will have to use your imagination to re-create the sound of the spoken medium. If you do get to see a performance of a play you are reading or to hear a recording of it, you will appreciate the extraordinary liveliness of dramatic literature when it is lifted from the page and provided with sound and action.

Reading a play does have some advantage over viewing a live performance. Unlike a theatergoer, a reader can stop and return to lines or speeches that seem especially complicated or meaningful. Close reading gives you the opportunity to examine and consider the playwright's exact words, which often fly by quickly, sometimes in altered form, in an actual performance.

Visualize the Scene

In addition to imagining the sound of the dialogue, you will also want to picture in your mind what the stage looks like. In a traditional theater the audience sits out front while the actors perform on a raised stage separated from the viewers by a curtain and perhaps an orchestra. The arch from which the curtain hangs is called the *proscenium*; the space extending from the bottom of the curtain to the footlights is the *apron*. The stage directions (printed in italics) indicate where the playwright wants the actors to move. *Upstage* means toward the back; *downstage* means toward the apron. A traditional set, made of canvas-covered frames called *flats*, will look like a room — with one wall removed for the audience to see through. Sometimes the set will be constructed to resemble the battlements of a castle, an opening in a forest, or a lifeboat on the ocean. Occasionally the setting is only suggested: a character climbs a ladder to deliver lines supposedly from a balcony or from an upstairs room. In one modern play, the two protagonists are presented on a bare stage speaking throughout the production (with only their heads visible) from inside garbage cans.

Another kind of stage, called *theater in the round* or an *arena stage*, puts the audience in raised seats on all sides with the players performing in the round space in the middle. After the audience is seated, the lights are extinguished, and the actors enter through the same aisles used earlier by the audience. When the actors are in position, the lights come up, illuminating only the stage, and the play begins. At the end of a scene or an act, the lights go down again, signifying the fall of the curtain and allowing the actors to leave. Stagehands come on between acts or scenes, if needed, to rearrange the setting. Not all plays are suited to this intimate staging, of course, but the audience at an arena production gains an immediacy, a feeling almost of being involved in the action, that cannot be achieved in a traditional theater.

Envision the Action

Poet and playwright Ezra Pound pointed out that the "medium of drama is not words, but persons moving about on a stage using words." This observation underlines the importance of movement, gesture, and setting in the performance of a play. These nonverbal elements of the language of drama are sometimes described in the author's stage directions. Oftentimes, though, you will find the cues for gestures, movements, and facial expressions in the words themselves, just as the director and the actors do when they are preparing a script for production. For example, these lines of Othello, spoken when he has been roused from his bed by a fight among his men, suggest the physical performance that would accompany the words:

> Why, how now, ho! from whence ariseth this?
> Are we turn'd Turks, and to ourselves do that
> Which heaven hath forbid the Ottomites?
> For Christian shame, put by this barbarous brawl:
> He that stirs next to carve for his own rage
> Holds his soul light; he dies upon his motion.
> Silence that dreadful bell.

Reading this speech with an actor's or director's imagination, you can see in your mind the character stride angrily into the fight scene, gesture threateningly at the men who are poised to continue the fight, and then point suddenly off-stage in the direction of the clamoring alarm bell. Such a detailed reading will take time, but you will be rewarded by the fun and satisfaction of catching the full dramatic quality of the play.

In more recent years, playwrights like Arthur Miller and Tennessee Williams have tried to keep artistic control over the interpretations of their works by including detailed stage directions in the scripts. The extensive production notes for Williams's *The Glass Menagerie* sometimes read like descriptions from a novel or poem:

> Friday evening. It is about five o'clock of a late spring evening which comes "scattering poems in the sky." A delicate lemony light is in the Wingfield apartment. . . . A fragile, unearthly prettiness has come out in Laura: she is like a piece of translucent glass touched by light, given a momentary radiance, not actual, not lasting.

With or without notes like this, your imagination will be working full time when you read a play. You will not be at the mercy of some designer's taste or the personal interpretation of a director or actor. You will be free to produce the play in the theater of your mind.

CHART 14–1 Critical Questions for Reading Plays

Before planning an analysis of any of the plays in this text, write out your answers to the following questions to be sure you understand the play and to help you generate material for your paper.

1. What is the central conflict in the play? How is it resolved?

2. Does the play contain any secondary conflicts (subplots)? How do they relate to the main conflict?

3. Does the play follow a traditional dramatic structure (see Chapter 15)? What is the climax? Is there a denouement?

4. Who is the main character or protagonist (see Chapter 15)? What sort of person is he or she? Does this protagonist have a fatal flaw? Is the protagonist a hero (see Chapter 16)?

5. Is the antagonist (the one who opposes the protagonist) a person, an environment, or a social force (see Chapter 15)? If a person, does the antagonist cause conflict intentionally?

6. Do the other characters provide exposition (background information)? Are they used as *foils* to oppose, contrast, criticize, and thus help develop the main characters?

7. What are the time and setting of the play? How important are these elements? Could the play be set just as effectively in another time or place?

8. Does the title provide any clues to an understanding of the play? If you had to give the play another title, what would it be?

9. What is the theme of the play? Can you state it in a single sentence?

10. Is the play a tragedy, a comedy, or a mixture (see Chapter 16)? Is this classification important?

11. Is the presentation realistic? Does the playwright use any special theatrical devices (such as lighting, music, costumes, distinctive or surreal settings)? If so, what effect do they have on your impression of the play?

15

Writing About Dramatic Structure

Drama is not as flexible as other forms of literature. A writer of fiction can take as much time as needed to inform the reader about character, setting, motivation, or theme. The dramatist must do everything quickly and clearly. Audiences will not sit through a tedious first act; neither can they stop the play, pick it up tomorrow, or go back to Act 1 to refresh their memories. Even with the technology of video recording, most plays, including film and television drama, are seen in a single, relatively brief sitting.

What Is Dramatic Structure?

More than two thousand years ago the Greek philosopher Aristotle pointed out that the most important element of drama is the *fable*, what we call the *story*, or *plot*. The fable, said Aristotle, has to have a beginning, a middle, and an end. As obvious as this observation seems, it emphasizes the dramatist's special need to engage an audience early and keep it engaged until the conclusion of the play.

Recognizing the drama's strict time limits, Aristotle set down a number of conditions for developing the fable, or plot, in a clear and interesting way. According to Aristotle, the heart of the dramatic story is the *agon*, or *argument*, and the conflict surrounding this argument creates tension and incites interest. The two sides of the conflict, the pros and cons of the argument, are represented on stage by the *protagonist* and the *antagonist*. The protagonist may be one person or many, and the antagonist may be a person, a group, a thing, or a force (supernatural or natural). We often call the protagonist of a play its *hero* or *heroine*, and sometimes the antagonist is also the *villain*.

The fundamental struggle between the protagonist and the antagonist is developed according to a set pattern that theater audiences have come to recognize and expect. This conventional structure can be varied, of course, but most dramatic literature contains the following components:

1. *Point of attack* — the starting point from which the dramatist leads the audience into the plot. A playwright can begin at the story's beginning and allow the audience to discover what is going on at the same time the characters do; or the writer can begin in the middle of things (*in medias res*), or even near the end, and gradually reveal the events that have already taken place.

2. *Exposition* — the revelation of facts, circumstances, and past events. Establishing the essential facts about the characters and the conflict can be accomplished in a number of ways: from having minor characters reveal information through conversation to plunging the audience right into the action.

3. *Rising action* — the building of interest through complication of the conflict. In this stage the protagonist and antagonist move steadily toward a confrontation.

4. *Climax* — the play's high point, the decisive showdown between protagonist and antagonist. The climax — the play's turning point — can be a single moment or a series of events, but once reached, it becomes a point of no return.

5. *Falling action* — the unraveling of the plot, where events fall into place and the conflict moves toward final resolution.

6. *Denouement* — the play's conclusion; the explanation or outcome of the action. The term *denouement* (literally an "untying") may be applied to both comedy and tragedy, but the Greeks used the word *catastrophe* for a tragic denouement, probably because it involved the death of the hero or heroine.

Whatever it is called, the denouement marks the end of the play: the lovers kiss, the bodies are carried off the stage, and the audience goes home. Most dramatists employ this traditional pattern. Even when they mix in other devices, rearrange elements, and invent new ways to exhibit their materials, dramatists still establish a conflict, develop both sides of the argument, and reach a credible conclusion. After centuries of theater history, the basic structure of drama has changed very little.

Looking at Dramatic Structure

As you read *Antigone*, written in 442 B.C., notice that the play's central conflict is introduced, developed, and resolved according to the pattern we have just described.

Although written first, *Antigone* is the third and last play in the chronology of events that concern Sophocles' Oedipus cycle, which also includes *Oedipus Rex* and *Oedipus at Colonus*. According to Greek legend, King Laius of Thebes and his descendants were doomed by the god Apollo. Warned by the Oracle of Delphi that his own son would kill him, Laius leaves the son, Oedipus, to die in the mountains. But Oedipus survives and unknowingly kills his father, whom he encounters on the road to Thebes. Oedipus solves the riddle of the Sphinx for the Thebans and becomes their king, marrying his mother, the widow Jocasta. Several years later, when he learns what he has done, Oedipus blinds himself and leaves Thebes. His two sons, Eteocles and Polyneices, quarrel over the succession, and Polyneices is driven out of the city. He returns with an army, but he and Eteocles kill each other in battle, while Creon, brother of Jocasta, succeeds to the throne. Antigone and Ismene, daughters of Oedipus, are discussing Creon's first official decree as the play opens.

Sophocles *ca. 496–ca. 405* B.C.

ANTIGONE

An English version by Dudley Fitts and Robert Fitzgerald

THE CHARACTERS

ANTIGONE, *daughter of Oedipus, former banished king.*

ISMENE, *her elder sister.*

CREON, *their maternal uncle, now King of Thebes.*

HAIMON, *Creon's son, beloved of Antigone.*

EURYDICE, *the Queen, his mother, whose other son has*

just been killed defending Thebes from attack.

TEIRESIAS, *the old and blind seer or prophet.*

A SENTRY *and* A MESSENGER

THE CHORUS *of fifteen Thebans, elder citizens, among whom the*

CHORAGOS *is the leader.*

TIME: *The legendary past of Ancient Greece.*
PLACE: *The walled city of Thebes with its seven gates.*

PROLOGUE

SCENE

Before the palace of CREON, *King of Thebes. A central double door, and two lateral doors. A platform extends the length of the façade, and from this platform three steps lead down into the "orchestra," or chorus-ground. Time: Dawn of the day after the repulse of the Argive army from the assault on Thebes.*

[ANTIGONE *and* ISMENE *enter from the central door of the Palace.*]

ANTIGONE. Ismenê, dear sister,
  You would think that we had already suffered enough
  For the curse on Oedipus:
  I cannot imagine any grief
  That you and I have not gone through. And now—
  Have they told you of the new decree of our King Creon?
ISMENE. I have heard nothing: I know
  That two sisters lost two brothers, a double death
  In a single hour; and I know that the Argive army
  Fled in the night; but beyond this, nothing.
ANTIGONE. I thought so. And that is why I wanted you   10
  To come out here with me. There is something we must do.

ISMENE. Why do you speak so strangely?
ANTIGONE. Listen, Ismenê:
  Creon buried our brother Eteoclês
  With military honors, gave him a soldier's funeral,
  And it was right that he should; but Polyneicês,
  Who fought as bravely and died as miserably,—
  They say that Creon has sworn
  No one shall bury him, no one mourn for him,   20
  But his body must lie in the fields, a sweet treasure
  For carrion birds to find as they search for food.
  That is what they say, and our good Creon is coming here
  To announce it publicly; and the penalty—
  Stoning to death in the public square! There it is,
  And now you can prove what you are:
  A true sister, or a traitor to your family.
ISMENE. Antigonê, you are mad! What could I possibly do?
ANTIGONE. You must decide whether you will help me or not.
ISMENE. I do not understand you. Help you in what?   30
ANTIGONE. Ismenê, I am going to bury him. Will you come?
ISMENE. Bury him! You have just said the new law forbids it.
ANTIGONE. He is my brother. And he is your brother, too.
ISMENE. But think of the danger! Think what Creon will do!
ANTIGONE. Creon is not strong enough to stand in my way.
ISMENE. Ah sister!
  Oedipus died, everyone hating him
  For what his own search brought to light, his eyes
  Ripped out by his own hand; and Jocastê died,
  His mother and wife at once: she twisted the cords   40
  That strangled her life; and our two brothers died,
  Each killed by the other's sword. And we are left:
  But oh, Antigonê,
  Think how much more terrible than these
  Our own death would be if we should go against Creon
  And do what he has forbidden! We are only women,
  We cannot fight with men, Antigonê!
  The law is strong, we must give in to the law
  In this thing, and in worse. I beg the Dead
  To forgive me, but I am helpless: I must yield   50
  To those in authority. And I think it is dangerous business
  To be always meddling.
ANTIGONE.   If that is what you think,
  I should not want you, even if you asked to come.
  You have made your choice, you can be what you want to be.
  But I will bury him; and if I must die,
  I say that this crime is holy: I shall lie down
  With him in death, and I shall be as dear
  To him as he to me.
         It is the dead,
  Not the living, who make the longest demands:
  We die for ever . . .

                                    You may do as you like,   60
Since apparently the laws of the gods mean nothing to you.
ISMENE. They mean a great deal to me; but I have no strength
   To break laws that were made for the public good.
ANTIGONE. That must be your excuse, I suppose. But as for me,
   I will bury the brother I love.
ISMENE.   Antigonê,
   I am so afraid for you!
ANTIGONE.   You need not be:
   You have yourself to consider, after all.
ISMENE. But no one must hear of this, you must tell no one!
   I will keep it a secret, I promise!
ANTIGONE. Oh, tell it! Tell everyone!   70
   Think how they'll hate you when it all comes out
   If they learn that you knew about it all the time!
ISMENE. So fiery! You should be cold with fear.
ANTIGONE. Perhaps. But I am doing only what I must.
ISMENE. But can you do it? I say that you cannot.
ANTIGONE. Very well: when my strength gives out, I shall do no more.
ISMENE. Impossible things should not be tried at all.
ANTIGONE. Go away, Ismenê:
   I shall be hating you soon, and the dead will too,
   For your words are hateful. Leave me my foolish plan: 80
   I am not afraid of the danger; if it means death,
   It will not be the worst of deaths — death without honor.
ISMENE. Go then, if you feel that you must.
   You are unwise,
   But a loyal friend indeed to those who love.
                              [*Exit into the Palace.* ANTIGONE *goes off, L.*]

                        [*Enter the* CHORUS.]

PÁRODOS

                                                                       [*strophe 1*]

CHORUS. Now the long blade of the sun, lying
   Level east to west, touches with glory
   Thebes of the Seven Gates. Open, unlidded
   Eye of golden day! O marching light
   Across the eddy and rush of Dircê's stream,
   Striking the white shields of the enemy
   Thrown headlong backward from the blaze of morning!
CHORAGOS. Polyneicês their commander
   Roused them with windy phrases,
   He the wild eagle screaming
   Insults above our land,   10
   His wings their shields of snow,
   His crest their marshaled helms.

[*antistrophe 1*]

CHORUS. Against our seven gates in a yawning ring
 The famished spears came onward in the night;
 But before his jaws were sated with our blood,
 Or pinefire took the garland of our towers,
 He was thrown back; and as he turned, great Thebes—
 No tender victim for his noisy power—
 Rose like a dragon behind him, shouting war.   20
CHORAGOS. For God hates utterly
 The bray of bragging tongues;
 And when he beheld their smiling,
 Their swagger of golden helms,
 The frown of his thunder blasted
 Their first man from our walls.

[*strophe 2*]

CHORUS. We heard his shout of triumph high in the air
 Turn to a scream; far out in a flaming arc
 He fell with his windy torch, and the earth struck him. 30
 And others storming in fury no less than his
 Found shock of death in the dusty job of battle.
CHORAGOS. Seven captains at seven gates
 Yielded their clanging arms to the god
 That bends the battle-line and breaks it.
 These two only, brothers in blood,
 Face to face in matchless rage,
 Mirroring each of the other's death,
 Clashed in long combat.

Brothers fight

[*antistrophe 2*]

CHORUS. But now in the beautiful morning of victory
 Let Thebes of the many chariots sing for joy!
 With hearts dancing we'll take leave of war: 40
 Our temples shall be sweet with hymns of praise,
 And the long night shall echo with our chorus.

SCENE i

CHORAGOS. But now at last our new King is coming:
 Creon of Thebes, Menoiceus' son.
 In this auspicious dawn of his reign
 What are the new complexities
 That shifting Fate has woven for him?
 What is his counsel? Why has he summoned
 The old men to hear him?

[*Enter* CREON *from the Palace, C. He addresses the* CHORUS *from the top step.*]

CREON. Gentlemen: I have the honor to inform you that our Ship of State, which recent storms have threatened to destroy, has come safely to harbor at last, guided by the merciful wisdom of Heaven. I have summoned you 10 here this morning because I know that I can depend upon you: your devotion to King Laïos was absolute; you never hesitated in your duty to our late ruler Oedipus; and when Oedipus died, your loyalty was transferred to his children. Unfortunately, as you know, his two sons, the princes Eteoclês and Polyneicês, have killed each other in battle; and I, as the next in blood, have succeeded to the full power of the throne.

I am aware, of course, that no Ruler can expect complete loyalty from his subjects until he has been tested in office. Nevertheless, I say to you at the very outset that I have nothing but contempt for the kind of Governor who is afraid, for whatever reason, to follow the course that he knows 20 is best for the State; and as for the man who sets private friendship above the public welfare, — I have no use for him, either. I call God to witness that if I saw my country headed for ruin, I should not be afraid to speak out plainly; and I need hardly remind you that I would never have any dealings with an enemy of the people. No one values friendship more highly than I; but we must remember that friends made at the risk of wrecking our Ship are not real friends at all.

These are my principles, at any rate, and that is why I have made the following decision concerning the sons of Oedipus: Eteoclês, who died as a man should die, fighting for his country, is to be buried with full military honors, with all the ceremony that is usual when the greatest heroes 30 die; but his brother Polyneicês, who broke his exile to come back with fire and sword against his native city and the shrines of his fathers' gods, whose one idea was to spill the blood of his blood and sell his own people into slavery — Polyneicês, I say, is to have no burial: no man is to touch him or say the least prayer for him; he shall lie on the plain, unburied; and the birds and the scavenging dogs can do with him whatever they like.

This is my command, and you can see the wisdom behind it. As long as I am King, no traitor is going to be honored with the loyal man. But whoever shows by word and deed that he is on the side of the State, — he shall have my respect while he is living, and my reverence when he is dead.   40

CHORAGOS. If that is your will, Creon son of Menoiceus,
 You have the right to enforce it: we are yours.
CREON. That is my will. Take care that you do your part.
CHORAGOS. We are old men: let the younger ones carry it out.
CREON. I do not mean that: the sentries have been appointed.
CHORAGOS. Then what is it that you would have us do?
CREON. You will give no support to whoever breaks this law.
CHORAGOS. Only a crazy man is in love with death!
CREON. And death it is; yet money talks, and the wisest
 Have sometimes been known to count a few coins too many.   50

[Enter SENTRY *from L.]*

SENTRY. I'll not say that I'm out of breath from running, King, because every time I stopped to think about what I have to tell you, I felt like going back. And all the time a voice kept saying, "You fool, don't you know you're walking straight into trouble?"; and then another voice: "Yes, but if you let somebody else get the news to Creon first, it will be even worse than that for you!" But good sense won out, at least I hope it was good sense, and here I am with a story that makes no sense at all; but I'll tell it anyhow, because, as they say, what's going to happen's going to happen, and—

CREON. Come to the point. What have you to say?

SENTRY. I did not do it. I did not see who did it. You must not punish   60
me for what someone else has done.

CREON. A comprehensive defense! More effective, perhaps,
If I knew its purpose. Come: what is it?

SENTRY. A dreadful thing . . . I don't know how to put it—

CREON. Out with it!

SENTRY.   Well, then;
The dead man—

                Polyneicês—

[*Pause. The* SENTRY *is overcome, fumbles for words.* CREON
waits impassively.]

                              out there—

                              someone,—   70
New dust on the slimy flesh!
[*Pause. No sign from* CREON.]
Someone has given it burial that way, and
Gone . . .
[*Long pause.* CREON *finally speaks with deadly control.*]

CREON. And the man who dared do this?

SENTRY.   I swear I
Do not know! You must believe me!

                        Listen:
The ground was dry, not a sign of digging, no,
Not a wheeltrack in the dust, no trace of anyone.
It was when they relieved us this morning: and one of them,   80
The corporal, pointed to it.

                        There it was,
The strangest—

        Look:
The body, just mounded over with light dust: you see?
Not buried really, but as if they'd covered it
Just enough for the ghost's peace. And no sign
Of dogs or any wild animal that had been there.

And then what a scene there was! Every man of us
Accusing the other: we all proved the other man did it,   90
We all had proof that we could not have done it,
We were ready to take hot iron in our hands,
Walk through fire, swear by all the gods,
It was not I!
I do not know who it was, but it was not I!

[CREON'S *rage has been mounting steadily, but the* SENTRY *is too intent upon his
story to notice it.*]

And then, when this came to nothing, someone said
A thing that silenced us and made us stare
Down at the ground: you had to be told the news,
And one of us had to do it! We threw the dice,
And the bad luck fell to me. So here I am,   100

[handwritten margin note: reports burial attempt *]*

No happier to be here than you are to have me:
Nobody likes the man who brings bad news.

CHORAGOS. I have been wondering, King: can it be that the gods have done
this?

CREON [*furiously*]. Stop.
　　Must you doddering wrecks
Go out of your heads entirely? "The gods!"
Intolerable!
The gods favor this corpse? Why? How had he served them?
Tried to loot their temples, burn their images,
Yes, and the whole State, and its laws with it!   110
Is it your senile opinion that the gods love to honor bad men?
A pious thought!—
　　　　　　　　　No, from the very beginning
There have been those who have whispered together,
Stiff-necked anarchists, putting their heads together,
Scheming against me in alleys. These are the men,
And they have bribed my own guard to do this thing.
[*Sententiously*]   Money!
There's nothing in the world so demoralising as money.
Down go your cities,   120
Homes gone, men gone, honest hearts corrupted,
Crookedness of all kinds, and all for money!
[*To* SENTRY]   But you—!
I swear by God and by the throne of God,
The man who has done this thing shall pay for it!
Find that man, bring him here to me, or your death
Will be the least of your problems: I'll string you up
Alive, and there will be certain ways to make you
Discover your employer before you die;
And the process may teach you a lesson you seemed to have missed: 130
The dearest profit is sometimes all too dear:
That depends on the source. Do you understand me?
A fortune won is often misfortune.

SENTRY. King, may I speak?

CREON.   Your very voice distresses me.

SENTRY. Are you sure that it is my voice, and not your conscience?

CREON. By God, he wants to analyse me now!

SENTRY. It is not what I say, but what has been done, that hurts you.

CREON. You talk too much.

SENTRY. Maybe; but I've done nothing.   140

CREON. Sold your soul for some silver: that's all you've done.

SENTRY. How dreadful it is when the right judge judges wrong!

CREON. Your figures of speech
May entertain you now; but unless you bring me the man,
You will get little profit from them in the end.
　　　　　　　　　　　　　　　　　　　[*Exit* CREON *into the Palace.*]

SENTRY. "Bring me the man"—!
I'd like nothing better than bringing him the man!

But bring him or not, you have seen the last of me here.
At any rate, I am safe!

[*Exit* SENTRY.]

ODE I

[*strophe 1*]

CHORUS. Numberless are the world's wonders, but none
  More wonderful than man; the stormgray sea
  Yields to his prows, the huge crests bear him high;
  Earth, holy and inexhaustible, is graven
  With shining furrows where his plows have gone
  Year after year, the timeless labor of stallions.

[*antistrophe 1*]

  The lightboned birds and beasts that cling to cover,
  The lithe fish lighting their reaches of dim water,
  All are taken, tamed in the net of his mind;
  The lion on the hill, the wild horse windy-maned,
  Resign to him; and his blunt yoke has broken
  The sultry shoulders of the mountain bull.

[*strophe 2*]

  Words also, and thought as rapid as air,
  He fashions to his good use; statecraft is his,
  And his the skill that deflects the arrows of snow,
  The spears of winter rain: from every wind
  He has made himself secure—from all but one:
  In the late wind of death he cannot stand.

[*antistrophe 2*]

  O clear intelligence, force beyond all measure!
  O fate of man, working both good and evil!
  When the laws are kept, how proudly his city stands!
  When the laws are broken, what of his city then?
  Never may the anarchic man find rest at my hearth,
  Never be it said that my thoughts are his thoughts.

basically laws are good

SCENE ii

[*Re-enter* SENTRY *leading* ANTIGONE.]

CHORAGOS. What does this mean? Surely this captive woman
  Is the Princess, Antigonê. Why should she be taken?
SENTRY. Here is the one who did it! We caught her
  In the very act of burying him.—Where is Creon?
CHORAGOS. Just coming from the house.

[*Enter* CREON, C.]

CREON.   What has happened?
  Why have you come back so soon?
SENTRY [*expansively*].   O King,
  A man should never be too sure of anything:
  I would have sworn
  That you'd not see me here again: your anger
  Frightened me so, and the things you threatened me with;   10

But how could I tell then
That I'd be able to solve the case so soon?
No dice-throwing this time: I was only too glad to come!
Here is this woman. She is the guilty one:
We found her trying to bury him.
Take her, then; question her; judge her as you will.
I am through with the whole thing now, and glad of it.
CREON. But this is Antigonê! Why have you brought her here?
SENTRY. She was burying him, I tell you!
CREON [*severely*].   Is this the truth?
SENTRY. I saw her with my own eyes. Can I say more?   20
CREON. The details: come, tell me quickly!
SENTRY.   It was like this:
After those terrible threats of yours, King,
We went back and brushed the dust away from the body.
The flesh was soft by now, and stinking,
So we sat on a hill to windward and kept guard.
No napping this time! We kept each other awake.
But nothing happened until the white round sun
Whirled in the center of the round sky over us:
Then, suddenly,
A storm of dust roared up from the earth, and the sky   30
Went out, the plain vanished with all its trees
In the stinging dark. We closed our eyes and endured it.
The whirlwind lasted a long time, but it passed;
And then we looked, and there was Antigonê!
I have seen
A mother bird come back to a stripped nest, heard
Her crying bitterly a broken note or two
For the young ones stolen. Just so, when this girl
Found the bare corpse, and all her love's work wasted,
She wept, and cried on heaven to damn the hands   40
That had done this thing.
                          And then she brought more dust
And sprinkled wine three times for her brother's ghost.
We ran and took her at once. She was not afraid,
Not even when we charged her with what she had done.
She denied nothing.
                    And this was a comfort to me,
And some uneasiness: for it is a good thing
To escape from death, but it is no great pleasure
To bring death to a friend.
                          Yet I always say
There is nothing so comfortable as your own safe skin!
CREON [*slowly, dangerously*]. And you, Antigonê?   50
You with your head hanging,—do you confess this thing?
ANTIGONE. I do. I deny nothing.
CREON [*to* SENTRY].   You may go.
                                                    [*Exit* SENTRY.]

[*To* ANTIGONE.] Tell me, tell me briefly:
Had you heard my proclamation touching this matter?

ANTIGONE. It was public. Could I help hearing it?
CREON. And yet you dared defy the law.
ANTIGONE.   I dared.
  It was not God's proclamation. That final Justice
  That rules the world below makes no such laws.
  Your edict, King, was strong,
  But all your strength is weakness itself against   60
  The immortal unrecorded laws of God.
  They are not merely now: they were, and shall be,
  Operative for ever, beyond man utterly.   *about death*
  I knew I must die, even without your decree:
  I am only mortal. And if I must die
  Now, before it is my time to die,
  Surely this is no hardship: can anyone
  Living, as I live, with evil all about me,
  Think Death less than a friend? This death of mine
  Is of no importance; but if I had left my brother   70
  Lying in death unburied, I should have suffered.
  Now I do not.
                You smile at me. Ah Creon,
  Think me a fool, if you like; but it may well be
  That a fool convicts me of folly.
CHORAGOS. Like father, like daughter: both headstrong, deaf to reason!
  She has never learned to yield.
CREON.   She has much to learn.
  The inflexible heart breaks first, the toughest iron
  Cracks first, and the wildest horses bend their necks
  At the pull of the smallest curb.
                    Pride? In a slave?
  This girl is guilty of a double insolence,   80
  Breaking the given laws and boasting of it.
  Who is the man here,
  She or I, if this crime goes unpunished?
  Sister's child, or more than sister's child,
  Or closer yet in blood—she and her sister
  Win bitter death for this!
  [*To* SERVANTS.]   Go, some of you,   *calls to arrest ismene*
  Arrest Ismenê. I accuse her equally.
  Bring her: you will find her sniffling in the house there.
  Her mind's a traitor: crimes kept in the dark
  Cry for light, and the guardian brain shudders;   90
  But how much worse than this
  Is brazen boasting of barefaced anarchy!
ANTIGONE. Creon, what more do you want than my death?
CREON.   Nothing.
  That gives me everything.
ANTIGONE. Then I beg you: kill me.
  This talking is a great weariness: your words
  Are distasteful to me, and I am sure that mine
  Seem so to you. And yet they should not seem so:
  I should have praise and honor for what I have done.

All these men here would praise me   100
Were their lips not frozen shut with fear of you.
[*Bitterly.*] Ah the good fortune of kings,
Licensed to say and do whatever they please!
CREON. You are alone here in that opinion.
ANTIGONE. No, they are with me.
  But they keep their tongues in leash.
CREON. Maybe. But you are guilty, and they are not.
ANTIGONE. There is no guilt in reverence for the dead.
CREON. But Eteoclês—was he not your brother too?
ANTIGONE. My brother too.
CREON.   And you insult his memory?   110
ANTIGONE [*softly*]. The dead man would not say that I insult it.
CREON. He would: for you honor a traitor as much as him.
ANTIGONE. His own brother, traitor or not, and equal in blood.
CREON. He made war on his country.
  Eteoclês defended it.
ANTIGONE. Nevertheless, there are honors due all the dead.
CREON. But not the same for the wicked as for the just.
ANTIGONE. Ah Creon, Creon.
  Which of us can say what the gods hold wicked?
CREON. An enemy is an enemy, even dead.   120
ANTIGONE. It is my nature to join in love, not hate.
CREON [*finally losing patience*]. Go join them, then; if you must have your love,
  Find it in hell!
CHORAGOS.   But see, Ismenê comes:

[*Enter* ISMENE, *guarded.*]

Those tears are sisterly, the cloud
That shadows her eyes rains down gentle sorrow.
CREON. You too, Ismenê,
  Snake in my ordered house, sucking my blood
  Stealthily—and all the time I never knew
  That these two sisters were aiming at my throne!
                              Ismenê,
Do you confess your share in this crime, or deny it?   130
  Answer me.
ISMENE. Yes, if she will let me say so. I am guilty.
ANTIGONE [*coldly*]. No, Ismenê. You have no right to say so.
  You would not help me, and I will not have you help me.
ISMENE. But now I know what you meant; and I am here
  To join you, to take my share of punishment.
ANTIGONE. The dead man and the gods who rule the dead
  Know whose act this was. Words are not friends.
ISMENE. Do you refuse me, Antigonê? I want to die with you:
  I too have a duty that I must discharge to the dead.   140
ANTIGONE. You shall not lessen my death by sharing it.
ISMENE. What do I care for life when you are dead?
ANTIGONE. Ask Creon. You're always hanging on his opinions.
ISMENE. You are laughing at me. Why, Antigonê?
ANTIGONE. It's a joyless laughter, Ismenê.

ISMENE.   But can I do nothing?
ANTIGONE. Yes. Save yourself. I shall not envy you.
  There are those who will praise you; I shall have honor, too.
ISMENE. But we are equally guilty!
ANTIGONE.   No more, Ismenê.
  You are alive, but I belong to Death.
CREON [*to the* CHORUS]. Gentlemen, I beg you to observe these girls: 150
  One has just now lost her mind; the other,
  It seems, has never had a mind at all.
ISMENE. Grief teaches the steadiest minds to waver, King.
CREON. Yours certainly did, when you assumed guilt with the guilty!
ISMENE. But how could I go on living without her?
CREON.   You are.
  She is already dead.
ISMENE.   But, your own son's bride!
CREON. There are places enough for him to push his plow.
  I want no wicked women for my sons!
ANTIGONE. O dearest Haimon, how your father wrongs you!
CREON. I've had enough of your childish talk of marriage!   160
CHORAGOS. Do you really intend to steal this girl from your son?
CREON. No; Death will do that for me.
CHORAGOS.   Then she must die?
CREON [*ironically*]. You dazzle me.
                              —But enough of this talk!
  [*To* GUARDS.] You, there, take them away and guard them well:
  For they are but women, and even brave men run
  When they see Death coming.
                              [*Exeunt* ISMENE, ANTIGONE *and* GUARDS.]

ODE II

[*strophe 1*]

CHORUS. Fortunate is the man who has never tasted God's vengeance!
  Where once the anger of heaven has struck, that house is shaken
  For ever: damnation rises behind each child
  Like a wave cresting out of the black northeast,
  When the long darkness under sea roars up
  And bursts drumming death upon the windwhipped sand.

[*antistrophe 1*]

  I have seen this gathering sorrow from time long past
  Loom upon Oedipus' children: generation from generation
  Takes the compulsive rage of the enemy god.
  So lately this last flower of Oedipus' line   10
  Drank the sunlight! but now a passionate word
  And a handful of dust have closed up all its beauty.

[*strophe 2*]

      What mortal arrogance
      Transcends the wrath of Zeus?
  Sleep cannot lull him, nor the effortless long months

Of the timeless gods: but he is young for ever,
And his house is the shining day of high Olympos.
    All that is and shall be,
    And all the past, is his.
No pride on earth is free of the curse of heaven.   20

                                                    [*antistrophe 2*]

    The straying dreams of men
    May bring them ghosts of joy:
But as they drowse, the waking embers burn them;
Or they walk with fixed éyes, as blind men walk.
But the ancient wisdom speaks for our own time:
    Fate works most for woe
    With Folly's fairest show.
— Man's little pleasure is the spring of sorrow. —

                        SCENE iii

CHORAGOS. But here is Haimon, King, the last of all your sons.
    Is it grief for Antigonê that brings him here,
    And bitterness at being robbed of his bride?

                    [*Enter* HAIMON.]
CREON. We shall soon see, and no need of diviners.
                                            —Son,
    You have heard my final judgment on that girl:
    Have you come here hating me, or have you come
    With deference and with love, whatever I do?
HAIMON. I am your son, father. You are my guide.
    You make things clear for me, and I obey you.
    No marriage means more to me than your continuing wisdom.   10
CREON. Good. That is the way to behave: subordinate
    Everything else, my son, to your father's will.
    This is what a man prays for, that he may get
    Sons attentive and dutiful in his house,
    Each one hating his father's enemies,
    Honoring his father's friends. But if his sons
    Fail him, if they turn out unprofitably,
    What has he fathered but trouble for himself
    And amusement for the malicious?
                        So you are right   20
    Not to lose your head over this woman.
    Your pleasure with her would soon grow cold, Haimon,
    And then you'd have a hellcat in bed and elsewhere.
    Let her find her husband in Hell!
    Of all the people in this city, only she
    Has had contempt for my law and broken it.
    Do you want me to show myself weak before the people?
    Or to break my sworn word? No, and I will not.
    The woman dies.
    I suppose she'll plead "family ties." Well, let her.
    If I permit my own family to rebel,   30
    How shall I earn the world's obedience?

Show me the man who keeps his house in hand,
He's fit for public authority.
                              I'll have no dealings
With law-breakers, critics of the government:
Whoever is chosen to govern shall be obeyed—
Must be obeyed, in all things, great and small,
Just and unjust! O Haimon,
The man who knows how to obey, and that man only,
Knows how to give commands when the time comes.
You can depend on him, no matter how fast   40
The spears come: he's a good soldier, he'll stick it out.
Anarchy, anarchy! Show me a greater evil!
This is why cities tumble and the great houses rain down,
This is what scatters armies!
No, no: good lives are made so by discipline.
We keep the laws then, and the lawmakers,
And no woman shall seduce us. If we must lose,
Let's lose to a man, at least! Is a woman stronger than we?
CHORAGOS. Unless time has rusted my wits,
What you say, King, is said with point and dignity.
HAIMON [*boyishly earnest*].   Father.   50
Reason is God's crowning gift to man, and you are right
To warn me against losing mine. I cannot say—
I hope that I shall never want to say—that you
Have reasoned badly. Yet there are other men
Who can reason, too; and their opinions might be helpful.
You are not in a position to know everything
That people say or do, or what they feel:
Your temper terrifies them—everyone
Will tell you only what you like to hear.
But I, at any rate, can listen; and I have heard them   60
Muttering and whispering in the dark about this girl.
They say no woman has ever, so unreasonably,
Died so shameful a death for a generous act:
"She covered her brother's body. Is this indecent?
"She kept him from dogs and vultures. Is this a crime?
"Death?—She should have all the honor that we can give her!"
This is the way they talk out there in the city.
You must believe me:
Nothing is closer to me than your happiness.
What could be closer? Must not any son   70
Value his father's fortune as his father does his?
I beg you, do not be unchangeable:
Do not believe that you alone can be right.
The man who thinks that,
The man who maintains that only he has the power
To reason correctly, the gift to speak, the soul—
A man like that, when you know him, turns out empty.
It is not reason never to yield to reason!
In flood time you can see how some trees bend,

And because they bend, even their twigs are safe,   80
While stubborn trees are torn up, roots and all.
And the same thing happens in sailing:
Make your sheet fast, never slacken,—and over you go,
Head over heels and under: and there's your voyage.
Forget you are angry! Let yourself be moved!
I know I am young; but please let me say this:
The ideal condition
Would be, I admit, that men should be right by instinct;
But since we are all too likely to go astray,
The reasonable thing is to learn from those who can teach.   90

CHORAGOS. You will do well to listen to him, King,
If what he says is sensible. And you, Haimon,
Must listen to your father.—Both speak well.

CREON. You consider it right for a man of my years and experience
To go to school to a boy?

HAIMON.   It is not right
If I am wrong. But if I am young, and right,
What does my age matter?

CREON. You think it right to stand up for an anarchist?

HAIMON. Not at all. I pay no respect to criminals.

CREON. Then she is not a criminal?   100

HAIMON. The City would deny it, to a man.

CREON. And the City proposes to teach me how to rule?

HAIMON. Ah. Who is it that's talking like a boy now?

CREON. My voice is the one voice giving orders in this City!

HAIMON. It is no City if it takes orders from one voice.

CREON. The State is the King!

HAIMON. Yes, if the State is a desert.

                                                        [*Pause.*]

CREON. This boy, it seems, has sold out to a woman.

HAIMON. If you are a woman: my concern is only for you.

CREON. So? Your "concern"! In a public brawl with your father!   110

HAIMON. How about you, in a public brawl with justice?

CREON. With justice, when all that I do is within my rights?

HAIMON. You have no right to trample on God's right.

CREON [*completely out of control*]. Fool, adolescent fool! Taken in by a woman!

HAIMON. You'll never see me taken in by anything vile.

CREON. Every word you say is for her!

HAIMON [*quietly, darkly*]. And for you.
And for me. And for the gods under the earth.

CREON. You'll never marry her while she lives.

HAIMON. Then she must die.—But her death will cause another.   120

CREON. Another?
Have you lost your senses? Is this an open threat?

HAIMON. There is no threat in speaking to emptiness.

CREON. I swear you'll regret this superior tone of yours!
You are the empty one!

HAIMON. If you were not my father, I'd say you were perverse.

CREON. You girlstruck fool, don't play at words with me!

HAIMON. I am sorry. You prefer silence.

CREON.   Now, by God—!
I swear, by all the gods in heaven above us,
You'll watch it, I swear you shall!
[*To the* SERVANTS]   Bring her out!   130
Bring the woman out! Let her die before his eyes!
Here, this instant, with her bridegroom beside her!

HAIMON. Not here, no; she will not die here, King.
And you will never see my face again.
Go on raving as long as you've a friend to endure you.

                                       [*Exit* HAIMON.]

CHORAGOS.   Gone, gone.
Creon, a young man in a rage is dangerous!

CREON. Let him do, or dream to do, more than a man can.
He shall not save these girls from death.

CHORAGOS.   These girls?
You have sentenced them both?

CREON.   No, you are right.
I will not kill the one whose hands are clean.   140

CHORAGOS. But Antigonê?

CREON [*somberly*].   I will carry her far away
Out there in the wilderness and lock her
Living in a vault of stone. She shall have food,
As the custom is, to absolve the State of her death.
And there let her pray to the gods of hell:
They are her only gods:
Perhaps they will show her an escape from death,
Or she may learn, though late,
That piety shown the dead is pity in vain.

                                     [*Exit* CREON.]

ODE III

                                        [*strophe*]

CHORUS. Love, unconquerable
   Waster of rich men, keeper
   Of warm lights and all-night vigil
   In the soft face of a girl:
   Sea-wanderer, forest-visitor!
   Even the pure Immortals cannot escape you,
   And mortal man, in his one day's dusk,
   Trembles before your glory.

                                       [*antistrophe*]

   Surely you swerve upon ruin
   The just man's consenting heart,
   As here you have made bright anger
   Strike between father and son—
   And none has conquered but Love!

A girl's glánce wórking the will of heaven:
Pleasure to her alone who mocks us,
Merciless Aphroditê.[1]

SCENE IV

[ANTIGONE *enters guarded.*]

CHORAGAOS. But I can no longer stand in awe of this,
　Nor, seeing what I see, keep back my tears.
　Here is Antigonê, passing to that chamber
　Where all find sleep at last.

[*strophe 1*]

ANTIGONE. Look upon me, friends, and pity me
　Turning back at the night's edge to say
　Goodbye to the sun that shines for me no longer;
　Now sleepy Death
　Summons me down to Acheron,[1] that cold shore:
　There is no bridesong there, nor any music.   10
CHORUS. Yet not unpraised, not without a kind of honor.
　You walk at last into the underworld;
　Untouched by sickness, broken by no sword.
　What woman has ever found your way to death?

[*antistrophe 1*]

ANTIGONE. How often I have heard the story of Niobê,
　Tantalos' wretched daughter, how the stone
　Clung fast about her, ivy-close: and they say
　The rain falls endlessly
　And sifting soft snow; her tears are never done.[2]
　I feel the loneliness of her death in mine.   20
CHORUS. But she was born of heaven, and you
　Are woman, woman-born. If her death is yours,
　A mortal woman's, is this not for you
　Glory in our world and in the world beyond?

[*strophe 2*]

ANTIGONE. You laugh at me. Ah, friends, friends,
　Can you not wait until I am dead? O Thebes,
　O men many-charioted, in love with Fortune,
　Dear springs of Dircê, sacred Theban grove,
　Be witness for me, denied all pity,
　Unjustly judged! and think a word of love   30
　For hèr whose path turns
　Under dark earth, where there are no more tears.
CHORUS. You have passed beyond human daring and come at last
　Into a place of stone where Justice sits.
　I cannot tell
　What shape of your father's guilt appears in this.

[1]Goddess of love.
[1]The river over which the souls cross into Hades.
[2]Niobe wept ceaselessly over the loss of her children and was eventually turned into stone.

[*antistrophe 2*]

ANTIGONE. You have touched it at last: that bridal bed
  Unspeakable, horror of son and mother mingling:
  Their crime, infection of all our family!
  O Oedipus, father and brother!
  Your marriage strikes from the grave to murder mine.   40
  I have been a stranger here in my own land:
  All my life
  The blasphemy of my birth has followed me.
CHORUS. Reverence is a virtue, but strength
  Lives in established law: that must prevail.
  You have made your choice,
  Your death is the doing of your conscious hand.

[*epode*]

ANTIGONE. Then let me go, since all your words are bitter,
  And the very light of the sun is cold to me.   50
  Lead me to my vigil, where I must have
  Neither love nor lamentation; no song, but silence.
  [CREON *interrupts impatiently.*]
CREON. If dirges and planned lamentations could put off death,
  Men would be singing for ever.
  [*To the* SERVANTS]   Take her, go!
  You know your orders: take her to the vault
  And leave her alone there. And if she lives or dies,
  That's her affair, not ours: our hands are clean.
ANTIGONE. O tomb, vaulted bridebed in eternal rock,
  Soon I shall be with my own again
  Where Persephonê[3] welcomes the thin ghosts underground: 60
  And I shall see my father again, and you, mother,
  And dearest Polyneicês —
                        dearest indeed
  To me, since it was my hand
  That washed him clean and poured the ritual wine:
  And my reward is death before my time!
  And yet, as men's hearts know, I have done no wrong,
  I have not sinned before God. Or if I have,
  I shall know the truth in death. But if the guilt
  Lies upon Creon who judged me, then, I pray,
  May his punishment equal my own.
CHORAGOS.   O passionate heart,   70
  Unyielding, tormented still by the same winds!
CREON. Her guards shall have good cause to regret their delaying.
ANTIGONE. Ah! That voice is like the voice of death!
CREON. I can give you no reason to think you are mistaken.
ANTIGONE. Thebes, and you my fathers' gods,
  And rulers of Thebes, you see me now, the last
  Unhappy daughter of a line of kings,

---

[3]Daughter of Demeter, goddess of fertility and marriage in Greek mythology, Persephone was
kidnapped by Hades, god of the underworld, and taken to the underworld to become his wife.

Your kings led away to death. You will remember
What things I suffer, and at what men's hands,
Because I would not transgress the laws of heaven.   80
[*To the* GUARDS, *simply*] Come: let us wait no longer.

[*Exit* ANTIGONE, *L., guarded*]

ODE IV

[*strophe 1*]

CHORUS. All Danaê's beauty was locked away
　　In a brazen cell where the sunlight could not come:
　　A small room, still as any grave, enclosed her.
　　Yet she was a princess too,
　　And Zeus in a rain of gold poured love upon her.[4]
　　O child, child,
　　No power in wealth or war
　　Or tough sea-blackened ships
　　Can prevail against untiring Destiny!

[*antistrophe 1*]

And Dryas' son also, that furious king,   10
　　Bore the god's prisoning anger for his bride:
　　Sealed up by Dionysos in deaf stone,
　　His madness died among echoes.
　　So at the last he learned what dreadful power
　　His tongue had mocked:
　　For he had profaned the revels,
　　And fired the wrath of the nine
　　Implacable Sisters that love the sound of the flute.[5]

[*strophe 2*]

And old men tell a half-remembered tale
　　Of horror done where a dark ledge splits the sea   20
　　And a double surf beats on the gráy shóres:
　　How a king's new woman, sick
　　With hatred for the queen he had imprisoned,
　　Ripped out his two sons' eyes with her bloody hands
　　While grinning Arês[6] watched the shuttle plunge
　　Four times: four blind wounds crying for revenge,

[*antistrophe 2*]

Crying, tears and blood mingled. — Piteously born,
　　Those sons whose mother was of heavenly birth!
　　Her father was the god of the North Wind
　　And she was cradled by gales,
　　She raced with young colts on the glittering hills   30
　　And walked untrammeled in the open light:

[4]Danaê was the mother of Perseus by Zeus, who visited her in the form of a shower of gold during her imprisonment.
[5]Dryas' son, Lycurgus, opposed Dionysus and was punished by madness and imprisonment.
[6]the god of war.

But in her marriage deathless Fate found means
To build a tomb like yours for all her joy.[7]

SCENE V

[*Enter blind* TEIRESIAS,[1] *led by a boy. The opening speeches of* TEIRESIAS *should
be in singsong contrast to the realistic lines of* CREON.]

TEIRESIAS. This is the way the blind man comes, Princess, Princess,
    Lock-step, two heads lit by the eyes of one.
CREON. What new thing have you to tell us, old Teiresias?
TEIRESIAS. I have much to tell you: listen to the prophet, Creon.
CREON. I am not aware that I have ever failed to listen.
TEIRESIAS. Then you have done wisely, King, and ruled well.
CREON. I admit my debt to you. But what have you to say?
TEIRESIAS. This, Creon: you stand once more on the edge of fate.
CREON. What do you mean? Your words are a kind of dread.
TEIRESIAS. Listen, Creon: 10
    I was sitting in my chair of augury, at the place
    Where the birds gather about me. They were all a-chatter,
    As is their habit, when suddenly I heard
    A strange note in their jangling, a scream, a
    Whirring fury; I knew that they were fighting,
    Tearing each other, dying
    In a whirlwind of wings clashing. And I was afraid.
    I began the rites of burnt-offering at the altar,
    But Hephaistos[2] failed me: instead of bright flame,
    There was only the sputtering slime of the fat thigh-flesh   20
    Melting: the entrails dissolved in gray smoke,
    The bare bone burst from the welter. And no blaze!
    This was a sign from heaven. My boy described it,
    Seeing for me as I see for others.
    I tell you Creon, you yourself have brought
    This new calamity upon us. Our hearths and altars
    Are stained with the corruption of dogs and carrion birds
    That glut themselves on the corpse of Oedipus' son.
    The gods are deaf when we pray to them, their fire
    Recoils from our offering, their birds of omen   30
    Have no cry of comfort, for they are gorged
    With the thick blood of the dead.
O my son,
    These are no trifles! Think: all men make mistakes,
    But a good man yields when he knows his course is wrong,
    And repairs the evil. The only crime is pride.
    Give in to the dead man, then: do not fight with a corpse—
    What glory is it to kill a man who is dead?

---

[7]The second wife of King Phineus blinded her stepsons; their mother, Cleopatra, the daughter of the North Wind, was imprisoned in a cave.

[1]the old blind prophet of Thebes, who frequently appears in Greek literature.

[2]god of fire and metal-working.

Think, I beg you:
It is for your own good that I speak as I do.
You should be able to yield for your own good.   40
CREON. It seems that prophets have made me their especial province.
All my life long
I have been a kind of butt for the dull arrows
Of doddering fortune-tellers!
           No, Teiresias:
If your birds—if the great eagles of God himself
Should carry him stinking bit by bit to heaven,
I would not yield. I am not afraid of pollution:
No man can defile the gods.
              Do what you will,
Go into business, make money, speculate
In India gold or that synthetic gold from Sardis,   50
Get rich otherwise than by my consent to bury him.
Teiresias, it is a sorry thing when a wise man
Sells his wisdom, lets out his words for hire!
TEIRESIAS. Ah Creon! Is there no man left in the world—
CREON. To do what—Come, let's have the aphorism!
TEIRESIAS. No man who knows that wisdom outweighs any wealth?
CREON. As surely as bribes are baser than any baseness.
TEIRESIAS. You are sick, Creon! You are deathly sick!
CREON. As you say: it is not my place to challenge a prophet.
TEIRESIAS. Yet you have said my prophecy is for sale.   60
CREON. The generation of prophets has always loved gold.
TEIRESIAS. The generation of kings has always loved brass.
CREON. You forget yourself! You are speaking to your King.
TEIRESIAS. I know it. You are a king because of me.
CREON. You have a certain skill; but you have sold out.
TEIRESIAS. King, you will drive me to words that—
CREON.   Say them, say them!
   Only remember: I will not pay you for them.
TEIRESIAS. No, you will find them too costly.
CREON.   No doubt. Speak:
   Whatever you say, you will not change my will.
TEIRESIAS. Then take this, and take it to heart!   70
   The time is not far off when you shall pay back
   Corpse for corpse, flesh of your own flesh.
   You have thrust the child of this world into living night,
   You have kept from the gods below the child that is theirs:
   The one in a grave before her death, the other,
   Dead, denied the grave. This is your crime:
   And the Furies[3] and the dark gods of Hell
   Are swift with terrible punishment for you.
   Do you want to buy me now, Creon?
                Not many days,

[3] The three spirits who pursue and punish doers of unavenged crimes.

And your house will be full of men and women weeping,   80
And curses will be hurled at you from far
Cities grieving for sons unburied, left to rot
Before the walls of Thebes.
These are my arrows, Creon: they are all for you.
[*To* BOY] But come, child: lead me home
Let him waste his fine anger upon younger men.
Maybe he will learn at last
To control a wiser tongue in a better head.

[*Exit* TEIRESIAS.]

CHORAGOS. The old man has gone, King, but his words
  Remain to plague us. I am old, too,   90
  But I cannot remember that he was ever false.
CREON. That is true. . . . It troubles me.
  Oh it is hard to give in! but it is worse
  To risk everything for stubborn pride.
CHORAGOS. Creon: take my advice.
CREON.   What shall I do?
CHORAGOS. Go quickly: free Antigonê from her vault
  And build a tomb for the body of Polyneicês.
CREON. You would have me do this?
CHORAGOS.   Creon, yes!
  And it must be done at once: God moves
  Swiftly to cancel the folly of stubborn men.   100
CREON. It is hard to deny the heart! But I
  Will do it: I will not fight with destiny.
CHORAGOS. You must go yourself, you cannot leave it to others.
CREON. I will go.
         —Bring axes, servants:
Come with me to the tomb. I buried her, I
Will set her free.
         —Oh, quickly!
My mind misgives—
The laws of the gods are mighty, and a man must serve them   110
To the last day of his life!

[*Exit* CREON.]

PAEAN

[*strophe 1*]

CHORAGOS. God of many names
CHORUS.   O Iacchos
             son
  of Cadmeian Sémelê
        O born of the Thunder!
  Guardian of the West
        Regent
  of Eleusis' plain

O Prince of mænad Thebes
and the Dragon Field by rippling Ismenos:

[antistrophe 1]

CHORAGOS. God of many names[4]
CHORUS.   the flame of torches
    flares on our hills
                    the nymphs of Iacchos
    dance at the spring of Castalia:
    from the vine-close mountain
                            come ah come in ivy:
    Evohé evohé! sings through the streets of Thebes   10

[strophe 2]

CHORAGOS. God of many names
CHORUS.   Iacchos of Thebes
    heavenly child
                of Sémelê bride of the Thunderer!
    The shadow of plague is upon us:
                                come
    with clement feet
                    oh come from Parnasos
    down the long slopes
                        across the lamenting water

[antistrophe 2]

CHORAGOS. Iô Fire! Chorister of the throbbing stars!
    O purest among the voices of the night!
    Thou son of God, blaze for us!
CHORUS. Come with choric rapture of circling Mænads[5]
    Who cry *Iô Iacche!*
                    God of many names!   20

ÉXODOS

[Enter MESSENGER, L.]

MESSENGER. Men of the line of Cadmos, you who live
    Near Amphion's citadel:
                        I cannot say
    Of any condition of human life, "This is fixed,
    This is clearly good, or bad." Fate raises up,
    And Fate casts down the happy and unhappy alike:
    No man can foretell his Fate.
                            Take the case of Creon:
    Creon was happy once, as I count happiness:
    Victorious in battle, sole governor of the land,
    Fortunate father of children nobly born.
    And now it has all gone from him! Who can say   10
    That a man is still alive when his life's joy fails?

---

[4]Dionysus, the god of wine and of an orgiastic religion celebrating the power and fertility of
nature, was also called Bacchus as well as the many names and epithets given in these lines.
[5]Female members of the cult of Dionysus.

He is a walking dead man. Grant him rich,
Let him live like a king in his great house:
If his pleasure is gone, I would not give
So much as the shadow of smoke for all he owns.
CHORAGOS. Your words hint at sorrow: what is your news for us?
MESSENGER. They are dead. The living are guilty of their death.
CHORAGOS. Who is guilty? Who is dead? Speak!
MESSENGER.   Haimon. *suicide*
    Haimon is dead; and the hand that killed him
    Is his own hand.
CHORAGOS.   His father's? or his own?   20
MESSENGER. His own, driven mad by the murder his father had done.
CHORAGOS. Teiresias, how clearly you saw it all!
MESSENGER. This is my news: you must draw what conclusions you can from it.
CHORAGOS. But look: Eurydicê, our Queen:
    Has she overheard us?

[*Enter* EURYDICE *from the Palace, C.*]

EURYDICE. I have heard something, friends:
    As I was unlocking the gate of Pallas' shrine,
    For I needed her help today, I heard a voice
    Telling of some sorrow. And I fainted
    There at the temple with all my maidens about me.   30
    But speak again: whatever it is, I can bear it:
    Grief and I are no strangers.
MESSENGER.   Dearest Lady,
    I will tell you plainly all that I have seen.
    I shall not try to comfort you: what is the use,
    Since comfort could lie only in what is not true?
 ✗ The truth is always best.
                              I went with Creon   *Narrative*
    To the outer plain where Polyneicês was lying,
    No friend to pity him, his body shredded by dogs.
    We made our prayers in that place to Hecatê
    And Pluto, that they would be merciful. And we bathed   40
    The corpse with holy water, and we brought
    Fresh-broken branches to burn what was left of it,
    And upon the urn we heaped up a towering barrow
    Of the earth of his own land.
                              When we were done, we ran
    To the vault where Antigonê lay on her couch of stone.
    One of the servants had gone ahead,
    And while he was yet far off he heard a voice
    Grieving within the chamber, and he came back
    And told Creon. And as the King went closer,
    The air was full of wailing, the words lost,   50
    And he begged us to make all haste. "Am I a prophet?"
    He said, weeping, "And must I walk this road,
    "The saddest of all that I have gone before?
    "My son's voice calls me on. Oh quickly, quickly!
    "Look through the crevice there, and tell me

"If it is Haimon, or some deception of the gods!"
We obeyed; and in the cavern's farthest corner
We saw her lying:
She had made a noose of her fine linen veil   *one – suicide*
And hanged herself. Haimon lay beside her,   60
His arms about her waist, lamenting her,
His love lost under ground, crying out
That his father had stolen her away from him.
When Creon saw him the tears rushed to his eyes
And he called to him: "What have you done, child? Speak to me.
"What are you thinking that makes your eyes so strange?
"O my son, my son, I come to you on my knees!"
But Haimon spat in his face. He said not a word,
Staring—   *It attacks &*
          And suddenly drew his sword   *& misses*
And lunged. Creon shrank back, the blade missed; and the boy,   70
Desperate against himself, drove it half its length   *& then*
Into his own side, and fell. And as he died   *kills himself*
He gathered Antigonê close in his arms again,
Choking, his blood bright red on her white cheek.
And now he lies dead with the dead, and she is his
At last, his bride in the houses of the dead.

> [*Exit* EURYDICE *into the Palace.*]

CHORAGOS. *queen* She has left us without a word. What can this mean?
MESSENGER. It troubles me, too; yet she knows what is best,
  Her grief is too great for public lamentation,
  And doubtless she has gone to her chamber to weep   80
  For her dead son, leading her maidens in his dirge.
CHORAGOS. It may be so: but I fear this deep silence.   [*Pause.*]
MESSENGER. I will see what she is going. I will go in.

> [*Exit* MESSENGER *into the Palace.*]

> [*Enter* CREON *with attendants, bearing* HAIMON'S *body.*]
CHORAGOS. But here is the King himself: oh look at him,
  Bearing his own damnation in his arms.
CREON. Nothing you say can touch me any more.
  My own blind heart has brought me
  From darkness to final darkness. Here you see
  The father murdering, the murdered son—
  And all my civic wisdom!   90
  Haimon my son, so young, so young to die,
  I was the fool, not you; and you died for me.
CHORAGOS. That is the truth; but you were late in learning it.
CREON. This truth is hard to bear. Surely a god
  Has crushed me beneath the hugest weight of heaven,
  And driven me headlong a barbaric way
  To trample out the thing I held most dear.
  The pains that men will take to come to pain!

> [*Enter* MESSENGER *from the Palace.*]

MESSENGER. The burden you carry in your hands is heavy,
But it is not all: you will find more in your house.   100
CREON. What burden worse than this shall I find there?   *queen dead*
MESSENGER. The Queen is dead.
CREON.   O port of death, deaf world,
Is there no pity for me? And you, Angel of evil,
I was dead, and your words are death again.
Is it true, boy? Can it be true?
Is my wife dead? Has death bred death?
MESSENGER. You can see for yourself.
   [*The doors are opened, and the body of* EURYDICE *is disclosed within.*]
CREON. Oh pity!
All true, all true, and more than I can bear!
O my wife, my son!
MESSENGER. She stood before the altar, and her heart   *suicide*   110
Welcomed the knife her own hand guided,
And a great cry burst from her lips for Megareus dead,
And for Haimon dead, her sons; and her last breath
Was a curse for their father, the murderer of her sons.
And she fell, and the dark flowed in through her closing eyes.
CREON. Oh God, I am sick with fear.
Are there no swords here? Has no one a blow for me?
MESSENGER. Her curse is upon you for the deaths of both.
CREON. It is right that it should be. I alone am guilty.
I know it, and I say it. Lead me in,   120
Quickly, friends.
I have neither life nor substance. Lead me in.
CHORAGOS. You are right, if there can be right in so much wrong.
The briefest way is best in a world of sorrow.
CREON.   Let it come,
Let death come quickly, and be kind to me.
I would not ever see the sun again.
CHORAGOS. All that will come when it will; but we, meanwhile,
Have much to do. Leave the future to itself.
CREON. All my heart was in that prayer!
CHORAGOS. Then do not pray any more: the sky is deaf.   130
CREON. Lead me away. I have been rash and foolish.
I have killed my son and my wife.
I look for comfort; my comfort lies here dead.
Whatever my hands have touched has come to nothing.
Fate has brought all my pride to a thought of dust.
[*As* CREON *is being led into the house, the* CHORAGOS *advances and speaks directly
to the audience.*]
CHORAGOS. There is no happiness where there is no wisdom;
No wisdom but in submission to the gods.   ✗ *moral*
Big words are always punished,
And proud men in old age learn to be wise.

                                                (ca. 442 B.C.)

Prewriting

Now that you have read *Antigone* and have some sense of its basic structure, read the play again carefully and write out the answers to the questions below. Your responses will not only help you to sharpen your understanding of dramatic structure; they will also lead you to clarify your reactions to *Antigone*'s characters and themes.

Analyzing Dramatic Structure

1. What background are we given in the Prologue? List the main points of information that this scene between Antigone and Ismene reveals.

2. What exposition do the Chorus and the Choragos (the leader of the chorus) give in the section called the Parados (pages 636–641)?

3. How does Sophocles use the Sentry in Scene I? Does this character provide more than factual exposition?

4. What do you think the main conflict is? State it as specifically as you can in a single sentence.

5. Identify the protagonist and the antagonist. Is it fair to apply the labels *heroine* or *villain* to them?

6. Where does the climax occur? Identify the scene and describe what happens. Why do you think this is the play's turning point?

7. Does the climax seem to come early in the play? How does Sophocles maintain interest after the turning point? Did you expect such dramatic developments after the climax? Do you think Creon expected them?

8. When does the catastrophe occur? Was this outcome inevitable? Did you feel different about the outcome the second time you read the play?

9. State what you consider the play's theme to be.

10. A *foil* is a contrasting character who sets off or helps to define another character. How is Ismene a foil to Antigone? Are there any foils to Creon?

11. Why is Eurydice included in the plot? How do you feel about her fate?

Having answered these questions about the structure of *Antigone*, devise a graph or chart that illustrates the pattern of events in the play. Make sure your graph shows the six structural components discussed on page 632.

Writing

Your understanding of the structure of *Antigone* will enable you to write more easily about the play's arguments. As you watched the conflict develop between Antigone and Creon, you undoubtedly became aware of the opposing values that these two characters represent. As one critic has observed about *Antigone,* "the characters *are* the issues, and the issues the characters."[1] It is now your turn to examine these issues and decide where you stand.

Discovering a Workable Argumentative Thesis

Argument means dispute; it implies that there are opposing sides. Any matter worth arguing will involve at least one "issue"—that is, an essential point in question or disagreement. You need not always take sides, but once you have decided what issues are involved in an argument, you can write an effective paper by taking a stand and explaining why you have chosen one side over the other.

Your approach to *Antigone* will have to take into account the controversial nature of the play's conflict. Review your responses to the prewriting questions about the disagreement and about the antagonist and protagonist. Can you identify an issue that you think is central to the play's meaning? Are there other issues involved in the conflict? Try to get the main issues stated as clearly and specifically as you can before you begin to write. The ideas for writing that follow should help you to work out the important issues of the play.

You can argue an issue in two ways. You can take an affirmative position on one side of the question and present reasons and evidence to support your stand. Or you can anticipate the arguments of the opposing side and show how the evidence does not support this side, indicating where the fallacies or errors lie in the opposition's reasoning. You will probably want to combine both techniques in writing about *Antigone.*

Whatever your approach, you need to study the evidence and examine the ideas on both sides for flaws in logical thinking. One way to make this examination involves listing the main arguments, pro and con, in two columns on a sheet of paper:

Creon	*Antigone*
Public interest outweighs private loyalties	Eternal unwritten laws take precedence.
Polyneices made war on his own country.	All the dead deserve honor.

You can make a similar listing of speeches or lines from the play that serve as evidence for the two sides of the argument. For instance, you may want to note such revealing statements by Creon as these:

---

[1] Charles Paul Segal, "Sophocles' Praise of Man and the Conflicts of *Antigone,*" *Sophocles: A Collection of Critical Essays,* ed. T. Woodward (Englewood Cliffs: Prentice Hall, 1966), 63.

"Whoever is chosen to govern should be obeyed."
"If we must lose, / Let's lose to a man, at least! Is a woman stronger than we?"
"The State is the King!"

Compare these lists and see which side has the stronger arguments and the greater amount of evidence. You can then decide which side you are going to support; you also have a convenient listing of specific ideas and quotations to use in developing your essay.

Quoting from a Play

When writing a paper on a single play, you need to cite your source in a note only the first time you quote from the play. For subsequent quotations give act and scene numbers in parentheses at the end of the quoted material; for verse plays give act, scene, and line numbers. Because *Antigone* is not divided into acts, give the scene and line numbers for the quotations you use. Long quotations (more than two lines) should be indented with *no* quotation marks. Also, indicate the speaker when quoting a passage in which more than one character speaks. Here are some samples:

> It is up to Ismene to point out the obvious: "We are only women,
> We cannot fight with the men, Antigone!" (Pro. 46–47).

[Only two lines quoted — separated with a slash and enclosed in quotation marks]

> Creon's speeches show his contempt for women:
>> Gentlemen, I beg you to observe these girls:
>> One has just now lost her mind; the other,
>> It seems, has never had a mind at all. (2.148–49)

[Long quotation — indented, no quotation marks]

> Iago is a master of understatement and insinuation:
>> *Othello.* Is he not honest?
>> *Iago.* Honest, my lord!
>> *Othello.* Honest! ay, honest.
>> *Iago.* My lord, for aught I know.
>> *Othello.* What dost thou think?
>> *Iago.* Think, my lord! (3.3.103–105)

[Change of speakers indicated]

Remember to introduce each quotation carefully. You may want to review the material in Chapter 5 on integrating quotations gracefully (page 70).

Ideas for Writing
Ideas for Responsive Writing

1. Do you see yourself as approving of or opposing the rules and norms of the society you live in? How do you support, change, or disobey these rules and norms? Write about one rule or group of related rules (for example, sex roles or parent–child relationships) that you accept or reject.

2. In modern society, what might Creon and Antigone disagree about? Write an essay explaining where the two characters would probably stand on one of today's issues.

Ideas for Critical Writing

1. Is Creon a politician concerned with imposing and maintaining order? Is Antigone an anarchist whose action will destroy that order? Or is she a private citizen determined to follow the dictates of her personal beliefs? Write about the issues in *Antigone* as a struggle between public policy and individual conscience, supporting the side that you think is "right."

2. Can you analyze the conflict between Antigone and Creon as a psychological clash between a woman and a man? Write an essay that focuses on the male–female opposition in the play. You may want to work Ismene, Haimon, and Eurydice into your scheme of opposing values.

Rewriting

You will want to be certain that your arguments about *Antigone* are perfectly clear. Take some time to ensure that what you have written cannot be misunderstood. If you can, coax a friend or classmate into reading your first draft; ask your reader to point out sentences that do not make sense or are unclear.

Avoiding Unclear Language

Multisyllabic words and long, involved sentences may dazzle your readers, but they also hinder clear communication. Your first goal in writing should be to convey ideas and information. Trying to impress your readers with big words and fancy phrases may lead to one or more forms of unclear expression:

1. *Engfish:* Writing specialist Ken Macrorie uses this term to call attention to artificial language that does not represent a writer's own experience and education. Engfish is phony, pretentious, stuffy, and

often impossible to decode. Writers use Engfish, it seems, when they are unsure of which attitude to take toward their subject and their audience. The student who wrote

> Antigone's unacceptable posture toward the designated governmental powers inevitably entailed the termination of her existence,

no doubt thought that this inflated diction was appropriate for a serious paper on a classical play. But most readers probably would prefer to see that sentence revised to read more clearly, like this:

> Antigone's defiance led to her death.

In the long run, clarity will impress your readers more than Engfish ever can.

2. *Jargon:* This term applies to the specialized language used by a particular group of people. Computer operators, sociologists, teenagers, architects, hockey players, mobsters — all sorts of interest groups and professions — employ words and terms that relate only to their particular activities. The problem with jargon is that outsiders do not understand it. Writing about a "love game" or the "ad court" will be all right for an audience of tennis buffs, but you will have to change your language for more general readers. Jargon may not come up in your essay about *Antigone,* but it can creep in from other sources. For instance, the student who wrote

> Antigone's behavior is marked by regressive reaction formation toward authoritarian figures.

was apparently influenced by the jargon of her psychology class. Unless you are writing for an audience of fellow psychoanalysts, you would do better to say the following:

> Antigone sometimes acted liked a disobedient daughter.

3. *Abstract words:* Abstract terms and general expressions do not automatically make your writing intellectual and impressive. Although it is true that writing an argumentative essay requires using abstract ideas, your paper will still be more persuasive if it is factual, concrete, and clear. Abstractions tend to be hazy and difficult to define. Words like *duty, anarchy, patriotism,* and *truth* have different meanings for different people. When writing about an abstract concept, make certain that you have a definite meaning in your own mind. If, for instance, you write that

> Antigone is a woman of honor,

it is a good idea to check the dictionary to see if your understanding of the word *honor* coincides with a standard definition. *The American Heritage Dictionary* gives thirteen entries for *honor.* Which one does the above sentence convey? Would "a woman's chastity" be accurate in this context? It might be more meaningful to say

Antigone is a woman of principle and integrity,

although those words are also abstract. Try, if possible, to specify the meaning you want when using an abstract term:

Above all, Creon is a master politician—a man of ambition intent on holding his power.

Sample Student Paper on Drama

The following paper analyzing the power struggle between male and female in *Antigone* was written by Laurie Dahlberg, a student at Illinois State University. Notice how she uses and documents quoted material from the play. Your Work Cited section at the end belongs on a separate page.

Laurie Dahlberg

English 102

April 2, 1990

"A Woman Stronger Than We?": Gender Conflict

in Antigone

Antigone is a drama built around two basic conflicts. Beneath the more obvious conflict of the individual versus the state lies a struggle of male against female. The protagonist, Antigone, becomes a criminal by choice, but a feminist by chance. The antagonist, Creon, is fighting to retain control over Antigone, not only as king over subject but also as man over woman.

Antigone knows that she has violated the king's order not to bury her brother Polyneices, but she seems not to notice that she has also violated the social code by stepping outside the boundaries of acceptable feminine behavior. Her act of defiance is courageous, self-reliant, and completely contrary to the obedience expected of women in her society. She

fearlessly assures her sister, Ismene, that "Creon is not
strong enough to stand in my way."[1] (Pro 35). It is up to
Ismene, then, to point out the obvious: "We are only women, /We
cannot fight with men, Antigone!" (Pro. 46-47). A perfect foil
for Antigone, Ismene epitomizes the good Theban woman--she is
deferential, passive, and timid. Though she loves Antigone
dearly, Ismene is still bound to her male masters and cannot
follow her sister: "I must yield to those in authority," she
says. "And I think it is a dangerous business to be always
meddling." (Pro. 50-51). Eventually, Ismene is rewarded for
her passivity when Creon spares her life.

When Antigone is arrested, King Creon expresses shock that
a woman in his court has committed the crime. But his disbelief
soon turns to perverse pleasure at the opportunity to punish
this woman for her audacity. Creon's speeches show his contempt
for women:

> Gentlemen, I beg you to observe these girls:
> One has just now lost her mind; the other,
> It seems, has never had a mind at all. (2.150-51)

Antigone, however, rises above the pettiness of sexual
rivalry by responding only to the conflict between king and
subject. Unlike Creon, Antigone acts out of a heartfelt moral
obligation, not pride: ''There is no guilt in reverence for the
dead,'' she cries (2.108). As Antigone calmly and eloquently
argues the righteousness of her action, instead of quivering
with fear under Creon's threats, the king's feeling of triumph
slowly turns to rage. At the close of her defense, Antigone
states:

> You smile at me. Ah Creon,
> Think me a fool, if you like; but it may well be
> That a fool convicts me of folly. (2.72-74)

To which Creon angrily replies:

> Pride? In a slave?
> This girl is guilty of a double insolence,

Breaking the given laws and boasting of it.
Who is the man here,
She or I, if this crime goes unpunished? (2.79-83)

Though Antigone's illegal act is punishable by death, it
is the fact that a mere woman has defied him that enrages Creon.
Her death alone will not satisfy him. He needs to master her
willfulness and make her regret her arrogance. Instead of
killing her, he entombs her, where she will die slowly. This
method of execution, Creon says, will teach the woman a lesson:

> And there let her pray to the gods of hell:
> They are her only gods:
> Perhaps they will show her an escape from death,
> Or she may learn, though late,
> That piety shown the dead is pity in vain. (3.145-49)

The key to Creon's personality is found in his comment to
Haimon when he is explaining why he (the king) has sentenced his
son's bride to death:

> We keep the laws then, and the lawmakers,
> And no woman shall seduce us. If we must lose,
> Let's lose to a man, at least! Is a woman stronger than
> we? (3.46-48)

Creon refuses to listen to Haimon's reasoning, and the young
man, disgusted by his father's cruelty, rejects him. This
rejection makes the king even more bitter. Creon's pride has
made him blind to his mistake.

Throughout the course of the play, Creon changes from a
strict but competent leader to a wildly insecure man, plagued
by imaginary enemies. He has come to suspect that anyone who
disagrees with him is involved in a plot against him:

> You, too, Ismene,
> Snake in my ordered house, sucking my blood,
> Stealthily--and all the time I never knew
> That these two sisters were aiming at my
> throne! (2.126-29)

Creon has mistaken Antigone's act of piety
for a wild attempt by a power-hungry woman to undermine his
rule. Out of his own fear of being beaten by a woman, Creon
begins a chain of events which finally destroy him, fulfilling
Antigone's prediction:

> . . . if the guilt
> Lies upon Creon who judged me, then, I pray,
> May his punishment equal my own. (4.66-70)

Work Cited

[1]Sophocles, <u>Antigone</u>. Trans. Dudley Fitts and Robert
    Fitzgerald. <u>Literature and the Writing Process</u>. Ed.
    Elizabeth McMahan, Susan Day, and Robert Funk. 3rd ed. New
    York: Macmillan, 1993: Prologue, line 35.

Questions for Discussion

1. Do you think this essay overemphasizes the gender issue in analyzing the conflict between Creon and Antigone? Has the author slighted or ignored more important issues?

2. Can you find any additional evidence which the author of the essay overlooked or chose not to use? Would the case be strengthened by including Eurydice in the analysis?

3. The author says that Antigone rises above sexual rivalry in her defiant behavior. Is this view entirely true? Can you find any evidence to suggest that Antigone is also caught up in the power struggle between male and female?

4. In carrying out her approach, the author of the essay analyzes Creon more than Antigone. Why is that? Is this strategy productive? Do you agree with the conclusion about Creon's character development?

16

Writing About Character

Pondering people's characters comes quite naturally and easily. You will remember that we began our approach to literature with the study of character in the short story. Drama also provides us with carefully drawn examples of human speech and behavior. Whether the presentation is realistic or not, the characters are at the heart of the play.

What Is the Modern Hero?

In everyday life, we use the word *heroic* to describe people who save others' lives while risking their own, acts of great self-sacrifice or self-control, feats that we hold in awe. Before you read on, think of the last time you remember calling something heroic or referring to someone as a hero. Note the situation, and think about what you meant by the word. We often use it lightly — the person who supplies a much needed extension cord or an emergency ten dollar loan may temporarily be a hero. But drama practically forces us into deeper consideration of what a hero is.

The Classical Tragic Hero

In the fourth century B.C. Aristotle described the classic concept of the tragic hero. He wrote that the hero must be someone "who is highly renowned and prosperous." Classical tragedy involves the inevitable destruction of a noble person by means of a character flaw, usually a disproportionate measure of a specific human attribute such as pride or jealousy or indecision. The Aristotelian definition implies a basic premise that there is a natural, right ordering and proportion of traits within the human being which, if violated, produces calamity. Many critics cite Antigone's "difficult willfulness" as the explanation of her fate. Charles Segal claims that "she can assert what she is only by staking her entire being, her life. It is by this extreme defense of her beliefs that she rises to heroic and deeply tragic stature."[1]

The Modern Tragic Hero

In 1949, the famous playwright Arthur Miller described what he considered a new kind of hero. In an article called "Tragedy and the Common Man" (*New York Times*, 27 Feb. 1949, 3.1.3.), he challenged Aristotle's idea that the hero must be a "highly renowned and prosperous" figure who has a tragic flaw. In contrast to disorder exclusively within the personal traits of the hero, Miller's idea of the modern hero emphasizes a clash between the character and the environment, especially social environment. He says that each person has a chosen image of self and position and that tragedy results when the character's environment denies the fulfillment of this self-concept. The hero no longer must be born into the nobility but gains stature in the action of pitting self against cosmos. The tragedy is "the disaster inherent in being torn away from our chosen image of what and who we are in this world." Feelings of displacement and indignity, then, are the driving forces for Miller's modern tragic hero. In his own play *Death of a Salesman*, the character Willy Loman imagines himself as a well-liked, successful, worldly businessman. Tragically, he is really an object of ridicule and contempt, always on the edge of poverty. Such conflicts between ideal self-image and reality occur over and over in the modern play you are about to read.

Looking at the Modern Hero

As you read *Cat on a Hot Tin Roof* by Tennessee Williams for pleasure, take note of the characters especially. Who is the hero? the heroine? — or are there none? Which characters do you respond positively to? Are there any to whom you respond negatively?

---

[1]Charles Segal, "Sophocles' Praise of Man and the Conflicts of the *Antigone, Sophocles: A Collection of Critical Essays*, ed. T. Woodward (Englewood Cliffs, N.J.: Prentice-Hall," 1966): 65.

Tennessee Williams *1911–1983*

CAT ON A HOT TIN ROOF

CHARACTERS

MARGARET.
BRICK.
MAE, *sometimes called*
   SISTER WOMAN.
BIG MAMA.
DIXIE, *a little girl.*
BIG DADDY.
REVEREND TOOKER.

GOOPER, *sometimes called*
   BROTHER MAN.
DOCTOR BAUGH, *pronounced*
   "Baw."
LACEY, *a Negro servant.*
SOOKEY, *another.*
CHILDREN.

NOTES FOR THE DESIGNER

The set is the bed-sitting room of a plantation home in the Mississippi Delta. It is along an upstairs gallery which probably runs around the entire house; it has two pairs of very wide doors opening onto the gallery, showing white balustrades against a fair summer sky that fades into dusk and night during the course of the play, which occupies precisely the time of its performance, excepting, of course, the fifteen minutes of intermission.

Perhaps the style of the room is not what you would expect in the home of the Delta's biggest cotton-planter. It is Victorian with a touch of the Far East. It hasn't changed much since it was occupied by the original owners of the place, Jack Straw and Peter Ochello, a pair of old bachelors who shared this room all their lives together. In other words, the room must evoke some ghosts; it is gently and poetically haunted by a relationship that must have involved a tenderness which was uncommon. This may be irrelevant or unnecessary, but I once saw a reproduction of a faded photograph of the verandah of Robert Louis Stevenson's home on that Samoan Island where he spent his last years, and there was a quality of tender light on weathered wood, such as porch furniture made of bamboo and wicker, exposed to tropical suns and tropical rains, which came to mind when I thought about the set for this play, bringing also to mind the grace and comfort of light, the reassurance it gives, on a late and fair afternoon in summer, the way that no matter what, even dread of death, is gently touched and soothed by it. For the set is the background for a play that deals with human extremities of emotion, and it needs that softness behind it.

The bathroom door, showing only pale-blue tile and silver towel racks, is in one side wall; the hall door in the opposite wall. Two articles of furniture need mention: a big double bed which staging should make a functional part of the set as often as suitable, the surface of which should be slightly raked to make figures on it seen more easily; and against the wall space between the two huge double doors upstage: a monumental monstrosity peculiar to our times, a huge console combination of radio-phonograph (hi-fi with three speakers) TV set and liquor cabinet, bearing and containing many glasses and bottles, all in one piece, which is a combination of muted silver tones, and the opalescent tones of reflecting glass, a chromatic link, this thing, between the sepia (tawny gold) tones of the interior and the cool (white and blue) tones of the gallery and sky. This piece of furniture (?/!), this monument, is a very complete and compact little shrine to virtually all the comforts and illusions behind which we hide from such things as the characters in the play are faced with.

The set should be far less realistic than I have so far implied in this description of it. I think the walls below the ceiling should dissolve mysteriously into air; the set should be roofed by the sky; stars and moon suggested by traces of milky pallor, as if they were observed through a telescope lens out of focus.

Anything else I can think of? Oh, yes, fanlights (transoms shaped like an open glass fan) above all the doors in the set, with panes of blue and amber, and above all, the designer should take as many pains to give the actors room to move about freely (to show their restlessness, their passion for breaking out) as if it were a set for a ballet.

An evening in summer. The action is continuous, with two intermissions.

ACT I

[At the rise of the curtain someone is taking a shower in the bathroom, the door of which is half open. A pretty young woman, with anxious lines in her face, enters the bedroom and crosses to the bathroom door.]

MARGARET *[shouting above roar of water]*. One of those no-neck monsters hit me with a hot buttered biscuit so I have t' change!

*[*MARGARET*'s voice is both rapid and drawling. In her long speeches she has the vocal tricks of a priest delivering a liturgical chant, the lines are almost sung, always continuing a little beyond her breath so she has to gasp for another. Sometimes she intersperses the lines with a little wordless singing, such as "da-da-daaa!"]*

[Water turns off and BRICK *calls out to her, but is still unseen. A tone of politely feigned interest, masking indifference, or worse, is characteristic of his speech with* MARGARET.*]*

BRICK. Wha'd you say, Maggie? Water was on s' loud I couldn't hearya. . . .

MARGARET. Well, I! — just remarked that! — one of th' no-neck monsters messed up m'lovely lace dress so I got t' — cha-a-ange. . . . *[She opens and kicks shut drawers of the dresser.]*

BRICK. Why d'ya call Gooper's kiddies no-neck monsters?

MARGARET. Because they've got no necks! Isn't that a good enough reason?

BRICK. Don't they have any necks?

MARGARET. None visible. Their fat little heads are set on their fat little bodies without a bit of connection.

BRICK. That's too bad.

MARGARET. Yes, it's too bad because you can't wring their necks if they've got no necks to wring! Isn't that right, honey? [*She steps out of her dress, stands in a slip of ivory satin and lace.*] Yep, they're no-neck monsters, all no-neck people are monsters. . . .

[*Children shriek downstairs.*]

Hear them? Hear them screaming? I don't know where their voice boxes are located since they don't have necks. I tell you I got so nervous at that table tonight I thought I would throw back my head and utter a scream you could hear across the Arkansas border an' parts of Louisiana an' Tennessee. I said to your charming sister-in-law, Mae, honey, couldn't you feed those precious little things at a separate table with an oilcloth cover? They make such a mess an' the lace cloth looks *so* pretty! She made enormous eyes at me and said, "Ohhh, noooooo! On Big Daddy's birthday? Why, he would never forgive me!" Well, I want you to know, Big Daddy hadn't been at the table two minutes with those five no-neck monsters slobbering and drooling over their food before he threw down his fork an' shouted, "Fo' God's sake, Gooper, why don't you put them pigs at a trough in th' kitchen?"—Well, I swear, I simply could have di-ieed!

Think of it, Brick, they've got five of them and number six is coming. They've brought the whole bunch down here like animals to display at a county fair. Why, they have those children doin' tricks all the time! "Junior, show Big Daddy how you do this, show Big Daddy how you do that, say your little piece fo' Big Daddy, Sister. Show your dimples, Sugar. Brother, show Big Daddy how you stand on your head!"—It goes on all the time, along with constant little remarks and innuendos about the fact that you and I have not produced any children, are totally childless and therefore totally useless!—Of course it's comical but it's also disgusting since it's so obvious what they're up to!

BRICK [*without interest*]. What are they up to, Maggie?

MARGARET. Why, you know what they're up to!

BRICK [*appearing*]. No, I don't know what they're up to.

[*He stands there in the bathroom doorway drying his hair with a towel and hanging onto the towel rack because one ankle is broken, plastered and bound. He is still slim and firm as a boy. His liquor hasn't started tearing him down outside. He has the additional charm of that cool air of detachment that people have who have given up the struggle. But now and then, when disturbed, something flashes behind it, like lightning in a fair sky, which shows that at some deeper level he is far from peaceful. Perhaps in a stronger light he would show some signs of deliquescence, but the fading, still warm, light from the gallery treats him gently.*]

MARGARET. I'll tell you what they're up to, boy of mine!—They're up to cutting you out of your father's estate, and—

[*She freezes momentarily before her next remark. Her voice drops as if it were somehow a personally embarrassing admission.*]

—Now we know that Big Daddy's dyin' of—*cancer.* . . .

[*There are voices on the lawn below: long-drawn calls across distance.* MARGARET *raises her lovely bare arms and powders her armpits with a light sigh.*]

[*She adjusts the angle of a magnifying mirror to straighten an eyelash, then rises fretfully saying,*]

There's so much light in the room it—

BRICK [*softly but sharply*]. Do we?

MARGARET. Do we what?

BRICK. Know Big Daddy's dyin' of cancer?

MARGARET. Got the report today.

BRICK. Oh . . .

MARGARET [*letting down bamboo blinds which cast long, gold-fretted shadows over the room*]. Yep, got th' report just now . . . it didn't surprise me, Baby. . . .

[*Her voice has range, and music; sometimes it drops low as a boy's and you have a sudden image of her playing boy's games as a child.*]

I recognized the symptoms soon's we got here last spring, and I'm willin' to bet you that Brother Man and his wife were pretty sure of it, too. That more than likely explains why their usual summer migration to the coolness of the Great Smokies was passed up this summer in favor of—hustlin' down here ev'ry whipstitch with their whole screamin' tribe! And why so many allusions have been made to Rainbow Hill lately. You know what Rainbow Hill is? Place that's famous for treatin' alcoholics an' dope fiends in the movies!

BRICK. I'm not in the movies.

MARGARET. No, and you don't take dope. Otherwise you're a perfect candidate for Rainbow Hill, Baby, and that's where they aim to ship you—over my dead body! Yep, over my dead body they'll ship you there, but nothing would please them better. Then Brother Man could get a-hold of the purse strings and dole out remittances to us, maybe get power of attorney and sign checks for us and cut off our credit wherever, whenever he wanted! Son-of-a-bitch! How'd you like that, Baby?—Well, you've been doin' just about ev'rything in your power to bring it about, you've just been doin' ev'rything you can think of to aid and abet them in this scheme of theirs! Quittin' work, devoting yourself to the occupation of drinkin'!—Breakin' your ankle last night on the high school athletic field: doin' what? Jumpin' hurdles? At two or three in the morning? Just fantastic! Got in the paper. *Clarksdale Register* carried a nice little item about it, human interest story about a well-known former athlete stagin' a one-man track meet on the Glorious Hill High School athletic field last night, but was slightly out of condition and didn't clear the first hurdle! Brother Man Gooper claims he exercised his influence t' keep it from goin' out over AP or UP or every goddam "P."

But, Brick? You still have one big advantage!

[*During the above swift flood of words, BRICK has reclined with contrapuntal leisure on the snowy surface of the bed and has rolled over carefully on his side or belly.*]

BRICK [*wryly*]. Did you *say* something, Maggie?

MARGARET. Big Daddy dotes on you, honey. And he can't stand Brother Man and Brother Man's wife, that monster of fertility, Mae. Know how I know? By little expressions that flicker over his face when that woman is holding fo'th on one of her choice topics such as—how she refused twilight sleep!—when the twins were delivered! Because she feels motherhood's an experience that a woman ought to experience fully!—in order to fully appreciate the wonder and beauty of it! HAH!—and how she made Brother Man come in an' stand beside her in the delivery room so he would not miss out on the "wonder and beauty" of it either!—producin' those no-neck monsters. . . .

[*A speech of this kind would be antipathetic from almost anybody but MARGARET; she makes it oddly funny, because her eyes constantly twinkle and her voice shakes with laughter which is basically indulgent.*]

—Big Daddy shares my attitude toward those two! As for me, well—I give
him a laugh now and then and he tolerates me. In fact!—I sometimes suspect
that Big Daddy harbors a little unconscious "lech" fo' me. . . .

BRICK. What makes you think that Big Daddy has a lech for you, Maggie?

MARGARET. Way he always drops his eyes down my body when I'm talkin' to
him, drops his eyes to my boobs and licks his old chops! Ha Ha!

BRICK. That kind of talk is disgusting.

MARGARET. Did anyone ever tell you that you're an ass-aching Puritan, Brick?
I think it's mighty fine that that ole fellow, on the doorstep of death, still
takes in my shape with what I think is deserved appreciation!

And you wanta know something else? Big Daddy didn't know how many
little Maes and Goopers had been produced! "How many kids have you got?"
he asked at the table, just like Brother Man and his wife were new acquaintances to him! Big Mama said he was jokin', but that ole boy wasn't jokin',
Lord, no!

And when they infawmed him that they had five already and were turning
out number six!—the news seemed to come as a sort of unpleasant surprise. . . .

[*Children yell below.*]

Scream, monsters!

[*Turns to* BRICK *with a sudden, gay, charming smile which fades as she notices that
he is not looking at her but into fading gold space with a troubled expression.*]

[*It is constant rejection that makes her humor "bitchy."*]

Yes, you should of been at that supper-table, Baby.

[*Whenever she calls him "baby" the word is a soft caress.*]

Y'know, Big Daddy, bless his ole sweet soul, he's the dearest ole thing in the ·
world, but he does hunch over his food as if he preferred not to notice
anything else. Well, Mae an' Gooper were side by side at the table, direckly
across from Big Daddy, watchin' his face like hawks while they jawed an'
jabbered about the cuteness an' brilliance of th' no-neck monsters!

[*She giggles with a hand fluttering at her throat and her breast and her long throat
arched.*]

[*She comes downstage and recreates the scene with voice and gesture.*]

And the no-neck monsters were ranged around the table, some in high chairs
and some on th' *Books of Knowledge*, all in fancy little paper caps in honor of
Big Daddy's birthday, and all through dinner, well, I want you to know that
Brother Man an' his partner never once, for one moment, stopped exchanging
pokes an' pinches an' kicks an' signs an' signals!—Why, they were like a
couple of cardsharps fleecing a sucker.—Even Big Mama, bless her ole sweet
soul, she isn't th' quickest an' brightest thing in the world, she finally noticed,
at last, an' said to Gooper, "Gooper, what are you an' Mae makin' all these
signs at each other about?"—I swear t' goodness, I nearly choked on my
chicken!

[MARGARET, *back at the dressing table, still doesn't see* BRICK. *He is watching her
with a look that is not quite definable—Amused? shocked? contemptuous?—part
of those and part of something else.*]

Y'know—your brother Gooper still cherishes the illusion he took a giant
step up the social ladder when he married Miss Mae Flynn of the Memphis
Flynns.

But I have a piece of Spanish news for Gooper. The Flynns never had a thing in this world but money and they lost that, they were nothing at all but fairly successful climbers. Of course, Mae Flynn came out in Memphis eight years before I made my debut in Nashville, but I had friends at Ward-Belmont who came from Memphis and they used to come to see me and I used to go to see them for Christmas and spring vacations, and so I know who rates an' who doesn't rate in Memphis society. Why, y'know ole Papa Flynn, he barely escaped doing time in the Federal pen for shady manipulations on th' stock market when his chain stores crashed, and as for Mae having been a cotton carnival queen, as they remind us so often, lest we forget, well, that's one honor that I don't envy her for! — Sit on a brass throne on a tacky float an' ride down Main Street, smilin', bowin', and blowin' kisses to all the trash on the street —

[*She picks out a pair of jeweled sandals and rushes to the dressing table.*]

Why, year before last, when Susan McPheeters was singled out fo' that honor, y' know what happened to her? Y'know what happened to poor little Susie McPheeters?

BRICK [*absently*]. No. What happened to little Susie McPheeters?

MARGARET. Somebody spit tobacco juice in her face.

BRICK [*dreamily*]. Somebody spit tobacco juice in her face?

MARGARET. That's right, some old drunk leaned out of a window in the Hotel Gayoso and yelled, "Hey, Queen, hey, hey, there, Queenie!" Poor Susie looked up and flashed him a radiant smile and he shot out a squirt of tobacco juice right in poor Susie's face.

BRICK. Well, what d'you know about that.

MARGARET [*gaily*]. What do I know about it? I was there, I saw it!

BRICK [*absently*]. Must have been kind of funny.

MARGARET. Susie didn't think so. Had hysterics. Screamed like a banshee. They had to stop th' parade an' remove her from her throne an' go on with —

[*She catches sight of him in the mirror, gasps slightly, wheels about to face him. Count ten.*]

— Why are you looking at me like that?

BRICK [*whistling softly, now*]. Like what, Maggie?

MARGARET [*intensely, fearfully*]. The way y' were lookin' at me just now, befo' I caught your eye in the mirror and you started t' whistle! I don't know how t' describe it but it froze my blood! — I've caught you lookin' at me like that so often lately. What are you thinkin' of when you look at me like that?

BRICK. I wasn't conscious of lookin' at you, Maggie.

MARGARET. Well, I was conscious of it! What were you thinkin'?

BRICK. I don't remember thinking of anything, Maggie.

MARGARET. Don't you think I know that —? Don't you —? — Think I know that —?

BRICK [*cooly*]. Know *what*, Maggie?

MARGARET [*struggling for expression*]. That I've gone through this — hideous! — transformation, become — hard! Frantic! [*Then she adds, almost tenderly.*] — cruel!!

That's what you've been observing in me lately. How could y' help but observe it? That's all right. I'm not — thin-skinned any more, can't afford t' be thin-skinned any more. [*She is now recovering her power.*] — But Brick? Brick?

BRICK. Did you say something?

MARGARET. I was *goin'* t' say something; that I get — lonely. Very!

BRICK. Ev'rybody gets that. . . .

MARGARET. Living with someone you love can be lonelier — than living entirely *alone*! — if the one that y' love doesn't love you. . . .

[*There is a pause.* BRICK *hobbles downstage and asks, without looking at her.*]

BRICK. Would you like to live alone, Maggie?

[*Another pause: then — after she has caught a quick, hurt breath.*]

MARGARET. *No! — God! — I wouldn't!*

[*Another gasping breath. She forcibly controls what must have been an impulse to cry out. We see her deliberately, very forcibly, going all the way back to the world in which you can talk about ordinary matters.*]

Did you have a nice shower?

BRICK. Uh-huh.

MARGARET. Was the water cool?

BRICK. No.

MARGARET. But it made y' feel fresh, huh?

BRICK. Fresher. . . .

MARGARET. I know something would make y' feel *much* fresher!

BRICK. What?

MARGARET. An alcohol rub. Or cologne, a rub with cologne!

BRICK. That's good after a workout but I haven't been workin' out, Maggie.

MARGARET. You've kept in good shape, though.

BRICK [*indifferently*]. You think so, Maggie?

MARGARET. I always thought drinkin' men lost their looks, but I was plainly mistaken.

BRICK [*wryly*]. Why, thanks, Maggie.

MARGARET. You're the only drinkin' man I know that it never seems t' put fat on.

BRICK. I'm gettin' softer, Maggie.

MARGARET. Well, sooner or later it's bound to soften you up. It was just beginning to soften up Skipper when— [*She stops short.*] I'm sorry. I never could keep my fingers off a sore — I wish you *would* lose your looks. If you did it would make the martyrdom of Saint Maggie a little more bearable. But no such goddam luck. I actually believe you've gotten better looking since you've gone on the bottle. Yeah, a person who didn't know you would think you'd never had a tense nerve in your body or a strained muscle.

[*There are sounds of croquet on the lawn below: the click of mallets, light voices, near and distant.*]

Of course, you always had that detached quality as if you were playing a game without much concern over whether you won or lost, and now that you've lost the game, not lost but just quit playing, you have that rare sort of charm that usually only happens in very old or hopelessly sick people, the charm of the defeated. — You look so cool, so cool, so enviably cool.

REVEREND TOOKER [*off stage right*]. Now looka here, boy, lemme show you how to get outa that!

MARGARET. They're playing croquet. The moon has appeared and it's white, just beginning to turn a little bit yellow. . . .

You were a wonderful lover. . . .

Such a wonderful person to go to bed with, and I think mostly because you were really indifferent to it. Isn't that right? Never had any anxiety about it, did it naturally, easily, slowly, with absolute confidence and perfect calm, more like opening a door for a lady or seating her at a table than giving expression to any longing for her. Your indifference made you wonderful at lovemaking — *strange?* — but true. . . .

REVERED TOOKER. Oh! That's a beauty.

DOCTOR BAUGH. Yeah. I got you boxed.

MARGARET. You know, if I thought you would never, never, *never* make love to me again — I would go downstairs to the kitchen and pick out the longest and sharpest knife I could find and stick it straight into my heart, I swear that I would!

REVEREND TOOKER. Watch out, you're gonna miss it.

DOCTOR BAUGH. You just don't know me, boy!

MARGARET. But one thing I don't have is the charm of the defeated, my hat is still in the ring, and I am determined to win!

[*There is the sound of croquet mallets hitting croquet balls.*]

REVERED TOOKER. Mmm — You're too slippery for me.

MARGARET. — What is the victory of a cat on a hot tin roof? — I wish I knew. . . .

Just staying on it, I guess, as long as she can. . . .

DOCTOR BAUGH. Jus' like an eel, boy, jus' like an eel!

[*More croquet sounds.*]

MARGARET. Later tonight I'm going to tell you I love you an' maybe by that time you'll be drunk enough to believe me. Yes, they're playing croquet. . . .

Big Daddy is dying of cancer. . . .

What were you thinking of when I caught you looking at me like that? Were you thinking of Skipper?

[BRICK *takes up his crutch, rises.*]

Oh, excuse me, forgive me, but laws of silence don't work! No, laws of silence don't work. . . .

[BRICK *crosses to the bar, takes a quick drink, and rubs his head with a towel.*]

Laws of silence don't work. . . .

When something is festering in your memory or your imagination, laws of silence don't work, it's just like shutting a door and locking it on a house on fire in hope of forgetting that the house is burning. But not facing a fire doesn't put it out. Silence about a thing just magnifies it. It grows and festers in silence, becomes malignant. . . .

[*He drops his crutch.*]

BRICK. Give me my crutch.

[*He has stopped rubbing his hair dry but still stands hanging onto the towel rack in a white towel-cloth robe.*]

MARGARET. Lean on me.

BRICK. No, just give me my crutch.

MARGARET. Lean on my shoulder.

BRICK. *I don't want to lean on your shoulder, I want my crutch!*

[*This is spoken like sudden lightning.*]

Are you going to give me my crutch or do I have to get down on my knees on the floor and —

MARGARET. *Here, here, take it, take it!* [*She has thrust the crutch at him.*]

BRICK [*hobbling out*]. Thanks. . . .

MARGARET. We mustn't scream at each other, the walls in this house have ears. . . .

[*He hobbles directly to the liquor cabinet to get a new drink.*]

   —but that's the first time I've heard you raise your voice in a long time, Brick. A crack in the wall?—Of composure?

   —I think that's a good sign. . . .

   A sign of nerves in a player on the defensive!

[BRICK *turns and smiles at her cooly over his fresh drink.*]

BRICK. It just hasn't happened yet, Maggie.

MARGARET. What?

BRICK. The click I get in my head when I've had enough of this stuff to make me peaceful. . . .

   Will you do me a favor?

MARGARET. Maybe I will. What favor?

BRICK. Just, just keep your voice down!

MARGARET [*in a hoarse whisper*]. I'll do you that favor, I'll speak in a whisper, if not shut up completely, if *you* will do *me* a favor and make that drink your last one till after the party.

BRICK. What party?

MARGARET. Big Daddy's birthday party.

BRICK. Is this Big Daddy's birthday?

MARGARET. You know this is Big Daddy's birthday!

BRICK. No, I don't, I forgot it.

MARGARET. Well, I remembered it for you. . . .

[*They are both speaking as breathlessly as a pair of kids after a fight, drawing deep exhausted breaths and looking at each other with faraway eyes, shaking and panting together as if they had broken apart from a violent struggle.*]

BRICK. Good for you, Maggie.

MARGARET. You just have to scribble a few lines on this card.

BRICK. You scribble something, Maggie.

MARGARET. It's got to be your handwriting; it's your present, I've given him my present; it's got to be your handwriting!

[*The tension between them is building again, the voices becoming shrill once more.*]

BRICK. I didn't get him a present.

MARGARET. I got one for you.

BRICK. All right. You write the card, then.

MARGARET. And have him know you didn't remember his birthday?

BRICK. I didn't remember his birthday.

MARGARET. You don't have to prove you didn't!

BRICK. I don't want to fool him about it.

MARGARET. Just write "Love, Brick!" for God's—

BRICK. No.

MARGARET. You've *got* to!

BRICK. I don't have to do anything I don't want to do. You keep forgetting the conditions on which I agreed to stay on living with you.

MARGARET [*out before she knows it*]. I'm not living with you. We occupy the same cage.

BRICK. You've got to remember the conditions agreed on.

SONNY [*off stage*]. Mommy, give it to me. I had it first.

MAE. Hush.

MARGARET. They're impossible conditions!

BRICK. Then why don't you—?

SONNY. I want it, I want it!

MAE. Get away!

MARGARET. HUSH! Who is out there? Is somebody at the door?

[*There are footsteps in hall.*]

MAE [*outside*]. May I enter a moment?

MARGARET. OH, *you!* Sure. Come in, Mae.

[*Mae enters bearing aloft the bow of a young lady's archery set.*]

MAE. Brick, is this thing yours?

MARGARET. Why, Sister Woman—that's my Diana Trophy. Won it at the intercollegiate archery contest on the Ole Miss campus.

MAE. It's a mighty dangerous thing to leave exposed round a house full of nawmal rid-blooded children, attracted t'weapons.

MARGARET. "Nawmal rid-blooded children attracted t'weapons" ought t'be taught to keep their hands off things that don't belong to them.

MAE. Maggie, honey, if you had children of your own you'd know how funny that is. Will you please lock this up and put the key out of reach?

MARGARET. Sister Woman, nobody is plotting the destruction of your kiddies. —Brick and I still have our special archers' license. We're goin' deer-huntin' on Moon Lake as soon as the season starts. I love to run with dogs through chilly woods, run, run leap over obstructions—[*She goes into the closet carrying the bow.*]

MAE. How's the injured ankle, Brick?

BRICK. Doesn't hurt. Just itches.

MAE. Oh, my! Brick—Brick, you should've been downstairs after supper! Kiddies put on a show. Polly played the piano, Buster an' Sonny drums, an' then they turned out the lights an' Dixie an' Trixie puhfawmed a toe dance in fairy costume with *spahklus!* Big Daddy just beamed! He just beamed!

MARGARET [*from the closet with a sharp laugh*]. Oh, I bet. It breaks my heart that we missed it! [*She reenters.*] But Mae? Why did y'give dawgs' names to all your kiddies?

MAE. *Dogs'* names?

MARGARET [*sweetly*]. Dixie, Trixie, Buster, Sonny, Polly!—Sounds like four dogs and a parrot. . . .

MAE. Maggie?

[MARGARET *turns with a smile.*]

Why are you so catty?

MARGARET. Cause I'm a cat! But why can't *you* take a joke, Sister Woman?

MAE. Nothin' pleases me more than a joke that's funny. You know the real names of our kiddies. Buster's real name is Robert. Sonny's real name is Saunders. Trixie's real name is Marlene and Dixie's—

[GOOPER *downstairs calls for her. "Hey, Mae! Sister Woman, intermission is over!"—she rushes to door, saying.*]

Intermission is over! See ya later!

MARGARET. I wonder what Dixie's real name is?

BRICK. Maggie, being catty doesn't help things any. . . .

MARGARET. I know! *WHY!*—Am I so catty?—Cause I'm consumed with envy an' eaten up with longing?—Brick, I'm going to lay out your beautiful Shantung silk suit from Rome and one of your monogrammed silk shirts. I'll put your cuff links in it, those lovely star sapphires I get you to wear so rarely. . . .

BRICK. I can't get trousers on over this plaster cast.

MARGARET. Yes, you can, I'll help you.

BRICK. I'm not going to get dressed, Maggie.

MARGARET. Will you just put on a pair of white silk pajamas?

BRICK. Yes, I'll do that, Maggie.

MARGARET. *Thank* you, thank you so *much!*

BRICK. Don't mention it.

MARGARET. *Oh, Brick!* How long does it have t' go on? This punishment? Haven't I done time enough, haven't I served my term, can't I apply for a — pardon?

BRICK. Maggie, you're spoiling my liquor. Lately your voice always sounds like you'd been running upstairs to warn somebody that the house was on fire!

MARGARET. Well, no wonder, no wonder. Y'know what I feel like, Brick? *I feel all the time like a cat on a hot tin roof!*

BRICK. Then jump off the roof, jump off it, cats can jump off roofs and land on their four feet uninjured!

MARGARET. Oh, yes!

BRICK. Do it! — fo' God's sake, do it. . . .

MARGARET. Do what?

BRICK. Take a lover!

MARGARET. I can't see a man but you! Even with my eyes closed, I just see you! Why don't you get ugly, Brick, why don't you please get fat or ugly or something so I could stand it? [*She rushes to hall door, opens it, listens.*] The concert is still going on! Bravo, no-necks, bravo! [*She slams and locks door fiercely.*]

BRICK. What did you lock the door for?

MARGARET. To give us a little privacy for a while.

BRICK. You know better, Maggie.

MARGARET. No, I don't know better. . . .

[*She rushes to gallery doors, draws the rose-silk drapes across them.*]

BRICK. Don't make a fool of yourself.

MARGARET. I don't mind makin' a fool of myself over you!

BRICK. I mind, Maggie. I feel embarrassed for you.

MARGARET. Feel embarrassed! But don't continue my torture. I can't live on and on under these circumstances.

BRICK. You agreed to —

MARGARET. I know but —

BRICK. —Accept that condition!

MARGARET. *I CAN'T! I CAN'T! I CAN'T!* [*She seizes his shoulder.*]

BRICK. Let go!

[*He breaks away from her and seizes the small boudoir chair and raises it like a lion-tamer facing a big circus cat.*]

[*Count five. She stares at him with her fist pressed to her mouth, then bursts into shrill, almost hysterical laughter. He remains grave for a moment, then grins and puts the chair down.*]

[BIG MAMA *calls through closed door.*]

BIG MAMA. Son? Son? Son?

BRICK. What is it, Big Mama?

BIG MAMA [*outside*]. Oh, son! We got the most wonderful news about Big Daddy. I just had t' run up an' tell you right this — [*She rattles the knob.*] — What's this door doin', locked, faw? You all think there's robbers in the house?

MARGARET. Big Mama, Brick is dressin', he's not dressed yet.

BIG MAMA. That's all right, it won't be the first time I've seen Brick not dressed. Come on, open this door!

[MARGARET, *with a grimace, goes to unlock and open the hall door, as* BRICK *hobbles rapidly to the bathroom and kicks the door shut.* BIG MAMA *has disappeared from the hall.*

MARGARET. Big Mama?

[BIG MAMA *appears through the opposite gallery doors behind* MARGARET, *huffing and puffing like an old bulldog. She is a short, stout woman; her sixty years and 170 pounds have left her somewhat breathless most of the time; she's always tensed like a boxer, or rather, a Japanese wrestler. Her "family" was maybe a little superior to* BIG DADDY'S *but not much. She wears a black or silver lace dress and at least half a million in flashy gems. She is very sincere.*]

BIG MAMA [*loudly, startling* MARGARET]. Here—I come through Gooper's and Mae's gall'ry door. Where's Brick? *Brick*—Hurry on out of there, son, I just have a second and want to give you the news about Big Daddy.—I hate locked doors in a house. . . .

MARGARET [*with affected lightness*]. I've noticed you do, Big Mama, but people have got to have *some* moments of privacy, don't they?

BIG MAMA. No, ma'am, not in *my* house. [*Without pause.*] Whacha took off you' dress faw? I thought that little lace dress was so sweet on yuh, honey.

MARGARET. I thought it looked sweet on me, too, but one of m' cute little table-partners used it for a napkin so—!

BIG MAMA [*picking up stockings on floor*]. What?

MARGARET. You know, Big Mama, Mae and Gooper's so touchy about those children—thanks, Big Mama. . . .

[BIG MAMA *has thrust the picked-up stockings in* MARGARET'*s hand with a grunt.*]
—that you just don't dare to suggest there's any room for improvement in their—

BIG MAMA. Brick, hurry out!—Shoot, Maggie, you just don't like children.

MARGARET. I do SO like children! Adore them!—well brought up!

BIG MAMA [*gentle—loving*]. Well, why don't you have some and bring them up well, then, instead of all the time pickin' on Gooper's an' Mae's?

GOOPER [*shouting up the stairs*]. Hey, hey, Big Mama, Betsy an' Hugh got to go, waitin' t' tell yuh g'by!

BIG MAMA. Tell 'em to hold their hawses, I'll be right down in a jiffy!

GOOPER. Yes ma'am!

[*She turns to the bathroom door and calls out.*]

BIG MAMA. Son? Can you hear me in there?

[*There is a muffled answer.*]

We just got the full report from the laboratory at the Ochsner Clinic, completely negative, son, ev'rything negative, right on down the line! Nothin' a-tall's wrong with him but some little functional thing called a spastic colon. Can you hear me, son?

MARGARET. He can hear you, Big Mama.

BIG MAMA. Then why don't he say something? God Almighty, a piece of news like that should make him shout. It made *me* shout, I can tell you. I shouted and sobbed and fell right down on my knees!—Look! [*She pulls up her skirt.*]

See the bruises where I hit my kneecaps? Took both doctors to haul me back on my feet!

[*She laughs — she always laughs like hell at herself.*]

Big Daddy was furious with me! But ain't that wonderful news?

[*Facing bathroom again, she continues.*]

After all the anxiety we been through to git a report like that on Big Daddy's birthday? Big Daddy tried to hide how much of a load that news took off his mind, but didn't fool *me*. He was mighty close to crying about it *himself!*

[*Goodbyes are shouted downstairs, and she rushes to door.*]

GOOPER. Big Mama!

BIG MAMA. *Hold those people down there, don't let them go!* — Now, git dressed, we're comin' up to this room fo' Big Daddy's birthday party because of your ankle. — How's his ankle, Maggie?

MARGARET. Well, he broke it, Big Mama.

BIG MAMA. I know he broke it.

[*A phone is ringing in hall. A Negro voice answers: "Mistuh Polly's res'dence."*]

I mean does it hurt him much still.

MARGARET. I'm afraid I can't give you that information, Big Mama. You'll have to ask Brick if it hurts much still or not.

SOOKEY [*in the hall*]. It's Memphis, Mizz Polly, it's Miss Sally in Memphis.

BIG MAMA. Awright, Sookey.

[BIG MAMA *rushes into the hall and is heard shouting on the phone.*]

Hello, Miss Sally. How are you, Miss Sally? — Yes, well, I was just gonna call you about it. *Shoot!*

MARGARET. Brick, don't!

[BIG MAMA *raises her voice to a bellow.*]

BIG MAMA. *Miss Sally? Don't ever call me from the Gayoso Lobby, too much talk goes on in that hotel lobby, no wonder you can't hear me!* Now listen, Miss Sally. They's nothin' serious wrong with Big Daddy. We got the report just now, they's nothin' wrong but a thing called a — spastic! *SPASTIC!* — colon. . . . [*She appears at the hall door and calls to* MARGARET.] — Maggie, come out here and talk to that fool on the phone. I'm shouted breathless!

MARGARET [*goes out and is heard sweetly at phone*]. Miss Sally? This is Brick's wife, Maggie. So nice to hear your voice. Can you hear *mine?* Well, *good!* — Big Mama just wanted you to know that they've got the report from the Ochsner Clinic and what Big Daddy has is a spastic colon. Yes. Spastic colon, Miss Sally. That's right, spastic colon. *G'bye, Miss Sally, hope I'll see you real soon!*

[*Hangs up a little before* MISS SALLY *was probably ready to terminate the talk. She returns through the hall door.*]

She heard me perfectly. I've discovered with deaf people the thing to do is not shout at them but just enunciate clearly. My rich old Aunt Cornelia was deaf as the dead but I could make her hear me just by sayin' each word slowly, distinctly, close to her ear. I read her the *Commercial Appeal* ev'ry night, read her the classified ads in it, even, she never missed a word of it. But was she a mean ole thing! Know what I got when she died? Her unexpired subscriptions to five magazines and the Book-of-the-Month Club and a LIBRARY full of ev'ry dull book ever written! All else went to her hellcat of a sister . . . meaner than she was, even!

[BIG MAMA *has been straightening things up in the room during this speech.*]

BIG MAMA [*closing closet door on discarded clothes*]. *Miss Sally sure is a case!* Big Daddy says she's always got her hand out fo' something. He's not mistaken. That poor ole thing always has her hand out fo' somethin'. I don't think Big Daddy gives her as much as he should.

GOOPER. Big Mama! Come on now! Betsy and Hugh can't wait no longer!

BIG MAMA [*shouting*]. I'm comin'!

[*She starts out. At the hall door, turns and jerks a forefinger, first toward the bathroom door, then toward the liquor cabinet, meaning: "Has* BRICK *been drinking?"* MARGARET *pretends not to understand, cocks her head and raises her brows as if the pantomimic performance was completely mystifying to her.*]

[BIG MAMA *rushes back to* MARGARET.]

Shoot! Stop playin' so dumb! — I mean has he been drinkin' that stuff much yet?

MARGARET [*with a little laugh*]. Oh! I think he had a highball after supper.

BIG MAMA. Don't laugh about it! — some single men stop drinkin' when they git married and others start! Brick never touched liquor before he — !

MARGARET [*crying out*]. THAT'S NOT FAIR!

BIG MAMA. Fair or not fair I want to ask you a question, one question: D'you make Brick happy in bed?

MARGARET. Why don't you ask if he makes *me* happy in bed?

BIG MAMA. Because I know that —

MARGARET. *It works both ways!*

BIG MAMA. Something's not right! You're childless and my son drinks!

GOOPER. Come on, Big Mama!

[GOOPER *has called her downstairs and she has rushed to the door on the line above. She turns at the door and points at the bed.*]

— When a marriage goes on the rocks, the rocks are *there*, right *there!*

MARGARET. *That's* —

[BIG MAMA *has swept out of the room and slammed the door.*]

— not — *fair . . .*

[MARGARET *is alone, completely alone, and she feels it. She draws in, hunches her shoulders, raises her arms with fists clenched, shuts her eyes tight as a child about to be stabbed with a vaccination needle. When she opens her eyes again, what she sees is the long oval mirror and she rushes straight to it, stares into it with a grimace and says: "Who are you?" — Then she crouches a little and answers herself in a different voice which is high, thin, mocking: "I am Maggie the Cat!" — Straightens quickly as bathroom door opens a little and* BRICK *calls out to her.*]

BRICK. Has Big Mama gone?

MARGARET. She's gone.

[*He opens the bathroom door and hobbles out, with his liquor glass now empty, straight to the liquor cabinet. He is whistling softly.* MARGARET'S *head pivots on her long, slender throat to watch him.*]

[*She raises a hand uncertainly to the base of her throat, as if it was difficult for her to swallow, before she speaks.*]

You know, our sex life didn't just peter out in the usual way, it was cut off short, long before the natural time for it to, and it's going to revive again, just as sudden as that. I'm confident of it. That's what I'm keeping myself attractive for. For the time when you'll see me again like other men see me.

Yes, like other men see me. They still see me, Brick, and they like what they see. Uh-huh. Some of them would give their—
 Look, Brick!
[*She stands before the long oval mirror, touches her breast and then her hips with her two hands.*]
How high my body stays on me!—Nothing has fallen on me—not a fraction. . . .
[*Her voice is soft and trembling: a pleading child's. At this moment as he turns to glance at her—a look which is like a player passing a ball to another player, third down and goal to go—she has to capture the audience in a grip so tight that she can hold it till the first intermission without any lapse of attention.*]
Other men still want me. My face looks strained, sometimes, but I've kept my figure as well as you've kept yours, and men admire it. I still turn heads on the street. Why, last week in Memphis everywhere that I went men's eyes burned holes in my clothes, at the country club and in restaurants and department stores, there wasn't a man I met or walked by that didn't just eat me up with his eyes and turn around when I passed him and look back at me. Why, at Alice's party for her New York cousins, the best-lookin' man in the crowd— followed me upstairs and tried to force his way in the powder room with me, followed me to the door and tried to force his way in!

BRICK. Why didn't you let him, Maggie?

MARGARET. Because I'm not that common, for one thing. Not that I wasn't almost tempted to. You like to know who it was? It was Sonny Boy Maxwell, that's who!

BRICK. Oh, yeah, Sonny Boy Maxwell, he was a good end-runner but had a little injury to his back and had to quit.

MARGARET. He has no injury now and has no wife and still has a lech for me!

BRICK. I see no reason to lock him out of a powder room in that case.

MARGARET. And have someone catch me at it? I'm not that stupid. Oh, I might sometime cheat on you with someone, since you're so insultingly eager to have me do it!—But if I do, you can be damned sure it will be in a place and a time where no one but me and the man could possibly know. Because I'm not going to give you any excuse to divorce me for being unfaithful or anything else. . . .

BRICK. Maggie, I wouldn't divorce you for being unfaithful or anything else. Don't you know that? Hell. I'd be relieved to know that you'd found yourself a lover.

MARGARET. Well, I'm taking no chances. No, I'd rather stay on this hot tin roof.

BRICK. A hot tin roof's 'n uncomfo'table place t' stay on. . . . [*He starts to whistle softly.*]

MARGARET [*through his whistle*]. Yeah, but I can stay on it just as long as I have to.

BRICK. You could leave me, Maggie.

[*He resumes whistle. She wheels about to glare at him.*]

MARGARET. *Don't want to and will not!* Besides if I did, you don't have a cent to pay for it but what you get from Big Daddy and he's dying of cancer!

[*For the first time a realization of* BIG DADDY's *doom seems to penetrate to* BRICK's *consciousness, visibly, and he looks at* MARGARET.]

BRICK. Big Mama just said he *wasn't*, that the report was okay.

MARGARET. That's what she thinks because she got the same story that they gave Big Daddy. And was just as taken in by it as he was, poor ole things. . . . But tonight they're going to tell her the truth about it. When Big Daddy goes to bed, they're going to tell her that he is dying of cancer. [*She slams the dresser drawer.*]—It's malignant and it's terminal.

BRICK. Does Big Daddy know it?

MARGARET. Hell, do they *ever* know it? Nobody says, "You're dying." You have to fool them. They have to fool *themselves.*

BRICK. Why?

MARGARET. *Why?* Because human beings dream of life everlasting, that's the reason! But most of them want it on earth and not in heaven.

[*He gives a short, hard laugh at her touch of humor.*]

Well. . . . [*She touches up her mascara.*] That's how it is, anyhow. . . . [*She looks about.*] Where did I put down my cigarette? Don't want to burn up the home-place, at least not with Mae and Gooper and their five monsters in it!

[*She has found it and sucks at it greedily. Blows out smoke and continues.*]

So this is Big Daddy's last birthday. And Mae and Gooper, they know it, oh, *they* know it, all right. They got the first information from the Ochsner Clinic. That's why they rushed down here with their no-neck monsters. Because. Do you know something? Big Daddy's made no will? Big Daddy's never made out any will in his life, and so this campaign's afoot to impress him, forcibly as possible, with the fact that you drink and I've borne no children!

[*He continues to stare at her a moment, then mutters something sharp but not audible and hobbles rather rapidly out onto the long gallery in the fading, much faded, gold light.*]

MARGARET [*continuing her liturgical chant*]. Y'know, I'm *fond* of Big Daddy, I am genuinely fond of that old man, I really *am*, you know. . . .

BRICK [*faintly, vaguely*]. Yes, I know you are. . . .

MARGARET. I've always sort of admired him in spite of his coarseness, his four-letter words and so forth. Because Big Daddy *is* what he *is*, and he makes no bones about it. He hasn't turned gentleman farmer, he's still a Mississippi redneck, as much of a redneck as he must have been when he was just overseer here on the old Jack Straw and Peter Ochello place. But he got hold of it an' built it into th' biggest an' finest plantation in the Delta. — I've always *liked* Big Daddy. . . .

[*She crosses to the proscenium.*]

Well, this is Big Daddy's last birthday. I'm sorry about it. But I'm facing the facts. It takes money to take care of a drinker and that's the office that I've been elected to lately.

BRICK. You don't have to take care of me.

MARGARET. Yes, I do. Two people in the same boat have got to take care of each other. At least you want money to buy more Echo Spring when this supply is exhausted, or will you be satisfied with a ten-cent beer?

Mae an' Gooper are plannin' to freeze us out of Big Daddy's estate because you drink and I'm childless. But we can defeat that plan. We're *going* to defeat that plan!

Brick, y'know, I've been so God damn disgustingly poor all my life! — That's the *truth*, Brick!

BRICK. I'm not sayin' it isn't.

MARGARET. Always had to suck up to people I couldn't stand because they had money and I was poor as Job's turkey. You don't know what that's like. Well, I'll tell you, it's like you would feel a thousand miles away from Echo Spring! — And had to get back to it on that broken ankle . . . without a crutch!

That's how it feels to be as poor as Job's turkey and have to suck up to relatives that you hated because they had money and all you had was a bunch of hand-me-down clothes and a few old moldy three-per-cent government bonds. My daddy loved his liquor, he fell in love with his liquor the way you've fallen in love with Echo Spring! — And my poor Mama, having to maintain some semblance of social position, to keep appearances up, on an income of one hundred and fifty dollars a month on those old government bonds!

When I came out, the year that I made my debut, I had just two evening dresses! One Mother made me from a pattern in *Vogue*, the other a hand-me-down from a snotty rich cousin I hated!

— The dress that I married you in was my grandmother's weddin' gown. . . .

So that's why I'm like a cat on a hot tin roof!

[BRICK *is still on the gallery. Someone below calls up to him in a warm Negro voice,* "Hiya, Mistuh Brick, how yuh feelin'?" BRICK *raises his liquor glass as if that answered the question.*]

MARGARET. You can be young without money, but you can't be old without it. You've got to be old *with* money because to be old without it is just too awful, you've got to be one or the other, either *young* or *with money*, you can't be old and *without* it. — That's the *truth*, Brick. . . .

[BRICK *whistles softly, vaguely.*]

Well, now I'm dressed, I'm all dressed, there's nothing else for me to do. [*Forlornly, almost fearfully.*] I'm dressed, all dressed, nothing else for me to do. . . .

[*She moves about restlessly, aimlessly, and speaks, as if to herself.*]

What am I — ? Oh! — my bracelets. . . .

[*She starts working a collection of bracelets over her hands onto her wrists, about six on each, as she talks.*]

I've thought a whole lot about it and now I know when I made my mistake. Yes, I made my mistake when I told you the truth about that thing with Skipper. Never should have confessed it, a fatal error, tellin' you about that thing with Skipper.

BRICK. Maggie, shut up about Skipper. I mean it, Maggie; you got to shut up about Skipper.

MARGARET. You ought to understand that Skipper and I—

BRICK. You don't think I'm serious, Maggie? You're fooled by the fact that I am saying this quiet? Look, Maggie. What you're doing is a dangerous thing to do. You're — you're — you're — foolin' with something that — nobody ought to fool with.

MARGARET. This time I'm going to finish what I have to say to you. Skipper and I made love, if love you could call it, because it made both of us feel a little bit closer to you. You see, you son of a bitch, you asked too much of people, of me, of him, of all the unlucky poor damned sons of bitches that happen to love you, and there was a whole pack of them, yes, there was a pack of them besides me and Skipper, you asked too goddam much of people that loved you, you — superior creature! — you godlike being! — And so we made love to each other to dream it was you, both of us! Yes, yes, yes! Truth, truth! What's so awful about it? I like it, I think the truth is — yeah! I shouldn't have told you. . . .

BRICK [*holding his head unnaturally still and uptilted a bit*]. It was Skipper that told me about it. Not you, Maggie.

MARGARET. I told you!

BRICK. After he told me!

MARGARET. What does it matter who — ?

DIXIE. I got your mallet, I got your mallet.

TRIXIE. Give it to me, give it to me, IT's mine.

[BRICK *turns suddenly out upon the gallery and calls.*]

BRICK. Little girl! Hey, little girl!

LITTLE GIRL [*at a distance*]. What, Uncle Brick?

BRICK. Tell the folks to come up! — Bring everybody upstairs!

TRIXIE. It's mine, it's mine.

MARGARET. I can't stop myself! I'd go on telling you this in front of them all, if I had to!

BRICK. Little girl, Go on, go on, will you? Do what I told you, call them!

DIXIE. Okay.

MARGARET. Because it's got to be told and you, you — you never let me!

[*She sobs, then controls herself, and continues almost calmly.*]

It was one of those beautiful, ideal things, they tell about in the Greek legends, it couldn't be anything else, you being you, and that's what made it so sad, and that's what made it so awful, because it was love that never could be carried through to anything satisfying or even talked about plainly.

BRICK. Maggie, you gotta stop this.

MARGARET. Brick, I tell you, you got to believe me, Brick, I *do* understand all about it! I — I think it was — *noble!* Can't you tell I'm sincere when I say I respect it? My only point, the only point that I'm making, is life has got to be allowed to continue even after the *dream* of life is — all — over. . . .

[BRICK *is without his crutch. Leaning on furniture, he crosses to pick it up as she continues as if possessed by a will outside herself.*]

Why I remember when we double-dated at college, Gladys Fitzgerald and I and you and Skipper, it was more like a date between you and Skipper. Gladys and I were just sort of tagging along as if it was necessary to chaperone you! — to make a good public impression —

BRICK [*turns to face her, half lifting his crutch*]. Maggie, you want me to hit you with this crutch? Don't you know I could kill you with this crutch?

MARGARET. Good, Lord, man 'd' you think I'd care if you did?

BRICK. One man has one great good true thing in his life. One great good thing which is true! — I had friendship with Skipper. — You are naming it dirty!

MARGARET. I'm not naming it dirty! I am naming it clean.

BRICK. Not love with you, Maggie, but friendship with Skipper was that one great true thing, and you are naming it dirty!

MARGARET. Then you haven't been listenin', not understood what I'm saying! I'm naming it so damn clean that it killed poor Skipper! — You two had something that had to be kept on ice, yes, incorruptible, yes! — and death was the only icebox where you could keep it. . . .

BRICK. I married you, Maggie. Why would I marry you, Maggie, if I was—?
MARGARET. Brick, let me finish!—I know, believe me I know, that it was only
Skipper that harbored even any *unconscious* desire for anything not perfectly
pure between you two!—Now let me skip a little. You married me early that
summer we graduated out of Ole Miss, and we were happy, weren't we, we
were blissful, yes, hit heaven together ev'ry time that we loved! But that fall
you an' Skipper turned down wonderful offers of jobs in order to keep on
bein' football heroes—pro-football heroes. You organized the Dixie Stars
that fall, so you could keep on bein' teammates forever! But somethin' was not
right with it!—*Me included!*—between you. Skipper began hittin' the bottle . . . you got a spinal injury—couldn't play the Thanksgivin' game in
Chicago, watched it on TV from a traction bed in Toledo. I joined Skipper.
The Dixie Stars lost because poor Skipper was drunk. We drank together that
night all night in the bar of the Blackstone and when cold day was comin' up
over the Lake an' we were comin' out drunk to take a dizzy look at it, I said,
"SKIPPER! STOP LOVIN' MY HUSBAND OR TELL HIM HE'S GOT
TO LET YOU ADMIT IT TO HIM!"—one way or another!
    HE SLAPPED ME HARD ON THE MOUTH!—then turned and ran
without stopping once, I am sure, all the way back into his room at the
Blackstone. . . .
    —When I came to his room that night, with a little scratch like a shy little
mouse at his door, he made that pitiful, ineffectual little attempt to prove that
what I had said wasn't true. . . .
[BRICK *strikes at her with crutch, a blow that shatters the gemlike lamp on the table.*]
    —In this way, I destroyed him, by telling him truth that he and his world
which he was born and raised in, yours and his world, had told him could not
be told?
    From then on Skipper was nothing at all but a receptacle for liquor and
drugs. . . .
    —*Who shot cock robin? I with my*—[*She throws back her head with tight shut
eyes.*]—*merciful arrow!*
[BRICK *strikes at her; misses.*]
Missed me!—Sorry,—I'm not tryin' to whitewash my behavior, Christ, no!
Brick, I'm not good. I don't know why people have to pretend to be good,
nobody's good. The rich or the well-to-do can afford to respect moral
patterns, conventional moral patterns, but I could never afford to, yeah,
but—I'm honest! Give me credit for just that, will you *please?*—Born poor,
raised poor, expect to die poor unless I manage to get us something out of
what Big Daddy leaves when he dies of cancer! But Brick?!—*Skipper is dead!*
I'm alive! Maggie the cat is—
[BRICK *hops awkwardly forward and strikes at her again with his crutch.*]
    —*alive! I am alive, alive! I am* . . .
[*He hurls the crutch at her, across the bed she took refuge behind, and pitches forward
on the floor as she completes her speech.*]
    —*alive!*

[*A little girl,* DIXIE, *bursts into the room, wearing an Indian war bonnet and
    firing a cap pistol at* MARGARET *and shouting: "Bang, bang, bang!"*]
[*Laughter downstairs floats through the open hall door.* MARGARET *had crouched
grasping the bed at child's entrance. She now rises and says with cool fury.*]
Little girl, your mother or someone should teach you—[*gasping*]—to knock

at a door before you come into a room. Otherwise people might think that you — lack — good breeding. . . .

DIXIE. Yanh, yanh, yanh, what is Uncle Brick doin' on th' floor?

BRICK. I tried to kill your Aunt Maggie, but I failed — and I fell. Little girl, give me my crutch so I can get up off th' floor.

MARGARET. Yes, give your uncle his crutch, he's a cripple, honey, he broke his ankle last night jumping hurdles on the high school athletic field!

DIXIE. What were you jumping hurdles for, Uncle Brick?

BRICK. Because I used to jump them, and people like to do what they used to do, even after they've stopped being able to do it. . . .

MARGARET. That's right, that's your answer, now go away, little girl.

[DIXIE *fires cap pistol at* MARGARET *three times.*]

Stop, you stop that, monster! You little no-neck monster! [She seizes the cap pistol and hurls it through gallery door.]

DIXIE [*with a precocious instinct for the cruelest thing*]. You're *jealous!* — You're just jealous because you can't have babies!

[*She sticks out her tongue at* MARGARET *as she sashays past her with her stomach stuck out, to the gallery.* MARGARET *slams the gallery doors and leans panting against them. There is a pause.* BRICK *has replaced his spilt drink and sits, faraway, on the great four-poster bed.*]

MARGARET. You see? — they gloat over us being childless, even in front of their five little no-neck monsters!

[*Pause. Voices approach on the stairs.*]

Brick? — I've been to a doctor in Memphis, a — a gynecologist. . . .

I've been completely examined, and there is no reason why we can't have a child whenever we want one. And this is my time by the calendar to conceive. Are you listening to me? Are you? Are you LISTENING TO ME!

BRICK. Yes. I hear you, Maggie. [*His attention returns to her inflamed face.*] — But how in hell on earth do you imagine — that you're going to have a child by a man that can't stand you?

MARGARET. That's a problem that I will have to work out. [*She wheels about to face the hall door.*]

MAE [*off stage left*]. Come on, Big Daddy. We're all goin' up to Brick's room.

[*From off stage left, voices:* REVEREND TOOKER, DOCTOR BAUGH, MAE.]

MARGARET. *Here they come!*

[*The lights dim.*]

ACT II

[*There is no lapse of time.* MARGARET *and* BRICK *are in the same positions they held at the end of Act I.*]

MARGARET [*at door*]. *Here they come!*

[BIG DADDY *appears first, a tall man with a fierce, anxious look, moving carefully not to betray his weakness even, or especially, to himself.*]

GOOPER. I read in the *Register* that you're getting a new memorial window.

[*Some of the people are approaching through the hall, others along the gallery: voices from both directions.* GOOPER *and* REVEREND TOOKER *become visible outside gallery doors, and their voices come in clearly.*]

[*They pause outside as* GOOPER *lights a cigar.*]

REVEREND TOOKER [*vivaciously*]. Oh, but St. Paul's in Grenada has three memorial windows, and the latest one is a Tiffany stained-glass window that cost twenty-five hundred dollars, a picture of Christ the Good Shepherd with a Lamb in His arms.

MARGARET. Big Daddy.

BIG DADDY. Well, Brick.

BRICK. Hello Big Daddy. — Congratulations!

BIG DADDY. — Crap. . . .

GOOPER. Who give that window, Preach?

REVEREND TOOKER. Clyde Fletcher's widow. Also presented St. Paul's with a baptismal font.

GOOPER. Y'know what somebody ought t' give your church is a *coolin'* system, Preach.

MAE [*almost religiously*]. Let's see now, they've had their *tyyy*-phoid shots, and their tetanus shots, their diptheria shots and their hepatitis shots and their polio shots, they got *those* shots every month from May through September, and — Gooper? Hey! Gooper! — What all have the kiddies been shot faw?

REVEREND TOOKER. Yes, siree, Bob! And y'know what Gus Hamma's family gave in his memory to the church at Two Rivers? A complete new stone parish-house with a basketball court in the basement and a —

BIG DADDY [*uttering a loud barking laugh which is far from truly mirthful*]. Hey, Preach! What's all this talk about memorials, Preach? Y' think somebody's about t' kick off around here? 'S that it?

[*Startled by this interjection,* REVEREND TOOKER *decides to laugh at the question almost as loud as he can.*]

   [*How he would answer the question we'll never know, as he's spared that embarrassment by the voice of* GOOPER's *wife,* MAE, *rising high and clear as she appears with* "DOC" BAUGH, *the family doctor, through the hall door.*]

MARGARET [*overlapping a bit*]. Turn on the hi-fi, Brick! Let's have some music t' start th' party with!

BRICK. You turn it on, Maggie.

[*The talk becomes so general that the room sounds like a great aviary of chattering birds. Only* BRICK *remains unengaged, leaning upon the liquor cabinet with his faraway smile, an ice cube in a paper napkin with which he now and then rubs his forehead. He doesn't respond to* MARGARET's *command. She bounds forward and stoops over the instrument panel of the console.*]

GOOPER. We gave 'em that thing for a third anniversary present, got three speakers in it.

[*The room is suddenly blasted by the climax of a Wagnerian opera or a Beethoven symphony.*]

BIG DADDY. *Turn that damn thing off!*

   [*Almost instant silence, almost instantly broken by the shouting charge of* BIG MAMA, *entering through the hall door like a charging rhino.*]

BIG MAMA. *Wha's my Brick, wha's mah precious baby!!*

BIG DADDY. *Sorry! Turn it back on!*

[*Everyone laughs very loud.* BIG DADDY *is famous for his jokes at* BIG MAMA's *expense, and nobody laughs louder at these jokes than* BIG MAMA *herself, though* sometimes *they're pretty cruel and* BIG MAMA *has to pick up or fuss with something to cover the hurt that the loud laugh doesn't quite cover.*]

[*On this occasion, a happy occasion because the dread in her heart has also been lifted by the false report on* BIG DADDY'*s condition, she giggles, grotesquely, coyly, in* BIG DADDY'*s direction and bears down upon* BRICK, *all very quick and alive.*]

BIG MAMA. Here he is, here's my precious baby! What's that you've got in your hand? You put that liquor down, son, your hand was made fo' holdin' somethin' better than that!

GOOPER. Look at Brick put it down!

[BRICK *has obeyed* BIG MAMA *by draining the glass and handing it to her. Again everyone laughs, some high, some low.*]

BIG MAMA. Oh, you bad boy, you, you're my bad little boy. Give Big Mama a kiss, you bad boy, you!—Look at him shy away, will you? Brick never liked bein' kissed or made a fuss over, I guess because he's always had too much of it!

   Son, you turn that thing off!

[BRICK *has switched on the TV set.*]

   I can't stand TV, radio was bad enough but TV has gone it one better, I mean—[*plops wheezing in chair*]—one worse, ha ha! Now what'm I sittin' down here faw? I want t' sit next to my sweetheart on the sofa, hold hands with him and love him up a little!

[BIG MAMA *has on a black and white figured chiffon. The large irregular patterns, like the markings of some massive animal, the luster of her great diamonds and many pearls, the brilliants set in the silver frames of her glasses, her riotous voice, booming laugh, have dominated the room since she entered.* BIG DADDY *has been regarding her with a steady grimace of chronic annoyance.*]

BIG MAMA [*still louder*]. Preacher, Preacher, hey, Preach! Give me you' hand an' help me up from this chair!

REVEREND TOOKER. None of your tricks, Big Mama!

BIG MAMA. What tricks? You give me you' hand so I can get up an'—

[REVEREND TOOKER *extends her his hand. She grabs it and pulls him into her lap with a shrill laugh that spans an octave in two notes.*]

   Ever seen a preacher in a fat lady's lap? Hey, hey, folks! Ever seen a preacher in a fat lady's lap?

[BIG MAMA *is notorious throughout the Delta for this sort of inelegant horseplay.* MARGARET *looks on with indulgent humor, sipping Dubonnet "on the rocks" and watching* BRICK, *but* MAE *and* GOOPER *exchange signs of humorless anxiety over these antics, the sort of behavior which* MAE *thinks may account for their failure to quite get in with the smartest young married set in Memphis, despite all. One of the Negroes,* LACY *or* SOOKEY, *peeks in, cackling. They are waiting for a sign to bring in the cake and champagne. But* BIG DADDY'*s not amused. He doesn't understand why, in spite of the infinite mental relief he's received from the doctor's report, he still has these same old fox teeth in his guts. "This spastic condition is something else," he says to himself, but aloud he roars at* BIG MAMA.]

BIG DADDY. *BIG MAMA, WILL YOU QUIT HORSIN'?*—You're too old an' too fat fo' that sort of crazy kid stuff an' besides a woman with your blood pressure—she had two hundred last spring!—is riskin' a stroke when you mess around like that. . . .

[MAE *blows on a pitch pipe.*]

BIG MAMA. *Here comes Big Daddy's birthday!*

[*Negroes in white jackets enter with an enormous birthday cake ablaze with candles and carrying buckets of champagne with satin ribbons about the bottle necks.* MAE *and* GOOPER *strike up song, and everybody, including the* NEGROES *and* CHILDREN, *joins in. Only* BRICK *remains aloof.*]

EVERYONE.
    Happy birthday to you.
    Happy birthday to you.
    Happy Birthday, Big Daddy —
[*Some sing: "Dear, Big Daddy!"*]
    Happy birthday to you.
[*Some sing: "How old are you?"*]
[MAE *has come down center and is organizing her children like a chorus. She gives them a barely audible: "One, two, three!" and they are off in the new tune.*]
CHILDREN.
    Skinamarinka — dinka — dink
    Skinamarinka — do
    We love you.
    Skinamarinka — dinka — dink
    Skinamarinka — do.
[*All together, they turn to* BIG DADDY.]
    Big Daddy, you!
[*They turn back front, like a musical comedy chorus.*]
    We love you in the morning.
    We love you in the night.
    We love you when we're with you,
    And we love you out of sight.
    Skinamarinka — dinka — dink
    Skinamarinka — do.
[MAE *turns to* BIG MAMA.]
    Big Mama, too!
[BIG MAMA *bursts into tears. The* NEGROES *leave.*]
BIG DADDY. Now Ida, what the hell is the matter with you?
MAE. She's just so happy.
BIG MAMA. I'm just so happy, Big Daddy, I have to cry or something.
[*Sudden and loud in the hush.*]
    Brick, do you know the wonderful news that Doc Baugh got from the clinic about Big Daddy? Big Daddy's one hundred per cent!
MARGARET. Isn't that wonderful?
BIG MAMA. He's just one hundred per cent. Passed the examination with flying colors. Now that we know there's nothing wrong with Big Daddy but a spastic colon, I can tell you something. I was worried sick, half out of my mind, for fear Big Daddy might have a thing like —
[MARGARET *cuts through this speech, jumping up and exclaiming shrilly.*]
MARGARET. Brick, honey, aren't you going to give Big Daddy his birthday present?
[*Passing by him, she snatches his liquor glass from him.*]
[*She picks up a fancily wrapped package.*]
    Here it is, Big Daddy, this is from Brick!
BIG MAMA. This is the biggest birthday Big Daddy's ever had, a hundred presents and bushels of telegrams from —

MAE [*at same time*]. What is it, Brick?

GOOPER. I bet 500 to 50 that Brick don't *know* what it is.

BIG MAMA. The fun of presents is not knowing what they are till you open the package. Open your present, Big Daddy.

BIG DADDY. Open it you'self. I want to ask Brick somethin'! Come here, Brick.

MARGARET. Big Daddy's callin' you, Brick. [*She is opening the package.*]

BRICK. Tell Big Daddy I'm crippled.

BIG DADDY. I see you're crippled. I want to know how you got crippled.

MARGARET [*making diversionary tactics*]. *Oh, look, oh, look, why, it's a cashmere robe!* [*She holds the robe up for all to see.*]

MAE. You sound surprised, Maggie.

MARGARET. I never saw one before.

MAE. That's funny. — *Hah!*

MARGARET [*turning on her fiercely, with a brilliant smile*]. Why is it funny? All my family ever had was family — and luxuries such as cashmere robes still surprise me!

BIG DADDY [*ominously*]. Quiet!

MAE [*heedless in her fury*]. I don't see how you could be so surprised when you bought it yourself at Loewenstein's in Memphis last Saturday. You know how I know?

BIG DADDY. I said, Quiet!

MAE. — I know because the salesgirl that sold it to you waited on me and said, Oh, Mrs. Pollitt, your sister-in-law just bought a cashmere robe for your husband's father!

MARGARET. Sister Woman! Your talents are wasted as a housewife and mother, you really ought to be with the FBI or —

BIG DADDY. QUIET!

[REVEREND TOOKER's *reflexes are slower than the others'. He finishes a sentence after the bellow.*]

REVEREND TOOKER [*to* DOC BAUGH]. — the Stork and the Reaper are running neck and neck!

[*He starts to laugh gaily when he notices the silence and* BIG DADDY's *glare. His laugh dies falsely.*]

BIG DADDY. Preacher, I hope I'm not butting in on more talk about memorial stained-glass windows, am I, Preacher?

[REVEREND TOOKER *laughs feebly, then coughs dryly in the embarrassed silence.*] Preacher?

BIG MAMA. Now, Big Daddy, don't you pick on Preacher!

BIG DADDY [*raising his voice*]. You ever hear that expression all hawk and no spit? You bring that expression to mind with that little dry cough of yours, all hawk an' no spit. . . .

[*The pause is broken only by a short startled laugh from* MARGARET, *the only one there who is conscious of and amused by the grotesque.*]

MAE [*raising her arms and jangling her bracelets*]. I wonder if the mosquitoes are active tonight?

BIG DADDY. What's that, Little Mama? Did you make some remark?

MAE. Yes, I said I wondered if the mosquitoes would eat us alive if we went out on the gallery for a while.

BIG DADDY. Well, if they do, I'll have your bones pulverized for fertilizer!

BIG MAMA [*quickly*]. Last week we had an airplane spraying the place and I think it done some good, at least I haven't had a —

BIG DADDY [*cutting her speech*]. Brick, they tell me, if what they tell me is true, that you done some jumping last night on the high school athletic field?

BIG MAMA. Brick, Big Daddy is talking to you, son.

BRICK [*smiling vaguely over his drink*]. What was that, Big Daddy?

BIG DADDY. They said you done some jumping on the high school track field last night.

BRICK. That's what they told me, too.

BIG DADDY. Was it jumping or humping that you were doing out there? What were you doing out there at three A.M., layin' a woman on that cinder track?

BIG MAMA. Big Daddy, you are off the sick-list, now, and I'm not going to excuse you for talkin' so —

BIG DADDY. Quiet!

BIG MAMA. —*nasty* in front of Preacher and—

BIG DADDY. *QUIET!*—I ast you, Brick, if you was cuttin' you'self a piece o' poon-tang last night on that cinder track? I thought maybe you were chasin' poon-tang on that track an' tripped over something in the heat of the chase — 'sthat it?

[GOOPER *laughs, loud and false, others nervously following suit.* BIG MAMA *stamps her foot, and purses her lips, crossing to* MAE *and whispering something to her as* BRICK *meets his father's hard, intent, grinning stare with a slow, vague smile that he offers all situations from behind the screen of his liquor.*]

BRICK. No, sir, I don't think so. . . .

MAE [*at the same time, sweetly*]. Reverend Tooker, let's you and I take a stroll on the widow's walk.

[*She and the preacher go out on the gallery as* BIG DADDY *says.*]

BIG DADDY. Then what the hell were you doing out there at three o'clock in the morning?

BRICK. Jumping the hurdles, Big Daddy, runnin' and jumpin' the hurdles, but those high hurdles have gotten too high for me, now.

BIG DADDY. Cause you was drunk?

BRICK [*his vague smile fading a little*]. Sober I wouldn't have tried to jump the *low* ones. . . .

BIG MAMA [*quickly*]. Big Daddy, blow out the candles on your birthday cake!

MARGARET [*at the same time*]. I want to propose a toast to Big Daddy Pollitt on his sixty-fifth birthday, the biggest cotton planter in—

BIG DADDY [*bellowing with fury and disgust*]. *I told you to stop it, now stop it, quit this—!*

BIG MAMA [*coming in front of* BIG DADDY *with the cake*]. Big Daddy, I will not allow you to talk that way, not even on your birthday, I—

BIG DADDY. I'll talk like I want to on my birthday, Ida, or any other goddam day of the year and anybody here that don't like it knows what they can do!

BIG MAMA. You don't mean that!

BIG DADDY. What makes you think I don't mean it?

[*Meanwhile various discreet signals have been exchanged and* GOOPER *has also gone out on the gallery.*]

BIG MAMA. I just know you don't mean it.

BIG DADDY. You don't know a goddam thing and you never did!

BIG MAMA. Big Daddy, you don't mean that.

BIG DADDY. Oh, yes, I do, oh, yes, I do, I mean it! I put up with a whole lot of crap around here because I thought I was dying. And you thought I was dying and you started taking over, well, you can stop taking over now, Ida, because I'm not gonna die, you can just stop now this business of taking over because you're not taking over because I'm not dying, I went through the laboratory and the goddam exploratory operation and there's nothing wrong with me but a spastic colon. And I'm not dying of cancer which you thought I was dying of. Ain't that so? Didn't you think I was dying of cancer, Ida?

[*Almost everybody is out on the gallery but the two old people glaring at each other across the blazing cake.*]

[BIG MAMA's *chest heaves and she presses a fat fist to her mouth.*]

[BIG DADDY *continues, hoarsely.*]

Ain't that so, Ida? Didn't you have an idea I was dying of cancer and now you could take control of this place and everything on it? I got that impression, I seemed to get that impression. Your loud voice everywhere, your fat old body butting in here and there!

BIG MAMA. Hush! The Preacher!

BIG DADDY. Fuck the goddam preacher!

[BIG MAMA *gasps loudly and sits down on the sofa which is almost too small for her.*]

Did you hear what I said? I said fuck the goddam preacher!

[*Somebody closes the gallery doors from outside just as there is a burst of fireworks and excited cries from the children.*]

BIG MAMA. I never seen you act like this before and I can't think what's got in you!

BIG DADDY. I went through all that laboratory and operation and all just so I would know if you or me was boss here! Well, now it turns out that I am and you ain't—and that's my birthday present—and my cake and champagne!—because for three years now you been gradually taking over. Bossing. Talking. Sashaying your fat old body around the place I made! I made this place! I was overseer on it! I was the overseer on the old Straw and Ochello plantation. I quit school at ten! I quit school at ten years old and went to work like a nigger in the fields. And I rose to be overseer of the Straw and Ochello plantation. And old Straw died and I was Ochello's partner and the place got bigger and bigger and bigger and bigger and bigger! I did all that myself with no goddam help from you, and now you think you're just about to take over. Well, I am just about to tell you that you are not just about to take over, you are not just about to take over a God damn thing. Is that clear to you, Ida? Is that very plain to you, now? Is that understood completely? I been through the laboratory from A to Z. I've had the goddam exploratory operation, and nothing is wrong with me but a spastic colon—made spastic, I guess, by *disgust!* By all the goddam lies and liars that I have had to put up with, and all the goddam hypocrisy that I lived with all these forty years that we been livin' together!

Hey! Ida!! Blow out the candles on the birthday cake! Purse up your lips and draw a deep breath and blow out the goddam candles on the cake!

BIG MAMA. Oh, Big Daddy, oh, oh, oh, Big Daddy!

BIG DADDY. What's the matter with you?

BIG MAMA. *In all these years you never believed that I loved you??*

BIG DADDY. Huh?

BIG MAMA. *And I did. I did so much. I did love you!* — I even loved your hate and your hardness, Big Daddy! [*She sobs and rushes awkwardly out onto the gallery.*]

BIG DADDY [*to himself*]. Wouldn't it be funny if that was true. . . .

[*A pause is followed by a burst of light in the sky from the fireworks.*]
  BRICK! HEY, BRICK!
[*He stands over his blazing birthday cake.*]

[*After some moments,* BRICK *hobbles in on his crutch, holding his glass.*
MARGARET *follows him with a bright, anxious smile.*]
  I didn't call you, Maggie. I called Brick.
MARGARET. I'm just delivering him to you.
[*She kisses* BRICK *on the mouth which he immediately wipes with the back of his hand.*
  She flies girlishly back out. BRICK *and his father are alone.*]
BIG DADDY. Why did you do that?
BRICK. Do what, Big Daddy?
BIG DADDY. Wipe her kiss off your mouth like she'd spit on you.
BRICK. I don't know. I wasn't conscious of it.
BIG DADDY. That woman of yours has a better shape on her than Gooper's but
  somehow or other they got the same look about them.
BRICK. What sort of look is that, Big Daddy?
BIG DADDY. I don't know how to describe it but it's the same look.
BRICK. They don't look peaceful, do they?
BIG DADDY. No, they sure in hell don't.
BRICK. They look nervous as cats?
BIG DADDY. That's right, they look nervous as cats.
BRICK. Nervous as a couple of cats on a hot tin roof?
BIG DADDY. That's right, boy, they look like a couple of cats on a hot tin roof.
  It's funny that you and Gooper being so different would pick out the same
  type of woman.
BRICK. Both of us married into society, Big Daddy.
BIG DADDY. Crap . . . I wonder what gives them both that look?
BRICK. Well. They're sittin' in the middle of a big piece of land, Big Daddy,
  twenty-eight thousand acres is a pretty big piece of land and so they're
  squaring off on it, each determined to knock off a bigger piece of it than the
  other whenever you let it go.
BIG DADDY. I got a surprise for those women. I'm not gonna let it go for a long
  time yet if that's what they're waiting for.
BRICK. That's right, Big Daddy. You just sit tight and let them scratch each
  other's eyes out. . . .
BIG DADDY. You bet your life I'm going to sit tight on it and let those sons of
  bitches scratch their eyes out, ha ha ha. . . .
    But Gooper's wife's a good breeder, you got to admit she's fertile. Hell, at
  supper tonight she had them all at the table and they had to put a couple of
  extra leafs in the table to make room for them, she's got five head of them,
  now, and another one's comin'.
BRICK. Yep, number six is comin'. . . .
BIG DADDY. Six hell, she'll probably drop a litter next time. Brick, you know, I
  swear to God, I don't know the way it happens?
BRICK. The way what happens, Big Daddy?
BIG DADDY. You git you a piece of land, by hook or crook, an' things start
  growin' on it, things accumulate on it, and the first thing you know it's
  completely out of hand, completely out of hand!
BRICK. Well, they say nature hates a vacuum, Big Daddy.

BIG DADDY. That's what they say, but sometimes I think that a vacuum is a hell of a lot better than some of the stuff that nature replaces it with.

Is someone out there by that door?

GOOPER. Hey Mae.

BRICK. Yep.

BIG DADDY. Who? [*He has lowered his voice.*]

BRICK. Someone int'rested in what we say to each other.

BIG DADDY. Gooper? — *GOOPER!*

[*After a discreet pause,* MAE *appears in the gallery door.*]

MAE. Did you call Gooper, Big Daddy?

BIG DADDY. Aw, it was you.

MAE. Do you want Gooper, Big Daddy?

BIG DADDY. No, and I don't want you. I want some privacy here, while I'm having a confidential talk with my son Brick. Now it's too hot in here to close them doors, but if I have to close those fuckin' doors in order to have a private talk with my son Brick, just let me know and I'll close 'em. Because I hate eavesdroppers, I don't like any kind of sneakin' an' spyin'.

MAE. Why, Big Daddy —

BIG DADDY. You stood on the wrong side of the moon, it threw your shadow!

MAE. I was just —

BIG DADDY. You was just nothing but *spyin'* an' you *know* it!

MAE [*begins to sniff and sob*]. Oh, Big Daddy, you're so unkind for some reason to those that really love you!

BIG DADDY. Shut up, shut up, shut up! I'm going to move you and Gooper out of that room next to this! It's none of your goddam business what goes on in here at night between Brick an' Maggie. You listen at night like a couple of rutten peekhole spies and go and give a report on what you hear to Big Mama an' she comes to me and says they say such and such and so and so about what they heard goin' on between Brick an' Maggie, and Jesus, it makes me sick. I'm goin' to move you an' Gooper out of that room, I can't stand sneakin' an' spyin', it makes me puke. . . .

> [MAE *throws back her head and rolls her eyes heavenward and extends her arms as if invoking God's pity for this unjust martyrdom; then she presses a handkerchief to her nose and flies from the room with a loud swish of skirts.*]

BRICK [*now at the liquor cabinet*]. They listen, do they?

BIG DADDY. Yeah. They listen and give reports to Big Mama on what goes on in here between you and Maggie. They say that — [*He stops as if embarrassed.*] — You won't sleep with her, that you sleep on the sofa. Is that true or not true? If you don't like Maggie, get rid of Maggie! — What are you doin' there now?

BRICK. Fresh'nin up my drink.

BIG DADDY. Son, you know you got a real liquor problem?

BRICK. Yes, sir, yes, I know.

BIG DADDY. Is that why you quit sports-announcing, because of this liquor problem?

BRICK. Yes, sir, yes, sir, I guess so.

[*He smiles vaguely and amiably at his father across his replenished drink.*]

BIG DADDY. Son, don't guess about it, it's too important.

BRICK [*vaguely*]. Yes, sir.

BIG DADDY. And listen to me, don't look at the damn chandelier. . . .

[*Pause.* BIG DADDY'*s voice is husky.*]

—Somethin' else we picked up at th' big fire sale in Europe.

[*Another pause.*]

Life is important. There's nothing else to hold onto. A man that drinks is throwing his life away. Don't do it, hold onto your life. There's nothing else to hold onto. . . .

Sit down over here so we don't have to raise our voices, the walls have ears in this place.

BRICK [*hobbling over to sit on the sofa beside him*]. All right, Big Daddy.

BIG DADDY. Quit!—how'd that come about? Some disappointment?

BRICK. I don't know. Do you?

BIG DADDY. I'm askin' you, God damn it! How in hell would I know if you don't?

BRICK. I just got out there and found that I had a mouth full of cotton. I was always two or three beats behind what was goin' on on the field and so I—

BIG DADDY. Quit!

BRICK [*amiably*]. Yes, quit.

BIG DADDY. Son?

BRICK. Huh?

BIG DADDY [*inhales loudly and deeply from his cigar; then bends suddenly a little forward, exhaling loudly and raising a hand to his forehead*]. Whew!—ha ha!—I took in too much smoke, it made me a little lightheaded. . . .

[*The mantel clock chimes.*]

Why is it so damn hard for people to talk?

BRICK. Yeah. . . .

[*The clock goes on sweetly chiming till it has completed the stroke of ten.*]

—Nice peaceful-soundin' clock, I like to hear it all night. . . .

[*He slides low and comfortable on the sofa;* BIG DADDY *sits straight and rigid with some unspoken anxiety. All his gestures are tense and jerky as he talks. He wheezes and pants and sniffs through his nervous speech, glancing quickly, shyly, from time to time, at his son.*]

BIG DADDY. We got that clock the summer we wint to Europe, me an' Big Mama on that damn Cook's Tour, never had such an awful time in my life. I'm tellin' you, son, those gooks over there, they gouge your eyeballs out in their grand hotels. And Big Mama bought more stuff than you could haul in a couple of boxcars, that's no crap. Everywhere she wint on this whirlwind tour, she bought, bought, bought. Why, half that stuff she bought is still crated up in the cellar, under water last spring! [*He laughs.*]

That Europe is nothin' on earth but a great big auction, that's all it is, that bunch of old worn-out places, it's just a big firesale, the whole fuckin' thing, an' Big Mama wint wild in it, why, you couldn't hold that woman with a mule's harness! Bought, bought, bought!—lucky I'm a rich man, yes siree, Bob, an' half that stuff is mildewin' in th' basement. It's lucky I'm a rich man, it sure is lucky, well, I'm a rich man, Brick, yep, I'm a mighty rich man. [*His eyes light up for a moment.*]

Y'know how much I'm worth? Guess, Brick! Guess how much I'm worth!

[BRICK *smiles vaguely over his drink.*]

Close on ten million in cash an' blue-chip stocks, outside, mind you, of twenty-eight thousand acres of the richest land this side of the valley Nile!

But a man can't buy his life with it, he can't buy back his life with it when his life has been spent, that's one thing not offered in the Europe fire-sale or in the American markets or any markets on earth, a man can't buy his life with it, he can't buy back his life when his life is finished.

That's a sobering thought, a very sobering thought, and that's a thought that I was turning over in my head, over and over and over — until today. . . .

I'm wiser and sadder, Brick, for this experience which I just gone through. They's one thing else that I remember in Europe.

BRICK. What is that, Big Daddy?

BIG DADDY. The hills around Barcelona in the country of Spain and the children running over those bare hills in their bare skins beggin' like starvin' dogs with howls and screeches, and how fat the priests are on the streets of Barcelona, so many of them and so fat and so pleasant, ha ha! — Y'know I could feed that country? I got money enough to feed that goddam country, but the human animal is a selfish beast and I don't reckon the money I passed out there to those howling children in the hills around Barcelona would more than uphol-ster the chairs in this room, I mean pay to put a new cover on this chair!

Hell, I threw them money like you'd scatter feed corn for chickens, I threw money at them just to get rid of them long enough to climb back into th' car and — drive away. . . .

And then in Morocco, them Arabs, why, I remember one day in Marrakech, that old walled Arab city, I set on a broken-down wall to have a cigar, it was fearful hot there and this Arab woman stood in the road and looked at me till I was embarrassed, she stood stock still in the dusty hot road and looked at me till I was embarrassed. But listen to this. She had a naked child with her, a little naked girl with her, barely able to toddle, and after a while she set this child on the ground and give her a push and whispered something to her.

This child come toward me, barely able t' walk, come toddling up to me and —

Jesus, it makes you sick to' remember a thing like this!

It stuck out its hand and tried to unbutton my trousers!

That child was not yet five! Can you believe me? Or do you think that I am making this up? I wint back to the hotel and said to Big Mama, Git packed! We're clearing out of this country. . . .

BRICK. Big Daddy, you're on a talkin' jag tonight.

BIG DADDY [*ignoring this remark*]. Yes, sir, that's how it is, the human animal is a beast that dies but the fact that he's dying don't give him pity for others, no, sir, it —

— Did you say something?

BRICK. Yes.

BIG DADDY. What?

BRICK. Hand me over that crutch so I can get up.

BIG DADDY. Where you goin'?

BRICK. I'm takin' a little short trip to Echo Spring.

BIG DADDY. To where?

BRICK. Liquor cabinet. . . .

BIG DADDY. Yes, sir, boy — [*He hands* BRICK *the crutch*] — the human animal is
a beast that dies and if he's got money he buys and buys and buys and I think
the reason he buys everything he can buy is that in the back of his mind he has
the crazy hope that one of his purchases will be life everlasting! — Which it
never can be. . . . The human animal is a beast that —

BRICK [*at the liquor cabinet*]. Big Daddy, you sure are shootin' th' breeze here
tonight.

[*There is a pause and voices are heard outside.*]

BIG DADDY. I been quiet here lately, spoke not a word, just sat and stared into
space. I had something heavy weighing on my mind but tonight that load was
took off me. That's why I'm talking. — The sky looks diff'rent to me. . . .

BRICK. You know what I like to hear most?

BIG DADDY. What?

BRICK. Solid quiet. Perfect unbroken quiet.

BIG DADDY. Why?

BRICK. Because it's more peaceful.

BIG DADDY. Man, you'll hear a lot of that in the grave. [*He chuckles agreeably.*]

BRICK. Are you through talkin' to me?

BIG DADDY. Why are you so anxious to shut me up?

BRICK. Well, sir, ever so often you say to me, Brick, I want to have a talk with
you, but when we talk, it never materializes. Nothing is said. You sit in a chair
and gas about this and that and I look like I listen. I try to look like I listen, but
I don't listen, not much. Communication is — awful hard between people
an' — somehow between you and me, it just don't — happen.

BIG DADDY. Have you ever been scared? I mean have you ever felt downright
terror of something? [*He gets up.*] Just one moment. [*He looks off as if he were
going to tell an important secret.*]

BIG DADDY. Brick?

BRICK. What?

BIG DADDY. Son, I thought I had it!

BRICK. Had what? Had what, Big Daddy?

BIG DADDY. Cancer!

BRICK. Oh . . .

BIG DADDY. I thought the old man made out of bones had laid his cold and heavy
hand on my shoulder!

BRICK. Well, Big Daddy, you kept a tight mouth about it.

BIG DADDY. A pig squeals. A man keeps a tight mouth about it, in spite of a man
not having a pig's advantage.

BRICK. What advantage is that?

BIG DADDY. Ignorance — of mortality — is a comfort. A man don't have that
comfort, he's the only living thing that conceives of death, that knows what it
is. The others go without knowing which is the way that anything living
should go, go without knowing, without any knowledge of it, and yet a pig
squeals, but a man sometimes, he can keep a tight mouth about it. Sometimes
he —

[*There is a deep smoldering ferocity in the old man.*]

— can keep a tight mouth about it. I wonder if —

BRICK. What, Big Daddy?

BIG DADDY. A whiskey highball would injure this spastic condition?

BRICK. No, sir, it might do it good.

BIG DADDY [*grins suddenly, wolfishly*]. Jesus, I can't tell you! *The sky is open!* Christ, it's open again! It's open boy, it's open!

[BRICK *looks down at his drink.*]

BRICK. You feel better, Big Daddy?

BIG DADDY. Better? Hell! I can breathe — All of my life I been like a doubled up fist. . . . [*He pours a drink.*] — Poundin', smashin', drivin'! — now I'm going to loosen these doubled-up hands and touch things *easy* with them. . . .

[*He spreads his hands as if caressing the air.*]

You know what I'm contemplating?

BRICK [*vaguely*]. No, sir. What are you contemplating?

BIG DADDY. Ha ha! — *Pleasure!* — pleasure with *women!*

[BRICK's *smile fades a little but lingers.*]

— Yes, boy. I'll tell you something that you might not guess. I still have desire for women and this is my sixty-fifth birthday.

BRICK. I think that's mighty remarkable, Big Daddy.

BIG DADDY. Remarkable?

BRICK. *Admirable*, Big Daddy.

BIG DADDY. You're damn right it is, remarkable and admirable both. I realize now that I never had me enough. I let many chances slip by because of scruples about it, scruples, convention — crap. . . . All that stuff is bull, bull, bull! — It took the shadow of death to make me see it. Now that shadow's lifted, I'm going to cut loose and have, what is it they call it, have me a — ball!

BRICK. A ball, huh?

BIG DADDY. That's right, a ball, a ball! Hell! — I slept with Big Mama till, let's see, five years ago, till I was sixty and she was fifty-eight, and never even liked her, never did!

[*The phone has been ringing down the hall.* BIG MAMA *enters, exclaiming.*]

BIG MAMA. Don't you men hear that phone ring? I heard it way out on the gall'ry.

BIG DADDY. There's five rooms off this front gall'ry that you could go through. Why do you go through this one?

[BIG MAMA *makes a playful face as she bustles out the hall door.*]

Hunh! — Why, when Big Mama goes out of a room, I can't remember what that woman looks like —

BIG MAMA. Hello.

BIG DADDY. But when Big Mama comes back into the room, boy, then I see what she looks like, and I wish I didn't.

[*Bends over laughing at this joke till it hurts his guts and he straightens with a grimace. The laugh subsides to a chuckle as he puts the liquor glass a little distrustfully down on the table.*]

BIG MAMA. Hello, Miss Sally.

[BRICK *has risen and hobbled to the gallery doors.*]

BIG DADDY. Hey! Where you goin'?

BRICK. Out for a breather.

BIG DADDY. Not yet you ain't. Stay here till this talk is finished, young fellow.

BRICK. I thought it was finished, Big Daddy.

BIG DADDY. It ain't even begun.

BRICK. My mistake. Excuse me. I just wanted to feel that river breeze.

BIG DADDY. Set back in that chair.

[BIG MAMA'*s voice rises, carrying down the hall.*]
BIG MAMA. Miss Sally, you're a case! You're a caution, Miss Sally.
BIG DADDY. Jesus, she's talking to my old maid sister again.
BIG MAMA. Why didn't you give me a chance to explain it to you?
BIG DADDY. Brick, this stuff burns me.
BIG MAMA. Well, goodbye, now, Miss Sally. You come down real soon. Big
    Daddy's dying to see you.
BIG DADDY. Crap!
BIG MAMA. Yaiss, goodbye, Miss Sally. . . .
[*She hangs up and bellows with mirth.* BIG DADDY *groans and covers his ears as she
    approaches.*]
[*Bursting in*]
    Big Daddy, that was Miss Sally callin' from Memphis again! You know what
    she done, Big Daddy? She called her doctor in Memphis to git him to tell her
    what that spastic thing is! Ha-*HAAAA!*—And called back to tell me how
    relieved she was that—Hey! Let me in!
[BIG DADDY *has been holding the door half closed against her.*]
BIG DADDY. Naw I ain't. I told you not to come and go through this room. You
    just back out and go through those five other rooms.
BIG MAMA. Big Daddy? Big Daddy? Oh, Big Daddy!—You didn't mean those
    things you said to me, did you?
[*He shuts door firmly against her but she still calls.*]
    Sweetheart? Sweetheart? Big Daddy? You didn't mean those awful things you
    said to me?—I know you didn't. I know you didn't mean those things in your
    heart. . . .

> [*The childlike voice fades with a sob and her heavy
> footsteps retreat down the hall.* BRICK *has risen once
> more on his crutches and starts for the gallery again.*]

BIG DADDY. All I ask of that woman is that she leave me alone. But she can't
    admit to herself that she makes me sick. That comes of having slept with her
    too many years. Should of quit much sooner but that old woman she never got
    enough of it—and I was good in bed . . . I never should of wasted so much
    of it on her. . . . They say you got just so many and each one is numbered.
    Well, I got a few left in me, a few, and I'm going to pick me a good one to
    spend 'em on! I'm going to pick me a choice one, I don't care how much she
    costs, I'll smother her in—minks! Ha ha! I'll strip her naked and smother her
    in minks and choke her with diamonds! Ha ha! I'll strip her naked and choke
    her with diamonds and smother her with minks and hump her from hell to
    breakfast. *Ha aha ha ha ha!*
MAE [*gaily at door*]. Who's that laughin' in there?
GOOPER. Is Big Daddy laughin' in there?
BIG DADDY. Crap!—them two—*drips*. . . .
[*He goes over and touches* BRICK'*s shoulder.*]
    Yes, son. Brick, boy.—I'm *happy!* I'm happy, son, I'm happy!
[*He chokes a little and bites his under lip, pressing his head quickly, shyly against his
    son's head and then, coughing with embarrassment, goes uncertainly back to the
    table where he set down the glass. He drinks and makes a grimace as it burns his
    guts.* BRICK *sighs and rises with effort.*]
    What makes you so restless? Have you got ants in your britches?
BRICK. Yes, sir. . . .

BIG DADDY. Why?

BRICK. —Something—hasn't happened. . . .

BIG DADDY. Yeah? What is that!

BRICK [*sadly*]. —the click. . . .

BIG DADDY. Did you say click?

BRICK. Yes, click.

BIG DADDY. What click?

BRICK. A click that I get in my head that makes me peaceful.

BIG DADDY. I sure in hell don't know what you're talking about, but it disturbs me.

BRICK. It's just a mechanical thing.

BIG DADDY. What is a mechanical thing?

BRICK. This click that I get in my head that makes me peaceful. I got to drink till I get it. It's just a mechanical thing, something like a—like a—like a—

BIG DADDY. Like a—

BRICK. Switch clicking off in my head, turning the hot light off and the cool night on and—[*He looks up, smiling sadly.*]—all of a sudden there's—peace!

BIG DADDY [*whistles long and soft with astonishment; he goes back to* BRICK *and clasps his son's two shoulders*]. Jesus! I didn't know it had gotten that bad with you. Why, boy, you're—*alcoholic!*

BRICK. That's the truth, Big Daddy. I'm alcoholic.

BIG DADDY. This shows how I—let things go!

BRICK. I have to hear that little click in my head that makes me peaceful. Usually I hear it sooner than this, sometimes as early as—noon, but

—Today it's—dilatory. . . .

—I just haven't got the right level of alcohol in my bloodstream yet!

[*This last statement is made with energy as he freshens his drink.*]

BIG DADDY. Uh—huh. Expecting death made me blind. I didn't have no idea that a son of mine was turning into a drunkard under my nose.

BRICK [*gently*]. Well, now you do, Big Daddy, the news has penetrated. . . .

BIG DADDY. Uh-huh, yes, now I do. The news has penetrated.

BRICK. And so if you'll excuse me—

BIG DADDY. No, I won't excuse you.

BRICK. —I'd better sit by myself till I hear that click in my head, it's just a mechanical thing but it don't happen except when I'm alone or talking to no one. . . .

BIG DADDY. You got a long, long time to sit still, boy, and talk to no one, but now you're talkin' to me. At least I'm talking to you. And you set there and listen until I tell you the conversation is over!

BRICK. But this talk is like all the others we've ever had together in our lives! It's nowhere, nowhere!—it's—it's *painful*, Big Daddy. . . .

BIG DADDY. All right, then let it be painful, but don't you move from that chair!—I'm going to remove that crutch. . . . [*He seizes the crutch and tosses it across room.*]

BRICK. I can hop on one foot, and if I fall, I can crawl!

BIG DADDY. If you ain't careful you're gonna crawl off this plantation and then, by Jesus, you'll have to hustle your drinks along Skid Row!

BRICK. That'll come, Big Daddy.

BIG DADDY. Naw, it won't. You're my son and I'm going to straighten you out; now that *I'm* straightened out, I'm going to straighten out you!

BRICK. Yeah?

BIG DADDY. Today the report come in from Ochsner Clinic. Y'know what they told me? [*His face glows with triumph.*] The only thing that they could detect with all the instruments of science in that great hospital is a little spastic condition of the colon! And nerves torn to pieces by all that worry about it.

[*A little girl bursts into room with a sparkler clutched in each fist, hops and shrieks like a monkey gone mad and rushes back out again as* BIG DADDY *strikes at her.*]
[*Silence. The two men stare at each other. A woman laughs gaily outside.*]
I want you to know I breathed a sigh of relief almost as powerful as the Vicksburg tornado!
[*There is laughter outside, running footsteps, the soft, plushy sound and light of exploding rockets.*]

> [BRICK *stares at him soberly for a long moment; then makes a sort of startled sound in his nostrils and springs up on one foot and hops across the room to grab his crutch, swinging on the furniture for support. He gets the crutch and flees as if in horror for the gallery. His father seizes him by the sleeve of his white silk pajamas.*]

Stay here, you son of a bitch! — till I say go!
BRICK. I can't.
BIG DADDY. You sure in hell will, God damn it.
BRICK. No, I can't. We talk, you talk, in — circles! We get no where, no where! It's always the same, you say you want to talk to me and don't have a fuckin' thing to say to me!
BIG DADDY. Nothin' to say when I'm tellin' you I'm going to live when I thought I was dying?!
BRICK. Oh — *that* — Is that what you have to say to me?
BIG DADDY. Why, you son of a bitch! Ain't that, ain't that — *important?!*
BRICK. Well, you said that, that's said, and now *I* —
BIG DADDY. Now you set back down.
BRICK. You're all balled up, you —
BIG DADDY. I ain't all balled up!
BRICK. You are, you're all balled up!
BIG DADDY. Don't tell me what I am, you drunken whelp! I'm going to tear this coat sleeve off you if you don't set down!
BRICK. Big Daddy —
BIG DADDY. Do what I tell you! I'm the boss here, now! I want you to know I'm back in the driver's seat now!

[BIG MAMA *rushes in, clutching her great heaving bosom.*]
BIG MAMA. Big Daddy!
BIG DADDY. What in hell do you want in here, Big Mama?
BIG MAMA. Oh, Big Daddy! Why are you shouting like that? I just cain't stainnnnnnnd — it. . . .
BIG DADDY [*raising the back of his hand above his head*]. GIT! — outa here.
[*She rushes back out, sobbing.*]

BRICK [*softly, sadly*]. Christ. . . .
BIG DADDY [*fiercely*]. Yeah! Christ! — is right. . . .

[BRICK *breaks loose and hobbles toward the gallery.*]

[BIG DADDY *jerks his crutch from under* BRICK *so he steps with the injured ankle. He utters a hissing cry of anguish, clutches a chair and pulls it over on top of him on the floor.*]

Son of a—tub of—hog fat. . . .

BRICK. Big Daddy! Give me my crutch.

[BIG DADDY *throws the crutch out of reach.*]

Give me that crutch, Big Daddy.

BIG DADDY. Why do you drink?

BRICK. Don't know, give me my crutch!

BIG DADDY. You better think why you drink or give up drinking!

BRICK. Will you please give me my crutch so I can get up off this floor?

BIG DADDY. First you answer my question. Why do you drink? Why are you throwing your life away, boy, like somethin' disgusting you picked up on the street?

BRICK [*getting onto his knees*]. Big Daddy, I'm in pain, I stepped on that foot.

BIG DADDY. Good! I'm glad you're not too numb with the liquor in you to feel some pain!

BRICK. You—spilled my—drink. . . .

BIG DADDY. I'll make a bargain with you. You tell me why you drink and I'll hand you one. I'll pour the liquor myself and hand it to you.

BRICK. Why do I drink?

BIG DADDY. Yea! Why?

BRICK. Give me a drink and I'll tell you.

BIG DADDY. Tell me first!

BRICK. I'll tell you in one word.

BIG DADDY. What word?

BRICK. DISGUST!

[*The clock chimes, softly, sweetly.* BIG DADDY *gives it a short, outraged glance.*]

Now how about that drink?

BIG DADDY. What are you disgusted with? You got to tell me that, first. Otherwise being disgusted don't make no sense!

BRICK. Give me my crutch.

BIG DADDY. You heard me, you got to tell me what I asked you first.

BRICK. I told you, I said to kill my disgust!

BIG DADDY. DISGUST WITH WHAT!

BRICK. You strike a hard bargain.

BIG DADDY. What are you disgusted with?—an' I'll pass you the liquor.

BRICK. I can hop on one foot, and if I fall, I can crawl.

BIG DADDY. You want liquor that bad?

BRICK [*dragging himself up, clinging to bedstead*]. Yeah, I want it that bad.

BIG DADDY. If I give you a drink, will you tell me what it is you're disgusted with, Brick?

BRICK. Yes, sir, I will try to.

[*The old man pours him a drink and solemnly passes it to him.*]

[*There is a silence as* BRICK *drinks.*]

Have you ever heard the word "mendacity"?

BIG DADDY. Sure. Mendacity is one of them five dollar words that cheap politicians throw back and forth at each other.

BRICK. You know what it means?

BIG DADDY. Don't it mean lying and liars?
BRICK. Yes, sir, lying and liars.
BIG DADDY. Has someone been lying to you?
CHILDREN [*chanting in chorus offstage*].
   We want Big Dad-dee!
   We want Big Dad-dee

[GOOPER *appears in the gallery door.*]
GOOPER. Big Daddy, the kiddies are shouting for you out there.
BIG DADDY [*fiercely*]. Keep out, Gooper!
GOOPER. 'Scuse *me!*
[BIG DADDY *slams the doors after* GOOPER.]
BIG DADDY. Who's been lying to you, has Margaret been lying to you, has your
   wife been lying to you about something, Brick?
BRICK. Not her. That wouldn't matter.
BIG DADDY. Then who's been lying to you, and what about?
BRICK. No one single person and no one lie. . . .
BIG DADDY. Then what, what then, for Christ's sake?
BRICK. The whole, the whole — thing. . . .
BIG DADDY. Why are you rubbing your head? You got a headache?
BRICK. No, I'm tryin' to —
BIG DADDY. — Concentrate, but you can't because your brain's all soaked with
   liquor, is that the trouble? Wet brain! [*He snatches the glass from* BRICK's
   hand.] What do you know about this mendacity thing? Hell! I could write a
   book on it! Don't you know that? I could write a book on it and still not cover
   the subject. Well, I could, I could write a goddam book on it and still not
   cover the subject anywhere near enough!! — Think of all the lies I got to put
   up with! — Pretenses! Ain't that mendacity? Having to pretend stuff you don't
   think or feel or have any idea of? Having for instance to act like I care for Big
   Mama! — I haven't been able to stand the sight, sound, or smell of that woman
   for forty years now! — even when I *laid* her! — regular as a piston. . . .
      Pretend to love that son of a bitch of a Gooper and his wife Mae and those
   five same screechers out there like parrots in a jungle? Jesus! Can't stand to
   look at 'em!
      Church! — it bores the bejesus out of me but I go! — I go an' sit there and
   listen to the fool preacher!
      Clubs! — Elks! Masons! Rotary! — *crap!*
[*A spasm of pain makes him clutch his belly. He sinks into a chair and his voice is
   softer and hoarser.*]
You I *do* like for some reason, did always have some kind of real feeling
   for — affection — respect — yes, always. . . .
      You and being a success as a planter is all I ever had any devotion to in my
   whole life! — and that's the truth. . . .
      I don't know why, but it is!
      I've lived with mendacity! — Why can't *you* live with it? Hell, you *got* to
   live with it, there's nothing *else* to *live* with except mendacity, is there?
BRICK. Yes, sir. Yes, sir there is something else that you can live with!
BIG DADDY. What?
BRICK [*lifting his glass*]. This! — Liquor. . . .
BIG DADDY. That's not living, that's dodging away from life.

BRICK. I want to dodge away from it.

BIG DADDY. Then why don't you kill yourself, man?

BRICK. I like to drink. . . .

BIG DADDY. Oh, God, I can't talk to you. . . .

BRICK. I'm sorry, Big Daddy.

BIG DADDY. Not as sorry as I am. I'll tell you something. A little while back when I thought my number was up—

[*This speech should have torrential pace and fury.*]

    —before I found out it was just this—spastic—colon. I thought about you. Should I or should I not, if the jig was up, give you this place when I go—since I hate Gooper an' Mae an' know that they hate me, and since all five same monkeys are little Maes an' Goopers.—And I thought, No!—Then I thought, Yes!—I couldn't make up my mind. I hate Gooper and his five same monkeys and that bitch Mae! Why should I turn over twenty-eight thousand acres of the richest land this side of the valley Nile to not my kind?—But why in hell, on the other hand, Brick—should I subsidize a goddam fool on the bottle?—Liked or not liked, well, maybe even—*loved!* —Why should I do that?—Subsidize worthless behavior? Rot? Corruption?

BRICK [*smiling*]. I understand.

BIG DADDY. Well, if you do, you're smarter than I am. God damn it, because I don't understand. And this I will tell you frankly. I didn't make up my mind at all on that question and still to this day I ain't made out no will!—Well, now I don't *have* to. The pressure is gone. I can just wait and see if you pull yourself together or if you don't.

BRICK. That's right, Big Daddy.

BIG DADDY. You sound like you thought I was kidding.

BRICK [*rising*]. No, sir, I know you're not kidding.

BIG DADDY. But you don't care—?

BRICK [*hobbling toward the gallery door*]. No, sir, I don't care. . . .

[*He stands in the gallery doorway as the night sky turns pink and green and gold with successive flashes of light.*]

BIG DADDY. *WAIT!*—Brick. . . .

[*His voice drops. Suddenly there is something shy, tender, in his restraining gesture.*]

    Don't let's—leave it like this, like them other talks we've had, we've always—talked around things, we've—just talked around things for some fuckin' reason. I don't know what, it's always like something was left not spoken, something avoided because neither of us was honest enough with the—other. . . .

BRICK. I never lied to you, Big Daddy.

BIG DADDY. Did I ever to *you?*

BRICK. No, sir. . . .

BIG DADDY. Then there is at least two people that never lied to each other.

BRICK. But we've never *talked* to each other.

BIG DADDY. We can *now.*

BRICK. Big Daddy, there don't seem to be anything much to say.

BIG DADDY. You say that you drink to kill your disgust with lying.

BRICK. You said to give you a reason.

BIG DADDY. Is liquor the only thing that'll kill this disgust?

BRICK. Now. Yes.

BIG DADDY. But not once, huh?

BRICK. Not when I was still young an' believing. A drinking man's someone who wants to forget he isn't still young an' believing.

BIG DADDY. Believing what?

BRICK. Believing. . . .

BIG DADDY. Believing *what?*

BRICK [*stubbornly evasive*]. Believing. . . .

BIG DADDY. I don't know what the hell you mean by believing and I don't think you know what you mean by believing, but if you still got sports in your blood, go back to sports announcing and—

BRICK. Sit in a glass box watching games I can't play? Describing what I can't do while players do it? Sweating out their disgust and confusion in contests I'm not fit for? Drinkin' a coke, half bourbon, so I can stand it? That's no goddam good any more, no help—time just outran me, Big Daddy—got there first. . . .

BIG DADDY. I think you're passing the buck.

BRICK. You know many drinkin' men?

BIG DADDY [*with a slight, charming smile*]. I have known a fair number of that species.

BRICK. Could any of them tell you why he drank?

BIG DADDY. Yep, you're passin' the buck to things like time and disgust with "mendacity" and—crap!—if you got to use that kind of language about a thing, it's ninety-proof bull, and I'm not buying any.

BRICK. I had to give you a reason to get a drink!

BIG DADDY. You started drinkin' when your friend Skipper died.

[*Silence for five beats. Then* BRICK *makes a startled movement, reaching for his crutch.*]

BRICK. What are you suggesting?

BIG DADDY. I'm suggesting nothing.

[*The shuffle and clop of* BRICK'S *rapid hobble away from his father's steady, grave attention.*]

—But Gooper an' Mae suggested that there was something not right exactly in your—

BRICK [*stopping short downstage as if backed to a wall*]. "Not right?"

BIG DADDY. Not, well, exactly *normal* in your friendship with—

BRICK. They suggested that, too? I thought that was Maggie's suggestion.

[BRICK'S *detachment is at last broken through. His heart is accelerated; his forehead sweat-beaded; his breath becomes more rapid and his voice hoarse. The thing they're discussing, timidly and painfully on the side of* BIG DADDY, *fiercely, violently on* BRICK'S *side, is the inadmissible thing that* SKIPPER *died to disavow between them. The fact that if it existed it had to be disavowed to "keep face" in the world they lived in, may be at the heart of the "mendacity" that* BRICK *drinks to kill his disgust with. It may be the root of his collapse. Or maybe it is only a single manifestation of it, not even the most important. The bird that I hope to catch in the net of this play is not the solution of one man's psychological problem. I'm trying to catch the true quality of experience in a group of people, that cloudy, flickering, evanescent—fiercely charged!—interplay of live human beings in the thundercloud of a common crisis. Some mystery should be left in the revelation of characters in a play, just as a great deal of mystery is always left in the revelation of character in life, even in one's own character to himself. This does not absolve the playwright of his duty to observe and probe as clearly and deeply as he*] *legitimately can: but it should steer him away from "pat" conclusions, facile definitions which make a play just a play, not a snare for the truth of human experience.*]

[*The following scene should be played with great concentration, with most of the power leashed but palpable in what is left unspoken.*]

Who else's suggestion is it, is it *yours*? How many others thought that Skipper and I were—

BIG DADDY [*gently*]. Now, hold on, hold on a minute, son.—I knocked around in my time.

BRICK. What's that got to do with—

BIG DADDY. I said "Hold on!"—I bummed, I bummed this country till I was—

BRICK. Whose suggestion, who else's suggestion is it?

BIG DADDY. Slept in hobo jungles and railroad Y's and flophouses in all cities before I—

BRICK. Oh, *you* think so, too, you call me your son and a queer. Oh! Maybe that's why you put Maggie and me in this room that was Jack Straw's and Peter Ochello's, in which that pair of old sisters slept in a double bed where both of 'em died!

BIG DADDY. *Now just don't go throwing rocks at—*

[*Suddenly* REVEREND TOOKER *appears in the gallery doors, his head slightly, playfully, fatuously cocked, with a practised clergyman's smile, sincere as a bird call blown on a hunter's whistle, the living embodiment of the pious, conventional lie.*]

[BIG DADDY *gasps a little at this perfectly timed, but incongruous, apparition.*]
—What're you lookin' for, Preacher?

REVEREND TOOKER. The gentleman's lavatory, ha ha!—heh, heh . . .

BIG DADDY [*with strained courtesy*].—Go back out and walk down to the other end of the gallery, Reverend Tooker, and use the bathroom connected with my bedroom, and if you can't find it, ask them where it is!

REVEREND TOOKER. Ah, thanks. [*He goes out with a deprecatory chuckle.*]

BIG DADDY. It's hard to talk in this place. . . .

BRICK. Son of a—!

BIG DADDY [*leaving a lot unspoken*].—I seen all things and understood a lot of them, till 1910. Christ, the year that—I had worn my shoes through, hocked my—I hopped off a yellow dog freight car half a mile down the road, slept in a wagon of cotton outside the gin—Jack Straw an' Peter Ochello took me in. Hired me to manage this place which grew into this one.—When Jack Straw died—why, old Peter Ochello quit eatin' like a dog does when its master's dead, and died, too!

BRICK. Christ!

BIG DADDY. I'm just saying I understand such—

BRICK [*violently*]. Skipper is dead. I have not quit eating!

BIG DADDY. No, but you started drinking.

[BRICK *wheels on his crutch and hurls his glass across the room shouting.*]

BRICK. YOU THINK SO, TOO?

[*Footsteps run on the gallery. There are women's calls.*]

[BIG DADDY *goes toward the door.*]

[BRICK *is transformed, as if a quiet mountain blew suddenly up in volcanic flame.*]

BRICK. You think so, too? You think so, too? You think me an' Skipper did, did, did!—*sodomy!*—together?

BIG DADDY. Hold—!

BRICK. That what you—

BIG DADDY. —ON—a minute!

BRICK. You think we did dirty things between us, Skipper an'—

BIG DADDY. Why are you shouting like that? Why are you—

BRICK. —Me, is that what you think of Skipper, is that—

BIG DADDY. —so excited? I don't think nothing. I don't know nothing. I'm simply telling you what—

BRICK. You think that Skipper and me were a pair of dirty old men?

BIG DADDY. Now that's—

BRICK. Straw? Ochello? A couple of—

BIG DADDY. Now just—

BRICK. —fucking sissies? Queers? Is that what you—

BIG DADDY. Shhh.

BRICK. —think?

[*He loses his balance and pitches to his knees without noticing the pain. He grabs the bed and drags himself up.*]

BIG DADDY. Jesus!—Whew. . . . Grab my hand!

BRICK. Naw, I don't want your hand. . . .

BIG DADDY. Well, I want yours. Git up!

[*He draws him up, keeps an arm about him with concern and affection.*]

You broken out in a sweat! You're panting like you'd run a race with—

BRICK [*freeing himself from his father's hold*]. Big Daddy, you shock me, Big Daddy, you, you—*shock* me! Talkin' so—[*He turns away from his father.*]—casually!—about a—thing like that. . . .

—Don't you know how people *feel* about things like that? How, how *disgusted* they are by things like that? Why, at Ole Miss when it was discovered a pledge to our fraternity, Skipper's and mine, did a, *attempted* to do a, unnatural thing with—

We not only dropped him like a hot rock!—We told him to git off the campus, and he did, he got!—All the way to—[*He halts, breathless.*]

BIG DADDY. —Where?

BRICK. —North Africa, last I heard!

BIG DADDY. Well, I have come back from further away than that, I have just now returned from the other side of the moon, death's country, son, and I'm not easy to shock by anything here. [*He comes downstage and faces out.*] Always, anyhow, lived with too much space around me to be infected by ideas of other people. One thing you can grow on a big place more important than cotton!—is *tolerance!*—I grown it. [*He returns toward* BRICK.]

BRICK. Why can't exceptional friendship, *real, real, deep, deep friendship!* between two men be respected as something clean and decent without being thought of as—

BIG DADDY. It can, it is, for God's sake.

BRICK. —Fairies . . .

[*In his utterance of this word, we gauge the wide and profound reach of the conventional mores he got from the world that crowned him with early laurel.*]

BIG DADDY. I told Mae an' Gooper—

BRICK. Frig Mae and Gooper, frig all dirty lies and liars!—Skipper and me had a clean, true thing between us! — had a clean friendship, practically all our lives, till Maggie got the idea you're talking about. Normal? No! — it was too rare to be normal, any true thing between two people is too rare to be normal. Oh, once in a while he put his hand on my shoulder or I'd put mine on his, oh, maybe even, when we were touring the country in pro-football an' shared hotel-rooms we'd reach across the space between the two beds and shake hands to say goodnight, yeah, one or two times we —

BIG DADDY. Brick, nobody thinks that that's not normal!

BRICK. Well, they're mistaken, it was! It was a pure an' true thing an' that's not normal.

MAE [*off stage*]. Big Daddy, they're startin' the fireworks.

[*They both stare straight at each other for a long moment. The tension breaks and both turn away as if tired.*]

BIG DADDY. Yeah, it's — hard t' — talk. . . .

BRICK. All right, then, let's — let it go. . . .

BIG DADDY. Why did Skipper crack up? Why have you?

[BRICK *looks back at his father again. He has already decided, without knowing that he has made this decision, that he is going to tell his father that he is dying of cancer. Only this could even the score between them: one inadmissible thing in return for another.*]

BRICK [*ominously*]. All right. You're asking for it, Big Daddy. We're finally going to have that real true talk you wanted. It's too late to stop it, now, we got to carry it through and cover every subject.

[*He hobbles back to the liquor cabinet.*]

Uh-huh.

[*He opens the ice bucket and picks up the silver tongs with slow admiration of their frosty brightness.*]

Maggie declares that Skipper and I went into pro-football after we left "Ole Miss" because we were scared to grow up. . . .

[*He moves downstage with the shuffle and clop of a cripple on a crutch. As* MAR-GARET *did when her speech became "recitative," he looks out into the house, commanding its attention by his direct, concentrated gaze — a broken, "tragically elegant" figure telling simply as much as he knows of "the Truth."*]

— Wanted to — keep on tossing — those long, long! — high, high! — passes that — couldn't be intercepted except by time, the aerial attack that made us famous! And so we did, we did, we kept it up for one season, that aerial attack, we held it high! — Yeah, but —

— that summer, Maggie, she laid the law down to me, said, Now or never, and so I married Maggie. . . .

BIG DADDY. How was Maggie in bed?

BRICK [*wryly*]. Great! the greatest!

[BIG DADDY *nods as if he thought so.*]

She went on the road that fall with the Dixie Stars. Oh, she made a great show of being the world's best sport. She wore a — wore a — tall bearskin cap! A shako, they call it, a dyed moleskin coat, a moleskin coat dyed red! — Cut up crazy! Rented hotel ballrooms for victory celebrations, wouldn't cancel them when it — turned out — defeat. . . .

MAGGIE THE CAT! Ha Ha!

[BIG DADDY *nods.*]

— But Skipper, he had some fever which came back on him which doctors couldn't explain and I got that injury — turned out to be just a shadow on the X-ray plate — and a touch of bursitis. . . .

I lay in a hospital bed, watched our games on TV, saw Maggie on the bench next to Skipper when he was hauled out of a game for stumbles, fumbles! — Burned me up the way she hung on his arm! — Y'know, I think that Maggie had always felt sort of left out because she and me never got any closer together than two people just get in bed, which is not much closer than two cats on a — fence humping. . . .

So! She took this time to work on poor dumb Skipper. He was a less than average student at Ole Miss, you know that, don't you?! — Poured in his mind the dirty, false idea that what we were, him and me, was a frustrated case of that ole pair of sisters that lived in this room, Jack Straw and Peter Ochello! — He, poor Skipper, went to bed with Maggie to prove it wasn't true, and when it didn't work out, he thought it *was* true! — Skipper broke in two like a rotten stick — nobody ever turned so fast to a lush — or died of it so quick. . . .

— Now are you satisfied?

[BIG DADDY *has listened to this story, dividing the grain from the chaff. Now he looks at his son.*]

BIG DADDY. Are *you* satisfied?

BRICK. With what?

BIG DADDY. That half-ass story!

BRICK. What's half-ass about it?

BIG DADDY. Something's left out of that story. What did you leave out?

[*The phone has started ringing in the hall.*]

GOOPER [*off stage*]. Hello.

[*As if it reminded him of something* BRICK *glances suddenly toward the sound and says.*]

BRICK. Yes! — I left out a long-distance call which I had from Skipper —

GOOPER. Speaking, go ahead.

BRICK. — In which he made a drunken confession to me and on which I hung up!

GOOPER. No.

BRICK. Last time we spoke to each other in our lives. . . .

GOOPER. No, sir.

BIG DADDY. You musta said something to him before you hung up.

BRICK. What could I say to him?

BIG DADDY. Anything. Something.

BRICK. Nothing.

BIG DADDY. Just hung up?

BRICK. Just hung up.

BIG DADDY. Uh-huh. Anyhow now! — we have tracked down the lie with which you're disgusted and which you are drinking to kill your disgust with, Brick. You have been passing the buck. This disgust with mendacity is disgust with yourself.

You! — dug the grave of your friend and kicked him in it! — before you'd face truth with him!

BRICK. *His* truth, not *mine!*

BIG DADDY. His truth, okay! But you wouldn't face it with him!

BRICK. Who *can* face truth? Can *you?*

BIG DADDY. Now don't start passin' the rotten buck again, boy!

BRICK. *How about these birthday congratulations, these many, many happy returns of the day, when ev'rybody knows there won't be any except you!*

[GOOPER, *who has answered the hall phone, lets out a high, shrill laugh; the voice becomes audible saying: "No, no, you got it all wrong! Upside down. Are you crazy?"*]

[BRICK *suddenly catches his breath as he realizes that he has made a shocking disclosure. He hobbles a few paces, then freezes, and without looking at his father's shocked face, says.*]

Let's, let's — go out, now, and — watch the fireworks. Come on, Big Daddy.

[BIG DADDY *moves suddenly forward and grabs hold of the boy's crutch like it was a weapon for which they were fighting for possession.*]

BIG DADDY. Oh, no, no! No one's going out! What did you start to say?

BRICK. I don't remember.

BIG DADDY. "Many happy returns when they know there won't be any"?

BRICK. Aw, hell, Big Daddy, forget it. Come on out on the gallery and look at the fireworks they're shooting off for your birthday. . . .

BIG DADDY. First you finish that remark you were makin' before you cut off. "Many happy returns when they know there won't be any"? — Ain't that what you just said?

BRICK. Look, now. I can get around without that crutch if I have to but it would be a lot easier on the furniture an' glassware if I didn' have to go swinging along like Tarzan of th' —

BIG DADDY. FINISH! WHAT YOU WAS SAYIN'!

[*An eerie green glow shows in sky behind him.*]

BRICK [*sucking the ice in his glass, speech becoming thick*]. Leave th' place to Gooper and Mae an' their five little same little monkeys. All I want is —

BIG DADDY. "LEAVE TH' PLACE," did you say?

BRICK [*vaguely*]. All twenty-eight thousand acres of the richest land this side of the valley Nile.

BIG DADDY. Who said I was "leaving the place" to Gooper or anybody? This is my sixty-fifth birthday! I got fifteen years or twenty years left in me! I'll outlive *you!* I'll bury you an' have to pay for your coffin!

BRICK. Sure. Many happy returns. Now let's go watch the fireworks, come on, let's —

BIG DADDY. Lying, have they been lying? About the report from th' — clinic? Did they, did they — find something — *Cancer.* Maybe?

BRICK. Mendacity is a system that we live in. Liquor is one way out an' death's the other. . . .

[*He takes the crutch from* BIG DADDY's *loose grip and swings out on the gallery leaving the doors open.*]

[*A song, "Pick a Bale of Cotton," is heard.*]

MAE [*appearing in door*]. Oh, Big Daddy, the field hands are singin' fo' you!

BRICK. I'm sorry, Big Daddy. My head don't work any more and it's hard for me to understand how anybody could care if he lived or died or was dying or cared about anything but whether or not there was liquor left in the bottle and so I said what I said without thinking. In some ways I'm no better than the others, in some ways worse because I'm less alive. Maybe it's being alive that makes them lie, and being almost *not* alive makes me sort of accidentally truthful — I don't know but — anyway — we've been friends. . . .

— And being friends is telling each other the truth. . . .

[*There is a pause.*]

You told *me!* I told *you!*
BIG DADDY [*slowly and passionately*]. CHRIST—DAMN—
GOOPER [*off stage*]. Let her go!
[*Fireworks off stage right.*]
BIG DADDY. —ALL—LYING SONS OF—LYING BITCHES!
[*He straightens at last and crosses to the inside door. At the door he turns and looks back as if he had some desperate question he couldn't put into words. Then he nods reflectively and says in a hoarse voice.*]
Yes, all liars, all liars, all lying dying liars!
> [*This is said slowly, slowly, with a fierce revulsion. He goes on out.*]

—Lying! Dying! Liars!
[BRICK *remains motionless as the lights dim out and the curtain falls.*]

ACT III

> [*There is no lapse of time.* BIG DADDY *is seen leaving as at the end of ACT II.*]

BIG DADDY. ALL LYIN'—DYIN'!—LIARS!—LIARS!—LIARS!

[MARGARET *enters.*]
MARGARET. Brick, what in the name of God was goin' on in this room?

[DIXIE *and* TRIXIE *enter through the doors and circle around* MARGARET *shouting.* MAE *enters from the lower gallery window.*]
MAE. Dixie, Trixie, you quit that!

[GOOPER *enters through the doors.*]
Gooper, will y' please get these kiddies to bed right now!
GOOPER. Mae, you seen Big Mama?
MAE. Not yet.

[GOOPER *and kids exit through the doors.* REVEREND TOOKER *enters through the windows.*]
REVEREND TOOKER. Those kiddies are so full of vitality. I think I'll have to be starting back to town.
MAE. Not yet, Preacher. You know we regard you as a member of this family, one of our closest an' dearest, so you just got t' be with us when Doc Baugh gives Big Mama th' actual truth about th' report from the clinic.
MARGARET. Where do you think you're going?
BRICK. Out for some air.
MARGARET. Why'd Big Daddy shout "Liars"?
MAE. Has Big Daddy gone to bed, Brick?
GOOPER [*entering*]. Now where is that old lady?
REVEREND TOOKER. I'll look for her.
> [*He exits to the gallery.*]

MAE. Cain'tcha find her, Gooper?
GOOPER. She's avoidin' this talk.
MAE. I think she senses somethin'.

MARGARET [*going out to the gallery to* BRICK]. Brick, they're goin' to tell Big Mama the truth about Big Daddy and she's goin' to need you.

DOCTOR BAUGH. This is going to be painful.

MAE. Painful things cain't always be avoided.

REVEREND TOOKER. I see Big Mama.

GOOPER. Hey, Big Mama, come here.

MAE. Hush, Gooper, don't holler.

BIG MAMA [*entering*]. Too much smell of burnt fireworks makes me feel a little bit sick at my stomach. — Where is Big Daddy?

MAE. That's what I want to know, where has Big Daddy gone?

BIG MAMA. He must have turned in, I reckon he went to baid. . . .

GOOPER. Well, then, now we can talk.

BIG MAMA. What *is* this talk, *what* talk?

[MARGARET *appears on the gallery, talking to* DOCTOR BAUGH.]

MARGARET [*musically*]. My family freed their slaves ten years before abolition. My great-great-grandfather gave his slaves their freedom five years before the War between the States started!

MAE. Oh, for God's sake! Maggie's climbed back up in her family tree!

MARGARET [*sweetly*]. What, Mae?

[*The pace must be very quick: great Southern animation.*]

BIG MAMA [*addressing them all*]. I think Big Daddy was just worn out. He loves his family, he loves to have them around him, but it's a strain on his nerves. He wasn't himself tonight. Big Daddy wasn't himself, I could tell he was all worked up.

REVEREND TOOKER. I think he's remarkable.

BIG MAMA. Yaisss! Just remarkable. Did you all notice the food he ate at that table? Did you all notice the supper he put away? Why he ate like a hawss!

GOOPER. I hope he doesn't regret it.

BIG MAMA. What? Why that man — ate a huge piece of cawn bread with molasses on it! Helped himself twice to hoppin' John.

MARGARET. Big Daddy loves hoppin' John. — We had a real country dinner.

BIG MAMA [*overlapping* MARGARET]. Yaiss, he simply adores it! an' candied yams? Son? That man put away enough food at that table to stuff a *field* hand!

GOOPER [*with grim relish*]. I hope he don't have to pay for it later on. . . .

BIG MAMA [*fiercely*]. What's *that*, Gooper?

MAE. Gooper says he hopes Big Daddy doesn't suffer tonight.

BIG MAMA. Oh, shoot, Gooper says, Gooper says! Why should Big Daddy suffer for satisfying a normal appetite? There's nothin' wrong with that man but nerves, he's sound as a dollar! And now he knows he is an' that's why he ate such a supper. He had a big load off his mind, knowin' he wasn't doomed t' — what he thought he was doomed to. . . .

MARGARET [*sadly and sweetly*]. Bless his old sweet soul. . . .

BIG MAMA [*vaguely*]. Yais, bless his heart, where's Brick?

MAE. Outside.

GOOPER. — Drinkin'. . . .

BIG MAMA. I know he's drinkin'. Cain't I see he's drinkin' without you continually tellin' me that boy's drinkin'?

MARGARET. Good for you, Big Mama! [*She applauds.*]

BIG MAMA. Other people *drink* and *have* drunk an' will *drink*, as long as they make that stuff an' put it in bottles.

MARGARET. That's the truth. I never trusted a man that didn't drink.

BIG MAMA. *Brick? Brick!*

MARGARET. He's still on the gall'ry. I'll go bring him in so we can talk.

BIG MAMA [*worriedly*]. I don't know what this mysterious family conference is about.

[*Awkward silence.* BIG MAMA *looks from face to face, then belches slightly and mutters, "Excuse me . . . " She opens an ornamental fan suspended about her throat. A black lace fan to go with her black lace gown, and fans her wilting corsage, sniffing nervously and looking from face to face in the uncomfortable silence as* MARGARET *calls "Brick?" and* BRICK *sings to the moon on the gallery.*]

MARGARET. Brick, they're gonna tell Big Mama the truth an' she's gonna need you.

BIG MAMA. I don't know what's wrong here, you all have such long faces! Open that door on the hall and let some air circulate through here, will you please, Gooper?

MAE. I think we'd better leave that door closed, Big Mama, till after the talk.

MARGARET. Brick!

BIG MAMA. Reveren' Tooker, will *you* please open that door?

REVEREND TOOKER. I sure will, Big Mama.

MAE. I just didn't think we ought t' take any chance of Big Daddy hearin' a word of this discussion.

BIG MAMA. *I swan!* Nothing's going to be said in Big Daddy's house that he cain't hear if he want to!

GOOPER. Well, Big Mama, it's —

[MAE *gives him a quick, hard poke to shut him up. He glares at her fiercely as she circles before him like a burlesque ballerina, raising her skinny bare arms over her head, jangling her bracelets, exclaiming.*]

MAE. *A breeze! A breeze!*

REVEREND TOOKER. I think this house is the coolest house in the Delta. — Did you all know that Halsey Bank's widow put air-conditioning units in the church and rectory at Friar's Point in memory of Halsey?

[*General conversation has resumed; everybody is chatting so that the stage sounds like a bird cage.*]

GOOPER. Too bad nobody cools your church off for you. I bet you sweat in that pulpit these hot Sundays, Reverend Tooker.

REVEREND TOOKER. Yes, my vestments are drenched. Last Sunday the gold in my chasuble faded into the purple.

GOOPER. Reveren', you musta been preachin' hell's fire last Sunday.

MAE [*at the same time to* DOCTOR BAUGH]. You reckon those vitamin B12 injections are what they're cracked up t' be, Doc Baugh?

DOCTOR BAUGH. Well if you want to be stuck with something I guess they're as good to be stuck with as anything else.

BIG MAMA [*at the gallery door*]. *Maggie, Maggie, aren't you comin' with Brick?*

MAE [*suddenly and loudly, creating a silence*]. I have a strange feeling, I have a peculiar feeling!

BIG MAMA [*turning from the gallery*]. What feeling?

MAE. That Brick said somethin' he shouldn't of said t' Big Daddy.

BIG MAMA. Now what on earth could Brick of said t' Big Daddy that he shouldn't say?

GOOPER. Big Mama, there's somethin' —

MAE. NOW, WAIT!

[*She rushes up to* BIG MAMA *and gives her a quick hug and kiss.* BIG MAMA *pushes her impatiently off.*]

DOCTOR BAUGH. In my day they had what they call the Keeley cure for heavy drinkers.

BIG MAMA. Shoot!

DOCTOR BAUGH. But now I understand they just take some kind of tablets.

GOOPER. They call them "Annie Bust" tablets.

BIG MAMA. *Brick* don't need to take *nothin'*.

[BRICK *and* MARGARET *appear in gallery doors.* BIG MAMA *unaware of his presence behind her.*]

That boy is just broken up over Skipper's death. You know how poor Skipper died. They gave him a big, big dose of that sodium amytal stuff at his home and then they called the ambulance and give him another big, big dose of it at the hospital and that and all of the alcohol in his system fo' months an' months just proved too much for his heart. . . . I'm scared of needles! I'm more scared of a needle than the knife. . . . I think more people have been needled out of this world than — [*She stops short and wheels about.*]

Oh — here's Brick! My precious baby —

[*She turns upon* BRICK *with short, fat arms extended, at the same time uttering a loud, short sob, which is both comic and touching.* BRICK *smiles and bows slightly, making a burlesque gesture of gallantry for* MARGARET *to pass before him into the room. Then he hobbles on his crutch directly to the liquor cabinet and there is absolute silence, with everybody looking at* BRICK *as everybody has always looked at* BRICK *when he spoke or moved or appeared. One by one he drops ice cubes in his glass, then suddenly, but not quickly looks back over his shoulder with a wry, charming smile, and says.*]

BRICK. I'm sorry! Anyone else?

BIG MAMA [*sadly*]. No, son, I *wish* you wouldn't!

BRICK. I wish I didn't have to, Big Mama, but I'm still waiting for that click in my head which makes it all smooth out!

BIG MAMA. Ow, Brick, you — BREAK MY HEART!

MARGARET [*at same time*]. Brick, go sit with Big Mama!

BIG MAMA. I just cain't staiiiiiiii-nnnnnnnd-it . . . [*She sobs.*]

MAE. Now that we're all assembled —

GOOPER. We kin talk. . . .

BIG MAMA. Breaks my heart. . . .

MARGARET. Sit with Big Mama, Brick, and hold her hand.

[BIG MAMA *sniffs very loudly three times, almost like three drumbeats in the pocket of silence.*]

BRICK. You do that, Maggie. I'm a restless cripple. I got to stay on my crutch.

[BRICK *hobbles to the gallery door; leans there as if waiting.*]

[MAE *sits beside* BIG MAMA, *while* GOOPER *moves in front and sits on the end of the couch, facing her.* REVEREND TOOKER *moves nervously into the space between them; on the other side,* DOCTOR BAUGH *stands looking at nothing in particular and lights a cigar.* MARGARET *turns away.*]

BIG MAMA. Why're you all *surroundin'* me — like this? Why're you all starin' at me like this an' makin' signs at each other?

[REVEREND TOOKER *steps back startled.*]

MAE. Calm yourself, Big Mama.

BIG MAMA. Calm you'self, *you'self*, Sister Woman. How could I calm myself
   with everyone starin' at me as if big drops of blood had broken out on m'face?
   What's this all about, annh! What?

[GOOPER *coughs and takes a center position.*]

GOOPER. Now, Doc Baugh.

MAE. Doc Baugh?

GOOPER. Big Mama wants to know the complete truth about the report we got
   from the Ochsner Clinic.

MAE. [*eagerly*].—on Big Daddy's condition!

GOOPER. Yais, on Big Daddy's condition, we got to face it.

DOCTOR BAUGH. Well . . .

BIG MAMA [*terrified, rising*]. Is there? Something? Something that I? Don't
   —know?

[*In these few words, this startled, very soft question,* BIG MAMA *reviews the history
   of her forty-five years with* BIG DADDY, *her great almost embarrassingly true-
   hearted and simple-minded devotion to* BIG DADDY, *who must have had something* BRICK *has, who made himself loved so much by the "simple expedient" of not
   loving enough to disturb his charming detachment, also once coupled, like* BRICK,
   with virile beauty.]

[BIG MAMA *has a dignity at this moment; she almost stops being fat.*]

DOCTOR BAUGH [*after a pause, uncomfortably*]. Yes?—Well—

BIG MAMA. I!!!—want to—knowwwwww . . .

[*Immediately she thrusts her fist to her mouth as if to deny that statement. Then for
   some curious reason, she snatches the withered corsage from her breast and hurls it
   on the floor and steps on it with her short, fat feet.*]
   Somebody must be lyin'!—I want to know!

MAE. Sit down, Big Mama, sit down on this sofa.

MARGARET. Brick, go sit with Big Mama.

BIG MAMA. *What is it, what is it?*

DOCTOR BAUGH. I never have seen a more thorough examination than Big
   Daddy Pollitt was given in all my experience with the Ochsner Clinic.

GOOPER. It's one of the best in the country.

MAE. It's THE best in the country—bar *none!*

[*For some reason she gives* GOOPER *a violent poke as she goes past him. He slaps at
   her hand without removing his eyes from his mother's face.*]

DOCTOR BAUGH. Of course they were ninety-nine and nine-tenths per cent
   sure before they even started.

BIG MAMA. Sure of what, sure of what, sure of—*what?—what?*

[*She catches her breath in a startled sob.* MAE *kisses her quickly. She thrusts* MAE
   fiercely away from her, staring at the DOCTOR.]

MAE. Mommy, be a brave girl!

BRICK [*in the doorway, softly*]. "By the light, by the light, Of the sil-ve-ry
   mo-oo-n . . ."

GOOPER. Shut up!—Brick.

BRICK. Sorry . . . [*He wanders out on the gallery.*]

DOCTOR BAUGH. But, now, you see, Big Mama, they cut a piece off this
   growth, a specimen of the tissue and—

BIG MAMA. Growth? You told Big Daddy—

DOCTOR BAUGH. Now wait.

BIG MAMA [*fiercely*]. You told me and Big Daddy there wasn't a thing wrong with him but—

MAE. Big Mama, they always—

GOOPER. Let Doc Baugh talk, will yuh?

BIG MAMA. —little spastic condition of—[*Her breath gives out in a sob.*]

DOCTOR BAUGH. Yes, that's what we told Big Daddy. But we had this bit of tissue run through the laboratory and I'm sorry to say the test was positive on it. It's—well—malignant. . . .

[*Pause.*]

BIG MAMA. Cancer?! Cancer?!

[DOCTOR BAUGH *nods gravely.* BIG MAMA *gives a long gasping cry.*]

MAE AND GOOPER. Now, now, now. Big Mama, you had to know. . . .

BIG MAMA. WHY DIDN'T THEY CUT IT OUT OF HIM? HANH? HANH?

DOCTOR BAUGH. Involved too much, Big Mama, too many organs affected.

MAE. Big Mama, the liver's affected and so's the kidneys, both! It's gone way past what they call a—

GOOPER. A surgical risk.

MAE. —Uh-huh . . .

[BIG MAMA *draws a breath like a dying gasp.*]

REVEREND TOOKER. Tch, tch, tch, tch, tch!

DOCTOR BAUGH. Yes, it's gone past the knife.

MAE. *That's why he's turned yellow, Mommy!*

BIG MAMA. *Git away from me, git away from me, Mae!* [*She rises abruptly.*] I want Brick! Where's Brick? Where is my only son?

MAE. Mama! Did she say "*only* son"?

GOOPER. What does that make *me*?

MAE. A sober responsible man with five precious children!—*Six!*

BIG MAMA. I want Brick to tell me! Brick! Brick!

MARGARET [*rising from her reflections in a corner*]. Brick was so upset he went back out.

BIG MAMA. *Brick!*

MARGARET. Mama, let *me* tell you!

BIG MAMA. No, no, leave me alone, you're not my blood!

GOOPER. *Mama, I'm your son!* Listen to *me!*

MAE. Gooper's your son, he's your first-born!

BIG MAMA. Gooper never liked Daddy.

MAE [*as if terribly shocked*]. *That's not TRUE!*

[*There is a pause. The minister coughs and rises.*]

REVEREND TOOKER [*to* MAE]. I think I'd better slip away at this point. [*Discreetly.*] Good night, good night, everybody, and God bless you all . . . on this place. . . .

[*He slips out.*]

[MAE *coughs and points at* BIG MAMA.]

DOCTOR BAUGH. Well, Big Mama . . . [*He sighs.*]

BIG MAMA. It's all a mistake, I know it's just a bad dream.

DOCTOR BAUGH. We're gonna keep Big Daddy as comfortable as we can.

BIG MAMA. Yes, it's just a bad dream, that's all it is, it's just an awful dream.

GOOPER. In my opinion Big Daddy is having some pain but won't admit that he has it.

BIG MAMA. Just a dream, a bad dream.

DOCTOR BAUGH. That's what lots of them do, they think if they don't admit they're having the pain they can sort of escape the fact of it.

GOOPER [*with relish*]. Yes, they get sly about it, they get real sly about it.

MAE. Gooper and I think —

GOOPER. Shut up, Mae! Big Mama, I think — Big Daddy ought to be started on morphine.

BIG MAMA. Nobody's going to give Big Daddy morphine.

DOCTOR BAUGH. Now, Big Mama, when that pain strikes it's going to strike mighty hard and Big Daddy's going to need the needle to bear it.

BIG MAMA. I tell you, nobody's going to give him morphine.

MAE. Big Mama, you don't want to see Big Daddy suffer, you know you —

[GOOPER, *standing beside her, gives her a savage poke.*]

DOCTOR BAUGH [*placing a package on the table*]. I'm leaving this stuff here, so if there's a sudden attack you all won't have to send out for it.

MAE. I know how to give a hypo.

BIG MAMA. Nobody's gonna give Big Daddy morphine.

GOOPER. Mae took a course in nursing during the war.

MARGARET. Somehow I don't think Big Daddy would want Mae to give him a hypo.

MAE. You think he'd want *you* to do it?

DOCTOR BAUGH. Well . . .

[DOCTOR BAUGH *rises.*]

GOOPER. Doctor Baugh is goin'.

DOCTOR BAUGH. Yes, I got to be goin'. Well, keep your chin up, Big Mama.

GOOPER [*with jocularity*]. She's gonna keep *both* chins up, aren't you, Big Mama?

[BIG MAMA *sobs.*]

Now stop that, Big Mama.

GOOPER [*at the door with* DOCTOR BAUGH]. Well, Doc, we sure do appreciate all you done. I'm telling you, we're surely obligated to you for —

[DOCTOR BAUGH *has gone out without a glance at him.*]

— I guess that doctor has got a lot on his mind but it wouldn't hurt him to act a little more human. . . .

[BIG MAMA *sobs.*]

Now be a brave girl Mommy.

BIG MAMA. It's not true, I know that it's just not true!

GOOPER. Mama, those tests are infallible!

BIG MAMA. Why are you so determined to see your father daid?

MAE. Big Mama!

MARGARET [*gently*]. I know what Big Mama means.

MAE [*fiercely*]. Oh, do you?

MARGARET [*quietly and very sadly*]. Yes, I think I do.

MAE. For a newcomer in the family you sure do show a lot of understanding.

MARGARET. Understanding is needed on this place.

MAE. I guess you must have needed a lot of it in your family, Maggie, with your father's liquor problem and now you've got Brick with his!

MARGARET. Brick does not have a liquor problem at all. Brick is devoted to Big Daddy. This thing is a terrible strain on him.

BIG MAMA. Brick is Big Daddy's boy, but he drinks too much and it worries me and Big Daddy, and, Margaret, you've got to cooperate with us, you've got to co-operate with Big Daddy and me in getting Brick straightened out. Because it will break Big Daddy's heart if Brick don't pull himself together and take hold of things.

MAE. Take hold of *what* things, Big Mama?

BIG MAMA. The place.

[*There is a quick violent look between* MAE *and* GOOPER.]

GOOPER. Big Mama, you've had a shock.

MAE. Yais, we've all had a shock, but . . .

GOOPER. Let's be realistic —

MAE. Big Daddy would never, would *never*, be foolish enough to —

GOOPER. — put this place in irresponsible hands!

BIG MAMA. Big Daddy ain't going to leave the place in anybody's hands; Big Daddy is *not* going to die. I want you to get that in your heads, all of you!

MAE. Mommy, Mommy, Big Mama, we're just as hopeful an' optimistic as you are about Big Daddy's prospects, we have faith in *prayer* — but nevertheless there are certain matters that have to be discussed an' dealt with, because otherwise —

GOOPER. Eventualities have to be considered and now's the time. . . . Mae, will you please get my brief case out of our room?

MAE. Yes, honey.

[She rises and goes out through the hall door.]

GOOPER [*standing over* BIG MAMA]. Now, Big Mom. What you said just now was not at all true and you know it. I've always loved Big Daddy in my own quiet way. I never made a show of it, and I know that Big Daddy has always been fond of me in a quiet way, too, and he never made a show of it neither.

[MAE *returns with* GOOPER'*s brief case.*]

MAE. Here's your brief case, Gooper, honey.

GOOPER [*handing the brief case back to her*]. Thank you. . . . Of cou'se, my relationship with Big Daddy is different from Brick's.

MAE. You're eight years older'n Brick an' always had t' carry a bigger load of th' responsibilities than Brick ever had t' carry. He never carried a thing in his life but a football or a highball.

GOOPER. Mae, will y' let me talk, please?

MAE. Yes, honey.

GOOPER. Now, a twenty-eight-thousand-acre plantation's a mighty big thing t' run.

MAE. Almost singlehanded.

[MARGARET has gone onto the gallery and can be heard calling softly to BRICK.]

BIG MAMA. You never had to run this place! What are you talking about? As if Big Daddy was dead and in his grave, you had to run it? Why, you just helped him out with a few business details and had your law practice at the same time in Memphis!

MAE. Oh, Mommy, Mommy, Big Mommy! Let's be fair!

MARGARET. Brick!

MAE. Why, Gooper has given himself body and soul to keeping this place up for
the past five years since Big Daddy's health started failing.

MARGARET. Brick!

MAE. Gooper won't say it, Gooper never thought of it as a duty, he just did it.
And what did Brick do? Brick kept living in his past glory at college! Still a
football player at twenty-seven!

MARGARET [*returning alone*]. Who are you talking about now? Brick? A football player? He isn't a football player and you know it. Brick is a sports
announcer on T.V. and one of the best-known ones in the country!

MAE. I'm talking about what he was.

MARGARET. Well, I wish you would just stop talking about my husband.

GOOPER. I've got a right to discuss my brother with others members of MY
OWN family, which don't include *you*. Why don't you go out there and drink
with Brick?

MARGARET. I've never seen such malice toward a brother.

GOOPER. How about his for me? Why, he can't stand to be in the same room
with me!

MARGARET. This is a deliberate campaign of vilification for the most disgusting
and sordid reason on earth, and I know what it is! It's *avarice, greed, greed!*

BIG MAMA. *Oh, I'll scream! I will scream in a moment unless this stops!*

[GOOPER *has stalked up to* MARGARET *with clenched fists at his sides as if he would
strike her.* MAE *distorts her face again into a hideous grimace behind* MAR-
GARET's *back.*]

BIG MAMA [*sobs*]. Margaret. Child. Come here. Sit next to Big Mama.

MARGARET. Precious Mommy. I'm sorry, I'm, sorry, I—!

[*She bends her long graceful neck to press her forehead to* BIG MAMA's *bulging
shoulder under its black chiffon.*]

MAE. How beautiful, how touching, this display of devotion! Do you know why
she's childless? She's childless because that big beautiful athlete husband of
hers won't go to bed with her!

GOOPER. You jest won't let me do this in a nice way, will yah? Aw right—I
don't give a goddam if Big Daddy likes me or don't like me or did or never did
or will or will never! I'm just appealing to a sense of common decency and fair
play. I'll tell you the truth. I've resented Big Daddy's partiality to Brick ever
since Brick was born, and the way I've been treated like I was just barely good
enough to spit on and sometimes not even good enough for that. Big Daddy is
dying of cancer, and it's spread all through him and it's attacked all his vital
organs including the kidneys and right now he is sinking in uremia, and you
all know what uremia is, it's poisoning of the whole system due to the failure
of the body to eliminate its poisons.

MARGARET [*to herself, downstage, hissingly*]. *Poisons, poisons! Venomous thoughts
and words! In hearts and minds!—That's poisons!*

GOOPER [*overlapping her*]. I am asking for a square deal, and by God, I expect to
get one. But if I don't get one, if there's any peculiar shenanigans going on
around here behind my back, well, I'm not a corporation lawyer for nothing, I
know how to protect my own interests.

[BRICK *enters from the gallery with a tranquil, blurred smile, carrying an
empty glass with him.*]

BRICK. Storm coming up.

GOOPER. Oh! A late arrival!

MAE. Behold the conquering hero comes!

GOOPER. The fabulous Brick Pollitt! Remember him? — Who could forget him!

MAE. He looks like he's been injured in a game!

GOOPER. Yep, I'm afraid you'll have to warm the bench at the Sugar Bowl this year, Brick!

[MAE *laughs shrilly.*]

Or was it the Rose Bowl that he made that famous run in? —

[*Thunder.*]

MAE. The punch bowl, honey. It was in the punch bowl, the cut-glass punch bowl!

GOOPER. Oh, that's right, I'm getting the bowls mixed up!

MARGARET. Why don't you stop venting your malice and envy on a sick boy?

BIG MAMA. *Now you two hush, I mean it, hush, all of you, hush!*

DAISY, SOOKEY. Storm! Storm comin'! Storm! Storm!

LACEY. Brightie, close them shutters.

GOOPER. Lacey, put the top up on my Cadillac, will yuh?

LACEY. Yes, suh, Mistah Pollitt!

GOOPER [*at the same time*]. Big Mama, you know it's necessary for me t' go back to Memphis in th' mornin' t' represent the Parker estate in a lawsuit.

[MAE *sits on the bed and arranges papers she has taken from the brief case.*]

BIG MAMA. Is it, Gooper?

MAE. Yaiss.

GOOPER. That's why I'm forced to — to bring up a problem that —

MAE. Somethin' that's too important t' be put off!

GOOPER. If Brick was sober, he ought to be in on this.

MARGARET. Brick is present; we're present.

GOOPER. Well, good. I will now give you this outline my partner, Tom Bullitt, an' me have drawn up — a sort of dummy — trusteeship.

MARGARET. Oh, that's it! You'll be in charge an' dole out remittances, will you?

GOOPER. This we did as soon as we got the report on Big Daddy from th' Ochsner Laboratories. We did this thing, I mean we drew up this dummy outline with the advice and assistance of the Chairman of the Boa'd of Directors of th' Southern Plantahs Bank and Trust Company in Memphis, C. C. Bellowes, a man who handles estates for all th' prominent fam'lies in West Tennessee and th' Delta.

BIG MAMA. Gooper?

GOOPER [*crouching in front of* BIG MAMA]. Now this is not — not final, or anything like it. This is just a preliminary outline. But it does provide a basis — a design — a — possible, feasible — *plan!*

MARGARET. Yes, I'll bet it's a plan.

[*Thunder.*]

MAE. It's a plan to protect the biggest estate in the Delta from irresponsibility an' —

BIG MAMA. Now you listen to me, all of you, you listen here? They's not goin' to be any more catty talk in my house! And Gooper, you put that away before I grab it out of your hand and tear it right up! I don't know what the hell's in it, and I don't want to know what the hell's in it. I'm talkin' in Big Daddy's language now; I'm his *wife* not his *widow*, I'm still his *wife!* And I'm talkin' to you in his language an' —

GOOPER. Big Mama, what I have here is—

MAE [*at the same time*]. Gooper explained that it's just a plan. . . .

BIG MAMA. I don't care what you got there. Just put it back where it came from, an' don't let me see it again, not even the outside of the envelope of it! Is that understood? Basis! Plan! Preliminary! Design! I say—what is it Big Daddy always says when he's disgusted?

BRICK [*from the bar*]. Big Daddy says "crap" when he's disgusted.

BIG MAMA [*rising*]. That's right!—CRAP! I say CRAP too, like Big Daddy! [*Thunder.*]

MAE. Coarse language doesn't seem called for in this—

GOOPER. Somethin' in me is *deeply outraged* by hearin' you talk like this.

BIG MAMA. *Nobody's goin' to take nothin'!*—till Big Daddy lets go of it— maybe, just possibly, not—not even then! No, not even then! [*Thunder.*]

MAE. Sookey, hurry up an' git that po'ch furniture covahed; want th' paint to come off?

GOOPER. Lacey, put mah car away!

LACEY. Caint, Mistah Pollitt, you got the keys!

GOOPER. Naw, you got 'em, man. Where th' keys to th' car, honey?

MAE. You got 'em in your pocket!

BRICK. "You can always hear me singin' this song, Show me the way to go home."

[*Thunder distantly.*]

BIG MAMA. Brick! Come here, Brick, I need you. Tonight Brick looks like he used to look when he was a little boy, just like he did when he played wild games and used to come home when I hollered myself hoarse for him, all sweaty and pink cheeked and sleepy, with his—red curls shining. . . .

[BRICK *draws aside as he does from all physical contact and continues the song in a whisper, opening the ice bucket and dropping in the ice cubes one by one as if he were mixing some important chemical formula.*]

[*Distant thunder.*]

Time goes by so fast. Nothin' can outrun it. Death commences too early— almost before you're half acquainted with life—you meet the other. . . . Oh, you know we just got to love each other an' stay together, all of us, just as close as we can, especially now that such a *black* thing has come and moved into this place without invitation.

[*Awkwardly embracing* BRICK, *she presses her head to his shoulder.*]

[*A dog howls off stage.*]

Oh, Brick, son of Big Daddy, Big Daddy does so love you. Y'know what would be his fondest dream come true? If before he passed on, if Big Daddy has to pass on. . . .

[*A dog howls.*]

. . . you give him a child of yours, a grandson as much like his son as his son is like Big Daddy . . .

MARGARET. I know that's Big Daddy's dream.

BIG MAMA. That's his dream.

MAE. Such a pity that Maggie and Brick can't oblige.

BIG DADDY [*off down stage right on the gallery*]. Looks like the wind was takin' liberties with this place.

SERVANT [*off stage*]. Yes, sir, Mr. Pollitt.

MARGARET [*crossing to the right door*]. Big Daddy's on the gall'ry.
[BIG MAMA *has turned toward the hall door at the sound of* BIG DADDY'*s voice on the gallery*.]
BIG MAMA. I can't stay here. He'll see somethin' in my eyes.

[BIG DADDY *enters the room from up stage right*.]
BIG DADDY. Can I come in?
[*He puts his cigar in an ash tray*.]
MARGARET. Did the storm wake you up, Big Daddy?
BIG DADDY. Which stawm are you talkin' about — th' one outside or th' hulla-balloo in here?
[GOOPER *squeezes past* BIG DADDY.]
GOOPER. 'Scuse me.
[MAE *tries to squeeze past* BIG DADDY *to join* GOOPER, *but* BIG DADDY *puts his arm firmly around her*.]
BIG DADDY. I heard some mighty loud talk. Sounded like somethin' important was bein' discussed. What was the powwow about?
MAE [*flustered*]. Why — nothin', Big Daddy. . . .
BIG DADDY [*crossing to extreme left center, taking* MAE *with him*]. What is that pregnant-lookin' envelope you're puttin' back in your brief case, Gooper?
GOOPER [*at the foot of the bed, caught, as he stuffs papers into envelope*]. That? Nothin', suh — nothin' much of anythin' at all . . .
BIG DADDY. Nothin'? It looks like a whole lot of nothin'!
[*He turns up stage to the group*.]
You all know th' story about th' young married couple —
GOOPER. Yes, sir!
BIG DADDY. Hello, Brick —
BRICK. Hello, Big Daddy.
[*The group is arranged in a semicircle above* BIG DADDY, MARGARET *at the extreme right, then* MAE *and* GOOPER, *then* BIG MAMA, *with* BRICK *at the left*.]
BIG DADDY. Young married couple took Junior out to th' zoo one Sunday, inspected all of God's creatures in their cages, with satisfaction.
GOOPER. Satisfaction.
BIG DADDY [*crossing to up stage center, facing front*]. This afternoon was a warm afternoon in spring an' that ole elephant had somethin' else on his mind which was bigger'n peanuts. You know this story, Brick?
[GOOPER *nods*.]
BRICK. No, sir, I don't know it.
BIG DADDY. Y'see, in th' cage adjoinin' they was a young female elephant in heat!
BIG MAMA [*at* BIG DADDY'*s shoulder*]. Oh, Big Daddy!
BIG DADDY. What's the matter, preacher's gone, ain't he? All right. That female elephant in the next cage was permeatin' the atmosphere about her with a powerful and excitin' odor of female fertility! Huh! Ain't that a nice way to put it, Brick?
BRICK. Yes, sir, nothin' wrong with it!
BIG DADDY. Brick says th's nothin' wrong with it!
BIG MAMA. Oh, Big Daddy!
BIG DADDY [*crossing to down stage center*]. So this ole bull elephant still had a couple of fornications left in him. He reared back his trunk an' got a whiff of

that elephant lady next door! — began to paw at the dirt in his cage an' butt his head against the separatin' partition and, first thing y'know, there was a conspicuous change in his *profile* — very *conspicuous!* Ain't I tellin' this story in decent language, Brick?

BRICK. Yes, sir, too fuckin' decent!

BIG DADDY. So, the little boy pointed at it and said, "What's that?" His mama said, "Oh, that's — nothin'!" — His papa said, "She's spoiled!"

[BIG DADDY *crosses to* BRICK *at left.*]
You didn't laugh at that story, Brick.

[BIG MAMA *crosses to down stage right crying.* MARGARET *goes to her.* MAE *and* GOOPER *hold up stage right center.*]

BRICK. No, sir, I didn't laugh at that story.

BIG DADDY. What is the smell in this room? Don't you notice it, Brick? Don't you notice a powerful and obnoxious odor of mendacity in this room?

BRICK. Yes, sir, I think I do, sir.

GOOPER. Mae, Mae . . .

BIG DADDY. There is nothing more powerful. Is there, Brick?

BRICK. No, sir. No, sir there isn't, an' nothin' more obnoxious.

BIG DADDY. Brick agrees with me. The odor of mendacity is a powerful and obnoxious odor an' the stawm hasn't blown it away from this room yet. You notice it, Gooper?

GOOPER. What, sir?

BIG DADDY. How about you, Sister Woman? You notice the unpleasant odor of mendacity in this room?

MAE. Why, Big Daddy, I don't even know what that is.

BIG DADDY. You can smell it. Hell, it smells like death!

[BIG MAMA *sobs.* BIG DADDY *looks toward her.*]
What's wrong with that fat woman over there, loaded with diamonds? Hey, what's-your-name, what's the matter with you?

MARGARET [*crossing toward* BIG DADDY]. She had a slight dizzy spell, Big Daddy.

BIG DADDY. You better watch that, Big Mama. A stroke is a bad way to go.

MARGARET [*crossing to* BIG DADDY *at center.*]. Oh, Brick, Big Daddy has on your birthday present to him, Brick, he has on your cashmere robe, the softest material I have ever felt.

BIG DADDY. Yeah, this is my soft birthday, Maggie. . . . Not my gold or my silver birthday, but my soft birthday, everything's got to be soft for Big Daddy on his soft birthday.

[MARGARET *kneels before* BIG DADDY *at center.*]

MARGARET. Big Daddy's got on his Chinese slippers that I gave him, Brick. Big Daddy, I haven't given you my big present yet, but now I will, now's the time for me to present it to you! I have an announcement to make!

MAE. What? What kind of announcement?

GOOPER. A sports announcement, Maggie?

MARGARET. Announcement of life beginning! A child is coming, sired by Brick, and out of Maggie the Cat! I have Brick's child in my body, an' that's my birthday present to Big Daddy on this birthday!

[BIG DADDY *looks at* BRICK *who crosses behind* BIG DADDY *to down stage portal, left.*]

BIG DADDY. Get up, girl, get up off your knees, girl.

[BIG DADDY *helps* MARGARET *to rise. He crosses above her, to her right, bites off the end of a fresh cigar, taken from his bathrobe pocket, as he studies* MARGARET.] *Uh-huh, this girl has life in her body, that's no lie!*

BIG MAMA. BIG DADDY'S DREAM COME TRUE!

BRICK. JESUS!

BIG DADDY [*crossing right below wicker stand*]. Gooper, I want my lawyer in the mornin'.

BRICK. Where are you goin', Big Daddy?

BIG DADDY. Son, I'm goin' up on the roof, to the belvedere on th' roof to look over my kingdom before I give up my kingdom—twenty-eight thousand acres of th' richest land this side of the valley Nile!

[*He exits through right doors, and down right on the gallery.*]

BIG MAMA [*following*]. Sweetheart, sweetheart, sweetheart—can I come with you?

[*She exits down stage right.*]

[MARGARET *is down stage center in the mirror area.* MAE *has joined* GOOPER *and she gives him a fierce poke, making a low hissing sound and a grimace of fury.*]

GOOPER [*pushing her aside.*] Brick, could you possibly spare me one small shot of that liquor?

BRICK. Why, help yourself, Gooper boy.

GOOPER. I will.

MAE [*shrilly*]. Of course we know that this is—a lie.

GOOPER. *Be still, Mae.*

MAE. I won't be still! I know she's made this up!

GOOPER. Goddam it, I said shut up!

MARGARET. Gracious! I didn't know that my little announcement was going to provoke such a storm!

MAE. *That* woman isn't *pregnant!*

GOOPER. Who said she was?

MAE. *She* did.

GOOPER. The doctor didn't. Doc Baugh didn't.

MARGARET. I haven't gone to Doc Baugh.

GOOPER. Then who'd you go to, Maggie?

MARGARET. One of the best gynecologists in the South.

GOOPER. Uh huh, uh huh!—I see. . . . [*He takes out a pencil and notebook.*]— May we have his name, please?

MARGARET. No, you may not, Mister Prosecuting Attorney!

MAE. He doesn't have any name, he doesn't exist!

MARGARET. Oh, he exists all right, and so does my child, Brick's baby!

MAE. You can't conceive a child by a man that won't sleep with you unless you think you're—

[BRICK *has turned on the phonograph. A scat song cuts* MAE'S *speech.*]

GOOPER. *Turn that off!*

MAE. We know it's a lie because we hear you in here; he won't sleep with you, we hear you! So don't imagine you're going to put a trick over on us, to fool a dying man with a—

[*A long drawn cry of agony and rage fills the house.* MARGARET *turns the phonograph down to a whisper. The cry is repeated.*]

MAE. Did you hear that, Gooper, did you hear that?

GOOPER. Sounds like the pain has struck.

MAE. Go see, Gooper!

GOOPER. Come along and leave these lovebirds together in their nest!

[*He goes out first.* MAE *follows but turns at the door, contorting her face and hissing at* MARGARET.]

MAE. *Liar!*

[*She slams the door.*]

[MARGARET *exhales with relief and moves a little unsteadily to catch hold of* BRICK'S *arm.*]

MARGARET. Thank you for—keeping still. . . .

BRICK. O.K., Maggie.

MARGARET. It was gallant of you to save my face!

[*He now pours down three shots in quick succession and stands waiting, silent. All at once he turns with a smile and says.*]

BRICK. *There!*

MARGARET. What?

BRICK. The *click* . . .

[*His gratitude seems almost infinite as he hobbles out on the gallery with a drink. We hear his crutch as he swings out of sight. Then, at some distance, he begins singing to himself a peaceful song.* MARGARET *holds the big pillow forlornly as if it were her only companion, for a few moments, then throws it on the bed. She rushes to the liquor cabinet, gathers all the bottles in her arms, turns about undecidedly, then runs out of the room with them, leaving the door ajar on the dim yellow hall.* BRICK *is heard hobbling back along the gallery, singing his peaceful song. He comes back in, sees the pillow on the bed, laughs lightly, sadly, picks it up. He has it under his arm as* MARGARET *returns to the room.* MARGARET *softly shuts the door and leans against it, smiling softly at* BRICK.]

MARGARET. Brick, I used to think that you were stronger than me and I didn't want to be overpowered by you. But now, since you've taken to liquor—you know what?—I guess it's bad, but now I'm stronger than you and I can love you more truly! Don't move that pillow, I'll move it right back if you do!—Brick?

[*She turns out all the lamps but a single rose-silk-shaded one by the bed.*]

I really have been to a doctor and I know what to do and—Brick?—this is my time by the calendar to conceive?

BRICK. Yes, I understand, Maggie. But how are you going to conceive a child by a man in love with his liquor?

MARGARET. By locking his liquor up and making him satisfy my desire before I unlock it!

BRICK. Is that what you've done, Maggie?

MARGARET. Look and see. That cabinet's mighty empty compared to before!

BRICK. Well, I'll be a son of a—

[*He reaches for his crutch but she beats him to it and rushes out on the gallery, hurls the crutch over the rail and comes back in, panting.*]

MARGARET. And so tonight we're going to make the lie true, and when that's done, I'll bring the liquor back here and we'll get drunk together, here, tonight, in this place that death has come into. . . . —What do you say?

BRICK. I don't say anything. I guess there's nothing to say.

MARGARET. Oh, you weak people, you weak, beautiful people who give up with such grace. What you want is someone to—

[*She turns out the rose-silk lamp.*]
　　—take hold of you. — Gently, gently with love hand your life back to you, like somethin' gold you let go of. I *do* love you, Brick, I *do!*
BRICK [*smiling with charming sadness*]. Wouldn't it be funny if that was true?

(1955)

Prewriting

Begin your study of *Cat on a Hot Tin Roof* by writing about and discussing the following ideas.

Analyzing the Characters

1. One way to look at the characters in this play involves discovering that they are afraid to face the truth. List five truths that the characters in the play are afraid to confront. Compare your list with those of others in your class. Discuss how you would rank the seriousness or harmlessness of each example of self-delusion that you have identified.

2. Reread the opening scene between Maggie and Brick (up to the point of Mae's entrance). With a classmate, prepare an oral reading of the scene, choosing one quality to emphasize in each of the characters. Present the scene to your class, asking them beforehand to try to identify the qualities you chose to emphasize. Invite the other students to offer interpretations of the characters in this scene.

3. In Act II, Big Daddy says to Brick, "*I've* lived with mendacity! — Why can't *you* live with it? Hell, you *got* to live with it, there's nothing *else* to *live* with except mendacity, is there?" How does this attitude fit in with Miller's concept of the clash between a "heroic" character and his or her social environment? Find statements by each of the characters that imply their feelings of displacement or indignity. How are the characters in *Antigone* different from these in their attitudes toward life and social situations?

4. How are family and tradition important to the characters in both *Antigone* and *Cat on a Hot Tin Roof*?

5. Reread the closing dialogue between Brick and Maggie. How have these characters changed since the beginning of the play? Do you think the changes are lasting ones?

6. Choose a character from *Cat on a Hot Tin Roof*, and argue that he or she is the play's protagonist. Can you argue for more than one character?

Writing

In your prewriting, you gathered a list of truths that the characters in *Cat on a Hot Tin Roof* would not confront. Looking at this list, you may come up with a thesis for an essay on the play. "Being afraid to face the truth is an important element in *Cat on a Hot Tin Roof*" is a useful observation, but you can sharpen that idea by deciding *why* failure to confront the truth is important. Here are some possible thesis statements focusing on various interpretations of the general idea of avoiding truth that lies at the heart of the play:

> Although Brick's failure to face the truth is the most significant, every character in the play hides behind some falsehood. This pervasive use of protective lies tempers our attitude toward Brick and allows us to accept him as the play's hero.

> One of the moral questions addressed in *Cat on a Hot Tin Roof* is this: "Which is more damaging to the human spirit, lying to others or lying to one's self?"

> In *Cat on a Hot Tin Roof*, Tennessee Williams presents mendacity on all levels of seriousness, presenting a view of life as suffused with lies and sustained with illusions.

Choosing a Structure

Your choice of thesis should determine how you organize your material — in this case, your list of examples from the prewriting activity. Perhaps your list will look something like this:

Unfaced Truths
—*Big Daddy's cancer:* Big Mama and Big Daddy (for a while)
—*Brick:* won't talk about his relationship with Skipper; won't face what he did to Skipper; blames Maggie, hides behind booze; pretends not to care what happens to his father and the family's property
—*Maggie:* pretends to others that everything's all right between her and Brick
—*Big Mama:* doesn't accept how Big Daddy feels about her
—*Mae and Gooper:* act as if they love Big Mama and Big Daddy; really want a bigger share of the inheritance; use children to further their pretended love
—*Birthday party, fireworks:* shows of good feeling and celebration; hide true feelings of envy, hatred, etc.
—*Reverend Tooker:* pretends interest in Big Daddy's welfare; really wants memorial donation
—*Gooper:* tries to hide what he's doing from Big Daddy

Sorting and Grouping   This unorganized jumble can be structured in several ways, depending on the focus of your essay.

1. For the first thesis we just mentioned, you would probably sort the unfaced truths character by character, perhaps presenting Brick's first and then those of the others. Or you could conclude with Brick's failings and observe that his are no worse than the others'.

2. For the second thesis, you could separate lies to others from lies to self and devote a section of your essay to each type, closing with an evaluation of the spiritual damage done by each.

3. For the last thesis, you would have the challenging work of arranging the list from the most trivial to the most serious so that your readers would be impressed by Williams's portrayal of the full spectrum of life's illusions and deceptions.

Ideas for Writing
Ideas for Responsive Writing

1. Devise a scale for ranking your responses to the six main characters: Brick, Maggie, Mae, Gooper, Big Mama, Big Daddy. It could be something like "least admirable to most admirable," "most hateful to least hateful," or "most like me to most unlike me." Write a brief paragraph about each character to explain your placement of that character on your scale.

2. Write a farewell scene between Big Mama and Big Daddy.

Ideas for Critical Writing

1. Write an essay in which you argue that Big Daddy is the central character of the play. Consider his malignant influence upon all the members of his family.

2. Consider the three women in the play. Each is married to a male in the Pollitt family. What else do they have in common? How are they different? For example, you might write an essay in which you show how Mae and Big Mama serve as foils to Maggie. (A foil is a character who, through contrast, highlights the distinctive qualities of another.)

3. Analyze the extended conversation between Brick and Big Daddy in Act II. Is anything resolved between them? How does this scene sum up the play's major conflicts?

4. The entire set for the play is the bedroom where Brick and Maggie are staying. Analyze the symbolic implications of this setting. Why is it highly appropriate that all the struggles of the troubled Pollitt family take place within this room?

5. Key elements in drama and fiction are character development and change. Does the confrontation with Big Daddy change Brick? Do any of the other characters undergo change?

6. Explain the play's title.

7. Read, summarize, and apply Miller's concept of tragedy and the ordinary person to *Cat on a Hot Tin Roof*.

Rewriting

The more specifically you support your statements about the work, the more credible you will be to your reader. Reminding yourself to quote liberally from the play will prevent you from straying from the printed page into the fields of your own mind, which may be rich and green but not always relevant.

Developing Paragraphs Specifically

The following paragraph makes several good observations but lacks examples to prove its points:

> In many ways Brick Pollitt fulfills Arthur Miller's characterization of the modern tragic hero. His ideal image of himself has been frustrated by age and disappointment. He feels isolated, a victim of indignity. He is clearly at odds with his environment.

Although these statements are true, the writer of the paragraph has given us no particular cause to believe them. The claims should include details from the play to make them understandable and convincing. Compare the following revision:

> In many ways Brick Pollitt fulfills Arthur Miller's characterization of the modern tragic hero. Near the beginning of the play, Williams says that Brick has "that cool air of detachment that people have who have given up the struggle" (674). Brick's ideal image of himself has been frustrated by age and time. He is a former professional football player who quit his job as a sports announcer because he could not bear to watch games he could no longer play, to describe younger men doing what he could no longer do. As he says to Big Daddy, "time just outran me . . . — got there first" (710). Brick feels isolated, a victim of indignity. He will not have sex with his wife and refuses to take any interest in the disposition of his father's enormous estate. His only concern is drinking, and he consumes liquor until he hears "this click in my head that makes me peaceful" (705). Clearly, this is a man at odds with his environment.

The references to the words and details of the play specifically support the writer's contentions about Brick. The exercise that follows will give you practice in finding such support.

Exercise on Choosing Specific Evidence

For each general statement, provide appropriate quotations from the play. Some of these generalizations may give you further ideas for writing.

1. Maggie is the one character who seems unafraid to tell the truth.
2. Gooper resents his parents' treatment of him.
3. The characters in the play take both realistic and unrealistic action toward their goals.
4. Children are often the focus of the Pollitt family battles.
5. Many of the characters attempt to cover their pain and anger with humor.

CHAPTER

17

Drama for Writing: The Research Paper

Until now, we have been discussing and illustrating how to write papers supported with material from only a *primary source* (i.e., from the literary work under consideration). In this chapter we will focus on the process of writing a paper supported with primary material but also drawing on *secondary sources* (i.e., critical material from the library). As we explain how to incorporate other people's ideas into your own writing, we will also introduce you to a mid-twentieth century development in drama: "theater of the absurd." You will thus have two avenues to explore at the library. You may decide to seek further information about theater of the absurd, or you may prefer to examine critical opinions about an absurdist play. You may, perhaps, even become inspired to investigate both.

Keep in mind as you study this chapter that the process we describe here for writing about drama is essentially the same procedure you would employ when writing a documented paper on a work in any literary genre—a short story, a poem, a novel, or a play.

What Is Theater of the Absurd?

Primarily a British and European phenomenon, theater of the absurd departs markedly from the realistic representation of events presented on stage in plays such as *A Doll's House* and *Cat on a Hot Tin Roof.* The absurdist playwrights attempt to show that the human condition is itself absurd, pointless—especially when the social order is based on empty rituals that serve as insulation against life's unpleasant realities. Eugene Ionesco in *The Bald Soprano* emphasizes the banality of comfortable middle-class people by presenting characters who do nothing throughout the play except talk earnestly about the obvious—declaring as an observation of great insight, for instance, that life in the city is less peaceful than in the country. Samuel Beckett often departs from a realistic setting to exaggerate the absurdity of life that must end in death. In *Endgame* his two main characters inhabit garbage cans on an otherwise empty stage. Harold Pinter employs more realistic settings, but his plots involve the characters in menacing situations beyond their comprehension, and their incongruous behavior often lacks any conventional motivation. The mindset shared by absurdist playwrights is that the human predicament is anguished, meaningless, and futile.

Looking at Absurdist Drama

Although theater of the absurd sounds depressing and hopeless, the plays are often quite funny, brightened by morbid humor. In the following play, *Picnic on the Battlefield*, Fernando Arrabal, a Spanish playwright living in France, presents a ridiculous situation in which comical characters enact a brief, bizarre drama, illustrating a grimly serious theme.

Fernando Arrabal *1933*–

PICNIC ON THE BATTLEFIELD

CHARACTERS

ZAPO, *a soldier.*
MONSIEUR TÉPAN, *the sol-dier's father.*
MADAME TÉPAN, *the soldier's mother.*

ZÉPO, *an enemy soldier.*
FIRST STRETCHER BEARER
SECOND STRETCHER BEARER

A battlefield. The stage is covered with barbed wire and sandbags. The battle is at its height. Rifle shots, exploding bombs and machine guns can be heard.
ZAPO is alone on the stage, flat on his stomach, hidden among the sandbags. He is very frightened. The sound of the fighting stops. Silence.
ZAPO takes a ball of wool and some needles out of a canvas workbag and starts knitting a pullover, which is already quite far advanced. The field telephone, which is by his side, suddenly starts ringing.

ZAPO. Hallo, hallo . . . yes, Captain . . . yes, I'm the sentry of sector 47 . . . Nothing new, Captain . . . Excuse me, Captain, but when's the fighting going to start again? And what am I supposed to do with the hand-grenades? Do I chuck them in front of me or behind me? . . . Don't get me wrong. I didn't mean to annoy you . . . Captain, I really feel terribly lonely, couldn't you send me someone to keep me company? . . . even if it's only a nanny-goat? [*The* CAPTAIN *is obviously severely reprimanding him.*] Whatever you say, Captain, whatever you say. [ZAPO *hangs up. He mutters to himself. Silence. Enter* MONSIEUR *and* MADAME TÉPAN, *carrying baskets as if they were going on a picnic. They address their son, who has his back turned and doesn't see them come in.*]

MONS. T. [*ceremoniously.*] Stand up, my son, and kiss your mother on the brow. [*Zapo, surprised, gets up and kisses his mother very respectfully on the forehead. He is about to speak, but his father doesn't give him a chance.*] And now, kiss *me.*

ZAPO. But, dear Father and dear Mother, how did you dare to come all this way, to such a dangerous place? You must leave at once.

MONS. T. So you think you've got something to teach your father about war and danger, do you? All this is just a game to me. How many times — to take the first example that comes to mind — have I got off an underground train while it was still moving.

MME. T. We thought you must be bored, so we came to pay you a little visit. This war must be a bit tedious, after all.

ZAPO. It all depends.

MONS. T. I know exactly what happens. To start with you're attracted by the novelty of it all. It's fun to kill people, and throw hand-grenades about, and wear uniforms — you feel smart, but in the end you get bored stiff. You'd have found it much more interesting in my day. Wars were much more lively, much more highly colored. And then, the best thing was that there were horses, plenty of horses. It was a real pleasure; if the Captain ordered us to attack, there we all were immediately, on horseback, in our red uniforms. It was a sight to be seen. And then there were the charges at the gallop, sword in hand, and suddenly you found yourself face to face with the enemy, and he was equal to the occasion too — with his horses — there were always horses, lots of horses, with their well-rounded rumps — in his highly-polished boots, and his green uniform.

MME. T. No, no, the enemy uniform wasn't green. It was blue. I remember distinctly that it was blue.

Mons. T. I tell you it was green.

MME. T. When I was little, how many times did I go out on to the balcony to watch the battle and say to the neighbour's little boy: "I bet you a gum-drop the blues win." And the blues were our enemies.

Mons. T. Oh, well, you must be right, then.

MME. T. I've always liked battles. As a child I always said that when I grew up I wanted to be a Colonel of dragoons. But my mother wouldn't hear of it, you know how she will stick to her principles at all costs.

Mons. T. Your mother's just a half-wit.

ZAPO. I'm sorry, but you really must go. You can't come into a war unless you're a soldier.

Mons. T. I don't give a damn, we came here to have a picnic with you in the country and to enjoy our Sunday.

MME. T. And I've prepared an excellent meal, too. Sausage, hard-boiled eggs — you know how you like them! — ham sandwiches, red wine, salad, and cakes.

ZAPO. All right, let's have it your way. But if the Captain comes he'll be absolutely furious. Because he isn't at all keen on us having visits when we're at the front. He never stops telling us: "Discipline and hand-grenades are what's wanted in war, not visits."

Mons. T. Don't worry, I'll have a few words to say to your Captain.

ZAPO. And what if we have to start fighting again?

Mons. T. You needn't think that'll frighten me, it won't be the first fighting I've seen. Now if only it was battles on horseback! Times have changed, you can't understand. [*Pause.*] We came by motor bike. No one said a word to us.

ZAPO. They must have thought you were the referees.

Mons. T. We had enough trouble getting through, though. What with all the tanks and jeeps.

MME. T. And do you remember the bottle-neck that cannon caused, just when we got here?

Mons. T. You musn't be surprised at anything in wartime, everyone knows that.

MME. T. Good, let's start our meal.

Mons. T. You're quite right, I feel as hungry as a hunter. It's the smell of gunpowder.

MME. T. We'll sit on the rug while we're eating.

ZAPO. Can I bring my rifle with me?

MME. T. You leave your rifle alone. It's not good manners to bring your rifle to table with you. [*Pause.*] But you're absolutely filthy, my boy. How on earth did you get into such a state? Let's have a look at your hands.

ZAPO [*ashamed, holding out his hands*]. I had to crawl about on the ground during the manoeuvres.

MME. T. And what about your ears?

ZAPO. I washed them this morning.

MME. T. Well that's all right, then. And your teeth? [*He shows them.*] Very good. Who's going to give her little boy a great big kiss for cleaning his teeth so nicely? [*To her husband*] Well, go on, kiss your son for cleaning his teeth so nicely. [M. TÉPAN *kisses his son.*] Because, you know, there's one thing I *will* not have, and that's making fighting a war an excuse for not washing.

ZAPO. Yes, Mother. [*They eat.*]

MONS. T. Well, my boy, did you make a good score?

ZAPO. When?

MONS. T. In the last few days, of course.

ZAPO. Where?

MONS. T. At the moment, since you're fighting a war.

ZAPO. No, nothing much. I didn't make a good score. Hardly ever scored a bull.

MONS. T. Which are you best at shooting, enemy horses or soldiers?

ZAPO. No, not horses, there aren't any horses any more.

MONS. T. Well, soldiers then?

ZAPO. Could be.

MONS. T. Could be? Aren't you sure?

ZAPO. Well you see . . . I shoot without taking aim, [*pause*] and at the same time I say a Pater Noster for the chap I've shot.

MONS. T. You must be braver than that. Like your father.

MME. T. I'm going to put a record on. [*She puts a record on the gramophone—a pasodoble. All three are sitting on the ground, listening.*]

MONS. T. That really *is* music. Yes indeed, ole! [*The music continues. Enter an enemy soldier:* ZÉPO. *He is dressed like* ZAPO. *The only difference is the colour of their uniforms.* ZÉPO *is in green and* ZAPO *is in grey.* ZÉPO *listens to the music openmouthed. He is behind the family so they can't see him. The record ends. As he gets up* ZAPO *discovers* ZÉPO. *Both put their hands up.* M. *and* MME. TÉPAN *look at them in surprise.*] What's going on? [ZAPO *reacts—he hesitates. Finally, looking as if he's made up his mind, he points his rifle at* ZÉPO.]

ZAPO. Hands up! [ZÉPO *puts his hands up even higher, looking even more terrified.* ZAPO *doesn't know what to do. Suddenly he goes over quickly to* ZÉPO *and touches him gently on the shoulder, like a child playing a game of 'tag'.*] Got you! [*To his father, very pleased.*] There we are! A prisoner!

MONS. T. Fine. And now what're you going to do with him?

ZAPO. I don't know, but, well, could be—they might make me a corporal.

MONS. T. In the meantime, you'd better tie him up.

ZAPO. Tie him up? Why?

MONS. T. Prisoners always get tied up!

ZAPO. How?

MONS. T. Tie up his hands.

MME. T. Yes, there's no doubt about it, you must tie up his hands, I've always seen them do that.

ZAPO. Right. [*To his prisoner.*] Put your hands together, if you please.

ZÉPO. Don't hurt me too much.

ZAPO. I won't.

ZÉPO. Ow! You're hurting me.

MONS. T. Now now, don't maltreat your prisoner.

MME. T. Is that the way I brought you up? How many times have I told you that we must be considerate of our fellow-men?

ZAPO. I didn't do it on purpose. [*To* ZÉPO.] And like that, does it hurt?

ZÉPO. No, it's all right like that.

MONS. T. Tell him straight out, say what you mean, don't mind us.

ZÉPO. It's all right like that.

MONS. T. Now his feet.

ZAPO. His feet as well, whatever next?

MONS. T. Didn't they teach you the rules?

ZAPO. Yes.

MONS. T. Well then!

ZAPO. [*very politely, to* ZÉPO]. Would you be good enough to sit on the ground, please?

ZÉPO. Yes, but don't hurt me.

MME. T. You'll see, he'll take a dislike to you.

ZAPO. No he won't, no he won't. I'm not hurting you, am I?

ZÉPO. No, that's perfect.

ZAPO. Papa, why don't you take a photo of the prisoner on the ground and me with my foot on his stomach?

MONS. T. Oh, yes that'd look good.

ZÉPO. Oh no, not that!

MME. T. Say yes, don't be obstinate.

ZÉPO. No, I said no, and no it is.

MME. T. But just a little teeny weeny photo, what harm could that do you? And we could put it in the dining room, next to the life-saving certificate my husband won thirteen years ago.

ZÉPO. No—you won't shift me.

ZAPO. But why won't you let us?

ZÉPO. I'm engaged. And if she sees the photo one day, she'll say I don't know how to fight a war properly.

ZAPO. No she won't, all you'll need to say is that it isn't you, it's a panther.

MME. T. Come on, do say yes.

ZÉPO. All right then. But only to please you.

ZAPO. Lie down flat. [ZÉPO *lies down.* ZAPO *puts a foot on his stomach and grabs his rifle with a martial air.*]

MME. T. Stick your chest out a bit further.

ZAPO. Like this?

MME. T. Yes like that, and don't breathe.

MONS. T. Try to look like a hero.

ZAPO. What d'you mean, like a hero?

MONS. T. It's quite simple; try and look like the butcher does when he's boasting about his successes with the girls.

ZAPO. Like this?

MONS. T. Yes, like that.

MME. T. The most important thing is to puff your chest out and not breathe.

ZÉPO. Have you nearly finished?

MONS. T. Just be patient a moment. One . . . two . . . three.

ZAPO. I hope I'll come out well.

MME. T. Yes, you looked very martial.

MONS. T. You were fine.

MME. T. It makes me want to have my photo taken with you.

MONS. T. Now there's a good idea.

ZAPO. Right. I'll take it if you like.

MME. T. Give me your helmet to make me look like a soldier.

ZÉPO. I don't want any more photos. Even one's far too many.

ZAPO. Don't take it like that. After all, what harm can it do you?

ZÉPO. It's my last word.

MONS. T. [*to his wife*]. Don't press the point, prisoners are always very sensitive. If we go on he'll get cross and spoil our fun.

ZAPO. Right, what're we going to do with him, then?

MME. T. We could invite him to lunch. What do you say?

MONS. T. I don't see why not.

ZAPO. [*to* ZÉPO]. Well, will you have lunch with us, then?

ZÉPO. Er . . .

MONS. T. We brought a good bottle with us.

ZÉPO. Oh well, all right then.

MME. T. Make yourself at home, don't be afraid to ask for anything you want.

ZÉPO. All right.

MONS. T. And what about you, did you make a good score?

ZÉPO. When?

MONS. T. In the last few days, of course.

ZÉPO. Where?

MONS. T. At the moment, since you're fighting a war.

ZÉPO. No, nothing much. I didn't make a good score, hardly ever scored a bull.

MONS. T. Which are you best at shooting? Enemy horses or soldiers?

ZÉPO. No, not horses, they aren't any horses any more.

MONS. T. Well, soldiers, then?

ZÉPO. Could be.

MONS. T. Could be? Aren't you sure?

ZÉPO. Well you see . . . I shoot without taking aim [*pause*], and at the same time I say an Ave Maria for the chap I've shot.

ZAPO. An Ave Maria? I'd have thought you'd have said a Pater Noster.

ZÉPO. No, always an Ave Maria. [*Pause*] It's shorter.

MONS. T. Come come, my dear fellow, you must be brave.

MME. T. [*to* ZÉPO]. We can untie you if you like.

ZÉPO. No, don't bother, it doesn't matter.

MONS. T. Don't start getting stand-offish with us now. If you'd like us to untie you, say so.

MME. T. Make yourself comfortable.

ZÉPO. Well, if that's how you feel, you can untie my feet, but it's only to please you.

MONS. T. Zapo, untie him. [ZAPO *unties him.*]

MME. T. Well, do you feel better?

ZÉPO. Yes, of course. I really am putting you to a lot of inconvenience.

MONS. T. Not at all, just make yourself at home. And if you'd like us to untie your hands you only have to say so.

ZÉPO. No, not my hands, I don't want to impose upon you.

MONS. T. No no, my dear chap, no no. I tell you, it's no trouble at all.

ZÉPO. Right . . . Well then, untie my hands too. But only for lunch, eh? I don't want you think that you give me an inch and I take an ell.[1]

MONS. T. Untie his hands, son.

---

[1] A unit of measure equal to forty-five inches.

MME. T. Well, since our distinguished prisoner is so charming, we're going to have a marvellous day in the country.

ZÉPO. Don't call me your distinguished prisoner; just call me your prisoner.

MME. T. Won't that embarrass you?

ZÉPO. No, no, not at all.

MONS. T. Well, I must say you're modest. [*Noise of aeroplanes.*]

ZAPO. Aeroplanes. They're sure to be coming to bomb us. [ZAPO *and* ZÉPO *throw themselves on the sandbags and hide.*] [*To his parents*]. Take cover. The bombs will fall on you. [*The noise of the aeroplanes overpowers all the other noises. Bombs immediately start to fall. Shells explode very near the stage but not on it. A deafening noise.* ZAPO *and* ZÉPO *are cowering down between the sandbags.* M. TÉPAN *goes on talking calmly to his wife, and she answers in the same unruffled way. We can't hear what they are saying because of the bombing.* MME. TÉPAN *goes over to one of the baskets and takes an umbrella out of it. She opens it.* M. *and* MME. TÉPAN *shelter under it as if it were raining. They are standing up. They shift rhythmically from one foot to the other and talk about their personal affairs. The bombing continues. Finally the aeroplanes go away. Silence.* M. TÉPAN *stretches an arm outside the umbrella to make sure that nothing more is falling from the heavens.*]

MONS. T. [*to his wife*]. You can shut your umbrella. [MME. TÉPAN *does so. They both go over to their son and tap him lightly on the behind with the umbrella.*] Come on, out you come. The bombing's over. [ZAPO *and* ZÉPO *come out of their hiding place.*]

ZAPO. Didn't you get hit?

MONS. T. What d'you think could happen to your father? [*Proudly.*] Little bombs like that! Don't make me laugh! [*Enter, left, two* RED CROSS SOLDIERS. *They are carrying a stretcher.*]

1ST STRETCHER BEARER. Any dead here?

ZAPO. No, no one around these parts.

1ST STRETCHER BEARER. Are you sure you've looked properly?

ZAPO. Sure.

1ST STRETCHER BEARER. And there isn't a single person dead?

ZAPO. I've already told you there isn't.

1ST STRETCHER BEARER. No one wounded, even?

ZAPO. Not even that.

2ND STRETCHER BEARER [*to the* 1ST S. B.]. Well, now we're in a mess! [*To* ZAPO *persuasively.*] Just look again, search everywhere, and see if you can't find us a stiff.

1ST STRETCHER BEARER. Don't keep on about it, they've told you quite clearly there aren't any.

2ND STRETCHER BEARER. What a lousy trick!

ZAPO. I'm terribly sorry. I promise you I didn't do it on purpose.

2ND STRETCHER BEARER. That's what they all say. That no one's dead and that they didn't do it on purpose.

1ST STRETCHER BEARER. Oh, let the chap alone!

MONS. T. [*obligingly*]. We should be only too pleased to help you. At your service.

2ND STRETCHER BEARER. Well, really, if things go on like this I don't know what the Captain will say to us.

MONS. T. But what's it all about?

2ND STRETCHER BEARER. Quite simply that the others' wrists are aching with carting so many corpses and wounded men about, and that we haven't found any yet. And it's not because we haven't looked!

MONS. T. Well, yes, that really is annoying. [*To* ZAPO.] Are you quite sure no one's dead?

ZAPO. Obviously, Papa.

MONS. T. Have you looked under all the sandbags?

ZAPO. Yes, Papa.

MONS. T. [*angrily*]. Well then, you might as well say straight out that you don't want to lift a finger to help these gentlemen, when they're so nice, too!

1ST STRETCHER BEARER. Don't be angry with him. Let him be. We must just hope we'll have more luck in another trench and that all the lot'll be dead.

MONS. T. I should be delighted.

MME. T. Me too. There's nothing I like more than people who put their hearts into their work.

MONS. T. [*indignantly, addressing his remarks to the wings*]. Then is no one going to do anything for these gentlemen?

ZAPO. If it only rested with me, it'd already be done.

ZÉPO. I can say the same.

MONS. T. But look here, is neither of you even wounded?

ZAPO [*ashamed*]. No, not me.

MONS. T. [*to* ZÉPO]. What about you?

ZÉPO [*ashamed*]. Me neither. I never have any luck.

MME. T. [*pleased*]. Now I remember! This morning, when I was peeling the onions, I cut my finger. Will that do you?

MONS. T. Of course it will! [*Enthusiastically.*] They'll take you off at once!

1ST STRETCHER BEARER. No, that won't work. With ladies it doesn't work.

MONS. T. We're no further advanced, then.

1ST STRETCHER BEARER. Never mind.

2ND STRETCHER BEARER. We may be able to make up for it in the other trenches. [*They start to go off.*]

MONS. T. Don't worry! If we find a dead man we'll keep him for you! No fear of us giving him to anyone else!

2ND STRETCHER BEARER. Thank you very much, sir.

MONS. T. Quite all right, old chap, think nothing of it. [*The two stretcher bearers say goodbye. All four answer them. The stretcher bearers go out.*]

MME. T. That's what's so pleasant about spending a Sunday in the country. You always meet such nice people.

MONS. T. [*pause*]. But why are you enemies?

ZÉPO. I don't know, I'm not very well educated.

MME. T. Was it by birth, or did you become enemies afterwards?

ZÉPO. I don't know, I don't know anything about it.

MONS. T. Well then, how did you come to be in the war?

ZÉPO. One day, at home, I was just mending my mother's iron, a man came and asked me: "Are you Zépo?" "Yes." "Right, you must come to the war." And so I asked him: "But what war?" and he said: "Don't you read the papers then? You're just a peasant!" I told him I did read the papers but not the war bits. . . .

ZAPO. Just how it was with me—exactly how it was with me.

MONS. T. Yes, they came to fetch you too.

MME. T. No, it wasn't quite the same; that day you weren't mending an iron, you were mending the car.

MONS. T. I was talking about the rest of it. [*To* ZÉPO.] Go on, what happened then?

ZÉPO. Then I told him I had a fiancée and that if I didn't take her to the pictures on Sundays she wouldn't like it. He said that that wasn't the least bit important.

ZAPO. Just how it was with me — exactly how it was with me.

ZÉPO. And then my father came down, and he said I couldn't go to the war because I didn't have a horse.

ZAPO. Just what my father said.

ZÉPO. The man said you didn't need a horse any more, and I asked him if I could take my fiancée with me. He said no. Then I asked whether I could take my aunt with me so that she could make me one of her custards on Thursdays; I'm very fond of them.

MME. T. [*realizing that she'd forgotten it*]. Oh! The custard!

ZÉPO. He said no again.

ZAPO. Same as with me.

ZÉPO. And ever since then I've been alone in the trench nearly all the time.

MME. T. I think you and your distinguished prisoner might play together this afternoon, as you're so close to each other and so bored.

ZAPO. Oh no, Mother, I'm too afraid, he's an enemy.

MONS. T. Now now, you mustn't be afraid.

ZAPO. If you only knew what the General was saying about the enemy!

MME. T. What did he say?

ZAPO. He said the enemy are very nasty people. When they take prisoners they put little stones in their shoes so that it hurts them to walk.

MME. T. How awful! What barbarians!

MONS. T. [*indignantly, to* ZÉPO]. And aren't you ashamed to belong to an army of criminals?

ZÉPO. I haven't done anything. I don't do anybody any harm.

MME. T. He was trying to take us in, pretending to be such a little saint!

MONS. T. We oughtn't to have untied him. You never know, we only need to turn our backs and he'll be putting a stone in our shoes.

ZÉPO. Don't be so nasty to me.

MONS. T. What'd you think we *should* be, then? I'm indignant. I know what I'll do. I'll go and find the Captain and ask him to let me fight in the war.

ZAPO. He won't let you, you're too old.

MONS. T. Then I'll buy myself a horse and a sword and come and fight on my own account.

MME. T. Bravo! If I were a man I'd do the same.

ZÉPO. Don't be like that with me, Madame. Anyway I'll tell you something — our General told us the same thing about you.

MME. T. How could he dare tell such a lie!

ZAPO. No — but the same thing really?

ZÉPO. Yes, the same thing.

MONS. T. Perhaps it was the same man who talked to you both?

MME. T. Well if it was the same man he might at least have said something different. That's a fine thing — saying the same thing to everyone!

MONS. T. [*to* ZÉPO *in a different tone of voice*]. Another little drink?

MME. T. I hope you liked our lunch?

MONS. T. In any case, it was better than last Sunday.

ZÉPO. What happened?

MONS. T. Well, we went to the country and we put the food on the rug. While we'd got our backs turned a cow ate up all our lunch, and the napkins as well.

ZÉPO. What a greedy cow!

MONS. T. Yes, but afterwards, to get our own back, we ate the cow. [*They laugh.*]

ZAPO [*to* ZÉPO]. They couldn't have been very hungry after that!

MONS. T. Cheers! [*They all drink.*]

MME. T. [*to* ZÉPO]. And what do you do to amuse yourself in the trench?

ZÉPO. I spend my time making flowers out of rags, to amuse myself. I get terribly bored.

MME. T. And what do you do with the flowers?

ZÉPO. At the beginning I used to send them to my fianceé, but one day she told me that the greenhouse and the cellar were already full of them and that she didn't know what to do with them any more, and she asked me, if I didn't mind, to send her something else.

MME. T. And what did you do?

ZÉPO. I tried to learn to make something else, but I couldn't so I go on making rag flowers to pass the time.

MME. T. Do you throw them away afterwards, then?

ZÉPO. No, I've found a way to use them now. I give one flower for each pal who dies. That way I know that even if I make an awful lot there'll never be enough.

MONS. T. That's a good solution you've hit on.

ZÉPO [*shyly*]. Yes.

ZAPO. Well, what I do is knit, so as not to get bored.

MME. T. But tell me, are all the soldiers as bored as you?

ZÉPO. It all depends on what they do to amuse themselves.

ZAPO. It's the same on our side.

MONS. T. Then let's stop the war.

ZÉPO. How?

MONS. T. It's very simple. [*To* ZAPO.] You just tell your pals that the enemy soldiers don't want to fight a war, and you [*to* ZÉPO] say the same to your comrades. And then everyone goes home.

ZAPO. Marvellous!

MME. T. And then you'll be able to finish mending the iron.

ZAPO. How is it that no one thought of such a good idea before?

MME. T. Your father is the only one who's capable of thinking of such ideas; don't forget he's a former student of the École Normale, *and* a philatelist.[2]

ZÉPO. But what will the sergeant-majors and corporals do?

MONS. T. We'll give them some guitars and castanets to keep them quiet!

ZÉPO. Very good idea.

MONS. T. You see how easy it is. Everything's fixed.

ZÉPO. We shall have a tremendous success.

ZAPO. My pals will be terribly pleased.

---

[2] Student of the Teacher's College and a stamp collector.

MME. T. What d'you say to putting on the pasodoble we were playing just now, to celebrate?

ZÉPO. Perfect.

ZAPO. Yes, put the record on, Mother. [MME. TÉPAN *puts a record on. She turns the handle. She waits. Nothing can be heard.*]

MONS. T. I can't hear a thing.

MME. T. Oh, how silly of me! Instead of putting a record on I put on a beret. [*She puts the record on. A gay pasodoble is heard.* ZAPO *dances with* ZÉPO *and* MME. TÉPAN *with her husband. They are all very gay. The field telephone rings. None of the four hears it. They go on dancing busily. The telephone rings again. The dance continues.*

The battle starts up again with a terrific din of bombs, shots and bursts of machine-gun fire. None of the four has seen anything and they go on dancing merrily. A burst of machine-gun fire mows them all down. They fall to the ground, stone dead. A shot must have grazed the gramophone; the record keeps repeating the same thing, like a scratched record. The music of the scratched record can be heard till the end of the play. The two STRETCHER BEARERS *enter left. They are carrying the empty stretcher.*]

SUDDEN CURTAIN

(1959)

Using Library Sources in Your Writing

The ability to locate sources of information on a given subject and then incorporate the new ideas you find into your own writing is a valuable skill that every well-educated person needs to learn. In order to begin a documented paper about a literary work, you first should read carefully at least twice the primary source (the piece of literature about which you intend to do research). Our advice will use examples related to Arrabal's *Picnic on the Battlefield,* but remember that the process is the same for writing a library paper on any piece of literature you may choose.

Prewriting

The prewriting stage for a documented paper will necessarily be more complex than just gathering ideas for writing using only your own thoughts. You still need to understand completely the literary work before you begin, and your task will be complicated by the need to find, read, and assimilate the work of others, being careful all the while to credit these ideas when you incorporate them into your own writing.

Finding A Thesis

In order to write a good paper involving research, you should begin with a *thesis question,* which you can eventually turn into a thesis statement once you have discovered the information needed to provide the answer. You might want to approach the matter as a problem to be solved.

Pose Yourself a Problem   You will write with greater engagement if you can discover some problem concerning your chosen literary work that genuinely interests you and then set out to solve that problem. Do you wonder, for instance, why several of Arrabal's characters seem so callous toward extreme cruelty? By reading about his work, you can probably find the answer to that question and arrive at a more thorough understanding of his plays. The problem, then, that you would work on solving as you write your paper would be this:

> How can I explain convincingly the reasons for Arrabal's casual presentation of cruelty in *Picnic on the Battlefield?*

Your thesis statement involves your solution of that problem and might read something like this:

> Arrabal's casual presentation of cruelty in *Picnic on the Battlefield* underscores the evil of accepting brutal behavior as commonplace in society—an acceptance that ultimately allows us to tolerate, sometimes even to celebrate, war.

Perhaps you find yourself more interested in the techniques used by Arrabal and the absurdist dramatists than by their philosophical stance. If so, you might conceive your problem this way:

> How does Arrabal go about conveying to the audience his conviction that war is absurd?

After completing your background reading, your problem would become finding the most effective way to explain how Arrabal achieves his dramatic purpose by using a pointless plot, stereotypical characters, meaningless actions, and absurd dialogue.

Locating Sources

At some stage in the writing of a documented paper, you need to visit the library and find out what other people have said about the literary work you have chosen as your subject.

Using the Card Catalogue or the Computer File

If your research is going to focus on some aspect of Fernando Arrabal's work, you could profitably make your first stop at the library's card catalogue—or at the handy computer terminal that functions the same way. Each provides a listing of all books with call numbers indicating their locations. Because you will not at this point know the names of the books you want to use, you should look up *Arrabal, Fernando*, in the *subject index* to find books written about him and his work. You should also check *Arrabal* in the author index to discover possible collections of essays in which he may discuss his own plays or offer perceptive comments on theater of the absurd.

Using Bibliographies and Indexes

Even though you might find ample material in books to supply a wealth of documentation, your paper will not be well researched unless you also discover what articles and reviews are available by consulting bibliographies and indexes.

The *MLA International Bibliography* lists (year by year) articles from leading periodicals devoted to literary criticism and theory. You would look under *Arrabal* in the twentieth-century French section because his plays were first published in French. If you are doing research on an author of whose nationality or birth date you are unsure, you need to find out this information first because the bibliography is organized according to national literature and literary period. You can find the data you need by checking the *Dictionary of American Biography*, the *Dictionary of National Biography* (British), or *World Authors*. Your library may also have a computerized version of the *MLA Bibliography* (at least of articles published since 1981), which is extremely handy to use because it allows you to call up an author without knowing nationality or date. But sometimes it is woefully incomplete.

The *Reader's Guide to Periodical Literature* will enable you to locate theater or book reviews appearing in popular magazines such as *Harper's, The Atlantic, The New Yorker, Time, Newsweek, The Nation*, and *The New Republic*. Entries are listed both by author and by subject.

If you want to know what Hawthorne's, Twain's, or Wharton's contemporaries thought of their work, you can consult *Poole's Index to Periodical Literature*, which covers magazines published in the nineteenth century.

Your library will also have a number of guides and indexes to articles on literature divided according to genre. Some of the most useful ones appear in Chart 17–1.

Taking Notes

Once you have found titles of articles and reviews that sound pertinent, you need to locate the journal and see whether the actual article or review

---

CHART 17–1 Guides to Criticism of Poetry, Drama, and Fiction

GUIDES TO CRITICISM OF POETRY

Index to Criticism of British and American Poetry
Poetry Explication: A Checklist of Interpretation Since 1925 of British and American Poems, Past and Present
McGill's Critical Survey of Poetry

GUIDES TO CRITICISM OF DRAMA

New York Theater Critics' Reviews
New York Times Theater Reviews
Dramatic Criticism Index

GUIDES TO CRITICISM OF FICTION

Twentieth-Century Short Story Explication
Short Story Criticism
Book Review Digest

[Please note that you are not supposed to quote directly from the excerpts in *Short Story Criticism* or the summaries in *Book Review Digest*. With all such publications, you are expected to look up and read the original article or review in full. The source to cite will be the journal or magazine in which you find the complete article or review.]

---

lives up to the promise of its title. If the material proves useful, take notes. Be sure to record on each notecard the name of the journal, the volume number, date, and pages. You will need this information later in order to credit your sources.

Writing

Before you begin actually writing your first draft, you need to turn the thesis question you were investigating into a thesis statement—a sentence that conveys the point you want to make after studying your primary source and reading your secondary sources. If, for instance, you begin by investigating this question:

> Why do Arrabal's characters in *Picnic on the Battlefield* make such ridiculous statements and engage in such bizarre actions?

you might, after doing your research, end up with a thesis statement something like this:

> The ridiculous conversation and bizarre actions of the characters in *Picnic on the Battlefield* effectively convey Arrabal's conviction that war is absurd.

Your thesis may change, of course, as you work with your material, but you need a fairly clear idea of what you want to say and how you will go about saying it before you start.

Developing A Plan

Many people strongly recommend taking notes on three- by five-inch or five- by seven-inch notecards during the researching stage of writing a documented paper. These small cards make the material easy to organize. If you have, instead, pages of notes, you may find yourself wasting time as you shuffle through dozens of sheets trying to locate the note you need.

Using Notecards After completing your note-taking, you should read each card and try to select a word or two that summarizes the meaning of the passage on each card. Write that heading in the upper right-hand corner of the card. You can do this as you take notes, if you prefer. After all the cards have headings, read through these headings and group the cards with similar ideas together in stacks.

That's the easy part. Next, you must put your mind to work and decide on some reasonable order in which to present these ideas. Then, arrange the stacks according to your plan. As you write, following this plan, the necessary information will be in front of you ready to be incorporated into the first draft of your paper.

Writing Before Researching

If you are fired with enthusiasm for the literary work, if you have a number of significant observations that you want to express, you should go right ahead and devise a thesis, marshall your evidence, order your ideas, and write a first draft. Then you can go to the library, locate and read a number of pertinent *secondary sources* (articles, reviews, sections of books, perhaps even whole books if your research needs to be thorough), and incorporate ideas from this reading into your paper at the appropriate places. You may find — especially if you are writing about a popular work by a well-known author — that most of your cogent insights have already appeared in print. Try not to be disheartened. Grit your teeth and give credit to the person who published first.

Say, for example, you had made this comment in your first draft:

> Everyone in the play considers war a game.

After reading criticism on Arrabal's play, you would discover that one of the critics, Peter Podol, makes this same observation. Thus you would need to alter your statement to read something like this:

> As Podol observes, everyone in the play considers war a game (31).

Or, if a critic has made the point more effectively than you did, you might decide to scrap your sentence and quote the secondary source directly, like this:

> As Podol observes, "The *jeu*, or game, . . . plays a significant role in this first drama" (31).

After giving credit where credit is due throughout your paper, you may want to emphasize — if you can do so gracefully — the remaining ideas that are entirely yours:

> Zapo's knitting and Zépo's making rag flowers suggest, I think, a feminine gentleness quite in keeping with their refusal to shoot the enemy deliberately.

Some people find this method of "plugging in" ideas from their research the easiest way to handle a documented paper. If you are knowledgeable and enthusiastic about your topic, it may be the best way to proceed.

But, on the other hand, if after reading the primary source, you find yourself devoid of ideas, perhaps confused about the work, a better method is the one we described first: go to the library, locate the pertinent secondary sources, and study them carefully. Then, after having gained a thorough understanding of the primary source, you devise a thesis, choose your supporting material (both from the literary work and from the critics), arrange your ideas in an orderly way, and write your first draft.

Avoiding Plagiarism

Whenever you write a paper after consulting secondary sources, you must take scrupulous care to give credit to those sources for any ideas or phrasings that you may borrow.

Plagiarism involves carelessly — or, far worse, deliberately — presenting the words or ideas of another writer as your own.

You must be careful in taking notes to put quotation marks around any passages — or even phrases — that you copy word for word. Changing an occasional word here and there will not do, either: such close paraphrasing is still considered plagiarism. The examples below may help you to see the difference between plagiarism and paraphrasing (stating another's ideas in your own words), in case you are in doubt.

Original Passage:
"I hope that it transcends the personal and the private, and has something to do with the anguish of us all" (54).
— *Edward Albee on* The American Dream

Plagiarism:
Albee writes that he hopes his play transcends the personal and the private and has a lot to do with everyone's anguish (54).

Combined Paraphrase and Direct Quotation:
Albee writes that he wants the play to rise above "the personal and the private" to reveal "the anguish of us all" (54).

Paraphrase:
Albee says that he hopes the play goes beyond individual problems and deals with universal grief and pain (54).

Direct Quotation:
"I hope," writes Albee, "that [*The American Dream*] transcends the personal and the private, and has something to do with the anguish of us all" (54).

Introducing Quotations

Whether you are quoting directly or simply paraphrasing someone else's ideas, you should always give credit in the text of your paper to the person from whom you are borrowing. The MLA documentary style now requires you to do so. No longer will you be able to toss in a quotation, put a note number at the end, and trust your reader to fumble for the note page to discover your source. Because you now have to cite all sources within the paper, you need to exercise great skill in varying the way you introduce quotations and borrowed ideas.

As you read your secondary sources, pay attention to the various ways that these writers credit their sources. If you read widely enough, this graceful introducing of other people's ideas will become second nature to you. But in case you still have to work at introducing your quotations and paraphrases here are a few models for you to go by:

As critic Lawrence Stone explains, daughters in Shakespeare's England were "often unwanted and might be regarded as no more than a tiresome drain on the economic resources of the family" (112).

Henry James argues that "The dramatic current stagnates . . ." (654).

Kettle declares *Middlemarch* to be "the most impressive novel in our language" (1:160).

According to biographer Joan Givner, the failure of Porter's personal relationship with Josephson caused a temporary inability to write (221).

Novelist Alice Walker asserts that the mothers and grandmothers of black women were "driven to a numb and bleeding madness by the springs of creativity in them for which there was no release" (31).

As Rachel Brownstein points out, "A beautiful virgin walled off from an imperfect real world is the central figure in romance" (35).

"A beginning as simple as this," observes Mark Schorer, "must overcome corrupted reading habits of long standing . . ." (706–07).

Ideas for Researched Writing
About Short Stories

1. Discuss the "power of blackness" in Hawthorne's "Young Goodman Brown."
2. Discuss the autobiographical implications of Gilman's "The Yellow Wall-paper."
3. Compare Glaspell's short story "A Jury of Her Peers" with her dramatic version of the same work, *Trifles*, both of which appear in this text.
4. Discuss the working out of the quest myth in Welty's "A Worn Path."
5. Discuss the role of popular music in Oates's "Where Are You Going, Where Have You Been?"

About Poetry

1. Compare Marlowe's "The Passionate Shepherd to His Love" and Raleigh's "The Nymph's Reply to the Shepherd."
2. Compare Lovelace's "To Lucasta, on Going to the Wars" with Crane's "War Is Kind."
3. Discuss Whitman's handling of the trinity of symbols in "When Lilacs Last in the Dooryard Bloom'd."
4. Discuss the relationship of Yeats's "Leda and the Swan" to the myth of Leda and Zeus.
5. Discuss e e cummings's disregard for traditional form in his poetry.

About Drama

1. Examine closely the conversations in *Picnic on the Battlefield*. How does this language help convey Arrabal's theme?
2. How does the language of Albee's *The American Dream* illustrate the existential philosophy of the theater of the absurd?

3. How does the staging of *Picnic on the Battlefield* reflect the absurdist philosophy of the playwright?
4. Research the staging of *A Doll's House* and *Picnic on the Battlefield*. Discuss how the staging changes from the traditional to the absurdist.
5. Contrast the characters of Antigone, Desdemona, and Nora Helmer.

Rewriting

Many people who do researched writing make no attempt to provide complete, accurate documentation of sources in the first draft because pausing to do so interrupts the flow of ideas. You need, of course, to include at least the last name of the person whose words are quoted or paraphrased (or the title of an anonymous source), but you can fill in from your notes the remaining information as part of the revising process.

Citing Sources

Various academic disciplines use different documentation styles. Because you are writing about literature, the appropriate one for you to follow is the recently streamlined Modern Language Association style. Sample entries to illustrate the MLA format appear at the end of this chapter. You may also use as a model the documentation included in the two sample student research papers in the next section.

Be sure that you follow the models accurately. You should have all the necessary information recorded on your notecards. If you neglected to write down a page number or a date or a publisher, you must now trudge back to the library and track down the book or periodical again. You can see that taking care during the information-gathering stage will save you frustration later during the documenting stage.

Including Informational Notes

With the MLA style you no longer use footnotes or endnotes to credit your sources. Any numbered notes will be informational notes. Any brief comment that is important enough to include but that is not precisely to the point of your discussion can be placed in a note. When you type these informational notes, you should entitle them simply "Notes" and place them on a separate page at the end of the paper, just before the "Works Cited" page.

CHART 17 – 2 Checklist for Accurate Documentation

Besides following your usual procedures for proofreading and editing, you should take time to read through the paper one extra time, checking nothing but the way you have incorporated your sources. Ask yourself these questions:

1. Did I put quotation marks around all sentences and phrases borrowed from my reading?

2. Did I give credit in the text for all ideas borrowed from my reading, whether quoted directly or not?

3. Did I always put periods and commas before the quotation marks except when documentation in parentheses follows the quotation? Here's an example:

> "Arrabal's world," Esslin believes, "derives its absurdity . . . from the fact that his characters see the human situation with uncomprehending eyes of childlike simplicity" (217).

4. Did I include all the required information in the citations?

5. Did I use accurate paraphrases that are not too close to the original wording?

Then, take a few extra minutes to check carefully your "Works Cited" page. Ask yourself these questions:

1. Did I alphabetize correctly? (*A, an,* and *the* do not count when alphabetizing the title of an anonymous article.)

2. Did I use hanging indention (indent all lines of an entry five spaces except for the first line)?

3. Did I use colons where colons are needed, periods where periods are needed, parentheses where parentheses are needed?

4. Did I underline the titles of all books and the names of all magazines and scholarly journals?

5. Did I use quotation marks around the titles of articles and chapters from books?

6. Did I convert all Roman numerals to Arabic?

7. Did I include all the necessary data?

Editing

You must be particularly careful in proofreading and correcting a documented paper. Careless errors in typing will ruin your credibility—as well as your grade. Careless errors in crediting your sources could result in plagiarism, thus threatening your credibility, and your grade.

Sample Documented Papers by Students
Paper on Drama

The following paper was written by a student at Illinois State University. A complete guide to using the MLA system appears at the end of this chapter.

Laurie Dahlberg

English 102

March 12, 1992

An Analysis of Arrabal's Picnic on the Battlefield

Fernando Arrabal's play Picnic on the Battlefield may at first appear to be simply a war protest, but its simplicity can be misleading. Like other artists, Arrabal himself can be found at the center of the play, projecting his own dismal yet amusing view of human nature at war with itself. Though the playwright's purpose is to expose the utter stupidity of war[1] which, as critic Janet Diaz observes, is "forced on peace-loving men by their governments" (151-2), he nonetheless portrays his characters in a way which causes the audience to wonder whether these people deserve the dignity of peace. Arrabal portrays humanity as innocent yet

cruel. Examining the characterization in the play gives us
insight into its absurdist philosophical underpinnings.

Arrabal creates a world which is altogether bewildering to
its inhabitants and audience alike. "Paradoxes abound,"
writes Podol: "the lyrical is united with the cruel, humor is
combined with terror, innocence with depravity. . ."
(29). Though Picnic on the Battlefield includes layers of
often confusing paradoxes, Arrabal achieves unity through
repetition--of words, symbols, even characters. Zapo and Zépo
behave exactly alike in order to stress the absurdity of
fighting a war against someone who is no different from oneself.

Drama specialist Martin Esslin notes that the play's
absurdity derives largely from the characters who see their
situation "through uncomprehending eyes of childlike
simplicity" (217). Thus Zapo knits in the trenches, a prisoner
lunches politely with his captors, and the Tépans protect
themselves from bombs with an ordinary umbrella. Diaz comments
that the action seems illogical only until we recognize that
the "logic is not directly expressed, but symbolically embodied
in the action" (153). Thus, the play presents a highly
subjective form of reality which, in the words of critic Ruby
Cohn, "syncopate[s] incidents in a dream-like way . . . "
(29-30). The bouyant, giddy behavior of the characters
suggests a dream world, but elements of reality are strongly
present. As Arrabal himself has observed, he is a "realist
including the nightmare" (qtd. in Killinger 220).

The characters in the play behave like adult
children. Thomas Donahue notes that they "combine the
imaginative, playful, sadistically cruel behavior of the child
with the chronologically mature body of an adult" (8). They
seem almost blameless in their innocence. Esslin adds that
"Like children, they are often cruel because they have failed
to understand, or even to notice, the existence of a moral law;
and like children, they suffer the cruelty of the world as a

meaningless affliction" (217). These adult children vacillate between being playful and pouting, generous and inconsiderate. As the play opens, the lonely Zapo, who cannot understand the meaning of war, is plaintively asking his captain to send him someone to keep him company, "even if it's only a nanny goat." Genevieve Serreau observes that the simplicity of the language contributes greatly to the effectiveness of the play. The characters speak, she says, with "the poetic truth of the language of childhood, a speech as direct as a shower of stones . . . " (68).

Of course, Zapo, and his double, Zépo, are little more than children, perhaps eighteen years old. But they at least have enough understanding of the dangers of war to dive under the sandbags when bombs begin to fall. Mons. and Mme. Tépan, on the other hand, do not recognize the slightest danger as they stroll casually into the middle of a war zone to have a picnic with their son. Arrabal, in fact, seems to intensify the immaturity of the older couple, perhaps suggesting that the longer one is on earth, the more confusing it all becomes. His characters can only cope with the complexity of life by retreating into a shell of ignorance, like pulling the covers up over their heads.

Reacting to war with the incomprehension of children, the characters relegate war to the status of a childish game. According to critic Peter Podol, the game, or "jeu," provides a motif in which war is equated with "a broad range of playful competitions" (31). The equation of war and game is reiterated throughout the play, as when Zapo tags the enemy Zépo on the shoulder, instead of taking him prisoner at gunpoint. Both characters understand this gesture.

But Arrabal goes beyond the contrast between the innocence of the adult children and the cruelty of the real world. He quite honestly includes the darker side of human nature in order to make his characters not just naive, but morally

naive. This conflict between depravity and innocence is an
emerging force in the play. As T. J. Donahue explains,

> [The characters'] moral systems, if one can call
> them such, tend to be mechanistic. They shoot their
> so-called enemy and then quickly recite the Hail Mary
> or the Our Father. In their eyes, asking for pardon
> is a sufficient safeguard against guilt. . . . Yet
> their lack of guilt demonstrates that reality never
> penetrates the fiber of their lives. (8)

We get our first clue about the unfeeling nature of the
characters when Mme. Tépan remarks, "We thought you must be
bored, so we came to pay you a little visit. This war must be a
bit tedious, after all." Tedious is hardly an appropriate word
to use to describe a war. Later, she casually declares, "I've
always liked battles. As a child I always said that when I grew
up I wanted to be a Colonel of the dragoons."[2] The same callous
nature is revealed by degrees in each of the characters.
Gentle Zapo is eager to pose with the captured Zépo like a hunter
with his trophy. Death and destruction seem only to heighten
Mons. Tépan's appetite: "I feel hungry as a hunter. It's the
smell of gunpowder."

Arrabal brilliantly counterpoints this cruelly
indifferent attitude with the excessively polite etiquette
observed by the Tépans--with highly comic results. In theory,
social politeness (supposedly a proud product of
"civilization") grew out of the understanding of accepted
moral laws, like the Golden Rule. And although the Tépans
strictly adhere to the complicated structure of social decorum,
it becomes apparent that the morality which should underlie
this civility is absent, leaving a ridiculous shell of social
niceties devoid of any connection with the principles which
produced them. In a highly ironic scene, Mme. Tépan is more
interested in the cleanliness of her son than in his safety or

his well-being: " . . . you know, there's one thing I <u>will</u> not have, and that's making fighting a war an excuse for not washing."

Thus, despite the dull horror and grotesqueries, <u>Picnic on the Battlefield</u> is often hilariously funny. Donahue describes the appeal of the black humor this way:

> From the point of view of the
> spectator, . . . the distance that is established
> between what these hapless children want to be and
> what they really are, between what they strive to do
> and what they do, gives a comic luster . . .
> reminiscent of the type of comedy produced by the
> pratfalls of Chaplin's tramp. (24)

By making us laugh, Arrabal clearly hopes to make us see the flaws of society. As Podol illustrates, Arrabal depends heavily upon humor--on the "construction of incongruities"--in order to "render the idea of war totally ludicrous" (30). But he does not hold human beings to blame for the evils of the social system. He declares, "My characters are not familiar with the laws. They try to understand laws that serve no useful purpose whatsoever. Even in extreme cases, they are not guilty. It is not my characters who should be changed, but rather society" (qtd. in Espinasse 72).

Notes

[1]Fernando Arrabal, born in Spanish Morocco in 1933, lived
in Spain during the Spanish Civil War under a military
dictatorship, which may account for his strong anti-war
sentiments (Serreau 61).

[2]According to Podol, "Zapo's mother, Mme. Tépan, mirrors
Arrabal's own mother both in name (Teran) and in her blind
admiration for the military uniform and its aura" (30).

Works Cited

Cohn, Ruby. <u>Currents in Contemporary Drama</u>. Bloomington: Indiana UP, 1960.

Diaz, Janet W. "Theatre and Theories of Fernando Arrabal." <u>Kentucky Romance Quarterly</u> 2 (1969): 1143-54.

Donahue, Thomas John. <u>The Theatre of Fernando Arrabal</u>. New York: New York UP, 1980.

Espinasse, Francoise. "An Interview with Fernando Arrabal." <u>Evergreen Review</u> 71 (Oct. 1969): 43-47, 72-73.

Esslin, Martin. <u>The Theatre of the Absurd</u>. Garden City: Doubleday, 1969.

Killinger, John. "Arrabal and Surrealism." <u>Modern Drama</u> 14 (Sept. 1971): 210-23.

Podol, Peter L. <u>Fernando Arrabal</u>. Boston: G. K. Hall, 1978.

Serreau, Genevieve. "A New Comic Style: Arrabal." <u>Evergreen Review</u> 4 (Nov.-Dec. 1960): 61-69.

Remember that in your paper the "Notes," if you use them, and the "Works Cited" list will each appear on separate pages.

Paper on a Short Story

The following essay, analyzing a story that appears in Chapter 13, was written by a student at Illinois State University.

Mindy K. Thomas
English 102
April 3, 1992

The Evils of Ignorance: Shirley Jackson's "The Lottery"

Human beings have always feared the unknown. In order to explain our existence, people create gods. And, to insure the happiness of these gods and thus the continuation of human life, people devise rituals to follow in their worship. In many ancient civilizations human sacrifice was an integral part of this worship. Often the gods were appeased through the performance of scapegoat rituals requiring that one person be sacrificed to atone for the sins of the whole society. Helen Nebeker observes that "those chosen for sacrifice were not victims but saviors who would propitiate the gods, enticing them to bring rebirth, renewal, and thanking them with their blood" (104). These practices, rich with symbolic meaning, were an essential part of the culture. In "The Lottery" Shirley Jackson shows us such a ritual but one in which the essential meaning has long ago been lost.

Jackson's lottery is set in the present, but the ceremony is obviously one that has been performed for so long that no one can even remember its significance. The blackness of the box represents the evil of a community kept in darkness by its own ignorance. Nebeker explains the significance of the box this way:

> Jackson certainly suggests the body of
> tradition . . . which the dead hand of the past
> codified in religion, mores, government, and the rest
> of culture, and passed from generation to generation,
> letting it grow ever more cumbersome, meaningless,
> and indefensible. (103-04)

Jackson tells us that the box "grew shabbier each year . . . and in some places was faded and stained" (75). This deterioration of the box mirrors the moral degeneration of people who perform murder for reasons they can no longer remember.

This savagery, Jackson shows us, is inherent in all people and is hidden just beneath the surface of our seemingly civilized exteriors. The duality of human nature is exhibited through the characterization and actions of the villagers. As Brooks and Warren note, "The cruel stoning is carried out by 'decent' citizens who in many other respects show themselves kind and thoughtful" (75). When it was time for the scapegoat to be murdered, Mrs. Delacroix, who earlier had made neighborly conversation with Tessie, "selected a stone so large she had to pick it up with both hands" (79). Another villager, Mr. Adams, who had previously mentioned that people in another village were "talking of giving up the lottery," was standing "in the front of the crowd" ready to attack as Mr. Warner urged the others to "come on" and begin the slaughter (77, 79). Critic Shyamal Bagchee rightly says of the townspeople that "The spectacle of death does not cause any radical rethinking among the living" (8). And James Gibson concurs, observing that their world "has no moral rules, for the lottery has rendered them meaningless" (195).

Although the depiction of human nature in this story is a grim one, there is a small glimmer of hope. "Some places have already quit [the] lotteries" (77), indicating that while human beings do have a deeply rooted fear of change, change is at least possible. Nebeker comments on this need for change:

> Until enough [people] are touched strongly enough by
> the horror of their ritualistic, irrational actions
> to reject the long-perverted ritual, to destroy the
> box completely--or to make, if necessary, a new one
> reflective of their own conditions and needs of
> life--they will never free themselves from their
> primitive nature. . . . (107)

Jackson's powerful story is a plea for tolerance, for compassion
for others, and for progression toward a future in which the
practices of society reflect a healthy social conscience. She
wants us to see that we can rid ourselves of the evil that
ignorance perpetuates by examining the practices we repeat out
of unquestioning tradition.

Works Cited

Bagchee, Shyamal. "Design of Darkness in Shirley Jackson's
    'The Lottery.'" <u>Notes on Contemporary Literature</u> 9.4
    (1979): 8-9).

Brooks, Cleanth, and Robert Penn Warren. <u>Understanding
    Fiction</u>. New York: Appleton, 1959.

Gibson, James R. "An Old Testament Analogue for 'The
    Lottery.'" <u>Journal of American Literature</u> 2.1 (1984):
    193-95.

Jackson, Shirley. "The Lottery." <u>Literature and the Writing
    Process</u>. Ed. Elizabeth McMahan, Susan Day, and Robert
    Funk. New York: Macmillan, 1993. 74-75.

Nebeker, Helen E. "'The Lottery': Symbolic Tour de
    Force." <u>American Literature</u> 46 (1974): 100-07.

Explanation of the MLA Documentation Style

1. Your paper will end with an alphabetized list of "Works Cited" that includes all sources mentioned in your essay.

2. In citing primary sources (i.e., short stories, poems, novels, or plays), include author's name and page number (or line number, if a poem) in the text for the first entry. Thereafter, page number alone will suffice, unless your list of "Works Cited" includes more than one work by that author. You should include a shortened title if you have several works by the same author, like this: (Gissing, *Grub Street* 37).

A. Quotation from a novel or short story:

Rhoda Nunn emphasizes the importance of role models as she declares to Monica, "Your mistake was in looking only at the weak women" (316).

We are told that Dorie "loved that woman's husband with a fierce love that was itself a little ugly" (112).

The "Works Cited" entries are

Gissing, George. <u>The Odd Women</u>. 1893. Rpt. New York: Norton, 1977.

Oates, Joyce Carol. "Accomplished Desires." The Wheel of Love
and Other Stories. New York: Fawcett, 1972. 111–47.

B. Quotation from a poem:

Coleridge's assertion that poetic life is a "miracle of rare device / A
sunny pleasure dome with caves of ice" (35–36) proves paradoxical.

Do not include the words or the abbreviations for *line* or *lines*.

The "Works Cited" entry is

Coleridge, S. T. "Kubla Khan." Coleridge: Poetical Works. Ed.
Ernest H. Coleridge. London: Oxford UP, 1973. 297–98.

C. Quotation from a play:

In Othello, Iago's striking comment, "What you know, you know. /
From this time forth I will never speak a word" (5.2.299–300), serves
as a philosophic closure.

The ontological level of discourse can be seen in the words of Emilia,
who exclaims, "O, the more angel she, / And you the blacker devil!"
(Othello 5.1.129–30).

[The numbers separated by periods mean: Act 5, scene 1, lines 129
through 130.] In modern plays, you may simply cite page numbers,
as you would with a quotation from a novel or short story.]

The "Works Cited" entry is

Shakespeare, William. Othello. Literature: An Introduction to Fiction,
Poetry, and Drama. Ed. X. J. Kennedy. 3rd ed. Boston:
Little, Brown 1983. 875–958.

D. Quotations from essays are cited the same way as a novel.

3. Individual citations of secondary sources (books or articles considering the work under discussion) are inserted in the paper by author and
page number (or by author, shortened title, and page number if your
list of "Works Cited" includes more than one work by that person).

A. Quotation from a work in more than one volume:

Kettle declares Middlemarch to be "the most impressive novel in our
language" (1:160).

The "Works Cited" entry is

Kettle, Arnold. An Introduction to the English Novel. 2 vols. New
York: Harper, 1951.

B. Quotation from book with single author:

As Lawrence Stone explains, daughters in Shakespeare's England were
"often unwanted and might be regarded as no more than a tiresome
drain on the economic resources of the family" (112).

The "Works Cited" entry is

Stone, Lawrence. The Family, Sex and Marriage in England: 1500–1800. New York: Harper, 1977.

C. Quotation from an article:

As Michael Holzman reports, many of his students felt that "Expression and communication were reserved for speech" (235).

The "Works Cited" entry is

Holzman, Michael. "Teaching Is Remembering." College English 46 (184): 229–38.

According to Tanselle, "The basic technical problem of bibliographical description arises from the difficulty of expressing the visual in verbal terms" (71).

The "Works Cited" entry is

Tanselle, G. Thomas. "The Bibliographical Description of Patterns." Studies in Bibliography 23 (1970): 70–102.

4. Any notes in your paper will be informational; that is, they will contain material of interest that is not essential to your discussion. These content notes are included as "Notes" just before your list of "Works Cited."

5. Always use Arabic numbers, except when citing pages from a preface, introduction, or table of contents (vi) or when mentioning monarchs (James I, Elizabeth II).

6. If the place of publication of a book is a foreign city, cite the original name and add the English version in brackets: München [Munich].

7. Always omit the abbreviations *p.* and *pp.* (for page and pages).

8. In general, use lower case for *vol.*, *no.*, *chap.*, *trans.* in citations.

9. If you cite two or more entries by the same author, do not repeat the author's name. Instead use three hyphens, followed by a period. Then give the remaining information as usual.

Sample Entries for a "Works Cited" List

Remember: You must alphabetize your list and use hanging indention; that is, after the first line, indent subsequent lines five spaces.

A. Book with one author:

Rabkin, Norman. Shakespeare and the Problem of Meaning. Chicago: U of Chicago P, 1981.

B. Reprint of an earlier edition:

Partridge, Eric. Shakespeare's Bawdy. 1948. New York: Dutton, 1969.

C. Revised edition:

Howe, Irving. <u>William Faulkner: A Critical Study</u>. 3rd ed. Chicago: U of Chicago P, 1973.

D. Book with two authors:

Gilbert, Sandra, and Susan Gubar. <u>The Madwoman in the Attic: The Woman Writer and the Nineteenth-Century Literary Imagination</u>. New Haven: Yale UP, 1979.

E. Book with more than three authors or editors:

Spiller, Robert E. et al. <u>LHUS</u>. 3rd ed. London: Macmillan, 1969.

[*LHUS* means *Literary History of the United States* and is abbreviated in citations, as are *PMLA (Publication of the Modern Language Association)* and *TLS (London Times Literary Supplement).*]

F. Work in several volumes:

Kettle, Arnold. <u>An Introduction to the English Novel</u>. 2 vols. New York: Harper, 1951.

G. Essay in a collection, casebook, or critical edition:

(A Primary Work)

Crane, Stephen. "The Open Boat." <u>Anthology of American Literature</u>. Ed. George McMichael. 3rd ed. 2 vols. New York: Macmillan, 1989. 2: 858–73.

(A Secondary Source)

Geist, Stanley, "Portraits from a Family Album: Daisy Miller." <u>Hudson Review</u> 5 (Summer 1952): 203–206. Reprinted in <u>James's</u> Daisy Miller. Ed. William T. Stafford. New York: Scribner's, 1963. 131–33.

[If an underlined title contains another title usually underlined, leave the second title without underlining.]

H. Work in an anthology:

Arnold, Matthew. "Dover Beach." <u>The Norton Anthology of English Literature</u>. Ed. M. H. Abrams et al. 2 vols. New York: Norton, 1968. 2: 1039.

I. Work in translation:

Cirlot, J. E. <u>A Dictionary of Symbols</u>. Trans. Jack Sage. 2nd ed. New York: Philosophical Lib., 1976.

J. Anonymous book:

<u>The Statutes of the Realm</u>. London: Record Commissions, 1820–28; facsim. ed. 1968.

[facsim. — abbreviation for facsimile]

K. Anonymous article (magazine with no volume number):

"Speaking Softly, Carrying No Stick." Newsweek 11, Nov. 1991: 66.

L. Signed article (newspaper):

Harding, D. W. "Father and Daughter in Shakespeare's Last Plays." TLS 30 Nov. 1979: 59–61.

[*TLS* means the London *Times Literary Supplement.*]

Unsigned article (newspaper):

"College Grads Better Consumers." Chicago Tribune 3 May 1976: 2.3.

[means section 2, page 3]

M. Signed article (periodical with no volume number):

Heilbrun, Carolyn. "The Masculine Wilderness of the American Novel." Saturday Review 29 Jan. 1962: 41–44.

N. Signed article (periodical with continuous pagination):

Mason, John B. "Whitman's Catalogues: Rhetorical Means for Two Journeys in 'Song of Myself.'" American Literature 45 (1973): 34–49.

Signed article (periodical with each issue separately paged):

Frey, John R. "America and Her Literature Reviewed by Postwar Germany." American-German Review 10.5 (1954): 4–7.

[means vol. 10, issue 5]

O. Unsigned encyclopedia article:

"Abolitionists." Encyclopedia Americana. 1974 ed.

P. Signed encyclopedia article:

P[ar]k, T[homas]. "Ecology." Encyclopaedia Britannica. 1968 ed.

Q. Article from *Dictionary of American Biography:*

N[evins], A[llan]. "Warren Gamaliel Harding." DAB (1932).

[The article is signed with initials. The corresponding name is listed at the beginning of the volume.]

R. Anonymous pamphlet:

Preparing Your Dissertation for Microfilming. Ann Arbor: UMI, n.d.

[UMI means University Microfilms International. n.d. means no date given.]

S. Reference to the Bible:

The Bible.   Trans. J. M. P. Smith et al.   Chicago: U of Chicago P, 1939.

The Geneva Bible.   1560.   Facsim.   Rpt. Madison: U of Wisconsin
         P, 1961.

[Do not underline the King James version of the Bible, and do not
list the Bible unless you have used a version other than the King
James. Cite chapter and verse in parentheses in the text of your
paper this way: (Dan. 9.25 – 27)].

T. **Reference to a letter (in a published collection):**

Clemens, Samuel.   Mark Twain's Letters.   Ed. A. B. Paine.   2
         vols.   New York: Harper, 1917.

U. **Reference to a letter (unpublished or personal):**

Wharton, Edith.   Letter to William Brownell.   6 Nov.
         1907.   Wharton Archives.   Amherst College, Amherst, MA.

Vidal, Gore.   Letter to author.   2 June 1984.

V. **Personal or telephone interview:**

Kesey, Ken.   Personal interview.   28 May 1983.

Didion, Joan.   Telephone interview.   10 April 1982.

W. **Review (signed or unsigned):**

Updike, John.   "Who Wants to Know?"   Rev. of the Dragons of
         Eden, by Carl Sagan.   The New Yorker 22 Aug. 1977: 87 – 90.

Rev. of Ring, by Jonathan Yardley.   The New Yorker 12 Sept. 1977:
         159 – 60.

X. **Lecture:**

Axelrod, Rise.   "Who Did What with Whom?"   MLA Convention.
         Chicago, 30 Dec. 1977.

Y. **Film:**

Modern Times.   Dir. Charles Chaplin.   With Chaplin and Paulette
         Goddard.   United Artists, 1936.

[If you are discussing the contribution of an individual, begin with
that person's name.]

Z. **Document from ERIC (Education Resources Information Center):**

Cooper, Grace C.   "The Teaching of Composition and Different
         Cognitive Styles."   Mar. 1980.   Ed 186 915.

Anthology of Drama

William Shakespeare *1564–1616*

OTHELLO, THE MOOR OF VENICE

THE NAMES OF THE ACTORS

OTHELLO, *the Moor.*

BRABANTIO, *a senator, father to Desdemona.*

CASSIO, *an honourable lieutenant to Othello.*

IAGO, *Othello's ancient, a villain.*

RODERIGO, *a gulled gentleman.*

DUKE OF VENICE.

SENATORS *of Venice.*

MONTANO, *governor of Cyprus.*

LODOVICO *and* GRATIANO,

kinsmen to Brabantio, two noble Venetians.

SAILORS.

CLOWN.

DESDEMONA, *daughter to Brabantio and wife to Othello.*

EMILIA, *wife to Iago.*

BIANCA, *a courtezan and mistress to Cassio.*

MESSENGER, HERALD, OFFICERS, GENTLEMEN, MUSICIANS, *and* ATTENDANTS.

[SCENE: VENICE: A SEA-PORT IN CYPRUS]

ACT I

SCENE I *Venice. A street.*

[*Enter* RODERIGO *and* IAGO.]

ROD. Tush! never tell me; I take it much unkindly
That thou, Iago, who hast had my purse

As if the strings were thine, shouldst know of this.
IAGO. 'Sblood,[1] but you'll not hear me:
  If ever I did dream of such a matter,
  Abhor me.
ROD. Thou told'st me thou didst hold him in thy hate.
IAGO. Despise me, if I do not. Three great ones of the city,[2]
  In personal suit to make me his lieutenant,
  Off-capp'd to him:[3] and, by the faith of man,   10
  I know my price, I am worth no worse a place:
  But he, as loving his own pride and purposes,
  Evades them, with a bombast circumstance
  Horribly stuff'd with epithets of war;
  And, in conclusion,
  Nonsuits[4] my mediators; for, "Certes," says he,
  "I have already chose my officer."
  And what was he?
  Forsooth, a great arithmetician,[5]
  One Michael Cassio, a Florentine,   20
  A fellow almost damn'd in a fair wife;[6]
  That never set a squadron in the field,
  Nor the division[7] of a battle knows
  More than a spinster; unless the bookish theoric,[8]
  Wherein the toged[9] consuls can propose[10]
  As masterly as he: mere prattle, without practice,
  Is all his soldiership. But he, sir, had th' election:
  And I, of whom his eyes had seen the proof
  At Rhodes, at Cyprus[11] and on other grounds
  Christian and heathen, must be be-lee'd and calm'd   30
  By debitor and creditor: this counter-caster,[12]
  He, in good time,[13] must his lieutenant be,
  And I—God bless the mark![14]—his Moorship's ancient.[15]
ROD. By heaven, I rather would have been his hangman.

---

[1]**'Sblood** an oath, "by God's blood"
[2]**great ones of the city** Iago means to indicate his importance in the community; this is suggested also by his use of the word *worth* in line 11
[3]**him** Othello
[4]**Nonsuits** rejects
[5]**arithmetician** a man whose military knowledge was merely theoretical, based on books of tactics
[6]**A . . . wife** Cassio does not seem to be married, but his counterpart in Shakespeare's source did have a wife
[7]**division** disposition of a battle line
[8]**theoric** theory
[9]**toged** wearing the toga
[10]**propose** discuss
[11]**Rhodes, Cyprus** islands in the Mediterranean south of Asia Minor, long subject to contention between the Venetians and the Turks
[12]**counter-caster** a sort of bookkeeper; contemptuous term
[13]**in good time** forsooth
[14]**God bless the mark** anciently, a pious interjection to avert evil omens
[15]**ancient** standardbearer, ensign

IAGO. Why, there's no remedy; 'tis the curse of service,
  Preferment goes by letter and affection,
  And not by old gradation,[16] where each second
  Stood heir to th' first. Now, sir, be judge yourself,
  Whether I in any just term am affin'd[17]
  To love the Moor.
ROD.   I would not follow then.
IAGO. O, sir, content you;
  I follow him to serve my turn upon him:
  We cannot all be masters, nor all masters
  Cannot be truly follow'd. You shall mark
  Many a duteous and knee-crooking knave,
  That, doting on his own obsequious bondage,
  Wears out his time, much like his master's ass,
  For nought but provender, and when he's old, cashier'd:
  Whip me such honest knaves. Others there are
  Who, trimm'd in forms and visages of duty,
  Keep yet their hearts attending on themselves,
  And, throwing but shows of service on their lords,
  Do well thrive by them and when they have lin'd their coats
  Do themselves homage: these fellows have some soul;
  And such a one do I profess myself. For, sir,
  It is as sure as you are Roderigo,
  Were I the Moor, I would not be Iago:[18]
  In following him, I follow but myself;
  Heaven is my judge, not I for love and duty,
  But seeming so, for my peculiar end:
  For when my outward action doth demonstrate
  The native act and figure of my heart
  In compliment extern,[19] 'tis not long after
  But I will wear my heart upon my sleeve
  For daws to peck at: I am not what I am.
ROD. What a full fortune does the thick-lips[20] owe,
  If he can carry 't thus!
IAGO.   Call up her father,
  Rouse him: make after him, poison his delight,
  Proclaim him in the streets; incense her kinsmen,
  And, though he in a fertile climate dwell,
  Plague him with flies: though that his joy be joy,
  Yet throw such changes of vexation on 't,
  As it may lose some colour.
ROD. Here is her father's house; I'll call aloud.
IAGO. Do, with like timorous[21] accent and dire yell

---

[16]**old gradation** seniority; Iago here expresses a characteristic prejudice of professional soldiers
[17]**affin'd** bound
[18]**Were . . . Iago** Were I in the position of the Moor, I should not feel as Iago feels
[19]**compliment extern** outward civility
[20]**thick-lips** Elizabethans often applied the term *Moor* to Negroes
[21]**timorous** frightening

As when, by night and negligence, the fire
   Is spied in populous cities.
ROD. What, ho, Brabantio! Signior Brabantio, ho!
IAGO. Awake! what, ho, Brabantio! thieves! thieves! thieves!
   Look to your house, your daughter and your bags!   80
   Thieves! thieves!

[BRABANTIO *appears above at a window.*]
BRA. What is the reason of this terrible summons?
   What is the matter there?
ROD. Signior, is all your family within?
IAGO. Are your doors lock'd?
BRA.   Why, wherefore ask you this?
IAGO. 'Zounds, sir, y' are robb'd; for shame, put on your gown;
   Your heart is burst, you have lost half your soul;
   Even now, now, very now, an old black ram
   Is tupping your white ewe. Arise, arise:
   Awake the snorting[22] citizens with the bell,   90
   Or else the devil will make a grandsire of you:
   Arise, I say.
BRA.   What, have you lost your wits?
ROD. Most reverend signior, do you know my voice?
BRA. Not I: what are you?
ROD. My name is Roderigo.
BRA.   The worser welcome:
   I have charg'd thee not to haunt about my doors:
   In honest plainness thou has heard me say
   My daughter is not for thee; and now, in madness,
   Being full of supper and distemp'ring draughts,
   Upon malicious bravery,[23] doest thou come   100
   To start[24] my quiet.
ROD. Sir, sir, sir,—
BRA.   But thou must needs be sure
   My spirit and my place have in them power
   To make this bitter to thee.
ROD.   Patience, good sir.
BRA. What tell'st thou me of robbing? this is Venice;
   My house is not a grange.[25]
ROD.   Most grave Brabantio,
   In simple and pure soul I come to you.   110
IAGO. 'Zounds, sir, you are one of those that will not serve God, if the devil bid
   you. Because we come to do you service and you think we are ruffians, you'll
   have your daughter covered with a Barbary horse, you'll have your nephews[26]
   neigh to you; you'll have coursers for cousins and gennets[27] for germans.[28]

---

[22]**snorting** snoring
[23]**bravery** defiance, bravado
[24]**start** disrupt
[25]**grange** isolated farmhouse
[26]**nephews** grandsons
[27]**gennets** small Spanish horses
[28]**germans** near relatives

BRA. What profane wretch are thou?

IAGO. I am one, sir, that comes to tell you your daughter and the Moor are now
making the beast with two backs.

BRA. Thou art a villain.

IAGO.   You are—a senator.

BRA. This thou shalt answer; I know thee, Roderigo.

ROD. Sir, I will answer any thing. But, I beseech you,
If 't be your pleasure and most wise consent,
As partly I find it is, that your fair daughter,
At this odd-even[29] and dull watch o' th' night,   120
Transported, with no worse nor better guard
But with a knave of common hire, a gondolier,
To the gross clasps of a lascivious Moor,—
If this be known to you and your allowance,[30]
We then have done you bold and saucy wrongs;
But if you know not this, my manners tell me
We have your wrong rebuke. Do not believe
That, from[31] the sense of all civility,
I thus would play and trifle with your reverence:
Your daughter, if you have not given her leave,   130
I say again, hath made a gross revolt;
Tying her duty, beauty, wit and fortunes
In an extravagant[32] and wheeling[33] stranger
Of here and every where. Straight satisfy yourself:
If she be in her chamber or your house,
Let loose on me the justice of the state
For thus deluding you.

BRA.   Strike on the tinder,[34] ho!
Give me a taper! call up all my people!
This accident[35] is not unlike my dream:
Belief of it oppresses me already.
Light, I say! light!   140

                                                                        [*Exit above.*]

IAGO.   Farewell; for I must leave you:
It seems not meet, nor wholesome to my place,
To be produc'd—as, if I stay, I shall—
Against the Moor: for, I do know, the state,
However this may gall him with some check,[36]
Cannot with safety cast[37] him, for he's embark'd
With such loud reason to the Cyprus wars,
Which even now stand in act,[38] that, for their souls,

[29]**odd-even** between night and morning

[30]**allowance** permission

[31]**from** contrary to

[32]**extravagant** wandering

[33]**wheeling** vagabond

[34]**tinder** charred linen kept in a metal box, and ignited by a spark from flint and steel

[35]**accident** occurrence, event

[36]**check** rebuke

[37]**cast** dismiss

[38]**stand in act** are going on

Another of his fathom[39] they have none,   150
To lead their business: in which regard,
Though I do hate him as I do hell-pains,
Yet, for necessity of present life,
I must show out a flag and sign of love,
Which is indeed but sign. That you shall surely find him,
Lead to the Sagittary[40] the raised search:
And there will I be with him. So, farewell.   [*Exit.*]

[*Enter below* BRABANTIO, *with* SERVANTS *and torches.*]
BRA. It is too true an evil: gone she is;
    And what's to come of my despised time
    Is nought but bitterness. Now, Roderigo,
    Where didst thou see her? O unhappy girl!   160
    With the Moor, say'st thou? Who would be a father!
    How didst thou know 'twas she? O, she deceives me
    Past thought! What said she to you? Get moe[41] tapers:
    Raise all my kindred. Are they married, think you?
ROD. Truly, I think they are.
BRA. O heaven! How got she out? O treason of the blood!
    Fathers, from hence trust not your daughters' minds
    By what you see them act. Is[42] there not charms
    By which the property[43] of youth and maidhood
    May be abus'd? Have you not read, Roderigo,   170
    Of some such thing?
ROD.   Yes, sir, I have indeed.
BRA. Call up my brother. O, would you[44] had had her!
    Some one way, some another. Do you know
    Where we may apprehend her and the Moor?
ROD. I think I can discover him, if you please
    To get good guard and go along with me.
BRA. Pray you, lead on. At every house I'll call;
    I may command at most. Get weapons, ho!
    And raise some special officers of night.[45]
    On, good Roderigo: I will deserve your pains.   180
                                                                [*Exeunt.*]

SCENE II *Another street.*

[*Enter* OTHELLO, IAGO, ATTENDANTS *with torches.*]
IAGO. Though in the trade of war I have slain men,
    Yet do I hold it very stuff o' th' conscience
    To do no contriv'd murder: I lack iniquity

[39]**fathom** ability
[40]**Sagittary** probably an inn
[41]**moe** more
[42]**Is** are
[43]**property** special quality
[44]**you** Roderigo
[45]**officers of night** police

Sometime to do me service: nine or ten times
I had thought t' have yerk'd[46] him here under the ribs.
OTH. 'Tis better as it is.
IAGO.   Nay, but he prated,
And spoke such scurvy and provoking terms
Against your honour
That, with the little godliness I have,
I did full hard forbear him. But, I pray you, sir,
Are you fast married? Be assur'd of this,   10
That the magnifico[47] is much belov'd,
And hath in his effect[48] a voice potential[49]
As double[50] as the duke's: he will divorce you;
Or put upon you what restraint and grievance
The law, with all his might to enforce it on,
Will give him cable.
OTH.   Let him do his spite;
My services, which I have done the signiory[51]
Shall out-tongue his complaints. 'Tis yet to know —
Which, when I know that boasting is an honour,
I shall promulgate — I fetch my life and being   20
From men of royal siege,[52] and my demerits[53]
May speak unbonneted[54] to as proud a fortune
As this that I have reach'd: for know, Iago,
But that I love the gentle Desdemona,
I would not my unhoused free condition
Put into circumscription and confine
For the sea's worth. But, look! what lights come yond?
IAGO. Those are the raised father and his friends:
You were best go in.
OTH.   Not I; I must be found: 30
My parts, my title and my perfect soul[55]
Shall manifest me rightly. Is it they?
IAGO. By Janus, I think no.

[*Enter* CASSIO *and certain* OFFICERS *with torches.*]
OTH. The servants of the duke, and my lieutenant.
The goodness of the night upon you, friends!
What is the news?

[46]**yerk'd** stabbed
[47]**magnifico** Venetian grandee (i.e., Brabantio)
[48]**effect** influence
[49]**potential** powerful
[50]**double** twice as influential as most men's
[51]**signiory** Venetian government
[52]**siege** rank
[53]**demerits** deserts
[54]**unbonneted** on equal terms
[55]**perfect soul** unflawed conscience

CAS.   The duke does greet you, general,
  And he requires your haste-post-haste appearance,
  Even on the instant.
OTH.   What is the matter, think you?
CAS. Something from Cyprus, as I may divine:
  It is a business of some heat: the galleys   40
  Have sent a dozen sequent[56] messengers
  This very night at one another's heels,
  And many of the consuls,[57] rais'd and met,
  Are at the duke's already: you have been hotly call'd for;
  When, being not at your lodging to be found,
  The senate hath sent about three several[58] quests
  To search you out.
OTH.   'Tis well I am found by you.
  I will but spend a word here in the house.
  And go with you.   [*Exit.*]

CAS.   Ancient, what makes he here?
IAGO. 'Faith, he to-night hath boarded a land carack:[59]   50
  If it prove lawful prize, he's made for ever.
CAS. I do not understand.
IAGO.   He's married.
CAS.   To who?

  [*Enter* OTHELLO.]
IAGO. Marry, to—Come, captain, will you?
OTH.   Have with you.
CAS. Here comes another troop to seek for you.

  [*Enter* BRABANTIO, RODERIGO, *with* OFFICERS *and torches.*]
IAGO. It is Brabantio. General, be advis'd;
  He comes to bad intent.
OTH.   Holla! stand there!
ROD. Signior, it is the Moor.
BRA.   Down with him, thief!
[*They draw on both sides.*]
IAGO. You, Roderigo! come, sir, I am for you.
OTH. Keep up your bright swords, for the dew will rust them.
  Good Signior, you shall more command with years   60
  Than with your weapons.
BRA. O thou foul thief, where hast thou stow'd my daughter?
  Damn'd as thou art, thou has enchanted her;
  For I'll refer me to all things of sense,[60]
  If she in chains of magic were not bound,
  Whether a maid so tender, fair and happy,

[56]**sequent** successive
[57]**consuls** senators
[58]**several** separate
[59]**carack** large merchant ship
[60]**things of sense** commonsense understandings of the natural order

So opposite to marriage that she shunn'd
The wealthy curled darlings of our nation,
Would ever have, t' incur a general mock
Run from her guardage[61] to the sooty bosom   70
Of such a thing as thou, to fear, not to delight.
Judge me the world, if 'tis not gross in sense[62]
That thou has practis'd on her with foul charms,
Abus'd her delicate youth with drugs or minerals[63]
That weaken motion:[64] I'll have't disputed on;[65]
'Tis probable and palpable to thinking.
I therefore apprehend and do attach thee
For an abuser of the world,[66] a practiser
Of arts inhibited[67] and out of warrant.
Lay hold upon him: if he do resist,   80
Subdue him at his peril.

OTH.   Hold your hands,
Both you of my inclining,[68] and the rest:
Were it my cue to fight, I should have known it
Without a prompter. Wither will you that I go
To answer this charge?

BRA.   To prison, till fit time
Of law and course of direct session[69]
Call thee to answer.

OTH.   What if I do obey?
How may the duke be therewith satisfied,
Whose messengers are here about my side,
Upon some present business of the state
To bring me to him?   90

FIRST OFF.   'Tis true, most worthy signior;
The duke's in council, and your noble self,
I am sure, is sent for.

BRA.   How! the duke in council!
In this time of night! Bring him away:
Mine's not an idle cause: the duke himself,
Or any of my brothers of the state,
Cannot but feel this wrong as 'twere their own;
For if such actions may have passage free,
Bond-slaves and pagans[70] shall our statesmen be.

[*Exeunt.*]

---

[61]**guardage** guardianship
[62]**gross in sense** easily discernible in apprehension or perception
[63]**minerals** medicine, poison
[64]**motion** thought, reason
[65]**disputed on** argued in court by professional counsel
[66]**abuser of the world** corrupter of society
[67]**inhibited** prohibited
[68]**inclining** following, party
[69]**course of direct session** regular legal proceedings
[70]**Bond-slaves and pagans** contemptuous reference to Othello's past history

SCENE III *A council-chamber.*

[*Enter* DUKE, SENATORS *and* OFFICERS *set at a table, with lights and* ATTENDANTS.]

DUKE. There is no composition in these news
  That gives them credit.
FIRST SEN.   Indeed, they are disproportion'd;[71]
  My letters say a hundred and seven galleys.
DUKE. And mine, a hundred forty.
SEC. SEN.   And mine, two hundred:
  But though they jump[72] not on a just account,—
  As in these cases, where the aim[73] reports,
  'Tis oft with difference—yet do they all confirm
  A Turkish fleet, and bearing up to Cyprus. *×/ danger coming*
                               ← Venice wants / to fight fleet →
DUKE. Nay, it is possible enough to judgment:
  I do not so secure me[74] in the error,   10
  But the main article[75] I do approve
  In fearful sense.
SAILOR.   [*Within*] What, ho! what, ho! what, ho!
FIRST OFF. A messenger from the galleys.

[*Enter* SAILOR.]

DUKE.   Now, what's the business?
SAIL. The Turkish preparation makes for Rhodes; *(instead Cyprus)*
  So was I bid report here to the state
  By Signior Angelo.
DUKE. How say you by this change?
FIRST SEN.   This cannot be,
  By no assay[76] of reason: 'tis a pageant,
  To keep us in false gaze. When we consider
  Th' importancy of Cyprus to the Turk,   20
  And let outselves again but understand,
  That as it more concerns the Turk than Rhodes,
  So may he with more facile question[77] bear it,
  For that it stands not in such warlike brace,[78]
  But altogether lacks th' abilities
  That Rhodes is dress'd in: if we make thought of this,
  We must not think the Turk is so unskilful
  To leave that latest which concerns him first,
  Neglecting an attempt of ease and gain,
  To wake and wage a danger profitless.   30
DUKE. Nay, in all confidence, he's not for Rhodes.
FIRST OFF. Here is more news.

[71]**disproportion'd** inconsistent
[72]**jump** agree
[73]**aim** conjecture
[74]**secure me** feel myself secure
[75]**main article** i.e., that the Turkish fleet is threatening
[76]**assay** test
[77]**more facile question** greater facility of effort
[78]**brace** state of defense

[*Enter a* MESSENGER.]

MESS. The Ottomites, reverend and gracious,
    Steering with due course toward the isle of Rhodes,
    Have there injointed them with an after fleet.
FIRST SEN. Ay, so I thought. How many, as you guess?
MESS. Of thirty sail: and now they do re-stem[79]
    Their backward course, bearing with frank appearance
    Their purposes toward Cyprus. Signior Montano,
    Your trusty and most valiant servitor,   40
    With his free duty recommends you thus,
    And prays you to believe him.
DUKE. 'Tis certain, then, for Cyprus.
    Marcus Luccicos, is not he in town?
FIRST SEN. He's now in Florence.
DUKE. Write from us to him; post-post-haste dispatch.
FIRST SEN. Here comes Brabantio and the valiant Moor.

[*Enter* BRABANTIO, OTHELLO, CASSIO, IAGO, RODERIGO, *and* OFFICERS.]
DUKE. Valiant Othello, we must straight employ you
    Against the general enemy Ottoman.
[*To* BRABANTIO] I did not see you; welcome, gentle signior;   50
    We lack'd your counsel and your help to-night.
BRA. So did I yours. Good your grace, pardon me;
    Neither my place nor aught I heard of business
    Hath rais'd me from my bed, nor doth the general care
    Take hold on me, for my particular grief
    Is of so flood-gate and o'erbearing nature
    That it engluts[80] and swallows other sorrows
    And it is still itself.
DUKE.   Why, what's the matter?
BRA. My daughter! O, my daughter!
DUKE *and* SEN.   Dead?
BRA.   Ay, to me;
    She is abus'd, stol'n from me, and corrupted   60
    By spells and medicines bought of mountebanks;
    For nature so preposterously to err,
    Being not deficient, blind, or lame of sense,
    Sans witchcraft could not.
DUKE. Whoe'er he be that in this foul proceeding
    Hath thus beguil'd your daughter of herself
    And you of her, the bloody book of law
    You shall yourself read in the bitter letter
    After your own sense, yea, though our proper son
    Stood in your action.[81]
BRA.   Humbly I thank your grace.   70
    Here is the man, this Moor, whom now, it seems,

---

[79]**re-stem** steer again
[80]**engluts** engulfs
[81]**Stood . . . action** was under your accusation

Your special mandate for the state-affairs
Hath hither brought.
DUKE *and* SEN.   We are very sorry for 't.
DUKE [*To* OTHELLO]. What, in your own part, can you say to this?
BRA. Nothing, but this is so.
OTH. Most potent, grave, and reverend signiors,
    My very noble and approv'd good masters,
    That I have ta'en away this old man's daughter,
    It is most true; true, I have married her.
    The very head and front of my offending   80
    Hath this extent, no more. Rude am I in my speech,
    And little bless'd with the soft phrase of peace;
    For since these arms of mine had seven years' pith,[82]
    Till now some nine moons wasted, they have us'd
    Their dearest action in the tented field,
    And little of this great world can I speak,
    More than pertains to feats of broil and battle,
    And therefore little shall I grace my cause
    In speaking for myself. Yet, by your gracious patience,[83]
    I will a round unvarnish'd tale deliver   90
    Of my whole course of love; what drugs, what charms,
    What conjuration and what mighty magic,
    For such proceeding I am charg'd withal,
    I won his daughter.
BRA.   A maiden never bold;
    Of spirit so still and quiet, that her motion
    Blush'd at herself;[84] and she, in spite of nature,
    Of years, of country, credit, every thing,
    To fall in love with what she fear'd to look on!
    It is a judgement maim'd and most imperfect
    That will confess perfection so could err   100
    Against all rules of nature, and must be driven
    To find our practices of cunning hell,
    Why this should be. I therefore vouch[85] again
    That with some mixtures pow'rful o'er the blood,
    Or with some dram conjur'd to this effect,
    He wrought upon her.
DUKE.   To vouch this, is no proof,
    Without more wider and more overt test
    Than these thin habits and poor likelihoods
    Of modern seeming do prefer against him.
FIRST SEN. But, Othello, speak: 110
    Did you by indirect and forced courses
    Subdue and poison this young maid's affections?
    Or came it by request and such fair question
    As soul to soul affordeth?

[82]**pith** strength, vigor
[83]**patience** suffering, permission
[84]**motion . . . herself** inward impulses blushed at themselves
[85]**vouch** assert

OTH.   I do beseech you,
  Send for the lady to the Sagittary,
  And let her speak of me before her father:
  If you do find me foul in her report,
  The trust, the office I do hold of you,
  Not only take away, but let your sentence
  Even fall upon my life.
DUKE.   Fetch Desdemona hither.   120
OTH. Ancient, conduct them; you best know the place.
                                 [*Exeunt* IAGO *and* ATTENDANTS.]

  And, till she come, as truly as to heaven
  I do confess the vices of my blood,
  So justly to your grave ear I'll present
  How I did thrive in this fair lady's love,
  And she in mine.
DUKE. Say it, Othello.
OTH. Her father lov'd me; oft invited me;
  Still question'd me the story of my life,
  From year to year, the battles, sieges, fortunes,   130
  That I have pass'd.
  I ran it through, even from my boyish days,
  To th' very moment that he bade me tell it;
  Wherein I spake of most disastrous chances,
  Of moving accidents by flood and field,
  Of hair-breadth scapes i' th' imminent[86] deadly breach,
  Of being taken by the insolent foe
  And sold to slavery, of my redemption thence
  And portance[87] in my travels' history:
  Wherein of antres[88] vast and deserts idle,[89]   140
  Rough quarries, rocks and hills whose heads touch heaven,
  It was my hint[90] to speak, — such was the process;
  And of the Cannibals that each other eat,[91]
  The Anthropophagi[92] and men whose heads
  Do grow beneath their shoulders. This to hear
  Would Desdemona seriously incline:
  But still the house-affairs would draw her thence:
  Which ever as she could with haste dispatch,
  She 'ld come again, and with a greedy ear
  Devour up my discourse: which I observing,   150
  Took once a pliant hour, and found good means
  To draw from her a prayer of earnest heart
  That I would all my pilgrimage dilate,[93]

[86]**imminent** i.e., impending parts when a gap has been made in a fortification
[87]**portance** conduct
[88]**antres** caverns
[89]**idle** barren, unprofitable
[90]**hint** occasion
[91]**eat** ate
[92]**Anthropophagi** man-eaters
[93]**dilate** relate in detail

Whereof by parcels she had something heard,
But not intentively:[94] I did consent,
And often did beguile her of her tears,
When I did speak of some distressful stroke
That my youth suffer'd. My story being done,
She gave me for my pains a world of sighs:
She swore, in faith, 'twas strange, 'twas passing strange,   160
'Twas pitiful, 'twas wondrous pitiful:
She wish'd she had not heard it, yet she wish'd
That heaven had made her such a man: she thank'd me,
And bade me, if I had a friend that lov'd her,
I should but teach him how to tell my story,
And that would woo her. Upon this hint I spake:
She lov'd me for the dangers I had pass'd,
And I lov'd her that she did pity them.
This only is the witchcraft I have us'd:
Here comes the lady; let her witness it.   170

[*Enter* DESDEMONA, IAGO *and* ATTENDANTS.]

DUKE. I think this tale would win my daughter too.
  Good Brabantio,
  Take up this mangled matter at the best:
  Men do their broken weapons rather use
  Than their bare hands.
BRA.   I pray you, hear her speak:
  If she confess that she was half the wooer,
  Destruction on my head, if my bad blame
  Light on the man! Come hither, gentle mistress:
  Do you perceive in all this noble company
  Where most you owe obedience?
DES.   My noble father,   180
  I do perceive here a divided duty:[95]
  To you I am bound for life and education;
  My life and education both do learn me
  How to respect you; you are the lord of duty;
  I am hitherto your daughter: but here's my husband,
  And so much duty as my mother show'd
  To you, preferring you before her father,
  So much I challenge that I may profess
  Due to the Moor my lord.
BRA.   God be with you! I have done.
  Please it your grace, on to[96] the state-affairs: 190
  I had rather to adopt a child than get[97] it.
  Come hither, Moor:
  I here do give thee that with all my heart
  Which, but thou hast already, with all my heart

[94]**intentively** with full attention
[95]**divided duty** Desdemona recognizes that she still owes a duty to her father even after marriage
[96]**on to** i.e., proceed with
[97]**get** beget

I would keep from thee. For your sake,[98] jewel,
I am glad at soul I have no other child;
For thy escape would teach me tyranny,
To hang clogs on them. I have done, my lord.
DUKE. Let me speak like yourself,[99] and lay a sentence,[100]
    Which, as a grise[101] or step, may help these lovers   200
    Into your favour.
    When remedies are past, the griefs are ended
    By seeing the worst, which late on hopes depended.
    To mourn a mischief that is past and gone
    Is the next[102] way to draw new mischief on.
    What cannot be preserv'd when fortune takes,
    Patience her injury a mock'ry makes.
    The robb'd that smiles steals something from the thief;
    He robs himself that spends a bootless grief.
BRA. So let the Turk of Cyprus us beguile;   210
    We lost it not, so long as we can smile.
    He bears the sentence well that nothing bears
    But the free comfort[103] which from thence he hears,
    But he bears both the sentence and the sorrow
    That, to pay grief, must of poor patience borrow.
    These sentences, to sugar, or to gall,
    Being strong on both sides, are equivocal:
    But words are words; I never yet did hear
    That the bruis'd heart was pierced through the ear.
    I humbly beseech you, proceed to th' affairs of state.   220
DUKE. The Turk with a most mighty preparation makes for Cyprus. Othello,
the fortitude[104] of the place is best known to you; and though we have there a
substitute of most allowed[105] sufficiency, yet opinion, a sovereign mistress of
effects, throws a more safer voice on you:[106] you must therefore be content to
slubber[107] the gloss of your new fortunes with this more stubborn and boisterous expedition.
OTH. The tyrant custom, most grave senators,
    Hath made the flinty and steel couch of war
    My thrice-driven[108] bed of down: I do agnize[109]
    A natural and prompt alacrity   230
    I find in hardness[110] and do undertake

[98]**For your sake** on your account
[99]**like yourself** i.e., as you would, in your proper temper
[100]**sentence** maxim
[101]**grise** step
[102]**next** nearest
[103]**comfort** i.e., the consolation that it may be borne with patience
[104]**fortitude** strength
[105]**allowed** acknowledged
[106]**opinion . . . on you** public opinion, an important determiner of affairs, chooses you as the best man
[107]**slubber** soil, sully
[108]**thrice-driven** thrice sifted
[109]**agnize** know in myself
[110]**hardness** hardship

These present wars against the Ottomites.
Most humbly therefore bending to your state,
I crave fit disposition for my wife,
Due reference of place and exhibition,[111]
With such accommodation and besort[112]
As levels with her breeding.

DUKE.   If you please,
    Be 't at her father's.

BRA.   I'll not have it so.

OTH. Nor I.

DES.   Nor I; I would not there reside,
    To put my father in impatient thoughts   240
    By being in his eye. Most gracious duke,
    To my unfolding lend your prosperous[113]ear;
    And let me find a charter[114] in your voice,
    T' assist my simpleness.[115]

DUKE. What would you, Desdemona?

DES. That I did love the Moor to live with him,
    My downright violence and storm of fortunes
    May trumpet to the world: my heart's subdu'd
    Even to the very quality of my lord:
    I saw Othello's visage in his mind,   250
    And to his honours and his valiant parts
    Did I my soul and fortunes consecrate.
    So that, dear lords, if I be left behind,
    A moth of peace, and he go to the war,
    The rites for why I love him are bereft me,
    And I a heavy interim shall support
    By his dear absence. Let me go with him.

OTH. Let her have your voices.
    Vouch with me, heaven, I therefore beg it not,
    To please the palate of my appetite,   260
    Nor to comply with heat — the young affects[116]
    In me defunct — and proper satisfaction,
    But to be free and bounteous to her mind:
    And heaven defend your good souls, that you think
    I will your serious and great business scant
    When she is with me: no, when light-wing'd toys
    Of feather'd Cupid seel[117] with wanton dullness
    My speculative and offic'd instruments,[118]

---

[111]**exhibition** allowance
[112]**besort** suitable company
[113]**prosperous** propitious
[114]**charter** privilege
[115]**simpleness** simplicity
[116]**affects** inclinations, desires
[117]**seel** in falconry, to make blind by sewing up the eyes of the hawk in training
[118]**speculative . . . instruments** ability to see and reason clearly

That[119] my disports[120] corrupt and taint[121] my business,
Let housewives make a skillet of my helm,
And all indign[122] and base adversities   270
Make head against my estimation![123]
DUKE. Be it as you shall privately determine,
  Either for her stay or going: th' affair cries haste,
  And speed must answer it.
FIRST SEN. You must away to-night.
OTH.   With all my heart.
DUKE. At nine i' th' morning here we'll meet again.
  Othello, leave some officer behind,
  And he shall our commission bring to you;
  With such things else of quality and respect   280
  As doth import[124] you.
OTH.   So please your grace, my ancient;
  A man he is of honesty and trust:
  To his conveyance I assign my wife,
  With what else needful your good grace shall think
  To be sent after me.
DUKE.   Let it be so.
  Good night to every one. [*To* BRA.] And, noble signior,
  If virtue no delighted[125] beauty lack,
  Your son-in-law is far more fair than black.
FIRST SEN. Adieu, brave Moor; use Desdemona well.
BRA. Look to her, Moor, if thou hast eyes to see;   290
  She has deceiv'd her father, and may thee.
              [*Exeunt* DUKE, SENATORS, OFFICERS, *&c.*]

OTH. My life upon her faith! Honest Iago,[126]
  My Desdemona must I leave to thee:
  I prithee, let thy wife attend on her;
  And bring them after in the best advantage.
  Come, Desdemona; I have but an hour
  Of love, of worldly matters and direction,
  To spend with thee: we must obey the time.

              [*Exit with* DESDEMONA.]

ROD. Iago—
IAGO. What say'st thou, noble heart?
ROD. What will I do, thinkest thou?   300
IAGO. Why, go to bed, and sleep.
ROD. I will incontinently[127] drown myself.

---

[119]**That** so that
[120]**disports** pastimes
[121]**taint** impair
[122]**indign** unworthy, shameful
[123]**estimation** reputation
[124]**import** concern
[125]**delighted** delightful
[126]**Honest Iago** an evidence of Iago's carefully built reputation
[127]**incontinently** immediately

IAGO. If thou dost, I shall never love thee after. Why, thou silly gentleman!

ROD. It is silliness to live when to live is torment; and then have we a prescription to die when death is our physician.

IAGO. O villanous! I have looked upon the world for four times seven years; and since I could distinguish betwixt a benefit and an injury, I never found man that knew how to love himself. Ere I would say, I would drown myself for the love of a guinea-hen, I would change my humanity with a baboon.   310

ROD. What should I do? I confess it is my shame to be so fond; but it is not in my virtue[128] to amend it.

IAGO. Virtue! a fig! 'tis in ourselves that we are thus or thus. Our bodies are our gardens, to the which our wills are gardeners; so that if we will plant nettles, or sow lettuce, set hyssop[129] and weed up thyme, supply it with one gender[130] of herbs, or distract it with many, either to have it sterile with idleness,[131] or manured with industry, why, the power and corrigible authority[132] of this lies in our wills. If the balance of our lives had not one scale of reason to poise another of sensuality, the blood and baseness of our natures would conduct us to most preposterous conclusions:[133] but we have reason to cool our raging motions,[134] our carnal stings, our unbitted[135] lusts, whereof I take this that you call love to be a sect[136] or scion.   322

ROD. It cannot be.

IAGO. It is merely a lust of the blood and a permission of the will. Come, be a man. Drown thyself! drown cats and blind puppies. I have professed me thy friend and I confess me knit to thy deserving with cables of perdurable[137] toughness; I could never better stead thee than now. Put money in thy purse; follow thou the wars; defeat thy favour[138] with an usurped beard; I say, put money in thy purse. It cannot be that Desdemona should long continue her love to the Moor, — put money in thy purse, — nor he his to her: it was a violent commencement in her, and thou shalt see an answerable sequestration:[139] — put but money in thy purse. These Moors are changeable in their wills: — fill thy purse with money: — the food that to him now is as luscious as locusts,[140] shall be to him shortly as bitter as coloquintida.[141] She must change for youth: when she is sated with his body, she will find the error of her choice: she must have change, she must: therefore put money in thy

---

[128]**virtue** strength

[129]**hyssop** an herb of the mint family

[130]**gender** kind

[131]**idleness** want of cultivation

[132]**corrigible authority** the power to correct

[133]**reason . . . motions** Iago understands the warfare between reason and sensuality, but his ethics are totally inverted; reason works in him not good, as it should according to natural law, but evil, which he has chosen for his good

[134]**motions** appetites

[135]**unbitted** uncontrolled

[136]**sect** cutting

[137]**perdurable** very durable

[138]**defeat thy favour** disguise and disfigure thy face

[139]**answerable sequestration** a separation corresponding

[140]**locusts** of doubtful meaning; defined as fruit of the carob tree, as honeysuckle, and as lollipops or sugar sticks

[141]**coloquintida** colocynth, or bitter apple, a purgative

purse. If thou wilt needs damn thyself, do it a more delicate way than drowning. Make all the money thou canst: if sanctimony and a frail vow betwixt an erring[142] barbarian and a super-subtle Venetian be not too hard for my wits and all the tribe of hell, thou shalt enjoy her; therefore make money. A pox of drowning thyself! it is clean out of the way: seek thou rather to be hanged in compassing thy joy than to be drowned and go without her. 342

ROD. Wilt thou be fast to my hopes, if I depend on the issue?

IAGO. Thou art sure of me: — go, make money: — I have told thee often, and I re-tell thee again and again, I hate the Moor: my cause is hearted;[143] thine hath no less reason. Let us be conjunctive[144] in our revenge against him; if thou canst cuckold him, thou dost thyself a pleasure, me a sport. There are many events in the womb of time which will be delivered. Traverse![145] go, provide thy money. We will have more of this to-morrow. Adieu.

ROD. Where shall we meet i' the morning?   350

IAGO. At my lodging.

ROD. I'll be with thee betimes.

IAGO. Go to; farewell. Do you hear, Roderigo?

ROD. What say you?

IAGO. No more of drowning, do you hear?

ROD. I am changed: I'll go sell all my land.   [*Exit*]

IAGO. Thus do I ever make my fool my purse;
  For I mine own gain'd knowledge should profane,
  If I would time expend with such a snipe,[146]
  But for my sport and profit. I hate the Moor;   360
  And it is thought abroad, that 'twixt my sheets
  H' as done my office: I know not if 't be true;
  But I, for mere suspicion in that kind,
  Will do as if for surety. He holds me well;
  The better shall my purpose work on him.
  Cassio's a proper man: let me see now:
  To get his place and to plume up[147] my will
  In double knavery — How, how? — Let's see: —
  After some time, to abuse Othello's ears
  That he[148] is too familiar with his wife.   370
  He hath a person and a smooth dispose[149]
  To be suspected, fram'd to make women false.
  The Moor is of a free[150] and open nature,
  That thinks men honest that but seem to be so,
  And will as tenderly be led by th' nose
  As asses are.

[Marginal annotations: soliloquy; motive ①; Iago suspects wife + O; motive ②; suspects; plot]

142**erring** wandering
143**hearted** fixed in the heart
144**conjunctive** united
145**Traverse** go (military term)
146**snipe** gull, fool
147**plume up** glorify, gratify
148**he** i.e., Cassio
149**dispose** external manner
150**free** frank

I have 't. It is engend'red. Hell and night
Must bring this monstrous birth to the world's light.

[Exit.]

ACT II

SCENE I *A Sea-port in Cyprus. An open place near the quay.*

gov of cyprus

[*Enter* MONTANO *and two* GENTLEMEN.]

MON. What from the cape can you discern at sea?
FIRST GENT. Nothing at all: it is a high-wrought flood;
    I cannot, 'twixt the heaven and the main,
    Descry a sail.
MON. Methinks the wind hath spoke aloud at land;
    A fuller blast ne'er shook our battlements:
    If it hath ruffian'd[1] so upon the sea,
    What ribs of oak, when mountains melt on them,
    Can hold the mortise?[2] What shall we hear of this?
SEC. GENT. A segregation[3] of the Turkish fleet: 10
    For do but stand upon the foaming shore,
    The chidden billow seems to pelt the clouds:
    The wind-shak'd surge, with high and monstrous mane,
    Seems to cast water on the burning bear,[4]
    And quench the guards[5] of th' ever-fixed pole:
    I never did like molestation view
    On the enchafed[6] flood.
MON.   If that the Turkish fleet
    Be not enshelter'd and embay'd, they are drown'd;
    It is impossible they bear it out.

[*Enter a third* GENTLEMAN.]

THIRD GENT. News, lads! our wars are done
    The desperate tempest hath so bang'd the Turks,   *turks wrecked as seen by Os fleet*   20
    That their designment[7] halts: a noble ship of Venice
    Hath seen a grievous wrack and sufferance[8]
    On most part of their fleet.
MON. How! is this true?
THIRD GENT.   The ship is here put in,
    A Veronesa; Michael Cassio,
    Lieutenant to the warlike Moor Othello,
    Is come on shore: the Moor himself at sea,
    And is in full commission here for Cyprus.

---

[1]**ruffian'd** raged
[2]**mortise** the socket hollowed out in fitting timbers
[3]**segregation** dispersion
[4]**bear** a constellation
[5]**quench the guards** overwhelm the stars near the polestar
[6]**enchafed** angry
[7]**designment** enterprise
[8]**sufferance** disaster

MON. I am glad on 't; 'tis a worthy governor.   30
THIRD GENT. But this same Cassio, though he speak of comfort
  Touching the Turkish loss, yet he looks sadly,
  And prays the Moor be safe; for they were parted
  With foul and violent tempest.
MON.   Pray heavens he be;
  For I have serv'd him, and the man commands
  Like a full⁹ soldier. Let's to the seaside, ho!
  As well to see the vessel that's come in
  As to throw out our eyes for brave Othello,
  Even till we make the main and th' aerial blue
  And indistinct regard.¹⁰
THIRD GENT.   Come, let's do so;   40
  For every minute is expectancy
  Of more arrivance.¹¹

  [*Enter* CASSIO.]
CAS. Thanks, you the valiant of this warlike isle,
  That so approve the Moor! O, let the heavens
  Give him defence against the elements,
  For I have lost him on a dangerous sea.
MON. Is he well shipp'd?
CAS. His bark is stoutly timber'd, and his pilot
  Of very expert and approv'd allowance;¹²
  Therefore my hopes, not surfeited to death,   50
  Stand in bold cure. [*A cry within.*] "A sail, a sail, a sail!"

  [*Enter a fourth* GENTLEMAN.]
CAS. What noise?
FOURTH GENT. The town is empty; on the brow o' th' sea
  Stand ranks of people, and they cry "A sail!"
CAS. My hopes do shape him for the governor.   [*Guns heard.*]
SEC. GENT. They do discharge their shot of courtesy:
  Our friends at least.
CAS.   I pray you, sir, go forth,
  And give us truth who 'tis that is arriv'd.
SEC. GENT. I shall.
                                  [*Exit.*]

MON. But, good lieutenant, is your general wiv'd?   60
CAS. Most fortunately: he hath achiev'd a maid
  That paragons¹³ description and wild fame;
  One that excels the quirks¹⁴ of blazoning¹⁵ pens,

---

⁹**full** perfect
¹⁰**make . . . regard** cause the blue of the sea and the air to grow indistinguishable in our view
¹¹**arrivance** arrival
¹²**allowance** reputation
¹³**paragons** surpasses
¹⁴**quirks** witty conceits
¹⁵**blazoning** setting forth honorably in words

And in th' essential vesture of creation[16]
Does tire the ingener.[17]

[*Enter second* GENTLEMAN.]
                        How now! who has put in?
SEC. GENT. 'Tis one Iago, ancient to the general.
CAS. Has had most favourable and happy speed:
  Tempests themselves, high seas and howling winds,
  The gutter'd[18] rocks and congregated sands,—
  Traitors ensteep'd[19] to clog the guiltless keel,—   70
  As having sense of beauty, do omit
  Their mortal[20] natures, letting go safely by
  The divine Desdemona.
MON.   What is she?
CAS. She that I spake of, our great captain's captain,
  Left in the conduct of the bold Iago,
  Whose footing here anticipates our thoughts
  A se'nnight's[21] speed. Great Jove, Othello guard,
  And swell his sail with thine own powr'ful breath,
  That he may bless this bay with his tall ship,
  Make love's quick pants in Desdemona's arms,   80
  Give renew'd fire to our extincted spirits,
  And bring all Cyprus comfort!

[*Enter* DESDEMONA, IAGO, RODERIGO, *and* EMILIA *with* ATTENDANTS.]
                      O, behold,
  The riches of the ship is come on shore!
  You men of Cyprus, let her have your knees. *Kneel to?*
  Hail to thee, lady! and the grace of heaven,
  Before, behind thee and on every hand,
  Enwheel thee round!
DES.   I thank you, valiant Cassio.
  What tidings can you tell me of my lord?
CAS. He is not yet arriv'd: nor know I aught
  But that he's well and will be shortly here.   90
DES. O, but I fear—How lost you company?
CAS. The great contention of the sea and skies
  Parted our fellowship—But, hark! a sail.
[*Within*] "A sail, a sail!" [*Guns heard.*]
SEC. GENT. They give their greeting to the citadel:
  This likewise is a friend.
CAS.   See for the news.   [*Exit* GENTLEMAN.]

  Good ancient, you are welcome. [*To* EMILIA] Welcome, mistress:
  Let it not gall your patience, good Iago,

[16]**vesture of creation** the real qualities with which creation has invested her
[17]**ingener** inventor, praiser
[18]**gutter'd** jagged, trenched
[19]**ensteep'd** lying under water
[20]**mortal** deadly
[21]**se'nnight's** week's

That I extend my manners; 'tis my breeding
That gives me this bold show of courtesy. *Emilia* [*Kissing her.*]
IAGO. Sir, would she give you so much of her lips 101
As of her tongue she oft bestows on me,
You would have enough.
DES. Alas, she has no speech.
IAGO. In faith, too much;
I find it still, when I have list to sleep:
Marry, before your ladyship, I grant,
She puts her tongue a little in her heart,
And chides with thinking.
EMIL. You have little cause to say so.
IAGO. Come on, come on; you are pictures out of doors, 110
Bells in your parlours, wild-cats in your kitchens,
Saints in your injuries, devils being offended,
Players in your housewifery, and housewives[22] in your beds.
DES. O, fie upon thee, slanderer!
IAGO. Nay, it is true, or else I am a Turk:
You rise to play and go to bed to work.
EMIL. You shall not write my praise.
IAGO. No, let me not.
DES. What wouldst thou write of me, if thou shouldst praise me?
IAGO. O gentle lady, do not put me to 't;
For I am nothing, if not critical.[23] 120
DES. Come on, assay. There's one gone to the harbour?
IAGO. Ay, madam.
DES. I am not merry; but I do beguile
The thing I am, by seeming otherwise.
Come, how wouldst thou praise me?
IAGO. I am about it; but indeed my invention
Comes from my pate as birdlime[24] does from frieze;[25]
It plucks out brains and all: but my Muse labours,
And thus she is deliver'd.
If she be fair and wise, fairness and wit, *Iago's praise of Des* 130
The one's for use, the other useth it.
DES. Well praised! How if she be black and witty?
IAGO. If she be black, and thereto have a wit,
She'll find a white[26] that shall her blackness fit.
DES. Worse and worse.
EMIL. How if fair and foolish?
IAGO. She never yet was foolish that was fair;
For even her folly help'd her to an heir.
DES. These are old fond[27] paradoxes to make fools laugh i' the alehouse.
What miserable praise hast thou for her that's foul and foolish? 140

[22]**housewives** hussies
[23]**critical** censorious
[24]**birdlime** sticky substance smeared on twigs to catch small birds
[25]**frieze** coarse woolen cloth
[26]**white** a fair person, with a wordplay on *wight*
[27]**fond** foolish

IAGO. There's none so foul and foolish thereunto,
   But does foul pranks which fair and wise ones do.
DES. O heavy ignorance! thou praisest the worst best. But what praise couldst
   thou bestow on a deserving woman indeed, one that, in the authority of her
   merit, did justly put on the vouch[28] of her malice itself?
IAGO. She that was ever fair and never proud,
   Had tongue at will and yet was never loud,
   Never lack'd gold and yet went never gay,
   Fled from her wish and yet said "Now I may,"
   She that being ang'red, her revenge being nigh,   150
   Bade her wrong stay and her displeasure fly,
   She that in wisdom never was so frail
   To change the cod's head for the salmon's tail,[29]
   She that could think and ne'er disclose her mind,
   See suitors following and not look behind,
   She was a wight, if ever such wight were,—
DES. To do what?
IAGO. To suckle fools and chronicle small beer.[30]
DES. O most lame and impotent conclusion! Do not learn of him, Emilia, though
   he be thy husband. How say you, Cassio? is he not a most profane and liberal[31]
   counsellor?   161
CAS. He speaks home,[32] madam: you may relish him more in the soldier than in
   the scholar.
IAGO [*Aside*]. He takes her by the palm: ay, well said, whisper: with as little a
   web as this will I ensnare as great a fly as Cassio. Ay, smile upon her, do; I will
   gyve[33] thee in thine own courtship.[34] You say true; 'tis so, indeed: if such
   tricks as these strip you out of your lieutenantry, it had been better you had
   not kissed your three fingers[35] so oft, which now again you are most apt to
   play the sir[36] in. Very good; well kissed! an excellent courtesy! 'tis so, indeed.
   Yet again your fingers to your lips? would they were clyster-pipes[37] for your
   sake. [*Trumpet within.*] The Moor! I know his trumpet.   171
CAS. 'Tis truly so.
DES. Let's meet him and receive him.
CAS. Lo, where he comes!

[*Enter* OTHELLO *and* ATTENDANTS.]
OTH. O my fair warrior!
DES.   My dear Othello!
OTH. It gives me wonder great as my content
   To see you here before me. O my soul's joy!

---

[28]**put on the vouch** compel the approval
[29]**To change . . . tail** to exchange a delicacy for mere refuse
[30]**chronicle small beer** keep petty household accounts
[31]**liberal** licentious
[32]**speaks home** i.e., without reserve
[33]**gyve** fetter, shackle
[34]**courtship** courtesy
[35]**kissed your three fingers** he kisses his own hand as a token of reverence
[36]**the sir** i.e., the fine gentleman
[37]**clyster-pipes** tubes used for enemas

If after every tempest come such calms,   180
May the winds blow till they have waken'd death!
And let the labouring bark climb hills of seas
Olympus-high and duck again as low
As hell 's from heaven! If it were now to die,
'Twere now to be most happy; for, I fear,
My soul hath her content so absolute
That not another comfort like to this
Succeeds in unknown fate.

DES.   The heavens forbid
But that our loves and comforts should increase,
Even as our days do grow!

OTH.   Amen to that, sweet powers!   190
I cannot speak enough of this content;
It stops me here; it is too much of joy:
And this, and this, the greatest discords be [*Kissing her*]
That e'er our hearts shall make!

IAGO   [*Aside*]. O, you are well tun'd now!
But I'll set down the pegs[38] that make this music,
As honest as I am.

OTH.   Come, let us to the castle.
News, friends; our wars are done, the Turks are drowned.
How does my old acquaintance of this isle?
Honey, you shall be well desir'd in Cyprus;
I have found great love amongst them. O my sweet,   200
I prattle out of fashion, and I dote
In mine own comforts. I prithee, good Iago,
Go to the bay and disembark my coffers:
Bring thou the master to the citadel;
He is a good one, and his worthiness
Does challenge much respect. Come, Desdemona,
Once more, well met at Cyprus.

                          [*Exeunt* OTHELLO *and* DESDEMONA *and all but*
                          IAGO *and* RODERIGO.]

IAGO [*to an* ATTENDANT]. Do thou meet me presently at the harbour. [*To* ROD.]
Come hither. If thou be'st valiant,—as, they say, base men being in love have
then a nobility in their natures more than is native to them,—list me. The
lieutenant tonight watches on the court of guard.[39]—First, I must tell thee
this—Desdemona is directly in love with him.   212

ROD. With him! why 'tis not possible.

IAGO. Lay thy finger thus, and let thy soul be instructed. Mark me with what
violence she first loved the Moor, but for bragging and telling her fantastical
lies: and will she love him still for prating? let not thy discreet heart think it.
Her eye must be fed; and what delight shall she have to look on the devil?
When the blood is made dull with the act of sport, there should be, again to
inflame it and to give satiety a fresh appetite, loveliness in favour, sympathy in
years, manners and beauties; all which the Moor is defective in: now, for want

---

[38]**set down the pegs** lower the pitch of the strings, i.e., disturb the harmony
[39]**court of guard** guardhouse

of these required conveniences, her delicate tenderness will find itself abused, begin to heave the gorge, disrelish and abhor the Moor; very nature will instruct her in it and compel her to some second choice. Now, sir, this granted,—as it is a most pregnant and unforced position—who stands so eminent in the degree of this fortune as Cassio does? a knave very voluble; no further conscionable[40] than in putting on the mere form of civil and humane seeming, for the better compassing of his salt[41] and most hidden loose affection? why, none; why, none: a slipper[42] and subtle knave, a finder of occasions, that has an eye can stamp and counterfeit advantages, though true advantage never present itself; a devilish knave. Besides, the knave is handsome, young, and hath all those requisites in him that folly and green minds look after: a pestilent complete knave; and the woman hath found him already.

ROD. I cannot believe that in her; she's full of most blessed condition.

IAGO. Blessed fig's-end! the wine she drinks is made of grapes: if she had been blessed, she would never have loved the Moor. Blessed pudding! Didst thou not see her paddle with the palm of his hand? didst not mark that?

ROD. Yes, that I did; but that was but courtesy.   237

IAGO. Lechery, by this hand; an index and obscure prologue to the history of lust and foul thoughts. They met so near with their lips that their breaths embraced together. Villainous thoughts, Roderigo! when these mutualities so marshall the way, hard at hand comes the master and main exercise, the incorporate conclusion. Pish! But, sir, be you ruled by me: I have brought you from Venice. Watch you to-night; for the command, I'll lay't upon you. Cassio knows you not. I'll not be far from you: do you find some occasion to anger Cassio, either by speaking too loud, or tainting[43] his discipline; or from what other course you please, which the time shall more favourably minister.

ROD. Well.

IAGO. Sir, he is rash and very sudden in choler, and haply may strike at you: provoke him, that he may; for even out of that will I cause these of Cyprus to mutiny; whose qualification[44] shall come into no true taste again but by the displanting of Cassio. So shall you have a shorter journey to your desires by the means I shall then have to prefer them; and the impediment most profitably removed, without the which there were no expectation of our prosperity.

ROD. I will do this, if I can bring it to any opportunity.   247

IAGO. I warrant thee. Meet me by and by[45] at the citadel: I must fetch his necessaries ashore. Farewell.

ROD. Adieu.   [*Exit*]

IAGO. That Cassio loves her, I do well believe 't;
That she loves him, 'tis apt[46] and of great credit:[47]
The Moor, howbeit that I endure him not,   260
Is of a constant, loving, noble nature,

---

[40]**conscionable** conscientious
[41]**salt** licentious
[42]**slipper** slippery
[43]**tainting** disparaging
[44]**qualification** appeasement
[45]**by and by** immediately
[46]**apt** probable
[47]**credit** credibility

And I dare think he'll prove to Desdemona
A most dear husband. Now, I do love her too;
Not out of absolute lust, though peradventure
I stand accountant for as great a sin,
But partly led to diet my revenge,
For that I do suspect the lusty Moor
Hath leap'd into my seat; the thought whereof
Doth, like a poisonous mineral, gnaw my inwards;
And nothing can or shall content my soul   270
Till I am even'd with him, wife for wife,
Or failing so, yet that I put the Moor   *Iago's plan*
At least into a jealousy so strong
That judgement cannot cure. Which thing to do,
If this poor trash[48] of Venice, whom I trash[49]
For his quick hunting, stand the putting on,[50]
I'll have our Michael Cassio on the hip,[51]
Abuse him to the Moor in the rank garb —
For I fear Cassio with my night-cap too —
Make the Moor thank me, love me and reward me,   280
For making him egregiously an ass
And practicing upon his peace and quiet
Even to madness. 'Tis here, but yet confus'd:
Knavery's plain face is never seen till us'd.   [*Exit.*]

SCENE II *A street.*

[*Enter Othello's* HERALD *with a proclamation.*]

HER. It is Othello's pleasure, our noble and valiant general, that, upon certain tidings now arrived, importing the mere perdition[52] of the Turkish fleet, every man put himself into triumph; some to dance, some to make bonfires, each man to what sport and revels his addiction leads him: for, besides these beneficial news, it is the celebration of his nuptial. So much was his pleasure should be proclaimed. All offices[53] are open, and there is full liberty of feasting from this present hour of five till the bell have told eleven. Heaven bless the isle of Cyprus and our general Othello!   [*Exit.*]

SCENE III *A hall in the castle.*

[*Enter* OTHELLO, DESDEMONA, CASSIO, *and* ATTENDANTS.]

OTH. Good Michael, look you to the guard to-night:
Let's teach ourselves that honourable stop,[54]
Not to outsport discretion.
CAS. Iago hath direction what to do;
But, notwithstanding, with my personal eye
Will I look to 't.

[48]**trash** worthless thing (Roderigo)
[49]**trash** hold in check
[50]**putting on** incitement to quarrel
[51]**on the hip** at my mercy (wrestling term)
[52]**mere perdition** complete destruction
[53]**offices** rooms where food and drink were kept
[54]**stop** restraint

OTH.   Iago is most honest.
        Michael, goodnight: to-morrow with your earliest
        Let me have speech with you. [*To* DESDEMONA] Come, my dear love,
        The purchase made, the fruits are to ensue;
        That profit's yet to come 'tween me and you.   10
        Good night.   [*Exit* OTHELLO, *with* DESDEMONA *and*
                                   ATTENDANTS.]

        [*Enter* IAGO.]

CAS. Welcome, Iago; we must to the watch.
IAGO. Not this hour, lieutenant; 'tis not yet ten o' the clock. Our general cast[55]
        us thus early for the love of his Desdemona; who let us not therefore blame:
        he hath not yet made wanton the night with her; and she is sport for Jove.
CAS. She's a most exquisite lady.
IAGO. And, I'll warrant her, full of game.
CAS. Indeed, she's a most fresh and delicate creature.
IAGO. What an eye she has! methinks it sounds a parley of provocation.
CAS. An inviting eye; and yet methinks right modest.   20
IAGO. And when she speaks, is it not an alarum to love?
CAS. She is indeed perfection.
IAGO. Well, happiness to their sheets! Come, lieutenant, I have a stoup[56] of
        wine; and here without are a brace of Cyprus gallants that would fain have a
        measure to the health of black Othello.
CAS. Not to-night, good Iago: I have very poor and unhappy brains for drinking:
        I could well wish courtesy would invent some other custom of entertainment.
IAGO. O, they are our friends; but one cup: I'll drink for you.   28
CAS. I have drunk but one cup to-night, and that was craftily qualified[57] too, and,
        behold, what innovation[58] it makes here:[59] I am unfortunate in the infirmity,
        and dare not task my weakness with any more.
IAGO. What, man! 'tis a night of revels: the gallants desire it.
CAS. Where are they?
IAGO. Here at the door; I pray you, call them in.
CAS. I'll do 't; but it dislikes me.   [*Exit.*]

IAGO. If I can fasten but one cup upon him,
        With that which he hath drunk to-night already,
        He'll be as full of quarrel and offence
        As my young mistress' dog. Now, my sick fool Roderigo,
        Whom love hath turn'd almost the wrong side out,   40
        To Desdemona hath to-night carous'd
        Potations pottle-deep;[60] and he's to watch:
        Three lads of Cyprus, noble swelling spirits,
        That hold their honours in a wary distance,[61]

[55]**cast** dismissed
[56]**stoup** measure of liquor, two quarts
[57]**qualified** diluted
[58]**innovation** disturbance
[59]**here** i.e., in Cassio's head
[60]**pottle-deep** to the bottom of the tankard
[61]**hold . . . distance** i.e., are extremely sensitive of their honor

The very elements[62] of this warlike isle,
Have I to-night fluster'd with flowing cups,
And they watch[63] too. Now, 'mongst this flock of drunkards,
Am I to put our Cassio in some action
That may offend the isle. — But here they come:

[*Enter* CASSIO, MONTANO, *and* GENTLEMEN; SERVANTS *following with wine.*]

If consequence do but approve[64] my dream,   50
My boat sails freely, both with wind and stream.
CAS. 'Fore God, they have given me a rouse[65] already.
MON. Good faith, a little one; not past a pint, as I am a soldier.
IAGO. Some wine, ho!
   [*Sings*] And let me the canakin[66] clink, clink;
      And let me the canakin clink:
         A soldier's a man;
         A life 's but a span;
      Why, then, let a soldier drink.
   Some wine, boys!   60
CAS. 'Fore God, an excellent song.
IAGO. I learned it in England, where, indeed, they are most potent in potting:
your Dane, your German, and your swag-bellied Hollander — Drink, ho! —
are nothing to your English.
CAS. Is your Englishman so expert in his drinking?
IAGO. Why, he drinks you, with facility, your Dane dead drunk; he sweats not
to overthrow your Almain;[67] he gives your Hollander a vomit, ere the next
pottle can be filled.
CAS. To the health of our general!
MON. I am for it, lieutenant; and I'll do you justice.[68]   70
IAGO. O sweet England! [*Sings.*]
   King Stephen was a worthy peer,
      His breeches cost him but a crown;
   He held them sixpence all too dear,
      With that he call'd the tailor lown.[69]

   He was a wight of high renown,
      And thou art but of low degree:
   'Tis pride that pulls the country down;
      Then take thine auld cloak about thee.
   Some wine, ho!   80
CAS. Why, this is a more exquisite song than the other.

---

[62]**very elements** true representatives
[63]**watch** are members of the guard
[64]**approve** confirm
[65]**rouse** full draft of liquor
[66]**canakin** small drinking vessel
[67]**Almain** German
[68]**I'll . . . justice** i.e., drink as much as you
[69]**lown** lout, loon

IAGO. Will you hear 't again?

CAS. No; for I hold him to be unworthy of his place that does those things. Well, God's above all; and there be souls must be saved, and there be souls must not be saved.

IAGO. It's true, good lieutenant.

CAS. For mine own part, — no offence to the general, nor any man of quality, — I hope to be saved.

IAGO. And so do I too, lieutenant.   89

CAS. Ay, but, by your leave, not before me; the lieutenant is to be saved before the ancient. Let 's have no more of this; let 's to our affairs. — God forgive us our sins! — Gentlemen, let 's look to our business. Do not think, gentlemen, I am drunk: this is my ancient; this is my right hand, and this is my left: I am not drunk now; I can stand well enough, and speak well enough.

ALL. Excellent well.

CAS. Why, very well then; you must not think then that I am drunk.   [*Exit*]

MON. To th' platform, masters; come, let's set the watch.

IAGO. You see this fellow that is gone before;
He's soldier fit to stand by Caesar
And give direction: and do but see his vice;   100
'Tis to his virtue a just equinox,[70]
The one as long as th' other: 'tis pity of him.
I fear the trust Othello puts him in,
On some odd time of his infirmity,
Will shake this island.

MON.   But is he often thus?

IAGO. 'Tis evermore the prologue to his sleep:
He'll watch the horologe[71] a double set,[72]
If drink rock not his cradle.

MON.   It were well
The general were put in mind of it.
Perhaps he sees it not; or his good nature   110
Prizes the virtue that appears in Cassio,
And looks not on his evils: is not this true?

[*Enter* RODERIGO.]

IAGO [*Aside to him*]. How now, Roderigo!
I pray you, after the lieutenant; go.   [*Exit* RODERIGO.]

MON. And 'tis great pity that the noble Moor
Should hazard such a place as his own second
With one of an ingraft[73] infirmity:
It were an honest action to say
So to the Moor.

IAGO.   Not I, for this fair island:

---

[70]**equinox** equal length of days and nights; used figuratively to mean "counterpart"
[71]**horologe** clock
[72]**double set** twice around
[73]**ingraft** ingrafted, inveterate

I do love Cassio well; and would do much
  To cure him of this evil — But, hark! what noise? 120
[*Cry within:* "Help! help!"]

    [*Enter* CASSIO, *pursuing* RODERIGO.]
CAS. 'Zounds, you rogue! you rascal!
MON.   What's the matter, lieutenant?
CAS. A knave teach me my duty!
  I'll beat the knave into a twiggen[74] bottle.
ROD. Beat me!
CAS.   Dost thou prate, rogue?   [*Striking* RODERIGO.]
MON.   Nay, good lieutenant;   [*Staying him.*]
  I pray you, sir, hold your hand.
CAS.   Let me go, sir,
  Or I'll knock you o'er the mazzard.[75]
MON.   Come, come, you're drunk.
CAS. Drunk!   [*They fight.*]
IAGO [*aside to* RODERIGO]. Away, I say; go out, and cry a mutiny.
                                     [*Exit* RODERIGO.]

  Nay, good lieutenant, — God's will, gentlemen; —
  Help, ho! — Lieutenant, — sir, — Montano, — sir, — 130
  Help, masters! — Here's a goodly watch indeed!   [*Bell rings.*]
  Who's that which rings the bell? — Diablo,[76] ho!
  The town will rise:[77] God's will, lieutenant, hold!
  You'll be asham'd for ever.

    [*Enter* OTHELLO *and* ATTENDANTS.]
OTH.   What is the matter here?
MON. 'Zounds, I bleed still; I am hurt to th' death.
  He dies!   [*Thrusts at* CASSIO.]
  OTH. Hold, for your lives!
IAGO. Hold, ho! Lieutenant, — sir, — Montano, — gentlemen, —
  Have you forgot all sense of place and duty?
  Hold! the general speaks to you; hold, for shame! 140
OTH. Why, how now, ho! from whence ariseth this?
  Are we turn'd Turks[78] and to ourselves do that
  Which heaven hath forbid the Ottomites?
  For Christian shame, put by this barbarous brawl:
  He that stirs next to carve for[79] his own rage
  Holds his soul light; he dies upon his motion.
  Silence that dreadful bell: it frights the isle
  From her propriety.[80] What is the matter, masters?

[74]**twiggen** covered with woven twigs
[75]**mazzard** head
[76]**Diablo** the devil
[77]**rise** grow riotous
[78]**turn'd Turks** changed completely for the worse; proverbial
[79]**carve for** indulge
[80]**propriety** proper state or condition

Honest Iago, that looks dead with grieving,
Speak, who began this? on thy love, I charge thee.   150

IAGO. I do not know: friends all but now, even now,
In quarter,[81] and in terms like bride and groom
Devesting them for bed; and then, but now —
As if some planet had unwitted men —
Swords out, and tilting one at other's breast,
In opposition bloody. I cannot speak
Any beginning to this peevish odds;[82]
And would in action glorious I had lost
Those legs that brought me to a part of it!

OTH. How comes it, Michael, you are thus forgot?   160
CAS. I pray you, pardon me; I cannot speak.
OTH. Worthy Montano, you were wont be civil;
The gravity and stillness of your youth
The world hath noted, and your name is great
In mouths of wisest censure:[83] what's the matter,
That you unlace[84] your reputation thus
And spend your rich opinion for the name
Of a night-brawler? give me answer to it.

MON. Worthy Othello, I am hurt to danger:
Your officer, Iago, can inform you, —   170
While I spare speech, which something now offends me, —
Of all that I do know: nor know I aught
By me that's said or done amiss this night;
Unless self-charity be sometimes a vice,
And to defend ourselves it be a sin
When violence assails us.

OTH.   Now, by heaven,
My blood begins my safer guides to rule;
And passion, having my best judgement collied,[85]
Assays to lead the way: if I once stir,
Or do but lift this arm, the best of you   180
Shall sink in my rebuke. Give me to know
How this foul rout began, who set it on;
And he that is approv'd in[86] this offence,
Though he had twinn'd with me, both at a birth,
Shall lose me. What! in a town of war,
Yet wild, the people's hearts brimful of fear,
To manage private and domestic quarrel,
In night, and on the court and guard[87] of safety!
'Tis monstrous. Iago, who began 't?

---

[81]**In quarter** on terms
[82]**peevish odds** childish quarrel
[83]**censure** judgment
[84]**unlace** degrade
[85]**collied** darkened
[86]**approv'd in** found guilty of
[87]**court and guard** spot and guarding place, i.e., the main guardhouse

[handwritten: Cassio fired]

MON. If partially affin'd,[88] or leagu'd in office,   190
    Thou dost deliver more or less than truth,
    Thou art no soldier.
IAGO.   Touch me not so near: *[handwritten: two faced]*
    I had rather have this tongue cut from my mouth
    Than it should do offence to Michael Cassio; *[handwritten: answer]*
    Yet, I, persuade myself, to speak the truth
    Shall nothing wrong him. Thus it is, general.
    Montano and myself being in speech,
    There comes a fellow crying out for help;
    And Cassio following him with determin'd sword,
    To execute[89] upon him. Sir, this gentleman   200
    Steps in to Cassio, and entreats his pause:
    Myself the crying fellow did pursue,
    Lest by his clamour — as it so fell out —
    The town might fall in fright: he, swift of foot,
    Outran my purpose; and I return'd the rather
    For that I heard the clink and fall of swords,
    And Cassio high in oath; which till to-night
    I ne'er might say before. When I came back —
    For this was brief — I found them close together,
    At blow and thrust; even as again they were   210
    When you yourself did part them.
    More of this matter cannot I report:
    But men are men; the best sometimes forget:
    Though Cassio did some little wrong to him,
    As men in rage strike those that wish them best,
    Yet surely, Cassio, I believe, receiv'd
    From him that fled some strange indignity,
    Which patience could not pass.
OTH.   I know, Iago, *[handwritten: O dismisses Cassio]*
    Thy honesty and love doth mince this matter,
    Making it light to Cassio. Cassio, I love thee;   220
    But never more be officer of mine.

    [*Enter* DESDEMONA, *attended.*]
    Look, if my gentle love be not rais'd up!
    I'll make thee an example.
DES.   What's the matter?
OTH. All 's well now, sweeting; come away to bed.
    Sir, for your hurts, myself will be your surgeon:
    Lead him off.   [*To* MONTANO, *who is led off.*]
    Iago, look with care about the town,
    And silence those whom this vile brawl distracted.
    Come, Desdemona: 'tis the soldiers' life
    To have their balmy slumbers wak'd with strife.   230
                    [*Exit with all but* IAGO *and* CASSIO.]

---

[88]**affin'd** bound by a tie
[89]**execute** give effect to (his anger)

IAGO. What, are you hurt, lieutenant?

CAS. Ay, past all surgery.

IAGO. Marry, God forbid!

CAS. Reputation, reputation, reputation! O, I have lost my reputation! I have lost
the immortal part of myself, and what remains is bestial. My reputation, Iago,
my reputation!   236

IAGO. As I am an honest man, I thought you had received some bodily wound;
there is more sense in that than in reputation. Reputation is an idle and most
false imposition; oft got without merit, and lost without deserving: you have
lost no reputation at all, unless you repute yourself such a loser. What, man!
there are ways to recover the general again: you are but now cast in his mood,
a punishment more in policy than in malice; even so as one would beat his
offenceless dog to affright an imperious lion: sue to him again, and he 's
yours.

CAS. I will rather sue to be despised than to deceive so good a commander with
so slight, so drunken, and so indiscreet an officer. Drunk? and speak parrot?[90]
and squabble? swagger? swear? and discourse fustian[91] with one's own
shadow? O thou invisible spirit of wine, if thou hast no name to be known by,
let us call thee devil!   248

IAGO. What was he that you followed with your sword? What had he done to
you?

CAS. I know not.

IAGO. Is 't possible?

CAS. I remember a mass of things, but nothing distinctly; a quarrel, but nothing
wherefore. O God, that men should put an enemy in their mouths to steal
away their brains! that we should, with joy, pleasance, revel and applause,
transform ourselves into beasts!   256

IAGO. Why, but you are now well enough: how came you thus recovered?

CAS. It hath pleased the devil drunkenness to give place to the devil wrath: one
unperfectness[92] shows me another, to make me frankly despise myself.

IAGO. Come, you are too severe a moraler: as the time, the place, and the
condition of this country stands, I could heartily wish this had not befallen;
but, since it is as it is, mend it for your own good.

CAS. I will ask him for my place again; he shall tell me I am a drunkard! Had I as
many mouths as Hydra,[93] such an answer would stop them all. To be now a
sensible man, by and by a fool, and presently a beast! O strange! Every
inordinate cup is unblessed and the ingredient is a devil.   266

IAGO. Come, come, good wine is a good familiar creature, if it be well used:
exclaim no more against it. And, good lieutenant, I think you think I love you.

CAS. I have well approved[94] it, sir. I drunk!

IAGO. You or any man living may be a drunk at a time, man. I'll tell you what
you shall do. Our general's wife is now the general: I may say so in this
respect, for that he hath devoted and given up himself to the contemplation,

---

[90]**speak parrot** talk nonsense
[91]**discourse fustian** talked nonsense
[92]**unperfectness** imperfection
[93]**Hydra** a monster with many heads, slain by Hercules as the second of his twelve labors
[94]**approved** proved

mark, and denotement[95] of her parts and graces: confess yourself freely to her;
importune her help to put you in your place again: she is of so free, so kind, so
apt, so blessed a disposition, she holds it a vice in her goodness not to do more
than she is requested: this broken joint between you and her husband entreat
her to splinter;[96] and, my fortunes against any lay[97] worth naming, this crack
of your love shall grow stronger than it was before.   278

CAS. You advise me well.

IAGO. I protest, in the sincerity of love and honest kindness.

CAS. I think it freely; and betimes in the morning I will beseech the virtuous
Desdemona to undertake for me: I am desperate of my fortunes if they
check[98] me here.

IAGO. You are in the right. Good night, lieutenant; I must to the watch.

CAS. Good night, honest Iago.   [*Exit* CASSIO.]

IAGO. And what 's he then that says I play the villain?
When this advice is free I give and honest,
Probal[99] to thinking and indeed the course
To win the Moor again? For 'tis most easy
Th' inclining[100] Desdemona to subdue[101]   290
In any honest suit: she 's fram'd as fruitful
As the free elements. And then for her
To win the Moor—were 't to renounce his baptism,
All seals and symbols of redeemed sin,
His soul is so enfetter'd to her love,
That she may make, unmake, do what she list,
Even as her appetite shall play the god
With his weak function. How am I then a villain
To counsel Cassio to this parallel[102] course,
Directly to his good? Divinity of hell!   300
When devils will the blackest sins put on,[103]
They do suggest[104] at first with heavenly shows,
As I do now: for whiles this honest fool
Plies Desdemona to repair his fortunes
And she for him pleads strongly to the Moor,
I'll pour this pestilence into his ear,
That she repeals him[105] for her body's lust;
And by how much she strives to do him good,
She shall undo her credit with the Moor.
So will I turn her virtue into pitch,   310
And out of her own goodness make the net
That shall enmesh them all.

[95]**denotement** observation
[96]**splinter** bind with splints
[97]**lay** stake, wager.
[98]**check** repulse
[99]**Probal** probable
[100]**inclining** favorably disposed
[101]**subdue** persuade
[102]**parallel** probably, corresponding to his best interest
[103]**put on** further
[104]**suggest** tempt
[105]**repeals him** i.e., attempts to get him restored

[*Enter* RODERIGO.]
                                    How now, Roderigo!
ROD. I do not follow here in the chase, not like a hound that hunts, but one that
    fills up the cry.[106] My money is almost spent; I have been tonight exceedingly
    well cudgellèd; and I think the issue will be, I shall have so much experience
    for my pains, and so, with no money at all and a little more wit, return again to
    Venice.
IAGO. How poor are they that have not patience!
    What wound did ever heal but by degrees?
    Thou know'st we work by wit, and not by witchcraft;   320
    And wit depends on dilatory time.
    Does 't not go well? Cassio hath beaten thee,
    And thou, by that small hurt, hast cashier'd[107] Cassio:
    Though other things grow fair against the sun,
    Yet fruits that blossom first will first be ripe:
    Content thyself awhile. By th' mass, 'tis morning;
    Pleasure and action make the hours seem short.
    Retire thee; go where thou art billeted:
    Away, I say; thou shalt know more hereafter:
    Nay, get thee gone.   [*Exit* RODERIGO.]
                        Two things are to be done: 330
    My wife must move for Cassio to her mistress;
    I'll set her on;
    Myself the while to draw the Moor apart,
    And bring him jump[108] when he may Cassio find
    Soliciting his wife: ay, that's the way:
    Dull not device by coldness and delay.   [*Exit.*]

ACT III

SCENE I *Before the castle.*

[*Enter* CASSIO *and* MUSICIANS.]
CAS. Masters, play here; I will content[1] your pains;
    Something that 's brief; and bid "Good morrow, general."   [*They play.*]

[*Enter* CLOWN.]
CLO. Why, masters, have your instruments been in Naples, that they speak i'
    the nose[2] thus?
FIRST MUS. How, sir, how!
CLO. Are these, I pray you, wind-instruments?
FIRST MUS. Ay, marry, are they, sir.

---

[106]**cry** pack
[107]**cashier'd** dismissed from service
[108]**jump** precisely
[1]**content** reward
[2]**speak i' the nose** i.e., like Neapolitans, who spoke a nasal dialect (with a joke on syphilis, which
attacks the nose)

CLO. O, thereby hangs a tail.

FIRST MUS. Whereby hangs a tale,[3] sir?

CLO. Marry, sir, by many a wind-instrument that I know. But, masters, here 's
money for you: and the general so likes your music, that he desires you, for
love's sake, to make no more noise with it.   12

FIRST MUS. Well, sir, we will not.

CLO. If you have any music that may not be heard, to 't again: but, as they say, to
hear music the general does not greatly care.

FIRST MUS. We have none such, sir.

CLO. Then put up your pipes in your bag, for I'll away: go; vanish into air; away!
                                                              [*Exeunt* MUSICIANS.]

CAS. Dost thou hear, my honest friend?

CLO. No, I hear not your honest friend; I hear you.   19

CAS. Prithee, keep up thy quillets. There 's a poor piece of gold for thee: if the
gentlewoman that attends the general's wife be stirring, tell her there 's one
Cassio entreats her a little favour of speech: wilt thou do this?

CLO. She is stirring, sir: if she will stir hither, I shall seem to notify unto her.

CAS. Do, good my friend.   [*Exit* CLOWN.]

[*Enter* IAGO.]
                         In happy time, Iago.

IAGO. You have not been a-bed, then?

CAS. Why, no; the day had broke
Before we parted. I have made bold, Iago,
To send in to your wife: my suit to her
Is, that she will to virtuous Desdemona
Procure me some access.

IAGO.   I'll send her to you presently;   30
And I'll devise a means to draw the Moor
Out of the way, that your converse and business
May be more free.

CAS. I humbly thank you for 't.   [*Exit* IAGO.]
                         I never knew
A Florentine more kind and honest.

[*Enter* EMILIA.]

EMIL. Good morrow, good lieutenant: 1 am sorry
For your displeasure; but all will sure be well.
The general and his wife are talking of it;
And she speaks for you stoutly: the Moor replies,
That he you hurt is of great fame in Cyprus   40
And great affinity[4] and that in wholesome wisdom
He might not but refuse you, but he protests he loves you
And needs no other suitor but his likings
To take the safest occasion by the front[5]
To bring you in again.

---

[3]**tale** pun on *tail*, a wind instrument of sorts
[4]**affinity** kindred, family connection
[5]**by the front** i.e., by the forelock

CAS.   Yet, I beseech you,
  If you think fit, or that it may be done,
  Give me advantage of some brief discourse
  With Desdemona alone.
EMIL.   Pray you, come in:
  I will bestow you where you shall have time
  To speak your bosom freely.   50
CAS. I am much bound to you.   [*Exeunt.*]

SCENE II *A room in the castle.*

[*Enter* OTHELLO, IAGO, *and* GENTLEMEN.]
OTH. These letters give, Iago, to the pilot;
  And by him do my duties to the senate:
  That done, I will be walking on the works:[6]
  Repair there to me.
IAGO.   Well, my good lord, I'll do 't.
OTH. This fortification, gentlemen, shall we see't?
GENT. We'll wait upon your lordship.   [*Exeunt.*]

SCENE III *The garden of the castle.*

[*Enter* DESDEMONA, CASSIO, *and* EMILIA.]
DES. Be thou assur'd, good Cassio, I will do
  All my abilities in thy behalf.
EMIL. Good madam, do: I warrant it grieves my husband,
  As if the case were his.
DES. O, that 's an honest fellow. Do not doubt, Cassio,
  But I will have my lord and you again
  As friendly as you were.
CAS.   Bounteous madam,
  Whatever shall become of Michael Cassio,
  He's never any thing but your true servant.
DES. I know 't; I thank you. You do love my lord: 10
  You have known him long; and be you well assur'd
  He shall in strangeness[7] stand no farther off
  Than in a politic distance.
CAS.   Ay, but lady,
  That policy may either last so long
  Or feed upon such nice and waterish diet,
  Or breed itself so out of circumstance,[8]
  That, I being absent and my place supplied,
  My general will forget my love and service.
DES. Do not doubt[9] that; before Emilia here
  I give thee warrant of thy place: assure thee,   20
  If I do vow a friendship, I'll perform it
  To the last article: my lord shall never rest;

[6]**works** earthworks, fortifications
[7]**strangeness** distant behavior
[8]**breed . . . circumstance** increase itself so on account of accidents
[9]**doubt** fear

I'll watch him tame[10] and talk him out of patience;
His bed shall seem a school, his board a shrift;[11]
I'll intermingle every thing he does
With Cassio's suit: therefore be merry, Cassio;
For thy solicitor shall rather die
Than give thy cause away.[12]

[*Enter* OTHELLO *and* IAGO *at a distance.*]

EMIL. Madam, here comes my lord.
CAS. Madam, I'll take my leave.   30
DES. Why, stay, and hear me speak.
CAS. Madam, not now: I am very ill at ease,
  Unfit for mine own purposes.
DES. Well, do your discretion.   [*Exit* CASSIO.]

IAGO. Ha! I like not that.
OTH.   What dost thou say?
IAGO. Nothing, my lord: or if—I know not what.
OTH. Was not that Cassio parted from my wife?
IAGO. Cassio, my lord! No, sure, I cannot think it,
  That he would steal away so guilty-like,
  Seeing you coming.
OTH.   I do believe 'twas he.   40
DES. How now, my lord!
  I have been talking with a suitor here,
  A man that languishes in your displeasure.
OTH. Who is 't you mean?
DES. Why, your lieutenant, Cassio. Good my lord,
  If I have any grace or power to move you,
  His present reconciliation take;
  For if he be not one that truly loves you,
  That errs in ignorance and not in cunning,
  I have no judgement in an honest face: 50
  I prithee, call him back.
OTH.   Went he hence now?
DES. Ay, sooth; so humbled
  That he hath left part of his grief with me,
  To suffer with him. Good love, call him back.
OTH. Not now, sweet Desdemon; some other time.
DES. But shall 't be shortly?
OTH.   The sooner, sweet, for you.
DES. Shall 't be to-night at supper?
OTH.   No, not to-night.
DES. To-morrow dinner, then?
OTH.   I shall not dine at home;
  I meet the captains at the citadel.
DES. Why, then, to-morrow night; or Tuesday morn;   60

---

[10]**watch him tame** tame him by keeping him from sleeping (a term from falconry)
[11]**shrift** confessional
[12]**away** up

On Tuesday noon, or night; on Wednesday morn:
I prithee, name the time, but let it not
Exceed three days: in faith, he's penitent;
And yet his trespass, in our common reason[13]—
Save that, they say, the wars must make examples
Out of their best—is not almost a fault
T' incur a private check. When shall he come?
Tell me, Othello: I wonder in my soul,
What you would ask me, that I should deny,
Or stand so mamm'ring on.[14] What! Michael Cassio,   70
That came a-wooing with you, and so many a time,
When I have spoke of you dispraisingly,
Hath ta'en your part; to have so much to do
To bring him in! Trust me, I could do much,—
OTH. Prithee, no more: let him come when he will;
I will deny thee nothing.
DES.   Why, this is not a boon;
'Tis as I should entreat you wear your gloves,
Or feed on nourishing dishes, or keep you warm,
Or sue to you to do a peculiar profit
To your own person: nay, when I have a suit   80
Wherein I mean to touch your love indeed,
It shall be full of poise[15] and difficult weight
And fearful to be granted.
OTH.   I will deny thee nothing:
Whereon, I do beseech thee, grant me this,
To leave me but a little to myself.
DES. Shall I deny you? no: farewell, my lord.
OTH. Farewell, my Desdemona: I'll come to thee straight.
DES. Emilia, come. Be as your fancies teach you;
Whate'er you be, I am obedient.   [*Exit with* EMILIA.]

OTH. Excellent wretch![16] Perdition catch my soul,   90
But I do love thee! and when I love thee not,
Chaos is come again.
IAGO. My noble lord,—
OTH.   What dost thou say, Iago?
IAGO. Did Michael Cassio, when you woo'd my lady,
Know of your love?
OTH. He did, from first to last: why dost thou ask?
IAGO. But for a satisfaction of my thought;
No further harm.
OTH.   Why of thy thought, Iago?
IAGO. I did not think he had been acquainted with her.
OTH. O, yes; and went between us very oft.   100
IAGO. Indeed!

---

[13]**common reason** everyday judgments
[14]**mamm'ring on** wavering
[15]**poise** weight, heaviness
[16]**wretch** term of affectionate endearment with a connotation of pity

OTH. Indeed! ay, indeed: discern'st thou aught in that? *O doubts Cas*
   Is he not honest?
IAGO.   Honest, my lord!
OTH.   Honest! ay, honest.
IAGO. My lord, for aught I know.
OTH. What dost thou think?
IAGO.   Think, my lord!
OTH.   Think, my lord! *Iago's work*
   By heaven, he echoes me, *begins to*
   As if there were some monster in his thought *take root*
   Too hideous to be shown. Thou dost mean something:
   I heard thee say even now, thou lik'st not that,
   When Cassio left my wife: what didst not like? 110
   And when I told thee he was of my counsel
   In my whole course of wooing, thou criedst "Indeed!"
   And didst contract and purse thy brow together,
   As if thou then hadst shut up in thy brain
   Some horrible conceit: if thou dost love me,
   Show me thy thought.
IAGO. My lord, you know I love you.
OTH.   I think thou dost;
   And, for I know thou 'rt full of love and honesty,
   And weigh'st thy words before thou giv'st them breath,
   Therefore these stops of thine fright me the more: 120
   For such things in a false disloyal knave
   Are tricks of custom, but in a man that's just
   They 're close delations,[17] working from the heart
   That passion cannot rule.
IAGO.   For Michael Cassio,
   I dare be sworn I think that he is honest.
OTH. I think so too.
IAGO.   Men should be what they seem;
   Or those that be not, would they might seem none!
OTH. Certain, men should be what they seem.
IAGO. Why, then, I think Cassio 's an honest man.
OTH. Nay, yet there 's more in this: 130
   I prithee, speak to me as to thy thinkings,
   As thou dost ruminate, and give thy worst of thoughts
   The worst of words.
IAGO.   Good my lord, pardon me:
   Though I am bound to every act of duty,
   I am not bound to that all slaves are free to.
   Utter my thoughts? Why, say they are vile and false;
   As where 's that palace whereinto foul things
   Sometimes intrude not? who has a breast so pure,
   But some uncleanly apprehensions

[17]**close delations** secret or involuntary accusations

Keep leets[18] and law-days[19] and in sessions sit   140
     With meditations lawful?
OTH. Thou dost conspire against thy friend, Iago,
     If thou but think'st him wrong'd and mak'st his ear
     A stranger to thy thoughts.
IAGO.   I do beseech you—
     Though I perchance am vicious[20] in my guess,
     As, I confess, it is my nature's plague
     To spy into abuses, and oft my jealousy[21]
     Shapes faults that are not—that your wisdom yet,
     From one that so imperfectly conceits,[22]
     Would take no notice, nor build yourself a trouble   150
     Out of his scattering and unsure observance.
     It were not for your quiet nor your good,
     Nor for my manhood, honesty, or wisdom,
     To let you know my thoughts.
OTH.   What dost thou mean?
IAGO. Good name in man and woman, dear my lord,
     Is the immediate jewel of their souls:
     Who steals my purse steals trash: 'tis something, nothing;
     'Twas mine, 'tis his, and has been slave to thousands;
     But he that filches from me my good name
     Robs me of that which not enriches him   160
     And makes me poor indeed.
OTH. By heaven, I'll know thy thoughts.
IAGO. You cannot, if my heart were in your hand;
     Nor shall not, whilst 'tis in my custody.
OTH. Ha!
IAGO.   Oh, beware, my lord, of jealousy;
     It is the green-ey'd monster which doth mock
     The meat it feeds on: that cuckold lives in bliss
     Who, certain of his fate, loves not his wronger;
     But, O, what damned minutes tells he o'er
     Who dotes, yet doubts, suspects, yet strongly loves!   170
OTH. O misery!
IAGO. Poor and content is rich and rich enough,
     But riches fineless[23] is as poor as winter
     To him that ever fears he shall be poor.
     Good God, the souls of all my tribe defend
     From jealousy!
OTH.   Why, why is this?
     Think'st thou I'd make a life of jealousy,
     To follow still the changes of the moon
     With fresh suspicions? No; to be once in doubt

---

[18]**Keep leets** hold courts
[19]**law-days** court days
[20]**vicious** wrong
[21]**jealousy** suspicion of evil
[22]**conceits** judges
[23]**fineless** boundless

Is once to be resolv'd: exchange me for a goat,   180
When I shall turn the business of my soul
To such exsufflicate and blown[24] surmises,
Matching thy inference. 'Tis not to make me jealous
To say my wife is fair, feeds well, loves company,
Is free of speech, sings, plays and dances well;
Where virtue is, these are more virtuous;
Nor from mine own weak merits will I draw
The smallest fear or doubt of her revolt:
For she had eyes, and chose me. No, Iago;
I'll see before I doubt; when I doubt, prove;   190
And on the proof, there is no more but this, —
Away at once with love or jealousy!

IAGO. I am glad of this; for now I shall have reason
To show the love and duty that I bear you
With franker spirit: therefore, as I am bound,
Receive it from me. I speak not yet of proof.
Look to your wife; observe her well with Cassio;
Wear your eye thus, not jealous nor secure:[25]
I would not have your free and noble nature,
Out of self-bounty,[26] be abus'd; look to 't: 200
I know our country disposition well;
In Venice they do let heaven see the pranks
They dare not show their husbands; their best conscience
Is not to leave 't undone, but keep 't unknown.

OTH. Dost thou say so?

IAGO. She did deceive her father, marrying you;
And when she seem'd to shake and fear your looks,
She lov'd them most.

OTH.   And so she did.

IAGO.   Why, go to then;
She that, so young, could give out such a seeming,[27]
To seel[28] her father's eyes up close as oak —   210
He thought 'twas witchcraft — but I am much to blame;
I humbly do beseech you of your pardon
For too much loving you.

OTH.   I am bound to thee for ever.

IAGO. I see this hath a little dash'd your spirits.

OTH. Not a jot, not a jot.

IAGO.   I' faith, I fear it has.
I hope you will consider what is spoke
Comes from my love. But I do see y' are mov'd:
I am to pray you not to strain my speech

---

[24]**exsufflicate and blown** unsubstantial and inflated, flyblown
[25]**secure** free from uneasiness
[26]**self-bounty** inherent or natural goodness
[27]**seeming** false appearance
[28]**seel** blind (a term from falconry)

To grosser issues nor to larger reach[29]
  Than to suspicion.
OTH. I will not.
IAGO.   Should you do so, my lord,   220
  My speech should fall into such vile success
  As my thoughts aim not at. Cassio 's my worthy friend —
  My lord, I see y' are mov'd.
OTH.   No, not much mov'd:
  I do not think but Desdemona 's honest.
IAGO. Long live she so! and long live you to think so!
OTH. And yet, how nature erring from itself, —
IAGO. Ay, there 's the point: as — to be bold with you —
  Not to affect many proposed matches
  Of her own clime, complexion, and degree,   230
  Whereto we see in all things nature tends —
  Foh! one may smell in such a will[30] most rank,
  Foul disproportion,[31] thoughts unnatural.
  But pardon me; I do not in position[32]
  Distinctly speak of her; though I may fear
  Her will, recoiling to[33] her better judgment,
  May fall to match you with her country forms[34]
  And happily repent.[35]
OTH.   Farewell, farewell:
  If more thou dost perceive, let me know more;
  Set on thy wife to observe: leave me, Iago.   240
IAGO [going]. My lord, I take my leave.
OTH. Why did I marry? This honest creature doubtless
  Sees and knows more, much more, than he unfolds.
IAGO [returning]. My Lord, I would I might entreat your honour
  To scan this thing no farther; leave it to time:
  Although 'tis fit that Cassio have his place,
  For, sure, he fills it up with great ability,
  Yet, if you please to hold him off awhile,
  You shall by that perceive him and his means:
  Note, if your lady strain his entertainment[36]   250
  With any strong or vehement importunity;
  Much will be seen in that. In the mean time,
  Let me be thought too busy in my fears —
  As worthy cause I have to fear I am —
  And hold her free,[37] I do beseech your honour.

[29]**reach** meaning
[30]**will** sensuality
[31]**disproportion** abnormality
[32]**position** general argument
[33]**recoiling to** falling back upon, or recoiling against
[34]**fall . . . forms** happen to compare you with Venetian norms of handsomeness
[35]**repent** i.e., of her marriage
[36]**strain his entertainment** urge his reinstatement
[37]**hold her free** regard her as innocent

OTH. Fear not my government.[38]
IAGO. I once more take my leave. *[Exit.]*

OTH. This fellow 's of exceeding honesty,
And knows all qualities, with a learned spirit,
Of human dealings. If I do prove her haggard,[39]   260
Though that her jesses[40] were my dear heartstrings,
I 'ld whistle her off and let her down the wind,
To prey at fortune.[41] Haply, for I am black
And have not those soft parts of conversation
That chamberers[42] have, or for I am declin'd
Into the vale of years,—yet that 's not much—
She 's gone. I am abus'd: and my relief
Must be to loathe her. O curse of marriage,
That we can call these delicate creatures ours,
And not their appetites! I had rather be a toad,   270
And live upon the vapour of a dungeon,
Than keep a corner in the thing I love
For others' uses. Yet, 'tis the plague of great ones;
Prerogativ'd[43] are they less than the base;
'Tis destiny unshunnable, like death:
Even then this forked[44] plague is fated to us
When we do quicken.[45] Look where she comes:

[Enter DESDEMONA *and* EMILIA.]
If she be false, O, then heaven mocks itself!
I'll not believe 't.
DES.   How now, my dear Othello!
Your dinner, and the generous[46] islanders   280
By you invited, do attend your presence.
OTH. I am to blame.
DES.   Why do you speak so faintly?
Are you not well?
OTH. I have a pain upon my forehead here.
DES. 'Faith, that 's with watching;[47] 'twill away again:
Let me but bind it hard, within this hour
It will be well.
OTH.   Your napkin is too little:
[He puts the handkerchief from him; and it drops.]
Let it alone. Come, I'll go in with you.
DES. I am very sorry that you are not well.   *[Exit with* OTHELLO.]

[38]**government** self-control
[39]**haggard** a wild female duck
[40]**jesses** straps fastened around the legs of a trained hawk
[41]**at fortune** at random
[42]**chamberers** gallants
[43]**Prerogativ'd** privileged
[44]**forked** an allusion to the horns of the cuckold
[45]**quicken** receive life
[46]**generous** noble
[47]**watching** working late

EMIL. I am glad I have found this napkin: *handkerchief*   290
  This was her first remembrance from the Moor:
  My wayward husband hath a hundred times
  Woo'd me to steal it; but she so loves the token,
  For he conjur'd her she should ever keep it,
  That she reserves it evermore about her
  To kiss and talk to. I'll have the work ta'en out,[48]
  And give 't Iago: what he will do with it
  Heaven knows, not I;
  I nothing but to please his fantasy.

  [*Enter* IAGO.]
IAGO. How now! what do you here alone?   300
EMIL. Do not you chide; I have a thing for you.
IAGO. A thing for me? it is a common thing[49]—
EMIL. Ha!
IAGO. To have a foolish wife.
EMIL. O, is that all? What will you give me now
  For that same handkerchief?
IAGO.   What handkerchief?
EMIL. What handkerchief!
  Why, that the Moor first gave to Desdemona;
  That which so often you did bid me steal.
IAGO. Hast stol'n it from her?   310
EMIL. No, 'faith; she let it drop by negligence,
  And, to th' advantage, I, being here, took 't up.
  Look, here it is.
IAGO.   A good wench; give it me.
EMIL. What will you do with 't, that you have been so earnest
  To have me filch it?
IAGO.   [*Snatching it*] Why, what is that to you?
EMIL. If it be not for some purpose of import,
  Give 't me again: poor lady, she'll run mad
  When she shall lack it.
IAGO. Be not acknown on 't;[50] I have use for it.
  Go, leave me.   [*Exit* EMILIA.]

  I will in Cassio's lodging lose this napkin,   *Iago plans*   320
  And let him find it. Trifles light as air   *about*
  Are to the jealous confirmations strong   *napkin*
  As proofs of holy writ: this may do something.
  The Moor already changes with my poison:
  Dangerous conceits are, in their natures, poisons,
  Which at the first are scarce found to distaste,

---

[48]**work ta'en out** design copied

[49]**common thing** *common* suggests coarseness and availability to all, and *thing* is slang for female sexual organs

[50]**Be . . . on't** do not confess knowledge of it

But with a little act[51] upon the blood,
Burn like the mines of sulphur. I did say so:

[*Enter* OTHELLO.]

Look, where he comes! Not poppy, nor mandragora,   330
Nor all the drowsy syrups of the world,
Shall ever medicine thee to that sweet sleep
Which thou owedst yesterday.

OTH.   Ha! ha! false to me?

IAGO. Why, how now, general! no more of that.

OTH. Avaunt! be gone! thou has set me on the rack;
I swear 'tis better to be much abus'd
Than but to know 't a little.

IAGO.   How now, my lord!

OTH. What sense had I of her stol'n hours of lust?
I saw 't not, thought it not, it harm'd not me:
I slept the next night well, fed well, was free and merry;   340
I found not Cassio's kisses on her lips:
He that is robb'd, not wanting what is stol'n,
Let him not know 't, and he 's not robb'd at all.

IAGO. I am sorry to hear this.

OTH. I had been happy, if the general camp,
Pioners[52] and all, had tasted her sweet body,
So I had nothing known. O, now, for ever
Farewell the tranquil mind! farewell content!
Farewell the plumed troop, and the big wars,
That make ambition virtue! O, farewell!   350
Farewell the neighing steed, and the shrill trump,
The spirit-stirring drum, th' ear-piercing fife,
The royal banner, and all quality,
Pride, pomp and circumstance[53] of glorious war!
And, O you mortal engines,[54] whose rude throats
Th' immortal Jove's dread clamours counterfeit,
Farewell! Othello's occupation 's gone!

IAGO. Is 't possible, my lord?

OTH. Villain, be sure thou prove my love a whore,
Be sure of it; give me the ocular proof;   360
Or, by the worth of mine eternal soul,
Thou hadst been better have been born a dog
Than answer my wak'd wrath!

IAGO.   Is 't come to this?

OTH. Make me to see 't; or, at the least, so prove it,
That the probation bear no hinge nor loop
To hang a doubt on; or woe upon thy life!

IAGO. My noble lord,—

---

[51]**act** action, working
[52]**Pioners** sappers, a low grade of soldiers
[53]**circumstance** attendant fact; here, formal display
[54]**mortal engines** i.e., cannon

OTH. If thou dost slander her and torture me,
  Never pray more; abandon all remorse;
  On horror's head horrors[55] accumulate;   370
  Do deeds to make heaven weep, all earth amaz'd;
  For nothing canst thou to damnation add
  Greater than that.
IAGO.   O grace! O heaven forgive me!
  Are you a man? have you a soul or sense?
  God be wi' you; take mine office. O wretched fool,
  That liv'st to make thine honesty a vice!
  O monstrous world! Take note, take note, O world,
  To be direct and honest is not safe.
  I thank you for this profit; and from hence
  I'll love no friend, sith love breeds such offence.   380
OTH. Nay, stay: thou shouldst be honest.
IAGO. I should be wise, for honesty 's a fool
  And loses that it works for.
OTH.   By the world,
  I think my wife be honest and think she is not;
  I think that thou are just and think thou art not.
  I'll have some proof. Her name, that was as fresh
  As Dian's visage, is now begrim'd and black
  As mine own face. If there be cords, or knives,
  Poison, or fire, or suffocating streams,
  I'll not endure it. Would I were satisfied!   390
IAGO. I see, sir, you are eaten up with passion:
  I do repent me that I put it to you.
  You would be satisfied!
OTH.   Would! nay, I will.
IAGO. And may: but, how? how satisfied, my lord?
  Would you, the supervisor, grossly gape on—
  Behold her topp'd?
OTH.   Death and damnation! O!
IAGO. It were a tedious difficulty, I think,
  To bring them to that prospect: damn them then,   400
  If ever mortal eyes do see them bolster[56]
  More than their own! What then? how then?
  What shall I say? Where 's satisfaction?
  It is impossible you should see this,
  Were they as prime as goats, as hot as monkeys,
  As salt[57] as wolves in pride, and fools as gross
  As ignorance made drunk. But yet, I say,
  If imputation[58] and strong circumstances,
  Which lead directly to the door of truth,
  Will give you satisfaction, you may have 't.

---

[55]**horrors** object of *accumulate*
[56]**bolster** lie together
[57]**salt** wanton, sensual
[58]**imputation** i.e., opinion founded on strong circumstantial evidence

OTH. Give me a living reason she 's disloyal.
IAGO. I do not like the office: 410
But, sith I am ent'red in this cause so far,
Prick'd to 't by foolish honesty and love,
I will go on. I lay with Cassio lately;
And, being troubled with a raging tooth,
I could not sleep.
There are a kind of men so loose of soul,
That in their sleeps will mutter their affairs:
One of this kind is Cassio:
In sleep I heard him say "Sweet Desdemona, *Iago heard Cassio*
Let us be wary, let us hide our loves"; 420
And then, sir, would he grip and wring my hand,
Cry "O sweet creature!" and then kiss me hard,
As if he pluck'd up kisses by the roots
That grew upon my lips: then laid his leg
Over my thigh, and sigh'd, and kiss'd; and then
Cried "Cursed fate that gave thee to the Moor!"
OTH. O monstrous! monstrous!
IAGO.   Nay, this was but his dream.
OTH. But this denoted a foregone conclusion:[59]
'Tis a shrewd doubt, though it be but a dream.
IAGO. And this may help to thicken other proofs 430
That do demonstrate thinly.
OTH   I'll tear her all to pieces.
IAGO. Nay, but be wise: yet we see nothing done;
She may be honest yet. Tell me but this,
Have you not sometimes seen a handkerchief *handkerchief*
Spotted with strawberries in your wife's hand?
OTH. I gave her such a one; 'twas my first gift.
IAGO. I know not that: but such a handkerchief—
I am sure it was your wife's—did I to-day
See Cassio wipe his beard with.
OTH.   If it be that,—
IAGO. If it be that, or any that was hers, 440
It speaks against her with the other proofs.
OTH. O, that the slave had forty thousand lives!
One is too poor, too weak for my revenge.
Now do I see 'tis true. Look here, Iago;
All my fond love thus do I blow to heaven.
'Tis gone.
Arise, black vengeance, from the hollow hell!
Yield up, O love, thy crown and hearted[60] throne
To tyrannous hate! Swell, bosom, with thy fraught,[61]
For 'tis of aspics'[62] tongues!

---

[59]**foregone conclusion** previous trial or experience (not used in our sense)
[60]**hearted** fixed in the heart
[61]**fraught** freight, burden
[62]**aspics'** venemous serpents'

IAGO.   Yet be content.   450
OTH. O, blood, blood, blood!
IAGO. Patience, I say; your mind perhaps may change.
OTH. Never, Iago. Like to the Pontic sea,
   Whose icy current and compulsive course
   Ne'er feels retiring ebb, but keeps due on
   To the Propontic and the Hellespont,
   Even so my bloody thoughts, with violent pace,
   Shall ne'er look back, ne'er ebb to humble love,
   Till that a capable and wide revenge
   Swallow them up. Now, by yond marble[63] heaven,   460
   [*Kneels*] In the due reverence of a sacred vow
   I here engage my words.
IAGO.   Do not rise yet.
   [*Kneels*] Witness, you ever-burning lights above,
   You elements that clip us round about,
   Witness that here Iago doth give up
   The execution[64] of his wit, hands, heart,
   To wrong'd Othello's service! Let him command,
   And to obey shall be in me remorse,[65]
   What bloody business ever.   [*They rise.*]
OTH.   I greet thy love,
   Not with vain thanks, but with acceptance bounteous,   470
   And will upon the instant put thee to 't:
   Within these three days let me hear thee say
   That Cassio 's not alive.
IAGO. My friend is dead; 'tis done at your request:
   But let her live.
OTH. Damn her, lewd minx! O, damn her! damn her!
   Come, go with me apart; I will withdraw,
   To furnish me with some swift means of death
   For the fair devil. Now art thou my lieutenant.
IAGO. I am your own for ever.   [*Exeunt.*]

                    SCENE IV *Before the castle.*

[*Enter* DESDEMONA, EMILIA, *and* CLOWN.]
DES. Do you know, sirrah, where Lieutenant Cassio lies?
CLO. I dare not say he lies any where.
DES. Why, man?
CLO. He's a soldier, and for one to say a soldier lies, is stabbing.
DES. Go to: where lodges he?
CLO. To tell you where he lodges, is to tell you where I lie.
DES. Can any thing be made of this?
CLO. I know not where he lodges, and for me to devise a lodging and say he lies
   here or he lies there, were to lie in mine own throat.
DES. Can you inquire him out, and be edified by report?   10

---

[63]**marble** i.e., gleaming like marble
[64]**execution** exercise
[65]**remorse** pity for Othello's wrongs

CLO. I will catechize the world for him; that is, make questions, and by them answer.

DES. Seek him, bid him come hither: tell him I have moved my lord on his behalf, and hope all will be well.

CLO. To do this is within the compass of man's wit; and therefore I will attempt the doing it. [*Exit* CLOWN.]

DES. Where should I lose that handkerchief, Emilia? *missed handk*

EMIL. I know not, madam.

DES. Believe me, I had rather have lost my purse
Full of crusadoes:[66] and, but my noble Moor   20
Is true of mind and made of no such baseness
As jealous creatures are, it were enough
To put him to ill thinking.

EMIL.   Is he not jealous?

DES. Who, he? I think the sun where he was born
Drew all such humours from him.

EMIL.   Look, where he comes.

[*Enter* OTHELLO.]

DES. I will not leave him now till Cassio
Be call'd to him. — How is 't with you, my lord?

OTH. Well, my good lady. [*Aside*] O, hardness to dissemble! —
How do you, Desdemona?

DES.   Well, my good lord.

OTH. Give me your hand: this hand is moist, my lady.   30

DES. It yet hath felt no age nor known no sorrow.

OTH. This argues fruitfulness and liberal heart:
Hot, hot, and moist: this hand of yours requires
A sequester[67] from liberty, fasting and prayer,
Much castigation, exercise devout;
For here 's a young and sweating devil here,
That commonly rebels. 'Tis a good hand,
A frank one.

DES.   You may, indeed, say so:
For 'twas that hand that gave away my heart.

OTH. A liberal hand: the hearts of old gave hands;   40
But our new heraldry is hands, not hearts.[68]

DES. I cannot speak of this. Come now, your promise.

OTH. What promise, chuck?

DES. I have sent to bid Cassio come speak with you.

OTH. I have a salt and sorry rheum[69] offends me;
Lend my thy handkerchief.

DES.   Here, my lord.

OTH. That which I gave you.   *asks for handk.*

---

[66]**crusadoes** Portuguese gold coins
[67]**sequester** separation, sequestration
[68]**new . . . hearts** a current expression referring to marriages in which there is a joining of hands without the giving of hearts
[69]**sorry rheum** distressful head cold

DES.   I have it not about me.
OTH. Not?
DES.   No, indeed, my lord.
OTH.   That 's a fault.
  That handkerchief
  Did an Egyptian[70] to my mother give;   50
  She was a charmer, and could almost read
  The thoughts of people: she told her, while she kept it,
  'Twould make her amiable and subdue my father
  Entirely to her love, but if she lost it
  Or made a gift of it, my father's eye
  Should hold her loathed and his spirits should hunt
  After new fancies: she, dying, gave it me;
  And bid me, when my fate would have me wive,
  To give it her. I did so: and take heed on 't;
  Make it a darling like your precious eye;   60
  To lose 't or give 't away were such perdition
  As nothing else could match.
DES.   Is 't possible?
OTH. 'Tis true: there 's magic in the web of it:
  A sibyl, that had numb'red in the world
  The sun to course two hundred compasses,
  In her prophetic fury sew'd the work;
  The worms were hallow'd that did breed the silk;
  And it was dy'd in mummy[71] which the skilful
  Conserv'd of[72] maidens' hearts.
DES.   Indeed! is 't true?
OTH. Most veritable; therefore look to 't well.   70
DES. Then would to God that I had never seen 't!
OTH. Ha! wherefore?
DES. Why do you speak so startingly and rash?
OTH. Is 't lost? is 't gone? speak, is it out o' th' way?
DES. Heaven bless us!
OTH. Say you?
DES. It is not lost; but what an if it were?
OTH. How!
DES. I say, it is not lost.
OTH.   Fetch 't, let me see 't.
DES. Why, so I can, sir, but I will not now.   80
  This is a trick to put me from my suit:
  Pray you, let Cassio be receiv'd again.
OTH. Fetch me the handkerchief: my mind misgives.
DES. Come, come;
  You'll never meet a more sufficient man.
OTH. The handkerchief!
DES.   I pray, talk me of Cassio.

[70]Egyptian gypsy
[71]mummy medicinal or magical preparation drained from the flesh of mummified bodies
[72]Conserv'd of preserved out of

OTH. The handkerchief!
DES.   A man that all his time
  Hath founded his good fortunes on your love,
  Shar'd dangers with you,—
OTH. The handkerchief!
DES. In sooth, you are to blame.   90
OTH. Away!   [*Exit* OTHELLO.]

EMIL. Is not this man jealous?
DES. I ne'er saw this before.
  Sure, there 's some wonder in this handkerchief:
  I am most unhappy in the loss of it.
EMIL. 'Tis not a year or two shows us a man:
  They are all but stomachs, and we all but food;
  They eat us hungerly, and when they are full,
  They belch us.

[*Enter* IAGO *and* CASSIO.]
                    Look you, Cassio and my husband!   100
IAGO. There is no other way; 'tis she must do 't:
  And, lo, the happiness! go, and importune her.
DES. How now, good Cassio! what 's the news with you?
CAS. Madam, my former suit: I do beseech you
  That by your virtuous means I may again
  Exist, and be a member of his love
  Whom I with all the office of my heart
  Entirely honour: I would not be delay'd.
  If my offence be of such mortal kind
  That nor my service past, nor present sorrows,   110
  Nor purpos'd merit in futurity,
  Can ransom me into his love again,
  But to know so much be my benefit;[73]
  So shall I clothe me in a forc'd content,
  And shut myself up in some other course,
  To fortune's alms.
DES.   Alas, thrice-gentle Cassio!
  My advocation[74] is not now in tune;
  My lord is not my lord; nor should I know him,
  Were he in favour as in humour alter'd.
  So help me every spirit sanctified   120
  As I have spoken for you all my best
  And stood within the blank[75] of his displeasure
  For my free speech! You must awhile be patient:
  What I can do I will; and more I will
  Than for myself I dare: let that suffice you.
IAGO. Is my lord angry?

---

[73]**to know . . . benefit** to know that my case is hopeless will end my vain endeavor
[74]**advocation** advocacy
[75]**blank** white spot in the center of a target; here, range

EMIL. He went hence but now,
And certainly in strange unquietness.
IAGO. Can he be angry? I have seen the cannon,
When it hath blown his ranks into the air,
And, like the devil, from his very arm   130
Puff'd his own brother: — and can he be angry?
Something of moment then: I will go meet him:
There 's matter in 't indeed, if he be angry.
DES. I prithee, do so.   [*Exit* IAGO.]

Something, sure, of state,
Either from Venice, or some unhatch'd practice
Made demonstrable here in Cyprus to him,
Hath puddled[76] his clear spirit; and in such cases
Men's natures wrangle with inferior things,
Though great ones are their object. 'Tis even so;
For let our finger ache, and it indues[77]   140
Our other healthful members even to a sense
Of pain: nay, we must think men are not gods,
Nor of them look for such observancy
As fits the bridal. Beshrew me much, Emilia,
I was, unhandsome[78] warrior as I am,
Arraigning his unkindness with my soul;
But now I find I had suborn'd the witness,
And he 's indicted falsely.
EMIL. Pray heaven it be state-matters, as you think,
And no conception[79] nor no jealous toy   150
Concerning you.
DES. Alas the day! I never gave him cause.
EMIL. But jealous souls will not be answer'd so;
They are not ever jealous for the cause,
But jealous for they are jealous: 'tis a monster
Begot upon itself, born on itself.
DES. Heaven keep that monster from Othello's mind!
EMIL. Lady, amen.
DES. I will go seek him. Cassio, walk here about:
If I do find him fit, I'll move your suit   160
And seek to effect it to my uttermost.
CAS. I humbly thank your ladyship.   [*Exit* DESDEMONA *with* EMILIA.]

[*Enter* BIANCA.]
BIAN. Save you, friend Cassio!
CAS.   What make you from home?
How is 't with you, my most fair Bianca?
I' faith, sweet love, I was coming to your house.
BIAN. And I was going to your lodging, Cassio.

---

[76]**puddled** sullied the purity of
[77]**indues** brings to the same condition
[78]**unhandsome** unfair
[79]**conception** mere fancy

What, keep a week away? seven days and nights?
Eight score eight hours? and lovers' absent hours,
More tedious than the dial eight score times?
O weary reck'ning!

CAS.   Pardon me, Bianca.   170
I have this while with leaden thoughts been press'd;
But I shall, in a more continuate[80] time,
Strike off this score of absence. Sweet Bianca,
[*Giving her* DESDEMONA'*s handkerchief.*]
Take me this work out.[81]

BIAN.   O Cassio, whence came this?
This is some token from a newer friend:
To the felt absence now I feel a cause:
Is 't come to this? Well, well.

CAS.   Go to, woman!
Throw your vile guesses in the devil's teeth,
From whence you have them. You are jealous now
That this is from some mistress, some remembrance: 180
No, in good troth, Bianca.

BIAN.   Why, whose is it?

CAS. I know not, sweet: I found it in my chamber.
I like the work well: ere it be demanded—
As like enough it will—I would have it copied:
Take it, and do 't; and leave me for this time.

BIAN. Leave you! wherefore?

CAS. I do attend here on the general;
And think it no addition, nor my wish,
To have him see me woman'd.

BIAN.   Why, I pray you?

CAS. Not that I love you not.

BIAN.   But that you do not love me.   190
I pray you, bring me on the way a little,
And say if I shall see you soon at night.

CAS. 'Tis but a little way that I can bring you;
For I attend here: but I'll see you soon.

BIAN. 'Tis very good; I must be circumstance'd.[82]   [*Exeunt omnes.*]

ACT IV

SCENE I *Cyprus. Before the castle.*

[*Enter* OTHELLO *and* IAGO.]

IAGO. Will you think so?

OTH.   Think so, Iago!

IAGO.   What,
To kiss in private?

---

[80]**continuate** uninterrupted
[81]**Take . . . out** i.e., copy this embroidery for me
[82]**circumstance'd** governed by circumstances

OTH.   An unauthoriz'd kiss.
IAGO. Or to be naked with her friend in bed
    An hour or more, not meaning any harm?
OTH. Naked in bed, Iago, and not mean harm!
    It is hypocrisy against the devil:
    They that mean virtuously, and yet do so,
    The devil their virtue tempts, and they tempt heaven.
IAGO. So[1] they do nothing, 'tis a venial slip:
    But if I give my wife a handkerchief,—   10
OTH. What then?
IAGO. Why, then, 'tis hers, my lord: and, being hers,
    She may, I think, bestow 't on any man.
OTH. She is protectress of her honour too:
    May she give that?
IAGO. Her honour is an essence that 's not seen;
    They have it very oft that have it not:
    But, for the handkerchief,—
OTH. By heaven, I would most gladly have forgot it.
    Thou said'st—O, it comes o'er my memory,   20
    As doth the raven o'er the infected house,[2]
    Boding to all—he had my handkerchief.
IAGO. Ay, what of that?
OTH.   That 's not so good now.
IAGO.   What,
    If I had said I had seen him do you wrong?
    Or heard him say,—as knaves be such abroad,
    Who having, by their own importunate suit,
    Or voluntary dotage of some mistress,
    Convinced or supplied[3] them, cannot choose
    But they must blab—
OTH.   Hath he said any thing?
IAGO. He hath, my lord; but be you well assur'd,   30
    No more than he'll unswear.
OTH.   What hath he said?
IAGO. 'Faith, that he did—I know not what he did.
OTH. What? what?
IAGO. Lie—
OTH.   With her?
IAGO.   With her, on her; what you will.
OTH. Lie with her! lie on her! We say lie on her, when they belie her. Lie with
    her! that's fulsome.—Handkerchief—confessions—handkerchief!—To
    confess, and be hanged for his labour;—first, to be hanged, and then to
    confess.—I tremble at it. Nature would not invest herself in such shadowing
    passion without some instruction.[4] It is not words that shakes me thus. Pish!
    Noses, ears, and lips.—Is 't possible?—Confess—handkerchief—O devil!

---

[1]**So** so long as
[2]**raven . . . house** allusion to the belief that the raven hovered over a house of sickness or
infection
[3]**Convinced or supplied** i.e., mistresses gained by importunity and those who doted voluntarily
[4]**Nature . . . instruction** i.e., my jealousy cannot be merely the result of natural imagination, but
must have some foundation in fact

[Falls in a trance.]

IAGO. Work on, 42
My medicine, work! Thus credulous fools are caught;
And many worthy and chaste dames even thus,
All guiltless, meet reproach. What, ho! my lord!
My lord, I say! Othello!

[Enter CASSIO.]

                    How now, Cassio!
CAS. What 's the matter?
IAGO. My lord is fall'n into an epilepsy:
This is his second fit; he had one yesterday.
CAS. Rub him about the temples.
IAGO.   No, forbear; 50
The lethargy[5] must have his quiet course:
If not, he foams at mouth and by and by
breaks out to savage madness. Look, he stirs:
Do you withdraw yourself a little while,
He will recover straight: when he is gone,
I would on great occasion speak with you.   *[Exit CASSIO.]*

How is it, general? have you not hurt your head?
OTH. Dost thou mock me?
IAGO.   I mock you! no, by heaven.
Would you would bear your fortune like a man!
OTH. A horned man 's a monster and a beast. 60
IAGO. There 's many a beast then in a populous city,
And many a civil[6] monster.
OTH. Did he confess it?
IAGO.   Good sir, be a man;
Think every bearded fellow that 's but yok'd
May draw with you:[7] there 's millions now alive
That nightly lie in those unproper[8] beds
Which they dare swear peculiar:[9] your case is better.
O, 'tis the spite of hell, the fiend's arch-mock,
To lip a wanton in a secure couch,
And to suppose her chaste! No, let me know; 70
And knowing what I am, I know what she shall be.
OTH. O, thou are wise; 'tis certain.
IAGO.   Stand you awhile apart;
Confine yourself but in a patient list.[10]
Whilst you were here o'erwhelmed with your grief—
A passion most unsuiting such a man—
Cassio came hither: I shifted him away,
And laid good 'scuse upon your ecstasy,

---

[5]**lethargy** unconscious condition
[6]**civil** i.e., in civilized society
[7]**draw with you** i.e., share your fate as cuckold
[8]**unproper** not belonging exclusively to an individual
[9]**peculiar** private, one's own
[10]**patient list** within the bounds of patience

Bade him anon return and here speak with me;
The which he promis'd. Do but encave[11] yourself,
And mark the fleers,[12] the gibes, and notable scorns,   80
That dwell in every region of his face;
For I will make him tell the tale anew,
Where, how, how oft, how long ago, and when
He hath, and is again to cope your wife:
I say, but mark his gesture. Marry, patience;
Or I shall say y' are all in all in spleen,
And nothing of a man.
OTH.   Dost thou hear, Iago?
I will be found most cunning in my patience;
But—dost thou hear?—most bloody.
IAGO.   That 's not amiss;
But yet keep time[13] in all. Will you withdraw?   [OTHELLO *retires.*]   90

Now will I question Cassio of Bianca,
A housewife that by selling her desires
Buys herself bread and clothes: it is a creature
That dotes on Cassio; as 'tis the strumpet's plague
To beguile many and be beguil'd by one:
He, when he hears of her, cannot refrain
From the excess of laughter. Here he comes:

[*Enter* CASSIO.]
As he shall smile, Othello shall go mad;
And his unbookish[14] jealousy must conster[15]
Poor Cassio's smiles, gestures and light behaviour,   100
Quite in the wrong. How do you know, lieutenant?
CAS. The worser that you give me the addition[16]
Whose want even kills me.
IAGO. Ply Desdemona well, and you are sure on 't.
[*Speaking lower*] Now, if this suit lay in Bianca's power,
How quickly should you speed!
CAS.   Alas, poor caitiff!
OTH. Look, how he laughs already!
IAGO. I never knew woman love man so.
CAS. Alas, poor rogue! I think, i' faith, she loves me.
OTH. Now he denies it faintly, and laughs it out.   110
IAGO. Do you hear, Cassio?
OTH.   Now he importunes him
To tell o'er: go to; well said, well said.
IAGO. She gives it out that you shall marry her:
Do you intend it?
CAS. Ha, ha, ha!

[11]**encave** conceal
[12]**fleers** sneers
[13]**keep time** use judgment and order
[14]**unbookish** uninstructed
[15]**conster** construe
[16]**addition** title

OTH. Do you triumph, Roman?[17] do you triumph?

CAS. I marry her! what? a customer![18] Prithee, bear some charity to my wit; do not think it so unwholesome. Ha, ha, ha!

OTH. So, so, so, so: they laugh that win.

IAGO. 'Faith, the cry goes that you shall marry her.   120

CAS. Prithee, say true.

IAGO. I am a very villain else.

OTH. Have you scored me?[19] Well.

CAS. This is the monkey's own giving out: she is persuaded I will marry her, out of her own love and flattery, not out of my promise.

OTH. Iago beckons me; now he begins the story.

CAS. She was here even now; she haunts me in every place. I was the other day talking on the seabank with certain Venetians; and thither comes the bauble,[20] and, by this hand, she falls me thus about my neck—

OTH. Crying, 'O dear Cassio!' as it were: his gesture imports it.   130

CAS. So hangs, and lolls, and weeps upon me; so shakes, and pulls me: ha, ha, ha!

OTH. Now he tells how she plucked him to my chamber. O, I see that nose of yours, but not that dog I shall throw it to.

CAS. Well, I must leave her company.

IAGO. Before me![21] look, where she comes.

[*Enter* BIANCA.]

CAS. 'Tis such another fitchew![22] marry, a perfumed one.—What do you mean by this haunting of me?

BIAN. Let the devil and his dam haunt you! What did you mean by that same handkerchief you gave me even now? I was a fine fool to take it. I must take out the work?—A likely piece of work, that you should find it in your chamber, and not know who left it there! This is some minx's token, and I must take out the work? There; give it your hobby-horse:[23] wheresoever you had it, I'll take out no work on 't.   143

CAS. How now, my sweet Bianca! how now! how now!

OTH. By heaven, that should be my handkerchief!

BIAN. An you'll come to supper to-night, you may; an you will not, come when you are next prepared for.   [*Exit*]

IAGO. After her, after her.

CAS. 'Faith, I must; she'll rail in the street else.

IAGO. Will you sup there?   150

CAS. Yes, I intend so.

IAGO. Well, I may chance to see you; for I would very fain speak with you.

CAS. Prithee, come; will you?

IAGO. Go to; say no more.   [*Exit* CASSIO.]

OTH [*advancing*]. How shall I murder him, Iago?

[17]**Roman** epithet arising from the association of the Romans with the idea of triumph
[18]**customer** prostitute
[19]**scored me** made up my reckoning, or branded me
[20]**bauble** plaything
[21]**Before me!** On my soul!
[22]**fitchew** polecat (because of her strong perfume; also, slang word for a prostitute)
[23]**hobby-horse** harlot

IAGO. Did you perceive how he laughed at his vice?

OTH. O Iago!

IAGO. And did you see the handkerchief?

OTH. Was that mine?   159

IAGO. Yours, by this hand: and to see how he prizes the foolish woman your wife! She gave it him, and he hath given it his whore.

OTH. I would have him nine years a-killing. A fine woman! a fair woman! a sweet woman!

IAGO. Nay, you must forget that.

OTH. Ay, let her rot, and perish, and be damned to-night; for she shall not live: no, my heart is turned to stone; I strike it, and it hurts my hand. O, the world hath not a sweeter creature: she might lie by an emperor's side and command him tasks.

IAGO. Nay, that 's not your way.[24]   169

OTH. Hang her! I do but say what she is: so delicate with her needle: an admirable musician: O! she will sing the savageness out of a bear: of so high and plenteous wit and invention: —

IAGO. She 's the worse for all this.

OTH. O, a thousand thousand times: and then, of so gentle a condition!

IAGO. Ay, too gentle.

OTH. Nay, that 's certain: but yet the pity of it, Iago! O Iago, the pity of it, Iago!

IAGO. If you are so fond over her iniquity, give her patent[25] to offend; for, if it touch not you, it comes near nobody.

OTH. I will chop her into messes;[26] cuckold me!

IAGO. O, 'tis foul in her.   180

OTH. With mine officer!

IAGO. That 's fouler.

OTH. Get me some poison, Iago; this night: I'll not expostulate with her, lest her body and beauty unprovide[27] my mind again: this night, Iago.

IAGO. Do it not with poison, strangle her in her bed, even the bed she hath contaminated.

OTH. Good, good: the justice of it pleases: very good.

IAGO. And for Cassio, let me be his undertaker:[28] you shall hear more by midnight.

OTH. Excellent good. [*A trumpet within.*] What trumpet is that same?   190

IAGO. I warrant something from Venice.

[*Enter* LODOVICO, DESDEMONA, *and* ATTENDANTS.]
                                              'Tis Lodovico.
This comes from the duke: and, see, your wife's with him.

LOD. God save you, worthy general!

OTH.   With all my heart, sir.

LOD. The duke and the senators of Venice greet you.   [*Gives him a letter.*]

OTH. I kiss the instrument of their pleasures.   [*Opens the letter, and reads.*]

DES. And what 's the news, good cousin Lodovico?

---

[24]**your way** i.e., the way you should think of her

[25]**patent** license

[26]**messes** dishes of food

[27]**unprovide** weaken, unfit

[28]**let . . . undertaker** i.e., let me settle with him

IAGO. I am very glad to see you, signior;
  Welcome to Cyprus.
LOD. I thank you. How does Lieutenant Cassio?
IAGO. Lives, sir.
DES. Cousin, there 's fall'n between him and my lord   200
  An unkind breach: but you shall make all well.
OTH. Are you sure of that?
DES. My lord?
OTH [*reads*]. "This fail you not to do, as you will—"
LOD. He did not call; he 's busy in the paper.
  Is there division 'twixt my lord and Cassio?
DES. A most unhappy one: I would do much
  T' atone them, for the love I bear to Cassio.
OTH. Fire and brimstone!
DES.   My lord?
OTH.   Are you wise?   210
DES. What, is he angry?
LOD.   May be the letter mov'd him:
  For, as I think, they do command him home,
  Deputing Cassio in his government.[29]
DES. Trust me, I am glad on 't.
OTH.   Indeed!
DES.   My lord?
OTH. I am glad to see you mad.
DES.   Why, sweet Othello,—
OTH [*striking her*]. Devil!
DES. I have not deserv'd this.
LOD. My lord, this would not be believ'd in Venice,
  Though I should swear I saw 't; 'tis very much:
  Make her amends; she weeps.
OTH.   O devil, devil!   220
  If that the earth could teem with woman's tears,
  Each drop she falls would prove a crocodile.[30]
  Out of my sight!
DES.   I will not stay to offend you.   [*Going.*]
LOD. Truly, an obedient lady:
  I do beseech your lordship, call her back.
OTH. Mistress!
DES.   My lord?
OTH.   What would you with her, sir?
LOD. Who, I, my lord?
OTH. Ay; you did wish that I would make her turn:
  Sir, she can turn, and turn, and yet go on,
  And turn again; and she can weep, sir, weep;   230
  And she 's obedient, as you say, obedient,
  Very obedient. Proceed you in your tears.

[29]**government** office
[30]**prove a crocodile** i.e., by weeping crocodile tears; it was believed the crocodile shed tears over the body of the person it was eating

Concerning this, sir,— O well-painted passion,[31]!—
I am commanded home. Get you away;
I'll send for you anon. Sir, I obey the mandate,
And will return to Venice. Hence, avaunt!

[Exit DESDEMONA.]

Cassio shall have my place. And, sir, to-night,
I do entreat that we may sup together:
You are welcome, sir, to Cyprus.— Goats and monkeys!   [Exit.]

Lod. Is this the noble Moor whom our full senate   240
    Call all in all sufficient? Is this the nature
    Whom passion could not shake? whose solid virtue
    The shot of accident, nor dart of chance,
    Could neither graze nor pierce?
Iago.   He is much chang'd.
Lod. Are his wits safe? is he not light of brain?
Iago. He's that he is: I may not breathe my censure
    What he might be: if what he might he is not,
    I would to heaven he were!
Lod.   What, strike his wife!
Iago. 'Faith, that was not so well; yet would I knew
    That stroke would prove the worst!
Lod.   Is it his use?   250
    Or did the letters work upon his blood,
    And new-create this fault?
Iago   Alas, alas!
    It is not honesty in me to speak
    What I have seen and known. You shall observe him,
    And his own courses will denote him so
    That I may save my speech: do but go after,
    And mark how he continues.
Lod. I am sorry that I am deceiv'd in him.   [Exeunt.]

SCENE II A room in the castle.

[Enter OTHELLO and EMILIA.]
Oth. You have seen nothing then?
Emil. Nor ever heard, nor ever did suspect.
Oth. Yes, you have seen Cassio and she together.
Emil. But then I saw no harm, and then I heard
    Each syllable that breath made up between them.
Oth. What, did they never whisper?
Emil.   Never, my lord.
Oth. Nor send you out 'o th' way?
Emil. Never.
Oth. To fetch her fan, her gloves, her mask, nor nothing?
Emil. Never, my lord.   10
Oth. That's strange.
Emil. I durst, my lord, to wager she is honest,

---

[31]**well-painted passion** well-simulated emotion

Lay down my soul at stake: if you think other,
Remove your thought; it doth abuse your bosom.
If any wretch have put this in your head,
Let heaven requite it with the serpent's curse!
For, if she be not honest, chaste, and true,
There 's no man happy; the purest of their wives
Is foul as slander.

OTH.　　　　　　　Bid her come hither: go.

　　　　　　　　　　　　　　　　　　[*Exit* EMILIA.]

She says enough; yet she 's a simple bawd　　　　　　20
That cannot say as much. This is a subtle whore,
A closet lock and key[32] of villanous secrets:
And yet she'll kneel and pray; I have seen her do 't.

　　　[*Enter* DESDEMONA *and* EMILIA.]
DES. My lord, what is your will?
OTH.　　　　　　　　Pray, chuck, come hither.
DES. What is your pleasure?
OTH.　　　　　　　Let me see your eyes;
　Look in my face.
DES.　　　　　What horrible fancy 's this?
OTH [*to* EMILIA]. Some of your function,[33] mistress;
　Leave procreants[34] alone and shut the door;
　Cough, or cry "hem," if any body come:
　Your mystery, your mystery:[35] nay, dispatch.　　　30

　　　　　　　　　　　　　　　　　　[*Exit* EMILIA.]

DES. Upon my knees, what doth your speech import?
　I understand a fury in your words,
　But not the words.
OTH. Why, what art thou?
DES.　　　　　　Your wife, my lord; your true
　And loyal wife.
OTH.　　　　Come, swear it, damn thyself;
　Lest, being like one of heaven, the devils themselves
　Should fear to seize thee: therefore be double damn'd:
　Swear thou are honest.
DES.　　　　　　Heaven doth truly know it.
OTH. Heaven truly knows that thou are false as hell.
DES. To whom, my lord? with whom? how am I false?　　40
OTH. O Desdemon! away! away! away!
DES. Alas the heavy day! Why do you weep?
　Am I the motive of these tears, my lord?
　If haply you my father do suspect
　An instrument of this your calling back,

[32]**closet lock and key** complete storeroom
[33]**Some . . . function** i.e., set to work in your chosen profession, that of bawd
[34]**procreants** mating couples
[35]**mystery** trade, occupation

Lay not your blame on me: if you have lost him,
Why, I have lost him too.
OTH.   Had it pleas'd heaven
  To try me with affliction; had they[36] rain'd
  All kinds of sores and shames on my bare head,
  Steep'd me in poverty to the very lips,   50
  Given to captivity me and my utmost hopes,
  I should have found in some place of my soul
  A drop of patience: but, alas, to make me
  A fixed figure for the time of scorn
  To point his slow unmoving finger at![37]
  Yet could I bear that too; well, very well:
  But there, where I have garner'd up my heart,
  Where either I must live, or bear no life;
  The fountain from the which my current runs,
  Or else dries up; to be discarded thence!   60
  Or keep it as a cistern for foul toads
  To knot and gender[38] in! Turn thy complexion[39] there,
  Patience, thou young and rose-lipp'd cherubin,—
  Ay, there, look grim as hell!
DES. I hope my noble lord esteems me honest.
OTH. O, ay; as summer flies are in the shambles,[40]
  That quicken[41] even with blowing. O thou weed,
  Who are so lovely fair and smell'st so sweet
  That the sense aches at thee, would thou hads't ne'er been born!
DES. Alas, what ignorant sin have I committed?   70
OTH. Was this fair paper, this most goodly book,
  Made to write "whore" upon? What committed!
  Committed! O thou public commoner![42]
  I should make very forges of my cheeks,
  That would to cinders burn up modesty,
  Did I but speak thy deeds. What committed!
  Heaven stops the nose at it and the moon winks,
  The bawdy wind that kisses all it meets
  Is hush'd within the hollow mine of earth,
  And will not hear it. What committed!   80
  Impudent strumpet!
DES.   By heaven, you do me wrong.
OTH. Are not you a strumpet?
DES.   No, as I am a Christian:
  If to preserve this vessel[43] for my lord

[36]**they** heavenly powers
[37]**A . . . at** Othello possibly thinks of himself as a man set in a pillory at whom the scornful
world points in mockery. There seems to be a comparison with the sundial, whose gnomon, or
indicator, becomes the finger of scornful time
  [38]**gender** engender
  [39]**Turn thy complexion** grow pale
  [40]**shambles** slaughterhouse
  [41]**quicken** come to life
  [42]**commoner** prostitute
  [43]**vessel** body

From any other foul unlawful touch
  Be not to be a strumpet, I am none.
OTH. What, not a whore?
DES.   No, as I shall be sav'd.
OTH. Is 't possible?
DES. O, heaven forgive us!
OTH.   I cry you mercy, then:
  I took you for the cunning whore of Venice
  That married with Othello. [*Raising his voice*] You, mistress,   90
  That have the office opposite to Saint Peter,
  And keep the gate of hell!

  [*Enter* EMILIA.]
                    You, you, ay, you!
  We have done our course; there 's money for your pains:
  I pray you, turn the key and keep our counsel.   [*Exit.*]

EMIL. Alas, what does this gentleman conceive?
  How do you, madam? how do you, my good lady?
DES. 'Faith, half asleep.
EMIL. Good madam, what 's the matter with my lord?
DES. With who?
EMIL. Why, with my lord, madam.   100
DES. Who is thy lord?
EMIL.   He that is yours, sweet lady.
DES. I have none: do not talk to me, Emilia;
  I cannot weep; nor answers have I none,
  But what should go by water.[44] Prithee, tonight
  Lay on my bed my wedding sheets: remember;
  And call thy husband hither.
EMIL.   Here 's a change indeed!   [*Exit.*]
DES. 'Tis meet I should be us'd so, very meet.
  How have I been behav'd, that he might stick
  The small'st opinion on my least misuse?[45]

  [*Enter* IAGO *and* EMILIA.]
IAGO. What is your pleasure, madam? How is 't with you?   110
DES. I cannot tell. Those that do teach young babes
  Do it with gentle means and easy tasks:
  He might have chid me so; for, in good faith,
  I am a child to chiding.
IAGO.   What is the matter, lady?
EMIL. Alas, Iago, my lord hath so bewhor'd her,
  Thrown such despite[46] and heavy terms upon her,
  As true hearts cannot bear.
DES. Am I that name, Iago?
IAGO.   What name, fair lady?

---

[44]**go by water** be expressed by tears
[45]**misuse** evil conduct
[46]**despite** contempt, scorn

DES. Such as she said my lord did say I was.
EMIL. He call'd her whore: a beggar in his drink   120
  Could not have laid such terms upon his callet.[47]
IAGO. Why did he so?
DES. I do not know; I am sure I am none such.
IAGO. Do not weep, do not weep. Alas the day!
EMIL. Hath she forsook so many noble matches,
  Her father and her country and her friends,
  To be call'd whore? would it not make one weep?
DES. It is my wretched fortune.
IAGO.   Beshrew him for 't!
  How comes this trick upon him?
DES.   Nay, heaven doth know.
EMIL. I will be hang'd, if some eternal villain,   130
  Some busy and insinuating rogue,
  Some cogging,[48] cozening slave, to get some office,
  Have not devis'd this slander; I will be hang'd else.
IAGO. Fie, there is no such man; it is impossible.
DES. If any such there be, heaven pardon him!
EMIL. A halter pardon him! and hell gnaw his bones!
  Why should he call her whore? who keeps her company?
  What place? what time? what form? what likelihood?
  The Moor's abus'd by some most villainous knave,
  Some base notorious knave, some scurvy fellow.   140
  O heaven, that such companions thou 'ldst unfold,
  And put in every honest hand a whip
  To lash the rascals naked through the world
  Even from the east to th' west!
IAGO.   Speak within door.[49]
EMIL. O, fie upon them! Some such squire he was
  That turn'd your wit the seamy side without,
  And made you to suspect me with the Moor.
IAGO. You are a fool; go to.
DES.   Alas, Iago.
  What shall I do to win my lord again?
  Good friend, go to him; for, by this light of heaven,   150
  I know not how I lost him. Here I kneel:
  If e'er my will did trespass 'gainst his love,
  Either in discourse of thought or actual deed,
  Or that mine eyes, mine ears, or any sense,
  Delighted them in any other form;
  Or that I do not yet, and ever did,
  And ever will—though he do shake me off
  To beggarly divorcement—love him dearly,
  Comfort forswear me! Unkindness may do much;
  And his unkindness may defeat my life,   160

---

[47]**callet** lewd woman
[48]**cogging** cheating
[49]**Speak . . . door** i.e., not so loud

But never taint my lord. I cannot say "whore":
It doth abhor me now I speak the word;
To do the act that might the addition[50] earn
Not the world's mass of vanity could make me.
IAGO. I pray you, be content; 'tis but his humour:
The business of the state does him offence,
And he does chide with you.
DES. If 'twere no other,—
IAGO.   'Tis but so, I warrant.   [*Trumpets within.*]
Hark, how these instruments summon to supper!
The messengers of Venice stay the meat;[51]
Go in, and weep not; all things shall be well.   170
                              [*Exeunt* DESDEMONA *and* EMILIA.]

[*Enter* RODERIGO.] — *upset w/ Iago*
How now, Roderigo!
ROD. I do not find that thou dealest justly with me.
IAGO. What in the contrary?
ROD. Everyday thou daffest me[52] with some device, Iago; and rather, as it seems
to me now, keepest from me all conveniency[53] than suppliest me with the
least advantage of hope. I will indeed no longer endure it, nor am I yet
persuaded to put up[54] in peace what already I have foolishly suffered.
IAGO. Will you hear me, Roderigo?
ROD. 'Faith, I have heard too much, for your words and performances are no
kin together.   180
IAGO. You charge me most unjustly.
ROD. With nought but truth. I have wasted myself out of my means. The jewels
you have had from me to deliver to Desdemona would half have corrupted a
votarist:[55] you have told me she hath received them and returned me expecta-
tions and comforts of sudden respect and acquaintance, but I find none.
IAGO. Well; go to; very well.
ROD. Very well! go to! I cannot go to, man; nor 'tis not very well: nay, I think it
is scurvy, and begin to find myself fopped[56] in it.
IAGO. Very well.
ROD. I tell you 'tis not very well. I will make myself known to Desdemona: if
she will return me my jewels, I will give over my suit and repent my unlawful
solicitation; if not, assure yourself I will seek satisfaction of you.   192
IAGO. You have said now.[57]
ROD. Ay, and said nothing but what I protest intendment[58] of doing.
IAGO. Why, now I see there 's mettle in thee, and even from this instant do
build on thee a better opinion than ever before. Give my thy hand, Roderigo:

[50]**addition** title
[51]**stay the meat** are waiting for supper
[52]**daffest me** puts me off with an excuse
[53]**conveniency** advantage, opportunity
[54]**put up** submit to
[55]**votarist** nun
[56]**fopped** fooled
[57]**You . . . now** well said, quite right
[58]**intendment** purpose, intention

thou hast taken against me a most just exception; but yet, I protest, I have dealt most directly in thy affair.

Rod. It hath not appeared.

Iago. I grant indeed it hath not appeared, and your suspicion is not without wit and judgement. But, Roderigo, if thou hast that in thee indeed, which I have greater reason to believe now than ever, I mean purpose, courage and valour, this night show it: if thou the next night following enjoy not Desdemona, take me from this world with treachery and devise engines for[59] my life.   202

Rod. Well, what is it? is it within reason and compass?

Iago. Sir, there is especial commission come from Venice to depute Cassio in Othello's place.

Rod. Is that true? why, then Othello and Desdemona return again to Venice.

Iago. O, no; he goes into Mauritania[60] and takes away with him the fair Desdemona, unless his abode be lingered here by some accident: wherein none can be so determinate[61] as the removing of Cassio.

Rod. How do you mean, removing of him?

Iago. Why, by making him uncapable of Othello's place; knocking out his brains.

Rod. And that you would have me to do?   213

Iago. Ay, if you dare do yourself a profit and a right. He sups to-night with a harlotry,[62] and thither will I go to him: he knows not yet of his honourable fortune. If you will watch his going thence, which I will fashion to fall out between twelve and one, you may take him at your pleasure: I will be near to second your attempt, and he shall fall between us. Come, stand not amazed at it, but go along with me; I will show you such a necessity in his death that you shall think yourself bound to put it on him. It is now high[63] supper-time, and the night grows to waste: about it.

Rod. I will hear further reason for this.   222

Iago. And you shall be satisfied.   [*Exeunt.*]

SCENE III *Another room in the castle.*

[*Enter* Othello, Lodovico, Desdemona, Emilia, *and* Attendants.]

Lod. I do beseech you, sir, trouble yourself no further.

Oth. O, pardon me; 'twill do me good to walk.

Lod. Madam, good night; I humbly thank your ladyship.

Des. Your honour is most welcome.

Oth.   Will you walk, sir?

O, — Desdemona, —

Des. My lord?

Oth. Get you to bed on th' instant; I will be returned forthwith: dismiss your attendant there: look 't be done.

Des. I will, my lord.

[*Exit* Othello, *with* Lodovico *and* Attendants.]

---

[59]**engines for** plots against
[60]**Mauritania** Roman name of northwest Africa, supposed land of the Moors
[61]**determinate** decisive
[62]**harlotry** courtesan
[63]**high** quite

EMIL. How goes it now? he looks gentler than he did.   10
DES. He says he will return incontinent:[64]
  He hath commanded me to go to bed,
  And bade me to dismiss you.
EMIL.   Dismiss me!
DES. It was his bidding; therefore, good Emilia,
  Give me my nightly wearing, and adieu:
  We must not now displease him.
EMIL. I would you had never seen him!
DES. So would not I: my love doth so approve him,
  That even his stubbornness,[65] his checks,[66] his frowns,—
  Prithee, unpin me,—have grace and favour in them.   20
EMIL. I have laid those sheets you bade me on the bed.
DES. All 's one. Good faith, how foolish are our minds!
  If I do die before thee, prithee, shroud me
  In one of those same sheets.
EMIL.   Come, come, you talk.
DES. My mother had a maid call'd Barbary:
  She was in love, and he she lov'd prov'd mad
  And did forsake her: she had a song of 'willow';
  An old thing 'twas, but it express'd her fortune,
  And she died singing it: that song to-night
  Will not go from my mind; I have much to do,   30
  But to[67] go hang my head all at one side,
  And sing it like poor Barbary. Prithee, dispatch.
EMIL. Shall I go fetch your night-gown?[68]
DES.   No, unpin me here.
  This Lodovico is a proper man.
EMIL. A very handsome man.
DES. He speaks well.
EMIL. I know a lady in Venice would have walked barefoot to Palestine for a
  touch of his nether lip.
DES [*Singing*]. The poor soul sat sighing by a sycamore tree,
    Sing all a green willow;   40
  Her hand on her bosom, her head on her knee,
    Sing willow, willow, willow:
  The fresh streams ran by her, and murmur'd her moans;
    Sing willow, willow, willow;
  Her salt tears fell from her, and soft'ned the stones;—
  Lay by these:—
  [*Singing*] Sing willow, willow, willow;
  Prithee, hie thee; he'll come anon:—
  [*Singing*] Sing all a green willow must be my garland.
    Let nobody blame him; his scorn I approve,—   50
  Nay, that 's not next.—Hark! who is 't that knocks?

[64]**incontinent** immediately
[65]**stubbornness** harshness
[66]**checks** rebukes
[67]**But to** not to
[68]**night-gown** dressing gown

EMIL. It 's the wind.
DES [*Singing*]. I call'd my love false love; but what said he then?
    Sing willow, willow, willow:
  If I court moe women, you'll couch with moe men. —
So, get thee gone; good night. Mine eyes do itch;
Doth that bode weeping?
EMIL.   'Tis neither here nor there.
DES. I have heard it said so. O, these men, these men!
Dost thou in conscience think, — tell me, Emilia, —
That there be women do abuse their husbands   60
In such gross kind?
EMIL   There be some such, no question.
DES. Wouldst thou do such a deed for all the world?
EMIL. Why, would not you?
DES.   No, by this heavenly light!
EMIL. Nor I neither by this heavenly light; I might do 't as well i' the dark.
DES. Wouldst thou do such a deed for all the world?
EMIL. The world 's a huge thing: it is a great price
For a small vice.
DES. In troth, I think thou wouldst not.
EMIL. In troth, I think I should; and undo 't when I had done. Marry, I would
   not do such a thing for a joint-ring,[69] nor for measures of lawn, nor for
   gowns, petticoats, nor caps, nor any petty exhibition;[70] but, for all the whole
   world, — why, who would not make her husband a cuckold to make him a
   monarch? I should venture purgatory for 't.
DES. Beshrew me, if I would do such a wrong   74
For the whole world.
EMIL. Why, the wrong is but a wrong i' the world; and having the world for
   your labour, 'tis a wrong in your own world, and you might quickly make it
   right.
DES. I do not think there is any such woman.   80
EMIL. Yes, a dozen; and as many to the vantage[71] as would store the world they
   played for.
  But I do think it is their husband's faults
If wives do fall: say that they slack their duties,
And pour our treasures into foreign laps,[72]
Or else break out in peevish jealousies,
Throwing restraint upon us; or say they strike us,
Or scant our former having in despite;[73]
Why, we have galls,[74] and though we have some grace,[75]
Yet have we some revenge. Let husbands know
Their wives have sense like them: they see and smell   90

---

[69]**joint-ring** a ring made in separable halves as a lover's token
[70]**exhibition** gift, present
[71]**to the vantage** in addition
[72]**pour . . . laps** i.e., are unfaithful
[73]**scant . . . despite** reduce our allowance to spite us
[74]**have galls** are capable of resenting injury and insult
[75]**grace** i.e., to forgive

And have their palates both for sweet and sour,
As husbands have. What is it that they do
When they change us for others? Is it sport?
I think it is: and doth affection breed it?
I think it doth: is 't frailty that thus errs?
It is so too: and have not we affections,
Desires for sport, and frailty, as men have?
Then let them use us well: else let them know,
The ills we do, their ills instruct us so.
Des. Good night, good night: heaven me such uses send, 100
Not to pick bad from bad, but by bad mend!   [*Exeunt.*]

ACT V

SCENE I *Cyprus. A street.*

[*Enter* Iago *and* Roderigo.]

Iago. Here stand behind this bulk;[1] straight will he come:
Wear thy good rapier bare, and put it home:
Quick, quick; fear nothing; I'll be at thy elbow:
It makes us, or it mars us; think on that,
And fix most firm thy resolution.
Rod. Be near at hand; I may miscarry in 't.
Iago. Here, at thy hand: be bold, and take thy stand.   [*Retires.*]

Rod. I have no great devotion to the deed;
And yet he hath given me satisfying reasons:
'Tis but a man gone. Forth, my sword: he dies.   10
Iago. I have rubb'd this young quat[2] almost to the sense,[3]
And he grows angry. Now, whether he kill Cassio,
Or Cassio him, or each do kill the other,
Every way makes my gain: live Roderigo,
He calls me to a restitution large
Of gold and jewels that I bobb'd[4] from him, ✗
As gifts to Desdemona;
It must not be: if Cassio do remain,
He hath a daily beauty in his life
That makes me ugly; and, besides, the Moor   20
May unfold me to him; there stand I in much peril:
No, he must die. But so: I hear him coming.

[*Enter* Cassio.]
Rod. I know his gait, 'tis he. — Villain, thou diest!
                                      [*Makes a pass at* Cassio.]

---

[1]**bulk** framework projecting from the front of a shop
[2]**quat** pimple, pustule; used contemptuously
[3]**to the sense** to the quick
[4]**bobb'd** filched cunningly

CAS. That thrust had been mine enemy indeed,
   But that my coat[5] is better than thou know'st:
   I will make proof of thine.   [*Draws, and wounds* RODERIGO.]
ROD.   O, I am slain!
                   [IAGO *from behind wounds* CASSIO *in the leg, and exits.*]
CAS. I am maim'd for ever. Help, ho! murder! murder!   [*Falls.*]

   [*Enter* OTHELLO.]
OTH. The voice of Cassio: Iago keeps his word.
ROD. O, villain that I am!
OTH.   It is even so.
CAS. O, help, ho! light! a surgeon!   30
OTH. 'Tis he: — O brave Iago, honest and just,
   That hast such noble sense of thy friends's wrong!
   Thou teachest me. Minion, your dear lies dead,
   And your unblest fate hies: strumpet, I come.
   Forth of my heart those charms, thine eyes, are blotted;
   Thy bed, lust-stain'd, shall with lust's blood be spotted.

                                              [*Exit* OTHELLO.]

   [*Enter* LODOVICO *and* GRATIANO.]
CAS. What, ho! no watch? no passage?[6] murder! murder!
GRA. 'Tis some mischance; the cry is very direful.
Cas. O, help!
LOD. Hark!   40
ROD. O wretched villain!
LOD. Two or three groan: it is a heavy[7] night;
   These may be counterfeits: let 's think 't unsafe
   To come in to the cry without more help.
ROD. Nobody come? then shall I bleed to death.
LOD. Hark!

   [*Enter* IAGO *with a light.*]
GRA. Here 's one comes in his shirt, with light and weapons.
IAGO. Who 's there? whose noise is this that cries on[8] murder?
LOD. We do not know.
IAGO.   Did not you hear a cry?
CAS. Here, here! for heaven's sake, help me!
IAGO.   What 's the matter?   50
GRA. This is Othello's ancient, as I take it.
LOD. The same indeed; a very valiant fellow.
IAGO. What are you here that cry so grievously?
CAS. Iago? O, I am spoil'd, undone by villains!
   Give me some help.
IAGO. O me, lieutenant! what villains have done this?
CAS. I think that one of them is hereabout,
   And cannot make away.

---

[5]**coat** coat of mail
[6]**passage** people passing
[7]**heavy** thick, cloudy
[8]**cries on** cries out

IAGO.   O treacherous villains!
What are you there? come in, and give some help.

[*To* LODOVICO *and* GRATIANO.]

ROD. O, help me here!   60
CAS. That 's one of them.
IAGO.   O murd'rous slave! O villain!   [*Stabs* RODERIGO.]
ROD. O damn'd Iago! O inhuman dog!
IAGO. Kill men i' th' dark! — Where be these bloody thieves? —
   How silent in this town! — Ho! murder! murder! —
   What⁹ may you be? are you of good or evil?
LOD. As you shall prove us, praise us.
IAGO. Signior Lodovico?
LOD. He, sir.
IAGO. I cry you mercy. Here 's Cassio hurt by villains.
GRA. Cassio!   70
IAGO. How is 't, brother!
CAS. My leg is cut in two.
IAGO.   Marry, heaven forbid!
   Light, gentlemen: I'll bind it with my shirt.

[*Enter* BIANCA.]

BIAN. What is the matter, ho? who is 't that cried?
IAGO. Who is 't that cried?
BIAN. O my dear Cassio! my sweet Cassio!
   O Cassio, Cassio, Cassio!
IAGO. O notable strumpet! Cassio, may you suspect
   Who they should be that have thus mangled you?
CAS. No.   80
GRA. I am sorry to find you thus: I have been to seek you.
IAGO. Lend me a garter. So. O, for a chair,¹⁰
   To bear him easily hence!
BIAN. Alas, he faints! O Cassio, Cassio, Cassio!
IAGO. Gentlemen all, I do suspect this trash¹¹
   To be a party in this injury.
   Patience awhile, good Cassio. Come, come;
   Lend me a light. Know we this face or no?
   Alas, my friend and my dear countryman
   Roderigo! no: — yes, sure: — O heaven! Roderigo.   90
GRA. What, of Venice?
IAGO. Even he, sir: did you know him?
GRA.   Know him! ay.
IAGO. Signior Gratiano? I cry your gentle pardon;
   These bloody accidents must excuse my manners,
   That so neglected you.
GRA.   I am so glad to see you.
IAGO. How do you, Cassio? O, a chair, a chair!

---

⁹**What** who
¹⁰**chair** sedan chair
¹¹**trash** worthless thing. i.e., Bianca

GRA. Roderigo!
IAGO. He, he, 'tis he. [*A chair brought in.*] O, that's well said; the chair.
  Some good man bear him carefully from hence;
  I'll fetch the general's surgeon. [*To* BIANCA] For you, mistress,   100
  Save you your labour. He that lies slain here, Cassio,
  Was my dear friend: what malice was between you?
CAS. None in the world; nor do I know the man.
IAGO [*To* BIAN.]. What, look you pale? O, bear him out o' th' air.
                              [CASSIO *and* RODERIGO *are borne off.*]
  Stay you, good gentlemen. Look you pale, mistress?
  Do you perceive the gastness[12] of her eye?
  Nay, if you stare, we shall hear more anon.
  Behold her well; I pray you, look upon her:
  Do you see, gentlemen? nay, guiltiness will speak,
  Though tongues were out of use.   110

  [*Enter* EMILIA.]
EMIL. 'Las, what 's the matter? what 's the matter, husband?
IAGO. Cassio hath here been set on in the dark
  By Roderigo and fellows that are scap'd:
  He 's almost slain, and Roderigo dead.
EMIL. Alas, good gentlemen! alas, good Cassio!
IAGO. This is the fruit of whoring. Prithee, Emilia.
  Go know of Cassio where he supp'd to-night.
  [*To* BIANCA] What, do you shake at that?
BIAN. He supp'd at my house; but I therefore shake not.
IAGO. O, did he so? I charge you, go with me.   120
EMIL. Fie, fie upon thee, strumpet!
BIAN. I am no strumpet; but of life as honest
  As you that thus abuse me.
EMIL.   As I! foh! fie upon thee!
IAGO. Kind gentlemen, let 's go see poor Cassio dress'd.
  Come, mistress, you must tell 's another tale.
  Emilia, run you to the citadel,
  And tell my lord and lady what hath happ'd.
  Will you go on afore? [*Aside*] This is the night
  That either makes me or fordoes[13] me quite.   [*Exeunt.*]

        SCENE II *A bedchamber in the castle.*

  [*Enter* OTHELLO *with a light;* DESDEMONA *in her bed.*]
OTH. It is the cause, it is the cause,[14] my soul,—
  Let me not name it to you, you chaste stars!—
  It is the cause. Yet I'll not shed her blood;
  Nor scar that whiter skin of hers than snow,
  And smooth as monumental alabaster.
  Yet she must die, else she'll betray more men.

[12]**gastness** terror, ghastliness
[13]**fordoes** undoes, ruins
[14]**It is the cause** i.e., the cause of justice on which Othello must act, Desdemona's deed, which is
too unmentionable to be named to the chaste stars

Put out the light, and then put out the light:
If I quench thee, thou flaming minister,
I can again thy former light restore,
Should I repent me: but once put out thy light, 10
Thou cunning'st pattern of excelling nature,
I know not where is that Promethean heat[15]
That can thy light relume.[16] When I have pluck'd the rose,
I cannot give it vital growth again,
It needs must wither: I'll smell thee on the tree.   *[Kissing her.]*
O balmy breath, that dost almost persuade
Justice to break her sword! One more, one more.
Be thus when thou art dead, and I will kill thee,
And love thee after. One more, and that 's the last:
So sweet was ne'er so fatal. I must weep, 20
But they are cruel tears: this sorrow 's heavenly;[17]
It strikes where it doth love. She wakes.
DES. Who 's there? Othello?
OTH.   Ay, Desdemona.
DES. Will you come to bed, my lord?
OTH. Have you pray'd to-night, Desdemon?
DES.   Ay, my lord.
OTH. If you bethink yourself of any crime
  Unreconcil'd as yet to heaven and grace,
  Solicit for it straight.
DES. Alack, my lord, what may you mean by that?
OTH. Well, do it, and be brief; I will walk by: 30
  I would not kill thy unprepared spirit;
  No; heaven forfend! I would not kill thy soul.
DES. Talk you of killing?
OTH.   Ay, I do.
DES.   Then heaven
  Have mercy on me!
OTH.   Amen, with all my heart!
DES. If you say so, I hope you will not kill me.
OTH. Hum!
DES. And yet I fear you; for you 're fatal then
  When your eyes roll so: why I should fear I know not,
  Since guiltiness I know not; but yet I feel I fear.
OTH. Think on thy sins.
DES.   They are loves I bear to you. 40
OTH. Ay, and for that thou diest.
DES. That death 's unnatural that kills for loving.
  Alas, why gnaw you so your nether lip?
  Some bloody passion shakes your very frame:
  These are portents; but yet I hope, I hope,
  They do not point on me.

[15]**Promethean heat** divine fire; allusion to the theft of fire from heaven by Prometheus
[16]**relume** rekindle
[17]**this . . . heavenly** this tenderness, with which I lament the punishment which justice compels
me to inflict, is a holy passion

OTH.   Peace, and be still!
DES. I will so. What 's the matter?
OTH. That handkerchief which I so lov'd and gave thee
   Thou gav'st to Cassio.
DES.   No, by my life and soul!
   Send for the man, and ask him.
OTH.   Sweet soul, take heed,   50
   Take heed of perjury; thou are on thy deathbed.
DES. Ay, but not yet to die.
OTH.   Yes, presently:
   Therefore confess thee freely of thy sin;
   For to deny each article with oath
   Cannot remove nor choke the strong conception[18]
   That I do groan withal. Thou art to die.
DES. Then Lord have mercy on me!
OTH.   I say, amen.
DES. And have you mercy too! I never did
   Offend you in my life; never lov'd Cassio
   But with such general warranty of heaven   60
   As I might love; I never gave him token.
OTH. By heaven, I saw my handkerchief in 's hand.
   O perjur'd woman! thou dost stone[19] my heart,
   And makest me call what I intend to do
   A murder, which I thought a sacrifice:
   I saw the handkerchief.
DES.   He found it then;
   I never gave it him: send for him hither;
   Let him confess a truth.
OTH.   He hath confess'd.
DES. What, my Lord?
OTH. That he hath us'd thee.
DES.   How? unlawfully?
OTH.   Ay.   70
DES. He will not say so.
OTH.   No, his mouth is stopp'd;
   Honest Iago hath ta'en order[20] for 't.
DES. O! my fear interprets: what, is he dead?
OTH. Had all his hairs been lives, my great revenge
   Had stomach for them all.
DES. Alas! he is betray'd and I undone.
OTH. Out, strumpet! weep'st thou for him to my face?
DES. O, banish me, my lord, but kill me not!
OTH. Down, strumpet!
DES. Kill me to-morrow: let me live to-night!   80
OTH. Nay, if you strive,—

[18]**conception** plan, intention
[19]**stone** turn to stone, harden; Othello means that he will be tempted to kill her in sheer anger because of her perjury
[20]**ta'en order** taken measures

DES. But half an hour!

OTH.   Being done, there is no pause.[21]

DES. But while I say one prayer!

OTH.   It is too late.   [*Smothers her.*]

EMIL. [*at the door*]. My lord, my lord! what, ho! my lord, my lord!

OTH. What noise is this? Not dead? not yet quite dead?
  I that am cruel am yet merciful;
  I would not have thee linger in thy pain:
  So, so.

EMIL. [*within*]. What, ho! my lord, my lord!

OTH.   Who 's there?

EMIL. [*within*]. O, good my lord, I would speak a word with you!   90

OTH. Yes: 'tis Emilia. By and by. She 's dead.
  'Tis like she comes to speak of Cassio's death. —
  The noise was here. Ha! no more moving?
  Still as the grave. Shall she come in? were 't good? —
  I think she stirs again: — no. What 's best to do?
  If she come in, she'll sure speak to my wife:
  My wife! my wife! what wife? I have no wife.
  O, insupportable! O heavy hour!
  Methinks it should be now a huge eclipse
  Of sun and moon, and that th' affrighted globe   100
  Should yawn[22] at alteration.[23]

EMIL.   [*Within*] I do beseech you
  That I may speak with you, O, good my lord!

OTH. I had forgot thee: O, come in, Emilia:
  Soft; by and by. Let me the curtains draw.
  Where art thou?   [*Closes bed-curtains and opens door.*]

[*Enter* EMILIA.]
                    What 's the matter with thee now?

EMIL. O, my good lord, yonder's foul murders done!

OTH. What, now?

EMIL. But now, my lord.

OTH. It is the very error[24] of the moon;
  She comes more nearer earth than she was wont,   110
  And makes men mad.

EMIL. Cassio, my lord, hath kill'd a young Venetian
  Call'd Roderigo.

OTH.   Roderigo kill'd!
  And Cassio kill'd!

EMIL.   No, Cassio is not kill'd.

OTH. Not Cassio kill'd! then murder 's out of tune,
  And sweet revenge grows harsh.

DES. O, falsely, falsely murder'd!

EMIL.   Alas, what cry is that?

---

[21]**Being . . . pause** i.e., when the execution of the deed has once begun, there is no stopping
[22]**yawn** gape in amazement
[23]**at alteration** at the change
[24]**error** irregularity

OTH. That! what!

EMIL. Out, and alas! that was my lady's voice.
　　Help, help, ho! help. O lady, speak again!　　　　　　　　　　120
　　Sweet Desdemona! O sweet mistress, speak!

DES. A guiltless death I die.

EMIL. O, who hath done this deed?

DES. Nobody; I myself. Farewell:
　　Commend me to my kind lord: O, farewell!　　　　　　　　[*Dies*]

OTH. Why, how should she be murd'red?

EMIL.　　　　　　　　　　　　　　　　Alas, who knows?

OTH. You heard her say herself, it was not I.

EMIL. She said so: I must needs report the truth.

OTH. She's, like a liar, gone to burning hell:
　　'Twas I that kill'd her.

EMIL.　　　　　　　　　　O, the more angel she,　　　　　　130
　　And you the blacker devil!

OTH. She turn'd to folly,[25] and she was a whore.

EMIL. Thou dost belie her, and thou art a devil.

OTH. She was false as water.

EMIL.　　　　　　　　　　Thou art rash as fire, to say
　　That she was false: O, she was heavenly true!

OTH. Cassio did top her; ask thy husband else.
　　O, I were damned beneath all depth in hell,
　　But that I did proceed upon just grounds
　　To this extremity. Thy husband knew it all.

EMIL. My husband!　　　　　　　　　　　　　　　　　140

OTH. Thy husband.

EMIL. That she was false to wedlock?

OTH. Ay, with Cassio. Nay, had she been true,
　　If heaven would make me such another world
　　Of one entire and perfect chrysolite,[26]
　　I'ld not have sold her for it.

EMIL. My husband!

OTH.　　　　　　　　Ay, 'twas he that told me first:
　　An honest man he is, and hates the slime
　　That sticks on filthy deeds.

EMIL.　　　　　　　　　　My husband!

OTH. What needs this iterance,[27] woman? I say thy husband.　　150

EMIL. O mistress, villainy hath made mocks with[28] love!
　　My husband say that she was false!

OTH.　　　　　　　　　　He, woman;
　　I say thy husband: dost understand the word?
　　My friend, thy husband, honest, honest Iago.

EMIL. If he say so, may his pernicious soul
　　Rot half a grain a day! he lies to th' heart:
　　She was too fond of her most filthy bargain.

---

[25]**folly** unchastity

[26]**chrysolite** the golden stone; a name given to various precious stones of green color

[27]**iterance** iteration, repetition

[28]**made mocks with** derided, made sport of

OTH. Ha!

EMIL. Do thy worst:

    This deed of thine is no more worthy heaven 160

    Than thou wast worthy her.

OTH.   Peace, you were best.

EMIL. Thou hast not half that power to do me harm

    As I have to be hurt.[29] O gull! O dolt!

    As ignorant as dirt! thou hast done a deed—

    I care not for thy sword; I'll make thee known,

    Though I lost twenty lives.—Help! help, ho! help!

    The Moor hath kill'd my mistress! Murder! murder!

[*Enter* MONTANO, GRATIANO, *and* IAGO *with others.*]

MON. What is the matter! How now, general!

EMIL. O, are you come, Iago? you have done well,

    That men must lay their murders on your neck. 170

GRA. What is the matter?

EMIL. Disprove this villain, if thou be'st a man:

    He says thou told'st him that his wife was false:

    I know thou didst not, thou 'rt not such a villain:

    Speak, for my heart is full.

IAGO. I told him what I thought, and told no more

    Than what he found himself was apt[30] and true.

EMIL. But did you ever tell him she was false?

IAGO. I did.

EMIL. You told a lie; an odious, damned lie; 180

    Upon my soul, a lie, a wicked lie.

    She false with Cassio!—did you say with Cassio?

IAGO. With Cassio, mistress. Go to, charm[31] your tongue.

EMIL. I will not charm my tongue; I am bound to speak:

    My mistress here lies murdered in her bed,—

ALL. O heavens forfend!

EMIL. And your reports have set the murder on.

OTH. Nay, stare not, masters: it is true, indeed.

GRA. 'Tis a strange truth.

MON. O monstrous act!

EMIL.   Villainy, villainy, villainy! 190

    I think upon 't, I think: I smell 't: O villainy—

    I thought so then:[32] I'll kill myself for grief:—

    O villainy, villainy!

IAGO. What, are you mad? I charge you, get you home.

EMIL. Good gentlemen, let me have leave to speak:

    'Tis proper I obey him, but not now.

    Perchance, Iago, I will ne'er go home.

OTH. O! O! O!   [*He falls on the bed.*]

---

[29]**to be hurt** i.e., to endure hurting

[30]**apt** natural, likely

[31]**charm** keep silent

[32]**then** i.e., at some earlier time, probably IV, ii, when she suspected the machinations of *some eternal villain;* she did not, however, know that villain to be Iago until this moment

EMIL.   Nay, lay thee down and roar;
  For thou hast kill'd the sweetest innocent
  That e'er did lift up eye.
OTH.   [*Rising*] O, she was foul!   200
  I scarce did know you, uncle: there lies your niece,
  Whose breath, indeed, these hands have newly stopp'd:
  I know this act shows horrible and grim.
GRA. Poor Desdemon! I am glad thy father 's dead:
  Thy match was mortal to him, and pure grief
  Shore[33] his old thread in twain: did he live now,
  This sight would make him do a desperate turn,
  Yea, curse his better angel from his side,
  And fall to reprobation.[34]
OTH. 'Tis pitiful; but yet Iago knows   210
  That she with Cassio hath the act of shame
  A thousand times committed; Cassio confess'd it:
  And she did gratify his amorous works
  With that recognizance[35] and pledge of love
  Which I first gave her; I saw it in his hand:
  It was a handkerchief, an antique token
  My father gave my mother.
EMIL. O heaven! O heavenly pow'rs!
IAGO. Come, hold your peace.
EMIL.   'Twill out, 'twill out: I peace!
  No, I will speak as liberal as the north:[36]   220
  Let heaven and men and devils, let them all,
  All, all, cry shame against me, yet I'll speak.
IAGO. Be wise, and get you home.
EMIL.   I will not! [IAGO *offers to stab* EMILIA.]
GRA.   Fie!
  Your sword upon a woman?
EMIL. O thou dull Moor! that handkerchief thou speak'st of
  I found by fortune[37] and did give my husband;
  For often, with solemn earnestness,
  More than indeed belong'd to such a trifle,
  He begg'd me to steal it.
IAGO.   Villainous whore!
EMIL. She give it Cassio! no, alas! I found it,   230
  And I did give 't my husband.
IAGO.   Filth, thou liest!
EMIL. By heaven, I do not, I do not, gentlemen.
  O murd'rous coxsomb![38] what should such a fool
  Do with so good a wife!

---

[33]**Shore** cut
[34]**reprobation** damnation, rejection by God
[35]**recognizance** token
[36]**liberal as the north** freely as the north wind
[37]**fortune** chance
[38]**coxcomb** fool; addressed to Othello

OTH. Are there no stones in heaven[39]
But what serves for the thunder? — Precious villain!

[*He runs at* IAGO: IAGO, *from behind, stabs* EMILIA, *and exits.*]

GRA. The woman falls; sure, he hath kill'd his wife.

EMIL. Ay, ay: O, lay me by my mistress' side.

GRA. He 's gone, but his wife 's kill'd.

MON. 'Tis a notorious villain. Take you this weapon,
Which I have here recover'd from the Moor: 240
Come, guard the door without; let him not pass,
But kill him rather. I'll after that same villain,
For 'tis a damned slave. [*Exit with all but* OTHELLO *and* EMILIA.]

OTH. I am not valiant neither,
But every puny whipster[40] gets my sword:
But why should honour outlive honesty?[41]
Let it go all.

EMIL. What did thy song bode, lady?
Hark, canst thou hear me? I will play the swan,
And die in music. [*Singing*] Willow, willow, willow. —
Moor, she was chaste; she lov'd thee, cruel Moor;
So come my soul to bliss, as I speak true; 250
So speaking as I think, I die, I die. [*Dies.*]

OTH. I have another weapon in this chamber;
It is a sword of Spain, the ice-brook's temper[42]: —
O, here it is. Uncle, I must come forth.

GRA. [*within*]. If thou attempt it, it will cost thee dear:
Thou hast no weapon, and perforce must suffer.

OTH. Look in upon me then and speak with me,
Or, naked[43] as I am, I will assault thee.

[*Enter* GRATIANO.]

GRA. What is the matter?

OTH. Behold, I have a weapon;
A better never did itself sustain 260
Upon a soldier's thigh: I have seen the day,
That, with this little arm and this good sword,
I have made my way through more impediments
Than twenty times your stop:[44] but, O vain boast!
Who can control his fate? 'tis not so now.
Be not afraid, though you do see me weapon'd;
Here is my journey's end, here is my butt,[45]

---

[39]**stones in heaven** thunderbolts. It was supposed that real stones fell with the thunder and caused the damage

[40]**whipster** contemptible fellow

[41]**honour outlive honesty** Othello realizes that he has done a shameful deed; he asks why his reputation for valor should endure

[42]**ice-brook's temper** usually defined as "tempered in ice-cold water"

[43]**naked** unarmed

[44]**stop** power

[45]**butt** mark for archery, goal, limit

And very sea-mark[46] of my utmost sail.
Do you go back dismay'd? 'tis a lost fear;
Man[47] but a rush[48] against Othello's breast,   270
And he retires. Where should Othello go?
Now, how dost thou look now? O ill-starr'd wench!
Pale as thy smock! when we shall meet at compt,[49]
This look of thine will hurl my soul from heaven,
And fiends will snatch at it. Cold, cold, my girl!
Even like thy chastity. O cursed, cursed slave!
Whip me, ye devils,
From the possession of this heavenly sight!
Blow me about in winds! roast me in sulphur!
Wash me in steep-down gulfs of liquid fire!   280
O Desdemon! Dead Desdemon! dead!
Oh! Oh!

[*Enter* LODOVICO, CASSIO *carried in a chair,* MONTANO, *and* IAGO, *prisoner, with* OFFICERS.]

LOD. Where is this rash and most unfortunate man?
OTH. That 's he that was Othello: here I am.
LOD. Where is that viper? bring the villain forth.
OTH. I look down towards his feet;[50] but that 's a fable.
   If that thou be'st a devil, I cannot kill thee.   [*Wounds* IAGO.]
LOD. Wrench his sword from him.
IAGO.   I bleed sir; but not kill'd.
OTH. I am not sorry neither: I 'ld have thee live;
   For, in my sense, 'tis happiness to die.   290
LOD. O thou Othello, that wert once so good,
   Fall'n in the practice of a damned slave,
   What shall be said to thee?
OTH.   Why, any thing:
   An honourable murderer, if you will;
   For nought I did in hate, but all in honour.
LOD. This wretch hath part confess'd his villainy:
   Did you and he consent in Cassio's death?
OTH. Ay.
CAS. Dear general, I never gave you cause.
OTH. I do believe it, and I ask you pardon.   300
   Will you, I pray, demand that demi-devil
   Why he hath thus ensnar'd my soul and body?
IAGO. Demand me nothing: what you know, you know:
   From this time forth I never will speak word.
LOD. What, not to pray?
GRA.   Torments will ope your lips.
OTH. Well, thou dost best.

---

[46]**sea-mark** beacon (marking his destination or limit)
[47]**Man** provide, as in manning a gun
[48]**rush** reed
[49]**compt** account, judgment day
[50]**towards his feet** i.e., to see if they were cloven like a devil's

LOD. Sir, you shall understand what hath befall'n,
    Which, as I think, you know not. Here is a letter
    Found in the pocket of the slain Roderigo;
    And here another: the one of them imports   310
    The death of Cassio to be undertook
    By Roderigo.
OTH. O villain!
CAS.   Most heathenish and most gross!
LOD. Now here 's another discontented[51] paper,
    Found in his pocket too; and this, it seems,
    Roderigo meant t' have sent this damned villain;
    But that belike Iago in the interim
    Came in and satisfied him.
OTH.   O thou pernicious caitiff[52]!—
    How came you, Cassio, by that handkerchief
    That was my wife's?
CAS.   I found it in my chamber: 320
    And he himself confess'd but even now
    That there he dropp'd it for a special purpose
    Which wrought to his desire.
OTH.   O fool! O fool! fool!
CAS. There is besides in Roderigo's letter,
    How he upbraids Iago, that he made him
    Brave[53] me upon the watch; whereon it came
    That I was cast:[54] and even but now he spake,
    After long seeming dead, Iago hurt him,
    Iago set him on.
LOD. You must forsake this room, and go with us: 330
    Your power and your command is taken off,[55]
    And Cassio rules in Cyprus. For this slave,
    If there be any cunning cruelty
    That can torment him much and hold him long,
    It shall be his. You shall close prisoner rest,
    Till that the nature of your fault be known
    To the Venetian state. Come, bring him away.
OTH. Soft you; a word or two before you go.
    I have done the state some service, and they know 't.
    No more of that. I pray you, in your letters,   340
    When you shall these unlucky deeds relate,
    Speak of me as I am; nothing extenuate,[56]
    Nor set down aught in malice: then must you speak
    Of one that lov'd not wisely but too well;
    Of one not easily jealous, but being wrought,

---

[51]**discontented** expressing dissatisfaction
[52]**caitiff** wretch
[53]**Brave** defy
[54]**cast** dismissed
[55]**taken off** taken away
[56]**extenuate** diminish, depreciate; the idea is contrasted with the thought of *malice* in the following line

Perplex'd[57] in the extreme; of one whose hand,
Like the base Judean,[58] threw a pearl away
Richer than all his tribe; of one whose subdu'd eyes,
Albeit unused to the melting mood,
Drop tears as fast as the Arabian trees   350
Their medicinable gum. Set you down this;
And say besides, that in Aleppo[59] once,
Where a malignant and a turban'd Turk
Beat a Venetian and traduc'd the state,
I took by th' throat the circumcised dog,
And smote him, thus.   [*Stabs himself.*]
LOD. O bloody period![60]
GRA.   All that is spoke is marr'd.
OTH. I kiss'd thee ere I kill'd thee: no way but this;
Killing myself, to die upon a kiss.   [*Falls on the bed, and dies.*]
CAS. This did I fear, but thought he had no weapon;   360
For he was great of heart.
LOD.   [*To* IAGO] O Spartan dog,[61]
More fell than anguish, hunger, or the sea!
Look on the tragic loading of this bed;
This is thy work: the object poisons sight;
Let it be hid. Gratiano, keep the house,
And seize upon the fortunes of the Moor,
For they succeed on you. To you, lord governor,
Remains the censure of this hellish villain;
The time, the place, the torture: O, enforce it!
Myself will straight abroad; and to the state   370
This heavy act with heavy heart relate.   [*Exeunt.*]

                                                                            (1604)

[57]**Perplex'd** confounded, distracted
[58]**Judean** infidel or disbeliever
[59]**Aleppo** a Turkish city where the Venetians had special trading privileges. It is stated that it was immediate death for a Christian to strike a Turk in Aleppo; Othello risked his life for the honor of Venice
[60]**period** termination, conclusion
[61]**Spartan dog** Spartan dogs were noted for their savagery

Anton Chekhov *1860–1904*

THE MARRIAGE PROPOSAL

Translated by Ronald Hingley

CHARACTERS

STEPHEN CHUBUKOV, *a landowner.*

NATASHA, *his daughter, aged 25.*

IVAN LOMOV, *a landowning neighbor of Chubukov's, hefty and well-nourished, but a hypochondriac.*

The action takes place in the drawing-room of CHUBUKOV'S *country-house.*

SCENE I

CHUBUKOV *and* LOMOV; *the latter comes in wearing evening dress and white gloves.*

CHUBUKOV [*going to meet him*]. Why, it's Ivan Lomov — or do my eyes deceive me, old boy? Delighted. [*Shakes hands.*] I say, old bean, this is a surprise! How *are* you?

LOMOV. All right, thanks, And how might you be?

CHUBUKOV. Not so bad, dear boy. Good of you to ask and so on. Now, you simply must sit down. Never neglect the neighbours, old bean — what? But why so formal, old boy — the tails, the gloves and so on? Not going anywhere, are you, dear man?

LOMOV. Only coming here, my dear Chubukov.

CHUBUKOV. Then why the tails, my dear fellow? Why make such a great thing of it?

LOMOV. Well, look, the point is — . [*Takes his arm.*] I came to ask a favour, my dear Chubukov, if it's not too much bother. I have had the privilege of enlisting your help more than once, and you've always, as it were — but I'm so nervous, sorry. I'll drink some water, my dear Chubukov. [*Drinks water.*]

CHUBUKOV [*aside*]. He's come to borrow money. Well, there's nothing doing! [*To him.*] What's the matter, my dear fellow?

LOMOV. Well, you see, my dear Dubukov — my dear Chubukov, I mean, sorry — that's to say, I'm terribly jumpy, as you see. In fact only you can help me, though I don't deserve it, of course and, er, have no claims on you either.

CHUBUKOV. Now don't muck about with it, old bean. Let's have it. Well?

LOMOV. Certainly, this instant. The fact is, I'm here to ask for the hand of your daughter Natasha.

CHUBUKOV [*delightedly*]. My dear Lomov! Say that again, old horse, I didn't quite catch it.

LOMOV. I have the honour to ask —

CHUBUKOV [*interrupting him*]. My dear old boy! I'm delighted and so on, er,

857

and so forth — what? [*Embraces and kisses him.*] I've long wanted it, it's always been my wish. [*Sheds a tear.*] I've always loved you as a son, dear boy. May you both live happily ever after and so on. As for me, I've always wanted —. But why do I stand around like a blithering idiot? I'm tickled pink, I really am! Oh, I most cordially —. I'll go and call Natasha and so forth.

LOMOV [*very touched*]. My dear Chubukov, what do you think — can I count on a favourable response?

CHUBUKOV. What — her turn down a good-looking young fellow like you! Not likely! I bet she's crazy about you and so on. One moment. [*Goes out.*]

SCENE II

[LOMOV, *alone.*]

LOMOV. I feel cold, I'm shaking like a leaf. Make up your mind, that's the great thing. If you keep chewing things over, dithering on the brink, arguing the toss and waiting for your ideal woman or true love to come along, you'll never get hitched up. Brrr! I'm cold. Natasha's a good housewife. She's not bad-looking and she's an educated girl — what more can you ask? But I'm so jumpy, my ears have started buzzing. [*Drinks water.*] And get married I must. In the first place, I'm thirty-five years old — a critical age, so to speak. Secondly, I should lead a proper, regular life. I've heart trouble and constant palpitations, I'm irritable and nervous as a kitten. See how my lips are trembling now? See my right eyelid twitch? But my nights are the worst thing. No sooner do I get in bed and start dozing off than I have a sort of shooting pain in my left side. It goes right through my shoulder and head. Out I leap like a lunatic, walk about a bit, then lie down again — but the moment I start dropping off I get this pain in my side again. And it happens twenty times over.

SCENE III

[NATASHA *and* LOMOV.]

NATASHA [*comes in*]. Oh, it's you. That's funny, Father said it was a dealer collecting some goods or something. Good morning, Mr. Lomov.

LOMOV. And good morning to you, my dear Miss Chubukov.

NATASHA. Excuse my apron, I'm not dressed for visitors. We've been shelling peas — we're going to dry them. Why haven't you been over for so long? Do sit down. [*They sit.*] Will you have lunch?

LOMOV. Thanks, I've already had some.

NATASHA. Or a smoke? Here are some matches. It's lovely weather, but it rained so hard yesterday — the men were idle all day. How much hay have you cut? I've been rather greedy, you know — I mowed all mine, and now I'm none too happy in case it rots. I should have hung on. But what's this I see? Evening dress, it seems. That *is* a surprise! Going dancing or something? You're looking well, by the way — but why on earth go round in that get-up?

LOMOV [*agitated*]. Well, you see my dear Miss Chubukov. The fact is, I've decided to ask you to — er, lend me your ears. You're bound to be surprised — angry, even. But I —. [*Aside.*] I feel terribly cold.

NATASHA. What's up then? [*Pause.*] Well?

LOMOV. I'll try to cut it short. Miss Chubukov, you are aware that I have long been privileged to know your family — since I was a boy, in fact. My dear departed aunt and her husband — from whom, as you are cognizant, I inherited the estate — always entertained the deepest respect for your father and dear departed mother. We Lomovs and Chubukovs have always been on the friendliest terms — you might say we've been pretty thick. And what's more, as you are also aware, we own closely adjoining properties. You may recall that my land at Oxpen Field is right next to your birch copse.

NATASHA. Sorry to butt in, but you refer to Oxpen Field as "yours"? Surely you're not serious!

LOMOV. I am, madam.

NATASHA. Well, I like that! Oxpen Field is ours, it isn't yours.

LOMOV. You're wrong, my dear Miss Chubukov, that's my land.

NATASHA. This is news to me. How can it be yours?

LOMOV. How? What do you mean? I'm talking about Oxpen Field, that wedge of land between your birch copse and Burnt Swamp.

NATASHA. That's right. It's our land.

LOMOV. No, you're mistaken, my dear Miss Chubukov. It's mine.

NATASHA. Oh, come off it, Mr. Lomov. How long has it been yours?

LOMOV. How long? As long as I can remember — it's always been ours.

NATASHA. I say, this really is a bit steep!

LOMOV. But you have only to look at the deeds, my dear Miss Chubukov. Oxpen Field once *was* in dispute, I grant you, but it's mine now — that's common knowledge, and no argument about it. If I may explain, my aunt's grandmother made over that field rent free to your father's grandfather's labourers for their indefinite use in return for firing her bricks. Now, your great-grandfather's people used the place rent free for forty years or so, and came to look on it as their own. Then when the government land settlement was brought out —

NATASHA. No, that's all wrong. My grandfather and great-grandfather both claimed the land up to Burnt Swamp as theirs. So Oxpen Field was ours. Why argue? That's what I can't see. This is really rather aggravating.

LOMOV. I'll show you the deeds, Miss Chubukov.

NATASHA. Oh, you must be joking or having me on. This *is* a nice surprise! You own land for nearly three hundred years, then someone ups and tells you it's not yours! Mr. Lomov, I'm sorry, but I simply can't believe my ears. I don't mind about the field — it's only the odd twelve acres, worth the odd three hundred roubles. But it's so unfair — that's what infuriates me. I can't stand unfairness, I don't care what you say.

LOMOV. Do you hear me out, please! With due respect, your great-grandfather's people baked bricks for my aunt's grandmother, as I've already told you. Now, my aunt's grandmother wanted to do them a favour —

NATASHA. Grandfather, grandmother, aunt — it makes no sense to me. The field's ours, and that's that.

LOMOV. It's mine.

NATASHA. It's ours! Argue till the cows come home, put on tailcoats by the dozen for all I care — it'll still be ours, ours, ours! I'm not after your property, but I don't propose losing mine either, and I don't care what you think!

LOMOV. My dear Miss Chubukov, it's not that I need that field — it's the principle of the thing. If you want it, have it. Take it as a gift.

NATASHA. But it's mine to give *you* if I want — it's my property. This is odd, to put it mildly. We always thought you such a good neighbour and friend, Mr. Lomov. We lent you our threshing-machine last year, and couldn't get our own threshing done till November in consequence. We might be gipsies, the way you treat us. Making me a present of my own property! I'm sorry, but that's not exactly neighbourly of you. In fact, if you ask me, it's sheer howling cheek.

LOMOV. So I'm trying to pinch your land now, am I? It's not my habit, madam, to grab land that isn't mine, and I won't have anyone say it is! [*Quickly goes to the carafe and drinks some water.*] Oxpen Field belongs to me.

NATASHA. That's a lie, it's ours.

LOMOV. It's mine.

NATASHA. That's a lie and I'll nail it! I'll send my men to cut that field this very day.

LOMOV. What do you say?

NATASHA. My men will be out on that field today!

LOMOV. Too right, they'll be out! Out on their ear!

NATASHA. You'd never dare.

LOMOV [*clutches his heart*]. Oxpen Field belongs to me, do you hear? It's mine!

NATASHA. Kindly stop shouting. By all means yell yourself blue in the face when you're in your own home, but I'll thank you to keep a civil tongue in your head in this house.

LOMOV. Madam, if I hadn't got these awful, agonizing palpitations and this throbbing in my temples, I'd give you a piece of my mind! [*Shouts.*] Oxpen Field belongs to me.

NATASHA. To us, you mean!

LOMOV. It's mine!

NATASHA. It's ours!

LOMOV. Mine!

SCENE IV

[*The above and* CHUBUKOV]

CHUBUKOV [*coming in*]. What's going on, what's all the row in aid of?

NATASHA. Father, who owns Oxpen Field? Would you mind telling this gentleman? Is it his or ours?

CHUBUKOV [*to* LOMOV]. That field's ours, old cock!

LOMOV. Now look here, Chubukov, how can it be? You at least might show some sense! My aunt's grandmother made over that field to your grandfather's farm-labourers rent free on a temporary basis. Those villagers had the use of the land for forty years and came to think of it as theirs, but when the settlement came out —

CHUBUKOV. Now hang on, dear man, you forget one thing. That field was in dispute and so forth even in those days — and that's why the villagers paid your grandmother no rent and so on. But now it belongs to us, every dog in the district knows that, what? You can't have seen the plans.

LOMOV. It's mine and I'll prove it.

CHUBUKOV. Oh no you won't, my dear good boy.

LOMOV. Oh yes, I will.

CHUBUKOV. No need to shout, old bean. Shouting won't prove anything, what? I'm not after your property, but I don't propose losing mine, either. Why on earth should I? If it comes to that, old sausage, if you're set on disputing the field and so on, I'd rather give it to the villagers than you. So there.

LOMOV. This makes no sense to me. What right have you to give other people's property away?

CHUBUKOV. Permit me to be the best judge of that. Now, look here, young feller-me-lad—I'm not used to being spoken to like this, what? I'm twice your age, boy, and I'll thank you to talk to me without getting hot under the collar and so forth.

LOMOV. Oh, really, you must take me for a fool. You're pulling my leg. You say my land's yours, then you expect me to keep my temper and talk things over amicably. I call this downright unneighbourly, Chubukov. You're not a neighbour, you're a thoroughgoing shark!

CHUBUKOV. I *beg* your pardon! What did you say?

NATASHA. Father, send the men out to mow that field this very instant!

CHUBUKOV [*to* LOMOV]. What was it you said, sir?

NATASHA. Oxpen Field's ours and I won't let it go, I won't, I won't!

LOMOV. We'll see about that! I'll have the law on you!

CHUBUKOV. You will, will you? Then go right ahead, sir, and so forth, go ahead and sue, sir! Oh, I know your sort! Just what you're angling for and so on, isn't it—a court case, what? Quite the legal eagle, aren't you? Your whole family's always been litigation-mad, every last one of 'em!

LOMOV. I'll thank you not to insult my family. We Lomovs have always been honest, we've none of us been had up for embezzlement like your precious uncle.

CHUBUKOV. The Lomovs have always been mad as hatters!

NATASHA. Yes! All of you! Mad!

CHUBUKOV. Your grandfather drank like a fish, and your younger Aunt What's-her-name—Nastasya—ran off with an architect and so on.

LOMOV. And your mother was a cripple. [*Clutches his heart.*] There's that shooting pain in my side, and a sort of blow on the head. Heavens alive! Water!

CHUBUKOV. Your father gambled and ate like a pig!

NATASHA. Your aunt was a most frightful busybody!

LOMOV. My left leg's gone to sleep. And you're a very slippery customer. Oh my heart! And it's common knowledge that at election time you bri—. I'm seeing stars. Where's my hat?

NATASHA. What a rotten, beastly, filthy thing to say.

CHUBUKOV. You're a thoroughly nasty, cantankerous, hypocritical piece of work, what? Yes, sir!

LOMOV. Ah, there's my hat. My heart—. Which way do I go? Where's the door? Oh, I think I'm dying. I can hardly drag one foot after another. [*Moves to the door.*]

CHUBUKOV [*after him*]. You need never set either of those feet in my house again, sir.

NATASHA. Go ahead and sue, we'll see what happens.

[LOMOV *goes out staggering.*]

SCENE V

[CHUBUKOV *and* NATASHA.]

CHUBUKOV. Oh, blast it! [*Walks up and down in agitation.*]

NATASHA. The rotten cad! So much for trusting the dear neighbours!

CHUBUKOV. Scruffy swine!

NATASHA. He's an out-and-out monster! Pinches your land and then has the cheek to swear at you!

CHUBUKOV. And this monstrosity, this blundering oaf, has the immortal rind to come here with his proposal and so on, what? A proposal! I ask you!

NATASHA. A proposal, did you say?

CHUBUKOV. Not half I did! He came here to propose to you!

NATASHA. Propose? To me? Then why didn't you say so before?

CHUBUKOV. That's why he dolled himself up in tails. Damn popinjay! Twerp!

NATASHA. Me? Propose to me? Oh! [*Falls in an armchair and groans.*] Bring him back! Bring him back! Bring him back, I tell you!

CHUBUKOV. Bring who back?

NATASHA. Hurry up, be quick, I feel faint. Bring him back. [*Has hysterics.*]

CHUBUKOV. What's this? What do you want? [*Clutches his head.*] Oh, misery! I might as well go and boil my head! I'm fed up with them!

NATASHA. I'm dying. Bring him back!

CHUBUKOV. Phew! All right then. No need to howl. [*Runs out.*]

NATASHA [*alone, groans*]. What have we done! Bring him, bring him back!

CHUBUKOV [*runs in*]. He'll be here in a moment and so on, damn him! Phew! You talk to him—I don't feel like it, what?

NATASHA [*groans*]. Bring him back!

CHUBUKOV [*shouts*]. He's coming, I tell you
> "My fate, ye gods, is just too bad—
> To be a grown-up daughter's dad!"
I'll cut my throat, I'll make a point of it. We've sworn at the man, insulted him and kicked him out of the house. And it was all your doing.

NATASHA. It was *not*, it was yours!

CHUBUKOV. So now it's my fault, what?

[LOMOV *appears in the doorway.*]

CHUBUKOV. All right, now you talk to him. [*Goes out.*]

SCENE VI

[NATASHA *and* LOMOV.]

LOMOV [*comes in, exhausted*]. My heart's fairly thumping away, my leg's gone to sleep and there's this pain in my side—

NATASHA. I'm sorry we got a bit excited, Mr. Lomov. I've just remembered— Oxpen Field really does belong to you.

LOMOV. My heart's fairly thumping away. That field's mine. I've a nervous tic in both eyes.

NATASHA. The field *is* yours, certainly. Do sit down. [*They sit.*] We were mistaken.

LOMOV. This is a question of principle. It's not the land I mind about, it's the principle of the thing.

NATASHA. Just so, the principle. Now let's change the subject.

LOMOV. Especially as I can prove it. My aunt's grandmother gave your father's grandfather's villagers —

NATASHA. All right, that'll do. [*Aside.*] I don't know how to start. [*To him.*] Thinking of going shooting soon?

LOMOV. Yes, I'm thinking of starting on the woodcock after the harvest, my dear Miss Chubukov. I say, have you heard? What awful bad luck! You know my dog Tracker? He's gone lame.

NATASHA. Oh, I am sorry. How did it happen?

LOMOV. I don't know. Either it must be a sprain, or the other dogs bit him. [*Sighs.*] My best dog, to say nothing of what he set me back! Do you know, I gave Mironov a hundred and twenty-five roubles for him?

NATASHA. Then you were had, Mr. Lomov.

LOMOV. He came very cheap if you ask me — he's a splendid dog.

NATASHA. Father only gave eighty-five roubles for Rover. And Rover's a jolly sight better dog than Tracker, you'll agree.

LOMOV. Rover better than Tracker! Oh, come off it! [*Laughs.*] Rover a better dog than Tracker!

NATASHA. Of course he is. Rover's young, it's true, and not yet in his prime. But you could search the best kennels in the county without finding a nippier animal, or one with better points.

LOMOV. I am sorry, Miss Chubukov, but you forget he has a short lower jaw, and a dog like that can't grip.

NATASHA. Oh, can't he! That's news to me!

LOMOV. He has a weak chin, you can take that from me.

NATASHA. Why, have you measured it?

LOMOV. Yes, I have. Naturally he'll do for coursing, but when it comes to retrieving, that's another story.

NATASHA. In the first place, Rover has a good honest coat on him, and a pedigree as long as your arm. As for that mud-coloured, piebald animal of yours, his antecedents are anyone's guess, quite apart from him being ugly as a broken-down old cart-horse.

LOMOV. Old he may be, but I wouldn't swap him for a half dozen Rovers — not on your life! Tracker's a real dog, and Rover — why, it's absurd to argue. The kennels are lousy with Rovers, he'd be dear at twenty-five roubles.

NATASHA. You *are* in an awkward mood today, Mr. Lomov. First you decide our field is yours, now you say Tracker's better than Rover. I dislike people who won't speak their mind. Now, you know perfectly well that Rover's umpteen times better than that — yes, that stupid Tracker. So why say the opposite?

LOMOV. I see you don't credit me with eyes or brains, Miss Chubukov. Well, get it in your head that Rover has a weak chin.

NATASHA. That's not true.

LOMOV. Oh yes it is!

NATASHA [*shouts*]. Oh no it isn't!

LOMOV. Don't you raise your voice at me, madam.

NATASHA. Then don't you talk such utter balderdash! Oh, this is infuriating! It's time that measly Tracker was put out of his misery — and you compare him with Rover!

LOMOV. I can't go on arguing, sorry — it's my heart.

NATASHA. Men who argue most about sport, I've noticed, are always the worst sportsmen.

LOMOV. Will you kindly hold your trap, madam—my heart's breaking in two. [*Shouts.*] You shut up!

NATASHA. I'll do nothing of the sort till you admit Rover's a hundred times better than Tracker.

LOMOV. A hundred times worse, more like! I hope Rover drops dead! Oh, my head, my eye, my shoulder—

NATASHA. That half-wit Tracker doesn't need to drop dead—he's pretty well a walking corpse already.

LOMOV [*weeps*]. Shut up! I'm having a heart attack!

NATASHA. I will *not* shut up!

SCENE VII

[*The above and* CHUBUKOV.]

CHUBUKOV [*comes in*]. What is it this time?

NATASHA. Father, I want an honest answer: which is the better dog, Rover or Tracker?

LOMOV. Will you kindly tell us just one thing, Chubukov: has Rover got a weak chin or hasn't he? Yes or no?

CHUBUKOV. What if he has? As if that mattered! Seeing he's only the best dog in the county and so on.

LOMOV. Tracker's better, and you know it! Be honest!

CHUBUKOV. Keep your shirt on, dear man. Now look here. Tracker has got some good qualities, what? He's a pedigree dog, has firm paws, steep haunches and so forth. But that dog has two serious faults if you want to know, old bean: he's old and he's pug-nosed.

LOMOV. I'm sorry—it's my heart! Let's just look at the facts. You may recall that Tracker was neck and neck with the Count's Swinger on Maruskino Green when Rover was a good half-mile behind.

CHUBUKOV. He dropped back because the Count's huntsman fetched him a crack with his whip.

LOMOV. Serve him right. Hounds are all chasing the fox and Rover has to start worrying a sheep!

CHUBUKOV. That's not true, sir. I've got a bad temper, old boy, and the fact is—let's please stop arguing, what? He hit him because everyone hates the sight of another man's dog. Oh yes they do. Loathe 'em, they do. And you're no one to talk either, sir! The moment you spot a better dog than the wretched Tracker, you always try to start something and, er, so forth—what? I don't forget, you see.

LOMOV. Nor do I sir.

CHUBUKOV [*mimics him*]. "Nor do, I sir." What is it you don't forget then?

LOMOV. My heart! My leg's gone to sleep. I can't go on.

NATASHA [*mimics him*]. "My heart!" Call yourself a sportsman! You should be lying on the kitchen stove squashing black-beetles, not fox-hunting. His heart!

CHUBUKOV. Some sportsman, I must say! With that heart you should stay at home, not bob around in the saddle, what? I wouldn't mind if you hunted properly, but you only turn out to pick quarrels and annoy the hounds and so on. I have a bad temper, so let's change the subject. You're no sportsman, sir — what?

LOMOV. What about you then? You only turn out so you can get in the Count's good books and intrigue against people. Oh, my heart! You're a slippery customer, sir!

CHUBUKOV. What's that sir? Oh, I am, am I? [*Shouts.*] Hold your tongue!

LOMOV. You artful old dodger!

CHUBUKOV. Why, you young puppy!

LOMOV. Nasty old fogy! Canting hypocrite!

CHUBUKOV. Shut up, or I'll pot you like a ruddy partridge. And I'll use a dirty gun too, you idle gasbag!

LOMOV. And it's common knowledge that — oh, my heart — your wife used to beat you. Oh, my leg! My head! I can see stars! I can't stand up!

CHUBUKOV. And your housekeeper has you eating out of her hand!

LOMOV. Oh, oh! My heart's bursting. My shoulder seems to have come off — where is the thing? I'm dying. [*Falls into an armchair.*] Fetch a doctor. [*Faints.*]

CHUBUKOV. Why, you young booby! Hot air merchant! I think I'm going to faint. [*Drinks water.*] I feel unwell.

NATASHA. Calls himself a sportsman and can't even sit on a horse! [*To her father.*] Father, what's the matter with him? Father, have a look. [*Screeches.*] Mr. Lomov! He's dead!

CHUBUKOV. I feel faint. I can't breathe! Give me air!

NATASHA. He's dead. [*Tugs* LOMOV's *sleeve.*] Mr. Lomov, Mr. Lomov! What have we done? He's dead. [*Falls into an armchair.*] Fetch a doctor, a doctor! [*Has hysterics.*]

CHUBUKOV. Oh! What's happened? What's the matter?

NATASHA [*groans*]. He's dead! Dead!

CHUBUKOV. Who's dead? [*Glancing at* LOMOV.] My God, you're right! Water! A doctor! [*Holds a glass to* LOMOV's *mouth.*] Drink! No, he's not drinking. He must be dead, and so forth. Oh, misery, misery! Why don't I put a bullet in my brain? Why did I never get round to cutting my throat? What am I waiting for? Give me a knife! A pistol! [LOMOV *makes a movement.*] I think he's coming round. Drink some water! That's right.

LOMOV. I can see stars! There's a sort of mist. Where am I?

CHUBUKOV. Hurry up and get married and — oh, to hell with you! She says yes. [*Joins their hands.*] She says yes, and so forth. You have my blessing, and so on. Just leave me in peace, that's all.

LOMOV. Eh? What? [*Raising himself.*] Who?

CHUBUKOV. She says yes. Well, what about it? Kiss each other and — oh, go to hell!

NATASHA [*groans*]. He's alive. Yes, yes, yes! I agree.

CHUBUKOV. Come on, kiss.

LOMOV. Eh? Who? [*Kisses* NATASHA.] Very nice too. I say, what's all this about? Oh, I see — . My heart! I'm seeing stars! Miss Chubukov, I'm so happy. [*Kisses her hand.*] My leg's gone to sleep.

NATASHA. I, er, I'm happy too.

CHUBUKOV. Oh, what a weight off my mind! Phew!

NATASHA. Still, you must admit now that Tracker's not a patch on Rover.

LOMOV. Oh yes he is!

NATASHA. Oh no he isn't!

CHUBUKOV. You can see those two are going to live happily ever after! Champagne!

LOMOV. He's better.

NATASHA. He's worse, worse, worse.

CHUBUKOV [*trying to shout them down*]. Champagne, champagne, champagne!

CURTAIN

(1888–1889)

Henrik Ibsen *1828–1906*

A DOLL'S HOUSE

Translated and edited by James Walter McFarlane

CHARACTERS

TORVALD HELMER, *a lawyer.*
NORA, *his wife.*
DR. RANK.
MRS. KRISTINE LINDE.
NILS KROGSTAD.

ANNE MARIE, *the nursemaid.*
HELENE, *the maid.*
The Helmers' three children.
A Porter.

SCENE: *The action takes place in the Helmer's flat.*

ACT I

A pleasant room, tastefully but not expensively furnished. On the back wall, one door on the right leads to the entrance hall, a second door on the left leads to HELMER'S *study. Between these two doors, a piano. In the middle of the left wall, a door; and downstage from it, a window. Near the window a round table with armchairs and a small sofa. In the right wall, upstage, a door; and on the same wall downstage, a porcelain stove with a couple of armchairs and a rockingchair. Between the stove and the door a small table. Etchings on the walls. A whatnot with china and other small objets d'art; a small bookcase with books in handsome bindings. Carpet on the floor; a fire burns in the stove. A winter's day.*

The front door-bell rings in the hall; a moment later, there is the sound of the front door being opened. NORA *comes into the room, happily humming to herself. She is dressed in her outdoor things, and is carrying lots of parcels which she then puts down on the table, right. She leaves the door into the hall standing open; a* PORTER *can be seen outside holding a Christmas tree and a basket; he hands them to the* MAID *who has opened the door for them.*

NORA. Hide the Christmas tree away carefully, Helene. The children mustn't see it till this evening when it's decorated. [*To the* PORTER, *taking out her purse.*] How much?
PORTER. Fifty öre.
NORA. There's a crown. Keep the change.
[*The* PORTER *thanks her and goes.* NORA *shuts the door. She continues to laugh quietly and happily to herself as she takes off her things. She takes a bag of macaroons out of her pocket and eats one or two; then she walks stealthily across and listens at her husband's door.*]
NORA. Yes, he's in.
[*She begins humming again as she walks over to the table, right.*]

HELMER [*in his study*]. Is that my little sky-lark chirruping out there?

NORA [*busy opening some of the parcels*]. Yes, it is.

HELMER. Is that my little squirrel frisking about?

NORA. Yes!

HELMER. When did my little squirrel get home?

NORA. Just this minute. [*She stuffs the bag of macaroons in her pocket and wipes her mouth.*] Come on out, Torvald, and see what I've bought.

HELMER. I don't want to be disturbed! [*A moment later, he opens the door and looks out, his pen in his hand.*] "Bought," did you say? All that? Has my little spendthrift been out squandering money again?

NORA. But, Torvald, surely this year we can spread ourselves just a little. This is the first Christmas we haven't had to go carefully.

HELMER. Ah, but that doesn't mean we can afford to be extravagant, you know.

NORA. Oh yes, Torvald, surely we can afford to be just a little bit extravagant now, can't we? Just a teeny-weeny bit. You are getting quite a good salary now, and you are going to earn lots and lots of money.

HELMER. Yes, after the New Year. But it's going to be three whole months before the first pay check comes in.

NORA. Pooh! We can always borrow in the meantime.

HELMER. Nora! [*Crosses to her and takes her playfully by the ear.*] Here we go again, you and your frivolous ideas! Suppose I went and borrowed a thousand crowns today, and you went and spent it all over Christmas, then on New Year's Eve a slate fell and hit me on the head and there I was. . . .

NORA [*putting her hand over his mouth*]. Sh! Don't say such horrid things.

HELMER. Yes, but supposing something like that did happen . . . what then?

NORA. If anything as awful as that did happen, I wouldn't care if I owed anybody anything or not.

HELMER. Yes, but what about the people I'd borrowed from?

NORA. Them? Who cares about them! They are only strangers!

HELMER. Nora, Nora! Just like a woman! Seriously though, Nora, you know what I think about these things. No debts! Never borrow! There's always something inhibited, something unpleasant, about a home built on credit and borrowed money. We two have managed to stick it out so far, and that's the way we'll go on for the little time that remains.

NORA [*walks over to the stove*]. Very well, just as you say, Torvald.

HELMER [*following her*]. There, there! My little singing bird mustn't go drooping her wings, eh? Has it got the sulks, that little squirrel of mine? [*Takes out his wallet.*] Nora, what do you think I've got here?

NORA [*quickly turning around*]. Money!

HELMER. There! [*He hands her some notes.*] Good heavens, I know only too well how Christmas runs away with the housekeeping.

NORA [*counts*]. Ten, twenty, thirty, forty. Oh, thank you, thank you, Torvald! This will see me quite a long way.

HELMER. Yes, it'll have to.

NORA. Yes, yes, I'll see that it does. But come over here, I want to show you all the things I've bought. And so cheap! Look, some new clothes for Ivar . . . and a little sword. There's a horse and a trumpet for Bob. And a doll and a doll's cot for Emmy. They are not very grand but she'll have them all broken before long anyway. And I've got some dress material and some handkerchiefs for the maids. Though, really, dear old Anne Marie should have had something better.

HELMER. And what's in this parcel here?

NORA [*shrieking*]. No, Torvald! You mustn't see that till tonight!

HELMER. All right. But tell me now, what did my little spendthrift fancy for herself?

NORA. For me? Puh, I don't really want anything.

HELMER. Of course you do. Anything reasonable that you think you might like, just tell me.

NORA. Well, I don't really know. As a matter of fact, though, Torvald . . .

HELMER. Well?

NORA [*toying with his coat buttons, and without looking at him*]. If you did want to give me something, you could . . . you could always . . .

HELMER. Well, well, out with it!

NORA [*quickly*]. You could always give me money, Torvald. Only what you think you could spare. And then I could buy myself something with it later on.

HELMER. But Nora . . .

NORA. Oh, please, Torvald dear! Please! I beg you. Then I'd wrap the money up in some pretty gilt paper and hang it on the Christmas tree. Wouldn't that be fun?

HELMER. What do we call my pretty little pet when it runs away with all the money?

NORA. I know, I know, we call it a spendthrift. But please let's do what I said, Torvald. Then I'll have a bit of time to think about what I need most. Isn't that awfully sensible, now, eh?

HELMER [*smiling*]. Yes, it is indeed — that is, if only you really could hold on to the money I gave you, and really did buy something for yourself with it. But it just gets mixed up with the housekeeping and frittered away on all sorts of useless things, and then I have to dig into my pocket all over again.

NORA. Oh but, Torvald . . .

HELMER. You can't deny it, Nora dear. [*Puts his arm around her waist.*] My pretty little pet is very sweet, but it runs away with an awful lot of money. It's incredible how expensive it is for a man to keep such a pet.

NORA. For shame! How can you say such a thing? As a matter of fact I save everything I can.

HELMER [*laughs*]. Yes, you are right there. Everything you *can*. But you simply can't.

NORA [*hums and smiles quietly and happily*]. Ah, if you only knew how many expenses the likes of us sky-larks and squirrels have, Torvald!

HELMER. What a funny little one you are! Just like your father. Always on the look-out for money, wherever you can lay your hands on it; but as soon as you've got it, it just seems to slip through your fingers. You never seem to know what you've done with it. Well, one must accept you as you are. It's in the blood. Oh yes, it is, Nora. That sort of thing is hereditary.

NORA. Oh, I only wish I'd inherited a few more of Daddy's qualities.

HELMER. And I wouldn't want my pretty little song-bird to be the least bit different from what she is now. But come to think of it, you look rather . . . rather . . . how shall I put it? . . . rather guilty today. . . .

NORA. Do I?

HELMER. Yes, you do indeed. Look me straight in the eye.

NORA [*looks at him*]. Well?

HELMER [*wagging his finger at her*]. My little sweet-tooth surely didn't forget herself in town today?

NORA. No, whatever makes you think that?

HELMER. She didn't just pop into the confectioner's for a moment?

NORA. No, I assure you, Torvald . . . !

HELMER. Didn't try sampling the preserves?

NORA. No, really I didn't.

HELMER. Didn't go nibbling a macaroon or two?

NORA. No, Torvald, honestly, you must believe me . . . !

HELMER. All right then! It's really just my little joke. . . .

NORA [*crosses to the table*]. I would never dream of doing anything you didn't want me to.

HELMER. Of course not, I know that. And then you've given me your word. . . . [*Crosses to her.*] Well then, Nora dearest, you shall keep your little Christmas secrets. They'll all come out tonight, I dare say, when we light the tree.

NORA. Did you remember to invite Dr. Rank?

HELMER. No. But there's really no need. Of course he'll come and have dinner with us. Anyway, I can ask him when he looks in this morning. I've ordered some good wine. Nora, you can't imagine how I am looking forward to this evening.

NORA. So am I. And won't the children enjoy it, Torvald!

HELMER. Oh, what a glorious feeling it is, knowing you've got a nice, safe job, and a good fat income. Don't you agree? Isn't it wonderful, just thinking about it?

NORA. Oh, it's marvelous!

HELMER. Do you remember last Christmas? Three whole weeks beforehand you shut yourself up every evening till after midnight making flowers for the Christmas tree and all the other splendid things you wanted to surprise us with. Ugh, I never felt so bored in all my life.

NORA. I wasn't the least bit bored.

HELMER [*smiling*]. But it turned out a bit of an anticlimax, Nora.

NORA. Oh, you are not going to tease me about that again! How was I to know the cat would get in and pull everything to bits?

HELMER. No, of course you weren't. Poor little Nora! All you wanted was for us to have a nice time — and it's the thought behind it that counts, after all. All the same, it's a good thing we've seen the back of those lean times.

NORA. Yes, really it's marvelous.

HELMER. Now there's no need for me to sit here all on my own, bored to tears. And you don't have to strain your dear little eyes, and work those dainty little fingers to the bone. . . .

NORA [*clapping her hands*]. No, Torvald, I don't, do I? Not any more. Oh, how marvelous it is to hear that! [*Takes his arm.*] Now I want to tell you how I've been thinking we might arrange things, Torvald. As soon as Christmas is over. . . . [*The door-bell rings in the hall.*] Oh, there's the bell. [*Tidies one or two things in the room.*] It's probably a visitor. What a nuisance!

HELMER. Remember I'm not at home to callers.

MAID [*in the doorway*]. There's a lady to see you, ma'am.

NORA. Show her in, please.

MAID [*to* HELMER]. And the doctor's just arrived, too, sir.

HELMER. Did he go straight into my room?

MAID. Yes, he did sir.

[HELMER *goes into his study. The* MAID *shows in* MRS. LINDE, *who is in traveling clothes, and closes the door after her.*]

MRS. LINDE [*subdued and rather hesitantly*]. How do you do, Nora?

NORA [*uncertainly*]. How do you do?

MRS. LINDE. I'm afraid you don't recognize me.

NORA. No, I don't think I . . . And yet I seem to. . . . [*Bursts out suddenly.*] Why! Kristine! Is it really you?

MRS. LINDE. Yes, it's me.

NORA. Fancy not recognizing you again! But how was I to, when . . . [*Gently.*] How you've changed, Kristine!

MRS. LINDE. I dare say I have. In nine . . . ten years. . . .

NORA. Is it so long since we last saw each other? Yes, it must be. Oh, believe me these last eight years have been such a happy time. And now you've come up to town, too? All that long journey in wintertime. That took courage.

MRS. LINDE. I just arrived this morning on the steamer.

NORA. To enjoy yourself over Christmas, of course. How lovely! Oh, we'll have such fun, you'll see. Do take off your things. You are not cold, are you? [*Helps her.*] There now! Now let's sit down here in comfort beside the stove. No, here, you take the armchair, I'll sit here on the rocking-chair. [*Takes her hands.*] Ah, now you look a bit more like your old self again. It was just that when I first saw you. . . . But you are a little paler, Kristine . . . and perhaps even a bit thinner!

MRS. LINDE. And much, much older, Nora.

NORA. Yes, perhaps a little older . . . very, very little, not really very much. [*Stops suddenly and looks serious.*] Oh, what a thoughtless creature I am, sitting here chattering on like this! Dear, sweet Kristine, can you forgive me?

MRS. LINDE. What do you mean, Nora?

NORA [*gently*]. Poor Kristine, of course you're a widow now.

MRS. LINDE. Yes, my husband died three years ago.

NORA. Oh, I remember now. I read about it in the papers. Oh, Kristine, believe me I often thought at the time of writing to you. But I kept putting it off, something always seemed to crop up.

MRS. LINDE. My dear Nora, I understand so well.

NORA. No, it wasn't very nice of me, Kristine. Oh, you poor thing, what you must have gone through. And didn't he leave you anything?

MRS. LINDE. No.

NORA. And no children?

MRS. LINDE. No.

NORA. Absolutely nothing?

MRS. LINDE. Nothing at all . . . not even a broken heart to grieve over.

NORA [*looks at her incredulously*]. But, Kristine, is that possible?

MRS. LINDE [*smiles sadly and strokes* NORA's *hair*]. Oh, it sometimes happens, Nora.

NORA. So utterly alone. How terribly sad that must be for you. I have three lovely children. You can't see them for the moment, because they're out with their nanny. But now you must tell me all about yourself. . . .

MRS. LINDE. No, no, I want to hear about you.

NORA. No, you start. I won't be selfish today. I must think only about your affairs today. But there's just one thing I really must tell you. Have you heard about the great stroke of luck we've had in the last few days?

MRS. LINDE. No. What is it?

NORA. What do you think? My husband has just been made Bank Manager!

MRS. LINDE. Your husband? How splendid!

NORA. Isn't it tremendous! It's not a very steady way of making a living, you know, being a lawyer, especially if he refuses to take on anything that's the least bit shady — which of course is what Torvald does, and I think he's quite right. You can imagine how pleased we are! He starts at the Bank straight after New Year, and he's getting a big salary and lots of commission. From now on we'll be able to live quite differently . . . we'll do just what we want. Oh, Kristine, I'm so happy and relieved. I must say it's lovely to have plenty of money and not have to worry. Isn't it?

MRS. LINDE. Yes. It must be nice to have enough, at any rate.

NORA. No, not just enough, but pots and pots of money.

MRS. LINDE [*smiles*]. Nora, Nora, haven't you learned any sense yet? At school you used to be an awful spendthrift.

NORA. Yes, Torvald still says I am. [*Wags her finger.*] But little Nora isn't as stupid as everybody thinks. Oh, we haven't really been in a position where I could afford to spend a lot of money. We've both had to work.

MRS. LINDE. You too?

NORA. Yes, odd jobs — sewing, crochet-work, embroidery and things like that. [*Casually.*] And one or two other things, besides. I suppose you know that Torvald left the Ministry when we got married. There weren't any prospects of promotion in his department, and of course he needed to earn more money than he had before. But the first year he wore himself out completely. He had to take on all kinds of extra jobs, you know, and he found himself working all hours of the day and night. But he couldn't go on like that; and he became seriously ill. The doctors said it was essential for him to go South.

MRS. LINDE. Yes, I believe you spent a whole year in Italy, didn't you?

NORA. That's right. It wasn't easy to get away, I can tell you. It was just after I'd had Ivar. But of course we had to go. Oh, it was an absolutely marvelous trip. And it saved Torvald's life. But it cost an awful lot of money, Kristine.

MRS. LINDE. That I can well imagine.

NORA. Twelve hundred dollars. Four thousand eight hundred crowns. That's a lot of money, Kristine.

MRS. LINDE. Yes, but in such circumstances, one is very lucky if one has it.

NORA. Well, we got it from Daddy, you see.

MRS. LINDE. Ah, that was it. It was just about then your father died, I believe, wasn't it?

NORA. Yes, Kristine, just about then. And do you know, I couldn't even go and look after him. Here was I expecting Ivar any day. And I also had poor Torvald, gravely ill, on my hands. Dear, kind Daddy! I never saw him again, Kristine. Oh, that's the saddest thing that has happened to me in all my married life.

MRS. LINDE. I know you were very fond of him. But after that you left for Italy?

NORA. Yes, we had the money then, and the doctors said it was urgent. We left a month later.

MRS. LINDE. And your husband came back completely cured?

NORA. Fit as a fiddle!

MRS. LINDE. But . . . what about the doctor?

NORA. How do you mean?

MRS. LINDE. I thought the maid said something about the gentleman who came at the same time as me being a doctor.

NORA. Yes, that was Dr. Rank. But this isn't a professional visit. He's our best friend and he always looks in at least once a day. No, Torvald has never had a day's illness since. And the children are fit and healthy, and so am I. [*Jumps up and claps her hands.*] Oh God, oh God, isn't it marvelous to be alive, and to be happy, Kristine! . . . Oh but I ought to be ashamed of myself . . . Here I go on talking about nothing but myself. [*She sits on a low stool near* MRS. LINDE *and lays her arms on her lap.*] Oh, please, you mustn't be angry with me! Tell me, is it really true that you didn't love your husband? What made you marry him, then?

MRS. LINDE. My mother was still alive; she was bedridden and helpless. And then I had two young brothers to look after as well. I didn't think I would be justified in refusing him.

NORA. No, I dare say you are right. I suppose he was fairly wealthy then?

MRS. LINDE. He was quite well off, I believe. But the business was shaky. When he died, it went all to pieces, and there just wasn't anything left.

NORA. What then?

MRS. LINDE. Well, I had to fend for myself, opening a little shop, running a little school, anything I could turn my hand to. These last three years have been one long relentless drudge. But now it's finished, Nora. My poor dear mother doesn't need me any more, she's passed away. Nor the boys either; they're at work now, they can look after themselves.

NORA. What a relief you must find it. . . .

MRS. LINDE. No, Nora! Just unutterably empty. Nobody to live for any more. [*Stands up restlessly.*] That's why I couldn't stand it any longer being cut off up there. Surely it must be a bit easier here to find something to occupy your mind. If only I could manage to find a steady job of some kind, in an office perhaps. . . .

NORA. But, Kristine, that's terribly exhausting; and you look so worn out even before you start. The best thing for you would be a little holiday at some quiet little resort.

MRS. LINDE [*crosses to the window*]. I haven't any father I can fall back on for the money, Nora.

NORA [*rises*]. Oh, please, you mustn't be angry with me!

MRS. LINDE [*goes to her*]. My dear Nora, you mustn't be angry with me either. That's the worst thing about people in my position, they become so bitter. One has nobody to work for, yet one has to be on the look-out all the time. Life has to go on, and one starts thinking only of oneself. Believe it or not, when you told me the good news about your step up, I was pleased not so much for your sake as for mine.

NORA. How do you mean? Ah, I see. You think Torvald might be able to do something for you.

MRS. LINDE. Yes, that's exactly what I thought.

NORA. And so he shall, Kristine. Just leave things to me. I'll bring it up so cleverly. . . . I'll think up something to put him in a good mood. Oh, I do so much want to help you.

MRS. LINDE. It is awfully kind of you, Nora, offering to do all this for me, particularly in your case, where you haven't known much trouble or hardship in your own life.

NORA. When I . . . ? I haven't known much . . . ?

MRS. LINDE [*smiling*]. Well, good heavens, a little bit of sewing to do and a few things like that. What a child you are, Nora!

NORA [*tosses her head and walks across the room*]. I wouldn't be too sure of that, if I were you.

MRS. LINDE. Oh?

NORA. You're just like the rest of them. You all think I'm useless when it comes to anything really serious. . . .

MRS. LINDE. Come, come. . . .

NORA. You think I've never had anything much to contend with in this hard world.

MRS. LINDE. Nora dear, you've only just been telling me all the things you've had to put up with.

NORA. Pooh! They were just trivialities! [*Softly.*] I haven't told you about the really big thing.

MRS. LINDE. What big thing? What do you mean?

NORA. I know you rather tend to look down on me, Kristine. But you shouldn't, you know. You are proud of having worked so hard and so long for your mother.

MRS. LINDE. I'm sure I don't look down on anybody. But it's true what you say: I am both proud and happy when I think of how I was able to make Mother's life a little easier towards the end.

NORA. And you are proud when you think of what you have done for your brothers, too.

MRS. LINDE. I think I have every right to be.

NORA. I think so too. But now I'm going to tell you something, Kristine. I too have something to be proud and happy about.

MRS. LINDE. I don't doubt that. But what is it you mean?

NORA. Not so loud. Imagine if Torvald were to hear! He must never on any account . . . nobody must know about it, Kristine, nobody but you.

MRS. LINDE. But what is it?

NORA. Come over here. [*She pulls her down on the sofa beside her.*] Yes, Kristine, I too have something to be proud and happy about. I was the one who saved Torvald's life.

MRS. LINDE. Saved . . . ? How . . . ?

NORA. I told you about our trip to Italy. Torvald would never have recovered but for that. . . .

MRS. LINDE. Well? Your father gave you what money was necessary. . . .

NORA [*smiles*]. That's what Torvald thinks, and everybody else. But . . .

MRS. LINDE. But . . . ?

NORA. Daddy never gave us a penny. I was the one who raised the money.

MRS. LINDE. You? All that money?

NORA. Twelve hundred dollars. Four thousand eight hundred crowns. What do you say to that!

MRS. LINDE. But, Nora, how was it possible? Had you won a sweepstake or something?

NORA [*contemptuously*]. A sweepstake? Pooh! There would have been nothing to it then.

MRS. LINDE. Where did you get it from, then?

NORA [*hums and smiles secretively*]. H'm, tra-la-la!

MRS. LINDE. Because what you couldn't do was borrow it.

NORA. Oh? Why not?

MRS. LINDE. Well, a wife can't borrow without her husband's consent.

NORA [*tossing her head*]. Ah, but when it happens to be a wife with a bit of a sense for business . . . a wife who knows her way about things, then. . . .

MRS. LINDE. But, Nora, I just don't understand. . . .

NORA. You don't have to. I haven't said I did borrow the money. I might have got it some other way. [*Throws herself back on the sofa.*] I might even have got it from some admirer. Anyone as reasonably attractive as I am. . . .

MRS. LINDE. Don't be so silly!

NORA. Now you must be dying of curiosity, Kristine.

MRS. LINDE. Listen to me now, Nora dear—you haven't done anything rash, have you?

NORA [*sitting up again*]. Is it rash to save your husband's life?

MRS. LINDE. I think it was rash to do anything without telling him. . . .

NORA. But the whole point was that he mustn't know anything. Good heavens, can't you see! He wasn't even supposed to know how desperately ill he was. It was me the doctors came and told his life was in danger, that the only way to save him was to go South for a while. Do you think I didn't try talking him into it first? I began dropping hints about how nice it would be if I could be taken on a little trip abroad, like other young wives. I wept, I pleaded. I told him he ought to show some consideration for my condition, and let me have a bit of my own way. And then I suggested he might take out a loan. But at that he nearly lost his temper, Kristine. He said I was being frivolous, that it was his duty as a husband not to give in to all these whims and fancies of mine—as I do believe he called them. All right, I thought, somehow you've got to be saved. And it was then I found a way. . . .

MRS. LINDE. Did your husband never find out from your father that the money hadn't come from him?

NORA. No, never. It was just about the time Daddy died. I'd intended letting him into the secret and asking him not to give me away. But when he was so ill . . . I'm sorry to say it never became necessary.

MRS. LINDE. And you never confided in your husband?

NORA. Good heavens, how could you ever imagine such a thing! When he's so strict about such matters! Besides, Torvald is a man with a good deal of pride—it would be terribly embarrassing and humiliating for him if he thought he owed anything to me. It would spoil everything between us; this happy home of ours would never be the same again.

MRS. LINDE. Are you never going to tell him?

NORA [*reflectively, half-smiling*]. Oh yes, some day perhaps . . . in many years time, when I'm no longer as pretty as I am now. You mustn't laugh! What I mean of course is when Torvald isn't quite so much in love with me as he is now, when he's lost interest in watching me dance, or get dressed up, or recite. Then it might be a good thing to have something in reserve. . . . [*Breaks off.*] What nonsense! That day will never come. Well, what have you got to say to my big secret, Kristine? Still think I'm not much good for anything? One thing, though, it's meant a lot of worry for me, I can tell you. It hasn't always been easy to meet my obligations when the time came. You know in business there is something called quarterly interest, and other things called installments, and these are always terribly difficult things to cope with. So what I've had to do is save a little here and there, you see, wherever I could. I couldn't really save anything out of the housekeeping, because Torvald has to live in decent style. I couldn't let the children go about badly dressed either — I felt any money I got for them had to go on them alone. Such sweet little things!

MRS. LINDE. Poor Nora! So it had to come out of your own allowance?

NORA. Of course. After all, I was the one it concerned most. Whenever Torvald gave me money for new clothes and such-like, I never spent more than half. And always I bought the simplest and cheapest things. It's a blessing most things look well on me, so Torvald never noticed anything. But sometimes I did feel it was a bit hard, Kristine, because it is nice to be well dressed, isn't it?

MRS. LINDE. Yes, I suppose it is.

NORA. I have had some other sources of income, of course. Last winter I was lucky enough to get quite a bit of copying to do. So I shut myself up every night and sat and wrote through to the small hours of the morning. Oh, sometimes I was so tired, so tired. But it was tremendous fun all the same, sitting there working and earning money like that. It was almost like being a man.

MRS. LINDE. And how much have you been able to pay off like this?

NORA. Well, I can't tell exactly. It's not easy to know where you are with transactions of this kind, you understand. All I know is I've paid off just as much as I could scrape together. Many's the time I was at my wit's end. [*Smiles*] Then I used to sit here and pretend that some rich old gentleman had fallen in love with me. . . .

MRS. LINDE. What! What gentleman?

NORA. Oh, rubbish! . . . and that now he had died, and when they opened his will, there in big letters were the words: "My entire fortune is to be paid over, immediately and in cash, to charming Mrs. Nora Helmer."

MRS. LINDE. But my dear Nora — who *is* this man?

NORA. Good heavens, don't you understand? There never was any old gentleman; it was just something I used to sit here pretending, time and time again, when I didn't know where to turn next for money. But it doesn't make very much difference; as far as I'm concerned the old boy can do what he likes, I'm tired of him; I can't be bothered any more with him or his will. Because now all my worries are over. [*Jumping up.*] Oh God, what a glorious thought, Kristine! No more worries! Just think of being without a care in the world . . . being able to romp with the children, and making the house nice and attractive, and having things just as Torvald likes to have them! And then spring will soon be here, and blue skies. And maybe we can go away somewhere. I might even see something of the sea again. Oh yes! When you're happy, life is a wonderful thing!

[*The door-bell is heard in the hall.*]

MRS. LINDE [*gets up*]. There's the bell. Perhaps I'd better go.

NORA. No, do stay, please. I don't suppose it's for me; it's probably somebody for Torvald. . . .

MAID [*in the doorway*]. Excuse me, ma'am, but there's a gentleman here wants to see Mr. Helmer, and I didn't quite know . . . because the Doctor is in there. . . .

NORA. Who is the gentleman?

KROGSTAD [*in the doorway*]. It's me, Mrs. Helmer.

[MRS. LINDE *starts, then turns away to the window.*]

NORA [*tense, takes a step towards him and speaks in a low voice*]. You? What is it? What do you want to talk to my husband about?

KROGSTAD. Bank matters . . . in a manner of speaking. I work at the bank, and I hear your husband is to be the new manager. . . .

NORA. So it's . . .

KROGSTAD. Just routine business matters, Mrs. Helmer. Absolutely nothing else.

[*She nods impassively and shuts the hall door behind him; then she walks across and sees to the stove.*]

MRS. LINDE. Nora . . . who was that man?

NORA. His name is Krogstad.

MRS. LINDE. So it really was him.

NORA. Do you know the man?

MRS. LINDE. I used to know him . . . a good many years ago. He was a solicitor's clerk in our district for a while.

NORA. Yes, so he was.

MRS. LINDE. How he's changed!

NORA. His marriage wasn't a very happy one, I believe.

MRS. LINDE. He's a widower now, isn't he?

NORA. With a lot of children. There, it'll burn better now.

[*She closes the stove door and moves the rocking chair a little to one side.*]

MRS. LINDE. He does a certain amount of business on the side, they say?

NORA. Oh? Yes, it's always possible. I just don't know. . . . But let's not think about business . . . it's all so dull.

[DR. RANK *comes in from* HELMER's *study.*]

DR. RANK [*still in the doorway*]. No, no, Torvald, I won't intrude. I'll just look in on your wife for a moment. [*Shuts the door and notices* MRS. LINDE.] Oh, I beg your pardon. I'm afraid I'm intruding here as well.

NORA. No, not at all! [*Introduces them.*] Dr. Rank . . . Mrs. Linde.

RANK. Ah! A name I've often heard mentioned in this house. I believe I came past you on the stairs as I came in.

MRS. LINDE. I have to take things slowly going upstairs. I find it rather a trial.

NORA. Ah, some little disability somewhere, eh?

MRS. LINDE. Just a bit run down, I think, actually.

RANK. Is that all? Then I suppose you've come to town for a good rest — doing the rounds of the parties?

MRS. LINDE. I have come to look for work.

RANK. Is that supposed to be some kind of sovereign remedy for being run down?

MRS. LINDE. One must live, Doctor.

RANK. Yes, it's generally thought to be necessary.

NORA. Come, come, Dr. Rank. You are quite as keen to live as anybody.

RANK. Quite keen, yes. Miserable as I am, I'm quite ready to let things drag on as long as possible. All my patients are the same. Even those with a moral affliction are no different. As a matter of fact, there's a bad case of that kind in talking with Helmer at this very moment. . . .

MRS. LINDE [*softly*]. Ah!

NORA. Whom do you mean?

RANK. A person called Krogstad — nobody you would know. He's rotten to the core. But even he began talking about having to *live,* as though it were something terribly important.

NORA. Oh? And what did he want to talk to Torvald about?

RANK. I honestly don't know. All I heard was something about the Bank.

NORA. I didn't know that Krog . . . that this Mr. Krogstad had anything to do with the Bank.

RANK. Oh yes, he's got some kind of job down there. [*To* MRS. LINDE.] I wonder if you've got people in your part of the country too who go rushing round sniffing out cases of moral corruption, and then installing the individuals concerned in nice, well-paid jobs where they can keep them under observation. Sound, decent people have to be content to stay out in the cold.

MRS. LINDE. Yet surely it's the sick who most need to be brought in.

RANK [*shrugs his shoulders*]. Well, there we have it. It's that attitude that's turning society into a clinic.

[NORA, *lost in her own thoughts, breaks into smothered laughter and claps her hands.*]

RANK. Why are you laughing at that? Do you know in fact what society is?

NORA. What do I care about your silly old society? I was laughing about something quite different . . . something frightfully funny. Tell me, Dr. Rank, are all the people who work at the Bank dependent on Torvald now?

RANK. Is *that* what you find so frightfully funny?

NORA [*smiles and hums*]. Never you mind! Never you mind! [*Walks about the room.*] Yes, it really is terribly amusing to think that we . . . that Torvald now has power over so many people. [*She takes the bag out of her pocket.*] Dr. Rank, what about a little macaroon?

RANK. Look at this, eh? Macaroons. I thought they were forbidden here.

NORA. Yes, but these are some Kristine gave me.

MRS. LINDE. What? I . . . ?

NORA. Now, now, you needn't be alarmed. You weren't to know that Torvald had forbidden them. He's worried in case they ruin my teeth, you know. Still . . . what's it matter once in a while! Don't you think so, Dr. Rank? Here! [*She pops a macaroon into his mouth.*] And you too, Kristine. And I shall have one as well; just a little one . . . or two at the most [*She walks about the room again.*] Really I am so happy. There's just one little thing I'd love to do now.

RANK. What's that?

NORA. Something I'd love to say in front of Torvald.

RANK. Then why can't you?

NORA. No, I daren't. It's not very nice.

MRS. LINDE. Not very nice?

RANK. Well, in that case it might not be wise. But to us, I don't see why. . . . What is this you would love to say in front of Helmer?

NORA. I would simply love to say: "Damn."

RANK. Are you mad!

MRS. LINDE. Good gracious, Nora . . . !

RANK. Say it! Here he is!

NORA [*hiding the bag of macaroons*]. Sh! Sh!

[HELMER *comes out of his room, his overcoat over his arm and his hat in his hand.*]

NORA [*going over to him*]. Well, Torvald dear, did you get rid of him?

HELMER. Yes, he's just gone.

NORA. Let me introduce you. This is Kristine, who has just arrived in town. . . .

HELMER. Kristine . . . ? You must forgive me, but I don't think I know . . .

NORA. Mrs. Linde, Torvald dear. Kristine Linde.

HELMER. Ah, indeed. A school-friend of my wife's, presumably.

MRS. LINDE. Yes, we were girls together.

NORA. Fancy, Torvald, she's come all this long way just to have a word with you.

HELMER. How is that?

MRS. LINDE. Well, it wasn't really. . . .

NORA. The thing is, Kristine is terribly clever at office work, and she's frightfully keen on finding a job with some efficient man, so that she can learn even more. . . .

HELMER. Very sensible, Mrs. Linde.

NORA. And then when she read you'd been made Bank Manager — there was a bit in the paper about it — she set off at once. Torvald please! You *will* try and do something for Kristine, won't you? For my sake?

HELMER. Well, that's not altogether impossible. You are a widow, I presume?

MRS. LINDE. Yes.

HELMER. And you've had some experience in business?

MRS. LINDE. A fair amount.

HELMER. Well, it's quite probable I can find you a job, I think. . . .

NORA [*clapping her hands*]. There, you see!

HELMER. You have come at a fortunate moment, Mrs. Linde. . . .

MRS. LINDE. Oh, how can I ever thank you . . . ?

HELMER. Not a bit. [*He puts on his overcoat.*] But for the present I must ask you to excuse me. . . .

RANK. Wait. I'm coming with you.

[*He fetches his fur coat from the hall and warms it at the stove.*]

NORA. Don't be long, Torvald dear.

HELMER. Not more than an hour, that's all.

NORA. Are you leaving too, Kristine?

MRS. LINDE [*putting on her things*]. Yes, I must go and see if I can't find myself a room.

HELMER. Perhaps we can all walk down the road together.

NORA [*helping her*]. What a nuisance we are so limited for space here. I'm afraid it just isn't possible. . . .

MRS. LINDE. Oh, you mustn't dream of it! Goodbye, Nora dear, and thanks for everything.

NORA. Goodbye for the present. But . . . you'll be coming back this evening, of course. And you too, Dr. Rank? What's that? If you are up to it? Of course you'll be up to it. Just wrap yourself up well.

> [*They go out, talking, into the hall; children's voices can be heard on the stairs.*]

NORA. Here they are! Here they are! [*She runs to the front door and opens it. ANNE MARIE, the nursemaid, enters with the children.*] Come in! Come in! [*She bends down and kisses them.*] Ah! my sweet little darlings. . . . You see them, Kristine? Aren't they lovely!

RANK. Don't stand here chattering in this draft!

HELMER. Come along, Mrs. Linde. The place now becomes unbearable for anybody except mothers.

> [DR. RANK, HELMER *and* MRS. LINDE *go down the stairs: the* NURSEMAID *comes into the room with the children, then* NORA, *shutting the door behind her.*]

NORA. How fresh and bright you look! My, what red cheeks you've got! Like apples and roses. [*During the following, the children keep chattering away to her.*] Have you had a nice time? That's splendid. And you gave Emmy and Bob a ride on your sledge? Did you now! Both together! Fancy that! There's a clever boy, Ivar. Oh, let me take her a little while, Anne Marie. There's my sweet little baby-doll! [*She takes the youngest of the children from the nursemaid and dances with her.*] All right, Mummy will dance with Bobby too. What? You've been throwing snowballs? Oh, I wish I'd been there. No, don't bother, Anne Marie, I'll help them off with their things. No, please let me — I like doing it. You go on in, you look frozen. You'll find some hot coffee on the stove. [*The nursemaid goes into the room, left.* NORA *takes off the children's coats and hats and throws them down anywhere, while the children all talk at once.*] Really! A great big dog came running after you? But he didn't bite. No, the doggies wouldn't bite my pretty little dollies. You mustn't touch the parcels, Ivar! What are they? Wouldn't you like to know! No, no, that's nasty. Now? Shall we play something? What shall we play? Hide and seek? Yes, let's play hide and seek. Bob can hide first. Me first? All right, let me hide first.

[*She and the other children play, laughing and shrieking, in this room and in the adjacent room on the right. Finally* NORA *hides under the table; the children come rushing in to look for her but cannot find her; they hear her stifled laughter, rush to the table, lift up the tablecloth and find her. Tremendous shouts of delight. She creeps out and pretends to frighten them. More shouts. Meanwhile there has been a knock at the front door, which nobody has heard. The door half opens, and* KROGSTAD *can be seen. He waits a little; the game continues.*]

KROGSTAD. I beg your pardon, Mrs. Helmer. . . .

NORA [*turns with a stifled cry and half jumps up*]. Ah! What do you want?

KROGSTAD. Excuse me. The front door was standing open. Somebody must have forgotten to shut it. . . .

NORA [*standing up*]. My husband isn't at home, Mr. Krogstad.

KROGSTAD. I know.

NORA. Well . . . what are you doing here?

KROGSTAD. I want a word with you.

NORA. With . . . ? [*Quietly, to the children.*] Go to Anne Marie. What? No, the strange man won't do anything to Mummy. When he's gone we'll have another game. [*She leads the children into the room, left, and shuts the door after them; tense and uneasy.*] You want to speak to me?

KROGSTAD. Yes, I do.

NORA. Today? But it isn't the first of the month yet. . . .

KROGSTAD. No, it's Christmas Eve. It depends entirely on you what sort of Christmas you have.

NORA. What do you want? Today I can't possibly . . .

KROGSTAD. Let's not talk about that for the moment. It's something else. You've got a moment to spare?

NORA. Yes, I suppose so, though . . .

KROGSTAD. Good. I was sitting in Olsen's café, and I saw your husband go down the road. . . .

NORA. Did you?

KROGSTAD. . . . with a lady.

NORA. Well?

KROGSTAD. May I be so bold as to ask whether that lady was Mrs. Linde?

NORA. Yes.

KROGSTAD. Just arrived in town?

NORA. Yes, today.

KROGSTAD. And she's a good friend of yours?

NORA. Yes, she is. But I can't see . . .

KROGSTAD. I also knew her once.

NORA. I know.

KROGSTAD. Oh? So you know all about it. I thought as much. Well, I want to ask you straight: is Mrs. Linde getting a job in the Bank?

NORA. How dare you cross-examine me like this, Mr. Krogstad? You, one of my husband's subordinates? But since you've asked me, I'll tell you. Yes, Mrs. Linde *has* got a job. And I'm the one who got it for her, Mr. Krogstad. Now you know.

KROGSTAD. So my guess was right.

NORA [*walking up and down*]. Oh, I think I can say that some of us have a little influence now and again. Just because one happens to be a woman, that doesn't mean. . . . People in subordinate positions, ought to take care they don't offend anybody . . . who . . . hm . . .

KROGSTAD. . . . has influence?

NORA. Exactly.

KROGSTAD [*changing his tone*]. Mrs. Helmer, will you have the goodness to use your influence on my behalf?

NORA. What? What do you mean?

KROGSTAD. Will you be so good as to see that I keep my modest little job at the Bank?

NORA. What do you mean? Who wants to take it away from you?

KROGSTAD. Oh, you needn't try and pretend to me you don't know. I can quite see that this friend of yours isn't particularly anxious to bump up against me. And I can also see now whom I can thank for being given the sack.

NORA. But I assure you. . . .

KROGSTAD. All right, all right. But to come to the point: there's still time. And I advise you to use your influence to stop it.

NORA. But, Mr. Krogstad, I *have* no influence.

KROGSTAD. Haven't you? I thought just now you said yourself . . .

NORA. I didn't mean it that way, of course. Me? What makes you think I've got any influence of that kind over my husband?

KROGSTAD. I know your husband from our student days. I don't suppose he is any more steadfast than other married men.

NORA. You speak disrespectfully of my husband like that and I'll show you the door.

KROGSTAD. So the lady's got courage.

NORA. I'm not frightened of you any more. After New Year I'll soon be finished with the whole business.

KROGSTAD [*controlling himself*]. Listen to me, Mrs. Helmer. If necessary I shall fight for my little job in the Bank as if I were fighting for my life.

NORA. So it seems.

KROGSTAD. It's not just for the money, that's the last thing I care about. There's something else . . . well, I might as well out with it. You see it's like this. You know as well as anybody that some years ago I got myself mixed up in a bit of trouble.

NORA. I believe I've heard something of the sort.

KROGSTAD. It never got as far as the courts; but immediately it was as if all paths were barred to me. So I started going in for the sort of business you know about. I had to do something, and I think I can say I haven't been one of the worst. But now I have to get out of it. My sons are growing up; for their sake I must try and win back what respectability I can. That job in the Bank was like the first step on the ladder for me. And now your husband wants to kick me off the ladder again, back into the mud.

NORA. But in God's name, Mr. Krogstad, it's quite beyond my power to help you.

KROGSTAD. That's because you haven't the will to help me. But I have ways of making you.

NORA. You wouldn't go and tell my husband I owe you money?

KROGSTAD. Suppose I did tell him?

NORA. It would be a rotten shame. [*Half choking with tears.*] That secret is all my pride and joy — why should he have to hear about it in this nasty, horrid way . . . hear about it from *you*. You would make things horribly unpleasant for me. . . .

KROGSTAD. Merely unpleasant?

NORA [*vehemently*]. Go on, do it then! It'll be all the worse for you. Because then my husband will see for himself what a bad man you are, and then you certainly won't be able to keep your job.

KROGSTAD. I asked whether it was only a bit of domestic unpleasantness you were afraid of?

NORA. If my husband gets to know about it, he'll pay off what's owing at once. And then we'd have nothing more to do with you.

KROGSTAD [*taking a pace towards her*]. Listen, Mrs. Helmer, either you haven't a very good memory, or else you don't understand much about business. I'd better make the position a little bit clearer for you.

NORA. How do you mean?

KROGSTAD. When your husband was ill, you came to me for the loan of twelve hundred dollars.

NORA. I didn't know of anybody else.

KROGSTAD. I promised to find you the money. . . .

NORA. And you did find it.

KROGSTAD. I promised to find you the money on certain conditions. At the time you were so concerned about your husband's illness, and so anxious to get the money for going away with, that I don't think you paid very much attention to all the incidentals. So there is perhaps some point in reminding you of them.

Well, I promised to find you the money against an IOU which I drew up for you.

NORA. Yes, and which I signed.

KROGSTAD. Very good. But below that I added a few lines, by which your father was to stand security. This your father was to sign.

NORA. Was to . . . ? He did sign it.

KROGSTAD. I had left the date blank. The idea was that your father was to add the date himself when he signed it. Remember?

NORA. Yes, I think. . . .

KROGSTAD. I then gave you the IOU to post to your father. Wasn't that so?

NORA. Yes.

KROGSTAD. Which of course you did at once. Because only about five or six days later you brought it back to me with your father's signature. I then paid out the money.

NORA. Well? Haven't I paid the installments regularly?

KROGSTAD. Yes, fairly. But . . . coming back to what we were talking about . . . that was a pretty bad period you were going through then, Mrs. Helmer.

NORA. Yes, it was.

KROGSTAD. Your father was seriously ill, I believe.

NORA. He was very near the end.

KROGSTAD. And died shortly afterwards?

NORA. Yes.

KROGSTAD. Tell me, Mrs. Helmer, do you happen to remember which day your father died? The exact date, I mean.

NORA. Daddy died on 29 September.

KROGSTAD. Quite correct. I made some inquiries. Which brings up a rather curious point [*takes out a paper*] which I simply cannot explain.

NORA. Curious . . . ? I don't know . . .

KROGSTAD. The curious thing is, Mrs. Helmer, that your father signed this document three days after his death.

NORA. What? I don't understand. . . .

KROGSTAD. Your father died on 29 September. But look here. Your father has dated his signature 2 October. Isn't that rather curious, Mrs. Helmer? [NORA *remains silent.*] It's also remarkable that the words "2 October" and the year are not in your father's handwriting, but in a handwriting I rather think I recognize. Well, perhaps that could be explained. Your father might have forgotten to date his signature, and then somebody else might have made a guess at the date later, before the fact of your father's death was known. There is nothing wrong in that. What really matters is the signature. And *that* is of course genuine, Mrs. Helmer? It really was your father who wrote his name here?

NORA [*after a moment's silence, throws her head back and looks at him defiantly*]. No, it wasn't. It was me who signed father's name.

KROGSTAD. Listen to me. I suppose you realize that that is a very dangerous confession?

NORA. Why? You'll soon have all your money back.

KROGSTAD. Let me ask you a question: why didn't you send that document to your father?

NORA. It was impossible. Daddy was ill. If I'd asked him for his signature, I'd have had to tell him what the money was for. Don't you see, when he was as ill as that I couldn't go and tell him that my husband's life was in danger. It was simply impossible.

KROGSTAD. It would have been better for you if you had abandoned the whole trip.

NORA. No, that was impossible. This was the thing that was to save my husband's life. I couldn't give it up.

KROGSTAD. But did it never strike you that this was fraudulent . . . ?

NORA. That wouldn't have meant anything to me. Why should I worry about you? I couldn't stand you, not when you insisted on going through with all those cold-blooded formalities, knowing all the time what a critical state my husband was in.

KROGSTAD. Mrs. Helmer, it's quite clear you still haven't the faintest idea what it is you've committed. But let me tell you, my own offense was no more and no worse than that, and it ruined my entire reputation.

NORA. You? Are you trying to tell me that you once risked everything to save your wife's life?

KROGSTAD. The law takes no account of motives.

NORA. Then they must be very bad laws.

KROGSTAD. Bad or not, if I produce this document in court, you'll be condemned according to them.

NORA. I don't believe it. Isn't a daughter entitled to try and save her father from worry and anxiety on his deathbed? Isn't a wife entitled to save her husband's life? I might not know very much about the law, but I feel sure of one thing: it must say somewhere that things like this are allowed. You mean to say you don't know that—you, when it's your job? You must have been a rotten lawyer, Mr. Krogstad.

KROGSTAD. That may be. But when it comes to business transactions—like the sort between us two—perhaps you'll admit I know something about *them?* Good. Now you must please yourself. But I tell you this: if I'm pitched out a second time, you are going to keep me company.

[*He bows and goes out through the hall.*]

NORA [*stands thoughtfully for a moment, then tosses her head*]. Rubbish! He's just trying to scare me. I'm not such a fool as all that. [*Begins gathering up the children's clothes; after a moment she stops.*] Yet . . . ? No, it's impossible! I did it for love, didn't I?

THE CHILDREN [*in the doorway, left*]. Mummy, the gentleman's just gone out of the gate.

NORA. Yes, I know. But you musn't say anything to anybody about that gentleman. You hear? Not even to Daddy!

THE CHILDREN. All right, Mummy. Are you going to play again?

NORA. No, not just now.

THE CHILDREN. But Mummy, you promised!

NORA. Yes, but I can't just now. Off you go now, I have a lot to do. Off you go, my darlings. [*She herds them carefully into the other room and shuts the door behind them. She sits down on the sofa, picks up her embroidery and works a few stitches, but soon stops.*] No! [*She flings her work down, stands up, goes to the hall door and calls out.*] Helene! Fetch the tree in for me, please. [*She walks across to the table, left, and opens the drawer; again pauses.*] No, really, it's quite impossible!

MAID [*with the Christmas tree*]. Where shall I put it, ma'am?

NORA. On the floor there, in the middle.

MAID. Anything else you want me to bring?

NORA. No, thank you. I've got what I want.

[*The maid has put the tree down and goes out.*]

NORA [*busy decorating the tree*]. Candles here . . . and flowers here.— Revolting man! It's all nonsense! There's nothing to worry about. We'll have a lovely Christmas tree. And I'll do anything you want me to, Torvald; I'll sing for you, dance for you. . . .

[HELMER, *with a bundle of documents under his arm, comes in by the hall door.*]

NORA. Ah, back again already?

HELMER. Yes. Anybody been?

NORA. Here? No.

HELMER. That's funny. I just saw Krogstad leave the house.

NORA. Oh? O yes, that's right. Krogstad was here a minute.

HELMER. Nora, I can tell by your face he's been asking you to put a good word in for him.

NORA. Yes.

HELMER. And you were to pretend it was your own idea? You were to keep quiet about his having been here. He asked you to do that as well, didn't he?

NORA. Yes, Torvald. But . . .

HELMER. Nora, Nora, what possessed you to do a thing like that? Talking to a person like him, making him promises? And then on top of everything, to tell me a lie!

NORA. A lie . . . ?

HELMER. Didn't you say that nobody had been here? [*Wagging his finger at her.*] Never again must my little song-bird do a thing like that! Little song-birds must keep their pretty little beaks out of mischief; no chirruping out of tune! [*Puts his arm around her waist.*] Isn't that the way we want things to be? Yes, of course it is. [*Lets her go.*] So let's say no more about it. [*Sits down by the stove.*] Ah, nice and cozy here!

[*He glances through his papers.*]

NORA [*busy with the Christmas tree, after a short pause*]. Torvald!

HELMER. Yes.

NORA. I'm so looking forward to the fancy dress ball at the Stenborgs' on Boxing Day.[1]

HELMER. And I'm terribly curious to see what sort of surprise you've got for me.

NORA. Oh, it's too silly.

HELMER. Oh?

NORA. I just can't think of anything suitable. Everything seems so absurd, so pointless.

HELMER. Has my little Nora come to *that* conclusion?

NORA [*behind his chair, her arms on the chairback*]. Are you very busy, Torvald?

[1]The first weekday after Christmas.

HELMER. Oh . . .

NORA. What are all those papers?

HELMER. Bank matters.

NORA. Already?

HELMER. I have persuaded the retiring manager to give me authority to make any changes in organization or personnel I think necessary. I have to work on it over the Christmas week. I want everything straight by the New Year.

NORA. So that was why that poor Krogstad. . . .

HELMER. Hm!

NORA [*still leaning against the back of the chair, running her fingers through his hair*]. If you hadn't been so busy, Torvald, I'd have asked you to do me an awfully big favor.

HELMER. Let me hear it. What's it to be?

NORA. Nobody's got such good taste as you. And the thing is I do so want to look my best at the fancy dress ball. Torvald, couldn't you give me some advice and tell me what you think I ought to go as, and how I should arrange my costume?

HELMER. Aha! So my impulsive little woman is asking for somebody to come to her rescue, eh?

NORA. Please, Torvald, I never get anywhere without your help.

HELMER. Very well, I'll think about it. We'll find something.

NORA. That's sweet of you. [*She goes across to the tree again; pause.*] How pretty these red flowers look. — Tell me, was it really something terribly wrong this man Krogstad did?

HELMER. Forgery. Have you any idea what that means?

NORA. Perhaps circumstances left him no choice?

HELMER. Maybe. Or perhaps, like so many others, he just didn't think. I am not so heartless that I would necessarily want to condemn a man for a single mistake like that.

NORA. Oh no, Torvald, of course not!

HELMER. Many a man might be able to redeem himself, if he honestly confessed his guilt and took his punishment.

NORA. Punishment?

HELMER. But that wasn't the way Krogstad chose. He dodged what was due to him by a cunning trick. And that's what has been the cause of his corruption.

NORA. Do you think it would . . . ?

HELMER. Just think how a man with a thing like that on his conscience will always be having to lie and cheat and dissemble; he can never drop the mask, not even with his own wife and children. And the children — *that's* the most terrible part of it, Nora.

NORA. Why?

HELMER. A fog of lies like that in a household, and it spreads disease and infection to every part of it. Every breath the children take in that kind of house is reeking with evil germs.

NORA [*closer to him*]. Are you sure of that?

HELMER. My dear Nora, as a lawyer I know what I'm talking about. Practically all juvenile delinquents come from homes where the mother is dishonest.

NORA. Why mothers particularly?

HELMER. It's generally traceable to the mothers, but of course fathers can have the same influence. Every lawyer knows that only too well. And yet there's Krogstad been poisoning his own children for years with lies and deceit. That's the reason I call him morally depraved. [*Holds out his hands to her.*] That's why my sweet little Nora must promise me not to try putting in any more good words for him. Shake hands on it. Well? What's this? Give me your hand. There now! That's settled. I assure you I would have found it impossible to work with him. I quite literally feel physically sick in the presence of such people.

NORA [*draws her hand away and walks over to the other side of the Christmas tree*]. How hot it is in here! And I still have such a lot to do.

HELMER [*stands up and collects his papers together*]. Yes, I'd better think of getting some of this read before dinner. I must also think about your costume. And I might even be able to lay my hands on something to wrap in gold paper and hang on the Christmas tree. [*He lays his hand on her head.*] My precious little singing bird.

[*He goes into his study and shuts the door behind him.*]

NORA [*quietly, after a pause*]. Nonsense! It can't be. It's impossible. It *must* be impossible.

MAID [*in the doorway, left*]. The children keep asking so nicely if they can come in and see Mummy.

NORA. No, no, don't let them in! You stay with them, Anne Marie.

MAID. Very well, ma'am.

[*She shuts the door.*]

NORA [*pale with terror*]. Corrupt my children . . . ! Poison my home? [*Short pause; she throws back her head.*] It's not true! It could never, never be true!

ACT II

The same room. In the corner beside the piano stands the Christmas tree, stripped, bedraggled and with its candles burnt out. Nora's outdoor things lie on the sofa. NORA, alone there, walks about restlessly; at last she stops by the sofa and picks up her coat.

NORA [*putting her coat down again*]. Somebody's coming! [*Crosses to the door, listens.*] No, it's nobody. Nobody will come today, of course, Christmas Day — nor tomorrow, either. But perhaps. . . . [*She opens the door and looks out.*] No, nothing in the letter box; quite empty. [*Comes forward.*] Oh, nonsense! He didn't mean it seriously. Things like that *can't* happen. It's impossible! Why, I have three small children.

[*The* NURSEMAID *comes from the room, left, carrying a big cardboard box.*]

NURSEMAID. I finally found it, the box with the fancy dress costumes.

NORA. Thank you. Put it on the table, please.

NURSEMAID [*does this*]. But I'm afraid they are in an awful mess.

NORA. Oh, if only I could rip them up into a thousand pieces!

NURSEMAID. Good heavens, they can be mended all right, with a bit of patience.

NORA. Yes, I'll go over and get Mrs. Linde to help me.

NURSEMAID. Out again? In this terrible weather? You'll catch your death of cold, Ma'am.

NORA. Oh, worse things might happen.—How are the children?

NURSEMAID. Playing with their Christmas presents, poor little things, but . . .

NORA. Do they keep asking for me?

NURSEMAID. They are so used to being with their Mummy.

NORA. Yes, Anne Marie, from now on I can't be with them as often as I was before.

NURSEMAID. Ah well, children get used to anything in time.

NORA. Do you think so? Do you think they would forget their Mummy if she went away for good?

NURSEMAID. Good gracious—for good?

NORA. Tell me, Anne Marie—I've often wondered—how on earth could you bear to hand your child over to strangers?

NURSEMAID. Well, there was nothing else for it when I had to come and nurse my little Nora.

NORA. Yes but . . . how could you *bring* yourself to do it?

NURSEMAID. When I had the chance of such a good place? When a poor girl's been in trouble she must make the best of things. Because *he* didn't help, the rotter.

NORA. But your daughter will have forgotten you.

NURSEMAID. Oh no, she hasn't. She wrote to me when she got confirmed, and again when she got married.

NORA [*putting her arms around her neck*]. Dear old Anne Marie, you were a good mother to me when I was little.

NURSEMAID. My poor little Nora never had any other mother but me.

NORA. And if my little ones only had you, I know you would. . . . Oh, what am I talking about! [*She opens the box.*] Go in to them. I must . . . Tomorrow I'll let you see how pretty I am going to look. [*She goes into the room, left.*]

NORA [*begins unpacking the box, but soon throws it down*]. Oh, if only I dare go out. If only I could be sure nobody would come. And that nothing would happen in the meantime here at home. Rubbish—nobody's going to come. I mustn't think about it. Brush this muff. Pretty gloves, pretty gloves! I'll put it right out of my mind. One, two, three, four, five, six. . . . [*Screams.*] Ah, they are coming. . . . [*She starts towards the door, but stops irresolute.* MRS. LINDE *comes from the hall, where she has taken off her things.*] Oh, it's you, Kristine. There's nobody else out there, is there? I'm so glad you've come.

MRS. LINDE. I heard you'd been over looking for me.

NORA. Yes, I was just passing. There's something you must help me with. Come and sit beside me on the sofa here. You see, the Stenborgs are having a fancy dress party upstairs tomorrow evening, and now Torvald wants me to go as a Neapolitan fisher lass and dance the tarantella. I learned it in Capri, you know.

MRS. LINDE. Well, well! So you are going to do a party piece?

NORA. Torvald says I should. Look, here's the costume, Torvald had it made for me down there. But it's got all torn and I simply don't know. . . .

MRS. LINDE. We'll soon have that put right. It's only the trimming come away here and there. Got a needle and thread? Ah, here's what we are after.

NORA. It's awfully kind of you.

MRS. LINDE. So you are going to be all dressed up tomorrow, Nora? Tell you what — I'll pop over for a minute to see you in all your finery. But I'm quite forgetting to thank you for the pleasant time we had last night.

NORA [*gets up and walks across the room*]. Somehow I didn't think yesterday was as nice as things generally are. — You should have come to town a little earlier, Kristine. — Yes, Torvald certainly knows how to make things pleasant about the place.

MRS. LINDE. You too, I should say. You are not your father's daughter for nothing. But tell me, is Dr. Rank always as depressed as he was last night?

NORA. No, last night it was rather obvious. He's got something seriously wrong with him, you know. Tuberculosis of the spine, poor fellow. His father was a horrible man, who used to have mistresses and things like that. That's why the son was always ailing, right from being a child.

MRS. LINDE [*lowering her sewing*]. But my dear Nora, how do you come to know about things like that?

NORA [*walking about the room*]. Huh! When you've got three children, you get these visits from . . . women who have had a certain amount of medical training. And you hear all sorts of things from them.

MRS. LINDE [*begins sewing again; short silence*]. Does Dr. Rank call in every day?

NORA. Every single day. He was Torvald's best friend as a boy, and he's a good friend of *mine*, too. Dr. Rank is almost like one of the family.

MRS. LINDE. But tell me — is he really genuine? What I mean is: doesn't he sometimes rather turn on the charm?

NORA. No, on the contrary. What makes you think that?

MRS. LINDE. When you introduced me yesterday, he claimed he'd often heard my name in this house. Afterwards I noticed your husband hadn't the faintest idea who I was. Then how is it that Dr. Rank should. . . .

NORA. Oh yes, it was quite right what he said, Kristine. You see Torvald is so terribly in love with me that he says he wants me all to himself. When we were first married, it even used to make him sort of jealous if I only as much as mentioned any of my old friends from back home. So of course I stopped doing it. But I often talk to Dr. Rank about such things. He likes hearing about them.

MRS. LINDE. Listen, Nora! In lots of ways you are still a child. Now, I'm a good deal older than you, and a bit more experienced. I'll tell you something: I think you ought to give up all this business with Dr. Rank.

NORA. Give up what business?

MRS. LINDE. The whole thing, I should say. Weren't you saying yesterday something about a rich admirer who was to provide you with money. . . .

NORA. One who's never existed, I regret to say. But what of it?

MRS. LINDE. Has Dr. Rank money?

NORA. Yes, he has.

MRS. LINDE. And no dependents?

NORA. No, nobody. But . . . ?

MRS. LINDE. And he comes to the house every day?

NORA. Yes, I told you.

MRS. LINDE. But how can a man of his position want to pester you like this?

NORA. I simply don't understand.

MRS. LINDE. Don't pretend, Nora. Do you think I don't see now who you borrowed the twelve hundred from?

NORA. Are you out of your mind? Do you really think that? A friend of ours who comes here every day? The whole situation would have been absolutely intolerable.

MRS. LINDE. It *really* isn't him?

NORA. No, I give you my word. It would never have occurred to me for one moment. . . . Anyway, he didn't have the money to lend then. He didn't inherit it till later.

MRS. LINDE. Just as well for you, I'd say, my dear Nora.

NORA. No, it would never have occurred to me to ask Dr. Rank. . . . All the same I'm pretty certain if I were to ask him . . .

MRS. LINDE. But of course you won't.

NORA. No, of course not. I can't ever imagine it being necessary. But I'm quite certain if ever I were to mention it to Dr. Rank . . .

MRS. LINDE. Behind your husband's back?

NORA. I have to get myself out of that other business. That's also behind his back. I *must* get myself out of that.

MRS. LINDE. Yes, that's what I said yesterday. But . . .

NORA [*walking up and down*]. A man's better at coping with these things than a woman. . . .

MRS. LINDE. Your own husband, yes.

NORA. Nonsense! [*Stops.*] When you've paid everything you owe, you do get your IOU back again, don't you?

MRS. LINDE. Of course.

NORA. And you can tear it up into a thousand pieces and burn it — the nasty, filthy thing!

MRS. LINDE [*looking fixedly at her, puts down her sewing and slowly rises*]. Nora, you are hiding something from me.

NORA. Is it so obvious?

MRS. LINDE. Something has happened to you since yesterday morning. Nora, what is it?

NORA [*going towards her*]. Kristine! [*Listens.*] Hush! There's Torvald back. Look, you go and sit in there beside the children for the time being. Torvald can't stand the sight of mending lying about. Get Anne Marie to help you.

MRS. LINDE [*gathering a lot of things together*]. All right, but I'm not leaving until we have thrashed this thing out.

> [*She goes into the room, left; at the same time* HELMER *comes in from the hall.*]

NORA [*goes to meet him*]. I've been longing for you to be back, Torvald, dear.

HELMER. Was that the dressmaker . . . ?

NORA. No, it was Kristine; she's helping me with my costume. I think it's going to look very nice. . . .

HELMER. Wasn't that a good idea of mine, now?

NORA. Wonderful! But wasn't it also nice of me to let you have your way?

HELMER [*taking her under the chin*]. Nice of you — because you let your husband have his way? All right, you little rogue, I know you didn't mean it that way. But I don't want to disturb you. You'll be wanting to try the costume on, I suppose.

NORA. And I dare say you've got work to do?

HELMER. Yes. [*Shows her a bundle of papers.*] Look at this. I've been down at the Bank. . . .

[*He turns to go into his study.*]

NORA. Torvald!

HELMER [*stopping*]. Yes.

NORA. If a little squirrel were to ask ever so nicely . . . ?

HELMER. Well?

NORA. Would you do something for it?

HELMER. Naturally I would first have to know what it is.

NORA. Please, if only you would let it have its way, and do what it wants, it'd scamper about and do all sorts of marvelous tricks.

HELMER. What is it?

NORA. And the pretty little sky-lark would sing all day long. . . .

HELMER. Huh! It does that anyway.

NORA. I'd pretend I was an elfin child and dance a moonlight dance for you, Torvald.

HELMER. Nora—I hope it's not that business you started on this morning?

NORA [*coming closer*]. Yes, it is, Torvald. I implore you!

HELMER. You have the nerve to bring that up again?

NORA. Yes, yes, you *must* listen to me. You must let Krogstad keep his job at the Bank.

HELMER. My dear Nora, I'm giving his job to Mrs. Linde.

NORA. Yes, it's awfully sweet of you. But couldn't you get rid of somebody else in the office instead of Krogstad?

HELMER. This really is the most incredible obstinacy! Just because you go and make some thoughtless promise to put in a good word for him, you expect me . . .

NORA. It's not that, Torvald. It's for your own sake. That man writes in all the nastiest papers, you told me that yourself. He can do you no end of harm. He terrifies me to death. . . .

HELMER. Aha, now I see. It's your memories of what happened before that are frightening you.

NORA. What do you mean?

HELMER. It's your father you are thinking of.

NORA. Yes . . . yes, that's right. You remember all the nasty insinuations those wicked people put in the papers about Daddy? I honestly think they would have had him dismissed if the Ministry hadn't sent you down to investigate, and you hadn't been so kind and helpful.

HELMER. My dear little Nora, there is a considerable difference between your father and me. Your father's professional conduct was not entirely above suspicion. Mine is. And I hope it's going to stay that way as long as I hold this position.

NORA. But nobody knows what some of these evil people are capable of. Things could be so nice and pleasant for us here, in the peace and quiet of our home—you and me and the children, Torvald! That's why I implore you. . . .

HELMER. The more you plead for him, the more impossible you make it for me to keep him on. It's already known down at the Bank that I am going to give Krogstad his notice. If it ever got around that the new manager had been talked over by his wife. . . .

NORA. What of it?

HELMER. Oh, nothing! As long as the little woman gets her own stubborn way . . . ! Do you want me to make myself a laughing stock in the office? . . . Give the people the idea that I am susceptible to any kind of outside pressure? You can imagine how soon I'd feel the consequences of that! Anyway, there's one other consideration that makes it impossible to have Krogstad in the Bank as long as I am manager.

NORA. What's that?

HELMER. At a pinch I might have overlooked his past lapses. . . .

NORA. Of course you could, Torvald!

HELMER. And I'm told he's not bad at his job, either. But we knew each other rather well when we were younger. It was one of those rather rash friendships that prove embarrassing in later life. There's no reason why you shouldn't know we were once on terms of some familiarity. And he, in his tactless way, makes no attempt to hide the fact, particularly when other people are present. On the contrary, he thinks he has every right to treat me as an equal, with his "Torvald this" and "Torvald that" every time he opens his mouth. I find it extremely irritating, I can tell you. He would make my position at the Bank absolutely intolerable.

NORA. Torvald, surely you aren't serious?

HELMER. Oh? Why not?

NORA. Well, it's all so petty.

HELMER. What's that you say? Petty? Do you think I'm petty?

NORA. No, not at all, Torvald dear! And that's why . . .

HELMER. Doesn't make any difference! . . . You call my motives petty; so I must be petty too. Petty! Indeed! Well, we'll put a stop to that, once and for all. [*He opens the hall door and calls.*] Helene!

NORA. What are you going to do?

HELMER [*searching among his papers*]. Settle things. [THE MAID *comes in.*] See this letter? I want you to take it down at once. Get hold of a messenger and get him to deliver it. Quickly. The address is on the outside. There's the money.

MAID. Very good, sir.

[*She goes with the letter.*]

HELMER [*putting his papers together*]. There now, my stubborn little miss.

NORA [*breathless*]. Torvald . . . what was that letter?

HELMER. Krogstad's notice.

NORA. Get it back, Torvald! There's still time! Oh, Torvald, get it back! Please for my sake, for your sake, for the sake of the children! Listen, Torvald, please! You don't realize what it can do to us.

HELMER. Too late.

NORA. Yes, too late.

HELMER. My dear Nora, I forgive you this anxiety of yours, although it is actually a bit of an insult. Oh, but it is, I tell you! It's hardly flattering to suppose that anything this miserable pen-pusher wrote could frighten *me!* But I forgive you all the same, because it is rather a sweet way of showing how much you love me. [*He takes her in his arms.*] This is how things must be, my own darling Nora. When it comes to the point, I've enough strength and enough courage, believe me, for whatever happens. You'll find I'm man enough to take everything on myself.

NORA [*terrified*]. What do you mean?

HELMER. Everything, I said. . . .

NORA [*in command of herself*]. That is something you shall never, never do.

HELMER. All right, then we'll share it, Nora—as man and wife. That's what we'll do. [*Caressing her.*] Does that make you happy now? There, there, don't look at me with those eyes, like a little frightened dove. The whole thing is sheer imagination.—Why don't you run through the tarantella and try out the tambourine? I'll go into my study and shut both the doors, then I won't hear anything. You can make all the noise you want. [*Turns in the doorway.*] And when Rank comes, tell him where he can find me.

> [*He nods to her, goes with his papers into his room, and shuts the door behind him.*]

NORA [*wild-eyed with terror, stands as though transfixed*]. He's quite capable of doing it! He would do it! No matter what, he'd do it.—No, never in this world! Anything but that! Help? Some way out . . . ? [*The door-bell rings in the hall.*] Dr. Rank . . . ! Anything but that, *anything!* [*She brushes her hands over her face, pulls herself together and opens the door into the hall.* DR. RANK *is standing outside hanging up his fur coat. During what follows it begins to grow dark.*] Hello, Dr. Rank. I recognized your ring. Do you mind not going in to Torvald just yet, I think he's busy.

RANK. And you?

[DR. RANK *comes into the room and she closes the door behind him.*]

NORA. Oh, you know very well I've always got time for you.

RANK. Thank you. A privilege I shall take advantage of as long as I am able.

NORA. What do you mean—as long as you are able?

RANK. Does that frighten you?

NORA. Well, it's just that it sounds so strange. Is anything likely to happen?

RANK. Only what I have long expected. But I didn't think it would come quite so soon.

NORA [*catching at his arm*]. What have you found out? Dr. Rank, you must tell me!

RANK. I'm slowly sinking. There's nothing to be done about it.

NORA [*with a sigh of relief*]. Oh, it's *you* you're . . . ?

RANK. Who else? No point in deceiving oneself. I am the most wretched of all my patients, Mrs. Helmer. These last few days I've made a careful analysis of my internal economy. Bankrupt! Within a month I shall probably be lying rotting up there in the churchyard.

NORA. Come now, what a ghastly thing to say!

RANK. The whole damned thing is ghastly. But the worst thing is all the ghastliness that has to be gone through first. I only have one more test to make; and when that's done I'll know pretty well when the final disintegration will start. There's something I want to ask you. Helmer is a sensitive soul; he loathes anything that's ugly. I don't want him visiting me. . . .

NORA. But Dr. Rank. . . .

RANK. On no account must he. I won't have it. I'll lock the door on him.—As soon as I'm absolutely certain of the worst, I'll send you my visiting card with a black cross on it. You'll know then the final horrible disintegration has begun.

NORA. Really, you are being quite absurd today. And here I was hoping you would be in a thoroughly good mood.

RANK. With death staring me in the face? Why should I suffer for another man's sins? What justice is there in that? Somewhere, somehow, every single family must be suffering some such cruel retribution. . . .

NORA [*stopping up her ears*]. Rubbish! Do cheer up!

RANK. Yes, really the whole thing's nothing but a huge joke. My poor innocent spine must do penance for my father's gay subaltern life.

NORA [*by the table, left*]. Wasn't he rather partial to asparagus and *pâté de foie gras*?

RANK. Yes, he was. And truffles.

NORA. Truffles, yes. And oysters, too, I believe?

RANK. Yes, oysters, oysters, of course.

NORA. And all the port and champagne that goes with them. It does seem a pity all these delicious things should attack the spine.

RANK. Especially when they attack a poor spine that never had any fun out of them.

NORA. Yes, that is an awful pity.

RANK [*looks at her sharply*]. Hm . . .

NORA [*after a pause*]. Why did you smile?

RANK. No, it was you who laughed.

NORA. No, it was you who smiled, Dr. Rank!

RANK [*getting up*]. You are a bigger rascal than I thought you were.

NORA. I feel full of mischief today.

RANK. So it seems.

NORA [*putting her hands on his shoulders*]. Dear, dear Dr. Rank, you mustn't go and die on Torvald and me.

RANK. You wouldn't miss me for long. When you are gone, you are soon forgotten.

NORA [*looking at him anxiously*]. Do you think so?

RANK. People make new contacts, then . . .

NORA. Who make new contacts?

RANK. Both you and Helmer will, when I'm gone. You yourself are already well on the way, it seems to me. What was this Mrs. Linde doing here last night?

NORA. Surely you aren't jealous of poor Kristine?

RANK. Yes, I am. She'll be my successor in this house. When I'm done for, I can see this woman. . . .

NORA. Hush! Don't talk so loud, she's in there.

RANK. Today as well? There you are, you see!

NORA. Just to do some sewing on my dress. Good Lord, how absurd you are! [*She sits down on the sofa.*] Now Dr. Rank, cheer up. You'll see tomorrow how nicely I can dance. And you can pretend I'm doing it just for you — and for Torvald as well, of course. [*She takes various things out of the box.*] Come here, Dr. Rank. I want to show you something.

RANK [*sits*]. What is it?

NORA. Look!

RANK. Silk stockings.

NORA. Flesh-colored! Aren't they lovely! Of course, it's dark here now, but tomorrow. . . . No, no, no, you can only look at the feet. Oh well, you might as well see a bit higher up, too.

RANK. Hm . . .

NORA. Why are you looking so critical? Don't you think they'll fit?

RANK. I couldn't possibly offer any informed opinion about that.

NORA [*looks at him for a moment*]. Shame on you. [*Hits him lightly across the ear with the stockings.*] Take that! [*Folds them up again.*]

RANK. And what other delights am I to be allowed to see?

NORA. Not another thing. You are too naughty. [*She hums a little and searches among her things.*]

RANK [*after a short pause*]. Sitting here so intimately like this with you, I can't imagine . . . I simply cannot conceive what would have become of me if I had never come to this house.

NORA [*smiles*]. Yes, I rather think you do enjoy coming here.

RANK [*in a low voice, looking fixedly ahead*]. And the thought of having to leave it all . . .

NORA. Nonsense. You aren't leaving.

RANK [*in the same tone*]. . . . without being able to leave behind even the slightest token of gratitude, hardly a fleeting regret even . . . nothing but an empty place to be filled by the first person that comes along.

NORA. Supposing I were to ask you to . . . ? No . . .

RANK. What?

NORA. . . . to show me the extent of your friendship . . .

RANK. Yes?

NORA. I mean . . . to do me a tremendous favor. . . .

RANK. Would you really, for once, give me that pleasure?

NORA. You have no idea what it is.

RANK. All right, tell me.

NORA. No, really I can't, Dr. Rank. It's altogether too much to ask . . . because I need your advice and help as well. . . .

RANK. The more the better. I cannot imagine what you have in mind. But tell me anyway. You do trust me, don't you?

NORA. Yes, I trust you more than anybody I know. You are my best and my most faithful friend. I know that. So I will tell you. Well then, Dr. Rank, there is something you must help me to prevent. You know how deeply, how passionately Torvald is in love with me. He would never hesitate for a moment to sacrifice his life for my sake.

RANK [*bending towards her*]. Nora . . . do you think he's the only one who . . . ?

NORA [*stiffening slightly*]. Who . . . ?

RANK. Who wouldn't gladly give his life for your sake.

NORA [*sadly*]. Oh!

RANK. I swore to myself you would know before I went. I'll never have a better opportunity. Well, Nora! Now you know. And now you know too that you can confide in me as in nobody else.

NORA [*rises and speaks evenly and calmly*]. Let me past.

RANK [*makes way for her, but remains seated*]. Nora . . .

NORA [*in the hall doorway*]. Helene, bring the lamp in, please. [*Walks over to the stove.*] Oh, my dear Dr. Rank, that really was rather horrid of you.

RANK [*getting up*]. That I have loved you every bit as much as anybody? Is *that* horrid?

NORA. No, but that you had to go and tell me. When it was all so unnecessary. . . .

RANK. What do you mean? Did you know . . . ?

[THE MAID *comes in with the lamp, puts it on the table, and goes out again.*]

RANK. Nora . . . Mrs. Helmer . . . I'm asking you if you knew?

NORA. How can I tell whether I did or didn't. I simply can't tell you. . . . Oh, how could you be so clumsy, Dr. Rank! When everything was so nice.

RANK. Anyway, you know now that I'm at your service, body and soul. So you can speak out.

NORA [*looking at him*]. After this?

RANK. I beg you to tell me what it is.

NORA. I can tell you nothing now.

RANK. You must. You can't torment me like this. Give me a chance — I'll do anything that's humanly possible.

NORA. You can do nothing for me now. Actually, I don't really need any help. It's all just my imagination, really it is. Of course! [*She sits down in the rocking-chair, looks at him and smiles.*] I must say, you are a nice one, Dr. Rank! Don't you feel ashamed of yourself, now the lamp's been brought in?

RANK. No, not exactly. But perhaps I ought to go — for good?

NORA. No, you mustn't do that. You must keep coming just as you've always done. You know very well Torvald would miss you terribly.

RANK. And *you*?

NORA. I always think it's tremendous fun having you.

RANK. That's exactly what gave me the wrong ideas. I just can't puzzle you out. I often used to feel you'd just as soon be with me as with Helmer.

NORA. Well, you see, there are those people you love and those people you'd almost rather *be* with.

RANK. Yes, there's something in that.

NORA. When I was a girl at home, I loved Daddy best, of course. But I also thought it great fun if I could slip into the maids' room. For one thing they never preached at me. And they always talked about such exciting things.

RANK. Aha! So it's their role I've taken over!

NORA [*jumps up and crosses to him*]. Oh, my dear, kind Dr. Rank, I didn't mean that at all. But you can see how it's a bit with Torvald as it was with Daddy. . . .

[THE MAID *comes in from the hall.*]

MAID. Please, ma'am . . . !

[*She whispers and hands her a card.*]

NORA [*glances at the card*]. Ah!

[*She puts it in her pocket.*]

RANK. Anything wrong?

NORA. No, no, not at all. It's just . . . it's my new costume. . . .

RANK. How is that? There's your costume in there.

NORA. That one, yes. But this is another one. I've ordered it. Torvald mustn't hear about it. . . .

RANK. Ah, so that's the big secret, is it!

NORA. Yes, that's right. Just go in and see him, will you? He's in the study. Keep him occupied for the time being. . . .

RANK. Don't worry. He shan't escape me.

[*He goes into Helmer's study.*]

NORA [*to the maid*]. Is he waiting in the kitchen?

MAID. Yes, he came up the back stairs. . . .

NORA. But didn't you tell him somebody was here?

MAID. Yes, but it was no good.

NORA. Won't he go?

MAID. No, he won't till he's seen you.

NORA. Let him in, then. But quietly. Helene, you mustn't tell anybody about this. It's a surprise for my husband.

MAID. I understand, ma'am. . . .

[*She goes out.*]

NORA. Here it comes! What I've been dreading! No, no, it can't happen, it *can't* happen.

She walks over and bolts Helmer's door. The maid opens the hall door for KROGSTAD *and shuts it again behind him. He is wearing a fur coat, overshoes, and a fur cap.*]

NORA [*goes towards him*]. Keep your voice down, my husband is at home.

KROGSTAD. What if he is?

NORA. What do you want with me?

KROGSTAD. To find out something.

NORA. Hurry, then. What is it?

KROGSTAD. You know I've been given notice.

NORA. I couldn't prevent it, Mr. Krogstad. I did my utmost for you, but it was no use.

KROGSTAD. Has your husband so little affection for you? He knows what I can do to you, yet he dares. . . .

NORA. You don't imagine he knows about it!

KROGSTAD. No, I didn't imagine he did. It didn't seem a bit like my good friend Torvald Helmer to show that much courage. . . .

NORA. Mr. Krogstad, I must ask you to show some respect for my husband.

KROGSTAD. Oh, sure! All due respect! But since you are so anxious to keep this business quiet, Mrs. Helmer, I take it you now have a rather clearer idea of just what it is you've done, than you had yesterday.

NORA. Clearer than *you* could ever have given me.

KROGSTAD. Yes, being as I am such a rotten lawyer. . . .

NORA. What do you want with me?

KROGSTAD. I just wanted to see how things stood, Mrs. Helmer. I've been thinking about you all day. Even a mere money-lender, a hack journalist, a—well, even somebody like me has a bit of what you might call feeling.

NORA. Show it then. Think of my little children.

KROGSTAD. Did you or your husband think of mine? But what does it matter now? There was just one thing I wanted to say: you needn't take this business too seriously. I shan't start any proceedings, for the present.

NORA. Ah, I knew you wouldn't.

KROGSTAD. The whole thing can be arranged quite amicably. Nobody need know. Just the three of us.

NORA. My husband must never know.

KROGSTAD. How can you prevent it? Can you pay off the balance?

NORA. No, not immediately.

KROGSTAD. Perhaps you've some way of getting hold of the money in the next few days.

NORA. None I want to make use of.

KROGSTAD. Well, it wouldn't have been very much help to you if you had. Even if you stood there with the cash in your hand and to spare, you still wouldn't get your IOU back from me now.

NORA. What are you going to do with it?

KROGSTAD. Just keep it—have it in my possession. Nobody who isn't implicated need know about it. So if you are thinking of trying any desperate remedies . . .

NORA. Which I am. . . .

KROGSTAD. . . . or anything worse . . .

NORA. How did you know?

KROGSTAD. . . . forget it!

NORA. How did you know I was thinking of *that?*

KROGSTAD. Most of us think of *that,* to begin with. I did, too; but I didn't have the courage. . . .

NORA [*tonelessly*]. I haven't either.

KROGSTAD [*relieved*]. So you haven't the courage either, eh?

NORA. No, I haven't! I haven't!

KROGSTAD. It would also be very stupid. There'd only be the first domestic storm to get over. . . . I've got a letter to your husband in my pocket here. . . .

NORA. And it's all in there?

KROGSTAD. In as tactful a way as possible.

NORA [*quickly*]. He must never read that letter. Tear it up. I'll find the money somehow.

KROGSTAD. Excuse me, Mrs. Helmer, but I've just told you. . . .

NORA. I'm not talking about the money I owe you. I want to know how much you are demanding from my husband, and I'll get the money.

KROGSTAD. I want no money from your husband.

NORA. What do you want?

KROGSTAD. I'll tell you. I want to get on my feet again, Mrs. Helmer; I want to get to the top. And your husband is going to help me. For the last eighteen months I've gone straight; all that time it's been hard going; I was content to work my way up, step by step. Now I'm being kicked out, and I won't stand for being taken back again as an act of charity. I'm going to get to the top, I tell you. I'm going back into that Bank—with a better job. Your husband is going to create a new vacancy, just for me. . . .

NORA. He'll never do that!

KROGSTAD. He will do it. I know him. He'll do it without so much as a whimper. And once I'm in there with him, you'll see what's what. In less than a year I'll be his right-hand man. It'll be Nils Krogstad, not Torvald Helmer, who'll be running that Bank.

NORA. You'll never live to see that day!

KROGSTAD. You mean you . . . ?

NORA. Now I have the courage.

KROGSTAD. You can't frighten me! A precious pampered little thing like you. . . .

NORA. I'll show you! I'll show you!

KROGSTAD. Under the ice, maybe? Down in the cold, black water? Then being washed up in the spring, bloated, hairless, unrecognizable. . . .

NORA. You can't frighten me.

KROGSTAD. You can't frighten me, either. People don't do that sort of thing, Mrs. Helmer. There wouldn't be any point to it, anyway, I'd still have him in my pocket.

NORA. Afterwards? When I'm no longer . . .

KROGSTAD. Aren't you forgetting that your reputation would then be entirely in my hands? [NORA *stands looking at him, speechless.*] Well, I've warned you. Don't do anything silly. When Helmer gets my letter, I expect to hear from him. And don't forget: it's him who is forcing me off the straight and narrow again, your own husband! That's something I'll never forgive him for. Goodbye, Mrs. Helmer.

> [*He goes out through the hall.* NORA *crosses to the door, opens it slightly, and listens.*]

NORA. He's going. He hasn't left the letter. No, no, that would be impossible! [*Opens the door further and further.*] What's he doing? He's stopped outside. He's not going down the stairs. Has he changed his mind? Is he . . . ? [*A letter falls into the letter-box. Then* KROGSTAD's *footsteps are heard receding as he walks downstairs.* NORA *gives a stifled cry, runs across the room to the sofa table; pause.*] In the letter-box! [*She creeps stealthily across to the hall door.*] There it is! Torvald, Torvald! It's hopeless now!

MRS. LINDE [*comes into the room, left, carrying the costume*]. There, I think that's everything. Shall we try it on?

NORA [*in a low, hoarse voice*]. Kristine, come here.

MRS. LINDE [*throws the dress down on the sofa*]. What's wrong with you? You look upset.

NORA. Come here. Do you see that letter? *There*, look! Through the glass in the letter-box.

MRS. LINDE. Yes, yes, I can see it.

NORA. It's a letter from Krogstad.

MRS. LINDE. Nora! It was Krogstad who lent you the money!

NORA. Yes. And now Torvald will get to know everything.

MRS. LINDE. Believe me, Nora, it's best for you both.

NORA. But there's more to it than that. I forged a signature. . . .

MRS. LINDE. Heavens above!

NORA. Listen, I want to tell you something, Kristine, so you can be my witness.

MRS. LINDE. What do you mean "witness"? What do you want me to . . . ?

NORA. If I should go mad . . . which might easily happen . . .

MRS. LINDE. Nora!

NORA. Or if anything happened to me . . . which meant I couldn't be here. . . .

MRS. LINDE. Nora, Nora! Are you out of your mind?

NORA. And if somebody else wanted to take it all upon himself, the whole blame, you understand. . . .

MRS. LINDE. Yes, yes. But what makes you think . . . ?

NORA. Then you must testify that it isn't true, Kristine. I'm not out of my mind; I'm quite sane now. And I tell you this: nobody else knew anything, I alone was responsible for the whole thing. Remember that!

MRS. LINDE. I will. But I don't understand a word of it.

NORA. Why should you? You see something miraculous is going to happen.

MRS. LINDE. Something miraculous?

NORA. Yes, a miracle. But something so terrible as well, Kristine—oh, it must *never* happen, not for anything.

MRS. LINDE. I'm going straight over to talk to Krogstad.

NORA. Don't go. He'll only do you harm.

MRS. LINDE. There was a time when he would have done anything for me.

NORA. Him!

MRS. LINDE. Where does he live?

NORA. How do I know . . . ? Wait a minute. [*She feels in her pocket.*] Here's his card. But the letter, the letter . . . !

HELMER [*from his study, knocking on the door*]. Nora!

NORA [*cries out in terror*]. What's that? What do you want?

HELMER. Don't be frightened. We're not coming in. You've locked the door. Are you trying on?

NORA. Yes, yes, I'm trying on. It looks so nice on me, Torvald.

MRS. LINDE [*who has read the card*]. He lives just round the corner.

NORA. It's no use. It's hopeless. The letter is there in the box.

MRS. LINDE. Your husband keeps the key?

NORA. Always.

MRS. LINDE. Krogstad must ask for his letter back unread, he must find some sort of excuse. . . .

NORA. But this is just the time that Torvald generally . . .

MRS. LINDE. Put him off! Go in and keep him busy. I'll be back as soon as I can.

[*She goes out hastily by the hall door.* NORA *walks over to Helmer's door, opens it, and peeps in.*]

NORA. Torvald!

HELMER [*in the study*]. Well, can a man get into his own living room again now? Come along, Rank, now we'll see . . . [*In the doorway.*] But what's this?

NORA. What, Torvald dear?

HELMER. Rank led me to expect some kind of marvelous transformation.

RANK [*in the doorway*]. That's what I thought too, but I must have been mistaken.

NORA. I'm not showing myself off to anybody before tomorrow.

HELMER. Nora dear, you look tired. You haven't been practicing too hard?

NORA. No, I haven't practiced at all yet.

HELMER. You'll have to, though.

NORA. Yes, I certainly must, Torvald. But I just can't get anywhere without your help: I've completely forgotten it.

HELMER. We'll soon polish it up.

NORA. Yes, do help me, Torvald. Promise? I'm so nervous. All those people. . . . You must devote yourself exclusively to me this evening. Pens away! Forget all about the office! Promise me, Torvald dear!

HELMER. I promise. This evening I am wholly and entirely at your service . . . helpless little thing that you are. Oh, but while I remember, I'll just look first . . .

[*He goes towards the hall door.*]

NORA. What do you want out there?

HELMER. Just want to see if there are any letters.

NORA. No, don't, Torvald!

HELMER. Why not?

NORA. Torvald, *please!* There aren't any.

HELMER. Just let me see.

[*He starts to go.* NORA, *at the piano, plays the opening bars of the tarantella.*]

HELMER [*at the door, stops*]. Aha!

NORA. I shan't be able to dance tomorrow if I don't rehearse it with you.

HELMER [*walks to her*]. Are you really so nervous, Nora dear?

NORA. Terribly nervous. Let me run through it now. There's still time before supper. Come and sit here and play for me, Torvald dear. Tell me what to do, keep me right—as you always do.

HELMER. Certainly, with pleasure, if that's what you want.

[*He sits at the piano.* NORA *snatches the tambourine out of the box, and also a long gaily-colored shawl which she drapes around herself, then with a bound she leaps forward.*]

NORA [*shouts*]. Now play for me! Now I'll dance!

[HELMER *plays and* NORA *dances;* DR. RANK *stands at the piano behind Helmer and looks on.*]

HELMER [*playing*]. Not so fast! Not so fast!

NORA. I can't help it.

HELMER. Not so wild, Nora!

NORA. This is how it has to be.

HELMER [*stops*]. No, no, that won't do at all.

NORA [*laughs and swings the tambourine*]. Didn't I tell you?

RANK. Let me play for her.

HELMER [*gets up*]. Yes, do. Then I'll be better able to tell her what to do.

[RANK *sits down at the piano and plays.* NORA *dances more and more wildly.* HELMER *stands by the stove giving her repeated directions as she dances; she does not seem to hear them. Her hair comes undone and falls about her shoulders; she pays no attention and goes on dancing.* MRS. LINDE *enters.*]

MRS. LINDE [*standing as though spellbound in the doorway*]. Ah . . . !

NORA [*dancing*]. See what fun we are having, Kristine.

HELMER. But my dear darling Nora, you are dancing as though your life depended on it.

NORA. It does.

HELMER. Stop, Rank! This is sheer madness. Stop, I say.

[RANK *stops playing and* NORA *comes to a sudden halt.*]

HELMER [*crosses to her*]. I would never have believed it. You have forgotten everything I ever taught you.

NORA [*throwing away the tambourine*]. There you are, you see.

HELMER. Well, some more instruction is certainly needed there.

NORA. Yes, you see how necessary it is. You must go on coaching me right up to the last minute. Promise me, Torvald?

HELMER. You can rely on me.

NORA. You mustn't think about anything else but me until after tomorrow . . . mustn't open any letters . . . mustn't touch the letter-box.

HELMER. Ah, you are still frightened of what that man might . . .

NORA. Yes, yes, I am.

HELMER. I can see from your face there's already a letter there from him.

NORA. I don't know. I think so. But you mustn't read anything like that now. We don't want anything horrid coming between us until all this is over.

RANK [*softly to* HELMER]. I shouldn't cross her.

HELMER [*puts his arm around her*]. The child must have her way. But tomorrow night, when your dance is done. . . .

NORA. Then you are free.

MAID [*in the doorway, right*]. Dinner is served, madam.

NORA. We'll have champagne, Helene.

MAID. Very good, madam.

[*She goes.*]

HELMER. Aha! It's to be quite a banquet, eh?

NORA. With champagne flowing until dawn. [*Shouts.*] And some macaroons, Helene . . . lots of them, for once in a while.

HELMER [*seizing her hands*]. Now, now, not so wild and excitable! Let me see you being my own little singing bird again.

NORA. Oh yes, I will. And if you'll just go in . . . you, too, Dr. Rank. Kristine, you must help me to do my hair.

RANK [*softly, as they leave*]. There isn't anything . . . anything as it were, impending, is there?

HELMER. No, not at all, my dear fellow. It's nothing but these childish fears I was telling you about.

[*They go out to the right.*]

NORA. Well?

MRS. LINDE. He's left town.

NORA. I saw it in your face.

MRS. LINDE. He's coming back tomorrow evening. I left a note for him.

NORA. You shouldn't have done that. You must let things take their course. Because really it's a case for rejoicing, waiting like this for the miracle.

MRS. LINDE. What is it you are waiting for?

NORA. Oh, you wouldn't understand. Go and join the other two. I'll be there in a minute.

[MRS. LINDE *goes into the dining-room.* NORA *stands for a moment as though to collect herself, then looks at her watch.*]

NORA. Five. Seven hours to midnight. Then twenty-four hours till the next midnight. Then the tarantella will be over. Twenty-four and seven? Thirty-one hours to live.

HELMER [*in the doorway, right*]. What's happened to our little sky-lark?

NORA [*running towards him with open arms*]. Here she is!

ACT III

The same room. The round table has been moved to the center of the room, and the chairs placed round it. A lamp is burning on the table. The door to the hall stands open. Dance music can be heard coming from the floor above. MRS. LINDE *is sitting by the table, idly turning over the pages of a book; she tries to read, but does not seem able to concentrate. Once or twice she listens, tensely, for a sound at the front door.*

MRS. LINDE [*looking at her watch*]. Still not here. There isn't much time left. I only hope he hasn't . . . [*She listens again.*] Ah, there he is. [*She goes out into the hall, and cautiously opens the front door. Soft footsteps can be heard on the stairs. She whispers.*] Come in. There's nobody here.

KROGSTAD [*in the doorway*]. I found a note from you at home. What does it all mean?

MRS. LINDE. I *had* to talk to you.

KROGSTAD. Oh? And did it have to be here, in this house?

MRS. LINDE. It wasn't possible over at my place, it hasn't a separate entrance. Come in. We are quite alone. The maid's asleep and the Helmers are at a party upstairs.

KROGSTAD [*comes into the room*]. Well, well! So the Helmers are out dancing tonight! Really?

MRS. LINDE. Yes, why not?

KROGSTAD. Why not indeed!

MRS. LINDE. Well then, Nils. Let's talk.

KROGSTAD. Have we two anything more to talk about?

MRS. LINDE. We have a great deal to talk about.

KROGSTAD. I shouldn't have thought so.

MRS. LINDE. That's because you never really understood me.

KROGSTAD. What else was there to understand, apart from the old, old story? A heartless woman throws a man over the moment something more profitable offers itself.

MRS. LINDE. Do you really think I'm so heartless? Do you think I found it easy to break it off?

KROGSTAD. Didn't you?

MRS. LINDE. You didn't really believe that?

KROGSTAD. If that wasn't the case, why did you write to me as you did?

MRS. LINDE. There was nothing else I could do. If I had to make the break, I felt in duty bound to destroy any feeling that you had for me.

KROGSTAD [*clenching his hands*]. So that's how it was. And all that . . . was for money!

MRS. LINDE. You mustn't forget I had a helpless mother and two young brothers. We couldn't wait for you, Nils. At that time you hadn't much immediate prospect of anything.

KROGSTAD. That may be. But you had no right to throw me over for somebody else.

MRS. LINDE. Well, I don't know. Many's the time I've asked myself whether I was justified.

KROGSTAD [*more quietly*]. When I lost you, it was just as if the ground had slipped away from under my feet. Look at me now: a broken man clinging to the wreck of his life.

MRS. LINDE. Help might be near.

KROGSTAD. It *was* near. Then you came along and got in the way.

MRS. LINDE. Quite without knowing, Nils. I only heard today it's you I'm supposed to be replacing at the Bank.

KROGSTAD. If you say so, I believe you. But now you do know, aren't you going to withdraw?

MRS. LINDE. No, that wouldn't benefit you in the slightest.

KROGSTAD. Benefit, benefit . . . ! I would do it just the same.

MRS. LINDE. I have learned to go carefully. Life and hard, bitter necessity have taught me that.

KROGSTAD. And life has taught me not to believe in pretty speeches.

MRS. LINDE. Then life has taught you a very sensible thing. But deeds are something you surely must believe in?

KROGSTAD. How do you mean?

MRS. LINDE. You said you were like a broken man clinging to the wreck of his life.

KROGSTAD. And I said it with good reason.

MRS. LINDE. And I am like a broken woman clinging to the wreck of her life. Nobody to care about, and nobody to care for.

KROGSTAD. It was your own choice.

MRS. LINDE. At the time there was no other choice.

KROGSTAD. Well, what of it?

MRS. LINDE. Nils, what about us two castaways joining forces?

KROGSTAD. What's that you say?

MRS. LINDE. Two of us on *one* wreck surely stand a better chance than each on his own.

KROGSTAD. Kristine!

MRS. LINDE. Why do you suppose I came to town?

KROGSTAD. You mean, you thought of me?

MRS. LINDE. Without work I couldn't live. All my life I have worked, for as long as I can remember; that has always been my one great joy. But now I'm completely alone in the world, and feeling horribly empty and forlorn. There's no pleasure in working only for yourself. Nils, give me somebody and something to work for.

KROGSTAD. I don't believe all this. It's only a woman's hysteria, wanting to be all magnanimous and self-sacrificing.

MRS. LINDE. Have you ever known me hysterical before?

KROGSTAD. Would you really do this? Tell me — do you know all about my past?

MRS. LINDE. Yes.

KROGSTAD. And you know what people think about me?

MRS. LINDE. Just now you hinted you thought you might have been a different person with me.

KROGSTAD. I'm convinced I would.

MRS. LINDE. Couldn't it still happen?

KROGSTAD. Kristine! You know what you are saying, don't you? Yes, you do. I can see you do. Have you really the courage . . . ?

MRS. LINDE. I need someone to mother, and your children need a mother. We two need each other. Nils, I have faith in what, deep down, you are. With you I can face anything.

KROGSTAD [*seizing her hands*]. Thank you, thank you, Kristine. And I'll soon have everybody looking up to me, or I'll know the reason why. Ah, but I was forgetting. . . .

MRS. LINDE. Hush! The tarantella! You must go!

KROGSTAD. Why? What is it?

MRS. LINDE. You hear that dance upstairs? When it's finished they'll be coming.

KROGSTAD. Yes, I'll go. It's too late to do anything. Of course, you know nothing about what steps I've taken against the Helmers.

MRS. LINDE. Yes, Nils, I do know.

KROGSTAD. Yet you still want to go on. . . .

MRS. LINDE. I know how far a man like you can be driven by despair.

KROGSTAD. Oh, if only I could undo what I've done!

MRS. LINDE. You still can. Your letter is still there in the box.

KROGSTAD. Are you sure?

MRS. LINDE. Quite sure. But . . .

KROGSTAD [*regards her searching*]. Is that how things are? You want to save your friend at any price? Tell me straight. Is that it?

MRS. LINDE. When you've sold yourself *once* for other people's sake, you don't do it again.

KROGSTAD. I shall demand my letter back.

MRS. LINDE. No, no.

KROGSTAD. Of course I will, I'll wait here till Helmer comes. I'll tell him he has to give me my letter back . . . that it's only about my notice . . . that he mustn't read it. . . .

MRS. LINDE. No, Nils, don't ask for it back.

KROGSTAD. But wasn't that the very reason you got me here?

MRS. LINDE. Yes, that was my first terrified reaction. But that was yesterday, and it's quite incredible the things I've witnessed in this house in the last twenty-four hours. Helmer must know everything. This unhappy secret must come out. Those two must have the whole thing out between them. All this secrecy and deception, it just can't go on.

KROGSTAD. Well, if you want to risk it. . . . But one thing I can do, and I'll do it at once. . . .

MRS. LINDE [*listening*]. Hurry! Go, go! The dance has stopped. We aren't safe a moment longer.

KROGSTAD. I'll wait for you downstairs.

MRS. LINDE. Yes, do. You must see me home.

KROGSTAD. I've never been so incredibly happy before.

[*He goes out by the front door. The door out into the hall remains standing open.*]

MRS. LINDE [*tidies the room a little and gets her hat and coat ready*]. How things change! How things change! Somebody to work for . . . to live for. A home to bring happiness into. Just let me get down to it. . . . I wish they'd come. . . . [*Listens.*] Ah, there they are. . . . Get my things.

[*She takes her coat and hat. The voices of* HELMER *and* NORA *are heard outside. A key is turned and* HELMER *pushes* NORA *almost forcibly into the hall. She is dressed in the Italian costume, with a big black shawl over it. He is in evening dress, and over it a black cloak, open.*]

NORA [*still in the doorway, reluctantly*]. No, no, not in here! I want to go back up again. I don't want to leave so early.

HELMER. But my dearest Nora . . .

NORA. Oh, please, Torvald, I beg you. . . . *Please*, just for another hour.

HELMER. Not another minute, Nora my sweet. You remember what we agreed. There now, come along in. You'll catch cold standing there.

[*He leads her, in spite of her resistance, gently but firmly into the room.*]

MRS. LINDE. Good evening.

NORA. Kristine!

HELMER. Why, Mrs. Linde. You here so late?

MRS. LINDE. Yes. You must forgive me but I did so want to see Nora all dressed up.

NORA. Have you been sitting here waiting for me?

MRS. LINDE. Yes, I'm afraid I wasn't in time to catch you before you went upstairs. And I felt I couldn't leave again without seeing you.

HELMER [*removing* NORA's *shawl*]. Well take a good look at her. I think I can say she's worth looking at. Isn't she lovely, Mrs. Linde?

MRS. LINDE. Yes, I must say. . . .

HELMER. Isn't she quite extraordinarily lovely? That's what everybody at the party thought, too. But she's dreadfully stubborn . . . the sweet little thing! And what shall we do about that? Would you believe it, I nearly had to use force to get her away.

NORA. Oh Torvald, you'll be sorry you didn't let me stay, even for half an hour.

HELMER. You hear that, Mrs. Linde? She dances her tarantella, there's wild applause — which was well deserved, although the performance was perhaps rather realistic . . . I mean, rather more so than was strictly necessary from the artistic point of view. But anyway! The main thing is she was a success, a tremendous success. Was I supposed to let her stay after that? Spoil the effect? No, thank you! I took my lovely little Capri girl — my capricious little Capri girl, I might say — by the arm, whisked her once round the room, a curtsey all round, and then — as they say in novels — the beautiful vision vanished. An exit should always be effective, Mrs. Linde. But I just can't get Nora to see that. Phew! It's warm in here. [*He throws his cloak over a chair and opens the door to his study.*] What? It's dark. Oh yes, of course. Excuse me. . . .

[*He goes in and lights a few candles.*]

NORA [*quickly, in a breathless whisper*]. Well?

MRS. LINDE [*softly*]. I've spoken to him.

NORA. And . . . ?

MRS. LINDE. Nora . . . you must tell your husband everything.

NORA [*tonelessly*]. I knew it.

MRS. LINDE. You've got nothing to fear from Krogstad. But you must speak.

NORA. I won't

MRS. LINDE. Then the letter will.

NORA. Thank you, Kristine. Now I know what's to be done. Hush . . . !

HELMER [*comes in again*]. Well, Mrs. Linde, have you finished admiring her?

MRS. LINDE. Yes. And now I must say good night.

HELMER. Oh, already? Is this yours, this knitting?

MRS. LINDE [*takes it*]. Yes, thank you. I nearly forgot it.

HELMER. So you knit, eh?

MRS. LINDE. Yes.

HELMER. You should embroider instead, you know.

MRS. LINDE. Oh? Why?

HELMER. So much prettier. Watch! You hold the embroidery like this in the left hand, and then you take the needle in the right hand, like this, and you describe a long, graceful curve. Isn't that right?

MRS. LINDE. Yes, I suppose so. . . .

HELMER. Whereas knitting on the other hand just can't help being ugly. Look! Arms pressed into the sides, the knitting needles going up and down — there's something Chinese about it. . . . Ah, that was marvelous champagne they served tonight.

MRS. LINDE. Well, good night, Nora! And stop being so stubborn.

HELMER. Well said, Mrs. Linde!

MRS. LINDE. Good night, Mr. Helmer.

HELMER [*accompanying her to the door*]. Good night, good night! You'll get home all right, I hope? I'd be only too pleased to . . . But you haven't far to walk. Good night, good night! [*She goes; he shuts the door behind her and comes in again.*] There we are, got rid of her at last. She's a frightful bore, that woman.

NORA. Aren't you very tired, Torvald?

HELMER. Not in the least.

NORA. Not sleepy?

HELMER. Not at all. On the contrary, I feel extremely lively. What about you? Yes, you look quite tired and sleepy.

NORA. Yes, I'm very tired. I just want to fall straight off to sleep.

HELMER. There you are, you see! Wasn't I right in thinking we shouldn't stay any longer.

NORA. Oh, everything you do is right.

HELMER [*kissing her forehead*]. There's my little sky-lark talking common sense. Did you notice how gay Rank was this evening?

NORA. Oh, was he? I didn't get a chance to talk to him.

HELMER. I hardly did either. But it's a long time since I saw him in such a good mood. [*Looks at NORA for a moment or two, then comes nearer her.*] Ah, it's wonderful to be back in our own home again, and quite alone with you. How irresistibly lovely you are, Nora!

NORA. Don't look at me like that, Torvald!

HELMER. Can't I look at my most treasured possession? At all this loveliness that's mine and mine alone, completely and utterly mine.

NORA [*walks round to the other side of the table*]. You mustn't talk to me like that tonight.

HELMER [*following her*]. You still have the tarantella in your blood, I see. And that makes you even more desirable. Listen! The guests are beginning to leave now. [*Softly.*] Nora . . . soon the whole house will be silent.

NORA. I should hope so.

HELMER. Of course you do, don't you, Nora my darling? You know, whenever I'm out at a party with you . . . do you know why I never talk to you very much, why I always stand away from you and only steal a quick glance at you now and then . . . do you know why I do that? It's because I'm pretending we are secretly in love, secretly engaged and nobody suspects there is anything between us.

NORA. Yes, yes. I know your thoughts are always with me, of course.

HELMER. And when it's time to go, and I lay your shawl round those shapely, young shoulders, round the exquisite curve of your neck . . . I pretend that you are my young bride, that we are just leaving our wedding, that I am taking you to our new home for the first time . . . to be alone with you for the first time . . . quite alone with your young and trembling loveliness! All evening I've been longing for you, and nothing else. And as I watched you darting and swaying in the tarantella, my blood was on fire . . . I couldn't bear it any longer . . . and that's why I brought you down here with me so early. . . .

NORA. Go away, Torvald! Please leave me alone. I won't have it.

HELMER. What's this? It's just your little game isn't it, my little Nora. Won't! Won't! Am I not your husband . . . ?

[*There is a knock on the front door.*]

NORA [*startled*]. Listen . . . !

HELMER [*going towards the hall*]. Who's there?

RANK [*outside*]. It's me. Can I come in for a minute?

HELMER [*in a low voice, annoyed*]. Oh, what does he want now? [*Aloud.*] Wait a moment. [*He walks across and opens the door.*] How nice of you to look in on your way out.

RANK. I fancied I heard your voice and I thought I would just look in. [*He takes a quick glance round.*] Ah yes, this dear, familiar old place! How cozy and comfortable you've got things here, you two.

HELMER. You seemed to be having a pretty good time upstairs yourself.

RANK. Capital! Why shouldn't I? Why not make the most of things in this world? At least as much as one can, and for as long as one can. The wine was excellent. . . .

HELMER. Especially the champagne.

RANK. You noticed that too, did you? It's incredible the amount I was able to put away.

NORA. Torvald also drank a lot of champagne this evening.

RANK. Oh?

NORA. Yes, and that always makes him quite merry.

RANK. Well, why shouldn't a man allow himself a jolly evening after a day well spent?

HELMER. Well spent? I'm afraid I can't exactly claim that.

RANK [*clapping him on the shoulder*]. But I can, you see!

NORA. Dr. Rank, am I right in thinking you carried out a certain laboratory test today?

RANK. Exactly.

HELMER. Look at our little Nora talking about laboratory tests!

NORA. And may I congratulate you on the result?

RANK. You may indeed.

NORA. So it was good?

RANK. The best possible, for both doctor and patient—certainty!

NORA [*quickly and searchingly*]. Certainty?

RANK. Absolute certainty. So why shouldn't I allow myself a jolly evening after that?

NORA. Quite right, Dr. Rank.

HELMER. I quite agree. As long as you don't suffer for it in the morning.

RANK. Well, you never get anything for nothing in this life.

NORA. Dr. Rank . . . you are very fond of masquerades, aren't you?

RANK. Yes, when there are plenty of amusing disguises. . . .

NORA. Tell me, what shall we two go as next time?

HELMER. There's frivolity for you . . . thinking about the next time already!

RANK. We two? I'll tell you. You must go as Lady Luck. . . .

HELMER. Yes, but how do you find a costume to suggest *that*?

RANK. Your wife could simply go in her everyday clothes. . . .

HELMER. That was nicely said. But don't you know what you would be?

RANK. Yes, my dear friend, I know exactly what I shall be.

HELMER. Well?

RANK. At the next masquerade, I shall be invisible.

HELMER. That's a funny idea!

RANK. There's a big black cloak . . . haven't you heard of the cloak of invisibility? That comes right down over you, and then nobody can see you.

HELMER [*suppressing a smile*]. Of course, that's right.

RANK. But I'm clean forgetting what I came for. Helmer, give me a cigar, one of the dark Havanas.

HELMER. With the greatest of pleasure.

[*He offers his case.*]

RANK [*takes one and cuts the end off*]. Thanks.

NORA [*strikes a match*]. Let me give you a light.

RANK. Thank you. [*She holds out the match and he lights his cigar.*] And now, goodbye!

HELMER. Goodbye, goodbye, my dear fellow!

NORA. Sleep well, Dr. Rank.

RANK. Thank you for that wish.

NORA. Wish me the same.

RANK. You? All right, if you want me to. . . . Sleep well. And thanks for the light.

[*He nods to them both, and goes.*]

HELMER [*subdued*]. He's had a lot to drink.

NORA [*absently*]. Very likely.

[HELMER *takes a bunch of keys out of his pocket and goes out into the hall.*]

NORA. Torvald . . . what do you want there?

HELMER. I must empty the letter-box, it's quite full. There'll be no room for the papers in the morning. . . .

NORA. Are you going to work tonight?

HELMER. You know very well I'm not. Hello, what's this? Somebody's been at the lock.

NORA. At the lock?

HELMER. Yes, I'm sure of it. Why should that be? I'd hardly have thought the maids . . . ? Here's a broken hair-pin. Nora, it's one of yours. . . .

NORA [*quickly*]. It must have been the children. . . .

HELMER. Then you'd better tell them not to. Ah . . . there . . . I've managed to get it open. [*He takes the things out and shouts into the kitchen.*] Helene! . . . Helene, put the light out in the hall. [*He comes into the room again with the letters in his hand and shuts the hall door.*] Look how it all mounts up. [*Runs through them.*] What's this?

NORA. The letter! Oh no, Torvald, no!

HELMER. Two visiting cards . . . from Dr. Rank.

NORA. From Dr. Rank?

HELMER [*looking at them*]. Dr. Rank, Medical Practitioner. They were on top. He must have put them in as he left.

NORA. Is there anything on them?

HELMER. There's a black cross above his name. Look. What an uncanny idea. It's just as if he were announcing his own death.

NORA. He is.

HELMER. What? What do you know about it? Has he said anything to you?

NORA. Yes. He said when these cards came, he would have taken his last leave of us. He was going to shut himself up and die.

HELMER. Poor fellow! Of course I knew we couldn't keep him with us very long. But so soon. . . . And hiding himself away like a wounded animal.

NORA. When it has to happen, it's best that it should happen without words. Don't you think so, Torvald?

HELMER [*walking up and down*]. He had grown so close to us. I don't think I can imagine him gone. His suffering and his loneliness seemed almost to provide a background of dark cloud to the sunshine of our lives. Well, perhaps it's all for the best. For him at any rate. [*Pauses.*] And maybe for us as well, Nora. Now there's just the two of us. [*Puts his arms around her.*] Oh, my darling wife, I can't hold you close enough. You know, Nora . . . many's the time I wish you were threatened by some terrible danger so I could risk everything, body and soul, for your sake.

NORA [*tears herself free and says firmly and decisively*]. Now you must read your letters, Torvald.

HELMER. No, no, not tonight. I want to be with you, my darling wife.

NORA. Knowing all the time your friend is dying . . . ?

HELMER. You are right. It's been a shock to both of us. This ugly thing has come between us . . . thoughts of death and decay. We must try to free ourselves from it. Until then . . . we shall go our separate ways.

NORA [*her arms round his neck*]. Torvald . . . good night! Good night!

HELMER [*kisses her forehead*]. Goodnight, my little singing bird. Sleep well, Nora, I'll just read through my letters.

[*He takes the letters into his room and shuts the door behind him.*]

NORA [*gropes around her, wild-eyed, seizes Helmer's cloak, wraps it round herself, and whispers quickly, hoarsely, spasmodically*]. Never see him again. Never, never, never. [*Throws her shawl over her head.*] And never see the children again either. Never, never. Oh, that black icy water. Oh, that bottomless . . . ! If only it were all over! He's got it now. Now he's reading it. Oh no, no! Not yet! Torvald, goodbye . . . and my children. . . .

[*She rushes out in the direction of the hall; at the same moment* HELMER *flings open his door and stands there with an open letter in his hand.*]

HELMER. Nora!

NORA [*shrieks*]. Ah!

HELMER. What is this? Do you know what is in this letter?

NORA. Yes, I know. Let me go! Let me out!

HELMER [*holds her back*]. Where are you going?

NORA [*trying to tear herself free*]. You mustn't try to save me, Torvald!

HELMER [*reels back*]. True! Is it true what he writes? How dreadful! no, no, it can't possibly be true.

NORA. It *is* true. I loved you more than anything else in the world.

HELMER. Don't come to me with a lot of paltry excuses!

NORA [*taking a step towards him*]. Torvald . . . !

HELMER. Miserable woman . . . what is this you have done?

NORA. Let me go. I won't have you taking the blame for me. You mustn't take it on yourself.

HELMER. Stop play-acting! [*Locks the front door.*] You are staying here to give an account of yourself. Do you understand what you have done? Answer me? Do you understand?

NORA [*looking fixedly at him, her face hardening*]. Yes, now I'm really beginning to understand.

HELMER [*walking up and down*]. Oh, what a terrible awakening this is. All these eight years . . . this woman who was my pride and joy . . . a hypocrite, a liar, worse than that, a criminal! Oh, how utterly squalid it all is! Ugh! Ugh! [NORA *remains silent and looks fixedly at him.*] I should have realized something like this would happen. I should have seen it coming. All your father's irresponsible ways. . . . Quiet! All your father's irresponsible ways are coming out in you. No religion, no morals, no sense of duty. . . . Oh, this is my punishment for turning a blind eye to him. It was for your sake I did it, and this is what I get for it.

NORA. Yes, this.

HELMER. Now you have ruined my entire happiness, jeopardized my whole future. It's terrible to think of. Here I am, at the mercy of a thoroughly unscrupulous person; he can do whatever he likes with me, demand anything he wants, order me about just as he chooses . . . and I daren't even whimper. I'm done for, a miserable failure, and it's all the fault of a feather-brained woman!

NORA. When I've left this world behind, you will be free.

HELMER. Oh, stop pretending! Your father was just the same, always ready with fine phrases. What good would it do me if you left this world behind, as you put it? Not the slightest bit of good. He can still let it all come out, if he likes; and if he does, people might even suspect me of being an accomplice in these criminal acts of yours, they might even think I was the one behind it all, that it was I who pushed you into it! And it's you I have to thank for this . . . and when I've taken such good care of you, all our married life. Now do you understand what you have done to me?

NORA [*coldly and calmly*]. Yes.

HELMER. I just can't understand it, it's so incredible. But we must see about putting things right. Take that shawl off. Take it off, I tell you! I must see if I can't find some way or other of appeasing him. The thing must be hushed up at all costs. And as far as you and I are concerned, things must appear to go on exactly as before. But only in the eyes of the world, of course. In other words you'll go on living here; that's understood. But you will not be allowed to bring up the children, I can't trust you with them. . . . Oh, that I should have to say this to the woman I loved so dearly, the woman I still. . . . Well, that must be all over and done with. From now on, there can be no question of happiness. All we can do is save the bits and pieces from the wreck, preserve appearances. . . . [*The front door-bell rings.* HELMER *gives a start.*] What's that? So late? How terrible, supposing. . . . If he should . . . ? Hide, Nora! Say you are not well.

[NORA *stands motionless.* HELMER *walks across and opens the door into the hall.*]

MAID [*half dressed, in the hall*]. It's a note for Mrs. Helmer.

HELMER. Give it to me. [*He snatches the note and shuts the door.*] Yes, it's from him. You can't have it. I want to read it myself.

NORA. You read it then.

HELMER [*by the lamp*]. I hardly dare. Perhaps this is the end, for both of us. Well, I *must* know. [*He opens the note hurriedly, reads a few lines, looks at another enclosed sheet, and gives a cry of joy.*] Nora! [NORA *looks at him inquiringly.*] Nora! I must read it again. Yes, yes, it's true! I am saved! Nora, I am saved!

NORA. And me?

HELMER. You too, of course, we are both saved, you as well as me. Look, he's sent your IOU back. He sends his regrets and apologies for what he has done. . . . His luck has changed. . . . Oh, what does it matter what he says. We are saved, Nora! Nobody can do anything to you now. Oh, Nora, Nora . . . but let's get rid of this disgusting thing first. Let me see. . . . [*He glances at the IOU.*] No, I don't want to see it. I don't want it to be anything but a dream. [*He tears up the IOU and both letters, throws all the pieces into the stove and watches them burn.*] Well, that's the end of that. He said in his note you'd known since Christmas Eve. . . . You must have had three terrible days of it, Nora.

NORA. These three days haven't been easy.

HELMER. The agonies you must have gone through! When the only way out seemed to be. . . . No, let's forget the whole ghastly thing. We can rejoice and say: It's all over! It's all over! Listen to me, Nora! You don't seem to understand: it's all over! Why this grim look on your face? Oh, poor little Nora, of course I understand. You can't bring yourself to believe I've forgiven you. But I have. Nora, I swear it. I forgive you everything. I know you did what you did because you loved me.

NORA. That's true.

HELMER. You loved me as a wife should love her husband. It was simply that you didn't have the experience to judge what was the best way of going about things. But do you think I love you any the less for that; just because you don't know how to act on your own responsibility? No, no, you just lean on me. I shall give you all the advice and guidance you need. I wouldn't be a proper man if I didn't find a woman doubly attractive for being so obviously helpless. You mustn't dwell on the harsh things I said in the first moment of horror, when I thought everything was going to come crashing down about my ears. I have forgiven you, Nora, I swear it! I have forgiven you!

NORA. Thank you for your forgiveness.

[*She goes out through the door, right.*]

HELMER. No, don't go! [*He looks through the doorway.*] What are you doing in the spare room?

NORA. Taking off this fancy dress.

HELMER [*standing at the open door*]. Yes, do. You try and get some rest, and set your mind at peace again, my frightened little song-bird. Have a good long sleep; you know you are safe and sound under my wing. [*Walks up and down near the door.*] What a nice, cozy little home we have here, Nora! Here you can find refuge. Here I shall hold you like a hunted dove I have rescued unscathed from the cruel talons of the hawk, and calm your poor beating heart. And that will come, gradually, Nora, believe me. Tomorrow you'll see everything quite differently. Soon everything will be just as it was before. You won't need me to keep on telling you I've forgiven you: you'll feel convinced of it in your own heart. You don't really imagine me ever thinking of turning you out, or even of reproaching you? Oh, a real man isn't made that way, you know, Nora. For a man, there's something indescribably moving and very satisfying in knowing that he has forgiven his wife — forgiven her, completely and genuinely, from the depths of his heart. It's as though it made her his property in a double sense: he has, as it were, given her a new life, and she becomes in a way both his wife and at the same time his child. That is how you will seem to me after today, helpless, perplexed little thing that you are. Don't you worry your pretty little head about anything, Nora. Just you be frank with me, and I'll make all the decisions for you. . . . What's this? Not in bed? You've changed your things?

NORA [*in her everyday dress*]. Yes, Torvald, I've changed.

HELMER. What for? It's late.

NORA. I shan't sleep tonight.

HELMER. But my dear Nora. . . .

NORA [*looks at her watch*]. It's not so terribly late. Sit down, Torvald. We two have a lot to talk about.

[*She sits down at one side of the table.*]

HELMER. Nora, what is all this? Why so grim?

NORA. Sit down. It'll take some time. I have a lot to say to you.

HELMER [*sits down at the table opposite her*]. You frighten me, Nora. I don't understand you.

NORA. Exactly. You don't understand me. And I have never understood you, either — until tonight. No, don't interrupt. I just want you to listen to what I have to say. We are going to have things out, Torvald.

HELMER. What do you mean?

NORA. Isn't there anything that strikes you about the way we two are sitting here?

HELMER. What's that?

NORA. We have now been married eight years. Hasn't it struck you this is the first time you and I, man and wife, have had a serious talk together?

HELMER. Depends what you mean by "serious."

NORA. Eight whole years — no, more, ever since we first knew each other — and never have we exchanged one serious word about serious things.

HELMER. What did you want me to do? Get you involved in worries that you couldn't possibly help me to bear?

NORA. I'm not talking about worries. I say we've never once sat down together and seriously tried to get to the bottom of anything.

HELMER. But, my dear Nora, would that have been a thing for you?

NORA. That's just it. You have never understood me . . . I've been greatly wronged, Torvald. First by my father, and then by you.

HELMER. What! Us two! The two people who loved you more than anybody?

NORA [*shakes her head*]. You two never loved me. You only thought how nice it was to be in love with me.

HELMER. But, Nora, what's this you are saying?

NORA. It's right, you know, Torvald. At home, Daddy used to tell me what he thought, then I thought the same. And if I thought differently, I kept quiet about it, because he wouldn't have liked it. He used to call me his baby doll, and he played with me as I used to play with my dolls. Then I came to live in your house. . . .

HELMER. What way is that to talk about our marriage?

NORA [*imperturbably*]. What I mean is: I passed out of Daddy's hands into yours. You arranged everything to your tastes, and I acquired the same tastes. Or pretended to . . . I don't really know . . . I think it was a bit of both, sometimes one thing and sometimes the other. When I look back, it seems to me I have been living here like a beggar, from hand to mouth. I lived by doing tricks for you, Torvald. But that's the way you wanted it. You and Daddy did me a great wrong. It's your fault that I've never made anything of my life.

HELMER. Nora, how unreasonable . . . how ungrateful you are! Haven't you been happy here?

NORA. No, never. I thought I was, but I wasn't really.

HELMER. Not . . . not happy!

NORA. No, just gay. And you've always been so kind to me. But our house has never been anything but a play-room. I have been your doll wife, just as at home I was Daddy's doll child. And the children in turn have been my dolls. I thought it was fun when you came and played with me, just as they thought it was fun when I went and played with them. That's been our marriage, Torvald.

HELMER. There is some truth in what you say, exaggerated and hysterical though it is. But from now on it will be different. Play-time is over; now comes the time for lessons.

NORA. Whose lessons? Mine or the children's?

HELMER. Both yours and the children's, my dear Nora.

NORA. Ah, Torvald, you are not the man to teach me to be a good wife for you.

HELMER. How can you say that?

NORA. And what sort of qualifications have I to teach the children?

HELMER. Nora!

NORA. Didn't you say yourself, a minute or two ago, that you couldn't trust me with that job.

HELMER. In the heat of the moment! You shouldn't pay any attention to that.

NORA. On the contrary, you were quite right. I'm not up to it. There's another problem needs solving first. I must take steps to educate myself. You are not the man to help me there. That's something I must do on my own. That's why I'm leaving you.

HELMER [*jumps up*]. What did you say?

NORA. If I'm ever to reach any understanding of myself and the things around me, I must learn to stand alone. That's why I can't stay here with you any longer.

HELMER. Nora! Nora!

NORA. I'm leaving here at once. I dare say Kristine will put me up for to-night. . . .

HELMER. You are out of your mind! I won't let you! I forbid you!

NORA. It's no use forbidding me anything now. I'm taking with me my own personal belongings. I don't want anything of yours, either now or later.

HELMER. This is madness!

NORA. Tomorrow I'm going home — to what used to be my home, I mean. It will be easier for me to find something to do there.

HELMER. Oh, you blind, inexperienced . . .

NORA. I must set about *getting* experience, Torvald.

HELMER. And leave your home, your husband and your children? Don't you care what people will say?

NORA. That's no concern of mine. All I know is that this is necessary for *me*.

HELMER. This is outrageous! You are betraying your most sacred duty.

NORA. And what do you consider to be my most sacred duty?

HELMER. Does it take me to tell you that? Isn't it your duty to your husband and your children?

NORA. I have another duty equally sacred.

HELMER. You have not. What duty might *that* be?

NORA. My duty to myself.

HELMER. First and foremost, you are a wife and mother.

NORA. That I don't believe any more. I believe that first and foremost I am an individual, just as much as you are — or at least I'm going to try to be. I know most people agree with you, Torvald, and that's also what it says in books. But I'm not content any more with what most people say, or with what it says in books. I have to think things out for myself, and get things clear.

HELMER. Surely you are clear about your position in your own home? Haven't you an infallible guide in questions like these? Haven't you your religion?

NORA. Oh, Torvald, I don't really know what religion is.

HELMER. What do you say!

NORA. All I know is what Pastor Hansen said when I was confirmed. He said religion was this, that and the other. When I'm away from all this and on my own, I'll go into that, too. I want to find out whether what Pastor Hansen told me was right — or at least whether it's right for *me*.

HELMER. This is incredible talk from a young woman! But if religion cannot keep you on the right path, let me at least stir your conscience. I suppose you do have some moral sense? Or tell me — perhaps you don't?

NORA. Well, Torvald, that's not easy to say. I simply don't know. I'm really confused about such things. All I know is my ideas about such things are very different from yours. I've also learned that the law is different from what I thought; but I simply can't get it into my head that that particular law is right. Apparently a woman has no right to spare her old father on his death-bed, or to save her husband's life, even. I just don't believe it.

HELMER. You are talking like a child. You understand nothing about the society you live in.

NORA. No, I don't. But I shall go into that too. I must try to discover who is right, society or me.

HELMER. You are ill, Nora. You are delirious. I'm half inclined to think you are out of your mind.

NORA. Never have I felt so calm and collected as I do tonight.

HELMER. Calm and collected enough to leave your husband and children?

NORA. Yes.

HELMER. Then only one explanation is possible.

NORA. And that is?

HELMER. You don't love me any more.

NORA. Exactly.

HELMER. Nora! Can you say that!

NORA. I'm desperately sorry, Torvald. Because you have always been so kind to me. But I can't help it. I don't love you any more.

HELMER [*struggling to keep his composure*]. Is that also a "calm and collected" decision you've made?

NORA. Yes, absolutely calm and collected. That's why I don't want to stay here.

HELMER. And can you also account for how I forfeited your love?

NORA. Yes, very easily. It was tonight, when the miracle didn't happen. It was then I realized you weren't the man I thought you were.

HELMER. Explain yourself more clearly. I don't understand.

NORA. For eight years I have been patiently waiting. Because, heavens, I knew miracles didn't happen every day. Then this devastating business started, and I became absolutely convinced the miracle *would* happen. All the time Krogstad's letter lay there, it never so much as crossed my mind that you would ever submit to that man's conditions. I was absolutely convinced you would say to him: Tell the whole wide world if you like. And when that was done . . .

HELMER. Yes, then what? After I had exposed my wife to dishonor and shame . . . !

NORA. When that was done, I was absolutely convinced you would come forward and take everything on yourself, and say: I am the guilty one.

HELMER. Nora!

NORA. You mean I'd never let you make such a sacrifice for my sake? Of course not. But what would my story have counted for against yours? — That was the miracle I went in hope and dread of. It was to prevent it that I was ready to end my life.

HELMER. I would gladly toil day and night for you, Nora, enduring all manner of sorrow and distress. But nobody sacrifices his *honor* for the one he loves.

NORA. Hundreds and thousands of women have.

HELMER. Oh, you think and talk like a stupid child.

NORA. All right. But you neither think nor talk like the man I would want to share my life with. When you had got over your fright — and you weren't concerned about me but only about what might happen to you — and when all danger was past, you acted as though nothing had happened. I was your little sky-lark again, your little doll, exactly as before; except you would have to protect it twice as carefully as before, now that it had shown itself to be so weak and fragile. [*Rises.*] Torvald, that was the moment I realized that for eight years I'd been living with a stranger, and had borne him three children. . . . Oh, I can't bear to think about it! I could tear myself to shreds.

HELMER [*sadly*]. I see. I see. There is a tremendous gulf dividing us. But, Nora, is there no way we might bridge it?

NORA. As I am now, I am no wife for you.

HELMER. I still have it in me to change.

NORA. Perhaps . . . if you have your doll taken away.

HELMER. And be separated from you! No, no, Nora, the very thought of it is inconceivable.

NORA [*goes into the room, right*]. All the more reason why it must be done.

[*She comes back with her outdoor things and a small traveling bag which she puts on the chair beside the table.*]

HELMER. Nora, Nora, not now! Wait till the morning.

NORA [*putting on her coat*]. I can't spend the night in a strange man's room.

HELMER. Couldn't we go on living here like brother and sister . . . ?

NORA [*tying on her hat*]. You know very well that wouldn't last. [*She draws the shawl round her.*] Goodbye, Torvald. I don't want to see the children. I know they are in better hands than mine. As I am now, I can never be anything to them.

HELMER. But some day, Nora, some day . . . ?

NORA. How should I know? I've no idea what I might turn out to be.

HELMER. But you are my wife, whatever you are.

NORA. Listen, Torvald, from what I've heard, when a wife leaves her husband's house as I am doing now, he is absolved by law of all responsibility for her. I can at any rate free you from all responsibility. You must not feel in any way bound, any more than I shall. There must be full freedom on both sides. Look, here's your ring back. Give me mine.

HELMER. That too?

NORA. That too.

HELMER. There it is.

NORA. Well, that's the end of that. I'll put the keys down here. The maids know where everything is in the house — better than I do, in fact. Kristine will come in the morning after I've left to pack up the few things I brought with me from home. I want them sent on.

HELMER. The end! Nora, will you never think of me?

NORA. I dare say I'll often think about you and the children and this house.

HELMER. May I write to you, Nora?

NORA. No, never. I won't let you.

HELMER. But surely I can send you . . .

NORA. Nothing, nothing.

HELMER. Can't I help you if ever you need it?

NORA. I said "no." I don't accept things from strangers.

HELMER. Nora, can I never be anything more to you than a stranger?

NORA [*takes her bag*]. Ah, Torvald, only by a miracle of miracles. . . .

HELMER. Name it, this miracle of miracles!

NORA. Both you and I would have to change to the point where . . . Oh, Torvald, I don't believe in miracles any more.

HELMER. But I *will* believe. Name it! Change to the point where . . . ?

NORA. Where we could make a real marriage of our lives together. Goodbye!

[*She goes out through the hall door.*]

HELMER [*sinks down on a chair near the door, and covers his face with his hands*]. Nora! Nora! [*He rises and looks round.*] Empty! She's gone! [*With sudden hope.*] The miracle of miracles . . . ?

[*The heavy sound of a door being slammed is heard from below.*]

THE CURTAIN FALLS.

(1879)

Susan Glaspell *1882–1948*

TRIFLES

SCENE:

The kitchen in the now abandoned farmhouse of JOHN WRIGHT, *a gloomy kitchen, and left without having been put in order—the walls covered with a faded wallpaper. Down right is a door leading to the parlor. On the right wall above this door is a built-in kitchen cupboard with shelves in the upper portion and drawers below. In the rear wall at right, up two steps is a door opening onto stairs leading to the second floor. In the rear wall at left is a door to the shed and from there to the outside. Between these two doors is an old-fashioned black iron stove. Running along the left wall from the shed door is an old iron sink and sink shelf, in which is set a hand pump. Downstage of the sink is an uncurtained window. Near the window is an old wooden rocker. Center stage is an unpainted wooden kitchen table with straight chairs on either side. There is a small chair down right. Unwashed pans under the sink, a loaf of bread outside the breadbox, a dish towel on the table— other signs of incompleted work. At the rear the shed door opens and the* SHERIFF *comes in followed by the* COUNTY ATTORNEY *and* HALE. *The* SHERIFF *and* HALE *are men in middle life, the* COUNTY ATTORNEY *is a young man; all are much bundled up and go at once to the stove. They are followed by the two women— the* SHERIFF'S *wife,* MRS. PETERS, *first; she is a slight wiry woman, a thin nervous face.* MRS. HALE *is larger and would ordinarily be called more comfortable looking, but she is disturbed now and looks fearfully about as she enters. The women have come in slowly, and stand close together near the door.*

COUNTY ATTORNEY [*at the stove rubbing his hands*]. This feels good. Come up to the fire, ladies.

MRS. PETERS [*after taking a step forward*]. I'm not—cold.

SHERIFF [*unbuttoning his overcoat and stepping away from the stove to right of table as if to mark the beginning of official business*]. Now, Mr. Hale, before we move things about, you explain to Mr. Henderson just what you saw when you came here yesterday morning.

COUNTY ATTORNEY [*crossing down to left of the table*]. By the way, has anything been moved? Are things just as you left them yesterday?

SHERIFF [*looking about*]. It's just the same. When it dropped below zero last night I thought I'd better send Frank out this morning to make a fire for us—[*sits right of center table*] no use getting pneumonia with a big case on, but I told him not to touch anything except the stove—and you know Frank.

COUNTY ATTORNEY. Somebody should have been left here yesterday.

SHERIFF. Oh—yesterday. When I had to send Frank to Morris Center for that man who went crazy—I want you to know I had my hands full yesterday. I knew you could get back from Omaha by today and as long as I went over everything here myself—

COUNTY ATTORNEY. Well, Mr. Hale, tell just what happened when you came here yesterday morning.

HALE [*crossing down to above table*]. Harry and I had started to town with a load of potatoes. We came along the road from my place and as I got here I said, "I'm going to see if I can't get John Wright to go in with me on a party telephone." I spoke to Wright about it once before and he put me off, saying folks talked too much anyway, and all he asked was peace and quiet—I guess you know about how much he talked himself; but I thought maybe if I went to the house and talked about it before his wife, though I said to Harry that I didn't know as what his wife wanted made much difference to John—

COUNTY ATTORNEY. Let's talk about that later, Mr. Hale. I do want to talk about that, but tell now just what happened when you got to the house.

HALE. I didn't hear or see anything; I knocked at the door, and still it was all quiet inside. I knew they must be up, it was past eight o'clock. So I knocked again, and I thought I heard somebody say, "Come in." I wasn't sure, I'm not sure yet, but I opened the door—this door [*indicating the door by which the two women are still standing*] and there in that rocker—[*pointing to it*] sat Mrs. Wright. [*They all look at the rocker down left.*]

COUNTY ATTORNEY. What—what was she doing?

HALE. She was rockin' back and forth. She had her apron in her hand and was kind of—pleating it.

COUNTY ATTORNEY. And how did she—look?

HALE. Well, she looked queer.

COUNTY ATTORNEY. How do you mean—queer?

HALE. Well, as if she didn't know what she was going to do next. And kind of done up.

COUNTY ATTORNEY [*takes out notebook and pencil and sits left of center table*]. How did she seem to feel about your coming?

HALE. Why, I don't think she minded—one way or other. She didn't pay much attention. I said, "How do, Mrs. Wright, it's cold, ain't it?" And she said, "Is it?"—and went on kind of pleating at her apron. Well, I was surprised; she didn't ask me to come up to the stove, or to set down, but just sat there, not even looking at me, so I said, "I want to see John." And then she—laughed. I guess you would call it a laugh. I thought of Harry and the team outside, so I said a little sharp: "Can't I see John?" "No," she says, kind o' dull like. "Ain't he home?" says I. "Yes," says she, "he's home." "Then why can't I see him?" I asked her, out of patience. "'Cause he's dead," says she. "*Dead?*" says I. She just nodded her head, not getting a bit excited, but rockin' back and forth. "Why—where is he?" says I, not knowing what to say. She just pointed upstairs—like that. [*Himself pointing to the room above.*] I started for the stairs, with the idea of going up there. I walked from there to here—then I says, "Why, what did he die of?" "He died of a rope round his neck," says she, and just went on pleatin' at her apron. Well, I went out and called Harry. I thought I might—need help. We went upstairs and there he was lyin'—

COUNTY ATTORNEY. I think I'd rather have you go into that upstairs, where you can point it all out. Just go on now with the rest of the story.

HALE. Well, my first thought was to get that rope off. It looked . . . [*stops, his face twitches*] . . . but Harry, he went up to him, and he said, "No, he's dead all right, and we'd better not touch anything." So we went back downstairs. She was still sitting that same way. "Has anybody been notified?" I asked. "No," says she, unconcerned. "Who did this, Mrs. Wright?" said Harry. He said it business-like — and she stopped pleatin' on her apron. "I don't know," she says. "You don't *know?*" says Harry. "No," says she. "Weren't you sleepin' in the bed with him?" says Harry. "Yes," says she, "but I was on the inside." "Somebody slipped a rope round his neck and strangled him and you didn't wake up?" says Harry. "I didn't wake up," she said after him. We musta looked as if we didn't see how that could be, for after a minute she said, "I sleep sound." Harry was going to ask her more questions but I said maybe we ought to let her tell her story first to the coroner, or the sheriff, so Harry went fast as he could to Rivers' place, where there's a telephone.

COUNTY ATTORNEY. And what did Mrs. Wright do when she knew that you had gone for the coroner?

HALE. She moved from the rocker to that chair over there [*pointing to a small chair in the down right corner*] and just sat there with her hands held together and looking down. I got a feeling that I ought to make some conversation, so I said I had come in to see if John wanted to put in a telephone, and at that she started to laugh, and then she stopped and looked at me — scared. [*The* COUNTY ATTORNEY, *who has had his notebook out, makes a note.*] I dunno, maybe it wasn't scared. I wouldn't like to say it was. Soon Harry got back, and then Dr. Lloyd came, and you, Mr. Peters, and so I guess that's all I know that you don't.

COUNTY ATTORNEY [*rising and looking around*]. I guess we'll go upstairs first — and then out to the barn and around there. [*To the* SHERIFF] You're convinced that there was nothing important here — nothing that would point to any motive?

SHERIFF. Nothing here but kitchen things. [*The* COUNTY ATTORNEY, *after again looking around the kitchen, opens the door of a cupboard closet in right wall. He brings a small chair from right — gets up on it and looks on a shelf. Pulls his hand away, sticky.*]

COUNTY ATTORNEY. Here's a nice mess. [*The women draw nearer up center.*]

MRS. PETERS [*to the other woman*]. Oh, her fruit; it did freeze. [*To the* LAWYER] She worried about that when it turned so cold. She said the fire'd go out and her jars would break.

SHERIFF [*rises*]. Well, can you beat the women! Held for murder and worryin' about her preserves.

COUNTY ATTORNEY [*getting down from chair*]. I guess before we're through she may have something more serious than preserves to worry about. [*Crosses down right center.*]

HALE. Well, women are used to worrying over trifles. [*The two women move a little closer together.*]

COUNTY ATTORNEY [*with the gallantry of a young politician*]. And yet, for all their worries, what would we do without the ladies? [*The women do not unbend. He goes below the center table to the sink, takes a dipperful of water from the pail and pouring it into a basin, washes his hands. While he is doing this the* SHERIFF *and* HALE *cross to cupboard, which they inspect. The* COUNTY ATTORNEY *starts to wipe his hands on the roller towel, turns it for a cleaner place.*] Dirty towels! [*Kicks his foot against the pans under the sink.*] Not much of a housekeeper, would you say, ladies?

MRS. HALE [*stiffly*]. There's a great deal of work to be done on a farm.

COUNTY ATTORNEY. To be sure. And yet [*with a little bow to her*] I know there are some Dickson County farmhouses which do not have such roller towels. [*He gives it a pull to expose its full length again.*]

MRS. HALE. Those towels get dirty awful quick. Men's hands aren't always as clean as they might be.

COUNTY ATTORNEY. Ah, loyal to your sex, I see. But you and Mrs. Wright were neighbors. I suppose you were friends, too.

MRS. HALE [*shaking her head*]. I've not seen much of her of late years. I've not been in this house — it's more than a year.

COUNTY ATTORNEY [*crossing to women up center*]. And why was that? You didn't like her?

MRS. HALE. I liked her all well enough. Farmers' wives have their hands full, Mr. Henderson. And then —

COUNTY ATTORNEY. Yes——?

MRS. HALE [*looking about*]. It never seemed a very cheerful place.

COUNTY ATTORNEY. No — it's not cheerful. I shouldn't say she had the home-making instinct.

MRS. HALE. Well I don't know as Wright had, either.

COUNTY ATTORNEY. You mean that they didn't get on very well?

MRS. HALE. No, I don't mean anything. But I don't think a place'd be any cheerfuller for John Wright's being in it.

COUNTY ATTORNEY. I'd like to talk more of that a little later. I want to get the lay of things upstairs now. [*He goes past the women to up right where steps lead to a stair door.*]

SHERIFF. I suppose anything Mrs. Peters does'll be all right. She was to take in some clothes for her, you know, and a few little things. We left in such a hurry yesterday.

COUNTY ATTORNEY. Yes, but I would like to see what you take, Mrs. Peters, and keep an eye out for anything that might be of use to us.

MRS. PETERS. Yes, Mr. Henderson. [*The men leave by up right door to stairs. The women listen to the men's steps on the stairs, then look about the kitchen.*]

MRS. HALE [*crossing left to sink*]. I'd hate to have men coming into my kitchen, snooping around and criticizing. [*She arranges the pans under sink which the* LAWYER *had shoved out of place.*]

MRS. PETERS. Of course it's no more than their duty. [*Crosses to cupboard up right.*]

MRS. HALE. Duty's all right, but I guess that deputy sheriff that came out to make the fire might have got a little of this on. [*Gives the roller towel a pull.*] Wish I'd thought of that sooner. Seems mean to talk about her for not having things slicked up when she had to come away in such a hurry. [*Crosses right to* MRS. PETERS *at cupboard.*]

MRS. PETERS [*who has been looking through the cupboard, lifts one end of a towel that covers a pan*]. She had bread set. [*Stands still.*]

MRS. HALE [*eyes fixed on a loaf of bread beside the breadbox, which is on a low shelf of the cupboard*]. She was going to put this in there. [*Picks up loaf, then abruptly drops it. In a manner of returning to familiar things*] It's a shame about her fruit. I wonder if it's all gone. [*Gets up on the chair and looks.*] I think there's some here that's all right, Mrs. Peters. Yes — here; [*holding it toward the window*] this is cherries, too. [*Looking again.*] I declare I believe that's the only one. [*Gets down, jar in her hand. Goes to the sink and wipes it off on the outside.*] She'll feel awful bad after all her hard work in the hot weather. I remember the afternoon I put up my cherries last summer. [*She puts the jar on the big kitchen table, center of the room. With a sigh, is about to sit down in the rocking chair. Before she is seated realizes what chair it is; with a slow look at it, steps back. The chair which she has touched rocks back and forth.* MRS. PETERS *moves to center table and they both watch the chair rock for a moment or two.*]

MRS. PETERS [*shaking off the mood which the empty rocking chair has evoked. Now in a businesslike manner she speaks*]. Well, I must get those things from the front room closet. [*She goes to the door at the right, but, after looking into the other room, steps back.*] You coming with me, Mrs. Hale? You could help me carry them. [*They go in the other room; reappear,* MRS. PETERS *carrying a dress, petticoat and skirt,* MRS. HALE *following with a pair of shoes.*] My, it's cold in there. [*She puts the clothes on the big table, and hurries to the stove.*]

MRS. HALE [*right of center table examining the skirt*]. Wright was close. I think maybe that's why she kept so much to herself. She didn't even belong to the Ladies' Aid. I suppose she felt she couldn't do her part, and then you don't enjoy things when you feel shabby. I heard she used to wear pretty clothes and be lively, when she was Minnie Foster, one of the town girls singing in the choir. But that — oh, that was thirty years ago. This all you was to take in?

MRS. PETERS. She said she wanted an apron. Funny thing to want, for there isn't much to get you dirty in jail, goodness knows. But I suppose just to make her feel more natural. [*Crosses to cupboard.*] She said they was in the top drawer of this cupboard. Yes, here. And then her little shawl that always hung behind the door. [*Opens stair door and looks.*] Yes, here it is. [*Quickly shuts door leading upstairs.*]

MRS. HALE [*abruptly moving toward her*]. Mrs. Peters?

MRS. PETERS. Yes, Mrs. Hale? [*At up right door.*]

MRS. HALE. Do you think she did it?

MRS. PETERS [*in a frightened voice*]. Oh, I don't know.

MRS. HALE. Well, I don't think she did. Asking for an apron and her little shawl. Worrying about her fruit.

MRS. PETERS [*starts to speak, glances up, where footsteps are heard in the room above. In a low voice*]. Mr. Peters says it looks bad for her. Mr. Henderson is awful sarcastic in a speech and he'll make fun of her sayin' she didn't wake up.

MRS. HALE. Well, I guess John Wright didn't wake when they was slipping that rope under his neck.

MRS. PETERS [*crossing slowly to table and placing shawl and apron on table with other clothing*]. No, it's strange. It must have been done awful crafty and still. They say it was such a — funny way to kill a man, rigging it all up like that.

MRS. HALE [*crossing to left of* MRS. PETERS *at table*]. That's just what Mr. Hale said. There was a gun in the house. He says that's what he can't understand.

MRS. PETERS. Mr. Henderson said coming out that what was needed for the case was a motive; something to show anger, or — sudden feeling.

MRS. HALE [*who is standing by the table*]. Well, I don't see any signs of anger around here. [*She puts her hand on the dish towel which lies on the table, stands looking down at table, one-half of which is clean, the other half messy.*] It's wiped to here. [*Makes a move as if to finish work, then turns and looks at loaf of bread outside the breadbox. Drops towel. In that voice of coming back to familiar things*] Wonder how they are finding things upstairs. [*Crossing below table to down right.*] I hope she had it a little more red-up up there. You know, it seems kind of *sneaking*. Locking her up in town and then coming out here and trying to get her own house to turn against her!

MRS. PETERS. But, Mrs. Hale, the law is the law.

MRS. HALE. I s'pose 'tis. [*Unbuttoning her coat*] Better loosen up your things, Mrs. Peters. You won't feel them when you go out. [MRS. PETERS *takes off her fur tippet, goes to hang it on chair back left of table, stands looking at the work basket on floor near down left window.*]

MRS. PETERS. She was piecing a quilt. [*She brings the large sewing basket to the center table and they look at the bright pieces,* MRS. HALE *above the table and* MRS. PETERS *left of it.*]

MRS. HALE. It's a log cabin pattern. Pretty, isn't it? I wonder if she was goin' to quilt it or just knot it? [*Footsteps have been heard coming down the stairs. The* SHERIFF *enters followed by* HALE *and the* COUNTY ATTORNEY.]

SHERIFF. They wonder if she was going to quilt it or just knot it! [*The men laugh, the women look abashed.*]

COUNTY ATTORNEY [*rubbing his hands over the stove*]. Frank's fire didn't do much up there, did it? Well, let's go out to the barn and get that cleared up. [*The men go outside by up left door.*]

MRS. HALE [*resentfully*]. I don't know as there's anything so strange, our takin' up our time with little things while we're waiting for them to get the evidence. [*She sits in chair right of table smoothing out a block with decision.*] I don't see as it's anything to laugh about.

MRS. PETERS [*apologetically*]. Of course they've got awful important things on their minds. [*Pulls up a chair and joins* MRS. HALE *at the left of the table.*]

MRS. HALE [*examining another block*]. Mrs. Peters, look at this one. Here, this is the one she was working on, and look at the sewing! All the rest of it has been so nice and even. And look at this! It's all over the place! Why, it looks as if she didn't know what she was about! [*After she has said this they look at each other, then start to glance back at the door. After an instant* MRS. HALE *has pulled at a knot and ripped the sewing.*]

MRS. PETERS. Oh, what are you doing, Mrs. Hale?

MRS. HALE [*mildly*]. Just pulling out a stitch or two that's not sewed very good. [*Threading a needle.*] Bad sewing always made me fidgety.

MRS. PETERS [*with a glance at door, nervously*]. I don't think we ought to touch things.

MRS. HALE. I'll just finish up this end. [*Suddenly stopping and leaning forward*] Mrs. Peters?

MRS. PETERS. Yes, Mrs. Hale?

MRS. HALE. What do you suppose she was so nervous about?

MRS. PETERS. Oh — I don't know. I don't know as she was nervous. I sometimes sew awful queer when I'm just tired. [MRS. HALE *starts to say something, looks at* MRS. PETERS, *then goes on sewing.*] Well, I must get these things wrapped up. They may be through sooner than we think. [*Putting apron and other things together.*] I wonder where I can find a piece of paper, and string. [*Rises.*]

MRS. HALE. In that cupboard, maybe.

MRS. PETERS [*crosses right looking in cupboard*]. Why, here's a bird-cage. [*Holds it up.*] Did she have a bird, Mrs. Hale?

MRS. HALE. Why, I don't know whether she did or not — I've not been here for so long. There was a man around last year selling canaries cheap, but I don't know as she took one; maybe she did. She used to sing real pretty herself.

MRS. PETERS [*glancing around*]. Seems funny to think of a bird here. But she must have had one, or why would she have a cage? I wonder what happened to it?

MRS. HALE. I s'pose maybe the cat got it.

MRS. PETERS. No, she didn't have a cat. She's got that feeling some people have about cats — being afraid of them. My cat got in her room and she was real upset and asked me to take it out.

MRS. HALE. My sister Bessie was like that. Queer, ain't it?

MRS. PETERS [*examining the cage*]. Why, look at this door. It's broke. One hinge is pulled apart. [*Takes a step down to* MRS. HALE'*s right.*]

MRS. HALE [*looking too*]. Looks as if someone must have been rough with it.

MRS. PETERS. Why, yes. [*She brings the cage forward and puts it on the table.*]

MRS. HALE [*glancing toward up left door*]. I wish if they're going to find any evidence they'd be about it. I don't like this place.

MRS. PETERS. But I'm awful glad you came with me, Mrs. Hale. It would be lonesome for me setting here alone.

MRS. HALE. It would, wouldn't it? [*Dropping her sewing*] But I tell you what I do wish, Mrs. Peters. I wish I had come over sometimes when *she* was here. I — [*looking around the room*] — wish I had.

MRS. PETERS. But of course you were awful busy, Mrs. Hale — your house and your children.

MRS. HALE [*rises and crosses left*]. I could've come. I stayed away because it weren't cheerful — and that's why I ought to have come. I — [*looking out left window*] — I've never liked this place. Maybe because it's down in a hollow and you don't see the road. I dunno what it is, but it's a lonesome place and always was. I wish I had come over to see Minnie Foster sometimes. I can see now——[*Shakes her head.*]

MRS. PETERS [*left of table and above it*]. Well, you mustn't reproach yourself, Mrs. Hale. Somehow we just don't see how it is with other folks until — something turns up.

MRS. HALE. Not having children makes less work — but it makes a quiet house, and Wright out to work all day, and no company when he did come in. [*Turning from window*] Did you know John Wright, Mrs. Peters?

MRS. PETERS. Not to know him; I've seen him in town. They say he was a good man.

MRS. HALE. Yes — good; he didn't drink, and kept his word as well as most, I guess, and paid his debts. But he was a hard man, Mrs. Peters. Just to pass the time of day with him——[*Shivers.*] Like a raw wind that gets to the bone. [*Pauses, her eye falling on the cage.*] I should think she woulda wanted a bird. But what do you suppose went wrong with it?

MRS. PETERS. I don't know, unless it got sick and died. [*She reaches over and swings the broken door, swings it again, both women watch it.*]

MRS. HALE. You weren't raised round here, were you? [MRS. PETERS *shakes her head.*] You didn't know — her?

MRS. PETERS. Not till they brought her yesterday.

MRS. HALE. She — come to think of it, she was kind of like a bird herself — real sweet and pretty, but kind of timid and — fluttery. How — she — did —

change. [*Silence; then as if struck by a happy thought and relieved to get back to everyday things. Crosses right above* MRS. PETERS *to cupboard, replaces small chair used to stand on to its original place down right.*] Tell you what, Mrs. Peters, why don't you take the quilt in with you? It might take up her mind.

MRS. PETERS. Why, I think that's a real nice idea, Mrs. Hale. There couldn't possibly be any objection to it, could there? Now, just what would I take? I wonder if her patches are in here—and her things. [*They look in the sewing basket.*]

MRS. HALE [*crosses to right of table*]. Here's some red. I expect this has got sewing things in it. [*Brings out a fancy box.*] What a pretty box. Looks like something somebody would give you. Maybe her scissors are in here. [*Opens box. Suddenly puts her hand to her nose.*] Why——[MRS. PETERS *bends nearer, then turns her face away.*] There's something wrapped up in this piece of silk.

MRS. PETERS. Why, this isn't her scissors.

MRS. HALE [*lifting the silk*]. Oh, Mrs. Peters—it's——[MRS. PETERS *bends closer.*]

MRS. PETERS. It's the bird.

MRS. HALE. But, Mrs. Peters—look at it! Its neck! Look at its neck! It's all—other side *to*.

MRS. PETERS. Somebody—wrung—its—neck. [*Their eyes meet. A look of growing comprehension, of horror. Steps are heard outside.* MRS. HALE *slips box under quilt pieces, and sinks into her chair. Enter* SHERIFF *and* COUNTY ATTORNEY. MRS. PETERS *steps down left and stands looking out of window.*]

COUNTY ATTORNEY [*as one turning from serious things to little pleasantries*]. Well, ladies, have you decided whether she was going to quilt it or knot it? [*Crosses to center above table.*]

MRS. PETERS. We think she was going to—knot it. [SHERIFF *crosses to right of stove, lifts stove lid and glances at fire, then stands warming hands at stove.*]

COUNTY ATTORNEY. Well, that's interesting, I'm sure. [*Seeing the bird-cage.*] Has the bird flown?

MRS. HALE [*putting more quilt pieces over the box*]. We think the—cat got it.

COUNTY ATTORNEY [*preoccupied*]. Is there a cat? [MRS. HALE *glances in a quick covert way at* MRS. PETERS.]

MRS. PETERS [*turning from window takes a step in*]. Well, not *now*. They're superstitious, you know. They leave.

COUNTY ATTORNEY [*to* SHERIFF PETERS, *continuing an interrupted conversation*]. No sign at all of anyone having come from the outside. Their own rope. Now let's go up again and go over it piece by piece. [*They start upstairs.*] It would have to have been someone who knew just the——[MRS. PETERS *sits down left of table. The two women sit there not looking at one another, but as if peering into something and at the same time holding back. When they talk now it is in the manner of feeling their way over strange ground, as if afraid of what they are saying, but as if they cannot help saying it.*]

MRS. HALE [*hesitatively and in hushed voice*]. She liked the bird. She was going to bury it in that pretty box.

MRS. PETERS [*in a whisper*]. When I was a girl—my kitten—there was a boy took a hatchet, and before my eyes—and before I could get there——[*Covers her face an instant.*] If they hadn't held me back I would have—[*catches herself, looks upstairs where steps are heard, falters weakly*]—hurt him.

MRS. HALE [*with a slow look around her*]. I wonder how it would seem never to have had any children around. [*Pause.*] No, Wright wouldn't like the bird — a thing that sang. She used to sing. He killed that, too.

MRS. PETERS [*moving uneasily*]. We don't know who killed the bird.

MRS. HALE. I knew John Wright.

MRS. PETERS. It was an awful thing done in this house that night, Mrs. Hale. Killing a man while he slept, slipping a rope around his neck that choked the life out of him.

MRS. HALE. His neck. Choked the life out of him. [*Her hand goes out and rests on the bird-cage.*]

MRS. PETERS [*with rising voice*]. We don't know who killed him. We don't *know.*

MRS. HALE [*her own feeling not interrupted*]. If there'd been years and years of nothing, then a bird to sing to you, it would be awful — still, after the bird was still.

MRS. PETERS [*something within her speaking*]. I know what stillness is. When we homesteaded in Dakota, and my first baby died — after he was two years old, and me with no other then —

MRS. HALE [*moving*]. How soon do you suppose they'll be through looking for the evidence?

MRS. PETERS. I know what stillness is. [*Pulling herself back.*] The law has got to punish crime, Mrs. Hale.

MRS. HALE [*not as if answering that*]. I wish you'd seen Minnie Foster when she wore a white dress with blue ribbons and stood up there in the choir and sang. [*A look around the room.*] Oh, I *wish* I'd come over here once in a while! That was a crime! That was a crime! Who's going to punish that?

MRS. PETERS [*looking upstairs*]. We mustn't — take on.

MRS. HALE. I might have known she needed help! I know how things can be — for women. I tell you, it's queer, Mrs. Peters. We live close together and we live far apart. We all go through the same things — it's all just a different kind of the same thing. [*Brushes her eyes, noticing the jar of fruit, reaches out for it.*] If I was you I wouldn't tell her her fruit was gone. Tell her it *ain't.* Tell her it's all right. Take this in to prove it to her. She — she may never know whether it was broke or not.

MRS. PETERS [*takes the jar, looks about for something to wrap it in; takes petticoat from the clothes brought from the other room, very nervously begins winding this around the jar. In a false voice*]. My, it's a good thing the men couldn't hear us. Wouldn't they just laugh! Getting all stirred up over a little thing like a — dead canary. As if that could have anything to do with — with — wouldn't they *laugh!* [*The men are heard coming downstairs.*]

MRS. HALE [*under her breath*]. Maybe they would — maybe they wouldn't.

COUNTY ATTORNEY. No, Peters, it's all perfectly clear except a reason for doing it. But you know juries when it comes to women. If there was some definite thing. [*Crosses slowly to above table.* SHERIFF *crosses down right.* MRS. HALE *and* MRS. PETERS *remain seated at either side of table.*] Something to show — something to make a story about — a thing that would connect up with this strange way of doing it——[*The women's eyes meet for an instant. Enter* HALE *from outer door.*]

HALE [*remaining up left by door*]. Well, I've got the team around. Pretty cold out there.

COUNTY ATTORNEY. I'm going to stay awhile by myself. [*To the* SHERIFF] You can send Frank out for me, can't you? I want to go over everything. I'm not satisfied that we can't do better.

SHERIFF. Do you want to see what Mrs. Peters is going to take in? [*The* LAWYER *picks up the apron, laughs.*]

COUNTY ATTORNEY. Oh, I guess they're not very dangerous things the ladies have picked out. [*Moves a few things about, disturbing the quilt pieces which cover the box. Steps back.*] No, Mrs. Peters doesn't need supervising. For that matter a sheriff's wife is married to the law. Ever think of it that way, Mrs. Peters?

MRS. PETERS. Not—just that way.

SHERIFF [*chuckling*]. Married to the law. [*Moves to down right door to the other room.*] I just want you to come in here a minute, George. We ought to take a look at these windows.

COUNTY ATTORNEY [*scoffingly*]. Oh, windows!

SHERIFF. We'll be right out, Mr. Hale. (HALE *goes outside. The* SHERIFF *follows the* COUNTY ATTORNEY *into the other room. Then* MRS. HALE *rises, hands tight together, looking intensely at* MRS. PETERS, *whose eyes make a slow turn, finally meeting* MRS. HALE'*s. A moment* MRS. HALE *holds her, then her own eyes point the way to where the box is concealed. Suddenly* MRS. PETERS *throws back quilt pieces and tries to put the box in the bag she is carrying. It is too big. She opens box, starts to take bird out, cannot touch it, goes to pieces, stands there helpless. Sound of a knob turning in the other room.* MRS. HALE *snatches the box and puts it in the pocket of her big coat. Enter* COUNTY ATTORNEY *and* SHERIFF, *who remains down right.*]

COUNTY ATTORNEY [*crosses to up left door facetiously*]. Well, Henry, at least we found out that she was not going to quilt it. She was going to—what is it you call it, ladies?

MRS. HALE [*standing center below table facing front, her hand against her pocket*]. We call it—knot it, Mr. Henderson.

CURTAIN

(1916)

Edward Albee *1928–*

THE AMERICAN DREAM
A PLAY IN ONE SCENE

For David Diamond

THE PLAYERS:

MOMMY.
DADDY.
GRANDMA.

MRS. BARKER.
YOUNG MAN.

THE SCENE:

A living room. Two armchairs, one toward either side of the stage, facing each other diagonally out toward the audience. Against the rear wall, a sofa. A door, leading out from the apartment, in the rear wall, far stage-right. An archway, leading to other rooms, in the side wall, stage-left.

At the beginning, MOMMY *and* DADDY *are seated in the armchairs,* DADDY *in the armchair stage-left,* MOMMY *in the other. Curtain up. A silence. Then:*

MOMMY. I don't know what can be keeping them.

DADDY. They're late, naturally.

MOMMY. Of course, they're late; it never fails.

DADDY. That's the way things are today, and there's nothing you can do about it.

MOMMY. You're quite right.

DADDY. When we took this apartment, they were quick enough to have me sign the lease; they were quick enough to take my check for two months' rent in advance. . . .

MOMMY. And one month's security . . .

DADDY. . . . and one month's security. They were quick enough to check my references; they were quick enough about all that. But now! But now, try to get the icebox fixed, try to get the doorbell fixed, try to get the leak in the johnny fixed! Just try it . . . they aren't so quick about *that*.

MOMMY. Of course not; it never fails. People think they can get away with anything these days . . . and, of course they can. I went to buy a new hat yesterday.

[*Pause.*]

I said, I went to buy a new hat yesterday.

DADDY. Oh! Yes . . . yes.

MOMMY. Pay attention.

DADDY. I *am* paying attention, Mommy.

MOMMY. Well, be sure you do.

DADDY. Oh, I am.

MOMMY. All right, Daddy; now listen.

DADDY. I'm listening, Mommy.

MOMMY. You're sure!

DADDY. Yes . . . yes, I'm sure, I'm all ears.

MOMMY [*Giggles at the thought; then*]. All right, now. I went to buy a new hat yesterday and I said, "I'd like a new hat, please." And so, they showed me a few hats, green ones and blue ones, and I didn't like any of them, not one bit. What did I say? What did I just say?

DADDY. You didn't like any of them, not one bit.

MOMMY. That's right; you just keep paying attention. And then they showed me one that I did like. It was a lovely little hat, and I said, "Oh, this is a lovely little hat; I'll take this hat; oh my, it's lovely. What color is it?" And they said, "Why, this is beige; isn't it a lovely little beige hat?" And I said, "Oh, it's just lovely." And so, I bought it.

[*Stops, looks at* DADDY]

DADDY [*To show he is paying attention*]. And so you bought it.

MOMMY. And so I bought it, and I walked out of the store with the hat right on my head, and I ran spang into the chairman of our woman's club, and she said, "Oh, my dear, isn't that a lovely little hat? Where did you get that lovely little hat? It's the loveliest little hat; I've always wanted a wheat-colored hat *myself*." And, I said, "Why, no, my dear; this hat is beige; beige." And she laughed and said, "Why no, my dear, that's a wheat-colored hat . . . wheat. I know beige from wheat." And I said, "Well, my dear, I know beige from wheat, too." What did I say? What did I just say?

DADDY [*Tonelessly*]. Well, my dear, I know beige from wheat, too.

MOMMY. That's right. And she laughed, and she said, "Well, my dear, they certainly put one over on you. That's wheat if I ever saw wheat. But it's lovely, just the same." And then she walked off. She's a dreadful woman, you don't know her; she has dreadful taste, two dreadful children, a dreadful house, and an absolutely adorable husband who sits in a wheel chair all the time. You don't know him. You don't know anybody, do you? She's just a dreadful woman, but she *is* chairman of our woman's club, so naturally I'm terribly fond of her. So, I went right back into the hat shop, and I said, "Look here; what do you mean selling me a hat that you say is beige, when it's wheat all the time . . . wheat! I can tell beige from wheat any day in the week, but not in this artificial light of yours." They have artificial light, Daddy.

DADDY. Have they!

MOMMY. And I said, "The minute I got outside I could tell that it wasn't a beige hat at all; it was a wheat hat." And they said to me, "How could you tell that when you had the hat on the top of your head?" Well, that made me angry, and so I made a scene right there; I screamed as hard as I could; I took my hat off and I threw it down on the counter, and oh, I made a terrible scene. I said, I made a terrible scene.

DADDY [*Snapping to*]. Yes . . . yes . . . good for you!

MOMMY. And I made an absolutely terrible scene; and they became frightened, and they said, "Oh, madam; oh, madam." But I kept right on, and finally they admitted that they might have made a mistake; so they took my hat into the back, and then they came out again with a hat that looked exactly like it. I took one look at it, and I said, "This hat is wheat-colored; wheat." Well, of course, they said, "Oh, no, madam, this hat is beige; you go outside and see." So, I went outside, and lo and behold, it *was* beige. So I bought it.

DADDY [*Clearing his throat*]. I would imagine that it was the same hat they tried to sell you before.

MOMMY [*With a little laugh*]. Well, of course it was!

DADDY. That's the way things are today; you just can't get satisfaction; you just try.

MOMMY. Well, *I* got satisfaction.

DADDY. That's right, Mommy. *You did* get satisfaction, didn't you?

MOMMY. Why are they so late? I don't know what can be keeping them.

DADDY. I've been trying for two weeks to have the leak in the johnny fixed.

MOMMY. You can't get satisfaction; just try. *I* can get satisfaction, but you can't.

DADDY. I've been trying for two weeks and it isn't so much for my sake; I can always go to the club.

MOMMY. It isn't so much for my sake, either; I can always go shopping.

DADDY. It's really for Grandma's sake.

MOMMY. Of course it's for Grandma's sake. Grandma cries every time she goes to the johnny as it is; but now that it doesn't work it's even worse, it makes Grandma think she's getting feeble-headed.

DADDY. Grandma *is* getting feeble-headed.

MOMMY. Of course Grandma is getting feeble-headed, but not about her johnny-do's.

DADDY. No; that's true. I must have it fixed.

MOMMY. WHY are they so late? I don't know what can be keeping them.

DADDY. When they came here the first time, they were ten minutes early; they were quick enough about it then.

[*Enter* GRANDMA *from the archway, stage left. She is loaded down with boxes, large and small, neatly wrapped and tied.*]

MOMMY. Why Grandma, look at you! What *is* all that you're carrying?

GRANDMA. They're boxes. What do they look like?

MOMMY. Daddy! Look at Grandma; look at all the boxes she's carrying!

DADDY. My Goodness, Grandma; look at all those boxes.

GRANDMA. Where'll I put them?

MOMMY. Heavens! I don't know. Whatever are they for?

GRANDMA. That's nobody's damn business.

MOMMY. Well, in that case, put them down next to Daddy; there.

GRANDMA [*Dumping the boxes down, on and around* DADDY'*s feet*]. I sure wish you'd get the john fixed.

DADDY. Oh, I do wish they'd come and fix it. We hear you . . . for hours . . . whimpering away. . . .

MOMMY. Daddy! What a terrible thing to say to Grandma!

GRANDMA. Yeah. For shame, talking to me that way.

DADDY. I'm sorry, Grandma.

MOMMY. Daddy's sorry, Grandma.

GRANDMA. Well, all right. In that case I'll go get the rest of the boxes. I suppose I deserve being talked to that way. I've gotten so old. Most people think that when you get so old, you either freeze to death, or you burn up. But you don't. When you get so old, all that happens is that people talk to you that way.

DADDY [*Contrite*]. I said I'm sorry, Grandma.

MOMMY. Daddy said he was sorry.

GRANDMA. Well, that's all that counts. People being sorry. Makes you feel better; gives you a sense of dignity, and that's all that's important . . . a sense of dignity. And it doesn't matter if you don't care, or not, either. You got to have a sense of dignity, even if you don't care, 'cause, if you don't have that, civilization's doomed.

MOMMY. You've been reading my book club selections again!

DADDY. How dare you read Mommy's book club selections, Grandma!

GRANDMA. Because I'm old! When you're old you gotta do something. When you get old, you can't talk to people because people snap at you. When you get so old, people talk to you that way. That's why you become deaf, so you won't be able to hear people talking to you that way. And that's why you go and hide under the covers in the big soft bed, so you won't feel the house shaking from people talking to you that way. That's why old people die, eventually. People talk to them that way. I've got to go and get the rest of the boxes.

[GRANDMA *exits*]

DADDY. Poor Grandma, I didn't mean to hurt her.

MOMMY. Don't you worry about it; Grandma doesn't know what she means.

DADDY. She knows what she says, though.

MOMMY. Don't you worry about it; she won't know that soon. I love Grandma.

DADDY. I love her, too. Look how nicely she wrapped these boxes.

MOMMY. Grandma has always wrapped boxes nicely. When I was a little girl, I was very poor, and Grandma was very poor, too, because Grandpa was in heaven. And every day, when I went to school, Grandma used to wrap a box for me, and I used to take it with me to school; and when it was lunchtime, all the little boys and girls used to take out their boxes of lunch, and they weren't wrapped nicely at all, and they used to open them and eat their chicken legs and chocolate cakes; and I used to say, "Oh, look at my lovely lunch box; it's so nicely wrapped it would break my heart to open it." And so, I wouldn't open it.

DADDY. Because it was empty.

MOMMY. Oh no. Grandma always filled it up, because she never ate the dinner she cooked the evening before; she gave me all her food for my lunch box the next day. After school, I'd take the box back to Grandma, and she'd open it and eat the chicken legs and chocolate cake that was inside. Grandma used to say, "I love day-old cake." That's where the expression day-old cake came from. Grandma always ate everything a day late. I used to eat all the other little boys' and girls' food at school, because they thought my lunch box was empty. They thought my lunch box was empty, and that's why I wouldn't open it. They thought I suffered from the sin of pride, and since that made them better than me, they were very generous.

DADDY. You were a very deceitful little girl.

MOMMY. We were very poor! But then I married you, Daddy, and now we're very rich.

DADDY. Grandma isn't rich.

MOMMY. No, but you've been so good to Grandma she feels rich. She doesn't know you'd like to put her in a nursing home.

DADDY. I wouldn't!

MOMMY. Well, heaven knows, *I* would! I can't stand it, watching her do the cooking and the housework, polishing the silver, moving the furniture. . . .

DADDY. She likes to do that. She says it's the least she can do to earn her keep.

MOMMY. Well, she's right. You can't live off people. I can live off you, because I married you. And aren't you lucky all I brought with me was Grandma. A lot of women I know would have brought their whole families to live off you. All I brought was Grandma. Grandma is all the family I have.

DADDY. I feel very fortunate.

MOMMY. You should. I have a right to live off of you because I married you, and because I used to let you get on top of me and bump your uglies; and I have a right to all your money when you die. And when you do, Grandma and I can live by ourselves . . . if she's still here. Unless you have her put away in a nursing home.

DADDY. I have no intention of putting her in a nursing home.

MOMMY. Well, I wish somebody would do something with her!

DADDY. At any rate, you're very well provided for.

MOMMY. You're my sweet Daddy; that's very nice.

DADDY. I love my Mommy.

[*Enter* GRANDMA *again, laden with more boxes*]

GRANDMA [*Dumping the boxes on and around* DADDY's *feet*]. There; that's the lot of them.

DADDY. They're wrapped so nicely.

GRANDMA [*to* DADDY]. You won't get on my sweet side that way. . . .

MOMMY. Grandma!

GRANDMA. . . . telling me how nicely I wrap boxes. Not after what you said: how I whimpered for hours. . . .

MOMMY. Grandma!

GRANDMA [*to* MOMMY]. Shut up!

[*To* DADDY]

You don't have any feelings, that's what's wrong with you. Old people make all sorts of noises, half of them they can't help. Old people whimper, and cry, and belch, and make great hollow rumbling sounds at the table; old people wake up in the middle of the night screaming, and find out they haven't even been asleep; and when old people *are* asleep, they try to wake up, and they can't . . . not for the longest time.

MOMMY. Homilies, homilies!

GRANDMA. And there's more, too.

DADDY. I'm really very sorry, Grandma.

GRANDMA. I know you are, Daddy; it's Mommy over there makes all the trouble. If you'd listened to me, you wouldn't have married her in the first place. She was a tramp and a trollop and a trull to boot, and she's no better now.

MOMMY. Grandma!

GRANDMA [*to* MOMMY]. Shut up!

[*To* DADDY]

When she was no more than eight years old she used to climb up on my lap and say, in a sickening little voice, "When I gwo up, I'm going to mahwy a wich old man; I'm going to set my wittle were end right down in a tub o' butter, that's what I'm going to do." And I warned you, Daddy; I told you to stay away from her type. I told you to. I did.

MOMMY. You stop that! You're my mother, not his!

GRANDMA. I am?

DADDY. That's right, Grandma. Mommy's right.

GRANDMA. Well, how would you expect somebody as old as I am to remember a thing like that? You don't make allowances for people. I want an allowance. I want an allowance!

DADDY. All right, Grandma; I'll see to it.

MOMMY. Grandma! I'm ashamed of you.

GRANDMA. Humf! It's a fine time to say that. You should have gotten rid of me a long time ago if that's the way you feel. You should have had Daddy set me up in business somewhere. . . . I could have gone into the fur business, or I could have been a singer. But no; not you. You wanted me around so you could sleep in my room when Daddy got fresh. But now it isn't important, because Daddy doesn't want to get fresh with you any more, and I don't blame him. You'd rather sleep with me, wouldn't you, Daddy?

MOMMY. Daddy doesn't want to sleep with anyone. Daddy's been sick.

DADDY. I've been sick. I don't even want to sleep in the apartment.

MOMMY. See? I told you.

DADDY. I just want to get everything over with.

MOMMY. That's right. Why are they so late? Why can't they get here on time?

GRANDMA [*An owl*]. Who? Who? . . . Who? Who?

MOMMY. You know, Grandma.

GRANDMA. No, I don't.

MOMMY. Well, it doesn't really matter whether you do or not.

DADDY. Is that true?

MOMMY. Oh, more or less. Look how pretty Grandma wrapped these boxes.

GRANDMA. I didn't really like wrapping them; it hurt my fingers, and it frightened me. But it had to be done.

MOMMY. Why, Grandma?

GRANDMA. None of your damn business.

MOMMY. Go to bed.

GRANDMA. I don't want to go to bed. I just got up. I want to stay here and watch. Besides . . .

MOMMY. Go to bed.

DADDY. Let her stay up, Mommy; it isn't noon yet.

GRANDMA. I want to watch; besides . . .

DADDY. Let her watch, Mommy.

MOMMY. Well all right, you can watch; but don't you dare say a word.

GRANDMA. Old people are very good at listening; old people don't like to talk; old people have colitis and lavender perfume. Now I'm going to be quiet.

DADDY. She never mentioned she wanted to be a singer.

MOMMY. Oh, I forgot to tell you, but it was ages ago.

[*The doorbell rings*]

Oh, goodness! Here they are!

GRANDMA. Who? Who?

MOMMY. Oh, just some people.

GRANDMA. The van people? Is it the van people? Have you finally done it? Have you called the van people to come and take me away?

DADDY. Of course not, Grandma!

GRANDMA. Oh, don't be too sure. She'd have you carted off too, if she thought she could get away with it.

MOMMY. Pay no attention to her, Daddy.
[*An aside to* GRANDMA]
  My God, you're ungrateful!
[*The doorbell rings again*]
DADDY [*Wringing his hands*]. Oh dear; oh dear.
MOMMY [*Still to* GRANDMA]. Just you wait; I'll fix your wagon.
[*Now to* DADDY]
  Well, go let them in Daddy. What are you waiting for?
DADDY. I think we should talk about it some more. Maybe we've been
  hasty . . . a little hasty, perhaps.
[*Doorbell rings again*]
  I'd like to talk about it some more.
MOMMY. There's no need. You made up your mind; you were firm; you were
  masculine and decisive.
DADDY. We might consider the pros and the . . .
MOMMY. I won't argue with you; it has to be done; you were right. Open the
  door.
DADDY. But I'm not sure that . . .
MOMMY. Open the door.
DADDY. Was I firm about it?
MOMMY. Oh, so firm; so firm.
DADDY. And was I decisive?
MOMMY. SO decisive! Oh, I shivered.
DADDY. And masculine? Was I really masculine?
MOMMY. Oh, Daddy, you were so masculine; I shivered and fainted.
GRANDMA. Shivered and fainted, did she? Humf!
MOMMY. You be quiet.
GRANDMA. Old people have a right to talk to themselves; it doesn't hurt the
  gums, and it's comforting.
[*Doorbell rings again*]
DADDY. I shall now open the door.
MOMMY. WHAT a masculine Daddy! Isn't he a masculine Daddy?
GRANDMA. Don't expect me to say anything. Old people are obscene.
MOMMY. Some of your opinions aren't so bad. You know that?
DADDY [*Backing off from the door*]. Maybe we can send them away.
MOMMY. Oh, look at you! You're turning into jelly; you're indecisive; you're a
  woman.
DADDY. All right. Watch me now; I'm going to open the door. Watch. Watch!
MOMMY. We're watching; we're watching.
GRANDMA. *I'm* not.
DADDY. Watch now; it's opening.
[*He opens the door*]
  It's open!

[MRS. BARKER *steps into the room*]
  Here they are!
MOMMY. Here they are!
GRANDMA. Where?
DADDY. Come in. You're late. But, of course, we expected you to be late; we
  were saying that we expected you to be late.
MOMMY. Daddy, don't be rude! We were saying that you just can't get satisfac-

tion these days, and we were talking about you, of course. Won't you come in?

MRS. BARKER. Thank you. I don't mind if I do.

MOMMY. We're very glad that you're here, late as you are. You do remember us, don't you? You were here once before. I'm Mommy, and this is Daddy, and that's Grandma, doddering there in the corner.

MRS. BARKER. Hello, Mommy; hello, Daddy; and hello there, Grandma.

DADDY. Now that you're here, I don't suppose you could go away and maybe come back some other time.

MRS. BARKER. Oh no; we're much too efficient for that. I said, hello there, Grandma.

MOMMY. Speak to them, Grandma.

GRANDMA. I don't see them.

DADDY. For shame, Grandma; they're here.

MRS. BARKER. Yes, we're here, Grandma. I'm Mrs. Barker. I remember you; don't you remember me?

GRANDMA. I don't recall. Maybe you were younger, or something.

MOMMY. Grandma! What a terrible thing to say!

MRS. BARKER. Oh now, don't scold her, Mommy; for all she knows she may be right.

DADDY. Uh . . . Mrs. Barker, is it? Won't you sit down?

MRS. BARKER. I don't mind if I do.

MOMMY. Would you like a cigarette, and a drink, and would you like to cross your legs?

MRS. BARKER. You forget yourself, Mommy; I'm a professional woman. But I will cross my legs.

DADDY. Yes, make yourself comfortable.

MRS. BARKER. I don't mind if I do.

GRANDMA. Are they still here?

MOMMY. Be quiet, Grandma.

MRS. BARKER. Oh, we're still here. My, what an unattractive apartment you have!

MOMMY. Yes, but you don't know what a trouble it is. Let me tell you . . .

DADDY. I was saying to Mommy . . .

MRS. BARKER. Yes, I know. I was listening outside.

DADDY. About the icebox, and . . . the doorbell . . . and the . . .

MRS. BARKER. . . . and the johnny. Yes, we're very efficient; we have to know everything in our work.

DADDY. Exactly what do you do?

MOMMY. Yes, what is your work?

MRS. BARKER. Well, my dear, for one thing, I'm chairman of your woman's club.

MOMMY. Don't be ridiculous. I was talking to the chairman of my woman's club just yester— Why, so you are. You remember, Daddy, the lady I was telling you about? The lady with the husband who sits in the *swing?* Don't you remember?

DADDY. No . . . no. . . .

MOMMY. Of course you do. I'm sorry, Mrs. Barker. I would have known you anywhere, except in this artificial light. And look! You have a hat just like the one I bought yesterday.

MRS. BARKER [*With a little laugh*]. No, not really; this hat is cream.

MOMMY. Well, my dear, that may look like a cream hat to you, but I can . . .

MRS. BARKER. Now, now; you seem to forget who I am.

MOMMY. Yes, I do, don't I? Are you sure you're comfortable? Won't you take off your dress?

MRS. BARKER. I don't mind if I do.

[*She removes her dress*]

MOMMY. There. You must feel a great deal more comfortable.

MRS. BARKER. Well, I certainly *look* a great deal more comfortable.

DADDY. I'm going to blush and giggle.

MOMMY. Daddy's going to blush and giggle.

MRS. BARKER [*Pulling the hem of her slip above her knees*]. You're lucky to have such a man for a husband.

MOMMY. Oh, don't I know it!

DADDY. I just blushed and giggled and went sticky wet.

MOMMY. Isn't Daddy a caution, Mrs. Barker?

MRS. BARKER. Maybe if I smoked . . . ?

MOMMY. Oh, that isn't necessary.

MRS. BARKER. I don't mind if I do.

MOMMY. No; no, don't. Really.

MRS. BARKER. I don't mind. . . .

MOMMY. I won't have you smoking in my house, and that's that! You're a professional woman.

DADDY. Grandma drinks AND smokes; don't you Grandma?

GRANDMA. No.

MOMMY. Well, now, Mrs. Barker; suppose you tell us why you're here.

GRANDMA [*as* MOMMY *walks through the boxes*]. The boxes . . . the boxes . . .

MOMMY. Be quiet, Grandma.

DADDY. What did you say, Grandma?

GRANDMA [*as* MOMMY *steps on several of the boxes*]. The boxes, damn it!

MRS. BARKER. Boxes; she said boxes. She mentioned the boxes.

DADDY. What about the boxes, Grandma? Maybe Mrs. Barker is here because of the boxes. Is that what you meant, Grandma?

GRANDMA. I don't know if that's what I meant or not. It's certainly not what I *thought* I meant.

DADDY. Grandma is of the opinion that . . .

MRS. BARKER. Can we assume that the boxes are for us? I mean, can we assume that you had us come here for the boxes?

MOMMY. Are you in the habit of receiving boxes?

DADDY. A very good question.

MRS. BARKER. Well, that would depend on the reason we're here. I've got my fingers in so many little pies, you know. Now, I can think of one of my little activities in which we are in the habit of receiving *baskets;* but more in a literary sense than really. We *might* receive boxes, though, under very special circumstances. I'm afraid that's the best answer I can give you.

DADDY. It's a very interesting answer.

MRS. BARKER. *I* thought so. But, does it help?

MOMMY. No; I'm afraid not.

DADDY. I wonder if it might help us any if I said I feel misgivings, that I have definite qualms.

MOMMY. Where, Daddy?

DADDY. Well, mostly right here, right around where the stitches were.

MOMMY. Daddy had an operation, you know.

MRS. BARKER. Oh, you poor Daddy! I didn't know; but then, how could I?

GRANDMA. You might have asked; it wouldn't have hurt you.

MOMMY. Dry up, Grandma.

GRANDMA. There you go. Letting your true feelings come out. Old people aren't dry enough, I suppose. My sacks are empty, the fluid in my eyeballs is all caked on the inside edges, my spine is made of sugar candy, I breathe ice; but you don't hear me complain. Nobody hears old people complain because people think that's all old people do. And *that's* because old people are gnarled and sagged and twisted into the shape of a complaint.

[*Signs off*]

That's all.

MRS. BARKER. What was wrong, Daddy?

DADDY. Well, you know how it is: the doctors took out something that was there and put in something that wasn't there. An operation.

MRS. BARKER. You're very fortunate, I should say.

MOMMY. Oh, he is; he is. All his life, Daddy has wanted to be a United States Senator; but now . . . why now he's changed his mind, and for the rest of his life he's going to want to be Governor . . . it would be nearer the apartment, you know.

MRS. BARKER. You *are* fortunate, Daddy.

DADDY. Yes, indeed; except that I get these qualms now and then, definite ones.

MRS. BARKER. Well, it's just a matter of things settling; you're like an old house.

MOMMY. Why Daddy, thank Mrs. Barker.

DADDY. Thank you.

MRS. BARKER. Ambition! That's the ticket. I have a brother who's very much like you, Daddy . . . ambitious. Of course, he's a great deal younger than you; he's even younger than I am . . . if such a thing is possible. He runs a little newspaper. Just a little newspaper . . . but he runs it. He's chief cook and bottle washer of that little newspaper, which he calls *The Village Idiot*. He has such a sense of humor; he's so self-deprecating, so modest. And he'd never admit it himself, but he *is* the Village Idiot.

MOMMY. Oh, I think that's just grand. Don't you think so, Daddy?

DADDY. Yes, just grand.

MRS. BARKER. My brother's a dear man, and he has a dear little wife, whom he loves, dearly. He loves her so much he just can't get a sentence out without mentioning her. He wants everybody to know he's married. He's really a stickler on that point; he can't be introduced to anybody and say hello without adding, "Of course, I'm married." As far as I'm concerned, he's the chief exponent of Woman Love in this whole country; he's even been written up in psychiatric journals because of it.

DADDY. Indeed!

MOMMY. Isn't that lovely.

MRS. BARKER. Oh, I think so. There's too much woman hatred in this country, and that's a fact.

GRANDMA. Oh, I don't know.

MOMMY. Oh, I think that's just grand. Don't you think so, Daddy?

DADDY. Yes, just grand.

GRANDMA. In case anybody's interested . . .

MOMMY. Be quiet, Grandma.

GRANDMA. Nuts!

MOMMY. Oh, Mrs. Barker, you *must* forgive Grandma. She's rural.

MRS. BARKER. I don't mind if I do.

DADDY. Maybe Grandma has something to say.

MOMMY. Nonsense. Old people have nothing to say; and if old people *did* have something to say, nobody would listen to them.

[*To* GRANDMA]

You see? I can pull that stuff just as easy as you can.

GRANDMA. Well, you got the rhythm, but you don't really have the quality. Besides, you're middle-aged.

MOMMY. I'm proud of it!

GRANDMA. Look. I'll show you how it's really done. Middle-aged people think they can do anything, but the truth is that middle-aged people can't do most things as well as they used to. Middle-aged people think they're special because they're like everybody else. We live in the age of deformity. You see? Rhythm *and* content. You'll learn.

DADDY. I do wish I weren't surrounded by women; I'd like some men around here.

MRS. BARKER. You can say that again!

GRANDMA. I don't hardly count as a woman, so can I say my piece?

MOMMY. Go on. Jabber away.

GRANDMA. It's very simple; the fact is, these boxes don't have anything to do with why this good lady is come to call. Now, if you're interested in knowing why these boxes *are* here . . .

DADDY. I'm sure that must be all very true, Grandma, but what does it have to do with why . . . pardon me, what is that name again?

MRS. BARKER. Mrs. Barker.

DADDY. Exactly. What does it have to do with why . . . that name again?

MRS. BARKER. Mrs. Barker.

DADDY. Precisely. What does it have to do with why what's-her-name is here?

MOMMY. They're here because we asked them.

MRS. BARKER. Yes. That's why.

GRANDMA. Now if you're interested in knowing why these boxes *are* here . . .

MOMMY. Well, nobody *is* interested!

GRANDMA. You can be as snippety as you like for all the good it'll do you.

DADDY. You two will have to stop arguing.

MOMMY. I don't argue with her.

DADDY. It will just have to stop.

MOMMY. Well, why don't you call a van and have her taken away?

GRANDMA. Don't bother; there's no need.

DADDY. No, now, perhaps I can go away myself. . . .

MOMMY. Well, one or the other; the way things are now it's impossible. In the first place, it's too crowded in this apartment.

[*To* GRANDMA]

And it's you that takes up all the space, with your enema bottles, and your Pekinese, and God-only-knows-what-else . . . and now all these boxes. . . .

GRANDMA. These boxes are . . .

MRS. BARKER. I've never heard of enema *bottles*. . . .

GRANDMA. She means enema bags, but she doesn't know the difference.

Mommy comes from extremely bad stock. And besides, when Mommy was born . . . well, it was a difficult delivery, and she had a head shaped like a banana.

MOMMY. You ungrateful—Daddy? Daddy, you see how ungrateful she is after all these years, after all the things we've done for her?

[*To* GRANDMA]

One of these days you're going away in a van; that's what's going to happen to you!

GRANDMA. Do tell!

MRS. BARKER. Like a banana?

GRANDMA. Yup, just like a banana.

MRS. BARKER. My word!

MOMMY. You stop listening to her; she'll say anything. Just the other night she called Daddy a hedgehog.

MRS. BARKER. She didn't!

GRANDMA. That's right, baby; you stick up for me.

MOMMY. I don't know where she gets the words; on the television, maybe.

MRS. BARKER. Did you really call him a hedgehog?

GRANDMA. Oh look; what difference does it make whether I did or not?

DADDY. Grandma's right. Leave Grandma alone.

MOMMY [*to* DADDY]. How dare you!

GRANDMA. Oh, leave her alone, Daddy; the kid's all mixed up.

MOMMY. You see? I told you. It's all those television shows. Daddy, you go right into Grandma's room and take her television and shake all the tubes loose.

DADDY. Don't mention tubes to me.

MOMMY. Oh! Mommy forgot!

[*To* MRS. BARKER]

Daddy has tubes now, where he used to have tracts.

MRS. BARKER. Is that a fact!

GRANDMA. I know why this dear lady is here.

MOMMY. You be still.

MRS. BARKER. Oh, I do wish you'd tell me.

MOMMY. No! No! That wouldn't be fair at all.

DADDY. Besides, she knows why she's here; she's here because we called them.

MRS. BARKER. La! But that still leaves me puzzled. I know I'm here because you called us, but I'm such a busy girl, with this committee and that committee, and the Responsible Citizens Activities I indulge in.

MOMMY. Oh my; busy, busy.

MRS. BARKER. Yes, indeed. So I'm afraid you'll have to give me some help.

MOMMY. Oh, no. No, you must be mistaken. I can't believe we asked you here to give you any help. With the way taxes are these days, and the way you can't get satisfaction in ANYTHING . . . no, I don't believe so.

DADDY. And if you need help . . . why, I should think you'd apply for a Fulbright Scholarship. . . .

MOMMY. And if not that . . . why, then a Guggenheim Fellowship. . . .

GRANDMA. Oh, come on; why not shoot the works and try for the Prix de Rome.

[*Under her breath to* MOMMY *and* DADDY]

Beasts!

MRS. BARKER. Oh, what a jolly family. But let me think. I'm knee-deep in work these days; there's the Ladies' Auxiliary Air Raid Committee, for one thing; how do you feel about air raids?

MOMMY. Oh, I'd say we're hostile.

DADDY. Yes, definitely; we're hostile.

MRS. BARKER. Then, you'll be no help there. There's too much hostility in the world these days as it is; but I'll not badger you! There's a surfeit of badgers as well.

GRANDMA. While we're at it, there's been a run on old people, too. The Department of Agriculture, or maybe it wasn't the Department of Agriculture — anyway, it was some department that's run by a girl — put out figures showing that ninety per cent of the adult population of the country is over eighty years old . . . or eighty per cent is over ninety years old. . . .

MOMMY. You're such a liar! You just finished saying that everyone is middle-aged.

GRANDMA. I'm just telling you what the government says . . . that doesn't have anything to do with what . . .

MOMMY. It's that television! Daddy, go break her television.

GRANDMA. You won't find it.

DADDY [*Wearily getting up*]. If I must . . . I must.

MOMMY. And don't step on the Pekinese; it's blind.

DADDY. It may be blind, but Daddy isn't.

[*He exits, through the archway, stage left*]

GRANDMA. You won't find *it*, either.

MOMMY. Oh, I'm so fortunate to have such a husband. Just think; I could have a husband who was poor, or argumentative, or a husband who sat in a wheel chair all day . . . OOOOHHHH! *What* have I said? What *have* I said?

GRANDMA. You said you could have a husband who sat in a wheel . . .

MOMMY. I'm mortified! I could die! I could cut my tongue out! I could . . .

MRS. BARKER [*Forcing a smile*]. Oh, now . . . now . . . don't think about it. . . .

MOMMY. I could . . . why, I could . . .

MRS. BARKER. . . . don't think about it . . . really. . . .

MOMMY. You're quite right. I won't think about it, and that way I'll forget that I ever said it, and that way it will be all right.

[*Pause*]

There . . . I've forgotten. Well, now, now that Daddy is out of the room we can have some girl talk.

MRS. BARKER. I'm not sure that I . . .

MOMMY. You *do* want to have some girl talk, don't you?

MRS. BARKER. I was going to say I'm not sure that I wouldn't care for a glass of water. I feel a little faint.

MOMMY. Grandma, go get Mrs. Barker a glass of water.

GRANDMA. Go get it yourself. I quit.

MOMMY. Grandma loves to do little things around the house; it gives her a false sense of security.

GRANDMA. I quit! I'm through!

MOMMY. Now, you be a good Grandma, or you know what will happen to you. You'll be taken away in a van.

GRANDMA. You don't frighten me. I'm too old to be frightened. Besides . . .

MOMMY. WELL! I'll tend to you later. I'll hide your teeth . . . I'll . . .

GRANDMA. Everything's hidden.

MRS. BARKER. I *am* going to faint. I *am*.

MOMMY. Good heavens! I'll go myself.

[*As she exits, through the archway, stage-left*]

I'll fix you, Grandma. I'll take care of you later.

[*She exits*]

GRANDMA. Oh, go soak your head.

[*To* MRS. BARKER]

Well, dearie, how do you feel?

MRS. BARKER. A little better, I think. Yes, much better, thank you, Grandma.

GRANDMA. That's good.

MRS. BARKER. But . . . I feel so lost . . . not knowing why I'm here . . . and, on top of it, they say I was here before.

GRANDMA. Well, you were. You weren't *here*, exactly, because we've moved around a lot, from one apartment to another, up and down the social ladder like mice, if you like similes.

MRS. BARKER. I don't . . . particularly.

GRANDMA. Well, then, I'm sorry.

MRS. BARKER [*Suddenly*]. Grandma, I feel I can trust you.

GRANDMA. Don't be too sure; it's every man for himself around this place. . . .

MRS. BARKER. Oh . . . is it? Nonetheless, I really do feel that I can trust you. *Please* tell me why they called and asked us to come. I implore you!

GRANDMA. Oh my; that feels good. It's been so long since anybody implored me. Do it again. Implore me some more.

MRS. BARKER. You're your daughter's mother, all right!

GRANDMA. Oh, I don't mean to be hard. If you won't implore me, then beg me, or ask me, or entreat me . . . just anything like that.

MRS. BARKER. You're a dreadful old woman!

GRANDMA. You'll understand some day. Please!

MRS. BARKER. Oh, for heaven's sake! . . . I implore you . . . I beg you . . . I beseech you!

GRANDMA. Beseech! Oh, that's the nicest word I've heard in ages. You're a dear, sweet woman. . . . You . . . beseech . . . me. I can't resist that.

MRS. BARKER. Well, then . . . please tell me why they asked us to come.

GRANDMA. Well, I'll give you a hint. That's the best I can do, because I'm a muddleheaded old woman. Now listen, because it's important. Once upon a time, not too very long ago, but a long enough time ago . . . oh, about twenty years ago . . . there was a man very much like Daddy, and a woman very much like Mommy, who were married to each other, very much like Mommy and Daddy are married to each other; and they lived in an apartment very much like one that's very much like this one, and they lived there with an old woman who was very much like yours truly, only younger, because it was some time ago; in fact, they were all somewhat younger.

MRS. BARKER. How fascinating!

GRANDMA. Now, at the same time, there was a dear lady very much like you, only younger then, who did all sorts of Good Works. . . . And one of the Good Works this dear lady did was in something very much like a volunteer capacity for an organization very much like the Bye-Bye Adoption Service, which is nearby and which was run by a terribly deaf old lady very much like the Miss Bye-Bye who runs the Bye-Bye Adoption Service nearby.

MRS. BARKER. How enthralling!

GRANDMA. Well, be that as it may. Nonetheless, one afternoon this man, who was very much like Daddy, and this woman who was very much like Mommy came to see this dear lady who did all the Good Works, who was very much like you, dear, and they were very sad and very hopeful, and they cried and smiled and bit their fingers, and they said all the most intimate things.

MRS. BARKER. How spellbinding! What did they say?

GRANDMA. Well, it was very sweet. The woman, who was very much like Mommy, said that she and the man who was very much like Daddy had never been blessed with anything very much like a bumble of joy.

MRS. BARKER. A what?

GRANDMA. A bumble; a bumble of joy.

MRS. BARKER. Oh, like bundle.

GRANDMA. Well, yes; very much like it. Bundle, bumble; who cares? At any rate, the woman, who was very much like Mommy, said that they wanted a bumble of their own, but that the man, who was very much like Daddy, couldn't have a bumble; and the man, who was very much like Daddy, said that yes, they had wanted a bumble of their own, but that the woman, who was very much like Mommy, couldn't have one, and that now they wanted to buy something very much like a bumble.

MRS. BARKER. How engrossing!

GRANDMA. Yes. And the dear lady, who was very much like you, said something that was very much like, "Oh, what a shame; but take heart. . . . I think we have just the bumble *for* you." And, well, the lady, who was very much like Mommy, and the man, who was very much like Daddy, cried and smiled and bit their fingers, and said some more intimate things, which were totally irrelevant but which were pretty hot stuff, and so the dear lady, who was very much like you, and who had something very much like a penchant for pornography, listened with something very much like enthusiasm. "Whee," she said. "Whoooopeeeeee!" But that's beside the point.

MRS. BARKER. I suppose *so*. But how gripping!

GRANDMA. Anyway . . . they *bought* something very much like a bumble, and they took it away with them. But . . . things didn't work out very well.

MRS. BARKER. You mean there was trouble?

GRANDMA. You got it.

[*With a glance through the archway*]

But, I'm going to have to speed up now because I think I'm leaving soon.

MRS. BARKER. Oh. Are you really?

GRANDMA. Yup.

MRS. BARKER. But old people don't go anywhere; they're either taken places, or put places.

GRANDMA. Well, this old person is different. Anyway . . . things started going badly.

MRS. BARKER. Oh yes. Yes.

GRANDMA. Weeeeellll . . . in the first place, it turned out the bumble didn't look like either one of its parents. That was enough of a blow, but things got worse. One night, it cried its heart out, if you can imagine such a thing.

MRS. BARKER. Cried its heart out! Well!

GRANDMA. But that was only the beginning. Then it turned out it only had eyes for its Daddy.

MRS. BARKER. For its Daddy! Why, any self-respecting woman would have gouged those eyes right out of its head.

GRANDMA. Well, she did. That's exactly what she did. But then, it kept its nose up in the air.

MRS. BARKER. Ufggh! How disgusting!

GRANDMA. That's what they thought. But *then*, it began to develop an interest in its you-know-what.

MRS. BARKER. In its you-know-what! Well! I hope they cut its hands off at the wrists!

GRANDMA. Well, yes, they did that eventually. But first, they cut off its you-know-what.

MRS. BARKER. A much better idea!

GRANDMA. That's what they thought. But after they cut off its you-know-what, it *still* puts its hands under the covers, *looking* for its you-know-what. So, finally, they *had* to cut off its hands at the wrists.

MRS. BARKER. Naturally!

GRANDMA. And it was such a resentful bumble. Why, one day it called its Mommy a dirty name.

MRS. BARKER. Well, I hope they cut its tongue out!

GRANDMA. Of course. And then, as it got bigger, they found out all sorts of terrible things about it, like: it didn't have a head on its shoulders, it had no guts, it was spineless, its feet were made of clay . . . just dreadful things.

MRS. BARKER. Dreadful!

GRANDMA. So you can understand how they became discouraged.

MRS. BARKER. I certainly can! And what did they do?

GRANDMA. What did they do? Well, for the last straw, it finally up and died; and you can imagine how *that* made them feel, their having paid for it, and all. So, they called up the lady who sold them the bumble in the first place and told her to come right over to their apartment. They wanted satisfaction; they wanted their money back. That's what they wanted.

MRS. BARKER. My, my, my.

GRANDMA. How do you like *them* apples?

MRS. BARKER. My, my, my.

DADDY [*Off stage*]. Mommy! I can't find Grandma's television, and I can't find the Pekinese, either.

MOMMY [*Off stage*]. Isn't that funny! And I can't find the water.

GRANDMA. Heh, heh, heh. I told them everything was hidden.

MRS. BARKER. Did you hide the water, too?

GRANDMA [*Puzzled*]. No. No, I didn't do *that*.

DADDY [*Off stage*]. The truth of the matter is, I can't even find Grandma's room.

GRANDMA. Heh, heh, heh.

MRS. BARKER. My! You certainly did hide things, didn't you?

GRANDMA. Sure, kid, sure.

MOMMY [*Sticking her head in the room*]. Did you ever hear of such a thing, Grandma? Daddy can't find your television, and he can't find the Pekinese, and the truth of the matter is he can't even find your room.

GRANDMA. I told you. I hid everything.

MOMMY. Nonsense, Grandma! Just wait until I get my hands on you. You're a troublemaker . . . that's what you are.

GRANDMA. Well, I'll be out of here pretty soon, baby.

MOMMY. Oh, you don't know how right you are! Daddy's been wanting to send
you away for a long time now, but I've been restraining him. I'll tell you one
thing, though . . . I'm getting sick and tired of this fighting, and I might just
let him have his way. Then you'll see what'll happen. Away you'll go; in a van,
too. I'll let Daddy call the van man.

GRANDMA. I'm way ahead of you.

MOMMY. How can you be so old and so smug at the same time? You have no
sense of proportion.

GRANDMA. You just answered your own question.

MOMMY. Mrs. Barker, I'd much rather you came into the kitchen for that glass
of water, what with Grandma out here, and all.

MRS. BARKER. I don't see what Grandma has to do with it; and besides, I don't
think you're very polite.

MOMMY. You seem to forget that you're a guest in this house. . . .

GRANDMA. Apartment!

MOMMY. Apartment! And that you're a professional woman. So, if you'll be so
good as to come into the kitchen, I'll be more than happy to show you where
the water is, and where the glass is, and then you can put two and two
together, if you're clever enough.

[*She vanishes*]

MRS. BARKER [*After a moment's consideration*]. I suppose she's right.

GRANDMA. Well, that's how it is when people call you up and ask you over to
do something for them.

MRS. BARKER. I suppose you're right, too. Well, Grandma, it's been very nice
talking to you.

GRANDMA. And I've enjoyed listening. Say, don't tell Mommy or Daddy that I
gave you that hint, will you?

MRS. BARKER. Oh, dear me, the hint! I'd forgotten about it, if you can imagine
such a thing. No, I won't breathe a word of it to them.

GRANDMA. I don't know if it helped you any . . .

MRS. BARKER. I can't tell, yet. I'll have to . . . what *is* the word I
want? . . . I'll have to relate it . . . that's it . . . I'll have to relate it to
certain things that I *know*, and . . . draw . . . conclusions. . . . What I'll
really have to do is to see if it applies to anything. I mean, after all, I *do* do
volunteer work for an adoption service, but it isn't very much *like* the
Bye-Bye Adoption Service . . . it *is* the Bye-Bye Adoption Service . . . and
while I can remember Mommy and Daddy coming to see me, oh, about
twenty years ago, about buying a bumble, I can't quite remember anyone very
much *like* Mommy and Daddy coming to see me about buying a bumble. Don't
you see? It really presents quite a problem. . . . I'll have to think about
it . . . mull it . . . but at any rate, it was truly first-class of you to try to
help me. Oh, will you still be here after I've had my drink of water?

GRANDMA. Probably . . . I'm not as spry as I used to be.

MRS. BARKER. Oh. Well, I won't say good-by then.

GRANDMA. No. Don't.

[MRS. BARKER *exits through the archway*]

People don't say good-by to old people because they think they'll frighten
them. Lordy! If they only knew how awful "hello" and "My, you're looking

chipper" sounded, they wouldn't say those things either. The truth is, there isn't much you *can* say to old people that doesn't sound just terrible. [*The doorbell rings*].

Come on in!

[*The* YOUNG MAN *enters.* GRANDMA *looks him over*]

Well, now, aren't you a breath of fresh air!

YOUNG MAN. Hello there.

GRANDMA. My, my, my. Are you the van man?

YOUNG MAN. The what?

GRANDMA. The van man. The van man. Are you coming to take me away?

YOUNG MAN. I don't know what you're talking about.

GRANDMA. Oh.

[*Pause*]

Well.

[*Pause*]

My, my, aren't you something!

YOUNG MAN. Hm?

GRANDMA. I said, my, my, aren't you something.

YOUNG MAN. Oh. Thank you.

GRANDMA. You don't sound very enthusiastic.

YOUNG MAN. Oh, I'm . . . I'm used to it.

GRANDMA. Yup . . . yup. You know, if I were about a hundred and fifty years younger I could go for you.

YOUNG MAN. Yes, I imagine so.

GRANDMA. Unh-hunh . . . will you look at those muscles!

YOUNG MAN [*Flexing his muscles*]. Yes, they're quite good, aren't they?

GRANDMA. Boy, they sure are. They natural?

YOUNG MAN. Well the basic structure was there, but I've done some work, too . . . you know, in a gym.

GRANDMA. I'll bet you have. You ought to be in the movies, boy.

YOUNG MAN. I know.

GRANDMA. Yup! Right up there on the old silver screen. But I suppose you've heard that before.

YOUNG MAN. Yes, I have.

GRANDMA. You ought to try out for them . . . the movies.

YOUNG MAN. Well, actually, I may have a career there yet. I've lived out on the West Coast almost all my life . . . and I've met a few people who . . . might be able to help me. I'm not in too much of a hurry, though. I'm almost as young as I look.

GRANDMA. Oh, that's nice. And will you look at that face!

YOUNG MAN. Yes, it's quite good, isn't it? Clean-cut, midwest farm boy type, almost insultingly good-looking in a typically American way. Good profile, straight nose, honest eyes, wonderful smile. . . .

GRANDMA. Yup. Boy, you know what you are, don't you? You're the American Dream, that's what you are. All those other people, they don't know what they're talking about. You . . . *you* are the American Dream.

YOUNG MAN. Thanks.

MOMMY [*Off stage*]. Who rang the doorbell?

GRANDMA [*Shouting off-stage*]. The American Dream!

MOMMY [*Off stage*]. What? What was that, Grandma?

GRANDMA [*Shouting*]. The American Dream! The American Dream! Damn it!

DADDY [*Off stage*]. How's that, Mommy?

MOMMY [*Off stage*]. Oh, some gibberish; pay no attention. Did you find Grandma's room?

DADDY [*Off stage*]. No. I can't even find Mrs. Barker.

YOUNG MAN. What was all that?

GRANDMA. Oh, that was just the folks, but let's not talk about them, honey; let's talk about you.

YOUNG MAN. All right.

GRANDMA. Well, let's see. If you're not the van man, what are you doing here?

YOUNG MAN. I'm looking for work.

GRANDMA. Are you! Well, what kind of work?

YOUNG MAN. Oh, almost anything . . . almost anything that pays. I'll do almost anything for money.

GRANDMA. Will you . . . will you? Hmmmm. I wonder if there's anything you could do around here?

YOUNG MAN. There might be. It looked to be a likely building.

GRANDMA. It's always looked to be a rather unlikely building to me, but I suppose you'd know better than I.

YOUNG MAN. I can sense these things.

GRANDMA. There *might* be something you could do around here. Stay there! Don't come any closer.

YOUNG MAN. Sorry.

GRANDMA. I don't mean I'd *mind*. I don't know whether I'd mind, or not. . . . But it wouldn't look well; it would look just *awful*.

YOUNG MAN. Yes; I suppose so.

GRANDMA. Now, stay there, let me concentrate. What could you do? The folks have been in something of a quandary around here today, sort of a dilemma, and I wonder if you mightn't be some help.

YOUNG MAN. I hope so . . . if there's money in it. Do you have any money?

GRANDMA. Money! Oh, there's more money around here than you'd know what to do with.

YOUNG MAN. I'm not so sure.

GRANDMA. Well, maybe not. Besides, I've got money of my own.

YOUNG MAN. You have?

GRANDMA. Sure. Old people quite often have lots of money; more often than most people expect. Come here, so I can whisper to you . . . not too close. I might faint.

YOUNG MAN. Oh, I'm sorry.

GRANDMA. It's all right, dear. Anyway . . . have you ever heard of that big baking contest they run? The one where all the ladies get together in a big barn and bake away?

YOUNG MAN. I'm . . . not . . . sure. . . .

GRANDMA. Not so close. Well, it doesn't matter whether you've heard of it or not. The important thing is — and I don't want anybody to hear this . . . the folks think I haven't been out of the house in eight years — the important thing is that I won first prize in that baking contest this year. Oh, it was in all the papers; not under my own name, though. I used a *nom de boulangère*; I called myself Uncle Henry.

YOUNG MAN. Did you?

GRANDMA. Why not? I didn't see any reason not to. I look just as much like an old man as I do like an old woman. And you know what I called it . . . what I won for?

YOUNG MAN. No. What did you call it?

GRANDMA. I called it Uncle Henry's Day-Old Cake.

YOUNG MAN. That's a very nice name.

GRANDMA. And it wasn't any trouble, either. All I did was go out and get a store-bought cake, and keep it around for a while, and then slip it in, unbeknownst to anybody. Simple.

YOUNG MAN. You're a very resourceful person.

GRANDMA. Pioneer stock.

YOUNG MAN. Is all this true? Do you want me to believe all this?

GRANDMA. Well, you can believe it or not . . . it doesn't make any difference to me. All *I* know is, Uncle Henry's Day-Old Cake won me twenty-five thousand smackerolas.

YOUNG MAN. Twenty-five thou—

GRANDMA. Right on the old loggerhead. Now . . . how do you like them apples?

YOUNG MAN. Love 'em.

GRANDMA. I thought you'd be impressed.

YOUNG MAN. Money talks.

GRANDMA. Hey! You look familiar.

YOUNG MAN. Hm? Pardon?

GRANDMA. I said, you look familiar.

YOUNG MAN. Well, I've done some modeling.

GRANDMA. No . . . no. I don't mean that. You look familiar.

YOUNG MAN. Well, I'm a type.

GRANDMA. Yup; you sure are. Why do you say you'd do anything for money . . . if you don't mind my being nosy?

YOUNG MAN. No, no. It's part of the interviews. I'll be happy to tell you. It's that I have no talents at all, except what you see . . . my person; my body, my face. In every other way I am incomplete, and I must there-fore . . . compensate.

GRANDMA. What do you mean, incomplete? You look pretty complete to me.

YOUNG MAN. I think I can explain it to you, partially because you're very old, and very old people have perceptions they keep to themselves, because if they expose them to other people . . . well, you know what ridicule and neglect are.

GRANDMA. I do, child, I do.

YOUNG MAN. Then listen. My mother died the night that I was born, and I never knew my father; I doubt my mother did. But, I wasn't alone, because lying with me . . . in the placenta . . . there was someone else . . . my brother . . . my twin.

GRANDMA. Oh, my child.

YOUNG MAN. We were identical twins . . . he and I . . . not fraternal . . . identical; we were derived from the same ovum; and in *this,* in that we were twins not from separate ova but from the same one, we had a kinship such as you cannot imagine. We . . . we felt each other breathe . . . his heartbeats thundered in my temples . . . mine in his . . . our stomachs ached and we cried for feeding at the same time . . . are you old enough to understand?

GRANDMA. I think so, child; I think I'm nearly old enough.

YOUNG MAN. I hope so. But we were separated when we were still very young, my brother, my twin and I . . . inasmuch as you can separate one being. We were torn apart . . . thrown to opposite ends of the continent. I don't know what became of my brother . . . to the rest of myself . . . except that, from time to time, in the years that have passed, I have suffered losses . . . that I can't explain. A fall from grace . . . a departure of innocence . . . loss . . . loss. How can I put it to you? All right; like this: Once . . . it was as if all at once my heart . . . became numb . . . almost as though I . . . almost as though . . . just like that . . . it had been wrenched from my body . . . and from that time I have been unable to love. Once . . . I was asleep at the time . . . I awoke, and my eyes were burning. And since that time I have been unable to see anything, *anything*, with pity, with affection . . . with anything but . . . cool disinterest. And my groin . . . even there . . . since one time . . . one specific agony . . . since then I have not been able to *love* anyone with my body. And even my hands . . . I cannot touch another person and feel love. And there is more . . . there are more losses, but it all comes down to this: I no longer have the capacity to feel anything. I have no emotions. I have been drained, torn asunder . . . disemboweled. I have, now, only my person . . . my body, my face. I use what I have . . . I let people love me . . . I accept the syntax around me, for while I know I cannot relate . . . I know I must be related *to*. I let people love me . . . I let people touch me . . . I let them draw pleasure from my groin . . . from my presence . . . from the fact of me . . . but, that is all it comes to. As I told you, I am incomplete . . . I can feel nothing. I can feel nothing. And so . . . here I am . . . as you see me. I am . . . but this . . . what you see. And it will always be thus.

GRANDMA. Oh, my child; my child.

[*Long pause; then*]

I was mistaken . . . before. I don't know you from somewhere, but I knew . . . once . . . someone very much like you . . . or, very much as perhaps you were.

YOUNG MAN. Be careful; be very careful. What I have told you may not be true. In my profession . . .

GRANDMA. Shhhhhh.

[*The* YOUNG MAN *bows his head, in acquiescence*]

Someone . . . to be more precise . . . who might have turned out to be very much like you might have turned out to be. And . . . unless I'm terribly mistaken . . . you've found yourself a job.

YOUNG MAN. What are my duties?

MRS. BARKER [*Off stage*]. Yoo-hoo! Yoo-hoo!

GRANDMA. Oh-oh. You'll . . . you'll have to play it by ear, my dear . . . unless I get a chance to talk to you again. I've got to go into my act, now.

YOUNG MAN. But, I . . .

GRANDMA. Yoo-hoo!

MRS. BARKER [*Coming through archway*]. Yoo-hoo . . . oh, there you are, Grandma. I'm glad to see somebody. I can't find Mommy or Daddy.

[*Double takes*]

Well . . . who's this?

GRANDMA. This? Well . . . uh . . . oh, this is the . . . uh . . . the van man. That's who it is . . . the van man.

MRS. BARKER. So! It's true! They *did* call the van man. They *are* having you carted away.

GRANDMA [*Shrugging*]. Well, you know. It figures.

MRS. BARKER [*To* YOUNG MAN]. How dare you cart this poor old woman away!

YOUNG MAN [*After a quick look at* GRANDMA, *who nods*]. I do what I'm paid to do. I don't ask any questions.

MRS. BARKER [*After a brief pause*]. Oh.

[*Pause*]

Well, you're quite right, of course, and I shouldn't meddle.

GRANDMA [*To* YOUNG MAN]. Dear, will you take my things out to the van? [*She points to the boxes*]

YOUNG MAN [*After only the briefest hesitation*]. Why certainly.

GRANDMA [*As the* YOUNG MAN *takes up half the boxes, exits by the front door*]. Isn't that a nice young van man?

MRS. BARKER [*Shaking her head in disbelief, watching the* YOUNG MAN *exit*]. Unh-hunh . . . some things have changed for the better. I remember when I had *my* mother carted off . . . the van man who came for her wasn't anything near as nice as this one.

GRANDMA. Oh, did you have your mother carted off, too?

MRS. BARKER [*Cheerfully*]. Why certainly! Didn't you?

GRANDMA [*Puzzling*]. No . . . no, I didn't. At least, I can't remember. Listen dear; I got to talk to you for a second.

MRS. BARKER. Why certainly, Grandma.

GRANDMA. Now, listen.

MRS. BARKER. Yes, Grandma. Yes.

GRANDMA. Now listen carefully. You got this dilemma here with Mommy and Daddy. . . .

MRS. BARKER. Yes! I wonder where they've gone to?

GRANDMA. They'll be back in. Now, LISTEN!

MRS. BARKER. Oh, I'm sorry.

GRANDMA. Now, you got this dilemma here with Mommy and Daddy, and I think I got the way out for you.

[*The* YOUNG MAN *re-enters through the front door*]

Will you take the rest of my things out now, dear?

[*To* MRS. BARKER, *while the* YOUNG MAN *takes the rest of the boxes, exits again by the front door*]

Fine. Now listen, dear.

[*She begins to whisper in* MRS. BARKER'*s ear*]

MRS. BARKER. Oh! Oh! Oh! I don't think I could . . . do you really think I could? Well, why not? What a wonderful idea . . . what an absolutely wonderful idea!

GRANDMA. Well, yes, I thought it was.

MRS. BARKER. And you so old!

GRANDMA. Heh, heh, heh.

MRS. BARKER. Well, I think it's absolutely marvelous, anyway. I'm going to find Mommy and Daddy right now.

GRANDMA. Good. You do that.

MRS. BARKER. Well, now. I think I will say good-by. I can't thank you enough.
[*She starts to exit through the archway*]

GRANDMA. You're welcome. Say it!

MRS. BARKER. Huh? What?

GRANDMA. Say good-by.

MRS. BARKER. Oh. Good-by.

[*She exits*]

Mommy! I say, Mommy! Daddy!

GRANDMA. Good-by.
[*By herself now, she looks about*]
    Ah me.
[*Shakes her head*]
    Ah me.
[*Takes in the room*]
    Good-by.

[*The* YOUNG MAN *re-enters*]

GRANDMA. Oh, hello, there.

YOUNG MAN. All the boxes are outside.

GRANDMA [*A little sadly*]. I don't know why I bother to take them with me.
    They don't have much in them . . . some old letters, a couple of re-
    grets . . . Pekinese . . . blind at that . . . the television . . . my Sunday
    teeth . . . eighty-six years of living . . . some sounds . . . a few images, a
    little garbled by now . . . and, well . . .
[*She shrugs*]
    . . . you know . . . the things one accumulates.

YOUNG MAN. Can I get you . . . a cab, or something?

GRANDMA. Oh no, dear . . . thank you just the same. I'll take it from here.

YOUNG MAN. And what shall I do now?

GRANDMA. Oh, you stay here, dear. It will all become clear to you. It will be
    explained. You'll understand.

YOUNG MAN. Very well.

GRANDMA [*After one more look about*]. Well . . .

YOUNG MAN. Let me see you to the elevator.

GRANDMA. Oh . . . that *would* be nice, dear.

[*They both exit by the front door, slowly*]

[*Enter* MRS. BARKER, *followed by* MOMMY *and* DADDY]

MRS. BARKER. . . . and I'm happy to tell you that the whole thing's settled.
    Just like that.

MOMMY. Oh, we're so glad. We were afraid there might be a problem, what
    with delays, and all.

DADDY. Yes, we're very relieved.

MRS. BARKER. Well, now; that's what professional women are for.

MOMMY. Why . . . where's Grandma? Grandma's not here! Where's
    Grandma? And look! The boxes are gone, too. Grandma's gone, and so are the
    boxes. She's taken off, and she's stolen something! Daddy!

MRS. BARKER. Why, Mommy, the van man was here.

MOMMY [*Startled*]. The what?

MRS. BARKER. The van man. The van man was here.

[*The lights might dim a little, suddenly*]

MOMMY [*Shakes her head*]. No, that's impossible.

MRS. BARKER. Why, I saw him with my own two eyes.

MOMMY [*Near tears*]. No, no, that's impossible. No. There's no such thing as the van man. There is no van man. We . . . we made him up. Grandma? Grandma?

DADDY [*Moving to* MOMMY]. There, there, now.

MOMMY. Oh Daddy . . . where's Grandma?

DADDY. There, there, now.

[*While* DADDY *is comforting* MOMMY, GRANDMA *comes out, stage right, near the footlights*]

GRANDMA [*To the audience*]. Shhhhhh! I want to watch this.

[*She motions to* MRS. BARKER *who, with a secret smile, tiptoes to the front door and opens it. The* YOUNG MAN *is framed therein. Lights up full again as he steps into the room*]

MRS. BARKER. Surprise! Surprise! Here we are!

MOMMY. What? What?

DADDY. Hm? What?

MOMMY [*Her tears merely sniffles now*]. What surprise?

MRS. BARKER. Why, I told you. The surprise I told you about.

DADDY. You . . . you know, Mommy.

MOMMY. Sur . . . prise?

DADDY [*Urging her to cheerfulness*]. You remember, Mommy; why we asked . . . uh . . . what's-her-name to come here?

MRS. BARKER. Mrs. Barker, if you don't mind.

DADDY. Yes. Mommy? You remember now? About the bumble . . . about wanting satisfaction?

MOMMY [*Her sorrow turning into delight*]. Yes. Why yes! Of course! Yes! Oh, how wonderful!

MRS. BARKER [*To the* YOUNG MAN]. This is Mommy.

YOUNG MAN. How . . . how do you do?

MRS. BARKER [*Stage whisper*]. Her name's Mommy.

YOUNG MAN. How . . . how do you do, Mommy?

MOMMY. Well! Hello there!

MRS. BARKER [*To the* YOUNG MAN]. And that is Daddy.

YOUNG MAN. How do you do, sir?

DADDY. How do you do?

MOMMY [*Herself again, circling the* YOUNG MAN, *feeling his arm, poking him*]. Yes, sir! Yes, sirree! Now this is more like it. Now this is a great deal more like it! Daddy! Come see. Come see if this isn't a great deal more like it.

DADDY. I . . . I can see from here, Mommy. It does look a great deal more like it.

MOMMY. Yes, sir. Yes sirree! Mrs. Barker, I don't know *how* to thank you.

MRS. BARKER. Oh, don't worry about that. I'll send you a bill in the mail.

MOMMY. What this really calls for is a celebration. It calls for a drink.

MRS. BARKER. Oh, what a nice idea.

MOMMY. There's some sauterne in the kitchen.

YOUNG MAN. I'll go.

MOMMY. Will you? Oh, how nice. The kitchen's through the archway there.

[*As the* YOUNG MAN *exits: to* MRS. BARKER]

He's very nice. Really top notch; much better than the other one.

MRS. BARKER. I'm glad you're pleased. And I'm glad everything's all straightened out.

MOMMY. Well, at least we know why we sent for you. We're glad that's cleared up. By the way, what's his name?

MRS. BARKER. Ha! Call him whatever you like. He's yours. Call him what you called the other one.

MOMMY. Daddy? What did we call the other one?

DADDY [*Puzzles*]. Why . . .

YOUNG MAN [*Re-entering with a tray on which are a bottle of sauterne and five glasses*]. Here we are!

MOMMY. Hooray! Hooray!

MRS. BARKER. Oh, good!

MOMMY [*Moving to the tray*]. So, let's — Five glasses? Why five? There are only four of us. Why five?

YOUNG MAN [*Catches* GRANDMA'*s eye;* GRANDMA *indicates she is not there*]. Oh, I'm sorry.

MOMMY. You must learn to count. We're a wealthy family, and you must learn to count.

YOUNG MAN. I will.

MOMMY. Well, everybody take a glass.

[*They do*]

And we'll drink to celebrate. To satisfaction! Who says you can't get satisfaction these days!

MRS. BARKER. What dreadful sauterne!

MOMMY. Yes, isn't it?

[*To* YOUNG MAN, *her voice already a little fuzzy from the wine*]

You don't know how happy I am to see you! Yes sirree. Listen, that time we had with . . . with the other one. I'll tell you about it some time.

[*Indicates* MRS. BARKER]

After she's gone. She was responsible for all the trouble in the first place. I'll tell you all about it.

[*Sidles up to him a little*]

Maybe . . . maybe later tonight.

YOUNG MAN [*Not moving away*]. Why yes. That would be very nice.

MOMMY [*Puzzles*]. Something familiar about you . . . you know that? I can't quite place it. . . .

GRANDMA [*Interrupting . . . to audience*]. Well, I guess that just about wraps it up. I mean, for better or worse, this is a comedy, and I don't think we'd better go any further. No, definitely not. So, let's leave things as they are right now . . . while everybody's happy . . . while everybody's got what he wants . . . or everybody's got what he thinks he wants. Good night, dears.

CURTAIN

(1959–1960)

Lorraine Hansberry *1930–1965*

A RAISIN IN THE SUN

CHARACTERS IN ORDER OF APPEARANCE

RUTH YOUNGER *Walter's wife, about thirty*

TRAVIS YOUNGER *her son and Walter's*

WALTER LEE YOUNGER (BROTHER) *Ruth's husband, mid-thirties*

BENEATHA YOUNGER *Walter's sister, about twenty*

LENA YOUNGER (MAMA) *mother of Walter and Beneatha*

JOSEPH ASAGAI *Nigerian, Beneatha's suitor*

GEORGE MURCHISON *Beneatha's date, wealthy*

KARL LINDNER *white, chairman of the Clybourne Park New Neighbors Orientation Committee*

BOBO *one of Walter's business partners*

MOVING MEN

The action of the play is set in Chicago's Southside, sometime between World War II and the present.

ACT I

SCENE I. Friday morning
SCENE II. The following morning

ACT II

SCENE I. Later, the same day
SCENE II. Friday night, a few weeks later
SCENE III. Moving day, one week later.

ACT III

An hour later

ACT I

SCENE I

The Younger living room would be a comfortable and well-ordered room if it were not for a number of indestructible contradictions to this state of being. Its furnishings are typical and undistinguished and their primary feature now is that they have clearly had to accommodate the living of too many people for too many years—and they are tired. Still, we can see that at some time, a time probably no longer remembered by the family (except perhaps for MAMA) *the furnishings of this room were actually selected with care and love and even hope—and brought to this apartment and arranged with taste and pride.*

That was a long time ago. Now the once loved pattern of the couch upholstery has to fight to show itself from under acres of crocheted doilies and couch covers which have themselves finally come to be more important than the upholstery. And here a table or a chair has been moved to disguise the worn places in the carpet; but the carpet has fought back by showing its weariness, with depressing uniformity, elsewhere on its surface.

Weariness has, in fact, won in this room. Everything has been polished, washed, sat on, used, scrubbed too often. All pretenses but living itself have long since vanished from the very atmosphere of this room.

Moreover, a section of this room, for it is not really a room unto itself, though the landlord's lease would make it seem so, slopes backward to provide a small kitchen area, where the family prepares the meals that are eaten in the living room proper, which must also serve as dining room. The single window that has been provided for these "two" rooms is located in this kitchen area. The sole natural light the family may enjoy in the course of a day is only that which fights its way through this little window.

At left, a door leads to a bedroom which is shared by MAMA *and her daughter,* BENEATHA. *At right, opposite, is a second room (which in the beginning of the life of this apartment was probably a breakfast room) which serves as a bedroom for* WALTER *and his wife,* RUTH.

Time: Sometime between World War II and the present.

Place: Chicago's Southside.

At Rise: It is morning dark in the living room. TRAVIS *is asleep on the make-down bed at center. An alarm clock sounds from within the bedroom at right, and presently* RUTH *enters from that room and closes the door behind her. She crosses sleepily toward the window. As she passes her sleeping son she reaches down and shakes him a little. At the window she raises the shade and a dusky Southside morning light comes in feebly. She fills a pot with water and puts it on to boil. She calls to the boy, between yawns, in a slightly muffled voice.*

RUTH *is about thirty. We can see that she was a pretty girl, even exceptionally so, but now it is apparent that life has been little that she expected, and disappointment has already begun to hang in her face. In a few years, before thirty-five even, she will be known among her people as a "settled woman."*

She crosses to her son and gives him a good, final, rousing shake.

RUTH. Come on now, boy, it's seven thirty! [*Her son sits up at last, in a stupor of sleepiness*]. I say hurry up, Travis! You ain't the only person in the world got to use a bathroom! [*The child, a sturdy, handsome little boy of ten or eleven, drags himself out of the bed and almost blindly takes his towels and "today's clothes" from drawers and a closet and goes out to the bathroom, which is in an outside hall and which is shared by another family or families on the same floor.* RUTH *crosses to the bedroom door at right and opens it and calls in to her husband*] Walter Lee! . . . It's after seven thirty! Lemme see you do some waking up in there now! [*She waits*] You better get up from there, man! It's after seven thirty I tell you. [*She waits again*] All right, you just go ahead and lay there and next thing you know Travis be finished and Mr. Johnson'll be in there and you'll be fussing and cussing round here like a mad man! And be late too! [*She waits, at the end of patience*] Walter Lee—it's time for you to get up! [*She waits another second and then starts to go into the bedroom, but is apparently satisfied that her husband has begun to get up. She stops, pulls the door to, and returns to the kitchen area. She wipes her face with a moist cloth and runs her fingers through her sleep-disheveled hair in a vain effort and ties an apron around her housecoat. The bedroom door at right opens and her husband stands in the doorway in his pajamas, which are rumpled and mismated. He is a lean, intense young man in his middle thirties, inclined to quick nervous movements and erratic speech habits—and always in his voice there is a quality of indictment*]

WALTER. Is he out yet?

RUTH. What you mean *out?* He ain't hardly got in there good yet.

WALTER [*Wandering in, still more oriented to sleep than to a new day*]. Well, what was you doing all that yelling for if I can't even get in there yet? [*Stopping and thinking*] Check coming today?

RUTH. They *said* Saturday and this is just Friday and I hopes to God you ain't going to get up here first thing this morning and start talking to me 'bout no money—'cause I 'bout don't want to hear it.

WALTER. Something the matter with you this morning?

RUTH. No—I'm just sleepy as the devil. What kind of eggs you want?

WALTER. Not scrambled. [RUTH *starts to scramble eggs*] Paper come? [RUTH *points impatiently to the rolled up* Tribune *on the table, and he gets it and spreads it out and vaguely reads the front page*] Set off another bomb yesterday.

RUTH [*Maximum indifference*]. Did they?

WALTER [*Looking up*]. What's the matter with you?

RUTH. Ain't nothing the matter with me. And don't keep asking me that this morning.

WALTER. Ain't nobody bothering you. [*Reading the news of the day absently again*] Say Colonel McCormick is sick.

RUTH [*Affecting tea-party interest*]. Is he now? Poor thing.

WALTER [*Sighing and looking at his watch*]. Oh, me. [*He waits*] Now what is that boy doing in that bathroom all this time? He just going to have to start getting up earlier. I can't be being late to work on account of him fooling around in there.

RUTH [*Turning on him*]. Oh, no he ain't going to be getting up earlier no such thing! It ain't his fault that he can't get to bed no earlier nights 'cause he got a bunch of crazy good-for-nothing clowns sitting up running their mouths in what is supposed to be his bedroom after ten o'clock at night . . .

WALTER. That's what you mad about, ain't it? The things I want to talk about with my friends just couldn't be important in your mind, could they? [*He rises and finds a cigarette in her handbag on the table and crosses to the little window and looks out, smoking and deeply enjoying this first one*]

RUTH [*Almost matter of factly, a complaint too automatic to deserve emphasis*]. Why you always got to smoke before you eat in the morning?

WALTER [*At the window*]. Just look at 'em down there . . . Running and racing to work . . . [*He turns and faces his wife and watches her a moment at the stove, and then, suddenly*] You look young this morning, baby.

RUTH [*Indifferently*]. Yeah?

WALTER. Just for a second—stirring them eggs. It's gone now—just for a second it was—you looked real young again. [*Then, drily*] It's gone now—you look like yourself again.

RUTH. Man, if you don't shut up and leave me alone.

WALTER [*Looking out to the street again*]. First thing a man ought to learn in life is not to make love to no colored woman first thing in the morning. You all some evil people at eight o'clock in the morning. [TRAVIS *appears in the hall doorway, almost fully dressed and quite wide awake now, his towels and pajamas across his shoulders. He opens the door and signals for his father to make the bathroom in a hurry*]

TRAVIS [*Watching the bathroom*]. Daddy, come on! [WALTER *gets his bathroom utensils and flies out to the bathroom*]

RUTH. Sit down and have your breakfast, Travis.

TRAVIS. Mama, this is Friday. [*Gleefully*] Check coming tomorrow, huh?

RUTH. You get your mind off money and eat your breakfast.

TRAVIS [*Eating*]. This is the morning we supposed to bring the fifty cents to school.

RUTH. Well, I ain't got no fifty cents this morning.

TRAVIS. Teacher say we have to.

RUTH. I don't care what teacher say. I ain't got it. Eat your breakfast, Travis.

TRAVIS. I *am* eating.

RUTH. Hush up now and just eat! [*The boy gives her an exasperated look for her lack of understanding, and eats grudgingly*]

TRAVIS. You think Grandmama would have it?

RUTH. No! And I want you to stop asking your grandmother for money, you hear me?

TRAVIS [*Outraged*]. Gaaaleee! I don't ask her, she just gimme it sometimes!

RUTH. Travis Willard Younger—I got too much on me this morning to be—

TRAVIS. Maybe Daddy—

RUTH. *Travis!* [*The boy hushes abruptly. They are both quiet and tense for several seconds*]

TRAVIS [*Presently*]. Could I maybe go carry some groceries in front of the supermarket for a little while after school then?

RUTH. Just hush, I said. [TRAVIS *jabs his spoon into his cereal bowl viciously, and rests his head in anger upon his fists*] If you through eating, you can get over there and make up your bed. [*The boy obeys stiffly and crosses the room, almost mechanically, to the bed and more or less carefully folds the covering. He carries the bedding into his mother's room and returns with his books and cap*]

TRAVIS [*Sulking and standing apart from her unnaturally*]. I'm gone.

RUTH [*Looking up from the stove to inspect him automatically*]. Come here. [*He crosses to her and she studies his head*] If you don't take this comb and fix this here head, you better! [TRAVIS *puts down his books with a great sigh of oppression, and crosses to the mirror. His mother mutters under her breath about his "stubbornness"*] 'Bout to march out of here with that head looking just like chickens slept in it! I just don't know where you get your stubborn ways . . . And get your jacket, too. Looks chilly out this morning.

TRAVIS [*With conspicuously brushed hair and jacket*]. I'm gone.

RUTH. Get carfare and milk money—[*Waving one finger*]—and not a single penny for no caps, you hear me?

TRAVIS [*With sullen politeness*]. Yes'm. [*He turns in outrage to leave. His mother watches after him as in his frustration he approaches the door almost comically. When she speaks to him, her voice has become a very gentle tease*]

RUTH [*Mocking; as she thinks he would say it*]. Oh, Mama makes me so mad sometimes, I don't know what to do! [*She waits and continues to his back as he stands stock-still in front of the door*] I wouldn't kiss that woman good-bye for nothing in this world this morning! [*The boy finally turns around and rolls his eyes at her, knowing the mood has changed and he is vindicated; he does not, however, move toward her yet*] Not for nothing in this world! [*She finally laughs aloud at him and holds out her arms to him and we see that it is a way between them, very old and practiced. He crosses to her and allows her to embrace him warmly but keeps his face fixed with masculine rigidity. She holds him back from her presently and looks at him and runs her fingers over the features of his face. With utter gentleness—*] Now—whose little old angry man are you?

TRAVIS [*The masculinity and gruffness start to fade at last*]. Aw gaalee—Mama . . .

RUTH [*Mimicking*]. Aw—gaaaaalleeeee, Mama! [*She pushes him, with rough playfulness and finality, toward the door*] Get on out of here or you going to be late.

TRAVIS [*In the face of love, new aggressiveness*]. Mama, could I *please* go carry groceries?

RUTH. Honey, it's starting to get so cold evenings.

WALTER [*Coming in from the bedroom and drawing a make-believe gun from a make-believe holster and shooting at his son*]. What is it he wants to do?

RUTH. Go carry groceries after school at the supermarket.

WALTER. Well, let him go . . .

TRAVIS [*Quickly, to the ally*]. I *have* to—she won't gimme the fifty cents . . .

WALTER [*To his wife only*]. Why not?

RUTH [*Simply, and with flavor*]. 'Cause we don't have it.

WALTER [*To RUTH only*]. What you tell the boy things like that for? [*Reaching down into his pants with a rather important gesture*] Here, son—[*He hands the boy the coin, but his eyes are directed to his wife's. TRAVIS takes the money happily*]

TRAVIS. Thanks, Daddy. [*He starts out. RUTH watches both of them with murder in her eyes. WALTER stands and stares back at her with defiance, and suddenly reaches into his pocket again on an afterthought*]

WALTER [*Without even looking at his son, still staring hard at his wife*]. In fact, here's another fifty cents . . . Buy yourself some fruit today—or take a taxicab to school or something!

TRAVIS. Whoopee—[*He leaps up and clasps his father around the middle with his legs, and they face each other in mutual appreciation; slowly WALTER LEE peeks around the boy to catch the violent rays from his wife's eyes and draws his head back as if shot*]

WALTER. You better get down now—and get to school, man.

TRAVIS [*At the door*]. O.K. Good-bye. [*He exits*]

WALTER [*After him, pointing with pride*]. That's *my* boy. [*She looks at him in disgust and turns back to her work*] You know what I was thinking 'bout in the bathroom this morning?

RUTH. No.

WALTER. How come you always try to be so pleasant!

RUTH. What is there to be pleasant 'bout!

WALTER. You want to know what I was thinking 'bout in the bathroom or not!

RUTH. I know what you thinking 'bout.

WALTER [*Ignoring her*]. 'Bout what me and Willy Harris was talking about last night.

RUTH [*Immediately—a refrain*]. Willy Harris is a good-for-nothing loud mouth.

WALTER. Anybody who talks to me has got to be a good-for-nothing loud mouth, ain't he? And what you know about who is just a good-for-nothing loud mouth? Charlie Atkins was just a "good-for-nothing loud mouth" too, wasn't he! When he wanted me to go in the dry-cleaning business with him. And now—he's grossing a hundred thousand a year! A hundred thousand dollars a year! You still call *him* a loud mouth!

RUTH [*Bitterly*]. Oh, Walter Lee . . . [*She folds her head on her arms over the table*]

WALTER [*Rising and coming to her and standing over her*]. You tired, ain't you? Tired of everything. Me, the boy, the way we live—this beat-up hole—everything. Ain't you? [*She doesn't look up, doesn't answer*] So tired—moaning and groaning all the time, but you wouldn't do nothing to help, would you? You couldn't be on my side that long for nothing, could you?

RUTH. Walter, please leave me alone.

WALTER. A man needs for a woman to back him up . . .

RUTH. Walter—

WALTER. Mama would listen to you. You know she listen to you more than she do me and Bennie. She think more of you. All you have to do is just sit down with her when you drinking your coffee one morning and talking 'bout things like you do and—[*He sits down beside her and demonstrates graphically what he thinks her methods and tone should be*]—you just sip your coffee, see, and say easy like that you been thinking 'bout that deal Walter Lee is so interested in, 'bout the store and all, and sip some more coffee, like what you saying ain't really that important to you—And the next thing you know, she be listening good and asking you questions and when I come home—I can tell her the details. This ain't no fly-by-night proposition, baby. I mean we figured it out, me and Willy and Bobo.

RUTH [*With a frown*]. Bobo?

WALTER. Yeah. You see, this little liquor store we got in mind cost seventy-five thousand and we figured the initial investment on the place be 'bout thirty thousand, see. That be ten thousand each. Course, there's a couple of hundred you got to pay so's you don't spend your life just waiting for them clowns to let your license get approved—

RUTH. You mean graft?

WALTER [*Frowning impatiently*]. Don't call it that. See there, that just goes to show you what women understand about the world. Baby, don't *nothing* happen for you in this world 'less you pay *somebody* off!

RUTH. Walter, leave me alone! [*She raises her head and stares at him vigorously—then says, more quietly*] Eat your eggs, they gonna be cold.

WALTER [*Straightening up from her and looking off*]. That's it. There you are. Man say to his woman: I got me a dream. His woman say: Eat your eggs. [*Sadly, but gaining in power*] Man say: I got to take hold of this here world,

baby! And a woman will say: Eat your eggs and go to work. [*Passionately now*]
Man say: I got to change my life, I'm choking to death, baby! And his woman
say — [*In utter anguish as he brings his fists down on his thighs*] — Your eggs is
getting cold!

RUTH [*Softly*]. Walter, that ain't none of our money.

WALTER [*Not listening at all or even looking at her*]. This morning, I was lookin'
in the mirror and thinking about it . . . I'm thirty-five years old; I been
married eleven years and I got a boy who sleeps in the living room — [*Very,
very quietly*] — and all I got to give him is stories about how rich white people
live . . .

RUTH. Eat your eggs, Walter.

WALTER. *Damn my eggs . . . damn all the eggs that ever was!*

RUTH. Then go to work.

WALTER [*Looking up at her*]. See — I'm trying to talk to you 'bout myself —
[*Shaking his head with the repetition*] — and all you can say is eat them eggs and
go to work.

RUTH [*Wearily*]. Honey, you never say nothing new. I listen to you every day,
every night and every morning, and you never say nothing new. [*Shrugging*]
So you would rather *be* Mr. Arnold than be his chauffeur. So — I would *rather*
be living in Buckingham Palace.

WALTER. That is just what is wrong with the colored woman in this
world . . . Don't understand about building their men up and making 'em
feel like they somebody. Like they can do something.

RUTH [*Drily, but to hurt*]. There *are* colored men who do things.

WALTER. No thanks to the colored woman.

RUTH. Well, being a colored woman, I guess I can't help myself none. [*She rises
and gets the ironing board and sets it up and attacks a huge pile of rough-dried
clothes, sprinkling them in preparation for the ironing and then rolling them into
tight fat balls.*]

WALTER [*Mumbling*]. We one group of men tied to a race of women with small
minds. [*His sister BENEATHA enters. She is about twenty, as slim and intense as
her brother. She is not as pretty as her sister-in-law, but her lean, almost
intellectual face has a handsomeness of its own. She wears a bright-red flannel
nightie, and her thick hair stands wildly about her head. Her speech is a mixture of
many things; it is different from the rest of the family's insofar as education has
permeated her sense of English — and perhaps the Midwest rather than the South
has finally — at last — won out in her inflection; but not altogether, because over
all of it is a soft slurring and transformed use of vowels which is the decided
influence of the Southside. She passes through the room without looking at either
RUTH or WALTER and goes to the outside door and looks, a little blindly, out to
the bathroom. She sees that it has been lost to the Johnsons. She closes the door with
a sleepy vengeance and crosses to the table and sits down a little defeated*]

BENEATHA. I am going to start timing those people.

WALTER. You should get up earlier.

BENEATHA [*Her face in her hands. She is still fighting the urge to go back to
bed*]. Really — would you suggest dawn? Where's the paper?

WALTER [*Pushing the paper across the table to her as he studies her almost
clinically, as though he has never seen her before*]. You a horrible-looking chick
at this hour.

BENEATHA [*Drily*]. Good morning, everybody.

WALTER [*Senselessly*]. How is school coming?

BENEATHA [*In the same spirit*]. Lovely, Lovely. And you know, biology is the greatest. [*Looking up at him*] I dissected something that looked just like you yesterday.

WALTER. I just wondered if you've made up your mind and everything.

BENEATHA [*Gaining in sharpness and impatience*]. And what did I answer yesterday morning — and the day before that?

RUTH [*From the ironing board, like someone disinterested and old*]. Don't be so nasty, Bennie.

BENEATHA [*Still to her brother*]. And the day before that and the day before that!

WALTER [*Defensively*]. I'm interested in you. Something wrong with that? Ain't many girls who decide —

WALTER *and* BENEATHA [*In unison*]. — "to be a doctor." [*Silence*]

WALTER. Have we figured out yet just exactly how much medical school is going to cost?

RUTH. Walter Lee, why don't you leave that girl alone and get out of here to work?

BENEATHA [*Exits to the bathroom and bangs on the door*]. Come on out of there, please! [*She comes back into the room*]

WALTER [*Looking at his sister intently*]. You know the check is coming tomorrow.

BENEATHA [*Turning on him with a sharpness all her own*]. That money belongs to Mama, Walter, and it's for her to decide how she wants to use it. I don't care if she wants to buy a house or a rocket ship or just nail it up somewhere and look at it. It's hers. Not ours — *hers*.

WALTER [*Bitterly*]. Now ain't that fine! You just got your mother's interest at heart, ain't you, girl? You such a nice girl — but if Mama got that money she can always take a few thousand and help you through school too — can't she?

BENEATHA. I have never asked anyone around here to do anything for me!

WALTER. No! And the line between asking and just accepting when the time comes is big and wide — ain't it!

BENEATHA [*With fury*]. What do you want from me, Brother — that I quit school or just drop dead, which!

WALTER. I don't want nothing but for you to stop acting holy 'round here. Me and Ruth done made some sacrifices for you — why can't you do something for the family?

RUTH. Walter, don't be dragging me in it.

WALTER. You are in it — Don't you get up and go work in somebody's kitchen for the last three years to help put clothes on her back?

RUTH. Oh, Walter — that's not fair . . .

WALTER. It ain't that nobody expects you to get on your knees and say thank you, Brother; thank you, Ruth; thank you, Mama — and thank you, Travis, for wearing the same pair of shoes for two semesters —

BENEATHA [*Dropping to her knees*]. Well — I *do* — all right? — thank everybody . . . and forgive me for ever wanting to be anything at all . . . forgive me, forgive me!

RUTH. Please stop it! Your mama'll hear you.

WALTER. Who the hell told you you had to be a doctor? If you so crazy 'bout messing 'round with sick people — then go be a nurse like other women — or just get married and be quiet . . .

BENEATHA. Well — you finally got it said . . . It took you three years but you finally got it said. Walter, give up; leave me alone — it's Mama's money.

WALTER. *He was my father, too!*

BENEATHA. So what? He was mine, too — and Travis' grandfather — but the insurance money belongs to Mama. Picking on me is not going to make her give it to you to invest in any liquor stores — [*Underbreath, dropping into a chair*] — and I for one say, God bless Mama for that!

WALTER [*To* RUTH]. See — did you hear? Did you hear!

RUTH. Honey, please go to work.

WALTER. Nobody in this house is ever going to understand me.

BENEATHA. Because you're a nut.

WALTER. Who's a nut?

BENEATHA. You — you are a nut. Thee is mad, boy.

WALTER [*Looking at his wife and his sister from the door, very sadly*]. The world's most backward race of people, and that's a fact.

BENEATHA [*Turning slowly in her chair*]. And then there are all those prophets who would lead us out of the wilderness — [WALTER *slams out of the house*] — into the swamps!

RUTH. Bennie, why you always gotta be pickin' on your brother? Can't you be a little sweeter sometimes? [*Door opens.* WALTER *walks in*]

WALTER [*to* RUTH]. I need some money for carfare.

RUTH [*Looks at him, then warms; teasing, but tenderly*]. Fifty cents? [*She goes to her bag and gets money*] Here, take a taxi. [WALTER *exits.* MAMA *enters. She is a woman in her early sixties, full-bodied and strong. She is one of those women of a certain grace and beauty who wear it so unobtrusively that it takes a while to notice. Her dark-brown face is surrounded by the total whiteness of her hair, and, being a woman who has adjusted to many things in life and overcome many more, her face is full of strength. She has, we can see, wit and faith of a kind that keep her eyes lit and full of interest and expectancy. She is, in a word, a beautiful woman. Her bearing is perhaps most like the noble bearing of the women of the Hereros of Southwest Africa — rather as if she imagines that as she walks she still bears a basket or a vessel upon her head. Her speech, on the other hand, is as careless as her carriage is precise — she is inclined to slur everything — but her voice is perhaps not so much quiet as simply soft*]

MAMA. Who that 'round here slamming doors at this hour? [*She crosses through the room, goes to the window, opens it, and brings in a feeble little plant growing doggedly in a small pot on the window sill. She feels the dirt and puts in back out*]

RUTH. That was Walter Lee. He and Bennie was at it again.

MAMA. My children and they tempers. Lord, if this little old plant don't get more sun that it's been getting it ain't never going to see spring again. [*She turns from the window*] What's the matter with you this morning, Ruth? You looks right peaked. You aiming to iron all them things? Leave some for me. I'll get to 'em this afternoon. Bennie honey, it's too drafty for you to be sitting 'round half dressed. Where's your robe?

BENEATHA. In the cleaners.

MAMA. Well, go get mine and put it on.

BENEATHA. I'm not cold, Mama, honest.

MAMA. I know—but you so thin . . .

BENEATHA [*Irritably*]. Mama, I'm not cold.

MAMA [*Seeing the make-down bed as* TRAVIS *has left it*]. Lord have mercy, look at that poor bed. Bless his heart—he tries, don't he? [*She moves to the bed* TRAVIS *has sloppily made up*]

RUTH. No—he don't half try at all 'cause he knows you going to come along behind him and fix everything. That's just how come he don't know how to do nothing right now—you done spoiled that boy so.

MAMA. Well—he's a little boy. Ain't supposed to know 'bout housekeeping. My baby, that's what he is. What you fix for his breakfast this morning?

RUTH [*Angrily*]. I feed my son, Lena!

MAMA. I ain't meddling—[*Underbreath; busy-bodyish*]. I just noticed all last week he had cold cereal, and when it starts getting this chilly in the fall a child ought to have some hot grits or something when he goes out in the cold—

RUTH [*Furious*]. I gave him hot oats—is that all right!

MAMA. I ain't meddling. [*Pause*] Put a lot of nice butter on it? [RUTH *shoots her an angry look and does not reply*] He likes lots of butter.

RUTH [*Exasperated*]. Lena—

MAMA [*To* BENEATHA. MAMA *is inclined to wander conversationally sometimes*]. What was you and your brother fussing 'bout this morning?

BENEATHA. It's not important, Mama. [*She gets up and goes to look out at the bathroom, which is apparently free, and she picks up her towels and rushes out*]

MAMA. What was they fighting about?

RUTH. Now you know as well as I do.

MAMA [*Shaking her head*]. Brother still worrying hisself sick about that money?

RUTH. You know he is.

MAMA. You had breakfast?

RUTH. Some coffee.

MAMA. Girl, you better start eating and looking after yourself better. You almost thin as Travis.

RUTH. Lena—

MAMA. Uh-hunh?

RUTH. What are you going to do with it?

MAMA. Now don't you start, child. It's too early in the morning to be talking about money. It ain't Christian.

RUTH. It's just that he got his heart set on that store—

MAMA. You mean that liquor store that Willy Harris want him to invest in?

RUTH. Yes—

MAMA. We ain't no business people, Ruth. We just plain working folks.

RUTH. Ain't nobody business people till they go into business. Walter Lee say colored people ain't never going to start getting ahead till they start gambling on some different kinds of things in the world—investments and things.

MAMA. What done got into you, girl? Walter Lee done finally sold you on investing.

RUTH. No. Mama, something is happening between Walter and me. I don't know what it is—but he needs something—something I can't give him any more. He needs this chance, Lena.

MAMA [*Frowning deeply*]. But liquor, honey—

RUTH. Well—like Walter say—I spec people going to always be drinking themselves some liquor.

MAMA. Well—whether they drinks it or not ain't none of my business. But whether I go into business selling it to 'em *is*, and I don't want that on my ledger this late in life. [*Stopping suddenly and studying her daughter-in-law*] Ruth Younger, what's the matter with you today? You look like you could fall over right there.

RUTH. I'm tired.

MAMA. Then you better stay home from work today.

RUTH. I can't stay home. She'd be calling up the agency and screaming at them, "My girl didn't come in today—send me somebody! My girl didn't come in!" Oh, she just have a fit . . .

MAMA. Well, let her have it. I'll just call her up and say you got the flu—

RUTH [*Laughing*]. Why the flu?

MAMA. 'Cause it sounds respectable to 'em. Something white people get, too. They know 'bout the flu. Otherwise they think you been cut up or something when you tell 'em you sick.

RUTH. I got to go in. We need the money.

MAMA. Somebody would of thought my children done all but starved to death the way they talk about money here late. Child, we got a great big old check coming tomorrow.

RUTH [*Sincerely, but also self-righteously*]. Now that's your money. It ain't got nothing to do with me. We all feel like that—Walter and Bennie and me—even Travis.

MAMA [*Thoughtfully, and suddenly very far away*]. Ten thousand dollars—

RUTH. Sure is wonderful.

MAMA. Ten thousand dollars.

RUTH. You know what you should do, Miss Lena? You should take yourself a trip somewhere. To Europe or South America or someplace—

MAMA [*Throwing up her hands at the thought*]. Oh, child!

RUTH. I'm serious. Just pack up and leave! Go on away and enjoy yourself some. Forget about the family and have yourself a ball for once in your life—

MAMA [*Drily*]. You sound like I'm just about ready to die. Who'd go with me? What I look like wandering 'round Europe by myself?

RUTH. Shoot—these here rich white women do it all the time. They don't think nothing of packing up they suitcases and piling on one of them big steamships and—swoosh!—they gone, child.

MAMA. Something always told me I wasn't no rich white woman.

RUTH. Well—what are you going to do with it then?

MAMA. I ain't rightly decided. [*Thinking. She speaks now with emphasis*] Some of it got to be put away for Beneatha and her schoolin'—and ain't nothing going to touch that part of it. Nothing. [*She waits several seconds, trying to make up her mind about something, and looks at RUTH a little tentatively before going on*] Been thinking that we maybe could meet the notes on a little old two-story somewhere, with a yard where Travis could play in the summertime, if we use part of the insurance for a down payment and everybody kind of pitch in. I could maybe take on a little day work again, few days a week—

RUTH [*Studying her mother-in-law furtively and concentrating on her ironing, anxious to encourage without seeming to*]. Well, Lord knows, we've put enough rent into this here rat trap to pay for four houses by now . . .

MAMA [*Looking up at the words "rat trap" and then looking around and leaning back and sighing—in a suddenly reflective mood—*]. "Rat trap"—yes, that's all it is. [*Smiling*] I remember just as well the day me and Big Walter moved in here. Hadn't been married but two weeks and wasn't planning on living here no more than a year. [*She shakes her head at the dissolved dream*] We was going to set away, little by little, don't you know, and buy a little place out in Morgan Park. We had even picked out the house. [*Chuckling a little*] Looks right dumpy today. But Lord, child, you should know all the dreams I had 'bout buying that house and fixing it up and making me a little garden in the back — [*She waits and stops smiling*] And didn't none of it happen. [*Dropping her hands in a futile gesture*]

RUTH [*Keeps her head down, ironing*]. Yes, life can be a barrel of disappointments, sometimes.

MAMA. Honey, Big Walter would come in here some nights back then and slump down on that couch there and just look at the rug, and look at me and look at the rug and then back at me — and I'd know he was down then . . . really down. [*After a second very long and thoughtful pause; she is seeing back to times that only she can see*] And then, Lord, when I lost that baby — little Claude — I almost thought I was going to lose Big Walter too. Oh, that man grieved hisself! He was one man to love his children.

RUTH. Ain't nothin' can tear at you like losin' your baby.

MAMA. I guess that's how come that man finally worked hisself to death like he done. Likely he was fighting his own war with this here world that took his baby from him.

RUTH. He sure was a fine man, all right. I always liked Mr. Younger.

MAMA. Crazy 'bout his children! God knows there was plenty wrong with Walter Younger — hard-headed, mean, kind of wild with women — plenty wrong with him. But he sure loved his children. Always wanted them to have something — be something. That's where Brother gets all these notions, I reckon. Big Walter used to say, he'd get right wet in the eyes sometimes, lean his head back with the water standing in his eyes and say, "Seem like God didn't see fit to give the black man nothing but dreams — but He did give us children to make them dreams seem worth while." [*She smiles*] He could talk like that, don't you know.

RUTH. Yes, he sure could. He was a good man, Mr. Younger.

MAMA. Yes, a fine man — just couldn't never catch up with his dreams, that's all. [BENEATHA *comes in, brushing her hair and looking up to the ceiling, where the sound of a vacuum cleaner has started up*]

BENEATHA. What could be so dirty on that woman's rugs that she has to vacuum them every single day?

RUTH. I wish certain young women 'round here who I could name would take inspiration about certain rugs in a certain apartment I could also mention.

BENEATHA [*Shrugging*]. How much cleaning can a house need, for Christ's sakes?

MAMA [*Not liking the Lord's name used thus*]. Bennie!

RUTH. Just listen to her — just listen!

BENEATHA. Oh, God!

MAMA. If you use the Lord's name just one more time —

BENEATHA [*A bit of a whine*]. Oh, Mama —

RUTH. Fresh — just fresh as salt, this girl!

BENEATHA [*Drily*]. Well — if the salt loses its savor —

MAMA. Now that will do. I just ain't going to have you 'round here reciting the scriptures in vain — you hear me?

BENEATHA. How did I manage to get on everybody's wrong side by just walking into a room?

RUTH. If you weren't so fresh —

BENEATHA. Ruth, I'm twenty years old.

MAMA. What time you be home from school today?

BENEATHA. Kind of late. [*With enthusiasm*] Madeline is going to start my guitar lessons today. [MAMA *and* RUTH *look up with the same expression*]

MAMA. Your *what* kind of lessons?

BENEATHA. Guitar.

RUTH. Oh, Father!

MAMA. How come you done taken it in your mind to learn to play the guitar?

BENEATHA. I just want to, that's all.

MAMA [*Smiling*]. Lord, child, don't you know what to do with yourself? How long it going to be before you get tired of this now — like you got tired of that little play-acting group you joined last year? [*Looking at* RUTH] And what was it the year before that?

RUTH. The horseback-riding club for which she bought that fifty-five-dollar riding habit that's been hanging in the closet ever since!

MAMA [*To* BENEATHA]. Why you got to flit so from one thing to another, baby?

BENEATHA [*Sharply*]. I just want to learn to play the guitar. Is there anything wrong with that?

MAMA. Ain't nobody trying to stop you. I just wonders sometimes why you has to flit so from one thing to another all the time. You ain't never done nothing with all that camera equipment you brought home —

BENEATHA. I don't flit! I — I experiment with different forms of expression —

RUTH. Like riding a horse?

BENEATHA. — People have to express themselves one way or another.

MAMA. What is it you want to express?

BENEATHA [*Angrily*]. Me! [MAMA *and* RUTH *look at each other and burst into raucous laughter*] Don't worry — I don't expect you to understand.

MAMA [*To change the subject*]. Who you going out with tomorrow night?

BENEATHA [*With displeasure*]. George Murchison again.

MAMA [*Pleased*]. Oh — you getting a little sweet on him?

RUTH. You ask me, this child ain't sweet on nobody but herself — [*Underbreath*] Express herself! [*They laugh*]

BENEATHA. Oh — I like George all right, Mama. I mean I like him enough to go out with him and stuff, but —

RUTH [*For devilment*]. What does *and stuff* mean?

BENEATHA. Mind your own business.

MAMA. Stop picking at her now, Ruth. [*A thoughtful pause, and then a suspicious sudden look at her daughter as she turns in her chair for emphasis*] What *does* it mean?

BENEATHA [*Wearily*]. Oh, I just mean I couldn't ever really be serious about George. He's — he's so shallow.

RUTH. Shallow — what do you mean he's shallow? He's *Rich!*

MAMA. Hush, Ruth.

BENEATHA. I know he's rich. He knows he's rich, too.

RUTH. Well — what other qualities a man got to have to satisfy you, little girl?

BENEATHA. You wouldn't even begin to understand. Anybody who married Walter could not possibly understand.

MAMA [*Outraged*]. What kind of way is that to talk about your brother?

BENEATHA. Brother is a flip—let's face it.

MAMA [*To* RUTH, *helplessly*]. What's a flip?

RUTH [*Glad to add kindling*]. She's saying he's crazy.

BENEATHA. Not crazy. Brother isn't really crazy yet—he—he's an elaborate neurotic.

MAMA. Hush your mouth!

BENEATHA. As for George. Well. George looks good—he's got a beautiful car and he takes me to nice places and, as my sister-in-law says, he is probably the richest boy I will ever get to know and I even like him sometimes—but if the Youngers are sitting around waiting to see if their little Bennie is going to tie up the family with the Murchisons, they are wasting their time.

RUTH. You mean you wouldn't marry George Murchison if he asked you someday? That pretty, rich thing? Honey, I knew you was odd—

BENEATHA. No I would not marry him if all I felt for him was what I feel now. Besides, George's family wouldn't really like it.

MAMA. Why not?

BENEATHA. Oh, Mama—The Murchisons are honest-to-God-real-*live*-rich colored people, and the only people in the world who are more snobbish than rich white people are rich colored people. I thought everybody knew that. I've met Mrs. Murchison. She's a scene!

MAMA. You must not dislike people 'cause they well off, honey.

BENEATHA. Why not? It makes just as much sense as disliking people 'cause they are poor, and lots of people do that.

RUTH [*A wisdom-of-the-ages manner. To* MAMA]. Well, she'll get over some of this—

BENEATHA. Get over it? What are you talking about, Ruth? Listen, I'm going to be a doctor. I'm not worried about who I'm going to marry yet—if I ever get married.

MAMA *and* RUTH. If!

MAMA. Now, Bennie—

BENEATHA. Oh, I probably will . . . but first I'm going to be a doctor, and George, for one, still thinks that's pretty funny. I couldn't be bothered with that. I am going to be a doctor and everybody around here better understand that!

MAMA [*Kindly*]. 'Course you going to be a doctor, honey, God willing.

BENEATHA [*Drily*]. God hasn't got a thing to do with it.

MAMA. Beneatha—that just wasn't necessary.

BENEATHA. Well—neither is God. I get sick of hearing about God.

MAMA. Beneatha!

BENEATHA. I mean it! I'm just tired of hearing about God all the time. What has He got to do with anything? Does he pay tuition?

MAMA. You 'bout to get your fresh little jaw slapped!

RUTH. That's just what she needs, all right!

BENEATHA. Why? Why can't I say what I want to around here, like everybody else?

MAMA. It don't sound nice for a young girl to say things like that—you wasn't brought up that way. Me and your father went to trouble to get you and Brother to church every Sunday.

BENEATHA. Mama, you don't understand. It's all a matter of ideas, and God is just one idea I don't accept. It's not important. I am not going out and be immoral or commit crimes because I don't believe in God. I don't even think about it. It's just that I get tired of Him getting credit for all the things the human race achieves through its own stubborn effort. There simply is no blasted God—there is only man and it is he who makes miracles! [MAMA *absorbs this speech, studies her daughter and rises slowly and crosses to* BENEATHA *and slaps her powerfully across the face. After, there is only silence and the daughter drops her eyes from her mother's face, and* MAMA *is very tall before her*]

MAMA. Now—you say after me, in my mother's house there is still God. [*There is a long pause and* BENEATHA *stares at the floor wordlessly.* MAMA *repeats the phrase with precision and cool emotion*] In my mother's house there is still God.

BENEATHA. In my mother's house there is still God. [*A long pause*]

MAMA [*Walking away from* BENEATHA, *too disturbed for triumphant posture. Stopping and turning back to her daughter*]. There are some ideas we ain't going to have in this house. Not long as I am at the head of this family.

BENEATHA. Yes, ma'am. [MAMA *walks out of the room*]

RUTH [*Almost gently, with profound understanding*]. You think you a woman, Bennie—but you still a little girl. What you did was childish—so you got treated like a child.

BENEATHA. I see. [*Quietly*] I also see that everybody thinks it's all right for Mama to be a tyrant. But all the tyranny in the world will never put a God in the heavens! [*She picks up her books and goes out*]

RUTH [*Goes to* MAMA's *door*]. She said she was sorry.

MAMA [*Coming out, going to her plant*]. They frightens me, Ruth. My children.

RUTH. You got good children, Lena. They just a little off sometimes—but they're good.

MAMA. No—There's something come down between me and them that don't let us understand each other and I don't know what it is. One done almost lost his mind thinking 'bout money all the time and the other done commence to talk about things I can't seem to understand in no form or fashion. What is it that's changing, Ruth?

RUTH [*Soothingly, older than her years*]. Now . . . you taking it all too seriously. You just got strong-willed children and it takes a strong woman like you to keep 'em in hand.

MAMA [*Looking at her plant and sprinkling a little water on it*]. They spirited all right, my children. Got to admit they got spirit—Bennie and Walter. Like this little old plant that ain't never had enough sunshine or nothing—and look at it . . . [*She has her back to* RUTH, *who has had to stop ironing and lean against something and put the back of her hand to her forehead*]

RUTH [*Trying to keep* MAMA *from noticing*]. You . . . sure . . . loves that little old thing, don't you? . . .

MAMA. Well, I always wanted me a garden like I used to see sometimes at the back of the houses down home. This plant is close as I ever got to having one. [*She looks out of the window as she replaces the plant*] Lord, ain't nothing as dreary as the view from this window on a dreary day, is there? Why ain't you singing this morning, Ruth? Sing that "No Ways Tired." That song always lifts me up so—[*She turns at last to see that* RUTH *has slipped quietly into a chair, in a state of semiconsciousness*] Ruth! Ruth honey—what's the matter with you . . . Ruth!

CURTAIN

SCENE II

> It is the following morning; a Saturday morning, and house cleaning is in progress at the YOUNGERS. Furniture has been shoved hither and yon and MAMA is giving the kitchen-area walls a washing down. BENEATHA, in dungarees, with a handkerchief tied around her face, is spraying insecticide into the cracks in the walls. As they work, the radio is on and a Southside disk-jockey program is inappropriately filling the house with a rather exotic saxophone blues. TRAVIS, the sole idle one, is leaning on his arms, looking out of the window.

TRAVIS. Grandmama, that stuff Bennie is using smells awful. Can I go downstairs, please?

MAMA. Did you get all them chores done already? I ain't seen you doing much.

TRAVIS. Yes'm — finished early. Where did Mama go this morning?

MAMA [*Looking at* BENEATHA]. She had to go on a little errand.

TRAVIS. Where?

MAMA. To tend to her business.

TRAVIS. Can I go outside then?

MAMA. Oh, I guess so. You better stay right in front of the house, though . . . and keep a good lookout for the postman.

TRAVIS. Yes'm. [*He starts out and decides to give his* AUNT BENEATHA *a good swat on the legs as he passes her*] Leave them poor little old cockroaches alone, they ain't bothering you none. [*He runs as she swings the spray gun at him both viciously and playfully.* WALTER *enters from the bedroom and goes to the phone*]

MAMA. Look out there, girl, before you be spilling some of that stuff on that child!

TRAVIS [*Teasing*]. That's right — look out now! [*He exits*]

BENEATHA [*Drily*]. I can't imagine that it would hurt him — it has never hurt the roaches.

MAMA. Well, little boys' hides ain't as tough as Southside roaches.

WALTER [*Into phone*]. Hello — Let me talk to Willy Harris.

MAMA. You better get over there behind the bureau. I seen one marching out of there like Napoleon yesterday.

WALTER. Hello, Willy? It ain't come yet. It'll be here in a few minutes. Did the lawyer give you the papers?

BENEATHA. There's really only one way to get rid of them, Mama —

MAMA. How?

BENEATHA. Set fire to this building.

WALTER. Good. Good. I'll be right over.

BENEATHA. Where did Ruth go, Walter?

WALTER. I don't know. [*He exits abruptly*]

BENEATHA. Mama, where did Ruth go?

MAMA [*Looking at her with meaning*]. To the doctor, I think.

BENEATHA. The doctor? What's the matter? [*They exchange glances*] You don't think —

MAMA [*With her sense of drama*]. Now I ain't saying what I think. But I ain't never been wrong 'bout a woman neither. [*The phone rings*]

BENEATHA [*At the phone*]. Hay-lo . . . [*Pause, and a moment of recognition*] Well — when did you get back! . . . And how was it? . . . Of course I've missed you — in my way . . . This morning? No . . . house cleaning and all that and Mama hates it if I let people come over when the house is like this . . . You *have?* Well, that's different . . . What is it — Oh, what the hell, come on over . . . Right, see you then.

[*She hangs up*]

MAMA [*Who has listened vigorously, as is her habit*]. Who is that you inviting over here with this house looking like this? You ain't got the pride you was born with!

BENEATHA. Asagai doesn't care how houses look, Mama — he's an intellectual.

MAMA. *Who?*

BENEATHA. Asagai — Joseph Asagai. He's an African boy I met on campus. He's been studying in Canada all summer.

MAMA. What's his name?

BENEATHA. Asagai, Joseph. Ah-sah-guy . . . He's from Nigeria.

MAMA. Oh, that's the little country that was founded by slaves way back . . .

BENEATHA. No, Mama — that's Liberia.

MAMA. I don't think I never met no African before.

BENEATHA. Well, do me a favor and don't ask him a whole lot of ignorant questions about Africans. I mean, do they wear clothes and all that —

MAMA. Well, now, I guess if you think we so ignorant 'round here maybe you shouldn't bring your friends here —

BENEATHA. It's just that people ask such crazy things. All anyone seems to know about when it comes to Africa is Tarzan —

MAMA [*Indignantly*]. Why should I know anything about Africa?

BENEATHA. Why do you give money at church for the missionary work?

MAMA. Well, that's to help save people.

BENEATHA. You mean save them from *heathenism* —

MAMA [*Innocently*]. Yes.

BENEATHA. I'm afraid they need more salvation from the British and the French.

[RUTH *comes in forlornly and pulls off her coat with dejection. They both turn to look at her*]

RUTH [*Dispiritedly*]. Well, I guess from all the happy faces — everybody knows.

BENEATHA. You pregnant?

MAMA. Lord have mercy, I sure hope it's a little old girl. Travis ought to have a sister. [BENEATHA *and* RUTH *give her a hopeless look for this grandmotherly enthusiasm*]

BENEATHA. How far along are you?

RUTH. Two months

BENEATHA. Did you mean to? I mean did you plan it or was it an accident?

MAMA. What do you know about planning or not planning?

BENEATHA. Oh, Mama.

RUTH [*Wearily*]. She's twenty years old, Lena.

BENEATHA. Did you plan it, Ruth?

RUTH. Mind your own business.

BENEATHA. It is my business — where is he going to live, on the *roof?* [*There is silence following the remark as the three women react to the sense of it*] Gee — I didn't mean that, Ruth, honest. Gee, I don't feel like that at all. I — I think it is wonderful.

RUTH [*Dully*]. Wonderful.

BENEATHA. Yes — really.

MAMA [*Looking at* RUTH, *worried*]. Doctor say everything going to be all right?

RUTH [*Far away*]. Yes—she says everything is going to be fine . . .

MAMA [*Immediately suspicious*]. "She"—What doctor you went to? [RUTH *folds over, near hysteria*]

MAMA [*Worriedly hovering over* RUTH]. Ruth, honey—what's the matter with you—you sick? [RUTH *has her fists clenched on her thighs and is fighting hard to suppress a scream that seems to be rising in her*]

BENEATHA. What's the matter with her, Mama?

MAMA [*Working her fingers in* RUTH'S *shoulder to relax her*]. She be all right. Women gets right depressed sometimes when they get her way. [*Speaking softly, expertly, rapidly*] Now you just relax. That's right . . . just lean back, don't think 'bout nothing at all . . . nothing at all—

RUTH. I'm all right . . . [*The glassy-eyed look melts and then she collapses into a fit of heavy sobbing. The bell rings*]

BENEATHA. Oh, my God—that must be Asagai.

MAMA [*To* RUTH]. Come on now, honey. You need to lie down and rest awhile . . . then have some nice hot food. [*They exit,* RUTH'S *weight on her mother-in-law.* BENEATHA, *herself profoundly disturbed, opens the door to admit a rather dramatic-looking young man with a large package*]

ASAGAI. Hello, Alaiyo—

BENEATHA [*Holding the door open and regarding him with pleasure*]. Hello . . . [*Long pause*] Well—come in. And please excuse everything. My mother was very upset about my letting anyone come here with the place like this.

ASAGAI [*Coming into the room*]. You look disturbed too . . . Is something wrong?

BENEATHA [*Still at the door, absently*]. Yes . . . we've all got acute ghetto-itus. [*She smiles and comes toward him, finding a cigarette and sitting*] So—sit down! How was Canada?

ASAGAI [*A sophisticate*]. Canadian.

BENEATHA [*Looking at him*]. I'm very glad you are back.

ASAGAI [*Looking back at her in turn*]. Are you really?

BENEATHA. Yes—very.

ASAGAI. Why—you were quite glad when I went away. What happened?

BENEATHA. You went away.

ASAGAI. Ahhhhhhhh.

BENEATHA. Before—you wanted to be so serious before there was time.

ASAGAI. How much time must there be before one knows what one feels?

BENEATHA [*Stalling this particular conversation. Her hands pressed together, in a deliberately childish gesture*]. What did you bring me?

ASAGAI [*Handing her the package*]. Open it and see.

BENEATHA [*Eagerly opening the package and drawing out some records and the colorful robes of a Nigerian woman*]. Oh, Asagai! . . . You got them for me! . . . How beautiful . . . and the records too! [*She lifts out the robes and runs to the mirror with them and holds the drapery up in front of herself*]

ASAGAI [*Coming to her at the mirror*]. I shall have to teach you how to drape it properly. [*He flings the material about her for the moment and stands back to look at her*] Ah—Oh-pay-gay-day, oh-gbah-mu-shay. [*A Yoruba exclamation for admiration*] You wear it well . . . very well . . . mutilated hair and all.

BENEATHA [*Turning suddenly*]. My hair—what's wrong with my hair?

ASAGAI [*Shrugging*]. Were you born with it like that?

BENEATHA [*Reaching up to touch it*]. No . . . of course not. [*She looks back to the mirror, disturbed*]

ASAGAI [*Smiling*]. How then?

BENEATHA. You know perfectly well how . . . as crinkly as yours . . . that's how.

ASAGAI. And it is ugly to you that way?

BENEATHA [*Quickly*]. Oh, no — not ugly . . . [*More slowly, apologetically*] But it's so hard to manage when it's, well — raw.

ASAGAI. And so to accommodate that — you mutilate it every week?

BENEATHA. It's not mutilation!

ASAGAI [*Laughing aloud at her seriousness*]. Oh . . . please! I am only teasing you because you are so very serious about these things. [*He stands back from her and folds his arms across his chest as he watches her pulling at her hair and frowning in the mirror*] Do you remember the first time you met me at school? . . . [*He laughs*] You came up to me and said — and I thought you were the most serious little thing I had ever seen — you said: [*He imitates her*] "Mr. Asagai — I want very much to talk with you. About Africa. You see, Mr. Asagai, I am looking for my *identity!*" [*He laughs*]

BENEATHA [*Turning to him, not laughing*]. Yes — [*Her face is quizzical, profoundly disturbed*]

ASAGAI [*Still teasing and reaching out and taking her face in his hands and turning her profile to him*]. Well . . . it is true that this is not so much a profile of a Hollywood queen as perhaps a queen of the Nile — [*A mock dismissal of the importance of the question*] But what does it matter? Assimilationism is so popular in your country.

BENEATHA [*Wheeling, passionately, sharply*]. I am not an assimilationist!

ASAGAI [*The protest hangs in the room for a moment and* ASAGAI *studies her, his laughter fading*]. Such a serious one. [*There is a pause*] So — you like the robes? You must take excellent care of them — they are from my sister's personal wardrobe.

BENEATHA [*With incredulity*]. You — you sent all the way home — for me?

ASAGAI [*With charm*]. For you — I would do much more . . . Well, that is what I came for. I must go.

BENEATHA. Will you call me Monday?

ASAGAI. Yes . . . We have a great deal to talk about. I mean about identity and time and all that.

BENEATHA. Time?

ASAGAI. Yes. About how much time one needs to know what one feels.

BENEATHA. You never understood that there is more than one kind of feeling which can exist between a man and a woman — or, at least, there should be.

ASAGAI [*Shaking his head negatively but gently*]. No. Between a man and a woman there need be only one kind of feeling. I have that for you . . . Now even . . . right this moment . . .

BENEATHA. I know — and by itself — it won't do. I can find that anywhere.

ASAGAI. For a woman it should be enough.

BENEATHA. I know — because that's what it says in all the novels that men write. But it isn't. Go ahead and laugh — but I'm not interested in being someone's little episode in America or — [*With feminine vengeance*] — one of them! [ASAGAI *has burst into laughter again*] That's funny as hell, huh!

ASAGAI. It's just that every American girl I have known has said that to me. White—black—in this you are all the same. And the same speech, too!

BENEATHA [*Angrily*]. Yuk, yuk, yuk!

ASAGAI. It's how you can be sure that the world's most liberated women are not liberated at all. You all talk about it too much! [MAMA *enters and is immediately all social charm because of the presence of a guest*]

BENEATHA. Oh—Mama—this is Mr. Asagai.

MAMA. How do you do?

ASAGAI [*Total politeness to an elder*]. How do you do, Mrs. Younger. Please forgive me for coming at such an outrageous hour on a Saturday.

MAMA. Well, you are quite welcome. I just hope you understand that our house don't always look like this. [*Chatterish*] You must come again. I would love to hear all about—[*Not sure of the name*]—your country. I think it's so sad the way our American Negroes don't know nothing about Africa 'cept Tarzan and all that. And all that money they pour into these churches when they ought to be helping you people over there drive out them French and Englishmen done taken away your land. [*The mother flashes a slightly superior look at her daughter upon completion of the recitation*]

ASAGAI [*Taken aback by this sudden and acutely unrelated expression of sympathy*]. Yes . . . yes . . .

MAMA [*Smiling at him suddenly and relaxing and looking him over*]. How many miles is it from here to where you come from?

ASAGAI. Many thousands.

MAMA [*Looking at him as she would* WALTER]. I bet you don't half look after yourself, being away from your mama either. I spec you better come 'round here from time to time and get yourself some decent homecooked meals . . .

ASAGAI [*Moved*]. Thank you. Thank you very much. [*They are all quiet, then—*] Well . . . I must go. I will call you Monday, Alaiyo.

MAMA. What's that he call you?

ASAGAI. Oh—"Alaiyo." I hope you don't mind. It is what you would call a nickname, I think. It is a Yoruba word. I am a Yoruba.

MAMA [*Looking at* BENEATHA]. I—I thought he was from—

ASAGAI [*Understanding*]. Nigeria is my country. Yoruba is my tribal origin—

BENEATHA. You didn't tell us what Alaiyo means . . . for all I know, you might be calling me Little Idiot or something . . .

ASAGAI. Well . . . let me see . . . I do not know how just to explain it . . . The sense of a thing can be so different when it changes languages.

BENEATHA. You're evading.

ASAGAI. No—really it is difficult . . . [*Thinking*] It means . . . it means One for Whom Bread—Food—Is Not Enough. [*He looks at her*] Is that all right?

BENEATHA [*Understanding, softly*]. Thank you.

MAMA [*Looking from one to the other and not understanding any of it*]. Well . . . that's nice . . . You must come see us again—Mr.—

ASAGAI. Ah-sah-guy . . .

MAMA. Yes . . . Do come again.

ASAGAI. Good-bye. [*He exits*]

MAMA [*After him*]. Lord, that's a pretty thing just went out here! [*Insinuatingly, to her daughter*] Yes, I guess I see why we done commence to get so interested in Africa 'round here. Missionaries my aunt Jenny! [*She exits*]

BENEATHA. Oh, Mama! . . . [*She picks up the Nigerian dress and holds it up to her in front of the mirror again. She sets the headdress on haphazardly and then notices her hair again and clutches at it and then replaces the headdress and frowns at herself. Then she starts to wriggle in front of the mirror as she thinks a Nigerian woman might.* TRAVIS *enters and regards her*]

TRAVIS. You cracking up?

BENEATHA. Shut up. [*She pulls the headdress off and looks at herself in the mirror and clutches at her hair again and squinches her eyes as if trying to imagine something. Then, suddenly, she gets her raincoat and kerchief and hurriedly prepares for going out*]

MAMA [*Coming back into the room*]. She's resting now. Travis, baby, run next door and ask Miss Johnson to please let me have a little kitchen cleanser. This here can is empty as Jacob's kettle.

TRAVIS. I just came in.

MAMA. Do as you told. [*He exits and she looks at her daughter*] Where you going?

BENEATHA [*Halting at the door*]. To become a queen of the Nile! [*She exits in a breathless blaze of glory.* RUTH *appears in the bedroom doorway*]

MAMA. Who told you to get up?

RUTH. Ain't nothing wrong with me to be lying in no bed for. Where did Bennie go?

MAMA [*Drumming her fingers*]. Far as I could make out — to Egypt. [RUTH *just looks at her*] What time is it getting to?

RUTH. Ten twenty. And the mailman going to ring that bell this morning just like he done every morning for the last umpteen years. [TRAVIS *comes in with the cleanser can*]

TRAVIS. She say to tell you that she don't have much.

MAMA [*Angrily*]. Lord, some people I could name sure is tight-fisted! [*Directing her grandson*] Mark two cans of cleanser down on the list there. If she that hard up for kitchen cleanser, I sure don't want to forget to get her none!

RUTH. Lena — maybe the woman is just short on cleanser —

MAMA [*Not listening*]. — Much baking powder as she done borrowed from me all these years, she could of done gone into the baking business! [*The bell sounds suddenly and sharply and all three are stunned — serious and silent — mid-speech. In spite of all the other conversation and distractions of the morning, this is what they have been waiting for, even* TRAVIS, *who looks helplessly from his mother to his grandmother.* RUTH *is the first to come to life again*]

RUTH [*to* TRAVIS]. Get down them steps, boy! [TRAVIS *snaps to life and flies out to get the mail*]

MAMA [*Her eyes wide, her hand to her breast*]. You mean it done really come?

RUTH [*Excited*]. Oh, Miss Lena!

MAMA [*Collecting herself*]. Well . . . I don't know what we all so excited about 'round here for. We known it was coming for months.

RUTH. That's a whole lot different from having it come and being able to hold it in your hands . . . a piece of paper worth ten thousand dollars . . . [TRAVIS *bursts back into the room. He holds the envelope high above his head, like a little dancer, his face is radiant and he is breathless. He moves to his grandmother with sudden slow ceremony and puts the envelope into her hands. She accepts it, and then merely holds it and looks at it*] Come on! Open it . . . Lord have mercy, I wish Walter Lee was here!

TRAVIS. Open it, Grandmama!

MAMA [*Staring at it*]. Now you all be quiet. It's just a check.

RUTH. Open it . . .

MAMA [*Still staring at it*]. Now don't act silly . . . We ain't never been no people to act silly 'bout no money —

RUTH [*Swiftly*]. We ain't never had none before — *open it!* [MAMA *finally makes a good strong tear and pulls out the thin blue slice of paper and inspects it closely. The boy and his mother study it raptly over* MAMA'*s shoulders*]

MAMA. *Travis!* [*She is counting off with doubt*] Is that the right number of zeros?

TRAVIS. Yes'm . . . ten thousand dollars. Gaalee, Grandmama, you rich.

MAMA [*She holds the check away from her, still looking at it. Slowly her face sobers into a mask of unhappiness*]. Ten thousand dollars. [*She hands it to* RUTH] Put it away somewhere, Ruth. [*She does not look at* RUTH; *her eyes seem to be seeing something somewhere very far off*] Ten thousand dollars they give you. Ten thousand dollars.

TRAVIS [*To his mother, sincerely*]. What's the matter with Grandmama — don't she want to be rich?

RUTH [*Distractedly*]. You go on out and play now, baby. [TRAVIS *exits.* MAMA *starts wiping dishes absently, humming intently to herself.* RUTH *turns to her, with kind exasperation*] You've gone and got yourself upset.

MAMA [*Not looking at her*]. I spec if it wasn't for you all . . . I would just put that money away or give it to the church or something.

RUTH. Now what kind of talk is that. Mr. Younger would just be plain mad if he could hear you talking foolish like that.

MAMA [*Stopping and staring off*]. Yes . . . he sure would. [*Sighing*] We got enough to do with that money, all right. [*She halts then, and turns and looks at her daughter-in-law hard;* RUTH *avoids her eyes and* MAMA *wipes her hands with finality and starts to speak firmly to* RUTH] Where did you go today, girl?

RUTH. To the doctor.

MAMA [*Impatiently*]. Now, Ruth . . . you know better than that. Old Doctor Jones is strange enough in his way but there ain't nothing 'bout him make somebody slip and call him "she" — like you done this morning.

RUTH. Well, that's what happened — my tongue slipped.

MAMA. You went to see that woman, didn't you?

RUTH [*Defensively, giving herself away*]. What woman you talking about?

MAMA [*Angrily*]. That woman who — [WALTER *enters in great excitement*]

WALTER. Did it come?

MAMA [*Quietly*]. Can't you give people a Christian greeting before you start asking about money?

WALTER [*to* RUTH]. Did it come? [RUTH *unfolds the check and lays it quietly before him, watching him intently with thoughts of her own.* WALTER *sits down and grasps it close and counts off the zeros*] Ten thousand dollars — [*He turns suddenly, frantically to his mother and draws some papers out of his breast pocket*] Mama — look. Old Willy Harris put everything on paper —

MAMA. Son — I think you ought to talk to your wife . . . I'll go on out and leave you alone if you want —

WALTER. I can talk to her later — Mama, look —

MAMA. Son —

WALTER. WILL SOMEBODY PLEASE LISTEN TO ME TODAY!

MAMA [*Quietly*]. I don't 'low no yellin' in this house, Walter Lee, and you know it — [WALTER *stares at them in frustration and starts to speak several times*]

And there ain't going to be no investing in no liquor stores. I don't aim to have to speak on that again. [*A long pause*]

WALTER. Oh—so you don't aim to have to speak on that again? So *you* have decided . . . [*Crumpling his papers*]. Well, *you* tell that to my boy tonight when you put him to sleep on the living-room couch . . . [*Turning to* MAMA *and speaking directly to her*]. Yeah—and tell it to my wife, Mama, tomorrow when she has to go out of here to look after somebody else's kids. And tell it to *me*, Mama, every time we need a new pair of curtains and I have to watch *you* go out and work in somebody's kitchen. Yeah, you tell me then! [WALTER *starts out*]

RUTH. Where you going?

WALTER. I'm going out!

RUTH. Where?

WALTER. Just out of this house somewhere—

RUTH [*Getting her coat*]. I'll come too.

WALTER. I don't want you to come!

RUTH. I got something to talk to you about, Walter.

WALTER. That's too bad.

MAMA [*Still quietly*]. Walter Lee—[*She waits and he finally turns and looks at her*] Sit down.

WALTER. I'm a grown man, Mama.

MAMA. Ain't nobody said you wasn't grown. But you still in my house and my presence. And as long as you are—you'll talk to your wife civil. Now sit down.

RUTH [*Suddenly*]. Oh, let him go on out and drink himself to death! He makes me sick to my stomach! [*She flings her coat against him*]

WALTER [*Violently*]. And you turn mine, too, baby! [RUTH *goes into their bedroom and slams the door behind her.*] That was my greatest mistake—

MAMA [*Still quietly*]. Walter, what is the matter with you?

WALTER. Matter with me? Ain't nothing the matter with *me!*

MAMA. Yes there is. Something eating you up like a crazy man. Something more than me not giving you this money. The past few years I been watching it happen to you. You get all nervous acting and kind of wild in the eyes— [WALTER *jumps up impatiently at her words*] I said sit there now, I'm talking to you!

WALTER. Mama—I don't need no nagging at me today.

MAMA. Seem like you getting to a place where you always tied up in some kind of knot about something. But if anybody ask you 'bout it you just yell at 'em and bust out the house and go out and drink somewheres. Walter Lee, people can't live with that. Ruth's a good, patient girl in her way—but you getting to be too much. Boy, don't make the mistake of driving that girl away from you.

WALTER. Why—what she do for me?

MAMA. She loves you.

WALTER. Mama—I'm going out. I want to go off somewhere and be by myself for a while.

MAMA. I'm sorry 'bout your liquor store, son. It just wasn't the thing for us to do. That's what I want to tell you about—

WALTER. I got to go out, Mama—[*He rises*]

MAMA. It's dangerous, son.

WALTER. What's dangerous?

MAMA. When a man goes outside his home to look for peace.

WALTER [*Beseechingly*]. Then why can't there never be no peace in this house then?

MAMA. You done found it in some other house?

WALTER. No—there ain't no woman! Why do women always think there's a woman somewhere when a man gets restless. [*Coming to her*] Mama—Mama —I want so many things . . .

MAMA. Yes, son—

WALTER. I want so many things that they are driving me kind of crazy . . . Mama—look at me.

MAMA. I'm looking at you. You a good-looking boy. You got a job, a nice wife, a fine boy and—

WALTER. A job. [*Looks at her*] Mama, a job? I open and close car doors all day long. I drive a man around in his limousine and I say, "Yes, sir; no, sir; very good, sir; shall I take the Drive, sir?" Mama, that ain't no kind of job . . . that ain't nothing at all. [*Very quietly*] Mama, I don't know if I can make you understand.

MAMA. Understand what, baby?

WALTER [*Quietly*]. Sometimes it's like I can see the future stretched out in front of me—just plain as day. The future, Mama. Hanging over there at the edge of my days. Just waiting for me—a big, looming blank space—full of *nothing*. Just waiting for *me*. [*Pause*] Mama—sometimes when I'm downtown and I pass them cool, quiet-looking restaurants where them white boys are sitting back and talking 'bout things . . . sitting there turning deals worth millions of dollars . . . sometimes I see guys don't look much older than me—

MAMA. Son—how come you talk so much 'bout money?

WALTER [*With immense passion*]. Because it is life, Mama!

MAMA [*Quietly*]. Oh—[*Very quietly*] So now it's life. Money is life. Once upon a time freedom used to be life—now it's money. I guess the world really do change . . .

WALTER. No—it was always money, Mama. We just didn't know about it.

MAMA. No . . . something has changed. [*She looks at him*] You something new, boy. In my time we was worried about not being lynched and getting to the North if we could and how to stay alive and still have a pinch of dignity too . . . Now here come you and Beneatha—talking 'bout things we ain't never even thought about hardly, me and your daddy. You ain't satisfied or proud of nothing we done. I mean that you had a home; that we kept you out of trouble till you was grown; that you don't have to ride to work on the back of nobody's streetcar—You my children—but how different we done become.

WALTER. You just don't understand, Mama, you just don't understand.

MAMA. Son—do you know your wife is expecting another baby? [WALTER *stands, stunned, and absorbs what his mother has said*] That's what she wanted to talk to you about. [WALTER *sinks down into a chair*] This ain't for me to be telling—but you ought to know. [*She waits*] I think Ruth is thinking 'bout getting rid of that child.

WALTER [*Slowly understanding*]. No—no—Ruth wouldn't do that.

MAMA. When the world gets ugly enough—a woman will do anything for her family. *The part that's already living.*

WALTER. You don't know Ruth, Mama, if you think she would do that. [RUTH *opens the bedroom door and stands there a little limp*]

RUTH [*Beaten*]. Yes I would too, Walter. [*Pause*] I gave her a five-dollar down payment. [*There is total silence as the man stares at his wife and the mother stares at her son*]

MAMA [*Presently*]. Well—[*Tightly*] Well—son, I'm waiting to hear you say something . . . I'm waiting to hear how you be your father's son. Be the man he was . . . [*Pause*] Your wife say she going to destroy your child. And I'm waiting to hear you talk like him and say we a people who give children life, not who destroys them—[*She rises*] I'm waiting to see you stand up and look like your daddy and say we done give up one baby to poverty and that we ain't going to give up nary another one . . . I'm waiting.

WALTER. Ruth—

MAMA. If you a son of mine, tell her! [WALTER *turns, looks at her and can say nothing. She continues, bitterly*] You . . . you are a disgrace to your father's memory. Somebody get me my hat.

CURTAIN

ACT II

SCENE I

> *Time: Later the same day.*
> *At rise:* RUTH *is ironing again. She has the radio going. Presently* BENEATHA*'s bedroom door opens and* RUTH*'s mouth falls and she puts down the iron in fascination.*

RUTH. What have we got on tonight!

BENEATHA [*Emerging grandly from the doorway so that we can see her thoroughly robed in the costume* ASAGAI *brought.*] You are looking at what a well-dressed Nigerian woman wears—[*She parades for* RUTH, *her hair completely hidden by the headdress; she is coquettishly fanning herself with an ornate oriental fan, mistakenly more like Butterfly than any Nigerian that ever was*] Isn't it beautiful? [*She promenades to the radio and, with an arrogant flourish, turns off the good loud blues that is playing*] Enough of this assimilationist junk! [RUTH *follows her with her eyes as she goes to the phonograph and puts on a record and turns and waits ceremoniously for the music to come up. Then with a shout—*] OCOMOGOSIAY! [RUTH *jumps. The music comes up, a lovely Nigerian melody.* BENEATHA *listens, enraptured, her eyes far away—"back to the past." She begins to dance.* RUTH *is dumbfounded*]

RUTH. What kind of dance is that?

BENEATHA. A folk dance.

RUTH [*Pearl Bailey*]. What kind of folks do that, honey?

BENEATHA. It's from Nigeria. It's a dance of welcome.

RUTH. Who you welcoming?

BENEATHA. The men back to the village.

RUTH. Where they been?

BENEATHA. How should I know—out hunting or something. Anyway, they are coming back now . . .

RUTH. Well, that's good.

BENEATHA [*With the record*]. *Alundi, alundi*
Alundi alunya
Jop pu a jeepua
Ang gu soooooooooo
Ai yai yae . . .
Ayehaye—alundi . . . [WALTER *comes in during this performance; he has obviously been drinking. He leans against the door heavily and watches his sister, at first with distaste. Then his eyes look off—"back to the past"—as he lifts both his fists to the roof, screaming*]

WALTER. YEAH . . . AND ETHIOPIA STRETCH FORTH HER HANDS AGAIN! . . .

RUTH [*Drily, looking at him*]. Yes—and Africa sure is claiming her own tonight. [*She gives them both up and starts ironing again*]

WALTER [*All in a drunken, dramatic shout*]. Shut up! . . . I'm digging them drums . . . them drums move me! . . . [*He makes his weaving way to his wife's face and leans in close to her*] In my *heart of hearts*—[*He thumps his chest*]—I am much warrior!

RUTH [*Without even looking up*]. In your heart of hearts you are much drunkard.

WALTER [*Coming away from her and starting to wander around the room, shouting*]. Me and Jomo . . . [*Intently, in his sister's face. She has stopped dancing to watch him in this unknown mood*] That's my man, Kenyatta. [*Shouting and thumping his chest*] FLAMING SPEAR! HOT DAMN! [*He is suddenly in possession of an imaginary spear and actively spearing enemies all over the room*] *OCOMOGOSIAY* . . . THE LION IS WAKING . . . OWIMOWEH! [*He pulls his shirt open and leaps up on a table and gestures with his spear. The bell rings.* RUTH *goes to answer*]

BENEATHA [*To encourage* WALTER, *thoroughly caught up with this side of him*]. *OCOMOGOSIAY, FLAMING SPEAR!*

WALTER [*On the table, very far gone, his eyes pure glass sheets. He sees what we cannot, that he is a leader of his people, a great chief, a descendant of Chaka, and that the hour to march has come*]. Listen, my black brothers—

BENEATHA. OCOMOGOSIAY!

WALTER. —Do you hear the waters rushing against the shores of the coastlands—

BENEATHA. OCOMOGOSIAY!

WALTER. —Do you hear the screeching of the cocks in yonder hills beyond where the chiefs meet in council for the coming of the mighty war—

BENEATHA. OCOMOGOSIAY!

WALTER. —Do you hear the beating of the wings of the birds flying low over the mountains and the low places of our land—[RUTH *opens the door,* GEORGE MURCHISON *enters*]

BENEATHA. OCOMOGOSIAY!

WALTER. —Do you hear the singing of the women, singing the war songs of our fathers to the babies in the great houses . . . singing the sweet war songs? OH, DO YOU HEAR, MY BLACK BROTHERS?

BENEATHA [*Completely gone*]. We hear you, Flaming Spear—

WALTER. Telling us to prepare for the greatness of the time—[*To* GEORGE] Black Brother! [*He extends his hand for the fraternal clasp*]

GEORGE. Black Brother, hell!

RUTH [*Having had enough, and embarrassed for the family*]. Beneatha, you got company—what's the matter with you? Walter Lee Younger, get down off that table and stop acting like a fool . . . [WALTER *comes down off the table suddenly and makes a quick exit to the bathroom*]

RUTH. He's had a little to drink . . . I don't know what her excuse is.

GEORGE [*To* BENEATHA]. Look honey, we're going *to* the theatre—we're not going to be *in* it . . . so go change, huh?

RUTH. You expect this boy to go out with you looking like that?

BENEATHA [*Looking at* GEORGE]. That's up to George. If he's ashamed of his heritage—

GEORGE. Oh, don't be so proud of yourself, Bennie—just because you look eccentric.

BENEATHA. How can something that's natural be eccentric?

GEORGE. That's what being eccentric means—being natural. Get dressed.

BENEATHA. I don't like that, George.

RUTH. Why must you and your brother make an argument out of everything people say?

BENEATHA. Because I hate assimilationist Negroes!

RUTH. Will somebody please tell me what assimila-who-ever means!

GEORGE. Oh, it's just a college girl's way of calling people Uncle Toms—but that isn't what it means at all.

RUTH. Well, what does it mean?

BENEATHA [*Cutting* GEORGE *off and staring at him as she replies to* RUTH]. It means someone who is willing to give up his own culture and submerge himself completely in the dominant, and in this case, *oppressive* culture!

GEORGE. Oh, dear, dear, dear! Here we go! A lecture on the African past! On our Great West African Heritage! In one second we will hear all about the great Ashanti empires; the great Songhay civilizations; and the great sculpture of Bénin—and then some poetry in the Bantu—and the whole monologue will end with the word *heritage!* [*Nastily*] Let's face it, baby, your heritage is nothing but a bunch of raggedy-assed spirituals and some grass huts!

BENEATHA. *Grass huts!* [RUTH *crosses to her and forcibly pushes her toward the bedroom*] See there . . . you are standing there in your splendid ignorance talking about people who were the first to smelt iron on the face of the earth! [RUTH *is pushing her through the door*] The Ashanti were performing surgical operations when the English—[RUTH *pulls the door to, with* BENEATHA *on the other side, and smiles graciously at* GEORGE. BENEATHA *opens the door and shouts the end of the sentence defiantly at* GEORGE]—were still tattooing themselves with blue dragons . . . [*She goes back inside*]

RUTH. Have a seat, George. [*They both sit.* RUTH *folds her hands rather primly on her lap, determined to demonstrate the civilization of the family*] Warm, ain't it? I mean for September. [*Pause*] Just like they always say about Chicago weather: If it's too hot or cold for you, just wait a minute and it'll change. [*She smiles happily at this cliché of clichés*] Everybody say it's got to do with them bombs and things they keep setting off. [*Pause*] Would you like a nice cold beer?

GEORGE. No, thank you. I don't care for beer. [*He looks at his watch*] I hope she hurries up.

RUTH. What time is the show?

GEORGE. It's an eight-thirty curtain. That's just Chicago, though. In New York standard curtain time is eight forty. [*He is rather proud of this knowledge*]

RUTH [*Properly appreciating it*]. You get to New York a lot?

GEORGE [*Offhand*]. Few times a year.

RUTH. Oh — that's nice. I've never been to New York. [WALTER *enters. We feel he has relieved himself, but the edge of unreality is still with him*]

WALTER. New York ain't got nothing Chicago ain't. Just a bunch of hustling people all squeezed up together — being "Eastern." [*He turns his face into a screw of displeasure*]

GEORGE. Oh — you've been?

WALTER. *Plenty* of times.

RUTH [*Shocked at the lie*]. Walter Lee Younger!

WALTER [*Staring her down*]. Plenty! [*Pause*] What we got to drink in this house? Why don't you offer this man some refreshment. [*To* GEORGE] They don't know how to entertain people in this house, man.

GEORGE. Thank you — I don't really care for anything.

WALTER [*Feeling his head; sobriety coming*]. Where's Mama?

RUTH. She ain't come back yet.

WALTER [*Looking* MURCHISON *over from head to toe, scrutinizing his carefully casual tweed sports jacket over cashmere V-neck sweater over soft eyelet shirt and tie, and soft slacks, finished off with white buckskin shoes*]. Why all you college boys wear them fairyish-looking white shoes?

RUTH. Walter Lee! [GEORGE MURCHISON *ignores the remark*]

WALTER [*To* RUTH]. Well, they look crazy as hell — white shoes, cold as it is.

RUTH [*Crushed*]. You have to excuse him —

WALTER. No he don't! Excuse me for what? What you always excusing me for! I'll excuse myself when I needs to be excused! [*A pause*] They look as funny as them black knee socks Beneatha wears out of here all the time.

RUTH. It's the college *style*, Walter.

WALTER. Style, hell. She looks like she got burnt legs or something!

RUTH. Oh, Walter —

WALTER [*An irritable mimic*]. Oh, Walter! Oh, Walter! [*To* MURCHISON] How's your old man making out? I understand you all going to buy that big hotel on the Drive?[1] [*He finds a beer in the refrigerator, wanders over to* MURCHISON, *sipping and wiping his lips with the back of his hand, and straddling a chair backwards to talk to the other man*] Shrewd move. Your old man is all right, man. [*Tapping his head and half winking for emphasis*] I mean he knows how to operate. I mean he thinks *big*, you know what I mean, I mean for a *home*, you know?[2] But I think he's kind of running out of ideas now. I'd like

---

[1] **Drive:** Chicago's Outer Drive running along Lake Michigan.
[2] *Home:* Home-boy; one of us.

to talk to him. Listen, man, I got some plans that could turn this city upside down. I mean I think like he does. *Big.* Invest big, gamble big, hell, lose *big* if you have to, you know what I mean. It's hard to find a man on this whole Southside who understands my kind of thinking — you dig? [*He scrutinizes* MURCHISON *again, drinks his beer, squints his eyes and leans in close, confidential, man to man*] Me and you ought to sit down and talk sometimes, man. Man, I got me some ideas . . .

MURCHISON [*With boredom*]. Yeah — sometimes we'll have to do that, Walter.

WALTER [*Understanding the indifference, and offended*]. Yeah — well, when you get the time, man. I know you a busy little boy.

RUTH. Walter, please —

WALTER [*Bitterly, hurt*]. I know ain't nothing in this world as busy as you colored college boys with your fraternity pins and white shoes . . .

RUTH [*Covering her face with humiliation*]. Oh, Walter Lee —

WALTER. I see you all all the time — with the books tucked under your arms — going to your [*British A — a mimic*] "clahsses." And for what! What the hell you learning over there? Filling up your heads — [*Counting off on his fingers*] — with the sociology and the psychology — but they teaching you how to be a man? How to take over and run the world? They teaching you how to run a rubber plantation or a steel mill? Naw — just to talk proper and read books and wear white shoes . . .

GEORGE [*Looking at him with distaste, a little above it all*]. You're all wacked up with bitterness, man.

WALTER [*Intently, almost quietly, between the teeth, glaring at the boy*]. And you — ain't you bitter, man? Ain't you just about had it yet? Don't you see no stars gleaming that you can't reach out and grab? You happy? — You contented son-of-a-bitch — you happy? You got it made? Bitter? Man, I'm a volcano. Bitter? Here I am a giant — surrounded by ants! Ants who can't even understand what it is the giant is talking about.

RUTH [*Passionately and suddenly*]. Oh, Walter — ain't you with nobody!

WALTER [*Violently*]. No! 'Cause ain't nobody with me! Not even my own mother!

RUTH. Walter, that's a terrible thing to say! [BENEATHA *enters, dressed for the evening in a cocktail dress and earrings*]

GEORGE. Well — hey, you look great.

BENEATHA. Let's go, George. See you all later.

RUTH. Have a nice time.

GEORGE. Thanks. Good night. [*To* WALTER, *sarcastically*] Good night, *Prometheus.* [BENEATHA *and* GEORGE *exit*]

WALTER [*To* RUTH]. Who is Prometheus?

RUTH. I don't know. Don't worry about it.

WALTER [*In fury, pointing after* GEORGE]. See there — they get to a point where they can't insult you man to man — they got to go talk about something ain't nobody never heard of!

RUTH. How do you know it was an insult? [*To humor him*] Maybe Prometheus is a nice fellow.

WALTER. Prometheus! I bet there ain't even no such thing! I bet that simple-minded clown —

RUTH. Walter — [*She stops what she is doing and looks at him*]

WALTER [*Yelling*]. Don't start!

RUTH. Start what?

WALTER. Your nagging! Where was I? Who was I with? How much money did I spend?

RUTH [*Plaintively*]. Walter Lee—why don't we just try to talk about it . . .

WALTER [*Not listening*]. I been out talking with people who understand me. People who care about the things I got on my mind.

RUTH [*Wearily*]. I guess that means people like Willy Harris.

WALTER. Yes, people like Willy Harris

RUTH [*With a sudden flash of impatience*]. Why don't you all just hurry up and go into the banking business and stop talking about it!

WALTER. Why? You want to know why? 'Cause we all tied up in a race of people that don't know how to do nothing but moan, pray and have babies! [*The line is too bitter even for him and he looks at her and sits down*]

RUTH. Oh, Walter . . . [*Softly*] Honey, why can't you stop fighting me?

WALTER [*Without thinking*]. Who's fighting you? Who even cares about you? [*This line begins the retardation of his mood*]

RUTH. Well—[*She waits a long time, and then with resignation starts to put away her things*] I guess I might as well go on to bed . . . [*More or less to herself*] I don't know where we lost it . . . but we have . . . [*Then, to him*] I—I'm sorry about this new baby, Walter. I guess maybe I better go on and do what I started . . . I guess I just didn't realize how bad things was with us . . . I guess I just didn't really realize—[*She starts out to the bedroom and stops*] You want some hot milk?

WALTER. Hot milk?

RUTH. Yes—hot milk.

WALTER. Why hot milk?

RUTH. 'Cause after all that liquor you come home with you ought to have something hot in your stomach.

WALTER. I don't want no milk.

RUTH. You want some coffee then?

WALTER. No, I don't want no coffee. I don't want nothing hot to drink. [*Almost plaintively*] Why you always trying to give me something to eat?

RUTH [*Standing and looking at him helplessly*]. What else can I give you, Walter Lee Younger? [*She stands and looks at him and presently turns to go out again. He lifts his head and watches her going away from him in a new mood which began to emerge when he asked her "Who cares about you?"*]

WALTER. It's been rough, ain't it, baby? [*She hears and stops but does not turn around and he continues to her back*] I guess between two people there ain't never as much understood as folks generally thinks there is. I mean like between me and you—[*She turns to face him*] How we gets to the place where we scared to talk softness to each other. [*He waits, thinking hard himself*] Why you think it got to be like that? [*He is thoughtful, almost as a child would be*] Ruth, what is it gets into people ought to be close?

RUTH. I don't know, honey. I think about it a lot.

WALTER. On account of you and me, you mean? The way things are with us. The way something done come down between us.

RUTH. There ain't so much between us, Walter . . . Not when you come to me and try to talk to me. Try to be with me . . . a little even.

WALTER [*Total honesty*]. Sometimes . . . sometimes . . . I don't even know how to try.

RUTH. Walter—

WALTER. Yes?

RUTH [*Coming to him, gently and with misgiving, but coming to him*]. Honey . . . life don't have to be like this. I mean sometimes people can do things so that things are better . . . You remember how we used to talk when Travis was born . . . about the way we were going to live . . . the kind of house . . . [*She is stroking his head*] Well, it's all starting to slip away from us . . . [MAMA *enters, and* WALTER *jumps up and shouts at her*]

WALTER. Mama, where have you been?

MAMA. My—them steps is longer than they used to be. Whew! [*She sits down and ignores him*] How you feeling this evening, Ruth! [RUTH *shrugs, disturbed some at having been prematurely interrupted and watching her husband knowingly*]

WALTER. Mama, where have you been all day?

MAMA [*Still ignoring him and leaning on the table and changing to more comfortable shoes*]. Where's Travis?

RUTH. I let him go out earlier and he ain't come back yet. Boy, is he going to get it!

WALTER. Mama!

MAMA [*As if she has heard him for the first time*]. Yes, son?

WALTER. Where did you go this afternoon?

MAMA. I went downtown to tend to some business that I had to tend to.

WALTER. What kind of business?

MAMA. You know better than to question me like a child, Brother.

WALTER [*Rising and bending over the table*]. Where were you, Mama? [*Bringing his fists down and shouting*] Mama, you didn't go do something with that insurance money, something crazy? [*The front door opens slowly, interrupting him, and* TRAVIS *peeks his head in, less than hopefully*]

TRAVIS [*To his mother*]. Mama, I—

RUTH. "Mama I" nothing! You're going to get it, boy! Get on in that bedroom and get yourself ready!

TRAVIS. But I—

MAMA. Why don't you all never let the child explain hisself.

RUTH. Keep out of it now, Lena. [MAMA *clamps her lips together, and* RUTH *advances toward her son menacingly*]

RUTH. A thousand times I have told you not to go off like that—

MAMA [*Holding out her arms to her grandson*]. Well—at least let me tell him something. I want him to be the first one to hear . . . Come here, Travis. [*The boy obeys, gladly*] Travis—[*She takes him by the shoulder and looks into his face*]—you know that money we got in the mail this morning?

TRAVIS. Yes'm—

MAMA. Well—what you think your grandmama gone and done with that money?

TRAVIS. I don't know, Grandmama.

MAMA [*Putting her finger on his nose for emphasis*]. She went out and she bought you a house! [*The explosion comes from* WALTER *at the end of the revelation and he jumps up and turns away from all of them in a fury.* MAMA *continues, to*

TRAVIS] You glad about the house? It's going to be yours when you get to be a man.

TRAVIS. Yeah—I always wanted to live in a house.

MAMA. All right, gimme some sugar then—[TRAVIS *puts his arms around her neck as she watches her son over the boy's shoulder. Then, to* TRAVIS, *after the embrace*] Now when you say your prayers tonight, you thank God and your grandfather—'cause it was him who give you the house—in his way.

RUTH [*Taking the boy from* MAMA *and pushing him toward the bedroom*]. Now you get out of here and get ready for your beating.

TRAVIS. Aw, Mama—

RUTH. Get on in there—[*Closing the door behind him and turning radiantly to her mother-in-law*] So you went and did it!

MAMA [*Quietly, looking at her son with pain*]. Yes, I did.

RUTH [*Raising both arms classically*]. Praise God! [*Looks at* WALTER *a moment, who says nothing. She crosses rapidly to her husband*] Please, honey—let me be glad . . . you be glad too. [*She has laid her hands on his shoulders, but he shakes himself free of her roughly, without turning to face her*] Oh, Walter . . . a home . . . *a home*. [*She comes back to* MAMA] Well—where is it? How big is it? How much it going to cost?

MAMA. Well—

RUTH. When we moving?

MAMA [*Smiling at her*]. First of the month.

RUTH [*Throwing back her head with jubilance*]. Praise God!

MAMA [*Tentatively, still looking at her son's back turned against her and* RUTH]. It's—it's a nice house too . . . [*She cannot help speaking directly to him. An imploring quality in her voice, her manner, makes her almost like a girl now*] Three bedrooms—nice big one for you and Ruth . . . Me and Beneatha still have to share our room, but Travis have one of his own—and [*With difficulty*] I figure if the—new baby—is a boy, we could get one of them double-decker outfits . . . And there's a yard with a little patch of dirt where I could maybe get to grow me a few flowers . . . And a nice big basement . . .

RUTH. Walter honey, be glad—

MAMA [*Still to his back, fingering things on the table*]. 'Course I don't want to make it sound fancier than it is . . . It's just a plain little old house—but it's made good and solid—and it will be *ours*. Walter Lee—it makes a difference in a man when he can walk on floors that belong to *him* . . .

RUTH. Where is it?

MAMA [*Frightened at this telling*]. Well—well—it's out there in Clybourne Park—[RUTH'*s radiance fades abruptly, and* WALTER *finally turns slowly to face his mother with incredulity and hostility*]

RUTH. Where?

MAMA [*Matter-of-factly*]. Four o six Clybourne Street, Clybourne Park.

RUTH. Clybourne Park? Mama, there ain't no colored people living in Clybourne Park.

MAMA [*Almost idiotically*]. Well, I guess there's going to be some now.

WALTER [*Bitterly*]. So that's the peace and comfort you went out and bought for us today!

MAMA [*Raising her eyes to meet his finally*]. Son — I just tried to find the nicest place for the least amount of money for my family.

RUTH [*Trying to recover from the shock*]. Well — well — 'course I ain't one never been 'fraid of no crackers, mind you — but — well, wasn't there no other houses nowhere?

MAMA. Them houses they put up for colored in them areas way out all seem to cost twice as much as other houses. I did the best I could.

RUTH [*Struck senseless with the news, in its various degrees of goodness and trouble, she sits a moment, her fists propping her chin in thought, and then she starts to rise, bringing her fists down with vigor, the radiance spreading from cheek to cheek again*]. Well — well! — All I can say is — if this is my time in life — *my time* — to say good-bye — [*And she builds with momentum as she starts to circle the room with an exuberant, almost tearfully happy release*] — to these God-damned cracking walls! — [*She pounds the walls*] — and these marching roaches! — [*She wipes at an imaginary army of marching roaches*] — and this cramped little closet which ain't now or never was no kitchen! . . . then I say it loud and good, *Hallelujah! and good-bye misery . . . I don't never want to see your ugly face again!* [*She laughs joyously, having practically destroyed the apartment, and flings her arms up and lets them come down happily, slowly, reflectively, over her abdomen, aware for the first time perhaps that the life therein pulses with happiness and not despair*] Lena?

MAMA [*Moved, watching her happiness*]. Yes, honey?

RUTH [*Looking off*]. Is there — is there a whole lot of sunlight?

MAMA [*Understanding*]. Yes, child, there's a whole lot of sunlight. [*Long pause*]

RUTH [*Collecting herself and going to the door of the room* TRAVIS *is in*]. Well — I guess I better see 'bout TRAVIS. [*To* MAMA] Lord, I sure don't feel like whipping nobody today! [*She exits*]

MAMA [*The mother and son are left alone now and the mother waits a long time, considering deeply, before she speaks*]. Son — you — you understand what I done, don't you? [WALTER *is silent and sullen*] I — I just seen my family falling apart today . . . just falling to pieces in front of my eyes . . . We couldn't of gone on like we was today. We was going backwards 'stead of forwards — talking 'bout killing babies and wishing each other was dead . . . When it gets like that in life — you just got to do something different, push on out and do something bigger . . . [*She waits*] I wish you say something, son . . . I wish you'd say how deep inside you you think I done the right thing —

WALTER [*Crossing slowly to his bedroom door and finally turning there and speaking measuredly*]. What you need me to say you done right for? *You* the head of this family. You run our lives like you want to. It was your money and you did what you wanted with it. So what you need for me to say it was all right for? [*Bitterly, to hurt her as deeply as he knows is possible*] So you butchered up a dream of mine — you — who always talking 'bout your children's dreams . . .

MAMA. Walter Lee — [*He just closes the door behind him.* MAMA *sits alone, thinking heavily*]

CURTAIN

SCENE II

Time: Friday night. A few weeks later.
At rise: Packing crates mark the intention of the family to
move. BENEATHA *and* GEORGE *come in, presumably from an*
evening out again.]

GEORGE. O.K. . . . O.K., whatever you say . . . [*They both sit on the couch. He*
tries to kiss her. She moves away] Look, we've had a nice evening; let's not spoil
it, huh? . . . [*He again turns her head and tries to nuzzle in and she turns*
away from him, not with distaste but with momentary lack of interest; in a mood
to pursue what they were talking about]
BENEATHA. I'm *trying* to talk to you.
GEORGE. We always talk.
BENEATHA. Yes—and I love to talk.
GEORGE [*Exasperated; rising*]. I know it and I don't mind it sometimes . . . I
want you to cut it out, see—The moody stuff, I mean. I don't like it. You're a
nice-looking girl . . . all over. That's all you need, honey, forget the atmosphere. Guys aren't going to go for the atmosphere—they're going to go for
what they see. Be glad for that. Drop the Garbo routine. It doesn't go with
you. As for myself, I want a nice—[*Groping*]—simple [*Thoughtfully*]—
sophisticated girl . . . not a poet—O.K.? [*She rebuffs him again and he starts*
to leave]
BENEATHA. Why are you angry?
GEORGE. Because this is stupid! I don't go out with you to discuss the nature of
"quiet desperation" or to hear all about your thoughts—because the world
will go on thinking what it thinks regardless—
BENEATHA. Then why read books? Why go to school?
GEORGE [*With artificial patience, counting on his fingers*]. It's simple. You read
books—to learn facts—to get grades—to pass the course—to get a degree.
That's all—it has nothing to do with thoughts. [*A long pause*]
BENEATHA. I see. [*A longer pause as she looks at him*] Good night, George.
[GEORGE *looks at her a little oddly, and starts to exit. He meets* MAMA *coming*
in]
GEORGE. Oh—hello, Mrs. Younger.
MAMA. Hello, George, how you feeling?
GEORGE. Fine—fine, how are you?
MAMA. Oh, a little tired. You know them steps can get you after a day's work.
You all have a nice time tonight?
GEORGE. Yes—a fine time. Well, good night.
MAMA. Good night. [*He exits.* MAMA *closes the door behind her*] Hello, honey.
What you sitting like that for?
BENEATHA. I'm just sitting.
MAMA. Didn't you have a nice time?
BENEATHA. No.
MAMA. No? What's the matter?
BENEATHA. Mama, George is a fool—honest. [*She rises*]
MAMA [*Hustling around unloading the packages she has entered with. She stops*]. Is
he, baby?
BENEATHA. Yes. [BENEATHA *makes up* TRAVIS' *bed as she talks*]
MAMA. You sure?

BENEATHA. Yes.

MAMA. Well—I guess you better not waste your time with no fools. [BEN-EATHA *looks up at her mother, watching her put groceries in the refrigerator. Finally she gathers up her things and starts into the bedroom. At the door she stops and looks back at her mother*]

BENEATHA. Mama—

MAMA. Yes, baby—

BENEATHA. Thank you.

MAMA. For what?

BENEATHA. For understanding me this time. [*She exits quickly and the mother stands, smiling a little, looking at the place where* BENEATHA *had stood.* RUTH *enters*]

RUTH. Now don't you fool with any of this stuff, Lena—

MAMA. Oh, I just thought I'd sort a few things out. [*The phone rings.* RUTH *answers*]

RUTH [*At the phone*]. Hello—Just a minute. [*Goes to door*] Walter, it's Mrs. Arnold. [*Waits. Goes back to the phone. Tense*] Hello. Yes, this is his wife speaking . . . He's lying down now. Yes . . . well, he'll be in tomorrow. He's been very sick. Yes—I know we should have called, but we were so sure he'd be able to come in today. Yes—yes, I'm very sorry. Yes . . . Thank you very much. [*She hangs up.* WALTER *is standing in the doorway of the bedroom behind her*] That was Mrs. Arnold.

WALTER [*Indifferently*]. Was it?

RUTH. She said if you don't come in tomorrow that they are getting a new man . . .

WALTER. Ain't that sad—ain't that crying sad.

RUTH. She said Mr. Arnold has had to take a cab for three days . . . Walter, you ain't been to work for three days! [*This is a revelation to her*] Where you been, Walter Lee Younger? [WALTER *looks at her and starts to laugh*] You're going to lose your job.

WALTER. That's right . . .

RUTH. Oh, Walter, and with your mother working like a dog every day—

WALTER. That's sad too—Everything is sad.

MAMA. What you been doing for these three days, son?

WALTER. Mama—you don't know all the things a man what got leisure can find to do in this city . . . What's this—Friday night? Well—Wednesday I borrowed Willy Harris' car and I went for a drive . . . just me and myself and I drove and drove . . . Way out . . . way past South Chicago, and I parked the car and I sat and looked at the steel mills all day long. I just sat in the car and looked at them big black chimneys for hours. Then I drove back and I went to the Green Hat. [*Pause*] And Thursday—Thursday I borrowed the car again and I got in it and I pointed it the other way and I drove the other way—for hours—way, way up to Wisconsin, and I looked at the farms. I just drove and looked at the farms. Then I drove back and I went to the Green Hat. [*Pause*] And today—today I didn't get the car. Today I just walked. All over the Southside. And I looked at the Negroes and they looked at me and finally I just sat down on the curb at Thirty-ninth and South Parkway and I just sat there and watched the Negroes go by. And then I went to the Green Hat. You all sad? You all depressed? And you know where I am going right now—[RUTH *goes out quietly*]

MAMA. Oh, Big Walter, is this the harvest of our days?

WALTER. You know what I like about the Green Hat? [*He turns the radio on and a steamy, deep blues pours into the room*] I like this little cat they got there who blows a sax . . . He blows. He talks to me. He ain't but 'bout five feet tall and he's got a conked head and his eyes is always closed and he's all music —

MAMA [*Rising and getting some papers out of her handbag*]. Walter —

WALTER. And there's this other guy who plays the piano . . . and they got a sound. I mean they can work on some music . . . They got the best little combo in the world in the Green Hat . . . You can just sit there and drink and listen to them three men play and you realize that don't nothing matter worth a damn, but just being there —

MAMA. I've helped do it to you, haven't I, son? Walter, I been wrong.

WALTER. Naw — you ain't never been wrong about nothing, Mama.

MAMA. Listen to me, now. I say I been wrong, son. That I been doing to you what the rest of the world been doing to you. [*She stops and he looks up slowly at her and she meets his eyes pleadingly*] Walter — what you ain't understood is that I ain't got nothing, don't own nothing, ain't never really wanted nothing that wasn't for you. There ain't nothing as precious to me . . . There ain't nothing worth holding on to, money, dreams, nothing else — if it means — if it means it's going to destroy my boy. [*She puts her papers in front of him and he watches her without speaking or moving*] I paid the man thirty-five hundred dollars down on the house. That leaves sixty-five hundred dollars. Monday morning I want you to take this money and take three thousand dollars and put it in a savings account for Beneatha's medical schooling. The rest you put in a checking account — with your name on it. And from now on any penny that come out of it or that go in it is for you to look after. For you to decide. [*She drops her hands a little helplessly*] It ain't much, but it's all I got in the world and I'm putting it in your hands. I'm telling you to be the head of this family from now on like you supposed to be.

WALTER [*Stares at the money*]. You trust me like that, Mama?

MAMA. I ain't never stop trusting you. Like I ain't never stop loving you. [*She goes out, and* WALTER *sits looking at the money on the table as the music continues in its idiom, pulsing in the room. Finally, in a decisive gesture, he gets up, and, in mingled joy and desperation, picks up the money. At the same moment,* TRAVIS *enters for bed*]

TRAVIS. What's the matter, Daddy? You drunk?

WALTER [*Sweetly, more sweetly than we have ever known him*]. No, Daddy ain't drunk. Daddy ain't going to never be drunk again. . . .

TRAVIS. Well, good night, Daddy. [*The father has come from behind the couch and leans over, embracing his son*]

WALTER. Son, I feel like talking to you tonight.

TRAVIS. About what?

WALTER. Oh, about a lot of things. About you and what kind of man you going to be when you grow up. . . . Son — son, what do you want to be when you grow up?

TRAVIS. A bus driver.

WALTER [*Laughing a little*]. A what? Man, that ain't nothing to want to be!

TRAVIS. Why not?

WALTER. 'Cause, man — it ain't big enough — you know what I mean.

TRAVIS. I don't know then. I can't make up my mind. Sometimes Mama asks me that too. And sometimes when I tell her I just want to be like you — she says she don't want me to be like that and sometimes she says she does . . .

WALTER [*Gathering him up in his arms*]. You know what, Travis? In seven years you going to be seventeen years old. And things is going to be very different with us in seven years, Travis. . . . One day when you are seventeen I'll come home — home from my office downtown somewhere —

TRAVIS. You don't work in no office, Daddy.

WALTER. No — but after tonight. After what your daddy gonna do tonight, there's going to be offices — a whole lot of offices. . . .

TRAVIS. What you gonna do tonight, Daddy?

WALTER. You wouldn't understand yet, son, but your daddy's gonna make a transaction . . . a business transaction that's going to change our lives . . . That's how come one day when you 'bout seventeen years old I'll come home and I'll be pretty tired, you know what I mean, after a day of conferences and secretaries getting things wrong the way they do . . . 'cause an executive's life is hell, man — [*The more he talks the farther away he gets*] And I'll pull the car up on the driveway . . . just a plain black Chrysler, I think, with white walls — no — black tires. More elegant. Rich people don't have to be flashy . . . though I'll have to get something a little sportier for Ruth — maybe a Cadillac convertible to do her shopping in. . . . And I'll come up the steps to the house and the gardener will be clipping away at the hedges and he'll say, "Good evening, Mr. Younger." And I'll say, "Hello, Jefferson, how are you this evening?" And I'll go inside and Ruth will come downstairs and meet me at the door and we'll kiss each other and she'll take my arm and we'll go up to your room to see you sitting on the floor with the catalogues of all the great schools in America around you. . . . All the great schools in the world! And — and I'll say, all right son — it's your seventeenth birthday, what is it you've decided? . . . Just tell me where you want to go to school and you'll *go*. Just tell me, what it is you want to be — and you'll *be* it. . . . Whatever you want to be — Yessir! [*He holds his arms open for* TRAVIS] You just name it, son . . . [TRAVIS *leaps into them*] and I hand you the world! [WALTER'*s voice has risen in pitch and hysterical promise and on the last line he lifts* TRAVIS *high*]

BLACKOUT

SCENE III

    Time: Saturday, moving day, one week later.

    Before the curtain rises, RUTH'*s voice, a strident, dramatic church alto, cuts through the silence.*

    It is, in the darkness, a triumphant surge, a penetrating statement of expectation: "Oh, Lord, I don't feel no ways tired! Children, oh, glory hallelujah!"

    As the curtain rises we see that RUTH *is alone in the living room, finishing up the family's packing. It is moving day. She is nailing crates and tying cartons.* BENEATHA *enters, carrying a guitar case, and watches her exuberant sister-in-law.*

RUTH. Hey!

BENEATHA [*Putting away the case*]. Hi.

RUTH [*Pointing at a package*]. Honey—look in that package there and see what
I found on sale this morning at the South Center. [RUTH *gets up and moves to
the package and draws out some curtains*] Lookahere—hand-turned hems!

BENEATHA. How do you know the window size out there?

RUTH [*Who hadn't thought of that*]. Oh—Well, they bound to fit something in
the whole house. Anyhow, they was too good a bargain to pass up. [RUTH
slaps her head, suddenly remembering something] Oh, Bennie—I meant to put a
special note on that carton over there. That's your mama's good china and she
wants 'em to be very careful with it.

BENEATHA. I'll do it. [BENEATHA *finds a piece of paper and starts to draw large
letters on it*]

RUTH. You know what I'm going to do soon as I get in that new house?

BENEATHA. What?

RUTH. Honey—I'm going to run me a tub of water up to here . . . [*With her
fingers practically up to her nostrils*] And I'm going to get in it—and I am
going to sit . . . and sit . . . and sit in that hot water and the first person
who knocks to tell *me* to hurry up and come out—

BENEATHA. Gets shot at sunrise.

RUTH [*Laughing happily*]. You said it, sister! [*Noticing how large* BENEATHA *is
absent-mindedly making the note*] Honey, they ain't going to read that from no
airplane.

BENEATHA [*Laughing herself*]. I guess I always think things have more emphasis
if they are big, somehow.

RUTH [*Looking up at her and smiling*]. You and your brother seem to have that as
a philosophy of life. Lord, that man—done changed so 'round here. You
know—you know what we did last night? Me and Walter Lee?

BENEATHA. What?

RUTH [*Smiling to herself*]. We went to the movies. [*Looking at* BENEATHA *to see
if she understands*] We went to the movies. You know the last time me and
Walter went to the movies together?

BENEATHA. No.

RUTH. Me neither. That's how long it been. [*Smiling again*] But we went last
night. The picture wasn't much good, but that didn't seem to matter. We
went—and we held hands.

BENEATHA. Oh, Lord!

RUTH. We held hands—and you know what?

BENEATHA. What?

RUTH. When we come out of the show it was late and dark and all the stores
and things was closed up . . . and it was kind of chilly and there wasn't
many people on the streets . . . and we was still holding hands, me and
Walter.

BENEATHA. You're killing me. [WALTER *enters with a large package. His happiness is deep in him; he cannot keep still with his new-found exuberance. He is
singing and wiggling and snapping his fingers. He puts his package in a corner
and puts a phonograph record, which he has brought in with him, on the record
player. As the music comes up he dances over to* RUTH *and tries to get her to dance
with him. She gives in at last to his raunchiness and in a fit of giggling allows
herself to be drawn into his mood and together they deliberately burlesque an old
social dance of their youth*]

BENEATHA [*Regarding them a long time as they dance, then drawing in her breath for a deeply exaggerated comment which she does not particularly mean*]. Talk about — olddddddddddd — fashionedddddddd — Negroes!

WALTER [*Stopping momentarily*]. What kind of Negroes? [*He says this in fun. He is not angry with her today, nor with anyone. He starts to dance with his wife again*]

BENEATHA. Old-fashioned.

WALTER [*As he dances with* RUTH]. You know, when these *New Negroes* have their convention — [*Pointing at his sister*] — that is going to be the chairman of the Committee on Unending Agitation. [*He goes on dancing, then stops*] Race, race, race! . . . Girl, I do believe you are the first person in the history of the entire human race to successfully brainwash yourself. [BENEATHA *breaks up and he goes on dancing. He stops again, enjoying his tease*] Damn, even the N double A C P takes a holiday sometimes! [BENEATHA *and* RUTH *laugh. He dances with* RUTH *some more and starts to laugh and stops and pantomimes someone over an operating table*] I can just see that chick someday looking down at some poor cat on an operating table before she starts to slice him, saying . . . [*Pulling his sleeves back maliciously*] "By the way, what are your views on civil rights down there? . . . " [*He laughs at her again and starts to dance happily. The bell sounds*]

BENEATHA. Sticks and stones may break my bones but . . . words will never hurt me! [BENEATHA *goes to the door and opens it as* WALTER *and* RUTH *go on with the clowning.* BENEATHA *is somewhat surprised to see a quiet-looking middle-aged white man in a business suit holding his hat and a briefcase in his hand and consulting a small piece of paper*]

MAN. Uh — how do you do, miss. I am looking for a Mrs. — [*He looks at the slip of paper*] Mrs. Lena Younger?

BENEATHA [*Smoothing her hair with slight embarrassment*]. Oh — yes, that's my mother. Excuse me. [*She closes the door and turns to quiet the other two*] Ruth! Brother! Somebody's here. [*Then she opens the door. The man casts a curious quick glance at all of them*] Uh — come in please.

MAN [*Coming in*]. Thank you.

BENEATHA. My mother isn't here just now. Is it business?

MAN. Yes . . . well, of a sort.

WALTER [*Freely, the Man of the House*]. Have a seat. I'm Mrs. Younger's son. I look after most of her business matters. [RUTH *and* BENEATHA *exchange amused glances*]

MAN [*Regarding* WALTER, *and sitting*]. Well — My name is Karl Lindner . . .

WALTER [*Stretching out his hand*]. Walter Younger. This is my wife — [RUTH *nods politely*] — and my sister.

LINDNER. How do you do.

WALTER [*Amiably, as he sits himself easily on a chair, leaning with interest forward on his knees and looking expectantly into the newcomer's face*]. What can we do for you, Mr. Lindner!

LINDNER [*Some minor shuffling of the hat and briefcase on his knees*]. Well — I am a representative of the Clybourne Park Improvement Association —

WALTER [*Pointing*]. Why don't you sit your things on the floor?

LINDNER. Oh — yes. Thank you. [*He slides the briefcase and hat under the chair*] And as I was saying — I am from the Clybourne Park Improvement Association and we have had it brought to our attention at the last meeting that you people — or at least your mother — has bought a piece of residential property at — [*He digs for the slip of paper again*] — four o six at Clybourne Street . . .

WALTER. That's right. Care for something to drink? Ruth, get Mr. Lindner a beer.

LINDNER [*Upset for some reason*]. Oh — no, really. I mean thank you very much, but no thank you.

RUTH [*Innocently*]. Some coffee?

LINDNER. Thank you, nothing at all. [BENEATHA *is watching the man carefully*]

LINDNER. Well, I don't know how much you folks know about our organization. [*He is a gentle man; thoughtful and somewhat labored in his manner*] It is one of these community organizations set up to look after — oh, you know, things like block upkeep and special projects and we also have what we call our New Neighbors Orientation Committee . . .

BENEATHA [*Drily*]. Yes — and what do they do?

LINDNER [*Turning a little to her and then returning the main force to* WALTER]. Well — it's what you might call a sort of welcoming committee, I guess. I mean they, we, I'm the chairman of the committee — go around and see the new people who move into the neighborhood and sort of give them the lowdown on the way we do things out in Clybourne Park.

BENEATHA [*With appreciation of the two meanings, which escape* RUTH *and* WALTER]. Uh-huh.

LINDNER. And we also have the category of what the association calls — [*He looks elsewhere*] — uh — special community problems . . .

BENEATHA. Yes — and what are some of those?

WALTER. Girl, let the man talk.

LINDNER [*With understated relief*]. Thank you. I would sort of like to explain this thing in my own way. I mean I want to explain to you in a certain way.

WALTER. Go ahead.

LINDNER. Yes. Well. I'm going to try to get right to the point. I'm sure we'll all appreciate that in the long run.

BENEATHA. Yes.

WALTER. Be still now!

LINDNER. Well —

RUTH [*Still innocently*]. Would you like another chair — you don't look comfortable.

LINDNER [*More frustrated than annoyed*]. No, thank you very much. Please. Well — to get right to the point I — [*A great breath, and he is off at last*] I am sure you people must be aware of some of the incidents which have happened in various parts of the city when colored people have moved into certain areas — [BENEATHA *exhales heavily and starts tossing a piece of fruit up and down in the air*] Well — because we have what I think is going to be a unique type of organization in American community life — not only do we deplore that kind of thing — but we are trying to do something about it. [BENEATHA *stops tossing and turns with a new and quizzical interest to the man*] We feel — [*Gaining confidence in his mission because of the interest in the faces of the people he is talking to*] — we feel that most of the trouble in this world, when you come right down to it — [*He hits his knee for emphasis*] — most of the trouble exists because people just don't sit down and talk to each other.

RUTH [*Nodding as she might in church, pleased with the remark*]. You can say that again, mister.

LINDNER [*More encouraged by such affirmation*]. That we don't try hard enough in this world to understand the other fellow's problem. The other guy's point of view.

RUTH. Now that's right. [BENEATHA *and* WALTER *merely watch and listen with genuine interest*]

LINDNER. Yes — that's the way we feel out in Clybourne Park. And that's why I was elected to come here this afternoon and talk to you people. Friendly like, you know, the way people should talk to each other and see if we couldn't find some way to work this thing out. As I say, the whole business is a matter of *caring* about the other fellow. Anybody can see that you are a nice family of folks, hard working and honest I'm sure. [BENEATHA *frowns slightly, quizzically, her head tilted regarding him*] Today everybody knows what it means to be on the outside of *something.* And of course, there is always somebody who is out to take the advantage of people who don't always understand.

WALTER. What do you mean?

LINDNER. Well — you see our community is made of people who've worked hard as the dickens for years to build up that little community. They're not rich and fancy people; just hard-working, honest people who don't really have much but those little homes and a dream of the kind of community they want to raise their children in. Now, I don't say we are perfect and there is a lot wrong in some of the things they want. But you've got to admit that a man, right or wrong, has the right to want to have the neighborhood he lives in a certain kind of way. And at the moment the overwhelming majority of our people out there feel that people get along better, take more of a common interest in the life of the community, when they share a common background. I want you to believe me when I tell you that race prejudice simply doesn't enter into it. It is a matter of the people of Clybourne Park believing, rightly or wrongly, as I say, that for the happiness of all concerned that our Negro families are happier when they live in their *own* communities.

BENEATHA [*With a grand and bitter gesture*]. This, friends, is the Welcoming Committee!

WALTER [*Dumbfounded, looking at* LINDNER]. Is this what you came marching all the way over here to tell us?

LINDNER. Well, now we've been having a fine conversation. I hope you'll hear me all the way through.

WALTER [*Tightly*]. Go ahead, man.

LINDNER. You see — in the face of all things I have said, we are prepared to make your family a very generous offer . . .

BENEATHA. Thirty pieces and not a coin less!

WALTER. Yeah?

LINDNER [*Putting on his glasses and drawing a form out of the briefcase*]. Our association is prepared, through the collective effort of our people, to buy the house from you at a financial gain to your family.

RUTH. Lord have mercy, ain't this the living gall!

WALTER. All right, you through?

LINDNER. Well, I want to give you the exact terms of the financial arrangement —

WALTER. We don't want to hear no exact terms of no arrangements. I want to know if you got any more to tell us 'bout getting together?

LINDNER [*Taking off his glasses*]. Well—I don't suppose that you feel . . .

WALTER. Never mind how I feel—you got any more to say 'bout how people ought to sit down and talk to each other? . . . Get out of my house, man. [*He turns his back and walks to the door*]

LINDNER [*Looking around at the hostile faces and reaching and assembling his hat and briefcase*]. Well—I don't understand why you people are reacting this way. What do you think you are going to gain by moving into a neighborhood where you just aren't wanted and where some elements—well—people can get awful worked up when they feel that their whole way of life and everything they've ever worked for is threatened.

WALTER. Get out.

LINDNER [*At the door, holding a small card*]. Well—I'm sorry it went like this.

WALTER. Get out.

LINDNER [*Almost sadly regarding* WALTER]. You just can't force people to change their hearts, son. [*He turns and put his card on a table and exits.* WALTER *pushes the door to with stinging hatred, and stands looking at it.* RUTH *just sits and* BENEATHA *just stands. They say nothing.* MAMA *and* TRAVIS *enter*]

MAMA. Well—this all the packing got done since I left out of here this morning. I testify before God that my children got all the energy of the dead. What time the moving men due?

BENEATHA. Four o'clock. You had a caller, Mama. [*She is smiling, teasingly*]

MAMA. Sure enough—who?

BENEATHA [*Her arms folded saucily*]. The Welcoming Committee. [WALTER *and* RUTH *giggle*]

MAMA [*Innocently*]. Who?

BENEATHA. The Welcoming Committee. They said they're sure going to be glad to see you when you get there.

WALTER [*Devilishly*]. Yeah, they said they can't hardly wait to see your face. [*Laughter*]

MAMA [*Sensing their facetiousness*]. What's the matter with you all?

WALTER. Ain't nothing the matter with us. We just telling you 'bout the gentleman who came to see you this afternoon. From the Clybourne Park Improvement Association.

MAMA. What he want?

RUTH [*In the same mood as* BENEATHA *and* WALTER]. To welcome you, honey.

WALTER. He said they can't hardly wait. He said the one thing they don't have, that they just *dying* to have out there is a fine family of colored people! [*To* RUTH *and* BENEATHA] Ain't that right!

RUTH *and* BENEATHA [*Mockingly*]. Yeah! He left his card in case—[*They indicate the card, and* MAMA *picks it up and throws it on the floor—understanding and looking off as she draws her chair up to the table on which she has put her plant and some sticks and some cord*]

MAMA. Father, give us strength. [*Knowingly—and without fun*] Did he threaten us?

BENEATHA. Oh—Mama—they don't do it like that any more. He talked Brotherhood. He said everybody ought to learn how to sit down and hate each other with good Christian fellowship. [*She and* WALTER *shake hands to ridicule the remark*]

MAMA [*Sadly*]. Lord, protect us . . .

RUTH. You should hear the money those folks raised to buy the house from us. All we paid and then some.

BENEATHA. What they think we going to do — eat 'em?

RUTH. No, honey, marry 'em.

MAMA [*Shaking her head*]. Lord, Lord, Lord . . .

RUTH. Well — that's the way the crackers crumble. Joke.

BENEATHA [*Laughingly noticing what her mother is doing*]. Mama, what are you doing?

MAMA. Fixing my plant so it won't get hurt none on the way . . .

BENEATHA. Mama, you going to take *that* to the new house?

MAMA. Un-huh —

BENEATHA. That raggedy-looking old thing?

MAMA [*Stopping and looking at her*]. It expresses *me*.

RUTH [*With delight, to* BENEATHA]. So there, Miss Thing! [WALTER *comes to* MAMA *suddenly and bends down behind her and squeezes her in his arms with all his strength. She is overwhelmed by the suddenness of it and, though delighted, her manner is like that of* RUTH *with* TRAVIS]

MAMA. Look out now, boy! You make me mess up my thing here!

WALTER [*His face lit, he slips down on his knees beside her, his arms still about her*]. Mama . . . you know what it means to climb up in the chariot?

MAMA [*Gruffly, very happy*]. Get on away from me now . . .

RUTH [*Near the gift-wrapped package, trying to catch* WALTER'*s eye*]. Psst —

WALTER. What the old song say, Mama . . .

RUTH. Walter — Now? [*She is pointing at the package*]

WALTER [*Speaking the lines, sweetly, playfully, in his mother's face*].
I got wings . . . you got wings . . .
All God's children got wings . . .

MAMA. Boy — get out of my face and do some work . . .

WALTER.
When I get to heaven gonna put on my wings,
Gonna fly all over God's heaven . . .

BENEATHA [*Teasingly, from across the room*]. Everybody talking 'bout heaven ain't going there!

WALTER [*To* RUTH, *who is carrying the box across to them*]. I don't know, you think we ought to give her that . . . Seems to me she ain't been very appreciative around here.

MAMA [*Eying the box, which is obviously a gift*]. What is that?

WALTER [*Taking it from* RUTH *and putting it on the table in front of* MAMA]. Well — what you all think? Should we give it to her?

RUTH. Oh — she was pretty good today.

MAMA. I'll good you — [*She turns her eyes to the box again*]

BENEATHA. Open it, Mama. [*She stands up, looks at it, turns and looks at all of them, and then presses her hands together and does not open the package*]

WALTER [*Sweetly*]. Open it, Mama. It's for you. [MAMA *looks in his eyes. It is the first present in her life without its being Christmas. Slowly she opens her package and lifts out, one by one, a brand-new sparkling set of gardening tools.* WALTER *continues, prodding*] Ruth made up the note — read it . . .

MAMA [*Picking up the card and adjusting her glasses*]. "To our own Mrs. Miniver — Love from Brother, Ruth and Beneatha." Ain't that lovely . . .

TRAVIS [*Tugging at his father's sleeve*]. Daddy, can I give her mine now?

WALTER. All right, son. [TRAVIS *flies to get his gift*] Travis didn't want to go in with the rest of us, Mama. He got his own. [*Somewhat amused*] We don't know what it is . . .

TRAVIS [*Racing back in the room with a large hatbox and putting it in front of his grandmother*]. Here!

MAMA. Lord have mercy, baby. You done gone and bought your grandmother a hat?

TRAVIS [*Very proud*]. Open it! [*She does and lifts out an elaborate, but very elaborate, wide gardening hat, and all the adults break up at the sight of it*]

RUTH. Travis, honey, what is that?

TRAVIS [*Who thinks it is beautiful and appropriate*]. It's a gardening hat! Like the ladies always have on in the magazines when they work in their gardens.

BENEATHA [*Giggling fiercely*]. Travis — we were trying to make Mama Mrs. Miniver — not Scarlett O'Hara!

MAMA [*Indignantly*]. What's the matter with you all! This here is a beautiful hat! [*Absurdly*] I always wanted me one just like it! [*She pops it on her head to prove it to her grandson, and the hat is ludicrous and considerably oversized*]

RUTH. Hot dog! Go, Mama!

WALTER [*Doubled over with laughter*]. I'm sorry, Mama — but you look like you ready to go out and chop you some cotton sure enough! [*They all laugh except MAMA, out of deference to TRAVIS's feelings*]

MAMA [*Gathering the boy up to her*]. Bless your heart — this is the prettiest hat I ever owned — [WALTER, RUTH *and* BENEATHA *chime in — noisily, festively and insincerely congratulating* TRAVIS *on his gift*] What are we all standing around here for? We ain't finished packin' yet. Bennie, you ain't packed one book. [*The bell rings*]

BENEATHA. That couldn't be the movers . . . it's not hardly two o'clock yet — [BENEATHA *goes into her room.* MAMA *starts for door*]

WALTER [*Turning, stiffening*]. Wait — wait — I'll get it. [*He stands and looks at the door*]

MAMA. You expecting company, son?

WALTER [*Just looking at the door*]. Yeah — yeah . . . [MAMA *looks at* RUTH, *and they exchange innocent and unfrightened glances*]

MAMA [*Not understanding*]. Well, let them in, son.

BENEATHA [*From her room*]. We need some more string.

MAMA. Travis — you run to the hardware and get me some string cord. [MAMA *goes out and* WALTER *turns and looks at* RUTH. TRAVIS *goes to a dish for money*]

RUTH. Why don't you answer the door, man?

WALTER [*Suddenly bounding across the floor to her*]. 'Cause sometimes it hard to let the future begin! [*Stooping down in her face*]
I got wings! You got wings!
All God's children got wings!

[*He crosses to the door and throws it open. Standing there is a very slight little man in a not too prosperous business suit and with haunted frightened eyes and a hat pulled down tightly, brim up, around his forehead.* TRAVIS *passes between the men and exits.* WALTER *leans deep in the man's face, still in his jubilance*]
When I get to heaven gonna put on my wings,
Gonna fly all over God's heaven . . .
[*The little man just stares at him*]

Heaven—

[*Suddenly he stops and looks past the little man into the empty hallway*] Where's Willy, man?

BOBO. He ain't with me.

WALTER [*Not disturbed*]. Oh—come on in. You know my wife.

BOBO [*Dumbly, taking off his hat*]. Yes—h'you, Miss Ruth.

RUTH [*Quietly, a mood apart from her husband already, seeing* BOBO]. Hello, Bobo.

WALTER. You right on time today . . . Right on time. That's the way! [*He slaps* BOBO *on his back*] Sit down . . . lemme hear. [RUTH *stands stiffly and quietly in back of them, as though somehow she senses death, her eyes fixed on her husband*]

BOBO [*His frightened eyes on the floor, his hat in his hands*]. Could I please get a drink of water, before I tell you about it, Walter Lee? [WALTER *does not take his eyes off the man.* RUTH *goes blindly to the tap and gets a glass of water and brings it to* BOBO]

WALTER. There ain't nothing wrong, is there?

BOBO. Lemme tell you—

WALTER. Man—didn't nothing go wrong?

BOBO. Lemme tell you—Walter Lee. [*Looking at* RUTH *and talking to her more than to* WALTER] You know how it was. I got to tell you how it was. I mean first I got to tell you how it was all the way . . . I mean about the money I put in, Walter Lee . . .

WALTER [*With taut agitation now*]. What about the money you put in?

BOBO. Well—it wasn't much as we told you—me and Willy—[*He stops*] I'm sorry, Walter. I got a bad feeling about it. I got a real bad feeling about it . . .

WALTER. Man, what you telling me about all this for? . . . Tell me what happened in Springfield . . .

BOBO. Springfield.

RUTH [*Like a dead woman*]. What was supposed to happen in Springfield?

BOBO [*To her*]. This deal that me and Walter went into with Willy—Me and Willy was going to go down to Springfield and spread some money 'round so's we wouldn't have to wait so long for the liquor license . . . That's what we were going to do. Everybody said that was the way you had to do, you understand, Miss Ruth?

WALTER. Man—what happened down there?

BOBO [*A pitiful man, near tears*]. I'm trying to tell you, Walter.

WALTER [*Screaming at him suddenly*]. THEN TELL ME, GODDAMMIT . . . WHAT'S THE MATTER WITH YOU?

BOBO. Man . . . I didn't go to no Springfield, yesterday.

WALTER [*Halted, life hanging in the moment*]. Why not?

BOBO [*The long way, the hard way to tell*]. 'Cause I didn't have no reasons to . . .

WALTER. Man, what are you talking about!

BOBO. I'm talking about the fact that when I got to the train station yesterday morning—eight o'clock like we planned . . . Man—*Willy didn't never show up.*

WALTER. Why . . . where was he . . . where is he?

BOBO. That's what I'm trying to tell you . . . I don't know . . . I waited six hours . . . I called his house . . . and I waited . . . six hours . . . I waited in that train station six hours . . . [*Breaking into tears*] That was all the extra money I had in the world . . . [*Looking up at* WALTER *with the tears running down his face*] Man, *Willy is gone.*

WALTER. Gone, what you mean Willy is gone? Gone where? You mean he went by himself. You mean he went off to Springfield by himself—to take care of getting the license—[*Turns and looks anxiously at* RUTH] You mean maybe he didn't want too many people in on the business down there? [*Looks to* RUTH *again, as before*] You know Willy got his own ways. [*Looks back to* BOBO] Maybe you was late yesterday and he just went on down there without you. Maybe—maybe—he's been callin' you at home tryin' to tell you what happened or something. Maybe—maybe—he just got sick. He's somewhere —he's got to be somewhere. We just got to find him—me and you got to find him. [*Grabs* BOBO *senselessly by the collar and starts to shake him*] We got to!

BOBO [*In sudden angry, frightened agony*]. What's the matter with you, Walter! *When a cat take off with your money he don't leave you no maps!*

WALTER [*Turning madly, as though he is looking for* WILLY *in the very room*]. Willy! . . . Willy . . . don't do it . . . Please don't do it . . . Man, not with that money . . . Man, please, not with that money . . . Oh, God . . . Don't let it be true . . . [*He is wandering around, crying out for* WILLY *and looking for him or perhaps for help from God*] Man . . . I trusted you . . . Man, I put my life in your hands . . . [*He starts to crumple down on the floor as* RUTH *just covers her face in horror.* MAMA *opens the door and comes into the room, with* BENEATHA *behind her*] Man . . . [*He starts to pound the floor with his fists, sobbing wildly*] That money is made out of my father's flesh . . .

BOBO [*Standing over him helplessly*]. I'm sorry, Walter . . . [*Only* WALTER'*s sobs reply.* BOBO *puts on his hat*] I had my life staked on this deal, too . . . [*He exits*]

MAMA [*To* WALTER]. Son—[*She goes to him, bends down to him, talks to his bent head*] Son . . . Is it gone? Son, I gave you sixty-five hundred dollars. Is it gone? All of it? Beneatha's money too?

WALTER [*Lifting his head slowly*]. Mama . . . I never . . . went to the bank at all . . .

MAMA [*Not wanting to believe him*]. You mean . . . your sister's school money . . . you used that too . . . Walter? . . .

WALTER. Yessss! . . . All of it . . . It's all gone . . .

[*There is total silence.* RUTH *stands with her face covered with her hands;* BENEATHA *leans forlornly against a wall, fingering a piece of red ribbon from the mother's gift.* MAMA *stops and looks at her son without recognition and then, quite without thinking about it, starts to beat him senselessly in the face.* BENEATHA *goes to them and stops it*]

BENEATHA. Mama! [MAMA *stops and looks at both of her children and rises slowly and wanders vaguely, aimlessly away from them*]

MAMA. I seen . . . him . . . night after night . . . come in . . . and look at that rug . . . and then look at me . . . the red showing in his eyes . . . the veins moving in his head . . . I seen him grow thin and old before he was forty . . . working and working and working like somebody's old

horse . . . killing himself . . . and you—you give it all away in a
day . . .

BENEATHA. Mama—

MAMA. Oh, God . . . [*She looks up to Him*] Look down here—and show me
the strength.

BENEATHA. Mama—

MAMA [*Folding over*]. Strength . . .

BENEATHA [*Plaintively*]. Mama . . .

MAMA. Strength!

CURTAIN

ACT III

An hour later.

*At curtain, there is a sullen light of gloom in the living room,
gray light not unlike that which began the first scene of Act I. At
left we can see* WALTER *within his room, alone with himself. He is
stretched out on the bed, his shirt out and open, his arms under his
head. He does not smoke, he does not cry out, he merely lies there,
looking up at the ceiling, much as if he were alone in the world.*

In the living room BENEATHA *sits at the table, still surrounded
by the now almost ominous packing crates. She sits looking off. We
feel that this is a mood struck perhaps an hour before, and it lingers
now, full of the empty sound of profound disappointment. We see
on a line from her brother's bedroom the sameness of their attitudes. Presently the bell rings and* BENEATHA *rises without ambition or interest in answering. It is* ASAGAI, *smiling broadly,
striding into the room with energy and happy expectation and
conversation.*

ASAGAI. I came over . . . I had some free time. I thought I might help with the
packing. Ah, I like the look of packing crates! A household in preparation for
a journey! It depresses some people . . . but for me . . . it is another feeling. Something full of the flow of life, do you understand? Movement,
progress . . . It makes me think of Africa.

BENEATHA. Africa!

ASAGAI. What kind of a mood is this? Have I told you how deeply you move
me?

BENEATHA. He gave away the money, Asagai . . .

ASAGAI. Who gave away what money?

BENEATHA. The insurance money. My brother gave it away.

ASAGAI. Gave it away?

BENEATHA. He made an investment! With a man even Travis wouldn't have
trusted.

ASAGAI. And it's gone?

BENEATHA. Gone!

ASAGAI. I'm very sorry . . . And you, now?

BENEATHA. Me? . . . Me? . . . Me I'm nothing . . . Me. When I was very small . . . we used to take our sleds out in the wintertime and the only hills we had were the ice-covered stone steps of some houses down the street. And we used to fill them in with snow and make them smooth and slide down them all day . . . and it was very dangerous you know . . . far too steep . . . and sure enough one day a kid named Rufus came down too fast and hit the sidewalk . . . and we saw his face just split open right there in front of us . . . And I remember standing there looking at his bloody open face thinking that was the end of Rufus. But the ambulance came and they took him to the hospital and they fixed the broken bones and they sewed it all up . . . and the next time I saw Rufus he just had a little line down the middle of his face . . . I never got over that . . . [WALTER *sits up, listening on the bed. Throughout this scene it is important that we feel his reaction at all times, that he visibly respond to the words of his sister and* ASAGAI]

ASAGAI. What?

BENEATHA. That that was what one person could do for another, fix him up — sew up the problem, make him all right again. That was the most marvelous thing in the world . . . I wanted to do that. I always thought it was the one concrete thing in the world that a human being could do. Fix up the sick, you know — and make them whole again. This was truly being God . . .

ASAGAI. You wanted to be God?

BENEATHA. No — I wanted to cure. It used to be so important to me. I wanted to cure. It used to matter. I used to care. I mean about people and how their bodies hurt . . .

ASAGAI. And you've stopped caring?

BENEATHA. Yes — I think so.

ASAGAI. Why? [WALTER *rises, goes to the door of his room and is about to open it, then stops and stands listening, leaning on the door jamb*]

BENEATHA. Because it doesn't seem deep enough, close enough to what ails mankind — I mean this thing of sewing up bodies or administering drugs. Don't you understand? It was a child's reaction to the world. I thought that doctors had the secret to all the hurts . . . That's the way a child sees things — or an idealist.

ASAGAI. Children see things very well sometimes — and idealists even better.

BENEATHA. I know that's what you think. Because you are still where I left off — you still care. This is what you see for the world, for Africa. You with the dreams of the future will patch up all Africa — you are going to cure the Great Sore of colonialism with Independence —

ASAGAI. Yes!

BENEATHA. Yes — and you think that one word is the penicillin of the human spirit: "Independence!" But then what?

ASAGAI. That will be the problem for another time. First we must get there.

BENEATHA. And where does it end?

ASAGAI. End? Who even spoke of an end? To life? To living?

BENEATHA. An end to misery!

ASAGAI [*Smiling*]. You sound like a French intellectual.

BENEATHA. No! I sound like a human being who just had her future taken right out of her hands! While I was sleeping in my bed in there, things were happening in this world that directly concerned me — and nobody asked me,

consulted me—they just went out and did things—and changed my life.
Don't you see there isn't any real progress, Asagai, there is only one large
circle that we march in, around and around, each of us with our own little
picture—in front of us—our own little mirage that we think is the future.

ASAGAI. That is the mistake.

BENEATHA. What?

ASAGAI. What you just said—about the circle. It isn't a circle—it is simply a
long line—as in geometry, you know, one that reaches into infinity. And
because we cannot see the end—we also cannot see how it changes. And it is
very odd but those who see the changes are called "idealists"—and those who
cannot, or refuse to think, they are the "realists." It is very strange, and
amusing too, I think.

BENEATHA. You—you are almost religious.

ASAGAI. Yes . . . I think I have the religion of doing what is necessary in the
world—and of worshipping man—because he is so marvelous, you see.

BENEATHA. Man is foul! And the human race deserves its misery!

ASAGAI. You see: *you* have become the religious one in the old sense. Already,
and after such a small defeat, you are worshipping despair.

BENEATHA. From now on, I worship the truth—and the truth is that people are
puny, small and selfish . . .

ASAGAI. Truth? Why is it that you despairing ones always think that only you
have the truth? I never thought to see *you* like that. You! Your brother made a
stupid, childish mistake—and you are grateful to him. So that now you can
give up the ailing human race on account of it. You talk about what good is
struggle; what good is anything? Where are we all going? And why are we
bothering?

BENEATHA. *And you cannot answer it!* All your talk and dreams about Africa and
Independence. Independence and then what? What about all the crooks and
petty thieves and just plain idiots who will come into power to steal and
plunder the same as before—only now they will be black and do it in the
name of the new Independence—You cannot answer that.

ASAGAI [*Shouting over her*]. *I live the answer!* [*Pause*] In my village at home it is
the exceptional man who can even read a newspaper . . . or who ever *sees* a
book at all. I will go home and much of what I will have to say will seem
strange to the people of my village . . . But I will teach and work and things
will happen, slowly and swiftly. At times it will seem that nothing changes at
all . . . and then again . . . the sudden dramatic events which make history
leap into the future. And then quiet again. Retrogression even. Guns, murder,
revolution. And I even will have moments when I wonder if the quiet was not
better than all that death and hatred. But I will look about my village at the
illiteracy and disease and ignorance and I will not wonder long. And perhaps . . . perhaps I will be a great man . . . I mean perhaps I will hold on
to the substance of truth and find my way always with the right
course . . . and perhaps for it I will be butchered in my bed some night by
the servants of empire . . .

BENEATHA. *The martyr!*

ASAGAI. . . . or perhaps I shall live to be a very old man, respected and esteemed in my new nation . . . And perhaps I shall hold office and this is
what I'm trying to tell you, Alaiyo; perhaps the things I believe now for my
country will be wrong and outmoded, and I will not understand and do

terrible things to have things my way or merely to keep my power. Don't you see that there will be young men and women, not British soldiers then, but my own black countrymen . . . to step out of the shadows some evening and slit my then useless throat? Don't you see they have always been there . . . that they always will be. And that such a thing as my own death will be an advance? They who might kill me even . . . actually replenish me!

BENEATHA. Oh, Asagai, I know all that.

ASAGAI. Good! Then stop moaning and groaning and tell me what you plan to do.

BENEATHA. Do?

ASAGAI. I have a bit of a suggestion.

BENEATHA. What?

ASAGAI [*Rather quietly for him*]. That when it is all over—that you come home with me—

BENEATHA [*Slapping herself on the forehead with exasperation born of misunderstanding*]. Oh—Asagai—at this moment you decide to be romantic!

ASAGAI [*Quickly understanding the misunderstanding*]. My dear, young creature of the New World—I do not mean across the city—I mean across the ocean; home—to Africa.

BENEATHA [*Slowly understanding and turning to him with murmured amazement*]. To—to Nigeria?

ASAGAI. Yes! . . . [*Smiling and lifting his arms playfully*]. Three hundred years later the African Prince rose up out of the seas and swept the maiden back across the middle passage over which her ancestors had come—

BENEATHA [*Unable to play*]. Nigeria?

ASAGAI. Nigeria. Home. [*Coming to her with genuine romantic flippancy*] I will show you our mountains and our stars; and give you cool drinks from gourds and teach you the old songs and the ways of our people—and, in time, we will pretend that—[*Very softly*]—you have only been away for a day—[*She turns her back to him, thinking. He swings her around and takes her full in his arms in a long embrace which proceeds to passion*]

BENEATHA [*Pulling away*]. You're getting me all mixed up—

ASAGAI. Why?

BENEATHA. Too many things—too many things have happened today. I must sit down and think. I don't know what I feel about anything right this minute. [*She promptly sits down and props her chin on her fist*]

ASAGAI [*Charmed*]. All right, I shall leave you. No—don't get up. [*Touching her, gently, sweetly*] Just sit awhile and think . . . Never be afraid to sit awhile and think. [*He goes to door and looks at her*] How often I have looked at you and said, "Ah—so this is what the New World hath finally wrought . . ." [*He exits. BENEATHA sits on alone. Presently WALTER enters from his room and starts to rummage through things, feverishly looking for something. She looks up and turns in her seat*]

BENEATHA [*Hissingly*]. Yes—just look at what the New World hath wrought! . . . Just look! [*She gestures with bitter disgust*] There he is! *Monsieur le petit bougeois noir*—himself! There he is—Symbol of a Rising Class! Entrepreneur! Titan of the system! [*WALTER ignores her completely and continues frantically and destructively looking for something and hurling things to the floor and tearing things out of their place in his search. BENEATHA ignores the *eccentricity of his actions and goes on with the monologue of insult*] Did you dream of yachts on Lake Michigan, Brother? Did you see yourself on that Great Day sitting down at the Conference Table, surrounded by all the mighty bald-headed men in America? All halted, waiting, breathless, waiting for your pronouncements on industry? Waiting for you — Chairman of the Board? [WALTER *finds what he is looking for — a small piece of white paper — and pushes it in his pocket and puts on his coat and rushes out without ever having looked at her. She shouts after him*] I look at you and I see the final triumph of stupidity in the world! [*The door slams and she returns to just sitting again.* RUTH *comes quickly out of* MAMA's *room*]

RUTH. Who was that?

BENEATHA. Your husband.

RUTH. Where did he go?

BENEATHA. Who knows — maybe he has an appointment at U.S. Steel.

RUTH [*Anxiously, with frightened eyes*]. You didn't say nothing bad to him, did you?

BENEATHA. Bad? Say anything bad to him? No — I told him he was a sweet boy and full of dreams and everything is strictly peachy keen, as the ofay[3] kids say! [MAMA *enters from her bedroom. She is lost, vague, trying to catch hold, to make some sense of her former command of the world, but it still eludes her. A sense of waste overwhelms her gait; a measure of apology rides on her shoulders. She goes to her plant, which has remained on the table, looks at it, picks it up and takes it to the window sill and sets it outside, and she stands and looks at it a long moment. Then she closes the window, straightens her body with effort and turns around to her children*]

MAMA. Well — ain't it a mess in here, though? [*A false cheerfulness, a beginning of something*] I guess we all better stop moping around and get some work done. All this unpacking and everything we got to do. [RUTH *raises her head slowly in response to the sense of the line; and* BENEATHA *in similar manner turns very slowly to look at her mother*] One of you all better call the moving people and tell 'em not to come.

RUTH. Tell 'em not to come?

MAMA. Of course, baby. Ain't no need in 'em coming all the way here and having to go back. They charges for that too. [*She sits down, fingers to her brow, thinking*] Lord, ever since I was a little girl, I always remembers people saying, "Lena — Lena Eggleston, you aims too high all the time. You needs to slow down and see life a little more like it is. Just slow down some." That's what they always used to say down home — "Lord, that Lena Eggleston is a high-minded thing. She'll get her due one day!"

RUTH. No, Lena . . .

MAMA. Me and Big Walter just didn't never learn right.

RUTH. Lena, no! We gotta go. Bennie — tell her . . . [*She rises and crosses to* BENEATHA *with her arms outstretched.* BENEATHA *doesn't respond*] Tell her we can still move . . . the notes ain't but a hundred and twenty-five a month. We got four grown people in this house — we can work . . .

MAMA [*To herself*]. Just aimed too high all the time —

RUTH [*Turning and going to* MAMA *fast — the words pouring out with urgency and desperation*]. Lena — I'll work . . . I'll work twenty hours a day in all the

[3]**ofay**: white (pig Latin meaning *foe*).

kitchens in Chicago . . . I'll strap my baby on my back if I have to and scrub all the floors in America and wash all the sheets in America if I have to — but we got to move . . . We got to get out of here . . . [MAMA *reaches out absently and pats* RUTH'*s hand*]

MAMA. No — I sees things differently now. Been thinking 'bout some of the things we could do to fix this place up some. I seen a second-hand bureau over on Maxwell Street just the other day that could fit right there. [*She points to where the new furniture might go.* RUTH *wanders away from her*] Would need some new handles on it and then a little varnish and then it look like something brand-new. And — we can put up them new curtains in the kitchen . . . Why this place be looking fine. Cheer us all up so that we forget trouble ever came . . . [*To* RUTH] And you could get some nice screens to put up in your room round the baby's bassinet . . . [*She looks at both of them, pleadingly*] Sometimes you just got to know when to give up some things . . . and hold on to what you got. [WALTER *enters from the outside, looking spent and leaning against the door, his coat hanging from him*]

MAMA. Where you been, son?

WALTER [*Breathing hard*]. Made a call.

MAMA. To who, son?

WALTER. To The Man.

MAMA. What man, baby?

WALTER. The Man, Mama. Don't you know who The Man is?

RUTH. Walter Lee?

WALTER. *The Man.* Like the guys in the street say — *The Man.* Captain Boss — Mistuh Charley . . . Old Captain Please Mr. Bossman . . .

BENEATHA [*Suddenly*]. Lindner!

WALTER. That's right! That's good. I told him to come right over.

BENEATHA [*Fiercely, understanding*]. For what? What do you want to see him for?

WALTER [*Looking at his sister*]. We are going to do business with him.

MAMA. What you talking 'bout, son?

WALTER. Talking 'bout life, Mama. You all always telling me to see life like it is. Well — I laid in there on my back today . . . and I figured it out. Life just like it is. Who gets and who don't get. [*He sits down with his coat on and laughs*] Mama, you know it's all divided up. Life is. Sure enough. Between the takers and the "tooken." [*He laughs*] I've figured it out finally. [*He looks around at them*] Yeah. Some of us always getting "tooken." [*He laughs*] People like Willy Harris, they don't never get "tooken." And you know why the rest of us do? 'Cause we all mixed up. Mixed up bad. We get to looking 'round for the right and the wrong; and we worry about it and cry about it and stay up nights trying to figure out 'bout the wrong and the right of things all the time . . . And all the time, man, them takers is out there operating, just taking and taking. Willy Harris? Shoot — Willy Harris don't even count. He don't even count in the big scheme of things. But I'll say one thing for old Willy Harris . . . he's taught me something. He's taught me to keep my eye on what counts in this world. Yeah — [*Shouting out a little*] Thanks, Willy!

RUTH. What did you call that man for, Walter Lee!

WALTER. Called him to tell him to come on over to the show. Gonna put on a show for the man. Just what he wants to see. You see, Mama, the man came here today and he told us that them people out there where you want us to move — well they so upset they willing to pay us not to move out there. [*He laughs again*] And — and oh, Mama — you would of been proud of the way me and Ruth and Bennie acted. We told him to get out . . . Lord have mercy! We told the man to get out. Oh, we was some proud folks this afternoon, yeah. [*He lights a cigarette*] We were still full of that old-time stuff . . .

RUTH [*Coming toward him slowly*]. You talking 'bout taking them people's money to keep us from moving in that house?

WALTER. I ain't just talking 'bout it, baby — I'm telling you that's what's going to happen.

BENEATHA. Oh, God! Where is the bottom! Where is the real honest-to-God bottom so he can't go any farther!

WALTER. See — that's the old stuff. You and that boy that was here today. You all want everybody to carry a flag and a spear and sing some marching songs, huh? You wanna spend your life looking into things and trying to find the right and the wrong part, huh? Yeah. You know what's going to happen to that boy someday — he'll find himself sitting in a dungeon, locked in forever — and the takers will have the key! Forget it, baby! There ain't no causes — there ain't nothing but taking in this world, and he who takes most is smartest — and it don't make a damn bit of difference *how*.

MAMA. You making something inside me cry, son. Some awful pain inside me.

WALTER. Don't cry, Mama. Understand. That white man is going to walk in that door able to write checks for more money than we ever had. It's important to him and I'm going to help him . . . I'm going to put on the show, Mama.

MAMA. Son — I come from five generations of people who was slaves and sharecroppers — but ain't nobody in my family never let nobody pay 'em no money that was a way of telling us we wasn't fit to walk the earth. We ain't never been that poor. [*Raising her eyes and looking at him*] We ain't never been that dead inside.

BENEATHA. Well — we are dead now. All the talk about dreams and sunlight that goes on in this house. All dead.

WALTER. What's the matter with you all! I didn't make this world! It was give to me this way! Hell, yes, I want me some yachts someday! Yes, I want to hang some real pearls 'round my wife's neck. Ain't she supposed to wear no pearls? Somebody tell me — tell me, who decides which women is suppose to wear pearls in this world. I tell you I am a *man* — and I think my wife should wear some pearls in this world! [*This last line hangs a good while and* WALTER *begins to move about the room. The word "Man" has penetrated his consciousness; he mumbles it to himself repeatedly between strange agitated pauses as he moves about*]

MAMA. Baby, how you going to feel on the inside?

WALTER. Fine! . . . Going to feel fine . . . a man . . .

MAMA. You won't have nothing left then, Walter Lee.

WALTER [*Coming to her*]. I'm going to feel fine, Mama. I'm going to look that son-of-a-bitch in the eyes and say — [*He falters*] — and say, "All right, Mr. Lindner — [*He falters even more*] — that's your neighborhood out there. You got the right to keep it like you want. You got the right to have it like you want. Just write the check and — the house is yours." And, and I am going to say — [*His voice almost breaks*] And you — you people just put the money in my hand and you won't have to live next to this bunch of stinking niggers! . . . [*He straightens up and moves away from his mother, walking around the room*] Maybe — maybe I'll just get down on my black knees . . . [*He does so;* RUTH *and* BENNIE *and* MAMA *watch him in frozen horror*] Captain, Mistuh, Bossman. [*He starts crying*] A-hee-hee-hee! [*Wringing his hands in profoundly anguished imitation*] Yasssssuh! Great White Father, just gi' ussen de money, fo' God's sake, and we's ain't gwine come out deh and dirty up yo' white folks neighborhood . . . [*He breaks down completely, then gets up and goes into the bedroom*]

BENEATHA. That is not a man. That is nothing but a toothless rat.

MAMA. Yes — death done come in this here house. [*She is nodding, slowly, reflectively*] Done come walking in my house. On the lips of my children. You what supposed to be my beginning again. You — what supposed to be my harvest. [*To* BENEATHA] You — you mourning your brother?

BENEATHA. He's no brother of mine.

MAMA. What you say?

BENEATHA. I said that that individual in that room is no brother of mine.

MAMA. That's what I thought you said. You feeling like you better than he is today? [BENEATHA *does not answer*] Yes? What you tell him a minute ago? That he wasn't a man? Yes? You give him up for me? You done wrote his epitaph too — like the rest of the world? Well, who give you the privilege?

BENEATHA. Be on my side for once! You saw what he just did, Mama! You saw him — down on his knees. Wasn't it you who taught me — to despise any man who would do that? Do what he's going to do.

MAMA. Yes — I taught you that. Me and your daddy. But I thought I taught you something else too . . . I thought I taught you to love him.

BENEATHA. Love him? There is nothing left to love.

MAMA. There is always something left to love. And if you ain't learned that, you ain't learned nothing. [*Looking at her*] Have you cried for that boy today? I don't mean for yourself and for the family 'cause we lost the money. I mean for him; what he been through and what it done to him. Child, when do you think is the time to love somebody the most; when they done good and made things easy for everybody? Well then, you ain't through learning — because that ain't the time at all. It's when he's at his lowest and can't believe in hisself 'cause the world done whipped him so. When you starts measuring somebody, measure him right, child, measure him right. Make sure you done taken into account what hills and valleys he come through before he got to wherever he is. [TRAVIS *bursts into the room at the end of the speech, leaving the door open*]

TRAVIS. Grandmama — the moving men are downstairs! The truck just pulled up.

MAMA [*Turning and looking at him*]. Are they, baby? They downstairs? [*She sighs and sits.* LINDNER *appears in the doorway. He peers in and knocks lightly, to gain attention, and comes in. All turn to look at him*]

LINDNER [*Hat and briefcase in hand*]. Uh — hello . . . [RUTH *crosses mechanically to the bedroom door and opens it and lets it swing open freely and slowly as the lights come up on* WALTER *within, still in his coat, sitting at the far corner of the room. He looks up and out through the room to* LINDNER]

RUTH. He's here. [*A long minute passes and* WALTER *slowly gets up*]

LINDNER [*Coming to the table with efficiency, putting his briefcase on the table and starting to unfold papers and unscrew fountain pens*]. Well, I certainly was glad to hear from you people. [WALTER *has begun the trek out of the room, slowly and awkwardly, rather like a small boy, passing the back of his sleeve across his mouth from time to time*] Life can really be so much simpler than people let it be most of the time. Well — with whom do I negotiate? You, Mrs. Younger, or your son here? [MAMA *sits with her hands folded on her lap and her eyes closed as* WALTER *advances.* TRAVIS *goes close to* LINDNER *and looks at the papers curiously*] Just some official papers, sonny.

RUTH. Travis, you go downstairs.

MAMA [*Opening her eyes and looking into* WALTER'*s*]. No. Travis, you stay right here. And you make him understand what you doing. Walter Lee. You teach him good. Like Willy Harris taught you. You show where our five generations done come to. Go ahead, son —

WALTER [*Looks down into his boy's eyes.* TRAVIS *grins at him merrily and* WALTER *draws him beside him with his arm lightly around his shoulders*]. Well, Mr. Lindner. [BENEATHA *turns away*] We called you — [*There is a profound, simple groping quality in his speech*] — because, well, me and my family [*He looks around and shifts from one foot to the other*] Well — we are very plain people . . .

LINDNER. Yes —

WALTER. I mean — I have worked as a chauffeur most of my life — and my wife here, she does domestic work in people's kitchens. So does my mother. I mean — we are plain people . . .

LINDNER. Yes, Mr. Younger —

WALTER [*Really like a small boy, looking down at his shoes and then up at the man*]. And — uh — well, my father, well, he was a laborer most of his life.

LINDNER [*Absolutely confused*]. Uh, yes —

WALTER [*Looking down at his toes once again*]. My father almost beat a man to death once because this man called him a bad name or something, you know what I mean?

LINDNER. No, I'm afraid I don't

WALTER [*Finally straightening up*]. Well, what I mean is that we come from people who had a lot of pride. I mean — we are very proud people. And that's my sister over there and she's going to be a doctor — and we are very proud —

LINDNER. Well — I am sure that is very nice, but —

WALTER [*Starting to cry and facing the man eye to eye*]. What I am telling you is that we called you over here to tell you that we are very proud and that this is — this is my son, who makes the sixth generation of our family in this country, and that we have all thought about your offer and we have decided to move into our house because my father — my father — he earned it. [MAMA *has her eyes closed and is rocking back and forth as though she were in church, with her head nodding the amen yes*] We don't want to make no trouble for nobody or fight no causes — but we will try to be good neighbors. That's all we got to say. [*He looks the man absolutely in the eyes*] We don't want your money. [*He turns and walks away from the man*]

LINDNER [*Looking around at all of them*]. I take it then that you have decided to occupy.

BENEATHA. That's what the man said.

LINDNER [*To* MAMA *in her reverie*]. Then I would like to appeal to you, Mrs. Younger. You are older and wiser and understand things better I am sure . . .

MAMA [*Rising*]. I am afraid you don't understand. My son said we was going to move and there ain't nothing left for me to say. [*Shaking her head with double meaning*] You know how these young folks is nowadays, mister. Can't do a thing with 'em. Good-bye.

LINDNER [*Folding up his materials*]. Well—if you are that final about it . . . There is nothing left for me to say. [*He finishes. He is almost ignored by the family, who are concentrating on* WALTER LEE. *At the door* LINDNER *halts and looks around*] I sure hope you people know what you're doing. [*He shakes his head and exits*]

RUTH [*Looking around and coming to life*]. Well, for God's sake—if the moving men are here—LET'S GET THE HELL OUT OF HERE!

MAMA [*Into action*]. Ain't it the truth! Look at all this here mess. Ruth, put Travis' good jacket on him . . . Walter Lee, fix your tie and tuck your shirt in, you look just like somebody's hoodlum. Lord have mercy, where is my plant? [*She flies to get it amid the general bustling of the family, who are deliberately trying to ignore the nobility of the past moment*] You all start on down . . . Travis child, don't go empty-handed . . . Ruth, where did I put that box with my skillets in it? I want to be in charge of it myself . . . I'm going to make us the biggest dinner we ever ate tonight . . . Beneatha, what's the matter with them stockings? Pull them things up, girl . . . [*The family starts to file out as two moving men appear and begin to carry out the heavier pieces of furniture, bumping into the family as they move about*]

BENEATHA. Mama, Asagai—asked me to marry him today and go to Africa—

MAMA [*In the middle of her getting-ready activity*]. He did? You ain't old enough to marry nobody—[*Seeing the moving men lifting one of her chairs precariously*] Darling, that ain't no bale of cotton, please handle it so we can sit in it again. I had that chair twenty-five years . . . [*The movers sigh with exasperation and go on with their work*]

BENEATHA [*Girlishly and unreasonably trying to pursue the conversation*]. To go to Africa, Mama—be a doctor in Africa . . .

MAMA [*Distracted*]. Yes, baby—

WALTER. Africa! What he want to go to Africa for?

BENEATHA. To practice there . . .

WALTER. Girl, if you don't get all them silly ideas out your head! You better marry yourself a man with some loot . . .

BENEATHA [*Angrily, precisely as in the first scene of the play*]. What have you go to do with who I marry!

WALTER. Plenty. Now I think George Murchison—[*He and* BENEATHA *go out yelling at each other vigorously;* BENEATHA *is heard saying that she would not marry* GEORGE MURCHISON *if he were Adam and she were Eve, etc. The anger is loud and real till their voices diminish.* RUTH *stands at the door and turns to* MAMA *and smiles knowingly*]

MAMA [*Fixing her hat at last*]. Yeah—they something all right, my children . . .

RUTH. Yeah—they're something. Let's go, Lena.

MAMA [*Stalling, starting to look around at the house*]. Yes—I'm coming. Ruth—

RUTH. Yes?

MAMA [*Quietly, woman to woman*]. He finally come into his manhood today, didn't he? Kind of like a rainbow after the rain . . .

RUTH [*Biting her lip lest her own pride explode in front of* MAMA]. Yes, Lena. [WALTER'*s voice calls for them raucously*]

MAMA [*Waving* RUTH *out vaguely*]. All right, honey—go on down. I be down directly. [RUTH *hesitates, then exits.* MAMA *stands, at last alone in the living room, her plant on the table before her as the lights start to come down. She looks around at all the walls and ceilings and suddenly, despite herself, while the children call below, a great heaving thing rises in her and she puts her fist to her mouth, takes a final desperate look, pulls her coat about her, pats her hat and goes out. The lights dim down. The door opens and she comes back in, grabs her plant, and goes out for the last time*]

CURTAIN

(1958)

PART V

The Editing Process

The following material provides a concise Handbook for Correcting Errors and a handy Glossary of Rhetorical and Literary Terms.

A Handbook for Correcting Errors

Once you have become a good editor and proofreader, you will find editing the easiest part of the writing process. But just because locating and correcting errors is less taxing than composing the paper, do not consider it unimportant. Correcting errors is crucial. Errors will lower your grades in college and undermine the confidence of your readers in any writing that you do.

Proofreading

As we suggested in Chapter 3, you will need to proofread at least twice, concentrating on catching different types of errors each time. Here are some general rules to follow:

1. Read the essay aloud to catch words accidentally repeated or left out.
2. Read sentence by sentence from the bottom of the page to the top (to keep your attention focused on finding errors).
3. Read again, looking for any particular errors that you know you tend to make: fragments, comma splices, typical misspellings, and so on.
4. Go over each page using an index card with a small rectangle cut in the middle. This will force you to look at only a few words at a time to catch typographical errors and misspellings.
5. When in doubt about either spelling or meaning, use your dictionary.
6. If the piece of writing is important, find a literate friend to read it over for mistakes after you have completed all of the above.

CHART A. Examples of Phrases and Clauses

PHRASES

to the lighthouse
having been converted
a still, eerie, deserted beach

Phrases do not have subject and verb combinations.

CLAUSES

Independent	Dependent (incomplete sentences)
Clarissa finished.	after Clarissa finished
She completed her essay.	which completed the essay
John gave her the assignment.	because John gave her the assignment

All clauses have subject and verb combinations.

Correcting Sentence Boundary Errors

Probably the most serious errors you need to check for are those that involve faulty sentence punctuation: fragments, comma splices, and run-on sentences. These errors reflect uncertainty or carelessness about the acceptable boundaries for written sentences.

Phrases and Clauses

To punctuate correctly, you need to know the difference between phrases and clauses. Charts A through C on these following pages will help you remember.

Fragments

As the term suggests, a sentence *fragment* is an incomplete group of words punctuated as a complete sentence. Fragments occur frequently in speech and are often used by professional writers for emphasis and convenience. But a fragmentary sentence may also represent a fragmentary idea that would be more effective if it were completed or connected to another idea.

The following are examples of typical sentence fragments that need to be revised.

1. **Phrases that can be joined to the preceding sentence:**

CHART B. Kinds of Phrases

PHRASE: a string of related words that does not contain a subject and verb combination

1. *Noun phrase:* a noun plus modifiers

   an old yellowed photograph

2. *Prepositional phrase:* a preposition plus its object and modifiers of the object

   against the dusty curtains

3. *Verbal phrase:* a verbal (word derived from a verb) plus modifiers and objects or completers

   A. *Infinitive* (verb with *to* before it)

   to leave her father

   B. *Gerund* (*-ing* word used as a noun)

   leaving her father

   C. *Participle* (*-ing* or *-ed* word used as an adjective)

   leaning against the curtains
   frightened by her father

4. *Verb phrase:* an action or being verb plus its auxiliary verbs

   have been
   might be leaving
   will go

(*Questionable fragment*)   Eveline gripped the iron railing and stared ahead. With no glimmer of "love or recognition" in her eyes.

[The fragment is a prepositional phrase without a subject or verb; see Charts A and B]

(*Revision*)   Eveline gripped the iron railing and stared ahead with no glimmer of "love or recognition" in her eyes.

2. **Explanatory phrases that begin with such expressions as *for example*, *that is*, and *such as* and belong in the sentence with the material they are explaining:**

   (*Questionable fragment*)   As Eveline looked around the room, she noticed familiar objects that she might never see again. For instance, the yellowing photograph of the priest and the broken harmonium.

   (*Revision*)   As Eveline looked around the room, she noticed familiar objects that she might never see again — for instance, the yellowing photograph of the priest and the broken harmonium.

CHART C. Kinds of Clauses

CLAUSE: a group of related words containing a subject and verb combination

1. *Independent (main) clause:*

   subject + verb: Her hands trembled.

   subject + verb + completer: Her hands gripped the railing.

2. *Dependent (subordinate) clause:* incomplete sentence that depends on an independent clause to complete its meaning

   A. *Noun clause:* used as a noun

   She could not believe *what Frank told her.*
   (direct object)
   Whoever called her did not identify himself.
   (subject)

   B. *Adjective clause:* modifies a noun or pronoun

   The promise *that Eveline made to her mother* weighed heavily on her conscience.

   She loved her younger brother, *who had died some years ago.*

   An adjective clause is introduced by a relative pronoun: *who, which, that, whose, whom.*

   C. *Adverb clause:* modifies a verb, adjective, or adverb

   After Eveline wrote the letters, she held them in her lap.
   She could not leave with Frank *because she was afraid.*

   An adverb clause is introduced by a subordinating conjunction: *after, although, as, as if, because, before, if, only, since, so as, as far as, so that, than, though, till, unless, until, when, whenever, while, whereas.*

3. **Dependent (or subordinate) clauses that can be added to another sentence or rewritten as complete sentences:**

   (*Questionable fragment*)   Eveline decided to stay with her family. Even though she felt she could forget her worries and be happy forever with Frank. [adverb clause, beginning with *even though;* see Chart C]

   (*Revision*)   Even though she felt she could forget her worries and be happy forever with Frank, Eveline decided to stay with her family.

   (*Questionable fragment*)   Frank had told Eveline numerous stories about his adventures on the high seas. Many of which seemed suspiciously vague and predictably romantic. [adjective clause, indicated by *which;* see Chart C]

(*Revision*)   Frank had told Eveline numerous stories about his adventures on the high seas. Many of his tales seemed suspiciously vague and predictably romantic.

Note: In English we typically begin sentences with adverbial clauses. But if you often write fragments, you may not be attaching those dependent clauses to independent clauses.

Remember that a group of words beginning with a subordinating word like *although, if, because, since, unless, when, which,* or *who* will be a fragment unless connected to an independent clause. If you typically have problems with fragments, put a bookmark at page 1015 and consult Chart B and Chart C.

4. Verbal phrases that do not contain a complete verb:

(*Questionable fragment*)   Eveline sat by the window and thought about her home and family. Leaning her head against the dusty curtains. [The second group of words is a participle phrase; *leaning* is not a complete verb. See Chart B.]

(*Revision*)   Leaning her head against the dusty curtains, Eveline sat by the window and thought about her home and family.

Note: Words ending in *-ing* or *-ed* sound like verbs, but often they are *verbals* (verb forms used as adjectives or nouns) and do not function as full verbs for a sentence.

5. Semicolon fragments:

(*Questionable fragment*)   Eveline was fearful of her father and helplessly trapped; feeling immobile, like the dust on the curtains. [The words which follow the semicolon do not constitute a full sentence. See Chart B.]

(*Revision*)   Eveline was fearful of her father and helplessly trapped; she felt immobile, like the dust on the curtains.

Note: A semicolon is often used as a weak period to separate independent clauses that are closely related. Be sure you have written an independent clause before and after a semicolon (unless the semicolon separates items in a series which themselves contain commas).

Comma Splices

A comma splice (or comma fault or comma blunder) occurs when a writer places two independent clauses together with only a comma between them. Because the result appears to be a single sentence, it can momentarily confuse the reader:

(*Comma Splice*)   Frank has become the Prince Charming in Eveline's fairy tale world, the other man in her life is much more real.

Because the two clauses joined here are independent (i.e., each could stand alone as a sentence), the two clauses should be linked by a stronger mark than a comma. Here are some options:

1. **Punctuate both clauses as complete sentences.**

   > Frank has become the Prince Charming in Eveline's fairy tale world. The other man in her life is much more real.

2. **Use a semicolon.**

   > Frank has become the Prince Charming in Eveline's fairy tale world; the other man in her life is much more real.

3. **Keep the comma and add a coordinating conjunction** (*and, but, or, nor, for, yet, so*).

   > Frank has become the Prince Charming in Eveline's fairy tale world, but the other man in her life is much more real.

4. **Subordinate one of the independent clauses.**

   > Although Frank has become the Prince Charming in Eveline's fairy tale world, the other man in her life is much more real.

To avoid comma splices, follow this general advice:

1. Be careful with commas.

   If you understand sentence structure, your writing probably won't contain many comma splices. But if you are not paying attention to sentence boundaries, you may be joining independent clauses without realizing it and separating them with commas.

2. Check your conjunctive adverbs.

   Transitional expressions like *indeed, however, thus, therefore, nevertheless, furthermore,* and *consequently* may lead you to use just a comma when connecting two independent clauses with these words. Do not do it. These words are called *conjunctive adverbs;* they do not serve to join clauses the way coordinating conjunctions do. Their main force is adverbial. Thus, you still need a semicolon (or a period and a capital letter) when you use these connectives:

   > (*Comma splice*)   Eveline's father is violent and overbearing, however, he is the man who really loves her.

   > (*Correct*)   Eveline's father is violent and overbearing; however, he is the man who really loves her.

3. Use commas with short clauses.

   Although we advise you not to use commas to join independent clauses, many professional writers intentionally violate this advice if the clauses are short, if they are parallel in structure, if they are antithetical, or if there is no chance of misunderstanding:

> He's not brave, he's crazy.
> She felt one way, she acted another.
> It was sunny, it was crisp, it was a perfect day.

Exercise on Comma Splices

If any of the following sentences contain comma splices, correct the flawed sentence twice: once by adding a suitable coordinating conjunction (*and, but, or, for, nor, yet, so*) and once by changing the comma to a semicolon.

1. Clyde is constantly revising his essays, thus he turns in fine finished papers.
2. Your analysis is flawed in several ways, because you need to rewrite it, let's discuss your problems.
3. You have written an excellent analysis, Bertha, you should read it to the class.
4. Monroe complains that he never understands the stories, yet he only reads them through once, hastily.
5. Plot is the main element in this story, as far as one can tell, characterization is scarcely important at all.

Run-On Sentences

A run-on sentence (also called a fused sentence) is similar to a comma splice, except that there is no punctuation at all to separate the independent clauses:

> Eveline realizes that she leads a dull and unhappy home life she is also safely and securely encircled in her own little world.

Few writers ignore sentence boundaries so completely. Most people at least put a comma in (and thus produce a comma splice). When you edit, make sure that you have not run any sentences together. Run-ons will confuse and annoy your readers.

Clearing Up Confused Sentences

Sometimes you can get careless and lose track of the way a sentence is developing. The result is called a confused sentence or a mixed construction. Repunctuating will not correct this kind of error. You will have to rewrite the garbled passage into readable prose:

> (*Confused*)   One reason to conclude Eveline's hopeless situation would have to be related to her indecisive and timid lifestyle.

(*Revised*)   One reason for Eveline's hopeless situation is her indecisive and timid personality.

Sentences can go astray in many ways. The only sure defense against sentence confusion is to understand the basic principles of sentence structure. Checking your writing carefully and reading your sentences aloud will also help.

Solving Faulty Predication Problems

Another kind of sentence confusion occurs when you carelessly complete a linking verb (*is, am, are, was, were, will be, has been, becomes, appears,* etc.[1]) with a predicate noun or predicate adjective that does not match the subject of the sentence. This error is called *faulty predication*. In this kind of sentence the linking verb acts as an equals sign and sets up a verbal equation: the subject = the predicate noun (or predicate adjective).

(*Logical*)   Eveline is a passive, sheltered young woman.

(*Logical*)   At least at home Eveline would be secure.

In the first sentence, Eveline = young woman; and in the second, "secure" (predicate adjective) logically modifies "Eveline" (the subject). Here are some faulty predications followed by logical revisions:

(*Faulty*)   The importance of religion in the story is crucial to Eveline's decision.

(*Logical*)   Religion is important to Eveline's decision.

(*Faulty*)   The theme of the poem is thousands of dead soldiers.

(*Logical*)   The theme of the poem is the deplorable slaughter of thousands of soldiers.

(*Faulty*)   The setting for the advertisement is a man and a woman walking through a jungle in safari suits.

(*Logical*)   The setting for the advertisement is a jungle; a man and a woman in safari suits are walking through it.

The phrases "is where" and "is when" are likely culprits in producing faulty predication. Remember, "where" refers to a place, and "when" refers to a time. Use those words only in a place or time context, not in a context that equates them with an abstract quality. Here are examples:

(*Faulty*)   Dramatic irony is when Jim says Whitey is a card.

(*Logical*)   We recognize the dramatic irony when Jim says Whitey is a card.

---

[1]The most common linking verb is *be* in its various forms: *is, are, was, were, has been, will be, might be.* Other linking verbs include *seem* and *appear* and, in some instances, *feel, grow, act, look, smell, taste,* and *sound.*

(*Faulty*)   Visual imagery is where Owen describes the soldier's death.
(*Logical*)   Owen uses visual imagery to describe the soldier's death.

Exercise on Faulty Predication

Revise the following sentences to eliminate faulty predications and confused constructions.

1. The changes of tone are used in a way where the characters singing the jingle dance.
2. Lyrics to country music are broken hearts and forgotten dreams.
3. By using a psychological approach to the modern novel can provide significant insights.
4. The fact that Chicano poets reflect their Aztec heritage describes the culture they depict in their works.
5. The reason Wharton's fiction is becoming more respected is a result of the woman's movement.

Fixing Subject–Verb Agreement Errors

1. **Verbs agree with their subjects in number** (that is, being either singular or plural).

   Victorian *novels are* usually long.
   A Victorian *novel is* often moral.
   A Victorian *novel* and a post-modernist *novel are* radically different.

2. **Be sure to find the grammatical subject.**

A. Sometimes a clause or phrase comes between the subject and verb to confuse you, like this:

   (*Wrong*)   The good movies that come out in the fall makes up for the summer's trash.

   The clause — *that come out in the fall* — intervenes between the subject *movies* and the verb, which should be *make* (plural to agree with *movies*):

   (*Right*)   The good movies that come out in the fall make up for the summer's trash.

Note: The plural form of the verb drops the *s*, unlike nouns, which add an *s* to form the plural (one villain lies, two villains lie).

B. Sometimes — especially in questions — the subject will come after the verb, like this:

(*Right*)   Why *are Romeo* and *Juliet* so impetuous?
(*Right*)   From boredom, restlessness, and ignorance *comes* an
otherwise senseless *crime*.

C. If you begin a sentence with *here, there, what, where, when,* or *why,*
these words can rarely be subjects. Find the real subject (or subjects)
and make the verb agree.

(*Wrong*)   Where is the climax and the denouement?
(*Wrong*)   There is suspense and tension in DuMaurier's novel.

The subjects in both of those examples are compound, requiring a
plural verb:

(*Right*)   Where *are* the *climax* and the *denouement?*
(*Right*)   There *are suspense* and *tension* in DuMaurier's novel.

3. **Compound singular subjects connected by correlative conjunctions**
(*either . . . or, not only . . . but also, neither . . . nor, not . . .*
but, etc.) **require a singular verb.**

(*Right*)   Either *Antigone* or *Creon* is going to prevail.
(*Right*)   Not a *beau* but a *husband* is what Amanda wants for Laura.

If both subjects are plural, make the verb plural:

(*Right*)   Either *poems* or *stories are* fine with me.

If one subject is singular and the other one plural, make the verb agree
with the subject closer to it:

(*Right*)   Either *poems* or a *story* is a good choice.
(*Right*)   Either a *story* or some *poems are* fine.

4. **Some prepositions sound like conjunctions**—*with, like, along with,*
as well as, no less than, including, besides—**and may appear to connect**
compound subjects, but they do not; the subject, if singular, re-
mains singular.

(*Right*)   My *career,* as well as my reputation, *is* lost.
(*Right*)   *Alcohol,* together with my passion for filmy underthings, *is*
responsible.
(*Right*)   My *mother,* like my aunt Chloe, my uncle Zeke, and my
cousin Zelda, *is* not speaking to me.

5. **Collective nouns (like** *jury, family, company, staff, group, committee*)
take either singular or plural verbs, depending on your meaning.

If the group is acting in unison, use the singular:

(*Right*)   The *jury has* agreed upon a verdict.

If the group is behaving like separate individuals, use the plural:

(*Right*)   The *jury* still *are* not in agreement.

Or avoid the problem this way:

(*Right*)   The *members* of the jury still *are* not in agreement.

Fixing Pronoun Errors

1. Avoid ambiguous or unclear pronoun reference.

(*Ambiguous*)   Marvin gave Tom *his* pen back, but *he* swore it wasn't *his*.
(*Clear*)   Marvin gave Tom's pen back, but Tom swore it wasn't his.

Sometimes it is necessary to replace an inexact pronoun with a noun:

(*Unclear*)   She did not know how to make quiche until I wrote *it* out for her.
(*Clear*)   She did not know how to make quiche until I wrote out *the recipe* for her.

2. Use *this* and *which* with care.

These pronouns often refer to whole ideas or situations, and the reference is sometimes not clear:

(*Unclear*)   Renaldo runs three miles a day and works out with weights twice a week. He says *this* controls his high blood pressure and prevents heart attacks.
(*Clear*)   Renaldo runs three miles a day and works out with weights twice a week. He says *this exercise program* controls his high blood pressure and prevents heart attacks.

Avoid using *this* without a noun following it. Get in the habit of writing *this idea, this point,* or *this remark,* instead of having a pronoun that means nothing in particular.

The pronoun *which* can cause similar problems:

(*Unclear*)   Craig told me that he didn't like the movie, *which* upset me.
(*Clear*)   Craig told me that he didn't like the movie. His opinion upset me.
(*Clear*)   Craig told me that he didn't like the movie. The film upset me, too.

3. Be sure your pronouns agree with their antecedents in number (singular or plural).

Agreement errors occur when the pronoun is separated from its antecedent (the preceding noun which the pronoun replaces):

(*Incorrect*)   Although the average *American* believes in the ideal of justice for all, *they* do not always practice it.

(*Correct*)   Although most *Americans* believe in the ideal of justice for all, *they* do not always practice it.

4. Take care with indefinite pronouns.

Many indefinite pronouns sound plural but are considered grammatically singular: *anybody, anyone, everyone, everybody, someone, none, no one, neither, either*. If you follow this grammatical guideline in all cases, you may produce an illogical sentence:

Everybody applauded my speech, and I was glad *he* did.

It is now acceptable to use plural pronouns when referring to indefinite words:

Everyone should have *their* own pinking shears.
None of the students would admit *they* were cheating.

Some readers still question this practice and will insist that you refer to *everyone* and *none* with singular pronouns. This dilemma can sometimes be avoided by recasting your sentence or by writing in the plural:

(*Recast*)   None of the students would admit to cheating.

(*Questionable*)   *Each* of the contestants must supply *their* own water skis.

(*No question*)   *All contestants* must supply *their* own water skis.

If you prefer to write in the singular, you may have to revise sentences with indefinite pronouns or stick to the old rule of referring to such words as *anyone, somebody, everyone, none*, and *neither* with singular pronouns:

(*Singular agreement*)   *Neither* of the drivers escaped the crash with *his* life.

That sentence is all right if both drivers were indeed males. But if one was a woman or if you are not sure of the gender of both drivers, you may want to use *his or her* to make your statement completely accurate. Or you can revise and avoid the problem altogether.

(*Revised*)   Neither driver survived the crash.

5. Choose the proper case.

Except for possessives and plurals, nouns do not change form when used in different ways in a sentence. You can write "Ernie was watching the new kitten" or "The new kitten was watching Ernie" and neither noun (Ernie, kitten) changes. But pronouns do change with their function:

> *He* watched the kitten.
> The kitten watched *him*.

In the first sentence the subjective form (he) is used because the pronoun acts as the subject. In the second sentence the pronoun is the direct object of *watched*, so the objective form (him) is used. (The objective form is used for any objects — of prepositions, indirect objects, and direct objects.) The forms vary according to the *case* of the pronoun; in English there are three cases of pronouns:

Subjective	*Objective*	*Possessive*
I	me	mine
he	him	his
she	her	hers
you	your	yours
it	it	its
we	us	ours
they	them	theirs
who	whom	whose
whoever	whomever	whosever

You probably select the correct case for most of the pronouns you use, but you may need to keep the following warnings in mind:

A. Do not confuse the possessive *its* with the contraction *it's*.

If you look at the list of case forms above, you will notice that possessive pronouns do *not* include an apostrophe. This information may confuse you because the possessives of nouns and indefinite words *do* contain an apostrophe:

    my mother's jewels
    the students' books
    everyone's appetite

Remember that *it's* is a contraction of *it is* and that *its* is a possessive like *his, her,* and *ours.*

B. Be careful of pronouns in compound subjects and objects:

(*Faulty*)   Nanouchka and *me* went to the movies.

(*Preferred*)   Nanouchka and *I* went to the movies.

(*Faulty*)   Shelly went with Nan and *I*.

(*Preferred*)   Shelly went with Nan and *me*.

If you are uncertain about which pronoun to use, drop the first part of the compound and see how the pronoun sounds alone:

    I went? or *me* went?
    with *I*? or with *me*?

You will recognize at once that "me went" and "with I" are not standard constructions.

C. **Watch out for pronouns used with appositives.** The pronoun should be in the same case as the word it is in apposition with:

(*Faulty*)   *Us* video game addicts are slaves to our hobby.
(*Preferred*)   *We* video game addicts are slaves to our hobby.

(*Faulty*)   Video games are serious business to *we* addicts.
(*Preferred*)   Video games are serious business to *us* addicts.

Again, you can test this construction by dropping the noun and letting the sound guide you: "us are slaves" and "to we" should sound unacceptable to you.

D. **Take care with pronouns in comparisons:**

(*Faulty*)   Ernie is a lot stronger than *me*.
(*Preferred*)   Ernie is a lot stronger than *I*.

This comparison is not complete. There is an implied (or understood) verb after *than:* "stronger than I am." If you complete such comparative constructions in your mind, you will be able to choose the appropriate case for the pronoun.

E. **Choose carefully between *who* and *whom:***

(*Preferred*)   My ex-roommate was a con artist *whom* we all trusted too much.

Although informal usage would allow you to use *who* in this sentence, the objective case form (*whom*) is preferred in most writing because the pronoun is the direct object in the clause it introduces: "we all trusted *him* too much." You can get around the choice between *who* and *whom* in this instance by using *that:*

(*Acceptable*)   My ex-roommate was a con artist *that* we all trusted too much.

Some people will still insist that you use *whom* in this sentence, even though the use of *that* is now considered standard. But you should not substitute *which* for *who* or *whom*, because standard usage does not permit *which* to refer to people:

(*Preferred*)   the taxidermist *whom* I often dated
(*Acceptable*)   the taxidermist *that* I often dated
(*Faulty*)   the taxidermist *which* I often dated

Exercise on Pronoun Errors

Rewrite the following sentences to avoid vague pronoun reference.

1. The policeman yelled at Walter Mitty. This irritated him very much.
2. A good dramatist always respects the intelligence of his audience.
3. A perfectly clear story can be made obscure by a literary critic. They use abstract words and vague terms.
4. You should reread the story and underline key words, which will help you analyze it better.
5. An optimist and a pessimist will always be able to find examples of poetry to support their point of view.

Correcting Shifts in Person

1. **Decide before you begin writing whether to use first, second, or third person, and then be consistent.**

A. Formal usage requires third person:

> The reader senses foreboding in Poe's opening lines.
> One senses foreboding in Poe's opening lines.

or first person plural:

> We sense foreboding in Poe's opening lines.

B. Informal usage allows first person singular:

> I find his characters too one-dimensional.

and many readers accept second person (as long as *you* means you, the reader):

> If you examine his plots, you discover that the success of his tales lies elsewhere.

C. Do not switch person carelessly once you have begun:

> (*Wrong*) The *reader* feels the tension mount as *you* wait for the beast to spring.
> (*Right*) *We* feel the tension mount as *we* wait for the beast to spring.

Exercise on Shifts in Person

We have added shifts in person to this paragraph (which was originally written correctly by one of our students). Edit the passage to correct the unwarranted shifts in person.

In Willa Cather's short story, "Neighbor Rosicky," we see a comparison between the debilitating life of the city and the harsh life of the country. Yet you notice a difference in the quality of these lifestyles. Through Rosicky, Cather shows us the stagnant, draining effects of urban life, which serve to enhance the birth-death-rebirth theme of the story. Rosicky, one can easily observe, is a gentle, loving, and tender person. Through the trials of city living and country living, he has, you know, gained knowledge about the meaning of true happiness. We see him, in his gentle, unobtrusive manner, try to share his enlightenment with those around him. If one observes closely, you notice that even a minor character, Dr. Ed, is affected by Rosicky's example. By examining this relationship, we see Cather put forth a plea for tasting the simple pleasures your life has to offer. Education, wealth, and career cannot guarantee you happiness. Cather wants us to realize that the enjoyment of one's life makes living worthwhile.

Correcting Shifts in Tense

1. Stay in the same tense unless you have cause to change.

A. Sometimes you need to switch tenses because you are discussing events that happened (or will happen) at different times (past, present, or future), like this:

>   (*Right*)   Although I *saw* the Split Banana in concert last week, I *am going* to hear them again tonight when they *perform* in Chicago.

B. Do not change tense, though, without a reason:

>   (*Wrong*)   The group *appears* on stage, obviously drunk; the drummer *dropped* his sticks, the lead singer *trips* over the microphone cord, and the bass player *had* his back to the audience during the entire show.

C. When writing about literature, use the historical present tense even when discussing authors long dead:

>   (*Right*)   Hawthorne, in the opening scene of *The Scarlet Letter*, creates a somber setting relieved only by the flowers on a single rosebush.

Or you may write in the past tense:

>   (*Right*)   Hawthorne, in the opening scene of *The Scarlet Letter*, created a somber setting.

But do not switch carelessly back and forth:

>   (*Wrong*)   Hawthorne *creates* a somber setting into which Hester *stepped* with Pearl in her arms.

Exercise on Shifts in Tense

Make the tense consistent wherever appropriate in the following sentences.

1. Dudley Randall's shocking images included "a stub, a stump, a butt, a scab, a knob" as he describes the possible victim of mercy killing.

2. When Dickinson writes, "To ache is human—not polite," she made a statement about the nature of politeness as well as humanity.

3. The relationship between the ideal lovers in Donne's poem is illuminated by a comparison between the two legs of a compass, whose interdependence was emphasized.

4. In "Design," Frost pondered the possible meanings of a chance meeting of a spider, a flower, and a moth and makes the apparent coincidence seem ominous.

5. The first line of Donald Hall's poem sets up the paradox the persona expressed: he finds his own mortality brought home to him by his new baby, an "instrument of immortality."

Finding Modifier Mistakes

A modifier is a word, phrase, or clause that describes, limits, or qualifies something else in the sentence. Be sure that every modifier has only one thing to refer to and that the relationship is clear.

1. Avoid dangling modifiers.

An introductory adjective phrase that does not modify the subject of the sentence is called a *dangling modifier:*

(*Dangling*)   Wheezing and shivering from the cold, the warm fire slowly revived Orville.

(*Improved*)   Wheezing and shivering from the cold, Orville slowly revived in front of the warm fire.

Sometimes you need to add a subject, making the phrase into a clause:

(*Dangling*)   While asleep in class, the instructor called on Jocasta to recite.

(*Improved*)   While Jocasta was asleep in class, the instructor called on her to recite.

2. Avoid misplaced modifiers.

Do not allow modifiers to stray too far from the thing they modify or you may produce confusing (and sometimes unintentionally amusing) sentences:

(*Misplaced*)   I can jog to the grocery store; then we can have lox and bagels for breakfast in just three minutes.

(*Improved*)   In just three minutes I can jog to the grocery store; then we can have lox and bagels for breakfast.

(*Dangling*)   Seymour was caught taking a nap in the restroom where he works.

(*Improved*)   While supposedly working, Seymour was caught taking a nap in the restroom.

3. Avoid squinting modifiers.

Be sure your modifiers have only one possible word to modify, or you may puzzle your readers:

(*Squinting*)   Arvilla suspects privately Agnes reads Harlequin romances.

(*Improved*)   Arvilla privately suspects that Agnes reads Harlequin romances.

(*Improved*)   Arvilla suspects that Agnes privately reads Harlequin romances.

Exercise on Modifier Mistakes

In the following sentences, move any misplaced modifier so that the statements make better sense. You may have to rewrite the sentences that have dangling or squinting modifiers.

1. Antigone's faith without doubt sustained her in her struggle with Creon.
2. After attempting to kill his father, Haimon's sword becomes the instrument of his own death.
3. Ismene feels in her heart Antigone is right.
4. Creon has no illusions about the stupidity of the populace, thinking the edict is good enough for them.
5. Antigone wants to bury her brother Polyneices in the opening scene.
6. Championing unwritten universal laws, the burial of Polyneices turns Antigone into an enemy of the state in Creon's eyes.

Coping with Irregular Verbs

Some verbs are irregular; their principal parts must be memorized. Here is a list of the most common ones.

Present	Past	Past participle
begin	began	begun
break	broke	broken
burst	burst	burst (not busted)
choose	chose	chosen
come	came	come
do	did	done
drag	dragged	dragged (not drug)

drink	drank	drunk
forget	forgot	forgotten (or forgot)
get	got	got (or gotten)
lay	laid	laid (meaning "placed")
lead	led	led
lie	lay	lain (meaning "reclined")
ride	rode	ridden
rise	rose	risen
run	ran	run
see	saw	seen
swim	swam	swum
take	took	taken
wake	waked (or woke)	waked (or woke)

If you find yourself wondering whether someone's heart was *broke* or *broken*, whether the sun has *rose* or *risen*, your dictionary can clear up your difficulty. Each dictionary has a guide to itself in the front, explaining how to use it and how the entries are arranged. You need to look up *inflected forms* and *principal parts of verbs* in this guide. Those sections will tell you how your dictionary lists irregular verb forms. Usually, the past and past participle are given in boldface type within the entry for the present tense verb.

Exercise on Irregular Verbs

Fill in the proper forms of the verbs in the following sentences.

1. None of the characters in *The Glass Menagerie* seems to be living lives they have [choose] themselves.
2. Amanda had [begin] to worry about Laura's becoming an old maid.
3. Tom was [wake] from a sound sleep by the resounding "Rise and shine!" of Amanda's voice.
4. Laura had [lay] the glass unicorn on a small table.
5. Once when Tom had [drink] too much, he lost his apartment keys.

Setting Verbs Right

Even regular verbs sometimes cause trouble for two reasons.

1. The third person *singular* adds an *-s* (or *-es*), whereas with nouns, the plural adds an *-s* or *-es:*

   (*Plural*)   two aardvarks, ten kisses
   (*Singular verbs*)   cream rises, a horse gallops, a goose hisses

2. The regular *-ed* ending that forms the past tense often is not heard in speech:

> talked deliberately
> used to go
> supposed to come
> locked the gate

Writing in Active Voice

Unless you have a clear reason for using passive voice, use *active voice*. Active voice usually leads you to write stronger, less wordy sentences. In passive voice, the grammatical subject of the sentence does *not* perform the action suggested by the verb; frequently, the performer is tacked onto the sentence in a separate phrase:

> In the story "Everyday Use," the quilts are coveted by both sisters.

Who covets the quilts? Both sisters, even though *quilts* is the subject of the sentence. In active voice, the sentence reads this way:

> In the story "Everyday Use," both sisters covet the quilts.

This version cuts two words and emphasizes the sisters' rivalry. (If you had some reason to emphasize the quilts instead, the first version would be better.)

All passive verbs use at least two words: some form of the *to be* verb as an auxiliary and the past participle of a verb. Even when the sentence is in the present tense, the past participle is there:

> The meaning of Stephen Crane's poem *is communicated* by the word "bitter."

The emphasis shifts when the sentence is written in active voice:

> The word "bitter" communicates the meaning of Stephen Crane's poem.

Exercise on Using Active Voice

Rewrite the following passive sentences, using active voice. Add, change, and delete words freely to strengthen the sentences while retaining their basic meanings. (Remember, passive voice form = *be* auxiliary + past participle.)

1. The play was concerned with the problem of male impotence.
2. The story line was embellished with shocking sexual revelations.
3. The limerick is enlivened by silly, outrageous rhymes and puns.
4. The comedy is made more complicated by several mistaken identities.
5. The main conflict of the story will not be revealed until the second act.

6. The meaning has been obscured by too many strange symbols.

7. The ending might be misinterpreted by an inattentive reader.

Solving Punctuation Problems

The most direct approach to punctuating your writing involves two questions:

1. What kinds of word groups are concerned?

2. What pieces of punctuation are standard and appropriate for this situation?

To answer question one, you need to remember the terms *phrase, dependent clause,* and *independent clause.* See Charts A, B, and C on pages 1014–1016 for a refresher. Using these terms, you can probably identify any group of words you are trying to punctuate and classify it into one of the four writing situations we describe in the following section. Under each situation, we list guidelines for deciding what punctuation to use.

1. Punctuation between two independent clauses:

A *period*, usually:

> I enjoy a strong plot in a novel. Allen cares about style more than plot.

A *comma*, only if the two independent clauses are connected by *and, or, for, but, nor, yet,* and *so*:

> I enjoy a strong plot in a novel, so I liked *The Skull Beneath the Skin*.

A *semicolon*, to show a close relationship in meaning between the two:

> I enjoy a strong plot in a novel; however, Allen cares more about style.

A *colon*, if the second independent clause restates or exemplifies the first:

> I enjoy a strong plot in a novel: I read *The Skull Beneath the Skin* in just three days.

2. Punctuation between a phrase or dependent clause and an independent clause:

A *comma*, if the phrase or dependent clause comes first and is long or transitional:

> When we were discussing epidemics this morning, Helen provided some new information. In fact, she had researched the subject recently. As a result, her knowledge was up-to-date.

No punctuation, usually, if the independent clause comes first:

> Helen described recent research when we were discussing epidemics this morning.

A *comma,* if the independent clause comes first and is followed by a transitional phrase or a tacked-on thought:

> She had researched the subject recently, in fact. She told us what she had found out, at least the main points.

3. **Punctuation in an independent clause interrupted by a phrase or dependent clause:**

No punctuation if the interrupter (italicized in the example) limits the meaning of the word before it:

> Students *who are living alone for the first time* make several mistakes. Mistakes *that make them feel foolish* include accidentally dyeing all their underwear blue. Mistakes *that are more serious* include not budgeting their time and money.

Commas on both ends of the interrupter (italicized) if it simply adds information or detail about the word before it:

> Students, *who usually lead hectic lives,* must learn to budget their time and money. A night of cramming, *no matter how thorough,* cannot substitute for seven weeks of steady studying. And snacks at fast food restaurants, *which seem cheap,* can be expensive if they are a nightly habit.

Parentheses to play down the interrupter:

> Sue went to the concert with Pam (her friend from Denver) to hear the all-female rock 'n' roll band.

Dashes to emphasize the interrupter:

> The music—although some might call it noise—made Sue and Pam get up and dance.

4. **Punctuation in a list or series of words, phrases, or clauses:**

A *comma* between all parallel items:

> Pam planned to trim Sue's hair, do some paperwork, make dinner for seven, and take her granddaughter shopping all in the same day.

A *semicolon* to separate each of the items when one of them already has a comma in it:

> To me, the ideal novel has a strong plot; is intelligent, touching, and funny; and involves characters I would like to know personally.

A *colon* after an independent clause followed by a list:

I usually read three kinds of fiction for pleasure: detective stories, feminist science fiction, and long nineteenth-century novels.

Using Necessary Commas Only

Commas *are* necessary to separate certain sentence elements. In brief, we need them in the following situations:

1. To set off transitional or dependent elements before the main clause —

As a matter of fact, Frank is an imaginary hero.

After Eveline finally decides to run away with Frank, she finds herself unable to do so.

2. To set off elements that interrupt the main sentence:

I told you, Frank, not to set foot on that boat without me.

My mother, a devout Catholic, made me promise to take care of my insufferable father.

3. To separate two independent clauses (sentences) when they are connected with *and, or, nor, yet, but, so,* or *for*:

No one will listen to you, so you will have to go talk to your horse.

Does this wallpaper look odd to you, or am I just seeing things?

4. To separate two or more items in a series:

I am writing about the relationship between setting, atmosphere, and structure in the story "A Hunger Artist."

Those boys are famous for staying up all night, hooting like owls, and setting fire to barns.

5. To mark off an element tacked on at the end of the main clause:

It sure looks like Emily, doesn't it?

The setting of the story is Japan, making it even harder to understand.

Sometimes commas are needed for clarity: to keep the reader from running words together inappropriately, for example. But many writers clutter their prose with unnecessary commas. These extra commas crop up frequently between the main parts of a subject–verb–object sentence.

1. Do not place a comma between the subject and the verb if no interrupter needing commas intervenes.

(*Faulty*)   The key to understanding difficult poetry, lies in finding a central image.

(*Revised*)   The key to understanding difficult poetry lies in finding a cental image.

2. **Do not place a comma between the verb and its object if no interrupter needing commas intervenes.**

(*Faulty*)   Eveline's problem with leaving her dull home was, that she felt too guilty.

(*Revised*)   Eveline's problem with leaving her dull home was that she felt too guilty.

(*Revised more fully*)   Eveline's problem with leaving her dull home was her feeling of overwhelming guilt.

3. **Do not place a comma before a coordinating conjunction (*and, but, or, nor, for, yet,* or *so*) unless it marks the conclusion of a series or the division between two complete sentences.**

(*Faulty*)   Women from certain backgrounds can understand Aunt Jennifer, and know the reasons for her timidity.

(*Revised*)   Women from certain backgrounds can understand Aunt Jennifer and know the reasons for her timidity.

Note: These three places where unnecessary commas creep in have something in common: they are places where someone might pause in speaking the sentences aloud. Perhaps the extra commas are a remnant of an old prescription to put commas wherever you would pause in speech. That old prescription expired many years ago.

Using Apostrophes

1. **Use an apostrophe to indicate the possessive form of nouns.**

A. Use an apostrophe followed by *s* to form the possessive of a singular noun or a plural noun not ending in *s:*

> a child's toy
> the boss's tie
> the children's toys
> Tom's parents

B. Use an apostrophe without *s* to form the possessive of a plural noun that ends in *s:*

> the boys' locker room
> my parents' house

C. Use an apostrophe with *s* or use the apostrophe alone to form the possessive of proper nouns ending in *s:*

> James's hat or James' hat
> the Jones's car or the Jones' car

D. Use an apostrophe with *s* to indicate the possessive of indefinite pronouns:

> everybody's business
> someone's book

E. Do *not* use an apostrophe for possessive pronouns:

> his   its   yours   whose
> hers   ours   theirs

2. Use an apostrophe to indicate that some letters or figures have been omitted in contractions.

> isn't   it's   I'll
> the best film of '68   o'clock   class of '82

3. An apostrophe is optional in forming the plural of letters, figures, and words referred to as words.

> Your 2's look like 7's. *or* Your 2s look like 7s.
> You use too many *and*'s in your sentences. *or* You use too many *and*s.
> Dot your *i*'s and cross your *t*'s.

Integrating Quotations Gracefully

In any literary essay you will need quotations from the text of the work you are examining. Be sure that you enclose these borrowings in quotation marks as you gracefully introduce them or integrate them into your own sentences, like this:

> We feel the danger of Edna's relationship with Arobin when the excitement of an afternoon with him is described as "a remittent fever" (217).

> Underscoring the physical dimension of the relationship, Chopin writes that "the touch of his [Arobin's] lips upon her hand had acted like a narcotic upon her" (218).

That last example shows how you may add your own words to explain a possibly confusing word in the quotation: use brackets. Most of the time, though, you can avoid this awkwardness by rewriting the sentence:

> The physical dimension of the relationship between Edna and Arobin is underscored by Chopin's imagery: "The touch of his lips upon her hand had acted like a narcotic upon her" (218).

Quoting from a Story: Crediting Sources

When writing a paper on a single literary source, you should place the specific page number or numbers of the quotation in parentheses, like this:

> Early on, we doubt Arobin's sincerity: "Alcée Arobin's manner was so genuine that it often deceived even himself" (218).

Then, at the end of your paper, provide a "Works Cited" page with complete publication information for the source you used:

> Chopin, Kate. "The Awakening." *Literature and the Writing Process.* Ed. Elizabeth McMahan, Susan Day, and Robert Funk. 3rd ed. New York: Macmillan, 1993: 162–247.

If you use only one source, put the page number in parentheses after the first quotation. If you use more than one source, use the relevant author's last name in the parentheses, as well, and list all sources on the "Works Cited" page. Notice that when giving credit within the paper, you close the quotation, put in the parentheses, and end with the period:

> Arobin is decidedly "prolific with pretexts" (218).

(Otherwise, remember that commas and periods go *inside* the quotation marks.)

If you use a long quotation (over four lines of type), indent the whole thing ten spaces from the left margin, omit the quotation marks, and leave the numbers in parentheses *outside* the closing punctuation. Double space the quotation. Here is an example of a long quotation used within a paper:

> Chopin allows the women's clothing to help define their characters. She contrasts Madame Ratignolle's attire with Edna Pontellier's:
>
> > Madame Ratignolle, more careful of her complexion, had twined a gauze veil about her head. She wore doeskin gloves, with gauntlets that protected her wrists. She was dressed in pure white, with a fluffiness of ruffles that became her. (172)

Notice again that in the case of a long indented quotation, no quotation marks are used unless they appear in the work itself. Also, in this case *only*, the numbers in parentheses appear *after* the closing punctuation.

Quoting from a Poem

1. **When quoting poetry, be sure to reproduce capitalization and punctuation exactly within each line, but adjust punctuation at the end of your quotation to suit your sentence.**

A. If quoting only a couple of lines, use a slash mark to indicate the end of each line (except the last):

Blake reminds us of the traditional repression of sexuality by the church when he observes, "And the gates of this chapel were shut, / And 'thou shalt not' writ over the door."

B. If quoting several lines of poetry, indent and single-space without quotation marks:

Blake's persona emphasizes the sexual restrictions imposed by Christian doctrine as he looks at the ruined Garden of Love:

And I saw it was filled with graves,
And tombstones where flowers should be,
And priests in black gowns were walking their rounds,
And binding with briars my joy & desires.

C. Use ellipsis marks to show omissions when quoting poetry, just as you would if quoting prose:

When Blake's persona revisits the Garden of Love, he sees "priests in black gowns . . . walking their rounds" instead of the lush, sensual flowers he remembers.

Quoting from a Play

When writing a paper on a play arranged in verse with line numbers, you need to cite your source using act, scene, and line numbers. For nonverse plays, simply give act and scene numbers in parentheses at the end of the quoted material. Because *Antigone* is not divided into acts, give the scene and line numbers for the quotations you use. Long quotations (more than two lines) should be indented with *no* quotation marks. Also, indicate the speaker when quoting a passage in which more than one character speaks. Here are some samples:

It is up to Ismene to point out the obvious: "We are only women / We cannot fight with the men, Antigone!" (Pro. 46–47).

[Only two lines quoted—separated with a slash and enclosed in quotation marks]

Creon's speeches show his contempt for women:

Gentlemen, I beg you to observe these girls:
One has just now lost her mind; the other,
It seems, has never had a mind at all. (2.148–49)

[Long quotation—indented, no quotation marks]

Iago is a master of understatement and insinuation:

Othello. Is he not honest?
Iago. Honest, my lord!
Othello. Honest! ay, honest.
Iago. My lord, for aught I know.

Othello. What dost thou think?
Iago. Think, my lord! (3.3.103–105)

[Change of speakers indicated]

Remember to introduce each quotation carefully. You may want to review the material in Chapter 5 on integrating quotations gracefully (page 70).

Punctuating Quoted Material

1. **Put quotation marks around words that you copy from any source.**

   A. Quoted complete sentence using a comma:

   > As Joan Didion points out, "Almost everything can trigger an attack of migraine: stress, allergy, fatigue, an abrupt change in barometric pressure, a contretemps over a parking ticket"(103).

   B. Quoted complete sentence introduced by *that* (without a comma):

   > Didion asserts that "Migraine is something more than the fancy of a neurotic imagination" (102).

   C. Quoted partial sentence that readers can clearly tell is a partial sentence:

   > Didion explains that migraines stem from various causes, even so minor a trauma as "a contretemps over a parking ticket" (103).

   > Didion is clearly irritated by people who attribute migraine to "the fancy of a neurotic imagination" (102).

   D. Quoted partial sentence in which readers *cannot* tell something has been omitted; use ellipsis dots (three spaced periods) to show the omission:

   > According to Didion, "Once the attack is under way . . . , no drug touches it" (104).

   > [*Original sentence:*   "Once the attack is under way, however, no drug touches it."]

   > Didion complains that ". . . nothing so tends to prolong an attack as the accusing eye of someone who has never had a headache" (104).

   > [*Original sentence:*   "My husband also has migraine, which is unfortunate for him but fortunate for me: perhaps nothing so tends to prolong an attack as the accusing eye of someone who has never had a headache."]

   > Didion attests that "All of us who have migraine suffer not only from the attacks themselves but from this common conviction that we are perversely refusing to cure ourselves by taking a couple of aspirin . . ." (104).

> [*Original sentence:*   "All of us who have migraine suffer not only from the attacks themselves but from this common conviction that we are perversely refusing to cure ourselves by taking a couple of aspirin, that we are making ourselves sick, that we 'bring it on ourselves.'"]

Note: When the omission occurs at the end of the sentence, use *four* dots, not three. The extra dot is the period.

2. **When you quote material already containing quotation marks, use single quotation marks or indent the passage.**

   A. If quoted material within quotation marks is short, enclose within single quotation marks, using the apostrophe on your keyboard:

   > Didion observes, "There certainly is what doctors call a 'migraine personality,' and that personality tends to be ambitious, inward, intolerant of error, rather rigidly organized, perfectionist" (103).

   B. If quoting extensive conversation, set off the entire passage by indenting *ten spaces* and double-spacing the quotation:

   > Howell's attitude toward the sentimental novel is made clear when the dinner conversation turns to discussion of a current bestseller, *Tears, Idle Tears:*
   >
   > > "Ah, that's the secret of its success," said Bromfield Corey. "It flatters the reader by painting the characters collosal, but with his limp and stoop, so that he feels himself of their supernatural proportions. You've read it, Nanny?"
   > > "Yes," said his daughter. "It ought to have been called *Slop, Silly Slop.*" (237)
   >
   > This same scorn for sentimentality is reflected in the subplot involving Lapham's daughters.

   C. If quoted conversation is *brief,* use single quotation marks within double ones:

   > We soon realize that the characters are hopelessly lost: "'It's a funny thing,' said Rabbit ten minutes later, 'how everything looks the same in a mist. Have you noticed it, Pooh?'" (142).

3. **Put periods and commas inside quotation marks, except when citing a page or line number in parentheses at the end of a quotation:**

   > Kurt Vonnegut advises that "Simplicity of language is not only reputable, but perhaps even sacred."

   > "Simplicity of language," advises Kurt Vonnegut, "is not only reputable, but perhaps even sacred."

   > As Kurt Vonnegut advises, "Simplicity of language is not only reputable, but perhaps even sacred" (113).

Iago, in soliloquy, reveals his devious intentions toward Othello early in the play: "Though I do hate him as I do hell-pains,/Yet, for necessity of present life,/I must show out a flag and sign of love,/Which is indeed but sign" (I.i.152–55).

4. **Put question marks and exclamation marks inside the quotation marks if they belong with the quotation; put these marks *outside* if they punctuate the whole sentence:**

   Is this an exact quotation from Twain, "Truth is more of a stranger than fiction"?

   E. M. Forster asks, "How do I know what I think until I see what I say?"

5. **Put colons, semicolons, and dashes outside the quotation marks.**

   Avoid cliches like these in stating the theme of a work: "Appearances can be deceiving"; "Do unto others . . ."; "The love of money is the root of all evil."

6. **Put quotation marks (or underline to indicate italics) around words used as words.**

   The term "sentimentality" carries a negative meaning when applied to literature.

7. **Put quotation marks around the titles of works that are short (essays and articles in magazines, short stories and poems, chapters in books).**

   "A Hanging" (essay by George Orwell)
   "Rope" (short story by Katherine Anne Porter)
   "Living in Sin" (poem by Adrienne Rich)
   "Paper Pills" (chapter title in Sherwood Anderson's *Winesburg, Ohio*)

8. **Underline the titles of works that are long (books, movies, plays, long poems, names of magazines and newspapers).**

   Adventures of Huckleberry Finn
   Casablanca
   Death of a Salesman
   Paradise Lost
   Sports Illustrated
   The Detroit *Free Press*

Note: Do not underline or put in quotation marks the title of your own essay.

9. **Put square brackets around words or letters that you add to clarify a quotation or change the verb tense.**

> Iago early declares his ill feelings: "Though I do hate [Othello] as I do hell-pains,/Yet, for necessity of present life,/I must show out a flag and sign of love. . . ."

> The crowd is hushed; then "Mr. Graves open[s] the slip of paper and there [is] a general sigh through the crowd . . . ," as his proves to be blank.

Writing Smooth Transitions

The transitions between paragraphs serve to set up expectations in your reader about what will follow—expectations that you will then fulfill. Look at these transitions and state what you would expect from a paragraph opening with each:

> On the other hand,
> Furthermore,
> In brief,

Probably you would expect a paragraph opening with "On the other hand" to provide some contrast with the topic of the paragraph before it. But "Furthermore" suggests that the new paragraph will add development along the same lines as the paragraph just above it. "In brief" would lead you to expect a summary of earlier points. In fact, if the paragraphs did *not* fulfill the expectations elicited by the transitions, you would feel decidedly unsatisfied with the writing.

Transitions in good essays not only set up accurate expectations but also do so gracefully. Experienced writers use the *echo transition* to achieve this purpose. This technique echoes a word, phrase, or idea from the last sentence of one paragraph to provide the transition at the beginning of the next. Here is an example, beginning with the closing of a paragraph and showing the transition to the next:

> Throughout the story, the husband's word is considered law, and the wife barely dares to question it.
>   *This unequal marriage* fits perfectly into the historical period of the setting.

The words *this unequal marriage* echo the inequality described in the previous sentence. Another echo transition might reuse exact words in this way:

> Throughout the story, the husband's word is considered law, and the wife barely dares to question it.
>   This *husband–wife relationship* fits perfectly into the historical period of the setting.

Consider for a moment the information given by the sample transitional sentences above. The echo of "this unequal marriage" or "this husband–wife relationship" suggests that the subject matter is similar to the subject of the preceding paragraph, while the rest of the sentence leads you to expect material linking the marriage to its historical context. Rework at least a few of your own paragraph transitions so that they will provide such subtle but easily followed continuity.

Catching Careless Mistakes

These are errors that you make, even though you know better, because you are paying more attention to your thoughts than to the mechanical act of getting them down properly. In the rough drafts, careless mistakes are no real problem, but in a finished paper, they are an extreme embarrassment. Some of the most common ones follow.

1. Skipping a word or letter:

As you race along on an inspired part, your thoughts run ahead of your hand, and you may write sentences like

> Without knowing it, Emilia been an aid to an evil plot.

leaving the auxiliary verb *has* out before the *been*. Or you could end up with

> Five of the main characters die violently befor the end of the play.

2. Repeating a word:

Most people have pens or keyboards that stutter sometimes, producing sentences like

> The characters who survive are are dramatically altered.

Short words like *the* and *of* seem to invite careless repetition more than long ones do.

3. Creative capitalization:

Out of habit or due to the idiosyncracies of your handwriting, you sometimes capitalize or fail to capitalize on impulse rather than by the rules. For example, one student wrote,

> Last thursday I took my Final Exam in History.

Though the capitalization surely reflects what the student considers important in the sentence, it should be altered to conform to standard capitalization. These rules are listed in the front of your collegiate dictionary.

4. Typographical errors:

In a final draft, there's no such thing as "*just* a typing error." Most readers are irritated, some even offended, by negligent proofreading. Correct typographical errors neatly in ink. Reading your manuscript aloud sometimes allows you to catch a number of careless surface errors, as well as more serious problems like sentence fragments.

Glossary of Literary and Rhetorical Terms

Allegory A form of symbolism in which ideas or abstract qualities are represented as characters or events in a story, novel, or play. For example, in the medieval drama *Everyman*, Fellowship, Kindred, and Goods, the friends of the title character, will not accompany him on his end-of-life journey, and he must depend on Good Works, whom he has previously neglected.

Alliteration Repetition of the same consonant sounds, usually at the beginning of words:

> Should the glee — glaze —
> In Death's — stiff — stare —
> — *Emily Dickinson*

Allusion An indirect reference to some character or event in literature, history, or mythology that enriches the meaning of the passage. For example, the title of W. H. Auden's poem "The Unknown Citizen" is an ironic allusion to the Tomb of the Unknown Soldier.

Ambiguity Something that may be validly interpreted in more than one way; double meaning.

Anapest *See* Meter.

Antagonist The character (or a force such as war or poverty) in a drama, poem, or work of fiction whose actions oppose those of the protagonist (hero or heroine).

Anticlimax A trivial event following immediately after significant events.

Apostrophe A poetic figure of speech in which a personification is addressed:

> You sea! I resign myself to you also — I guess what you mean.
> — *Walt Whitman*

Archetype A recurring character type, plot, symbol, or theme of seemingly universal significance: the blind prophet figure, the journey to the underworld, the sea as source of life, the initiation theme.

1047

Assonance The repetition of similar vowel sounds within syllables:

> On desperate seas long wont to roam
> —*Edgar Allan Poe*

Atmosphere *See* Mood.

Audience In composition, the readers for whom a piece of writing is intended.

Ballad A narrative poem in four-line stanzas, rhyming *xaxa*, often sung or recited as a folk tale. The *x* means that those two lines do not rhyme.

Blank Verse Unrhymed iambic pentameter, the line that most closely resembles speech in English:

> When I see birches bend to left and right
> Across the lines of straighter darker trees,
> I like to think some boy's been swinging them.
> —*Robert Frost*

Carpe Diem Literally, seize the day, a phrase applicable to many lyric poems advocating lustful living:

> Gather ye rosebuds while ye may,
> Old time is still a-flying:
> And this same flower that smiles today
> Tomorrow will be dying.
> —*Robert Herrick*

Catharsis In classical tragedy, the purging of pity and fear experienced by the audience at the end of the play; a "there but for the grace of the gods go I" sense of relief.

Chorus In Greek drama, a group (often led by an individual) who comments on or interprets the action of the play.

Climax The point toward which the action of a plot builds as the conflicts become increasingly intense or complex; the turning point.

Coherence In good writing, the orderly, logical relationship among the many parts — the smooth moving forward of ideas through clearly related sentences. *Also see* Unity.

Comedy A play, light in tone, designed to amuse and entertain, that usually ends happily, often with a marriage.

Comedy of Manners A risqué play satirizing the conventions of courtship and marriage.

Complication The rising action of a plot during which the conflicts build toward the climax.

Conceit A highly imaginative, often startling, figure of speech drawing an analogy between two unlike things in an ingenious way:

> In this sad state, God's tender bowels run
> Out streams of grace. . . .
> —*Edward Taylor*

Concrete That which can be touched, seen, or tasted; not abstract. Concrete illustrations make abstractions easier to understand.

Conflict The antagonism between opposing characters or forces that causes tension or suspense in the plot.

Connotation The associations that attach themselves to many words, deeply affecting their literal meanings (e.g., *politician, statesman*).

Consonance Close repetition of the same consonant sounds preceded by different vowel sounds (*flesh/flash* or *breed/bread*). At the end of lines of poetry, this pattern produces half-rhyme.

Controlling Idea *See* Thesis.

Controlling Image In a short story, novel, play, or poem, an image that recurs and carries such symbolic significance that it embodies the theme of the work, as the wallpaper does in Gilman's "The Yellow Wall-Paper," as the quilts do in Walker's "Everyday Use," and as the grass does in Whitman's "Leaves of Grass."

Convention An accepted improbability in a literary work, such as the dramatic aside, in which an actor turns from the stage and addresses the audience.

Couplet Two rhymed lines of poetry:

> For thy sweet love remembered such wealth brings
> That then I scorn to change my state with kings.
> — *William Shakespeare*

Crisis *See* Plot.

Dactyl *See* Meter.

Denotation The literal dictionary meaning of a word.

Denouement Literally, the "untying"; the resolution of the conflicts following the climax (or crisis) of a plot.

Diction Words chosen in writing or speaking.

Double Entendre A double meaning, one of which usually carries sexual suggestions, as in the country-western song about a truck driver who calls his wife long distance to say he is bringing his "big ol' engine" home to her.

Dramatic Irony *See* Irony.

Dramatic Monologue A poem consisting of a self-revealing speech delivered by one person to a silent listener; for instance, Robert Browning's "My Last Duchess."

Dramatic Point of View *See* Point of View.

Elegy A poem commemorating someone's death but usually encompassing a larger issue as well.

Empathy Literally, "feeling in"; the emotional identification that a reader or an audience feels with a character.

English Sonnet *See* Sonnet.

Epigram A short, witty saying that often conveys a bit of wisdom:

> Heaven for climate; hell for society.
> — *Mark Twain*

Epigraph A quotation at the beginning of a poem, novel, play, or essay that suggests the theme of the work.

Epilogue The concluding section of a literary work, usually a play, in which loose threads are tied together or a moral is drawn.

Epiphany A moment of insight in which something simple and commonplace is seen in a new way and, as James Joyce said, "its soul, its whatness leaps to us from the vestment of its appearance."

Episode In a narrative, a unified sequence of events; in Greek drama, the action between choruses.

Exposition That part of a plot devoted to supplying background information, explaining events that happened before the current action.

Extended Metaphor *See* Metaphor.

Fable A story, usually using symbolic characters and settings, designed to teach a lesson.

Falling Action In classical dramatic structure, the part of a play after the climax, in which the consequences of the conflict are revealed. *Also see* Denouement.

Figurative Language Words that carry suggestive or symbolic meaning beyond the literal level.

First Person Point of View *See* Point of View.

Flashback Part of a narrative that interrupts the chronological flow by relating events from the past.

Flat Character In contrast to a well-developed round character, a flat one is stereotyped or shallow, not seeming as complex as real people; flat characters are often created deliberately to give them a symbolic role, like Faith in "Young Goodman Brown."

Foil A character, usually a minor one, who emphasizes the qualities of another one through implied contrast between the two.

Foot A unit of poetic rhythm. *See* Meter.

Foreshadowing Early clues about what will happen later in a narrative or play.

Formal Writing The highest level of usage, in which no slang, contractions, or fragments are used.

Free Verse Poetry that does not have regular rhythm, rhyme, or standard form.

Free Writing Writing without regard to coherence or correctness, intended to relax the writer and produce ideas for further writing.

Genre A classification of literature: drama, novel, short story, poem.

Hero/Heroine The character intended to engage most fully the audience's or reader's sympathies and admiration. *Also see* Protagonist.

Hubris Unmitigated pride, often the cause of the hero's downfall in Greek tragedy.

Hyperbole A purposeful exaggeration.

Iamb *See* Meter.

Image/Imagery Passages or words that stir feelings or memories through an appeal to the senses.

Informal Writing The familiar, everyday level of usage, which includes contractions and perhaps slang but precludes nonstandard grammar and punctuation.

Internal Rhyme The occurrence of similar sounds within the lines of a poem rather than just at the ends of lines:

> Too bright for our infirm delight
> — *Emily Dickinson*

Invention The process of generating subjects, topics, details, and plans for writing.

Irony Incongruity between expectation and actuality. *Verbal irony* involves a discrepancy between the words spoken and the intended meaning, as in sarcasm. *Dramatic irony* involves the difference between what a character believes true and what the better-informed reader or audience knows to be true. *Situational irony* involves the contrast between characters' hopes and fears and their eventual fate.

Italian Sonnet *See* Sonnet.

Jargon The specialized words and expressions belonging to certain professions, sports, hobbies, or social groups. Sometimes any tangled and incomprehensible prose is called jargon.

Juxtaposition The simultaneous presentation of two conflicting images or ideas, designed to make a point of the contrast: for example, an elaborate and well-kept church surrounded by squalorous slums.

Limited Point of View *See* Point of View.

Lyric A poem that primarily expresses emotion.

Metaphor A figure of speech that makes an imaginative comparison between two literally unlike things:

> Sylvia's face was a pale star.

Metaphysical Poetry A style of poetry (usually associated with seventeenth century poet John Donne) that boasts intellectual, complex, and even strained images (called *conceits*) which frequently link the personal and familiar to the cosmic and mysterious. *Also see* Conceit.

Meter Recurring patterns of stressed and unstressed syllables in poetry. A metrical unit is called a *foot*. There are four basic patterns of stress: an *iamb*, or *iambic foot*, which consists of an unstressed syllable followed by a stressed one (bĕfóre, rĕtúrn); a *trochee*, or *trochaic foot*, which consists of a stressed syllable followed by an unstressed one (fúnnÿ, dóublĕ); an *anapest*, or *anapestic foot*, which consists of two unstressed syllables followed by a stressed one (cŏntrădíct); and a *dactyl*, or *dactylic* foot, which consists of a stressed syllable followed by two unstressed ones (mérrĭlÿ, sýllăblĕ). One common variation is the *spondee*, or *spondaic* foot, which consists of two stressed syllables (moónshíne, foótbáll).

Lines are classified according to the number of metrical feet they contain: *monometer* (one foot), *dimeter* (two feet), *trimeter* (three feet), *tetrameter* (four feet), *pentameter* (five feet), *hexameter* (six feet), and so on.

Metonymy A figure of speech in which the name of one thing is substituted for that of something else closely associated with it—for example, *the White House* (meaning the President or the whole executive branch), or *the pen is mightier than the sword* (meaning written words are more powerful than military force).

Mood The emotional content of a scene or setting, usually described in terms of feeling: somber, gloomy, joyful, expectant. *Also see* Tone.

Motif A pattern of identical or similar images recurring throughout a passage or entire work.

Myth A traditional story involving deities and heroes, usually expressing and inculcating the established values of a culture.

Narrative A story line in prose or verse.

Narrator The person who tells the story to the audience or reader. *Also see* Unreliable Narrator.

Objective Point of View *See* Point of View.

Ode A long, serious lyric focusing on a stated theme: "Ode on a Grecian Urn."

Omniscient Point of View *See* Point of View.

Onomatopoeia A word that sounds like what it names: whoosh, clang, babble.

Oxymoron A single phrase that juxtaposes opposite terms:

the lonely crowd, a roaring silence.

Parable A story designed to demonstrate a principle or lesson using symbolic characters, details, and plot lines.

Paradox An apparently contradictory statement that, upon examination, makes sense:

> Time held me green and dying
> —*Dylan Thomas, "Fern Hill"*

Paraphrase In prose, a restatement in different words, usually briefer than the original version; in poetry, a statement of the literal meaning of the poem in everyday language.

Parody An imitation of a piece of writing, copying some features such as diction, style, and form, but changing or exaggerating other features for humorous effect.

Pentameter A line of poetry that contains five metrical feet. *See* Meter.

Persona The person created by the writer to be the speaker of the poem or story. The persona is not usually identical to the writer: for example, a personally optimistic writer could create a cynical persona to narrate a story.

Personification Giving human qualities to nonhuman things:

> The craft pranced and reared, and plunged like an animal.
> —*Stephen Crane*

Plagiarism Carelessly or deliberately presenting the words or ideas of another writer as your own; literary theft.

Plot A series of causally related events or episodes that occur in a narrative or play. *Also see* Climax, Complication, Conflict, Denouement, Falling Action, Resolution, and Rising Action.

Point of View The angle or perspective from which a story is reported and interpreted. There are four common points of view that authors use: *First Person* — someone, often the main character, tells the story as he or she experienced it (and uses the pronoun *I*). *Omniscient* — the narrator knows everything about the characters and events and can move about in time and place and into the minds of all the characters. *Limited* — the story is limited to the observations, thoughts, and feelings of a single character (not identified as *I*). *Objective* or *dramatic* — the actions and conversations are presented in detail, as they occur, more or less objectively, without any comment from the author or a narrator.

Prewriting The process that writers use to gather ideas, consider audience, determine purpose, develop a thesis and tentative structure (plan), and generally prepare for the actual writing stage.

Protagonist The main character in drama or fiction, sometimes called the hero or heroine.

Pun A verbal joke based on the similarity of sound between words that have different meanings:

> They went and *told* the sexton and the sexton *tolled* the bell.
> — *Thomas Hood*

Quatrain A four-line stanza of poetry, with any number of rhyme schemes.

Resolution The conclusion of the conflict in a fictional or dramatic plot. *Also see* Denouement *and* Falling Action.

Rhyme Similar or identical sounds between words, usually the end sounds in lines of verse (brain/strain; liquor/quicker).

Rhythm The recurrence of stressed and unstressed syllables in a regular pattern. *Also see* Meter.

Rising Action The complication and development of the conflict leading to the climax in a plot.

Round Character A literary character with sufficient complexity to be convincing, true to life.

Sarcasm A form of *verbal irony* that presents caustic and bitter disapproval in the guise of praise. *Also see* Irony.

Satire Literary expression that uses humor and wit to attack and expose human folly and weakness. *Also see* Parody.

Sentimentality The attempt to produce an emotional response that exceeds the circumstances and to draw from the readers a stock response instead of a genuine emotional response.

Setting The time and place in which a story, play, or novel occurs. *Also see* Mood.

Shakespearean Sonnet *See* Sonnet.

Simile A verbal comparison in which a similarity is expressed directly, using *like* or *as*:

> houses leaning together like conspirators.
> —*James Joyce*

Also see Metaphor.

Situational Irony *See* Irony.

Soliloquy A speech in which a dramatic character reveals what is going through the mind by talking aloud to the self. *Also see* Dramatic Monologue.

Sonnet A poem of fourteen ten-syllable lines, arranged in a pattern of rhyme schemes. The *English* or *Shakespearean* sonnet uses seven rhymes that divide the poem into three quatrains and a couplet: abab, cdcd, efef, gg. The *Italian* sonnet usually divides into an octave (eight lines) and a sestet (six lines) by using only five rhymes: abba, abba, cdecde. (The rhyme scheme of the sestet varies widely from sonnet to sonnet.)

Speaker The voice or person presenting a poem.

Spondee *See* Meter.

Standard English The language that is written and spoken by most educated persons.

Stereotype An oversimplified, commonly held image or opinion about a person, a race, an issue.

Stilted Language Words and expressions that are too formal for the writing situation; unnatural, artificial language.

Structure The general plan, framework, or form of a piece of writing.

Style Individuality of expression, achieved in writing through the selection and arrangement of words and punctuation.

Symbol Something that suggests or stands for an idea, quality, or concept larger than itself: the lion is a symbol of courage; a voyage or journey can symbolize life; water suggests spirituality; dryness the lack thereof.

Synecdoche A figure of speech in which some prominent feature is used to name the whole, or vice versa — for example, *a sail in the harbor* (meaning a ship), or *call the law* (meaning call the law enforcement officers).

Synesthesia Figurative language in which two or more sense impressions are combined:

> blue uncertain stumbling buzz
> — *Emily Dickinson*

Syntax Sentence structure; the relationship between words and among word groups in sentences.

Theme The central or dominating idea advanced by a literary work.

Thesis The main point or position that a writer develops and supports in a composition.

Tone The attitude a writer conveys toward his or her subject and audience. In poetry this attitude is sometimes called *voice*.

Tragedy A serious drama that relates the events in the life of a protagonist, or *tragic hero*, whose error in judgment, dictated by a *tragic flaw*, results in the hero's downfall and culminates in catastrophe. In less classical terms, any serious drama, novel, or short story that ends with the death or defeat of the main character may be called tragic.

Trochee *See* Meter.

Type Character A literary character who embodies a number of traits that are common to a particular group or class of people (a rebellious daughter, a stern father, a jealous lover); all of the characters in Albee's *An American Dream* are types.

Understatement A form of ironic expression that intentionally minimizes the importance of an idea or fact.

Unity The fitting together or harmony of all elements in a piece of writing. *Also see* Coherence.

Unreliable Narrator A viewpoint character who presents a biased or erroneous report that may mislead or distort a reader's judgments about other characters and actions; sometimes the unreliable narrator may be self-deceived.

Usage The actual or express way in which a language is used.

Verbal Irony *See* Irony.

Verisimilitude The appearance of truth or believability in a literary work.

Versification The mechanics of poetic composition, including such elements as rhyme, rhythm, meter, and stanza form.

Biographical Notes

CHINUA ACHEBE (1930–) started as a writer for the Nigerian Broadcasting Corporation, but his first novel, *Things Fall Apart* (1958), which depicts the conflicts of African and European culture in Nigeria, brought him international success. His fiction often deals with the legacy of colonialism in Africa, reflecting the civil war and violence that have wracked Nigeria since it gained independence from British rule in 1963. Achebe has taught in Canada and at the University of Connecticut.

EDWARD ALBEE (1928–) was adopted in infancy by wealthy parents. He was expelled from two prep schools, dropped out of college, and moved to Greenwich Village where he worked at odd jobs. His first play, *The Zoo Story* (1958), was performed in West Berlin before beginning its successful run in New York. Albee's plays often explore the strife inherent in family relationships. His most famous play, *Who's Afraid of Virginia Woolf?*, won several awards and was made into a film featuring Elizabeth Taylor and Richard Burton.

SHERWOOD ANDERSON (1876–1941) delved into the dark side of small-town American life, exposing the psychological deformity and frustration beneath the placid surface. His greatest work, *Winesburg, Ohio* (1919), a collection of twenty-three linked stories, explores this theme to great effect. His other short story collections include *The Triumph of the Egg* (1921), *Horses and Men* (1923), and *Death in the Woods* (1933).

MATTHEW ARNOLD (1822–1888), born in Middlesex, England, studied classics at Oxford and later taught there. He was appointed inspector of schools for England and remained in that post for thirty-five years. As a poet, Arnold took his inspiration from Greek tragedies, Keats, and Wordsworth. An eminent social and literary critic in later years, he lectured in America in 1883 and 1886. His essay "The Function of Criticism" explains his shift from poet to critic.

FERNANDO ARRABAL (1933–   ) was born in Spanish Morocco but moved to France in 1955. He writes in Spanish, though his works, translated by his wife, appeared first in French. He wrote his first play, *Picnic on the Battlefield*, at age fourteen. His most powerful political play, *And They Put Handcuffs on the Flowers* (1969), was inspired by his experience as a prisoner in post–Civil War Spain.

W. H. AUDEN (1907–1973) was born in England but became a U.S. citizen in 1946. An extremely talented poet, he was the major literary voice of the 1930s, an "age of anxiety" that faced war and world-wide depression. Influenced by Freud, Auden often wrote about human guilt and fear, but he also celebrated the power of love to overcome anxiety. His volume of poetry *The Age of Anxiety* (1947) won the Pulitzer Prize. Auden also collaborated on verse plays and wrote librettos for operas.

JIMMY SANTIAGO BACA (1952–   ) endured a family life shattered by matricide, a childhood in a state orphanage, and years in a state prison for supposed drug crimes. Baca managed to teach himself to read and write while receiving the state-ordered electroshock treatments that had been prescribed to curb his combative nature. His poetry, especially that about prison life, has won him critical acclaim.

IMAMU AMIRI BARAKA (1934–   ) was born LeRoi Jones in Newark, New Jersey. He attended Rutgers, graduated from Howard University, and spent three years in the Air Force. In the 1960s he became involved with black nationalist politics, changed his name to Imamu Amiri Baraka, and founded the Black Arts Theater in Harlem. His anger at the privileged status of whites is expressed in such plays as *Dutchman* and *The Slave* (both 1964) and in his collection of poetry *Black Magic* (1967).

JOHN BERRYMAN (1914–1972) was born in Oklahoma. He is noted for his complex, dramatic verse, which combines bleak introspection with giddy comedy. Thrice married and twice divorced, an alcoholic who could not control his drinking for more than a few months at a time, Berryman ended his difficult life in suicide, an act often contemplated in his poetry. Berryman's *77 Dream Songs* (1964) won a Pulitzer Prize. Other works include *Homage to Mistress Bradstreet* (1956) and *Delusions, Etc.* (1972).

WILLIAM BLAKE (1757–1827) was both artist and poet, though he achieved little success as either during his lifetime. Of the more than half dozen books he wrote and illustrated, only one of them was published conventionally; his wife helped him print the rest. A mystic and visionary, Blake created his own mythology, complete with illustrations. His best-known works are *Songs of Innocence* (1789) and *Songs of Experience* (1794).

ARNA BONTEMPS (1902–1973), a black writer and historian, was born in Louisiana, educated at the University of Chicago, and became a librarian at Fisk University. His passion for history led him to write *Black Thunder* (1936), a novel that focuses on a slave rebellion that occurred in Virginia in 1800. With Countee Cullen, Bontemps turned his novel *God Sends Sunday* (1931) into a Broadway musical called *St. Louis Woman* (1946).

GWENDOLYN BROOKS (1917–   ) is an African-American poet whose work often focuses on ghetto life. Although she came from a middle-class family, Brooks has identified with poor blacks, and the simplicity of her poetic voice often mirrors the meager circumstances of her subjects. Her second book of poetry, *Annie Allen* (1949), won the Pulitzer Prize in 1950, making Brooks the first African-American woman to receive this award. Brooks was named poet laureate of Illinois in 1969.

ROBERT BROWNING (1812–1889) was an English poet who experimented with diction and rhythm as well as with psychological portraits in verse. He secretly married Elizabeth Barrett, and they moved to Italy in 1846, partly to avoid her domineering father. Browning was a master of dramatic monologues, a talent exemplified in "My Last Duchess" and "Porphyria's Lover." After the death of his wife, Browning returned to England where he wrote what some consider his masterwork, *The Ring and the Book* (1868–1869).

ROBERT BURNS (1759–1796) was raised on a farm in Scotland. In rural isolation, he read extensively, and he began writing poetry at an early age. In 1786 he published *Poems, Chiefly in the Scottish Dialect*, which depicted Scottish rural life with humor and exuberance. The book was an immense success, and Burns remained in Scotland for the rest of his life. Although he failed at farming, he produced such favorite songs as "Auld Lang Syne," "Comin' thro' the Rye," and "Flow Gently, Sweet Afton."

GEORGE GORDON, LORD BYRON (1788–1824) was born in London of an aristocratic family and educated at Cambridge. He became a public figure, as much for his scandalous personal life as for his irreverent, satiric poetry. Rumors about an affair with his half-sister forced him to leave England in 1816. Byron died in Greece from a fever that he contracted while fighting for Greek independence. His masterpiece is the comic epic poem *Don Juan*, begun in 1819 and still unfinished when he died.

RAYMOND CARVER (1938–1988) grew up in Yakima, Washington. Married at nineteen and a father of two by twenty, he moved to California, worked nights, and attended Chico State College. Carver's stories describe the frustrations and loneliness of blue-collar Americans living on the West Coast, where glamour and affluence belong to someone else. Carver published four collections of stories, including *Cathedral* (1982) and *Where I'm Calling From* (1988), before dying of lung cancer.

ANTON CHEKOV (1860–1904), a multitalented man whose gifts were matched by his humanitarianism, was born in southern Russia, studied medicine in Moscow, and supported himself by writing humorous sketches. Later he ran a free clinic for peasants while gaining fame as a playwright. He established close ties with the famous Moscow Art Theater, where his great plays, *Three Sisters* (1901) and *The Cherry Orchard* (1904), were produced. His emphasis on characterization and tragicomedy has influenced a generation of modern dramatists.

KATE CHOPIN (1851–1904), born Kate O'Flaherty in St. Louis, was raised by her mother, grandmother, and great-grandmother, all widows, after her father's death when she was four. In 1870 she married Oscar Chopin and moved to New Orleans. Although she published numerous short stories in popular magazines, Chopin made her greatest impact with *The Awakening* (1899), a short novel. Her explorations of female sexuality and her championing of women's self-worth, themes which outraged readers at the turn of the century, are now highly regarded.

SAMUEL TAYLOR COLERIDGE (1772–1834) was a friend of William Wordsworth and collaborated with him on the landmark work *Lyrical Ballads* (1798), which introduced Romanticism to England. Erratic in his university career and, indeed, throughout most of his life, Coleridge was a brilliant lecturer and wrote on subjects ranging from philosophy to literature. "The Rime of the Ancient Mariner" and "Kubla Khan" are his best known shorter works.

STEPHEN CRANE (1871–1900) was born in Newark, the fourteenth child of a Methodist minister who died when Crane was nine. Leaving college early, he moved to New York City, where he observed firsthand the boozers and prostitutes who inhabited the slums. His first novel, *Maggie: A Girl of the Streets* (1893), drew on these observations. At age twenty-four, and with no military experience, he wrote *The Red Badge of Courage* (1895), a Civil War novel that made Crane famous and became an American classic.

COUNTEE CULLEN (1903–1946) was adopted by a Methodist minister and raised in Harlem. His first volume of poems, *Color* (1925), was published when he was a student at New York University. His early work established him as a leader of the Harlem Renaissance, but his collection *Copper Sun* (1927), which featured love poems, disappointed black nationalists. Cullen stopped writing poetry after he published *The Black Christ* in 1929. He taught school in New York City for the rest of his life.

e e cummings (1894–1962), born Edward Estlin Cummings in Cambridge, Massachusetts, is perhaps best known for his eccentric antipathy toward capital letters — a style copied by many poetry students. His volumes of poetry include *Tulips and Chimneys* (1923) and *95 Poems* (1958). During World War I, Cummings served as an ambulance driver in France and was mistakenly committed to a French prison camp for three months, an experience he recounted in the prose journal *The Enormous Room* (1922).

JAMES DICKEY (1923–) was born in Atlanta, played football in college, served in the Army Air Force in World War II, worked in advertising, taught at several universities, and is poet-in-residence at the University of South Carolina. Dickey's poems are usually wedded to personal incident and project an almost demonic view of life. His several volumes of poetry include *Buckdancer's Choice* (1965), winner of the National Book Award. He also wrote the best-selling novel *Deliverance* (1970).

EMILY DICKINSON (1830–1886) is among the greatest of American poets. During most of her adult life, she was a recluse, confining herself to her father's Amherst, Massachusetts, home, wearing only white, and shunning company. She produced over 1,700 lyrics, which are characterized by startling imagery, ellipses, and unexpected juxtapositions. Only seven of her poems were published in her lifetime — and those without her permission. Her influence is still felt in modern poetry.

JOHN DONNE (1572–1631) was the first and perhaps greatest of the metaphysical poets. In his youth, he wrote erotic lyrics and cynical love poems. A politically disastrous marriage ruined his civil career, but in 1615 he converted to Anglicanism and later became dean of St. Paul's Cathedral and the most influential preacher in England. In later years, he wrote religious sonnets, elegies, epigrams, and verse letters. Donne's use of complex conceits and compressed phrasing has influenced many twentieth-century poets, especially T. S. Eliot.

H.D. (1886–1961) was born Hilda Doolittle in Pennsylvania. While at Bryn Mawr, she met and fell in love with Ezra Pound, but her father put an end to the affair. She went to Europe in 1911, married poet Richard Aldington, and had several other love relationships, the most enduring one with novelist Winifred Bryher. H. D. wrote articles for the early film journal *Close Up* and underwent psychoanalysis with Freud. Her poetry combines the clarity of Imagist technique with themes from classical myth.

ANDRÉ DUBUS (1936–) was born in Lake Charles, Louisiana, served in the U.S. Marine Corps, and rose to the rank of captain. He then received an MFA from the University of Iowa and taught for eighteen years at Bradford College, in Massachusetts, before an automobile accident forced him to retire. Drawing on his experiences in the military, Dubus wrote the novel *The Lieutenant* (1967).

He is best known for his short stories, which often involve hard moral choices and violent situations.

PAUL LAURENCE DUNBAR (1872–1906) was born in Dayton, Ohio, the son of former slaves. He graduated from high school but could not afford college and worked instead as an elevator operator. He published his first two books of poetry with his own money. He finally found a major publisher for *Lyrics of Lowly Life* (1896) and became the first African-American poet to win national recognition. Although the public seemed to prefer his dialect poems, Dunbar favored those, like "We Wear the Mask," that are written in literary English.

T. S. ELIOT (1888–1965) was born in St. Louis, studied at Harvard, and emigrated to London, where he worked as a bank clerk and as an editor. In 1927 he became a British citizen and joined the Church of England. His landmark poem *The Wasteland* (1922) influenced a generation of young poets. As a critic, he revived interest in John Donne and other metaphysical poets. In later years, he wrote verse plays, such as *Murder in the Cathedral* (1935) and *The Cocktail Party* (1950). He won the Nobel Prize for Literature in 1948.

LOUISE ERDRICH (1954–   ) was born in Minnesota, of native American and German heritage, and she grew up in North Dakota as a member of the Turtle Mountain Chippewas. Her fiction captures both the comedy and the poignancy of cultural loss and fragmentation. Her novels *Love Medicine* (1984), *The Beet Queen* (1986), and *Tracks* (1988) form a cycle about contemporary Native American life and have established Erdrich as one of the country's most important writers.

WILLIAM FAULKNER (1897–1962), one of the great novelists of this century, was born in New Albany, Mississippi. He used a dense and varied style, often experimenting with point of view and stream of consciousness, to probe the turbid depths of Southern life. He received two Pulitzer Prizes, for *A Fable* (1954) and *The Reivers* (1962), and was also awarded the Nobel Prize for Literature in 1949. His many other works include *The Sound and the Fury* (1929), *As I Lay Dying* (1930), and *Light in August* (1932).

ANNE FINCH, COUNTESS OF WINCHILSEA (1661–1720) came from a distinguished family in England. She married an associate of the Duke of York (later King James II), and her husband encouraged her poetic pursuits, even though such activity was frowned upon for women at that time. Being childless, she had the leisure to write and to support the rights of women to express themselves.

ROBERT FROST (1874–1963) is probably one of the most popular and respected of American poets. He was born in San Francisco, but when he was a young boy his family moved to New England. His poems are characterized by colloquial, restrained language that implies messages rather than openly stating them. His works include *A Boy's Will* (1913), *New Hampshire* (1923), *A Witness Tree* (1942), *Steeple Bush* (1947), and *In the Clearing* (1962). Frost was awarded four Pulitzer Prizes for his poetry.

CHARLOTTE PERKINS GILMAN (1860–1935) is probably best known for her promotion of feminism. Her first major work, *Women and Economics* (1898), makes an appeal for the financial independence of women, and in *Concerning Children* (1900) she proposes that children be cared for collectively by women best suited for parenting. She co-founded the Women's Peace Party in 1915. Her success came only after she recovered from a mental illness and left her husband and child.

ALLEN GINSBERG (1926–) grew up in Paterson, New Jersey, where his father taught high school English. After attending Columbia University, Ginsberg moved to San Francisco in the early 1950s and began his relationship with poet Peter Orlovsky. The appearance of the controversial *Howl and Other Poems* (1956) established Ginsberg as a major "Beat" poet. In the 1960s, he gave public readings and became a prominent figure in civil rights rallies, the war resistance movement, and gay liberation. His other works include *Kaddish* (1961), *Reality Sandwiches* (1963), and *Collected Poems* (1980).

NIKKI GIOVANNI (1943–) is noted for her often joyous poetry, which she shares, enthusiastically, with large audiences. She contributed to the outpouring of militant black poetry in the 1960s and 1970s, but she has since focused on writing about love and relationships. She has recorded over five albums of her poetry, one of which uses gospel music in the background because she wanted her grandmother to like it. Giovanni's works include *Black Feeling, Black Talk* (1968) and *A Poetic Equation* (1974).

SUSAN GLASPELL (1882–1948), born and raised in Davenport, Iowa, began her career writing fiction for popular magazines. In 1915 she became one of the founders of the Provincetown Players, an experimental theater group. *Trifles* was written to be performed with several one-act plays by Eugene O'Neill at the company's summer playhouse. Some of her other plays include *Suppressed Desires* (1915), *The Verge* (1921), and *Alison's House* (1930), a Pulitzer Prize-winning drama based on the life of Emily Dickinson.

SUSAN GRIFFIN (1943–) was born in California, graduated from San Francisco State University, and has worked as a waitress, teacher, house painter, and switchboard operator to support her writing and her daughter. Her collections of poetry include *Dear Sky* (1971) and *Like the Iris of an Eye* (1976). Griffin has also written two works of feminist social criticism, *Woman and Nature* (1978) and *Pornography and Silence* (1981).

THOM GUNN (1929–   ) was born in England, but after the publication of his first volume of poems, *Fighting Terms* (1954), he took a fellowship at Stanford University and in 1960 settled permanently in San Francisco, gradually giving up his academic career for full-time writing. Gunn's poetry is marked by a careful craftsmanship that strives for exact images rather than flamboyance. Collections of his poems include *The Sense of Movement* (1957), *My Sad Captains* (1961), and *Moly* (1971).

DONALD HALL (1928–   ) was born in Connecticut and attended both Harvard and Oxford universities. He was poetry editor of the *Paris Review* and professor of English at the University of Michigan before moving to rural New Hampshire. His first book of poems, *Exiles and Marriages* (1955), won several awards, including the Millay Award of the Poetry Society of America. Hall has also written children's books, several college textbooks, and a book about baseball.

LORRAINE HANSBERRY (1930–1965) was born to a middle-class African-American family on Chicago's south side. She studied painting in Chicago and abroad before moving to New York City. Her *A Raisin in the Sun* was the first play by a black woman to be produced on Broadway; it won the New York Drama Critics Award in 1959. Hansberry died of cancer on the day her second play, *The Sign in Sidney Brustein's Window* (1964), closed on Broadway.

THOMAS HARDY (1840–1928) was an architect in London when he first became interested in literature. At age thirty he began to write novels and produced sixteen of them. When his novel *Jude, the Obscure* (1896) was called immoral for criticizing marriage, Hardy became so angry that he wrote nothing but poetry for the rest of his life. Among his best-known novels are *The Return of the Native* (1878) and *Tess of the D'Urbervilles* (1928).

NATHANIEL HAWTHORNE (1804–1864) ranks with the great writers of fiction in English. His first publication, *Twice-Told Tales* (1837), a volume of richly symbolic tales about moral duty and human guilt, helped to establish the short story as a legitimate literary form. The appearance of his masterpiece of hidden guilt and redemption, *The Scarlet Letter* (1850), secured his position as America's foremost romancer. His other major novels are *The House of the Seven Gables* (1851) and *The Blithedale Romance* (1852).

ROBERT HAYDEN (1913–1980), born Asa Bundy Sheffey in Detroit, was renamed by his foster parents. In the poetry of his first collection, *Heart-Shape in the Dust* (1940), he used facts about African-American history that he unearthed as a researcher for the Federal Writers' Project (1936–1940). Educated at Wayne State and the

University of Michigan, Hayden taught at Fisk University and later returned to teach at Michigan. He considered his writing "a form of prayer—a prayer for illumination, perfection."

SEAMUS HEANEY (1939–   ) has been cited as Ireland's best poet since Yeats. Heaney was born on a farm in Northern Ireland, and his early poetry communicates a strong sense of the physical environment of his youth. His later work, often dense and poignant, concerns the cultural implications of words and their historical contexts. Heaney now divides his time between Dublin and America, where he teaches at Harvard. His most recent books of poetry are *Station Island* (1985) and *The Haw Lantern* (1987).

ERNEST HEMINGWAY (1899–1961) began his professional writing career as a reporter for newspapers in Kansas City and Toronto. In the 1920s he became a voice for the Lost Generation of expatriated Americans living in Paris. His direct, forceful style is exhibited in short stories and novels, which include *A Farewell to Arms* (1929), *For Whom the Bell Tolls* (1940), and *The Old Man and the Sea* (1954), which won the Pulitzer Prize. Hemingway was awarded the Nobel Prize for Literature in 1954.

GERARD MANLEY HOPKINS (1844–1889) was, like Emily Dickinson, a major poet who was not recognized during his lifetime. Born in Essex, England, he attended Oxford, converted to Catholicism, and became a Jesuit priest. He died of typhoid fever at age forty-four. Nearly thirty years later, his friend Robert Bridges published Hopkins' *Poems* (1918), having thought them too demanding for earlier readers. Hopkins developed his own theory of meter, called "sprung rhythm," which focuses on the number of stressed syllables in a line and disregards the unstressed syllables.

A. E. HOUSMAN (1859–1936), after failing his finals at Oxford, became a clerk in the London Patent Office. An extremely capable scholar, he began publishing his studies of classical authors and was eventually appointed professor of Latin at London University and then at Cambridge. Housman's own poetry, admired for its exquisite simplicity and penetrating feeling, often deals with the tragedy of doomed youth. His poetic works include *A Shropshire Lad* (1896) and *Last Poems* (1922).

LANGSTON HUGHES (1902–1967), born in Joplin, Missouri, became a major contributor to the Harlem Renaissance by writing about black urban life. In his writing he achieved a cultivated artlessness by incorporating spirituals and blues into traditional verse forms. Hughes was the first black writer to make a living by composing radio plays, song lyrics, novels, plays, poetry, and children's books. His poetry collections include *The Weary Blues* (1926) and *One-Way Ticket* (1949).

TED HUGHES (1930–   ) was born in Yorkshire, England. He writes poetry and children's books. His style is characterized by a tightly ordered form in poetry and by imaginative explorations of the psyche in children's books. Hughes was married to the American poet Sylvia Plath. His works include *The Hawk in the Rain* (1957), *Lupercal* (1960), *Crow* (1971), and *Moortown* (1980).

ZORA NEALE HURSTON (1901–1960), born in Eatonville, Florida, was a writer and folklorist. She studied anthropology at Columbia University and collected stories in Jamaica, Haiti, Bermuda, and Honduras, which she transformed into novels and plays, including musicals. Her best known novel, *Their Eyes Were Watching God* (1937), came from her sharp eye for detail, from her willingness to be bawdy, and from being comfortable with being black at a time when others were not.

HENRIK IBSEN (1828–1906), a Norwegian dramatist, was one of the most influential figures in modern theater. He worked as a stage manager, playwright, and director, and he is best known for breaking away from the romantic tradition in drama in order to portray life realistically. His social plays, such as *A Doll's House* (1879), *Ghosts* (1881), and *Hedda Gabler* (1890), shocked audiences with subject matter (venereal disease, suicide, women's independence) that was considered unmentionable in public.

SHIRLEY JACKSON (1919–1965) did not receive attention as a writer until 1948 when *The New Yorker* published "The Lottery." The magazine reported that no other story had ever received such a strong response. Although known for her tales of supernatural terror, such as *We Have Always Lived in the Castle* (1962) and *The Haunting of Hill House* (1959), she also wrote humorous chronicles of family life, such as *Life Among the Savages* (1953) and *Raising Demons* (1957).

RANDALL JARRELL (1914–1965) is recognized as one of the most powerful commentators on war in American literature. He flew as a pilot during World War II, and two of his collections of poetry — *Little Friend, Little Friend* (1945) and *Losses* (1948) — describe the war's profound effect on him. After the war he returned to his life as professor, poet, and critic. In later years he wrote four books for children, including *The Bat Poet* (1964). Jarrell was struck and killed by an automobile in 1965.

JAMES JOYCE (1882–1941) rejected his Irish Catholic heritage and left his homeland at age twenty. Though an expatriate most of his adult life, Joyce wrote almost exclusively about his native Dublin. His first book, *Dubliners* (1914), was a series of sharply drawn vignettes based on his experiences in Ireland, the homeland he later described as "a sow that eats its own farrow." His novel *Ulysses* (1933) was banned for a time in the U.S. because of its coarse language and frank treatment of sexuality.

DONALD JUSTICE (1925–) is a poet often praised for his control over the technical aspects of his craft. His mastery of form led critic Cathrael Kazin to remark, "Justice has come to be recognized not only as one of America's most elegant and distinctive contemporary poets but also as one of its most significant." Born in Florida and educated at Miami University, North Carolina, and Iowa, Justice teaches college writing. His *Selected Poems* won a Pulitzer Prize in 1980.

FRANZ KAFKA (1883–1924) was born into a middle-class Jewish family in Prague. He earned a law degree, worked in an insurance office, and lived with a domineering father who belittled his literary endeavors. Despite these conditions, Kafka produced a remarkable body of original work in his short life, including the powerful novels *The Trial* (1925) and *The Castle* (1926). His starkly realistic stories take place in nightmarish worlds where people are demeaned and intimidated by an unfeeling bureaucracy.

JOHN KEATS (1795–1821) was a major figure in the romantic period of English poetry. His potential was cut short when he died of tuberculosis in Italy at the age of twenty-five. He began writing when he was eighteen, already having seen his mother die of consumption; his brother was to follow. Perhaps the haunting disease provided the spur to Keats's uncanny development. His poems, which are rich in imagery and dignified in expression, include "Ode on a Grecian Urn," "To Autumn," and "The Eve of St. Agnes."

CLAIRE KEMP (1936–) was born in Worcester, Massachusetts; she now lives and works in South Pasadena, Florida. Two of her short stories, "Early Frost" and "Keeping Company," were selected by the PEN Fiction Syndicate for publication, and both appeared in the *Chicago Tribune Magazine*. Kemp is currently completing a novel and also working on a collection of short stories.

MAXINE KUMIN (1925–) was born Maxine Winokur in Philadelphia and attended Radcliffe. She lives on a farm in New Hampshire where she breeds horses. Kumin likes to write about what she calls "small overlooked things," bringing them "back to the world's attention." She has published several poetry collections, including the Pulitzer Prize-winning *Up Country* (1972), four novels, short stories, and more than twenty children's books, three of them in collaboration with poet Anne Sexton.

RING LARDNER (1885–1933) is best known for his satirical stories of American life in the early twentieth century, told in the language of baseball players, boxers, stockbrokers, chorus girls, etc. Born in Niles, Michigan, Lardner worked as a reporter for various newspapers in Chicago, St. Louis, and Boston. At one time his syndicated column appeared in over 150 newspapers. He published more than twenty volumes of stories, including *You Know Me Al* (1916) and *Love Nest and Other Stories* (1926).

PHILIP LARKIN (1922 – 1985) came from a working-class background in the north of England. His past is reflected in his first volume of poems, *The North Ship* (1946), and his first two novels, *Jill* (1946) and *A Girl in Winter* (1947). Larkin, who once said, "Form holds little interest for me," became the leader of the British anti-romantic movement. His poetry collection *The Less Deceived* (1955) treats conventional themes, like love and death, with searing wit and sophisticated roughness.

D. H. LAWRENCE (1885 – 1930), born David Herbert Lawrence, was a celebrated British poet, novelist, essayist, and short-story writer. Lawrence regarded sex, the primitive subconscious, and nature as cures for what he saw as the dehumanization of modern society. He expressed many of his views in his novels *The Rainbow* (1915) and *Women in Love* (1920). He never ceased to rebel against puritanism and social conventions, a rebellion that led to some of the most famous censorship trials of the twentieth century.

URSULA LE GUIN (1929 –   ), a popular writer of science fiction and fantasy, was born in Berkeley, California, the daughter of a psychologist mother and an anthropologist father. Le Guin attended Radcliffe and Columbia, went to France, married, and returned to Oregon to begin her prolific writing career. She has created a series of imaginative worlds, combining myth, anthropology, and psychology to present a vision of balance and wholeness. Her novel *The Left Hand of Darkness* (1969) explores gender relations on a planet where all the inhabitants are androgynous.

JOHN LENNON (1940 – 1980) was the acknowledged leader of the British rock group, the Beatles. He described himself as the "hip" and "hallucinatory" side of the Lennon-McCartney composing team, and his hand was most evident in such songs as "Help!," "Strawberry Fields," and "Revolution." After teaming with his second wife, Yoko Ono, he recorded a number of political songs, such as "Imagine," "Give Peace a Chance," and "Come Together." Lennon was shot outside his New York City apartment.

DENISE LEVERTOV (1923 –   ) was born in England and educated by her mother, who was Welsh, and her father, an Anglican priest converted from Judaism. She was a nurse in World War II, married an American novelist, and moved to the United States, where she discovered the work of William Carlos Williams and other free-form poets. Although her poetry focuses on politics, especially concern for women and the Third World, much of it remains personal. Her collections include *The Jacob's Ladder* (1961), *The Freeing of the Dust* (1975), and *A Door in the Hive* (1989).

AUDRE LORDE (1934 –   ) was born of West Indian parents in New York City. She was educated at the National University of Mexico, Hunter College, and Columbia University. Her poetry is passionate about love, angry about race, and feminist. Her first major work of prose, *The Cancer Journals* (1980), depicts her struggle with breast cancer and mastectomy and carries her message of the strength of women. *The Black Unicorn* (1978) is a volume of poems about Africa.

RICHARD LOVELACE (1618–1657) was a wealthy, handsome, elegant Cavalier poet. Because of his loyal support of King Charles I, Lovelace was twice imprisoned by the Puritan Parliament during the English Civil War. He died in poverty in a London slum. Much of Lovelace's poetry is labored and lifeless, but he did write several charming, graceful lyrics, such as "To Althea from Prison," "To Amarantha, That She Would Dishevel Her Hair," and "To Lucasta, on Going to the Wars."

AMY LOWELL (1874–1925) was born in Brookline, Massachusetts, into one of New England's most prominent families. She rejected her upbringing and devoted herself to modern poetry and the company of gifted women. As the chief advocate for a new kind of verse that rejected traditional forms and utilized the suggestiveness of vivid imagery, Lowell helped to bring American poetry into the twentieth century. Her best poems contain evocative images that recall the impressionist painters and composers she admired.

ARCHIBALD MacLEISH (1892–1982) was born in Illinois and attended Yale and Harvard Law School. After serving in World War I, he began writing poetry to express his postwar disillusionment and his concern about the rise of fascism. He was Librarian of Congress from 1939 to 1944. Although his verse play *J.B.* (1958) won a Pulitzer Prize and a Tony Award, MacLeish's reputation rests on his poetry. His epic about the conquest of Mexico, *Conquistador* (1932), won the Pulitzer Prize, as did *Collected Poems 1917–1952*.

CHRISTOPHER MARLOWE (1564–1593), the son of a Canterbury shoemaker, was one of the leading poets and dramatists of his day. His major plays, which include *Tamburlaine the Great* (1587), *Dr. Faustus* (1588), and *Edward II* (1592), concern heroic figures who are brought down by their own extravagant passions. He was one of the first to use blank verse in his plays, a practice that Shakespeare perfected. Marlowe's lyric poetry is graceful and warmly sensuous. He was killed in a quarrel over a tavern bill.

ANDREW MARVELL (1621–1678), though not a Puritan himself, supported the Puritan cause in the English Civil War. He held a number of posts during the Commonwealth and was instrumental in saving John Milton from punishment after the Restoration. One of the metaphysical poets, Marvell is best known for his witty lyrics that often present a tacit debate about opposing values. He has been called "the most major minor poet" in English.

PAUL McCARTNEY (1942–   ) is the most successful survivor of the legendary rock group, the Beatles. He and the late John Lennon established themselves as one of the century's best-loved songwriting teams, turning out an extraordinary number of pop standards within a very few years. Following the Beatles' breakup, McCartney continued as a solo artist and as the leader of the band Wings. The *Guiness Book of Records* lists him as the best-selling composer and recording artist of all time.

CLAUDE McKAY (1890–1948) was born in Sunny Ville, Jamaica. At the age of twenty-three, he moved to the U.S. where he experienced the strong racial prejudice so prevalent during this period. A prominent figure in the Harlem Renaissance, McKay was a catalyst among African-American writers, preaching black vitality and social reform. He wrote four volumes of poetry, including *If We Must Die* (1919); a novel, *Home to Harlem* (1928); and his autobiography, *A Long Way from Home* (1937).

EDNA ST. VINCENT MILLAY (1892–1950) was born in Maine and educated at Vassar. In 1917 she moved to Greenwich Village and published her first book of poetry, *Renascence and Other Poems*. She won the Pulitzer Prize for *The Harp-Weaver* (1922), a collection of sonnets that deal wittily and flippantly with love. Although Millay became politically involved and used her poetry to speak out for social causes, she is known best for her poems about the bittersweet emotions of love and the brevity of life.

MARIANNE MOORE (1887–1972) was born in Kirkwood, Missouri, and graduated from Bryn Mawr. For a time she taught business at the Carlisle Indian School. By 1915, her witty, innovative poems began to appear in *Poetry* magazine. Her *Collected Poems* (1951) won a Pulitzer Prize. Moore lived in Brooklyn most of her adult life, taking care of her mother, writing poems and reviews, editing *The Dial* (a literary magazine that published some of the best poets of the day), and attending baseball games.

ALBERTO MORAVIA (1907–1990) was born in Rome. His first novel, *Time of Indifference* (1929), was a great success. His writings also brought him into conflict with Italy's Fascist regime, and he had to flee the country when the Germans occupied Rome. The acknowledged leader of the "neorealists" who emerged in Italy after World War II, Moravia wrote about the inability of modern humanity to understand and connect with reality. His best-known works are *The Woman of Rome* (1947) and *The Conformist* (1951).

ALICE MUNRO (1931–   ), a Canadian writer who grew up in rural Ontario, focuses on small-town life, particularly on the lives of women. Although her characters seem ordinary and self-conscious, they possess emotional lives of surprising depth. Munro specializes in short stories, claiming they allow her to present "intense, but not connected, moments of experience." Her collections include *Lives of Girls and Women* (1971), *The Progress of Love* (1986), and *Friends of My Youth* (1990).

PABLO NERUDA (1904–1973) was born in Parral, Chile. Despite his reputation as one of the greatest Spanish-American poets in history, few of his works have been translated into English. Neruda was a radical poet who mixed meditations on political oppression with intensely personal lyrics about romantic love. He was awarded the Nobel Prize for Literature in 1971.

JOYCE CAROL OATES (1938–) was born in Lockport, New York, graduated from Syracuse University, and now teaches at Princeton. Fascinated by psychological and social disorder, Oates often explores the relationship between violence and love in American society. She has written over one hundred stories and nearly forty novels, as well as literary criticism and essays on boxing. Among her works are *A Garden of Earthly Delights* (1967), *them* (1969), *Bellefleur* (1980), and *Last Days* (1984).

FLANNERY O'CONNOR (1925–1964), afflicted with lupus erythematosus, spent most of her short life in Milledgeville, Georgia. After earning an M.F.A. from the University of Iowa, she returned to the family farm to raise peacocks and write about contemporary Southern life in grotesquely comic terms. She produced two novels, *Wise Blood* (1952) and *The Violent Bear It Away* (1960), and two volumes of short stories, *A Good Man Is Hard to Find* (1955) and *Everything That Rises Must Converge* (1965).

SHARON OLDS (1942–), born in San Francisco and educated at Stanford University, is the author of three books of poetry: *Satan Says* (1980), *The Dead and the Living* (1983; National Book Award), and *The Gold Cell* (1987). Because of its intense focus on family and sexual relationships, her poetry is often compared to that of confessional poets Sylvia Plath and Anne Sexton. Olds teaches creative writing at New York University and at the Goldwater Hospital, a facility for the physically disabled.

TILLIE OLSEN (1913–) emphasizes, in her book *Silences* (1978), how gender, race, and class can render people inarticulate. Her own life illustrates the problem. She began working on a novel before she was twenty, but then she married, had four children, worked, participated in union activities, and did not resume writing until the 1950s. The completed novel, *Yonnondio*, was finally published in 1974. Her long story "Tell Me a Riddle" won the O. Henry Prize in 1961.

WILFRED OWEN (1893–1918) began writing poetry at the University of London. After teaching English in France for a few years, Owen returned to England and joined the army. He was wounded in 1917 and killed in action a few days before the armistice was declared in 1918. Owen's poems, published only after his death, are some of the most powerful and vivid accounts of the horrors of war to emerge from World War I.

DOROTHY PARKER (1893–1967), known best for her acerbic wit, was actually a serious editor and writer. Fired from *Vanity Fair* for writing harsh theater reviews, she reviewed books for *The New Yorker*, which also published her stories, poems, and articles for over thirty years. Her lasting literary contributions include short stories such as "Big Blonde" and "The Waltz" and several collections of sardonic verse.

MARGE PIERCY (1936–   ) was born in Detroit, Michigan. Concerned with depicting and dignifying women's experiences, Piercy has been accused of politicizing her work. In the introduction to her book of poetry *Circles on the Water* (1982), she explains how her writing can be "of use" to women: "To find ourselves spoken for in art gives dignity to our pain, our anger, our lust, our losses." Among her popular novels are *Small Changes* (1973), *Woman on the Edge of Time* (1976), and *Gone to Soldiers* (1987).

SYLVIA PLATH (1932–1963) was born in Boston, the daughter of German immigrants who taught at Boston University. Her early years were filled with honors and awards. She won a Fulbright Scholarship to Cambridge, where she met and married English poet Ted Hughes. But beneath the conventional success was a woman whose acute perceptions and intolerable pain led her to commit suicide at age thirty. Plath produced three volumes of powerful poetry and an autobiographical novel, *The Bell Jar* (1963).

EDGAR ALLAN POE (1809–1849) played a key role in developing the short story. He was born in Boston, orphaned at age two, and adopted by the Allans of Richmond. He attended the University of Virginia, served in the army, and went to West Point—but was expelled for not attending classes. After marrying his thirteen-year-old cousin, Poe wrote and worked as a journalist and editor. He died under mysterious circumstances. His best tales, such as "The Fall of the House of Usher" and "The Tell-Tale Heart," skillfully probe the dark recesses of the human mind.

KATHERINE ANNE PORTER (1890–1980) specialized in short fiction. She worked for several newspapers and did some acting until she was able to survive on her earnings as an author. Nurtured by academia, she received a number of honors and lectured at more than 200 universities and colleges. Her finest collections are *Flowering Judas* (1930) and *Pale Horse, Pale Rider* (1939). Her only novel, *Ship of Fools* (1962), was made into an award-winning film. *The Collected Stories* (1965) won a Pulitzer Prize.

EZRA POUND (1885–1972), one of the most influential and controversial poets of our time, was born in Idaho, left America in 1908, and lived in Europe for much of his life. Pound's colossal ambition led him to found the Imagist movement in poetry, to advise a galaxy of great writers (Eliot, Joyce, Yeats, Frost), and to write numerous critical works. It also led to a charge of treason (for broadcasting propaganda for Mussolini) and to twelve years in a mental hospital. His poetry is collected in *Personae* (1949) and *The Cantos* (1976).

SIR WALTER RALEIGH (1552–1618) was an English soldier, explorer, courtier, and man of letters. A favorite of Queen Elizabeth I, he organized the colonizing expeditions to North America that ended tragically with the "lost colony" of Roanoke Island. Imprisoned for thirteen years in the Tower of London by James I, Raleigh was released to search for gold in South America. When he returned empty-handed, he was executed. A true court poet, he circulated his poems in manuscript. As a result, only a few have survived.

DUDLEY RANDALL (1914–   ) was born in Washington, D.C., and graduated from Wayne State and the University of Michigan. A pioneer in the movement to publish the work of African-American writers, Randall founded one of the most influential small publishing houses in America—Broadside Press. Collections of his work include *Cities Burning* (1968), *After the Killing* (1973), and *A Litany of Friends: New and Selected Poems* (1981).

ISHMAEL REED (1938–   ) was born in Chattanooga, grew up in Buffalo, and attended the State University of New York. In 1965 he co-founded the *East Village Other*, an outlet for experimental writing. Reed's poetry demonstrates an interest in Egyptian symbolism and in American and African-American history. He has written several novels and prose satires, including *The Terrible Twos* (1982), which combines a deconstruction of Christmas customs with an allegory of the Reagan presidency.

ADRIENNE RICH (1929–   ), who was born in Baltimore, graduated from Radcliffe College in 1951, the same year that her first book of poetry, *A Change of World*, appeared in the Yale Series of Younger Poets. The Vietnam War and her experience in teaching minority youth in New York City heightened Rich's political awareness, and she became increasingly involved in the women's movement. Her poetry often concerns the tension between artistic achievement and the demands of female roles.

EDWIN ARLINGTON ROBINSON (1869–1935) was born in Tide Head, Maine. Though now considered an important poet, Robinson spent many years depending on friends for a livelihood. The publication of his narrative poem *Tristram* (1927) brought him wide recognition and some measure of financial independence. Although his verse is traditional in form, he anticipated many twentieth century poets with his emphasis on themes of alienation and failure. His poetry won three Pulitzer Prizes—in 1921, 1924, and 1927.

THEODORE ROETHKE (1908–1963) was born in Saginaw, Michigan, where he grew up surrounded by his father's twenty-five-acre greenhouse complex. While an undergraduate at the University of Michigan, he decided to pursue both poetry and teaching. A preoccupation with literal and symbolic growth pervades his poetry, as does a concern for nature and childhood. His collection *The Waking* (1953) won the Pulitzer Prize, and *Words for the Wind* (1958) received the National Book Award.

CHRISTINA ROSSETTI (1830–1894) has been called the finest woman poet England has yet produced. Sister to poet-painter Dante Gabriel Rossetti, she grew up in a liberal household where few conversational topics were forbidden. Her ardent Anglicanism drove her to break off plans for marriage twice. Her lyric poetry typically expresses frustration and parting in relationships, rarely happiness and fulfillment. Her works include *The Goblin Market and Other Poems* (1862).

CARL SANDBURG (1878–1967) was born in Galesburg, Illinois, and worked as a day laborer, soldier, political activist, and journalist. These experiences provided a rich palette of poetic colors to select from, and Sandburg painted boldly in vigorous free verse. His works include *Chicago Poems* (1916), *Cornhuskers* (1918), *The People, Yes* (1936), and *Harvest Poems* (1960). He also wrote a six-volume biography of Abraham Lincoln and four children's books, including the *Rootabaga Stories* (1922).

DELMORE SCHWARTZ (1913–1966), born in Brooklyn, was a poet, short story writer, and editor who was plagued by instability and unhappiness. His genius crossed pop culture with the insights of Freud and Marx. Once timed to have talked for eight hours straight, Schwartz was no stranger to sanatoriums. His volume *Summer Knowledge: New and Selected Poems* (1959) won the Bollingen Prize. He was fictionalized by Saul Bellow as the main character in the novel *Humboldt's Gift* (1975).

ANNE SEXTON (1928–1974) once wrote that poetry "should be a shock to the senses. It should hurt." Born in Newton, Massachusetts, Sexton attended college, married, worked as a fashion model, and wrote highly introspective poetry that won her a wide and loyal audience. She committed suicide at age forty-six. Her collection of poems *Live or Die* (1966) won a Pulitzer Prize. Other works include *To Bedlam and Part Way Back* (1960), *Transformations* (1971), and three volumes of verse for children.

WILLIAM SHAKESPEARE (1554–1616) is the most widely known author in all English literature. He was born in Stratford-on-Avon, probably attended grammar school there, and at eighteen married Anne Hathaway, who bore him three children. In 1585 or shortly thereafter, he went to London and began his apprenticeship as an actor. By 1594 he had won recognition as a poet, but it was in the theater that he made his strongest reputation. Shakespeare produced perhaps thirty-five plays in twenty-five years, including historical dramas, comedies, romances, and the great tragedies: *Hamlet* (1602), *Othello* (1604), *King Lear* (1605), and *Macbeth* (1606). His 154 sonnets are supreme examples of the form.

KARL SHAPIRO (1913–) is best known for his antiwar poetry and for his critical essays. While serving in the Pacific in World War II, Shapiro wrote *V-Letter and Other Poems* (1944), for which he received the Pulitzer Prize. In addition to editing *Poetry* magazine, he has taught at the University of Nebraska and other schools. His *Selected Poems* appeared in 1968. Shapiro's critical works include *Beyond Criticism* (1953) and *To Abolish Children and Other Essays* (1968).

PERCY BYSSHE SHELLEY (1792–1822) married sixteen-year-old Harriet Westbrook in 1811, the same year he was expelled from Oxford for writing a pamphlet on atheism. In 1814 he went to France with Mary Wollstonecraft, later famous for writing *Frankenstein* (1818). They were married in 1816, after Harriet committed suicide, and settled in Italy, where Shelley wrote some of his best lyrics, including "Ozymandias." His other works include "Ode to the West Wind" and *Adonais*, an elegy to John Keats.

PAUL SIMON (1942–) was born in Newark, New Jersey, and attended Queens College, where he majored in English. In 1964 he teamed with Art Garfunkel to form one of the most successful singing duos in rock history, recording such hits as "Mrs. Robinson," "Bridge over Troubled Waters," and "The Sounds of Silence." The team split in 1971. Simon's solo albums include *Still Crazy After All These Years* (1975) and *Graceland* (1986). He was inducted into the Rock & Roll Hall of Fame in 1990.

STEVIE SMITH (1902–1971) was born Florence Margaret Smith in Hull, England. She worked as a secretary and occasionally as a writer and broadcaster for the BBC. She began publishing verse, which she often illustrated herself, in the 1930s but did not gain much recognition until 1962, when her *Selected Poems* appeared. Noted for her eccentricity and humor, Smith often aimed her satirical barbs at religion and made unexpected use of traditional hymns, songs, and nursery rhymes in her poems.

W.D. SNODGRASS (1926–) is one of the original "confessional" poets. His poems often contain references to the wives and children from his three marriages. Born in Pennsylvania, Snodgrass served in the navy before studying at the University of Iowa; he has taught at many universities. His works include the Pulitzer Prize-winning *Heart's Needle* (1959) and *The Führer Bunker: A Cycle of Poems in*

Progress (1977), which uses the imagined voices of prominent Nazis in dramatic juxtaposition.

SOPHOCLES (c. 496–405 B.C.) wrote more than 120 plays but only seven have survived. Born in Colonus, near Athens, he studied under Aeschylus, the master of Greek tragedy. Sophocles did not question the justice of the gods; his plays assume a divine order that humans must follow. His strong-willed protagonists end tragically because of pride and lack of self-knowledge. His works include *Oedipus Rex, Antigone, Electra,* and *Ajax.*

WOLE SOYINKA (1934–   ) was born in Isara, Nigeria. An outspoken social critic, Soyinka has had to flee Nigeria several times for criticizing the government, and he has been jailed twice. Educated at Leeds University in England, he has written fifteen plays along with two novels and three books of poetry. His works often concern the difficult struggle between tradition and modernization in Africa. Soyinka won the Nobel Prize for Literature in 1986.

JOHN STEINBECK (1902–1968) was born in Salinas, California, where he worked as a fruit-picker and hod-carrier. Seeing firsthand the grief and misery caused by agricultural exploitation, he incorporated his sympathetic observations about oppressed workers into several novels including *The Grapes of Wrath,* which won the Pulitzer Prize in 1940. Other novels include *Of Mice and Men* (1937), *Cannery Row* (1945), and *East of Eden* (1952). Steinbeck was awarded the Nobel Prize for Literature in 1962.

WALLACE STEVENS (1879–1955), born in Reading, Pennsylvania, was an insurance executive who wrote poetry almost as a hobby. He was forty-four when he published his first book of poems, *Harmonium* (1923). His elegant images often give substance to such abstract concepts as time, being, and meaning. A key figure in modernist literature, Stevens profoundly affected the writing of poetry in America. His *Collected Poems* (1954) won the Pulitzer Prize.

MAY SWENSON (1919–1989) grew up in Logan, Utah, but later settled in New York City, where she became an editor at New Directions Publishing. Poet Elizabeth Bishop has described Swenson's verse as direct and optimistic: the poet "looks, and sees, and rejoices in what she sees." Sometimes she arranged the words of poems to create a pictorial shape. Her works include *Another Animal* (1954), *To Mix with Time* (1963), *Iconographs* (1970), and *Poems to Solve* (1966), a volume of verse for children.

ALFRED, LORD TENNYSON (1809–1892), one of the most popular poets in Victorian England, showed his talents early, publishing his first volume at age eighteen. Encouraged to devote himself to poetry by friends at Cambridge, he was particularly close to Arthur Hallam, whose sudden death inspired the long elegy *In Memoriam* (1850).

This work brought Tennyson lasting recognition: he was appointed poet laureate the year it appeared. His other works include *Locksley Hall* (1842) and *Idylls of the King* (1859–1885).

DYLAN THOMAS (1914–1953) was born in Wales. Shunning school to pursue a writing career, he published his first book of poetry at age twenty. Limited by his lack of a degree, he had trouble making a living as a writer, and his early life was marked by poverty and heavy drinking. Calling his poetry a "record of my struggle from darkness towards some measure of light," Thomas delighted in sound, sometimes at the expense of sense. His play *Under Milk Wood* (1954) is filled with his private, onomatopoetic language.

JEAN TOOMER (1894–1967) grew up in Washington, D.C., attended several colleges, and worked briefly as the headmaster of a black school in Georgia. His best-known work, *Cane* (1923), combines poetry, fiction, and drama into an artistic vision of the black American experience. Widely acclaimed for its innovative style and penetrating insights, *Cane* is one of the most important works of the Harlem Renaissance, though Toomer later disavowed any connection with the Harlem movement.

JOHN UPDIKE (1932–   ) grew up in Pennsylvania, graduated from Harvard, studied art at Oxford, and worked on the staff of *The New Yorker*. Although his first published work was a collection of verse, he is best known for his fiction, including the novels *The Witches of Eastwick* (1984), which was made into a successful motion picture, and *Rabbit at Rest*, which won the Pulitzer Prize in 1991. Updike's stories contain little external action, emphasizing feelings and insight instead of plot.

MONA VAN DUYN (1921–   ) was born in Waterloo, Iowa, and educated at Iowa State Teachers' College. Most of her poems concern love, social situations, and everyday experience. A meticulous craftsman, Van Duyn has published several volumes of poetry, including *To See, To Take* (1970), which won the National Book Award, and *Near Changes* (1990), which won the Pulitzer Prize. She is presently poet laureate of the United States.

ALICE WALKER (1944–   ) was born in Eatonton, Georgia, the daughter of sharecroppers. She attended Spelman and Sarah Lawrence colleges and was active in the civil rights movement. Walker has taught at several universities, contributes to *Ms.* magazine, and works with the Wild Trees Press. Her novel *The Color Purple* won the 1983 Pulitzer Prize and was made into a popular film. She also writes stories (*You Can't Keep a Good Woman Down*, 1981) and essays (*In Search of Our Mothers' Gardens*, 1983).

EDMUND WALLER (1606–1687) was an English poet and a wealthy member of Parliament. Despite a turbulent political career, he managed to write poetry that is smooth and effortlessly clear. His most famous poems include "Song" (1645), "On a Girdle" (1686), and "Of the Last Verses in the Book" (1686).

EUDORA WELTY (1909–), one of America's most distinguished writers of fiction, was born in Jackson, Mississippi, and attended the University of Wisconsin and Columbia University. Returning to Jackson in 1932, she worked for a radio station, several newspapers, and the WPA, before launching her literary career. Welty's humor and astute observations give her portraits of small-town life a universal reality. Her awards include three O. Henry Prizes, a Pulitzer Prize (for *The Optimist's Daughter*, 1972), and the Howells Medal (for her *Collected Stories*, 1980).

EDITH WHARTON (1862–1937), a novelist and short story writer, was born in New York into great wealth and social position. She won a Pulitzer Prize in 1921 for *The Age of Innocence* (1920), one of twenty novels, most of which provide insight into the role of women in a society that repressed and neglected them. The most celebrated woman writer of her time, Wharton spent the last half of her life in France, where she was awarded the Legion of Honor for her selfless work with refugees during World War I.

WALT WHITMAN (1819–1892) was born on Long Island and worked as a printer, teacher, journalist, and carpenter. *Leaves of Grass* (1855) established his reputation after it was praised by Ralph Waldo Emerson. Whitman's celebration of human sexuality, expressed in experimental free verse, shocked his contemporaries. He revised *Leaves of Grass* throughout his lifetime, bringing out numerous editions. A great lover of his native land, Whitman honors America in his poetry and in his essay *Democratic Vistas* (1871). His influence on modern poetry is inestimable.

RICHARD WILBUR (1921–), the son of a portrait artist, was born in New York City and educated at Amherst College. After serving as a staff sergeant in World War II, he earned an M.A. from Harvard, taught English at Wellesley College and Wesleyan University, and was named writer-in-residence at Smith College. Winner of the 1957 Pulitzer Prize in poetry for *Things of This World*, Wilbur also translated Moliere's *The Misanthrope* and wrote the lyrics for the Broadway musical based on *Candide*.

TENNESSEE WILLIAMS (1911–1983) was born Thomas Lanier Williams in Columbus, Mississippi, but grew up in St. Louis. When his mother gave him a typewriter for his eleventh birthday, he began to write — and continued to write for the rest of his life. He dropped out of the University of Missouri, worked at a shoe company, later attended the University of Iowa, and won a grant for promising playwrights. The promise was fulfilled in 1945 with the performance of *The Glass Menagerie*. His remarkably successful career included two Pulitzer-Prize winning plays, *A Streetcar Named Desire* (1947) and *Cat on a Hot Tin Roof* (1955).

WILLIAM CARLOS WILLIAMS (1883 – 1963) spent almost his entire life as a physician in Rutherford, New Jersey. The "inarticulate poems" that he heard in the words of his patients inspired him to write, jotting down lines and phrases whenever he could find a moment. Williams wrote about common objects and experiences and imbued them with spiritual qualities. His works include *Pictures from Brueghel* (1962), which won a Pulitzer Prize, and his masterpiece, *Paterson* (1946 – 1958), a poem in five volumes.

WILLIAM WORDSWORTH (1770 – 1850) was an English poet recognized for his use of common language and for his love of nature. Educated at Cambridge University, he lived for a time in France, where he fathered an illegitimate daughter and experienced the French Revolution firsthand. When he returned to England, he began writing in earnest. His works include *Lyrical Ballads* (1798), *Poems in Two Volumes* (1807), and *The Excursion* (1814). A leader of English Romanticism, Wordsworth was named poet laureate in 1843.

JAMES WRIGHT (1927 – 1980) was born in Martins Ferry, Ohio. After studying with Theodore Roethke at the University of Washington, Wright taught at a number of colleges, wrote several volumes of poetry, and translated the poems of Cesar Valejo, Pablo Neruda, and George Trakl. His *Collected Poems* received the Pulitzer Prize in 1972. His work dealt increasingly with a homeless, lonely persona confronted by an overwhelming, godless universe.

RICHARD WRIGHT (1908 – 1960) was born near Natchez, Mississippi, attended school in Jackson, and moved to Memphis, where he worked odd jobs and began to write. In 1927, he moved to Chicago and joined the Federal Writers' Project in the 1930s. Like many writers of the time, Wright joined the Communist Party but quit after several years. In 1946, he moved to Paris. His works include story collections, *Uncle Tom's Children* (1938) and *Eight Men* (1961); a novel, *Native Son* (1940); and a two-part autobiography, *Black Boy* (1945) and *American Hunger* (1977).

THOMAS WYATT (1503 – 1542), like many of his peers, wrote poems of great charm and wit while pursuing a career as a politician and diplomat. He was rumored to have been Anne Boleyn's lover before she married King Henry VIII. On a diplomatic mission to Italy, he became acquainted with the poetry of Petrarch and, as a result, was one of the first poets to compose sonnets in English.

HISAYE YAMAMOTO (1921 –) was born in Redondo Beach, California. Before World War II she wrote for the Japan-California *Daily News*. When the U.S. entered the war, she and her family, like others of Japanese ancestry, were interned in a relocation center.

After the war she wrote for the Los Angeles *Tribune*, a black weekly. She published her first short story in *The Partisan Review* in 1948. Yamamoto's stories usually concern rural Japanese-Americans during the Depression or the 1940s.

WILLIAM BUTLER YEATS (1865 – 1939), one of the most important poets of the twentieth century, was born near Dublin, attended art school for a time, but quit to devote himself to poetry. His early work is full of Irish myth, but he later turned to actual events and real people to speak for a "New Ireland" that "longs for psychological truth." He helped found the Irish National Theatre and served as a senator in the Irish Free State (1922 – 1928). Yeats was awarded the Nobel Prize for Literature in 1923.

Index of Authors, Titles, and First Lines of Poems

NOTE: First lines are set in roman type; all titles are italicized.

Subject Index